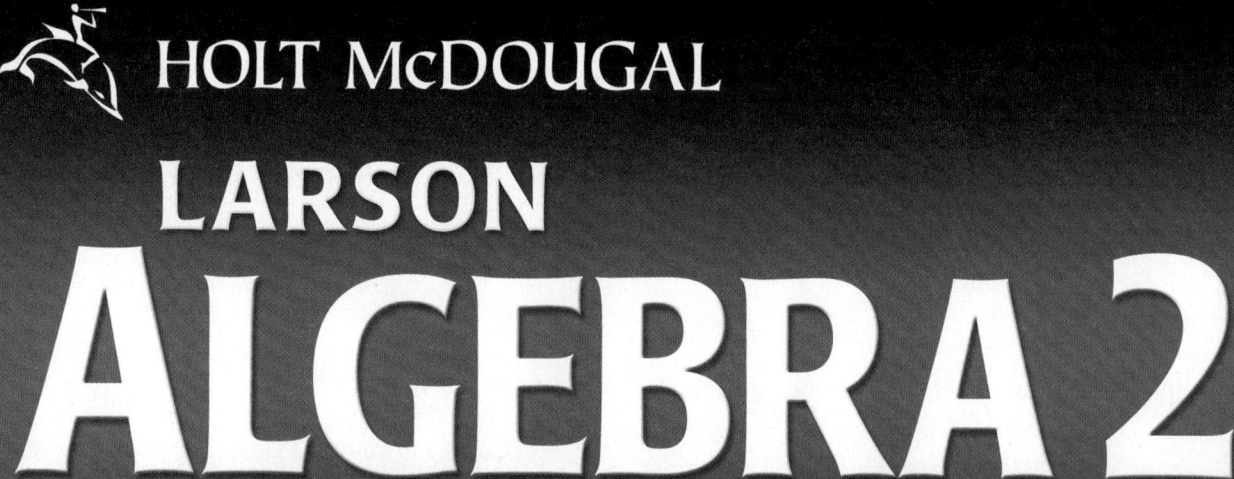

HOLT McDOUGAL

LARSON
ALGEBRA 2

Ron Larson

Laurie Boswell

Timothy D. Kanold

Lee Stiff

HOLT McDOUGAL

HOUGHTON MIFFLIN HARCOURT

COMMON CORE

EDITION

About *Larson Algebra 2*

The content of *Algebra 2* is organized around families of functions, including linear, quadratic, exponential, logarithmic, radical, and rational functions. As you study each family of functions, you will learn to represent them in multiple ways—as verbal descriptions, equations, tables, and graphs. You will also learn to model real-world situations using functions in order to solve problems arising from those situations.

In addition to its algebra content, *Algebra 2* includes lessons on probability and data analysis as well as numerous examples and exercises involving geometry and trigonometry. These math topics often appear on standardized tests, so maintaining your familiarity with them is important. To help you prepare for standardized tests, *Algebra 2* provides instruction and practice on standardized test questions in a variety of formats—multiple choice, short response, extended response, and so on. Technology support for both learning algebra and preparing for standardized tests is available at my.hrw.com.

© Michael Wong/Corbis

About the Authors

Ron Larson

"My goal is to write books that are mathematically correct, instructionally sound, and student friendly."

I think of myself as a facilitator of teaching and learning—writing instructional materials that teachers have told me they need. Over the years, my greatest input has come from the thousands of teachers that have used our books in real classes with real students. Based on this input, we have written books that meet a variety of teaching and learning needs.

Ron Larson is a professor of mathematics at Penn State University at Erie, where he has taught since receiving his Ph.D. in mathematics from the University of Colorado. Dr. Larson is well known as the author of a comprehensive program for mathematics that spans middle school, high school, and college courses. Dr. Larson's numerous professional activities keep him in constant touch with the needs of teachers and supervisors. He closely follows developments in mathematics standards and assessment.

Laurie Boswell

"To reach all students, you need to address different learning styles."

As a mathematics teacher, I quickly learned that to engage all students, I needed to provide for different learning styles. I also learned the importance of designing lessons that would challenge and motivate students. Using a balance of direct instruction, student-engaged activities, and meaningful communication has enabled me to help all students learn.

Laurie Boswell is a mathematics teacher at The Riverside School in Lyndonville, Vermont, as well as a Regional Director of the National Council of Supervisors of Mathematics. She has taught mathematics at all levels, elementary through college. She is the recipient of the Presidential Award for Excellence in Mathematics and Science Teaching, and a past president of the Council for Presidential Awardees in Mathematics. She served on the NCTM Board of Directors (2002–2005), and she speaks frequently at regional and national conferences.

Timothy D. Kanold

"Relevance and meaning are key to successful learning."

Key to creating a mathematics program that will help students be successful are relevance and meaningfulness. Student access to relevant and meaningful mathematics is a critical equity issue in this decade. Our authorship team has worked hard to ensure that we present a balanced curriculum that builds mathematical skills and conceptual understanding simultaneously. We believe students should experience lessons considered to be important, engaging, and meaningful to the context and culture of the student.

Timothy D. Kanold is a past president of the NCSM and a former superintendent of Adlai E. Stevenson High School District 125 in Lincolnshire, Illinois, where he also taught and directed mathematics and science for 22 years. He received a Presidential Award for Excellence in Mathematics and Science Teaching. He also received the prestigious 2010 Damen Award from Loyola University Chicago, for outstanding contributions to education, including work with professional learning communities and the common core state standards recommendations.

Lee Stiff

"All students must have opportunities to take rigorous, high-quality mathematics."

I am proud to be a part of an author team that shares my goals and commitment to setting high mathematics standards for all students. Our focus in writing this program has been to help all students acquire the knowledge, skills, and problem-solving abilities they need in order to become successful adults.

Lee Stiff is a professor of mathematics education in the College of Education of North Carolina State University at Raleigh and has taught mathematics at the high school and middle school levels. He served on the NCTM Board of Directors and was elected President of NCTM for the years 2000–2002. He was a Fulbright Scholar to the University of Ghana and a recipient of the W. W. Rankin Award for Excellence in Mathematics Education presented by the North Carolina Council of Teachers of Mathematics.

Advisers and Reviewers

Curriculum Advisers and Reviewers

Randy Daniels
Mathematics Department Chair
Ankeny High School
Ankeny, IA

Bonnie Davis
Mathematics Consultant (retired)
Gilmer Independent School District
Gilmer, TX

Brett Duffney
Mathematics Teacher
Preble High School
Green Bay, WI

Nancy L. Fisher
Mathematics Teacher
Hilliard Davidson High School
Hilliard, OH

Lois M. McCarty
Mathematics Chair and Teacher
Midland Independent School District
Midland, TX

Dr. Anne Papakonstantinou
Director, School Mathematics Project
Rice University
Houston, TX

Richard Parr
Associate Director for Curricular
  and Instructional Programs,
  School Mathematics Project
Rice University
Houston, TX

Teacher Panels

Craig Edward Auten
Mathematics Chair and Teacher
Walled Lake Central High School
Walled Lake, MI

Barbara J. Brooks
Mathematics Teacher
Mumford High School
Detroit, MI

Ronnee Sue Carpenter
Mathematics Teacher
Flint Southwestern Academy High School
Flint, MI

Robert W. Ewing
Mathematics Teacher
Austin High School
El Paso, TX

Teacher Panels *(Continued)*

Diana Hart
Mathematics Teacher
Romeo Engineering and Technology Center
Washington, MI

Kristen Karbon
Mathematics Teacher
Troy High School
Troy, MI

David Kaynor
Mathematics Teacher
Roseville High School
Roseville, MI

Kathryn Laster
Mathematics Teacher
Lake Highlands High School
Dallas, TX

Kelly Leal
Mathematics Teacher
The Colony High School
The Colony, TX

Jamie K. Luellen
Math Facilitator
Lakeview Centennial High School
Garland, TX

Mohammad Moshfeghian
Mathematics Department Chair
Homer Hanna High School
Brownsville, TX

Susan B. Nelson
Team Leader
Spring High School
Spring, TX

Joseph F. Pawloski
Mathematics Teacher
Brighton High School
Brighton, MI

Donald J. Pratt
Mathematics Teacher (retired)
Huron High School
Ann Arbor, MI

Michael Schulte
Assistant Principal
Warren Consolidated Schools
Warren, MI

Denise Weatherford
Mathematics Teacher
Fredericksburg High School
Fredericksburg, TX

Dianne Young
Mathematics Teacher
Midland High School
Midland, TX

Complex Numbers, p. 48
$$f(z) = z^2 + c$$

Quadratic Functions and Factoring

Mandy Collins/Alamy

Polynomial Functions, p. 98
$E = 0.0029s^4$

Polynomials and Polynomial Functions

COMMON
CORE

Dave Bjorn/Photo Resource Hawaii

Square Root Functions, p. 203

$$v_t = 33.7\sqrt{\frac{W}{A}}$$

Rational Exponents and Radical Functions

COMMON CORE

Joe McBride/Getty Images

Power Functions, p. 270
$y = 0.0784x^{2.5}$

Exponential and Logarithmic Functions

Rational Equations, p. 316

$$t = \frac{1000}{0.6T + 331}$$

Rational Functions

COMMON CORE

Ralph Wetmore/Getty Images

Solving Counting Problems, p. 383
$$_{20}P_4 = 116{,}280 \text{ or } _{20}C_4 = 4845$$

Data Analysis and Statistics

COMMON CORE

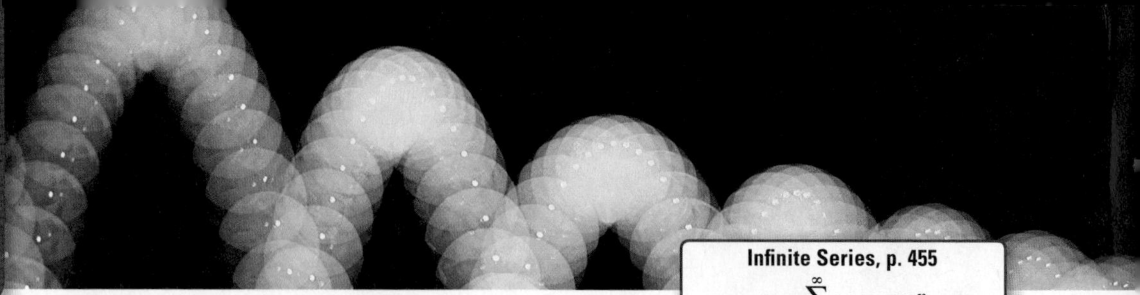

Infinite Series, p. 455

$$8 + \sum_{n=1}^{\infty} 16(0.75)^n$$

Sequences and Series

COMMON CORE

Ted Kinsman/Photo Researchers, Inc.

Classify Conic Sections, p. 532
$$21y^2 - 210y - 4x^2 = -441$$

Quadratic Relations and Conic Sections

COMMON
CORE

Law of Cosines, p. 597
$$a^2 = b^2 + c^2 - 2bc \cos A$$

Trigonometric Ratios and Functions

COMMON CORE

David Madison/Getty Images

CHAPTER

10

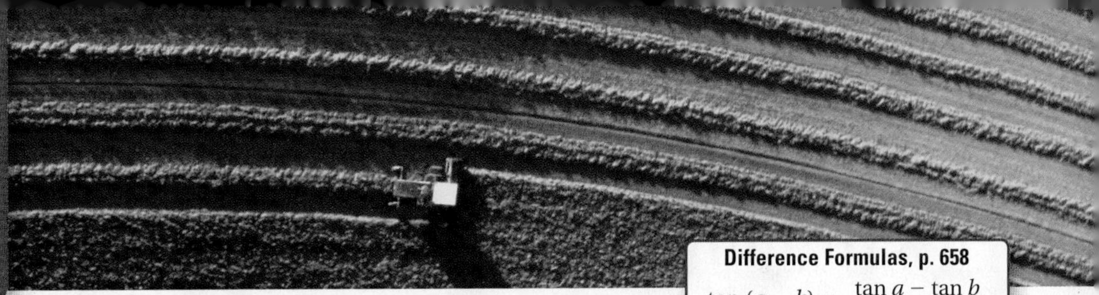

Difference Formulas, p. 658

$$\tan(a - b) = \frac{\tan a - \tan b}{1 + \tan a \tan b}$$

Trigonometric Graphs, Identities, and Equations

COMMON CORE

Thorney Lieberman/Getty Images

Contents
of Student Resources

Using Your Textbook

Your textbook contains many resources that you can use for reference when you are studying or doing your homework.

IN EVERY CHAPTER

BIG IDEAS The second page of every chapter includes a list of important ideas developed in the chapter. More information about these ideas appears in the Chapter Summary page at the end of the chapter.

KEY CONCEPTS The Key Concept notebook displays in every lesson present the main ideas of the lesson. You may want to copy these ideas into your notes.

VOCABULARY New words and review words are listed in a column on the first page of every lesson. Vocabulary terms appear highlighted and in bold print within the lesson. A list of vocabulary appears in the Chapter Review at the end of each chapter.

STUDENT RESOURCES AT THE BACK OF THE BOOK

SKILLS REVIEW HANDBOOK Use the Skills Review Handbook topics to review material learned in previous courses.

EXTRA PRACTICE Use the Extra Practice for more exercises or to review a chapter before a test.

TABLES Refer to the tables for information about mathematical symbols, measures, formulas, and properties.

GLOSSARY Use the English-Spanish Glossary to see definitions in English and Spanish, as well as examples illustrating vocabulary.

INDEX Look up items in the alphabetical Index to find where a particular math topic is covered in the book.

WORKED-OUT SOLUTIONS In each lesson, exercises identified by a red circle have complete worked-out solutions. These provide a model for what a full solution should include.

SELECTED ANSWERS Use the Selected Answers to check your work.

Use Properties of Complex Numbers

GOAL Use the commutative, associative, and distributive properties to perform operations on complex numbers.

CC.9-12.N.CN.2 Use the relation $i^2 = -1$ and the commutative, associative, and distributive properties to add, subtract, and multiply complex numbers.

The properties that you have used to perform operations on real numbers apply more generally to complex numbers (remember that the set of real numbers is a subset of the set of complex numbers). The definitions for adding, subtracting, multiplying, and dividing complex numbers that you learned are written in such a way that you obtain the same results using the commutative, associative, and distributive properties.

EXAMPLE 1 Add and subtract complex numbers

Find the sum or difference. Name each property you use.

a. $(6 + 4i) + (3 - 2i)$ **b.** $(3 - 7i) - (5 + 5i)$

Solution

a. $(6 + 4i) + (3 - 2i) = 6 + (4i + 3) - 2i$ Associative property

$= 6 + (3 + 4i) - 2i$ Commutative property

$= (6 + 3) + (4i - 2i)$ Associative property

$= (6 + 3) + (4 - 2)i$ Distributive property

$= 9 + 2i$ Simplify.

b. $(3 - 7i) - (5 + 5i) = (3 - 7i) + (-5 - 5i)$ Distributive property

$= 3 + [-7i + (-5)] + (-5i)$ Associative property

$= 3 + [-5 + (-7i)] + (-5i)$ Commutative property

$= [3 + (-5)] + [-7i + (-5i)]$ Associative property

$= [3 + (-5)] + (-7 - 5)i$ Distributive property

$= -2 - 12i$ Simplify.

EXAMPLE 2 Multiply pure imaginary numbers

Find the product $(5i)(7i)$. Name each property you use.

THE IMAGINARY UNIT
Remember that i is defined as $i = \sqrt{-1}$, and $i^2 = -1$.

$(5i)(7i) = 5(i \bullet 7)i$ Associative property

$= 5(7 \bullet i)i$ Commutative property

$= (5 \bullet 7)i^2$ Associative property

$= -35$ Simplify.

MULTIPLYING COMPLEX NUMBERS Using the associative property, it is easy to see that the product of a real number a and a pure imaginary number bi is $(ab)i$. Example 2 illustrates the fact that the product of two pure imaginary numbers bi and di is $-bd$. You can use these facts, the distributive property, and the definitions of complex number addition and subtraction illustrated in Example 1 to multiply complex numbers.

EXAMPLE 3 **Multiply complex numbers**

Find the product. Name each property you use.

a. $(4 + 2i)(3 + 6i)$ **b.** $(3 - i)(7 - 2i)$

Solution

a. $(4 + 2i)(3 + 6i) = 4(3 + 6i) + 2i(3 + 6i)$	**Distributive property**
$= 4 \cdot 3 + 4 \cdot 6i + 2i \cdot 3 + 2i \cdot 6i$	**Distributive property**
$= 12 + 24i + 6i - 12$	**Simplify.**
$= (12 + 24i) + (-12 + 6i)$	**Commutative property**
$= [12 + (-12)] + (24 + 6)i$	**Definition of addition**
$= 30i$	**Simplify.**
b. $(3 - i)(7 - 2i) = 3(7 - 2i) - i(7 - 2i)$	**Distributive property**
$= 3 \cdot 7 + 3 \cdot (-2i) - i \cdot 7 - i \cdot (-2i)$	**Distributive property**
$= 21 - 6i - 7i - 2$	**Simplify.**
$= (21 - 6i) + (-2 - 7i)$	**Commutative property**
$= [21 + (-2)] + (-6 - 7)i$	**Definition of addition**
$= 19 - 13i$	**Simplify.**

AVOID ERRORS
Be careful with the sign of the term that includes i^2: $-i(-2i)$ $= -(-2)(i^2) = 2(-1) = -2$

PRACTICE

EXAMPLE 1
for Exs. 1–12

Find the sum or difference. Name each property you use.

1. $(2 + 3i) + (9 - 2i)$ **2.** $(6 - 8i) + (-2 + 5i)$ **3.** $(-7 + i) + (-4 + 3i)$

4. $(-8 - 2i) + (13 - 5i)$ **5.** $(5 + 11i) + 12i$ **6.** $(9 + 2i) + (7 + i)$

7. $(4 + 5i) - (3 - 2i)$ **8.** $(15 - 6i) - (15 + 4i)$ **9.** $5i - (8 - 2i)$

10. $(-7 - 10i) - (6 - 10i)$ **11.** $7i - (4 - 7i)$ **12.** $(-1 - 15i) - (1 + i)$

EXAMPLES 2 AND 3
for Exs. 13–24

Find the product. Name each property you use.

13. $(2i)(9i)$ **14.** $(12i)(3i)$ **15.** $(-4i)(-5i)$

16. $(6i)(-3i)$ **17.** $(7i)^2$ **18.** $(-3i)^2$

19. $(2 + 7i)(3 - 2i)$ **20.** $(1 - 2i)(4 + 4i)$ **21.** $(9 + i)(4 - 5i)$

22. $(-6 + 5i)(3 - 4i)$ **23.** $(2 + 5i)^2$ **24.** $(6 - 2i)^2$

Use Polynomial Identities

GOAL Prove polynomial identities and use them to describe numerical relationships.

Recall that a *Pythagorean triple* is a set of positive integers a, b, and c such that $a^2 + b^2 = c^2$. For example, because $3^2 + 4^2 = 5^2$ and $5^2 + 12^2 = 13^2$, the sets 3, 4, 5 and 5, 12, 13 are Pythagorean triples. You can generate Pythagorean triples by choosing positive integers x and y, with $x > y$, then using the polynomial identity

INTERPRET AN IDENTITY
This identity states that the sum of the squares of the expressions in parentheses on the left is equal to the square of the expression in parentheses on the right.

$$(x^2 - y^2)^2 + (2xy)^2 = (x^2 + y^2)^2.$$

To form a Pythagorean triple, let $a = x^2 - y^2$, $b = 2xy$, and $c = x^2 + y^2$. The identity guarantees that $a^2 + b^2 = c^2$.

CC.9-12.A.APR.4 Prove polynomial identities and use them to describe numerical relationships.

USE AN IDENTITY
When you first learned to square binomials, you learned polynomial identities for the square of a binomial difference and the square of a binomial sum:
$(a - b)^2 = a^2 - 2ab + b^2$
$(a + b)^2 = a^2 + 2ab + b^2$

EXAMPLE 1   Prove and use a polynomial identity

Prove the polynomial identity $(x^2 - y^2)^2 + (2xy)^2 = (x^2 + y^2)^2$. Then use it to generate a Pythagorean triple.

Solution

STEP 1 **Prove** the polynomial identity by showing that each side is equal to the other. First, expand and simplify the left side of the equation.

$(x^2 - y^2)^2 + (2xy)^2$ **Write the left side of the identity.**

$= \left[(x^2)^2 - 2x^2y^2 + (y^2)^2 \right] + (2xy)^2$ **Square the binomial.**

$= x^4 - 2x^2y^2 + y^4 + 4x^2y^2$ **Simplify and evaluate $(2xy)^2$.**

$= x^4 + 2x^2y^2 + y^4$ **Combine like terms.**

Now expand and simplify the expression on the right side of the equation.

$(x^2 + y^2)^2$ **Write the right side of the identity.**

$= (x^2)^2 + 2x^2y^2 + (y^2)^2$ **Square the binomial.**

$= x^4 + 2x^2y^2 + y^4$ **Simplify.**

Because the simplified expressions for the left and right sides are the same, the statement $(x^2 - y^2)^2 + (2xy)^2 = (x^2 + y^2)^2$ is true.

STEP 2 **Use** the identity to generate a Pythagorean triple. Choose positive integers x and y with $x > y$. For example, let $x = 4$ and $y = 3$.

$a = x^2 - y^2 = 4^2 - 3^2 = 16 - 9 = 7$

$b = 2xy = 2 \cdot 4 \cdot 3 = 24$

$c = x^2 + y^2 = 4^2 + 3^2 = 16 + 9 = 25$

So, using $x = 4$ and $y = 3$ generates the Pythagorean triple 7, 24, 25.

EXAMPLE 2   **Prove and use a polynomial identity**

Prove the polynomial identity for the product of the sum and difference of the same two terms: $(x - y)(x + y) = x^2 - y^2$. Then explain how you can use the identity to calculate $18 \cdot 22$.

Solution

STEP 1   **Prove** the polynomial identity.

Simplify the expression on the left side of the equation.

$$(x - y)(x + y) \overset{?}{=} x^2 - y^2 \qquad \text{Write original identity.}$$

$$x(x + y) - y(x + y) \overset{?}{=} x^2 - y^2 \qquad \text{Distributive property}$$

$$x^2 + xy - yx - y^2 \overset{?}{=} x^2 - y^2 \qquad \text{Distributive property}$$

$$x^2 - y^2 = x^2 - y^2 \checkmark \qquad \text{Simplify. Both sides are equal.}$$

Both sides of the equation are equal, so the identity $(x - y)(x + y) = x^2 - y^2$ is true.

STEP 2   **Use** the identity to calculate $18 \cdot 22$.

Write each factor as a sum or difference of the same two integers.

$$18 \cdot 22 = (20 - 2)(20 + 2) \qquad 18 = 20 - 2 \text{ and } 22 = 20 + 2$$

$$= 20^2 - 2^2 \qquad \text{Use the polynomial identity.}$$

$$= 400 - 4 = 396 \qquad \text{Simplify.}$$

PRACTICE

EXAMPLE 1
for Ex. 1

1. You can also generate Pythagorean triples by choosing a positive integer x ($x > 1$) and using the polynomial identity $(2x)^2 + (x^2 - 1)^2 = (x^2 + 1)^2$. To generate a Pythagorean triple, let $a = 2x$, $b = x^2 - 1$, and $c = x^2 + 1$. Prove the polynomial identity $(2x)^2 + (x^2 - 1)^2 = (x^2 + 1)^2$. Then use it to generate a Pythagorean triple.

EXAMPLE 2
for Ex. 2

2. Prove the polynomial identity $(x + y)^3 = x^3 + 3x^2y + 3xy^2 + y^3$. Then explain how you can use it as an easy way to calculate 11^3.

3. **MENTAL MATH** You have been asked to order textbooks for your class. You need to order 29 textbooks that cost $31 each. Explain how you can use the polynomial identity $(x - y)(x + y) = x^2 - y^2$ and mental math to find the total cost of the textbooks.

4. **REASONING** When you use $(x^2 - y^2)^2 + (2xy)^2 = (x^2 + y^2)^2$ to generate a Pythagorean triple, why must you choose x and y such that $x > y$?

5. **OPEN-ENDED** Give an example of two whole numbers greater than 10 that can be multiplied easily using mental math and the identity $(x - y)(x + y) = x^2 - y^2$. Explain your reasoning.

Advanced Proof Techniques

GOAL Use proof by contradiction and mathematical induction to prove theorems.

Key Vocabulary
- proof by contradiction
- mathematical induction

CC.9-12.N.CN.9 (+) Know the Fundamental Theorem of Algebra; show that it is true for quadratic polynomials.
CC.9-12.A.APR.5 (+) Know and apply the Binomial Theorem for the expansion of $(x + y)^n$ in powers of x and y for a positive integer n, where x and y are any numbers, with coefficients determined, for example, by Pascal's Triangle. (The Binomial Theorem can be proved by mathematical induction or by a combinatorial argument.)

To write a **proof by contradiction** (a type of *indirect proof*), you first make a temporary assumption that the desired conclusion is false. Then you use logical reasoning to show that this assumption leads to a contradiction of known facts.

KEY CONCEPT   *For Your Notebook*

Writing a Proof by Contradiction

STEP 1 **Identify** the statement you want to prove. **Assume** temporarily that the statement is false by assuming its opposite is true.

STEP 2 **Reason** logically until you reach a contradiction of known facts.

STEP 3 **Conclude** that the statement you want to prove must be true because the contradiction shows that your temporary assumption must be false.

EXAMPLE 1 Write a proof by contradiction

A corollary to the fundamental theorem of algebra states that if $f(x)$ is a polynomial of degree $n > 0$, then the equation $f(x) = 0$ has exactly n solutions, or roots, given that you count repeated roots individually. Prove that this corollary is true for quadratic equations.

Solution

STEP 1 You can use the quadratic formula to find two roots of any quadratic equation $ax^2 + bx + c = 0$ if you count repeated roots twice. So, you know that there are *at least* two roots. You want to prove that there are *exactly* two roots. To use proof by contradiction, assume that a quadratic equation can have *more than* two roots: Assume that $f(x)$ is a quadratic polynomial for which $f(x) = 0$ has 3 roots: a, b, and c.

CHOOSE A SIMPLE CASE
Assuming $f(x)$ has 3 roots is the simplest case of "more than 2." The argument is the same for any number greater than 3.

STEP 2 Since a is a solution of $f(x) = 0$, you know that $f(a) = 0$. By the factor theorem, $x - a$ is a factor of $f(x)$. Similarly, $x - b$ and $x - c$ are factors of $f(x)$. So, we can rewrite $f(x)$ in factored form as $f(x) = q(x)(x - a)(x - b)(x - c)$ where $q(x)$ is the quotient polynomial. (Note that $q(x)$ could just be 1 or another constant, but cannot be zero, or $f(x)$ would be 0, which is not quadratic.)

Because multiplying shows that $(x - a)(x - b)(x - c)$ is a polynomial of degree 3, $f(x)$ must have a degree of *at least* 3. This contradicts the original fact that $f(x)$ is a quadratic polynomial.

STEP 3 The assumption that a quadratic equation can have more than two roots must be false. Because a quadratic equation has at least two roots, but never more than two roots, it must have *exactly* two roots.

MATHEMATICAL INDUCTION The rule below gives the sum of the first n positive integers.

$$\sum_{i=1}^{n} i = 1 + 2 + \cdots + n = \frac{n(n + 1)}{2}$$

For example, when $n = 5$, the formula gives $1 + 2 + 3 + 4 + 5 = \frac{5(6)}{2} = 15$. You can use **mathematical induction** to prove statements about positive integers.

KEY CONCEPT   *For Your Notebook*

Mathematical Induction

To show that a statement is true for all positive integers n, perform these steps:

Basis Step: Show that the statement is true for $n = 1$.

Inductive Step: Assume that the statement is true for $n = k$, where k is any positive integer. Then show that this implies the statement is true for $n = k + 1$.

EXAMPLE 2   **Use mathematical induction**

Use mathematical induction to prove that $1 + 2 + \cdots + n = \frac{n(n + 1)}{2}$.

Solution

Basis Step: Check that the formula works for $n = 1$.

$$1 \stackrel{?}{=} \frac{1(1 + 1)}{2} \quad\longrightarrow\quad 1 = 1 \ \checkmark$$

Inductive Step: Assume that the formula is true for $n = k$, that is, that $1 + 2 + \cdots + k = \frac{k(k + 1)}{2}$. We want to show that this implies that the formula is true for $n = \boldsymbol{k + 1}$, that is, that $1 + 2 + \cdots + k + (\boldsymbol{k + 1}) = \frac{(\boldsymbol{k + 1})[(\boldsymbol{k + 1}) + 1]}{2}$.

$$1 + 2 + \cdots + k = \frac{k(k + 1)}{2} \qquad \text{Assume true for } n = k.$$

$$1 + 2 + \cdots + k + (k + 1) = \frac{k(k + 1)}{2} + (k + 1) \qquad \text{Add } k + 1 \text{ to each side.}$$

$$= \frac{k(k + 1) + 2(k + 1)}{2} \qquad \text{Add.}$$

$$= \frac{(k + 1)(k + 2)}{2} \qquad \text{Factor out } k + 1.$$

$$= \frac{(k + 1)[(k + 1) + 1]}{2} \qquad \text{Rewrite } k + 2 \text{ as } (k + 1) + 1.$$

Therefore, $1 + 2 + \cdots + n = \frac{n(n + 1)}{2}$ for all positive integers n.

UNDERSTAND INDUCTION

If you know from the basis step that a statement is true for $n = 1$, then the inductive step implies that it is true for $n = 2$, and therefore for $n = 3$, for $n = 4$, and so on for all positive integers n.

EXAMPLE 3 Use mathematical induction

The binomial theorem states that for any positive integer n,

$$(a + b)^n = {}_nC_0a^nb^0 + {}_nC_1a^{n-1}b^1 + {}_nC_2a^{n-2}b^2 + \cdots + {}_nC_na^0b^n.$$

Use mathematical induction to prove the binomial theorem.

Solution

Basis Step: Check that the formula works for $n = 1$.

$$(a + b)^1 \stackrel{?}{=} {}_1C_0a^1b^0 + {}_1C_1a^0b^1 \qquad \text{Write the formula with } n = 1.$$

$$= a + b \; \checkmark \qquad {}_1C_0 = {}_1C_1 = 1 \text{ and } b^0 = a^0 = 1$$

Inductive Step: Assume that the formula is true for $n = k$, that is, that

$$(a + b)^k = {}_kC_0a^kb^0 + {}_kC_1a^{k-1}b^1 + {}_kC_2a^{k-2}b^2 + \cdots + {}_kC_ka^0b^k.$$

We want to show that this implies that the formula is true for $n = k + 1$, that is, that

$$(a + b)^{k+1} = {}_{k+1}C_0a^{k+1}b^0 + {}_{k+1}C_1a^kb^1 + {}_{k+1}C_2a^{k-1}b^2 + \cdots + {}_{k+1}C_{k+1}a^0b^{k+1}.$$

GOAL STATEMENT

This statement is what we want to prove. Use it to help guide your steps as you simplify below.

Rewrite $(a + b)^{k+1}$ so you can use the assumption in the inductive step. Then simplify.

$$(a + b)^{k+1} = (a + b)(a + b)^k$$

$$= (a + b)({}_kC_0a^kb^0 + {}_kC_1a^{k-1}b^1 + {}_kC_2a^{k-2}b^2 + \cdots + {}_kC_ka^0b^k)$$

$$= ({}_kC_0a^{k+1}b^0 + {}_kC_1a^kb^1 + {}_kC_2a^{k-1}b^2 + \cdots + {}_kC_ka^1b^k) +$$
$$({}_kC_0a^kb^1 + {}_kC_1a^{k-1}b^2 + {}_kC_2a^{k-2}b^3 + \cdots + {}_kC_ka^0b^{k+1})$$

$$= {}_kC_0a^{k+1}b^0 + [{}_kC_0 + {}_kC_1]a^kb^1 + [{}_kC_1 + {}_kC_2]a^{k-1}b^2 + \cdots + {}_kC_ka^0b^{k+1}$$

DISTRIBUTIVE PROPERTY

Using the laws of exponents, multiply each term of the expression for $(a + b)^k$ by a and then by b. Then simplify by combining like terms.

Notice that the subscript before each C in the last line above is k, but in the goal statement it is $k + 1$. Remember that ${}_nC_0 = 1$ and ${}_nC_n = 1$ for every whole number n. This lets us perform a "trick" by substituting ${}_{k+1}C_0$ for ${}_kC_0$ in the first term above (since both equal 1), and substituting ${}_{k+1}C_{k+1}$ for ${}_kC_k$ in the last term above.

$$(a + b)^{k+1} = {}_{k+1}C_0a^{k+1}b^0 + [{}_kC_0 + {}_kC_1]a^kb^1 + [{}_kC_1 + {}_kC_2]a^{k-1}b^2 + \cdots +$$
$$\qquad {}_{k+1}C_{k+1}a^0b^{k+1}$$

In Example 4, you will prove Pascal's identity. Pascal's identity states that

$$_nC_k + {}_nC_{k+1} = {}_{n+1}C_{k+1}.$$

PASCAL'S IDENTITY

This statement just expresses what you know about Pascal's triangle: To find the value of a term in the triangle, add the two consecutive terms diagonally above it in the previous row.

Now apply Pascal's identity to the coefficients in square brackets to rewrite the last expression for $(a + b)^{k+1}$:

$$(a + b)^{k+1} = {}_{k+1}C_0a^{k+1}b^0 + {}_{k+1}C_1a^kb^1 + {}_{k+1}C_2a^{k-1}b^2 + \cdots + {}_{k+1}C_{k+1}a^0b^{k+1}.$$

Notice that this matches the goal statement. So, for all positive integers n,

$$(a + b)^n = {}_nC_0a^nb^0 + {}_nC_1a^{n-1}b^1 + {}_nC_2a^{n-2}b^2 + \cdots + {}_nC_na^0b^n.$$

EXAMPLE 4   **Prove Pascal's Identity**

Prove that $_nC_k + {_nC_{k+1}} = {_{n+1}C_{k+1}}$.

Solution

$_nC_k + {_nC_{k+1}}$

$$= \frac{n!}{(n-k)!k!} + \frac{n!}{(n-(k+1))!(k+1)!}$$

$_nC_r = \dfrac{n!}{(n-r)! \cdot r!}$

FACTORIAL NOTATION

Notice that $(n-k)! = (n-k)(n-(k+1))!$. For example, $(8-3)! = 5 \cdot 4!$.
Also, $(k+1)! = (k+1) \cdot k!$.
For example, $(3+1)! = 4 \cdot 3!$.

$$= \frac{n!}{(n-k)(n-(k+1))!k!} + \frac{n!}{(n-(k+1))!(k+1)k!}$$

Rewrite denominators.

$$= \frac{n!(k+1)}{(n-k)(n-(k+1))!k!(k+1)} + \frac{n!(n-k)}{(n-(k+1))!(k+1)k!(n-k)}$$

Form common denominator.

$$= \frac{n!(k+1) + n!(n-k)}{(n-k)(n-(k+1))!(k+1)k!}$$

Add.

$$= \frac{n!(k+1+n-k)}{(n-k)!(k+1)!}$$

Factor numerator; simplify denominator.

CLARIFY THE GOAL

Up to this step we have just added and simplified. We want to prove that this expression is equivalent to $_{n+1}C_{k+1} = \dfrac{(n+1)!}{((n+1)-(k+1))! \cdot (k+1)!}$.

$$= \frac{n!(n+1)}{(n-k)!(k+1)!}$$

Simplify.

$$= \frac{(n+1)!}{((n+1)-(k+1))!(k+1)!}$$

$n!(n+1) = (n+1)!$ and $n-k = (n+1)-(k+1)$

$$= {_{n+1}C_{k+1}}$$

Definition

PRACTICE

EXAMPLE 1
for Exs. 1–3

Write a proof by contradiction for the statement.

1. An odd number is not divisible by 4.

2. The sum of an even number and an odd number is odd.

3. For any positive integer n, if n^2 is odd, then n is odd.

EXAMPLES 2, 3, AND 4
for Exs. 4–8

Use mathematical induction to prove the statement.

4. $2 + 4 + 6 + \cdots + 2n = n(n+1)$

5. $(ab)^n = a^n b^n$

6. $1^3 + 2^3 + 3^3 + \cdots + n^3 = \dfrac{n^2(n+1)^2}{4}$

7. $1^2 + 2^2 + 3^2 + \cdots + n^2 = \dfrac{n(n+1)(2n+1)}{6}$

8. If you make n straight cuts across a pizza, the greatest number of pieces you can form is $\dfrac{n(n+1)}{2} + 1$. (*Hint*: The $(k+1)$st cut adds $k+1$ new pieces to the total number of pieces that existed after k cuts when it crosses each of the first k cuts.)

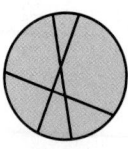
3 cuts
7 pieces

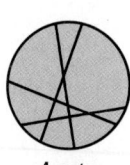
4 cuts
11 pieces

Make and Analyze Decisions

CC.9-12.S.MD.6 (+) Use probabilities to make fair decisions (e.g., drawing by lots, using a random number generator).*

CC.9-12.S.MD.7 (+) Analyze decisions and strategies using probability concepts (e.g., product testing, medical testing, pulling a hockey goalie at the end of a game).*

GOAL Use probability and random processes to make decisions.

Probabilities can help in making fair decisions, as when using a process with equally likely outcomes to select a contest winner. Probabilities also underlie all kinds of real-world decisions in business, science, agriculture, and so on.

EXAMPLE 1 Use probability to make a decision

Twenty students, including Noe, volunteer to present the "Best Teacher" award at a school banquet. Describe a process that gives Noe a fair chance to be chosen, and find the probability, if (a) "fair" means equally likely, and (b) "fair" means proportional to how many banquet prep hours the volunteer worked. Each volunteer worked at least one hour, Noe worked four hours, and, in all, the 20 students worked 45 hours.

Solution

a. Write the names on slips of paper, place them in a box, and draw a slip at random. The probability is 1 out of 20, or 5%.

b. Write the names on slips of paper, but for each hour more than one that a student worked, write their name on an extra slip. Then draw as in part (a). The probability is 4 out of 45, or about 8.9%.

EXAMPLE 2 Use probability to make a decision

Your company must produce 50,000 non-defective cell phones using a component from one of the suppliers below.

	Price per 1000	P(defective)	P(working)
Supplier *X*	$740.00	4.0%	96.0%
Supplier *Y*	$800.00	1.9%	98.1%

Each defective component bought results in $2.20 in extra cost to your company. From which supplier should you buy?

Solution

Use the probability that a component is defective to estimate the total cost.

$$\text{Total cost} = \frac{\text{Cost to get 50,000}}{\text{working components}} + \frac{\text{Extra cost from}}{\text{defective components}}$$

X: Solving $0.96x = 50{,}000$ gives $x = 52{,}083$. You must buy 53,000 components.
Total cost = 53,000($.74) + (0.04)(53,000)($2.20) = $39,220 + $4664 = $43,884

Y: Solving $0.981y = 50{,}000$ gives $y = 50{,}968$. You must buy 51,000 components.
Total cost = 51,000($.80) + (0.019)(51,000)($2.20) = $40,800 + $2132 = $42,932

▶ For the lowest total cost, you should buy from supplier Y.

EXAMPLE 1
for Ex. 1

1. A teacher tells students, "For each puzzler you complete, I will assign you a prize entry." In all, 10 students complete 53 puzzlers. Leon completed 7. To award the prize, the teacher sets a calculator to generate a random integer from 1 to 53. Leon is assigned 18 to 24 as "winners." Is this fair to Leon according to the original instructions? *Explain*.

EXAMPLE 2
for Exs. 2–4

2. A company creates a new brand of a snack, N, and tests it against the current market leader, L. The table shows the results.

	Prefer L	Prefer N
Current L consumer	72	46
Not current L consumer	52	114

Use probability to explain how the company's decisions about whether to try to improve the snack before marketing it and to which consumers it should aim its marketing might differ if the total size of the snack's market is expected to (a) change very little, and (b) expand very rapidly.

3. The Redbirds trail the Bluebirds by 1 goal with 1 minute left in the hockey game. The coach must decide whether to remove the goalie and add a frontline player. The only way the Redbirds can tie the game is for them to score and for the Bluebirds not to score. The probabilities are shown below.

	Goalie	No Goalie
Redbirds score	0.1	0.3
Bluebirds score	0.1	0.6

a. Find the probability that the Redbirds score and the Bluebirds do not score if the coach leaves the goalie in.

b. Find the probability that the Redbirds score and the Bluebirds do not score if the coach takes the goalie out.

c. Based on parts (a) and (b), what should the coach do?

4. A farmer is offered a contract that guarantees him $11.00 per bushel for his entire soybean crop when it is harvested in three months. Below are predictions for the market price m per of soybeans in three months.

$P(m \le \$9.00) = 10\%$ $P(m \ge \$10.50) = 50\%$
$P(m \ge \$12.50) = 20\%$

The farmer predicts a total crop of 20,000 bushels, with a 30% chance of less than 15,000 bushels, and a 20% chance of at least 25,000 bushels.

a. Find the probability and income range for (i) the best case: the farmer declines the contract, the price is highest, and the harvest is largest; and (ii) the worst case: he declines the contract, the price is lowest, and the harvest is smallest. (Assume harvest size and price are independent.)

b. How much will the farmer make if he accepts the contract and his total crop prediction is accurate? How might this and the answers to part (a) affect the decision of whether or not to accept the contract?

Standards for Mathematical Content
Correlation for Holt McDougal Larson Algebra 1, Geometry, Algebra 2

Standards	Descriptor	Algebra 1	Geometry	Algebra 2
Standards for Mathematical Content				
(+ = advanced; * = also a Modeling Standard)				
Number and Quantity				
CC.9-12.N.RN.1	Explain how the definition of the meaning of rational exponents follows from extending the properties of integer exponents to those values, allowing for a notation for radicals in terms of rational exponents.	SE: 459–460		SE: 166–171, 211, 218, 221, 473, EP4
CC.9-12.N.RN.2	Rewrite expressions involving radicals and rational exponents using the properties of exponents.	SE: 459–460	SE: 129, 419, 447, 453–455	SE: 172–179, 219, 221, 257, EP4
CC.9-12.N.RN.3	Explain why the sum or product of two rational numbers is rational; that the sum of a rational number and an irrational number is irrational; and that the product of a nonzero rational number and an irrational number is irrational.	SE: 80–81		
CC.9-12.N.Q.1	Use units as a way to understand problems and to guide the solution of multi-step problems; choose and interpret units consistently in formulas; choose and interpret the scale and the origin in graphs and data displays.*	SE: 17–18, 19–20, 27, 43, 48, 50–51, 53, 54, 87, 90–91, 165–166, 168–170, 373, 376–377, 555, 558–559, 560, 611, 613–614, 690, 691–696, 697, 700	SE: 53, 58, 64, 68, 87, 150, 187, 319, 525, 699, 715–720, 723–729, 731, 735–736, 743, 753, 754, 756–761, 763, 767–774, 779–785, 790–794, 797, 799, 801, 802–803, 804, 810–811, SR10, SR20–SR21, EP3, EP23–EP24	SE: 5, 8–9, 30, 103, 114, 116, 374, 492, 494–495, 500–501, 507, SR13, SR17–SR19, SR21

SE = Student Edition

Standards	Descriptor	Algebra 1	Geometry	Algebra 2
Standards for Mathematical Content				
(+ = advanced; * = also a Modeling Standard)				
Number and Quantity				
CC.9-12.N.Q.2	Define appropriate quantities for the purpose of descriptive modeling.*	SE: 168, 279, 284, 692, 695, 697		SE: 5, 20, 27, 28, 114, 131, 147, 312, 469
CC.9-12.N.Q.3	Choose a level of accuracy appropriate to limitations on measurement when reporting quantities.*	SE: 35–40	SE: 478, 731, 733–736	
CC.9-12.N.CN.1	Know there is a complex number i such that $i^2 = -1$, and every complex number has the form $a + bi$ with a and b real.			SE: 41–42
CC.9-12.N.CN.2	Use the relation $i^2 = -1$ and the commutative, associative, and distributive properties to add, subtract, and multiply complex numbers.			SE: 42–44, 45–47, 57, 78–79, 81, 93, EP2
CC.9-12.N.CN.3	(+) Find the conjugate of a complex number; use conjugates to find moduli and quotients of complex numbers.			SE: 44–46, 57, 79, 81, EP2
CC.9-12.N.CN.4	(+) Represent complex numbers on the complex plane in rectangular and polar form (including real and imaginary numbers), and explain why the rectangular and polar forms of a given complex number represent the same number.			SE: 44–46
CC.9-12.N.CN.5	(+) Represent addition, subtraction, multiplication, and conjugation of complex numbers geometrically on the complex plane; use properties of this representation for computation.			SE: 47, 48

SE = Student Edition

Standards	Descriptor	Algebra 1	Geometry	Algebra 2
Standards for Mathematical Content				
(+ = advanced; * = also a Modeling Standard)				
Number and Quantity				
CC.9-12.N.CN.6	(+) Calculate the distance between numbers in the complex plane as the modulus of the difference, and the midpoint of a segment as the average of the numbers at its endpoints.			SE: 47, 48
CC.9-12.N.CN.7	Solve quadratic equations with real coefficients that have complex solutions.			SE: 41, 45, 57, 81, 85, EP2
CC.9-12.N.CN.8	(+) Extend polynomial identities to the complex numbers.			SE: 138–140, 142, 159
CC.9-12.N.CN.9	(+) Know the Fundamental Theorem of Algebra; show that it is true for quadratic polynomials.			SE: 137–143, 157, 159, AL6–AL7
CC.9-12.N.VM.1	(+) Recognize vector quantities as having both magnitude and direction. Represent vector quantities by directed line segments, and use appropriate symbols for vectors and their magnitudes (e.g., v, $|v|$, $\|v\|$, v).	*This standard is outside the Common Core college and career ready standards.*		
CC.9-12.N.VM.2	(+) Find the components of a vector by subtracting the coordinates of an initial point from the coordinates of a terminal point.	*This standard is outside the Common Core college and career ready standards.*		
CC.9-12.N.VM.3	(+) Solve problems involving velocity and other quantities that can be represented by vectors.	*This standard is outside the Common Core college and career ready standards.*		

SE = Student Edition

Standards	Descriptor	Algebra 1	Geometry	Algebra 2
Standards for Mathematical Content				
(+ = advanced; * = also a Modeling Standard)				
Number and Quantity				
CC.9-12.N.VM.4	(+) Add and subtract vectors. a. Add vectors end-to-end, component-wise, and by the parallelogram rule. Understand that the magnitude of a sum of two vectors is typically not the sum of the magnitudes. b. Given two vectors in magnitude and direction form, determine the magnitude and direction of their sum. c. Understand vector subtraction $v - w$ as $v + (-w)$, where $-w$ is the additive inverse of w, with the same magnitude as w and pointing in the opposite direction. Represent vector subtraction graphically by connecting the tips in the appropriate order, and perform vector subtraction component-wise.	*This standard is outside the Common Core college and career ready standards.*		
CC.9-12.N.VM.5	(+) Multiply a vector by a scalar. a. Represent scalar multiplication graphically by scaling vectors and possibly reversing their direction; perform scalar multiplication component-wise, e.g., as $c(v_x, v_y) = (cv_x, cv_y)$. b. Compute the magnitude of a scalar multiple cv using $\|cv\| = |c|v$. Compute the direction of cv knowing that when $|c|v \neq 0$, the direction of cv is either along v (for $c > 0$) or against v (for $c < 0$).	*This standard is outside the Common Core college and career ready standards.*		
CC.9-12.N.VM.6	(+) Use matrices to represent and manipulate data, e.g., to represent payoffs or incidence relationships in a network.		SE: 577, 580–581	

SE = Student Edition

Standards	Descriptor	Algebra 1	Geometry	Algebra 2
Standards for Mathematical Content				
(+ = advanced; * = also a Modeling Standard)				
Number and Quantity				
CC.9-12.N.VM.7	(+) Multiply matrices by scalars to produce new matrices, e.g., as when all of the payoffs in a game are doubled.		SE: 621–625, 633, EP20	
CC.9-12.N.VM.8	(+) Add, subtract, and multiply matrices of appropriate dimensions.		SE: 575, 578–579, 581, EP19	
CC.9-12.N.VM.9	(+) Understand that, unlike multiplication of numbers, matrix multiplication for square matrices is not a commutative operation, but still satisfies the associative and distributive properties.		SE: 576–577, 580, 581, EP19	
CC.9-12.N.VM.10	(+) Understand that the zero and identity matrices play a role in matrix addition and multiplication similar to the role of 0 and 1 in the real numbers. The determinant of a square matrix is nonzero if and only if the matrix has a multiplicative inverse.	*This standard is outside the Common Core college and career ready standards.*		
CC.9-12.N.VM.11	(+) Multiply a vector (regarded as a matrix with one column) by a matrix of suitable dimensions to produce another vector. Work with matrices as transformations of vectors.		SE: 576, 586–588, 594, 597	
CC.9-12.N.VM.12	(+) Work with 2 × 2 matrices as a transformations of the plane, and interpret the absolute value of the determinant in terms of area.		SE: 586–588, 594, 597	

SE = Student Edition

Standards	Descriptor	Algebra 1	Geometry	Algebra 2
Standards for Mathematical Content				
(+ = advanced; * = also a Modeling Standard)				
Algebra				
CC.9-12.A.SSE.1	Interpret expressions that represent a quantity in terms of its context.* a. Interpret parts of an expression, such as terms, factors, and coefficients. b. Interpret complicated expressions by viewing one or more of their parts as a single entity.	SE: 78, 182–183, 185–187, 191, 193, 194	SE: 429–431, 433, 435, 653–654, 693–694, 715, 717, 723–725, 731, 756–758, 798	SE: 5, 20, 27, 28, 95, 105, 114, 131, 147, 183, 469
CC.9-12.A.SSE.2	Use the structure of an expression to identify ways to rewrite it.	SE: 501–502, 507, 508–509, 515–516, 528, 529–530, 532–534, 538, 539–540, 542–543, 546–547, 549–550, 552–554, 556	SE: 96, 707, 755–758, 767–769, SR4, SR5	SE: 18–19, 21–22, 25–26, 29–30, 31, 77–78, 81, 104–105, 111–113, 114–115
CC.9-12.A.SSE.3	Choose and produce an equivalent form of an expression to reveal and explain properties of the quantity represented by the expression. a. Factor a quadratic expression to reveal the zeros of the function it defines. b. Complete the square in a quadratic expression to reveal the maximum or minimum value of the function it defines. c. Use the properties of exponents to transform expressions for exponential functions.	SE: 466, 478, 539, 540, 541, 543, 544, 547, 548, 549, 550, 553, 555, 558, 587–588, 593, 615–616		SE: 11–12, 14, 15, 21–22, 27–28, 53, 55–56, 240–241, 242–243, 248
CC.9-12.A.SSE.4	Derive the formula for the sum of a finite geometric series (when the common ratio is not 1), and use the formula to solve problems.			SE: 452–453, 455–457, 458, 460, 479, 481, 483, 487, 576, EP8

SE = Student Edition

Standards	Descriptor	Algebra 1	Geometry	Algebra 2
Standards for Mathematical Content				
(+ = advanced; * = also a Modeling Standard)				
Algebra				
CC.9-12.A.APR.1	Understand that polynomials form a system analogous to the integers, namely, they are closed under the operations of addition, subtraction, and multiplication; add, subtract, and multiply polynomials.	SE: 500–502, 503–505, 507, 508–511, 512–514, 515–517, 518–520, 526, 527, 535, 551, 561, 562–563, 567, 570, AL10–AL11		SE: 104–106, 107–110, 126, 127, 155, 159, 179, 343–344, AL2–AL3
CC.9-12.A.APR.2	Know and apply the Remainder Theorem: For a polynomial $p(x)$ and a number a, the remainder on division by $x - a$ is $p(a)$, so $p(a) = 0$ if and only if $(x - a)$ is a factor of $p(x)$.			SE: 121–123, 124–125, 129–131, 132–133, 156, 159, 163, 203, EP3
CC.9-12.A.APR.3	Identify zeros of polynomials when suitable factorizations are available, and use the zeros to construct a rough graph of the function defined by the polynomial.	SE: 553, 587–588		SE: 111–114, 115–117, 120–123, 124–126, 127, 128–131, 132–135, 138, 140, 142, 145, 148–149, 153, 156–157, 159, 171, 203
CC.9-12.A.APR.4	Prove polynomial identities and use them to describe numerical relationships.	SE: 515–517, 518–520, 546–548, 549–551		SE: 105–106, 107–108, 111–113, 114–117, AL4–AL5
CC.9-12.A.APR.5	(+) Know and apply the Binomial Theorem for the expansion of $(x + y)^n$ in powers of x and y for a positive integer n, where x and y are any numbers, with coefficients determined for example by Pascal's Triangle. (The Binomial Theorem can be proved by mathematical induction or by a combinatorial argument.)			SE: 381–382, 383, 385, AL8–AL11, EP7

SE = Student Edition

Standards	Descriptor	Algebra 1	Geometry	Algebra 2
Standards for Mathematical Content				
(+ = advanced; * = also a Modeling Standard)				
Algebra				
CC.9-12.A.APR.6	Rewrite simple rational expressions in different forms; write $a(x)/b(x)$ in the form $q(x) + r(x)/b(x)$, where $a(x)$, $b(x)$, $q(x)$, and $r(x)$ are polynomials with the degree of $r(x)$ less than the degree of $b(x)$, using inspection, long division, or, for the more complicated examples, a computer algebra system.			SE: 120–122, 124, 135, 156, 159, 317–318, EP3
CC.9-12.A.APR.7	(+) Understand that rational expressions form a system analogous to the rational numbers, closed under addition, subtraction, multiplication, and division by a nonzero rational expression; add, subtract, multiply, and divide rational expressions.	SE: 762		SE: 327–331, 332–334, 335, 336–339, 340–342, 343–344, 351, 366, 369, 371, 501, EP6
CC.9-12.A.CED.1	Create equations and inequalities in one variable and use them to solve problems. Include equations arising from linear and quadratic functions, and simple rational and exponential functions.*	SE: 87, 88–90, 93, 95–96, 100, 102–103, 105, 108–109, 302, 304–305, 309, 311–312, 315, 316–318, 324–325, 327, 329–330	SE: 13, 16, 19, 26, 30, 36, 39, 41, 45, 54, 55, 59, 311, 313, 315, 327, 332, 334, 341, 347, 350, 685–687, 688–689	SE: 35, 36–37, 56, 61, 72, 114, 131, 134, 268, 350–351, 356, 641
CC.9-12.A.CED.2	Create equations in two or more variables to represent relationships between quantities; graph equations on coordinate axes with labels and scales.*	SE: 43, 45–46, 156, 157–159, 164–166, 167–170, 183, 185–187, 192–193, 195–197, 201, 203, 205–206, 225–227, 228–231, 234–237, 238–241, 245–247, 248–250, 255, 257–258	SE: 163–164, 165–167, 170–173, 174–177	SE: 3–9, 11–17, 95–102, 103, 145–150, 198–203, 228–235, 236–241, 251–257, 281–288, 496–501, 502–508, 510–515, 518–524

SE = Student Edition

Standards	Descriptor	Algebra 1	Geometry	Algebra 2
Standards for Mathematical Content				
(+ = advanced; * = also a Modeling Standard)				
Algebra				
CC.9-12.A.CED.3	Represent constraints by equations or inequalities, and by systems of equations and/or inequalities, and interpret solutions as viable or nonviable options in a modeling context.*	SE: 29, 32–33, 43, 45–46, 100, 102–103, 227, 230–231, 352, 354–355, 381, 382, 384–385, 397, 400–401, 418, 421–422, 423		SE: 3–9, 11–17, 95–102, 103, 145–150, 198–203, 228–235, 236–241, 251–257, 281–288, 496–501, 502–508, 510–515, 518–524
CC.9-12.A.CED.4	Rearrange formulas to highlight a quantity of interest, using the same reasoning as in solving equations.*	SE: 126–128, 129–131, 132, 133, 138, 139, 141, 152, EP3	SE: 479, 482–483, 783, SR9	
CC.9-12.A.REI.1	Explain each step in solving a simple equation as following from the equality of numbers asserted at the previous step, starting from the assumption that the original equation has a solution. Construct a viable argument to justify a solution method.	SE: 84–86, 87–88, 91–93, 94, 98–99, 100, 104–106, 111–112, 120–121, 126–128, 133, 134–138	SE: 94, 95–96, 98–99, 101, 109, 126, 128, 168, 202, SR21	
CC.9-12.A.REI.2	Solve simple rational and radical equations in one variable, and give examples showing how extraneous solutions may arise.	SE: 762		SE: 204–207, 208–211, 212–213, 214–215, 216, 217, 220, 221, 225, 250, 265, 309, 345–348, 349–351, 352–353, 354–355, 356, 365, 366, 370, 371, 495

SE = Student Edition

Standards	Descriptor	Algebra 1	Geometry	Algebra 2
Standards for Mathematical Content				
(+ = advanced; * = also a Modeling Standard)				
Algebra				
CC.9-12.A.REI.3	Solve linear equations and inequalities in one variable, including equations with coefficients represented by letters.	SE: 82–83, 84–87, 88–90, 91–93, 94–96, 98–100, 101–103, 104–106, 107–109, 110, 113, 115–116, 117–119, 125, 126–128, 129–131, 132, 133, 134–136, 138, 139, 298, 300–302, 303–305, 306, 307–309, 310–312, 313–315, 316–318, 321–322, 324–327, 328–331, 332, 334–336, 337–339	SE: 16, 26, 29, 37, 44, 74, 79, 81, 145, 148, 151, 176, 219, 266, 268, 305, 313, 325, 332, 341, 379	
CC.9-12.A.REI.4	Solve quadratic equations in one variable. a. Use the method of completing the square to transform any quadratic equation in x into an equation of the form $(x - p)^2 = q$ that has the same solutions. Derive the quadratic formula from this form. b. Solve quadratic equations by inspection (e.g., for $x^2 = 49$), taking square roots, completing the square, the quadratic formula and factoring, as appropriate to the initial form of the equation. Recognize when the quadratic formula gives complex solutions and write them as $a \pm bi$ for real numbers a and b.	SE: 531, 532, 535, 541–542, 543, 545, 548, 549, 551, 559, 564–565, 567, 568–569, 598–600, 601–604, 605, 607, 610–611, 612–614, 617–619, 620–622, 623, 651, 654–655, 657, 658–659, 663	SE: 495, SR14–SR15	SE: 18–21, 22–24, 25–28, 29–31, 32–35, 36–37, 38–39, 40, 48, 50–52, 54–57, 58–61, 62–65, 77–79, 81
CC.9-12.A.REI.5	Prove that, given a system of two equations in two variables, replacing one equation by the sum of that equation and a multiple of the other produces a system with the same solutions.	SE: 402–403		

SE = Student Edition

Standards	Descriptor	Algebra 1	Geometry	Algebra 2
Standards for Mathematical Content				
(+ = advanced; * = also a Modeling Standard)				
Algebra				
CC.9-12.A.REI.6	Solve systems of linear equations exactly and approximately (e.g., with graphs), focusing on pairs of linear equations in two variables.	SE: 370, 371–374, 375–377, 378, 379–382, 383–385, 386, 387, 388–390, 391–394, 395–398, 399–401, 404, 405–407, 408–411, 422, 423, 424, 425–428, 429, 430–431, 432–433, 435, 458	SE: 173, 176, SR12	
CC.9-12.A.REI.7	Solve a simple system consisting of a linear equation and a quadratic equation in two variables algebraically and graphically.	SE: 625–631		SE: 534–537, 538–540, 543, 548, 549, 550–551, 553, EP9
CC.9-12.A.REI.8	(+) Represent a system of linear equations as a single matrix equation in a vector variable.	*This standard is outside the Common Core college and career ready standards.*		
CC.9-12.A.REI.9	(+) Find the inverse of a matrix if it exists and use it to solve systems of linear equations (using technology for matrices of dimension 3×3 or greater).	*This standard is outside the Common Core college and career ready standards.*		
CC.9-12.A.REI.10	Understand that the graph of an equation in two variables is the set of all its solutions plotted in the coordinate plane, often forming a curve (which could be a line).	SE: 153		

SE = Student Edition

Standards	Descriptor	Algebra 1	Geometry	Algebra 2
Standards for Mathematical Content				
(+ = advanced; * = also a Modeling Standard)				
Algebra				
CC.9-12.A.REI.11	Explain why the *x*-coordinates of the points where the graphs of the equations $y = f(x)$ and $y = g(x)$ intersect are the solutions of the equation $f(x) = g(x)$; find the solutions approximately, e.g., using technology to graph the functions, make tables of values, or find successive approximations. Include cases where $f(x)$ and/or $g(x)$ are linear, polynomial, rational, absolute value, exponential, and logarithmic functions.*	SE: 189–190, 207–208, 589–592, 593–595, 597, 600		SE: 38–39, 118–119, 130, 132–133, 140–141, 145, 207, 212–213, 270, 275–277, 278–309, 635, 638, 642–643
CC.9-12.A.REI.12	Graph the solutions to a linear inequality in two variables as a half-plane (excluding the boundary in the case of a strict inequality), and graph the solution set to a system of linear inequalities in two variables as the intersection of the corresponding half-planes.	SE: 348, 349–352, 353–356, 357, 362, 363, 366–367, 411, 416–418, 419–422, 423, 424, 428, 429, 444, 505, 514, 526	SE: 197, SR13	SE: 57, 65
Functions				
CC.9-12.F.IF.1	Understand that a function from one set (called the domain) to another set (called the range) assigns to each element of the domain exactly one element of the range. If *f* is a function and *x* is an element of its domain, then $f(x)$ denotes the output of *f* corresponding to the input *x*. The graph of *f* is the graph of the equation $y = f(x)$.	SE: 41–42, 44, 49–51, 54, 55–56, 58, 62, 65, 119, 201, 202, 204–206		
CC.9-12.F.IF.2	Use function notation, evaluate functions for inputs in their domains, and interpret statements that use function notation in terms of a context.	SE: 200–203, 204–206, 209, 214, 215, 219, 272, 340–341, EP4		SE: 24, 31, 57, 73, 137–141, 142–143, 146–147, 148–149, 171, 180–183, 184–186, 187, 189, 191–193, 195, 197

SE = Student Edition

Standards	Descriptor	Algebra 1	Geometry	Algebra 2
Standards for Mathematical Content				
(+ = advanced; * = also a Modeling Standard)				
Functions				
CC.9-12.F.IF.3	Recognize that sequences are functions, sometimes defined recursively, whose domain is a subset of the integers.	SE: 251–252, 481–482, 463–485	SE: 68	SE: 434, 466, 467–470, 471–473, 475, 478, 479, 482, 483, 484, 486–487, EP8
CC.9-12.F.IF.4	For a function that models a relationship between two quantities, interpret key features of graphs and tables in terms of the quantities, and sketch graphs showing key features given a verbal description of the relationship. Key features include: intercepts; intervals where the function is increasing, decreasing, positive, or negative; relative maximums and minimums; symmetries; end behavior; and periodicity.*	SE: 165–166, 168–170, 171, 176, 179–180, 205, 255, 257, 277–279, 281–283, 577, 579–580, 583, 585–586, 592, 594–595, 642–648		SE: 5, 7–9, 12–13, 16–17, 94, 97, 145–147, 148–150, 242–243, 357–364, 612–615, 616–618
CC.9-12.F.IF.5	Relate the domain of a function to its graph and, where applicable, to the quantitative relationship it describes.*	SE: 50–51, 52, 57, 62, 65, 155–156, 157–159, 166, 170, 171, 201, 205, 255, 257, 468, 577, 579		SE: 17, 102, 149, 198–201, 202–203, 229, 232, 234, 237–238, 239, 241, 245–246, 248, 250, 255, 256, 311–313, 314–315, 319, 615
CC.9-12.F.IF.6	Calculate and interpret the average rate of change of a function (presented symbolically or as a table) over a specified interval. Estimate the rate of change from a graph.*	SE: 175–176, 178–180, 209, 236–237, 241, 243, 246–247, 249, 268, 269–272, 649		SE: 357–364

SE = Student Edition

Standards	Descriptor	Algebra 1	Geometry	Algebra 2
Standards for Mathematical Content				
(+ = advanced; * = also a Modeling Standard)				
Functions				
CC.9-12.F.IF.7	Graph functions expressed symbolically and show key features of the graph, by hand in simple cases and using technology for more complicated cases.* a. Graph linear and quadratic functions and show intercepts, maxima, and minima. b. Graph square root, cube root, and piecewise-defined functions, including step functions and absolute value functions. c. Graph polynomial functions, identifying zeros when suitable factorizations are available, and showing end behavior. d. (+) Graph rational functions, identifying zeros and asymptotes when suitable factorizations are available, and showing end behavior. e. Graph exponential and logarithmic functions, showing intercepts and end behavior, and trigonometric functions, showing period, midline, and amplitude.	SE: 154–156, 157–158, 160, 163–166, 167–169, 182–184, 185–188, 189–190, 192, 195, 197, 200–203, 204–206, 209, 212–214, 215, 245, 248, 255, 257, 340–341, 413–414, 463, 466–467, 474–475, 477–478, 506, 574–577, 578–580, 581–582, 584, 587–588, 589–592, 593, 596–597, 615–616, 640–641	SE: 172, 175–176, 495, SR14–SR15	SE: 2–5, 6–9, 11–14, 15–17, 94, 97–99, 100–102, 103, 145–147, 148–150, 198–201, 202–203, 228–230, 232–234, 236–238, 239–241, 245–246, 248–249, 254–255, 256–257, 310–313, 314–315, 316, 319–321, 322–325, 612–616, 617–618, 619–623, 624–626
CC.9–12.F.IF.8	Write a function defined by an expression in different but equivalent forms to reveal and explain different properties of the function. a. Use the process of factoring and completing the square in a quadratic function to show zeros, extreme values, and symmetry of the graph, and interpret these in terms of a context. b. Use the properties of exponents to interpret expressions for exponential functions.	SE: 163–166, 167–168, 182–184, 185–188, 225–227, 228–231, 234–237, 238–241, 244–246, 247–250, 253–255, 256–258, 288, 464, 465, 476, 477, 581–582, 584–586, 587–588, 615–616		SE: 2–5, 6–9, 10, 11–14, 15–17, 31, 228–231, 232–233, 236, 239, 242–243

SE = Student Edition

Standards	Descriptor	Algebra 1	Geometry	Algebra 2
Standards for Mathematical Content				
(+ = advanced; * = also a Modeling Standard)				
Functions				
CC.9-12.F.IF.9	Compare properties of two functions each represented in a different way (algebraically, graphically, numerically in tables, or by verbal descriptions).	SE: 340–341, 463, 474, 574–576, 642–648		SE: 357–364
CC.9-12.F.BF.1	Write a function that describes a relationship between two quantities.* a. Determine an explicit expression, a recursive process, or steps for calculation from a context. b. Combine standard function types using arithmetic operations. c. (+) Compose functions.	SE: 227, 230–231, 236–237, 240–241, 246–247, 249–250, 255, 257–258, 268–269, 270–272, 273–274, 276, 277–280, 281–283, 284, 287, 292, 293, 296, 297, 462, 464–465, 466–467, 472, 473, 475, 477, 479, 634–635, 657, AL4–AL5		SE: 74, 80, 81, 85, 152, 158, 159, 162–163, 180–183, 184–186, 187, 280, 281–285, 286–288, 294, 295, 299, 422, 426, 427, 431, 466, 467–470, 471–473, 645–647, 648–651
CC.9-12.F.BF.2	Write arithmetic and geometric sequences both recursively and with an explicit formula, use them to model situations, and translate between the two forms.*	SE: 251–252, 481–482, 483–485, AL12–AL13		SE: 438, 442–444, 446–448, 450–452, 454–456, 466, 467–470, 471–473, 476–477, 478, 479, 481–482, 483, 484–485, 486
CC.9-12.F.BF.3	Identify the effect on the graph of replacing $f(x)$ by $f(x) + k$, $k f(x)$, $f(kx)$, and $f(x + k)$ for specific values of k (both positive and negative); find the value of k given the graphs. Experiment with cases and illustrate an explanation of the effects on the graph using technology. Include recognizing even and odd functions from their graphs and algebraic expressions for them.	SE: 201–203, 204–206, 209, 214, 232–233, 340–341, 463, 466, 474, 477–478, 615–616		SE: 2–3, 6, 11, 15, 198–200, 201–202, 229, 232, 237, 239, 242–243, 245, 248, 255, 256, 310–311, 313–314, 357–365, 613–616, 617, 619–623, 624–626, 645–647, 648–651

SE = Student Edition

Standards	Descriptor	Algebra 1	Geometry	Algebra 2
Standards for Mathematical Content				
(+ = advanced; * = also a Modeling Standard)				
Functions				
CC.9-12.F.BF.4	Find inverse functions. a. Solve an equation of the form $f(x) = c$ for a simple function f that has an inverse and write an expression for the inverse. b. (+) Verify by composition that one function is the inverse of another. c. (+) Read values of an inverse function from a graph or a table, given that the function has an inverse. d. (+) Produce an invertible function from a non-invertible function by restricting the domain.	SE: AL6–AL9	SE: 479, 481, 482–484	SE: 189, 190–194, 195–197, 205, 210, 251, 253–254, 258, 268, 271, 274, 578, 579–581, 582–584, 635–638, 639–641
CC.9-12.F.BF.5	(+) Understand the inverse relationship between exponents and logarithms and use this relationship to solve problems involving logarithms and exponents.			SE: 251–254, 255–257, 258, 263, 265, 268–271, 272–274, 282–284, 290, 293–294, 295, 297, 298, EP5
CC.9-12.F.LE.1	Distinguish between situations that can be modeled with linear functions and with exponential functions.* a. Prove that linear functions grow by equal differences over equal intervals, and that exponential functions grow by equal factors over equal intervals. b. Recognize situations in which one quantity changes at a constant rate per unit interval relative to another. c. Recognize situations in which a quantity grows or decays by a constant percent rate per unit interval relative to another.	SE: 462–465, 466–469, 473, 477, 481–482, 632–635, 636–639, 640–641, 642–648		SE: 449

SE = Student Edition

Standards	Descriptor	Algebra 1	Geometry	Algebra 2
Standards for Mathematical Content				
(+ = advanced; * = also a Modeling Standard)				
Functions				
CC.9-12.F.LE.2	Construct linear and exponential functions, including arithmetic and geometric sequences, given a graph, a description of a relationship, or two input-output pairs (include reading these from a table).*	SE: 50–51, 52–53, 225–227, 228–231, 234–237, 238–241, 244–247, 248–250, 251–252, 253–255, 256–258, 259, 260, 262, 263–264, 268, 269–272, 277–280, 281–283, 284, 462–465, 466–469, 472, 473–476, 477–480, 481–482, 483–485		SE: 230–231, 233–235, 238, 239–241, 247, 248–249, 280, 281–282, 285–287, 438, 442–444, 446–448, 450–452, 454–456, 466, 467–470, 471–473, 478, 479, 481–482, 483, 484–485, 486
CC.9-12.F.LE.3	Observe using graphs and tables that a quantity increasing exponentially eventually exceeds a quantity increasing linearly, quadratically, or (more generally) as a polynomial function.*	SE: 642–648		SE: 299, 357–364
CC.9-12.F.LE.4	For exponential models, express as *a* logarithm the solution to $ab^{ct} = d$ where *a*, *c*, and *d* are numbers and the base *b* is 2, 10, or *e*; evaluate the logarithm using technology.*			SE: 268, 272–274, 283, 288, 289, 290, 294, 295
CC.9-12.F.LE.5	Interpret the parameters in a linear or exponential function in terms of a context.*	SE: 227, 236–237, 241, 246, 269, 271–272, 464–465, 469, 475–476, 479		SE: 230–231, 232, 236, 239, 246
CC.9-12.F.TF.1	Understand radian measure of an angle as the length of the arc on the unit circle subtended by the angle.			SE: 564–566, 567–569

SE = Student Edition

Standards	Descriptor	Algebra 1	Geometry	Algebra 2
Standards for Mathematical Content				
(+ = advanced; * = also a Modeling Standard)				
Functions				
CC.9-12.F.TF.2	Explain how the unit circle in the coordinate plane enables the extension of trigonometric functions to all real numbers, interpreted as radian measures of angles traversed counterclockwise around the unit circle.			SE: 563–565, 570–574, 575–576, 603
CC.9-12.F.TF.3	(+) Use special triangles to determine geometrically the values of sine, cosine, tangent for $\pi/3$, $\pi/4$ and $\pi/6$, and use the unit circle to express the values of sine, cosines, and tangent for x, $\pi + x$, and $2\pi - x$ in terms of their values for x, where x is any real number.			SE: 557–558, 572, 578
CC.9-12.F.TF.4	(+) Use the unit circle to explain symmetry (odd and even) and periodicity of trigonometric functions.			SE: 570–574, 612–616, 628
CC.9-12.F.TF.5	Choose trigonometric functions to model periodic phenomena with specified amplitude, frequency, and midline.*			SE: 614–615, 617–618, 620, 625–626, 644, 645–647, 648–651, 652, 667, 671, 673, 676
CC.9-12.F.TF.6	(+) Understand that restricting a trigonometric function to a domain on which it is always increasing or always decreasing allows its inverse to be constructed.			SE: 579, 601, 603
CC.9-12.F.TF.7	(+) Use inverse functions to solve trigonometric equations that arise in modeling contexts; evaluate the solutions using technology, and interpret them in terms of the context.*			SE: 635–638, 639–641, 642–643, 644, 651, 658, 668, 671, 673, 677, EP11

SE = Student Edition

Standards	Descriptor	Algebra 1	Geometry	Algebra 2
Standards for Mathematical Content				
(+ = advanced; * = also a Modeling Standard)				
Functions				
CC.9-12.F.TF.8	Prove the Pythagorean identity $\sin^2(\theta) + \cos^2(\theta) = 1$ and use it to calculate trigonometric ratios.		SE: 474	SE: 628–631, 632–633, 638, 651, 658, 662, 670, 673, 677, EP11
CC.9-12.F.TF.9	(+) Prove the addition and subtraction formulas for sine, cosine, and tangent and use them to solve problems.			SE: 653–655, 656–658, 666, 668, 672, 673, 677, EP11
Geometry				
CC.9-12.G.CO.1	Know precise definitions of angle, circle, perpendicular line, parallel line, and line segment, based on the undefined notions of point, line, distance along a line, and distance around a circular arc.	SE: 184, 185, 260–261, 263	SE: 2–3, 24–25, 71, 72, 137, 645, 714–715, 717	SE: 563, 565
CC.9-12.G.CO.2	Represent transformations in the plane using, e.g., transparencies and geometry software; describe transformations as functions that take points in the plane as inputs and give other points as outputs. Compare transformations that preserve distance and angle to those that do not (e.g., translation versus horizontal stretch).		SE: 223–224, 225–230, 271, 273–275, 276–279, 285, 288, 291, 293, 402, 403–405, 406–409, 412, 417, 418, 423, 566–568, 570–573, 575, 579, 582, 583–584, 586, 587–588, 590, 591, 593–594, 596–597, 599, 600, 601, 602–603, 606–607, 609, 622, 624–625, 627	SE: SR14–SR15
CC.9-12.G.CO.3	Given a rectangle, parallelogram, trapezoid, or regular polygon, describe the rotations and reflections that carry it onto itself.		SE: 613–615, 617–618, 633, 634, 795–796	

SE = Student Edition

Standards	Descriptor	Algebra 1	Geometry	Algebra 2
Standards for Mathematical Content				
(+ = advanced; * = also a Modeling Standard)				
Geometry				
CC.9-12.G.CO.4	Develop definitions of rotations, reflections, and translations in terms of angles, circles, perpendicular lines, parallel lines, and line segments.		SE: 566–568, 570–573, 582, 583–586, 587–590, 592–595, 596–599, 601, 602–605, 606–609	
CC.9-12.G.CO.5	Given a geometric figure and a rotation, reflection, or translation, draw the transformed figure using, e.g., graph paper, tracing paper, or geometry software. Specify a sequence of transformations that will carry a given figure onto another.	SE: SR13	SE: 271, 273–275, 276, 278, 279, 280, 285, 288, 293, 566, 568, 570–572, 581, 582, 583–584, 587–588, 591, 592–593, 596–597, 600, 601, 602–605, 606–608, 610–612	
CC.9-12.G.CO.6	Use geometric descriptions of rigid motions to transform figures and to predict the effect of a given rigid motion on a given figure; given two figures, use the definition of congruence in terms of rigid motions to decide if they are congruent.		SE: 223–224, 225–230, 272–275, 276–279, 280, 285, 288, 291, 292–293, 566–569, 570–573, 575, 578–579, 581, 582, 583–586, 587–590, 591, 592–595, 596–599, 600, 601, 602–605, 606–609, 610–612, 628, 629, 630–632, 634	
CC.9-12.G.CO.7	Use the definition of congruence in terms of rigid motions to show that two triangles are congruent if and only if corresponding pairs of sides and corresponding pairs of angles are congruent.		SE: 223–224, 225–230	
CC.9-12.G.CO.8	Explain how the criteria for triangle congruence (ASA, SAS, and SSS) follow from the definition of congruence in terms of rigid motions.		SE: 254–255	

SE = Student Edition

Standards	Descriptor	Algebra 1	Geometry	Algebra 2
Standards for Mathematical Content				
(+ = advanced; * = also a Modeling Standard)				
Geometry				
CC.9-12.G.CO.9	Prove geometric theorems about lines and angles. Theorems include: vertical angles are congruent; when a transversal crosses parallel lines, alternate interior angles are congruent and corresponding angles are congruent; points on a perpendicular bisector of a line segment are exactly those equidistant from the segment's endpoints.		SE: 103–104, 108, 114–116, 119–120, 127, 143, 145–146, 149–150, 152–153, 158, 167, 180–182, 186, 305, 310	
CC.9-12.G.CO.10	Prove theorems about triangles. Theorems include: measures of interior angles of a triangle sum to 180°; base angles of isosceles triangles are congruent; the segment joining midpoints of two sides of a triangle is parallel to the third side and half the length; the medians of a triangle meet at a point.		SE: 206, 208–209, 214, 264–265, 269, 296, 297, 299, 302–303, 305–307, 310, 312, 314, 317–318, 320, 321–323, 325–326, 328–329, 330–331, 332, 336, 337, 340, 342–343	
CC.9-12.G.CO.11	Prove theorems about parallelograms. Theorems include: opposite sides are congruent, the diagonals of a parallelogram bisect each other, and conversely, rectangles are parallelograms with congruent diagonals.		SE: 510, 511–513, 514–517, 518–521, 522–525, 526–527, 529–532, 533–536, 546–547, 548–551, 553, 555–557, 558	
CC.9-12.G.CO.12	Make formal geometric constructions with a variety of tools and methods (compass and straightedge, string, reflective devices, paper folding, dynamic geometry software, etc.). Copying a segment; copying an angle; bisecting a segment; bisecting an angle; constructing perpendicular lines, including the perpendicular bisector of a line segment; and constructing a line parallel to a given line through a point not on the line.		SE: 33–34, 159, 188–189, 233, 258, 261–262, 307, 309, 314, 316, 325, 395, 402, 523, 619, 623, 659, 665, 735	

SE = Student Edition

Standards	Descriptor	Algebra 1	Geometry	Algebra 2
Standards for Mathematical Content				
(+ = advanced; * = also a Modeling Standard)				
Geometry				
CC.9-12.G.CO.13	Construct an equilateral triangle, a square, and a regular hexagon inscribed in a circle.		SE: 674–675, 735	
CC.9-12.G.SRT.1	Verify experimentally the properties of dilations given by a center and a scale factor: a. A dilation takes a line not passing through the center of the dilation to a parallel line, and leaves a line passing through the center unchanged. b. The dilation of a line segment is longer or shorter in the ratio given by the scale factor.		SE: 366, 367–373, 402, 408, 619, 625, 627	
CC.9-12.G.SRT.2	Given two figures, use the definition of similarity in terms of similarity transformations to decide if they are similar; explain using similarity transformations the meaning of similarity for triangles as the equality of all corresponding angles and the proportionality of all corresponding pairs of sides.		SE: 367–374	
CC.9-12.G.SRT.3	Use the properties of similarity transformations to establish the AA criterion for two triangles to be similar.		SE: 374	
CC.9-12.G.SRT.4	Prove theorems about triangles. Theorems include: a line parallel to one side of a triangle divides the other two proportionally, and conversely; the Pythagorean Theorem proved using triangle similarity.		SE: 382–384, 388–389, 391–392, 396–397, 444, 445, 448, 451–452, 453, 455, 459	

SE = Student Edition

Standards	Descriptor	Algebra 1	Geometry	Algebra 2
Standards for Mathematical Content				
(+ = advanced; * = also a Modeling Standard)				
Geometry				
CC.9-12.G.SRT.5	Use congruence and similarity criteria for triangles to solve problems and prove relationships in geometric figures.		SE: 215–218, 219–221, 232–234, 235–237, 238–240, 241–244, 246, 247–250, 251–253, 256–258, 259–263, 283–284, 288, 292–293, 302, 358–361, 362–365, 375–377, 378–381, 382–385, 386–389, 391–393, 394–397, 399, 412, 416–417, 418, 420, 422, 445–448, 449–452, 453–456, 457–460	
CC.9-12.G.SRT.6	Understand that by similarity, side ratios in right triangles are properties of the angles in the triangle, leading to definitions of trigonometric ratios for acute angles.		SE: 462–463, 465, 469, 473	SE: 556–557
CC.9-12.G.SRT.7	Explain and use the relationship between the sine and cosine of complementary angles.		SE: 476, AL2–AL3	SE: 628, 631–632, 670
CC.9-12.G.SRT.8	Use trigonometric ratios and the Pythagorean Theorem to solve right triangles in applied problems.		SE: 430, 433–435, 439, 441–442, 461, 464, 467–468, 470–472, 475–476, 478, 480–481, 483–484, 488, 492, 494, 496, 499	SE: 559, 561–562, 569, 581, 583–584, 600, 603, 605, 606–607, 618
CC.9-12.G.SRT.9	(+) Derive the formula $A = \frac{1}{2}\,ab\sin(C)$ for the area of a triangle by drawing an auxiliary line from a vertex perpendicular to the opposite side.		SE: 475	SE: 589, 591

SE = Student Edition

Standards	Descriptor	Algebra 1	Geometry	Algebra 2
Standards for Mathematical Content				
(+ = advanced; * = also a Modeling Standard)				
Geometry				
CC.9-12.G.SRT.10	(+) Prove the Laws of Sines and Cosines and use them to solve problems.		SE: 486–487, AL4–AL9, AL10–AL13	SE: 585, 586–588, 590–592, 593–595, 596–598, 600, 601, 604, 605, EP10
CC.9-12.G.SRT.11	(+) Understand and apply the Law of Sines and the Law of Cosines to find unknown measurements in right and non-right triangles (e.g., surveying problems, resultant forces).		SE: 486–487, AL4–AL9, AL10–AL13	SE: 585, 586–588, 590–592, 593–595, 596–598, 600, 601, 604, 605, EP10
CC.9-12.G.C.1	Prove that all circles are similar.		SE: 367–373	
CC.9-12.G.C.2	Identify and describe relationships among inscribed angles, radii, and chords. Include the relationship between central, inscribed, and circumscribed angles; inscribed angles on a diameter are right angles; the radius of a circle is perpendicular to the tangent where the radius intersects the circle.		SE: 644, 647–648, 650–652, 653–655, 656–657, 658–660, 661–664, 665, 666–669, 670–673, 699, 703–704, 706	
CC.9-12.G.C.3	Construct the inscribed and circumscribed circles of a triangle, and prove properties of angles for a quadrilateral inscribed in a circle.		SE: 308, 309, 314, 316, 669, 672	
CC.9-12.G.C.4	(+) Construct a tangent line from a point outside a given circle to the circle.		SE: 674–675	
CC.9-12.G.C.5	Derive using similarity the fact that the length of the arc intercepted by an angle is proportional to the radius, and define the radian measure of the angle as the constant of proportionality; derive the formula for the area of a sector.		SE: 715, 717, 721–722, 724, 726	SE: 564–565

SE = Student Edition

Standards	Descriptor	Algebra 1	Geometry	Algebra 2
Standards for Mathematical Content				
(+ = advanced; * = also a Modeling Standard)				
Geometry				
CC.9-12.G.GPE.1	Derive the equation of a circle of given center and radius using the Pythagorean Theorem; complete the square to find the center and radius of a circle given by an equation.		SE: 693, 697	SE: 502, 532, 540, 548, 549, EP9
CC.9-12.G.GPE.2	Derive the equation of a parabola given a focus and directrix.		SE: AL14–AL17	SE: 496–498
CC.9–12.G.GPE.3	(+) Derive the equations of ellipses and hyperbolas given foci and directrices.			SE: 514, 522
CC.9-12.G.GPE.4	Use coordinates to prove simple geometric theorems algebraically.		SE: 296, 298–299, 300–303, 304, 311, 318, 322–323, 324, 346, 352–353, 513, 514–515, 521, 522–523, 527, 528, 534, 538, 542–543, 545, 549	SE: 490, 493, 495
CC.9-12.G.GPE.5	Prove the slope criteria for parallel and perpendicular lines and use them to solve geometric problems (e.g., find the equation of line parallel or perpendicular to a given line that passes through a given point).	SE: 260–262, 263–265, 272, 287, 291, 293, 297	SE: 162–163, 165–166, 169, 170–171, 175–176, 183, 185, 187, 191, 194–195, 196, 199, 200–201	
CC.9-12.G.GPE.6	Find the point on a directed line segment between two given points that partitions the segment in a given ratio.		SE: 410–411	

SE = Student Edition

Standards	Descriptor	Algebra 1	Geometry	Algebra 2
Standards for Mathematical Content				
(+ = advanced; * = also a Modeling Standard)				
Geometry				
CC.9-12.G.GPE.7	Use coordinates to compute perimeters of polygons and areas of triangles and rectangles, e.g., using the distance formula.*		SE: 22, 48, 53	
CC.9-12.G.GMD.1	Give an informal argument for the formulas for the circumference of a circle, area of a circle, volume of a cylinder, pyramid, and cone. Use dissection arguments, Cavalieri's principle, and informal limit arguments.		SE: 729, 755–756, 766, 767	SE: 561
CC.9-12.G.GMD.2	(+) Give an informal argument using Cavalieri's principle for the formulas for the volume of a sphere and other solid figures.		SE: 757–758, 760, 763, 770, 774, 802	
CC.9-12.G.GMD.3	Use volume formulas for cylinders, pyramids, cones, and spheres to solve problems.*		SE: 755–758, 759–761, 762–763, 767–769, 770–774, 775, 780–781, 783–785, 794, 802–803, 810–811	SE: 90, 92–93, 108–109, 114, 115–117, 118–119, 125, 127, 131, 144, 147, 150, 152, 159, 160, 162, 321, 323–325, 328, 333–334, 365
CC.9-12.G.GMD.4	Identify the shapes of two-dimensional cross-sections of three-dimensional objects, and identify three-dimensional objects generated by rotations of two-dimensional objects.		SE: 749, 751–753, 754, 757, 761, 779	SE: 525, 533, 543
CC.9-12.G.MG.1	Use geometric shapes, their measures, and their properties to describe objects (e.g., modeling a tree trunk or a human torso as a cylinder).*	SE: 130–131, 444, 467	SE: 504, 506, 508, 513, 515–516, 519–520, 522, 524, 527, 528, 533, 535, 541, 651, 657, 659, 663, 668, 673, 678, 681, 711, 715, 719, 723, 728, 735, 748, 752, 754, 756, 759, 760–761, 768–769	

SE = Student Edition

Standards	Descriptor	Algebra 1	Geometry	Algebra 2
Standards for Mathematical Content				
(+ = advanced; * = also a Modeling Standard)				
Geometry				
CC.9-12.G.MG.2	Apply concepts of density based on area and volume in modeling situations (e.g., persons per square mile, BTUs per cubic foot).*	SE: 30, 103, 356, 674	SE: 762–765	
CC.9-12.G.MG.3	Apply geometric methods to solve design problems (e.g., designing an object or structure to satisfy physical constraints or minimize cost; working with typographic grid systems based on ratios).*		SE: 7, 23, 31, 48, 58, 97, 122, 141, 149, 160, 179, 203, 207, 213, 216, 220, 234, 236, 240, 269, 274, 278, 293, 297, 302, 319, 331, 344, 384, 412, 451, 484, 532, 535, 610–612, 671, 673, 725, 748, 775	
Statistics and Probability				
CC.9-12.S.ID.1	Represent data with plots on the real number line (dot plots, histograms, and box plots).*	SE: 684, 686–689, 690, 691–696, 697, 700, 757, 760–761, EP11	SE: SR20–SR21	SE: 388–394, 395, SR34–SR35
CC.9-12.S.ID.2	Use statistics appropriate to the shape of the data distribution to compare center (median, mean) and spread (interquartile range, standard deviation) of two or more different data sets.*	SE: 670, 671–674, 675–676, 687, 689, 691, 695–696, 697, 698–699, 757, SR10	SE: SR19	SE: 427, 431
CC.9-12.S.ID.3	Interpret differences in shape, center, and spread in the context of the data sets, accounting for possible effects of extreme data points (outliers).*	SE: 674, 676, 689, 692, 695, 696, 697, 700, 757, AL16–AL17		

SE = Student Edition

Standards	Descriptor	Algebra 1	Geometry	Algebra 2
Standards for Mathematical Content				
(+ = advanced; * = also a Modeling Standard)				
Statistics and Probability				
CC.9-12.S.ID.4	Use the mean and standard deviation of a data set to fit it to a normal distribution and to estimate population percentages. Recognize that there are data sets for which such a procedure is not appropriate. Use calculators, spreadsheets, and tables to estimate areas under the normal curve.*			SE: 397–398, 400–404, 425, 427, EP7
CC.9-12.S.ID.5	Summarize categorical data for two categories in two-way frequency tables. Interpret relative frequencies in the context of the data (including joint, marginal, and conditional relative frequencies). Recognize possible associations and trends in the data.*	SE: 679–683, 714, 717, 718, 731	SE: 810, 815, 816	SE: SR34
CC.9-12.S.ID.6	Represent data on two quantitative variables on a scatter plot, and describe how the variables are related.* a. Fit a function to the data; use functions fitted to data to solve problems in the context of the data. Use given functions or choose a function suggested by the context. Emphasize linear and exponential models. b. Informally assess the fit of a function by plotting and analyzing residuals. c. Fit a linear function for a scatter plot that suggests a linear association.	SE: 268–272, 273–274, 277–283, 284, 285–286, 287, 292, 293, 296–297, EP5		SE: 37, 81, 85, 152, 282, 284–287, 289, 295, 299, 426, 427, 431, 647, 650, 651, 673, EP3, EP7

SE = Student Edition

Standards	Descriptor	Algebra 1	Geometry	Algebra 2
Standards for Mathematical Content				
(+ = advanced; * = also a Modeling Standard)				
Statistics and Probability				
CC.9-12.S.ID.7	Interpret the slope (rate of change) and the intercept (constant term) of a linear model in the context of the data.*	SE: 175–176, 178–179, 183, 186–187, 246–247, 280, 282, 283, AL2–AL3	SE: 163, 167–168, 172, 176	
CC.9-12.S.ID.8	Compute (using technology) and interpret the correlation coefficient of a linear fit.*	SE: 274, 275		
CC.9-12.S.ID.9	Distinguish between correlation and causation.*	SE: 275		
CC.9-12.S.IC.1	Understand statistics as a process for making inferences about population parameters based on a random sample from that population.*	SE: 666–667, 670	SE: 817–818	SE: 410–411, 412–413
CC.9-12.S.IC.2	Decide if a specified model is consistent with results from a given data-generating process, e.g., using simulation.*	SE: 719–720	SE: 817–818	SE: 386–387
CC.9-12.S.IC.3	Recognize the purposes of and differences among sample surveys, experiments, and observational studies; explain how randomization relates to each.*	SE: 667, 669–670		SE: 406–407, 409, 414–419, 422, EP7
CC.9-12.S.IC.4	Use data from a sample survey to estimate a population mean or proportion; develop a margin of error through the use of simulation models for random sampling.*	SE: 666		SE: 408–411, 412–413, 422, 427, EP7
CC.9-12.S.IC.5	Use data from a randomized experiment to compare two treatments; use simulations to decide if differences between parameters are significant.*	SE: 670, 679–683, 720	SE: 810	SE: 420–421
CC.9-12.S.IC.6	Evaluate reports based on data.*	SE: 670		SE: 411, 414–419

SE = Student Edition

Standards	Descriptor	Algebra 1	Geometry	Algebra 2
Standards for Mathematical Content				
(+ = advanced; * = also a Modeling Standard)				
Statistics and Probability				
CC.9-12.S.CP.1	Describe events as subsets of a sample space (the set of outcomes) using characteristics (or categories) of the outcomes, or as unions, intersections, or complements of other events ("or," "and," "not").*	SE: 713, 716, 731, SR22–SR23	SE: 811–816, 819–823, 824–827, 831–837, 839–846	SE: 396, EP7
CC.9-12.S.CP.2	Understand that two events A and B are independent if the probability of A and B occurring together is the product of their probabilities, and use this characterization to determine if they are independent.*	SE: 735–742, 756, 757, 763, EP12	SE: 839–846	
CC.9-12.S.CP.3	Understand the conditional probability of A given B as P(A and B)/P(B), and interpret independence of A and B as saying that the conditional probability of A given B is the same as the probability of A, and the conditional probability of B given A is the same as the probability of B.*	SE: 735–742	SE: 839–846	
CC.9-12.S.CP.4	Construct and interpret two-way frequency tables of data when two categories are associated with each object being classified. Use the two-way table as a sample space to decide if events are independent and to approximate conditional probabilities.*	SE: 673–677, 714, 717–718	SE: 831–837, 839–846	
CC.9-12.S.CP.5	Recognize and explain the concepts of conditional probability and independence in everyday language and everyday situations.*	SE: 735–742	SE: 831–837, 839–846	
CC.9-12.S.CP.6	Find the conditional probability of A given B as the fraction of B's outcomes that also belong to A, and interpret the answer in terms of the model.*	SE: 735–742	SE: 839–846	

SE = Student Edition

Standards	Descriptor	Algebra 1	Geometry	Algebra 2
Standards for Mathematical Content				
(+ = advanced; * = also a Modeling Standard)				
Statistics and Probability				
CC.9-12.S.CP.7	Apply the Addition Rule, $P(A$ or $B) = P(A) + P(B) - P(A$ and $B)$, and interpret the answer in terms of the model.*	SE: 728–733, 756	SE: 831–837	
CC.9-12.S.CP.8	(+) Apply the general Multiplication Rule in a uniform probability model, $P(A$ and $B) = P(A)P(B\|A) = P(B)P(A\|B)$, and interpret the answer in terms of the model.*	SE: 735–742	SE: 839–846	
CC.9-12.S.CP.9	(+) Use permutations and combinations to compute probabilities of compound events and solve problems.*	SE: 723, 725, 727, 729	SE: 819–823, 824–827, 828, 831–837, 839–846	
CC.9-12.S.MD.1	(+) Define a random variable for a quantity of interest by assigning a numerical value to each event in a sample space; graph the corresponding probability distribution using the same graphical displays as for data distributions.*			SE: 388–389, 391–392
CC.9-12.S.MD.2	(+) Calculate the expected value of a random variable; interpret it as the mean of the probability distribution.*	*This standard is outside the Common Core college and career ready standards.*		
CC.9-12.S.MD.3	(+) Develop a probability distribution for a random variable defined for a sample space in which theoretical probabilities can be calculated; find the expected value. *			SE: 388–390, 391–394, 395, 396

SE = Student Edition

Standards	Descriptor	Algebra 1	Geometry	Algebra 2
Standards for Mathematical Content				
(+ = advanced; * = also a Modeling Standard)				
Statistics and Probability				
CC.9-12.S.MD.4	(+) Develop a probability distribution for a random variable defined for a sample space in which probabilities are assigned empirically; find the expected value.*			SE: 390–393
CC.9-12.S.MD.5	(+) Weigh the possible outcomes of a decision by assigning probabilities to payoff values and finding expected values.* a. Find the expected payoff for a game of chance. b. Evaluate and compare strategies on the basis of expected values.	*This standard is outside the Common Core college and career ready standards.*		
CC.9-12.S.MD.6	(+) Use probabilities to make fair decisions (e.g., drawing by lots, using a random number generator).*	SE: 125, 668, 743–744	SE: 819–823, 824–827, 831–837, 839–846, 847–848	SE: 406–407
CC.9-12.S.MD.7	(+) Analyze decisions and strategies using probability concepts (e.g., product testing, medical testing, pulling a hockey goalie at the end of a game).*	SE: 717, 743–744	SE: 819–823, 824–827, 831–837, 839–846, 847–848	

SE = Student Edition

MATHEMATICAL PRACTICES

Mastering the *Standards*

for Mathematical Practice

The topics described in the Standards for Mathematical Content will vary from year to year. However, the *way* in which you learn, study, and think about mathematics will not. The Standards for Mathematical Practice describe skills that you will use in all of your math courses. These pages show some features of your book that will help you gain these skills and use them to master this year's topics.

① Make sense of problems and persevere in solving them.

Mathematically proficient students start by explaining to themselves the meaning of a problem... They analyze givens, constraints, relationships, and goals. They make conjectures about the form... of the solution and plan a solution pathway...

In your book

Verbal Models and the **Problem Solving Plan** help you translate the information in a problem into a model and then analyze your solution.

② Reason abstractly and quantitatively.
③ Construct viable arguments and critique the reasoning of others.

Mathematically proficient students... justify their conclusions, [and]... distinguish correct... reasoning from that which is flawed.

In your book

What if?, **Error Analysis**, and **Reasoning** exercises ask you to evaluate statements, explain relationships, apply mathematical principles, and justify your reasoning.

WHAT IF? In Exercise 2, suppose the price of the 60 inch bookshelf was $99.30. Can you still solve the problem? *Explain.*

ERROR ANALYSIS *Describe* and correct the error in writing an equation of the line shown.

$$m = \frac{4 - 2}{4 - 1} = \frac{2}{3} \qquad y - 2 = \frac{2}{3}(x - 4)$$

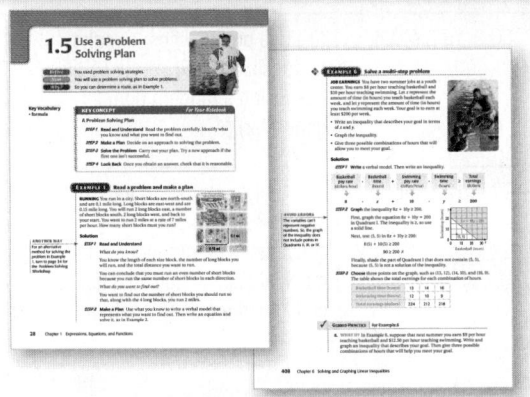

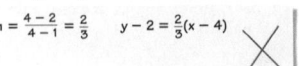

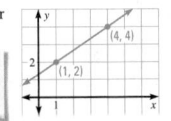

REASONING Give a counterexample for the following statement: If the graphs of the equations of a linear system have the same slope, then the linear system has no solution.

④ Model with mathematics.

Mathematically proficient students can apply... mathematics... to... problems... in everyday life, society, and the workplace...

In your book

Application exercises and **Mixed Reviews of Problem Solving** apply mathematics to other disciplines and in real-world scenarios.

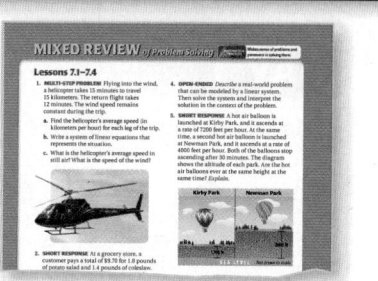

⑤ Use appropriate tools strategically.

Mathematically proficient students consider the available tools when solving a... problem... [and] are... able to use technological tools to explore and deepen their understanding...

In your book

Problem Solving Workshops explore alternative methods as tools for problem solving. A variety of **Activities** use concrete and technological tools to explore mathematical concepts.

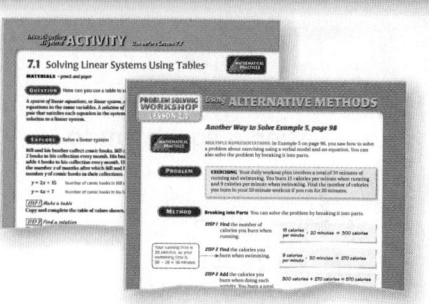

⑥ Attend to precision.

Mathematically proficient students... communicate precisely... with others and in their own reasoning... [They] give carefully formulated explanations...

In your book

Multiple Representations and **Extended Response exercises** ask you to explain your reasoning to help you learn to communicate mathematics precisely.

 **EXTENDED RESPONSE**

 **MULTIPLE REPRESENTATIONS**

⑦ Look for and make use of structure.
⑧ Look for and express regularity in repeated reasoning.

Mathematically proficient students... look both for general methods and for shortcuts...

In your book

Lesson examples group similar types of problems together, and the solutions are carefully stepped out. This allows you to make generalizations about—and notice variations in—the underlying structures.

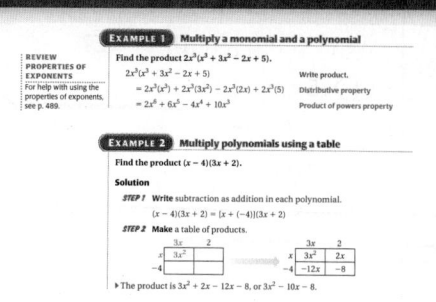

Countdown to Mastery

DAY 1

The figure shows a square within a square. Which expression represents the area of the shaded region of the figure in square units?

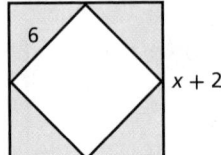

(A) $(x + 2)^2 - 36$ (C) $2(x + 2) - 12$

(B) $(x + 2) - 6$ (D) $(x + 2 - 6)^2$

DAY 2

If x is a nonzero real number, which expression is equivalent to $(x + 5) - 8$?

(F) $-8x + 5$

(G) $8 - (x + 5)$

(H) $x + (5 - 8)$

(J) $(x + 8) - 5$

DAY 3

If a, b, and c are positive integers, what is the greatest common factor of the expressions $18ab$ and $8abc$?

(A) 18

(B) ab

(C) $2ab$

(D) $72abc$

DAY 4

$\triangle ABC$ is a right triangle.

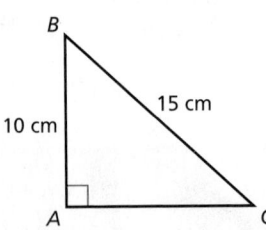

What is the length of $\overline{AC}$?

(F) 5 cm

(G) $5\sqrt{5}$ cm

(H) $5\sqrt{13}$ cm

(J) 25 cm

DAY 5

Simplify the expression $5(x^2 + 4x) + 3(x + 6)$.

(A) $12x^2 + 6$

(B) $12x^2 + 18$

(C) $5x^2 + 7x + 6$

(D) $5x^2 + 23x + 18$

DAY 1

The figure shows a right triangle. Which equation can be solved for the unknown side length c?

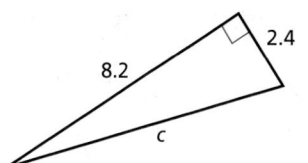

(A) $\sqrt{8.2^2 + 2.4^2} = c$

(B) $\sqrt{(8.2 + 2.4)^2} = c$

(C) $\sqrt{8.2^2 - 2.4^2} = c$

(D) $\sqrt{(8.2 - 2.4)^2} = c$

DAY 2

What is the perimeter in units of a rectangle with a length of $g + 8$ units and a width of $g - 6$ units?

(F) $4g + 2$

(G) $4g + 4$

(H) $g^2 - 16$

(J) $g^2 + 2g - 16$

DAY 3

Which expression is equivalent to $\dfrac{12x^4y^8}{9xy^4}$?

(A) $\dfrac{4}{3}xy^2$

(B) $\dfrac{4}{3}xy^4$

(C) $\dfrac{4}{3}x^3y^4$

(D) $\dfrac{4}{3}x^4y^2$

DAY 4

A particular hummingbird averages 60 wing beats per second. At this rate, how many times would the hummingbird beat its wings during an hour of flight?

(F) 2.16×10^3

(G) 2.16×10^4

(H) 2.16×10^5

(J) 2.16×10^6

DAY 5

A marathon is a 26.2-mile race. Kendra's average speed during marathons is 7.2 miles per hour. Which function d represents the distance in miles Kendra has left to run in a marathon t hours after the race begins?

(A) $d(t) = \dfrac{t}{7.2} - 26.2$

(B) $d(t) = 26.2 - \dfrac{t}{7.2}$

(C) $d(t) = 7.2t - 26.2$

(D) $d(t) = 26.2 - 7.2t$

DAY 1

Which of the following best represents the domain of the function shown in the graph?

Ⓐ $-2 \le x \le 2$

Ⓑ $-3 \le x \le 3$

Ⓒ $-4 \le x \le 4$

Ⓓ $-5 \le x \le 5$

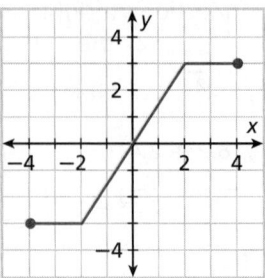

DAY 2

A diagonal of a rectangle measures 9 meters. The width of the rectangle is 6 meters. What is the length of the rectangle?

Ⓕ $3\sqrt{5}$ m

Ⓖ $9\sqrt{5}$ m

Ⓗ $\sqrt{15}$ m

Ⓙ $\sqrt{117}$ m

DAY 3

If a and b are integers, which expression is equivalent to $6^a \cdot 6^b$?

Ⓐ 6^{a+b}

Ⓑ $6^{a \cdot b}$

Ⓒ 36^{a+b}

Ⓓ $36^{a \cdot b}$

DAY 4

In the diagram, points W, X, Y, and Z are collinear, $WX = YZ$, and $XY = 25$. If WX is a whole number, which is NOT a possible value of WZ?

Ⓕ 27

Ⓖ 30

Ⓗ 35

Ⓙ 37

DAY 5

What is the parent function of the function shown in the graph?

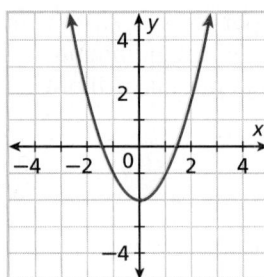

Ⓐ $f(x) = x$

Ⓑ $f(x) = x^2$

Ⓒ $f(x) = x^3$

Ⓓ $f(x) = \sqrt{x}$

DAY 1

Which graph best represents the function $f(x) = \frac{1}{2}x + 2$?

(A)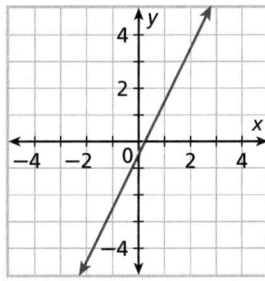

(C)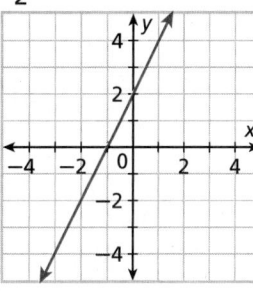

(B)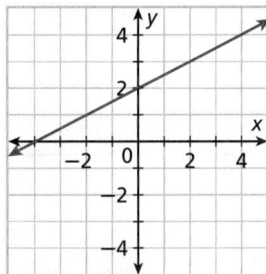

(D)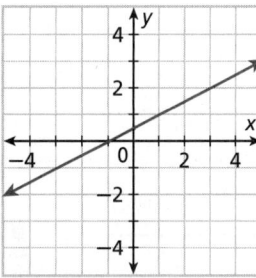

DAY 2

Given that $f(x) = -6x^2 - 12x + 3$, what is $f(-2)$?

(F) -45

(G) 0

(H) 3

(J) 51

DAY 3

What transformation is suggested by the spokes on a stationary bicycle tire?

(A) Rotation

(B) Reflection

(C) Dilation

(D) Translation

DAY 4

Which expression is equivalent to $\left(\dfrac{6x^2y^4}{x^4y^2}\right)^3$?

(F) $216xy^5$

(G) $216x^2y^{10}$

(H) $216x^{-5}y^5$

(J) $216x^{-6}y^6$

DAY 5

What is the parent function of the graph shown?

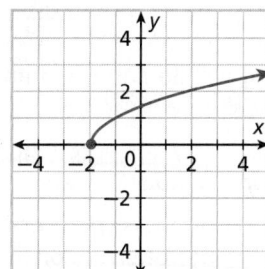

(A) $f(x) = x$ (C) $f(x) = x^3$

(B) $f(x) = x^2$ (D) $f(x) = \sqrt{x}$

DAY 1

Which graph best represents the function $f(x) = x^2$?

(A)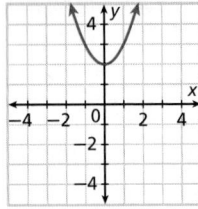

(C)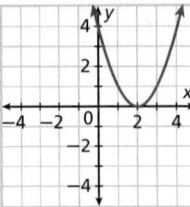

(B)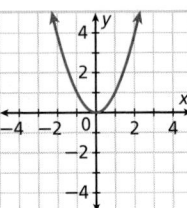

(D)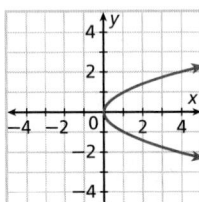

DAY 2

The graph of which function has the end behavior $f(x) \to -\infty$ as $x \to -\infty$ and $f(x) \to -\infty$ as $x \to +\infty$?

(F) $y = x^4 + x^3 + x^2 + 1$

(G) $y = 8x^5 + 2x^4 + 9$

(H) $y = -x^5 - x^3 - 3x - 5$

(J) $y = -9x^4 + 4x^3 + 16x$

DAY 3

Solve $4z + 16 - 3 = z - 7 + 5z$.

(A) $z = 0$

(B) $z = 2.5$

(C) $z = 10$

(D) $z = 20$

DAY 4

The scatter plot shown is most likely to represent which of the following sets of data?

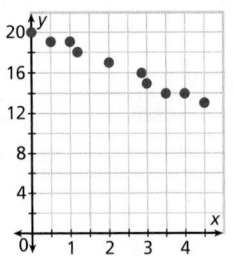

(F) The age of a child and the number of toys he or she owns

(G) The number of years in college and the amount of student loans

(H) The number of hours spent practicing and the number of errors on a typing test

(J) The duration of a movie and the cost in millions of dollars to produce it

DAY 5

What transformation of the graph of $f(x) = x$ is the graph of $g(x) = 4x$?

(A) Vertical stretch by a factor of 4

(B) Translation 4 units up

(C) Horizontal stretch by a factor of 4

(D) Translation 4 units right

DAY 1

If $A = \frac{1}{2}bh$, what is the value of A when $b = 10x^3y^2$ and $h = 15x^{-2}y^4$?

Ⓐ $75x^{-1}y^6$ Ⓒ $3xy^8$

Ⓑ $75xy^6$ Ⓓ $150x^5y^2$

DAY 2

What are all the real-number solutions of the equation $3x^4 - x^3 = 12x^2 - 4x$?

Ⓕ $-2, 0, 2$ Ⓗ $-2, 0, 2, 3$

Ⓖ $-2, -\frac{1}{3}, 0, 2$ Ⓙ $-2, \frac{1}{3}, 0, 2$

DAY 3

The graph shows the number of survival kits s a company sells after d days. Which function can best be used to model the data?

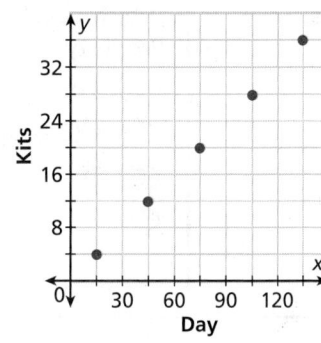

Ⓐ $s = \frac{1}{15}d + 4$ Ⓑ $s = \frac{1}{3}d - 1$ Ⓒ $s = \frac{4}{15}d$ Ⓓ $s = \frac{1}{5}d$

DAY 4

What is the equation of the graph shown?

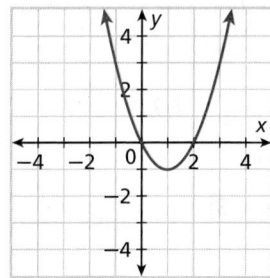

Ⓕ $y = (x - 1)^2 - 1$

Ⓖ $y = (x + 1)^2 - 1$

Ⓗ $y = (x - 1)^2 + 1$

Ⓙ $y = (x + 1)^2 + 1$

DAY 5

The graph represents which system of linear inequalities?

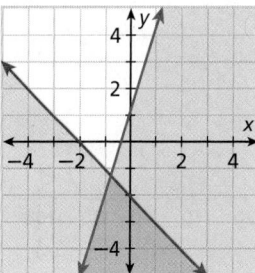

Ⓐ $\begin{cases} y \le 3x + 1 \\ y \le -x - 2 \end{cases}$ Ⓒ $\begin{cases} y < 3x + 1 \\ y < -x - 2 \end{cases}$

Ⓑ $\begin{cases} y \le x + 3 \\ y \le -2x - 1 \end{cases}$ Ⓓ $\begin{cases} y < x + 3 \\ y < -2x - 1 \end{cases}$

DAY 1

Which equation fits the data in the table?

x	−3	−1	1	3	5
y	0.125	0.5	2	8	32

(A) $y = 2x$ (B) $y = x^2$ (C) $y = 2^x$ (D) $\log_2 x$

DAY 2

A polynomial function of degree 6 has roots -1, 4, $2 - \sqrt{3}$, and $1 + 3i$. Which of the following is an additional real root?

(F) 1

(G) −4

(H) $2 + \sqrt{3}$

(J) $1 - 3i$

DAY 3

Which best illustrates the Associative Property?

(A) $3x^2 + 5x^2 - 6 = 3x^2 - 6 + 5x^2$

(B) $x^2(3 + 5) - 6 = (3x^2 + 5x^2) - 6$

(C) $3x^2 + (5x^2 - 6) = (3x^2 + 5x^2) - 6$

(D) $3x^2 + (5x^2 - 6) = (-6 + 3x^2) + 5x^2$

DAY 4

The position of a moving dot on a computer screen over time is given by the graph. What is the domain of this function?

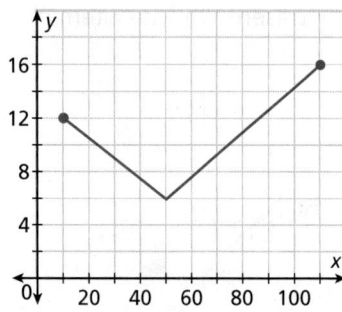

(F) $\{x \mid 5 \le x \le 40\}$

(G) $\{x \mid x \ge 10\}$

(H) $\{x \mid 12 \le x \le 16\}$

(J) $\{x \mid 10 \le x \le 110\}$

DAY 5

The graph shown represents which function?

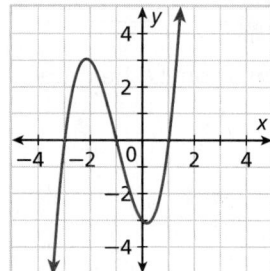

(A) $(x^2 - 1)(x + 3)$

(B) $(x^2 - 1)(x - 3)$

(C) $(x^2 - 9)(x - 1)$

(D) $(x^2 - 9)(x^2 - 1)$

DAY 1

What is the range of the function
$y = -(2x - 1)^2 + 3$?

Ⓐ $\{y \mid y \leq 3\}$

Ⓑ $\{y \mid y \geq 3\}$

Ⓒ all real numbers except $\frac{1}{2}$

Ⓓ all real numbers

DAY 2

By inspecting the polynomial function below, which of the following can you immediately rule out as a possible rational zero?

$$y = 3x^3 - 2x^2 + 2x + 3$$

Ⓕ 1

Ⓖ −3

Ⓗ $\frac{1}{3}$

Ⓙ $\frac{1}{2}$

DAY 3

Which is an extraneous solution obtained when you solve the radical equation $\sqrt{x - 3} + 2 = \sqrt{7 - x}$ by squaring?

Ⓐ 0

Ⓑ 3

Ⓒ 4

Ⓓ 7

DAY 4

Which ordered pair is the solution of the following system?

$$\begin{cases} 3x - 5y = 12 \\ 2x = 4 + 5y \end{cases}$$

Ⓕ $\left(8, 2\frac{2}{5}\right)$

Ⓖ $\left(3\frac{1}{5}, 2\frac{4}{5}\right)$

Ⓗ $\left(16, 7\frac{1}{5}\right)$

Ⓙ $\left(3\frac{2}{5}, \frac{12}{25}\right)$

DAY 5

Teresa has two identical CD binders that are partly filled with CDs.
How much does each binder weigh when empty, to the nearest ounce?

Ⓐ 1 oz   Ⓒ 24 oz

Ⓑ 2 oz   Ⓓ 26 oz

contains 30 CDs
weight: 41 oz

contains 75 CDs
weight: 66.5 oz

DAY 1

What is the range of the function
$f(x) = -2|x|$?

(A) $y > 0$

(B) $y \leq 0$

(C) $y \leq -2$

(D) All real numbers

DAY 2

What is the solution of the system?

$$\begin{cases} 0.5x + 2.5y = -6.4 \\ 2x - 5y = 19.4 \end{cases}$$

(F) $(10.7, 2.1)$

(G) $(4.\overline{3}, 2.15)$

(H) $(2.2, -3)$

(J) $(0.8, -3.56)$

DAY 3

The time to download a software update varies inversely with the speed of the
Internet connection. An update downloads in 1 minute 20 seconds when the
download speed is 1.5 megabytes per second. Which is the best prediction of the
time that will be required for the update to download on a high-speed connection
that has a speed of 24 megabytes per second?

(A) 3.3 s

(B) 5 s

(C) 53 s

(D) 21 min 20 s

DAY 4

What is the average rate of change over
the domain interval [4, 6] of a set of data
that can be modeled by the function
$y = -16t^2 + 36t + 400$ over the interval?

(F) 40

(G) −124

(H) −228

(J) −248

DAY 5

What is the equation of the line through
the origin that is perpendicular to $\overleftrightarrow{AB}$?

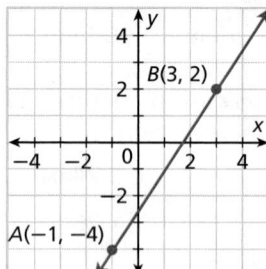

(A) $y = \frac{2}{3}x$

(C) $y = \frac{3}{2}x$

(B) $y = -\frac{2}{3}x$

(D) $y = -\frac{3}{2}x$

DAY 1

Which function is shown in the graph?

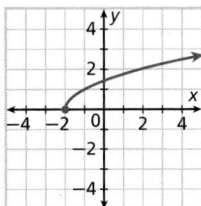

Ⓐ $f(x) = \sqrt{x} + 2$ Ⓒ $f(x) = 2\sqrt{x}$

Ⓑ $f(x) = \sqrt{x + 2}$ Ⓓ $f(x) = \sqrt{x - 2}$

DAY 2

Which equation represents the following relationship:

"p varies directly with q and inversely with r."

Ⓕ $p = \frac{kr}{q}$

Ⓖ $\frac{pq}{r} = k$

Ⓗ $\frac{pr}{q} = k$

Ⓙ $p = \frac{qr}{k}$

DAY 3

Which is the graph of $f(x) = 3x^2 - 1$?

Ⓐ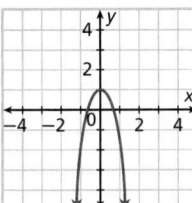

Ⓒ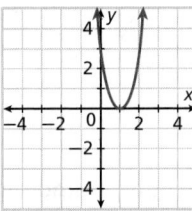

Ⓑ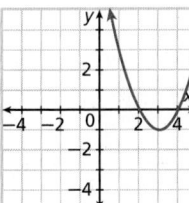

Ⓓ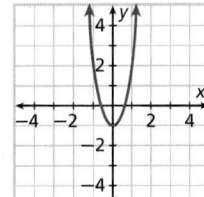

DAY 4

Between which two numbers does the polynomial function $2x^3 - 4x^2 + x - 5$ have a real zero?

Ⓕ $x = 0$ and $x = 1$

Ⓖ $x = 1$ and $x = 2$

Ⓗ $x = 2$ and $x = 3$

Ⓙ $x = 3$ and $x = 4$

DAY 5

The equation of a least-squares line is $y \approx 0.15x - 0.21$. Predict the x-value that corresponds to a y-value of 20.

Ⓐ 95.24

Ⓑ 131.93

Ⓒ 134.73

Ⓓ 175.13

DAY 1

What is the range of the function
$f(x) = -\frac{1}{4}|x - 2|$?

Ⓐ $y \le 0$

Ⓑ $y > 0$

Ⓒ $y \le -2$

Ⓓ $y > 2$

DAY 2

Which line is *not* an asymptote of the graph of the function $y = \frac{1.5\,(x - 1)(x + 3)}{x^2 - 4}$?

Ⓕ $x = 1$

Ⓖ $y = 1.5$

Ⓗ $x = -2$

Ⓙ $x = 2$

DAY 3

Which is a true statement about the rational function $f(x) = \frac{2x^3}{1 - x^2}$?

Ⓐ The function is an increasing function over all values of its domain.

Ⓑ The function is an even function.

Ⓒ The end behavior of the graph is $f(x) \to -\infty$ as $x \to -\infty$ and $f(x) \to +\infty$ as $x \to +\infty$.

Ⓓ The graph has two vertical asymptotes and one horizontal asymptote.

DAY 4

Which value is equivalent to
$30 \div 2 + \sqrt{64} - 4^3(8 - 4)^{-2}$?

Ⓕ -1

Ⓖ 13

Ⓗ 19

Ⓙ 535

DAY 5

The graph shown represents which parent function?

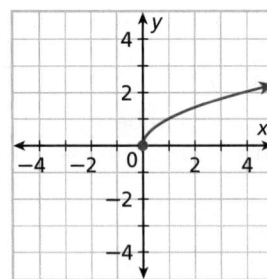

Ⓐ $f(x) = \sqrt{x}$

Ⓑ $f(x) = x^2$

Ⓒ $f(x) = 2$

Ⓓ $f(x) = x^3$

DAY 1

How is the graph of $g(x) = |x| - 4$ transformed from the graph of $f(x) = |x|$?

Ⓐ The graph of f is translated 4 units up.

Ⓑ The graph of f is translated 4 units down.

Ⓒ The graph of f is translated 4 units right.

Ⓓ The graph of f is translated 4 units left.

DAY 2

Which expression represents the coefficient of the sixth term in the expansion of $(m + n)^9$?

Ⓕ ${}_9C_5$

Ⓖ ${}_9C_6$

Ⓗ ${}_9C_7$

Ⓙ ${}_6C_9$

DAY 3

The following graph represents which table of data?

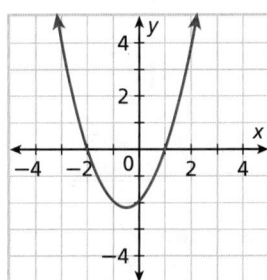

Ⓐ
x	−2	−1	0	1
$f(x)$	2	−2	2	1

Ⓒ
x	−2	−1	0	1
$f(x)$	0	−2	−2	0

Ⓑ
x	0	−2	−2	0
$f(x)$	−2	−1	0	1

Ⓓ
x	−2	−1	0	1
$f(x)$	−1	0	1	2

DAY 4

What is the domain of the function $f(x) = -\frac{1}{2}|x - 4|$?

Ⓕ All real numbers

Ⓖ $x < 0$

Ⓗ $x \geq -2$

Ⓙ $x > 4$

DAY 5

How is the graph of $g(x) = 2(x + 1)^2$ transformed from the graph of $f(x) = x^2$?

Ⓐ The graph of f is translated 2 units left and 1 unit up.

Ⓑ The graph of f is vertically compressed by a factor of $\frac{1}{2}$ and translated 1 unit left.

Ⓒ The graph of f is vertically stretched by a factor of 2 and translated 1 unit up.

Ⓓ The graph of f is vertically stretched by a factor of 2 and translated 1 unit left.

DAY 1

Which of the following best describes the correlation found in the scatter plot?

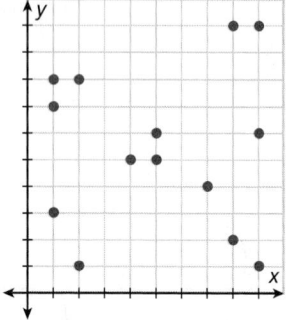

(A) Strong positive correlation

(B) Weak positive correlation

(C) No correlation

(D) Negative correlation

DAY 2

Which of the following best describes how to graph the function $f(x) = (x - 7)^2 + 3$?

(F) Move the parent function to the right 7 units and up 3 units.

(G) Move the parent function to the right 3 units and down 7 units.

(H) Move the parent function to the left 7 units and up 3 units.

(J) Move the parent function to the right 7 units and down 3 units.

DAY 3

Which situation is best represented by the data?

t	0	0.5	1	1.5	2	2.5
$f(t)$	112	108	96	76	48	12

(A) The distance decreases by 4 miles for every 30 seconds traveled.

(B) The height of an object above ground decreases nonlinearly over time.

(C) As the time increases, the speed of a car increases at a constant rate.

(D) As the time increases, the distance traveled decreases at a constant rate.

DAY 4

Which function is equivalent to $f(x) = 30x^2 + 2x - 56$?

(F) $f(x) = (3x - 4)(5x + 14)$

(G) $f(x) = 2(3x + 4)(5x - 7)$

(H) $f(x) = (6x - 4)(5x + 7)$

(J) $f(x) = 2(3x - 4)(5x + 7)$

DAY 5

The height h of a football t seconds after it is kicked is given by $h(t) = -16t^2 + 40t$. What is a reasonable real-world domain for the situation?

(A) all positive real numbers

(B) all real numbers between 0 and 3

(C) all real numbers between 0 and 2.5

(D) all real numbers between 0 and 1.25

DAY 1

The length x of a rectangle is 6 feet longer than its width. What is a reasonable domain for the function that represents the area of the rectangle?

Ⓐ all real numbers

Ⓑ all positive numbers

Ⓒ $x > 6$

Ⓓ $0 \le x \le 6$

DAY 2

Which quadratic equation has no real-number solutions?

Ⓕ $x^2 - 8x + 16 = 0$

Ⓖ $4x^2 - 12x + 9 = 0$

Ⓗ $-x^2 + 4x - 5 = 0$

Ⓙ $x^2 - 3x - 7 = 0$

DAY 3

The function $P = (h - 3)^2 + 174$ models the power, in megawatts, generated between midnight and noon by a power plant, where h represents hours after midnight. How would the graph of the function change if the minimum power generated increased to 250 megawatts?

Ⓐ The vertex would change to (3, 250).

Ⓑ The vertex would change to (250, 174).

Ⓒ The graph of the function would be reflected over the x-axis.

Ⓓ The graph of the function would be horizontally compressed.

DAY 4

To solve the equation $0 = x^2 + 7x - 26$ by completing the square, the first step is to add 26 to both sides of the equation. Which statement best describes the second step?

Ⓕ Add $\frac{9}{4}$ to both sides.

Ⓖ Square the product of 7 and 2.

Ⓗ Take half of 7 and square it.

Ⓙ Rewrite the perfect square trinomial as a binomial squared.

DAY 5

Which quadratic inequality best represents the graph?

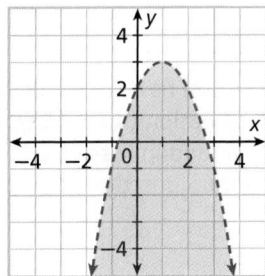

Ⓐ $y < -x^2 + 2x + 2$

Ⓑ $y > x^2 + 2x + 2$

Ⓒ $y \le -x^2 + 2x + 2$

Ⓓ $y < x^2 - 2x + 2$

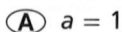

DAY 1

The equation of the graph shown has the form

$y = a\sqrt[3]{x} + b$, where a and b are constants. Which is true?

Ⓐ $a = 1$

Ⓑ $a < 0$

Ⓒ $b > 0$

Ⓓ $b = 0$

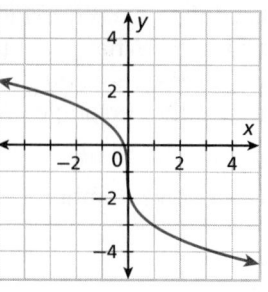

DAY 2

Which best describes $g(x) = \sqrt{2(x - 1)} + 4$ as a transformation of $f(x) = \sqrt{x}$?

Ⓕ g is f horizontally compressed by a factor of $\frac{1}{2}$ and translated left 1 unit and up 4 units.

Ⓖ g is f horizontally stretched by a factor of 2 and translated right 1 unit and up 4 units.

Ⓗ g is f horizontally compressed by a factor of $\frac{1}{2}$ and translated right 1 unit and up 4 units.

Ⓙ g is f horizontally stretched by a factor of 2 and translated left 1 unit and down 4 units.

DAY 3

Which statement is true of the function $f(x) = \frac{1}{5}x + 6$?

Ⓐ $f(x)$ is an odd function.

Ⓑ $f(x)$ is an always increasing function.

Ⓒ $f(x)$ is an always decreasing function.

Ⓓ $f(x)$ is always greater than x.

DAY 4

A normal distribution has a mean of 14 and a standard deviation of 2.5. What is the probability that a randomly-selected x-value from the distribution is in the interval [11.5, 19]?

Ⓕ 0.32

Ⓖ 0.68

Ⓗ 0.815

Ⓙ 0.95

DAY 5

A speaker wants to have a sample of the 400 people sitting in an audience answer a question. The speaker hands each of the 20 people in the first row a slip of paper with the question, and has them answer it and put the paper in a box. Which best describes the sample?

Ⓐ self-selected

Ⓑ random

Ⓒ convenience

Ⓓ systematic

DAY 1

What are the solutions of the equation $3x^2 - 6x - 7 = 0$?

(A) $x = \dfrac{3 \pm 2i\sqrt{3}}{3}$

(B) $x \approx 2.8$ and $x \approx -0.8$

(C) $x \approx 17$ and $x \approx -5$

(D) $x \approx 3.2$ and $x \approx -0.6$

DAY 2

Which function best represents the data in the table?

x	−2	−1	0	1	2	3
$f(x)$	25	13	5	1	1	5

(F) $f(x) = 2x^2 - 6x + 5$

(G) $f(x) = -2x^2 - 6x + 8$

(H) $f(x) = x^2 - 6x + 5$

(J) $f(x) = 2x^2 - 9x + 5$

DAY 3

The graph can be used to determine the solutions to which quadratic equation?

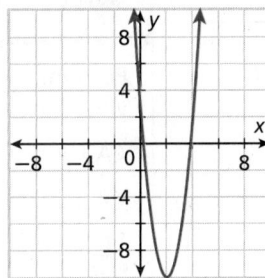

(A) $x^2 - 5x + 4 = 0$

(C) $3x^2 - 13x + 4 = 0$

(B) $3x^2 - 7x + 2 = 0$

(D) $3x^2 - 8x + 4 = 0$

DAY 4

At the beginning of a basketball game, the referee tosses the ball into the air with an initial vertical velocity of 24 feet per second. The ball's initial height is 5 feet above the floor. Which inequality can be used to find the time interval t for which the height of the ball is greater than 10 feet?

(F) $-16t^2 + 24t + 5 < 10$

(G) $-16t^2 + 24t + 5 > 10$

(H) $24t^2 - 16t + 5 > 10$

(J) $24t + 5 > 10$

DAY 5

The function $P = -16(c - 25)^2 + 10,000$ models the profit the student council makes from a dance, where c is the cost per ticket in dollars. How does the graph of the function change if the maximum profit is made by selling the tickets for $40?

(A) The graph of the function would be reflected over the y-axis.

(B) The vertex would change to $(25, 40)$.

(C) The vertex would change to $(40, 10,000)$.

(D) The graph of the function would not change.

DAY 1

Which graph could represent a polynomial function of degree 5 whose leading coefficient is positive?

(A)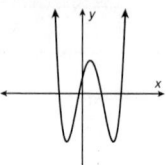

(C)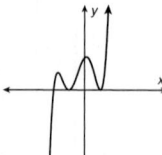

(B)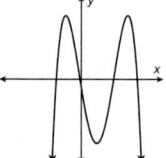

(D)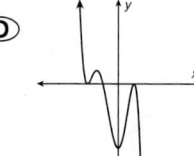

DAY 2

In chemistry, pH = $-\log[H^+]$, where $[H^+]$ is the hydrogen ion concentration of a solution in moles per liter. What is $[H^+]$ of a carbonated soda if its pH is 1.5?

(F) $10^{-1.5}$

(G) $10^{1.5}$

(H) $-\log 1.5$

(J) $-\log(-1.5)$

DAY 3

For which of the following functions does y vary inversely as x?

(A) $y = \frac{x}{2}$

(B) $y = -7x$

(C) $10 = xy$

(D) $y = x^0 - 15$

DAY 4

The distance a spring stretches varies directly as the amount of weight hanging from it. A weight of 60 pounds stretches the spring 15 centimeters. How heavy is the weight hanging on the spring when it stretches 12 centimeters?

(F) 3 pounds

(G) 12 pounds

(H) 48 pounds

(J) 52 pounds

DAY 5

The graph represents which parent function?

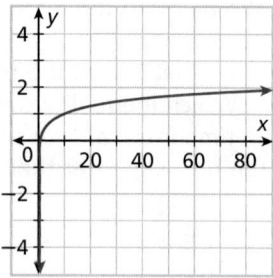

(A) $y = x^2$

(B) $y = x$

(C) $y = \log x$

(D) $y = e^x$

DAY 1

The area of a rectangular parking lot with a length of 1500 feet can be no more than 3,000,000 square feet. Which is the most reasonable domain of the function representing the parking lot's area A in square feet in terms of its width w in feet?

Ⓐ $0 < w \leq 1500$

Ⓑ $0 < w \leq 2000$

Ⓒ $1500 < w \leq 2000$

Ⓓ $1500 < w \leq 3,000,000$

DAY 2

Which ordered pair is NOT a solution of the exponential inequality shown in the graph?

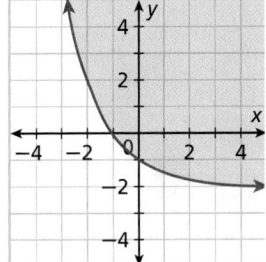

Ⓕ $(2, -2)$

Ⓖ $(5, 1)$

Ⓗ $(3, 3)$

Ⓙ $(0, 4)$

DAY 3

Which is *not* an essential characteristic of a randomized comparative experiment?

Ⓐ a statistical measure that can be tracked in a group over time

Ⓑ a randomly chosen control group composed of individuals to whom no treatment is applied

Ⓒ a randomly chosen experimental or treatment group composed of individuals to whom a treatment is applied

Ⓓ a statistical measure that can be compared between the control group and treatment group

DAY 4

Which function represents the graph of $f(x) = \ln x$ translated 2 units right and 5 units up?

Ⓕ $g(x) = \ln(x + 2) - 5$

Ⓖ $g(x) = \ln(x + 5) - 2$

Ⓗ $g(x) = \ln(x - 2) + 5$

Ⓙ $g(x) = \ln(x - 5) + 2$

DAY 5

Which ordered pair is a solution of the inequality $y > -(x - 3)^2 + 8$?

Ⓐ $(5, 0)$

Ⓑ $(5, 1)$

Ⓒ $(5, 4)$

Ⓓ $(5, 6)$

DAY 1

The radius of a circle can be determined by dividing the area by π and taking the square root of the result. Which graph best shows the radius as a function of the area?

(A)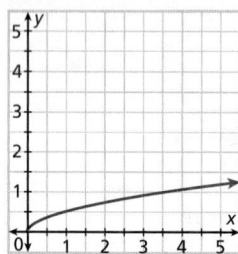

(C)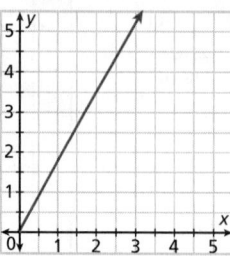

(B)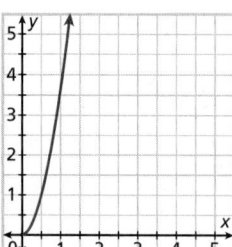

(D)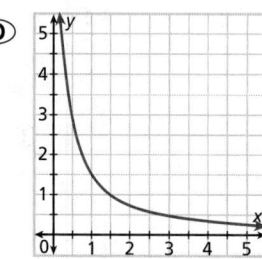

DAY 2

A section of seats in a stadium has 9 seats in the first row. With each successive row, the number of seats in the row increases by 2. There are 9 rows of seats in the section. How many seats are in the section in all?

(F) 136

(G) 153

(H) 162

(J) 180

DAY 3

What function best represents the data in the table?

x	f(x)
0	−2
1	−1
4	0
9	1
16	2

(A) $f(x) = x - 2$

(C) $f(x) = \sqrt{x - 2}$

(B) $f(x) = (x - 2)^2$

(D) $f(x) = \sqrt{x} - 2$

DAY 4

How does the graph of $g(x) = \sqrt{-x}$ differ from the graph of $f(x) = \sqrt{x}$?

(F) The graph is reflected across the x-axis.

(G) The graph is reflected across the y-axis.

(H) The graph is rotated 180° about the origin.

(J) The graph is shifted 4 units down.

DAY 5

Where does a hole occur in the graph of
$$f(x) = \frac{(x + 4)(x - 6)}{(x + 2)(x - 6)(x + 3)}?$$

(A) $x = 6$

(B) $x = 2$

(C) $x = -3$

(D) $x = -4$

DAY 1

The speed of a sound wave traveling through a thin rod is given by the formula $v = \sqrt{\dfrac{Y}{p}}$, where v is the speed of the waves in meters per second, Y is 8.0×10^{10} pascals, and p is the density of the rod in kilograms per cubic meter. If you know the value of v, which equation can you use to determine p?

(A) $p = \sqrt{\dfrac{Y}{v}}$

(B) $p = \dfrac{Y}{v^2}$

(C) $p = \dfrac{\sqrt{Y}}{v}$

(D) $p = (Yv)^2$

DAY 2

Martha invested $12,000 and earned $840 in interest in one year. She invested some of the money in an account that pays 8% per year and the rest of it in an account that pays 5% per year. Which system can be used to find the amount she invested at each rate?

(F) $\begin{cases} x - y = 12{,}000 \\ 0.08x - 0.05y = 840 \end{cases}$

(G) $\begin{cases} y = 12{,}000 - x \\ 0.08x + 0.05y = 12{,}000 - 840 \end{cases}$

(H) $\begin{cases} xy = 12{,}000 \\ 0.08x - 0.05y = 840 \end{cases}$

(J) $\begin{cases} y = 12{,}000 - x \\ 0.08x - 0.05y = 840 \end{cases}$

DAY 3

Which is the graph of $f(x) = \ln x$?

(A)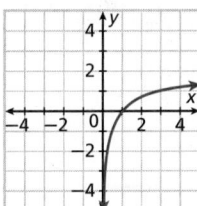

(C)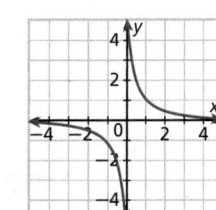

(B)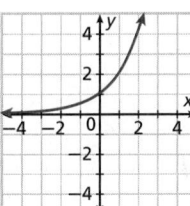

(D)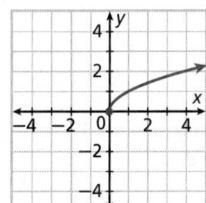

DAY 4

Which function represents a reflection of $f(x) = 2^x$ across the y-axis?

(F) $g(x) = -2^x$ (H) $g(x) = 2^{-x}$

(G) $g(x) = \left(\dfrac{1}{2}\right)^x$ (J) $g(x) = \left(\dfrac{1}{x}\right)^2$

DAY 5

Which equation is equivalent to $12^{-x} = 24$?

(A) $\log_{24} 12 = x$ (C) $\log_{12} 24 = -x$

(B) $\log_x 24 = 12$ (D) $\log_{-x} 12 = 24$

DAY 1

The range of a quadratic function is $\{y|y \le 4\}$. What is the range of the same function after a translation of 3 units up?

Ⓐ $\{y|y \le 1\}$

Ⓑ $\{y|y \ge 1\}$

Ⓒ $\{y|y \le 7\}$

Ⓓ $\{y|y \ge 7\}$

DAY 2

Which function represents a translation of $f(x) = 2^x$ six units right?

Ⓕ $g(x) = 2^x - 6$

Ⓖ $g(x) = 2^{x-x}$

Ⓗ $g(x) = 2^x + 6$

Ⓙ $g(x) = 2^{x+6}$

DAY 3

What is the domain of the function $f(x) = -\sqrt{7 - x}$?

Ⓐ $x \ge -7$

Ⓑ $x \le -7$

Ⓒ $x \ge 7$

Ⓓ $x \le 7$

DAY 4

Which transformation was NOT applied to the graph of $f(x) = \sqrt{x}$ to obtain $g(x) = -4\sqrt{6(x + 3)}$?

Ⓕ Vertical translation 3 units up

Ⓖ Reflection across the x-axis

Ⓗ Vertical stretch by a factor of 4

Ⓙ Horizontal compression by a factor of $\frac{1}{6}$.

DAY 5

Which quadratic function is represented by the graph?

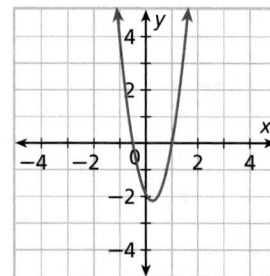

Ⓐ $f(x) = 4x^2 - 2x - 2$

Ⓑ $f(x) = x^2 - 2$

Ⓒ $f(x) = (x + 1)(x - 1)$

Ⓓ $f(x) = (x - 2)^2 - 2$

DAY 1

Francisco wants to make a scatter plot to determine if there is a correlation between duration of a construction highway project and the number of managers assigned to the project. Which table would be best for Francisco to organize his findings?

Ⓐ
Duration of Project			
Manager Names			

Ⓑ
Number of Managers			
Project Number			

Ⓒ
Duration of Project			
Number of Managers			

Ⓓ
Project Number			
Manager Names			

DAY 2

Bobby is on a biking trip that consists of 55 miles on paved roads and 18 miles on unpaved roads. He is able to bike twice as fast on paved roads as on unpaved roads. Which function represents the total time T in hours that Bobby needs to complete the trip in terms of his average speed on unpaved roads x in miles per hour?

Ⓕ $T(x) = \dfrac{55}{x} + \dfrac{18}{2x}$

Ⓖ $T(x) = \dfrac{55}{2x} + \dfrac{18}{x}$

Ⓗ $T(x) = \dfrac{55}{x} - \dfrac{37}{2x}$

Ⓙ $T(x) = \dfrac{55}{x} - \dfrac{18}{2x}$

DAY 3

The graph of the inequality $y \geq -(x - 3)^2 + 8$ is shown below. Which of the given points is not in the solution region?

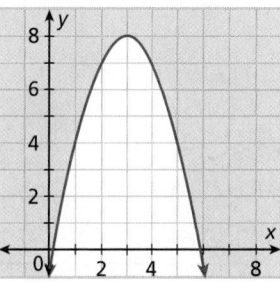

Ⓐ $(-2, -3)$ Ⓒ $(3, 4)$

Ⓑ $(1, 7)$ Ⓓ $(6, 5)$

DAY 4

Solve $\sqrt{x + 14} \leq x - 16$.

Ⓕ $x \geq 16$

Ⓖ $-16 \leq x \leq 22$

Ⓗ $x \leq -22$

Ⓙ $x \geq 22$

DAY 5

What is the relationship between the graph of the function $y = x^2 - 4x$ and the graph of its inverse?

Ⓐ Reflection across the line $y = x$

Ⓑ Translation of 4 units down

Ⓒ 180° rotation about the origin

Ⓓ Vertical stretch by a factor of 4

DAY 1

What is the domain of $f(x) = \dfrac{3x + 5}{x^2 + 3x - 18}$?

(A) All real numbers

(B) All real numbers except −6

(C) All real numbers except 3

(D) All real numbers except 3 and −6

DAY 2

Which is the sum of the geometric series represented by the expression

$$\sum_{i=1}^{8} 3(2)^{i-1}?$$

(F) 384

(G) 387

(H) 765

(J) 768

DAY 3

Which parent function is shown in the graph?

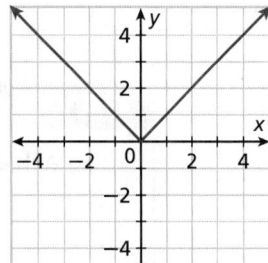

(A) $f(x) = e^x$

(B) $f(x) = \ln x$

(C) $f(x) = \sqrt{x}$

(D) $f(x) = |x|$

DAY 4

Which function does NOT include the values −2, 4, 8, and 12 in the domain?

(F) $f(x) = \sqrt{12x + 24}$

(G) $f(x) = \sqrt{7(x - 4)}$

(H) $f(x) = \sqrt{x^2 + 5x + 6}$

(J) $f(x) = \sqrt{\dfrac{2}{x^2 + 1}}$

DAY 5

A parabola is a conic section formed by the intersection of a plane and a(n) _____.

(A) circle

(B) hyperbola

(C) double cone

(D) ellipse

DAY 1

Which graph can be used to determine the solution of $x^2 = \sqrt{2x}$?

Ⓐ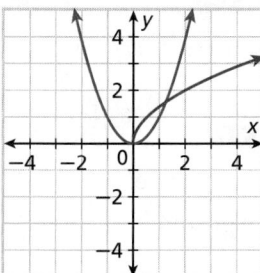

Ⓒ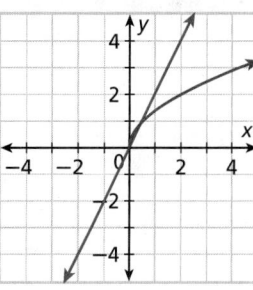

Ⓑ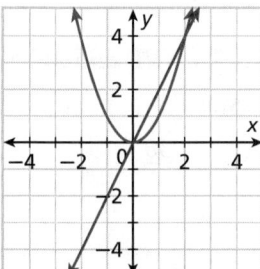

Ⓓ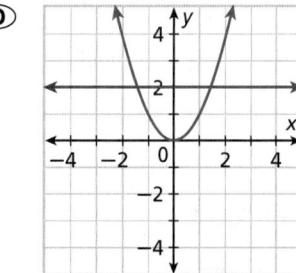

DAY 2

Solve $\dfrac{x}{x-2} = \dfrac{3x}{x+2}$.

Ⓕ $x = 2$ or $x = -2$

Ⓖ $x = 0$ or $x = 3$

Ⓗ $x = 0$ or $x = 4$

Ⓙ No real solution

DAY 3

The population of Warren County is 55,000 and is growing at a rate of 3.8% per decade. Which of the following expressions represents the population of Warren County after n decades?

Ⓐ $55{,}000(3.8)^n$

Ⓑ $55{,}000(1.38)^n$

Ⓒ $55{,}000(1.038)^n$

Ⓓ $55{,}000 + (3.8)^n$

DAY 4

What value of x makes the equation $3 = 1 + \log(2x)$ true?

Ⓕ 1

Ⓖ 10

Ⓗ 50

Ⓙ 100

DAY 5

The equation $\dfrac{x^2}{100} - \dfrac{y^2}{64} = 1$ represents which conic section?

Ⓐ Circle

Ⓑ Hyperbola

Ⓒ Parabola

Ⓓ Ellipse

Skills Readiness

Pre-Course Test

SQUARES AND SQUARE ROOTS

Find the square root.

1. $\sqrt{196}$ **2.** $\sqrt{121}$

EVALUATE POWERS

Find the value of the expression.

3. 3^4 **4.** $2^6 + 6^2$

FRACTIONS, DECIMALS, AND PERCENTS

Write the equivalent decimal and percent.

5. $\dfrac{76}{100}$ **6.** $\dfrac{15}{25}$

7. $\dfrac{4}{5}$ **8.** $\dfrac{3}{8}$

COMPARE AND ORDER REAL NUMBERS

Order the numbers from least to greatest.

9. $\dfrac{4}{10}$, 65%, $\dfrac{4}{5}$, 0.63

10. 1.8, $\dfrac{13}{7}$, 170%, $1\dfrac{3}{4}$

GRAPH NUMBERS ON A NUMBER LINE

Graph the numbers on the same number line.

11. 3.5 **12.** -0.5

13. 2.3 **14.** -1.2

CONVERT UNITS OF MEASURE

Convert the unit of measure.

15. 2.7 kilograms to grams

16. 4.5 feet to inches

SIMPLIFY RADICAL EXPRESSIONS

Simplify the expression.

17. $\sqrt{169} \cdot \sqrt{16}$ **18.** $\sqrt{\dfrac{36}{81}}$

ORDER OF OPERATIONS

Evaluate the expression.

19. $6 + 2 \cdot 3$ **20.** $(6 + 5)^2 - 8$

CONNECT WORDS AND ALGEBRA

21. Write an expression that represents a number x divided by 9.

22. Jaylynn collected 28 postcards. Every month, she collects 4 more postcards. Write an equation representing the number of postcards p that Jaylynn has collected at the end of m months.

PROPERTIES OF EXPONENTS

Simplify the expression.

23. $3b \cdot 4b^2$

24. $-6e^2 \cdot 4e$

25. $16g^2h \cdot 4gh$

26. $-6st \cdot 3t \cdot 4s$

MULTIPLY BINOMIALS

Multiply.

27. $(x + 2)(x + 7)$

28. $(y - 3)(y + 4)$

29. $(2z + 1)(2z - 5)$

SOLVE ONE-STEP EQUATIONS

Solve.

30. $g + 7 = -8$ **31.** $\frac{n}{5} = 15$

SOLVE MULTI-STEP EQUATIONS

Solve.

32. $6d + 9 = 45$ **33.** $7 + \frac{z}{4} = 14$

SOLVE EQUATIONS WITH VARIABLES ON BOTH SIDES

Solve.

34. $4h + 7 = 7h - 8$ **35.** $10j - 10 = 3j - 5$

SOLVE EQUATIONS WITH FRACTIONS

Solve.

36. $p - \frac{8}{10} = -\frac{3}{10}$ **37.** $\frac{4}{5}y + 8 = 20$

SOLVE AND GRAPH INEQUALITIES

Solve and graph the inequality.

38. $h - 3 > -7$ **39.** $-3j \leq -12$

GRAPH LINEAR FUNCTIONS

Graph the function.

40. $y = -3x + 5$ **41.** $y = \frac{2}{3}x - 5$

SLOPES OF PARALLEL AND PERPENDICULAR LINES

State whether the graphs of the linear equations in each pair are *parallel*, *perpendicular*, or *neither*.

42. $y = \frac{1}{5}x - 8$ **43.** $4y - 5x = 10$

$ y = -5x + 4$ $ 5y - 4x = -20$

44. $y = \frac{4}{5}x - 6$ **45.** $x = 1$

$ 5y = 4x - 15$ $ y = 2$

GRAPH FUNCTIONS

Graph the function for the given domain.

46. $y = (x + 3)^2$

D: $\{-5, -4, -3, -2, -1\}$

47. $y = x^2 - 4$

D: $\{-2, -1, 0, 1, 2\}$

SOLVE QUADRATIC EQUATIONS

Solve the equation.

48. $6x^2 = 96$

49. $5x^2 = 192 + 2x^2$

50. $3x^2 - 40 = 203$

1 Quadratic Functions and Factoring

COMMON CORE

Lesson
1.1 CC.9-12.F.IF.7a*
1.2 CC.9-12.F.IF.7a*
1.3 CC.9-12.A.SSE.3a*
1.4 CC.9-12.A.SSE.3a*
1.5 CC.9-12.A.REI.4b
1.6 CC.9-12.N.CN.2
1.7 CC.9-12.A.REI.4a
1.8 CC.9-12.N.CN.7
1.9 CC.9-12.A.REI.4b

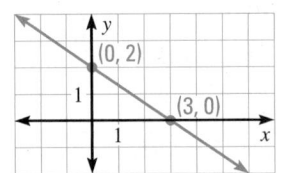

Before

Previously, you learned the following skills, which you'll use in this chapter: evaluating expressions, simplifying expressions, and solving equations.

Prerequisite Skills

VOCABULARY CHECK

Copy and complete the statement.

1. The **x-intercept** of the line shown is ___?___.

2. The **y-intercept** of the line shown is ___?___.

SKILLS CHECK

Evaluate the expression.

3. 1096^0 4. $(-5)^2$ 5. $7^2 + 2^0$ 6. $4^3 \div 2^3$

Simplify.

7. $(y + 3)(y + 2)$ 8. $(x - 4)(x + 6)$ 9. $(3h + 7)(h + 9)$ 10. $(4n - 10)(3n - 1)$

Solve the equation.

11. $2x + 1 = x$ 12. $5x - 7 = 2x$ 13. $4(x - 3) = x$ 14. $6(x - 5) = 4(2x - 1)$

In this chapter, you will apply the big ideas listed below and reviewed in the Chapter Summary. You will also use the key vocabulary listed below.

Big Ideas

1. Graphing and writing quadratic functions in several forms
2. Solving quadratic equations using a variety of methods
3. Performing operations with square roots and complex numbers

KEY VOCABULARY

- standard form of a quadratic function
- parabola
- vertex form
- intercept form
- quadratic equation

- root of an equation
- zero of a function
- square root
- complex number
- imaginary number

- completing the square
- quadratic formula
- discriminant

Why?

You can use quadratic functions to model the heights of projectiles. For example, the height of a baseball hit by a batter can be modeled by a quadratic function.

Animated Algebra

The animation illustrated below helps you answer a question from this chapter: How does changing the ball speed and hitting angle affect the maximum height of a baseball?

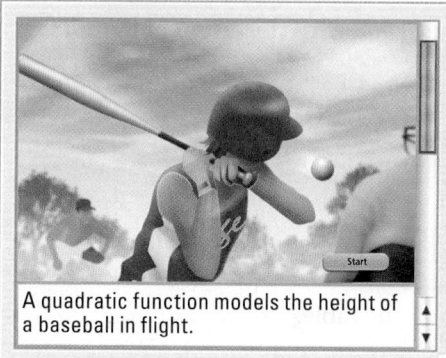

A quadratic function models the height of a baseball in flight.

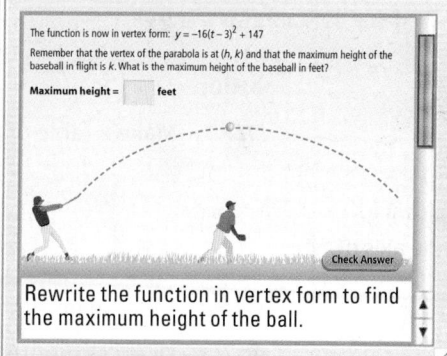

The function is now in vertex form: $y = -16(t - 3)^2 + 147$

Remember that the vertex of the parabola is at (h, k) and that the maximum height of the baseball in flight is k. What is the maximum height of the baseball in feet?

Maximum height = ____ feet

Check Answer

Rewrite the function in vertex form to find the maximum height of the ball.

Animated Algebra at my.hrw.com

1.1 Graph Quadratic Functions in Standard Form

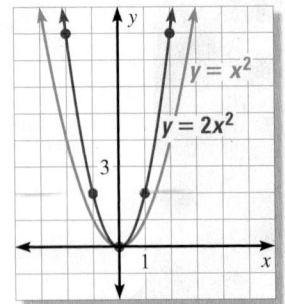

Before	You graphed linear functions.
Now	You will graph quadratic functions.
Why?	So you can model sports revenue, as in Example 5.

Key Vocabulary
- quadratic function
- parabola
- vertex
- axis of symmetry
- minimum value
- maximum value

CC.9-12.F.IF.7 Graph functions expressed symbolically and show key features of the graph, by hand in simple cases and using technology for more complicated cases.*
a. Graph linear and quadratic functions and show intercepts, maxima, and minima.

A **quadratic function** is a function that can be written in the **standard form** $y = ax^2 + bx + c$ where $a \neq 0$. The graph of a quadratic function is a **parabola**.

KEY CONCEPT   *For Your Notebook*

Parent Function for Quadratic Functions

The parent function for the family of all quadratic functions is $f(x) = x^2$. The graph of $f(x) = x^2$ is the parabola shown below.

The **lowest or highest point on a parabola is the vertex.** The vertex for $f(x) = x^2$ is (0, 0).

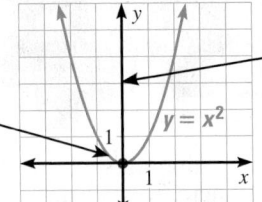

The **axis of symmetry** divides the parabola into mirror images and passes through the vertex.

For $f(x) = x^2$, and for any quadratic function $g(x) = ax^2 + bx + c$ where $b = 0$, the vertex lies on the y-axis and the axis of symmetry is $x = 0$.

EXAMPLE 1   Graph a function of the form $y = ax^2$

Graph $y = 2x^2$. Compare the graph with the graph of $y = x^2$.

Solution

STEP 1 **Make** a table of values for $y = 2x^2$.

SKETCH A GRAPH
Choose values of x on *both* sides of the axis of symmetry $x = 0$.

x	−2	−1	0	1	2
y	8	2	0	2	8

STEP 2 **Plot** the points from the table.

STEP 3 **Draw** a smooth curve through the points.

STEP 4 **Compare** the graphs of $y = 2x^2$ and $y = x^2$. Both open up and have the same vertex and axis of symmetry. The graph of $y = 2x^2$ is narrower than the graph of $y = x^2$.

EXAMPLE 2 **Graph a function of the form $y = ax^2 + c$**

Graph $y = -\frac{1}{2}x^2 + 3$. Compare the graph with the graph of $y = x^2$.

Solution

STEP 1 **Make** a table of values for $y = -\frac{1}{2}x^2 + 3$.

SKETCH A GRAPH
Choose values of x that are multiples of 2 so that the values of y will be integers.

x	−4	−2	0	2	4
y	−5	1	3	1	−5

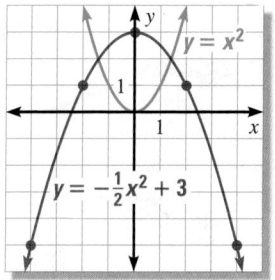

STEP 2 **Plot** the points from the table.

STEP 3 **Draw** a smooth curve through the points.

STEP 4 **Compare** the graphs of $y = -\frac{1}{2}x^2 + 3$ and $y = x^2$. Both graphs have the same axis of symmetry. However, the graph of $y = -\frac{1}{2}x^2 + 3$ opens down and is wider than the graph of $y = x^2$. Also, its vertex is 3 units higher.

✓ **GUIDED PRACTICE** for Examples 1 and 2

Graph the function. Compare the graph with the graph of $y = x^2$.

1. $y = -4x^2$ **2.** $y = -x^2 - 5$ **3.** $f(x) = \frac{1}{4}x^2 + 2$

GRAPHING ANY QUADRATIC FUNCTION You can use the following properties to graph *any* quadratic function $y = ax^2 + bx + c$, including a function where $b \neq 0$.

KEY CONCEPT *For Your Notebook*

Properties of the Graph of $y = ax^2 + bx + c$

$y = ax^2 + bx + c, a > 0$

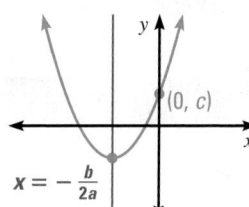

$y = ax^2 + bx + c, a < 0$

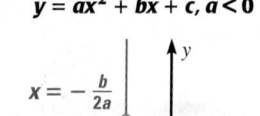
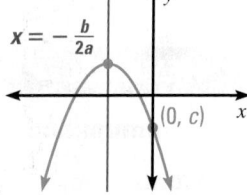

Characteristics of the graph of $y = ax^2 + bx + c$:

- The graph opens up if $a > 0$ and opens down if $a < 0$.
- The graph is narrower than the graph of $y = x^2$ if $|a| > 1$ and wider if $|a| < 1$.
- The axis of symmetry is $x = -\frac{b}{2a}$ and the vertex has x-coordinate $-\frac{b}{2a}$.
- The y-intercept is c. So, the point $(0, c)$ is on the parabola.

EXAMPLE 3 **Graph a function of the form** $y = ax^2 + bx + c$

Graph $y = 2x^2 - 8x + 6$.

Solution

STEP 1 **Identify** the coefficients of the function. The coefficients are $a = 2$, $b = -8$, and $c = 6$. Because $a > 0$, the parabola opens up.

STEP 2 **Find** the vertex. Calculate the x-coordinate.

$$x = -\frac{b}{2a} = -\frac{(-8)}{2(2)} = 2$$

Then find the y-coordinate of the vertex.

$$y = 2(2)^2 - 8(2) + 6 = -2$$

So, the vertex is $(2, -2)$. Plot this point.

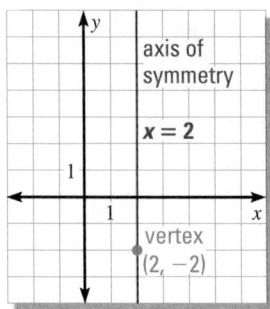

STEP 3 **Draw** the axis of symmetry $x = 2$.

STEP 4 **Identify** the y-intercept c, which is 6. Plot the point $(0, 6)$. Then reflect this point in the axis of symmetry to plot another point, $(4, 6)$.

STEP 5 **Evaluate** the function for another value of x, such as $x = 1$.

$$y = 2(1)^2 - 8(1) + 6 = 0$$

Plot the point $(1, 0)$ and its reflection $(3, 0)$ in the axis of symmetry.

STEP 6 **Draw** a parabola through the plotted points.

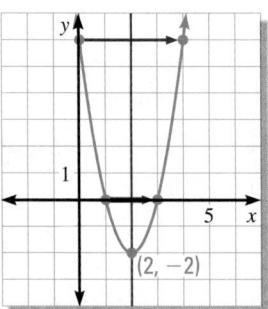

Animated Algebra at my.hrw.com

> **AVOID ERRORS**
> Be sure to include the negative sign before the fraction when calculating the x-coordinate of the vertex.

✔ **GUIDED PRACTICE** | for Example 3

Graph the function. Label the vertex and axis of symmetry.

4. $y = x^2 - 2x - 1$ **5.** $y = 2x^2 + 6x + 3$ **6.** $f(x) = -\frac{1}{3}x^2 - 5x + 2$

KEY CONCEPT   *For Your Notebook*

Minimum and Maximum Values

Words   For $y = ax^2 + bx + c$, the vertex's y-coordinate is the **minimum value** of the function if $a > 0$ and the **maximum value** if $a < 0$.

Graphs

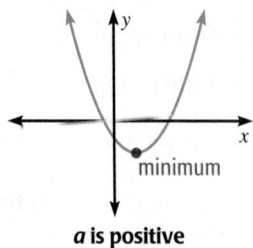

a is positive

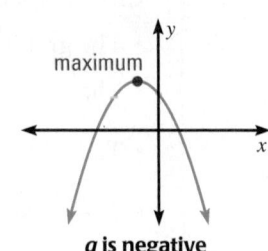

a is negative

❖ **EXAMPLE 4** **Find the minimum or maximum value**

Tell whether the function $y = 3x^2 - 18x + 20$ has a *minimum value* or a *maximum value*. Then find the minimum or maximum value.

Solution

Because $a > 0$, the function has a minimum value. To find it, calculate the coordinates of the vertex.

$$x = -\frac{b}{2a} = -\frac{(-18)}{2(3)} = 3$$

$$y = 3(3)^2 - 18(3) + 20 = -7$$

▶ The minimum value is $y = -7$. You can check the answer on a graphing calculator.

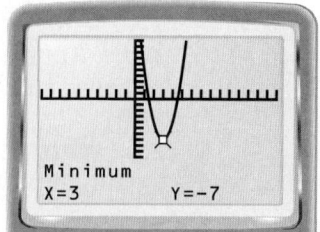

Minimum
X=3   Y=-7

EXAMPLE 5 **Solve a multi-step problem**

GO-CARTS A go-cart track has about 380 racers per week and charges each racer $35 to race. The owner estimates that there will be 20 more racers per week for every $1 reduction in the price per racer. How can the owner of the go-cart track maximize weekly revenue?

Solution

STEP 1 **Define** the variables. Let x represent the price reduction and $R(x)$ represent the weekly revenue.

STEP 2 **Write** a verbal model. Then write and simplify a quadratic function.

Revenue (dollars)	=	Price (dollars/racer)	·	Attendance (racers)

$$R(x) = (35 - x) \cdot (380 + 20x)$$
$$R(x) = 13{,}300 + 700x - 380x - 20x^2$$
$$R(x) = -20x^2 + 320x + 13{,}300$$

INTERPRET FUNCTIONS
Notice that $a = -20 < 0$, so the revenue function has a maximum value.

STEP 3 **Find** the coordinates $(x, R(x))$ of the vertex.

$$x = -\frac{b}{2a} = -\frac{320}{2(-20)} = 8 \qquad \text{Find } x\text{-coordinate.}$$

$$R(8) = -20(8)^2 + 320(8) + 13{,}300 = 14{,}580 \qquad \text{Evaluate } R(8).$$

▶ The vertex is $(8, 14{,}580)$, which means the owner should reduce the price per racer by $8 to increase the weekly revenue to $14,580.

✓ **GUIDED PRACTICE** for Examples 4 and 5

7. Find the minimum value of $y = 4x^2 + 16x - 3$.

8. **WHAT IF?** In Example 5, suppose each $1 reduction in the price per racer brings in 40 more racers per week. How can weekly revenue be maximized?

HOMEWORK KEY

○ = See WORKED-OUT SOLUTIONS
Exs. 15, 37, and 57

★ = STANDARDIZED TEST PRACTICE
Exs. 2, 39, 40, 43, 53, 58, and 60

◆ = MULTIPLE REPRESENTATIONS
Ex. 59

SKILL PRACTICE

1. **VOCABULARY** Copy and complete: The graph of a quadratic function is called a(n) __?__ .

2. ★ **WRITING** *Describe* how to determine whether a quadratic function has a minimum value or a maximum value.

EXAMPLE 1
for Exs. 3–12

USING A TABLE **Copy and complete the table of values for the function.**

3. $y = 4x^2$

x	−2	−1	0	1	2
y	?	?	?	?	?

4. $y = -3x^2$

x	−2	−1	0	1	2
y	?	?	?	?	?

5. $y = \frac{1}{2}x^2$

x	−4	−2	0	2	4
y	?	?	?	?	?

6. $y = -\frac{1}{3}x^2$

x	−6	−3	0	3	6
y	?	?	?	?	?

MAKING A GRAPH **Graph the function.** *Compare* **the graph with the graph of** $y = x^2$.

7. $y = 3x^2$

8. $y = 5x^2$

9. $y = -2x^2$

10. $y = -x^2$

11. $f(x) = \frac{1}{3}x^2$

12. $g(x) = -\frac{1}{4}x^2$

EXAMPLE 2
for Exs. 13–18

13. $y = 5x^2 + 1$

14. $y = 4x^2 + 1$

⃝15. $f(x) = -x^2 + 2$

16. $g(x) = -2x^2 - 5$

17. $f(x) = \frac{3}{4}x^2 - 5$

18. $g(x) = -\frac{1}{5}x^2 - 2$

ERROR ANALYSIS *Describe* **and correct the error in analyzing the graph of** $y = 4x^2 + 24x - 7$.

19.
The x-coordinate of the vertex is:

$x = \frac{b}{2a} = \frac{24}{2(4)} = 3$

20.
The y-intercept of the graph is the value of c, which is 7.

EXAMPLE 3
for Exs. 21–32

MAKING A GRAPH **Graph the function. Label the vertex and axis of symmetry.**

21. $y = x^2 + 2x + 1$

22. $y = 3x^2 - 6x + 4$

23. $y = -4x^2 + 8x + 2$

24. $y = -2x^2 - 6x + 3$

25. $g(x) = -x^2 - 2x - 1$

26. $f(x) = 6x^2 - 4x - 5$

27. $y = \frac{2}{3}x^2 - 3x + 6$

28. $y = -\frac{3}{4}x^2 - 4x - 1$

29. $g(x) = -\frac{3}{5}x^2 + 2x + 2$

30. $f(x) = \frac{1}{2}x^2 + x - 3$

31. $y = \frac{8}{5}x^2 - 4x + 5$

32. $y = -\frac{5}{3}x^2 - x - 4$

EXAMPLE 4
for Exs. 33–38

MINIMUMS OR MAXIMUMS Tell whether the function has a *minimum value* or a *maximum value.* Then find the minimum or maximum value.

33. $y = -6x^2 - 1$

34. $y = 9x^2 + 7$

35. $f(x) = 2x^2 + 8x + 7$

36. $g(x) = -3x^2 + 18x - 5$

37. $f(x) = \frac{3}{2}x^2 + 6x + 4$

38. $y = -\frac{1}{4}x^2 - 7x + 2$

39. ★ **MULTIPLE CHOICE** What is the effect on the graph of the function $y = x^2 + 2$ when it is changed to $y = x^2 - 3$?

(**A**) The graph widens.

(**B**) The graph narrows.

(**C**) The graph opens down.

(**D**) The vertex moves down the y-axis.

40. ★ **MULTIPLE CHOICE** Which function has the widest graph?

(**A**) $y = 2x^2$

(**B**) $y = x^2$

(**C**) $y = 0.5x^2$

(**D**) $y = -x^2$

IDENTIFYING COEFFICIENTS In Exercises 41 and 42, identify the values of a, b, and c for the quadratic function.

41. The path of a basketball thrown at an angle of 45° can be modeled by $y = -0.02x^2 + x + 6$.

42. The path of a shot put released at an angle of 35° can be modeled by $y = -0.01x^2 + 0.7x + 6$.

43. ★ **OPEN-ENDED MATH** Write three different quadratic functions whose graphs have the line $x = 4$ as an axis of symmetry but have different y-intercepts.

MATCHING In Exercises 44–46, match the equation with its graph.

44. $y = 0.5x^2 - 2x$

45. $y = 0.5x^2 + 3$

46. $y = 0.5x^2 - 2x + 3$

A.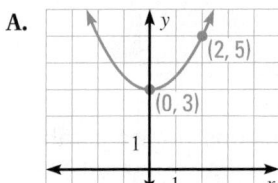

B.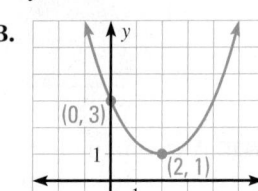

C.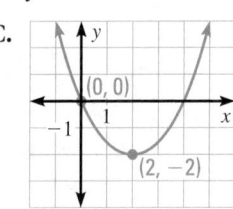

MAKING A GRAPH Graph the function. Label the vertex and axis of symmetry.

47. $f(x) = 0.1x^2 + 2$

48. $g(x) = -0.5x^2 - 5$

49. $y = 0.3x^2 + 3x - 1$

50. $y = 0.25x^2 - 1.5x + 3$

51. $f(x) = 4.2x^2 + 6x - 1$

52. $g(x) = 1.75x^2 - 2.5$

53. ★ **SHORT RESPONSE** The points $(2, 3)$ and $(-4, 3)$ lie on the graph of a quadratic function. *Explain* how these points can be used to find an equation of the axis of symmetry. Then write an equation of the axis of symmetry.

54. **CHALLENGE** For the graph of $y = ax^2 + bx + c$, show that the y-coordinate of the vertex is $-\frac{b^2}{4a} + c$.

EXAMPLE 5
for Exs. 55–58

55. ONLINE MUSIC An online music store sells about 4000 songs each day when it charges $1 per song. For each $.05 increase in price, about 80 fewer songs per day are sold. Use the verbal model and quadratic function to find how the store can maximize daily revenue.

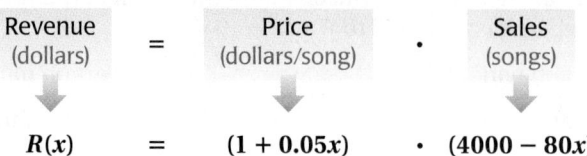

Revenue (dollars)	=	Price (dollars/song)	·	Sales (songs)
$R(x)$	=	$(1 + 0.05x)$	·	$(4000 - 80x)$

56. DIGITAL CAMERAS An electronics store sells about 70 of a new model of digital camera per month at a price of $320 each. For each $20 decrease in price, about 5 more cameras per month are sold. Write a function that models the situation. Then tell how the store can maximize monthly revenue from sales of the camera.

57. GOLDEN GATE BRIDGE Each cable joining the two towers on the Golden Gate Bridge can be modeled by the function

$$y = \frac{1}{9000}x^2 - \frac{7}{15}x + 500$$

where x and y are measured in feet. What is the height h above the road of a cable at its lowest point?

58. ★ SHORT RESPONSE A woodland jumping mouse hops along a parabolic path given by $y = -0.2x^2 + 1.3x$ where x is the mouse's horizontal position (in feet) and y is the corresponding height (in feet). Can the mouse jump over a fence that is 3 feet high? *Explain.*

59. ◆ MULTIPLE REPRESENTATIONS A community theater sells about 150 tickets to a play each week when it charges $20 per ticket. For each $1 decrease in price, about 10 more tickets per week are sold. The theater has fixed expenses of $1500 per week.

  a. Writing a Model Write a verbal model and a quadratic function to represent the theater's weekly profit.

  b. Making a Table Make a table of values for the quadratic function.

  c. Drawing a Graph Use the table to graph the quadratic function. Then use the graph to find how the theater can maximize weekly profit.

○ = **See WORKED-OUT SOLUTIONS** in Student Resources   ★ = **STANDARDIZED TEST PRACTICE**   ◆ = **MULTIPLE REPRESENTATIONS**

60. ★ **EXTENDED RESPONSE** In 1971, astronaut Alan Shepard hit a golf ball on the moon. The path of a golf ball hit at an angle of 45° and with a speed of 100 feet per second can be modeled by

$$y = -\frac{g}{10,000}x^2 + x$$

where x is the ball's horizontal position (in feet), y is the corresponding height (in feet), and g is the acceleration due to gravity (in feet per second squared).

a. Model Use the information in the diagram to write functions for the paths of a golf ball hit on Earth and a golf ball hit on the moon.

Earth: $g = 32$ ft/sec^2

Moon: $g = 5.3$ ft/sec^2

GRAPHING CALCULATOR

In part (b), use the calculator's *zero* feature to answer the questions.

b. Graphing Calculator Graph the functions from part (a) on a graphing calculator. How far does the golf ball travel on Earth? on the moon?

c. Interpret *Compare* the distances traveled by a golf ball on Earth and on the moon. Your answer should include the following:

- a calculation of the ratio of the distances traveled
- a discussion of how the distances and values of g are related

61. **CHALLENGE** Lifeguards at a beach want to rope off a rectangular swimming section. They have P feet of rope with buoys. In terms of P, what is the maximum area that the swimming section can have?

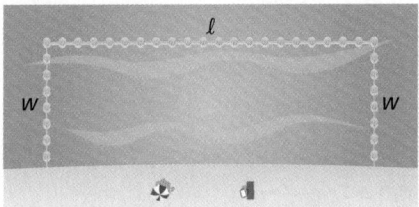

ℓ

w w

Find Maximum and Minimum Values

MATHEMATICAL PRACTICES

Use appropriate tools strategically.

QUESTION How can you use a graphing calculator to find the maximum or minimum value of a function?

EXAMPLE Find the maximum value of a function

Find the maximum value of $y = -2x^2 - 10x - 5$ and the value of x where it occurs.

STEP 1 *Graph function*

Graph the given function and select the *maximum* feature.

STEP 2 *Choose left bound*

Move the cursor to the left of the maximum point. Press ENTER .

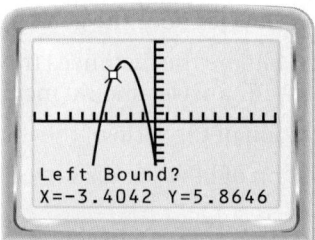

STEP 3 *Choose right bound*

Move the cursor to the right of the maximum point. Press ENTER .

STEP 4 *Find maximum*

Put the cursor approximately on the maximum point. Press ENTER .

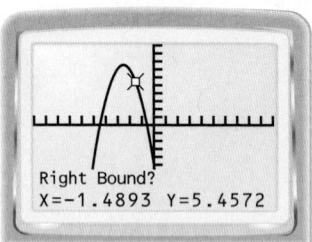

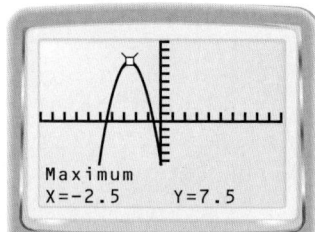

▸ The maximum value of the function is $y = 7.5$ and occurs at $x = -2.5$.

PRACTICE

Tell whether the function has a *maximum value* or a *minimum value*. Then find the maximum or minimum value and the value of x where it occurs.

1. $y = x^2 - 6x + 4$ 2. $f(x) = x^2 - 3x + 3$ 3. $y = -3x^2 + 9x + 2$

4. $y = 0.5x^2 + 0.8x - 2$ 5. $h(x) = \frac{1}{2}x^2 - 3x + 2$ 6. $y = -\frac{3}{8}x^2 + 6x - 5$

1.2 Graph Quadratic Functions in Vertex or Intercept Form

Before	You graphed quadratic functions in standard form.
Now	You will graph quadratic functions in vertex form or intercept form.
Why?	So you can find the height of a jump, as in Ex. 51.

Key Vocabulary
• vertex form
• intercept form

Previously, you learned that the standard form of a quadratic function is $y = ax^2 + bx + c$ where $a \neq 0$. Another useful form of a quadratic function is the **vertex form**, $y = a(x - h)^2 + k$.

KEY CONCEPT *For Your Notebook*

Graph of Vertex Form $y = a(x - h)^2 + k$

ANALYZE GRAPHS
The graph of a quadratic function $y = a(x - h)^2 + k$ where $a > 0$ is decreasing on the interval $(-\infty, h)$ and increasing on the interval $(h, +\infty)$.

COMMON CORE

CC.9-12.F.IF.7 Graph functions expressed symbolically and show key features of the graph, by hand in simple cases and using technology for more complicated cases.*
a. Graph linear and quadratic functions and show intercepts, maxima, and minima.

The graph of $y = a(x - h)^2 + k$ is the parabola $y = ax^2$ translated horizontally h units and vertically k units.

Characteristics of the graph of $y = a(x - h)^2 + k$:

• The vertex is (h, k).

• The axis of symmetry is $x = h$.

• The graph opens up if $a > 0$ and down if $a < 0$.

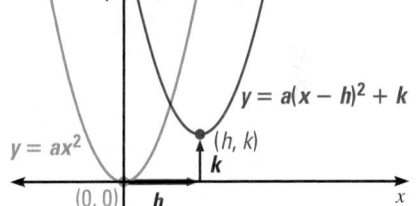

EXAMPLE 1 Graph a quadratic function in vertex form

Graph $y = -\dfrac{1}{4}(x + 2)^2 + 5$.

Solution

STEP 1 **Identify** the constants $a = -\dfrac{1}{4}$, $h = -2$, and $k = 5$. Because $a < 0$, the parabola opens down.

STEP 2 **Plot** the vertex $(h, k) = (-2, 5)$ and draw the axis of symmetry $x = -2$.

STEP 3 **Evaluate** the function for two values of x.

$$x = 0: \ y = -\frac{1}{4}(0 + 2)^2 + 5 = 4$$

$$x = 2: \ y = -\frac{1}{4}(2 + 2)^2 + 5 = 1$$

Plot the points $(0, 4)$ and $(2, 1)$ and their reflections in the axis of symmetry.

STEP 4 **Draw** a parabola through the plotted points.

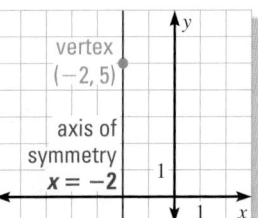

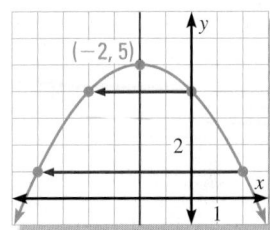

EXAMPLE 2   **Use a quadratic model in vertex form**

CIVIL ENGINEERING The Tacoma Narrows Bridge in Washington has two towers that each rise 307 feet above the roadway and are connected by suspension cables as shown. Each cable can be modeled by the function

$$y = \frac{1}{7000}(x - 1400)^2 + 27$$

where x and y are measured in feet. What is the distance d between the two towers?

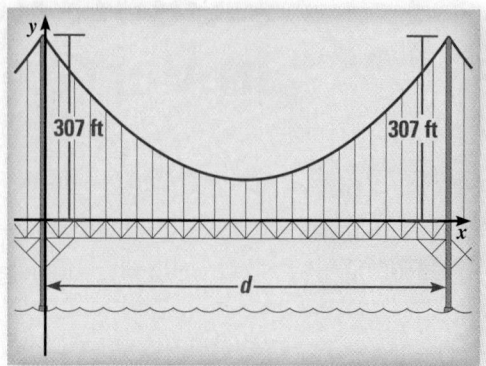

Not drawn to scale

Solution

The vertex of the parabola is (1400, 27). So, a cable's lowest point is 1400 feet from the left tower shown above. Because the heights of the two towers are the same, the symmetry of the parabola implies that the vertex is also 1400 feet from the right tower. So, the distance between the two towers is $d = 2(1400) = 2800$ feet.

 GUIDED PRACTICE   **for Examples 1 and 2**

Graph the function. Label the vertex and axis of symmetry.

1. $y = (x + 2)^2 - 3$

2. $y = -(x - 1)^2 + 5$

3. $f(x) = \frac{1}{2}(x - 3)^2 - 4$

4. **WHAT IF?** Suppose an architect designs a bridge with cables that can be modeled by $y = \frac{1}{6500}(x - 1400)^2 + 27$ where x and y are measured in feet. Compare this function's graph to the graph of the function in Example 2.

INTERCEPT FORM If the graph of a quadratic function has at least one x-intercept, then the function can be represented in **intercept form**, $y = a(x - p)(x - q)$.

KEY CONCEPT   *For Your Notebook*

Graph of Intercept Form $y = a(x - p)(x - q)$

Characteristics of the graph of $y = a(x - p)(x - q)$:

• The x-intercepts are p and q.

• The axis of symmetry is halfway between $(p, 0)$ and $(q, 0)$. It has equation $x = \dfrac{p + q}{2}$.

• The graph opens up if $a > 0$ and opens down if $a < 0$.

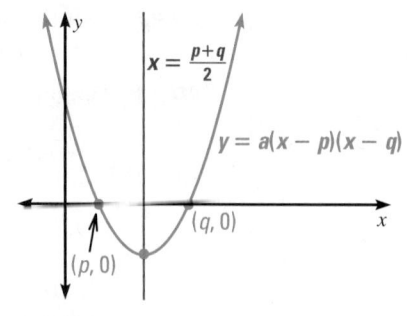

EXAMPLE 3 Graph a quadratic function in intercept form

Graph $y = 2(x + 3)(x - 1)$.

Solution

AVOID ERRORS
Remember that the x-intercepts for a quadratic function written in the form $y = a(x - p)(x - q)$ are p and q, not $-p$ and $-q$.

STEP 1 **Identify** the x-intercepts. Because $p = -3$ and $q = 1$, the x-intercepts occur at the points $(-3, 0)$ and $(1, 0)$.

STEP 2 **Find** the coordinates of the vertex.

$$x = \frac{p + q}{2} = \frac{-3 + 1}{2} = -1$$

$$y = 2(-1 + 3)(-1 - 1) = -8$$

So, the vertex is $(-1, -8)$.

STEP 3 **Draw** a parabola through the vertex and the points where the x-intercepts occur.

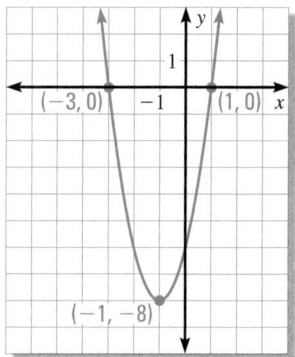

Animated Algebra at my.hrw.com

EXAMPLE 4 Use a quadratic function in intercept form

FOOTBALL The path of a placekicked football can be modeled by the function $y = -0.026x(x - 46)$ where x is the horizontal distance (in yards) and y is the corresponding height (in yards).

a. How far is the football kicked?

b. What is the football's maximum height?

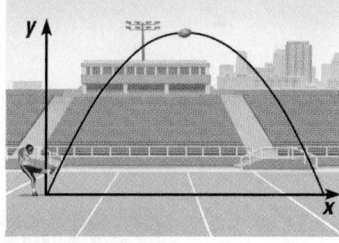

Solution

a. Rewrite the function as $y = -0.026(x - 0)(x - 46)$. Because $p = 0$ and $q = 46$, you know the x-intercepts are 0 and 46. So, you can conclude that the football is kicked a distance of 46 yards.

b. To find the football's maximum height, calculate the coordinates of the vertex.

$$x = \frac{p + q}{2} = \frac{0 + 46}{2} = 23$$

$$y = -0.026(23)(23 - 46) \approx 13.8$$

The maximum height is the y-coordinate of the vertex, or about 13.8 yards.

 GUIDED PRACTICE for Examples 3 and 4

Graph the function. Label the vertex, axis of symmetry, and x-intercepts.

5. $y = (x - 3)(x - 7)$ **6.** $f(x) = 2(x - 4)(x + 1)$ **7.** $y = -(x + 1)(x - 5)$

8. **WHAT IF?** In Example 4, what is the maximum height of the football if the football's path can be modeled by the function $y = -0.025x(x - 50)$?

1.2   Graph Quadratic Functions in Vertex or Intercept Form   **13**

FOIL METHOD You can change quadratic functions from intercept form or vertex form to standard form by multiplying algebraic expressions. One method for multiplying two expressions each containing two terms is *FOIL*.

KEY CONCEPT   *For Your Notebook*

FOIL Method

Words   To multiply two expressions that each contain two terms, add the products of the **F**irst terms, the **O**uter terms, the **I**nner terms, and the **L**ast terms.

Example   F   O   I   L

$(x + 4)(x + 7) = x^2 + 7x + 4x + 28 = x^2 + 11x + 28$

EXAMPLE 5   Change from intercept form to standard form

Write $y = -2(x + 5)(x - 8)$ in standard form.

$y = -2(x + 5)(x - 8)$	Write original function.
$= -2(x^2 - 8x + 5x - 40)$	Multiply using FOIL.
$= -2(x^2 - 3x - 40)$	Combine like terms.
$= -2x^2 + 6x + 80$	Distributive property

EXAMPLE 6   Change from vertex form to standard form

Write $f(x) = 4(x - 1)^2 + 9$ in standard form.

$f(x) = 4(x - 1)^2 + 9$	Write original function.
$= 4(x - 1)(x - 1) + 9$	Rewrite $(x - 1)^2$.
$= 4(x^2 - x - x + 1) + 9$	Multiply using FOIL.
$= 4(x^2 - 2x + 1) + 9$	Combine like terms.
$= 4x^2 - 8x + 4 + 9$	Distributive property
$= 4x^2 - 8x + 13$	Combine like terms.

✓ **GUIDED PRACTICE**   for Examples 5 and 6

Write the quadratic function in standard form.

9. $y = -(x - 2)(x - 7)$ **10.** $y = -4(x - 1)(x + 3)$

11. $f(x) = 2(x + 5)(x + 4)$ **12.** $y = -7(x - 6)(x + 1)$

13. $y = -3(x + 5)^2 - 1$ **14.** $g(x) = 6(x - 4)^2 - 10$

15. $f(x) = -(x + 2)^2 + 4$ **16.** $y = 2(x - 3)^2 + 9$

1.2 **EXERCISES**

HOMEWORK
KEY

○ = See WORKED-OUT SOLUTIONS
Exs. 19, 29, and 53

★ = STANDARDIZED TEST PRACTICE
Exs. 2, 12, 22, 54, and 55

SKILL PRACTICE

1. VOCABULARY Copy and complete: A quadratic function in the form $y = a(x - h)^2 + k$ is in ___?___ form.

2. ★ WRITING *Explain* how to find a quadratic function's maximum value or minimum value when the function is given in intercept form.

EXAMPLE 1
for Exs. 3–12

GRAPHING WITH VERTEX FORM **Graph the function. Label the vertex and axis of symmetry.**

3. $y = (x - 3)^2$

4. $y = (x + 4)^2$

5. $f(x) = -(x + 3)^2 + 5$

6. $y = 3(x - 7)^2 - 1$

7. $g(x) = -4(x - 2)^2 + 4$

8. $y = 2(x + 1)^2 - 3$

9. $f(x) = -2(x - 1)^2 - 5$

10. $y = -\frac{1}{4}(x + 2)^2 + 1$

11. $y = \frac{1}{2}(x - 3)^2 + 2$

12. ★ MULTIPLE CHOICE What is the vertex of the graph of the function $y = 3(x + 2)^2 - 5$?

Ⓐ $(2, -5)$ Ⓑ $(-2, -5)$ Ⓒ $(-5, 2)$ Ⓓ $(5, -2)$

EXAMPLE 3
for Exs. 13–23

GRAPHING WITH INTERCEPT FORM **Graph the function. Label the vertex, axis of symmetry, and *x*-intercepts.**

13. $y = (x + 3)(x - 3)$

14. $y = (x + 1)(x - 3)$

15. $y = 3(x + 2)(x + 6)$

16. $f(x) = 2(x - 5)(x - 1)$

17. $y = -(x - 4)(x + 6)$

18. $g(x) = -4(x + 3)(x + 7)$

19. $y = (x + 1)(x + 2)$

20. $f(x) = -2(x - 3)(x + 4)$

21. $y = 4(x - 7)(x + 2)$

22. ★ MULTIPLE CHOICE What is the vertex of the graph of the function $y = -(x - 6)(x + 4)$?

Ⓐ $(1, 25)$ Ⓑ $(-1, 21)$ Ⓒ $(-6, 4)$ Ⓓ $(6, -4)$

23. ERROR ANALYSIS *Describe* and correct the error in analyzing the graph of the function $y = 5(x - 2)(x + 3)$.

The x-intercepts of the graph are −2 and 3.

EXAMPLES 5 and 6
for Exs. 24–32

WRITING IN STANDARD FORM **Write the quadratic function in standard form.**

24. $y = (x + 4)(x + 3)$

25. $y = (x - 5)(x + 3)$

26. $h(x) = 4(x + 1)(x - 6)$

27. $y = -3(x - 2)(x - 4)$

28. $f(x) = (x + 5)^2 - 2$

29. $y = (x - 3)^2 + 6$

30. $g(x) = -(x + 6)^2 + 10$

31. $y = 5(x + 3)^2 - 4$

32. $f(x) = 12(x - 1)^2 + 4$

MINIMUM OR MAXIMUM VALUES **Find the minimum value or the maximum value of the function.**

33. $y = 3(x - 3)^2 - 4$

34. $g(x) = -4(x + 6)^2 - 12$

35. $y = 15(x - 25)^2 + 130$

36. $f(x) = 3(x + 10)(x - 8)$

37. $y = -(x - 36)(x + 18)$

38. $y = -12x(x - 9)$

39. $y = 8x(x + 15)$

40. $y = 2(x - 3)(x - 6)$

41. $g(x) = -5(x + 9)(x - 4)$

42. **GRAPHING CALCULATOR** Consider the function $y = a(x - h)^2 + k$ where $a = 1$, $h = 3$, and $k = -2$. Predict the effect of each change in a, h, or k described in parts (a)–(c). Use a graphing calculator to check your prediction by graphing the original and revised functions in the same coordinate plane.

   a. a changes to -3 **b.** h changes to -1 **c.** k changes to 2

MAKING A GRAPH Graph the function. Label the vertex and axis of symmetry.

43. $y = 5(x - 2.25)^2 - 2.75$ 44. $g(x) = -8(x + 3.2)^2 + 6.4$ 45. $y = -0.25(x - 5.2)^2 + 8.5$

46. $y = -\dfrac{2}{3}\left(x - \dfrac{1}{2}\right)^2 + \dfrac{4}{5}$ 47. $f(x) = -\dfrac{3}{4}(x + 5)(x + 8)$ 48. $g(x) = \dfrac{5}{2}\left(x - \dfrac{4}{3}\right)\left(x - \dfrac{2}{5}\right)$

49. **ANALYZING A GRAPH** On what interval(s) are the values of $f(x) = -2(x + 1)(x - 5)$ positive? negative?

50. **CHALLENGE** Write $y = a(x - h)^2 + k$ and $y = a(x - p)(x - q)$ in standard form. Knowing the vertex of the graph of $y = ax^2 + bx + c$ occurs at $x = -\dfrac{b}{2a}$, show that the vertex of the graph of $y = a(x - h)^2 + k$ occurs at $x = h$ and that the vertex of the graph of $y = a(x - p)(x - q)$ occurs at $x = \dfrac{p + q}{2}$.

PROBLEM SOLVING

EXAMPLES
2 and 4
for Exs. 51–54

51. **BIOLOGY** The function $y = -0.03(x - 14)^2 + 6$ models the jump of a red kangaroo where x is the horizontal distance (in feet) and y is the corresponding height (in feet). What is the kangaroo's maximum height? How long is the kangaroo's jump?

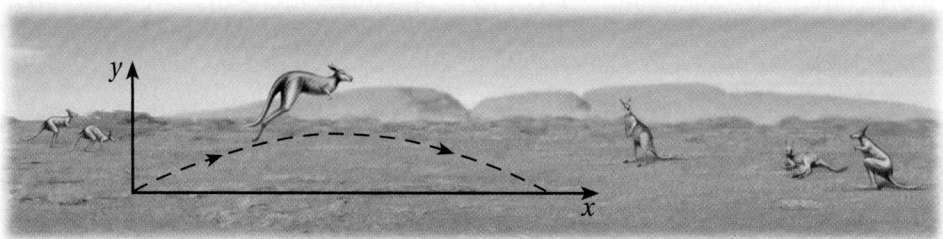

52. **CIVIL ENGINEERING** The arch of the Gateshead Millennium Bridge forms a parabola with equation $y = -0.016(x - 52.5)^2 + 45$ where x is the horizontal distance (in meters) from the arch's left end and y is the distance (in meters) from the base of the arch. What is the width of the arch?

53. **MULTI-STEP PROBLEM** Although a football field appears to be flat, its surface is actually shaped like a parabola so that rain runs off to both sides. The cross section of a field with synthetic turf can be modeled by

   $$y = -0.000234x(x - 160)$$

   where x and y are measured in feet.

   a. What is the field's width?

   b. What is the maximum height of the field's surface?

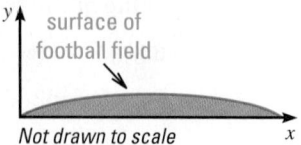

surface of football field

Not drawn to scale

54. ★ SHORT RESPONSE A jump on a pogo stick with a conventional spring can be modeled by $y = -0.5(x - 6)^2 + 18$, and a jump on a pogo stick with a bow spring can be modeled by $y = -1.17(x - 6)^2 + 42$, where x and y are measured in inches. *Compare* the maximum heights of the jumps on the two pogo sticks. Which constants in the functions affect the maximum heights of the jumps? Which do not?

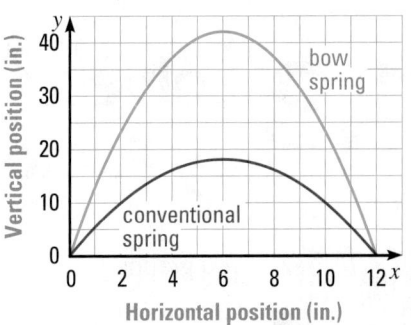

55. ★ EXTENDED RESPONSE A kernel of popcorn contains water that expands when the kernel is heated, causing it to pop. The equations below give the "popping volume" y (in cubic centimeters per gram) of popcorn with moisture content x (as a percent of the popcorn's weight).

Hot-air popping: $y = -0.761(x - 5.52)(x - 22.6)$

Hot-oil popping: $y = -0.652(x - 5.35)(x - 21.8)$

a. **Interpret** For hot-air popping, what moisture content maximizes popping volume? What is the maximum volume?

b. **Interpret** For hot-oil popping, what moisture content maximizes popping volume? What is the maximum volume?

c. **Graphing Calculator** Graph the functions in the same coordinate plane. What are the domain and range of each function in this situation? *Explain* how you determined the domain and range.

56. CHALLENGE Flying fish use their pectoral fins like airplane wings to glide through the air. Suppose a flying fish reaches a maximum height of 5 feet after flying a horizontal distance of 33 feet. Write a quadratic function $y = a(x - h)^2 + k$ that models the flight path, assuming the fish leaves the water at (0, 0). *Describe* how changing the value of a, h, or k affects the flight path.

1.3 Solve $x^2 + bx + c = 0$ by Factoring

Before	You graphed quadratic functions.
Now	You will solve quadratic equations.
Why?	So you can double the area of a picnic site, as in Ex. 42.

Key Vocabulary
- monomial
- binomial
- trinomial
- quadratic equation
- root of an equation
- zero of a function

A **monomial** is an expression that is either a number, a variable, or the product of a number and one or more variables. A **binomial**, such as $x + 4$, is the sum of two monomials. A **trinomial**, such as $x^2 + 11x + 28$, is the sum of three monomials.

You know how to use FOIL to write $(x + 4)(x + 7)$ as $x^2 + 11x + 28$. You can use factoring to write a trinomial as a product of binomials. To factor $x^2 + bx + c$, find integers m and n such that:

$$x^2 + bx + c = (x + m)(x + n)$$
$$= x^2 + (m + n)x + mn$$

So, the *sum* of m and n must equal b and the *product* of m and n must equal c.

CC.9-12.A.SSE.3a Factor a quadratic expression to reveal the zeros of the function it defines.*

EXAMPLE 1   Factor trinomials of the form $x^2 + bx + c$

Factor the expression.

a. $x^2 - 9x + 20$

b. $x^2 + 3x - 12$

Solution

a. You want $x^2 - 9x + 20 = (x + m)(x + n)$ where $mn = 20$ and $m + n = -9$.

AVOID ERRORS
When factoring $x^2 + bx + c$ where $c > 0$, you must choose factors $x + m$ and $x + n$ such that m and n have the same sign.

Factors of 20: *m, n*	1, 20	−1, −20	2, 10	−2, −10	4, 5	−4, −5
Sum of factors: *m + n*	21	−21	12	−12	9	−9

▸ Notice that $m = -4$ and $n = -5$. So, $x^2 - 9x + 20 = (x - 4)(x - 5)$.

b. You want $x^2 + 3x - 12 = (x + m)(x + n)$ where $mn = -12$ and $m + n = 3$.

Factors of −12: *m, n*	−1, 12	1, −12	−2, 6	2, −6	−3, 4	3, −4
Sum of factors: *m + n*	11	−11	4	−4	1	−1

▸ Notice that there are no factors m and n such that $m + n = 3$. So, $x^2 + 3x - 12$ cannot be factored.

 GUIDED PRACTICE   for Example 1

Factor the expression. If the expression cannot be factored, say so.

1. $x^2 - 3x - 18$ **2.** $n^2 - 3n + 9$ **3.** $r^2 + 2r - 63$

FACTORING SPECIAL PRODUCTS Factoring quadratic expressions often involves trial and error. However, some expressions are easy to factor because they follow special patterns.

KEY CONCEPT   *For Your Notebook*

Special Factoring Patterns

Pattern Name	Pattern	Example
Difference of Two Squares	$a^2 - b^2 = (a + b)(a - b)$	$x^2 - 4 = (x + 2)(x - 2)$
Perfect Square Trinomial	$a^2 + 2ab + b^2 = (a + b)^2$	$x^2 + 6x + 9 = (x + 3)^2$
	$a^2 - 2ab + b^2 = (a - b)^2$	$x^2 - 4x + 4 = (x - 2)^2$

EXAMPLE 2   **Factor with special patterns**

Factor the expression.

a. $x^2 - 49 = x^2 - 7^2$ Difference of two squares

$\qquad\quad = (x + 7)(x - 7)$

b. $d^2 + 12d + 36 = d^2 + 2(d)(6) + 6^2$ Perfect square trinomial

$\qquad\qquad\qquad = (d + 6)^2$

c. $z^2 - 26z + 169 = z^2 - 2(z)(13) + 13^2$ Perfect square trinomial

$\qquad\qquad\qquad\; = (z - 13)^2$

 GUIDED PRACTICE   for Example 2

Factor the expression.

4. $x^2 - 9$ **5.** $q^2 - 100$ **6.** $y^2 + 16y + 64$ **7.** $w^2 - 18w + 81$

SOLVING QUADRATIC EQUATIONS You can use factoring to solve certain *quadratic equations*. A **quadratic equation** in one variable can be written in the form $ax^2 + bx + c = 0$ where $a \neq 0$. This is called the **standard form** of the equation. The solutions of a quadratic equation are called the **roots** of the equation. If the left side of $ax^2 + bx + c = 0$ can be factored, then the equation can be solved using the *zero product property*.

KEY CONCEPT   *For Your Notebook*

Zero Product Property

Words   If the product of two expressions is zero, then one or both of the expressions equal zero.

Algebra   If A and B are expressions and $AB = 0$, then $A = 0$ or $B = 0$.

Example   If $(x + 5)(x + 2) = 0$, then $x + 5 = 0$ or $x + 2 = 0$. That is, $x = -5$ or $x = -2$.

EXAMPLE 3 **Standardized Test Practice**

What are the roots of the equation $x^2 - 5x - 36 = 0$?

(**A**) −4, −9   (**B**) 4, −9   (**C**) −4, 9   (**D**) 4, 9

Solution

$x^2 - 5x - 36 = 0$	Write original equation.
$(x - 9)(x + 4) = 0$	Factor.
$x - 9 = 0$ or $x + 4 = 0$	Zero product property
$x = 9$ or $x = -4$	Solve for *x*.

▸ The correct answer is C. Ⓐ Ⓑ ⓒ Ⓓ

EXAMPLE 4 **Use a quadratic equation as a model**

NATURE PRESERVE A town has a nature preserve with a rectangular field that measures 600 meters by 400 meters. The town wants to double the area of the field by adding land as shown. Find the new dimensions of the field.

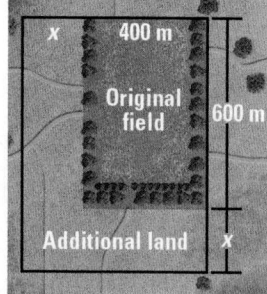

Solution

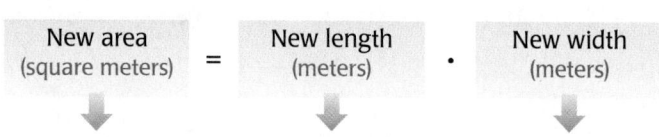

New area (square meters) = New length (meters) · New width (meters)

2(600)(400)	=	**(600 + x)** · **(400 + x)**

$480{,}000 = 240{,}000 + 1000x + x^2$	Multiply using FOIL.
$0 = x^2 + 1000x - 240{,}000$	Write in standard form.
$0 = (x - 200)(x + 1200)$	Factor.
$x - 200 = 0$ or $x + 1200 = 0$	Zero product property
$x = 200$ or $x = -1200$	Solve for *x*.

▸ Reject the negative value, −1200. The field's length and width should each be increased by 200 meters. The new dimensions are 800 meters by 600 meters.

 GUIDED PRACTICE   for Examples 3 and 4

8. Solve the equation $x^2 - x - 42 = 0$.

9. **WHAT IF?** In Example 4, suppose the field initially measures 1000 meters by 300 meters. Find the new dimensions of the field.

ZEROS OF A FUNCTION You know that the *x*-intercepts of the graph of $y = a(x - p)(x - q)$ are *p* and *q*. Because the function's value is zero when $x = p$ and when $x = q$, the numbers *p* and *q* are also called **zeros** of the function.

EXAMPLE 5 **Find the zeros of quadratic functions**

Find the zeros of the function by rewriting the function in intercept form.

a. $y = x^2 - x - 12$ **b.** $y = x^2 + 12x + 36$

Solution

UNDERSTAND REPRESENTATIONS
If a real number k is a zero of the function $y = ax^2 + bx + c$, then k is an x-intercept of this function's graph and k is also a root of the equation $ax^2 + bx + c = 0$.

a. $y = x^2 - x - 12$ **Write original function.**

     $= (x + 3)(x - 4)$ **Factor.**

The zeros of the function are -3 and 4.

CHECK Graph $y = x^2 - x - 12$. The graph passes through $(-3, 0)$ and $(4, 0)$.

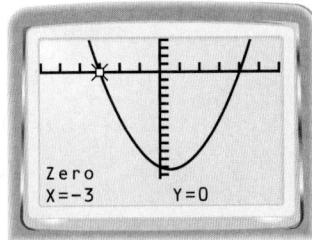

b. $y = x^2 + 12x + 36$ **Write original function.**

     $= (x + 6)(x + 6)$ **Factor.**

The zero of the function is -6.

CHECK Graph $y = x^2 + 12x + 36$. The graph passes through $(-6, 0)$.

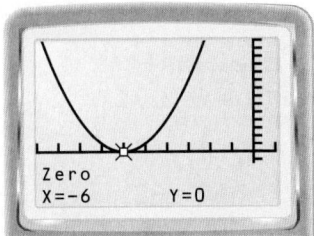

✓ **GUIDED PRACTICE**   **for Example 5**

Find the zeros of the function by rewriting the function in intercept form.

10. $y = x^2 + 5x - 14$ **11.** $y = x^2 - 7x - 30$ **12.** $f(x) = x^2 - 10x + 25$

1.3 EXERCISES

HOMEWORK KEY

○ = See WORKED-OUT SOLUTIONS
    Exs. 33, 47, and 67

★ = STANDARDIZED TEST PRACTICE
    Exs. 2, 41, 56, 58, 63, and 71

◆ = MULTIPLE REPRESENTATIONS
    Ex. 68

SKILL PRACTICE

1. **VOCABULARY** What is a zero of a function $y = f(x)$?

2. ★ **WRITING** *Explain* the difference between a monomial, a binomial, and a trinomial. Give an example of each type of expression.

EXAMPLE 1
for Exs. 3–14

FACTORING Factor the expression. If the expression cannot be factored, say so.

3. $x^2 + 6x + 5$ **4.** $x^2 - 7x + 10$ **5.** $a^2 - 13a + 22$

6. $r^2 + 15r + 56$ **7.** $p^2 + 2p + 4$ **8.** $q^2 - 11q + 28$

9. $b^2 + 3b - 40$ **10.** $x^2 - 4x - 12$ **11.** $x^2 - 7x - 18$

12. $c^2 - 9c - 18$ **13.** $x^2 + 9x - 36$ **14.** $m^2 + 8m - 65$

EXAMPLE 2
for Exs. 15–23

FACTORING WITH SPECIAL PATTERNS Factor the expression.

15. $x^2 - 36$

16. $b^2 - 81$

17. $x^2 - 24x + 144$

18. $t^2 - 16t + 64$

19. $x^2 + 8x + 16$

20. $c^2 + 28c + 196$

21. $n^2 + 14n + 49$

22. $s^2 - 26s + 169$

23. $z^2 - 121$

EXAMPLE 3
for Exs. 24–41

SOLVING EQUATIONS Solve the equation.

24. $x^2 - 8x + 12 = 0$

25. $x^2 - 11x + 30 = 0$

26. $x^2 + 2x - 35 = 0$

27. $a^2 - 49 = 0$

28. $b^2 - 6b + 9 = 0$

29. $c^2 + 5c + 4 = 0$

30. $n^2 - 6n = 0$

31. $t^2 + 10t + 25 = 0$

32. $w^2 - 16w + 48 = 0$

(33.) $z^2 - 3z = 54$

34. $r^2 + 2r = 80$

35. $u^2 = -9u$

36. $m^2 = 7m$

37. $14x - 49 = x^2$

38. $-3y + 28 = y^2$

ERROR ANALYSIS *Describe* and correct the error in solving the equation.

39.

$x^2 - x - 6 = 0$

$(x - 2)(x + 3) = 0$

$x - 2 = 0 \quad \text{or} \quad x + 3 = 0$

$x = 2 \quad \text{or} \quad x = -3$

40.

$x^2 + 7x + 6 = 14$

$(x + 6)(x + 1) = 14$

$x + 6 = 14 \quad \text{or} \quad x + 1 = 14$

$x = 8 \quad \text{or} \quad x = 13$

41. ★ **MULTIPLE CHOICE** What are the roots of the equation $x^2 + 2x - 63 = 0$?

(A) 7, −9

(B) −7, −9

(C) −7, 9

(D) 7, 9

EXAMPLE 4
for Exs. 42–43

WRITING EQUATIONS Write an equation that you can solve to find the value of x.

42. A rectangular picnic site measures 24 feet by 10 feet. You want to double the site's area by adding the same distance x to the length and the width.

43. A rectangular performing platform in a park measures 10 feet by 12 feet. You want to triple the platform's area by adding the same distance x to the length and the width.

EXAMPLE 5
for Exs. 44–55

FINDING ZEROS Find the zeros of the function by rewriting the function in intercept form.

44. $y = x^2 + 6x + 8$

45. $y = x^2 - 8x + 16$

46. $y = x^2 - 4x - 32$

(47.) $y = x^2 + 7x - 30$

48. $f(x) = x^2 + 11x$

49. $g(x) = x^2 - 8x$

50. $y = x^2 - 64$

51. $y = x^2 - 25$

52. $f(x) = x^2 - 12x - 45$

53. $g(x) = x^2 + 19x + 84$

54. $y = x^2 + 22x + 121$

55. $y = x^2 + 2x + 1$

56. ★ **MULTIPLE CHOICE** What are the zeros of $f(x) = x^2 + 6x - 55$?

(A) −11, −5

(B) −11, 5

(C) −5, 11

(D) 5, 11

57. **REASONING** Write a quadratic equation of the form $x^2 + bx + c = 0$ that has roots 8 and 11.

58. ★ **SHORT RESPONSE** For what integers b can the expression $x^2 + bx + 7$ be factored? *Explain.*

○ = See **WORKED-OUT SOLUTIONS** in Student Resources   ★ = **STANDARDIZED TEST PRACTICE**

GEOMETRY Find the value of *x*.

59. Area of rectangle = 36

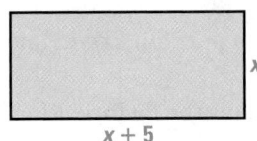

x

x + 5

60. Area of rectangle = 84

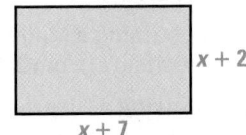

x + 2

x + 7

61. Area of triangle = 42

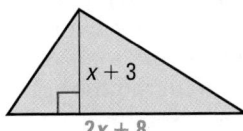

x + 3

2*x* + 8

62. Area of trapezoid = 32

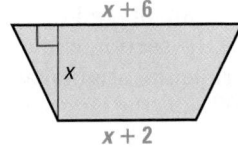

x + 6

x

x + 2

63. ★ **OPEN-ENDED MATH** Write a quadratic function with zeros that are equidistant from 10 on a number line.

64. **CHALLENGE** Is there a formula for factoring the *sum* of two squares? You will investigate this question in parts (a) and (b).

   a. Consider the sum of two squares $x^2 + 16$. If this sum can be factored, then there are integers m and n such that $x^2 + 16 = (x + m)(x + n)$. Write two equations that m and n must satisfy.

   b. Show that there are no integers m and n that satisfy both equations you wrote in part (a). What can you conclude?

PROBLEM SOLVING

EXAMPLE 4
for Exs. 65–67

65. **SKATE PARK** A city's skate park is a rectangle 100 feet long by 50 feet wide. The city wants to triple the area of the skate park by adding the same distance *x* to the length and the width. Write and solve an equation to find the value of *x*. What are the new dimensions of the skate park?

66. **ZOO** A rectangular enclosure at a zoo is 35 feet long by 18 feet wide. The zoo wants to double the area of the enclosure by adding the same distance *x* to the length and the width. Write and solve an equation to find the value of *x*. What are the new dimensions of the enclosure?

67. **MULTI-STEP PROBLEM** A museum has a café with a rectangular patio. The museum wants to add 464 square feet to the area of the patio by expanding the existing patio as shown.

   a. Find the area of the existing patio.

   b. Write a verbal model and an equation that you can use to find the value of *x*.

   c. Solve your equation. By what distance *x* should the length and the width of the patio be expanded?

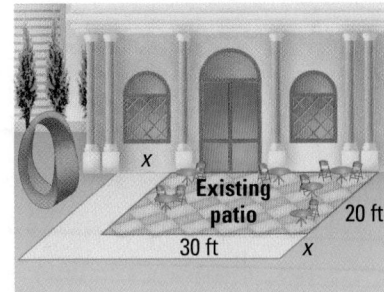

x

Existing patio

20 ft

30 ft

x

68. ◆ **MULTIPLE REPRESENTATIONS** Use the diagram shown.

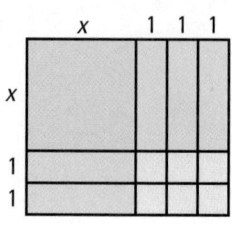

   a. Writing an Expression Write a quadratic trinomial that represents the area of the diagram.

   b. Describing a Model Factor the expression from part (a). *Explain* how the diagram models the factorization.

   c. Drawing a Diagram Draw a diagram that models the factorization $x^2 + 8x + 15 = (x + 5)(x + 3)$.

69. SCHOOL FAIR At last year's school fair, an 18 foot by 15 foot rectangular section of land was roped off for a dunking booth. The length and width of the section will each be increased by x feet for this year's fair in order to triple the original area. Write and solve an equation to find the value of x. What is the length of rope needed to enclose the new section?

70. RECREATION CENTER A rectangular deck for a recreation center is 21 feet long by 20 feet wide. Its area is to be halved by subtracting the same distance x from the length and the width. Write and solve an equation to find the value of x. What are the deck's new dimensions?

71. ★ SHORT RESPONSE A square garden has sides that are 10 feet long. A gardener wants to double the area of the garden by adding the same distance x to the length and the width. Write an equation that x must satisfy. Can you solve the equation you wrote by factoring? *Explain* why or why not.

72. CHALLENGE A grocery store wants to double the area of its parking lot by expanding the existing lot as shown. By what distance x should the lot be expanded?

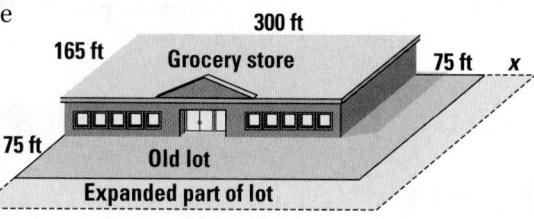

1.4 Solve $ax^2 + bx + c = 0$ by Factoring

Before	You used factoring to solve equations of the form $x^2 + bx + c = 0$.
Now	You will use factoring to solve equations of the form $ax^2 + bx + c = 0$.
Why?	So you can maximize a shop's revenue, as in Ex. 64.

Key Vocabulary
• monomial

CC.9-12.A.SSE.3a Factor a quadratic expression to reveal the zeros of the function it defines.*

FACTOR EXPRESSIONS
When factoring $ax^2 + bx + c$ where $a > 0$, it is customary to choose factors $kx + m$ and $lx + n$ such that k and l are positive.

To factor $ax^2 + bx + c$ when $a \neq 1$, find integers k, l, m, and n such that:

$$ax^2 + bx + c = (kx + m)(lx + n) = klx^2 + (kn + lm)x + mn$$

So, k and l must be factors of a, and m and n must be factors of c.

EXAMPLE 1 Factor $ax^2 + bx + c$ where $c > 0$

Factor $5x^2 - 17x + 6$.

Solution

You want $5x^2 - 17x + 6 = (kx + m)(lx + n)$ where k and l are factors of 5 and m and n are factors of 6. You can assume that k and l are positive and $k \geq l$. Because $mn > 0$, m and n have the same sign. So, m and n must both be negative because the coefficient of x, -17, is negative.

k, l	5, 1	5, 1	5, 1	5, 1
m, n	$-6, -1$	$-1, -6$	$-3, -2$	$-2, -3$
$(kx + m)(lx + n)$	$(5x - 6)(x - 1)$	$(5x - 1)(x - 6)$	$(5x - 3)(x - 2)$	$(5x - 2)(x - 3)$
$ax^2 + bx + c$	$5x^2 - 11x + 6$	$5x^2 - 31x + 6$	$5x^2 - 13x + 6$	$5x^2 - 17x + 6$

▶ The correct factorization is $5x^2 - 17x + 6 = (5x - 2)(x - 3)$.

EXAMPLE 2 Factor $ax^2 + bx + c$ where $c < 0$

Factor $3x^2 + 20x - 7$.

Solution

You want $3x^2 + 20x - 7 = (kx + m)(lx + n)$ where k and l are factors of 3 and m and n are factors of -7. Because $mn < 0$, m and n have opposite signs.

k, l	3, 1	3, 1	3, 1	3, 1
m, n	$7, -1$	$-1, 7$	$-7, 1$	$1, -7$
$(kx + m)(lx + n)$	$(3x + 7)(x - 1)$	$(3x - 1)(x + 7)$	$(3x - 7)(x + 1)$	$(3x + 1)(x - 7)$
$ax^2 + bx + c$	$3x^2 + 4x - 7$	$3x^2 + 20x - 7$	$3x^2 - 4x - 7$	$3x^2 - 20x - 7$

▶ The correct factorization is $3x^2 + 20x - 7 = (3x - 1)(x + 7)$.

✔ **GUIDED PRACTICE** for Examples 1 and 2

Factor the expression. If the expression cannot be factored, say so.

  1. $7x^2 - 20x - 3$ **2.** $5z^2 + 16z + 3$ **3.** $2w^2 + w + 3$

  4. $3x^2 + 5x - 12$ **5.** $4u^2 + 12u + 5$ **6.** $4x^2 - 9x + 2$

FACTORING SPECIAL PRODUCTS If the values of a and c in $ax^2 + bx + c$ are perfect squares, check to see whether you can use one of the special factoring patterns to factor the expression.

EXAMPLE 3 **Factor with special patterns**

Factor the expression.

  a. $9x^2 - 64 = (3x)^2 - 8^2$ Difference of two squares

  $\quad\quad\quad\quad = (3x + 8)(3x - 8)$

  b. $4y^2 + 20y + 25 = (2y)^2 + 2(2y)(5) + 5^2$ Perfect square trinomial

  $\quad\quad\quad\quad\quad\quad = (2y + 5)^2$

  c. $36w^2 - 12w + 1 = (6w)^2 - 2(6w)(1) + 1^2$ Perfect square trinomial

  $\quad\quad\quad\quad\quad\quad = (6w - 1)^2$

✔ **GUIDED PRACTICE** for Example 3

Factor the expression.

  7. $16x^2 - 1$ **8.** $9y^2 + 12y + 4$ **9.** $4r^2 - 28r + 49$

  10. $25s^2 - 80s + 64$ **11.** $49z^2 + 42z + 9$ **12.** $36n^2 - 9$

FACTORING OUT MONOMIALS When factoring an expression, first check to see whether the terms have a common monomial factor.

EXAMPLE 4 **Factor out monomials first**

Factor the expression.

AVOID ERRORS
Be sure to factor out the common monomial from all of the terms of the expression, not just the first term.

  a. $5x^2 - 45 = 5(x^2 - 9)$ **b.** $6q^2 - 14q + 8 = 2(3q^2 - 7q + 4)$

  $\quad\quad\quad\quad = 5(x + 3)(x - 3)$ $\quad\quad\quad\quad\quad\quad = 2(3q - 4)(q - 1)$

  c. $-5z^2 + 20z = -5z(z - 4)$ **d.** $12p^2 - 21p + 3 = 3(4p^2 - 7p + 1)$

 GUIDED PRACTICE for Example 4

Factor the expression.

  13. $3s^2 - 24$ **14.** $8t^2 + 38t - 10$ **15.** $6x^2 + 24x + 15$

  16. $12x^2 - 28x - 24$ **17.** $-16n^2 + 12n$ **18.** $6z^2 + 33z + 36$

SOLVING QUADRATIC EQUATIONS As you have seen, if the left side of the quadratic equation $ax^2 + bx + c = 0$ can be factored, then the equation can be solved using the zero product property.

EXAMPLE 5 Solve quadratic equations

Solve (a) $3x^2 + 10x - 8 = 0$ and (b) $5p^2 - 16p + 15 = 4p - 5$.

a. $3x^2 + 10x - 8 = 0$ Write original equation.

$(3x - 2)(x + 4) = 0$ Factor.

$3x - 2 = 0$ or $x + 4 = 0$ Zero product property

$x = \dfrac{2}{3}$ or $x = -4$ Solve for *x*.

b. $5p^2 - 16p + 15 = 4p - 5$ Write original equation.

$5p^2 - 20p + 20 = 0$ Write in standard form.

$p^2 - 4p + 4 = 0$ Divide each side by 5.

$(p - 2)^2 = 0$ Factor.

$p - 2 = 0$ Zero product property

$p = 2$ Solve for *p*.

INTERPRET EQUATIONS

If the square of an expression is zero, then the expression itself must be zero.

EXAMPLE 6 Use a quadratic equation as a model

QUILTS You have made a rectangular quilt that is 5 feet by 4 feet. You want to use the remaining 10 square feet of fabric to add a decorative border of uniform width to the quilt. What should the width of the quilt's border be?

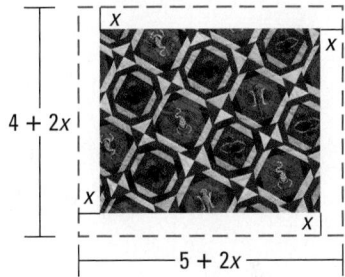

Solution

Write a verbal model. Then write an equation.

Area of border (square feet)	=	Area of quilt and border (square feet)	−	Area of quilt (square feet)

$10 \quad\quad = (5 + 2x)(4 + 2x) - \quad (5)(4)$

$10 = 20 + 18x + 4x^2 - 20$ Multiply using FOIL.

$0 = 4x^2 + 18x - 10$ Write in standard form.

$0 = 2x^2 + 9x - 5$ Divide each side by 2.

$0 = (2x - 1)(x + 5)$ Factor.

$2x - 1 = 0$ or $x + 5 = 0$ Zero product property

$x = \dfrac{1}{2}$ or $x = -5$ Solve for *x*.

▸ Reject the negative value, -5. The border's width should be $\dfrac{1}{2}$ ft, or 6 in.

FACTORING AND ZEROS To find the maximum or minimum value of a quadratic function, you can first use factoring to write the function in intercept form $y = a(x - p)(x - q)$. Because the function's vertex lies on the axis of symmetry $x = \dfrac{p + q}{2}$, the maximum or minimum occurs at the *average* of the zeros p and q.

EXAMPLE 7 **Solve a multi-step problem**

MAGAZINES A monthly teen magazine has 28,000 subscribers when it charges $10 per annual subscription. For each $1 increase in price, the magazine loses about 2000 subscribers. How much should the magazine charge to maximize annual revenue? What is the maximum annual revenue?

Solution

STEP 1 **Define** the variables. Let x represent the price increase and $R(x)$ represent the annual revenue.

STEP 2 **Write** a verbal model. Then write and simplify a quadratic function.

Annual revenue (dollars)	=	Number of subscribers (people)	·	Subscription price (dollars/person)

$$R(x) = (28{,}000 - 2000x) \cdot (10 + x)$$
$$R(x) = (-2000x + 28{,}000)(x + 10)$$
$$R(x) = -2000(x - 14)(x + 10)$$

STEP 3 **Identify** the zeros and find their average. Find how much each subscription should cost to maximize annual revenue.

The zeros of the revenue function are 14 and −10. The average of the zeros is $\dfrac{14 + (-10)}{2} = 2$. To maximize revenue, each subscription should cost $10 + $2 = $12.

STEP 4 **Find** the maximum annual revenue.

$$R(2) = -2000(2 - 14)(2 + 10) = \$288{,}000$$

▶ The magazine should charge $12 per subscription to maximize annual revenue. The maximum annual revenue is $288,000.

✓ **GUIDED PRACTICE** for Examples 5, 6, and 7

Solve the equation.

19. $6x^2 - 3x - 63 = 0$ **20.** $12x^2 + 7x + 2 = x + 8$ **21.** $7x^2 + 70x + 175 - 0$

22. **WHAT IF?** In Example 7, suppose the magazine initially charges $11 per annual subscription. How much should the magazine charge to maximize annual revenue? What is the maximum annual revenue?

1.4 EXERCISES

HOMEWORK KEY

◯ = See WORKED-OUT SOLUTIONS
Exs. 27, 39, and 63

★ = STANDARDIZED TEST PRACTICE
Exs. 2, 12, 64, 65, and 67

SKILL PRACTICE

1. **VOCABULARY** What is the greatest common monomial factor of the terms of the expression $12x^2 + 8x + 20$?

2. ★ **WRITING** *Explain* how the values of a and c in $ax^2 + bx + c$ help you determine whether you can use a perfect square trinomial factoring pattern.

EXAMPLES 1 and 2
for Exs. 3–12

FACTORING Factor the expression. If the expression cannot be factored, say so.

3. $2x^2 + 5x + 3$

4. $3n^2 + 7n + 4$

5. $4r^2 + 5r + 1$

6. $6p^2 + 5p + 1$

7. $11z^2 + 2z - 9$

8. $15x^2 - 2x - 8$

9. $4y^2 - 5y - 4$

10. $14m^2 + m - 3$

11. $9d^2 - 13d - 10$

12. ★ **MULTIPLE CHOICE** Which factorization of $5x^2 + 14x - 3$ is correct?

A $(5x - 3)(x + 1)$

B $(5x + 1)(x - 3)$

C $5(x - 1)(x + 3)$

D $(5x - 1)(x + 3)$

EXAMPLE 3
for Exs. 13–21

FACTORING WITH SPECIAL PATTERNS Factor the expression.

13. $9x^2 - 1$

14. $4r^2 - 25$

15. $49n^2 - 16$

16. $16s^2 + 8s + 1$

17. $49x^2 + 70x + 25$

18. $64w^2 + 144w + 81$

19. $9p^2 - 12p + 4$

20. $25t^2 - 30t + 9$

21. $36x^2 - 84x + 49$

EXAMPLE 4
for Exs. 22–31

FACTORING MONOMIALS FIRST Factor the expression.

22. $12x^2 - 4x - 40$

23. $18z^2 + 36z + 16$

24. $32v^2 - 2$

25. $6u^2 - 24u$

26. $12m^2 - 36m + 27$

27. $20x^2 + 124x + 24$

28. $21x^2 - 77x - 28$

29. $-36n^2 + 48n - 15$

30. $-8y^2 + 28y - 60$

31. **ERROR ANALYSIS** *Describe* and correct the error in factoring the expression.

$$4x^2 - 36 = 4(x^2 - 36)$$
$$= 4(x + 6)(x - 6)$$

EXAMPLE 5
for Exs. 32–40

SOLVING EQUATIONS Solve the equation.

32. $16x^2 - 1 = 0$

33. $11q^2 - 44 = 0$

34. $14s^2 - 21s = 0$

35. $45n^2 + 10n = 0$

36. $4x^2 - 20x + 25 = 0$

37. $4p^2 + 12p + 9 = 0$

38. $15x^2 + 7x - 2 = 0$

39. $6r^2 - 7r - 5 = 0$

40. $36z^2 + 96z + 15 = 0$

EXAMPLE 7
for Exs. 41–49

FINDING ZEROS Find the zeros of the function by rewriting the function in intercept form.

41. $y = 4x^2 - 19x - 5$

42. $g(x) = 3x^2 - 8x + 5$

43. $y = 5x^2 - 27x - 18$

44. $f(x) = 3x^2 - 3x$

45. $y = 11x^2 - 19x - 6$

46. $y = 16x^2 - 2x - 5$

47. $y = 15x^2 - 5x - 20$

48. $y = 18x^2 - 6x - 4$

49. $g(x) = 12x^2 + 5x - 7$

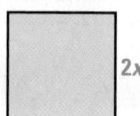 **GEOMETRY** Find the value of x.

50. Area of square = 36

51. Area of rectangle = 30

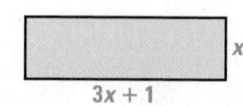

3x + 1

52. Area of triangle = 115

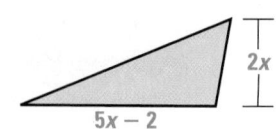

SOLVING EQUATIONS Solve the equation.

53. $2x^2 - 4x - 8 = -x^2 + x$

54. $24x^2 + 8x + 2 = 5 - 6x$

55. $18x^2 - 22x = 28$

56. $13x^2 + 21x = -5x^2 + 22$

57. $x = 4x^2 - 15x$

58. $(x + 8)^2 = 16 - x^2 + 9x$

CHALLENGE Factor the expression.

59. $2x^3 - 5x^2 + 3x$

60. $8x^4 - 8x^3 - 6x^2$

61. $9x^3 - 4x$

PROBLEM SOLVING

EXAMPLE 6
for Exs. 62–63

62. ARTS AND CRAFTS You have a rectangular stained glass window that measures 2 feet by 1 foot. You have 4 square feet of glass with which to make a border of uniform width around the window. What should the width of the border be?

63. URBAN PLANNING You have just planted a rectangular flower bed of red roses in a city park. You want to plant a border of yellow roses around the flower bed as shown. Because you bought the same number of red and yellow roses, the areas of the border and flower bed will be equal. What should the width of the border of yellow roses be?

EXAMPLE 7
for Exs. 64–65

64. ★ **MULTIPLE CHOICE** A surfboard shop sells 45 surfboards per month when it charges $500 per surfboard. For each $20 decrease in price, the store sells 5 more surfboards per month. How much should the shop charge per surfboard in order to maximize monthly revenue?

(A) $340

(B) $492

(C) $508

(D) $660

65. ★ **SHORT RESPONSE** A restaurant sells about 330 sandwiches each day at a price of $6 each. For each $.25 decrease in price, 15 more sandwiches are sold per day. How much should the restaurant charge to maximize daily revenue? *Explain* each step of your solution. What is the maximum daily revenue?

66. PAINTINGS You place a mat around a 25 inch by 21 inch painting as shown. The mat is twice as wide at the left and right of the painting as it is at the top and bottom of the painting. The area of the mat is 714 square inches. How wide is the mat at the left and right of the painting? at the top and bottom of the painting?

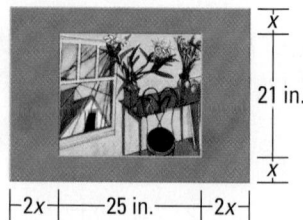

○ = See **WORKED-OUT SOLUTIONS** in Student Resources

★ = **STANDARDIZED TEST PRACTICE**

Seth Thompson/Getty Images

67. ★ **EXTENDED RESPONSE** A U.S. Postal Service guideline states that for a rectangular package like the one shown, the sum of the length and the girth cannot exceed 108 inches. Suppose that for one such package, the length is 36 inches and the girth is as large as possible.

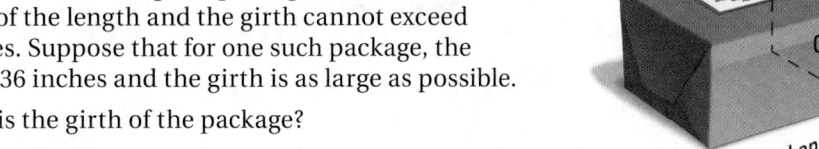

  a. What is the girth of the package?

  b. Write an expression for the package's width w in terms of h. Write an equation giving the package's volume V in terms of h.

  c. What height and width maximize the volume of the package? What is the maximum volume? *Explain* how you found it.

68. **CHALLENGE** Recall from geometry the theorem about the products of the lengths of segments of two chords that intersect in the interior of a circle. Use this theorem to find the value of x in the diagram.

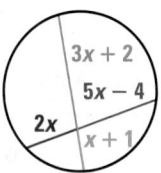

QUIZ

Graph the function. Label the vertex and axis of symmetry.

  1. $y = x^2 - 6x + 14$
  2. $y = 2x^2 + 8x + 15$
  3. $f(x) = -3x^2 + 6x - 5$

Write the quadratic function in standard form.

  4. $y = (x - 4)(x - 8)$
  5. $g(x) = -2(x + 3)(x - 7)$
  6. $y = 5(x + 6)^2 - 2$

Solve the equation.

  7. $x^2 + 9x + 20 = 0$
  8. $n^2 - 11n + 24 = 0$
  9. $z^2 - 3z - 40 = 0$
  10. $5s^2 - 14s - 3 = 0$
  11. $7a^2 - 30a + 8 = 0$
  12. $4x^2 + 20x + 25 = 0$

13. **DVD PLAYERS** A store sells about 50 of a new model of DVD player per month at a price of $140 each. For each $10 decrease in price, about 5 more DVD players per month are sold. How much should the store charge in order to maximize monthly revenue? What is the maximum monthly revenue?

1.5 Solve Quadratic Equations by Finding Square Roots

 **Before**	You solved quadratic equations by factoring.
Now	You will solve quadratic equations by finding square roots.
Why?	So you can solve problems about astronomy, as in Ex. 39.

Key Vocabulary
- **square root**
- **radical**
- **radicand**
- **rationalizing the denominator**
- **conjugates**

A number r is a **square root** of a number s if $r^2 = s$. A positive number s has two square roots, written as $\sqrt{s}$ and $-\sqrt{s}$. For example, because $3^2 = 9$ and $(-3)^2 = 9$, the two square roots of 9 are $\sqrt{9} = 3$ and $-\sqrt{9} = -3$. The positive square root of a number is also called the *principal* square root.

The expression $\sqrt{s}$ is called a **radical**. The symbol $\sqrt{}$ is a *radical sign*, and the number s beneath the radical sign is the **radicand** of the expression.

CC.9-12.A.REI.4b Solve quadratic equations by inspection (e.g., for $x^2 = 49$), taking square roots, completing the square, the quadratic formula and factoring, as appropriate to the initial form of the equation. Recognize when the quadratic formula gives complex solutions and write them as $a \pm bi$ for real numbers a and b.

KEY CONCEPT   *For Your Notebook*

Properties of Square Roots ($a > 0$, $b > 0$)

Product Property $\sqrt{ab} = \sqrt{a} \cdot \sqrt{b}$ **Example** $\sqrt{18} = \sqrt{9} \cdot \sqrt{2} = 3\sqrt{2}$

Quotient Property $\sqrt{\dfrac{a}{b}} = \dfrac{\sqrt{a}}{\sqrt{b}}$ **Example** $\sqrt{\dfrac{2}{25}} = \dfrac{\sqrt{2}}{\sqrt{25}} = \dfrac{\sqrt{2}}{5}$

SIMPLIFYING SQUARE ROOTS You can use the properties above to simplify expressions containing square roots. A square-root expression is simplified if:

- no radicand has a perfect-square factor other than 1, and

- there is no radical in a denominator

EXAMPLE 1   Use properties of square roots

Simplify the expression.

USE A CALCULATOR
You can use a calculator to approximate $\sqrt{s}$ when s is not a perfect square. For example, $\sqrt{80} \approx 8.944$.

a. $\sqrt{80} = \sqrt{16} \cdot \sqrt{5} = 4\sqrt{5}$ **b.** $\sqrt{6} \cdot \sqrt{21} = \sqrt{126} = \sqrt{9} \cdot \sqrt{14} = 3\sqrt{14}$

c. $\sqrt{\dfrac{4}{81}} = \dfrac{\sqrt{4}}{\sqrt{81}} = \dfrac{2}{9}$ **d.** $\sqrt{\dfrac{7}{16}} = \dfrac{\sqrt{7}}{\sqrt{16}} = \dfrac{\sqrt{7}}{4}$

 GUIDED PRACTICE   for Example 1

Simplify the expression.

1. $\sqrt{27}$ **2.** $\sqrt{98}$ **3.** $\sqrt{10} \cdot \sqrt{15}$ **4.** $\sqrt{8} \cdot \sqrt{28}$

5. $\sqrt{\dfrac{9}{64}}$ **6.** $\sqrt{\dfrac{15}{4}}$ **7.** $\sqrt{\dfrac{11}{25}}$ **8.** $\sqrt{\dfrac{36}{49}}$

NASA

RATIONALIZING THE DENOMINATOR
Suppose the denominator of a fraction has the form $\sqrt{b}$, $a + \sqrt{b}$, or $a - \sqrt{b}$ where a and b are rational numbers. The table shows how to eliminate the radical from the denominator. This is called **rationalizing the denominator**.

Form of the denominator	Multiply numerator and denominator by:
$\sqrt{b}$	$\sqrt{b}$
$a + \sqrt{b}$	$a - \sqrt{b}$
$a - \sqrt{b}$	$a + \sqrt{b}$

The expressions $a + \sqrt{b}$ and $a - \sqrt{b}$ are called **conjugates** of each other. Their product is always a rational number.

EXAMPLE 2 **Rationalize denominators of fractions**

Simplify (a) $\sqrt{\dfrac{5}{2}}$ and (b) $\dfrac{3}{7 + \sqrt{2}}$.

Solution

a. $\sqrt{\dfrac{5}{2}} = \dfrac{\sqrt{5}}{\sqrt{2}}$

$= \dfrac{\sqrt{5}}{\sqrt{2}} \cdot \dfrac{\sqrt{2}}{\sqrt{2}}$

$= \dfrac{\sqrt{10}}{2}$

b. $\dfrac{3}{7 + \sqrt{2}} = \dfrac{3}{7 + \sqrt{2}} \cdot \dfrac{7 - \sqrt{2}}{7 - \sqrt{2}}$

$= \dfrac{21 - 3\sqrt{2}}{49 - 7\sqrt{2} + 7\sqrt{2} - 2}$

$= \dfrac{21 - 3\sqrt{2}}{47}$

SOLVING QUADRATIC EQUATIONS You can use square roots to solve some types of quadratic equations. For example, if $s > 0$, then the equation $x^2 = s$ has two real-number solutions: $x = \sqrt{s}$ and $x = -\sqrt{s}$. These solutions are often written in condensed form as $x = \pm\sqrt{s}$ (read as "plus or minus the square root of s").

EXAMPLE 3 **Solve a quadratic equation**

Solve $3x^2 + 5 = 41$.

$3x^2 + 5 = 41$	Write original equation.
$3x^2 = 36$	Subtract 5 from each side.
$x^2 = 12$	Divide each side by 3.
$x = \pm\sqrt{12}$	Take square roots of each side.
$x = \pm\sqrt{4} \cdot \sqrt{3}$	Product property
$x = \pm 2\sqrt{3}$	Simplify.

AVOID ERRORS
When solving an equation of the form $x^2 = s$ where $s > 0$, make sure to find both the positive and negative solutions.

▶ The solutions are $2\sqrt{3}$ and $-2\sqrt{3}$.

CHECK Check the solutions by substituting them into the original equation.

$3x^2 + 5 = 41$ $3x^2 + 5 = 41$

$3\left(2\sqrt{3}\right)^2 + 5 \stackrel{?}{=} 41$ $3\left(-2\sqrt{3}\right)^2 + 5 \stackrel{?}{=} 41$

$3(12) + 5 \stackrel{?}{=} 41$ $3(12) + 5 \stackrel{?}{=} 41$

$41 = 41$ ✓ $41 = 41$ ✓

What are the solutions of the equation $\frac{1}{5}(z + 3)^2 = 7$?

(A) $-38, 32$

(B) $-3 - 5\sqrt{7}, -3 + 5\sqrt{7}$

(C) $-3 - \sqrt{35}, -3 + \sqrt{35}$

(D) $-3 - \dfrac{\sqrt{35}}{5}, -3 + \dfrac{\sqrt{35}}{5}$

Solution

$\frac{1}{5}(z + 3)^2 = 7$	Write original equation.
$(z + 3)^2 = 35$	Multiply each side by 5.
$z + 3 = \pm\sqrt{35}$	Take square roots of each side.
$z = -3 \pm \sqrt{35}$	Subtract 3 from each side.

The solutions are $-3 + \sqrt{35}$ and $-3 - \sqrt{35}$.

▶ The correct answer is C. Ⓐ Ⓑ ● Ⓓ

 GUIDED PRACTICE for Examples 2, 3, and 4

Simplify the expression.

9. $\sqrt{\dfrac{6}{5}}$ **10.** $\sqrt{\dfrac{9}{8}}$ **11.** $\sqrt{\dfrac{17}{12}}$ **12.** $\sqrt{\dfrac{19}{21}}$

13. $\dfrac{-6}{7 - \sqrt{5}}$ **14.** $\dfrac{2}{4 + \sqrt{11}}$ **15.** $\dfrac{-1}{9 + \sqrt{7}}$ **16.** $\dfrac{4}{8 - \sqrt{3}}$

Solve the equation.

17. $5x^2 = 80$ **18.** $z^2 - 7 = 29$ **19.** $3(x - 2)^2 = 40$

MODELING DROPPED OBJECTS When an object is dropped, its height h (in feet) above the ground after t seconds can be modeled by the function

$$h = -16t^2 + h_0$$

where h_0 is the object's initial height (in feet). The graph of $h = -16t^2 + 200$, representing the height of an object dropped from an initial height of 200 feet, is shown at the right.

The model $h = -16t^2 + h_0$ assumes that the force of air resistance on the object is negligible. Also, this model works only on Earth. For planets with stronger or weaker gravity, different models are used (see Exercise 39).

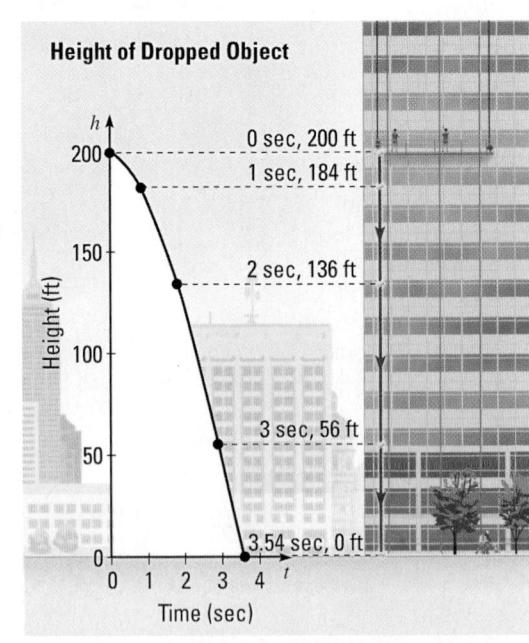

Height of Dropped Object

0 sec, 200 ft
1 sec, 184 ft
2 sec, 136 ft
3 sec, 56 ft
3.54 sec, 0 ft

Height (ft)

Time (sec)

EXAMPLE 5   Model a dropped object with a quadratic function

SCIENCE COMPETITION For a science competition, students must design a container that prevents an egg from breaking when dropped from a height of 50 feet. How long does the container take to hit the ground?

ANOTHER WAY

For alternative methods for solving the problem in Example 5, see the **Problem Solving Workshop**.

Solution

$$h = -16t^2 + h_0 \qquad \text{Write height function.}$$

$$0 = -16t^2 + 50 \qquad \text{Substitute 0 for } h \text{ and 50 for } h_0.$$

$$-50 = -16t^2 \qquad \text{Subtract 50 from each side.}$$

$$\frac{50}{16} = t^2 \qquad \text{Divide each side by } -16.$$

$$\pm\sqrt{\frac{50}{16}} = t \qquad \text{Take square roots of each side.}$$

$$\pm 1.8 \approx t \qquad \text{Use a calculator.}$$

▶ Reject the negative solution, −1.8, because time must be positive. The container will fall for about 1.8 seconds before it hits the ground.

Animated Algebra   at my.hrw.com

After a successful egg drop

✓ **GUIDED PRACTICE**   for Example 5

20. WHAT IF? In Example 5, suppose the egg container is dropped from a height of 30 feet. How long does the container take to hit the ground?

1.5 **EXERCISES**

HOMEWORK
KEY

◯ = See **WORKED-OUT SOLUTIONS**
      Exs. 17, 27, and 41

★ = **STANDARDIZED TEST PRACTICE**
      Exs. 2, 19, 34, 35, 36, 40, and 41

SKILL PRACTICE

1. **VOCABULARY** In the expression $\sqrt{72}$, what is 72 called?

2. ★ **WRITING** *Explain* what it means to "rationalize the denominator" of a quotient containing square roots.

EXAMPLES
1 and 2
for Exs. 3–20

SIMPLIFYING RADICAL EXPRESSIONS Simplify the expression.

3. $\sqrt{28}$

4. $\sqrt{192}$

5. $\sqrt{150}$

6. $\sqrt{3} \cdot \sqrt{27}$

7. $4\sqrt{6} \cdot \sqrt{6}$

8. $5\sqrt{24} \cdot 3\sqrt{10}$

9. $\sqrt{\dfrac{5}{16}}$

10. $\sqrt{\dfrac{35}{36}}$

11. $\dfrac{8}{\sqrt{3}}$

12. $\dfrac{7}{\sqrt{12}}$

13. $\sqrt{\dfrac{18}{11}}$

14. $\sqrt{\dfrac{13}{28}}$

15. $\dfrac{2}{1 - \sqrt{3}}$

16. $\dfrac{1}{5 + \sqrt{6}}$

(17.) $\dfrac{\sqrt{2}}{4 + \sqrt{5}}$

18. $\dfrac{3 + \sqrt{7}}{2 - \sqrt{10}}$

19. ★ **MULTIPLE CHOICE** What is a completely simplified expression for $\sqrt{108}$?

    (A) $2\sqrt{27}$ **(B)** $3\sqrt{12}$ **(C)** $6\sqrt{3}$ **(D)** $10\sqrt{8}$

ERROR ANALYSIS *Describe* and correct the error in simplifying the expression or solving the equation.

20.

$$\sqrt{96} = \sqrt{4} \cdot \sqrt{24}$$
$$= 2\sqrt{24}$$

21.

$$5x^2 = 405$$
$$x^2 = 81$$
$$x = 9$$

SOLVING QUADRATIC EQUATIONS Solve the equation.

EXAMPLES 3 and 4 for Exs. 21–34

22. $s^2 = 169$ **23.** $a^2 = 50$ **24.** $x^2 = 84$

25. $6z^2 = 150$ **26.** $4p^2 = 448$ **27.** $-3w^2 = -213$

28. $7r^2 - 10 = 25$ **29.** $\dfrac{x^2}{25} - 6 = -2$ **30.** $\dfrac{t^2}{20} + 8 = 15$

31. $4(x - 1)^2 = 8$ **32.** $7(x - 4)^2 - 18 = 10$ **33.** $2(x + 2)^2 - 5 = 8$

34. **SOLVING EQUATIONS AND INEQUALITIES** Solve the equation or inequality. Simplify any radical expressions.

    a. $\sqrt{12} - x\sqrt{2} \le \sqrt{3}$ **b.** $x\sqrt{3} > 2 + x$ **c.** $2\sqrt{5} = 4 + x\sqrt{8}$

35. ★ **SHORT RESPONSE** *Describe* two different methods for solving the equation $x^2 - 4 = 0$. Include the steps for each method.

36. ★ **OPEN-ENDED MATH** Write an equation of the form $x^2 = s$ that has **(a)** two real solutions, **(b)** exactly one real solution, and **(c)** no real solutions.

37. **CHALLENGE** Solve the equation $a(x + b)^2 = c$ in terms of a, b, and c.

PROBLEM SOLVING

EXAMPLE 5 for Exs. 38–39

38. **CLIFF DIVING** A cliff diver dives off a cliff 40 feet above water. Write an equation giving the diver's height h (in feet) above the water after t seconds. How long is the diver in the air?

39. **ASTRONOMY** On any planet, the height h (in feet) of a falling object t seconds after it is dropped can be modeled by $h = -\dfrac{g}{2}t^2 + h_0$ where h_0 is the object's initial height (in feet) and g is the acceleration (in feet per second squared) due to gravity. For each planet (or dwarf planet) in the table, find the time it takes for a rock dropped from a height of 150 feet to hit the surface.

Planet	Earth	Mars	Jupiter	Saturn	Pluto (dwarf planet)
g (ft/sec^2)	32	12	76	30	2

40. ★ **SHORT RESPONSE** The equation $h = 0.019s^2$ gives the height h (in feet) of the largest ocean waves when the wind speed is s knots. *Compare* the wind speeds required to generate 5 foot waves and 20 foot waves.

41. ★ **EXTENDED RESPONSE** You want to transform a square gravel parking lot with 10 foot sides into a circular lot. You want the circle to have the same area as the square so that you do not have to buy any additional gravel.

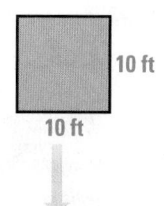
10 ft
10 ft
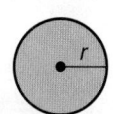

   a. **Model** Write an equation you can use to find the radius r of the circular lot.

   b. **Solve** What should the radius of the circular lot be?

   c. **Generalize** In general, if a square has sides of length s, what is the radius r of a circle with the same area? *Justify* your answer algebraically.

42. **BICYCLING** The air resistance R (in pounds) on a racing cyclist is given by the equation $R = 0.00829s^2$ where s is the bicycle's speed (in miles per hour).

   a. What is the speed of a racing cyclist who experiences 5 pounds of air resistance?

   b. What happens to the air resistance if the cyclist's speed doubles? *Justify* your answer algebraically.

43. **CHALLENGE** For a swimming pool with a rectangular base, Torricelli's law implies that the height h of water in the pool t seconds after it begins draining is given by $h = \left(\sqrt{h_0} - \dfrac{2\pi d^2 \sqrt{3}}{lw} t \right)^2$ where l and w are the pool's length and width, d is the diameter of the drain, and h_0 is the water's initial height. (All measurements are in inches.) In terms of l, w, d, and h_0, what is the time required to drain the pool when it is completely filled?

Using ALTERNATIVE METHODS

Another Way to Solve Example 5

Make sense of problems and persevere in solving them.

MULTIPLE REPRESENTATIONS In Example 5, you solved a quadratic equation by finding square roots. You can also solve a quadratic equation using a table or a graph.

PROBLEM

SCIENCE COMPETITION For a science competition, students must design a container that prevents an egg from breaking when dropped from a height of 50 feet. How long does the container take to hit the ground?

METHOD 1

Using a Table One alternative approach is to write a quadratic equation and then use a table of values to solve the equation. You can use a graphing calculator to make the table.

STEP 1 **Write** an equation that models the situation using the height function $h = -16t^2 + h_0$.

$$h = -16t^2 + h_0 \qquad \text{Write height function.}$$

$$0 = -16t^2 + 50 \qquad \text{Substitute 0 for } h \text{ and 50 for } h_0.$$

STEP 2 **Enter** the function $y = -16x^2 + 50$ into a graphing calculator. Note that time is now represented by x and height is now represented by y.

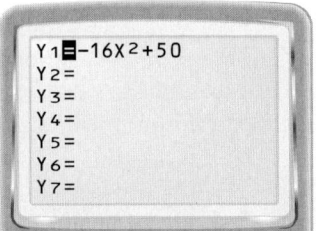

STEP 3 **Make** a table of values for the function. Set the table so that the x-values start at 0 and increase in increments of 0.1.

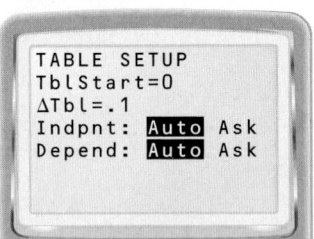

STEP 4 **Scroll** through the table to find the time x at which the height y of the container is 0 feet.

The table shows that $y = 0$ between $x = 1.7$ and $x = 1.8$ because y has a change of sign.

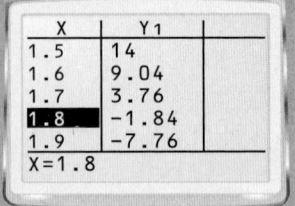

▶ The container hits the ground between 1.7 and 1.8 seconds after it is dropped.

METHOD 2

Using a Graph Another approach is to write a quadratic equation and then use a graph to solve the equation. You can use a graphing calculator to make the graph.

STEP 1 **Write** an equation that models the situation using the height function $h = -16t^2 + h_0$.

$$h = -16t^2 + h_0 \qquad \text{Write height function.}$$

$$0 = -16t^2 + 50 \qquad \text{Substitute 0 for } h \text{ and 50 for } h_0.$$

STEP 2 **Enter** the function $y = -16x^2 + 50$ into a graphing calculator. Note that time is now represented by x and height is now represented by y.

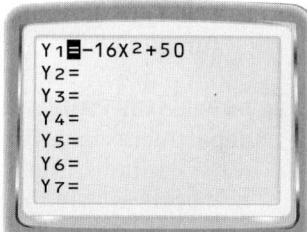

STEP 3 **Graph** the height function. Adjust the viewing window so that you can see the point where the graph crosses the positive x-axis. Find the positive x-value for which $y = 0$ using the *zero* feature. The graph shows that $y = 0$ when $x \approx 1.8$.

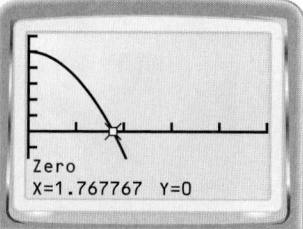

▶ The container hits the ground about 1.8 seconds after it is dropped.

PRACTICE

SOLVING EQUATIONS **Solve the quadratic equation using a table and using a graph.**

1. $2x^2 - 12x + 10 = 0$

2. $x^2 + 7x + 12 = 0$

3. $9x^2 - 30x + 25 = 0$

4. $7x^2 - 3 = 0$

5. $x^2 + 3x - 6 = 0$

6. **WHAT IF?** How long does it take for an egg container to hit the ground when dropped from a height of 100 feet? Find the answer using a table and using a graph.

7. **WIND PRESSURE** The pressure P (in pounds per square foot) from wind blowing at s miles per hour is given by $P = 0.00256s^2$. What wind speed produces a pressure of 30 lb/ft^2? Solve this problem using a table and using a graph.

8. **BIRDS** A bird flying at a height of 30 feet carries a shellfish. The bird drops the shellfish to break it and get the food inside. How long does it take for the shellfish to hit the ground? Find the answer using a table and using a graph.

9. **DROPPED OBJECT** You are dropping a ball from a window 29 feet above the ground to your friend who will catch it 4 feet above the ground. How long is the ball in the air before your friend catches it? Solve this problem using a table and using a graph.

10. **REASONING** *Explain* how to use the *table* feature of a graphing calculator to approximate the solution of the problem on the preceding page to the nearest hundredth of a second. Use this procedure to find the approximate solution.

MIXED REVIEW *of Problem Solving*

MATHEMATICAL PRACTICES — Make sense of problems and persevere in solving them.

1. **MULTI-STEP PROBLEM** A pinecone falls from a tree branch that is 20 feet above the ground.

   a. Write a function that models the height of the pinecone as it falls.

   b. Graph the function.

   c. After how many seconds does the pinecone hit the ground?

   d. What are the domain and range of the function?

2. **MULTI-STEP PROBLEM** Some harbor police departments have fire-fighting boats with water cannons. The boats are used to fight fires that occur within the harbor.

   a. The function $y = -0.0035x(x - 143.9)$ models the path of water shot by a water cannon where x is the horizontal distance (in feet) and y is the corresponding height (in feet). What are the domain and range of this function?

   b. How far does the water cannon shoot?

   c. What is the maximum height of the water?

3. **EXTENDED RESPONSE** The diagonal of the screen on a laptop computer measures 15 inches. The ratio of the screen's width w to its height h is $4:3$.

   a. Write an expression for w in terms of h.

   b. Use the Pythagorean theorem and the result from part (a) to write an equation that you can use to find h.

   c. Solve the equation from part (b). *Explain* why you must reject one of the solutions.

   d. What are the height, width, and area of the laptop screen?

4. **SHORT RESPONSE** You are creating a metal border of uniform width for a wall mirror that is 20 inches by 24 inches. You have 416 square inches of metal to use. Write and solve an equation to find the border's width. Does doubling the width require exactly twice as much metal? *Explain.*

   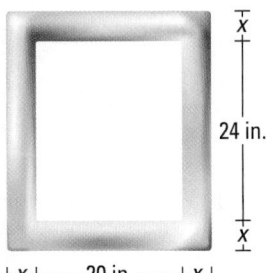

   24 in.

   ⊢x⊣— 20 in. —⊢x⊣

5. **EXTENDED RESPONSE** A pizza shop sells about 80 slices of pizza each day during lunch when it charges $2 per slice. For each $.25 increase in price, about 5 fewer slices are sold each day during lunch.

   a. Write a function that gives the pizza shop's revenue R if there are x price increases.

   b. What value of x maximizes R? *Explain* the meaning of your answer in this situation.

   c. Repeat parts (a) and (b) using the equivalent assumption that each $.25 *decrease* in price results in 5 *more* slices being sold. Why do you obtain a negative x-value in part (b)?

6. **GRIDDED ANSWER** You have a rectangular vegetable garden that measures 42 feet by 8 feet. You want to double the area of the garden by expanding the length and width as shown. Find the value of x.

   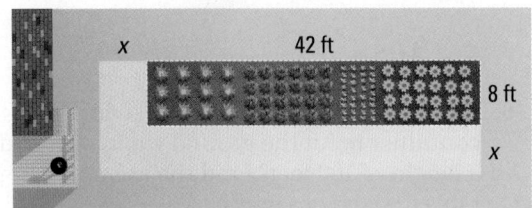

   x — 42 ft — 8 ft — x

7. **OPEN-ENDED** Write three different quadratic functions in standard form whose graphs have a vertex of $(-3, 2)$.

AP Images/Cheryl Hatch

1.6 Perform Operations with Complex Numbers

Before You performed operations with real numbers.

Now You will perform operations with complex numbers.

Why? So you can solve problems involving fractals, as in Ex. 76.

Key Vocabulary
- **imaginary unit** *i*
- **complex number**
- **imaginary number**
- **complex conjugates**
- **complex plane**
- **absolute value of a complex number**

CC.9-12. N.CN.2 Use the relation $i^2 = -1$ and the commutative, associative, and distributive properties to add, subtract, and multiply complex numbers.

Not all quadratic equations have real-number solutions. For example, $x^2 = -1$ has no real-number solutions because the square of any real number x is never a negative number.

To overcome this problem, mathematicians created an expanded system of numbers using the **imaginary unit *i***, defined as $i = \sqrt{-1}$. Note that $i^2 = -1$. The imaginary unit *i* can be used to write the square root of *any* negative number.

KEY CONCEPT
For Your Notebook

The Square Root of a Negative Number

Property

1. If *r* is a positive real number, then $\sqrt{-r} = i\sqrt{r}$.

2. By Property (1), it follows that $(i\sqrt{r})^2 = -r$.

Example

$\sqrt{-3} = i\sqrt{3}$

$(i\sqrt{3})^2 = i^2 \cdot 3 = -3$

EXAMPLE 1 Solve a quadratic equation

Solve $2x^2 + 11 = -37$.

$2x^2 + 11 = -37$	Write original equation.
$2x^2 = -48$	Subtract 11 from each side.
$x^2 = -24$	Divide each side by 2.
$x = \pm\sqrt{-24}$	Take square roots of each side.
$x = \pm i\sqrt{24}$	Write in terms of *i*.
$x = \pm 2i\sqrt{6}$	Simplify radical.

▶ The solutions are $2i\sqrt{6}$ and $-2i\sqrt{6}$.

✓ GUIDED PRACTICE for Example 1

Solve the equation.

1. $x^2 = -13$
2. $x^2 = -38$
3. $x^2 + 11 = 3$
4. $x^2 - 8 = -36$
5. $3x^2 - 7 = -31$
6. $5x^2 + 33 = 3$

COMPLEX NUMBERS A **complex number** written in **standard form** is a number $a + bi$ where a and b are real numbers. The number a is the *real part* of the complex number, and the number bi is the *imaginary part*.

If $b \neq 0$, then $a + bi$ is an **imaginary number**. If $a = 0$ and $b \neq 0$, then $a + bi$ is a **pure imaginary number**. The diagram shows how different types of complex numbers are related.

Two complex numbers $a + bi$ and $c + di$ are equal if and only if $a = c$ and $b = d$. For example, if $x + yi = 5 - 3i$, then $x = 5$ and $y = -3$.

Complex Numbers ($a + bi$)

Real Numbers ($a + 0i$)	Imaginary Numbers ($a + bi, b \neq 0$)
$-1 \quad \dfrac{5}{2}$ $\pi \quad \sqrt{2}$	$2 + 3i \quad 5 - 5i$ **Pure Imaginary Numbers** ($0 + bi, b \neq 0$) $-4i \quad 6i$

KEY CONCEPT   *For Your Notebook*

Sums and Differences of Complex Numbers

To add (or subtract) two complex numbers, add (or subtract) their real parts and their imaginary parts separately.

Sum of complex numbers: $(a + bi) + (c + di) = (a + c) + (b + d)i$

Difference of complex numbers: $(a + bi) - (c + di) = (a - c) + (b - d)i$

EXAMPLE 2   **Add and subtract complex numbers**

Write the expression as a complex number in standard form.

a. $(8 - i) + (5 + 4i)$ **b.** $(7 - 6i) - (3 - 6i)$ **c.** $10 - (6 + 7i) + 4i$

Solution

a. $(8 - i) + (5 + 4i) = (8 + 5) + (-1 + 4)i$ **Definition of complex addition**

$= 13 + 3i$ **Write in standard form.**

b. $(7 - 6i) - (3 - 6i) = (7 - 3) + (-6 + 6)i$ **Definition of complex subtraction**

$= 4 + 0i$ **Simplify.**

$= 4$ **Write in standard form.**

c. $10 - (6 + 7i) + 4i = [(10 - 6) - 7i] + 4i$ **Definition of complex subtraction**

$= (4 - 7i) + 4i$ **Simplify.**

$= 4 + (-7 + 4)i$ **Definition of complex addition**

$= 4 - 3i$ **Write in standard form.**

 GUIDED PRACTICE   for Example 2

Write the expression as a complex number in standard form.

7. $(9 - i) + (-6 + 7i)$ **8.** $(3 + 7i) - (8 - 2i)$ **9.** $-4 - (1 + i) - (5 + 9i)$

EXAMPLE 3 Use addition of complex numbers in real life

ELECTRICITY Circuit components such as resistors, inductors, and capacitors all oppose the flow of current. This opposition is called *resistance* for resistors and *reactance* for inductors and capacitors. A circuit's total opposition to current flow is *impedance*. All of these quantities are measured in ohms (Ω).

READING

Note that while a component's resistance or reactance is a real number, its impedance is a complex number.

Component and symbol	Resistor —W—	Inductor —ell—	Capacitor —⊣⊢—
Resistance or reactance	R	L	C
Impedance	R	Li	$-Ci$

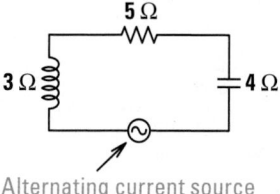

Alternating current source

The table shows the relationship between a component's resistance or reactance and its contribution to impedance. A *series circuit* is also shown with the resistance or reactance of each component labeled.

The impedance for a series circuit is the sum of the impedances for the individual components. Find the impedance of the circuit shown above.

Solution

The resistor has a resistance of 5 ohms, so its impedance is 5 ohms. The inductor has a reactance of 3 ohms, so its impedance is $3i$ ohms. The capacitor has a reactance of 4 ohms, so its impedance is $-4i$ ohms.

$$\text{Impedance of circuit} = 5 + 3i + (-4i) \qquad \textbf{Add the individual impedances.}$$

$$= 5 - i \qquad \textbf{Simplify.}$$

▶ The impedance of the circuit is $5 - i$ ohms.

MULTIPLYING COMPLEX NUMBERS To multiply two complex numbers, use the distributive property or the FOIL method just as you do when multiplying real numbers or algebraic expressions.

EXAMPLE 4 Multiply complex numbers

Write the expression as a complex number in standard form.

a. $4i(-6 + i)$ **b.** $(9 - 2i)(-4 + 7i)$

Solution

AVOID ERRORS

When simplifying an expression that involves complex numbers, be sure to simplify i^2 to -1.

a. $4i(-6 + i) = -24i + 4i^2$ **Distributive property**

$\qquad\qquad\quad = -24i + 4(-1)$ **Use $i^2 = -1$.**

$\qquad\qquad\quad = -24i - 4$ **Simplify.**

$\qquad\qquad\quad = -4 - 24i$ **Write in standard form.**

b. $(9 - 2i)(-4 + 7i) = -36 + 63i + 8i - 14i^2$ **Multiply using FOIL.**

$\qquad\qquad\qquad\qquad = -36 + 71i - 14(-1)$ **Simplify and use $i^2 = -1$.**

$\qquad\qquad\qquad\qquad = -36 + 71i + 14$ **Simplify.**

$\qquad\qquad\qquad\qquad = -22 + 71i$ **Write in standard form.**

COMPLEX CONJUGATES Two complex numbers of the form $a + bi$ and $a - bi$ are called **complex conjugates**. The product of complex conjugates is always a real number. For example, $(2 + 4i)(2 - 4i) = 4 - 8i + 8i + 16 = 20$. You can use this fact to write the quotient of two complex numbers in standard form.

EXAMPLE 5 Divide complex numbers

Write the quotient $\dfrac{7 + 5i}{1 - 4i}$ in standard form.

REWRITE QUOTIENTS
When a quotient has an imaginary number in the denominator, rewrite the denominator as a real number so you can express the quotient in standard form.

$\dfrac{7 + 5i}{1 - 4i} = \dfrac{7 + 5i}{1 - 4i} \cdot \dfrac{1 + 4i}{1 + 4i}$ Multiply numerator and denominator by $1 + 4i$, the complex conjugate of $1 - 4i$.

$= \dfrac{7 + 28i + 5i + 20i^2}{1 + 4i - 4i - 16i^2}$ Multiply using FOIL.

$= \dfrac{7 + 33i + 20(-1)}{1 - 16(-1)}$ Simplify and use $i^2 = 1$.

$= \dfrac{-13 + 33i}{17}$ Simplify.

$= -\dfrac{13}{17} + \dfrac{33}{17}i$ Write in standard form.

✓ **GUIDED PRACTICE**   for Examples 3, 4, and 5

10. **WHAT IF?** In Example 3, what is the impedance of the circuit if the given capacitor is replaced with one having a reactance of 7 ohms?

Write the expression as a complex number in standard form.

11. $i(9 - i)$ 12. $(3 + i)(5 - i)$ 13. $\dfrac{5}{1 + i}$ 14. $\dfrac{5 + 2i}{3 - 2i}$

COMPLEX PLANE Just as every real number corresponds to a point on the real number line, every complex number corresponds to a point in the **complex plane**. As shown in the next example, the complex plane has a horizontal axis called the *real axis* and a vertical axis called the *imaginary axis*.

EXAMPLE 6 Plot complex numbers

Plot the complex numbers in the same complex plane.

a. $3 - 2i$ **b.** $-2 + 4i$ **c.** $3i$ **d.** $-4 - 3i$

Solution

a. To plot $3 - 2i$, start at the origin, move 3 units to the right, and then move 2 units down.

b. To plot $-2 + 4i$, start at the origin, move 2 units to the left, and then move 4 units up.

c. To plot $3i$, start at the origin and move 3 units up.

d. To plot $-4 - 3i$, start at the origin, move 4 units to the left, and then move 3 units down.

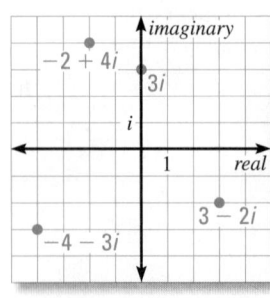

Absolute Value of a Complex Number

The **absolute value** of a complex number $z = a + bi$, denoted $|z|$, is a nonnegative real number defined as $|z| = \sqrt{a^2 + b^2}$. This is the distance between z and the the origin in the complex plane.

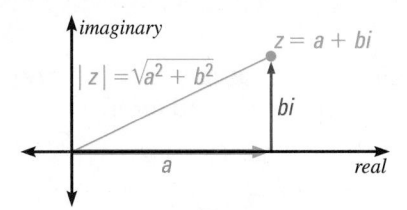

imaginary

$|z| = \sqrt{a^2 + b^2}$

$z = a + bi$

bi

a *real*

EXAMPLE 7   **Find absolute values of complex numbers**

Find the absolute value of (a) $-4 + 3i$ and (b) $-3i$.

a. $|-4 + 3i| = \sqrt{(-4)^2 + 3^2} = \sqrt{25} = 5$

b. $|-3i| = |0 + (-3i)| = \sqrt{0^2 + (-3)^2} = \sqrt{9} = 3$

Animated Algebra at my.hrw.com

✓ **GUIDED PRACTICE**   for Examples 6 and 7

Plot the complex numbers in the same complex plane. Then find the absolute value of each complex number.

15. $4 - i$ **16.** $-3 - 4i$ **17.** $2 + 5i$ **18.** $-4i$

1.6 EXERCISES

SKILL PRACTICE

1. VOCABULARY What is the complex conjugate of $a - bi$?

2. ★ WRITING Is every complex number an imaginary number? *Explain.*

EXAMPLE 1
for Exs. 3–11

SOLVING QUADRATIC EQUATIONS Solve the equation.

3. $x^2 = -28$ **4.** $r^2 = -624$ **5.** $z^2 + 8 = 4$

6. $s^2 - 22 = -112$ **7.** $2x^2 + 31 = 9$ **8.** $9 - 4y^2 = 57$

9. $6t^2 + 5 = 2t^2 + 1$ **10.** $3p^2 + 7 = -9p^2 + 4$ **11.** $-5(n - 3)^2 = 10$

EXAMPLE 2
for Exs. 12–21

ADDING AND SUBTRACTING Write the expression as a complex number in standard form.

12. $(6 - 3i) + (5 + 4i)$ **13.** $(9 + 8i) + (8 - 9i)$ **14.** $(-2 - 6i) - (4 - 6i)$

15. $(-1 + i) - (7 - 5i)$ **16.** $(8 + 20i) - (-8 + 12i)$ **17.** $(8 - 5i) - (-11 + 4i)$

18. $(10 - 2i) + (-11 - 7i)$ **19.** $(14 + 3i) + (7 + 6i)$ **20.** $(-1 + 4i) + (-9 - 2i)$

21. ★ MULTIPLE CHOICE What is the standard form of the expression $(2 + 3i) - (7 + 4i)$?

    (A) -4 **(B)** $-5 + 7i$ **(C)** $-5 - i$ **(D)** $5 + i$

EXAMPLES
4 and 5
for Exs. 22–33

MULTIPLYING AND DIVIDING Write the expression as a complex number in standard form.

22. $6i(3 + 2i)$ **23.** $-i(4 - 8i)$ **24.** $(1 - i)^3$

25. $(-2 + 5i)(-1 + 4i)$ **26.** $(-2i)^4$ **27.** $(8 - 3i)(8 + 3i)$

28. $\dfrac{7i}{8 + i}$ **(29.)** $\dfrac{6i}{3 - i}$ **30.** $\dfrac{-2 - 5i}{3i}$

31. $\dfrac{4 + 9i}{12i}$ **32.** $\dfrac{7 + 4i}{2 - 3i}$ **33.** $\dfrac{-1 - 6i}{5 + 9i}$

EXAMPLE 6
for Exs. 34–41

PLOTTING COMPLEX NUMBERS Plot the numbers in the same complex plane.

34. $1 + 2i$ **35.** $-5 + 3i$ **36.** $-6i$ **37.** $4i$

38. $-7 - i$ **39.** $5 - 5i$ **40.** 7 **41.** -2

EXAMPLE 7
for Exs. 42–50

FINDING ABSOLUTE VALUE Find the absolute value of the complex number.

42. $4 + 3i$ **43.** $-3 + 10i$ **44.** $10 - 7i$ **45.** $-1 - 6i$

46. $-8i$ **47.** $4i$ **48.** $-4 + i$ **49.** $7 + 7i$

50. ★ MULTIPLE CHOICE What is the absolute value of $9 + 12i$?

    (A) 7 **(B)** 15 **(C)** 108 **(D)** 225

STANDARD FORM Write the expression as a complex number in standard form.

51. $-8 - (3 + 2i) - (9 - 4i)$ **52.** $(3 + 2i) + (5 - i) + 6i$ **53.** $5i(3 + 2i)(8 + 3i)$

54. $(1 - 9i)(1 - 4i)(4 - 3i)$ **55.** $\dfrac{(5 - 2i) + (5 + 3i)}{(1 + i) - (2 - 4i)}$ **56.** $\dfrac{(10 + 4i) - (3 - 2i)}{(6 - 7i)(1 - 2i)}$

ERROR ANALYSIS *Describe* and correct the error in simplifying the expression.

57.
$$(1 + 2i)(4 - i)$$
$$= 4 - i + 8i - 2i^2$$
$$= -2i^2 + 7i + 4$$

58.
$$|2 - 3i| = \sqrt{2^2 - 3^2}$$
$$= \sqrt{-5}$$
$$= i\sqrt{5}$$

59. ADDITIVE AND MULTIPLICATIVE INVERSES The additive inverse of a complex number z is a complex number z_a such that $z + z_a = 0$. The multiplicative inverse of z is a complex number z_m such that $z \cdot z_m = 1$. Find the additive and multiplicative inverses of each complex number.

    a. $z = 2 + i$ **b.** $z = 5 - i$ **c.** $z = -1 + 3i$

60. ★ OPEN-ENDED MATH Find two imaginary numbers whose sum is a real number. How are the imaginary numbers related?

CHALLENGE Write the expression as a complex number in standard form.

61. $\dfrac{a + bi}{c + di}$ **62.** $\dfrac{a - bi}{c - di}$ **63.** $\dfrac{a + bi}{c - di}$ **64.** $\dfrac{a - bi}{c + di}$

○ = See **WORKED-OUT SOLUTIONS** in Student Resources   ★ = **STANDARDIZED TEST PRACTICE**

EXAMPLE 3
for Exs. 65–67

CIRCUITS In Exercises 65–67, each component of the circuit has been labeled with its resistance or reactance. Find the impedance of the circuit.

65.
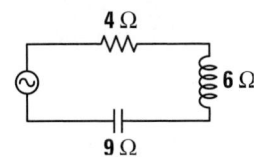

66.
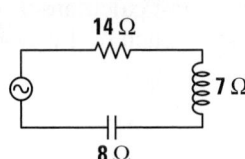

67.
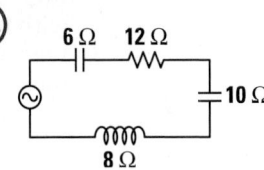

68. **VISUAL THINKING** The graph shows how you can geometrically add two complex numbers (in this case, 4 + *i* and 2 + 5*i*) to find their sum (in this case, 6 + 6*i*). Find each of the following sums by drawing a graph.

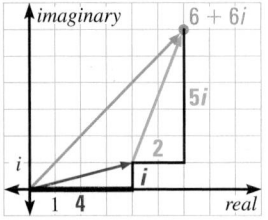

   a. $(5 + i) + (1 + 4i)$ **b.** $(-7 + 3i) + (2 - 2i)$

   c. $(3 - 2i) + (-1 - i)$ **d.** $(4 + 2i) + (-5 - 3i)$

69. ★ **SHORT RESPONSE** Make a table that shows the powers of *i* from i^1 to i^8 in the first row and the simplified forms of these powers in the second row. *Describe* the pattern you observe in the table. Verify that the pattern continues by evaluating the next four powers of *i*.

In Exercises 70–73, use the given numbers to verify that the given property extends to the complex numbers. Refer to the example.

EXAMPLE **Extend real number properties**

The associative property of addition for real numbers can be extended to the complex numbers. Verify this property for the numbers $2 + i$, $1 - 2i$, and $3i$.

Solution

The associative property of addition for real numbers states that for real numbers a, b, and c, $(a + b) + c = a + (b + c)$.

$$[(2 + i) + (1 - 2i)] + 3i = [(2 + 1) + (1 - 2)i] + 3i$$
$$= (3 - i) + 3i$$
$$= 3 + (-1 + 3)i$$
$$= 3 + 2i$$
$$(2 + i) + [(1 - 2i) + 3i] = (2 + i) + [1 + (-2 + 3)i]$$
$$= (2 + i) + (1 + i)$$
$$= (2 + 1) + (1 + 1)i$$
$$= 3 + 2i$$

▶ Because the sums are equal, the property is verified for the given numbers.

70. $4 - 2i$, $-3 + i$; commutative property of multiplication

71. $7 - 2i$, i, $-1 + i$; associative property of multiplication

72. $-2i$, $3 + 2i$, $5 + i$; distributive property

73. $a + bi$, $c + di$; commutative property of addition

74. **★ SHORT RESPONSE** Evaluate $\sqrt{-4} \cdot \sqrt{-25}$ and $\sqrt{100}$. Does the rule $\sqrt{a} \cdot \sqrt{b} = \sqrt{ab}$ hold when a and b are negative numbers?

75. **PARALLEL CIRCUITS** In a *parallel circuit*, there is more than one pathway through which current can flow. To find the impedance Z of a parallel circuit with two pathways, first calculate the impedances Z_1 and Z_2 of the pathways separately by treating each pathway as a series circuit. Then apply this formula:

$$Z = \frac{Z_1 Z_2}{Z_1 + Z_2}$$

What is the impedance of each parallel circuit shown below?

a.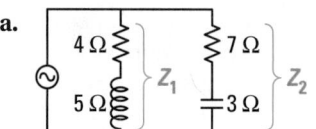

b.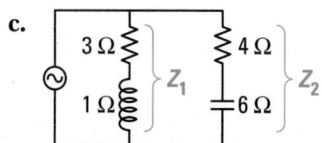

c.

76. **CHALLENGE** *Julia sets* are fractals defined on the complex plane. For every complex number c, there is an associated Julia set determined by the function $f(z) = z^2 + c$.

For example, the Julia set corresponding to $c = 1 + i$ is determined by the function $f(z) = z^2 + 1 + i$. A number z_0 is a member of this Julia set if the absolute values of the numbers $z_1 = f(z_0)$, $z_2 = f(z_1)$, $z_3 = f(z_2)$, ... are all less than some fixed number N, and z_0 is not a member if these absolute values grow infinitely large.

Tell whether the given number z_0 belongs to the Julia set associated with the function $f(z) = z^2 + 1 + i$.

A Julia set

a. $z_0 = i$ b. $z_0 = 1$ c. $z_0 = 2i$ d. $z_0 = 2 + 3i$

Using Algebra Tiles to Complete the Square

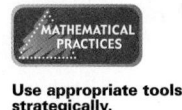

MATHEMATICAL PRACTICES

Use appropriate tools strategically.

MATERIALS · algebra tiles

QUESTION How can you use algebra tiles to complete the square for a quadratic expression?

If you are given an expression of the form $x^2 + bx$, you can add a constant c to the expression so that the result $x^2 + bx + c$ is a perfect square trinomial. This process is called *completing the square*.

EXPLORE Complete the square for the expression $x^2 + 6x$

STEP 1

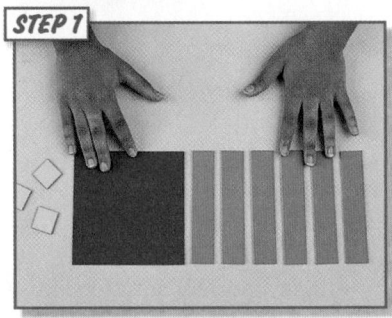

STEP 2

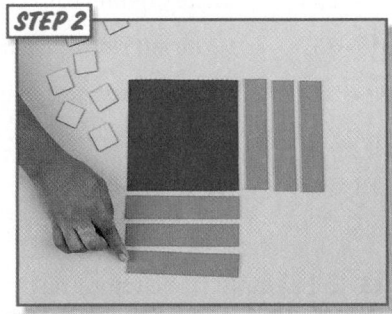

STEP 3

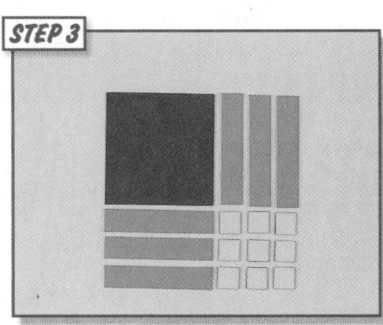

Model the expression

Use algebra tiles to model the expression $x^2 + 6x$. You will need to use one x^2-tile and six x-tiles for this expression.

Make a square

Arrange the tiles in a square. You want the length and width of the square to be equal. Your arrangement will be incomplete in one of the corners.

Complete the square

Find the number of 1-tiles needed to complete the square. By adding nine 1-tiles, you can see that $x^2 + 6x + 9$ is equal to $(x + 3)^2$.

DRAW CONCLUSIONS Use your observations to complete these exercises

1. Copy and complete the table at the right by following the steps above.

2. Look for patterns in the last column of your table. Consider the general statement $x^2 + bx + c = (x + d)^2$.

   a. How is d related to b in each case?

   b. How is c related to d in each case?

   c. How can you obtain the numbers in the table's second column directly from the coefficients of x in the expressions from the first column?

Completing the Square		
Expression	Number of 1-tiles needed to complete the square	Expression written as a square
$x^2 + 2x +$ <u>?</u>	?	?
$x^2 + 4x +$ <u>?</u>	?	?
$x^2 + 6x +$ <u>?</u>	9	$x^2 + 6x + 9$ $= (x + 3)^2$
$x^2 + 8x +$ <u>?</u>	?	?
$x^2 + 10x +$ <u>?</u>	?	?

1.7 Complete the Square

Before	You solved quadratic equations by finding square roots.
Now	You will solve quadratic equations by completing the square.
Why?	So you can find a baseball's maximum height, as in Example 7.

Key Vocabulary
• completing the square

Previously, you have solved equations of the form $x^2 = k$ by finding square roots. This method also works if one side of an equation is a perfect square trinomial.

EXAMPLE 1 **Solve a quadratic equation by finding square roots**

Solve $x^2 - 8x + 16 = 25$.

$$x^2 - 8x + 16 = 25 \qquad \text{Write original equation.}$$

$$(x - 4)^2 = 25 \qquad \text{Write left side as a binomial squared.}$$

$$x - 4 = \pm 5 \qquad \text{Take square roots of each side.}$$

$$x = 4 \pm 5 \qquad \text{Solve for } x.$$

▶ The solutions are $4 + 5 = 9$ and $4 - 5 = -1$.

ANOTHER WAY

You can also find the solutions by writing the given equation as $x^2 - 8x - 9 = 0$ and solving this equation by factoring.

COMMON CORE

CC.9-12.A.REI.4a Use the method of completing the square to transform any quadratic equation in x into an equation of the form $(x - p)^2 = q$ that has the same solutions. Derive the quadratic formula from this form.

PERFECT SQUARES In Example 1, the trinomial $x^2 - 8x + 16$ is a perfect square because it equals $(x - 4)^2$. Sometimes you need to add a term to an expression $x^2 + bx$ to make it a square. This process is called **completing the square**.

KEY CONCEPT *For Your Notebook*

Completing the Square

Words To complete the square for the expression $x^2 + bx$, add $\left(\dfrac{b}{2}\right)^2$.

Diagrams In each diagram, the combined area of the shaded regions is $x^2 + bx$. Adding $\left(\dfrac{b}{2}\right)^2$ completes the square in the second diagram.

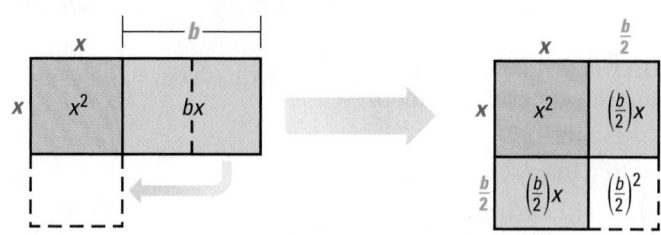

Algebra $x^2 + bx + \left(\dfrac{b}{2}\right)^2 = \left(x + \dfrac{b}{2}\right)\left(x + \dfrac{b}{2}\right) = \left(x + \dfrac{b}{2}\right)^2$

EXAMPLE 2 **Make a perfect square trinomial**

Find the value of c that makes $x^2 + 16x + c$ a perfect square trinomial. Then write the expression as the square of a binomial.

Solution

STEP 1 **Find** half the coefficient of x. $\dfrac{16}{2} = 8$

STEP 2 **Square** the result of Step 1. $8^2 = 64$

STEP 3 **Replace** c with the result of Step 2. $x^2 + 16x + 64$

▶ The trinomial $x^2 + 16x + c$ is a perfect square when $c = 64$. Then $x^2 + 16x + 64 = (x + 8)(x + 8) = (x + 8)^2$.

	x	8
x	x^2	$8x$
8	$8x$	64

✔ **GUIDED PRACTICE**   for Examples 1 and 2

Solve the equation by finding square roots.

1. $x^2 + 6x + 9 = 36$ **2.** $x^2 - 10x + 25 = 1$ **3.** $x^2 - 24x + 144 = 100$

Find the value of c that makes the expression a perfect square trinomial. Then write the expression as the square of a binomial.

4. $x^2 + 14x + c$ **5.** $x^2 + 22x + c$ **6.** $x^2 - 9x + c$

SOLVING EQUATIONS The method of completing the square can be used to solve *any* quadratic equation. When you complete a square as part of solving an equation, you must add the same number to *both* sides of the equation.

❖ **EXAMPLE 3** **Solve $ax^2 + bx + c = 0$ when $a = 1$**

Solve $x^2 - 12x + 4 = 0$ by completing the square.

$x^2 - 12x + 4 = 0$ Write original equation.

$x^2 - 12x = -4$ Write left side in the form $x^2 + bx$.

$x^2 - 12x + 36 = -4 + 36$ Add $\left(\dfrac{-12}{2}\right)^2 = (-6)^2 = 36$ to each side.

$(x - 6)^2 = 32$ Write left side as a binomial squared.

$x - 6 = \pm\sqrt{32}$ Take square roots of each side.

$x = 6 \pm \sqrt{32}$ Solve for x.

$x = 6 \pm 4\sqrt{2}$ Simplify: $\sqrt{32} = \sqrt{16} \cdot \sqrt{2} = 4\sqrt{2}$

▶ The solutions are $6 + 4\sqrt{2}$ and $6 - 4\sqrt{2}$.

CHECK You can use algebra or a graph.

Algebra Substitute each solution in the original equation to verify that it is correct.

Graph Use a graphing calculator to graph $y = x^2 - 12x + 4$. The x-intercepts are about $0.34 \approx 6 - 4\sqrt{2}$ and $11.66 \approx 6 + 4\sqrt{2}$.

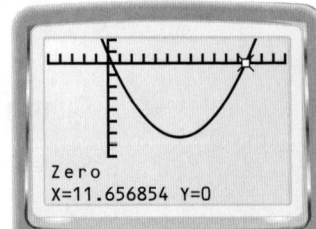

Zero
X=11.656854 Y=0

EXAMPLE 4 Solve $ax^2 + bx + c = 0$ when $a \neq 1$

Solve $2x^2 + 8x + 14 = 0$ by completing the square.

$2x^2 + 8x + 14 = 0$	Write original equation.
$x^2 + 4x + 7 = 0$	Divide each side by the coefficient of x^2.
$x^2 + 4x = -7$	Write left side in the form $x^2 + bx$.
$x^2 + 4x + 4 = -7 + 4$	Add $\left(\dfrac{4}{2}\right)^2 = 2^2 = 4$ to each side.
$(x + 2)^2 = -3$	Write left side as a binomial squared.
$x + 2 = \pm\sqrt{-3}$	Take square roots of each side.
$x = -2 \pm \sqrt{-3}$	Solve for x.
$x = -2 \pm i\sqrt{3}$	Write in terms of the imaginary unit i.

▶ The solutions are $-2 + i\sqrt{3}$ and $-2 - i\sqrt{3}$.

EXAMPLE 5 Standardized Test Practice

The area of the rectangle shown is 72 square units. What is the value of x?

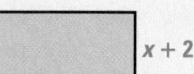

Ⓐ −6   Ⓑ 4

Ⓒ 8.48   Ⓓ −6 or 4

ELIMINATE CHOICES
You can eliminate choices A and D because the side lengths are negative when $x = -6$.

Solution

Use the formula for the area of a rectangle to write an equation.

$3x(x + 2) = 72$	Length × Width = Area
$3x^2 + 6x = 72$	Distributive property
$x^2 + 2x = 24$	Divide each side by the coefficient of x^2.
$x^2 + 2x + 1 = 24 + 1$	Add $\left(\dfrac{2}{2}\right)^2 = 1^2 = 1$ to each side.
$(x + 1)^2 = 25$	Write left side as a binomial squared.
$x + 1 = \pm 5$	Take square roots of each side.
$x = -1 \pm 5$	Solve for x.

So, $x = -1 + 5 = 4$ or $x = -1 - 5 = -6$. You can reject $x = -6$ because the side lengths would be −18 and −4, and side lengths cannot be negative.

▶ The value of x is 4. The correct answer is B. Ⓐ **Ⓑ** Ⓒ Ⓓ

 GUIDED PRACTICE for Examples 3, 4, and 5

Solve the equation by completing the square.

7. $x^2 + 6x + 4 = 0$

8. $x^2 - 10x + 8 = 0$

9. $2n^2 - 4n - 14 = 0$

10. $3x^2 + 12x - 18 = 0$

11. $6x(x + 8) = 12$

12. $4p(p - 2) = 100$

VERTEX FORM Recall that the vertex form of a quadratic function is $y = a(x - h)^2 + k$ where (h, k) is the vertex of the function's graph. To write a quadratic function in vertex form, use completing the square.

EXAMPLE 6 Write a quadratic function in vertex form

Write $y = x^2 - 10x + 22$ in vertex form. Then identify the vertex.

$y = x^2 - 10x + 22$	Write original function.
$y + \boxed{?} = (x^2 - 10x + \boxed{?}) + 22$	Prepare to complete the square.
$y + 25 = (x^2 - 10x + 25) + 22$	Add $\left(\dfrac{-10}{2}\right)^2 = (-5)^2 = 25$ to each side.
$y + 25 = (x - 5)^2 + 22$	Write $x^2 - 10x + 25$ as a binomial squared.
$y = (x - 5)^2 - 3$	Solve for y.

▶ The vertex form of the function is $y = (x - 5)^2 - 3$. The vertex is $(5, -3)$.

EXAMPLE 7 Find the maximum value of a quadratic function

BASEBALL The height y (in feet) of a baseball t seconds after it is hit is given by this function:

$$y = -16t^2 + 96t + 3$$

Find the maximum height of the baseball.

Solution

The maximum height of the baseball is the y-coordinate of the vertex of the parabola with the given equation.

$y = -16t^2 + 96t + 3$	Write original function.
$y = -16(t^2 - 6t) + 3$	Factor -16 from first two terms.
$y + (-16)(\boxed{?}) = -16(t^2 - 6t + \boxed{?}) + 3$	Prepare to complete the square.
$y + (-16)(9) = -16(t^2 - 6t + 9) + 3$	Add $(-16)(9)$ to each side.
$y - 144 = -16(t - 3)^2 + 3$	Write $t^2 - 6t + 9$ as a binomial squared.
$y = -16(t - 3)^2 + 147$	Solve for y.

AVOID ERRORS
When you complete the square, be sure to add $(-16)(9) = -144$ to each side, not just 9.

▶ The vertex is $(3, 147)$, so the maximum height of the baseball is 147 feet.

Animated Algebra at my.hrw.com

✓ **GUIDED PRACTICE** for Examples 6 and 7

Write the quadratic function in vertex form. Then identify the vertex.

13. $y = x^2 - 8x + 17$ **14.** $y = x^2 + 6x + 3$ **15.** $f(x) = x^2 - 4x - 4$

16. WHAT IF? In Example 7, suppose the height of the baseball is given by $y = -16t^2 + 80t + 2$. Find the maximum height of the baseball.

1.7 EXERCISES

HOMEWORK
KEY

◯ = See WORKED-OUT SOLUTIONS
Exs. 27, 45, and 65

★ = STANDARDIZED TEST PRACTICE
Exs. 2, 12, 34, 58, 59, and 67

◆ = MULTIPLE REPRESENTATIONS
Ex. 66

SKILL PRACTICE

1. **VOCABULARY** What is the difference between a binomial and a trinomial?

2. ★ **WRITING** *Describe* what completing the square means for an expression of the form $x^2 + bx$.

EXAMPLE 1
for Exs. 3–12

SOLVING BY SQUARE ROOTS Solve the equation by finding square roots.

3. $x^2 + 4x + 4 = 9$

4. $x^2 + 10x + 25 = 64$

5. $n^2 + 16n + 64 = 36$

6. $m^2 - 2m + 1 = 144$

7. $x^2 - 22x + 121 = 13$

8. $x^2 - 18x + 81 = 5$

9. $t^2 + 8t + 16 = 45$

10. $4u^2 + 4u + 1 = 75$

11. $9x^2 - 12x + 4 = -3$

12. ★ **MULTIPLE CHOICE** What are the solutions of $x^2 - 4x + 4 = -1$?

   A $2 \pm i$ **B** $-2 \pm i$ **C** $-3, -1$ **D** $1, 3$

EXAMPLE 2
for Exs. 13–21

FINDING C Find the value of c that makes the expression a perfect square trinomial. Then write the expression as the square of a binomial.

13. $x^2 + 6x + c$

14. $x^2 + 12x + c$

15. $x^2 - 24x + c$

16. $x^2 - 30x + c$

17. $x^2 - 2x + c$

18. $x^2 + 50x + c$

19. $x^2 + 7x + c$

20. $x^2 - 13x + c$

21. $x^2 - x + c$

EXAMPLES 3 and 4
for Exs. 22–34

COMPLETING THE SQUARE Solve the equation by completing the square.

22. $x^2 + 4x = 10$

23. $x^2 + 8x = -1$

24. $x^2 + 6x - 3 = 0$

25. $x^2 + 12x + 18 = 0$

26. $x^2 - 18x + 86 = 0$

27. $x^2 - 2x + 25 = 0$

28. $2k^2 + 16k = -12$

29. $3x^2 + 42x = -24$

30. $4x^2 - 40x - 12 = 0$

31. $3s^2 + 6s + 9 = 0$

32. $7t^2 + 28t + 56 = 0$

33. $6r^2 + 6r + 12 = 0$

34. ★ **MULTIPLE CHOICE** What are the solutions of $x^2 + 10x + 8 = -5$?

   A $5 \pm 2\sqrt{3}$ **B** $5 \pm 4\sqrt{3}$ **C** $-5 \pm 2\sqrt{3}$ **D** $-5 \pm 4\sqrt{3}$

EXAMPLE 5
for Exs. 35–38

GEOMETRY Find the value of x.

35. Area of rectangle = 50

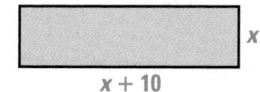

36. Area of parallelogram = 48

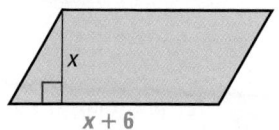

37. Area of triangle = 40

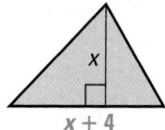

38. Area of trapezoid = 20

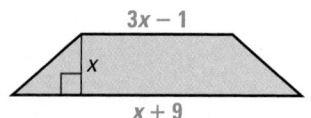

FINDING THE VERTEX In Exercises 39 and 40, use completing the square to find the vertex of the given function's graph. Then tell what the vertex represents.

125 ft

39. At Buckingham Fountain in Chicago, the water's height h (in feet) above the main nozzle can be modeled by $h = -16t^2 + 89.6t$ where t is the time (in seconds) since the water has left the nozzle.

40. When you walk x meters per minute, your rate y of energy use (in calories per minute) can be modeled by $y = 0.0085x^2 - 1.5x + 120$.

Buckingham Fountain

EXAMPLES
6 and 7
for Exs. 41–49

WRITING IN VERTEX FORM Write the quadratic function in vertex form. Then identify the vertex.

41. $y = x^2 - 8x + 19$ 42. $y = x^2 - 4x - 1$ 43. $y = x^2 + 12x + 37$

44. $y = x^2 + 20x + 90$ 45. $f(x) = x^2 - 3x + 4$ 46. $g(x) = x^2 + 7x + 2$

47. $y = 2x^2 + 24x + 25$ 48. $y = 5x^2 + 10x + 7$ 49. $y = 2x^2 - 28x + 99$

ERROR ANALYSIS *Describe* and correct the error in solving the equation.

50.

$x^2 + 10x + 13 = 0$

$x^2 + 10x = -13$

$x^2 + 10x + 25 = -13 + 25$

$(x + 5)^2 = 12$

$x + 5 = \pm\sqrt{12}$

$x = -5 \pm \sqrt{12}$

$x = -5 \pm 4\sqrt{3}$

51.

$4x^2 + 24x - 11 = 0$

$4(x^2 + 6x) = 11$

$4(x^2 + 6x + 9) = 11 + 9$

$4(x + 3)^2 = 20$

$(x + 3)^2 = 5$

$x + 3 = \pm\sqrt{5}$

$x = -3 \pm \sqrt{5}$

COMPLETING THE SQUARE Solve the equation by completing the square.

52. $x^2 + 9x + 20 = 0$ 53. $x^2 + 3x + 14 = 0$ 54. $7q^2 + 10q = 2q^2 + 155$

55. $3x^2 + x = 2x - 6$ 56. $0.1x^2 - x + 9 = 0.2x$ 57. $0.4v^2 + 0.7v = 0.3v - 2$

58. ★ **OPEN-ENDED MATH** Write a quadratic equation with real-number solutions that can be solved by completing the square but not by factoring.

59. ★ **SHORT RESPONSE** In this exercise, you will investigate the graphical effect of completing the square.

  a. Graph each pair of functions in the same coordinate plane.

   $y = x^2 + 2x$ $y = x^2 + 4x$ $y = x^2 - 6x$

   $y = (x + 1)^2$ $y = (x + 2)^2$ $y = (x - 3)^2$

  b. *Compare* the graphs of $y = x^2 + bx$ and $y = \left(x + \dfrac{b}{2}\right)^2$. What happens to the graph of $y = x^2 + bx$ when you complete the square?

60. **REASONING** For what value(s) of k does $x^2 + bx + \left(\dfrac{b}{2}\right)^2 = k$ have exactly 1 real solution? 2 real solutions? 2 imaginary solutions?

61. **CHALLENGE** Solve $x^2 + bx + c = 0$ by completing the square. Your answer will be an expression for x in terms of b and c.

Rion Watts/Corbis

EXAMPLE 7
for Exs. 62–65

62. DRUM MAJOR While marching, a drum major tosses a baton into the air and catches it. The height h (in feet) of the baton after t seconds can be modeled by $h = -16t^2 + 32t + 6$. Find the maximum height of the baton.

63. VOLLEYBALL The height h (in feet) of a volleyball t seconds after it is hit can be modeled by $h = -16t^2 + 48t + 4$. Find the volleyball's maximum height.

64. SKATEBOARD REVENUE A skateboard shop sells about 50 skateboards per week for the price advertised. For each \$1 decrease in price, about 1 more skateboard per week is sold. The shop's revenue can be modeled by $y = (70 - x)(50 + x)$. Use vertex form to find how the shop can maximize weekly revenue.

SKATEBOARDS
Quality Skateboards for $70

65. VIDEO GAME REVENUE A store sells about 40 video game systems each month when it charges \$200 per system. For each \$10 increase in price, about 1 less system per month is sold. The store's revenue can be modeled by $y = (200 + 10x)(40 - x)$. Use vertex form to find how the store can maximize monthly revenue.

66. ◆ MULTIPLE REPRESENTATIONS The path of a ball thrown by a softball player can be modeled by the function

$$y = -0.0110x^2 + 1.23x + 5.50$$

where x is the softball's horizontal position (in feet) and y is the corresponding height (in feet).

a. Rewriting a Function Write the given function in vertex form.

b. Making a Table Make a table of values for the function. Include values of x from 0 to 120 in increments of 10.

c. Drawing a Graph Use your table to graph the function. What is the maximum height of the softball? How far does it travel?

67. ★ EXTENDED RESPONSE Your school is adding a rectangular outdoor eating section along part of a 70 foot side of the school. The eating section will be enclosed by a fence along its three open sides. The school has 120 feet of fencing and plans to use 1500 square feet of land for the eating section.

a. Write an equation for the area of the eating section.

b. Solve the equation. *Explain* why you must reject one of the solutions.

c. What are the dimensions of the eating section?

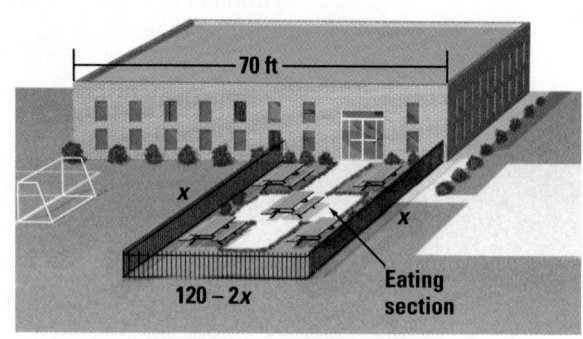

70 ft

x

x

$120 - 2x$

Eating section

○ = See **WORKED-OUT SOLUTIONS** in Student Resources   ★ = **STANDARDIZED TEST PRACTICE**   ◆ = **MULTIPLE REPRESENTATIONS**

68. ⚠ **CHALLENGE** In your pottery class, you are given a lump of clay with a volume of 200 cubic centimeters and are asked to make a cylindrical pencil holder. The pencil holder should be 9 centimeters high and have an inner radius of 3 centimeters. What thickness x should your pencil holder have if you want to use all of the clay?

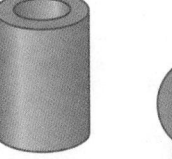

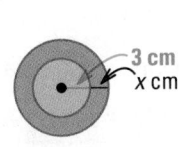

Top view

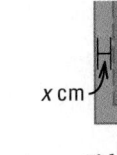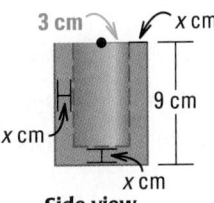

Side view

QUIZ

Solve the equation.

1. $4x^2 = 64$

2. $3(p - 1)^2 = 15$

3. $16(m + 5)^2 = 8$

4. $-2z^2 = 424$

5. $s^2 + 12 = 9$

6. $7x^2 - 4 = -6$

Write the expression as a complex number in standard form.

7. $(5 - 3i) + (-2 + 5i)$

8. $(-2 + 9i) - (7 + 8i)$

9. $3i(7 - 9i)$

10. $(8 - 3i)(-6 - 10i)$

11. $\dfrac{4i}{-6 - 11i}$

12. $\dfrac{3 - 2i}{-8 + 5i}$

Write the quadratic function in vertex form. Then identify the vertex.

13. $y = x^2 - 4x + 9$

14. $y = x^2 + 14x + 45$

15. $f(x) = x^2 - 10x + 17$

16. $g(x) = x^2 - 2x - 7$

17. $y = x^2 + x + 1$

18. $y = x^2 + 9x + 19$

19. FALLING OBJECT A student drops a ball from a school roof 45 feet above ground. How long is the ball in the air?

1.8 Use the Quadratic Formula and the Discriminant

Before	You solved quadratic equations by completing the square.
Now	You will solve quadratic equations using the quadratic formula.
Why?	So you can model the heights of thrown objects, as in Example 5.

Key Vocabulary
- quadratic formula
- discriminant

Previously, you solved quadratic equations by completing the square for *each equation separately*. By completing the square *once* for the general equation $ax^2 + bx + c = 0$, you can develop a formula that gives the solutions of *any* quadratic equation. The formula for the solutions is called the **quadratic formula**.

CC.9-12.N.CN.7 Solve quadratic equations with real coefficients that have complex solutions.

KEY CONCEPT   *For Your Notebook*

The Quadratic Formula

Let a, b, and c be real numbers such that $a \neq 0$. The solutions of the quadratic equation $ax^2 + bx + c = 0$ are $x = \dfrac{-b \pm \sqrt{b^2 - 4ac}}{2a}$.

❖ **EXAMPLE 1** Solve an equation with two real solutions

Solve $x^2 + 3x = 2$.

AVOID ERRORS
Remember to write the quadratic equation in standard form before applying the quadratic formula.

$$x^2 + 3x = 2 \qquad \text{Write original equation.}$$

$$x^2 + 3x - 2 = 0 \qquad \text{Write in standard form.}$$

$$x = \frac{-b \pm \sqrt{b^2 - 4ac}}{2a} \qquad \text{Quadratic formula}$$

$$x = \frac{-3 \pm \sqrt{3^2 - 4(1)(-2)}}{2(1)} \qquad a = 1, b = 3, c = -2$$

$$x = \frac{-3 \pm \sqrt{17}}{2} \qquad \text{Simplify.}$$

▸ The solutions are $x = \dfrac{-3 + \sqrt{17}}{2} \approx 0.56$ and $x = \dfrac{-3 - \sqrt{17}}{2} \approx -3.56$.

CHECK Graph $y = x^2 + 3x - 2$ and note that the x-intercepts are about 0.56 and about -3.56. ✓

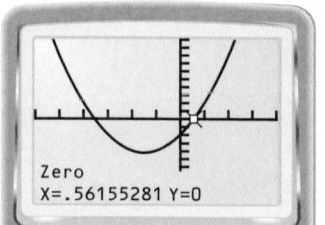

Zero
X=.56155281 Y=0

Mike Yamashita/Corbis

 **EXAMPLE 2** **Solve an equation with one real solution**

Solve $25x^2 - 18x = 12x - 9$.

ANOTHER WAY
....
You can also use factoring to solve this equation because the left side factors as $(5x - 3)^2$.

$25x^2 - 18x = 12x - 9$ Write original equation.

$25x^2 - 30x + 9 = 0$ Write in standard form.

$$x = \frac{30 \pm \sqrt{(-30)^2 - 4(25)(9)}}{2(25)}$$ $a = 25, b = -30, c = 9$

$$x = \frac{30 \pm \sqrt{0}}{50}$$ Simplify.

$$x = \frac{3}{5}$$ Simplify.

▶ The solution is $\frac{3}{5}$.

CHECK   Graph $y = 25x^2 - 30x + 9$ and note that the only x-intercept is $0.6 = \frac{3}{5}$. ✓

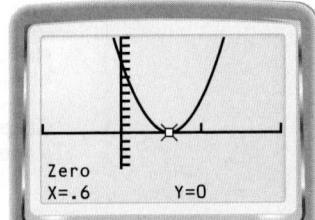

Zero
X=.6   Y=0

 **EXAMPLE 3** **Solve an equation with imaginary solutions**

Solve $-x^2 + 4x = 5$.

$-x^2 + 4x = 5$ Write original equation.

$-x^2 + 4x - 5 = 0$ Write in standard form.

$$x = \frac{-4 \pm \sqrt{4^2 - 4(-1)(-5)}}{2(-1)}$$ $a = -1, b = 4, c = -5$

$$x = \frac{-4 \pm \sqrt{-4}}{-2}$$ Simplify.

$$x = \frac{-4 \pm 2i}{-2}$$ Rewrite using the imaginary unit i.

$$x = 2 \pm i$$ Simplify.

▶ The solutions are $2 + i$ and $2 - i$.

CHECK   Graph $y = -x^2 + 4x - 5$. There are no x-intercepts. So, the original equation has no real solutions. The algebraic check for the imaginary solution $2 + i$ is shown.

$$-(2 + i)^2 + 4(2 + i) \stackrel{?}{=} 5$$

$$-3 - 4i + 8 + 4i \stackrel{?}{=} 5$$

$$5 = 5 ✓$$

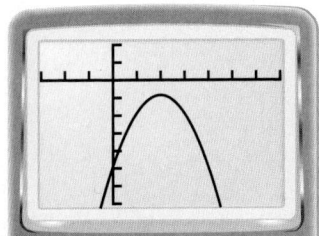

 GUIDED PRACTICE   for Examples 1, 2, and 3

Use the quadratic formula to solve the equation.

1. $x^2 = 6x - 4$ **2.** $4x^2 - 10x = 2x - 9$ **3.** $7x - 5x^2 - 4 = 2x + 3$

DISCRIMINANT In the quadratic formula, the expression $b^2 - 4ac$ is called the **discriminant** of the associated equation $ax^2 + bx + c = 0$.

$$x = \frac{-b \pm \sqrt{b^2 - 4ac}}{2a} \quad \longleftarrow \quad \text{discriminant}$$

You can use the discriminant of a quadratic equation to determine the equation's number and type of solutions.

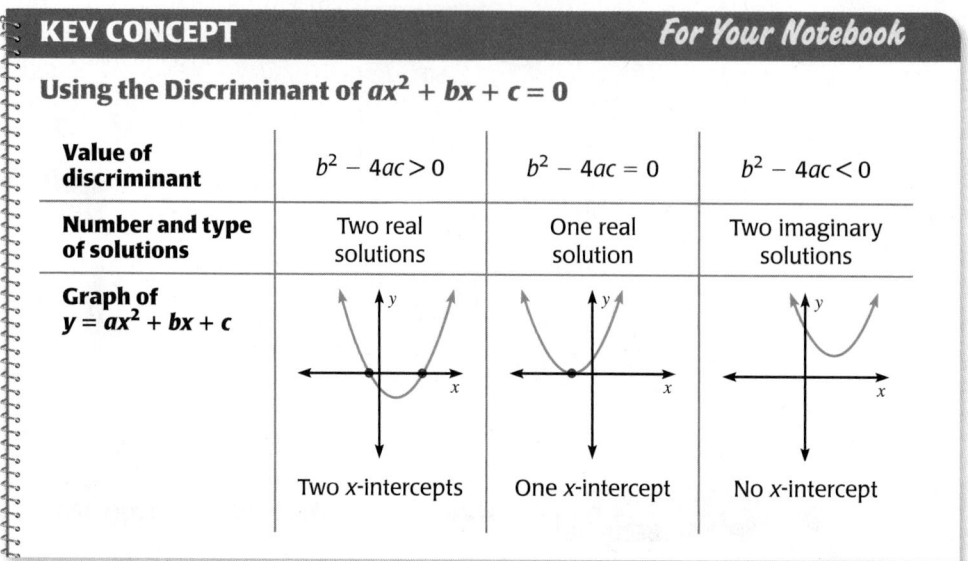

KEY CONCEPT *For Your Notebook*

Using the Discriminant of $ax^2 + bx + c = 0$

Value of discriminant	$b^2 - 4ac > 0$	$b^2 - 4ac = 0$	$b^2 - 4ac < 0$
Number and type of solutions	Two real solutions	One real solution	Two imaginary solutions
Graph of $y = ax^2 + bx + c$	Two x-intercepts	One x-intercept	No x-intercept

EXAMPLE 4 Use the discriminant

Find the discriminant of the quadratic equation and give the number and type of solutions of the equation.

a. $x^2 - 8x + 17 = 0$ **b.** $x^2 - 8x + 16 = 0$ **c.** $x^2 - 8x + 15 = 0$

Solution

Equation $ax^2 + bx + c = 0$	Discriminant $b^2 - 4ac$	Solution(s) $x = \dfrac{-b \pm \sqrt{b^2 - 4ac}}{2a}$
a. $x^2 - 8x + 17 = 0$	$(-8)^2 - 4(1)(17) = -4$	Two imaginary: $4 \pm i$
b. $x^2 - 8x + 16 = 0$	$(-8)^2 - 4(1)(16) = 0$	One real: 4
c. $x^2 - 8x + 15 = 0$	$(-8)^2 - 4(1)(15) = 4$	Two real: 3, 5

 GUIDED PRACTICE for Example 4

Find the discriminant of the quadratic equation and give the number and type of solutions of the equation.

4. $2x^2 + 4x - 4 = 0$ **5.** $3x^2 + 12x + 12 = 0$ **6.** $8x^2 = 9x - 11$

7. $7x^2 - 2x = 5$ **8.** $4x^2 + 3x + 12 = 3 - 3x$ **9.** $3x - 5x^2 + 1 = 6 - 7x$

MODELING LAUNCHED OBJECTS The function $h = -16t^2 + h_0$ is used to model the height of a *dropped* object. For an object that is *launched or thrown*, an extra term v_0t must be added to the model to account for the object's initial vertical velocity v_0 (in feet per second). Recall that h is the height (in feet), t is the time in motion (in seconds), and h_0 is the initial height (in feet).

$$h = -16t^2 + h_0 \qquad \text{Object is dropped.}$$

$$h = -16t^2 + v_0t + h_0 \qquad \text{Object is launched or thrown.}$$

As shown below, the value of v_0 can be positive, negative, or zero depending on whether the object is launched upward, downward, or parallel to the ground.

$v_0 > 0$ $\qquad\qquad$ $v_0 < 0$ $\qquad\qquad$ $v_0 = 0$

EXAMPLE 5 **Solve a vertical motion problem**

JUGGLING A juggler tosses a ball into the air. The ball leaves the juggler's hand 4 feet above the ground and has an initial vertical velocity of 40 feet per second. The juggler catches the ball when it falls back to a height of 3 feet. How long is the ball in the air?

Solution

Because the ball is thrown, use the model $h = -16t^2 + v_0t + h_0$. To find how long the ball is in the air, solve for t when $h = 3$.

$h = -16t^2 + v_0t + h_0$ $\qquad$ **Write height model.**

$3 = -16t^2 + 40t + 4$ $\qquad$ **Substitute 3 for *h*, 40 for *v$_0$*, and 4 for *h$_0$*.**

$0 = -16t^2 + 40t + 1$ $\qquad$ **Write in standard form.**

$t = \dfrac{-40 \pm \sqrt{40^2 - 4(-16)(1)}}{2(-16)}$ $\qquad$ **Quadratic formula**

$t = \dfrac{-40 \pm \sqrt{1664}}{-32}$ $\qquad$ **Simplify.**

$t \approx -0.025 \text{ or } t \approx 2.5$ $\qquad$ **Use a calculator.**

▶ Reject the solution -0.025 because the ball's time in the air cannot be negative. So, the ball is in the air for about 2.5 seconds.

✓ **GUIDED PRACTICE** for Example 5

10. **WHAT IF?** In Example 5, suppose the ball leaves the juggler's hand with an initial vertical velocity of 50 feet per second. How long is the ball in the air?

1.8 EXERCISES

HOMEWORK KEY

$\bigcirc$ = See WORKED-OUT SOLUTIONS
Exs. 19, 39, and 71

★ = STANDARDIZED TEST PRACTICE
Exs. 2, 12, 51, 55, 62, 69, 72, and 73

SKILL PRACTICE

1. **VOCABULARY** Copy and complete: You can use the __?__ of a quadratic equation to determine the equation's number and type of solutions.

2. ★ **WRITING** *Describe* a real-life situation in which you can use the model $h = -16t^2 + v_0 t + h_0$ but not the model $h = -16t^2 + h_0$.

EXAMPLES
1, 2, and 3
for Exs. 3–30

EQUATIONS IN STANDARD FORM Use the quadratic formula to solve the equation.

3. $x^2 - 4x - 5 = 0$

4. $x^2 - 6x + 7 = 0$

5. $t^2 + 8t + 19 = 0$

6. $x^2 - 16x + 7 = 0$

7. $8w^2 - 8w + 2 = 0$

8. $5p^2 - 10p + 24 = 0$

9. $4x^2 - 8x + 1 = 0$

10. $6u^2 + 4u + 11 = 0$

11. $3r^2 - 8r - 9 = 0$

12. ★ **MULTIPLE CHOICE** What are the complex solutions of the equation $2x^2 - 16x + 50 = 0$?

(A) $4 + 3i, 4 - 3i$

(B) $4 + 12i, 4 - 12i$

(C) $16 + 3i, 16 - 3i$

(D) $16 + 12i, 16 - 12i$

EQUATIONS NOT IN STANDARD FORM Use the quadratic formula to solve the equation.

13. $3w^2 - 12w = -12$

14. $x^2 + 6x = -15$

15. $s^2 = -14 - 3s$

16. $-3y^2 = 6y - 10$

17. $3 - 8v - 5v^2 = 2v$

18. $7x - 5 + 12x^2 = -3x$

19. $4x^2 + 3 = x^2 - 7x$

20. $6 - 2t^2 = 9t + 15$

21. $4 + 9n - 3n^2 = 2 - n$

SOLVING USING TWO METHODS Solve the equation using the quadratic formula. Then solve the equation by factoring to check your solution(s).

22. $z^2 + 15z + 24 = -32$

23. $x^2 - 5x + 10 = 4$

24. $m^2 + 5m - 99 = 3m$

25. $s^2 - s - 3 = s$

26. $r^2 - 4r + 8 = 5r$

27. $3x^2 + 7x - 24 = 13x$

28. $45x^2 + 57x + 1 = 5$

29. $5p^2 + 40p + 100 = 25$

30. $9n^2 - 42n - 162 = 21n$

EXAMPLE 4
for Exs. 31–39

USING THE DISCRIMINANT Find the discriminant of the quadratic equation and give the number and type of solutions of the equation.

31. $x^2 - 8x + 16 = 0$

32. $s^2 + 7s + 11 = 0$

33. $8p^2 + 8p + 3 = 0$

34. $-4w^2 + w - 14 = 0$

35. $5x^2 + 20x + 21 = 0$

36. $8z - 10 = z^2 - 7z + 3$

37. $8n^2 - 4n + 2 = 5n - 11$

38. $5x^2 + 16x = 11x - 3x^2$

39. $7r^2 - 5 = 2r + 9r^2$

SOLVING QUADRATIC EQUATIONS Solve the equation using any method.

40. $16t^2 - 7t = 17t - 9$

41. $7x - 3x^2 = 85 + 2x^2 + 2x$

42. $4(x - 1)^2 = 6x + 2$

43. $25 - 16v^2 = 12v(v + 5)$

44. $\frac{3}{2}y^2 - 6y = \frac{3}{4}y - 9$

45. $3x^2 + \frac{9}{2}x - 4 = 5x + \frac{3}{4}$

46. $1.1(3.4x - 2.3)^2 = 15.5$

47. $19.25 = -8.5(2r - 1.75)^2$

48. $4.5 = 1.5(3.25 - s)^2$

ERROR ANALYSIS *Describe* and correct the error in solving the equation.

49.

$$3x^2 + 6x + 15 = 0$$

$$x = \frac{-6 \pm \sqrt{6^2 - 4(3)(15)}}{2(3)}$$

$$= \frac{-6 \pm \sqrt{-144}}{6}$$

$$= \frac{-6 \pm 12}{6}$$

$$= 1 \text{ or } -3 \qquad \times$$

50.

$$x^2 + 6x + 8 = 2$$

$$x = \frac{-6 \pm \sqrt{6^2 - 4(1)(8)}}{2(1)}$$

$$= \frac{-6 \pm \sqrt{4}}{2}$$

$$= \frac{-6 \pm 2}{2}$$

$$= -2 \text{ or } -4 \qquad \times$$

51. ★ **SHORT RESPONSE** For a quadratic equation $ax^2 + bx + c = 0$ with two real solutions, show that the mean of the solutions is $-\dfrac{b}{2a}$. How is this fact related to the symmetry of the graph of $y = ax^2 + bx + c$?

VISUAL THINKING In Exercises 52–54, the graph of a quadratic function $y = ax^2 + bx + c$ is shown. Tell whether the discriminant of $ax^2 + bx + c = 0$ is *positive*, *negative*, or *zero*.

52.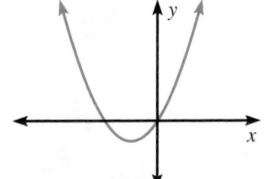

53.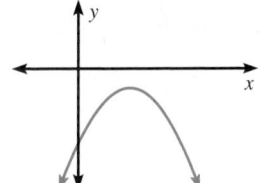

54.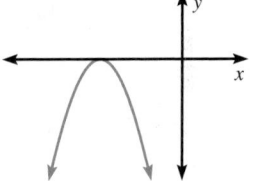

55. ★ **MULTIPLE CHOICE** What is the value of c if the discriminant of $2x^2 + 5x + c = 0$ is -23?

Ⓐ -23 Ⓑ -6 Ⓒ 6 Ⓓ 14

THE CONSTANT TERM Use the discriminant to find all values of c for which the equation has (a) two real solutions, (b) one real solution, and (c) two imaginary solutions.

56. $x^2 - 4x + c = 0$ 57. $x^2 + 8x + c = 0$ 58. $-x^2 + 16x + c = 0$

59. $3x^2 + 24x + c = 0$ 60. $-4x^2 - 10x + c = 0$ 61. $x^2 - x + c = 0$

62. ★ **OPEN-ENDED MATH** Write a quadratic equation in standard form that has a discriminant of -10.

WRITING EQUATIONS Write a quadratic equation in the form $ax^2 + bx + c = 0$ such that $c = 4$ and the equation has the given solutions.

63. -4 and 3 64. $-\dfrac{4}{3}$ and -1 65. $-1 + i$ and $-1 - i$

66. **REASONING** Show that there is no quadratic equation $ax^2 + bx + c = 0$ such that a, b, and c are real numbers and $3i$ and $-2i$ are solutions.

67. **CHALLENGE** Solve the equation.

 a. $|x^2 - 3x - 14| = 4$ b. $x^2 = |x| + 6$

EXAMPLE 5
for Exs. 68–69

68. FOOTBALL In a football game, a defensive player jumps up to block a pass by the opposing team's quarterback. The player bats the ball downward with his hand at an initial vertical velocity of −50 feet per second when the ball is 7 feet above the ground. How long do the defensive player's teammates have to intercept the ball before it hits the ground?

69. ★ **MULTIPLE CHOICE** For the period 1990–2002, the number S (in thousands) of cellular telephone subscribers in the United States can be modeled by $S = 858t^2 + 1412t + 4982$ where t is the number of years since 1990. In what year did the number of subscribers reach 50 million?

(A) 1991   (B) 1992   (C) 1996   (D) 2000

70. MULTI-STEP PROBLEM A stunt motorcyclist makes a jump from one ramp 20 feet off the ground to another ramp 20 feet off the ground. The jump between the ramps can be modeled by $y = -\frac{1}{640}x^2 + \frac{1}{4}x + 20$ where x is the horizontal distance (in feet) and y is the height above the ground (in feet).

a. What is the motorcycle's height r when it lands on the ramp?

b. What is the distance d between the ramps?

c. What is the horizontal distance h the motorcycle has traveled when it reaches its maximum height?

d. What is the motorcycle's maximum height k above the ground?

71. BIOLOGY The number S of ant species in Kyle Canyon, Nevada, can be modeled by the function $S = -0.000013E^2 + 0.042E - 21$ where E is the elevation (in meters). Predict the elevation(s) at which you would expect to find 10 species of ants.

72. ★ **SHORT RESPONSE** A city planner wants to create adjacent sections for athletics and picnics in the yard of a youth center. The sections will be rectangular and will be surrounded by fencing as shown. There is 900 feet of fencing available. Each section should have an area of 12,000 square feet.

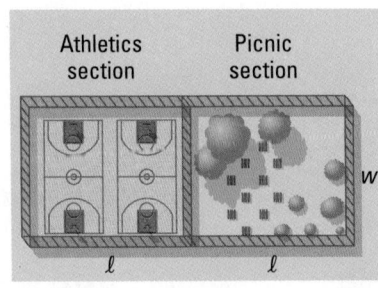

a. Show that $w = 300 - \frac{4}{3}\ell$.

b. Find the possible dimensions of each section.

○ = See WORKED-OUT SOLUTIONS in Student Resources   ★ = STANDARDIZED TEST PRACTICE

73. ★ **EXTENDED RESPONSE** You can model the position (x, y) of a moving object using a pair of *parametric equations*. Such equations give x and y in terms of a third variable t that represents time. For example, suppose that when a basketball player attempts a free throw, the path of the basketball can be modeled by the parametric equations

$$x = 20t$$

$$y = -16t^2 + 21t + 6$$

where x and y are measured in feet, t is measured in seconds, and the player's feet are at $(0, 0)$.

a. Evaluate Make a table of values giving the position (x, y) of the basketball after 0, 0.25, 0.5, 0.75, and 1 second.

b. Graph Use your table from part (a) to graph the parametric equations.

c. Solve The position of the basketball rim is $(15, 10)$. The top of the backboard is $(15, 12)$. Does the player make the free throw? *Explain.*

74. **CHALLENGE** The Stratosphere Tower in Las Vegas is 921 feet tall and has a "needle" at its top that extends even higher into the air. A thrill ride called the Big Shot catapults riders 160 feet up the needle and then lets them fall back to the launching pad.

Big Shot ride

a. The height h (in feet) of a rider on the Big Shot can be modeled by $h = -16t^2 + v_0 t + 921$ where t is the elapsed time (in seconds) after launch and v_0 is the initial vertical velocity (in feet per second). Find v_0 using the fact that the maximum value of h is $921 + 160 = 1081$ feet.

b. A brochure for the Big Shot states that the ride up the needle takes two seconds. *Compare* this time with the time given by the model $h = -16t^2 + v_0 t + 921$ where v_0 is the value you found in part (a). Discuss the model's accuracy.

Ben Mangor/SuperStock

1.9 Graph and Solve Quadratic Inequalities

Before   You graphed and solved linear inequalities.

Now   You will graph and solve quadratic inequalities.

Why?   So you can model the strength of a rope, as in Example 2.

Key Vocabulary
- quadratic inequality in two variables
- quadratic inequality in one variable

CC.9-12.A.REI.4b Solve quadratic equations by inspection (e.g., for $x^2 = 49$), taking square roots, completing the square, the quadratic formula and factoring, as appropriate to the initial form of the equation. Recognize when the quadratic formula gives complex solutions and write them as $a \pm bi$ for real numbers a and b.

A **quadratic inequality in two variables** can be written in one of the following forms:

$$y < ax^2 + bx + c \qquad y \leq ax^2 + bx + c \qquad y > ax^2 + bx + c \qquad y \geq ax^2 + bx + c$$

The graph of any such inequality consists of all solutions (x, y) of the inequality.

KEY CONCEPT   *For Your Notebook*

Graphing a Quadratic Inequality in Two Variables

To graph a quadratic inequality in one of the forms above, follow these steps:

STEP 1   **Graph** the parabola with equation $y = ax^2 + bx + c$. Make the parabola *dashed* for inequalities with < or > and *solid* for inequalities with ≤ or ≥.

STEP 2   **Test** a point (x, y) inside the parabola to determine whether the point is a solution of the inequality.

STEP 3   **Shade** the region inside the parabola if the point from Step 2 is a solution. Shade the region outside the parabola if it is not a solution.

EXAMPLE 1   Graph a quadratic inequality

Graph $y > x^2 + 3x - 4$.

Solution

AVOID ERRORS
Be sure to use a dashed parabola if the symbol is > or < and a solid parabola if the symbol is ≥ or ≤.

STEP 1   **Graph** $y = x^2 + 3x - 4$. Because the inequality symbol is >, make the parabola dashed.

STEP 2   **Test** a point inside the parabola, such as $(0, 0)$.

$$y > x^2 + 3x - 4$$

$$0 \overset{?}{>} 0^2 + 3(0) - 4$$

$$0 > -4 \checkmark$$

So, $(0, 0)$ is a solution of the inequality.

STEP 3   **Shade** the region inside the parabola.

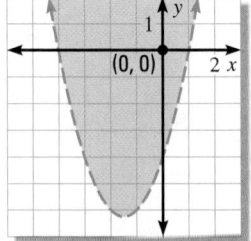

Animated Algebra   at my.hrw.com

©Photodisc/Getty Images

EXAMPLE 2 Use a quadratic inequality in real life

RAPPELLING A manila rope used for rappelling down a cliff can safely support a weight W (in pounds) provided

$$W \le 1480d^2$$

where d is the rope's diameter (in inches). Graph the inequality.

Solution

Graph $W = 1480d^2$ for nonnegative values of d. Because the inequality symbol is $\le$, make the parabola solid. Test a point inside the parabola, such as (1, 2000).

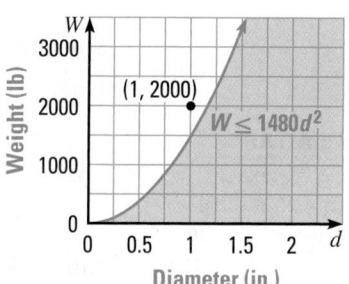

$$W \le 1480d^2$$

$$2000 \overset{?}{\le} 1480(1)^2$$

$$2000 \le 1480 \text{ ✗}$$

Because (1, 2000) is not a solution, shade the region below the parabola.

SYSTEMS OF QUADRATIC INEQUALITIES Graphing a *system* of quadratic inequalities is similar to graphing a system of linear inequalities. First graph each inequality in the system. Then identify the region in the coordinate plane common to all of the graphs. This region is called the *graph of the system.*

EXAMPLE 3 Graph a system of quadratic inequalities

Graph the system of quadratic inequalities.

$y \le -x^2 + 4$ **Inequality 1**
$y > x^2 - 2x - 3$ **Inequality 2**

Solution

STEP 1 **Graph** $y \le -x^2 + 4$. The graph is the red region inside and including the parabola $y = -x^2 + 4$.

STEP 2 **Graph** $y > x^2 - 2x - 3$. The graph is the blue region inside (but not including) the parabola $y = x^2 - 2x - 3$.

STEP 3 **Identify** the **purple region** where the two graphs overlap. This region is the graph of the system.

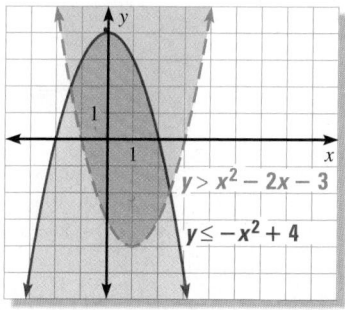

✓ **GUIDED PRACTICE** for Examples 1, 2, and 3

Graph the inequality.

1. $y > x^2 + 2x - 8$ **2.** $y \le 2x^2 - 3x + 1$ **3.** $y < -x^2 + 4x + 2$

4. Graph the system of inequalities consisting of $y \ge x^2$ and $y < -x^2 + 5$.

ONE-VARIABLE INEQUALITIES A **quadratic inequality in one variable** can be written in one of the following forms:

$$ax^2 + bx + c < 0 \qquad ax^2 + bx + c \le 0 \qquad ax^2 + bx + c > 0 \qquad ax^2 + bx + c \ge 0$$

You can solve quadratic inequalities using tables, graphs, or algebraic methods.

EXAMPLE 4 Solve a quadratic inequality using a table

Solve $x^2 + x \le 6$ using a table.

Solution

Rewrite the inequality as $x^2 + x - 6 \le 0$. Then make a table of values.

MAKE A TABLE
To give the exact solution, your table needs to include the x-values for which the value of the quadratic expression is 0.

x	−5	−4	−3	−2	−1	0	1	2	3	4
$x^2 + x - 6$	14	6	0	−4	−6	−6	−4	0	6	14

Notice that $x^2 + x - 6 \le 0$ when the values of x are between −3 and 2, inclusive.

▶ The solution of the inequality is $-3 \le x \le 2$.

GRAPHING TO SOLVE INEQUALITIES Another way to solve $ax^2 + bx + c < 0$ is to first graph the related function $y = ax^2 + bx + c$. Then, because the inequality symbol is $<$, identify the x-values for which the graph lies *below* the x-axis. You can use a similar procedure to solve quadratic inequalities that involve $\le$, $>$, or $\ge$.

EXAMPLE 5 Solve a quadratic inequality by graphing

Solve $2x^2 + x - 4 \ge 0$ by graphing.

Solution

The solution consists of the x-values for which the graph of $y = 2x^2 + x - 4$ lies on or above the x-axis. Find the graph's x-intercepts by letting $y = 0$ and using the quadratic formula to solve for x.

$$0 = 2x^2 + x - 4$$

$$x = \frac{-1 \pm \sqrt{1^2 - 4(2)(-4)}}{2(2)}$$

$$x = \frac{-1 \pm \sqrt{33}}{4}$$

$$x \approx 1.19 \text{ or } x \approx -1.69$$

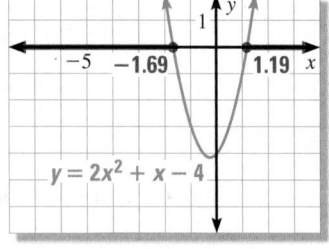

Sketch a parabola that opens up and has 1.19 and −1.69 as x-intercepts. The graph lies on or above the x-axis to the left of (and including) $x = -1.69$ and to the right of (and including) $x = 1.19$.

▶ The solution of the inequality is approximately $x \le -1.69$ or $x \ge 1.19$.

✓ **GUIDED PRACTICE** for Examples 4 and 5

5. Solve the inequality $2x^2 + 2x \le 3$ using a table and using a graph.

EXAMPLE 6 Use a quadratic inequality as a model

ROBOTICS The number T of teams that have participated in a robot-building competition for high school students can be modeled by

$$T(x) = 7.51x^2 - 16.4x + 35.0,\, 0 \le x \le 9$$

where x is the number of years since 1992. For what years was the number of teams greater than 100?

Solution

You want to find the values of x for which:

$$T(x) > 100$$
$$7.51x^2 - 16.4x + 35.0 > 100$$
$$7.51x^2 - 16.4x - 65 > 0$$

Graph $y = 7.51x^2 - 16.4x - 65$ on the domain $0 \le x \le 9$. The graph's x-intercept is about 4.2. The graph lies above the x-axis when $4.2 < x \le 9$.

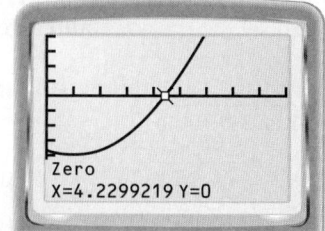

Zero
X=4.2299219 Y=0

▶ There were more than 100 teams participating in the years 1997–2001.

EXAMPLE 7 Solve a quadratic inequality algebraically

Solve $x^2 - 2x > 15$ algebraically.

Solution

First, write and solve the equation obtained by replacing > with =.

$$x^2 - 2x = 15 \qquad \text{Write equation that corresponds to original inequality.}$$
$$x^2 - 2x - 15 = 0 \qquad \text{Write in standard form.}$$
$$(x + 3)(x - 5) = 0 \qquad \text{Factor.}$$
$$x = -3 \text{ or } x = 5 \qquad \text{Zero product property}$$

The numbers -3 and 5 are the *critical x-values* of the inequality $x^2 - 2x > 15$. Plot -3 and 5 on a number line, using open dots because the values do not satisfy the inequality. The critical x-values partition the number line into three intervals. Test an x-value in each interval to see if it satisfies the inequality.

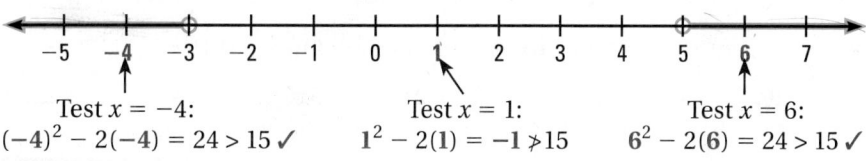

Test $x = -4$:
$(-4)^2 - 2(-4) = 24 > 15$ ✓

Test $x = 1$:
$1^2 - 2(1) = -1 \not> 15$

Test $x = 6$:
$6^2 - 2(6) = 24 > 15$ ✓

▶ The solution is $x < -3$ or $x > 5$.

✓ **GUIDED PRACTICE** for Examples 6 and 7

6. **ROBOTICS** Use the information in Example 6 to determine in what years at least 200 teams participated in the robot-building competition.

7. Solve the inequality $2x^2 - 7x > 4$ algebraically.

1.9 EXERCISES

HOMEWORK
KEY

○ = See WORKED-OUT SOLUTIONS
Exs. 17, 39, and 73

★ = STANDARDIZED TEST PRACTICE
Exs. 2, 44, 45, 68, and 73

◆ = MULTIPLE REPRESENTATIONS
Ex. 74

SKILL PRACTICE

1. **VOCABULARY** Give an example of a quadratic inequality in one variable and an example of a quadratic inequality in two variables.

2. ★ **WRITING** *Explain* how to solve $x^2 + 6x - 8 < 0$ using a table, by graphing, and algebraically.

EXAMPLE 1
for Exs. 3–19

MATCHING INEQUALITIES WITH GRAPHS Match the inequality with its graph.

3. $y \le x^2 + 4x + 3$

4. $y > -x^2 + 4x - 3$

5. $y < x^2 - 4x + 3$

A.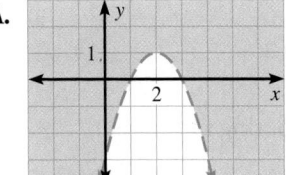

B.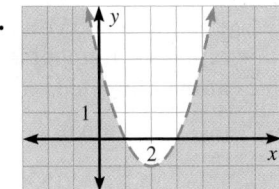

C.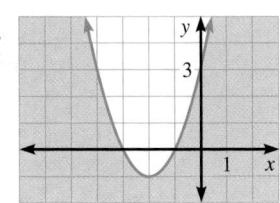

GRAPHING QUADRATIC INEQUALITIES Graph the inequality.

6. $y < -x^2$

7. $y \ge 4x^2$

8. $y > x^2 - 9$

9. $y \le x^2 + 5x$

10. $y < x^2 + 4x - 5$

11. $y > x^2 + 7x + 12$

12. $y \le -x^2 + 3x + 10$

13. $y \ge 2x^2 + 5x - 7$

14. $y \ge -2x^2 + 9x - 4$

15. $y < 4x^2 - 3x - 5$

16. $y > 0.1x^2 - x + 1.2$

17. $y \le -\frac{2}{3}x^2 + 3x + 1$

ERROR ANALYSIS Describe and correct the error in graphing $y \ge x^2 + 2$.

18.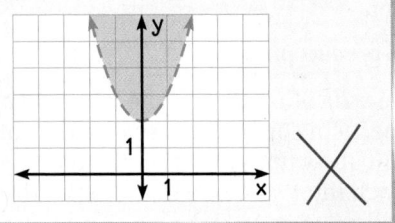

19.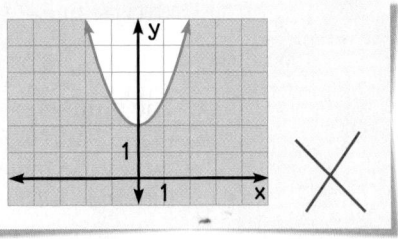

EXAMPLE 3
for Exs. 20–25

GRAPHING SYSTEMS Graph the system of inequalities.

20. $y \ge 2x^2$
$y < -x^2 + 1$

21. $y > -5x^2$
$y > 3x^2 - 2$

22. $y \ge x^2 - 4$
$y \le -2x^2 + 7x + 4$

23. $y \le -x^2 + 4x - 4$
$y < 2x^2 + x - 8$

24. $y > 3x^2 + 3x - 5$
$y < -x^2 + 5x + 10$

25. $y \ge x^2 - 3x - 6$
$y \ge 2x^2 + 7x + 6$

EXAMPLE 4
for Exs. 26–34

SOLVING USING A TABLE Solve the inequality using a table.

26. $x^2 - 5x < 0$

27. $x^2 + 2x - 3 > 0$

28. $x^2 + 3x \le 10$

29. $x^2 - 2x \ge 8$

30. $-x^2 + 15x - 50 > 0$

31. $x^2 - 10x < -16$

32. $x^2 - 4x > 12$

33. $3x^2 - 6x - 2 \le 7$

34. $2x^2 - 6x - 9 \ge 11$

70 Chapter 1 Quadratic Functions and Factoring

EXAMPLE 5
for Exs. 35–43

SOLVING BY GRAPHING Solve the inequality by graphing.

35. $x^2 - 6x < 0$

36. $x^2 + 8x \leq -7$

37. $x^2 - 4x + 2 > 0$

38. $x^2 + 6x + 3 > 0$

39. $3x^2 + 2x - 8 \leq 0$

40. $3x^2 + 5x - 3 < 1$

41. $-6x^2 + 19x \geq 10$

42. $-\frac{1}{2}x^2 + 4x \geq 1$

43. $4x^2 - 10x - 7 < 10$

44. ★ **MULTIPLE CHOICE** What is the solution of $3x^2 - x - 4 > 0$?

Ⓐ $x < -1$ or $x > \frac{4}{3}$

Ⓑ $-1 < x < \frac{4}{3}$

Ⓒ $x < -\frac{4}{3}$ or $x > 1$

Ⓓ $1 < x < \frac{4}{3}$

45. ★ **MULTIPLE CHOICE** What is the solution of $2x^2 + 9x \leq 56$?

Ⓐ $x \leq -8$ or $x \geq 3.5$

Ⓑ $-8 \leq x \leq 3.5$

Ⓒ $x \leq 0$ or $x \geq 4.5$

Ⓓ $0 \leq x \leq 4.5$

EXAMPLE 7
for Exs. 46–57

SOLVING ALGEBRAICALLY Solve the inequality algebraically.

46. $4x^2 < 25$

47. $x^2 + 10x + 9 < 0$

48. $x^2 - 11x \geq -28$

49. $3x^2 - 13x > 10$

50. $2x^2 - 5x - 3 \leq 0$

51. $4x^2 + 8x - 21 \geq 0$

52. $-4x^2 - x + 3 \leq 0$

53. $5x^2 - 6x - 2 \leq 0$

54. $-3x^2 + 10x > -2$

55. $-2x^2 - 7x \geq 4$

56. $3x^2 + 1 < 15x$

57. $6x^2 - 5 > 8x$

58. **GRAPHING CALCULATOR** In this exercise, you will use a different graphical method to solve Example 6.

    a. Enter the equations $y = 7.51x^2 - 16.4x + 35.0$ and $y = 100$ into a graphing calculator.

    b. Graph the equations from part (a) for $0 \leq x \leq 9$ and $0 \leq y \leq 300$.

    c. Use the *intersect* feature to find the point where the graphs intersect.

    d. During what years was the number of participating teams greater than 100? *Explain* your reasoning.

CHOOSING A METHOD Solve the inequality using any method.

59. $8x^2 - 3x + 1 < 10$

60. $4x^2 + 11x + 3 \geq -3$

61. $-x^2 - 2x - 1 > 2$

62. $-3x^2 + 4x - 5 \leq 2$

63. $x^2 - 7x + 4 > 5x - 2$

64. $2x^2 + 9x - 1 \geq -3x + 1$

65. $3x^2 - 2x + 1 \leq -x^2 + 1$

66. $5x^2 + x - 7 < 3x^2 - 4x$

67. $6x^2 - 5x + 2 < -3x^2 + x$

68. ★ **OPEN-ENDED MATH** Write a quadratic inequality in one variable that has a solution of $x < -2$ or $x > 5$.

69. **CHALLENGE** The area A of the region bounded by a parabola and a horizontal line is given by $A = \frac{2}{3}bh$ where b and h are as defined in the diagram. Find the area of the region determined by each pair of inequalities.

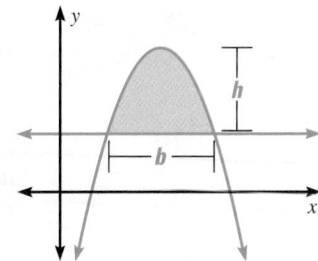

    a. $y \leq -x^2 + 4x$
        $y \geq 0$

    b. $y \geq x^2 - 4x - 5$
        $y \leq 3$

EXAMPLE 2
for Exs. 70–71

70. **ENGINEERING** A wire rope can safely support a weight W (in pounds) provided $W \le 8000d^2$ where d is the rope's diameter (in inches). Graph the inequality.

71. **WOODWORKING** A hardwood shelf in a wooden bookcase can safely support a weight W (in pounds) provided $W \le 115x^2$ where x is the shelf's thickness (in inches). Graph the inequality.

EXAMPLE 6
for Exs. 72–74

72. **ARCHITECTURE** The arch of the Sydney Harbor Bridge in Sydney, Australia, can be modeled by $y = -0.00211x^2 + 1.06x$ where x is the distance (in meters) from the left pylons and y is the height (in meters) of the arch above the water. For what distances x is the arch above the road?

73. ★ **SHORT RESPONSE** The length L (in millimeters) of the larvae of the black porgy fish can be modeled by

$$L(x) = 0.00170x^2 + 0.145x + 2.35, \ 0 \le x \le 40$$

where x is the age (in days) of the larvae. Write and solve an inequality to find at what ages a larvae's length tends to be greater than 10 millimeters. *Explain* how the given domain affects the solution.

74. ◆ **MULTIPLE REPRESENTATIONS** A study found that a driver's reaction time $A(x)$ to audio stimuli and his or her reaction time $V(x)$ to visual stimuli (both in milliseconds) can be modeled by

$$A(x) = 0.0051x^2 - 0.319x + 15, \ 16 \le x \le 70$$
$$V(x) = 0.005x^2 - 0.23x + 22, \ 16 \le x \le 70$$

where x is the driver's age (in years).

a. **Writing an Inequality** Write an inequality that you can use to find the x-values for which $A(x)$ is less than $V(x)$.

b. **Making a Table** Use a table to find the solution of the inequality from part (a). Your table should contain x-values from 16 to 70 in increments of 6.

c. **Drawing a Graph** Check the solution you found in part (b) by using a graphing calculator to solve the inequality $A(x) < V(x)$ graphically. *Describe* how you used the domain $16 \le x \le 70$ to determine a reasonable solution.

d. **Interpret** Based on your results from parts (b) and (c), do you think a driver would react more quickly to a traffic light changing from green to yellow or to the siren of an approaching ambulance? *Explain*.

○ = See **WORKED-OUT SOLUTIONS** in Student Resources   ★ = **STANDARDIZED TEST PRACTICE**   ◆ = **MULTIPLE REPRESENTATIONS**

Paul Steel/The Stock Market/Corbis

75. SOCCER The path of a soccer ball kicked from the ground can be modeled by

$$y = -0.0540x^2 + 1.43x$$

where x is the horizontal distance (in feet) from where the ball was kicked and y is the corresponding height (in feet).

   a. A soccer goal is 8 feet high. Write and solve an inequality to find at what values of x the ball is low enough to go into the goal.

   b. A soccer player kicks the ball toward the goal from a distance of 15 feet away. No one is blocking the goal. Will the player score a goal? *Explain* your reasoning.

76. MULTI-STEP PROBLEM A truck that is 11 feet tall and 7 feet wide is traveling under an arch. The arch can be modeled by

$$y = -0.0625x^2 + 1.25x + 5.75$$

where x and y are measured in feet.

   a. Will the truck fit under the arch? *Explain* your reasoning.

   b. What is the maximum width that a truck 11 feet tall can have and still make it under the arch?

   c. What is the maximum height that a truck 7 feet wide can have and still make it under the arch?

77. CHALLENGE For clear blue ice on lakes and ponds, the maximum weight w (in tons) that the ice can support is given by

$$w(x) = 0.1x^2 - 0.5x - 5$$

where x is the thickness of the ice (in inches).

   a. Calculate What thicknesses of ice can support a weight of 20 tons?

   b. Interpret *Explain* how you can use the graph of $w(x)$ to determine the minimum x-value in the domain for which the function gives meaningful results.

QUIZ

Use the quadratic formula to solve the equation.

   1. $x^2 - 4x + 5 = 0$
   2. $2x^2 - 8x + 1 = 0$
   3. $3x^2 + 5x + 4 = 0$

Graph the inequality.

   4. $y < -3x^2$
   5. $y > -x^2 + 2x$
   6. $y \geq -x^2 + 2x + 3$

Solve the inequality.

   7. $0 \geq x^2 + 5$
   8. $12 \leq x^2 - 7x$
   9. $2x^2 + 2 > -5x$

Find the discriminant of the quadratic equation and give the number and type of solutions of the equation.

   10. $0 = 2x^2 - 3x + 10$
   11. $0 = -x^2 - 4x - 4$
   12. $0 = x^2 - 6$

13. SPORTS A person throws a baseball into the air with an initial vertical velocity of 30 feet per second and then lets the ball hit the ground. The ball is released 5 feet above the ground. How long is the ball in the air?

MIXED REVIEW *of Problem Solving*

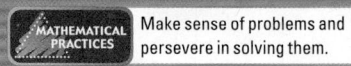

MATHEMATICAL PRACTICES   Make sense of problems and persevere in solving them.

1. **MULTI-STEP PROBLEM** You are playing a lawn version of tic-tac-toe in which you toss bean bags onto a large board. One of your tosses can be modeled by $y = -0.12x^2 + 1.2x + 2$ where x is the bean bag's horizontal position (in feet) and y is the corresponding height (in feet).

   a. Write the given function in vertex form.

   b. Graph the function.

   c. What is the bean bag's maximum height?

2. **SHORT RESPONSE** Given the functions $f(x) = x^2$ and $g(x) = (x - 1)^2 + 2$, compare the graph of $g(x)$ with the graph of $f(x)$.

3. **EXTENDED RESPONSE** The table shows the average price of a car part from 2003 through 2008.

Years since 2003, t	Price (dollars), p
0	133
1	102
2	81
3	71
4	61
5	61

   a. Graph the price of the part versus time.

   b. Describe the shape the data appear to follow. What kind of equation would model this shape?

   c. Do you think such a model will give a good estimate of the price of the part in 2015? *Explain.*

4. **OPEN-ENDED** Name three different complex numbers with an absolute value of 25. Then plot your answers in the same complex plane.

5. **GRIDDED ANSWER** What is the product of $5 - 9i$ and its complex conjugate?

6. **GRIDDED RESPONSE** An interior designer is making a hanging glass lamp, modeled on the equation $y = -0.63x^2 + 3.17x$. If each unit represents 2 inches, how wide is the base of the lamp, to the nearest tenth of an inch?

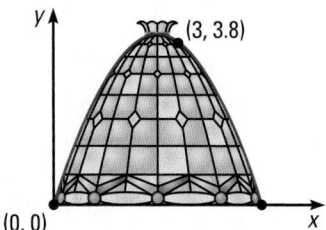

7. **EXTENDED RESPONSE** You throw a ball to your friend. The ball leaves your hand 5 feet above the ground and has an initial vertical velocity of 50 feet per second. Your friend catches the ball when it falls to a height of 3 feet.

   a. Write a function that gives the ball's height h (in feet) t seconds after you throw it.

   b. How long is the ball in the air?

   c. *Describe* three methods you could use to find the maximum height of the ball. Then find the maximum height using each method.

8. **SHORT RESPONSE** You are designing notepaper with a solid stripe along the paper's top and left sides as shown. The stripes will take up one third of the area of the paper. The paper measures 5 inches by 8 inches. What will the width x of the stripes be? *Explain* why you must reject one of the solutions.

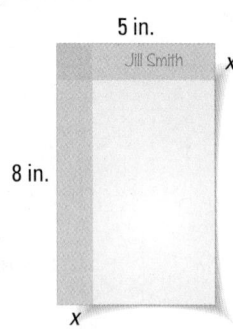

9. **GRIDDED ANSWER** What is the discriminant of the equation $3x^2 + 5x - 2 = 0$?

CHAPTER SUMMARY

Animated Algebra
my.hrw.com
Electronic Function Library

BIG IDEAS
For Your Notebook

Big Idea 1

Graphing and Writing Quadratic Functions in Several Forms

You can graph or write a quadratic function in standard form, vertex form, or intercept form.

Form	Equation	Information about quadratic function
Standard form	$y = ax^2 + bx + c$	• The x-coordinate of the vertex is $-\dfrac{b}{2a}$. • The axis of symmetry is $x = -\dfrac{b}{2a}$.
Vertex form	$y = a(x - h)^2 + k$	• The vertex is (h, k). • The axis of symmetry is $x = h$.
Intercept form	$y = a(x - p)(x - q)$	• The x-intercepts are p and q. • The axis of the symmetry is $x = \dfrac{p + q}{2}$.

Big Idea 2

Solving Quadratic Equations Using a Variety of Methods

There are several different methods you can use to solve a quadratic equation.

Equation contains:	Example	Method
Binomial without x-term	$5x^2 - 45 = 0$	Isolate the x^2-term. Then take square roots of each side.
Factorable trinomial	$x^2 - 5x + 6 = 0$	Factor the trinomial. Then use the zero product property.
Unfactorable trinomial	$x^2 - 8x + 35 = 0$	Complete the square, *or* use the quadratic formula.

Big Idea 3

Performing Operations with Square Roots and Complex Numbers

You can use the following properties to simplify expressions involving square roots or complex numbers.

Square roots	If $a > 0$ and $b > 0$, then $\sqrt{ab} = \sqrt{a} \cdot \sqrt{b}$ and $\sqrt{\dfrac{a}{b}} = \dfrac{\sqrt{a}}{\sqrt{b}}$.
Complex numbers	• The imaginary unit i is defined as $i = \sqrt{-1}$, so that $i^2 = -1$. • If r is a positive real number, then $\sqrt{-r} = i\sqrt{r}$ and $(i\sqrt{r})^2 = -r$. • $(a + bi) + (c + di) = (a + c) + (b + d)i$ • $(a + bi) - (c + di) = (a - c) + (b - d)i$ • $|a + bi| = \sqrt{a^2 + b^2}$

REVIEW KEY VOCABULARY

- quadratic function
- standard form of a quadratic function
- parabola
- vertex
- axis of symmetry
- minimum, maximum value
- vertex form
- intercept form
- monomial, binomial, trinomial
- quadratic equation

- standard form of a quadratic equation
- root of an equation
- zero of a function
- square root
- radical, radicand
- rationalizing the denominator
- conjugates
- imaginary unit i
- complex number
- standard form of a complex number

- imaginary number
- pure imaginary number
- complex conjugates
- complex plane
- absolute value of a complex number
- completing the square
- quadratic formula
- discriminant
- quadratic inequality in two variables
- quadratic inequality in one variable

VOCABULARY EXERCISES

1. **WRITING** Given a quadratic function in standard form, explain how to determine whether the function has a maximum value or a minimum value.

2. Copy and complete: A(n) __?__ is a complex number $a + bi$ where $a = 0$ and $b \neq 0$.

3. Copy and complete: A function of the form $y = a(x - h)^2 + k$ is written in __?__.

4. Give an example of a quadratic equation that has a negative discriminant.

REVIEW EXAMPLES AND EXERCISES

Use the review examples and exercises below to check your understanding of the concepts you have learned in each lesson of this chapter.

1.1 Graph Quadratic Functions in Standard Form

EXAMPLE

Graph $y = -x^2 - 4x - 5$.

Because $a < 0$, the parabola opens down. Find and plot the vertex $(-2, -1)$. Draw the axis of symmetry $x = -2$. Plot the y-intercept at $(0, -5)$, and plot its reflection $(-4, -5)$ in the axis of symmetry. Plot two other points: $(-1, -2)$ and its reflection $(-3, -2)$ in the axis of symmetry. Draw a parabola through the plotted points.

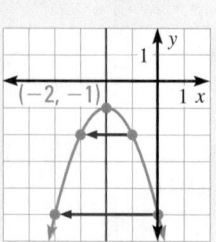

EXERCISES

EXAMPLE 3
for Exs. 5–7

Graph the function. Label the vertex and axis of symmetry.

5. $y = x^2 + 2x - 3$

6. $y = -3x^2 + 12x - 7$

7. $f(x) = -x^2 - 2x - 6$

1.2 Graph Quadratic Functions in Vertex or Intercept Form

EXAMPLE

Graph $y = (x - 4)(x + 2)$.

Identify the x-intercepts. The quadratic function is in intercept form $y = a(x - p)(x - q)$ where $a = 1$, $p = 4$, and $q = -2$. Plot the x-intercepts at $(4, 0)$ and $(-2, 0)$.

Find the coordinates of the vertex.

$$x = \frac{p + q}{2} = \frac{4 + (-2)}{2} = 1$$
$$y = (1 - 4)(1 + 2) = -9$$

Plot the vertex at $(1, -9)$. Draw a parabola through the plotted points as shown.

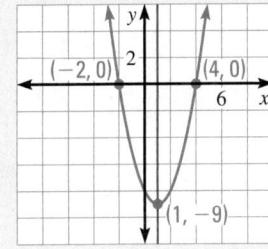

EXERCISES

Graph the function. Label the vertex and axis of symmetry.

EXAMPLES 1, 3, and 4
for Exs. 8–14

8. $y = (x - 1)(x + 5)$ **9.** $g(x) = (x + 3)(x - 2)$ **10.** $y = -3(x + 1)(x - 6)$

11. $y = (x - 2)^2 + 3$ **12.** $f(x) = (x + 6)^2 + 8$ **13.** $y = -2(x + 8)^2 - 3$

14. BIOLOGY A flea's jump can be modeled by the function $y = -0.073x(x - 33)$ where x is the horizontal distance (in centimeters) and y is the corresponding height (in centimeters). How far did the flea jump? What was the flea's maximum height?

1.3 Solve $x^2 + bx + c = 0$ by Factoring

EXAMPLE

Solve $x^2 - 13x - 48 = 0$.

Use factoring to solve for x.

$x^2 - 13x - 48 = 0$	Write original equation.
$(x - 16)(x + 3) = 0$	Factor.
$x - 16 = 0$ or $x + 3 = 0$	Zero product property
$x = 16$ or $x = -3$	Solve for x.

EXERCISES

Solve the equation.

EXAMPLE 3
for Exs. 15–21

15. $x^2 + 5x = 0$ **16.** $z^2 = 63z$ **17.** $s^2 - 6s - 27 = 0$

18. $k^2 + 12k - 45 = 0$ **19.** $x^2 + 18x = -81$ **20.** $n^2 + 5n = 24$

21. URBAN PLANNING A city wants to double the area of a rectangular playground that is 72 feet by 48 feet by adding the same distance x to the length and the width. Write and solve an equation to find the value of x.

CHAPTER REVIEW

1.4 Solve $ax^2 + bx + c = 0$ by Factoring

EXAMPLE

Solve $-30x^2 + 9x + 12 = 0$.

$-30x^2 + 9x + 12 = 0$	Write original equation.
$10x^2 - 3x - 4 = 0$	Divide each side by -3.
$(5x - 4)(2x + 1) = 0$	Factor.
$5x - 4 = 0$ or $2x + 1 = 0$	Zero product property
$x = \dfrac{4}{5}$ or $x = -\dfrac{1}{2}$	Solve for x.

EXAMPLE 5
for Exs. 22–24

EXERCISES

Solve the equation.

22. $16 = 38r - 12r^2$ **23.** $3x^2 - 24x - 48 = 0$ **24.** $20a^2 - 13a - 21 = 0$

1.5 Solve Quadratic Equations by Finding Square Roots

EXAMPLE

Solve $4(x - 7)^2 = 80$.

$4(x - 7)^2 = 80$	Write original equation.
$(x - 7)^2 = 20$	Divide each side by 4.
$x - 7 = \pm\sqrt{20}$	Take square roots of each side.
$x = 7 \pm 2\sqrt{5}$	Add 7 to each side and simplify.

EXAMPLES
3 and 4
for Exs. 25–28

EXERCISES

Solve the equation.

25. $3x^2 = 108$ **26.** $5y^2 + 4 = 14$ **27.** $3(p + 1)^2 = 81$

28. GEOGRAPHY The total surface area of Earth is 510,000,000 square kilometers. Use the formula $S = 4\pi r^2$, which gives the surface area of a sphere with radius r, to find the radius of Earth.

1.6 Perform Operations with Complex Numbers

EXAMPLE

Write $(6 - 4i)(1 - 3i)$ as a complex number in standard form.

$(6 - 4i)(1 - 3i) = 6 - 18i - 4i + 12i^2$	Multiply using FOIL.
$= 6 - 22i + 12(-1)$	Simplify and use $i^2 = -1$.
$= -6 - 22i$	Write in standard form.

EXAMPLES
2, 4, and 5
for Exs. 29–34

EXERCISES

Write the expression as a complex number in standard form.

29. $-9i(2 - i)$

30. $(5 + i)(4 - 2i)$

31. $(2 - 5i)(2 + 5i)$

32. $(8 - 6i) + (7 + 4i)$

33. $(2 - 3i) - (6 - 5i)$

34. $\dfrac{4i}{-3 + 6i}$

1.7 | ## Complete the Square

EXAMPLE

Solve $x^2 - 8x + 13 = 0$ by completing the square.

$x^2 - 8x + 13 = 0$ Write original equation.

$x^2 - 8x = -13$ Write left side in the form $x^2 + bx$.

$x^2 - 8x + 16 = -13 + 16$ Add $\left(\dfrac{-8}{2}\right)^2 = (-4)^2 = 16$ to each side.

$(x - 4)^2 = 3$ Write left side as a binomial squared.

$x - 4 = \pm\sqrt{3}$ Take square roots of each side.

$x = 4 \pm\sqrt{3}$ Solve for x.

EXAMPLES
3 and 4
for Exs. 35–37

EXERCISES

Solve the equation by completing the square.

35. $x^2 - 6x - 15 = 0$

36. $3x^2 - 12x + 1 = 0$

37. $x^2 + 3x - 1 = 0$

1.8 | ## Use the Quadratic Formula and the Discriminant

EXAMPLE

Solve $3x^2 + 6x = -2$.

$3x^2 + 6x = -2$ Write original equation.

$3x^2 + 6x + 2 = 0$ Write in standard form.

$x = \dfrac{-6 \pm \sqrt{6^2 - 4(3)(2)}}{2(3)}$ Use $a = 3$, $b = 6$, and $c = 2$ in quadratic formula.

$x = \dfrac{-3 \pm \sqrt{3}}{3}$ Simplify.

EXAMPLES
1, 2, 3, and 5
for Exs. 38–41

EXERCISES

Use the quadratic formula to solve the equation.

38. $x^2 + 4x - 3 = 0$

39. $9x^2 = -6x - 1$

40. $6x^2 - 8x = -3$

41. VOLLEYBALL A person spikes a volleyball over a net when the ball is 9 feet above the ground. The volleyball has an initial vertical velocity of -40 feet per second. The volleyball is allowed to fall to the ground. How long is the ball in the air after it is spiked?

1.9 Graph and Solve Quadratic Inequalities

EXAMPLE

Solve $-2x^2 + 2x + 5 \leq 0$.

The solution consists of the x-values for which the graph of $y = -2x^2 + 2x + 5$ lies on or below the x-axis. Find the graph's x-intercepts by letting $y = 0$ and using the quadratic formula to solve for x.

$$x = \frac{-2 \pm \sqrt{2^2 - 4(-2)(5)}}{2(-2)}$$

$$= \frac{-2 \pm \sqrt{44}}{-4} = \frac{-1 \pm \sqrt{11}}{-2}$$

$$x \approx -1.16 \text{ or } x \approx 2.16$$

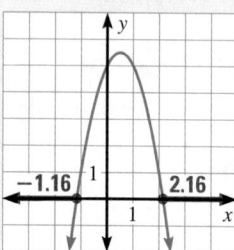

Sketch a parabola that opens down and has -1.16 and 2.16 as x-intercepts. The solution of the inequality is approximately $x \leq -1.16$ or $x \geq 2.16$.

EXERCISES

EXAMPLE 5
for Exs. 42–44

Solve the inequality by graphing.

42. $2x^2 - 11x + 5 < 0$

43. $-x^2 + 4x + 3 \geq 0$

44. $\frac{1}{2}x^2 + 3x - 6 > 0$

1

Graph the function. Label the vertex and axis of symmetry.

1. $y = x^2 - 8x - 20$

2. $y = -(x + 3)^2 + 5$

3. $f(x) = 2(x + 4)(x - 2)$

Factor the expression.

4. $x^2 - 11x + 30$

5. $z^2 + 2z - 15$

6. $n^2 - 64$

7. $2s^2 + 7s - 15$

8. $9x^2 + 30x + 25$

9. $6t^2 + 23t + 20$

Solve the equation.

10. $x^2 - 3x - 40 = 0$

11. $r^2 - 13r + 42 = 0$

12. $2w^2 + 13w - 7 = 0$

13. $10y^2 + 11y - 6 = 0$

14. $2(m - 7)^2 = 16$

15. $(x + 2)^2 - 12 = 36$

Write the expression as a complex number in standard form.

16. $(3 + 4i) - (2 - 5i)$

17. $(2 - 7i)(1 + 2i)$

18. $\dfrac{3 + i}{2 - 3i}$

Solve the equation by completing the square.

19. $x^2 + 4x - 14 = 0$

20. $x^2 - 10x - 7 = 0$

21. $4x^2 + 8x + 3 = 0$

Use the quadratic formula to solve the equation.

22. $3x^2 + 10x - 5 = 0$

23. $2x^2 - x + 6 = 0$

24. $5x^2 + 2x + 5 = 0$

Graph the inequality.

25. $y \geq x^2 - 8$

26. $y < x^2 + 4x - 21$

27. $y > -x^2 + 5x + 50$

Graph the system of quadratic inequalities.

28. $y \leq 3 - x^2$
$y \geq x^2$

29. $y < 2 - (x + 1)^2$
$y \geq \frac{1}{2}x^2 + 1$

30. $y < x^2$
$y \geq \frac{1}{2}(x + 1)^2$

31. ASPECT RATIO The *aspect ratio* of a widescreen TV is the ratio of the screen's width to its height, or 16 : 9. What are the width and the height of a 32 inch widescreen TV? (*Hint:* Use the Pythagorean theorem and the fact that TV sizes such as 32 inches refer to the length of the screen's diagonal.)

CONTEXT-BASED MULTIPLE CHOICE QUESTIONS

Some of the information you need to solve a context-based multiple choice question may appear in a table, a diagram, or a graph.

PROBLEM 1

The area of the shaded region is 56 square meters. What is the height of the trapezoid?

(A) 3 meters   (B) 4 meters

(C) 6 meters   (D) 7.5 meters

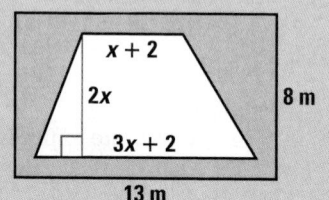

Plan

INTERPRET THE DIAGRAM You know the area of the shaded region. Use the diagram to find the area of the rectangle, and write an expression for the area of the trapezoid. The difference of these two areas is the area of the shaded region.

Solution

STEP 1
Find expressions for the two areas.

Area of rectangle:

$A = \ell w$

$= 13(8)$

$= 104 \text{ m}^2$

Area of trapezoid:

$A = \frac{1}{2}(b_1 + b_2)h$

$= \frac{1}{2}[(x + 2) + (3x + 2)](2x)$

$= \frac{1}{2}(2x)(4x + 4)$

$= x(4x + 4)$

$= 4x^2 + 4x$

STEP 2
Write an equation for the area of the shaded region and solve by factoring.

Area of shaded region = Area of rectangle − Area of trapezoid

$56 = 104 - (4x^2 + 4x)$ **Substitute.**

$-48 = -4x^2 - 4x$ **Subtract 104 from each side.**

$4x^2 + 4x - 48 = 0$ **Write in standard form.**

$x^2 + x - 12 = 0$ **Divide each side by 4.**

$(x - 3)(x + 4) = 0$ **Factor.**

$x = 3 \text{ or } x = -4$ **Zero product property**

STEP 3
Find the possible heights.

The height of the trapezoid is given by the expression $2x$. Therefore, the possible heights are $2(3) = 6$ meters and $2(-4) = -8$ meters.

STEP 4
Reject the negative height.

Because height cannot be negative, the height of the trapezoid is 6 meters.

▸ The correct answer is C. (A) (B) (C) (D)

The height h (in feet) of a lobbed tennis ball after t seconds is shown by the graph. What is the initial vertical velocity of the tennis ball?

(A) 3 feet/second   **(B)** 16 feet/second

(C) 37.5 feet/second   **(D)** 47 feet/second

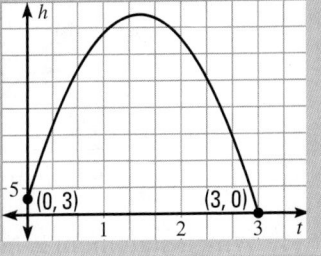

Plan

INTERPRET THE GRAPH The graph is a parabola passing through the points $(0, 3)$ and $(3, 0)$. In order to find the initial vertical velocity of the tennis ball, you must write an equation of the parabola.

Solution

STEP 1
Write the model for an object that is launched.

Because the tennis ball is launched, the parabola has an equation of the form $h = -16t^2 + v_0t + h_0$ where v_0 is the initial vertical velocity and h_0 is the initial height of the tennis ball.

STEP 2
Use the initial height in your model.

The graph passes through $(0, 3)$, so the initial height of the tennis ball is 3 feet. When you substitute 3 for h_0 in the model, you obtain $h = -16t^2 + v_0t + 3$.

STEP 3
Find the initial vertical velocity by substituting a point on the parabola.

Use the fact that the graph of $h = -16t^2 + v_0t + 3$ passes through $(3, 0)$ to find the initial vertical velocity v_0.

$0 = -16(3)^2 + v_0(3) + 3$	**Substitute 0 for h and 3 for t.**
$0 = -141 + 3v_0$	**Simplify.**
$47 = v_0$	**Solve for v_0.**

The initial vertical velocity is 47 feet per second.

▶ The correct answer is D. **(A)** **(B)** **(C)** **(D)**

PRACTICE

In Exercises 1 and 2, use the graph in Problem 2.

1. What is the maximum height of the tennis ball to the nearest tenth of a foot?

   (A) 36.3 feet   **(B)** 36.8 feet   **(C)** 37.5 feet   **(D)** 38.0 feet

2. What does the x-coordinate of the vertex of the graph represent?

   (A) The maximum height of the tennis ball

   (B) The number of seconds the ball is in the air

   (C) The number of seconds it takes the ball to reach its maximum height

   (D) The initial height of the tennis ball

CONTEXT-BASED MULTIPLE CHOICE

In Exercises 1 and 2, use the parabola below.

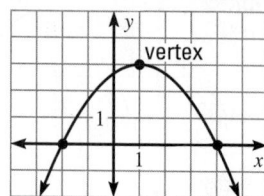

1. Which statement is *not* true about the parabola?

   (A) The x-intercepts are -2 and 4.

   (B) The y-intercept is -2.

   (C) The maximum value is 3.

   (D) The axis of symmetry is $x = 1$.

2. What is an equation of the parabola?

   (A) $y = (x - 2)(x + 4)$

   (B) $y = -\frac{1}{3}(x + 2)(x - 4)$

   (C) $y = -(x + 2)(x - 4)$

   (D) $y = -3(x + 2)(x - 4)$

3. You are using glass tiles to make a picture frame for a square photograph with sides 10 inches long. You want the frame to form a uniform border around the photograph. You have enough tiles to cover 300 square inches. What is the largest possible frame width x?

   (A) 3.6 inches

   (B) 5 inches

   (C) 7.3 inches

   (D) 15 inches

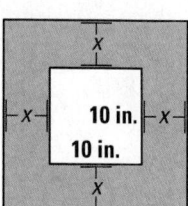

4. At a flea market held each weekend, an artist sells handmade earrings. The table below shows the average number of pairs of earrings sold for several prices. Given the pattern in the table, how much should the artist charge to maximize revenue?

Price	$15	$14	$13	$12
Pairs sold	50	60	70	80

   (A) $5   (B) $7.50   (C) $10   (D) $15

5. The graph of which inequality is shown?

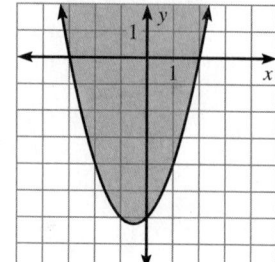

   (A) $y \geq -x^2 - x + 6$ (B) $y \geq x^2 + x - 6$

   (C) $y > 2x^2 + 2x - 12$ (D) $y \geq -2x^2 - 2x + 12$

In Exercises 6 and 7, use the information below.

The graph shows the height h (in feet) after t seconds of a horseshoe tossed during a game of horseshoes. The initial vertical velocity of the horseshoe is 30 feet per second.

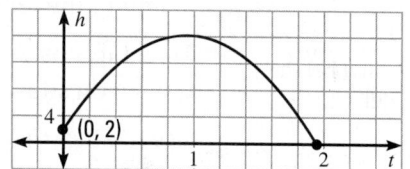

6. To the nearest tenth of a second, how long is the horseshoe in the air?

   (A) 0.1 seconds   (B) 1.9 seconds

   (C) 2.1 seconds   (D) 3.9 seconds

7. To the nearest tenth of a foot, what is the maximum height of the horseshoe?

   (A) 15.9 feet   (B) 16.1 feet

   (C) 29.2 feet   (D) 32.2 feet

8. The diagram shows a circle inscribed in a square. The area of the shaded region is 21.5 square inches. To the nearest tenth of an inch, how long is a side of the square?

   (A) 4.6 inches

   (B) 8.7 inches

   (C) 9.7 inches

   (D) 10.0 inches

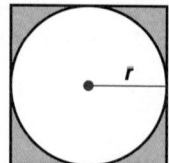

GRIDDED ANSWER

9. What is the value of k in the equation $6x^2 - 11x - 10 = (3x + 2)(2x - k)$?

10. What is the real part of the standard form of the expression $(5 + i)(10 - i)$?

11. For what value of c is $x^2 - 7x + c$ a perfect square trinomial?

12. What is the maximum value of the function $y = -3(x - 2)^2 + 6$?

13. What is the greatest zero of the function $y = x^2 - 25x + 66$?

14. What is the absolute value of $-5 + 12i$?

15. What is the x-coordinate of the vertex of the parabola that passes through the points $(0, -22)$, $(2, -6)$, and $(5, -12)$?

16. What is the minimum value of the function $f(x) = 4x^2 + 24x + 39$?

SHORT RESPONSE

17. Solve $3x^2 + 6x + 14 = 0$ by completing the square. *Explain* all of your steps.

18. The surface area y of a cube is given by the function $y = 6x^2$ where x is an edge length. Graph the function. *Compare* this graph to the graph of $y = x^2$.

19. The height h (in feet) of an object after it is launched is given by the function

$$h = -16t^2 + v_0 t + h_0$$

where v_0 is the initial vertical velocity, h_0 is the initial height of the object, and t is the time (in seconds) after the object is launched. *Explain* how this function is related to the general function for a dropped object.

20. At what two points do the graphs of $y = 2x^2 - 5x - 12$ and $y = \frac{1}{2}x^2 - 3x + 4$ intersect? *Explain* your reasoning.

EXTENDED RESPONSE

21. The table below shows the New York Yankees' payroll (in millions of dollars) from 1989 through 2004.

Years since 1989	0	1	2	3	4	5	6	7
Payroll	21	21	28	36	41	45	47	52
Years since 1989	8	9	10	11	12	13	14	15
Payroll	59	63	88	93	112	126	153	184

a. Make a scatter plot of the data.

b. Draw the parabola that you think best fits the data.

c. Estimate the coordinates of three points on the parabola from part (b). Then use a system of equations to write a quadratic model for the data.

d. Use your model from part (c) to make a table of data for the years listed in the original table. *Compare* the numbers given by your model with the actual data. Assess the accuracy of your model.

22. A volleyball is hit upward by a player in a game. The height h (in feet) of the volleyball after t seconds is given by the function $h = -16t^2 + 30t + 6$.

a. What is the maximum height of the volleyball? *Explain* your reasoning.

b. After how many seconds does the volleyball reach its maximum height?

c. After how many seconds does the volleyball hit the ground?

2 Polynomials and Polynomial Functions

COMMON CORE

Lesson
2.1   CC.9-12.N.RN.1
2.2   CC.9-12.F.IF.7c*
2.3   CC.9-12.A.APR.1
2.4   CC.9-12.A.SSE.2
2.5   CC.9-12.A.APR.2
2.6   CC.9-12.A.APR.2
2.7   CC.9-12.N.CN.9 (+)
2.8   CC.9-12.F.IF.7c*

Before

Previously, you learned the following skills, which you'll use in this chapter: simplifying expressions, finding volume, and factoring.

Prerequisite Skills

VOCABULARY CHECK

Copy and complete the statement.

1. The **zeros** of the function graphed are __?__.

2. The **maximum value** of the function graphed is __?__.

3. The **standard form** of a quadratic equation in one variable is __?__ where $a \neq 0$.

SKILLS CHECK

Simplify the expression.

4. 4^3

5. $(-2)^4 + 3^2$

6. 12^0

Find the volume of the solid.

7. a sphere with radius 6 cm

8. a cube with side length 4 in.

Factor the expression.

9. $x^2 + 9x + 20$

10. $x^2 + 13x + 30$

11. $x^2 + 8x + 12$

In this chapter, you will apply the big ideas listed below and reviewed in the Chapter Summary. You will also use the key vocabulary listed below.

Big Ideas

1 **Graphing polynomial functions**

2 **Performing operations with polynomials**

3 **Solving polynomial equations and finding zeros**

KEY VOCABULARY

- polynomial
- polynomial function
- synthetic substitution
- end behavior

- factored completely
- factor by grouping
- quadratic form
- polynomial long division

- synthetic division
- repeated solution
- local maximum
- local minimum
- finite differences

Why?

You can use polynomial functions to model real-life situations. For example, you can use a polynomial function to model the relationship between the speed of an object and the power needed to maintain that speed.

Animated Algebra

The animation illustrated below helps you answer a question from this chapter: How does the power needed to keep a bicycle moving at a constant speed change as the conditions change?

The power exerted by a bicyclist depends on speed and resistance.

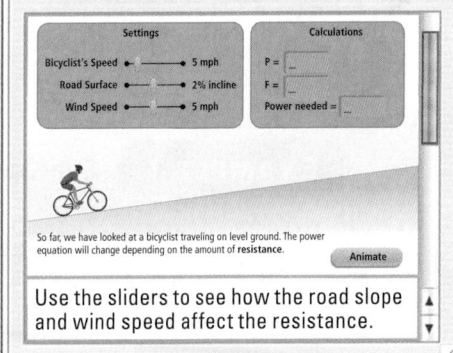

Use the sliders to see how the road slope and wind speed affect the resistance.

Animated Algebra at my.hrw.com

2.1 Use Properties of Exponents

Before	You evaluated powers.
Now	You will simplify expressions involving powers.
Why?	So you can compare the volumes of two stars, as in Example 5.

Key Vocabulary
• scientific notation

CC.9-12.N.RN.1 Explain how the definition of the meaning of rational exponents follows from extending the properties of integer exponents to those values, allowing for a notation for radicals in terms of rational exponents.

AVOID ERRORS
When you multiply powers, do not multiply the bases. For example, $3^2 \cdot 3^5 \neq 9^7$.

Consider what happens when you multiply two powers that have the same base:

$$2^3 \cdot 2^5 = (2 \cdot 2 \cdot 2) \cdot (2 \cdot 2 \cdot 2 \cdot 2 \cdot 2) = 2^8$$

Note that the exponent 8 in the product is the sum of the exponents 3 and 5 in the factors. This property is one of several properties of exponents shown below.

KEY CONCEPT
For Your Notebook

Properties of Exponents

Let a and b be real numbers and let m and n be integers.

Property Name	Definition	Example
Product of Powers	$a^m \cdot a^n = a^{m+n}$	$5^3 \cdot 5^{-1} = 5^{3+(-1)} = 5^2 = 25$
Power of a Power	$(a^m)^n = a^{mn}$	$(3^3)^2 = 3^{3 \cdot 2} = 3^6 = 729$
Power of a Product	$(ab)^m = a^m b^m$	$(2 \cdot 3)^4 = 2^4 \cdot 3^4 = 1296$
Negative Exponent	$a^{-m} = \dfrac{1}{a^m}, a \neq 0$	$7^{-2} = \dfrac{1}{7^2} = \dfrac{1}{49}$
Zero Exponent	$a^0 = 1, a \neq 0$	$(-89)^0 = 1$
Quotient of Powers	$\dfrac{a^m}{a^n} = a^{m-n}, a \neq 0$	$\dfrac{6^{-3}}{6^{-6}} = 6^{-3-(-6)} = 6^3 = 216$
Power of a Quotient	$\left(\dfrac{a}{b}\right)^m = \dfrac{a^m}{b^m}, b \neq 0$	$\left(\dfrac{4}{7}\right)^2 = \dfrac{4^2}{7^2} = \dfrac{16}{49}$

EXAMPLE 1 Evaluate numerical expressions

a. $\left(-4 \cdot 2^5\right)^2 = (-4)^2 \cdot \left(2^5\right)^2$ **Power of a product property**

$= 16 \cdot 2^{5 \cdot 2}$ **Power of a power property**

$= 16 \cdot 2^{10} = 16{,}384$ **Simplify and evaluate power.**

b. $\left(\dfrac{11^5}{11^8}\right)^{-1} = \dfrac{11^8}{11^5}$ **Negative exponent property**

$= 11^{8-5}$ **Quotient of powers property**

$= 11^3 = 1331$ **Simplify and evaluate power.**

NASA/Corbis

SCIENTIFIC NOTATION A number is expressed in **scientific notation** if it is in the form $c \times 10^n$ where $1 \le c < 10$ and n is an integer. When you work with numbers in scientific notation, the properties of exponents can make calculations easier.

EXAMPLE 2 Use scientific notation in real life

LOCUSTS A swarm of locusts may contain as many as 85 million locusts per square kilometer and cover an area of 1200 square kilometers. About how many locusts are in such a swarm?

Solution

$$\text{Number of locusts} = \text{Locusts per square kilometer} \times \text{Number of square kilometers}$$

$= 85{,}000{,}000 \times 1200$ **Substitute values.**

$= (8.5 \times 10^7)(1.2 \times 10^3)$ **Write in scientific notation.**

$= (8.5 \times 1.2)(10^7 \times 10^3)$ **Use multiplication properties.**

$= 10.2 \times 10^{10}$ **Product of powers property**

$= 1.02 \times 10^1 \times 10^{10}$ **Write 10.2 in scientific notation.**

$= 1.02 \times 10^{11}$ **Product of powers property**

▶ The number of locusts is about 1.02×10^{11}, or about 102,000,000,000.

REVIEW SCIENTIFIC NOTATION
For help with scientific notation, see p. SR8.

✓ **GUIDED PRACTICE** for Examples 1 and 2

Evaluate the expression. Tell which properties of exponents you used.

1. $\left(4^2\right)^3$ **2.** $(-8)(-8)^3$ **3.** $\left(\dfrac{2}{9}\right)^3$ **4.** $\dfrac{6 \cdot 10^{-4}}{9 \cdot 10^7}$

SIMPLIFYING EXPRESSIONS You can use the properties of exponents to simplify algebraic expressions. A simplified expression contains only positive exponents.

EXAMPLE 3 Simplify expressions

a. $b^{-4}b^6b^7 = b^{-4\,+\,6\,+\,7} = b^9$ **Product of powers property**

INTERPRET BASES
In this book, it is assumed that any base with a zero or negative exponent is nonzero.

b. $\left(\dfrac{r^{-2}}{s^3}\right)^{-3} = \dfrac{(r^{-2})^{-3}}{(s^3)^{-3}}$ **Power of a quotient property**

$= \dfrac{r^6}{s^{-9}}$ **Power of a power property**

$= r^6 s^9$ **Negative exponent property**

c. $\dfrac{16m^4 n^{-5}}{2n^{-5}} = 8m^4 n^{-5\,-\,(-5)}$ **Quotient of powers property**

$= 8m^4 n^0 = 8m^4$ **Zero exponent property**

 Animated Algebra at my.hrw.com

right Reuters/Corbis; left Dex Image/Getty Images

EXAMPLE 4 **Standardized Test Practice**

What is the simplified form of $\dfrac{(x^{-3}y^3)^2}{x^5y^6}$?

(A) x^{11} (B) $\dfrac{1}{x^{11}}$ (C) $\dfrac{1}{x^6y}$ (D) $\dfrac{1}{x^{11}y}$

Solution

$$\dfrac{(x^{-3}y^3)^2}{x^5y^6} = \dfrac{(x^{-3})^2(y^3)^2}{x^5y^6}$$ Power of a product property

$$= \dfrac{x^{-6}y^6}{x^5y^6}$$ Power of a power property

$$= x^{-6-5}y^{6-6}$$ Quotient of powers property

$$= x^{-11}y^0$$ Simplify exponents.

$$= x^{-11} \cdot 1$$ Zero exponent property

$$= \dfrac{1}{x^{11}}$$ Negative exponent property

▶ The correct answer is B. (A) (B) (C) (D)

EXAMPLE 5 **Compare real-life volumes**

ASTRONOMY Betelgeuse is one of the stars found in the constellation Orion. Its radius is about 1500 times the radius of the sun. How many times as great as the sun's volume is Betelgeuse's volume?

Betelgeuse

Solution

Let r represent the sun's radius. Then $1500r$ represents Betelgeuse's radius.

$$\dfrac{\text{Betelgeuse's volume}}{\text{Sun's volume}} = \dfrac{\frac{4}{3}\pi(1500r)^3}{\frac{4}{3}\pi r^3}$$ The volume of a sphere is $\frac{4}{3}\pi r^3$.

$$= \dfrac{\frac{4}{3}\pi 1500^3 r^3}{\frac{4}{3}\pi r^3}$$ Power of a product property

$$= 1500^3 r^0$$ Quotient of powers property

$$= 1500^3 \cdot 1$$ Zero exponent property

$$= 3,375,000,000$$ Evaluate power.

▶ Betelgeuse's volume is about 3.4 billion times as great as the sun's volume.

GUIDED PRACTICE for Examples 3, 4, and 5

Simplify the expression. Tell which properties of exponents you used.

5. $x^{-6}x^5x^3$ **6.** $(7y^2z^5)(y^{-4}z^{-1})$ **7.** $\left(\dfrac{s^3}{t^{-4}}\right)^2$ **8.** $\left(\dfrac{x^4y^{-2}}{x^3y^6}\right)^3$

2.1 EXERCISES

HOMEWORK KEY   ◯ = See WORKED-OUT SOLUTIONS
Exs. 17, 31, and 51

★ = STANDARDIZED TEST PRACTICE
Exs. 2, 36, 46, 51, and 53

SKILL PRACTICE

1. **VOCABULARY** State the name of the property illustrated.

   a. $a^m \cdot a^n = a^{m+n}$ **b.** $a^{-m} = \dfrac{1}{a^m}, a \neq 0$ **c.** $(ab)^m = a^m b^m$

2. ★ **WRITING** Is the number 25.2×10^{-3} in scientific notation? *Explain.*

EXAMPLE 1
for Exs. 3–14

EVALUATING NUMERICAL EXPRESSIONS Evaluate the expression. Tell which properties of exponents you used.

3. $3^3 \cdot 3^2$ **4.** $(4^{-2})^3$ **5.** $(-5)(-5)^4$ **6.** $(2^4)^2$

7. $\dfrac{5^2}{5^5}$ **8.** $\left(\dfrac{3}{5}\right)^4$ **9.** $\left(\dfrac{2}{7}\right)^{-3}$ **10.** $9^3 \cdot 9^{-1}$

11. $\dfrac{3^4}{3^{-2}}$ **12.** $\left(\dfrac{2}{3}\right)^{-5}\left(\dfrac{2}{3}\right)^4$ **13.** $6^3 \cdot 6^0 \cdot 6^{-5}$ **14.** $\left(\left(\dfrac{1}{2}\right)^{-5}\right)^2$

EXAMPLE 2
for Exs. 15–23

SCIENTIFIC NOTATION Write the answer in scientific notation.

15. $(4.2 \times 10^3)(1.5 \times 10^6)$ **16.** $(1.2 \times 10^{-3})(6.7 \times 10^{-7})$ **17.** $(6.3 \times 10^5)(8.9 \times 10^{-12})$

18. $(7.2 \times 10^9)(9.4 \times 10^8)$ **19.** $(2.1 \times 10^{-4})^3$ **20.** $(4.0 \times 10^3)^4$

21. $\dfrac{8.1 \times 10^{12}}{5.4 \times 10^9}$ **22.** $\dfrac{1.1 \times 10^{-3}}{5.5 \times 10^{-8}}$ **23.** $\dfrac{(7.5 \times 10^8)(4.5 \times 10^{-4})}{1.5 \times 10^7}$

EXAMPLES 3 and 4
for Exs. 24–39

SIMPLIFYING ALGEBRAIC EXPRESSIONS Simplify the expression. Tell which properties of exponents you used.

24. $\dfrac{w^{-2}}{w^6}$ **25.** $(2^2y^3)^5$ **26.** $(p^3q^2)^{-1}$ **27.** $(w^3x^{-2})(w^6x^{-1})$

28. $(5s^{-2}t^4)^{-3}$ **29.** $(3a^3b^5)^{-3}$ **30.** $\dfrac{x^{-1}y^2}{x^2y^{-1}}$ **31.** $\dfrac{3c^3d}{9cd^{-1}}$

32. $\dfrac{4r^4s^5}{24r^4s^{-5}}$ **33.** $\dfrac{2a^3b^{-4}}{3a^5b^{-2}}$ **34.** $\dfrac{y^{11}}{4z^3} \cdot \dfrac{8z^7}{y^7}$ **35.** $\dfrac{x^2y^{-3}}{3y^2} \cdot \dfrac{y^2}{x^{-4}}$

36. ★ **MULTIPLE CHOICE** What is the simplified form of $\dfrac{2x^2y}{6xy^{-1}}$?

   Ⓐ $\dfrac{y^2}{3}$ **Ⓑ** $\dfrac{xy^2}{3}$ **Ⓒ** $\dfrac{x}{3}$ **Ⓓ** $\dfrac{1}{3}$

ERROR ANALYSIS *Describe* and correct the error in simplifying the expression.

37.

$$\frac{x^{10}}{x^2} = x^5 \quad \times$$

38.

$$x^5 \cdot x^3 = x^{15} \quad \times$$

39.

$$(-3)^2(-3)^4 = 9^6 \quad \times$$

GEOMETRY Write an expression for the figure's area or volume in terms of x.

40. $A = \dfrac{\sqrt{3}}{4}s^2$

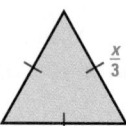

41. $V = \pi r^2 h$

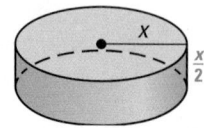

42. $V = \ell w h$

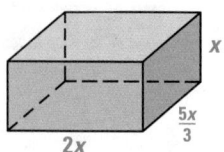

REASONING Write an expression that makes the statement true.

43. $x^{15}y^{12}z^8 = x^4y^7z^{11} \cdot \underline{?}$

44. $3x^3y^2 = \dfrac{12x^2y^5}{?}$

45. $(a^5b^4)^2 = a^{14}b^{-1} \cdot \underline{?}$

46. ★ **OPEN-ENDED MATH** Find three different ways to complete the following statement so that it is true: $x^{12}y^{16} = (x^?y^?)(x^?y^?)$.

CHALLENGE Refer to the properties of exponents.

47. Show how the negative exponent property can be derived from the quotient of powers property and the zero exponent property.

48. Show how the quotient of powers property can be derived from the product of powers property and the negative exponent property.

PROBLEM SOLVING

EXAMPLE 2
for Exs. 49–50

49. **OCEAN VOLUME** The table shows the surface areas and average depths of four oceans. Calculate the volume of each ocean by multiplying the surface area of each ocean by its average depth. Write your answers in scientific notation.

Ocean	Surface area (square meters)	Average depth (meters)
Pacific	1.56×10^{14}	4.03×10^3
Atlantic	7.68×10^{13}	3.93×10^3
Indian	6.86×10^{13}	3.96×10^3
Arctic	1.41×10^{13}	1.21×10^3

50. **EARTH SCIENCE** The continents of Earth move at a very slow rate. The South American continent has been moving about 0.000022 mile per year for the past 125,000,000 years. How far has the continent moved in that time? Write your answer in scientific notation.

○ = **See WORKED-OUT SOLUTIONS** in Student Resources

★ = **STANDARDIZED TEST PRACTICE**

EXAMPLE 5
for Exs. 51–52

51. ★ **SHORT RESPONSE** A typical cultured black pearl is made by placing a bead with a diameter of 6 millimeters inside an oyster. The resulting pearl has a diameter of about 9 millimeters. *Compare* the volume of the resulting pearl with the volume of the bead.

52. **MULTI-STEP PROBLEM** A can of tennis balls consists of three spheres of radius r stacked vertically inside a cylinder of radius r and height h.

   a. Write an expression for the total volume of the three tennis balls in terms of r.

   b. Write an expression for the volume of the cylinder in terms of r and h.

   c. Write an expression for h in terms of r using the fact that the height of the cylinder is the sum of the diameters of the three tennis balls.

   d. What fraction of the can's volume is taken up by the tennis balls?

53. ★ **EXTENDED RESPONSE** You can think of a penny as a cylinder with a radius of about 9.53 millimeters and a height of about 1.55 millimeters.

   a. **Calculate** Approximate the volume of a penny. Give your answer in cubic meters.

   b. **Estimate** Approximate the volume of your classroom in cubic meters. *Explain* how you obtained your answer.

   c. **Interpret** Use your results from parts (a) and (b) to estimate how many pennies it would take to fill your classroom. Do you think your answer is an overestimate or an underestimate? *Explain*.

54. **CHALLENGE** Earth's core is approximately spherical in shape and is divided into a solid inner core (the yellow region in the diagram shown) and a liquid outer core (the dark orange region in the diagram).

   a. Earth's radius is about 5 times as great as the radius of Earth's inner core. Find the ratio of Earth's total volume to the volume of Earth's inner core.

   b. Find the ratio of the volume of Earth's outer core to the volume of Earth's inner core.

End Behavior of Polynomial Functions

MATHEMATICAL PRACTICES

Use appropriate tools strategically.

MATERIALS · graphing calculator

QUESTION How is the end behavior of a polynomial function related to the function's equation?

Functions of the form $f(x) = \pm x^n$, where n is a positive integer, are examples of *polynomial functions*. (They are also examples of *power functions*, which are discussed in the lesson *Perform Function Operations and Composition*.) The *end behavior* of a polynomial function's graph is its behavior as x approaches positive infinity ($+\infty$) or as x approaches negative infinity ($-\infty$).

EXPLORE Investigate the end behavior of $f(x) = \pm x^n$ where n is even

Graph the function. Describe the end behavior of the graph.

  a. $f(x) = x^4$ **b.** $f(x) = -x^4$

STEP 1 *Graph functions* Graph each function on a graphing calculator.

a.

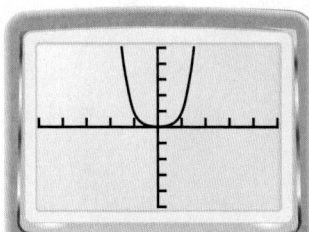

b.

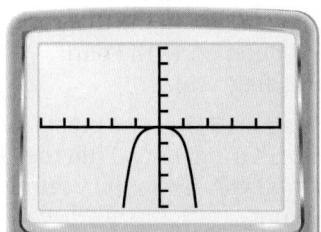

STEP 2 *Describe end behavior* Summarize the end behavior of each function.

Function	As x approaches $-\infty$	As x approaches $+\infty$
a. $f(x) = x^4$	$f(x)$ approaches $+\infty$	$f(x)$ approaches $+\infty$
b. $f(x) = -x^4$	$f(x)$ approaches $-\infty$	$f(x)$ approaches $-\infty$

DRAW CONCLUSIONS Use your observations to complete these exercises

Graph the function. Then describe its end behavior as shown above.

  1. $f(x) = x^5$ **2.** $f(x) = -x^5$ **3.** $f(x) = x^6$ **4.** $f(x) = -x^6$

  5. Make a conjecture about the end behavior of each family of functions.

    a. $f(x) = x^n$ where n is odd   **b.** $f(x) = -x^n$ where n is odd

    c. $f(x) = x^n$ where n is even   **d.** $f(x) = -x^n$ where n is even

  6. Make a conjecture about the end behavior of the function $f(x) = x^6 - x$. *Explain* your reasoning.

2.2 Evaluate and Graph Polynomial Functions

Before	You evaluated and graphed linear and quadratic functions.
Now	You will evaluate and graph other polynomial functions.
Why?	So you can model skateboarding participation, as in Ex. 55.

Key Vocabulary
- **polynomial**
- **polynomial function**
- **synthetic substitution**
- **end behavior**

CC.9-12.F.IF.7 Graph functions expressed symbolically and show key features of the graph, by hand in simple cases and using technology for more complicated cases.*
c. Graph polynomial functions, identifying zeros when suitable factorizations are available, and showing end behavior.

Recall that a monomial is a number, a variable, or a product of numbers and variables. A **polynomial** is a monomial or a sum of monomials. A **polynomial function** is a function of the form

$$f(x) = a_n x^n + a_{n-1} x^{n-1} + \cdots + a_1 x + a_0$$

where $a_n \neq 0$, the exponents are all whole numbers, and the coefficients are all real numbers. For this function, a_n is the leading coefficient, n is the degree, and a_0 is the constant term. A polynomial function is in **standard form** if its terms are written in descending order of exponents from left to right.

Common Polynomial Functions			
Degree	**Type**	**Standard form**	**Example**
0	Constant	$f(x) = a_0$	$f(x) = -14$
1	Linear	$f(x) = a_1 x + a_0$	$f(x) = 5x - 7$
2	Quadratic	$f(x) = a_2 x^2 + a_1 x + a_0$	$f(x) = 2x^2 + x - 9$
3	Cubic	$f(x) = a_3 x^3 + a_2 x^2 + a_1 x + a_0$	$f(x) = x^3 - x^2 + 3x$
4	Quartic	$f(x) = a_4 x^4 + a_3 x^3 + a_2 x^2 + a_1 x + a_0$	$f(x) = x^4 + 2x - 1$

EXAMPLE 1 Identify polynomial functions

Decide whether the function is a polynomial function. If so, write it in standard form and state its degree, type, and leading coefficient.

a. $h(x) = x^4 - \frac{1}{4}x^2 + 3$

b. $g(x) = 7x - \sqrt{3} + \pi x^2$

c. $f(x) = 5x^2 + 3x^{-1} - x$

d. $k(x) = x + 2^x - 0.6x^5$

Solution

a. The function is a polynomial function that is already written in standard form. It has degree 4 (quartic) and a leading coefficient of 1.

b. The function is a polynomial function written as $g(x) = \pi x^2 + 7x - \sqrt{3}$ in standard form. It has degree 2 (quadratic) and a leading coefficient of π.

c. The function is not a polynomial function because the term $3x^{-1}$ has an exponent that is not a whole number.

d. The function is not a polynomial function because the term 2^x does not have a variable base and an exponent that is a whole number.

EXAMPLE 2 Evaluate by direct substitution

Use direct substitution to evaluate $f(x) = 2x^4 - 5x^3 - 4x + 8$ when $x = 3$.

$f(x) = 2x^4 - 5x^3 - 4x + 8$ Write original function.

$f(3) = 2(3)^4 - 5(3)^3 - 4(3) + 8$ Substitute 3 for x.

$ = 162 - 135 - 12 + 8$ Evaluate powers and multiply.

$ = 23$ Simplify.

✓ **GUIDED PRACTICE** for Examples 1 and 2

Decide whether the function is a polynomial function. If so, write it in standard form and state its degree, type, and leading coefficient.

1. $f(x) = 13 - 2x$ **2.** $p(x) = 9x^4 - 5x^{-2} + 4$ **3.** $h(x) = 6x^2 + \pi - 3x$

Use direct substitution to evaluate the polynomial function for the given value of x.

4. $f(x) = x^4 + 2x^3 + 3x^2 - 7; x = -2$ **5.** $g(x) = x^3 - 5x^2 + 6x + 1; x = 4$

SYNTHETIC SUBSTITUTION Another way to evaluate a polynomial function is to use **synthetic substitution**. This method, shown in the next example, involves fewer operations than direct substitution.

EXAMPLE 3 Evaluate by synthetic substitution

Use synthetic substitution to evaluate $f(x)$ from Example 2 when $x = 3$.

Solution

AVOID ERRORS
The row of coefficients for $f(x)$ must include a coefficient of 0 for the "missing" x^2-term.

STEP 1 Write the coefficients of $f(x)$ in order of descending exponents. Write the value at which $f(x)$ is being evaluated to the left.

      x-value → 3 | 2   −5   0   −4   8   ← **coefficients**

STEP 2 **Bring down** the leading coefficient. **Multiply** the leading coefficient by the *x*-value. Write the product under the second coefficient. **Add.**

      3 | 2   −5   0   −4   8
                     6
         2   1

STEP 3 **Multiply** the previous sum by the *x*-value. Write the product under the third coefficient. **Add.** Repeat for all of the remaining coefficients. The final sum is the value of $f(x)$ at the given *x*-value.

      3 | 2   −5   0   −4   8
                 6   3   9   15
         2   1   3   5   **23**

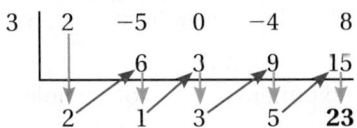

▶ Synthetic substitution gives $f(3) = 23$, which matches the result in Example 2.

END BEHAVIOR The **end behavior** of a function's graph is the behavior of the graph as x approaches positive infinity $(+\infty)$ or negative infinity $(-\infty)$. For the graph of a polynomial function, the end behavior is determined by the function's degree and the sign of its leading coefficient.

KEY CONCEPT *For Your Notebook*

End Behavior of Polynomial Functions

Degree: odd
Leading coefficient: positive

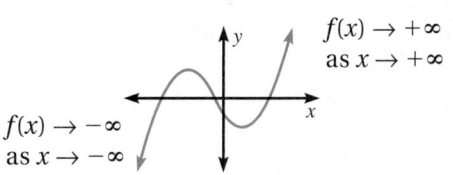

$f(x) \rightarrow +\infty$
as $x \rightarrow +\infty$

$f(x) \rightarrow -\infty$
as $x \rightarrow -\infty$

Degree: odd
Leading coefficient: negative

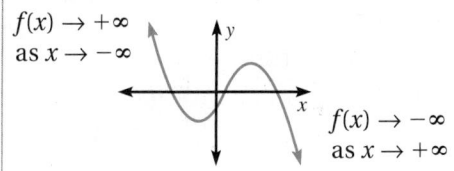

$f(x) \rightarrow +\infty$
as $x \rightarrow -\infty$

$f(x) \rightarrow -\infty$
as $x \rightarrow +\infty$

Degree: even
Leading coefficient: positive

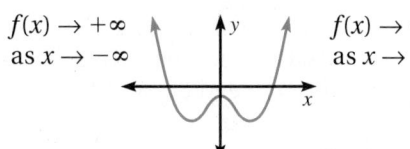

$f(x) \rightarrow +\infty$
as $x \rightarrow -\infty$

$f(x) \rightarrow +\infty$
as $x \rightarrow +\infty$

Degree: even
Leading coefficient: negative

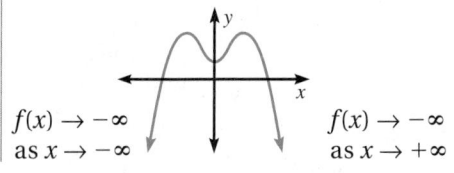

$f(x) \rightarrow -\infty$
as $x \rightarrow -\infty$

$f(x) \rightarrow -\infty$
as $x \rightarrow +\infty$

EXAMPLE 4 **Standardized Test Practice**

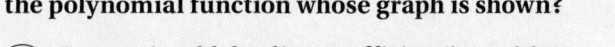

What is true about the degree and leading coefficient of the polynomial function whose graph is shown?

Ⓐ Degree is odd; leading coefficient is positive

Ⓑ Degree is odd; leading coefficient is negative

Ⓒ Degree is even; leading coefficient is positive

Ⓓ Degree is even; leading coefficient is negative

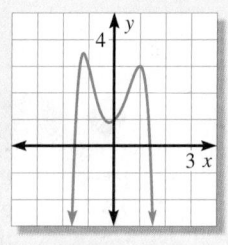

From the graph, $f(x) \rightarrow -\infty$ as $x \rightarrow -\infty$ and $f(x) \rightarrow -\infty$ as $x \rightarrow +\infty$. So, the degree is even and the leading coefficient is negative.

▶ The correct answer is D. Ⓐ Ⓑ Ⓒ **Ⓓ**

 GUIDED PRACTICE for Examples 3 and 4

Use synthetic substitution to evaluate the polynomial function for the given value of x.

6. $f(x) = 5x^3 + 3x^2 - x + 7$; $x = 2$

7. $g(x) = -2x^4 - x^3 + 4x - 5$; $x = -1$

8. *Describe* the degree and leading coefficient of the polynomial function whose graph is shown.

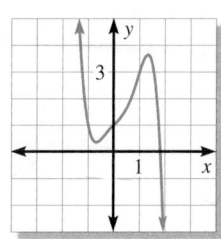

GRAPHING POLYNOMIAL FUNCTIONS To graph a polynomial function, first plot points to determine the shape of the graph's middle portion. Then use what you know about end behavior to sketch the ends of the graph.

EXAMPLE 5 Graph polynomial functions

Graph (a) $f(x) = -x^3 + x^2 + 3x - 3$ and (b) $f(x) = x^4 - x^3 - 4x^2 + 4$.

Solution

a. To graph the function, make a table of values and plot the corresponding points. Connect the points with a smooth curve and check the end behavior.

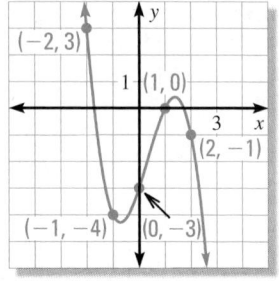

x	−3	−2	−1	0	1	2	3
y	24	3	−4	−3	0	−1	−12

The degree is odd and leading coefficient is negative. So, $f(x) \to +\infty$ as $x \to -\infty$ and $f(x) \to -\infty$ as $x \to +\infty$.

b. To graph the function, make a table of values and plot the corresponding points. Connect the points with a smooth curve and check the end behavior.

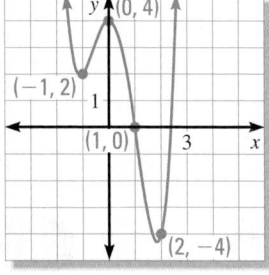

x	−3	−2	−1	0	1	2	3
y	76	12	2	4	0	−4	22

The degree is even and leading coefficient is positive. So, $f(x) \to +\infty$ as $x \to -\infty$ and $f(x) \to +\infty$ as $x \to +\infty$.

Animated Algebra at my.hrw.com

EXAMPLE 6 Solve a multi-step problem

PHYSICAL SCIENCE The energy E (in foot-pounds) in each square foot of a wave is given by the model $E = 0.0029s^4$ where s is the wind speed (in knots). Graph the model. Use the graph to estimate the wind speed needed to generate a wave with 1000 foot-pounds of energy per square foot.

Solution

STEP 1 **Make** a table of values. The model only deals with positive values of s.

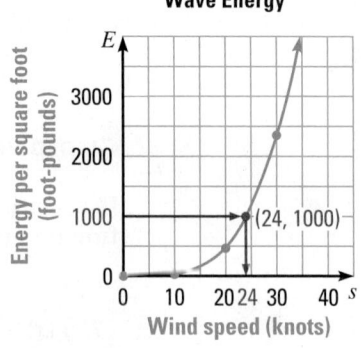

s	0	10	20	30	40
E	0	29	464	2349	7424

STEP 2 **Plot** the points and connect them with a smooth curve. Because the leading coefficient is positive and the degree is even, the graph rises to the right.

STEP 3 **Examine** the graph to see that $s \approx 24$ when $E = 1000$.

▸ The wind speed needed to generate the wave is about 24 knots.

Graph the polynomial function.

9. $f(x) = x^4 + 6x^2 - 3$ **10.** $f(x) = -x^3 + x^2 + x - 1$ **11.** $f(x) = 4 - 2x^3$

12. WHAT IF? If wind speed is measured in miles per hour, the model in Example 6 becomes $E = 0.0051s^4$. Graph this model. What wind speed is needed to generate a wave with 2000 foot-pounds of energy per square foot?

2.2 EXERCISES

HOMEWORK KEY

○ = See WORKED-OUT SOLUTIONS
Exs. 21, 27, and 57

★ = STANDARDIZED TEST PRACTICE
Exs. 2, 24, 37, 50, 52, and 59

◆ = MULTIPLE REPRESENTATIONS
Ex. 56

SKILL PRACTICE

1. VOCABULARY Identify the degree, type, leading coefficient, and constant term of the polynomial function $f(x) = 6 + 2x^2 - 5x^4$.

2. ★ WRITING *Explain* what is meant by the end behavior of a polynomial function.

EXAMPLE 1
for Exs. 3–8

POLYNOMIAL FUNCTIONS Decide whether the function is a polynomial function. If so, write it in standard form and state its degree, type, and leading coefficient.

3. $f(x) = 8 - x^2$ **4.** $f(x) = 6x + 8x^4 - 3$ **5.** $g(x) = \pi x^4 + \sqrt{6}$

6. $h(x) = x^3\sqrt{10} + 5x^{-2} + 1$ **7.** $h(x) = -\dfrac{5}{2}x^3 + 3x - 10$ **8.** $g(x) = 8x^3 - 4x^2 + \dfrac{2}{x}$

EXAMPLE 2
for Exs. 9–14

DIRECT SUBSTITUTION Use direct substitution to evaluate the polynomial function for the given value of x.

9. $f(x) = 5x^3 - 2x^2 + 10x - 15;\ x = -1$ **10.** $f(x) = 8x + 5x^4 - 3x^2 - x^3;\ x = 2$

11. $g(x) = 4x^3 - 2x^5;\ x = -3$ **12.** $h(x) = 6x^3 - 25x + 20;\ x = 5$

13. $h(x) = x + \dfrac{1}{2}x^4 - \dfrac{3}{4}x^3 + 10;\ x = -4$ **14.** $g(x) = 4x^5 + 6x^3 + x^2 - 10x + 5;\ x = -2$

EXAMPLE 3
for Exs. 15–23

SYNTHETIC SUBSTITUTION Use synthetic substitution to evaluate the polynomial function for the given value of x.

15. $f(x) = 5x^3 - 2x^2 - 8x + 16;\ x = 3$ **16.** $f(x) = 8x^4 + 12x^3 + 6x^2 - 5x + 9;\ x = -2$

17. $g(x) = x^3 + 8x^2 - 7x + 35;\ x = -6$ **18.** $h(x) = -8x^3 + 14x - 35;\ x = 4$

19. $f(x) = -2x^4 + 3x^3 - 8x + 13;\ x = 2$ **20.** $g(x) = 6x^5 + 10x^3 - 27;\ x = -3$

㉑. $h(x) = -7x^3 + 11x^2 + 4x;\ x = 3$ **22.** $f(x) = x^4 + 3x - 20;\ x = 4$

23. ERROR ANALYSIS *Describe* and correct the error in evaluating the polynomial function $f(x) = -4x^4 + 9x^2 - 21x + 7$ when $x = -2$.

$$\begin{array}{r|rrrr} -2 & -4 & 9 & -21 & 7 \\ & & 8 & -34 & 110 \\ \hline & -4 & 17 & -55 & 117 \end{array} \quad \times$$

EXAMPLE 4
for Exs. 24–27

24. ★ **MULTIPLE CHOICE** The graph of a polynomial function is shown. What is true about the function's degree and leading coefficient?

Ⓐ The degree is odd and the leading coefficient is positive.

Ⓑ The degree is odd and the leading coefficient is negative.

Ⓒ The degree is even and the leading coefficient is positive.

Ⓓ The degree is even and the leading coefficient is negative.

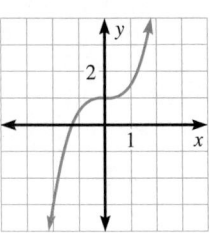

USING END BEHAVIOR *Describe* the degree and leading coefficient of the polynomial function whose graph is shown.

25.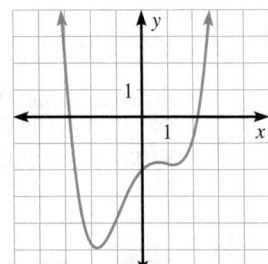

26.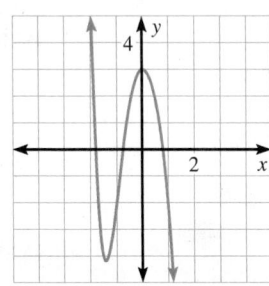

27.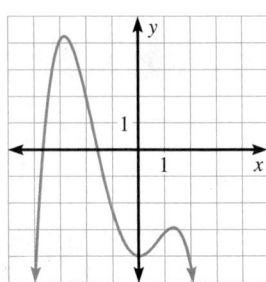

DESCRIBING END BEHAVIOR *Describe* the end behavior of the graph of the polynomial function by completing these statements: $f(x) \to$ _?_ as $x \to -\infty$ and $f(x) \to$ _?_ as $x \to +\infty$.

28. $f(x) = 10x^4$

29. $f(x) = -x^6 + 4x^3 - 3x$

30. $f(x) = -2x^3 + 7x - 4$

31. $f(x) = x^7 + 3x^4 - x^2$

32. $f(x) = 3x^{10} - 16x$

33. $f(x) = -6x^5 + 14x^2 + 20$

34. $f(x) = 0.2x^3 - x + 45$

35. $f(x) = 5x^8 + 8x^7$

36. $f(x) = -x^{273} + 500x^{271}$

37. ★ **OPEN-ENDED MATH** Write a polynomial function f of degree 5 such that the end behavior of the graph of f is given by $f(x) \to +\infty$ as $x \to -\infty$ and $f(x) \to -\infty$ as $x \to +\infty$. Then graph the function to verify your answer.

EXAMPLE 5
for Exs. 38–50

GRAPHING POLYNOMIALS Graph the polynomial function.

38. $f(x) = x^3$

39. $f(x) = -x^4$

40. $f(x) = x^5 + 3$

41. $f(x) = x^4 - 2$

42. $f(x) = -x^3 + 5$

43. $f(x) = x^3 - 5x$

44. $f(x) = -x^4 + 8x$

45. $f(x) = x^5 + x$

46. $f(x) = -x^3 + 3x^2 - 2x + 5$

47. $f(x) = x^5 + x^2 - 4$

48. $f(x) = x^4 - 5x^2 + 6$

49. $f(x) = -x^4 + 3x^3 - x + 1$

50. ★ **MULTIPLE CHOICE** Which function is represented by the graph shown?

Ⓐ $f(x) = \frac{1}{3}x^3 + 1$ Ⓑ $f(x) = -\frac{1}{3}x^3 + 1$

Ⓒ $f(x) = \frac{1}{3}x^3 - 1$ Ⓓ $f(x) = -\frac{1}{3}x^3 - 1$

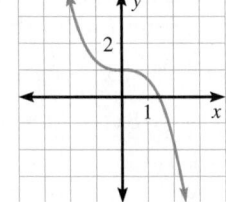

51. **VISUAL THINKING** Suppose $f(x) \to +\infty$ as $x \to -\infty$ and $f(x) \to -\infty$ as $x \to +\infty$. *Describe* the end behavior of $g(x) = -f(x)$.

52. ★ **SHORT RESPONSE** A cubic polynomial function f has leading coefficient 2 and constant term -5. If $f(1) = 0$ and $f(2) = 3$, what is $f(-5)$? *Explain* how you found your answer.

○ = **See WORKED-OUT SOLUTIONS** in Student Resources

★ = **STANDARDIZED TEST PRACTICE**

◆ = **MULTIPLE REPRESENTATIONS**

53. **CHALLENGE** The graph of a function is *symmetric with respect to the y-axis* if for each point (a, b) on the graph, $(-a, b)$ is also a point on the graph. The graph of a function is *symmetric with respect to the origin* if for each point (a, b) on the graph, $(-a, -b)$ is also a point on the graph.

   a. Use a graphing calculator to graph the function $y = x^n$ when $n = 1, 2, 3, 4, 5,$ and 6. In each case, identify what symmetry the graph has.

   b. Predict what symmetry the graphs of $y = x^{10}$ and $y = x^{11}$ each have. Explain your reasoning, and then confirm your predictions by graphing.

   c. If n is a positive integer, determine the values of n for which the graph of $y = x^{-n}$ is symmetric with respect to the y-axis as well as the values of n for which the graph is symmetric with respect to the origin.

PROBLEM SOLVING

EXAMPLE 6
for Exs. 54–59

54. **DIAMONDS** The weight of an ideal round-cut diamond can be modeled by

$$w = 0.0071d^3 - 0.090d^2 + 0.48d$$

where w is the diamond's weight (in carats) and d is its diameter (in millimeters). According to the model, what is the weight of a diamond with a diameter of 15 millimeters?

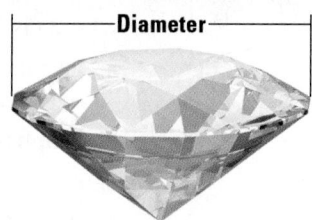

Diameter

55. **SKATEBOARDING** From 1992 to 2003, the number of people in the United States who participated in skateboarding can be modeled by

$$S = -0.0076t^4 + 0.14t^3 - 0.62t^2 + 0.52t + 5.5$$

where S is the number of participants (in millions) and t is the number of years since 1992. Graph the model. Then use the graph to estimate the first year that the number of skateboarding participants was greater than 8 million.

56. ◆ **MULTIPLE REPRESENTATIONS** From 1987 to 2003, the number of indoor movie screens M in the United States can be modeled by

$$M = -11.0t^3 + 267t^2 - 592t + 21{,}600$$

where t is the number of years since 1987.

   a. Classifying a Function State the degree and type of the function.

   b. Making a Table Make a table of values for the function.

   c. Sketching a Graph Use your table to graph the function.

57. **SNOWBOARDING** From 1992 to 2003, the number of people in the United States who participated in snowboarding can be modeled by

$$S = 0.0013t^4 - 0.021t^3 + 0.084t^2 + 0.037t + 1.2$$

where S is the number of participants (in millions) and t is the number of years since 1992. Graph the model. Use the graph to estimate the first year that the number of snowboarding participants was greater than 2 million.

58. MULTI-STEP PROBLEM From 1980 to 2002, the number of quarterly periodicals P published in the United States can be modeled by

$$P = 0.138t^4 - 6.24t^3 + 86.8t^2 - 239t + 1450$$

where t is the number of years since 1980.

  a. *Describe* the end behavior of the graph of the model.

  b. Graph the model on the domain $0 \leq t \leq 22$.

  c. Use the model to predict the number of quarterly periodicals in the year 2010. Is it appropriate to use the model to make this prediction? *Explain*.

59. ★ EXTENDED RESPONSE The weights of Sarus crane chicks S and hooded crane chicks H (both in grams) during the 10 days following hatching can be modeled by the functions

$$S = -0.122t^3 + 3.49t^2 - 14.6t + 136$$

$$H = -0.115t^3 + 3.71t^2 - 20.6t + 124$$

where t is the number of days after hatching.

  a. Calculate According to the models, what is the difference in weight between 5-day-old Sarus crane chicks and hooded crane chicks?

  b. Graph Sketch the graphs of the two models.

  c. Apply A biologist finds that the weight of a crane chick 3 days after hatching is 130 grams. What species of crane is the chick more likely to be? *Explain* how you found your answer.

60. CHALLENGE The weight y (in pounds) of a rainbow trout can be modeled by $y = 0.000304x^3$ where x is the length of the trout (in inches).

  a. Write a function that relates the weight y and length x of a rainbow trout if y is measured in kilograms and x is measured in centimeters. Use the fact that 1 kilogram ≈ 2.20 pounds and 1 centimeter ≈ 0.394 inch.

  b. Graph the original function and the function from part (a) in the same coordinate plane. What type of transformation can you apply to the graph of $y = 0.000304x^3$ to produce the graph from part (a)?

Set a Good Viewing Window

MATHEMATICAL
PRACTICES

**Use appropriate tools
strategically.**

QUESTION   What is a good viewing window for a polynomial function?

When you graph a function with a graphing calculator, you should choose a
viewing window that displays the important characteristics of the graph.

EXAMPLE   Graph a polynomial function

Graph $f(x) = 0.2x^3 - 5x^2 + 38x - 97$.

STEP 1 *Graph the function*	STEP 2 *Adjust horizontally*	STEP 3 *Adjust vertically*
Graph the function in the standard viewing window.	Adjust the horizontal scale so that the end behavior of the graph as $x \to +\infty$ is visible.	Adjust the vertical scale so that the turning points and end behavior of the graph as $x \to -\infty$ are visible.

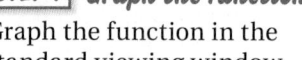

$-10 \leq x \leq 10, -10 \leq y \leq 10$

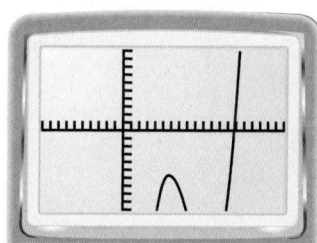

$-10 \leq x \leq 20, -10 \leq y \leq 10$

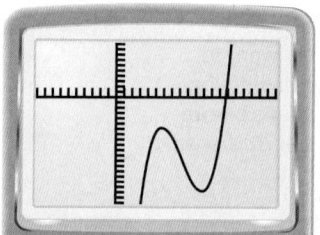

$-10 \leq x \leq 20, -20 \leq y \leq 10$

PRACTICE

**Find intervals for x and y that describe a good viewing window for the graph
of the polynomial function.**

1. $f(x) = x^3 + 4x^2 - 8x + 11$

2. $f(x) = -x^3 + 36x^2 - 10$

3. $f(x) = x^4 - 4x^2 + 2$

4. $f(x) = -x^4 - 2x^3 + 3x^2 - 4x + 5$

5. $f(x) = -x^4 + 3x^3 + 15x$

6. $f(x) = 2x^4 - 7x^3 + x - 8$

7. $f(x) = -x^5 + 9x^3 - 12x + 18$

8. $f(x) = x^5 - 7x^4 + 25x^3 - 40x^2 + 13x$

9. **REASONING** Let $g(x) = f(x) + c$ where $f(x)$ and $g(x)$ are polynomial functions
    and c is a positive constant. How is a good viewing window for the graph of
    $f(x)$ related to a good viewing window for the graph of $g(x)$?

10. **BASEBALL** From 1994 to 2003, the average salary S (in thousands of dollars)
    for major league baseball players can be modeled by

    $$S(x) = -4.10x^3 + 67.4x^2 - 121x + 1170$$

    where x is the number of years since 1994. Find intervals for the horizontal
    and vertical axes that describe a good viewing window for the graph of S.

2.3 Add, Subtract, and Multiply Polynomials

Before	You evaluated and graphed polynomial functions.
Now	You will add, subtract, and multiply polynomials.
Why?	So you can model collegiate sports participation, as in Ex. 63.

Key Vocabulary
• like terms

To add or subtract polynomials, add or subtract the coefficients of like terms. You can use a vertical or horizontal format.

EXAMPLE 1 — Add polynomials vertically and horizontally

a. Add $2x^3 - 5x^2 + 3x - 9$ and $x^3 + 6x^2 + 11$ in a vertical format.

b. Add $3y^3 - 2y^2 - 7y$ and $-4y^2 + 2y - 5$ in a horizontal format.

Solution

REVIEW SIMPLIFYING
You may want to review simplifying expressions before adding and subtracting polynomials.

a.
$$
\begin{array}{r}
2x^3 - 5x^2 + 3x - 9 \\
+\quad x^3 + 6x^2\quad\ + 11 \\
\hline
3x^3 +\ x^2 + 3x + 2
\end{array}
$$

b. $(3y^3 - 2y^2 - 7y) + (-4y^2 + 2y - 5)$
$= 3y^3 - 2y^2 - 4y^2 - 7y + 2y - 5$
$= 3y^3 - 6y^2 - 5y - 5$

COMMON CORE

CC.9-12.A.APR.1 Understand that polynomials form a system analogous to the integers, namely, they are closed under the operations of addition, subtraction, and multiplication; add, subtract, and multiply polynomials.

EXAMPLE 2 — Subtract polynomials vertically and horizontally

a. Subtract $3x^3 + 2x^2 - x + 7$ from $8x^3 - x^2 - 5x + 1$ in a vertical format.

b. Subtract $5z^2 - z + 3$ from $4z^2 + 9z - 12$ in a horizontal format.

Solution

a. Align like terms, then add the opposite of the subtracted polynomial.

$$
\begin{array}{r}
8x^3 -\ x^2 - 5x + 1 \\
-\ (3x^3 + 2x^2 -\ x + 7) \\
\hline
\end{array}
\quad\longrightarrow\quad
\begin{array}{r}
8x^3 -\ x^2 - 5x + 1 \\
+\ -3x^3 - 2x^2 +\ x - 7 \\
\hline
5x^3 - 3x^2 - 4x - 6
\end{array}
$$

b. Write the opposite of the subtracted polynomial, then add like terms.

$(4z^2 + 9z - 12) - (5z^2 - z + 3) = 4z^2 + 9z - 12 - 5z^2 + z - 3$
$\qquad\qquad\qquad\qquad\qquad = 4z^2 - 5z^2 + 9z + z - 12 - 3$
$\qquad\qquad\qquad\qquad\qquad = -z^2 + 10z - 15$

✓ **GUIDED PRACTICE** for Examples 1 and 2

Find the sum or difference.

1. $(t^2 - 6t + 2) + (5t^2 - t - 8)$

2. $(8d - 3 + 9d^3) - (d^3 - 13d^2 - 4)$

AP Images/Tim Larsen

MULTIPLYING POLYNOMIALS To multiply two polynomials, you multiply each term of the first polynomial by each term of the second polynomial.

EXAMPLE 3 Multiply polynomials vertically and horizontally

a. Multiply $-2y^2 + 3y - 6$ and $y - 2$ in a vertical format.

b. Multiply $x + 3$ and $3x^2 - 2x + 4$ in a horizontal format.

Solution

a.
$$
\begin{array}{r}
-2y^2 + 3y - 6 \\
\times \qquad\quad y - 2 \\
\hline
4y^2 - 6y + 12 \\
-2y^3 + 3y^2 - 6y \\
\hline
-2y^3 + 7y^2 - 12y + 12
\end{array}
$$

Multiply $-2y^2 + 3y - 6$ by -2.

Multiply $-2y^2 + 3y - 6$ by y.

Combine like terms.

b. $(x + 3)(3x^2 - 2x + 4) = (x + 3)3x^2 - (x + 3)2x + (x + 3)4$

$\qquad\qquad\qquad\qquad\qquad = 3x^3 + 9x^2 - 2x^2 - 6x + 4x + 12$

$\qquad\qquad\qquad\qquad\qquad = 3x^3 + 7x^2 - 2x + 12$

EXAMPLE 4 Multiply three binomials

Multiply $x - 5$, $x + 1$, and $x + 3$ in a horizontal format.

$(x - 5)(x + 1)(x + 3) = (x^2 - 4x - 5)(x + 3)$

$\qquad\qquad\qquad\qquad = (x^2 - 4x - 5)x + (x^2 - 4x - 5)3$

$\qquad\qquad\qquad\qquad = x^3 - 4x^2 - 5x + 3x^2 - 12x - 15$

$\qquad\qquad\qquad\qquad = x^3 - x^2 - 17x - 15$

PRODUCT PATTERNS Some binomial products occur so frequently that it is worth memorizing their patterns. You can verify these product patterns by multiplying.

KEY CONCEPT   *For Your Notebook*

Special Product Patterns

Sum and Difference   **Example**

$(a + b)(a - b) = a^2 - b^2$ $(x + 4)(x - 4) = x^2 - 16$

AVOID ERRORS
In general,
$(a \pm b)^2 \neq a^2 \pm b^2$
and
$(a \pm b)^3 \neq a^3 \pm b^3$.

Square of a Binomial   **Example**

$(a + b)^2 = a^2 + 2ab + b^2$ $(y + 3)^2 = y^2 + 6y + 9$

$(a - b)^2 = a^2 - 2ab + b^2$ $(3z^2 - 5)^2 = 9z^4 - 30z^2 + 25$

Cube of a Binomial   **Example**

$(a + b)^3 = a^3 + 3a^2b + 3ab^2 + b^3$ $(x + 2)^3 = x^3 + 6x^2 + 12x + 8$

$(a - b)^3 = a^3 - 3a^2b + 3ab^2 - b^3$ $(p - 3)^3 = p^3 - 9p^2 + 27p - 27$

EXAMPLE 5 Use special product patterns

a. $(3t + 4)(3t - 4) = (3t)^2 - 4^2$ **Sum and difference**

$= 9t^2 - 16$

b. $(8x - 3)^2 = (8x)^2 - 2(8x)(3) + 3^2$ **Square of a binomial**

$= 64x^2 - 48x + 9$

c. $(pq + 5)^3 = (pq)^3 + 3(pq)^2(5) + 3(pq)(5)^2 + 5^3$ **Cube of a binomial**

$= p^3q^3 + 15p^2q^2 + 75pq + 125$

✓ **GUIDED PRACTICE** for Examples 3, 4, and 5

Find the product.

3. $(x + 2)(3x^2 - x - 5)$ **4.** $(a - 5)(a + 2)(a + 6)$ **5.** $(xy - 4)^3$

EXAMPLE 6 Use polynomial models

PETROLEUM Since 1980, the number W (in thousands) of United States wells producing crude oil and the average daily oil output per well O (in barrels) can be modeled by

$$W = -0.575t^2 + 10.9t + 548 \quad \text{and} \quad O = -0.249t + 15.4$$

where t is the number of years since 1980. Write a model for the average *total* amount T of crude oil produced per day. What was the average total amount of crude oil produced per day in 2000?

Oil refinery in
Long Beach, California

DETERMINE SIGNIFICANT DIGITS
When multiplying models, round your result so that its terms have the same number of significant digits as the model with the fewest significant digits.

Solution

To find a model for T, multiply the two given models.

$$
\begin{array}{r}
-0.575t^2 + \quad 10.9t + \quad 548 \\
\times \qquad\qquad\qquad - \quad 0.249t + \quad 15.4 \\
\hline
- \quad 8.855t^2 + \quad 167.86t + 8439.2 \\
0.143175t^3 - \quad 2.7141t^2 - 136.452t \\
\hline
0.143175t^3 - 11.5691t^2 + \quad 31.408t + 8439.2
\end{array}
$$

▶ Total daily oil output can be modeled by $T = 0.143t^3 - 11.6t^2 + 31.4t + 8440$ where T is measured in thousands of barrels. By substituting $t = 20$ into the model, you can estimate that the average total amount of crude oil produced per day in 2000 was about 5570 thousand barrels, or 5,570,000 barrels.

✓ **GUIDED PRACTICE** for Example 6

6. INDUSTRY The models below give the average depth D (in feet) of new wells drilled and the average cost per foot C (in dollars) of drilling a new well. In both models, t represents the number of years since 1980. Write a model for the average *total* cost T of drilling a new well.

$$D = 109t + 4010 \quad \text{and} \quad C = 0.542t^2 - 7.16t + 79.4$$

2.3 EXERCISES

HOMEWORK KEY

○ = See WORKED-OUT SOLUTIONS
Exs. 11, 21, and 61

★ = STANDARDIZED TEST PRACTICE
Exs. 2, 15, 47, 56, and 63

SKILL PRACTICE

1. **VOCABULARY** When you add or subtract polynomials, you add or subtract the coefficients of __?__ .

2. ★ **WRITING** *Explain* how a polynomial subtraction problem is equivalent to a polynomial addition problem.

EXAMPLES 1 and 2
for Exs. 3–15

ADDING AND SUBTRACTING POLYNOMIALS Find the sum or difference.

3. $(3x^2 - 5) + (7x^2 - 3)$

4. $(x^2 - 3x + 5) - (-4x^2 + 8x + 9)$

5. $(4y^2 + 9y - 5) - (4y^2 - 5y + 3)$

6. $(z^2 + 5z - 7) + (5z^2 - 11z - 6)$

7. $(3s^3 + s) + (4s^3 - 2s^2 + 7s + 10)$

8. $(2a^2 - 8) - (a^3 + 4a^2 - 12a + 4)$

9. $(5c^2 + 7c + 1) + (2c^3 - 6c + 8)$

10. $(4t^3 - 11t^2 + 4t) - (-7t^2 - 5t + 8)$

11. $(5b - 6b^3 + 2b^4) - (9b^3 + 4b^4 - 7)$

12. $(3y^2 - 6y^4 + 5 - 6y) + (5y^4 - 6y^3 + 4y)$

13. $(x^4 - x^3 + x^2 - x + 1) + (x + x^4 - 1 - x^2)$

14. $(8v^4 - 2v^2 + v - 4) - (3v^3 - 12v^2 + 8v)$

15. ★ **MULTIPLE CHOICE** What is the result when $2x^4 - 8x^2 - x + 10$ is subtracted from $8x^4 - 4x^3 - x + 2$?

Ⓐ $-6x^4 + 4x^3 - 8x^2 + 8$

Ⓑ $6x^4 - 4x^3 + 8x^2 - 8$

Ⓒ $10x^4 - 8x^3 - 4x^2 + 12$

Ⓓ $6x^4 + 4x^3 - 2x - 8$

EXAMPLE 3
for Exs. 16–25

MULTIPLYING POLYNOMIALS Find the product of the polynomials.

16. $x(2x^2 - 5x + 7)$

17. $5x^2(6x + 2)$

18. $(y - 7)(y + 6)$

19. $(3z + 1)(z - 3)$

20. $(w + 4)(w^2 + 6w - 11)$

21. $(2a - 3)(a^2 - 10a - 2)$

22. $(5c^2 - 4)(2c^2 + c - 3)$

23. $(-x^2 + 4x + 1)(x^2 - 8x + 3)$

24. $(-d^2 + 4d + 3)(3d^2 - 7d + 6)$

25. $(3y^2 + 6y - 1)(4y^2 - 11y - 5)$

ERROR ANALYSIS *Describe* and correct the error in simplifying the expression.

26.
$$(x^2 - 3x + 4) - (x^3 + 7x - 2)$$
$$= x^2 - 3x + 4 - x^3 + 7x - 2$$
$$= -x^3 + x^2 + 4x + 2$$

27.
$$(2x - 7)^3 = (2x)^3 - 7^3$$
$$= 8x^3 - 343$$

EXAMPLE 4
for Exs. 28–37

MULTIPLYING THREE BINOMIALS Find the product of the binomials.

28. $(x + 4)(x - 6)(x - 5)$

29. $(x + 1)(x - 7)(x + 3)$

30. $(z - 4)(-z + 2)(z + 8)$

31. $(a - 6)(2a + 5)(a + 1)$

32. $(3p + 1)(p + 3)(p + 1)$

33. $(b - 2)(2b - 1)(-b + 1)$

34. $(2s + 1)(3s - 2)(4s - 3)$

35. $(w - 6)(4w - 1)(-3w + 5)$

36. $(4x - 1)(-2x - 7)(-5x - 4)$

37. $(3q - 8)(-9q + 2)(q - 2)$

EXAMPLE 5
. . . .
for Exs. 38–47

SPECIAL PRODUCTS **Find the product.**

38. $(x + 5)(x - 5)$ **39.** $(w - 9)^2$ **40.** $(y + 4)^3$

41. $(2c + 5)^2$ **42.** $(3t - 4)^3$ **43.** $(5p - 3)(5p + 3)$

44. $(7x - y)^3$ **45.** $(2a + 9b)(2a - 9b)$ **46.** $(3z + 7y)^3$

47. ★ **MULTIPLE CHOICE** Which expression is equivalent to $(3x - 2y)^2$?

Ⓐ $9x^2 - 4y^2$ Ⓑ $9x^2 + 4y^2$

Ⓒ $9x^2 + 12xy + 4y^2$ Ⓓ $9x^2 - 12xy + 4y^2$

GEOMETRY **Write the figure's volume as a polynomial in standard form.**

48. $V = \ell wh$
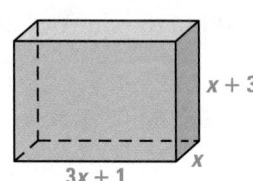

49. $V = \pi r^2 h$
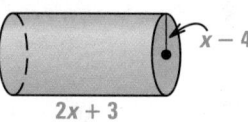

50. $V = s^3$
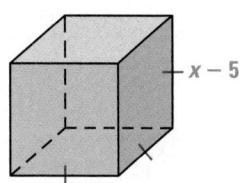

51. $V = \frac{1}{3}Bh$
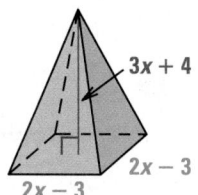

SPECIAL PRODUCTS **Verify the special product pattern by multiplying.**

52. $(a + b)(a - b) = a^2 - b^2$ **53.** $(a + b)^2 = a^2 + 2ab + b^2$

54. $(a + b)^3 = a^3 + 3a^2b + 3ab^2 + b^3$ **55.** $(a - b)^3 = a^3 - 3a^2b + 3ab^2 - b^3$

56. ★ **EXTENDED RESPONSE** Let $p(x) = x^4 - 7x + 14$ and $q(x) = x^2 - 5$.

a. What is the degree of the polynomial $p(x) + q(x)$?

b. What is the degree of the polynomial $p(x) - q(x)$?

c. What is the degree of the polynomial $p(x) \cdot q(x)$?

d. In general, if $p(x)$ and $q(x)$ are polynomials such that $p(x)$ has degree m, $q(x)$ has degree n, and $m > n$, what are the degrees of $p(x) + q(x)$, $p(x) - q(x)$, and $p(x) \cdot q(x)$?

57. **FINDING A PATTERN** Look at the following polynomial factorizations.

$x^2 - 1 = (x - 1)(x + 1)$

$x^3 - 1 = (x - 1)(x^2 + x + 1)$

$x^4 - 1 = (x - 1)(x^3 + x^2 + x + 1)$

a. Factor $x^5 - 1$ and $x^6 - 1$ into the product of $x - 1$ and another polynomial. Check your answers by multiplying.

b. In general, how can $x^n - 1$ be factored? Show that this factorization works by multiplying the factors.

58. **CHALLENGE** Suppose $f(x) = (x + a)(x + b)(x + c)(x + d)$. If $f(x)$ is written in standard form, show that the coefficient of x^3 is the sum of a, b, c, and d, and the constant term is the product of a, b, c, and d.

EXAMPLE 6
for Exs. 59–61

59. HIGHER EDUCATION Since 1970, the number (in thousands) of males M and females F attending institutes of higher education can be modeled by

$$M = 0.091t^3 - 4.8t^2 + 110t + 5000 \quad \text{and} \quad F = 0.19t^3 - 12t^2 + 350t + 3600$$

where t is the number of years since 1970. Write a model for the total number of people attending institutes of higher education.

60. ELECTRONICS From 1999 to 2004, the number of DVD players D (in millions) sold in the United States and the average price per DVD player P (in dollars) can be modeled by

$$D = 4.11t + 4.44 \quad \text{and} \quad P = 6.82t^2 - 61.7t + 265$$

where t is the number of years since 1999. Write a model for the total revenue R from DVD sales. According to the model, what was the total revenue in 2002?

61. BICYCLING The equation $P = 0.00267sF$ gives the power P (in horsepower) needed to keep a certain bicycle moving at speed s (in miles per hour), where F is the force (in pounds) of road and air resistance. On level ground, the equation

$$F = 0.0116s^2 + 0.789$$

models the force F. Write a model (in terms of s only) for the power needed to keep the bicycle moving at speed s on level ground. How much power is needed to keep the bicycle moving at 10 miles per hour?

Animated **Algebra** at my.hrw.com

62. MULTI-STEP PROBLEM A dessert is made by taking a hemispherical mound of marshmallow on a 0.5 centimeter thick cookie and covering it with a chocolate shell 1 centimeter thick. Use the diagrams to write two polynomial functions in standard form: $M(r)$ for the combined volume of the marshmallow plus cookie, and $D(r)$ for the volume of the entire dessert. Then use $M(r)$ and $D(r)$ to write a function $C(r)$ for the volume of the chocolate.

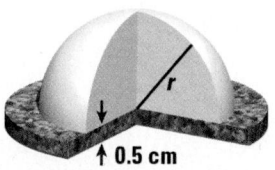

1 cm

0.5 cm

Marshmallow on cookie   Chocolate layer added

63. ★ SHORT RESPONSE From 1997 to 2002, the number of NCAA lacrosse teams for men L_m and women L_w, as well as the average size of a men's team S_m and a women's team S_w, can be modeled by

$$L_m = 5.57t + 182 \quad \text{and} \quad S_m = -0.127t^3 + 0.822t^2 - 1.02t + 31.5$$
$$L_w = 12.2t + 185 \quad \text{and} \quad S_w = -0.0662t^3 + 0.437t^2 - 0.725t + 22.3$$

where t is the number of years since 1997. Write a model for the *total* number of people N on NCAA lacrosse teams. *Explain* how you obtained your model.

64. CHALLENGE From 1970 to 2002, the circulation C (in millions) of Sunday newspapers in the United States can be modeled by

$$C = -0.00105t^3 + 0.0281t^2 + 0.465t + 48.8$$

where t is the number of years since 1970. Rewrite C as a function of s, where s is the number of years since 1975.

QUIZ

Evaluate the expression.

1. $3^5 \cdot 3^{-1}$

2. $\left(2^4\right)^2$

3. $\left(\dfrac{2}{3^{-2}}\right)^2$

4. $\left(\dfrac{3}{5}\right)^{-2}$

Simplify the expression.

5. $\left(x^4 y^{-2}\right)\left(x^{-3} y^8\right)$

6. $\left(a^2 b^{-5}\right)^{-3}$

7. $\dfrac{x^3 y^7}{x^{-4} y^0}$

8. $\dfrac{c^3 d^{-2}}{c^5 d^{-1}}$

Graph the polynomial function.

9. $g(x) = 2x^3 - 3x + 1$

10. $h(x) = x^4 - 4x + 2$

11. $f(x) = -2x^3 + x^2 - 5$

Perform the indicated operation.

12. $(x^3 + x^2 - 6) - (2x^2 + 4x - 8)$

13. $(-3x^2 + 4x - 10) + (x^2 - 9x + 15)$

14. $(x - 5)(x^2 - 5x + 7)$

15. $(x + 3)(x - 6)(3x - 1)$

16. NATIONAL DEBT On July 21, 2004, the national debt of the United States was about \$7,282,000,000,000. The population of the United States at that time was about 294,000,000. Suppose the national debt was divided evenly among everyone in the United States. How much would each person owe?

See **EXTRA PRACTICE** in Student Resources   ⟫ **ONLINE QUIZ** at my.hrw.com

2.4 Factor and Solve Polynomial Equations

Before You factored and solved quadratic equations.

Now You will factor and solve other polynomial equations.

Why? So you can find dimensions of archaeological ruins, as in Ex. 58.

Key Vocabulary
- **factored completely**
- **factor by grouping**
- **quadratic form**

CC.9-12.A.SSE.2 Use the structure of an expression to identify ways to rewrite it.

Previously, you learned how to factor the following types of quadratic expressions.

Type	Example
General trinomial	$2x^2 - 3x - 20 = (2x + 5)(x - 4)$
Perfect square trinomial	$x^2 + 8x + 16 = (x + 4)^2$
Difference of two squares	$9x^2 - 1 = (3x + 1)(3x - 1)$
Common monomial factor	$8x^2 + 20x = 4x(2x + 5)$

You can also factor polynomials with degree greater than 2. Some of these polynomials can be *factored completely* using techniques you have previously learned.

KEY CONCEPT *For Your Notebook*

Factoring Polynomials

Definition

A factorable polynomial with integer coefficients is **factored completely** if it is written as a product of unfactorable polynomials with integer coefficients.

Examples

$2(x + 1)(x - 4)$ and $5x^2(x^2 - 3)$ are factored completely.

$3x(x^2 - 4)$ is *not* factored completely because $x^2 - 4$ can be factored as $(x + 2)(x - 2)$.

EXAMPLE 1 Find a common monomial factor

Factor the polynomial completely.

a. $x^3 + 2x^2 - 15x = x(x^2 + 2x - 15)$ Factor common monomial.

         $= x(x + 5)(x - 3)$ Factor trinomial.

b. $2y^5 - 18y^3 = 2y^3(y^2 - 9)$ Factor common monomial.

         $= 2y^3(y + 3)(y - 3)$ Difference of two squares

c. $4z^4 - 16z^3 + 16z^2 = 4z^2(z^2 - 4z + 4)$ Factor common monomial.

         $= 4z^2(z - 2)^2$ Perfect square trinomial

FACTORING PATTERNS In part (b) of Example 1, the special factoring pattern for the difference of two squares is used to factor the expression completely. There are also factoring patterns that you can use to factor the sum or difference of two *cubes*.

KEY CONCEPT *For Your Notebook*

Special Factoring Patterns

Sum of Two Cubes

$a^3 + b^3 = (a + b)(a^2 - ab + b^2)$

Example

$8x^3 + 27 = (2x)^3 + 3^3$

$\qquad\qquad = (2x + 3)(4x^2 - 6x + 9)$

Difference of Two Cubes

$a^3 - b^3 = (a - b)(a^2 + ab + b^2)$

Example

$64x^3 - 1 = (4x)^3 - 1^3$

$\qquad\qquad = (4x - 1)(16x^2 + 4x + 1)$

EXAMPLE 2 **Factor the sum or difference of two cubes**

Factor the polynomial completely.

a. $x^3 + 64 = x^3 + 4^3$ Sum of two cubes

$\qquad\quad = (x + 4)(x^2 - 4x + 16)$

b. $16z^5 - 250z^2 = 2z^2(8z^3 - 125)$ Factor common monomial.

$\qquad\qquad\quad = 2z^2\left[(2z)^3 - 5^3\right]$ Difference of two cubes

$\qquad\qquad\quad = 2z^2(2z - 5)(4z^2 + 10z + 25)$

✔ **GUIDED PRACTICE** for Examples 1 and 2

Factor the polynomial completely.

1. $x^3 - 7x^2 + 10x$ **2.** $3y^5 - 75y^3$ **3.** $16b^5 + 686b^2$ **4.** $w^3 - 27$

FACTORING BY GROUPING For some polynomials, you can **factor by grouping** pairs of terms that have a common monomial factor. The pattern for factoring by grouping is shown below.

$$ra + rb + sa + sb = r(a + b) + s(a + b)$$
$$= (r + s)(a + b)$$

EXAMPLE 3 **Factor by grouping**

AVOID ERRORS

An expression is not factored completely until *all* factors, such as $x^2 - 16$, cannot be factored further.

Factor the polynomial $x^3 - 3x^2 - 16x + 48$ completely.

$x^3 - 3x^2 - 16x + 48 = x^2(x - 3) - 16(x - 3)$ Factor by grouping.

$\qquad\qquad\qquad\qquad = (x^2 - 16)(x - 3)$ Distributive property

$\qquad\qquad\qquad\qquad = (x + 4)(x - 4)(x - 3)$ Difference of two squares

QUADRATIC FORM An expression of the form $au^2 + bu + c$, where u is any expression in x, is said to be in **quadratic form**. The factoring techniques you studied in previous chapter can sometimes be used to factor such expressions.

EXAMPLE 4 Factor polynomials in quadratic form

Factor completely: (a) $16x^4 - 81$ and (b) $2p^8 + 10p^5 + 12p^2$.

IDENTIFY QUADRATIC FORM
The expression $16x^4 - 81$ is in quadratic form because it can be written as $u^2 - 81$ where $u = 4x^2$.

a. $16x^4 - 81 = (4x^2)^2 - 9^2$ Write as difference of two squares.

$\qquad\qquad = (4x^2 + 9)(4x^2 - 9)$ Difference of two squares

$\qquad\qquad = (4x^2 + 9)(2x + 3)(2x - 3)$ Difference of two squares

b. $2p^8 + 10p^5 + 12p^2 = 2p^2(p^6 + 5p^3 + 6)$ Factor common monomial.

$\qquad\qquad = 2p^2(p^3 + 3)(p^3 + 2)$ Factor trinomial in quadratic form.

 GUIDED PRACTICE for Examples 3 and 4

Factor the polynomial completely.

5. $x^3 + 7x^2 - 9x - 63$ **6.** $16g^4 - 625$ **7.** $4t^6 - 20t^4 + 24t^2$

SOLVING POLYNOMIAL EQUATIONS You have learned how to use the zero product property to solve factorable quadratic equations. You can extend this technique to solve some higher-degree polynomial equations.

EXAMPLE 5 Standardized Test Practice

What are the real-number solutions of the equation $3x^5 + 15x = 18x^3$?

(A) $0, 1, 3, 5$ **(B)** $-1, 0, 1$

(C) $0, 1, \sqrt{5}$ **(D)** $-\sqrt{5}, -1, 0, 1, \sqrt{5}$

Solution

AVOID ERRORS
Do not divide each side of an equation by a variable or a variable expression, such as $3x$. Doing so will result in the loss of solutions.

$\qquad\qquad 3x^5 + 15x = 18x^3$ Write original equation.

$\qquad\qquad 3x^5 - 18x^3 + 15x = 0$ Write in standard form.

$\qquad\qquad 3x(x^4 - 6x^2 + 5) = 0$ Factor common monomial.

$\qquad\qquad 3x(x^2 - 1)(x^2 - 5) = 0$ Factor trinomial.

$\qquad\qquad 3x(x + 1)(x - 1)(x^2 - 5) = 0$ Difference of two squares

$\qquad x = 0, x = -1, x = 1, x = \sqrt{5}, \text{ or } x = -\sqrt{5}$ Zero product property

▶ The correct answer is D. **(A)** **(B)** **(C)** **(D)**

 GUIDED PRACTICE for Example 5

Find the real-number solutions of the equation.

8. $4x^5 - 40x^3 + 36x = 0$ **9.** $2x^5 + 24x = 14x^3$ **10.** $-27x^3 + 15x^2 = -6x^4$

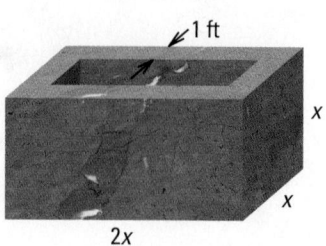
1 ft

x

x

2x

EXAMPLE 6   Solve a polynomial equation

CITY PARK You are designing a marble basin that will hold a fountain for a city park. The basin's sides and bottom should be 1 foot thick. Its outer length should be twice its outer width and outer height.

What should the outer dimensions of the basin be if it is to hold 36 cubic feet of water?

ANOTHER WAY

For alternative methods to solving the problem in Example 6, see the **Problem Solving Workshop**.

Solution

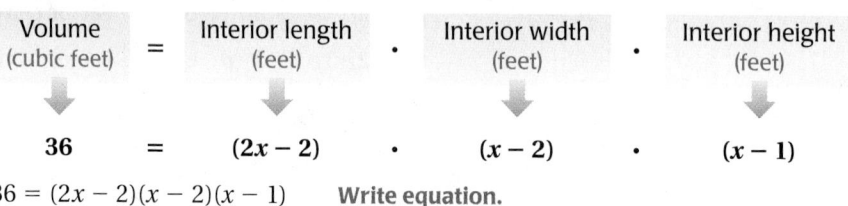

Volume (cubic feet)	=	Interior length (feet)	·	Interior width (feet)	·	Interior height (feet)
36	=	$(2x - 2)$	·	$(x - 2)$	·	$(x - 1)$

$36 = (2x - 2)(x - 2)(x - 1)$ **Write equation.**

$0 = 2x^3 - 8x^2 + 10x - 40$ **Write in standard form.**

$0 = 2x^2(x - 4) + 10(x - 4)$ **Factor by grouping.**

$0 = (2x^2 + 10)(x - 4)$ **Distributive property**

▸ The only real solution is $x = 4$. The basin is 8 ft long, 4 ft wide, and 4 ft high.

✓ **GUIDED PRACTICE**   for Example 6

11. WHAT IF? In Example 6, what should the basin's dimensions be if it is to hold 40 cubic feet of water and have outer length $6x$, width $3x$, and height x?

2.4 EXERCISES

HOMEWORK KEY

◯ = See WORKED-OUT SOLUTIONS
Exs. 7, 23, and 61

★ = STANDARDIZED TEST PRACTICE
Exs. 2, 9, 41, 63, and 64

SKILL PRACTICE

1. **VOCABULARY** The expression $8x^6 + 10x^3 - 3$ is in __?__ form because it can be written as $2u^2 + 5u - 3$ where $u = 2x^3$.

2. ★ **WRITING** What condition must the factorization of a polynomial satisfy in order for the polynomial to be factored completely?

EXAMPLE 1
for Exs. 3–9

MONOMIAL FACTORS **Factor the polynomial completely.**

3. $14x^2 - 21x$ 4. $30b^3 - 54b^2$ 5. $c^3 + 9c^2 + 18c$

6. $z^3 - 6z^2 - 72z$ ⑦ $3y^5 - 48y^3$ 8. $54m^5 + 18m^4 + 9m^3$

9. ★ **MULTIPLE CHOICE** What is the complete factorization of $2x^7 - 32x^3$?

   Ⓐ $2x^3(x + 2)(x - 2)(x^2 + 4)$ Ⓑ $2x^3(x^2 + 2)(x^2 - 2)$

   Ⓒ $2x^3(x^2 + 4)^2$ Ⓓ $2x^3(x + 2)^2(x - 2)^2$

EXAMPLE 2
for Exs. 10–17

SUM OR DIFFERENCE OF CUBES Factor the polynomial completely.

10. $x^3 + 8$

11. $y^3 - 64$

12. $27m^3 + 1$

13. $125n^3 + 216$

14. $27a^3 - 1000$

15. $8c^3 + 343$

16. $192w^3 - 3$

17. $-5z^3 + 320$

EXAMPLE 3
for Exs. 18–23

FACTORING BY GROUPING Factor the polynomial completely.

18. $x^3 + x^2 + x + 1$

19. $y^3 - 7y^2 + 4y - 28$

20. $n^3 + 5n^2 - 9n - 45$

21. $3m^3 - m^2 + 9m - 3$

22. $25s^3 - 100s^2 - s + 4$

23. $4c^3 + 8c^2 - 9c - 18$

EXAMPLE 4
for Exs. 24–29

QUADRATIC FORM Factor the polynomial completely.

24. $x^4 - 25$

25. $a^4 + 7a^2 + 6$

26. $3s^4 - s^2 - 24$

27. $32z^5 - 2z$

28. $36m^6 + 12m^4 + m^2$

29. $15x^5 - 72x^3 - 108x$

EXAMPLE 5
for Exs. 30–41

ERROR ANALYSIS *Describe* and correct the error in finding all real-number solutions.

30.
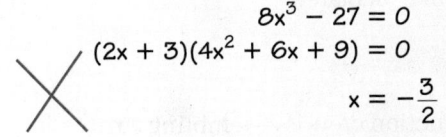
$$8x^3 - 27 = 0$$
$$(2x + 3)(4x^2 + 6x + 9) = 0$$
$$x = -\frac{3}{2}$$

31.
$$3x^3 - 48x = 0$$
$$3x(x^2 - 16) = 0$$
$$x^2 - 16 = 0$$
$$x = -4 \text{ or } x = 4$$

SOLVING EQUATIONS Find the real-number solutions of the equation.

32. $y^3 - 5y^2 = 0$

33. $18s^3 = 50s$

34. $g^3 + 3g^2 - g - 3 = 0$

35. $m^3 + 6m^2 - 4m - 24 = 0$

36. $4w^4 + 40w^2 - 44 = 0$

37. $4z^5 = 84z^3$

38. $5b^3 + 15b^2 + 12b = -36$

39. $x^6 - 4x^4 - 9x^2 + 36 = 0$

40. $48p^5 = 27p^3$

41. ★ **MULTIPLE CHOICE** What are the real-number solutions of the equation
$3x^4 - 27x^2 + 9x = x^3$?

(A) $-1, 0, 3$

(B) $-3, 0, 3$

(C) $-3, 0, \frac{1}{3}, 3$

(D) $-3, -\frac{1}{3}, 0, 3$

CHOOSING A METHOD Factor the polynomial completely using any method.

42. $16x^3 - 44x^2 - 42x$

43. $n^4 - 4n^2 - 60$

44. $-4b^4 - 500b$

45. $36a^3 - 15a^2 + 84a - 35$

46. $18c^4 + 57c^3 - 10c^2$

47. $2d^4 - 13d^2 - 45$

48. $32x^5 - 108x^2$

49. $8y^6 - 38y^4 - 10y^2$

50. $z^5 - 3z^4 - 16z + 48$

GEOMETRY Find the possible value(s) of x.

51. Area = 48

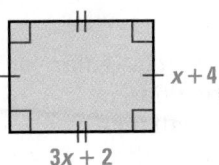

52. Volume = 40

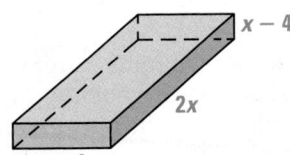

53. Volume = 125π

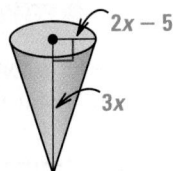

CHOOSING A METHOD Factor the polynomial completely using any method.

54. $x^3y^6 - 27$

55. $7ac^2 + bc^2 - 7ad^2 - bd^2$

56. $x^{2n} - 2x^n + 1$

57. **CHALLENGE** Factor $a^5b^2 - a^2b^4 + 2a^4b - 2ab^3 + a^3 - b^2$ completely.

EXAMPLE 6
for Exs. 58–63

58. ARCHAEOLOGY At the ruins of Caesarea, archaeologists discovered a huge hydraulic concrete block with a volume of 945 cubic meters. The block's dimensions are x meters high by $12x - 15$ meters long by $12x - 21$ meters wide. What is the height of the block?

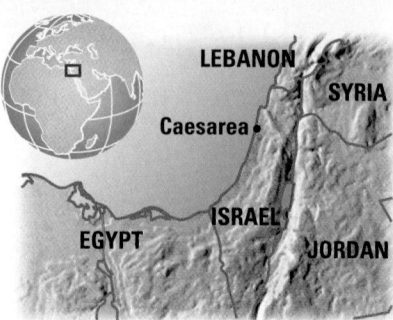

59. CHOCOLATE MOLD You are designing a chocolate mold shaped like a hollow rectangular prism for a candy manufacturer. The mold must have a thickness of 1 centimeter in all dimensions. The mold's outer dimensions should also be in the ratio $1 : 3 : 6$. What should the outer dimensions of the mold be if it is to hold 112 cubic centimeters of chocolate?

60. MULTI-STEP PROBLEM A production crew is assembling a three-level platform inside a stadium for a performance. The platform has the dimensions shown in the diagrams, and has a total volume of 1250 cubic feet.

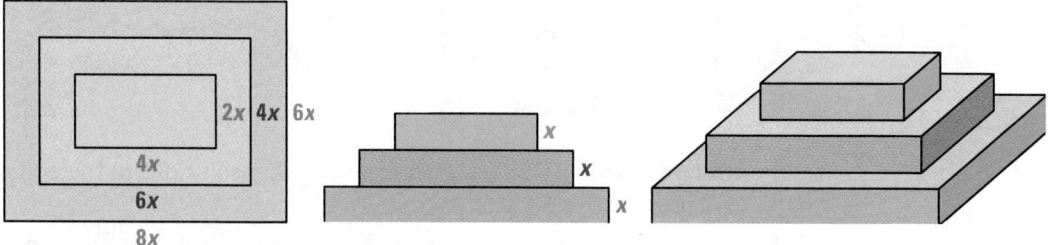

a. **Write Expressions** What is the volume, in terms of x, of each of the three levels of the platform?

b. **Write an Equation** Use what you know about the total volume to write an equation involving x.

c. **Solve** Solve the equation from part (b). Use your solution to calculate the dimensions of each of the three levels of the platform.

61. SCULPTURE Suppose you have 250 cubic inches of clay with which to make a sculpture shaped as a rectangular prism. You want the height and width each to be 5 inches less than the length. What should the dimensions of the prism be?

62. MANUFACTURING A manufacturer wants to build a rectangular stainless steel tank with a holding capacity of 670 gallons, or about 89.58 cubic feet. The tank's walls will be one half inch thick, and about 6.42 cubic feet of steel will be used for the tank. The manufacturer wants the outer dimensions of the tank to be related as follows:

• The width should be 2 feet less than the length.
• The height should be 8 feet more than the length.

What should the outer dimensions of the tank be?

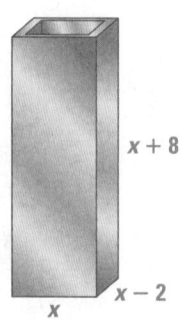

○ = See WORKED-OUT SOLUTIONS in Student Resources

★ = STANDARDIZED TEST PRACTICE

63. ★ **SHORT RESPONSE** A platform shaped like a rectangular prism has dimensions $x - 2$ feet by $3 - 2x$ feet by $3x + 4$ feet. *Explain* why the volume of the platform cannot be $\frac{7}{3}$ cubic feet.

64. ★ **EXTENDED RESPONSE** In 2000 B.C., the Babylonians solved polynomial equations using tables of values. One such table gave values of $y^3 + y^2$. To be able to use this table, the Babylonians sometimes had to manipulate the equation, as shown below.

$$ax^3 + bx^2 = c \qquad \text{Original equation}$$

$$\frac{a^3x^3}{b^3} + \frac{a^2x^2}{b^2} = \frac{a^2c}{b^3} \qquad \text{Multiply each side by } \frac{a^2}{b^3}.$$

$$\left(\frac{ax}{b}\right)^3 + \left(\frac{ax}{b}\right)^2 = \frac{a^2c}{b^3} \qquad \text{Rewrite cubes and squares.}$$

They then found $\frac{a^2c}{b^3}$ in the $y^3 + y^2$ column of the table. Because the corresponding y-value was $y = \frac{ax}{b}$, they could conclude that $x = \frac{by}{a}$.

a. Calculate $y^3 + y^2$ for $y = 1, 2, 3, \ldots, 10$. Record the values in a table.

b. Use your table and the method described above to solve $x^3 + 2x^2 = 96$.

c. Use your table and the method described above to solve $3x^3 + 2x^2 = 512$.

d. How can you modify the method described above for equations of the form $ax^4 + bx^3 = c$?

65. CHALLENGE Use the diagram to complete parts (a)–(c).

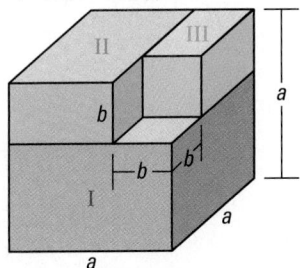

a. *Explain* why $a^3 - b^3$ is equal to the sum of the volumes of solid I, solid II, and solid III.

b. Write an algebraic expression for the volume of each of the three solids. Leave your expressions in factored form.

c. Use the results from parts (a) and (b) to derive the factoring pattern for $a^3 - b^3$.

Using ALTERNATIVE METHODS

Another Way to Solve Example 6

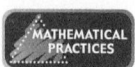

Make sense of problems and persevere in solving them.

MULTIPLE REPRESENTATIONS In Example 6, you solved a polynomial equation by factoring. You can also solve a polynomial equation using a table or a graph.

PROBLEM

CITY PARK You are designing a marble basin that will hold a fountain for a city park. The basin's sides and bottom should be 1 foot thick. Its outer length should be twice its outer width and outer height.

What should the outer dimensions of the basin be if it is to hold 36 cubic feet of water?

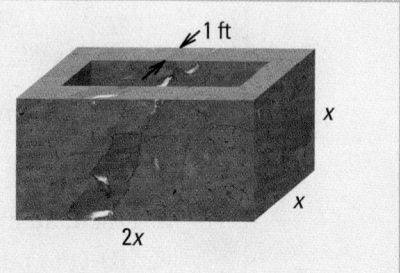

METHOD 1

Using a Table One alternative approach is to write a function for the volume of the basin and make a table of values for the function. Using the table, you can find the value of x that makes the volume of the basin 36 cubic feet.

STEP 1 **Write** the function. From the diagram, you can see that the volume y of water the basin can hold is given by this function:

$$y = (2x - 2)(x - 2)(x - 1)$$

STEP 2 **Make** a table of values for the function. Use only positive values of x because the basin's dimensions must be positive.

STEP 3 **Identify** the value of x for which $y = 36$. The table shows that $y = 36$ when $x = 4$.

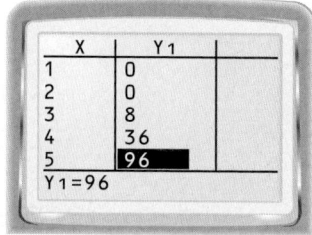

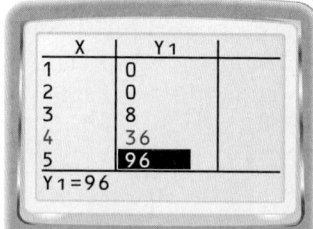

▶ The volume of the basin is 36 cubic feet when x is 4 feet. So, the outer dimensions of the basin should be as follows:

Length = $2x$ = 8 feet

Width = x = 4 feet

Height = x = 4 feet

METHOD 2 **Using a Graph** Another approach is to make a graph. You can use the graph to find the value of x that makes the volume of the basin 36 cubic feet.

STEP 1 **Write** the function. From the diagram, you can see that the volume y of water the basin can hold is given by this function:

$$y = (2x - 2)(x - 2)(x - 1)$$

STEP 2 **Graph** the equations $y = 36$ and $y = (x - 1)(2x - 2)(x - 2)$. Choose a viewing window that shows the intersection of the graphs.

STEP 3 **Identify** the coordinates of the intersection point. On a graphing calculator, you can use the *intersect* feature. The intersection point is (4, 36).

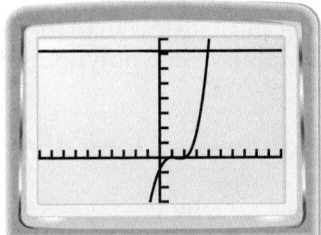
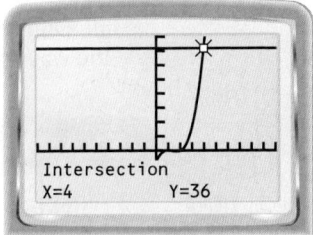

▸ The volume of the basin is 36 cubic feet when x is 4 feet. So, the outer dimensions of the basin should be as follows:

$$\text{Length} = 2x = 8 \text{ feet}$$
$$\text{Width} = x = 4 \text{ feet}$$
$$\text{Height} = x = 4 \text{ feet}$$

PRACTICE

SOLVING EQUATIONS Solve the polynomial equation using a table or using a graph.

1. $x^3 + 4x^2 - 8x = 96$

2. $x^3 - 9x^2 - 14x + 7 = -33$

3. $2x^3 - 11x^2 + 3x + 5 = 59$

4. $x^4 + x^3 - 15x^2 - 8x + 6 = -45$

5. $-x^4 + 2x^3 + 6x^2 + 17x - 4 = 32$

6. $-3x^4 + 4x^3 + 8x^2 + 4x - 11 = 13$

7. $4x^4 - 16x^3 + 29x^2 - 95x = -150$

8. **WHAT IF?** In example 6 of this lesson, suppose the basin is to hold 200 cubic feet of water. Find the outer dimensions of the basin using a table and using a graph.

9. **PACKAGING** A factory needs a box that has a volume of 1728 cubic inches. The width should be 4 inches less than the height, and the length should be 6 inches greater than the height. Find the dimensions of the box using a table and using a graph.

10. **AGRICULTURE** From 1970 to 2002, the average yearly pineapple consumption P (in pounds) per person in the United States can be modeled by the function

$$P(x) = 0.0000984x^4 - 0.00712x^3 + 0.162x^2 - 1.11x + 12.3$$

where x is the number of years since 1970. In what year was the pineapple consumption about 9.97 pounds per person? Solve the problem using a table and a graph.

2.5 Apply the Remainder and Factor Theorems

Before	You used special patterns to factor polynomials.
Now	You will use theorems to factor polynomials.
Why?	So you can determine attendance at sports games, as in Ex. 43.

Key Vocabulary
- polynomial long division
- synthetic division

When you divide a polynomial $f(x)$ by a divisor $d(x)$, you get a quotient polynomial $q(x)$ and a remainder polynomial $r(x)$.

$$\frac{f(x)}{d(x)} = q(x) + \frac{r(x)}{d(x)}$$

The degree of the remainder must be less than the degree of the divisor. One way to divide polynomials is called **polynomial long division**.

CC.9-12.A.APR.2 Know and apply the Remainder Theorem: For a polynomial $p(x)$ and a number a, the remainder on division by $x - a$ is $p(a)$, so $p(a) = 0$ if and only if $(x - a)$ is a factor of $p(x)$.

EXAMPLE 1 Use polynomial long division

Divide $f(x) = 3x^4 - 5x^3 + 4x - 6$ by $x^2 - 3x + 5$.

Solution

Write polynomial division in the same format you use when dividing numbers. Include a "0" as the coefficient of x^2 in the dividend. At each stage, divide the term with the highest power in what is left of the dividend by the first term of the divisor. This gives the next term of the quotient.

$$
\begin{array}{r}
3x^2 + 4x - 3 \quad \longleftarrow \textbf{quotient} \\
x^2 - 3x + 5 \overline{)\ 3x^4 - 5x^3 + 0x^2 + 4x - 6}
\end{array}
$$

$3x^4 - 9x^3 + 15x^2$	**Multiply divisor by $3x^4/x^2 = 3x^2$.**
$4x^3 - 15x^2 + 4x$	**Subtract. Bring down next term.**
$4x^3 - 12x^2 + 20x$	**Multiply divisor by $4x^3/x^2 = 4x$.**
$-3x^2 - 16x - 6$	**Subtract. Bring down next term.**
$-3x^2 + 9x - 15$	**Multiply divisor by $-3x^2/x^2 = -3$.**
$-25x + 9 \longleftarrow$ **remainder**	

$$\frac{3x^4 - 5x^3 + 4x - 6}{x^2 - 3x + 5} = 3x^2 + 4x - 3 + \frac{-25x + 9}{x^2 - 3x + 5}$$

AVOID ERRORS

The expression added to the quotient in the result of the long division problem is $\frac{r(x)}{d(x)}$, not $r(x)$.

CHECK You can check the result of a division problem by multiplying the quotient by the divisor and adding the remainder. The result should be the dividend.

$$(3x^2 + 4x - 3)(x^2 - 3x + 5) + (-25x + 9)$$
$$= 3x^2(x^2 - 3x + 5) + 4x(x^2 - 3x + 5) - 3(x^2 - 3x + 5) - 25x + 9$$
$$= 3x^4 - 9x^3 + 15x^2 + 4x^3 - 12x^2 + 20x - 3x^2 + 9x - 15 - 25x + 9$$
$$= 3x^4 - 5x^3 + 4x - 6 \checkmark$$

AP Images/Orlin Wagner

EXAMPLE 2 **Use polynomial long division with a linear divisor**

Divide $f(x) = x^3 + 5x^2 - 7x + 2$ by $x - 2$.

$$
\begin{array}{r}
x^2 + 7x + 7 \quad \leftarrow \text{quotient} \\
x - 2 \,\overline{\big)\, x^3 + 5x^2 - 7x + 2}
\end{array}
$$

$\underline{x^3 - 2x^2}$	Multiply divisor by $x^3/x = x^2$.
$7x^2 - 7x$	Subtract.
$\underline{7x^2 - 14x}$	Multiply divisor by $7x^2/x = 7x$.
$7x + 2$	Subtract.
$\underline{7x - 14}$	Multiply divisor by $7x/x = 7$.
$16 \quad \leftarrow \text{remainder}$	

▶ $\dfrac{x^3 + 5x^2 - 7x + 2}{x - 2} = x^2 + 7x + 7 + \dfrac{16}{x - 2}$

✓ **GUIDED PRACTICE** for Examples 1 and 2

Divide using polynomial long division.

1. $(2x^4 + x^3 + x - 1) \div (x^2 + 2x - 1)$ **2.** $(x^3 - x^2 + 4x - 10) \div (x + 2)$

SYNTHETIC DIVISION If you use synthetic substitution to evaluate $f(x)$ in Example 2 when $x = 2$, as shown below, you can see that $f(2)$ equals the remainder when $f(x)$ is divided by $x - 2$. Also, the other values below the line match the coefficients of the quotient. For this reason, synthetic substitution is sometimes called **synthetic division**. Synthetic division can be used to divide any polynomial by a divisor of the form $x - k$.

$$
\begin{array}{r|rrrr}
2 & 1 & 5 & -7 & 2 \\
 &   & 2 & 14 & 14 \\
\hline
 & 1 & 7 & 7 & 16
\end{array}
$$

coefficients of quotient $\longrightarrow$ 1   7   7   16 $\leftarrow$ remainder

---

KEY CONCEPT   *For Your Notebook*

Remainder Theorem

If a polynomial $f(x)$ is divided by $x - k$, then the remainder is $r = f(k)$.

EXAMPLE 3 **Use synthetic division**

DIVIDE POLYNOMIALS
Because the divisor is $x + 3 = x - (-3)$, evaluate the dividend when $x = -3$.

Divide $f(x) = 2x^3 + x^2 - 8x + 5$ by $x + 3$ using synthetic division.

$$
\begin{array}{r|rrrr}
-3 & 2 & 1 & -8 & 5 \\
 &   & -6 & 15 & -21 \\
\hline
 & 2 & -5 & 7 & -16
\end{array}
$$

▶ $\dfrac{2x^3 + x^2 - 8x + 5}{x + 3} = 2x^2 - 5x + 7 - \dfrac{16}{x + 3}$

FACTOR THEOREM Suppose the remainder is 0 when a polynomial $f(x)$ is divided by $x - k$. Then

$$\frac{f(x)}{x - k} = q(x) + \frac{0}{x - k} = q(x)$$

where $q(x)$ is the quotient polynomial. Therefore, $f(x) = (x - k) \cdot q(x)$, so that $x - k$ is a factor of $f(x)$. This result is summarized by the *factor theorem*.

KEY CONCEPT *For Your Notebook*

Factor Theorem

A polynomial $f(x)$ has a factor $x - k$ if and only if $f(k) = 0$.

The factor theorem can be used to solve a variety of problems.

Problem	Example
Given one *factor* of a polynomial, find the other *factors*.	See Example 4 below.
Given one *zero* of a polynomial function, find the other *zeros*.	See Example 5.
Given one *solution* of a polynomial equation, find the other *solutions*.	See Example 6.

EXAMPLE 4 **Factor a polynomial**

Factor $f(x) = 3x^3 - 4x^2 - 28x - 16$ completely given that $x + 2$ is a factor.

Solution

AVOID ERRORS

The remainder after using synthetic division should always be zero when you are dividing a polynomial by one of its factors.

Because $x + 2$ is a factor of $f(x)$, you know that $f(-2) = 0$. Use synthetic division to find the other factors.

$$
\begin{array}{r|rrrr}
-2 & 3 & -4 & -28 & -16 \\
   &   & -6 & 20 & 16 \\
\hline
   & 3 & -10 & -8 & 0 \\
\end{array}
$$

Use the result to write $f(x)$ as a product of two factors and then factor completely.

$f(x) = 3x^3 - 4x^2 - 28x - 16$ **Write original polynomial.**

$\quad = (x + 2)(3x^2 - 10x - 8)$ **Write as a product of two factors.**

$\quad = (x + 2)(3x + 2)(x - 4)$ **Factor trinomial.**

✓ **GUIDED PRACTICE** for Examples 3 and 4

Divide using synthetic division.

3. $(x^3 + 4x^2 - x - 1) \div (x + 3)$ **4.** $(4x^3 + x^2 - 3x + 7) \div (x - 1)$

Factor the polynomial completely given that $x - 4$ is a factor.

5. $f(x) = x^3 - 6x^2 + 5x + 12$ **6.** $f(x) = x^3 - x^2 - 22x + 40$

EXAMPLE 5 **Standardized Test Practice**

One zero of $f(x) = x^3 - 2x^2 - 23x + 60$ is $x = 3$. What is another zero of f?

(A) −5 **(B)** −4 **(C)** 2 **(D)** 5

Solution

Because $f(3) = 0$, $x - 3$ is a factor of $f(x)$. Use synthetic division.

```
3 | 1   -2   -23    60
  |      3     3   -60
  ---------------------
    1    1   -20     0
```

Use the result to write $f(x)$ as a product of two factors. Then factor completely.

$f(x) = x^3 - 2x^2 - 23x + 60 = (x - 3)(x^2 + x - 20) = (x - 3)(x + 5)(x - 4)$

The zeros are 3, −5, and 4.

▶ The correct answer is A. **(A)** **(B)** **(C)** **(D)**

EXAMPLE 6 **Use a polynomial model**

BUSINESS The profit P (in millions of dollars) for a shoe manufacturer can be modeled by $P = -21x^3 + 46x$ where x is the number of shoes produced (in millions). The company now produces 1 million shoes and makes a profit of \$25,000,000, but would like to cut back production. What lesser number of shoes could the company produce and still make the same profit?

Solution

$25 = -21x^3 + 46x$ Substitute 25 for P in $P = -21x^3 + 46x$.

$0 = 21x^3 - 46x + 25$ Write in standard form.

You know that $x = 1$ is one solution of the equation. This implies that $x - 1$ is a factor of $21x^3 - 46x + 25$. Use synthetic division to find the other factors.

```
1 | 21    0   -46    25
  |       21   21   -25
  ---------------------
    21    21  -25     0
```

So, $(x - 1)(21x^2 + 21x - 25) = 0$. Use the quadratic formula to find that $x \approx 0.7$ is the other positive solution.

▶ The company could still make the same profit producing about 700,000 shoes.

✓ **GUIDED PRACTICE** for Examples 5 and 6

Find the other zeros of f given that $f(-2) = 0$.

7. $f(x) = x^3 + 2x^2 - 9x - 18$ **8.** $f(x) = x^3 + 8x^2 + 5x - 14$

9. **WHAT IF?** In Example 6, how does the answer change if the profit for the shoe manufacturer is modeled by $P = -15x^3 + 40x$?

© Fuse/Jupiterimages

2.5 Apply the Remainder and Factor Theorems **123**

2.5 EXERCISES

HOMEWORK KEY

◯ = See WORKED-OUT SOLUTIONS
Exs. 17, 25, and 43

★ = STANDARDIZED TEST PRACTICE
Exs. 2, 35, 39, 44, and 45

◆ = MULTIPLE REPRESENTATIONS
Ex. 38

SKILL PRACTICE

1. **VOCABULARY** State the remainder theorem.

2. ★ **WRITING** Synthetic division has been used to divide $f(x) = x^4 - 5x^2 + 8x - 2$ by $x + 3$. *Explain* what the colored numbers represent in the division problem.

$$
\begin{array}{r|rrrrr}
-3 & 1 & 0 & -5 & 8 & -2 \\
   &   & -3 & 9 & -12 & 12 \\
\hline
   & 1 & -3 & 4 & -4 & 10
\end{array}
$$

EXAMPLES 1 and 2 for Exs. 3–10

USING LONG DIVISION Divide using polynomial long division.

3. $(x^2 + x - 17) \div (x - 4)$

4. $(3x^2 - 11x - 26) \div (x - 5)$

5. $(x^3 + 3x^2 + 3x + 2) \div (x - 1)$

6. $(8x^2 + 34x - 1) \div (4x - 1)$

7. $(3x^3 + 11x^2 + 4x + 1) \div (x^2 + x)$

8. $(7x^3 + 11x^2 + 7x + 5) \div (x^2 + 1)$

9. $(5x^4 - 2x^3 - 7x^2 - 39) \div (x^2 + 2x - 4)$

10. $(4x^4 + 5x - 4) \div (x^2 - 3x - 2)$

EXAMPLE 3 for Exs. 11–20

USING SYNTHETIC DIVISION Divide using synthetic division.

11. $(2x^2 - 7x + 10) \div (x - 5)$

12. $(4x^2 - 13x - 5) \div (x - 2)$

13. $(x^2 + 8x + 1) \div (x + 4)$

14. $(x^2 + 9) \div (x - 3)$

15. $(x^3 - 5x^2 - 2) \div (x - 4)$

16. $(x^3 - 4x + 6) \div (x + 3)$

17. $(x^4 - 5x^3 - 8x^2 + 13x - 12) \div (x - 6)$

18. $(x^4 + 4x^3 + 16x - 35) \div (x + 5)$

ERROR ANALYSIS *Describe* and correct the error in using synthetic division to divide $x^3 - 5x + 3$ by $x - 2$.

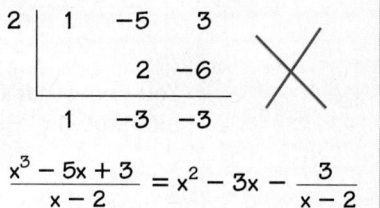

19.
$$
\begin{array}{r|rrrr}
2 & 1 & 0 & -5 & 3 \\
  &   & 2 & 4 & -2 \\
\hline
  & 1 & 2 & -1 & 1
\end{array}
$$

$$\frac{x^3 - 5x + 3}{x - 2} = x^3 + 2x^2 - x + 1$$

20.
$$
\begin{array}{r|rrr}
2 & 1 & -5 & 3 \\
  &   & 2 & -6 \\
\hline
  & 1 & -3 & -3
\end{array}
$$

$$\frac{x^3 - 5x + 3}{x - 2} = x^2 - 3x - \frac{3}{x - 2}$$

EXAMPLE 4 for Exs. 21–28

FACTOR Given polynomial $f(x)$ and a factor of $f(x)$, factor $f(x)$ completely.

21. $f(x) = x^3 - 10x^2 + 19x + 30; x - 6$

22. $f(x) = x^3 + 6x^2 + 5x - 12; x + 4$

23. $f(x) = x^3 - 2x^2 - 40x - 64; x - 8$

24. $f(x) = x^3 + 18x^2 + 95x + 150; x + 10$

25. $f(x) = x^3 + 2x^2 - 51x + 108; x + 9$

26. $f(x) = x^3 - 9x^2 + 8x + 60; x + 2$

27. $f(x) = 2x^3 - 15x^2 + 34x - 21; x - 1$

28. $f(x) = 3x^3 - 2x^2 - 61x - 20; x - 5$

EXAMPLE 5 for Exs. 29–35

FIND ZEROS Given polynomial function f and a zero of f, find the other zeros.

29. $f(x) = x^3 - 2x^2 - 21x - 18; -3$

30. $f(x) = 4x^3 - 25x^2 - 154x + 40; 10$

31. $f(x) = 10x^3 - 81x^2 + 71x + 42; 7$

32. $f(x) = 3x^3 + 34x^2 + 72x - 64; -4$

33. $f(x) = 2x^3 - 10x^2 - 71x - 9; 9$

34. $f(x) = 5x^3 - x^2 - 18x + 8; -2$

35. ★ **MULTIPLE CHOICE** One zero of $f(x) = 4x^3 + 15x^2 - 63x - 54$ is $x = -6$. What is another zero of f?

    Ⓐ -9 Ⓑ -3 Ⓒ -1 Ⓓ 3

🔷 **GEOMETRY** **You are given an expression for the volume of the rectangular prism. Find an expression for the missing dimension.**

36. $V = 2x^3 + 17x^2 + 46x + 40$

37. $V = x^3 + 13x^2 + 34x - 48$

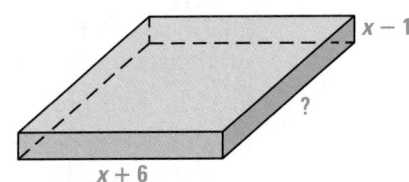

$x + 2$

$x + 4$

?

$x - 1$

?

$x + 6$

38. 🔶 **MULTIPLE REPRESENTATIONS** Consider the polynomial function $f(x) = x^3 - 5x^2 - 12x + 36$.

  a. **Zeros of a Function** Given that $f(2) = 0$, find the other zeros of f.

  b. **Factors of an Expression** Based on your results from part (a), what are the factors of the polynomial $x^3 - 5x^2 - 12x + 36$?

  c. **Solutions of an Equation** What are the solutions of the polynomial equation $x^3 - 5x^2 - 12x + 36 = 0$?

39. ★ **MULTIPLE CHOICE** What is the value of k such that $x - 5$ is a factor of $x^3 - x^2 + kx - 30$?

    Ⓐ -14 Ⓑ -2 Ⓒ 26 Ⓓ 32

40. **CHALLENGE** It can be shown that $2x - 1$ is a factor of the polynomial function $f(x) = 30x^3 + 7x^2 - 39x + 14$.

  a. What can you conclude is a zero of f?

  b. Use synthetic division to write $f(x)$ in the form $(x - k) \cdot q(x)$.

  c. Write $f(x)$ as the product of linear factors with integer coefficients.

PROBLEM SOLVING

EXAMPLE 6
for Exs. 41–43

41. **CLOTHING** The profit P (in millions of dollars) for a T-shirt manufacturer can be modeled by $P = -x^3 + 4x^2 + x$ where x is the number of T-shirts produced (in millions). Currently, the company produces 4 million T-shirts and makes a profit of $4,000,000. What lesser number of T-shirts could the company produce and still make the same profit?

42. **MP3 PLAYERS** The profit P (in millions of dollars) for a manufacturer of MP3 players can be modeled by $P = -4x^3 + 12x^2 + 16x$ where x is the number of MP3 players produced (in millions). Currently, the company produces 3 million MP3 players and makes a profit of $48,000,000. What lesser number of MP3 players could the company produce and still make the same profit?

AP Images/Joe Cavarotta

43. **WOMEN'S BASKETBALL** From 1985 to 2003, the total attendance A (in thousands) at NCAA women's basketball games and the number T of NCAA women's basketball teams can be modeled by

$$A = -1.95x^3 + 70.1x^2 - 188x + 2150 \qquad \text{and} \qquad T = 14.8x + 725$$

where x is the number of years since 1985. Write a function for the average attendance per team from 1985 to 2003.

44. ★ **EXTENDED RESPONSE** The price p (in dollars) that a radio manufacturer is able to charge for a radio is given by $p = 40 - 4x^2$ where x is the number (in millions) of radios produced. It costs the company $15 to make a radio.

   a. Write an expression for the company's total revenue in terms of x.

   b. Write a function for the company's profit P by subtracting the total cost to make x radios from the expression in part (a).

   c. Currently, the company produces 1.5 million radios and makes a profit of $24,000,000. Write and solve an equation to find a lesser number of radios that the company could produce and still make the same profit.

   d. Do all the solutions in part (c) make sense in this situation? *Explain.*

45. ★ **SHORT RESPONSE** Since 1990, overnight stays S and total visits V (both in millions) to national parks can be modeled by

$$S = -0.00722x^4 + 0.176x^3 - 1.40x^2 + 3.39x + 17.6$$

$$V = 3.10x + 256$$

where x is the number of years since 1990. Write a function for the percent of visits to national parks that were overnight stays. *Explain* how you constructed your function.

Joshua Tree National Park, California

46. **CHALLENGE** The profit P (in millions of dollars) for a DVD manufacturer can be modeled by $P = -6x^3 + 72x$ where x is the number of DVDs produced (in millions). Show that 2 million DVDs is the only production level for the company that yields a profit of $96,000,000.

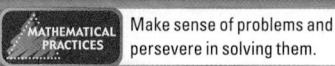
1. **MULTI-STEP PROBLEM** The average distance between Earth and the sun is 164,000,000,000 yards.

   a. Write the distance in scientific notation.

   b. The length of a football field, including the end zones, is 1.20×10^2 yards. How many football fields stretched end-to-end would it take to reach from Earth to the sun?

2. **MULTI-STEP PROBLEM** You are designing a rectangular picnic cooler with length 4 times its width and height 2 times its width. The cooler has insulation that is 1 inch thick on each of the four sides and 2 inches thick on the top and bottom.

   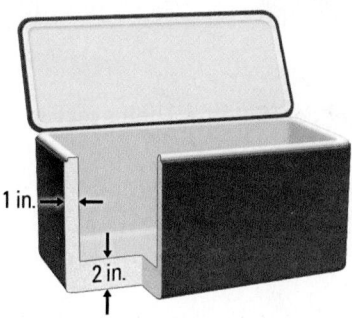

   a. Let x represent the width of the cooler. Write a polynomial function $T(x)$ in standard form for the volume of the rectangular prism formed by the cooler's outer surfaces.

   b. Write a polynomial function $C(x)$ in standard form for the volume of the inside of the cooler.

   c. Let $I(x)$ be a polynomial function for the volume of insulation. How is $I(x)$ related to $T(x)$ and $C(x)$?

   d. Write $I(x)$ in standard form. What is the volume of the insulation when $x = 8$ inches?

3. **SHORT RESPONSE** In biology, a cell with a higher surface area-to-volume ratio can exchange materials with its environment faster than a cell with a lower ratio. *Explain* whether a cubic cell with side length x or a spherical cell with diameter x can exchange materials with its environment faster.

4. **OPEN-ENDED** Write a polynomial function that has degree 4 and end behavior given by $f(x) \to -\infty$ as $x \to -\infty$ and $f(x) \to -\infty$ as $x \to +\infty$. Then graph the function to check your answer.

5. **EXTENDED RESPONSE** From 1995 to 2003, the average monthly cell phone bill C (in dollars) for subscribers in the United States can be modeled by

   $$C = -0.027t^4 + 0.32t^3 - 0.25t^2 - 4.9t + 51$$

   where t is the number of years since 1995.

   a. Classify the function by degree and type.

   b. Make a table of values for the function.

   c. Sketch a graph of the function. Do you think the model will accurately predict cell phone bills for years beyond 2003? *Explain.*

6. **EXTENDED RESPONSE** The price p (in dollars) that a camera manufacturer is able to charge for a camera is given by $p = 100 - 10x^2$ where x is the number (in millions) of cameras produced. It costs the company $30 to make a camera. Currently, the company produces 2 million cameras and makes a profit of $60,000,000.

   a. Write a function that gives the total revenue R in terms of x.

   b. Write a function that gives the company's profit P in terms of x.

   c. Write and solve an equation to find other values of x that yield a profit of $60,000,000.

   d. Do all the solutions in part (c) make sense in this situation? *Explain.*

7. **GRIDDED ANSWER** For the city park commission, you are designing a marble sculpture in the shape of a pyramid with a square base, as shown below. The volume of the sculpture is 48 cubic feet. What is the height x in feet of the sculpture?

   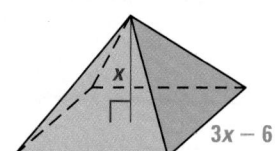

2.6 Find Rational Zeros

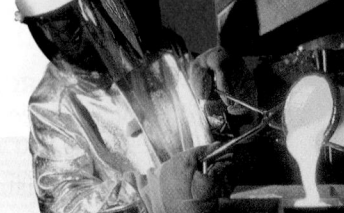

Before You found the zeros of a polynomial function given one zero.

Now You will find all real zeros of a polynomial function.

Why? So you can model manufacturing processes, as in Ex. 45.

Key Vocabulary
- zero of a function
- constant term
- leading coefficient

The polynomial function $f(x) = 64x^3 + 152x^2 - 62x - 105$ has $-\frac{5}{2}$, $-\frac{3}{4}$, and $\frac{7}{8}$ as its zeros. Notice that the numerators of these zeros (-5, -3, and 7) are factors of the constant term, -105. Also notice that the denominators (2, 4, and 8) are factors of the leading coefficient, 64. These observations are generalized by the *rational zero theorem*.

CC.9-12.A.APR.2 *Know and apply the Remainder Theorem: For a polynomial p(x) and a number a, the remainder on division by x − a is p(a), so p(a) = 0 if and only if (x − a) is a factor of p(x).*

> **KEY CONCEPT** *For Your Notebook*
>
> **The Rational Zero Theorem**
>
> If $f(x) = a_n x^n + \cdots + a_1 x + a_0$ has *integer* coefficients, then every rational zero of f has the following form:
>
> $$\frac{p}{q} = \frac{\text{factor of constant term } a_0}{\text{factor of leading coefficient } a_n}$$

EXAMPLE 1 List possible rational zeros

List the possible rational zeros of f using the rational zero theorem.

AVOID ERRORS
Be sure your lists include both the positive and negative factors of the constant term and the leading coefficient.

a. $f(x) = x^3 + 2x^2 - 11x + 12$

Factors of the constant term: $\pm 1, \pm 2, \pm 3, \pm 4, \pm 6, \pm 12$

Factors of the leading coefficient: ± 1

Possible rational zeros: $\pm\frac{1}{1}, \pm\frac{2}{1}, \pm\frac{3}{1}, \pm\frac{4}{1}, \pm\frac{6}{1}, \pm\frac{12}{1}$

Simplified list of possible zeros: $\pm 1, \pm 2, \pm 3, \pm 4, \pm 6, \pm 12$

b. $f(x) = 4x^4 - x^3 - 3x^2 + 9x - 10$

Factors of the constant term: $\pm 1, \pm 2, \pm 5, \pm 10$

Factors of the leading coefficient: $\pm 1, \pm 2, \pm 4$

Possible rational zeros:

$\pm\frac{1}{1}, \pm\frac{2}{1}, \pm\frac{5}{1}, \pm\frac{10}{1}, \pm\frac{1}{2}, \pm\frac{2}{2}, \pm\frac{5}{2}, \pm\frac{10}{2}, \pm\frac{1}{4}, \pm\frac{2}{4}, \pm\frac{5}{4}, \pm\frac{10}{4}$

Simplified list of possible zeros: $\pm 1, \pm 2, \pm 5, \pm 10, \pm\frac{1}{2}, \pm\frac{5}{2}, \pm\frac{1}{4}, \pm\frac{5}{4}$

List the possible rational zeros of f using the rational zero theorem.

1. $f(x) = x^3 + 9x^2 + 23x + 15$ **2.** $f(x) = 2x^3 + 3x^2 - 11x - 6$

VERIFYING ZEROS   Recall that you have found zeros of polynomial functions when one zero was known. The rational zero theorem is a starting point for finding zeros when no zeros are known.

However, the rational zero theorem lists only *possible* zeros. In order to find the *actual* zeros of a polynomial function f, you must test values from the list of possible zeros. You can test a value by evaluating $f(x)$ using the test value as x.

EXAMPLE 2   **Find zeros when the leading coefficient is 1**

Find all real zeros of $f(x) = x^3 - 8x^2 + 11x + 20$.

Solution

STEP 1   **List** the possible rational zeros. The leading coefficient is 1 and the constant term is 20. So, the possible rational zeros are:

$$x = \pm\frac{1}{1}, \ \pm\frac{2}{1}, \ \pm\frac{4}{1}, \ \pm\frac{5}{1}, \ \pm\frac{10}{1}, \ \pm\frac{20}{1}$$

AVOID ERRORS
Notice that not every *possible* zero generated by the rational zero theorem is an *actual* zero of f.

STEP 2   **Test** these zeros using synthetic division.

Test $x = 1$:

$$
\begin{array}{r|rrrr}
1 & 1 & -8 & 11 & 20 \\
  &   & 1 & -7 & 4 \\
\hline
  & 1 & -7 & 4 & 24 \\
\end{array}
$$

└─ 1 is not a zero.

Test $x = -1$:

$$
\begin{array}{r|rrrr}
-1 & 1 & -8 & 11 & 20 \\
   &   & -1 & 9 & -20 \\
\hline
   & 1 & -9 & 20 & 0 \\
\end{array}
$$

└─ −1 is a zero.

Because -1 is a zero of f, you can write $f(x) = (x + 1)(x^2 - 9x + 20)$.

STEP 3   **Factor** the trinomial in $f(x)$ and use the factor theorem.

$$f(x) = (x + 1)(x^2 - 9x + 20) = (x + 1)(x - 4)(x - 5)$$

▶ The zeros of f are -1, 4, and 5.

Animated Algebra   at my.hrw.com

✓ **GUIDED PRACTICE**   for Example 2

Find all real zeros of the function.

3. $f(x) = x^3 - 4x^2 - 15x + 18$ **4.** $f(x) = x^3 - 8x^2 + 5x + 14$

LIMITING THE SEARCH FOR ZEROS   In Example 2, the leading coefficient of the polynomial function is 1. When the leading coefficient is not 1, the list of possible rational zeros can increase dramatically. In such cases, the search can be shortened by sketching the function's graph.

EXAMPLE 3   **Find zeros when the leading coefficient is not 1**

Find all real zeros of $f(x) = 10x^4 - 11x^3 - 42x^2 + 7x + 12$.

Solution

STEP 1   **List** the possible rational zeros of f: $\pm\dfrac{1}{1}, \pm\dfrac{2}{1}, \pm\dfrac{3}{1}, \pm\dfrac{4}{1}, \pm\dfrac{6}{1}, \pm\dfrac{12}{1}$,

$\pm\dfrac{1}{2}, \pm\dfrac{3}{2}, \pm\dfrac{1}{5}, \pm\dfrac{2}{5}, \pm\dfrac{3}{5}, \pm\dfrac{4}{5}, \pm\dfrac{6}{5}, \pm\dfrac{12}{5}, \pm\dfrac{1}{10}, \pm\dfrac{3}{10}$

STEP 2   **Choose** reasonable values from the list above to check using the graph of the function. For f, the values

$x = -\dfrac{3}{2}, x = -\dfrac{1}{2}, x = \dfrac{3}{5}$, and $x = \dfrac{12}{5}$

are reasonable based on the graph shown at the right.

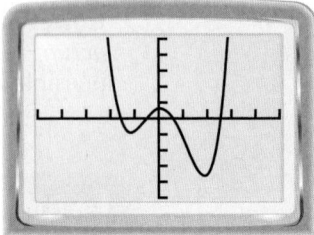

STEP 3   **Check** the values using synthetic division until a zero is found.

$-\dfrac{3}{2}$	10	-11	-42	7	12
		-15	39	$\dfrac{9}{2}$	$-\dfrac{69}{4}$
	10	-26	-3	$\dfrac{23}{2}$	$-\dfrac{21}{4}$

$-\dfrac{1}{2}$	10	-11	-42	7	12
			-5	8	17	-12
	10	-16	-34	24	**0**

$-\dfrac{1}{2}$ is a zero.

STEP 4   **Factor** out a binomial using the result of the synthetic division.

$f(x) = \left(x + \dfrac{1}{2}\right)(10x^3 - 16x^2 - 34x + 24)$ **Write as a product of factors.**

$= \left(x + \dfrac{1}{2}\right)(2)(5x^3 - 8x^2 - 17x + 12)$ **Factor 2 out of the second factor.**

$= (2x + 1)(5x^3 - 8x^2 - 17x + 12)$ **Multiply the first factor by 2.**

STEP 5   **Repeat** the steps above for $g(x) = 5x^3 - 8x^2 - 17x + 12$. Any zero of g will also be a zero of f. The possible rational zeros of g are:

$x = \pm1, \pm2, \pm3, \pm4, \pm6, \pm12, \pm\dfrac{1}{5}, \pm\dfrac{2}{5}, \pm\dfrac{3}{5}, \pm\dfrac{4}{5}, \pm\dfrac{6}{5}, \pm\dfrac{12}{5}$

The graph of g shows that $\dfrac{3}{5}$ may be a zero. Synthetic division shows that $\dfrac{3}{5}$ *is a zero* and $g(x) = \left(x - \dfrac{3}{5}\right)(5x^2 - 5x - 20) = (5x - 3)(x^2 - x - 4)$. It follows that:

$f(x) = (2x + 1) \cdot g(x) = (2x + 1)(5x - 3)(x^2 - x - 4)$

STEP 6   **Find** the remaining zeros of f by solving $x^2 - x - 4 = 0$.

$x = \dfrac{-(-1) \pm \sqrt{(-1)^2 - 4(1)(-4)}}{2(1)}$ **Substitute 1 for a, -1 for b, and -4 for c in the quadratic formula.**

$x = \dfrac{1 \pm \sqrt{17}}{2}$ **Simplify.**

▶ The real zeros of f are $-\dfrac{1}{2}, \dfrac{3}{5}, \dfrac{1 + \sqrt{17}}{2}$, and $\dfrac{1 - \sqrt{17}}{2}$.

Find all real zeros of the function.

5. $f(x) = 48x^3 + 4x^2 - 20x + 3$ **6.** $f(x) = 2x^4 + 5x^3 - 18x^2 - 19x + 42$

EXAMPLE 4 **Solve a multi-step problem**

ICE SCULPTURES Some ice sculptures are made by filling a mold with water and then freezing it. You are making such an ice sculpture for a school dance. It is to be shaped like a pyramid with a height that is 1 foot greater than the length of each side of its square base. The volume of the ice sculpture is 4 cubic feet. What are the dimensions of the mold?

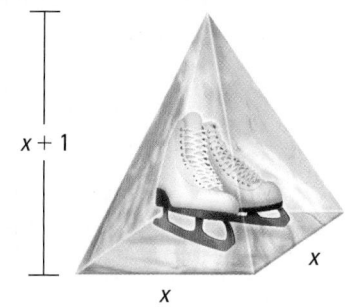

Solution

STEP 1 **Write** an equation for the volume of the ice sculpture.

Volume (cubic feet)	=	$\frac{1}{3}$	·	Area of base (square feet)	·	Height (feet)
4	=	$\frac{1}{3}$	·	x^2	·	$(x + 1)$

$4 = \frac{1}{3}x^2(x + 1)$ **Write equation.**

$12 = x^3 + x^2$ **Multiply each side by 3 and simplify.**

$0 = x^3 + x^2 - 12$ **Subtract 12 from each side.**

STEP 2 **List** the possible rational solutions: $\pm\frac{1}{1}, \pm\frac{2}{1}, \pm\frac{3}{1}, \pm\frac{4}{1}, \pm\frac{6}{1}, \pm\frac{12}{1}$

STEP 3 **Test** possible solutions. Only positive x-values make sense.

```
1 | 1   1   0   -12        2 | 1   1   0   -12
  |     1   2    2           |     2   6    12
  ---------------------      ---------------------
    1   2   2   -10            1   3   6    0
```
                                              └─ **2 is a solution.**

STEP 4 **Check** for other solutions. The other two solutions, which satisfy $x^2 + 3x + 6 = 0$, are $x = \dfrac{-3 \pm i\sqrt{15}}{2}$ and can be discarded because they are imaginary numbers.

▶ The only reasonable solution is $x = 2$. The base of the mold is 2 feet by 2 feet. The height of the mold is $2 + 1 = 3$ feet.

7. **WHAT IF?** In Example 4, suppose the base of the ice sculpture has sides that are 1 foot longer than the height. The volume of the ice sculpture is 6 cubic feet. What are the dimensions of the mold?

2.6 EXERCISES

HOMEWORK
KEY

○ = See WORKED-OUT SOLUTIONS
Exs. 7, 21, and 47

★ = STANDARDIZED TEST PRACTICE
Exs. 2, 23, 38, 39, 40, and 50

SKILL PRACTICE

1. **VOCABULARY** Copy and complete: If a polynomial function has integer coefficients, then every rational zero of the function has the form $\frac{p}{q}$, where p is a factor of the __?__ and q is a factor of the __?__.

2. ★ **WRITING** *Describe* a method you can use to shorten the list of possible rational zeros when using the rational zero theorem.

EXAMPLE 1
for Exs. 3–10

LISTING RATIONAL ZEROS **List the possible rational zeros of the function using the rational zero theorem.**

3. $f(x) = x^3 - 3x + 28$

4. $g(x) = x^3 - 4x^2 + x - 10$

5. $f(x) = 2x^4 + 6x^3 - 7x + 9$

6. $h(x) = 2x^3 + x^2 - x - 18$

7. $g(x) = 4x^5 + 3x^3 - 2x - 14$

8. $f(x) = 3x^4 + 5x^3 - 3x + 42$

9. $h(x) = 8x^4 + 4x^3 - 10x + 15$

10. $h(x) = 6x^3 - 3x^2 + 12$

EXAMPLE 2
for Exs. 11–18

FINDING REAL ZEROS **Find all real zeros of the function.**

11. $f(x) = x^3 - 12x^2 + 35x - 24$

12. $f(x) = x^3 - 5x^2 - 22x + 56$

13. $g(x) = x^3 - 31x - 30$

14. $h(x) = x^3 + 8x^2 - 9x - 72$

15. $h(x) = x^4 + 7x^3 + 26x^2 + 44x + 24$

16. $f(x) = x^4 - 2x^3 - 9x^2 + 10x - 24$

17. $f(x) = x^4 + 2x^3 - 9x^2 - 2x + 8$

18. $g(x) = x^4 - 16x^2 - 40x - 25$

EXAMPLE 3
for Exs. 19–35

ELIMINATING POSSIBLE ZEROS **Use the graph to shorten the list of possible rational zeros of the function. Then find all real zeros of the function.**

19. $f(x) = 4x^3 - 20x + 16$

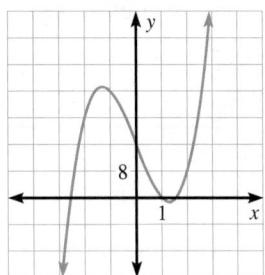

20. $f(x) = 4x^3 - 12x^2 - x + 15$

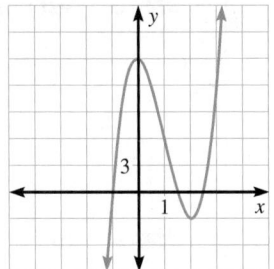

21. $f(x) = 6x^3 + 25x^2 + 16x - 15$

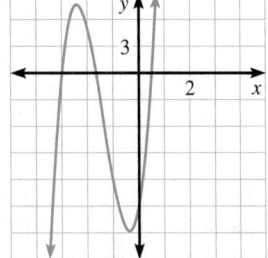

22. $f(x) = -3x^3 + 20x^2 - 36x + 16$

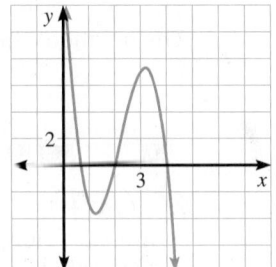

23. ★ **MULTIPLE CHOICE** According to the rational zero theorem, which is *not* a possible zero of the function $f(x) = 2x^4 - 5x^3 + 10x^2 - 9$?

     (A) -9 **(B)** $-\frac{1}{2}$ **(C)** $\frac{5}{2}$ **(D)** 3

FINDING REAL ZEROS Find all real zeros of the function.

24. $f(x) = 2x^3 + 2x^2 - 8x - 8$ **25.** $g(x) = 2x^3 - 7x^2 + 9$

26. $h(x) = 2x^3 - 3x^2 - 14x + 15$ **27.** $f(x) = 3x^3 + 4x^2 - 35x - 12$

28. $f(x) = 3x^3 + 19x^2 + 4x - 12$ **29.** $g(x) = 2x^3 + 5x^2 - 11x - 14$

30. $g(x) = 2x^4 + 9x^3 + 5x^2 + 3x - 4$ **31.** $h(x) = 2x^4 - x^3 - 7x^2 + 4x - 4$

32. $h(x) = 3x^4 - 6x^3 - 32x^2 + 35x - 12$ **33.** $f(x) = 2x^4 - 9x^3 + 37x - 30$

34. $f(x) = x^5 - 3x^4 - 5x^3 + 15x^2 + 4x - 12$ **35.** $h(x) = 2x^5 + 5x^4 - 3x^3 - 2x^2 - 5x + 3$

ERROR ANALYSIS *Describe* and correct the error in listing the possible rational zeros of the function.

36.
> $f(x) = x^3 + 7x^2 + 2x + 14$
>
> Possible zeros:
>
> 1, 2, 7, 14   ✗

37.
> $f(x) = 6x^3 - 3x^2 + 12x + 5$
>
> Possible zeros:
>
> $\pm 1, \pm 2, \pm 3, \pm 6, \pm\frac{1}{5}, \pm\frac{2}{5}, \pm\frac{3}{5}, \pm\frac{6}{5}$ ✗

38. ★ **OPEN-ENDED MATH** Write a polynomial function f that has a leading coefficient of 4 and has 12 possible rational zeros according to the rational zero theorem.

39. ★ **MULTIPLE CHOICE** Which of the following is *not* a zero of the function $f(x) = 40x^5 - 42x^4 - 107x^3 + 107x^2 + 33x - 36$?

     (A) $-\frac{3}{2}$ **(B)** $-\frac{3}{8}$ **(C)** $\frac{3}{4}$ **(D)** $\frac{4}{5}$

40. ★ **SHORT RESPONSE** Let a_n be the leading coefficient of a polynomial function f and a_0 be the constant term. If a_n has r factors and a_0 has s factors, what is the largest number of possible rational zeros of f that can be generated by the rational zero theorem? *Explain* your reasoning.

MATCHING Find all real zeros of the function. Then match each function with its graph.

41. $f(x) = x^3 - 2x^2 - x + 2$ **42.** $g(x) = x^3 - 3x^2 + 2$ **43.** $h(x) = x^3 + x^2 - x + 2$

A. 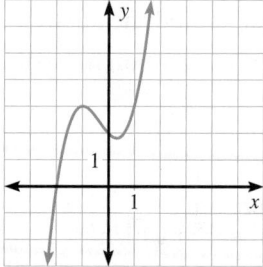   **B.** 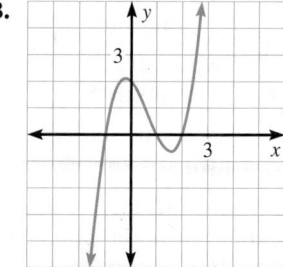   **C.**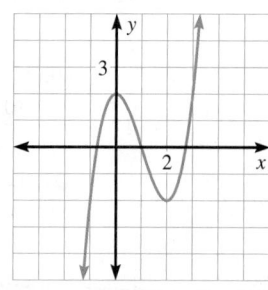

44. **CHALLENGE** Is it possible for a cubic function to have more than three real zeros? Is it possible for a cubic function to have no real zeros? *Explain.*

EXAMPLE 4
for Exs. 45–48

45. **MANUFACTURING** At a factory, molten glass is poured into molds to make paperweights. Each mold is a rectangular prism with a height 4 inches greater than the length of each side of its square base. Each mold holds 63 cubic inches of molten glass. What are the dimensions of the mold?

46. **SWIMMING POOL** You are designing a rectangular swimming pool that is to be set into the ground. The width of the pool is 5 feet more than the depth, and the length is 35 feet more than the depth. The pool holds 2000 cubic feet of water. What are the dimensions of the pool?

GEOMETRY In Exercises 47 and 48, write a polynomial equation to model the situation. Then list the possible rational solutions of the equation.

47. A rectangular prism has edges of lengths x, $x - 1$, and $x - 2$ and a volume of 24.

48. A pyramid has a square base with sides of length x, a height of $2x - 5$, and a volume of 3.

49. **MULTI-STEP PROBLEM** From 1994 to 2003, the amount of athletic equipment E (in millions of dollars) sold domestically can be modeled by

$$E(t) = -10t^3 + 140t^2 - 20t + 18{,}150$$

where t is the number of years since 1994. Use the following steps to find the year when about $20,300,000,000 of athletic equipment was sold.

   a. Write a polynomial equation that can be used to find the answer.

   b. List the possible whole-number solutions of the equation in part (a) that are less than 10.

   c. Use synthetic division to determine which of the possible solutions in part (b) is an actual solution. Then calculate the year which corresponds to the solution.

50. ★ **EXTENDED RESPONSE** Since 1990, the number of U.S. travelers to foreign countries F (in thousands) can be modeled by

$$F(t) = 12t^4 - 264t^3 + 2028t^2 - 3924t + 43{,}916$$

where t is the number of years since 1990. Use the following steps to find the year when there were about 56,300,000 travelers.

   a. Write a polynomial equation that can be used to find the answer.

   b. List the possible whole-number solutions of the equation in part (a) that are less than or equal to 10.

   c. Use synthetic division to determine which of the possible solutions in part (b) is an actual solution.

   d. Graph the function $F(t)$ and explain why there are no other reasonable solutions. Then calculate the year which corresponds to the solution.

○ = See WORKED-OUT SOLUTIONS in Student Resources   ★ = STANDARDIZED TEST PRACTICE

51. CHALLENGE You are building a pair of ramps for a loading platform. The left ramp is twice as long as the right ramp. If 150 cubic feet of concrete are used to build the two ramps, what are the dimensions of each ramp?

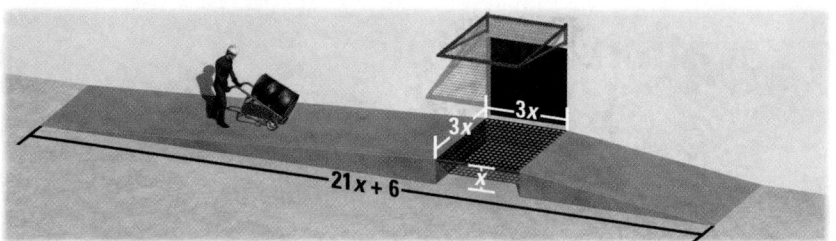

QUIZ

Factor the polynomial completely.

1. $2x^3 - 54$
2. $x^3 - 3x^2 + 2x - 6$
3. $x^3 + x^2 + x + 1$
4. $6x^5 - 150x$
5. $3x^4 - 24x^2 + 48$
6. $2x^3 - 3x^2 - 12x + 18$

Divide using polynomial long division or synthetic division.

7. $(x^4 + x^3 - 8x^2 + 5x + 5) \div (x^2 + 5x - 2)$
8. $(4x^3 + 27x^2 + 3x + 64) \div (x + 7)$

Find all real zeros of the function.

9. $f(x) = 2x^3 - 19x^2 + 50x + 30$
10. $f(x) = x^3 - 4x^2 - 25x - 56$
11. $f(x) = x^4 + 4x^3 - 13x^2 - 4x + 12$
12. $f(x) = 4x^4 - 5x^2 + 42x - 20$

13. **LANDSCAPING** You are a landscape artist designing a square patio that is to be made from 128 cubic feet of concrete. The thickness of the patio is 15.5 feet less than each side length. What are the dimensions of the patio?

my.hrw.com
Keystrokes

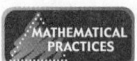

Use the Location Principle

MATHEMATICAL PRACTICES

Use appropriate tools strategically.

QUESTION How can you use the Location Principle to identify zeros of a polynomial function?

You can use the following result, called the *Location Principle*, to help you find zeros of polynomial functions:

> If f is a polynomial function and a and b are two numbers such that $f(a) < 0$ and $f(b) > 0$, then f has at least one real zero between a and b.

EXAMPLE Find zeros of a polynomial function

Find all real zeros of $f(x) = 6x^3 + 5x^2 - 17x - 6$.

STEP 1 *Enter values for x*

Enter "x" into cell A1. Enter "0" into cell A2. Type "=A2+1" into cell A3. Select cells A3 through A7, and use the *fill down* command to fill in values of x.

	A	B
1	x	
2	0	
3	1	
4	2	
5	3	
6	4	
7	5	

STEP 2 *Enter values for f(x)*

Enter "$f(x)$" into cell B1. Enter "=6*A2^3+5*A2^2−17*A2−6" into cell B2. Select cells B2 through B7, and use the *fill down* command to fill in the values of $f(x)$.

	A	B
1	x	f(x)
2	0	−6
3	1	−12
4	2	28
5	3	150
6	4	390
7	5	784

STEP 3 *Use Location Principle*

The spreadsheet in Step 2 shows that $f(1) < 0$ and $f(2) > 0$. So, by the Location Principle, f has a zero between 1 and 2. The rational zero theorem shows that the only possible *rational* zero between 1 and 2 is $\frac{3}{2}$. Synthetic division confirms that $\frac{3}{2}$ is a zero and that f can be factored as:

$$f(x) = \left(x - \frac{3}{2}\right)(6x^2 + 14x + 4) = (2x - 3)(3x^2 + 7x + 2) = (2x - 3)(3x + 1)(x + 2)$$

▶ The zeros of f are $\frac{3}{2}$, $-\frac{1}{3}$, and -2.

PRACTICE

Find all real zeros of the function.

1. $f(x) = 6x^3 - 10x^2 - 6x + 10$

2. $f(x) = 24x^4 - 38x^3 - 191x^2 - 157x - 28$

3. $f(x) = 36x^3 + 109x^2 - 341x + 70$

4. $f(x) = 12x^4 + 25x^3 - 160x^2 - 305x - 132$

2.7 Apply the Fundamental Theorem of Algebra

Before	You found zeros using the rational zero theorem.
Now	You will classify the zeros of polynomial functions.
Why?	So you can determine boat speed, as in Example 6.

Key Vocabulary
- **repeated solution**
- **irrational conjugates**
- **complex conjugates**

The equation $x^3 - 5x^2 - 8x + 48 = 0$, which becomes $(x + 3)(x - 4)^2 = 0$ when factored, has only two distinct solutions: -3 and 4. Because the factor $x - 4$ appears twice, however, you can count the solution 4 twice. So, with 4 counted as a **repeated solution**, this *third*-degree equation has *three* solutions: -3, 4, and 4.

The previous result is generalized by the *fundamental theorem of algebra*, first proved by the German mathematician Karl Friedrich Gauss (1777–1855).

CC.9-12.N.CN.9 (+) Know the Fundamental Theorem of Algebra; show that it is true for quadratic polynomials.

KEY CONCEPT   *For Your Notebook*

The Fundamental Theorem of Algebra

Theorem: If $f(x)$ is a polynomial of degree n where $n > 0$, then the equation $f(x) = 0$ has at least one solution in the set of complex numbers.

Corollary: If $f(x)$ is a polynomial of degree n where $n > 0$, then the equation $f(x) = 0$ has exactly n solutions provided each solution repeated twice is counted as 2 solutions, each solution repeated three times is counted as 3 solutions, and so on.

The corollary to the fundamental theorem of algebra also implies that an nth-degree polynomial function f has exactly n zeros.

EXAMPLE 1 Find the number of solutions or zeros

a. How many solutions does the equation $x^3 + 5x^2 + 4x + 20 = 0$ have?

b. How many zeros does the function $f(x) = x^4 - 8x^3 + 18x^2 - 27$ have?

Solution

a. Because $x^3 + 5x^2 + 4x + 20 = 0$ is a polynomial equation of degree 3, it has three solutions. (The solutions are -5, $-2i$, and $2i$.)

b. Because $f(x) = x^4 - 8x^3 + 18x^2 - 27$ is a polynomial function of degree 4, it has four zeros. (The zeros are -1, 3, 3, and 3.)

✓ **GUIDED PRACTICE**   for Example 1

1. How many solutions does the equation $x^4 + 5x^2 - 36 = 0$ have?

2. How many zeros does the function $f(x) = x^3 + 7x^2 + 8x - 16$ have?

EXAMPLE 2   **Find the zeros of a polynomial function**

Find all zeros of $f(x) = x^5 - 4x^4 + 4x^3 + 10x^2 - 13x - 14$.

Solution

STEP 1   **Find** the rational zeros of f. Because f is a polynomial function of degree 5, it has 5 zeros. The possible rational zeros are ± 1, ± 2, ± 7, and ± 14. Using synthetic division, you can determine that -1 is a zero repeated twice and 2 is also a zero.

STEP 2   **Write** $f(x)$ in factored form. Dividing $f(x)$ by its known factors $x + 1$, $x + 1$, and $x - 2$ gives a quotient of $x^2 - 4x + 7$. Therefore:

$$f(x) = (x + 1)^2(x - 2)(x^2 - 4x + 7)$$

STEP 3   **Find** the complex zeros of f. Use the quadratic formula to factor the trinomial into linear factors.

$$f(x) = (x + 1)^2(x - 2)\left[x - \left(2 + i\sqrt{3}\right)\right]\left[x - \left(2 - i\sqrt{3}\right)\right]$$

▶ The zeros of f are -1, -1, 2, $2 + i\sqrt{3}$, and $2 - i\sqrt{3}$.

BEHAVIOR NEAR ZEROS   The graph of f in Example 2 is shown at the right. Note that only the *real* zeros appear as x-intercepts. Also note that the graph is tangent to the x-axis at the repeated zero $x = -1$, but crosses the x-axis at the zero $x = 2$. This concept can be generalized as follows:

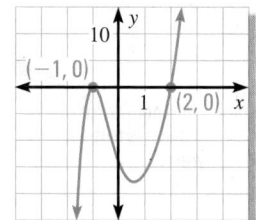

- When a factor $x - k$ of a function f is raised to an odd power, the graph of f crosses the x-axis at $x = k$.

- When a factor $x - k$ of a function f is raised to an even power, the graph of f is tangent to the x-axis at $x = k$.

✓   **GUIDED PRACTICE**   for Example 2

Find all zeros of the polynomial function.

3. $f(x) = x^3 + 7x^2 + 15x + 9$ **4.** $f(x) = x^5 - 2x^4 + 8x^2 - 13x + 6$

REVIEW COMPLEX NUMBERS

For help with complex conjugates, you may want to review the lesson *Perform Operations with Complex Numbers.*

COMPLEX CONJUGATES   Also in Example 2, notice that the zeros $2 + i\sqrt{3}$ and $2 - i\sqrt{3}$ are complex conjugates. This illustrates the first theorem given below. A similar result applies to irrational zeros of polynomial functions, as shown in the second theorem below.

KEY CONCEPT   *For Your Notebook*

Complex Conjugates Theorem

If f is a polynomial function with real coefficients, and $a + bi$ is an imaginary zero of f, then $a - bi$ is also a zero of f.

Irrational Conjugates Theorem

Suppose f is a polynomial function with rational coefficients, and a and b are rational numbers such that $\sqrt{b}$ is irrational. If $a + \sqrt{b}$ is a zero of f, then $a - \sqrt{b}$ is also a zero of f.

EXAMPLE 3 **Use zeros to write a polynomial function**

Write a polynomial function f of least degree that has rational coefficients, a leading coefficient of 1, and 3 and $2 + \sqrt{5}$ as zeros.

Solution

Because the coefficients are rational and $2 + \sqrt{5}$ is a zero, $2 - \sqrt{5}$ must also be a zero by the irrational conjugates theorem. Use the three zeros and the factor theorem to write $f(x)$ as a product of three factors.

$$f(x) = (x - 3)\left[x - \left(2 + \sqrt{5}\right)\right]\left[x - \left(2 - \sqrt{5}\right)\right] \quad \text{Write } f(x) \text{ in factored form.}$$

$$= (x - 3)\left[(x - 2) - \sqrt{5}\right]\left[(x - 2) + \sqrt{5}\right] \quad \text{Regroup terms.}$$

$$= (x - 3)[(x - 2)^2 - 5] \quad \text{Multiply.}$$

$$= (x - 3)[(x^2 - 4x + 4) - 5] \quad \text{Expand binomial.}$$

$$= (x - 3)(x^2 - 4x - 1) \quad \text{Simplify.}$$

$$= x^3 - 4x^2 - x - 3x^2 + 12x + 3 \quad \text{Multiply.}$$

$$= x^3 - 7x^2 + 11x + 3 \quad \text{Combine like terms.}$$

CHECK You can check this result by evaluating $f(x)$ at each of its three zeros.

$$f(3) = 3^3 - 7(3)^2 + 11(3) + 3 = 27 - 63 + 33 + 3 = 0 \checkmark$$

$$f\left(2 + \sqrt{5}\right) = \left(2 + \sqrt{5}\right)^3 - 7\left(2 + \sqrt{5}\right)^2 + 11\left(2 + \sqrt{5}\right) + 3$$

$$= 38 + 17\sqrt{5} - 63 - 28\sqrt{5} + 22 + 11\sqrt{5} + 3$$

$$= 0 \checkmark$$

Since $f\left(2 + \sqrt{5}\right) = 0$, by the irrational conjugates theorem $f\left(2 - \sqrt{5}\right) = 0$. $\checkmark$

 GUIDED PRACTICE for Example 3

Write a polynomial function f of least degree that has rational coefficients, a leading coefficient of 1, and the given zeros.

5. $-1, 2, 4$ **6.** $4, 1 + \sqrt{5}$ **7.** $2, 2i, 4 - \sqrt{6}$ **8.** $3, 3 - i$

DESCARTES' RULE OF SIGNS French mathematician René Descartes (1596–1650) found the following relationship between the coefficients of a polynomial function and the number of positive and negative zeros of the function.

KEY CONCEPT *For Your Notebook*

Descartes' Rule of Signs

Let $f(x) = a_n x^n + a_{n-1} x^{n-1} + \cdots + a_2 x^2 + a_1 x + a_0$ be a polynomial function with real coefficients.

- The number of *positive real zeros* of f is equal to the number of changes in sign of the coefficients of $f(x)$ or is less than this by an even number.

- The number of *negative real zeros* of f is equal to the number of changes in sign of the coefficients of $f(-x)$ or is less than this by an even number.

EXAMPLE 4   **Use Descartes' rule of signs**

Determine the possible numbers of positive real zeros, negative real zeros, and imaginary zeros for $f(x) = x^6 - 2x^5 + 3x^4 - 10x^3 - 6x^2 - 8x - 8$.

Solution

$$f(x) = x^6 - 2x^5 + 3x^4 - 10x^3 - 6x^2 - 8x - 8$$

The coefficients in $f(x)$ have **3 sign changes**, so f has 3 or 1 positive real zero(s).

$$f(-x) = (-x)^6 - 2(-x)^5 + 3(-x)^4 - 10(-x)^3 - 6(-x)^2 - 8(-x) - 8$$
$$= x^6 + 2x^5 + 3x^4 + 10x^3 - 6x^2 + 8x - 8$$

The coefficients in $f(-x)$ have **3 sign changes**, so f has 3 or 1 negative real zero(s).

The possible numbers of zeros for f are summarized in the table below.

Positive real zeros	Negative real zeros	Imaginary zeros	Total zeros
3	3	0	6
3	1	2	6
1	3	2	6
1	1	4	6

✓ **GUIDED PRACTICE**   for Example 4

Determine the possible numbers of positive real zeros, negative real zeros, and imaginary zeros for the function.

9. $f(x) = x^3 + 2x - 11$ **10.** $g(x) = 2x^4 - 8x^3 + 6x^2 - 3x + 1$

APPROXIMATING ZEROS All of the zeros of the function in Example 4 are irrational or imaginary. Irrational zeros can be approximated using technology.

EXAMPLE 5   **Approximate real zeros**

Approximate the real zeros of $f(x) = x^6 - 2x^5 + 3x^4 - 10x^3 - 6x^2 - 8x - 8$.

Solution

ANOTHER WAY
In Example 5, you can also approximate the zeros of f using the calculator's *trace* feature. However, this generally gives less precise results than the *zero* (or *root*) feature.

Use the *zero* (or *root*) feature of a graphing calculator, as shown below.

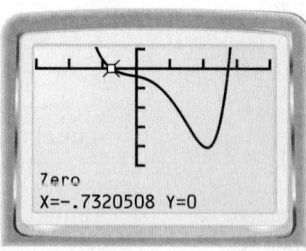

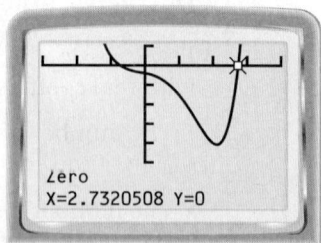

▶ From these screens, you can see that the zeros are $x \approx -0.73$ and $x \approx 2.73$.

EXAMPLE 6 **Approximate real zeros of a polynomial model**

TACHOMETER A tachometer measures the speed (in revolutions per minute, or RPMs) at which an engine shaft rotates. For a certain boat, the speed x of the engine shaft (in 100s of RPMs) and the speed s of the boat (in miles per hour) are modeled by

$$s(x) = 0.00547x^3 - 0.225x^2 + 3.62x - 11.0$$

What is the tachometer reading when the boat travels 15 miles per hour?

Solution

Substitute 15 for $s(x)$ in the given function. You can rewrite the resulting equation as:

$$0 = 0.00547x^3 - 0.225x^2 + 3.62x - 26.0$$

Then, use a graphing calculator to approximate the real zeros of $f(x) = 0.00547x^3 - 0.225x^2 + 3.62x - 26.0$.

From the graph, there is one real zero: $x \approx 19.9$.

▶ The tachometer reading is about 1990 RPMs.

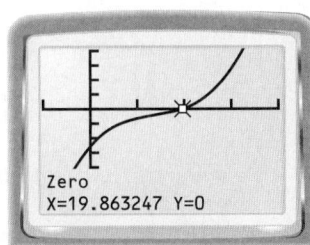

Zero
X=19.863247 Y=0

✓ **GUIDED PRACTICE** for Examples 5 and 6

11. Approximate the real zeros of $f(x) = 3x^5 + 2x^4 - 8x^3 + 4x^2 - x - 1$.

12. WHAT IF? In Example 6, what is the tachometer reading when the boat travels 20 miles per hour?

2.7 **EXERCISES**

HOMEWORK KEY

○ = See WORKED-OUT SOLUTIONS
Exs. 15, 37, and 61

★ = STANDARDIZED TEST PRACTICE
Exs. 2, 9, 33, 51, 52, 63, and 64

SKILL PRACTICE

1. VOCABULARY Copy and complete: For the equation $(x - 1)^2(x + 2) = 0$, a(n) __?__ solution is 1 because the factor $x - 1$ appears twice.

2. ★ WRITING *Explain* the difference between complex conjugates and irrational conjugates.

EXAMPLE 1
for Exs. 3–9

NUMBER OF SOLUTIONS OR ZEROS Identify the number of solutions or zeros.

3. $x^4 + 2x^3 - 4x^2 + x - 10 = 0$

4. $5y^3 - 3y^2 + 8y = 0$

5. $9t^6 - 14t^3 + 4t - 1 = 0$

6. $f(z) = -7z^4 + z^2 - 25$

7. $g(s) = 12s^7 - 9s^6 + 4s^5 - s^3 - 20s + 50$

8. $h(x) = -x^{12} + 7x^8 + 5x^4 - 8x + 6$

9. ★ MULTIPLE CHOICE How many zeros does the function $f(x) = 16x - 22x^3 + 6x^6 + 19x^5 - 3$ have?

   (A) 1   **(B)** 3   **(C)** 5   **(D)** 6

©Photodisc/Getty Images

EXAMPLE 2
for Exs. 10–19

FINDING ZEROS Find all zeros of the polynomial function.

10. $f(x) = x^4 - 6x^3 + 7x^2 + 6x - 8$

11. $f(x) = x^4 + 5x^3 - 7x^2 - 29x + 30$

12. $g(x) = x^4 - 9x^2 - 4x + 12$

13. $h(x) = x^3 + 5x^2 - 4x - 20$

14. $f(x) = x^4 + 15x^2 - 16$

15. $f(x) = x^4 + x^3 + 2x^2 + 4x - 8$

16. $h(x) = x^4 + 4x^3 + 7x^2 + 16x + 12$

17. $g(x) = x^4 - 2x^3 - 3x^2 + 2x + 2$

18. $g(x) = 4x^4 + 4x^3 - 11x^2 - 12x - 3$

19. $h(x) = 2x^4 + 13x^3 + 19x^2 - 10x - 24$

EXAMPLE 3
for Exs. 20–32

WRITING POLYNOMIAL FUNCTIONS Write a polynomial function f of least degree that has rational coefficients, a leading coefficient of 1, and the given zeros.

20. $1, 2, 3$

21. $-2, 1, 3$

22. $-5, -1, 2$

23. $-3, 1, 6$

24. $2, -i, i$

25. $3i, 2 - i$

26. $-1, 2, -3i$

27. $5, 5, 4 + i$

28. $4, -\sqrt{5}, \sqrt{5}$

29. $-4, 1, 2 - \sqrt{6}$

30. $-2, -1, 2, 3, \sqrt{11}$

31. $3, 4 + 2i, 1 + \sqrt{7}$

32. ERROR ANALYSIS *Describe* and correct the error in writing a polynomial function with rational coefficients and zeros 2 and $1 + i$.

$$f(x) = (x - 2)[x - (1 + i)]$$
$$= x(x - 1 - i) - 2(x - 1 - i)$$
$$= x^2 - x - ix - 2x + 2 + 2i$$
$$= x^2 - (3 + i)x + (2 + 2i)$$

33. ★ OPEN-ENDED MATH Write a polynomial function of degree 5 with zeros 1, 2, and $-i$.

EXAMPLE 4
for Exs. 34–41

CLASSIFYING ZEROS Determine the possible numbers of positive real zeros, negative real zeros, and imaginary zeros for the function.

34. $f(x) = x^4 - x^2 - 6$

35. $g(x) = -x^3 + 5x^2 + 12$

36. $g(x) = x^3 - 4x^2 + 8x + 7$

37. $h(x) = x^5 - 2x^3 - x^2 + 6x + 5$

38. $h(x) = x^5 - 3x^3 + 8x - 10$

39. $f(x) = x^5 + 7x^4 - 4x^3 - 3x^2 + 9x - 15$

40. $g(x) = x^6 + x^5 - 3x^4 + x^3 + 5x^2 + 9x - 18$

41. $f(x) = x^7 + 4x^4 - 10x + 25$

EXAMPLE 5
for Exs. 42–49

APPROXIMATING ZEROS Use a graphing calculator to graph the function. Then use the *zero* (or *root*) feature to approximate the real zeros of the function.

42. $f(x) = x^3 - x^2 - 8x + 5$

43. $f(x) = -x^4 - 4x^2 + x + 8$

44. $g(x) = x^3 - 3x^2 + x + 6$

45. $h(x) = x^4 - 5x - 3$

46. $h(x) = 3x^3 - x^2 - 5x + 3$

47. $g(x) = x^4 - x^3 + 2x^2 - 6x - 3$

48. $f(x) = 2x^6 + x^4 + 31x^2 - 35$

49. $g(x) = x^5 - 16x^3 - 3x^2 + 42x + 30$

50. REASONING Two zeros of $f(x) = x^3 - 6x^2 - 16x + 96$ are 4 and -4. *Explain* why the third zero must also be a real number.

51. ★ SHORT RESPONSE *Describe* the possible numbers of positive real, negative real, and imaginary zeros for a cubic function with rational coefficients.

52. ★ MULTIPLE CHOICE Which is *not* a possible classification of the zeros of $f(x) = x^5 - 4x^3 + 6x^2 + 12x - 6$ according to Descartes' rule of signs?

   Ⓐ 3 positive real zeros, 2 negative real zeros, and 0 imaginary zeros

   Ⓑ 3 positive real zeros, 0 negative real zeros, and 2 imaginary zeros

   Ⓒ 1 positive real zero, 4 negative real zeros, and 0 imaginary zeros

   Ⓓ 1 positive real zero, 2 negative real zeros, and 2 imaginary zeros

◯ = See **WORKED-OUT SOLUTIONS** in Student Resources   ★ = **STANDARDIZED TEST PRACTICE**

CLASSIFYING ZEROS Determine the numbers of positive real zeros, negative real zeros, and imaginary zeros for the function with the given degree and graph. *Explain* your reasoning.

53. Degree: 3

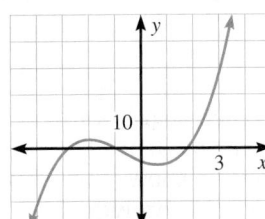

54. Degree: 4

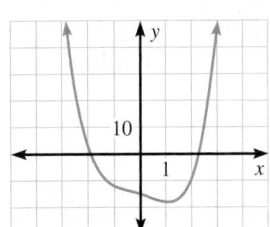

55. Degree: 5

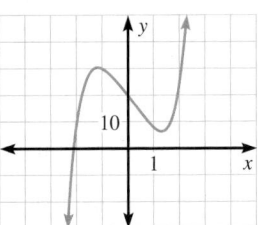

CHALLENGE Show that the given number is a zero of the given function but that the conjugate of the number is *not* a zero.

56. $f(x) = x^3 - 2x^2 + 2x + 5i; 2 - i$

57. $g(x) = x^3 + 2x^2 + 2i - 2; -1 + i$

58. *Explain* why the results of Exercises 56 and 57 do not contradict the complex conjugate theorem.

PROBLEM SOLVING

EXAMPLE 6
for Exs. 59–62

59. BUSINESS For the 12 years that a grocery store has been open, its annual revenue R (in millions of dollars) can be modeled by the function

$$R = 0.0001(-t^4 + 12t^3 - 77t^2 + 600t + 13{,}650)$$

where t is the number of years since the store opened. In which year(s) was the revenue $1.5 million?

60. ENVIRONMENT From 1990 to 2003, the number N of inland lakes in Michigan infested with zebra mussels can be modeled by the function

$$N = -0.028t^4 + 0.59t^3 - 2.5t^2 + 8.3t - 2.5$$

where t is the number of years since 1990. In which year did the number of infested inland lakes first reach 120?

Pipe clogged with zebra mussels

61. PHYSIOLOGY A study group found that a person's score S on a step-climbing exercise test was related to his or her amount of hemoglobin x (in grams per 100 milliliters of blood) by this function:

$$S = -0.015x^3 + 0.6x^2 - 2.4x + 19$$

Given that the normal range of hemoglobin is 12–18 grams per 100 milliliters of blood, what is the most likely amount of hemoglobin for a person who scores 75?

62. POPULATION From 1890 to 2000, the American Indian, Eskimo, and Aleut population P (in thousands) can be modeled by the function

$$P = 0.0035t^3 - 0.235t^2 + 4.87t + 243$$

where t is the number of years since 1890. In which year did the population first reach 722,000?

63. ★ **SHORT RESPONSE** A 60-inch-long bookshelf is warped under 180 pounds of books. The deflection d of the bookshelf (in inches) is given by

$$d = (2.724 \times 10^{-7})x^4 - (3.269 \times 10^{-5})x^3 + (9.806 \times 10^{-4})x^2$$

where x is the distance (in inches) from the bookshelf's left end. Approximate the real zeros of the function on the domain $0 \le x \le 60$. *Explain* why all your answers make sense in this situation.

64. ★ **EXTENDED RESPONSE** You plan to save $1000 each year towards buying a used car in four years. At the end of each summer, you deposit $1000 earned from summer jobs into your bank account. The table shows the value of your deposits over the four year period. In the table, g is the growth factor $1 + r$ where r is the annual interest rate expressed as a decimal.

	Year 1	Year 2	Year 3	Year 4
Value of 1st deposit	1000	$1000g$	$1000g^2$	$1000g^3$
Value of 2nd deposit	–	1000	?	?
Value of 3rd deposit	–	–	1000	?
Value of 4th deposit	–	–	–	1000

  a. Apply Copy and complete the table.

  b. Model Write a polynomial function that gives the value v of your account at the end of the fourth summer in terms of g.

  c. Reasoning You want to buy a car that costs about $4300. What growth factor do you need to obtain this amount? What annual interest rate do you need? *Explain* how you found your answers.

65. CHALLENGE A monument with the dimensions shown is to be built using 1000 cubic feet of marble. What is the value of x?

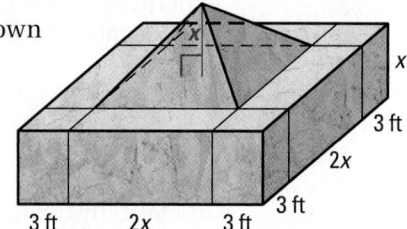

2.8 Analyze Graphs of Polynomial Functions

Before	You graphed polynomial functions by making tables.
Now	You will use intercepts to graph polynomial functions.
Why?	So you can maximize the volume of structures, as in Ex. 42.

Key Vocabulary
• local maximum
• local minimum

CC.9-12.F.IF.7 Graph functions expressed symbolically and show key features of the graph, by hand in simple cases and using technology for more complicated cases.*
c. Graph polynomial functions, identifying zeros when suitable factorizations are available, and showing end behavior.

In this chapter you have learned that zeros, factors, solutions, and x-intercepts are closely related concepts. The relationships are summarized below.

CONCEPT SUMMARY   *For Your Notebook*

Zeros, Factors, Solutions, and Intercepts

Let $f(x) = a_n x^n + a_{n-1} x^{n-1} + \cdots + a_1 x + a_0$ be a polynomial function. The following statements are equivalent.

Zero: k is a zero of the polynomial function f.

Factor: $x - k$ is a factor of the polynomial $f(x)$.

Solution: k is a solution of the polynomial equation $f(x) = 0$.

x-intercept: If k is a real number, k is an x-intercept of the graph of the polynomial function f. The graph of f passes through $(k, 0)$.

EXAMPLE 1   Use x-intercepts to graph a polynomial function

Graph the function $f(x) = \frac{1}{6}(x + 3)(x - 2)^2$.

Solution

STEP 1   **Plot** the intercepts. Because -3 and 2 are zeros of f, plot $(-3, 0)$ and $(2, 0)$.

STEP 2   **Plot** points between and beyond the x-intercepts.

x	-2	-1	0	1	3
y	$\frac{8}{3}$	3	2	$\frac{2}{3}$	1

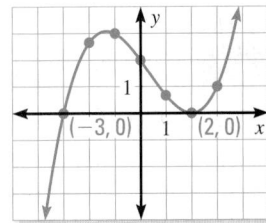

STEP 3   **Determine** end behavior. Because f has three factors of the form $x - k$ and a constant factor of $\frac{1}{6}$, it is a cubic function with a positive leading coefficient. So, $f(x) \to -\infty$ as $x \to -\infty$ and $f(x) \to +\infty$ as $x \to +\infty$.

STEP 4   **Draw** the graph so that it passes through the plotted points and has the appropriate end behavior.

TURNING POINTS Another important characteristic of graphs of polynomial functions is that they have *turning points* corresponding to local maximum and minimum values.

- The *y*-coordinate of a turning point is a **local maximum** of the function if the point is higher than all nearby points.

- The *y*-coordinate of a turning point is a **local minimum** of the function if the point is lower than all nearby points.

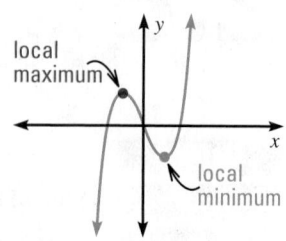

ANALYZE GRAPHS

The turning points of a graph help determine the intervals for which a function is increasing or decreasing. You can write these intervals using *interval notation*.

KEY CONCEPT   *For Your Notebook*

Turning Points of Polynomial Functions

1. The graph of every polynomial function of degree *n* has *at most n − 1* turning points.

2. If a polynomial function has *n* distinct real zeros, then its graph has *exactly n − 1* turning points.

EXAMPLE 2   **Find turning points**

Graph the function. Identify the *x*-intercepts and the points where the local maximums and local minimums occur.

a. $f(x) = x^3 - 3x^2 + 6$ b. $g(x) = x^4 - 6x^3 + 3x^2 + 10x - 3$

Solution

a. Use a graphing calculator to graph the function.

Notice that the graph of *f* has one *x*-intercept and two turning points.

FIND MAXIMUMS AND MINIMUMS

For help with using the *maximum* and *minimum* features of a graphing calculator, see the Graphing Calculator Activity used after the lesson *Graph Quadratic Functions in Standard Form*.

You can use the graphing calculator's *zero*, *maximum*, and *minimum* features to approximate the coordinates of the points.

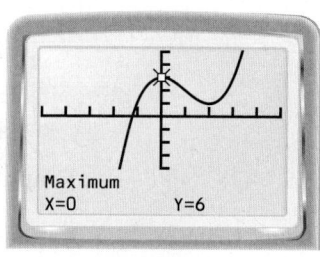

▶ The *x*-intercept of the graph is $x \approx -1.20$. The function has a local maximum at **(0, 6)** and a local minimum at **(2, 2)**.

b. Use a graphing calculator to graph the function.

Notice that the graph of *g* has four *x*-intercepts and three turning points.

You can use the graphing calculator's *zero*, *maximum*, and *minimum* features to approximate the coordinates of the points.

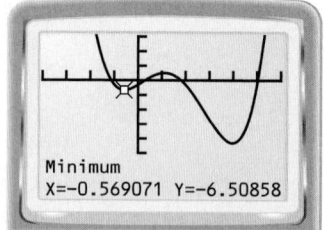

▶ The *x*-intercepts of the graph are $x \approx -1.14$, $x \approx 0.29$, $x \approx 1.82$, and $x \approx 5.03$. The function has a local maximum at **(1.11, 5.11)** and local minimums at **(−0.57, −6.51)** and **(3.96, −43.04)**.

Animated Algebra at my.hrw.com

◆ **EXAMPLE 3** **Maximize a polynomial model**

ARTS AND CRAFTS You are making a rectangular box out of a 16-inch-by-20-inch piece of cardboard. The box will be formed by making the cuts shown in the diagram and folding up the sides. You want the box to have the greatest volume possible.

• How long should you make the cuts?

• What is the maximum volume?

• What will the dimensions of the finished box be?

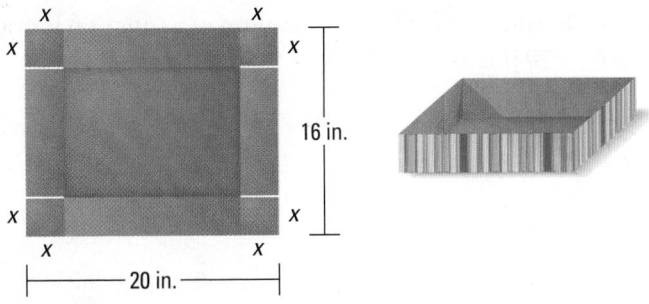

Solution

Write a verbal model for the volume. Then write a function.

Volume (cubic inches)	=	Length (inches)	·	Width (inches)	·	Height (inches)

$$V = (20 - 2x) \cdot (16 - 2x) \cdot x$$

$$= (320 - 72x + 4x^2)x \qquad \text{Multiply binomials.}$$

$$= 4x^3 - 72x^2 + 320x \qquad \text{Write in standard form.}$$

To find the maximum volume, graph the volume function on a graphing calculator, as shown at the right. Consider only the interval $0 < x < 8$ because this describes the physical restrictions on the size of the flaps.

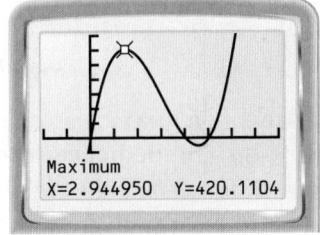

From the graph, you can see that the maximum volume is about 420 and occurs when $x \approx 2.94$.

▶ You should make the cuts about 3 inches long. The maximum volume is about 420 cubic inches. The dimensions of the box with this volume will be about 3 inches by 10 inches by 14 inches.

✓ **GUIDED PRACTICE** for Examples 1, 2, and 3

Graph the function. Identify the *x*-intercepts and the points where the local maximums and local minimums occur.

1. $f(x) = 0.25(x + 2)(x - 1)(x - 3)$ **2.** $g(x) = 2(x - 1)^2(x - 4)$

3. $h(x) = 0.5x^3 + x^2 - x + 2$ **4.** $f(x) = x^4 + 3x^3 - x^2 - 4x - 5$

5. **WHAT IF?** In Example 3, how do the answers change if the piece of cardboard is 10 inches by 15 inches?

2.8 EXERCISES

HOMEWORK
KEY

◯ = See WORKED-OUT SOLUTIONS
   Exs. 3, 19, and 41

★ = STANDARDIZED TEST PRACTICE
   Exs. 2, 21, 30, 32, 33, and 43

◆ = MULTIPLE REPRESENTATIONS
   Ex. 42

SKILL PRACTICE

1. **VOCABULARY** Copy and complete: A local maximum or local minimum of a polynomial function occurs at a __?__ point of the function's graph.

2. ★ **WRITING** *Explain* what a local maximum of a function is and how it may be different from the maximum value of the function.

EXAMPLE 1
for Exs. 3–14

GRAPHING POLYNOMIAL FUNCTIONS **Graph the function.**

3. $f(x) = (x - 2)^2(x + 1)$

4. $f(x) = (x + 1)^2(x - 1)(x - 3)$

5. $g(x) = \frac{1}{3}(x - 5)(x + 2)(x - 3)$

6. $h(x) = \frac{1}{12}(x + 4)(x + 8)(x - 1)$

7. $h(x) = 4(x + 1)(x + 2)(x - 1)$

8. $f(x) = 0.2(x - 4)^2(x + 1)^2$

9. $f(x) = 2(x + 2)^2(x + 4)^2$

10. $h(x) = 5(x - 1)(x - 2)(x - 3)$

11. $g(x) = (x - 3)(x^2 + x + 1)$

12. $h(x) = (x - 4)(2x^2 - 2x + 1)$

ERROR ANALYSIS *Describe* and correct the error in graphing *f*.

13. $f(x) = (x + 2)(x - 1)^2$

14. $f(x) = x(x - 3)^3$

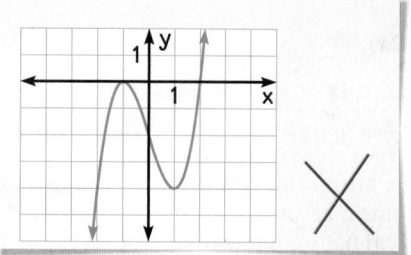

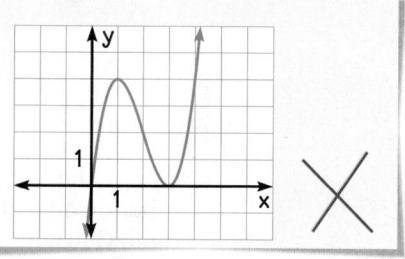

EXAMPLE 2
for Exs. 15–30

ANALYZING GRAPHS **Estimate the coordinates of each turning point and state whether each corresponds to a local maximum or a local minimum. Then estimate all real zeros and determine the least degree the function can have.**

15.

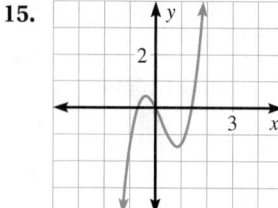

16.

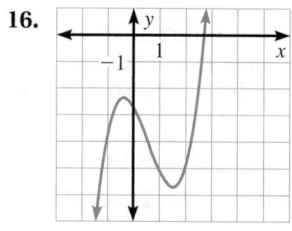

17.

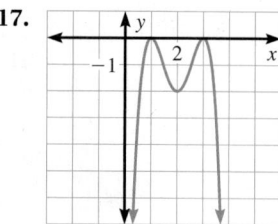

18.

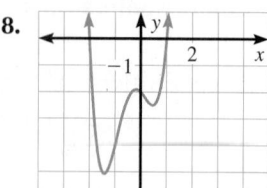

19.

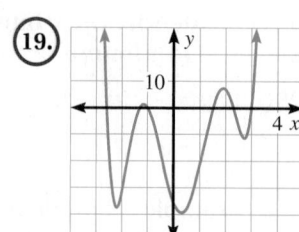

20.

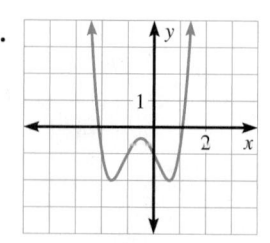

21. ★ **MULTIPLE CHOICE** Which point is a local maximum of the function $f(x) = 0.25(x + 2)(x - 1)^2$?

(A) $(-2, 0)$ **(B)** $(-1, 1)$ **(C)** $(1, 0)$ **(D)** $(2, 1)$

GRAPHING CALCULATOR Use a graphing calculator to graph the polynomial function. Identify the x-intercepts and the points where the local maximums and local minimums occur.

22. $f(x) = 2x^3 + 8x^2 - 3$ **23.** $g(x) = 0.5x^3 - 2x + 2.5$

24. $h(x) = -x^4 + 3x$ **25.** $f(x) = x^5 - 4x^3 + x^2 + 2$

26. $g(x) = x^4 - 3x^2 + x$ **27.** $h(x) = x^4 - 5x^3 + 2x^2 + x - 3$

28. $h(x) = x^5 + 2x^2 - 17x - 4$ **29.** $g(x) = 0.7x^4 - 8x^3 + 5x$

30. ★ **MULTIPLE CHOICE** What is a turning point of the graph of the function $g(x) = x^4 - 9x^2 + 4x + 12$?

(A) $(-3, 0)$ **(B)** $(-1, 0)$ **(C)** $(0, 12)$ **(D)** $(2, 0)$

31. **REASONING** Why is the adjective *local*, used to describe the maximums and minimums of cubic functions, not required for quadratic functions?

32. ★ **SHORT RESPONSE** Does a cubic function *always*, *sometimes*, or *never* have a turning point? *Justify* your answer.

33. ★ **OPEN-ENDED MATH** Choose one of the functions from Exercises 22–29. On what interval(s) is the function positive? negative? increasing? decreasing?

DOMAIN AND RANGE Graph the function. Then identify its domain and range.

34. $f(x) = x(x - 3)^2$ **35.** $f(x) = x^2(x - 2)(x - 4)(x - 5)$

36. $f(x) = (x + 1)^3(x - 1)$ **37.** $f(x) = (x + 2)(x + 1)(x - 1)^2(x - 2)^2$

38. **CHALLENGE** In general, what can you say about the domain and range of odd-degree polynomial functions? What can you say about the domain and range of even-degree polynomial functions?

PROBLEM SOLVING

EXAMPLE 3
for Exs. 39–40

In Exercises 39 and 40, assume that the box is constructed using the method illustrated in Example 3 of this lesson.

39. **POSTCARDS** Marcie wants to make a box to hold her postcard collection from a piece of cardboard that is 10 inches by 18 inches. What are the dimensions of the box with the maximum volume? What is the maximum volume of the box?

40. **COIN COLLECTION** Jorge is making a box for his coin collection from a piece of cardboard that is 30 centimeters by 40 centimeters. What are the dimensions of the box with the maximum volume? What is the maximum volume of the box?

41. **SWIMMING** For a swimmer doing the breaststroke, the function

$$S = -241t^7 + 1060t^6 - 1870t^5 + 1650t^4 - 737t^3 + 144t^2 - 2.43t$$

models the swimmer's speed S (in meters per second) during one complete stroke, where t is the number of seconds since the start of the stroke. Graph the function. According to the model, at what time during the stroke is the swimmer going the fastest?

42. ◆ **MULTIPLE REPRESENTATIONS** You have 600 square feet of material for building a greenhouse that is shaped like half a cylinder.

a. **Writing an Expression** The surface area S of the greenhouse is given by $S = \pi r^2 + \pi r \ell$. Substitute 600 for S and then write an expression for ℓ in terms of r.

b. **Writing a Function** The volume V of the greenhouse is given by $V = \frac{1}{2}\pi r^2 \ell$. Write an equation that gives V as a polynomial function of r alone.

c. **Graphing a Function** Graph the volume function from part (b). What are the dimensions r and ℓ that maximize the volume of the greenhouse? What is the maximum volume?

43. ★ **EXTENDED RESPONSE** From 1960 to 2001, the number of students S (in thousands) enrolled in public schools in the United States can be modeled by $S = 1.64x^3 - 102x^2 + 1710x + 36,300$ where x is the number of years since 1960.

a. Graph the function.

b. Identify any turning points on the domain $0 \le x \le 41$. What real-life meaning do these points have?

c. What is the range of the function for the domain $0 \le x \le 41$?

44. **CHALLENGE** A cylinder is inscribed in a sphere of radius 8. Write an equation for the volume of the cylinder as a function of h. Find the value of h that maximizes the volume of the inscribed cylinder. What is the maximum volume of the cylinder?

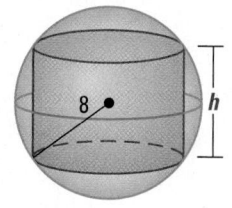

QUIZ

Find all zeros of the polynomial function.

1. $f(x) = x^3 - 4x^2 - 11x + 30$

2. $f(x) = 2x^4 - 2x^3 - 49x^2 + 9x + 180$

Write a polynomial function f of least degree that has rational coefficients, a leading coefficient of 1, and the given zeros.

3. $-4, -1, 2$

4. $4, 1 + i$

5. $-3, 5, 7 + \sqrt{2}$

6. $1, -2i, 3 - \sqrt{6}$

Graph the function.

7. $f(x) = -(x - 3)(x - 2)(x + 2)$

8. $f(x) = 3(x - 1)(x + 1)(x - 4)$

9. $f(x) = x(x - 4)(x - 1)(x + 2)$

10. $f(x) = (x - 3)(x + 2)^2(x + 3)^2$

See **EXTRA PRACTICE** in Student Resources   ⤳ **ONLINE QUIZ** at my.hrw.com

Mastering the Standards

for Mathematical Practice

The topics described in the Standards for Mathematical Content will vary from year to year. However, the *way* in which you learn, study, and think about mathematics will not. The Standards for Mathematical Practice describe skills that you will use in all of your math courses.

Mathematical Practices

1. *Make sense of problems and persevere in solving them.*
2. *Reason abstractly and quantitatively.*
3. *Construct viable arguments and critique the reasoning of others.*
4. *Model with mathematics.*
5. *Use appropriate tools strategically.*
6. *Attend to precision.*
7. *Look for and make use of structure.*
8. *Look for and express regularity in repeated reasoning.*

① Make sense of problems and persevere in solving them.

Mathematically proficient students start by explaining to themselves the meaning of a problem... They analyze givens, constraints, relationships, and goals. They make conjectures about the form... of the solution and plan a solution pathway...

In your book

Verbal Models and the **Problem Solving Plan** help you translate the information in a problem into a model and then analyze your solution.

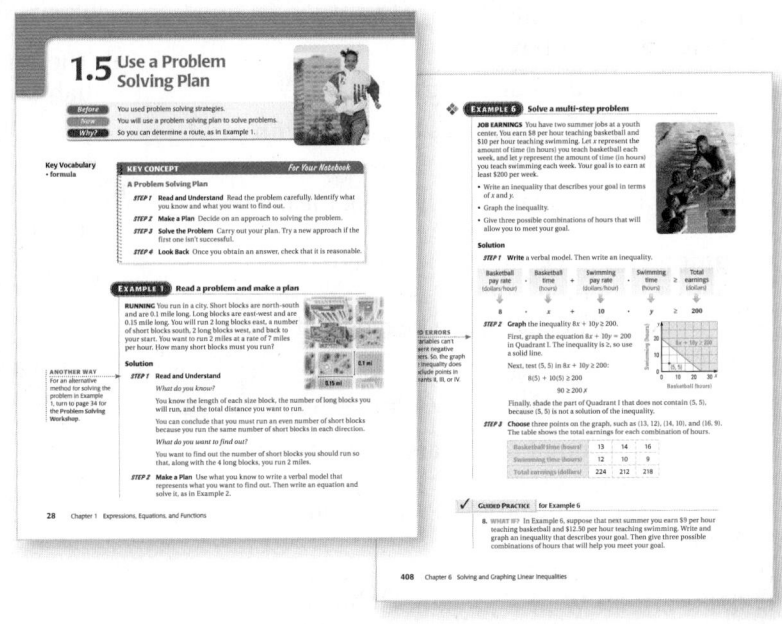

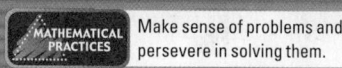

1. **MULTI-STEP PROBLEM** The volume of the rectangular prism shown is 180 cubic inches.

   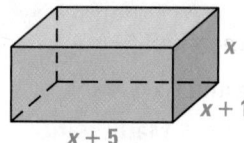

   a. Write a polynomial equation that you can use to find the value of x.

   b. Identify the possible rational solutions of the equation in part (a).

   c. Use synthetic division to find a rational solution of the equation. Show that no other real solutions exist.

   d. What are the dimensions of the prism?

2. **MULTI-STEP PROBLEM** You want to make an open box from a piece of cardboard to hold your school supplies. The box will be formed using the method described in Example 3. The original piece of cardboard is 20 inches by 30 inches.

   a. Write a polynomial function for the volume of the box.

   b. Graph the function in part (a).

   c. What are the dimensions of the box with the maximum volume?

   d. What is the maximum volume of the box?

3. **GRIDDED ANSWER** From 1980 to 2002, the number R (in thousands) of retirees receiving Social Security benefits can be modeled by the function

   $$R = 0.629t^3 - 27.8t^2 + 744t + 19{,}600$$

   where t is the number of years since 1980. In which year was the number of retirees receiving Social Security benefits about 26,900,000?

4. **OPEN-ENDED** Write a polynomial function with real coefficients that has degree 4 and zeros -2, 1, and $4 - i$.

5. **OPEN-ENDED** Write a polynomial function with rational coefficients that has 16 *possible* rational zeros according to the rational zero theorem, but has no actual rational zeros.

6. **EXTENDED RESPONSE** You are making a sculpture that is a pyramid with a square base. You want the height of the pyramid to be 4 inches less than the length of a side of the base. You want the volume of the sculpture to be 200 cubic inches.

   a. Let x represent the length (in inches) of a side of the sculpture's base. Draw a diagram of the sculpture, and label the dimensions in terms of x.

   b. Write a function that gives the volume V of the sculpture in terms of x.

   c. Graph the function in part (b). Use the graph to estimate the value of x for the sculpture.

   d. Write and solve an equation to find the value of x. *Compare* your answer with your estimate from part (c). What are the dimensions of the sculpture?

7. **MULTI-STEP PROBLEM** A zookeeper is building a cylindrical habitat for alligators. He has 4000 square feet of waterproof material to use. The habitat will not need a roof.

   a. The surface area (in square feet) of the habitat is given by $S = \pi r^2 + 2\pi rh$. Substitute 4000 for S and then write an expression for h in terms of r.

   b. The volume (in cubic feet) of the habitat is given by $V = \pi r^2 h$. Write an equation that gives V as a polynomial function of r alone.

   c. Graph the volume function from part (b). What are the dimensions r and h that maximize the volume of the habitat? What is the maximum volume?

   d. Which value of r did you have to reject when finding the maximum volume? Why?

BIG IDEAS
For Your Notebook

Big Idea ①

Graphing Polynomial Functions

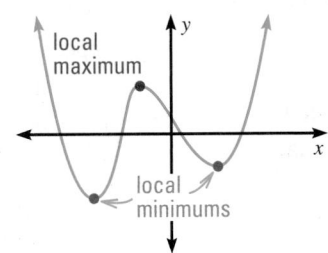

local maximum

local minimums

The end behavior of the graph of $f(x)$ is

$f(x) \to +\infty$ as $x \to -\infty$ and $f(x) \to +\infty$ as $x \to +\infty$

so $f(x)$ is of even degree and has a positive leading coefficient.

The graph has 3 turning points, so the degree of $f(x)$ is *at least* 4 and $f(x)$ has *at least* 4 zeros.

Big Idea ②

Performing Operations with Polynomials

You can add, subtract, multiply, and divide polynomials. You can also factor polynomials using any combination of the methods below.

Factoring method	Example
General trinomial	$6x^2 - 7x - 3 = (3x + 1)(2x - 3)$
Perfect square trinomial	$x^2 + 10x + 25 = (x + 5)^2$
Difference of two squares	$x^2 - 49 = (x + 7)(x - 7)$
Common monomial factor	$15x^3 + 9x^2 = 3x^2(5x + 3)$
Sum or difference of two cubes	$8x^3 - 27 = (2x - 3)(4x^2 + 6x + 9)$
Factor by grouping	$x^3 - 5x^2 + 9x - 45 = x^2(x - 5) + 9(x - 5) = (x^2 + 9)(x - 5)$

Big Idea ③

Solving Polynomial Equations and Finding Zeros

The terms *zero*, *factor*, *solution*, and *x-intercept* are closely related. Consider the function $f(x) = 2x^3 - x^2 - 13x - 6$.

-2 is a **zero** of f.	$f(-2) = 2(-2)^3 - (-2)^2 - 13(-2) - 6 = 0$
$x + 2$ is a **factor** of $f(x)$.	$2x^3 - x^2 - 13x - 6 = (x + 2)(x - 3)(2x + 1)$
$x = -2$ is a **solution** of the equation $f(x) = 0$.	$2(-2)^3 - (-2)^2 - 13(-2) - 6 = 0$
-2 is an **x-intercept** of the graph of f.	

CHAPTER REVIEW

2

@HomeTutor

my.hrw.com
• Multi-Language Glossary
• Vocabulary practice

REVIEW KEY VOCABULARY

- scientific notation
- polynomial
- polynomial function
- leading coefficient
- degree
- constant term

- standard form of a polynomial function
- synthetic substitution
- end behavior
- factored completely
- factor by grouping
- quadratic form

- polynomial long division
- synthetic division
- repeated solution
- local maximum
- local minimum

VOCABULARY EXERCISES

1. Copy and complete: At each of its turning points, the graph of a polynomial function has a(n) _?_ or a(n) _?_ .

2. **WRITING** *Explain* how you can tell whether a solution of a polynomial equation is a repeated solution when the equation is written in factored form.

3. **WRITING** *Explain* how you can tell whether a number is expressed in scientific notation.

4. Let f be a fourth-degree polynomial function with four distinct real zeros. How many turning points does the graph of f have?

REVIEW EXAMPLES AND EXERCISES

Use the review examples and exercises below to check your understanding of the concepts you have learned in each lesson of this chapter.

2.1 Use Properties of Exponents

EXAMPLE

Simplify the expression.

$$(x^2y^3)^3x^4 = (x^2)^3(y^3)^3x^4 \qquad \text{Power of a product property}$$
$$= x^6y^9x^4 \qquad \text{Power of a power property}$$
$$= x^{6+4}y^9 \qquad \text{Product of powers property}$$
$$= x^{10}y^9 \qquad \text{Simplify exponent.}$$

EXERCISES

EXAMPLES
1, 2, 3, and 4
for Exs. 5–12

Evaluate or simplify the expression. Tell which properties of exponents you used.

5. $2^2 \cdot 2^5$

6. $(3^2)^{-3}(3^3)$

7. $(x^{-2}y^5)^2$

8. $(3x^4y^{-2})^{-3}$

9. $\left(\dfrac{3}{4}\right)^{-2}$

10. $\dfrac{8 \times 10^7}{2 \times 10^3}$

11. $\left(\dfrac{x^2}{y^{-2}}\right)^{-4}$

12. $\dfrac{2x^{-6}y^5}{16x^3y^{-2}}$

2.2 Evaluate and Graph Polynomial Functions

EXAMPLE

Graph the polynomial function $f(x) = x^3 - 2x^2 + 3$.

Make a table of values.

x	−2	−1	0	1	2	3
$f(x)$	−13	0	3	2	3	12

Plot the points, connect the points with a smooth curve, and check the end behavior.

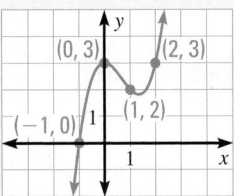

The degree is odd and the leading coefficient is positive, so $f(x) \to -\infty$ as $x \to -\infty$ and $f(x) \to +\infty$ as $x \to +\infty$.

EXERCISES

**EXAMPLES
5 and 6**
for Exs. 13–16

Graph the polynomial function.

13. $f(x) = -x^4$

14. $f(x) = x^3 - 4$

15. $f(x) = x^3 + 2x + 3$

16. FISH CONSUMPTION From 1990 to 2002, the amount of fish F (in millions of pounds) caught for human consumption in the United States can be modeled by

$$F = -0.907t^4 + 28.0t^3 - 258t^2 + 902t + 12{,}700$$

where t is the number of years since 1990. Graph the function. Use the graph to estimate the year when the amount of fish caught first was greater than 14.5 *billion* pounds.

2.3 Add, Subtract, and Multiply Polynomials

EXAMPLE

Perform the indicated operation.

a. $(3x^3 - 6x^2 - 7x + 5) + (x^3 + 8x + 3) = 3x^3 + x^3 - 6x^2 - 7x + 8x + 5 + 3$
$$= 4x^3 - 6x^2 + x + 8$$

b. $(x - 4)(2x^2 - 7x + 5) = (x - 4)2x^2 - (x - 4)7x + (x - 4)5$
$$= 2x^3 - 8x^2 - 7x^2 + 28x + 5x - 20$$
$$= 2x^3 - 15x^2 + 33x - 20$$

EXERCISES

**EXAMPLES
1, 2, 4, and 5**
for Exs. 17–20

Perform the indicated operation.

17. $(5x^3 - x + 3) + (x^3 - 9x^2 + 4x)$

18. $(x^3 + 4x^2 - 5x) - (4x^3 + x^2 - 7)$

19. $(x - 6)(5x^2 + x - 8)$

20. $(x - 4)(x + 7)(5x - 1)$

2.4 Factor and Solve Polynomial Equations

EXAMPLE

Factor the polynomial completely.

a. $x^3 + 125 = x^3 + 5^3 = (x + 5)(x^2 - 5x + 25)$ **Sum of two cubes**

b. $x^3 + 5x^2 - 9x - 45 = x^2(x + 5) - 9(x + 5)$ **Factor by grouping.**

$= (x^2 - 9)(x + 5)$ **Distributive property**

$= (x + 3)(x - 3)(x + 5)$ **Difference of two squares**

c. $3x^6 + 12x^4 - 96x^2 = 3x^2(x^4 + 4x^2 - 32)$ **Factor common monomial.**

$= 3x^2(x^2 - 4)(x^2 + 8)$ **Factor trinomial in quadratic form.**

$= 3x^2(x + 2)(x - 2)(x^2 + 8)$ **Difference of two squares**

EXERCISES

EXAMPLES
2, 3, 4, and 6
for Exs. 21–24

Factor the polynomial completely.

21. $64x^3 - 8$ **22.** $2x^5 - 12x^3 + 10x$ **23.** $2x^3 - 7x^2 - 8x + 28$

24. SCULPTURE You have 240 cubic inches of clay with which to make a sculpture shaped as a rectangular prism. You want the width to be 4 inches less than the length and the height to be 2 inches more than 3 times the length. What should the dimensions of the sculpture be?

2.5 Apply the Remainder and Factor Theorems

EXAMPLE

Divide $f(x) = 4x^4 + 29x^3 + 4x^2 - 14x + 37$ by $x + 7$.

Rewrite the divisor in the form $x - k$. Because $x + 7 = x - (-7)$, $k = -7$.

$$
\begin{array}{r|rrrrr}
-7 & 4 & 29 & 4 & -14 & 37 \\
   &   & -28 & -7 & 21 & -49 \\
\hline
   & 4 & 1 & -3 & 7 & -12
\end{array}
$$

So, $\dfrac{4x^4 + 29x^3 + 4x^2 - 14x + 37}{x + 7} = 4x^3 + x^2 - 3x + 7 - \dfrac{12}{x + 7}$.

EXERCISES

EXAMPLES
1, 3, and 4
for Exs. 25–32

Divide.

25. $(x^3 - 3x^2 - x - 10) \div (x^2 + 3x - 1)$ **26.** $(4x^4 - 17x^2 + 9x - 18) \div (2x^2 - 2)$

27. $(2x^3 - 11x^2 + 13x - 44) \div (x - 5)$ **28.** $(5x^4 + 2x^2 - 15x + 10) \div (x + 2)$

Given polynomial $f(x)$ and a factor of $f(x)$, factor $f(x)$ completely.

29. $f(x) = x^3 - 5x^2 - 2x + 24; \ x + 2$ **30.** $f(x) = x^3 - 11x^2 + 14x + 80; \ x - 8$

31. $f(x) = 9x^3 - 9x^2 - 4x + 4; \ x - 1$ **32.** $f(x) = 2x^3 + 7x^2 - 33x - 18; \ x + 6$

2.6 Find Rational Zeros

EXAMPLE

Find all real zeros of $f(x) = x^3 + 6x^2 + 5x - 12$.

The leading coefficient is 1 and the constant term is -12.

Possible rational zeros: $x = \pm\frac{1}{1}, \pm\frac{2}{1}, \pm\frac{3}{1}, \pm\frac{4}{1}, \pm\frac{6}{1}, \pm\frac{12}{1}$

Test these zeros using synthetic division. Test $x = 1$:

```
1 | 1   6    5    -12
  |      1    7     12
  ----------------------
    1   7   12     0   ←—  1 is a zero.
```

You can write $f(x) = (x - 1)(x^2 + 7x + 12)$. Factor the trinomial.

$f(x) = (x - 1)(x^2 + 7x + 12) = (x - 1)(x + 3)(x + 4)$

The zeros of f are 1, -3, and -4.

**EXAMPLES
2 and 3**
for Exs. 33–34

EXERCISES

Find all real zeros of the function.

33. $f(x) = x^3 - 4x^2 - 11x + 30$

34. $f(x) = 2x^4 - x^3 - 42x^2 + 16x + 160$

2.7 Apply the Fundamental Theorem of Algebra

EXAMPLE

Write a polynomial function f of least degree that has rational coefficients, a leading coefficient of 1, and -4 and $5 + \sqrt{2}$ as zeros.

Because $5 + \sqrt{2}$ is a zero, $5 - \sqrt{2}$ must also be a zero.

$f(x) = (x + 4)\left[x - \left(5 + \sqrt{2}\right)\right]\left[x - \left(5 - \sqrt{2}\right)\right]$ Write $f(x)$ in factored form.

$= (x + 4)\left[(x - 5) - \sqrt{2}\right]\left[(x - 5) + \sqrt{2}\right]$ Regroup terms.

$= (x + 4)[(x - 5)^2 - 2]$ Multiply.

$= x^3 - 6x^2 - 17x + 92$ Multiply.

EXERCISES

**EXAMPLES
3 and 6**
for Exs. 35–38

Write a polynomial function f of least degree that has rational coefficients, a leading coefficient of 1, and the given zeros.

35. $-4, 1, 5$

36. $-1, -1, 6, 3i$

37. $2, 7, 3 - \sqrt{5}$

38. ECONOMICS For the 15 years that a computer store has been open, its annual revenue R (in millions of dollars) can be modeled by

$$R = -0.0040t^4 + 0.088t^3 - 0.36t^2 - 0.55t + 5.8$$

where t is the number of years since the store opened. In what year was the revenue first greater than $7 million?

2.8 Analyze Graphs of Polynomial Functions

EXAMPLE

Graph the function $f(x) = x^3 - 4x + 2$. Identify the x-intercepts and the points where the local maximums and local minimums occur.

Use a graphing calculator to graph the function.

Notice that the graph has three x-intercepts and two turning points. You can use the graphing calculator's *zero*, *maximum*, and *minimum* features to approximate the coordinates of the points.

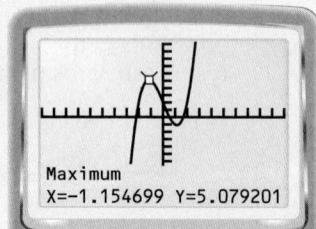

Maximum
X=-1.154699 Y=5.079201

The x-intercepts of the graph are about -2.21, 0.54, and 1.68. The function has a local maximum at $(-1.15, 5.08)$ and a local minimum at $(1.15, -1.08)$.

EXERCISES

EXAMPLE 2
for Exs. 39–40

Use a graphing calculator to graph the function. Identify the x-intercepts and the points where the local maximums and local minimums occur.

39. $f(x) = -2x^3 - 3x^2 - 1$

40. $f(x) = x^4 + 3x^3 - x^2 - 8x + 2$

CHAPTER TEST

2

Simplify the expression. Tell which properties of exponents you used.

1. $x^3 \cdot x^2 \cdot x^{-4}$

2. $(2x^{-2}y^3)^{-5}$

3. $\left(\dfrac{x^{-4}}{y^2}\right)^{-2}$

4. $\dfrac{3(xy)^3}{27x - 5y^3}$

Graph the polynomial function.

5. $f(x) = -x^3$

6. $f(x) = x^4 - 2x^2 - 5x + 1$

7. $f(x) = x^5 - x^4 - 9$

Perform the indicated operation.

8. $(2x^3 + 5x^2 - 7x + 4) + (x^3 - 3x^2 - 4x)$

9. $(3x^3 - 4x^2 + 3x - 5) - (x^2 + 4x - 8)$

10. $(3x - 2)(x^2 + 4x - 7)$

11. $(3x - 5)^3$

12. $(3x^3 - 14x^2 + 16x - 22) \div (x - 4)$

13. $(6x^4 + 7x^2 + 4x - 17) \div (3x^2 - 3x + 2)$

Factor the polynomial completely.

14. $8x^3 + 27$

15. $x^4 + 5x^2 - 6$

16. $x^3 - 3x^2 - 4x + 12$

Find all real zeros of the function.

17. $f(x) = x^3 + x^2 - 22x - 40$

18. $f(x) = 4x^4 - 8x^3 - 19x^2 + 23x - 6$

Write a polynomial function f of least degree that has rational coefficients, a leading coefficient of 1, and the given zeros.

19. $-1, 3, 4$

20. $6, 2i$

21. $-3, -1, 1 - \sqrt{5}$

22. $1 + 3i, 4 + \sqrt{10}$

Use a graphing calculator to graph the function. Identify the x-intercepts and the points where the local maximums and local minimums occur.

23. $f(x) = x^3 - 5x^2 + 3x + 4$

24. $f(x) = x^4 + 3x^3 - x^2 - 6x + 2$

Plot the points in each table of values. What is the lowest degree of polynomial that the data could represent?

25.

x	1	2	3	4	5	6
$f(x)$	3	1	1	3	7	13

26.

x	1	2	3	4	5	6
$f(x)$	−4	5	0	−7	−4	21

27. GROSS DOMESTIC PRODUCT In 2003, the gross domestic product (GDP) of the United States was about 1.099×10^{13} dollars. The population of the U.S. in 2003 was about 2.91×10^8. What was the per capita GDP in 2003?

28. Mario made an error in listing the possible rational zeros of the function. Find and correct his error.

$$f(x) = -8x^6 + 7x^5 - 3x^4 + 45x^3 - 1500x^2 + 16x$$

Possible zeros:

$$\pm 1, \pm 2, \pm 4, \pm 8, \pm \tfrac{1}{4}, \pm \tfrac{1}{2}, \pm \tfrac{1}{16}, \pm \tfrac{1}{8}$$

29. **GEOMETRY** A rectangular prism has edges of lengths x, $x + 2$, and $2x - 3$ inches. The volume of the prism is 1040 cubic inches. Write a polynomial equation that models the prism's volume. What are the prism's dimensions?

SHORT RESPONSE QUESTIONS

PROBLEM

The width of a rectangular prism is 2 meters less than its length, and the height is 1 meter less than its width. The volume of the prism is 30 cubic meters. Find the dimensions of the prism. *Explain* your reasoning.

Below are sample solutions to the problem. Read each solution and the comments on the left to see why the sample represents full credit, partial credit, or no credit.

SAMPLE 1: Full credit solution

The expressions for the dimensions are clearly explained.

> Let the length of the prism be x.
> The width is 2 meters less than the length, so width = $x - 2$.
> The height is 1 meter less than the width, so height = $(x - 2) - 1 = x - 3$.
>
> The volume of a rectangular prism is the product of its length, width, and height.

The equation is correct and all steps are clearly shown.

> | | |
> |---|---|
> | $30 = x(x - 2)(x - 3)$ | **Write equation.** |
> | $30 = x(x^2 - 5x + 6)$ | **Multiply binomials.** |
> | $0 = x^3 - 5x^2 + 6x - 30$ | **Write in standard form.** |
> | $0 = x^2(x - 5) + 6(x - 5)$ | **Factor by grouping.** |
> | $0 = (x^2 + 6)(x - 5)$ | **Distributive property** |

The solution of the equation is correct.

> The only real solution is $x = 5$. The factor $x^2 + 6$ does not produce any real solutions.
>
> Use substitution to find the dimensions: length = x = **5** meters
>
> width = $x - 2 = 5 - 2 = 3$ meters
>
> height = $x - 3 = 5 - 3 = 2$ meters

The dimensions are correct.

> The prism is 5 meters long, 3 meters wide, and 2 meters high.

SAMPLE 2: Partial credit solution

The equation is correct.

Imaginary solutions should be discarded. Dimensions are not given.

> Let length = x, width = $x - 2$, and height = $x - 3$.
>
> $30 = x(x - 2)(x - 3)$
>
> $0 = x^3 - 5x^2 + 6x - 30$
>
> $0 = (x^2 + 6)(x - 5)$
>
> $x = \pm i\sqrt{6}$ or $x = 5$

SAMPLE 3: No credit solution

The volume of a prism is the length cubed.

$$x^3 = 30$$

$$x \approx 3.11$$

The length of the prism is 3.11 meters.

The equation is incorrect.

The answer is incorrect.

PRACTICE Apply the Scoring Rubric

Use the rubric to score the solution to the problem below as *full credit*, *partial credit*, or *no credit*. *Explain* your reasoning.

PROBLEM The volume of a sphere with radius *r* is given by the function $V = \frac{4}{3}\pi r^3$. Graph the function. Then use the graph to estimate the radius of a sphere with a volume of 750 cubic feet.

1. The table shows the volumes of spheres with radii from 0 to 7 feet. Only positive *r*-values make sense.

r	0	1	2	3	4	5	6	7
V	0	4.189	33.51	113.1	268.1	523.6	904.8	1437

From the graph, you can see that the r-coordinate that corresponds to a V-coordinate of 750 is about 5.6.

A sphere with a volume of 750 cubic feet has a radius of about 5.6 feet.

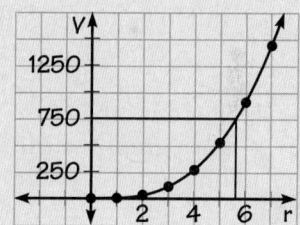

2. The table shows the volume *V* of a sphere with radius *r*.

r	0	2	4	6	8	10
V	0	10.67	85.33	288.0	682.7	1333

The r-coordinate that corresponds to a V-coordinate of 750 is 8.2, so the radius of a sphere with a volume of 750 cubic feet is about 8.2 feet.

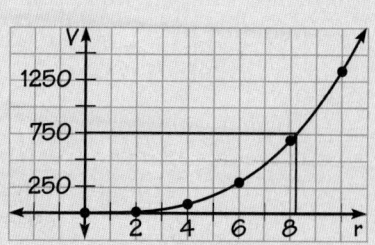

SHORT RESPONSE

1. Since 1960, the number of voters y (in millions) in United States federal elections can be modeled by the function

   $y = -0.0006x^3 + 0.0383x^2 + 0.383x + 68.6$

   where x is the number of years since 1960. According to the model, how many more people voted in 1980 than in 1960? *Explain* your reasoning.

2. Show two different ways to evaluate the polynomial $-3x^4 - 2x^3 + 7x^2 - 9$ when $x = -4$.

3. What does the graph of the polynomial function tell you about the sign of the leading coefficient, the degree of the function, and the number of real zeros? *Explain* your reasoning.

   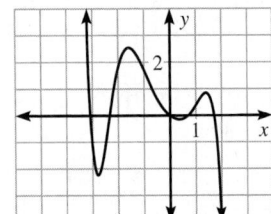

4. Since 1970, the average fuel efficiency E (in miles per gallon) for all vehicles in the United States can be modeled by the function

   $E = -0.0007t^3 + 0.0278t^2 - 0.0843t + 12.0$

   where t is the number of years since 1970. Use a graphing calculator to graph the function, and identify any turning points on the interval $0 \le t \le 30$. What real-life meaning does a turning point have in this situation?

5. Can you use the rational zero theorem to find the zeros of the polynomial function $f(x) = 3x^4 - 2x^3 + 1.5x^2 - 9$? *Explain* why or why not.

6. The profit P (in millions of dollars) for a manufacturer of winter coats can be modeled by $P = -x^3 + 3x^2 + 15x$ where x is the number of winter coats produced (in millions). Currently, the company produces 5 million winter coats and makes a profit of $25,000,000. *Explain* how the company can make the same profit by producing a lesser number of coats.

7. The volume of the rectangular prism shown below is given by the expression $2x^3 + 5x^2 - 19x - 42$.

   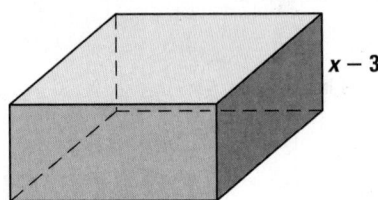

   Write a polynomial in standard form that represents the area of the base of the prism. Show all of your steps.

8. From 1990 to 2003, the number of CD singles (in millions) sold in the United States can be modeled by the polynomial function

   $y = 0.014x^5 - 0.40x^4 + 3.8x^3 - 13x^2 + 15x + 1.2$

   where x is the number of years since 1990.

   a. Use a graphing calculator to graph the function on the domain $0 \le x \le 13$. According to the model, in which year were the most CD singles sold?

   b. Do you think that sales will continue to follow the model indefinitely? *Explain* your reasoning.

9. Use finite differences and a system of equations to find a polynomial function that fits the data in each table. Then find $f(x) + g(x)$. *Explain* all of your steps.

x	1	2	3	4	5	6
$f(x)$	4	9	26	57	104	169

x	1	2	3	4	5	6
$g(x)$	-2	-2	12	52	130	258

10. The population of the United States in 1800 was 5.308×10^6, and the land area was 8.647×10^5 square miles. By 2000, the population had increased to 2.814×10^8, and the land area was 3.537×10^6 square miles. By how many people per square mile of land did the population density increase from 1800 to 2000? *Explain* your reasoning.

MULTIPLE CHOICE

11. Which expression is equivalent to $\dfrac{x^2y}{z^4}$?

Ⓐ $\dfrac{z^{-4}y^0}{x^{-2}}$

Ⓑ $xyz \cdot \dfrac{x}{z^{-3}}$

Ⓒ $(x^{-1}y^2z^2)^2(x^{-1}y^1z^2)^{-4}$

Ⓓ $\dfrac{(x^2yz)^3}{x^4y^2z^7}$

12. What are all the real solutions of the equation $x^4 = 125x$?

Ⓐ 0

Ⓑ 0, 5, −5

Ⓒ 0, 5

Ⓓ 0, 5i, −5i

13. Which polynomial function has −1, 3, and −4i as zeros?

Ⓐ $f(x) = x^4 - 2x^3 + 13x^2 - 32x - 48$

Ⓑ $f(x) = x^4 + 2x^3 + 13x^2 + 32x - 48$

Ⓒ $f(x) = x^4 - 2x^3 - 19x^2 + 32x + 48$

Ⓓ $f(x) = x^4 + 2x^3 + 19x^2 - 32x + 48$

GRIDDED ANSWER

14. Given that $p(x)$ is a polynomial of degree 6 and $q(x)$ is a polynomial of degree 3, what is the degree of the polynomial defined by $3 \cdot p(x) - 2 \cdot q(x)$?

15. How many *real* zeros does the function $f(x) = 2x^4 + 3x^2 - 1$ have?

16. Evaluate the expression $\left(\dfrac{3}{2}\right)^{-2}$.

17. What is the value of the function $f(x) = 4x^4 - x^3 + 2x^2 - 3$ when $x = 4$?

18. The graph of a quartic function is shown. How many imaginary zeros does the function have?

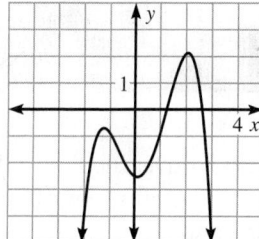

19. Use the rational zero theorem to determine the number of *possible* rational zeros for the function $f(x) = 15x^4 + 6x^3 - 8x^2 - 9$.

EXTENDED RESPONSE

20. You are making an open box to hold paper clips out of a piece of cardboard that is 5 inches by 8 inches. The box will be formed by making the cuts shown in the diagram and folding up the sides. You want the box to have the greatest volume possible.

a. Use a graphing calculator to find how long you should make the cuts. *Explain* your reasoning.

b. What is the maximum volume of the box?

c. What will the dimensions of the finished box be?

21. From 1980 to 2002, the number of hospitals H in the United States and the average number of hospital beds B in each hospital can be modeled by

$$H = -58.7t + 7070 \qquad \text{and} \qquad B = 0.0066t^3 - 0.192t^2 - 0.174t + 196$$

where t is the number of years since 1980.

a. Write a model for the total number of hospital beds in U.S. hospitals.

b. According to the model, how many beds were in U.S. hospitals in 1995?

c. How does the model change if you want to find the number of hospital beds *in thousands*? *Explain* your reasoning.

3 Rational Exponents and Radical Functions

COMMON CORE

Lesson
3.1 CC.9-12.N.RN.1
3.2 CC.9-12.N.RN.2
3.3 CC.9-12.F.BF.1*
3.4 CC.9-12.F.BF.4
3.5 CC.9-12.F.IF.7b*
3.6 CC.9-12.A.REI.2

Before

Previously, you learned the following skills, which you'll use in this chapter: simplifying expressions involving exponents, rewriting equations, and squaring binomials.

Prerequisite Skills

VOCABULARY CHECK

Copy and complete the statement.

1. The **square roots** of 81 are __?__ and __?__.

2. In the expression 2^5, the **exponent** is __?__.

3. For the polynomial function whose graph is shown, the sign of the **leading coefficient** is __?__.

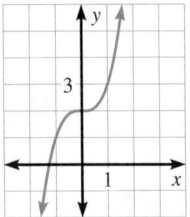

SKILLS CHECK

Simplify the expression.

4. $\dfrac{5x^2y}{15x^3y}$

5. $\dfrac{32x^3y^4}{24x^3y^2} \cdot \dfrac{3x}{9y}$

6. $(2x^5y^3)^3$

Solve the equation for y.

7. $-2x - 5y = 10$

8. $x - \dfrac{1}{3}y = -1$

9. $8x - 4xy = 3$

Simplify.

10. $(3x + 4)^2$

11. $(2x + 5)^2$

12. $(7x + 9)^2$

In this chapter, you will apply the big ideas listed below and reviewed in the Chapter Summary. You will also use the key vocabulary listed below.

Big Ideas

1. Using rational exponents
2. Performing function operations and finding inverse functions
3. Graphing radical functions and solving radical equations

KEY VOCABULARY

- nth root of a
- index of a radical
- simplest form of a radical
- like radicals

- power function
- composition
- inverse relation
- inverse function

- radical function
- radical equation

Why?

You can use a radical function to model the time you are suspended in the air during a jump. For example, the hang time of a basketball player can be modeled by a radical function.

Animated Algebra

The animation illustrated below helps you answer a question from this chapter: What is the relationship between the height of a jump and the time the jumper is suspended in air?

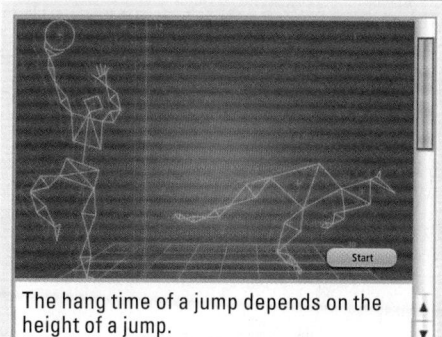

The hang time of a jump depends on the height of a jump.

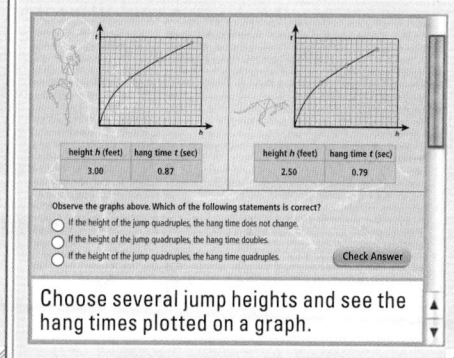

Choose several jump heights and see the hang times plotted on a graph.

Animated Algebra at my.hrw.com

3.1 Evaluate *n*th Roots and Use Rational Exponents

Before	You evaluated square roots and used properties of exponents.
Now	You will evaluate *n*th roots and study rational exponents.
Why?	So you can find the radius of a spherical object, as in Ex. 60.

Key Vocabulary
- *n*th root of *a*
- index of a radical

CC.9-12.N.RN.1 Explain how the definition of the meaning of rational exponents follows from extending the properties of integer exponents to those values, allowing for a notation for radicals in terms of rational exponents.

You can extend the concept of a square root to other types of roots. For example, 2 is a cube root of 8 because $2^3 = 8$. In general, for an integer *n* greater than 1, if $b^n = a$, then *b* is an **nth root of a**. An *n*th root of *a* is written as $\sqrt[n]{a}$ where *n* is the **index** of the radical.

You can also write an *n*th root of *a* as a power of *a*. If you assume the power of a power property applies to rational exponents, then the following is true:

$$\left(a^{1/2}\right)^2 = a^{(1/2) \cdot 2} = a^1 = a$$

$$\left(a^{1/3}\right)^3 = a^{(1/3) \cdot 3} = a^1 = a$$

$$\left(a^{1/4}\right)^4 = a^{(1/4) \cdot 4} = a^1 = a$$

Because $a^{1/2}$ is a number whose square is *a*, you can write $\sqrt{a} = a^{1/2}$. Similarly, $\sqrt[3]{a} = a^{1/3}$ and $\sqrt[4]{a} = a^{1/4}$. In general, $\sqrt[n]{a} = a^{1/n}$ for any integer *n* greater than 1.

KEY CONCEPT   *For Your Notebook*

Real *n*th Roots of *a*

Let *n* be an integer ($n > 1$) and let *a* be a real number.

n is an even integer.	**n is an odd integer.**
a < 0 No real *n*th roots.	**a < 0** One real *n*th root: $\sqrt[n]{a} = a^{1/n}$
a = 0 One real *n*th root: $\sqrt[n]{0} = 0$	**a = 0** One real *n*th root: $\sqrt[n]{0} = 0$
a > 0 Two real *n*th roots: $\pm\sqrt[n]{a} = \pm a^{1/n}$	**a > 0** One real *n*th root: $\sqrt[n]{a} = a^{1/n}$

EXAMPLE 1   Find *n*th roots

Find the indicated real *n*th root(s) of *a*.

a. $n = 3, a = -216$ **b.** $n = 4, a = 81$

Solution

a. Because $n = 3$ is odd and $a = -216 < 0$, -216 has one real cube root. Because $(-6)^3 = -216$, you can write $\sqrt[3]{-216} = -6$ or $(-216)^{1/3} = -6$.

b. Because $n = 4$ is even and $a = 81 > 0$, 81 has two real fourth roots. Because $3^4 = 81$ and $(-3)^4 = 81$, you can write $\pm\sqrt[4]{81} = \pm 3$ or $\pm 81^{1/4} = \pm 3$.

Javier Soriano/AFP/Getty Images

RATIONAL EXPONENTS A rational exponent does not have to be of the form $\frac{1}{n}$. Other rational numbers such as $\frac{3}{2}$ and $-\frac{1}{2}$ can also be used as exponents. Two properties of rational exponents are shown below.

KEY CONCEPT *For Your Notebook*

Rational Exponents

Let $a^{1/n}$ be an nth root of a, and let m be a positive integer.

$$a^{m/n} = \left(a^{1/n}\right)^m = \left(\sqrt[n]{a}\right)^m$$

$$a^{-m/n} = \frac{1}{a^{m/n}} = \frac{1}{\left(a^{1/n}\right)^m} = \frac{1}{\left(\sqrt[n]{a}\right)^m}, \; a \neq 0$$

EXAMPLE 2 **Evaluate expressions with rational exponents**

Evaluate (a) $16^{3/2}$ and (b) $32^{-3/5}$.

Solution

Rational Exponent Form	**Radical Form**
a. $16^{3/2} = \left(16^{1/2}\right)^3 = 4^3 = 64$	$16^{3/2} = \left(\sqrt{16}\right)^3 = 4^3 = 64$
b. $32^{-3/5} = \frac{1}{32^{3/5}} = \frac{1}{\left(32^{1/5}\right)^3} = \frac{1}{2^3} = \frac{1}{8}$	$32^{-3/5} = \frac{1}{32^{3/5}} = \frac{1}{\left(\sqrt[5]{32}\right)^3} = \frac{1}{2^3} = \frac{1}{8}$

AVOID ERRORS

Be sure to use parentheses to enclose a rational exponent: $9\wedge(1/5) \approx 1.552$. Without them, the calculator evaluates a power and then divides: $9\wedge1/5 = 1.8$.

EXAMPLE 3 **Approximate roots with a calculator**

Expression	Keystrokes	Display
a. $9^{1/5}$	9 $\boxed{\wedge}$ $\boxed{(}$ 1 $\boxed{\div}$ 5 $\boxed{)}$ $\boxed{\text{ENTER}}$	1.551845574
b. $12^{3/8}$	12 $\boxed{\wedge}$ $\boxed{(}$ 3 $\boxed{\div}$ 8 $\boxed{)}$ $\boxed{\text{ENTER}}$	2.539176951
c. $\left(\sqrt[4]{7}\right)^3 = 7^{3/4}$	7 $\boxed{\wedge}$ $\boxed{(}$ 3 $\boxed{\div}$ 4 $\boxed{)}$ $\boxed{\text{ENTER}}$	4.303517071

✓ **GUIDED PRACTICE** for Examples 1, 2, and 3

Find the indicated real nth root(s) of a.

1. $n = 4, a = 625$ **2.** $n = 6, a = 64$

3. $n = 3, a = -64$ **4.** $n = 5, a = 243$

Evaluate the expression without using a calculator.

5. $4^{5/2}$ **6.** $9^{-1/2}$ **7.** $81^{3/4}$ **8.** $1^{7/8}$

Evaluate the expression using a calculator. Round the result to two decimal places when appropriate.

9. $4^{2/5}$ **10.** $64^{-2/3}$ **11.** $\left(\sqrt[4]{16}\right)^5$ **12.** $\left(\sqrt[3]{-30}\right)^2$

EXAMPLE 4 **Solve equations using *n*th roots**

Solve the equation.

a. $4x^5 = 128$

$x^5 = 32$ Divide each side by 4.

$x = \sqrt[5]{32}$ Take fifth root of each side.

$x = 2$ Simplify.

b. $(x - 3)^4 = 21$

AVOID ERRORS
When *n* is even and *a* > 0, be sure to consider both the positive and negative *n*th roots of *a*.

$x - 3 = \pm\sqrt[4]{21}$ Take fourth roots of each side.

$x = \pm\sqrt[4]{21} + 3$ Add 3 to each side.

$x = \sqrt[4]{21} + 3$ or $x = -\sqrt[4]{21} + 3$ Write solutions separately.

$x \approx 5.14$ or $x \approx 0.86$ Use a calculator.

EXAMPLE 5 **Use *n*th roots in problem solving**

BIOLOGY A study determined that the weight *w* (in grams) of coral cod near Palawan Island, Philippines, can be approximated using the model

$$w = 0.0167\ell^3$$

where ℓ is the coral cod's length (in centimeters). Estimate the length of a coral cod that weighs 200 grams.

Solution

$w = 0.0167\ell^3$ Write model for weight.

$200 = 0.0167\ell^3$ Substitute 200 for *w*.

$11{,}976 \approx \ell^3$ Divide each side by 0.0167.

$\sqrt[3]{11{,}976} \approx \ell$ Take cube root of each side.

$22.9 \approx \ell$ Use a calculator.

▶ A coral cod that weighs 200 grams is about 23 centimeters long.

 GUIDED PRACTICE   for Examples 4 and 5

Solve the equation. Round the result to two decimal places when appropriate.

13. $x^3 = 64$ **14.** $\frac{1}{2}x^5 = 512$ **15.** $3x^2 = 108$

16. $\frac{1}{4}x^3 = 2$ **17.** $(x - 2)^3 = -14$ **18.** $(x + 5)^4 = 16$

19. WHAT IF? Use the information from Example 5 to estimate the length of a coral cod that has the given weight.

     a. 275 grams   **b.** 340 grams   **c.** 450 grams

3.1 EXERCISES

HOMEWORK KEY

◯ = See WORKED-OUT SOLUTIONS
Exs. 9, 25, and 63

★ = STANDARDIZED TEST PRACTICE
Exs. 2, 33, 46, 47, and 65

SKILL PRACTICE

1. **VOCABULARY** Copy and complete: In the expression $\sqrt[4]{10{,}000}$, the number 4 is called the __?__.

2. ★ **WRITING** *Explain* how the sign of a determines the number of real fourth roots of a and the number of real fifth roots of a.

EXAMPLE 1
for Exs. 3–20

MATCHING EXPRESSIONS Match the expression in rational exponent notation with the equivalent expression in radical notation.

3. $2^{1/3}$

4. $2^{3/2}$

5. $2^{2/3}$

6. $2^{1/2}$

A. $\left(\sqrt{2}\right)^3$

B. $\sqrt{2}$

C. $\sqrt[3]{2}$

D. $\left(\sqrt[3]{2}\right)^2$

USING RATIONAL EXPONENT NOTATION Rewrite the expression using rational exponent notation.

7. $\sqrt[3]{12}$

8. $\sqrt[5]{8}$

9. $\sqrt{x^5}$

10. $\sqrt[5]{(y + 2)^2}$

USING RADICAL NOTATION Rewrite the expression using radical notation.

11. $5^{1/4}$

12. $7^{1/3}$

13. $(2t)^{1/3}$

14. $x^{7/6}$

FINDING NTH ROOTS Find the indicated real nth root(s) of a.

15. $n = 2, a = 64$

16. $n = 3, a = -27$

17. $n = 4, a = 0$

18. $n = 3, a = 343$

19. $n = 4, a = -16$

20. $n = 5, a = -32$

EXAMPLE 2
for Exs. 21–33

EVALUATING EXPRESSIONS Evaluate the expression without using a calculator.

21. $\sqrt[6]{64}$

22. $8^{1/3}$

23. $16^{3/2}$

24. $\sqrt[3]{-125}$

25. $27^{2/3}$

26. $(-243)^{1/5}$

27. $\left(\sqrt[3]{8}\right)^{-2}$

28. $\left(\sqrt[3]{-64}\right)^4$

29. $\left(\sqrt[4]{16}\right)^{-7}$

30. $25^{3/2}$

31. $64^{-2/3}$

32. $\dfrac{1}{81^{-3/4}}$

33. ★ **MULTIPLE CHOICE** What is the value of $128^{5/7}$?

Ⓐ 8   Ⓑ 16   Ⓒ 32   Ⓓ 64

EXAMPLE 3
for Exs. 34–46

APPROXIMATING ROOTS Evaluate the expression using a calculator. Round the result to two decimals places when appropriate.

34. $\sqrt[5]{32{,}768}$

35. $\sqrt[7]{1695}$

36. $\sqrt[9]{-230}$

37. $85^{1/6}$

38. $25^{-1/3}$

39. $20{,}736^{1/4}$

40. $\left(\sqrt[4]{187}\right)^3$

41. $\left(\sqrt{6}\right)^{-5}$

42. $\left(\sqrt[5]{-8}\right)^8$

43. $86^{-5/6}$

44. $1974^{2/7}$

45. $\dfrac{1}{(-17)^{3/5}}$

46. ★ **MULTIPLE CHOICE** Which expression has the greatest value?

Ⓐ $27^{3/5}$ Ⓑ $5^{3/2}$ Ⓒ $\sqrt[3]{81}$ Ⓓ $\left(\sqrt[3]{2}\right)^8$

47. **REASONING** Between which two consecutive integers does $\sqrt[4]{125}$ lie? *Explain.*

EXAMPLE 4
....
for Exs. 48–58

ERROR ANALYSIS *Describe* and correct the error in solving the equation.

48.

$x^3 = 27$

$x = \sqrt[3]{27}$

$x = 9$

49.

$x^4 = 81$

$x = \sqrt[4]{81}$

$x = 3$

SOLVING EQUATIONS Solve the equation. Round the result to two decimal places when appropriate.

50. $x^3 = 125$

51. $5x^3 = 1080$

52. $x^6 + 36 = 100$

53. $(x - 5)^4 = 256$

54. $x^5 = -48$

55. $7x^4 = 56$

56. $x^3 + 40 = 25$

57. $(x + 10)^5 = 70$

58. $x^6 - 34 = 181$

59. CHALLENGE The general shape of the graph of $y = x^n$, where n is a positive *even* integer, is shown in red.

   a. *Explain* how the graph justifies the results in the first Key Concept box within this lesson when n is a positive *even* integer.

   b. Draw a similar graph that justifies the results in the Key Concept box when n is a positive *odd* integer.

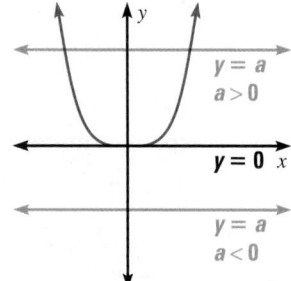

$y = a$
$a > 0$

$y = 0 \ x$

$y = a$
$a < 0$

PROBLEM SOLVING

EXAMPLE 5
....
for Exs. 60–65

60. SHOT PUT The shot used in men's shot put has a volume of about 905 cubic centimeters. Find the radius of the shot. (*Hint:* Use the formula $V = \frac{4}{3}\pi r^3$ for the volume of a sphere.)

61. BOWLING A bowling ball has a surface area of about 232 square inches. Find the radius of the bowling ball. (*Hint:* Use the formula $S = 4\pi r^2$ for the surface area of a sphere.)

62. INFLATION If the average price of an item increases from p_1 to p_2 over a period of n years, the annual rate of inflation r (expressed as a decimal) is given by $r = \left(\dfrac{p_2}{p_1}\right)^{1/n} - 1$. Find the rate of inflation for each item in the table. Write each answer as a percent rounded to the nearest tenth.

Item	Price in 1950	Price in 1990
Butter (lb)	$.7420	$2.195
Chicken (lb)	$.4430	$1.087
Eggs (dozen)	$.6710	$1.356
Sugar (lb)	$.0936	$.4560

63. MULTI-STEP PROBLEM The power p (in horsepower) used by a fan with rotational speed s (in revolutions per minute) can be modeled by the formula $p = ks^3$ for some constant k. A certain fan uses 1.2 horsepower when its speed is 1700 revolutions per minute. First find the value of k for this fan. Then find the speed of the fan if it uses 1.5 horsepower.

○ = See WORKED-OUT SOLUTIONS
in Student Resources

★ = STANDARDIZED
TEST PRACTICE

64. WATER RATE A *weir* is a dam that is built across a river to regulate the flow of water. The flow rate Q (in cubic feet per second) can be calculated using the formula $Q = 3.367\ell h^{3/2}$ where ℓ is the length (in feet) of the bottom of the spillway and h is the depth (in feet) of the water on the spillway. Determine the flow rate of a weir with a spillway that is 20 feet long and has a water depth of 5 feet.

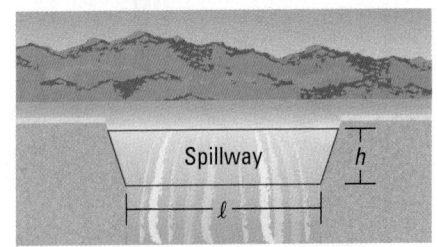

65. ★ **EXTENDED RESPONSE** Some games use dice in the shape of regular polyhedra. You are designing dice and want them all to have the same volume as a cube with an edge length of 16 millimeters.

Name	Tetrahedron	Octahedron	Dodecahedron	Icosahedron
Number of faces	4	8	12	20
Volume formula	$V = 0.118x^3$	$V = 0.471x^3$	$V = 7.663x^3$	$V = 2.182x^3$

  a. Find the volume of a cube with an edge length of 16 millimeters.

  b. Find the edge length x for each of the polyhedra shown in the table.

  c. Does the polyhedron with the greatest number of faces have the smallest edge length? *Explain.*

66. CHALLENGE The mass of the particles that a river can transport is proportional to the sixth power of the speed of the river. A certain river normally flows at a speed of 1 meter per second. What must its speed be in order to transport particles that are twice as massive as usual? 10 times as massive? 100 times as massive?

3.2 Apply Properties of Rational Exponents

Before	You simplified expressions involving integer exponents.
Now	You will simplify expressions involving rational exponents.
Why?	So you can find velocities, as in Ex. 84.

Key Vocabulary
- **simplest form of a radical**
- **like radicals**

CC.9-12.N.RN.2 Rewrite expressions involving radicals and rational exponents using the properties of exponents.

The properties of integer exponents that you have previously learned can also be applied to rational exponents.

KEY CONCEPT *For Your Notebook*

Properties of Rational Exponents

Let a and b be real numbers and let m and n be rational numbers. The following properties have the same names as those listed, but now apply to rational exponents as illustrated.

Property	Example
1. $a^m \cdot a^n = a^{m+n}$	$5^{1/2} \cdot 5^{3/2} = 5^{(1/2 + 3/2)} = 5^2 = 25$
2. $(a^m)^n = a^{mn}$	$(3^{5/2})^2 = 3^{(5/2 \cdot 2)} = 3^5 = 243$
3. $(ab)^m = a^m b^m$	$(16 \cdot 9)^{1/2} = 16^{1/2} \cdot 9^{1/2} = 4 \cdot 3 = 12$
4. $a^{-m} = \dfrac{1}{a^m}, \; a \neq 0$	$36^{-1/2} = \dfrac{1}{36^{1/2}} = \dfrac{1}{6}$
5. $\dfrac{a^m}{a^n} = a^{m-n}, \; a \neq 0$	$\dfrac{4^{5/2}}{4^{1/2}} = 4^{(5/2 - 1/2)} = 4^2 = 16$
6. $\left(\dfrac{a}{b}\right)^m = \dfrac{a^m}{b^m}, \; b \neq 0$	$\left(\dfrac{27}{64}\right)^{1/3} = \dfrac{27^{1/3}}{64^{1/3}} = \dfrac{3}{4}$

EXAMPLE 1 Use properties of exponents

Use the properties of rational exponents to simplify the expression.

a. $7^{1/4} \cdot 7^{1/2} = 7^{(1/4 + 1/2)} = 7^{3/4}$

b. $(6^{1/2} \cdot 4^{1/3})^2 = (6^{1/2})^2 \cdot (4^{1/3})^2 = 6^{(1/2 \cdot 2)} \cdot 4^{(1/3 \cdot 2)} = 6^1 \cdot 4^{2/3} = 6 \cdot 4^{2/3}$

c. $(4^5 \cdot 3^5)^{-1/5} = [(4 \cdot 3)^5]^{-1/5} = (12^5)^{-1/5} = 12^{[5 \cdot (-1/5)]} = 12^{-1} = \dfrac{1}{12}$

d. $\dfrac{5}{5^{1/3}} = \dfrac{5^1}{5^{1/3}} = 5^{(1 - 1/3)} = 5^{2/3}$

e. $\left(\dfrac{42^{1/3}}{6^{1/3}}\right)^2 = \left[\left(\dfrac{42}{6}\right)^{1/3}\right]^2 = (7^{1/3})^2 = 7^{(1/3 \cdot 2)} = 7^{2/3}$

EXAMPLE 2 **Apply properties of exponents**

BIOLOGY A mammal's surface area S (in square centimeters) can be approximated by the model $S = km^{2/3}$ where m is the mass (in grams) of the mammal and k is a constant. The values of k for some mammals are shown below. Approximate the surface area of a rabbit that has a mass of 3.4 kilograms (3.4×10^3 grams).

Mammal	Sheep	Rabbit	Horse	Human	Monkey	Bat
k	8.4	9.75	10.0	11.0	11.8	57.5

Solution

$S = km^{2/3}$	Write model.
$= 9.75(3.4 \times 10^3)^{2/3}$	Substitute 9.75 for k and 3.4×10^3 for m.
$= 9.75(3.4)^{2/3}(10^3)^{2/3}$	Power of a product property
$\approx 9.75(2.26)(10^2)$	Power of a power property
≈ 2200	Simplify.

▶ The rabbit's surface area is about 2200 square centimeters.

 GUIDED PRACTICE for Examples 1 and 2

Simplify the expression.

1. $(5^{1/3} \cdot 7^{1/4})^3$ 2. $2^{3/4} \cdot 2^{1/2}$ 3. $\dfrac{3}{3^{1/4}}$ 4. $\left(\dfrac{20^{1/2}}{5^{1/2}}\right)^3$

5. **BIOLOGY** Use the information in Example 2 to approximate the surface area of a sheep that has a mass of 95 kilograms (9.5×10^4 grams).

PROPERTIES OF RADICALS The third and sixth properties can be expressed using radical notation when $m = \dfrac{1}{n}$ for some integer n greater than 1.

KEY CONCEPT *For Your Notebook*

Properties of Radicals

Product property of radicals

$$\sqrt[n]{a \cdot b} = \sqrt[n]{a} \cdot \sqrt[n]{b}$$

Quotient property of radicals

$$\sqrt[n]{\dfrac{a}{b}} = \dfrac{\sqrt[n]{a}}{\sqrt[n]{b}}, b \neq 0$$

EXAMPLE 3 **Use properties of radicals**

Use the properties of radicals to simplify the expression.

a. $\sqrt[3]{12} \cdot \sqrt[3]{18} = \sqrt[3]{12 \cdot 18} = \sqrt[3]{216} = 6$ Product property

b. $\dfrac{\sqrt[4]{80}}{\sqrt[4]{5}} = \sqrt[4]{\dfrac{80}{5}} = \sqrt[4]{16} = 2$ Quotient property

SIMPLEST FORM A radical with index *n* is in **simplest form** if the radicand has no perfect *n*th powers as factors and any denominator has been rationalized.

EXAMPLE 4 Write radicals in simplest form

Write the expression in simplest form.

a. $\sqrt[3]{135} = \sqrt[3]{27 \cdot 5}$ Factor out perfect cube.

         $= \sqrt[3]{27} \cdot \sqrt[3]{5}$ Product property

         $= 3\sqrt[3]{5}$ Simplify.

REVIEW RADICALS
You may wish to review rationalizing denominators of radical expressions.

b. $\dfrac{\sqrt[5]{7}}{\sqrt[5]{8}} = \dfrac{\sqrt[5]{7}}{\sqrt[5]{8}} \cdot \dfrac{\sqrt[5]{4}}{\sqrt[5]{4}}$ Make denominator a perfect fifth power.

         $= \dfrac{\sqrt[5]{28}}{\sqrt[5]{32}}$ Product property

         $= \dfrac{\sqrt[5]{28}}{2}$ Simplify.

LIKE RADICALS Radical expressions with the same index and radicand are **like radicals**. To add or subtract like radicals, use the distributive property.

EXAMPLE 5 Add and subtract like radicals and roots

Simplify the expression.

a. $\sqrt[4]{10} + 7\sqrt[4]{10} = (1 + 7)\sqrt[4]{10} = 8\sqrt[4]{10}$

b. $2(8^{1/5}) + 10(8^{1/5}) = (2 + 10)(8^{1/5}) = 12(8^{1/5})$

c. $\sqrt[3]{54} - \sqrt[3]{2} = \sqrt[3]{27} \cdot \sqrt[3]{2} - \sqrt[3]{2} = 3\sqrt[3]{2} - \sqrt[3]{2} = (3 - 1)\sqrt[3]{2} = 2\sqrt[3]{2}$

 GUIDED PRACTICE   for Examples 3, 4, and 5

Simplify the expression.

6. $\sqrt[4]{27} \cdot \sqrt[4]{3}$ **7.** $\dfrac{\sqrt[3]{250}}{\sqrt[3]{2}}$ **8.** $\sqrt[5]{\dfrac{3}{4}}$ **9.** $\sqrt[3]{5} + \sqrt[3]{40}$

VARIABLE EXPRESSIONS The properties of rational exponents and radicals can also be applied to expressions involving variables. Because a variable can be positive, negative, or zero, sometimes absolute value is needed when simplifying a variable expression.

	Rule	Example
When *n* is odd	$\sqrt[n]{x^n} = x$	$\sqrt[7]{5^7} = 5$ and $\sqrt[7]{(-5)^7} = -5$
When *n* is even	$\sqrt[n]{x^n} = \lvert x \rvert$	$\sqrt[4]{3^4} = 3$ and $\sqrt[4]{(-3)^4} = 3$

Absolute value is not needed when all variables are assumed to be positive.

EXAMPLE 6 Simplify expressions involving variables

Simplify the expression. Assume all variables are positive.

a. $\sqrt[3]{64y^6} = \sqrt[3]{4^3(y^2)^3} = \sqrt[3]{4^3} \cdot \sqrt[3]{(y^2)^3} = 4y^2$

b. $(27p^3q^{12})^{1/3} = 27^{1/3}(p^3)^{1/3}(q^{12})^{1/3} = 3p^{(3 \cdot 1/3)}q^{(12 \cdot 1/3)} = 3pq^4$

WHAT IF?

If you do not put any restriction on the values of m and n in part (c) other than $n \neq 0$, the simplified expression would be written $\dfrac{|m|}{n^2}$. (You do not need to take the absolute value of n because n is being squared.)

c. $\sqrt[4]{\dfrac{m^4}{n^8}} = \dfrac{\sqrt[4]{m^4}}{\sqrt[4]{n^8}} = \dfrac{\sqrt[4]{m^4}}{\sqrt[4]{(n^2)^4}} = \dfrac{m}{n^2}$

d. $\dfrac{14xy^{1/3}}{2x^{3/4}z^{-6}} = 7x^{(1 - 3/4)}y^{1/3}z^{-(-6)} = 7x^{1/4}y^{1/3}z^6$

EXAMPLE 7 Write variable expressions in simplest form

Write the expression in simplest form. Assume all variables are positive.

a. $\sqrt[5]{4a^8b^{14}c^5} = \sqrt[5]{4a^5a^3b^{10}b^4c^5}$ Factor out perfect fifth powers.

    $= \sqrt[5]{a^5b^{10}c^5} \cdot \sqrt[5]{4a^3b^4}$ Product property

    $= ab^2c\sqrt[5]{4a^3b^4}$ Simplify.

AVOID ERRORS

You must multiply both the numerator *and* denominator of the fraction by y so that the value of the fraction does not change.

b. $\sqrt[3]{\dfrac{x}{y^8}} = \sqrt[3]{\dfrac{x \cdot y}{y^8 \cdot y}}$ Make denominator a perfect cube.

    $= \sqrt[3]{\dfrac{xy}{y^9}}$ Simplify.

    $= \dfrac{\sqrt[3]{xy}}{\sqrt[3]{y^9}}$ Quotient property

    $= \dfrac{\sqrt[3]{xy}}{y^3}$ Simplify.

EXAMPLE 8 Add and subtract expressions involving variables

Perform the indicated operation. Assume all variables are positive.

a. $\dfrac{1}{5}\sqrt{w} + \dfrac{3}{5}\sqrt{w} = \left(\dfrac{1}{5} + \dfrac{3}{5}\right)\sqrt{w} = \dfrac{4}{5}\sqrt{w}$

b. $3xy^{1/4} - 8xy^{1/4} = (3 - 8)xy^{1/4} = -5xy^{1/4}$

c. $12\sqrt[3]{2z^5} - z\sqrt[3]{54z^2} = 12z\sqrt[3]{2z^2} - 3z\sqrt[3]{2z^2} = (12z - 3z)\sqrt[3]{2z^2} = 9z\sqrt[3]{2z^2}$

✓ **GUIDED PRACTICE**   for Examples 6, 7, and 8

Simplify the expression. Assume all variables are positive.

10. $\sqrt[3]{27q^9}$ **11.** $\sqrt[5]{\dfrac{x^{10}}{y^5}}$ **12.** $\dfrac{6xy^{3/4}}{3x^{1/2}y^{1/2}}$ **13.** $\sqrt{9w^5} - w\sqrt{w^3}$

3.2 EXERCISES

HOMEWORK KEY

◯ = See WORKED-OUT SOLUTIONS
Exs. 5, 27, and 85

★ = STANDARDIZED TEST PRACTICE
Exs. 2, 23, 51, 69, 86, and 89

SKILL PRACTICE

1. VOCABULARY Are $2\sqrt{5}$ and $2\sqrt[3]{5}$ like radicals? *Explain* why or why not.

2. ★ WRITING Under what conditions is a radical expression in simplest form?

EXAMPLE 1
for Exs. 3–14

PROPERTIES OF RATIONAL EXPONENTS Simplify the expression.

3. $5^{3/2} \cdot 5^{1/2}$

4. $\left(6^{2/3}\right)^{1/2}$

5. $3^{1/4} \cdot 27^{1/4}$

6. $\dfrac{9}{9^{-4/5}}$

7. $\dfrac{80^{1/4}}{5^{-1/4}}$

8. $\left(\dfrac{7^3}{4^3}\right)^{-1/3}$

9. $\dfrac{11^{2/5}}{11^{4/5}}$

10. $\left(12^{3/5} \cdot 8^{3/5}\right)^5$

11. $\dfrac{120^{-2/5} \cdot 120^{2/5}}{7^{-3/4}}$

12. $\dfrac{64^{5/9} \cdot 64^{2/9}}{4^{3/4}}$

13. $\left(16^{5/9} \cdot 5^{7/9}\right)^{-3}$

14. $\dfrac{13^{3/7}}{13^{5/7}}$

EXAMPLE 3
for Exs. 15–22

PROPERTIES OF RADICALS Simplify the expression.

15. $\sqrt{20} \cdot \sqrt{5}$

16. $\sqrt[3]{16} \cdot \sqrt[3]{4}$

17. $\sqrt[4]{8} \cdot \sqrt[4]{8}$

18. $\left(\sqrt[3]{3} \cdot \sqrt[4]{3}\right)^{12}$

19. $\dfrac{\sqrt[5]{64}}{\sqrt[5]{2}}$

20. $\dfrac{\sqrt{3}}{\sqrt{75}}$

21. $\dfrac{\sqrt[4]{36} \cdot \sqrt[4]{9}}{\sqrt[4]{4}}$

22. $\dfrac{\sqrt[4]{8} \cdot \sqrt[4]{16}}{\sqrt[8]{2} \cdot \sqrt[8]{3}}$

EXAMPLE 4
for Exs. 23–31

23. ★ MULTIPLE CHOICE What is the simplest form of the expression $3\sqrt[4]{32} \cdot \left(-6\sqrt[4]{5}\right)$?

(A) $\sqrt[4]{10}$

(B) $-18\sqrt[4]{10}$

(C) $-36\sqrt[4]{10}$

(D) $36\sqrt[8]{10}$

SIMPLEST FORM Write the expression in simplest form.

24. $\sqrt{72}$

25. $\sqrt[6]{256}$

26. $\sqrt[3]{108} \cdot \sqrt[3]{4}$

27. $5\sqrt[4]{64} \cdot 2\sqrt[4]{8}$

28. $\sqrt[3]{\dfrac{1}{6}}$

29. $\dfrac{3}{\sqrt[4]{144}}$

30. $\sqrt[6]{\dfrac{81}{4}}$

31. $\dfrac{\sqrt[3]{9}}{\sqrt[5]{27}}$

EXAMPLE 5
for Exs. 32–41

COMBINING RADICALS AND ROOTS Simplify the expression.

32. $2\sqrt[6]{3} + 7\sqrt[6]{3}$

33. $\dfrac{3}{5}\sqrt[3]{5} - \dfrac{1}{5}\sqrt[3]{5}$

34. $25\sqrt[5]{2} - 15\sqrt[5]{2}$

35. $\dfrac{1}{8}\sqrt[4]{7} + \dfrac{3}{8}\sqrt[4]{7}$

36. $6\sqrt[3]{5} + 4\sqrt[3]{625}$

37. $-6\sqrt[7]{2} + 2\sqrt[7]{256}$

38. $12\sqrt[4]{2} - 7\sqrt[4]{512}$

39. $2\sqrt[4]{1250} - 8\sqrt[4]{32}$

40. $5\sqrt[3]{48} - \sqrt[3]{750}$

ERROR ANALYSIS *Describe* and correct the error in simplifying the expression.

41.

$$2\sqrt[3]{10} + 6\sqrt[3]{5} = (2 + 6)\sqrt[3]{15}$$
$$= 8\sqrt[3]{15}$$ ✗

42.

$$\sqrt[3]{\dfrac{x}{y^2}} = \sqrt[3]{\dfrac{x}{y^2 \cdot y}} = \sqrt[3]{\dfrac{x}{y^3}}$$
$$= \dfrac{\sqrt[3]{x}}{y}$$ ✗

EXAMPLE 6
for Exs. 43–51

VARIABLE EXPRESSIONS **Simplify the expression. Assume all variables are positive.**

43. $x^{1/4} \cdot x^{1/3}$

44. $\left(y^4\right)^{1/6}$

45. $\sqrt[4]{81x^4}$

46. $\dfrac{2}{x^{-3/2}}$

47. $\dfrac{x^{2/5}y}{xy^{-1/3}}$

48. $\sqrt[3]{\dfrac{x^{15}}{y^6}}$

49. $\left(\sqrt[3]{x^2} \cdot \sqrt[6]{x^4}\right)^{-3}$

50. $\dfrac{\sqrt[3]{x} \cdot \sqrt{x^5}}{\sqrt{25x^{16}}}$

51. ★ **OPEN-ENDED MATH** Write two variable expressions with noninteger exponents whose quotient is $x^{3/4}$.

EXAMPLE 7
for Exs. 52–59

SIMPLEST FORM **Write the expression in simplest form. Assume all variables are positive.**

52. $\sqrt{49x^5}$

53. $\sqrt[4]{12x^2y^6z^{12}}$

54. $\sqrt[3]{4x^3y^5} \cdot \sqrt[3]{12y^2}$

55. $\sqrt{x^2yz^3} \cdot \sqrt{x^3z^5}$

56. $\dfrac{-3}{\sqrt[5]{x^6}}$

57. $\sqrt[3]{\dfrac{x^3}{y^4}}$

58. $\sqrt{\dfrac{20x^3y^2}{9xz^3}}$

59. $\dfrac{\sqrt[4]{x^6}}{\sqrt[7]{x^5}}$

EXAMPLE 8
for Exs. 60–65

COMBINING VARIABLE EXPRESSIONS **Perform the indicated operation. Assume all variables are positive.**

60. $3\sqrt[5]{x} + 9\sqrt[5]{x}$

61. $\dfrac{3}{4}y^{3/2} - \dfrac{1}{4}y^{3/2}$

62. $-7\sqrt[3]{y} + 16\sqrt[3]{y}$

63. $\left(x^4y\right)^{1/2} + \left(xy^{1/4}\right)^2$

64. $x\sqrt{9x^3} - 2\sqrt{x^5}$

65. $y\sqrt[4]{32x^6} + \sqrt[4]{162x^2y^4}$

GEOMETRY **Find simplified expressions for the perimeter and area of the given figure.**

66.
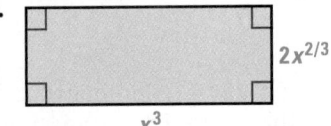
$2x^{2/3}$
x^3

67.
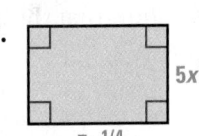
$5x^{1/4}$
$7x^{1/4}$

68.
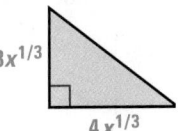
$3x^{1/3}$
$4x^{1/3}$

69. ★ **MULTIPLE CHOICE** What is the simplified form of $-\dfrac{1}{6}\sqrt{4x} - \dfrac{1}{6}\sqrt{9x}$?

(A) $-\dfrac{1}{3}\sqrt{x}$

(B) $-\dfrac{1}{3}\sqrt{36x}$

(C) $-\dfrac{5}{6}\sqrt{x}$

(D) $-\dfrac{5}{6}\sqrt{36x}$

DECIMAL EXPONENTS **Simplify the expression. Assume all variables are positive.**

70. $x^{0.5} \cdot x^2$

71. $y^{-0.6} \cdot y^{-6}$

72. $\left(x^6y^2\right)^{-0.75}$

73. $\dfrac{x^{0.3}}{x^{1.5}}$

74. $\left(x^5y^{-3}\right)^{-0.25}$

75. $\dfrac{y^{-0.5}}{y^{0.8}}$

76. $10x^{0.6} + \left(4x^{0.3}\right)^2$

77. $15z^{0.3} - \left(2z^{0.1}\right)^3$

IRRATIONAL EXPONENTS **The properties in this lesson can also be applied to irrational exponents. Simplify the expression. Assume all variables are positive.**

78. $\dfrac{x^{5\sqrt{3}}}{x^{2\sqrt{3}}}$

79. $\left(x^{\sqrt{2}}\right)^{\sqrt{3}}$

80. $\left(\dfrac{x^\pi}{x^{\pi/3}}\right)^2$

81. $x^2y^{\sqrt{2}} + 3x^2y^{\sqrt{2}}$

82. **CHALLENGE** Assume the variables can take any value for which the expression is defined. Simplify, using absolute value *only where necessary*.

a. $\sqrt[4]{32x^4y^5}$

b. $\sqrt[5]{x^{10}y^5}$

c. $\left(8x^3y^7\right)^{2/3}$

d. $\left(16x^9y^2\right)^{3/4}$

EXAMPLE 2
for Exs. 83–84

83. **BIOLOGY** Look back at Example 2. Use the model $S = km^{2/3}$ to approximate the surface area of the mammal given its mass.

    a. Bat: 32 grams

    b. Human: 59 kilograms

84. **AIRPLANE VELOCITY** The velocity v (in feet per second) of a jet can be approximated by the model

$$v = 8.8\sqrt{\frac{L}{A}}$$

where A is the area of the wings (in square feet) and L is the lift (in Newtons). Find the velocity of a jet with a wing area of 5.5×10^3 square feet and a lift of 1.4×10^7 Newtons.

85. **PINHOLE CAMERA** The optimum diameter d (in millimeters) of the pinhole in a pinhole camera can be modeled by

$$d = 1.9\left[(5.5 \times 10^{-4})\ell\right]^{1/2}$$

where ℓ is the length of the camera box (in millimeters). Find the optimum pinhole diameter for a camera box with a length of 10 centimeters.

86. ★ **SHORT RESPONSE** Show that the hypotenuse of an isosceles right triangle with legs of length x is $x\sqrt{2}$.

87. **STAR MAGNITUDE** The *apparent magnitude* of a star is a number that indicates how faint the star is in relation to other stars. The expression $\frac{2.512^{m_1}}{2.512^{m_2}}$ tells how many times fainter a star with magnitude m_1 is than a star with magnitude m_2.

    a. How many times fainter is Altair than Vega?

    b. How many times fainter is Deneb than Altair?

    c. How many times fainter is Deneb than Vega?

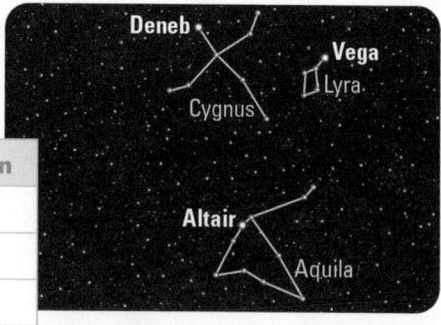

Star	Apparent magnitude	Constellation
Vega	0.03	Lyra
Altair	0.77	Aquila
Deneb	1.25	Cygnus

88. **PHYSICAL SCIENCE** The maximum horizontal distance d that an object can travel when launched at an optimum angle of projection is given by

$$d = \frac{v_0\sqrt{(v_0)^2 + 2gh_0}}{g}$$

where h_0 is the object's initial height, v_0 is its initial speed, and g is the acceleration due to gravity. Simplify the model when $h_0 = 0$.

○ = See **WORKED-OUT SOLUTIONS**
   in Student Resources

★ = **STANDARDIZED TEST PRACTICE**

89. ★ **EXTENDED RESPONSE** You have filled two round balloons with water. One balloon contains twice as much water as the other balloon.

a. Solve the formula for the volume of a sphere, $V = \frac{4}{3}\pi r^3$, for r.

b. Substitute the expression for r from part (a) into the formula for the surface area of a sphere, $S = 4\pi r^2$. Simplify to show that $S = (4\pi)^{1/3}(3V)^{2/3}$.

c. *Compare* the surface areas of the two water balloons using the formula from part (b).

90. CHALLENGE Substitute different combinations of odd and even positive integers for m and n in the expression $\sqrt[n]{x^m}$. If x is not always positive, when is absolute value needed in simplifying the expression?

QUIZ

Evaluate the expression without using a calculator.

1. $36^{3/2}$ **2.** $64^{-2/3}$ **3.** $-\left(625^{3/4}\right)$ **4.** $(-32)^{2/5}$

Solve the equation. Round your answer to two decimal places when appropriate.

5. $x^4 = 20$ **6.** $x^5 = -10$ **7.** $x^6 + 5 = 26$ **8.** $(x + 3)^3 = -16$

Simplify the expression. Assume all variables are positive.

9. $\sqrt[4]{32} \cdot \sqrt[4]{8}$ **10.** $\left(\sqrt{10} \cdot \sqrt[3]{10}\right)^8$ **11.** $\left(x^6 y^4\right)^{1/8} + 2\left(x^{1/3} y^{1/4}\right)^2$

12. $\dfrac{3\sqrt{7^3} + 4\sqrt{7^3}}{\sqrt{7^5}}$ **13.** $\dfrac{2\sqrt{x} \cdot \sqrt{x^3}}{\sqrt{64x^{15}}}$ **14.** $y^2 \sqrt[5]{64x^6} - 6\sqrt[5]{2x^6 y^{10}}$

15. 🔷 **GEOMETRY** Find a radical expression for the perimeter of the red triangle inscribed in the square shown to the right. Simplify the expression.

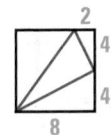

3.3 Perform Function Operations and Composition

Before	You performed operations with algebraic expressions.
Now	You will perform operations with functions.
Why?	So you can model biological processes, as in Example 3.

Key Vocabulary
- **power function**
- **composition**

CC.9-12.F.BF.1 Write a function that describes a relationship between two quantities.*
b. Combine standard function types using arithmetic operations.
c. (+) Compose functions.

You have learned how to add, subtract, multiply, and divide polynomial functions. These operations can be defined for any number of functions.

KEY CONCEPT *For Your Notebook*

Operations on Functions

Let f and g be any two functions. A new function h can be defined by performing any of the four basic operations on f and g.

Operation	Definition	Example: $f(x) = 5x$, $g(x) = x + 2$
Addition	$h(x) = f(x) + g(x)$	$h(x) = 5x + (x + 2) = 6x + 2$
Subtraction	$h(x) = f(x) - g(x)$	$h(x) = 5x - (x + 2) = 4x - 2$
Multiplication	$h(x) = f(x) \cdot g(x)$	$h(x) = 5x(x + 2) = 5x^2 + 10x$
Division	$h(x) = \dfrac{f(x)}{g(x)}$	$h(x) = \dfrac{5x}{x + 2}$

The domain of h consists of the x-values that are in the domains of both f and g. Additionally, the domain of the quotient does not include x-values for which $g(x) = 0$.

POWER FUNCTIONS So far you have studied several types of functions, including linear functions, quadratic functions, and polynomial functions of higher degree. Another common type of function is a **power function**, which has the form $y = ax^b$ where a is a real number and b is a rational number.

EXAMPLE 1 Add and subtract functions

Let $f(x) = 4x^{1/2}$ and $g(x) = -9x^{1/2}$. Find the following.

a. $f(x) + g(x)$ **b.** $f(x) - g(x)$ **c.** the domains of $f + g$ and $f - g$

Solution

a. $f(x) + g(x) = 4x^{1/2} + \left(-9x^{1/2}\right) = [4 + (-9)]x^{1/2} = -5x^{1/2}$

b. $f(x) - g(x) = 4x^{1/2} - \left(-9x^{1/2}\right) = [4 - (-9)]x^{1/2} = 13x^{1/2}$

c. The functions f and g each have the same domain: all nonnegative real numbers. So, the domains of $f + g$ and $f - g$ also consist of all nonnegative real numbers.

EXAMPLE 2 **Multiply and divide functions**

Let $f(x) = 6x$ and $g(x) = x^{3/4}$. Find the following.

a. $f(x) \cdot g(x)$

b. $\dfrac{f(x)}{g(x)}$

c. the domains of $f \cdot g$ and $\dfrac{f}{g}$

Solution

a. $f(x) \cdot g(x) = (6x)(x^{3/4}) = 6x^{(1 + 3/4)} = 6x^{7/4}$

b. $\dfrac{f(x)}{g(x)} = \dfrac{6x}{x^{3/4}} = 6x^{(1 - 3/4)} = 6x^{1/4}$

c. The domain of f consists of all real numbers, and the domain of g consists of all nonnegative real numbers. So, the domain of $f \cdot g$ consists of all nonnegative real numbers. Because $g(0) = 0$, the domain of $\dfrac{f}{g}$ is restricted to all *positive* real numbers.

EXAMPLE 3 **Solve a multi-step problem**

RHINOS For a white rhino, heart rate r (in beats per minute) and life span s (in minutes) are related to body mass m (in kilograms) by these functions:

$$r(m) = 241m^{-0.25} \qquad s(m) = (6 \times 10^6)m^{0.2}$$

• Find $r(m) \cdot s(m)$.

• Explain what this product represents.

Solution

STEP 1 **Find** and simplify $r(m) \cdot s(m)$.

$r(m) \cdot s(m) = 241m^{-0.25}\left[(6 \times 10^6)m^{0.2}\right]$ **Write product of $r(m)$ and $s(m)$.**

$= 241(6 \times 10^6)m^{(-0.25 + 0.2)}$ **Product of powers property**

$= (1446 \times 10^6)m^{-0.05}$ **Simplify.**

$= (1.446 \times 10^9)m^{-0.05}$ **Use scientific notation.**

STEP 2 **Interpret** $r(m) \cdot s(m)$.

Multiplying heart rate by life span gives the total number of heartbeats for a white rhino over its entire lifetime.

✓ **GUIDED PRACTICE**   for Examples 1, 2, and 3

Let $f(x) = -2x^{2/3}$ and $g(x) = 7x^{2/3}$. Find the following.

1. $f(x) + g(x)$

2. $f(x) - g(x)$

3. the domains of $f + g$ and $f - g$

Let $f(x) = 3x$ and $g(x) = x^{1/5}$. Find the following.

4. $f(x) \cdot g(x)$

5. $\dfrac{f(x)}{g(x)}$

6. the domains of $f \cdot g$ and $\dfrac{f}{g}$

7. **RHINOS** Use the result of Example 3 to find a white rhino's number of heartbeats over its lifetime if its body mass is 1.7×10^5 kilograms.

COMPOSITION OF FUNCTIONS Another operation that can be performed with two functions is *composition*.

KEY CONCEPT *For Your Notebook*

Composition of Functions

The **composition** of a function g with a function f is:

$$h(x) = g(f(x))$$

The domain of h is the set of all x-values such that x is in the domain of f and $f(x)$ is in the domain of g.

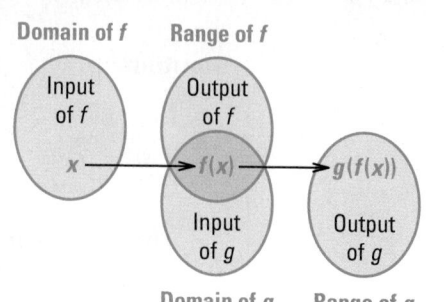

★ **EXAMPLE 4** **Standardized Test Practice**

Let $f(x) = 2x - 7$ and $g(x) = x^2 + 4$. What is the value of $g(f(3))$?

  (A) -5 **(B)** -3 **(C)** 3 **(D)** 5

Solution

To evaluate $g(f(3))$, you first must find $f(3)$.

$$f(3) = 2(3) - 7 = -1$$

Then $g(f(3)) = g(-1) = (-1)^2 + 4 = 1 + 4 = 5$.

So, the value of $g(f(3))$ is 5.

▶ The correct answer is D. **(A) (B) (C) ●**

EXAMPLE 5 **Find compositions of functions**

Let $f(x) = 4x^{-1}$ and $g(x) = 5x - 2$. Find the following.

  a. $f(g(x))$ **b.** $g(f(x))$

  c. $f(f(x))$ **d.** the domain of each composition

Solution

  a. $f(g(x)) = f(5x - 2) = 4(5x - 2)^{-1} = \dfrac{4}{5x - 2}$

  b. $g(f(x)) = g(4x^{-1}) = 5(4x^{-1}) - 2 = 20x^{-1} - 2 = \dfrac{20}{x} - 2$

  c. $f(f(x)) = f(4x^{-1}) = 4(4x^{-1})^{-1} = 4(4^{-1}x) = 4^0 x = x$

  d. The domain of $f(g(x))$ consists of all real numbers except $x = \dfrac{2}{5}$ because $g\left(\dfrac{2}{5}\right) = 0$ is not in the domain of f. (Note that $f(0) = \dfrac{4}{0}$, which is undefined.) The domains of $g(f(x))$ and $f(f(x))$ consist of all real numbers except $x = 0$, again because 0 is not in the domain of f.

EXAMPLE 6   Solve a multi-step problem

PAINT STORE You have a $10 gift certificate to a paint store. The store is offering 15% off your entire purchase of any paints and painting supplies. You decide to purchase a $30 can of paint and $25 worth of painting supplies.

Use composition of functions to do the following:

• Find the sale price of your purchase when the $10 gift certificate is applied before the 15% discount.

• Find the sale price of your purchase when the 15% discount is applied before the $10 gift certificate.

Solution

STEP 1   **Find** the total amount of your purchase. The total amount for the paint and painting supplies is $30 + $25 = $55.

STEP 2   **Write** functions for the discounts. Let x be the regular price, $f(x)$ be the price after the $10 gift certificate is applied, and $g(x)$ be the price after the 15% discount is applied.

Function for $10 gift certificate: $f(x) = x - 10$

Function for 15% discount: $g(x) = x - 0.15x = 0.85x$

STEP 3   **Compose** the functions.

The composition $g(f(x))$ represents the sale price when the $10 gift certificate is applied before the 15% discount.

$g(f(x)) = g(x - 10) = 0.85(x - 10)$

The composition $f(g(x))$ represents the sale price when the 15% discount is applied before the $10 gift certificate.

$f(g(x)) = f(0.85x) = 0.85x - 10$

STEP 4   **Evaluate** the functions $g(f(x))$ and $f(g(x))$ when $x = 55$.

$g(f(\mathbf{55})) = 0.85(\mathbf{55} - 10) = 0.85(45) = \$38.25$

$f(g(\mathbf{55})) = 0.85(\mathbf{55}) - 10 = 46.75 - 10 = \$36.75$

▸ The sale price is $38.25 when the $10 gift certificate is applied before the 15% discount. The sale price is $36.75 when the 15% discount is applied before the $10 gift certificate.

Animated Algebra at my.hrw.com

✓   **GUIDED PRACTICE**   for Examples 4, 5, and 6

Let $f(x) = 3x - 8$ and $g(x) = 2x^2$. Find the following.

  8. $g(f(5))$ **9.** $f(g(5))$ **10.** $f(f(5))$ **11.** $g(g(5))$

12. Let $f(x) = 2x^{-1}$ and $g(x) = 2x + 7$. Find $f(g(x))$, $g(f(x))$, and $f(f(x))$. Then state the domain of each composition.

13. WHAT IF? In Example 6, how do your answers change if the gift certificate to the paint store is $15 and the store discount is 20%?

3.3 EXERCISES

HOMEWORK KEY

○ = See WORKED-OUT SOLUTIONS
Exs. 3, 13, and 45

★ = STANDARDIZED TEST PRACTICE
Exs. 2, 11, 38, 39, and 44

◆ = MULTIPLE REPRESENTATIONS
Ex. 46

SKILL PRACTICE

1. **VOCABULARY** Copy and complete: The function $h(x) = g(f(x))$ is called the __?__ of the function g with the function f.

2. ★ **WRITING** Tell whether the sum of two power functions is *sometimes*, *always*, or *never* a power function. *Explain* your reasoning.

EXAMPLE 1
for Exs. 3–11

ADD AND SUBTRACT FUNCTIONS Let $f(x) = -3x^{1/3} + 4x^{1/2}$ and $g(x) = 5x^{1/3} + 4x^{1/2}$. **Perform the indicated operation and state the domain.**

3. $f(x) + g(x)$ 4. $g(x) + f(x)$ 5. $f(x) + f(x)$ 6. $g(x) + g(x)$

7. $f(x) - g(x)$ 8. $g(x) - f(x)$ 9. $f(x) - f(x)$ 10. $g(x) - g(x)$

11. ★ **MULTIPLE CHOICE** What is $f(x) + g(x)$ if $f(x) = -7x^{2/3} - 1$ and $g(x) = 2x^{2/3} + 6$?

   (A) $5x^{2/3} - 5$ (B) $-5x^{2/3} + 5$ (C) $9x^{2/3} + 7$ (D) $-9x^{2/3} - 7$

EXAMPLE 2
for Exs. 12–19

MULTIPLY AND DIVIDE FUNCTIONS Let $f(x) = 4x^{2/3}$ and $g(x) = 5x^{1/2}$. **Perform the indicated operation and state the domain.**

12. $f(x) \cdot g(x)$ 13. $g(x) \cdot f(x)$ 14. $f(x) \cdot f(x)$ 15. $g(x) \cdot g(x)$

16. $\dfrac{f(x)}{g(x)}$ 17. $\dfrac{g(x)}{f(x)}$ 18. $\dfrac{f(x)}{f(x)}$ 19. $\dfrac{g(x)}{g(x)}$

EXAMPLE 4
for Exs. 20–27

EVALUATE COMPOSITIONS OF FUNCTIONS Let $f(x) = 3x + 2$, $g(x) = -x^2$, and $h(x) = \dfrac{x-2}{5}$. **Find the indicated value.**

20. $f(g(-3))$ 21. $g(f(2))$ 22. $h(f(-9))$ 23. $g(h(8))$

24. $h(g(5))$ 25. $f(f(7))$ 26. $h(h(-4))$ 27. $g(g(-5))$

EXAMPLE 5
for Exs. 28–38

FIND COMPOSITIONS OF FUNCTIONS Let $f(x) = 3x^{-1}$, $g(x) = 2x - 7$, and $h(x) = \dfrac{x+4}{3}$. **Perform the indicated operation and state the domain.**

28. $f(g(x))$ 29. $g(f(x))$ 30. $h(f(x))$ 31. $g(h(x))$

32. $h(g(x))$ 33. $f(f(x))$ 34. $h(h(x))$ 35. $g(g(x))$

ERROR ANALYSIS Let $f(x) = x^2 - 3$ and $g(x) = 4x$. *Describe* and correct the error in the composition.

36.
$$f(g(x)) = f(4x)$$
$$= (x^2 - 3)(4x)$$
$$= 4x^3 - 12x$$
✗

37.
$$g(f(x)) = g(x^2 - 3)$$
$$= 4x^2 \quad 3$$
✗

38. ★ **MULTIPLE CHOICE** What is $g(f(x))$ if $f(x) = 7x^2$ and $g(x) = 3x^{-2}$?

Ⓐ $\dfrac{3}{49x^4}$ **Ⓑ** 21 **Ⓒ** $21x^4$ **Ⓓ** $\dfrac{7}{9x^4}$

39. ★ **OPEN-ENDED MATH** Find two different functions f and g such that $f(g(x)) = g(f(x))$.

CHALLENGE Find functions f and g such that $f(g(x)) = h(x)$, $g(x) \neq x$, and $f(x) \neq x$.

40. $h(x) = \sqrt[3]{x + 2}$ **41.** $h(x) = \dfrac{4}{3x^2 + 7}$ **42.** $h(x) = |2x + 9|$

PROBLEM SOLVING

EXAMPLE 3
for Exs. 43, 46

43. **BIOLOGY** For a mammal that weighs w grams, the volume b (in milliliters) of air breathed in and the volume d (in milliliters) of "dead space" (the portion of the lungs not filled with air) can be modeled by:

$$b(w) = 0.007w \qquad d(w) = 0.002w$$

The breathing rate r (in breaths per minute) of a mammal that weighs w grams can be modeled by:

$$r(w) = \frac{1.1w^{0.734}}{b(w) - d(w)}$$

Simplify $r(w)$ and calculate the breathing rate for body weights of 6.5 grams, 300 grams, and 70,000 grams.

EXAMPLE 6
for Exs. 44–45

44. ★ **SHORT RESPONSE** The cost (in dollars) of producing x sneakers in a factory is given by $C(x) = 60x + 750$. The number of sneakers produced in t hours is given by $x(t) = 50t$. Find $C(x(t))$. Evaluate $C(x(5))$ and explain what this number represents.

45. **MULTI-STEP PROBLEM** An online movie store is having a sale. You decide to open a charge account and buy four DVDs.

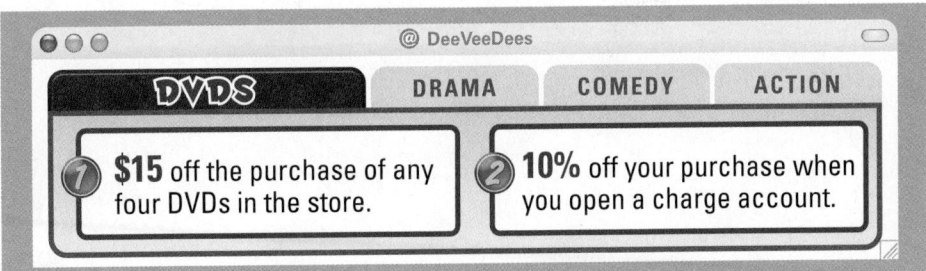

a. Use composition of functions to find the sale price of $85 worth of DVDs when the $15 discount is applied before the 10% discount.

b. Use composition of functions to find the sale price of $85 worth of DVDs when the 10% discount is applied before the $15 discount.

c. Which order of discounts gives you a better deal? *Explain.*

46. ◆ **MULTIPLE REPRESENTATIONS** A mathematician at a lake throws a tennis ball from point *A* along the water's edge to point *B* in the water, as shown. His dog, Elvis, first runs along the beach from point *A* to point *D* and then swims to fetch the ball at point *B*.

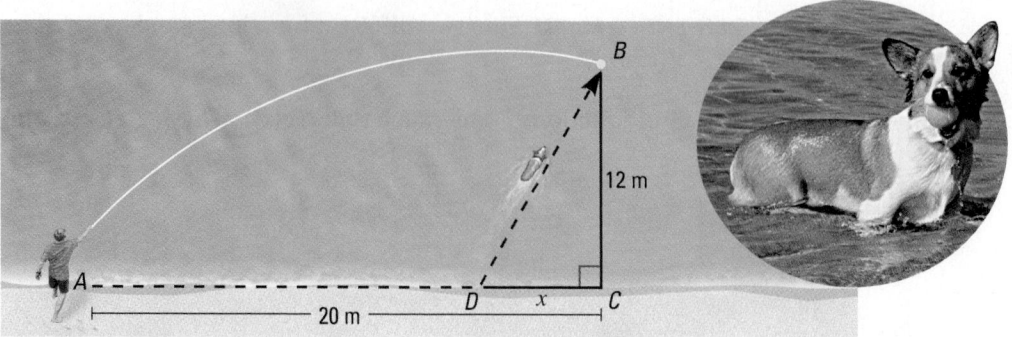

a. **Using a Diagram** Elvis's running speed is about 6.4 meters per second. Write a function $r(x)$ for the time he spends running from point *A* to point *D*. Elvis's swimming speed is about 0.9 meter per second. Write a function $s(x)$ for the time he spends swimming from point *D* to point *B*.

b. **Writing a Function** Write a function $t(x)$ that represents the total time Elvis spends traveling from point *A* to point *D* to point *B*.

c. **Using a Graph** Use a graphing calculator to graph $t(x)$. Find the value of *x* that minimizes $t(x)$. *Explain* the meaning of this value.

47. **CHALLENGE** To approximate the square root of a number *n*, the Babylonians used a method that involves starting with an initial guess *x* and calculating a sequence of values that approaches the exact answer. Their method was based on the function shown at the right.

$$f(x) = \frac{x + \frac{n}{x}}{2}$$

a. Let $n = 2$, and choose $x = 1$ as an initial guess for $\sqrt{n} = \sqrt{2}$. Calculate $f(x)$, $f(f(x))$, $f(f(f(x)))$, and $f(f(f(f(x))))$.

b. How many times do you need to compose the function in order for the result to approximate $\sqrt{2}$ to three decimal places? six decimal places?

my.hrw.com
Keystrokes

Use Operations with Functions

MATHEMATICAL PRACTICES

Use appropriate tools strategically.

QUESTION How can you use a graphing calculator to perform operations with functions?

EXAMPLE Perform function operations

Let $f(x) = x^2 - 3x + 6$ and $g(x) = x - 4$. Find $f(4) + g(4)$ and $f(g(-2))$.

STEP 1 *Form sum*

Enter $y_1 = x^2 - 3x + 6$ and $y_2 = x - 4$. The sum can be entered as $y_3 = y_1 + y_2$. To do so, press **VARS**, choose the Y-Vars menu, and select Function.

STEP 2 *Evaluate sum*

On the home screen, enter $y_3(4)$ and press **ENTER**. The screen shows that $y_3(4) = 10$, so $f(4) + g(4) = 10$.

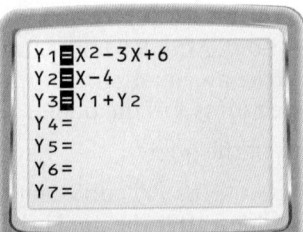

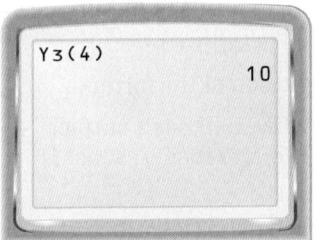

STEP 3 *Form composition*

The composition $f(g(x))$ can be entered as $y_3 = y_1(y_2)$.

STEP 4 *Evaluate composition*

On the home screen, enter $y_3(-2)$ and press **ENTER**. The screen shows that $y_3(-2) = 60$, so $f(g(-2)) = 60$.

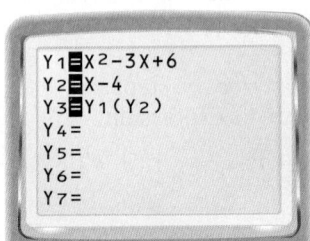

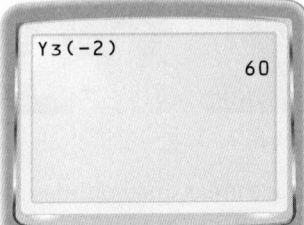

PRACTICE

Use a graphing calculator and the functions f and g to find the indicated value.

1. $f(x) = x^3 + 5x - 3$, $g(x) = -3x^2 - x$: $g(7) + f(7)$

2. $f(x) = x^{1/3}$, $g(x) = 9x$: $\dfrac{f(-8)}{g(-8)}$

3. $f(x) = 5x^3 - 3x^2$, $g(x) = -2x^2 - 5$: $g(2) - f(2)$

4. $f(x) = 2x^2 + 7x - 2$, $g(x) = x - 6$: $f(g(5))$

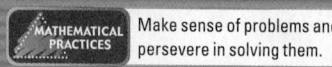
1. **MULTI-STEP PROBLEM** A circle is inscribed in a square, as shown.

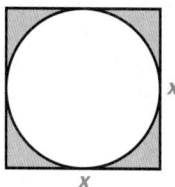

   a. Write a function $s(x)$ for the area of the square.

   b. Write a function $c(x)$ for the area of the circle.

   c. Write and simplify a function $r(x)$ for the area of the shaded region.

2. **MULTI-STEP PROBLEM** The formula for the volume V of a sphere in terms of its surface area S is $V = 3^{-1}(4\pi)^{-1/2}(S^3)^{1/2}$.

   a. Simplify the right side of the formula.

   b. A candlepin bowling ball has a surface area of about 79 square inches. What is its volume?

   c. A 10-pin bowling ball has a surface area of about 232 square inches. What is its volume?

Ten-pin bowling ball

   d. *Compare* the surface areas and volumes of the two bowling balls.

3. **SHORT RESPONSE** You are working as a sales representative for a clothing manufacturer. You are paid an annual salary plus a bonus of 3% of your sales over $100,000. Consider these two functions:

   $$f(x) = x - 100,000 \qquad g(x) = 0.03x$$

   Which composition, $f(g(x))$ or $g(f(x))$, represents your bonus if $x > 100,000$? *Explain*.

4. **EXTENDED RESPONSE** A cylindrical above-ground pool has a height of 5 feet and a radius of x feet.

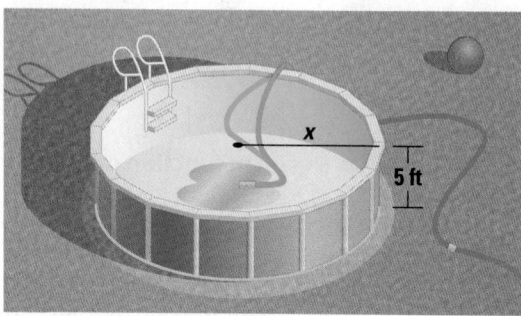

   a. Write an equation that gives the volume V of the pool as a function of the radius x. Use 3.14 for π.

   b. You use a hose to fill the pool with water. Water flows from the hose at a rate of 128 cubic feet per hour. After 8.8 hours the pool is half full. Write an equation that you can use to find the radius x of the pool.

   c. What is the radius of the pool?

   d. A second hose that outputs 104 cubic feet of water per hour is added after the pool is half full. Find the total number of hours it will take to fill $\frac{4}{5}$ of the pool. Your answer should include the 8.8 hours it took to fill the bottom half of the pool in part (b).

5. **OPEN-ENDED** Find two different functions $f(x)$ such that $f(f(x)) = x$.

6. **SHORT RESPONSE** *Describe* the steps you would use to simplify this expression:

   $$\left(\frac{16^{1/2}}{4^{1/2}} \right)^5$$

   Is there another set of steps you could use to simplify the expression? *Explain* your reasoning.

7. **GRIDDED ANSWER** The volume of a sphere is 900 cubic inches. Use the formula for the volume of a sphere, $V = \frac{4}{3}\pi r^3$, to find the radius r to the nearest tenth of an inch. Use 3.14 for π.

Exploring Inverse Functions

MATERIALS • graph paper • straightedge

Reason abstractly and quantitatively.

QUESTION How are a function and its *inverse* related?

EXPLORE Find the inverse of $f(x) = \dfrac{x - 3}{2}$

STEP 1 *Graph function* Choose values of x and find the corresponding values of $y = f(x)$. Plot the points and draw the line that passes through them.

STEP 2 *Interchange coordinates* Interchange the x- and y-coordinates of the ordered pairs found in Step 1. Plot the new points and draw the line that passes through them.

STEP 3 *Write equation* Write an equation of the line from Step 2. Call this function g.

STEP 4 *Compare graphs* Fold your graph paper so that the graphs of f and g coincide. How are the graphs geometrically related?

STEP 5 *Describe functions* In words, f is the function that subtracts 3 from x and then divides the result by 2. Describe the function g in words.

STEP 6 *Find compositions* Predict what the compositions $f(g(x))$ and $g(f(x))$ will be. Confirm your predictions by finding $f(g(x))$ and $g(f(x))$.

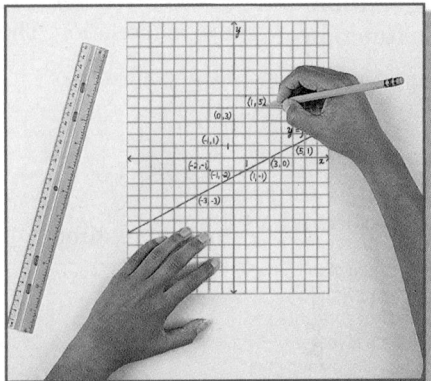

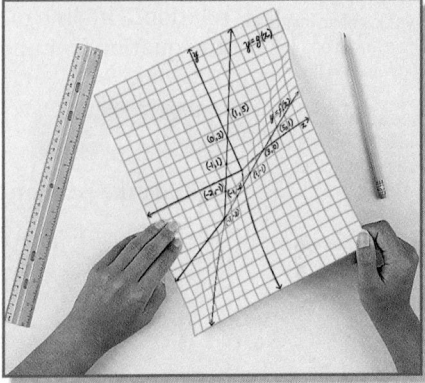

The functions f and g are called *inverses* of each other.

DRAW CONCLUSIONS Use your observations to complete these exercises

Complete Exercises 1–3 for each function below.

$$f(x) = 3x + 2 \qquad f(x) = \frac{x - 1}{6} \qquad f(x) = 4 - \frac{3}{2}x$$

1. Complete Steps 1–3 above to find the inverse of the function.

2. Complete Step 4. How can you graph the inverse of a function without first finding ordered pairs (x, y)?

3. Complete Steps 5 and 6. How can you test to see if the function you found in Exercise 1 is indeed the inverse of the original function?

3.4 Use Inverse Functions

Before You performed operations with functions.

Now You will find inverse functions.

Why? So you can convert temperatures, as in Ex. 48.

Key Vocabulary
• inverse relation
• inverse function

COMMON CORE

CC.9-12.F.BF.4 Find inverse functions.
a. Solve an equation of the form $f(x) = c$ for a simple function f that has an inverse and write an expression for the inverse.
b. (+) Verify by composition that one function is the inverse of another.
c. (+) Read values of an inverse function from a graph or a table, given that the function has an inverse.
d. (+) Produce an invertible function from a non-invertible function by restricting the domain.

Recall that you learned that a relation is a pairing of input values with output values. An **inverse relation** interchanges the input and output values of the original relation. This means that the domain and range are also interchanged.

Original relation

x	0	1	2	3	4
y	6	4	2	0	−2

Inverse relation

x	6	4	2	0	−2
y	0	1	2	3	4

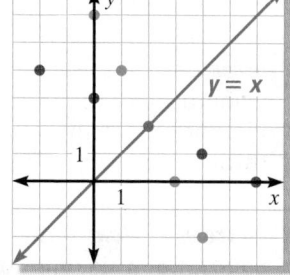

The graph of an inverse relation is a *reflection* of the graph of the original relation. The line of reflection is $y = x$. To find the inverse of a relation given by an equation in x and y, switch the roles of x and y and solve for y.

EXAMPLE 1 Find an inverse relation

Find an equation for the inverse of the relation $y = 3x - 5$.

$y = 3x - 5$	Write original relation.
$x = 3y - 5$	Switch x and y.
$x + 5 = 3y$	Add 5 to each side.
$\frac{1}{3}x + \frac{5}{3} = y$	Solve for y. This is the inverse relation.

In Example 1, both the original relation and the inverse relation happen to be functions. In such cases, the two functions are called **inverse functions**.

READING
The symbol −1 in f^{-1} is not to be interpreted as an exponent. In other words, $f^{-1}(x) \neq \frac{1}{f(x)}$.

KEY CONCEPT   *For Your Notebook*

Inverse Functions

Functions f and g are inverses of each other provided:

$$f(g(x)) = x \quad \text{and} \quad g(f(x)) = x$$

The function g is denoted by f^{-1}, read as "f inverse."

Paul A. Souders/Corbis

EXAMPLE 2 Verify that functions are inverses

Verify that $f(x) = 3x - 5$ and $f^{-1}(x) = \frac{1}{3}x + \frac{5}{3}$ are inverse functions.

Solution

STEP 1 Show that $f(f^{-1}(x)) = x$.

$$f(f^{-1}(x)) = f\left(\frac{1}{3}x + \frac{5}{3}\right)$$

$$= 3\left(\frac{1}{3}x + \frac{5}{3}\right) - 5$$

$$= x + 5 - 5$$

$$= x \checkmark$$

STEP 2 Show that $f^{-1}(f(x)) = x$.

$$f^{-1}(f(x)) = f^{-1}(3x - 5)$$

$$= \frac{1}{3}(3x - 5) + \frac{5}{3}$$

$$= x - \frac{5}{3} + \frac{5}{3}$$

$$= x \checkmark$$

EXAMPLE 3 Solve a multi-step problem

FITNESS Elastic bands can be used in exercising to provide a range of resistance. A band's resistance R (in pounds) can be modeled by $R = \frac{3}{8}L - 5$ where L is the total length of the stretched band (in inches).

*   Find the inverse of the model.

*   Use the inverse function to find the length at which the band provides 19 pounds of resistance.

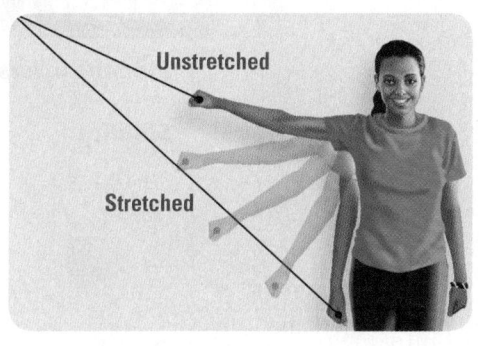

Unstretched

Stretched

Solution

FIND INVERSES
Notice that you do not switch the variables when you are finding inverses of models. This would be confusing because the letters are chosen to remind you of the real-life quantities they represent.

STEP 1 Find the inverse function.

$$R = \frac{3}{8}L - 5 \qquad \text{Write original model.}$$

$$R + 5 = \frac{3}{8}L \qquad \text{Add 5 to each side.}$$

$$\frac{8}{3}R + \frac{40}{3} = L \qquad \text{Multiply each side by } \frac{8}{3}.$$

STEP 2 Evaluate the inverse function when $R = 19$.

$$L = \frac{8}{3}R + \frac{40}{3} = \frac{8}{3}(19) + \frac{40}{3} = \frac{152}{3} + \frac{40}{3} = \frac{192}{3} = 64$$

▶ The band provides 19 pounds of resistance when it is stretched to 64 inches.

✓ **GUIDED PRACTICE** for Examples 1, 2, and 3

Find the inverse of the given function. Then verify that your result and the original function are inverses.

  1. $f(x) = x + 4$ **2.** $f(x) = 2x - 1$ **3.** $f(x) = -3x + 1$

  4. FITNESS Use the inverse function in Example 3 to find the length at which the band provides 13 pounds of resistance.

INVERSES OF NONLINEAR FUNCTIONS The graphs of the power functions $f(x) = x^2$ and $g(x) = x^3$ are shown below along with their reflections in the line $y = x$. Notice that the inverse of $g(x) = x^3$ is a function, but that the inverse of $f(x) = x^2$ is *not* a function.

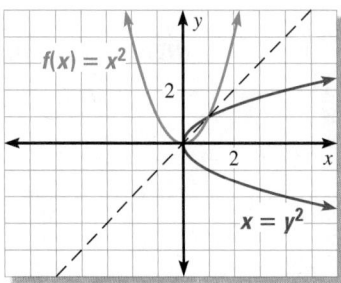

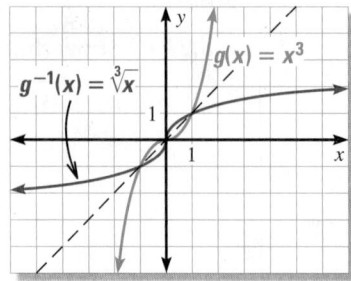

If the domain of $f(x) = x^2$ is *restricted* to only nonnegative real numbers, then the inverse of f *is* a function.

❖ **EXAMPLE 4** **Find the inverse of a power function**

Find the inverse of $f(x) = x^2$, $x \geq 0$. Then graph f and f^{-1}.

Solution

$$f(x) = x^2 \qquad \text{Write original function.}$$

$$y = x^2 \qquad \text{Replace } f(x) \text{ with } y.$$

$$x = y^2 \qquad \text{Switch } x \text{ and } y.$$

$$\pm\sqrt{x} = y \qquad \text{Take square roots of each side.}$$

The domain of f is restricted to nonnegative values of x. So, the range of f^{-1} must also be restricted to nonnegative values, and therefore the inverse is $f^{-1}(x) = \sqrt{x}$. (If the domain was restricted to $x \leq 0$, you would choose $f^{-1}(x) = -\sqrt{x}$.)

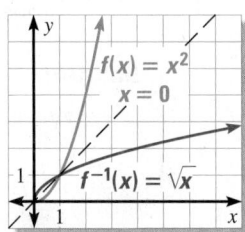

HORIZONTAL LINE TEST You can use the graph of a function f to determine whether the inverse of f is a function by applying the *horizontal line test*.

KEY CONCEPT *For Your Notebook*

Horizontal Line Test

The inverse of a function f is also a function if and only if no horizontal line intersects the graph of f more than once.

Inverse is a function

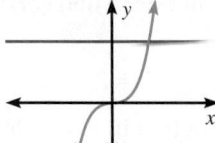

Inverse is not a function

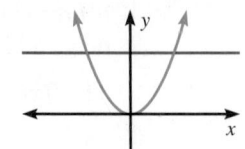

EXAMPLE 5 **Find the inverse of a cubic function**

Consider the function $f(x) = 2x^3 + 1$. Determine whether the inverse of f is a function. Then find the inverse.

Solution

Graph the function f. Notice that no horizontal line intersects the graph more than once. So, the inverse of f is itself a function. To find an equation for f^{-1}, complete the following steps:

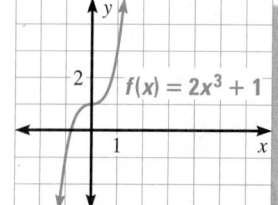

$$f(x) = 2x^3 + 1 \qquad \text{Write original function.}$$

$$y = 2x^3 + 1 \qquad \text{Replace } f(x) \text{ with } y.$$

$$x = 2y^3 + 1 \qquad \text{Switch } x \text{ and } y.$$

$$x - 1 = 2y^3 \qquad \text{Subtract 1 from each side.}$$

$$\frac{x - 1}{2} = y^3 \qquad \text{Divide each side by 2.}$$

$$\sqrt[3]{\frac{x - 1}{2}} = y \qquad \text{Take cube root of each side.}$$

▸ The inverse of f is $f^{-1}(x) = \sqrt[3]{\dfrac{x - 1}{2}}$.

✓ **GUIDED PRACTICE**   for Examples 4 and 5

Find the inverse of the function. Then graph the function and its inverse.

5. $f(x) = x^6, x \geq 0$

6. $g(x) = \dfrac{1}{27}x^3$

7. $f(x) = -\dfrac{64}{125}x^3$

8. $f(x) = -x^3 + 4$

9. $f(x) = 2x^5 + 3$

10. $g(x) = -7x^5 + 7$

EXAMPLE 6 **Find the inverse of a power model**

TICKET PRICES The average price P (in dollars) for a National Football League ticket can be modeled by

$$P = 35t^{0.192}$$

where t is the number of years since 1995. Find the inverse model that gives time as a function of the average ticket price.

Solution

$$P = 35t^{0.192} \qquad \text{Write original model.}$$

$$\frac{P}{35} = t^{0.192} \qquad \text{Divide each side by 35.}$$

$$\left(\frac{P}{35}\right)^{1/0.192} = \left(t^{0.192}\right)^{1/0.192} \qquad \text{Raise each side to the power } \dfrac{1}{0.192}.$$

$$\left(\frac{P}{35}\right)^{5.2} \approx t \qquad \text{Simplify. This is the inverse model.}$$

AP Images/Gail Burton

EXAMPLE 7 **Use an inverse power model to make a prediction**

Use the inverse power model from Example 6 to predict the year when the average ticket price will reach $58.

Solution

$$t = \left(\frac{P}{35}\right)^{5.2}$$ Write inverse power model.

$$= \left(\frac{58}{35}\right)^{5.2}$$ Substitute 58 for P.

$$\approx 14$$ Use a calculator.

▸ You can predict that the average ticket price will reach $58 about 14 years after 1995, or in 2009.

✓ **GUIDED PRACTICE**   for Examples 6 and 7

11. TICKET PRICES The average price P (in dollars) for a Major League Baseball ticket can be modeled by $P = 10.7t^{0.272}$ where t is the number of years since 1995. Write the inverse model. Then use the inverse to predict the year when the average ticket price will reach $25.

3.4 **EXERCISES**

HOMEWORK KEY   ○ = See **WORKED-OUT SOLUTIONS**
   Exs. 7, 15, and 49
★ = **STANDARDIZED TEST PRACTICE**
   Exs. 2, 14, 21, 28, and 48

SKILL PRACTICE

1. **VOCABULARY** State the definition of an inverse relation.

2. ★ **WRITING** *Explain* how to determine whether a function g is an inverse of f.

EXAMPLE 1
for Exs. 3–13

INVERSE RELATIONS **Find an equation for the inverse relation.**

3. $y = 4x - 1$

4. $y = -2x + 5$

5. $y = 7x - 6$

6. $y = 10x - 28$

7. $y = 12x + 7$

8. $y = -18x - 5$

9. $y = 5x + \frac{1}{3}$

10. $y = -\frac{2}{3}x + 2$

11. $y = -\frac{3}{5}x + \frac{7}{5}$

ERROR ANALYSIS *Describe* and correct the error in finding the inverse of the relation.

12.
$$y = 6x - 11$$
$$x = 6y - 11$$
$$x + 11 = 6y$$
$$\frac{x}{6} + 11 = y$$

13.
$$y = -x + 3$$
$$-x = y + 3$$
$$-x - 3 = y$$

14. ★ **OPEN-ENDED MATH** Write a function f such that the graph of f^{-1} is a line with a slope of 3.

EXAMPLE 2
for Exs. 15–21

VERIFYING INVERSE FUNCTIONS Verify that f and g are inverse functions.

15. $f(x) = x + 4$, $g(x) = x - 4$

16. $f(x) = 2x + 3$, $g(x) = \frac{1}{2}x - \frac{3}{2}$

17. $f(x) = \frac{1}{4}x^3$, $g(x) = (4x)^{1/3}$

18. $f(x) = \frac{1}{5}x - 1$, $g(x) = 5x + 5$

19. $f(x) = 4x + 9$, $g(x) = \frac{1}{4}x - \frac{9}{4}$

20. $f(x) = 5x^2 - 2$, $x \geq 0$; $g(x) = \left(\frac{x + 2}{5}\right)^{1/2}$

21. ★ **MULTIPLE CHOICE** What is the inverse of the function whose graph is shown?

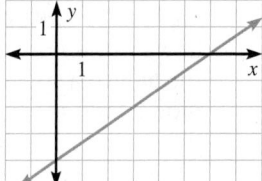

A $g(x) = \frac{3}{2}x - 6$

B $g(x) = \frac{3}{2}x + 6$

C $g(x) = \frac{2}{3}x - 6$

D $g(x) = \frac{3}{2}x + 12$

EXAMPLE 4
for Exs. 22–28

INVERSES OF POWER FUNCTIONS Find the inverse of the power function.

22. $f(x) = x^7$

23. $f(x) = 4x^4$, $x \geq 0$

24. $f(x) = -10x^6$, $x \leq 0$

25. $f(x) = 32x^5$

26. $f(x) = -\frac{2}{5}x^3$

27. $f(x) = \frac{16}{25}x^2$, $x \leq 0$

28. ★ **MULTIPLE CHOICE** What is the inverse of $f(x) = -\frac{1}{64}x^3$?

A $g(x) = -4x^3$

B $g(x) = 4\sqrt[3]{x}$

C $g(x) = -4\sqrt[3]{x}$

D $g(x) = \sqrt[3]{-4x}$

EXAMPLE 5
for Exs. 29–43

HORIZONTAL LINE TEST Graph the function f. Then use the graph to determine whether the inverse of f is a function.

29. $f(x) = 3x + 1$

30. $f(x) = -x - 5$

31. $f(x) = \frac{1}{4}x^2 - 1$

32. $f(x) = -6x^2$, $x \geq 0$

33. $f(x) = \frac{1}{3}x^3$

34. $f(x) = x^3 - 2$

35. $f(x) = (x - 4)(x + 1)$

36. $f(x) = |x| + 4$

37. $f(x) = 4x^4 - 5x^2 - 6$

INVERSES OF NONLINEAR FUNCTIONS Find the inverse of the function.

38. $f(x) = \frac{3}{2}x^4$, $x \geq 0$

39. $f(x) = x^3 - 2$

40. $f(x) = \frac{3}{4}x^5 + 5$

41. $f(x) = -\frac{2}{5}x^6 + 8$, $x \leq 0$

42. $f(x) = \frac{2x^3 - 6}{9}$

43. $f(x) = x^4 - 9$, $x \geq 0$

44. **REASONING** Determine whether the statement is *true* or *false*. *Explain* your reasoning.

  a. If $f(x) = x^n$ where n is a positive even integer, then the inverse of f is a function.

  b. If $f(x) = x^n$ where n is a positive odd integer, then the inverse of f is a function.

45. **CHALLENGE** Show that the inverse of any linear function $f(x) = mx + b$, where $m \neq 0$, is also a linear function. Give the slope and y-intercept of the graph of f^{-1} in terms of m and b.

EXAMPLE 3
for Exs. 46–48

46. **EXCHANGE RATES** The *euro* is the unit of currency for the European Union. On a certain day, the number E of euros that could be obtained for D dollars was given by this function:

$$E = 0.81419D$$

Find the inverse of the function. Then use the inverse to find the number of dollars that could be obtained for 250 euros on that day.

47. **MULTI-STEP PROBLEM** When calibrating a spring scale, you need to know how far the spring stretches for various weights. Hooke's law states that the length a spring stretches is proportional to the weight attached to it. A model for one scale is $\ell = 0.5w + 3$ where ℓ is the total length (in inches) of the stretched spring and w is the weight (in pounds) of the object.

  a. Find the inverse of the given model.

  b. If you place a weight on the scale and the spring stretches to a total length of 6.5 inches, how heavy is the weight?

48. ★ **EXTENDED RESPONSE** At the start of a dog sled race in Anchorage, Alaska, the temperature was 5°C. By the end of the race, the temperature was −10°C. The formula for converting temperatures from degrees Fahrenheit F to degrees Celsius C is $C = \frac{5}{9}(F - 32)$.

  a. Find the inverse of the given model. *Describe* what information you can obtain from the inverse.

  b. Find the Fahrenheit temperatures at the start and end of the race.

  c. Use a graphing calculator to graph the original function and its inverse. Find the temperature that is the same on both temperature scales.

EXAMPLES
6 and 7
for Exs. 49–50

(49.) **BOAT SPEED** The maximum hull speed v (in knots) of a boat with a displacement hull can be approximated by

$$v = 1.34\sqrt{\ell}$$

where ℓ is the length (in feet) of the boat's waterline. Find the inverse of the model. Then find the waterline length needed to achieve a maximum speed of 7.5 knots.

waterline length

Animated Algebra at my.hrw.com

50. **BIOLOGY** The body surface area A (in square meters) of a person with a mass of 60 kilograms can be approximated by the model

$$A = 0.2195h^{0.3964}$$

where h is the person's height (in centimeters). Find the inverse of the model. Then estimate the height of a 60 kilogram person who has a body surface area of 1.6 square meters.

○ = See WORKED-OUT SOLUTIONS   ★ = STANDARDIZED
   in Student Resources   TEST PRACTICE

AP Images/Rod Taylor

51. CHALLENGE Consider the function $g(x) = -x$.

    a. Graph $g(x) = -x$ and explain why it is its own inverse. Also verify that $g(x) = g^{-1}(x)$ algebraically.

    b. Graph other linear functions that are their own inverses. Write equations of the lines you graphed.

    c. Use your results from part (b) to write a general equation describing the family of linear functions that are their own inverses.

QUIZ

Let $f(x) = 4x^2 - x$ and $g(x) = 2x^2$. **Perform the indicated operation and state the domain.**

1. $f(x) + g(x)$ **2.** $g(x) - f(x)$ **3.** $f(x) \cdot g(x)$ **4.** $\dfrac{f(x)}{g(x)}$

5. $f(g(x))$ **6.** $g(f(x))$ **7.** $f(f(x))$ **8.** $g(g(x))$

Verify that f and g are inverse functions.

9. $f(x) = x - 9$, $g(x) = x + 9$ **10.** $f(x) = 5x^3$, $g(x) = \sqrt[3]{\dfrac{x}{5}}$

11. $f(x) = -\dfrac{3}{2}x + \dfrac{1}{4}$, $g(x) = -\dfrac{2}{3}x + \dfrac{1}{6}$ **12.** $f(x) = 6x^2 + 1$, $x \geq 0$; $g(x) = \left(\dfrac{x-1}{6}\right)^{1/2}$

Find the inverse of the function.

13. $f(x) = -\dfrac{1}{3}x + 5$ **14.** $f(x) = x^2 - 16$, $x \geq 0$ **15.** $f(x) = -\dfrac{2}{9}x^5$

16. $f(x) = 5x + 12$ **17.** $f(x) = -3x^3 - 4$ **18.** $f(x) = 9x^4 - 49$, $x \leq 0$

19. GASOLINE COSTS The cost (in dollars) of g gallons of gasoline can be modeled by $C(g) = 2.15g$. The amount of gasoline used by a car can be modeled by $g(d) = 0.02d$ where d is the distance (in miles) that the car has been driven. Find $C(g(d))$ and $C(g(400))$. What does $C(g(400))$ represent?

3.5 Graph Square Root and Cube Root Functions

Before	You graphed polynomial functions.
Now	You will graph square root and cube root functions.
Why?	So you can graph the speed of a racing car, as in Ex. 38.

Key Vocabulary
• radical function
• parent function

Previously, you saw the graphs of $y = \sqrt{x}$ and $y = \sqrt[3]{x}$. These are examples of **radical functions**. In this lesson, you will learn to graph functions of the form $y = a\sqrt{x - h} + k$ and $y = a\sqrt[3]{x - h} + k$.

CC.9-12.F.IF.7 Graph functions expressed symbolically and show key features of the graph, by hand in simple cases and using technology for more complicated cases.*
b. Graph square root, cube root, and piecewise-defined functions, including step functions and absolute value functions.

KEY CONCEPT
For Your Notebook

Parent Functions for Square Root and Cube Root Functions

The parent function for the family of square root functions is $f(x) = \sqrt{x}$.

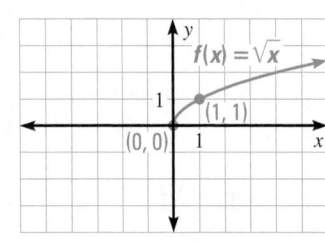

Domain: $x \geq 0$, Range: $y \geq 0$

The parent function for the family of cube root functions is $g(x) = \sqrt[3]{x}$.

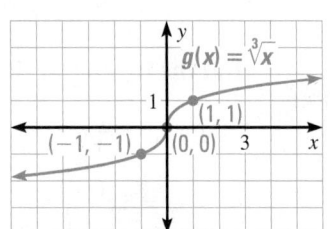

Domain and range: all real numbers

EXAMPLE 1   Graph a square root function

Graph $y = \frac{1}{2}\sqrt{x}$, and state the domain and range. Compare the graph with the graph of $y = \sqrt{x}$.

Solution

Make a table of values and sketch the graph.

x	0	1	2	3	4
y	0	0.5	0.71	0.87	1

The radicand of a square root must be nonnegative. So, the domain is $x \geq 0$. The range is $y \geq 0$.

The graph of $y = \frac{1}{2}\sqrt{x}$ is a vertical shrink of the graph of $y = \sqrt{x}$ by a factor of $\frac{1}{2}$.

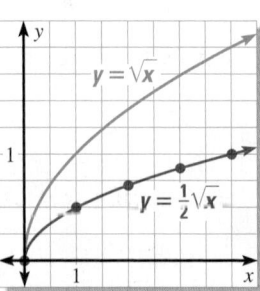

EXAMPLE 2 Graph a cube root function

Graph $y = -3\sqrt[3]{x}$, and state the domain and range. Compare the graph with the graph of $y = \sqrt[3]{x}$.

Solution

Make a table of values and sketch the graph.

x	−2	−1	0	1	2
y	3.78	3	0	−3	−3.78

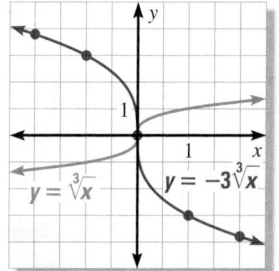

The domain and range are all real numbers.

The graph of $y = -3\sqrt[3]{x}$ is a vertical stretch of the graph of $y = \sqrt[3]{x}$ by a factor of 3 followed by a reflection in the x-axis.

EXAMPLE 3 Solve a multi-step problem

PENDULUMS The *period* of a pendulum is the time the pendulum takes to complete one back-and-forth swing. The period T (in seconds) can be modeled by $T = 1.11\sqrt{\ell}$ where ℓ is the pendulum's length (in feet).

- Use a graphing calculator to graph the model.

- How long is a pendulum with a period of 3 seconds?

Solution

STEP 1 **Graph** the model. Enter the equation $y = 1.11\sqrt{x}$. The graph is shown below.

STEP 2 **Use** the *trace* feature to find the value of x when $y = 3$. The graph shows $x \approx 7.3$.

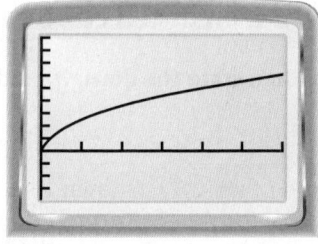

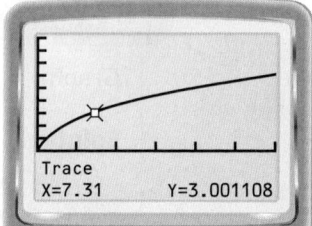

Trace
X=7.31   Y=3.001108

▸ A pendulum with a period of 3 seconds is about 7.3 feet long.

✓ **GUIDED PRACTICE** for Examples 1, 2, and 3

Graph the function. Then state the domain and range.

1. $y = -3\sqrt{x}$ 　　**2.** $f(x) = \frac{1}{4}\sqrt{x}$ 　　**3.** $y = -\frac{1}{2}\sqrt[3]{x}$ 　　**4.** $g(x) = 4\sqrt[3]{x}$

5. WHAT IF? Use the model in Example 3 to find the length of a pendulum with a period of 1 second.

TRANSLATIONS OF RADICAL FUNCTIONS The procedure for graphing functions of the form $y = a\sqrt{x - h} + k$ and $y = a\sqrt[3]{x - h} + k$ is described below.

KEY CONCEPT   *For Your Notebook*

Graphs of Radical Functions

To graph $y = a\sqrt{x - h} + k$ or $y = a\sqrt[3]{x - h} + k$, follow these steps:

STEP 1 **Sketch** the graph of $y = a\sqrt{x}$ or $y = a\sqrt[3]{x}$.

STEP 2 **Translate** the graph horizontally h units and vertically k units.

EXAMPLE 4 **Graph a translated square root function**

Graph $y = -2\sqrt{x - 3} + 2$. Then state the domain and range.

Solution

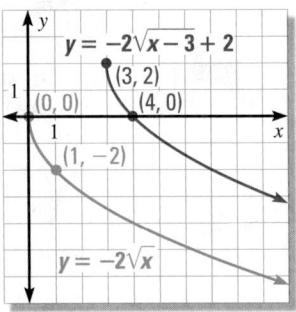

STEP 1 **Sketch** the graph of $y = -2\sqrt{x}$ (shown in blue). Notice that it begins at the origin and passes through the point $(1, -2)$.

STEP 2 **Translate** the graph. For $y = -2\sqrt{x - 3} + 2$, $h = 3$ and $k = 2$. So, shift the graph of $y = -2\sqrt{x}$ right 3 units and up 2 units. The resulting graph starts at $(3, 2)$ and passes through $(4, 0)$.

From the graph, you can see that the domain of the function is $x \geq 3$ and the range of the function is $y \leq 2$.

Animated Algebra at my.hrw.com

EXAMPLE 5 **Graph a translated cube root function**

Graph $y = 3\sqrt[3]{x + 4} - 1$. Then state the domain and range.

Solution

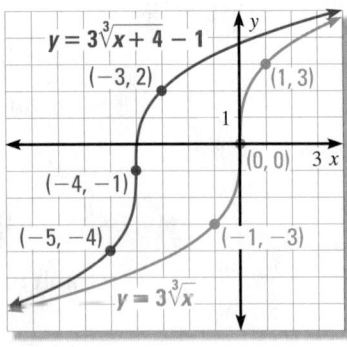

STEP 1 **Sketch** the graph of $y = 3\sqrt[3]{x}$ (shown in blue). Notice that it passes through the origin and the points $(-1, -3)$ and $(1, 3)$.

STEP 2 **Translate** the graph. Note that for $y = 3\sqrt[3]{x + 4} - 1$, $h = -4$ and $k = -1$. So, shift the graph of $y = 3\sqrt[3]{x}$ left 4 units and down 1 unit. The resulting graph passes through the points $(-5, -4)$, $(-4, -1)$, and $(-3, 2)$.

From the graph, you can see that the domain and range of the function are both all real numbers.

Animated Algebra at my.hrw.com

GUIDED PRACTICE for Examples 4 and 5

Graph the function. Then state the domain and range.

6. $y = -4\sqrt{x} + 2$ 7. $y = 2\sqrt{x+1}$ 8. $f(x) = \frac{1}{2}\sqrt{x-3} - 1$

9. $y = 2\sqrt[3]{x-4}$ 10. $y = \sqrt[3]{x} - 5$ 11. $g(x) = -\sqrt[3]{x+2} - 3$

3.5 EXERCISES

HOMEWORK KEY

○ = See WORKED-OUT SOLUTIONS
Exs. 11, 17, and 37

★ = STANDARDIZED TEST PRACTICE
Exs. 2, 9, 25, 27, and 37

◆ = MULTIPLE REPRESENTATIONS
Ex. 39

SKILL PRACTICE

1. **VOCABULARY** Copy and complete: Square root functions and cube root functions are examples of __?__ functions.

2. ★ **WRITING** The graph of $y = \sqrt{x}$ is the graph of $y = a\sqrt{x-h} + k$ with $a = 1$, $h = 0$, and $k = 0$. Predict how the graph of $y = \sqrt{x}$ will change if:
   a. $a = -3$ b. $h = 2$ c. $k = 4$

EXAMPLE 1
for Exs. 3–9

SQUARE ROOT FUNCTIONS Graph the function. Then state the domain and range.

3. $y = -4\sqrt{x}$ 4. $f(x) = \frac{1}{2}\sqrt{x}$ 5. $y = -\frac{4}{5}\sqrt{x}$

6. $y = -6\sqrt{x}$ 7. $y = 5\sqrt{x}$ 8. $g(x) = 9\sqrt{x}$

9. ★ **MULTIPLE CHOICE** The graph of which function is shown?

Ⓐ $y = \frac{3}{4}\sqrt{x}$ Ⓑ $y = -\frac{3}{4}\sqrt{x}$

Ⓒ $y = \frac{3}{2}\sqrt{x}$ Ⓓ $y = -\frac{3}{2}\sqrt{x}$

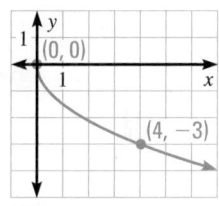

EXAMPLE 2
for Exs. 10–15

CUBE ROOT FUNCTIONS Graph the function. Then state the domain and range.

10. $y = \frac{1}{4}\sqrt[3]{x}$ 11. $y = 2\sqrt[3]{x}$ 12. $f(x) = -5\sqrt[3]{x}$

13. $h(x) = -\frac{1}{7}\sqrt[3]{x}$ 14. $g(x) = 6\sqrt[3]{x}$ 15. $y = \frac{7}{9}\sqrt[3]{x}$

EXAMPLES 4 and 5
for Exs. 16–24

RADICAL FUNCTIONS Graph the function. Then state the domain and range.

16. $f(x) = 2\sqrt{x-1} + 3$ 17. $y = (x+1)^{1/2} + 8$ 18. $y = -4\sqrt{x-5} + 1$

19. $y = \frac{3}{4}x^{1/3} - 1$ 20. $y = -2\sqrt[3]{x+5} + 5$ 21. $h(x) = -3\sqrt[3]{x+7} - 6$

22. $y = -\sqrt{x-4} - 7$ 23. $g(x) = -\frac{1}{3}\sqrt[3]{x} - 6$ 24. $y = 4\sqrt[3]{x-4} + 5$

25. ★ **SHORT RESPONSE** *Explain* why there are limitations on the domain and range of the function $y = \sqrt{x-5} + 4$.

26. ERROR ANALYSIS A student tried to explain how the graphs of $y = -2\sqrt[3]{x}$ and $y = -2\sqrt[3]{x+1} - 3$ are related. *Describe* and correct the error.

> The graph of $y = -2\sqrt[3]{x+1} - 3$ is the graph of $y = -2\sqrt[3]{x}$ translated right 1 unit and down 3 units.

27. ★ MULTIPLE CHOICE If the graph of $y = 3\sqrt[3]{x}$ is shifted left 2 units, what is the equation of the translated graph?

  A $y = 3\sqrt[3]{x} - 2$ **B** $y = 3\sqrt[3]{x} - 2$ **C** $y = 3\sqrt[3]{x+2}$ **D** $y = 3\sqrt[3]{x} + 2$

REASONING **Find the domain and range of the function without graphing.** *Explain* **how you found your answers.**

28. $y = \sqrt{x+5}$

29. $y = \sqrt{x-12}$

30. $y = \frac{1}{3}\sqrt{x} - 4$

31. $y = \frac{1}{2}\sqrt[3]{x+7}$

32. $g(x) = \sqrt[3]{x+7}$

33. $f(x) = \frac{1}{4}\sqrt{x-3} + 6$

34. CHALLENGE Graph $y = \sqrt[4]{x}$, $y = \sqrt[5]{x}$, $y = \sqrt[6]{x}$, and $y = \sqrt[7]{x}$ on a graphing calculator. Make generalizations about the graph of $y = \sqrt[n]{x}$ when n is even and when n is odd.

PROBLEM SOLVING

EXAMPLE 3
for Exs. 35–36

35. INDIRECT MEASUREMENT The distance d (in miles) that a pilot can see to the horizon can be modeled by $d = 1.22\sqrt{a}$ where a is the plane's altitude (in feet above sea level). Graph the model on a graphing calculator. Then determine at what altitude the pilot can see 8 miles.

36. PENDULUMS Use the model $T = 1.11\sqrt{\ell}$ for the period of a pendulum from Example 3.

  a. Find the period of a pendulum with a length of 2 feet.

  b. Find the length of a pendulum with a period of 2 seconds.

37. ★ SHORT RESPONSE The speed v (in meters per second) of sound waves in air depends on the temperature K (in kelvins) and can be modeled by:

$$v = 331.5\sqrt{\frac{K}{273.15}}, \ K \geq 0$$

  a. Kelvin temperature K is related to Celsius temperature C by the formula $K = 273.15 + C$. Write an equation that gives the speed v of sound waves in air as a function of the temperature C in degrees Celsius.

  b. What are a reasonable domain and range for the function from part (a)?

○ = See **WORKED-OUT SOLUTIONS** in Student Resources   ★ = **STANDARDIZED TEST PRACTICE**   ◆ = **MULTIPLE REPRESENTATIONS**

38. **DRAG RACING** For a given total weight, the speed of a car at the end of a drag race is a function of the car's power. For a car with a total weight of 3500 pounds, the speed s (in miles per hour) can be modeled by $s = 14.8\sqrt[3]{p}$ where p is the power (in horsepower). Graph the model. Then determine the power of a 3500 pound car that reaches a speed of 200 miles per hour.

39. ◆ **MULTIPLE REPRESENTATIONS** Under certain conditions, a skydiver's terminal velocity v_t (in feet per second) is given by

$$v_t = 33.7\sqrt{\frac{W}{A}}$$

where W is the weight of the skydiver (in pounds) and A is the skydiver's cross-sectional surface area (in square feet). Note that skydivers can vary their cross-sectional surface area by changing positions as they fall.

   a. **Writing an Equation** Write an equation that gives v_t as a function of A for a skydiver who weighs 165 pounds.

   b. **Making a Table** Make a table of values for the equation from part (a).

   c. **Drawing a Graph** Use your table to graph the equation.

40. **CHALLENGE** The surface area S of a right circular cone with a slant height of 1 unit is given by $S = \pi r + \pi r^2$ where r is the cone's radius.

   a. Use completing the square to show the following:

$$r = \frac{1}{\sqrt{\pi}}\sqrt{S + \frac{\pi}{4}} - \frac{1}{2}$$

   b. Graph the equation from part (a) using a graphing calculator.

   c. Find the radius of a right circular cone with a slant height of 1 unit and a surface area of $\frac{3\pi}{4}$ square units.

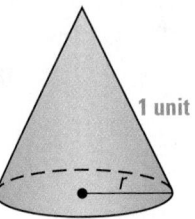

1 unit

r

3.6 Solve Radical Equations

Before	You solved polynomial equations.
Now	You will solve radical equations.
Why?	So you can calculate hang time, as in Ex. 60.

Key Vocabulary
• radical equation
• extraneous solution

CC.9-12.A.REI.2 Solve simple rational and radical equations in one variable, and give examples showing how extraneous solutions may arise.

Equations with radicals that have variables in their radicands are called **radical equations**. An example of a radical equation is $\sqrt[3]{2x + 7} = 3$.

KEY CONCEPT *For Your Notebook*

Solving Radical Equations

To solve a radical equation, follow these steps:

STEP 1 **Isolate** the radical on one side of the equation, if necessary.

STEP 2 **Raise** each side of the equation to the same power to eliminate the radical and obtain a linear, quadratic, or other polynomial equation.

STEP 3 **Solve** the polynomial equation using techniques you learned in previous chapters. Check your solution.

EXAMPLE 1 Solve a radical equation

Solve $\sqrt[3]{2x + 7} = 3$.

$\sqrt[3]{2x + 7} = 3$	Write original equation.
$(\sqrt[3]{2x + 7})^3 = 3^3$	Cube each side to eliminate the radical.
$2x + 7 = 27$	Simplify.
$2x = 20$	Subtract 7 from each side.
$x = 10$	Divide each side by 2.

CHECK Check $x = 10$ in the original equation.

$\sqrt[3]{2(10) + 7} \overset{?}{=} 3$	Substitute 10 for x.
$\sqrt[3]{27} \overset{?}{=} 3$	Simplify.
$3 = 3 \checkmark$	Solution checks.

✓ **GUIDED PRACTICE** for Example 1

Solve the equation. Check your solution.

1. $\sqrt[3]{x} - 9 = -1$ **2.** $\sqrt{x + 25} = 4$ **3.** $2\sqrt[3]{x - 3} = 4$

204 Chapter 3 Rational Exponents and Radical Functions

Cathrine Wessel/Corbis

EXAMPLE 2 Solve a radical equation given a function

WIND VELOCITY In a hurricane, the mean sustained wind velocity v (in meters per second) is given by

$$v(p) = 6.3\sqrt{1013 - p}$$

where p is the air pressure (in millibars) at the center of the hurricane. Estimate the air pressure at the center of a hurricane when the mean sustained wind velocity is 54.5 meters per second.

ANOTHER WAY

For alternative methods for solving the problem in Example 2, see the **Problem Solving Workshop**.

Solution

$v(p) = 6.3\sqrt{1013 - p}$	Write given function.
$54.5 = 6.3\sqrt{1013 - p}$	Substitute 54.5 for $v(p)$.
$8.65 \approx \sqrt{1013 - p}$	Divide each side by 6.3.
$(8.65)^2 \approx \left(\sqrt{1013 - p}\right)^2$	Square each side.
$74.8 \approx 1013 - p$	Simplify.
$-938.2 \approx -p$	Subtract 1013 from each side.
$938.2 \approx p$	Divide each side by -1.

▸ The air pressure at the center of the hurricane is about 938 millibars.

✓ **GUIDED PRACTICE** | for Example 2

4. WHAT IF? Use the function in Example 2 to estimate the air pressure at the center of a hurricane when the mean sustained wind velocity is 48.3 meters per second.

RATIONAL EXPONENTS When an equation contains a power with a rational exponent, you can solve the equation using a procedure similar to the one for solving radical equations. In this case, you first isolate the power and then raise each side of the equation to the reciprocal of the rational exponent.

★ EXAMPLE 3 Standardized Test Practice

What are the solutions of the equation $4x^{2/3} = 36$?

(A) ± 3 (B) ± 6 (C) ± 21 (D) ± 27

AVOID ERRORS

You can think of $x^{2/3} = 9$ as $(x^{1/3})^2 = 9$ and undo each power separately:

$$(x^{1/3})^2 = 9$$
$$x^{1/3} = \pm 3$$
$$x = \pm 27$$

Solution

$4x^{2/3} = 36$	Write original equation.
$x^{2/3} = 9$	Divide each side by 4.
$\left(x^{2/3}\right)^{3/2} = 9^{3/2}$	Raise each side to the power $\frac{3}{2}$.
$x = \pm 27$	Simplify.

▸ The correct answer is D. (A) (B) (C) **(D)**

Philippe Giraud/Corbis Sygma

EXAMPLE 4 Solve an equation with a rational exponent

Solve $(x + 2)^{3/4} - 1 = 7$.

$(x + 2)^{3/4} - 1 = 7$	Write original equation.
$(x + 2)^{3/4} = 8$	Add 1 to each side.
$\left[(x + 2)^{3/4}\right]^{4/3} = 8^{4/3}$	Raise each side to the power $\frac{4}{3}$.
$x + 2 = \left(8^{1/3}\right)^4$	Apply properties of exponents.
$x + 2 = 2^4$	Simplify.
$x + 2 = 16$	Simplify.
$x = 14$	Subtract 2 from each side.

▶ The solution is 14. Check this in the original equation.

GUIDED PRACTICE for Examples 3 and 4

Solve the equation. Check your solution.

5. $3x^{3/2} = 375$

6. $-2x^{3/4} = -16$

7. $-\frac{2}{3}x^{1/5} = -2$

8. $(x + 3)^{5/2} = 32$

9. $(x - 5)^{4/3} = 81$

10. $(x + 2)^{2/3} + 3 = 7$

EXTRANEOUS SOLUTIONS Raising each side of an equation to the same power may introduce extraneous solutions. When you use this procedure, you should always check each apparent solution in the *original* equation.

EXAMPLE 5 Solve an equation with an extraneous solution

Solve $x + 1 = \sqrt{7x + 15}$.

$x + 1 = \sqrt{7x + 15}$	Write original equation.
$(x + 1)^2 = \left(\sqrt{7x + 15}\right)^2$	Square each side.
$x^2 + 2x + 1 = 7x + 15$	Expand left side and simplify right side.
$x^2 - 5x - 14 = 0$	Write in standard form.
$(x - 7)(x + 2) = 0$	Factor.
$x - 7 = 0 \quad \text{or} \quad x + 2 = 0$	Zero-product property
$x = 7 \quad \text{or} \qquad x = -2$	Solve for x.

CHECK

Check $x = 7$ in the original equation.

$x + 1 = \sqrt{7x + 15}$

$7 + 1 \overset{?}{=} \sqrt{7(7) + 15}$

$8 \overset{?}{=} \sqrt{64}$

$8 = 8 \checkmark$

Check $x = -2$ in the original equation.

$x + 1 = \sqrt{7x + 15}$

$-2 + 1 \overset{?}{=} \sqrt{7(-2) + 15}$

$-1 \overset{?}{=} \sqrt{1}$

$-1 \neq 1$

▶ The only solution is 7. (The apparent solution -2 is extraneous.)

SQUARING TWICE When an equation contains two radicals, you may need to square each side twice in order to eliminate both radicals.

 EXAMPLE 6 **Solve an equation with two radicals**

Solve $\sqrt{x + 2} + 1 = \sqrt{3 - x}$.

Solution

METHOD 1 **Solve** using algebra.

REVIEW
FOIL METHOD
For help with multiplying algebraic expressions using the FOIL method, you may want to review the lesson *Graph Quadratic Functions in Vertex or Intercept Form.*

$\sqrt{x + 2} + 1 = \sqrt{3 - x}$	Write original equation.
$\left(\sqrt{x + 2} + 1\right)^2 = \left(\sqrt{3 - x}\right)^2$	Square each side.
$x + 2 + 2\sqrt{x + 2} + 1 = 3 - x$	Expand left side and simplify right side.
$2\sqrt{x + 2} = -2x$	Isolate radical expression.
$\sqrt{x + 2} = -x$	Divide each side by 2.
$\left(\sqrt{x + 2}\right)^2 = (-x)^2$	Square each side again.
$x + 2 = x^2$	Simplify.
$0 = x^2 - x - 2$	Write in standard form.
$0 = (x - 2)(x + 1)$	Factor.
$x - 2 = 0 \quad \text{or} \quad x + 1 = 0$	Zero-product property
$x = 2 \quad \text{or} \quad x = -1$	Solve for x.

Check $x = 2$ in the original equation.

$\sqrt{x + 2} + 1 = \sqrt{3 - x}$

$\sqrt{2 + 2} + 1 \stackrel{?}{=} \sqrt{3 - 2}$

$\sqrt{4} + 1 \stackrel{?}{=} \sqrt{1}$

$3 \neq 1$

Check $x = -1$ in the original equation.

$\sqrt{x + 2} + 1 = \sqrt{3 - x}$

$\sqrt{-1 + 2} + 1 \stackrel{?}{=} \sqrt{3 - (-1)}$

$\sqrt{1} + 1 \stackrel{?}{=} \sqrt{4}$

$2 = 2 \checkmark$

▶ The only solution is −1. (The apparent solution 2 is extraneous.)

METHOD 2 **Use** a graph to solve the equation.

Use a graphing calculator to graph $y_1 = \sqrt{x + 2} + 1$ and $y_2 = \sqrt{3 - x}$. Then find the intersection points of the two graphs by using the *intersect* feature. You will find that the only point of intersection is (−1, 2). Therefore, −1 is the only solution of the equation $\sqrt{x + 2} + 1 = \sqrt{3 - x}$.

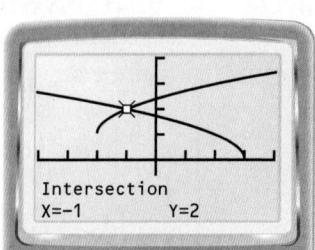

 GUIDED PRACTICE for Examples 5 and 6

Solve the equation. Check for extraneous solutions.

11. $x - \frac{1}{2} = \sqrt{\frac{1}{4}x}$

12. $\sqrt{10x + 9} = x + 3$

13. $\sqrt{2x + 5} = \sqrt{x + 7}$

14. $\sqrt{x + 6} - 2 = \sqrt{x - 2}$

3.6 EXERCISES

SKILL PRACTICE

1. **VOCABULARY** Copy and complete: When you solve an equation algebraically, an apparent solution that must be rejected because it does not satisfy the original equation is called a(n) __?__ solution.

2. ★ **WRITING** A student was asked to solve $\sqrt{3x-1} - \sqrt{9x-5} = 0$. His first step was to square each side. While trying to isolate x, he gave up in frustration. What could the student have done to avoid this situation?

EXAMPLE 1
for Exs. 3–21

EQUATIONS WITH SQUARE ROOTS Solve the equation. Check your solution.

3. $\sqrt{5x+1} = 6$

4. $\sqrt{3x+10} = 8$

5. $\sqrt{9x} + 11 = 14$

6. $\sqrt{2x} - \dfrac{2}{3} = 0$

7. $-2\sqrt{24x} + 13 = -11$

8. $8\sqrt{10x} - 7 = 9$

9. $\sqrt{x-25} + 3 = 5$

10. $-4\sqrt{x} - 6 = -20$

11. $\sqrt{-2x+3} - 2 = 10$

12. ★ **MULTIPLE CHOICE** What is the solution of $\sqrt{8x+3} = 3$?

Ⓐ $-\dfrac{3}{4}$
Ⓑ 0
Ⓒ $\dfrac{3}{4}$
Ⓓ $\dfrac{9}{8}$

EQUATIONS WITH CUBE ROOTS Solve the equation. Check your solution.

13. $\sqrt[3]{x} - 10 = -3$

14. $\sqrt[3]{x-16} = 2$

15. $\sqrt[3]{12x} - 13 = -7$

16. $3\sqrt[3]{16x} - 7 = 17$

17. $-5\sqrt[3]{8x} + 12 = -8$

18. $\sqrt[3]{4x+5} = \dfrac{1}{2}$

19. $\sqrt[3]{x-3} + 2 = 4$

20. $\sqrt[3]{4x+2} - 6 = -10$

21. $-4\sqrt[3]{x+10} + 3 = 15$

22. ★ **OPEN-ENDED MATH** Write a radical equation of the form $\sqrt[3]{ax+b} = c$ that has -3 as a solution. *Explain* the method you used to find your equation.

EXAMPLES 3 and 4
for Exs. 23–33

EQUATIONS WITH RATIONAL EXPONENTS Solve the equation. Check your solution.

23. $2x^{2/3} = 32$

24. $\dfrac{1}{2}x^{5/2} = 16$

25. $9x^{2/5} = 36$

26. $(8x)^{4/3} + 44 = 300$

27. $\dfrac{1}{7}(x+9)^{3/2} = 49$

28. $(x-5)^{5/3} - 73 = 170$

29. $\left(\dfrac{1}{3}x - 11\right)^{1/2} = 5$

30. $(5x-19)^{5/6} = 32$

31. $(3x+43)^{2/3} + 22 = 38$

ERROR ANALYSIS *Describe* and correct the error in solving the equation.

32.
$$\sqrt[3]{x} + 2 = 4$$
$$(\sqrt[3]{x} + 2)^3 = 4^3$$
$$x + 8 = 64$$
$$x = 56$$

33.
$$(x+7)^{1/2} = 5$$
$$[(x+7)^{1/2}]^2 = 5$$
$$x + 7 = 5$$
$$x = -2$$

EXAMPLE 5
for Exs. 34–44

SOLVING RADICAL EQUATIONS Solve the equation. Check for extraneous solutions.

34. $x - 6 = \sqrt{3x}$

35. $x - 10 = \sqrt{9x}$

36. $x = \sqrt{16x + 225}$

37. $\sqrt{21x + 1} = x + 5$

38. $\sqrt{44 - 2x} = x - 10$

39. $\sqrt{x^2 + 4} = x + 5$

40. $x - 2 = \sqrt{\dfrac{3}{2}x - 2}$

41. $\sqrt[4]{3 - 8x^2} = 2x$

42. $\sqrt[3]{8x^3 - 1} = 2x - 1$

43. ★ **MULTIPLE CHOICE** What is (are) the solution(s) of $\sqrt{32x - 64} = 2x$?

(A) 4   (B) −16   (C) 4, −16   (D) 1, 3

44. ★ **SHORT RESPONSE** *Explain* how you can tell that $\sqrt{x + 4} = -5$ has no solution without solving it.

EXAMPLE 6
for Exs. 45–52

EQUATIONS WITH TWO RADICALS Solve the equation. Check for extraneous solutions.

45. $\sqrt{4x + 1} = \sqrt{x + 10}$

46. $\sqrt[3]{12x - 5} - \sqrt[3]{8x + 15} = 0$

47. $\sqrt{3x - 8} + 1 = \sqrt{x + 5}$

48. $\sqrt{\dfrac{2}{3}x - 4} = \sqrt{\dfrac{2}{5}x - 7}$

49. $\sqrt{x + 2} = 2 - \sqrt{x}$

50. $\sqrt{2x + 3} + 2 = \sqrt{6x + 7}$

51. $\sqrt{2x + 5} = \sqrt{x + 2} + 1$

52. $\sqrt{5x + 6} + 3 = \sqrt{3x + 3} + 4$

SOLVING SYSTEMS Solve the system of equations.

53. $3\sqrt{x} + 5\sqrt{y} = 31$
    $5\sqrt{x} - 5\sqrt{y} = -15$

54. $5\sqrt{x} - 2\sqrt{y} = 4\sqrt{2}$
    $2\sqrt{x} + 3\sqrt{y} = 13\sqrt{2}$

55. **CHALLENGE** Give an example of a radical equation that has two extraneous solutions.

PROBLEM SOLVING

EXAMPLE 2
for Exs. 56–57

56. **MAXIMUM SPEED** In an amusement park ride called the Sky Flyer, a rider suspended by a cable swings back and forth like a pendulum from a tall tower. A rider's maximum speed v (in meters per second) occurs at the bottom of each swing and can be approximated by $v = \sqrt{2gh}$ where h is the height (in meters) at the top of each swing and g is the acceleration due to gravity $(g \approx 9.8 \text{ m/sec}^2)$. If a rider's maximum speed was 15 meters per second, what was the rider's height at the top of the swing?

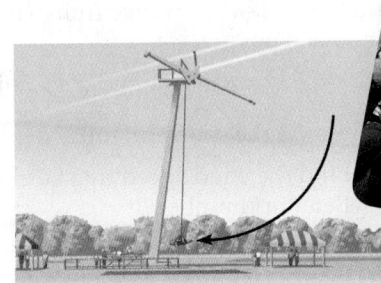

57. BURNING RATE A burning candle has a radius of r inches and was initially h_0 inches tall. After t minutes, the height of the candle has been reduced to h inches. These quantities are related by the formula

$$r = \sqrt{\frac{kt}{\pi(h_0 - h)}}$$

where k is a constant. How long will it take for the entire candle to burn if its radius is 0.875 inch, its initial height is 6.5 inches, and $k = 0.04$?

58. CONSTRUCTION The length ℓ (in inches) of a standard nail can be modeled by $\ell = 54d^{3/2}$ where d is the diameter (in inches) of the nail. What is the diameter of a standard nail that is 3 inches long?

(59.) ★ **SHORT RESPONSE** Biologists have discovered that the shoulder height h (in centimeters) of a male African elephant can be modeled by

$$h = 62.5\sqrt[3]{t} + 75.8$$

where t is the age (in years) of the elephant. *Compare* the ages of two elephants, one with a shoulder height of 150 centimeters and the other with a shoulder height of 250 centimeters.

60. ★ **EXTENDED RESPONSE** "Hang time" is the time you are suspended in the air during a jump. Your hang time t (in seconds) is given by the function $t = 0.5\sqrt{h}$ where h is the height of the jump (in feet). A basketball player jumps and has a hang time of 0.81 second. A kangaroo jumps and has a hang time of 1.12 seconds.

a. Solve Find the heights that the basketball player and the kangaroo jumped.

b. Calculate Double the hang times of the basketball player and the kangaroo and calculate the corresponding heights of each jump.

c. Interpret If the hang time doubles, does the height of the jump double? *Explain*.

Animated **Algebra** at my.hrw.com

61. MULTI-STEP PROBLEM The Beaufort wind scale was devised to measure wind speed. The Beaufort numbers B, which range from 0 to 12, can be modeled by

$$B = 1.69\sqrt{s + 4.25} - 3.55$$

where s is the speed (in miles per hour) of the wind.

a. Find the wind speed that corresponds to the Beaufort number $B = 0$.

b. Find the wind speed that corresponds to the Beaufort number $B = 12$.

c. Write an inequality that describes the range of wind speeds represented by the Beaufort model.

Beaufort Wind Scale	
Beaufort number	Force of wind
0	Calm
3	Gentle breeze
6	Strong breeze
9	Strong gale
12	Hurricane

○ = See **WORKED-OUT SOLUTIONS** in Student Resources   ★ = **STANDARDIZED TEST PRACTICE**

Digital Vision/Getty Images

62. CHALLENGE You are trying to determine a truncated pyramid's height, which cannot be measured directly. The height h and slant height ℓ of the truncated pyramid are related by the formula shown below.

$$\ell = \sqrt{h^2 + \frac{1}{4}(b_2 - b_1)^2}$$

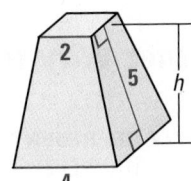

In the given formula, b_1 and b_2 are the side lengths of the upper and lower bases of the pyramid, respectively. If $\ell = 5$, $b_1 = 2$, and $b_2 = 4$, what is the height of the pyramid?

QUIZ

Graph the function. Then state the domain and range.

1. $y = 4\sqrt{x}$

2. $y = \sqrt{x} + 3$

3. $g(x) = \sqrt{x + 2} - 5$

4. $y = -\frac{1}{2}\sqrt[3]{x}$

5. $f(x) = \sqrt[3]{x} - 4$

6. $y = \sqrt[3]{x - 3} + 2$

Solve the equation. Check for extraneous solutions.

7. $\sqrt{6x + 15} = 9$

8. $\frac{1}{4}(7x + 8)^{3/2} = 54$

9. $\sqrt[3]{3x + 5} + 2 = 5$

10. $x - 3 = \sqrt{10x - 54}$

11. $\sqrt{4x - 4} = \sqrt{5x - 1} - 1$

12. $\sqrt[3]{\frac{4}{5}x - 9} = \sqrt[3]{x - 6}$

13. ASTRONOMY According to Kepler's third law of planetary motion, the function $P = 0.199a^{3/2}$ relates a planet's orbital period P (in days) to the length a (in millions of kilometers) of the orbit's minor axis. The orbital period of Mars is about 1.88 years. What is the length of the orbit's minor axis?

Using **ALTERNATIVE METHODS**

Another Way to Solve Example 2

Make sense of problems and persevere in solving them.

MULTIPLE REPRESENTATIONS In Example 2, you solved a radical equation algebraically. You can also solve a radical equation using a table or a graph.

PROBLEM

WIND VELOCITY In a hurricane, the mean sustained wind velocity v (in meters per second) is given by

$$v(p) = 6.3\sqrt{1013 - p}$$

where p is the air pressure (in millibars) at the center of the hurricane. Estimate the air pressure at the center of a hurricane when the mean sustained wind velocity is 54.5 meters per second.

METHOD 1

Using a Table The problem requires solving the radical equation $6.3\sqrt{1013 - p} = 54.5$. One way to solve this equation is to make a table of values. You can use a graphing calculator to make the table.

STEP 1 **Enter** the function $y = 6.3\sqrt{1013 - x}$ into a graphing calculator. Note that x represents air pressure and y represents wind velocity. Set up a table to display x-values starting at 900 and increasing in increments of 10.

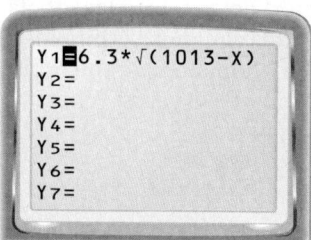
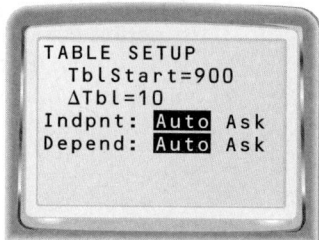

STEP 2 **Make** a table of values for the function. The first table below shows that $y = 54.5$ between $x = 930$ and $x = 940$. To approximate x more precisely, set up the table to display x-values starting at 930 and increasing in increments of 1. The second table below shows that $y = 54.5$ between $x = 938$ and $x = 939$.

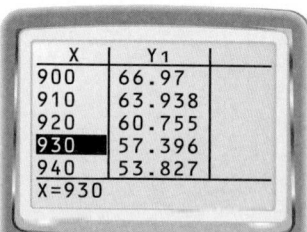
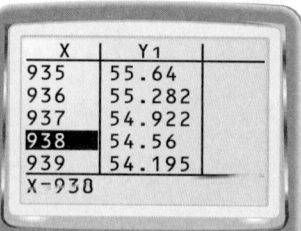

▶ The mean sustained wind velocity is 54.5 meters per second when the air pressure is between 938 and 939 millibars.

METHOD 2

Using a Graph You can also use a graph to solve the equation $6.3\sqrt{1013 - p} = 54.5$.

STEP 1 **Enter** the functions $y = 6.3\sqrt{1013 - x}$ and $y = 54.5$ into a graphing calculator.

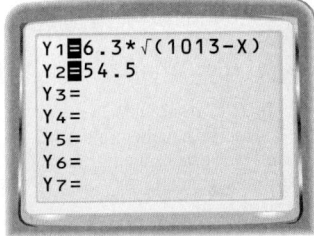

```
Y1■6.3*√(1013-X)
Y2■54.5
Y3=
Y4=
Y5=
Y6=
Y7=
```

STEP 2 **Graph** the functions from Step 1. Adjust the viewing window so that it shows the interval $800 \le x \le 1100$ with a scale of 50 and the interval $25 \le y \le 75$ with a scale of 5.

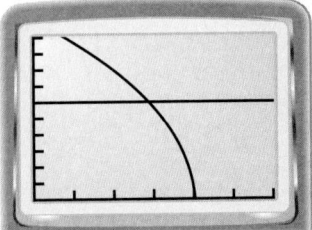

STEP 3 **Find** the intersection point of the two graphs using the *intersect* feature. The graphs intersect at about (938, 54.5).

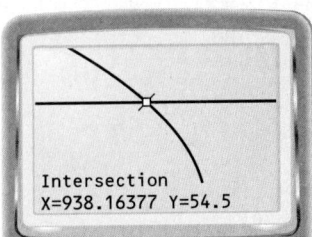

```
Intersection
X=938.16377  Y=54.5
```

▶ The mean sustained wind velocity is 54.5 meters per second when the air pressure is about 938 millibars.

PRACTICE

SOLVING EQUATIONS **Solve the radical equation using a table and using a graph.**

1. $\sqrt{25 - x} = 8$

2. $2.3\sqrt{x - 1} = 11.5$

3. $4.3\sqrt{x - 7} = 30$

4. $6\sqrt{2 - 7x} - 1.2 = 22.8$

5. ROCKETS A model rocket is launched 25 feet from you. When the rocket is at height h, the distance d between you and the rocket is given by $d = \sqrt{625 + h^2}$ where h and d are measured in feet. What is the rocket's height when the distance between you and the rocket is 100 feet?

6. WHAT IF? In example 2 of this lesson, what is the air pressure at the center of a hurricane when the mean sustained wind velocity is 25 meters per second?

7. GEOMETRY The lateral surface area L of a right circular cone is given by

$$L = \pi r\sqrt{r^2 + h^2}$$

where r is the radius and h is the height. Find the height of a right circular cone with a radius of 7.5 centimeters and a lateral surface area of 900 square centimeters.

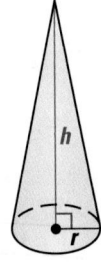

Solve Radical Inequalities

GOAL Solve radical inequalities by using tables and graphs.

COMMON CORE

CC.9-12.A.REI.2 Solve simple rational and radical equations in one variable, and give examples showing how extraneous solutions may arise.

Recall that you learned how to use tables and graphs to solve quadratic inequalities. You can also use tables and graphs to solve radical inequalities.

EXAMPLE 1 Solve a radical inequality using a table

Use a table to solve $3\sqrt{x} - 1 \le 11$.

Solution

STEP 1 **Enter** the function $y = 3\sqrt{x} - 1$ into a graphing calculator.

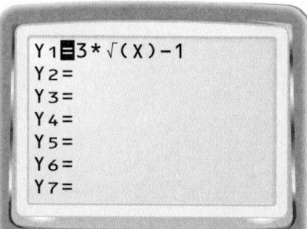

STEP 2 **Set up** the table to display x-values starting at 0 and increasing in increments of 1.

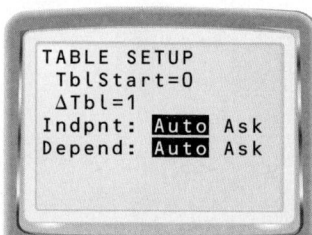

STEP 3 **Make** the table of values for $y = 3\sqrt{x} - 1$. Scroll through the table to find the x-value for which $y = 11$. This x-value is 16. It appears that $3\sqrt{x} - 1 \le 11$ when $x \le 16$.

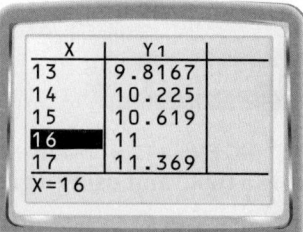

STEP 4 **Check** the domain of $y = 3\sqrt{x} - 1$. The domain is $x \ge 0$, so the solutions of $3\sqrt{x} - 1 \le 11$ cannot be negative. (This is indicated by the word ERROR next to the negative x-values.)

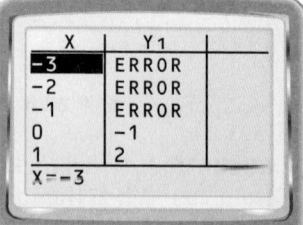

▶ The solution of the inequality is $x \le 16$ *and* $x \ge 0$, which you can write as $0 \le x \le 16$.

EXAMPLE 2 **Solve a radical inequality using a graph**

Use a graph to solve $\sqrt{x-5} > 3$.

Solution

STEP 1 **Enter** the functions $y = \sqrt{x-5}$ and $y = 3$ into a graphing calculator.

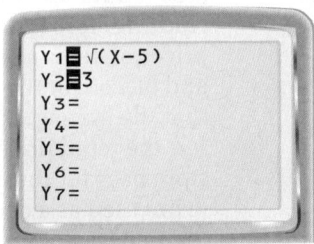

STEP 2 **Graph** the functions from Step 1. Adjust the viewing window so that the x-axis shows $0 \le x \le 30$ with a scale of 5 and the y-axis shows $-3 \le y \le 8$ with a scale of 1.

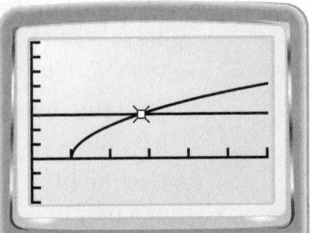

INTERPRET DOMAIN

In Example 2, note that the domain of $y = \sqrt{x-5}$ is $x \ge 5$. Therefore, the domain does not affect the solution.

STEP 3 **Identify** the x-values for which the graph of $y = \sqrt{x-5}$ lies above the graph of $y = 3$. You can use the *intersect* feature to show that the graphs intersect when $x = 14$. The graph of $y = \sqrt{x-5}$ lies above the graph of $y = 3$ when $x > 14$.

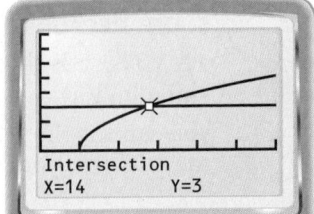

▶ The solution of the inequality is $x > 14$.

PRACTICE

EXAMPLE 1
for Exs. 1–6

Use a table to solve the inequality.

1. $2\sqrt{x} - 5 \ge 3$

2. $\sqrt{x-4} \le 5$

3. $4\sqrt{x} + 1 \le 9$

4. $\sqrt{x+7} \ge 3$

5. $\sqrt{x} + \sqrt{x+3} \ge 3$

6. $\sqrt{x} + \sqrt{x-5} \le 5$

EXAMPLE 2
for Exs. 7–12

Use a graph to solve the inequality.

7. $2\sqrt{x} + 3 \le 8$

8. $\sqrt{x+3} \ge 2.6$

9. $7\sqrt{x} + 1 < 9$

10. $4\sqrt{3x-7} > 7.8$

11. $\sqrt{x} - \sqrt{x+5} < -1$

12. $\sqrt{x+2} + \sqrt{x-1} \le 9$

13. SAILBOAT RACE In order to compete in the America's Cup sailboat race, a boat must satisfy the rule

$$\ell + 1.25\sqrt{s} - 9.8\sqrt[3]{d} \le 16$$

where ℓ is the length (in meters) of the boat, s is the area (in square meters) of the sails, and d is the volume (in cubic meters) of water displaced by the boat. A boat has a length of 20 meters and displaces 27 cubic meters of water. What is the maximum allowable value for s?

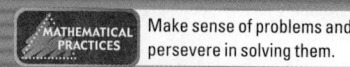

1. **MULTI-STEP PROBLEM** A manager at a clothing store is determining the retail prices of items so that they can be tagged and placed on the sales floor. The equation that the manager uses is $R = C + MC$ where R is the retail price, C is the cost that the store pays for the item, and M is the percent (expressed as a decimal) that the item is marked up.

   a. The markup for women's athletic shoes is 40%. Write a function that gives the retail price R in terms of the cost C.

   b. Find the inverse of the function from part (a).

   c. Use the inverse function to find the cost of a pair of women's athletic shoes that has a retail price of $60.

2. **SHORT RESPONSE** The graph of $y = \sqrt{3x - 5}$ is shown below. Solve the equation $\sqrt{3x - 5} = 4$. *Explain* how you can use the graph of $y = \sqrt{3x - 5}$ to verify that your solution is correct.

   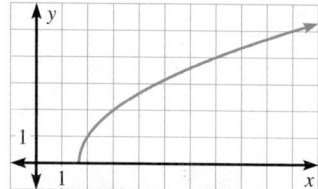

3. **OPEN-ENDED** Write a radical equation whose only solution is -5.

4. **EXTENDED RESPONSE** On a certain day, the function that gives Swedish kronor in terms of U.S. dollars is $k = 7.463d$ where k represents kronor and d represents U.S. dollars.

   a. Find the inverse function.

   b. How many U.S. dollars do you receive for 25 kronor?

   c. Express what the inverse function means in words.

5. **SHORT RESPONSE** Find a square root function that passes through the points $(-14, 0)$ and $(-13, 1)$. Are there other square root functions that pass through these points? *Explain.*

6. **OPEN-ENDED** Write two functions whose graphs are translations of the graph of $y = \sqrt{x}$. The first function should have a domain of $x \geq 4$. The second function should have a range of $y \geq -2$.

7. **SHORT RESPONSE** An object is launched upward from ground level and reaches a maximum height of h feet. The initial velocity v (in feet per second) of the object is given by the function $v = 8\sqrt{h}$.

   a. Find the inverse function.

   b. Write a problem that can be solved using the inverse function. Show how to solve the problem.

8. **GRIDDED ANSWER** Your friend releases a weather balloon 50 feet from you. When the balloon is at height h, the distance d between you and the balloon is given by $d = \sqrt{2500 + h^2}$ where h and d are measured in feet. To the nearest foot, what is the height of the balloon when the distance between you and the balloon is 100 feet?

   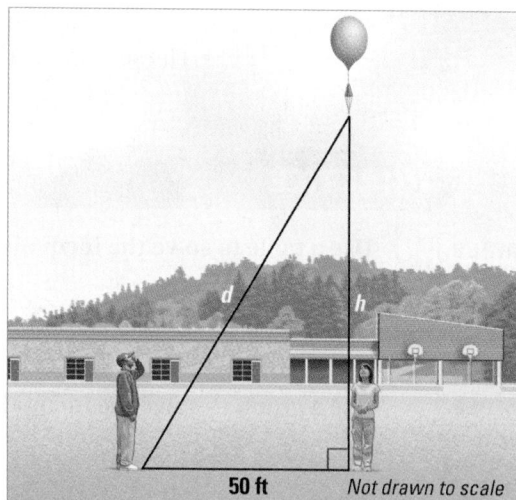

   50 ft   *Not drawn to scale*

9. **SHORT RESPONSE** You drop a pebble into a calm pond, causing ripples of concentric circles. The radius r (in feet) of the outer ripple is given by $r(t) = 6t$ where t is the time (in seconds) after the pebble hits the water. The area A (in square feet) of the outer ripple is given by $A(r) = \pi r^2$. Find $A(r(t))$ and evaluate $A(r(2))$. What does $A(r(2))$ represent?

3 CHAPTER SUMMARY

Animated Algebra
my.hrw.com
Electronic Function Library

BIG IDEAS

For Your Notebook

Big Idea 1

Using Rational Exponents

The following are properties of rational exponents. Let a and b be real numbers and let m and n be rational numbers.

Property	Example
$a^m \cdot a^n = a^{m+n}$	$4^{5/2} \cdot 4^{1/2} = 4^3 = 64$
$(a^m)^n = a^{mn}$	$(2^8)^{1/4} = 2^2 = 4$
$(ab)^m = a^m b^m$	$(25 \cdot 4)^{1/2} = 25^{1/2} \cdot 4^{1/2} = 5 \cdot 2 = 10$
$a^{-m} = \dfrac{1}{a^m}, a \neq 0$	$8^{-1/3} = \dfrac{1}{8^{1/3}} = \dfrac{1}{2}$
$\dfrac{a^m}{a^n} = a^{m-n}, a \neq 0$	$\dfrac{9^{5/8}}{9^{1/8}} = 9^{4/8} = 9^{1/2} = 3$
$\left(\dfrac{a}{b}\right)^m = \dfrac{a^m}{b^m}, b \neq 0$	$\left(\dfrac{16}{81}\right)^{1/4} = \dfrac{16^{1/4}}{81^{1/4}} = \dfrac{2}{3}$

Big Idea 2

Performing Function Operations and Finding Inverse Functions

Operation	Definition	Example: $f(x) = 2x$, $g(x) = x - 5$
Addition	$h(x) = f(x) + g(x)$	$h(x) = 2x + (x - 5) = 3x - 5$
Subtraction	$h(x) = f(x) - g(x)$	$h(x) = 2x - (x - 5) = x + 5$
Multiplication	$h(x) = f(x) \cdot g(x)$	$h(x) = 2x(x - 5) = 2x^2 - 10x$
Division	$h(x) = \dfrac{f(x)}{g(x)}$	$h(x) = \dfrac{2x}{x - 5}$
Composition	$h(x) = g(f(x))$	$h(x) = 2x - 5$
Inverse	$h(x) = g^{-1}(x)$	$h(x) = x + 5$

Big Idea 3

Graphing Radical Functions and Solving Radical Equations

To **graph** radical functions, use the graph of the parent functions. For example, to graph $y = \sqrt{x + 1} - 2$, translate the graph of $y = \sqrt{x}$ left 1 unit and down 2 units.

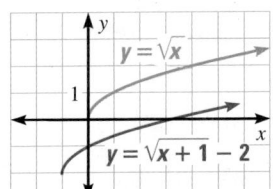

To **solve** a radical equation, first isolate the radical. Then raise each side of the equation to the same power and solve the polynomial equation.

$\sqrt{2x - 5} - 3 = 2$	Write equation.
$\sqrt{2x - 5} = 5$	Isolate radical.
$(\sqrt{2x - 5})^2 = 5^2$	Square each side.
$2x - 5 = 25$	Simplify.
$x = 15$	Solve.

3 CHAPTER REVIEW

my.hrw.com
• Multi-Language Glossary
• Vocabulary practice

REVIEW KEY VOCABULARY

• *n*th root of *a*
• index of a radical
• simplest form of a radical
• like radicals

• power function
• composition
• inverse relation

• inverse function
• radical function
• radical equation

VOCABULARY EXERCISES

1. Copy and complete: The index of the radical $\sqrt[4]{7}$ is __?__.

2. List two different pairs of like radicals.

3. Copy and complete: A(n) __?__ function has the form $y = ax^b$ where *a* is a real number and *b* is a rational number.

4. **WRITING** *Explain* how the graph of a function and the graph of its inverse are related.

5. **WRITING** *Explain* how to use the horizontal line test to determine whether the inverse of a function *f* is also a function.

6. **WRITING** *Describe* how the graph of $y = \sqrt[3]{x - 4} + 5$ is related to the graph of the parent function $y = \sqrt[3]{x}$.

7. **REASONING** A student began solving the equation $x^{2/3} = 5$ by cubing each side. What will the student have to do next? What could the student have done to solve the equation in just one step?

REVIEW EXAMPLES AND EXERCISES

Use the review examples and exercises below to check your understanding of the concepts you have learned in each lesson of this chapter.

3.1 Evaluate *n*th Roots and Use Rational Exponents

EXAMPLE

Evaluate the expression.

a. $\left(\sqrt[4]{16}\right)^5 = 2^5 = 32$

b. $27^{-4/3} = \dfrac{1}{27^{4/3}} = \dfrac{1}{(27^{1/3})^4} = \dfrac{1}{3^4} = \dfrac{1}{81}$

EXERCISES

EXAMPLE 2
for Exs. 8–15

Evaluate the expression without using a calculator.

8. $81^{1/4}$

9. $0^{1/3}$

10. $\sqrt[3]{-64}$

11. $\sqrt[3]{125}$

12. $256^{3/4}$

13. $27^{-2/3}$

14. $\left(\sqrt[3]{8}\right)^7$

15. $\dfrac{1}{\left(\sqrt[5]{-32}\right)^{-3}}$

218   Chapter 3   Rational Exponents and Radical Functions

3.2 Apply Properties of Rational Exponents

EXAMPLE

Write the expression in simplest form. Assume all variables are positive.

a. $\sqrt[3]{48} = \sqrt[3]{8 \cdot 6} = \sqrt[3]{8} \cdot \sqrt[3]{6} = 2\sqrt[3]{6}$

b. $\left(\dfrac{x^4}{y^8}\right)^{1/2} = \dfrac{(x^4)^{1/2}}{(y^8)^{1/2}} = \dfrac{x^{4 \cdot 1/2}}{y^{8 \cdot 1/2}} = \dfrac{x^2}{y^4}$

EXERCISES

**EXAMPLES
4, 6, and 7
for Exs. 16–19**

Write the expression in simplest form. Assume all variables are positive.

16. $\sqrt[3]{80}$ **17.** $(3^4 \cdot 5^4)^{-1/4}$ **18.** $(25a^{10}b^{16})^{1/2}$ **19.** $\sqrt{\dfrac{18x^5y^4}{49xz^3}}$

3.3 Perform Function Operations and Composition

EXAMPLE

Let $f(x) = 3x^2 + 1$ and $g(x) = x + 4$. Perform the indicated operation.

a. $f(x) + g(x) = (3x^2 + 1) + (x + 4) = 3x^2 + x + 5$

b. $f(x) \cdot g(x) = (3x^2 + 1)(x + 4) = 3x^3 + 12x^2 + x + 4$

c. $f(g(x)) = f(x + 4) = 3(x + 4)^2 + 1 = 3(x^2 + 8x + 16) + 1 = 3x^2 + 24x + 49$

EXERCISES

**EXAMPLES
1, 2, and 5
for Exs. 20–23**

Let $f(x) = 4x - 6$ and $g(x) = x + 8$. Perform the indicated operation.

20. $f(x) + g(x)$ **21.** $f(x) - g(x)$ **22.** $f(x) \cdot g(x)$ **23.** $f(g(x))$

3.4 Use Inverse Functions

EXAMPLE

Find the inverse of the function $y = 3x + 7$.

$y = 3x + 7$	Write original function.
$x = 3y + 7$	Switch x and y.
$x - 7 = 3y$	Subtract 7 from each side.
$\dfrac{1}{3}x - \dfrac{7}{3} = y$	Divide each side by 3.

EXERCISES

**EXAMPLES
1, 4, and 5
for Exs. 24–26**

Find the inverse of the function.

24. $y = \dfrac{1}{3}x + 4$ **25.** $y = 4x^2 + 9, x \geq 0$ **26.** $f(x) = x^3 - 4$

3.5 Graph Square Root and Cube Root Functions

EXAMPLE

Graph $y = -\sqrt{x - 3} + 2$.

Sketch the graph of $y = -\sqrt{x}$. Notice that it begins at the origin and passes through the point $(1, -1)$.

For $y = -\sqrt{x - 3} + 2$, $h = 3$, and $k = 2$. So, shift the graph of $y = -\sqrt{x}$ right 3 units and up 2 units. The resulting graph begins at the point $(3, 2)$ and passes through the point $(4, 1)$.

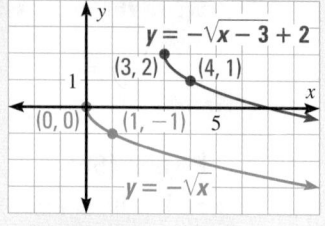

EXAMPLE

Graph $y = \sqrt[3]{x + 2} - 4$.

Sketch the graph of $y = \sqrt[3]{x}$. Notice that it passes through the points $(-1, -1)$, $(0, 0)$, and $(1, 1)$.

For $y = \sqrt[3]{x + 2} - 4$, $h = -2$ and $k = -4$. So, shift the graph of $y = \sqrt[3]{x}$ left 2 units and down 4 units. The resulting graph passes through the points $(-3, -5)$, $(-2, -4)$, and $(-1, -3)$.

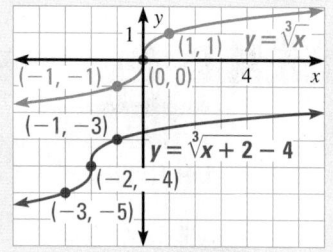

EXAMPLES
4 and 5
for Exs. 27–29

EXERCISES

Graph the function. Then state the domain and range.

27. $y = \sqrt{x + 3} + 5$

28. $y = 3\sqrt{x + 1} - 4$

29. $y = \sqrt[3]{x - 4} - 5$

3.6 Solve Radical Equations

EXAMPLE

Solve $\sqrt{4x + 9} = 5$.

$\sqrt{4x + 9} = 5$ Write original equation.

$\left(\sqrt{4x + 9}\right)^2 = 5^2$ Square each side to eliminate the radical.

$4x + 9 = 25$ Simplify.

$4x = 16$ Subtract 9 from each side.

$x = 4$ Divide each side by 4.

CHECK   Check $x = 4$ in the original equation.

$\sqrt{4x + 9} = \sqrt{4(4) + 9} = \sqrt{25} = 5$ ✓

EXAMPLES
1, 3, and 5
for Exs. 30–32

EXERCISES

Solve the equation. Check for extraneous solutions.

30. $\sqrt[3]{5x - 4} = 2$

31. $3x^{3/4} = 24$

32. $\sqrt{x^2 - 10} = \sqrt{3x}$

Evaluate the expression without using a calculator.

1. $-125^{1/3}$

2. $32^{1/5}$

3. $\sqrt[4]{81}$

4. $\sqrt[3]{27}$

5. $8^{5/3}$

6. $16^{-3/2}$

7. $\left(\sqrt[3]{-27}\right)^2$

8. $\left(\sqrt[3]{64}\right)^{-4}$

Write the expression in simplest form. Assume all variables are positive.

9. $\sqrt[3]{88}$

10. $\sqrt[5]{16} \cdot \sqrt[5]{8}$

11. $\sqrt{\dfrac{12}{49}}$

12. $\dfrac{\sqrt[3]{24}}{\sqrt[3]{9}}$

13. $\sqrt[3]{64x^4y^2}$

14. $\sqrt[4]{2x^6y^8z}$

15. $\sqrt[5]{\dfrac{x^6}{y^4}}$

16. $\sqrt{\dfrac{75x^5y^6}{36xz^5}}$

Let $f(x) = 2x + 9$ and $g(x) = 3x - 1$. Perform the indicated operation and state the domain.

17. $f(x) + g(x)$

18. $f(x) - g(x)$

19. $f(x) \cdot g(x)$

20. $\dfrac{f(x)}{g(x)}$

21. $f(g(x))$

22. $g(f(x))$

23. $f(f(x))$

24. $g(g(x))$

Find the inverse of the function.

25. $y = -2x + 5$

26. $y = \dfrac{1}{3}x + 4$

27. $f(x) = 5x - 12$

28. $y = \dfrac{1}{2}x^4, \ x \geq 0$

29. $f(x) = x^3 + 5$

30. $f(x) = -2x^3 + 1$

Graph the function. Then state the domain and range.

31. $y = -6\sqrt[3]{x}$

32. $y = \sqrt{x - 4} - 2$

33. $f(x) = -\sqrt[3]{x + 3} + 4$

Solve the equation. Check for extraneous solutions.

34. $\sqrt{3x + 7} = 4$

35. $\sqrt{3x} - \sqrt{x + 6} = 0$

36. $x - 3 = \sqrt{x - 1}$

37. **KINETIC ENERGY** The kinetic energy E (in joules) of a 1250 kilogram compact car is given by the equation $E = 625s^2$ where s is the speed of the car (in meters per second).

   a. Write an inverse model that gives the speed of the car as a function of its kinetic energy.

   b. Use the inverse model to find the speed of the car if its kinetic energy is 120,000 joules. Give the speed in kilometers per hour.

   c. If the kinetic energy doubles, will the speed double? *Explain* why or why not.

38. **BOWLING SCORES** In bowling, a *handicap* is a change in score to adjust for differences in players' abilities. You belong to a bowling league in which each bowler's handicap h is determined by his or her average a using this formula:

$$h = 0.9(200 - a)$$

   If a bowler's average is over 200, the handicap is 0. Find the inverse of the model. Then find your average if your handicap is 36.

EXTENDED RESPONSE QUESTIONS

PROBLEM

For a type of dinosaur called a theropod, the height at the hip h (in centimeters) can be modeled by $h(\ell) = 3.49\ell^{1.14}$ where ℓ is the length (in centimeters) of the dinosaur's instep.

The length of the instep can be modeled by $\ell(p) = 1.2p$ where p is the footprint length (in centimeters).

a. Find and simplify $h(\ell(p))$.

b. Evaluate $h(\ell(20))$.

c. Explain the meaning of $h(\ell(20))$.

Below are sample solutions to the problem. Read each solution and the comments on the left to see why the sample represents full credit, partial credit, or no credit.

SAMPLE 1: Full credit solution

The composition is formed and simplified correctly.

a. $h(\ell(p)) = h(1.2p)$
$\qquad = 3.49(1.2p)^{1.14}$
$\qquad = 3.49(1.2)^{1.14}p^{1.14}$
$\qquad \approx 4.30p^{1.14}$

The value of $h(\ell(20))$ is correctly determined, and a clear explanation of its meaning is given.

b. To evaluate $h(\ell(20))$, substitute 20 for p.
$\qquad 4.30p^{1.14} = 4.30(\mathbf{20})^{1.14} \approx 4.30(30.4) \approx 131$

c. The composition $h(\ell(p))$ represents the height at the hip h of a theropod as a function of the footprint length p. Therefore, $h(\ell(20)) \approx 131$ means that a theropod with a footprint length of 20 centimeters had an approximate height at the hip of 131 centimeters.

SAMPLE 2: Partial credit solution

The student does not apply the power of a product property correctly.

a. $h(\ell(p)) = h(1.2p)$
$\qquad = 3.49(1.2p)^{1.14}$
$\qquad = 3.49(1.2)p^{1.14}$
$\qquad \approx 4.19p^{1.14}$

The student evaluates the composition correctly and explains its meaning.

b. To evaluate $h(\ell(20))$, substitute 20 for p.
$\qquad 4.19p^{1.14} = 4.19(\mathbf{20})^{1.14} \approx 4.19(30.4) \approx 127$

c. The value of $h(\ell(20))$ is the height at the hip of a theropod with a footprint length of 20 centimeters.

SAMPLE 3: No credit solution

a. $h(\ell(p)) = h(3.49\ell^{1.14})$

$= 1.2(3.49\ell^{1.14})$

$= 1.2(\mathbf{3.49})^{\mathbf{1.14}}\ell^{1.14}$

$\approx 1.2(\mathbf{4.16})\ell^{\mathbf{1.14}}$

$\approx 4.99\ell^{1.14}$

> The composition is formed and simplified incorrectly.

b. To evaluate $h(\ell(20))$, substitute 20 for ℓ.

$4.99\ell^{1.14} = 4.99(\mathbf{20})^{1.14}$

$\approx 4.99(30.4)$

≈ 152

> The student substitutes 20 for ℓ rather than p.

c. The composition $h(\ell(p))$ represents the height of a theropod as a function of the instep length. So, $h(\ell(20)) \approx 152$ means that a theropod with an instep length of 152 centimeters is 20 centimeters tall.

> The student's description of $h(\ell(20))$ is incorrect.

PRACTICE   Apply the Scoring Rubric

Score each of the following solutions to the problem on the previous page as *full credit*, *partial credit*, or *no credit*. *Explain* your reasoning. If you choose *partial credit* or *no credit*, explain how you would change the solution so that it earns a score of full credit.

1. **a.** $h(\ell(p)) = h(1.2p)$

$= 3.49(1.2p)^{1.14}$

$= 3.49(1.2)^{1.14}(p)^{1.14}$

$\approx 4.3p^{1.14}$

b. $h(\ell(20)) = 4.3(20)^{1.14}$

$\approx 4.3(30.4)$

≈ 160

c. The value of $h(\ell(20))$ means that a theropod with a footprint 20 centimeters long had a height at the hip of 160 centimeters.

2. **a.** $h(\ell(p)) = h(1.2p)$

$= 3.49(1.2p)$

$\approx 4.19p$

b. Substitute 10 for p.

$h(\ell(10)) = 4.19(10)$

$= 41.9$

c. If a theropod has a footprint length of 41.9 centimeters, then the theropod was 10 centimeters tall.

3 ★ Standardized TEST PRACTICE

EXTENDED RESPONSE

1. The *gear ratio* of a bicycle is the number of teeth in the chainwheel divided by the number of teeth in the freewheel. The number w of rear-wheel revolutions is equal to the product of the gear ratio and the number p of pedal revolutions.

   a. A bicycle in first gear has 24 teeth in the chainwheel and 32 teeth in the freewheel. Write a function that gives w in terms of p.

   b. The distance d (in inches) a bicycle travels after w rear-wheel revolutions is given by the function $d = 220w$. Use composition of functions to find a function that gives d in terms of p.

   c. The gear ratio changes when the gear is shifted. Copy and complete the table. *Explain* how the distance traveled per pedal revolution changes as you shift gears.

Gear	5th	10th	15th
Teeth in chainwheel	24	40	50
Teeth in freewheel	19	22	19
Distance per pedal revolution	?	?	?

2. In rowing, a boat's speed s (in meters per second) can be modeled by the equation $s = 4.62\sqrt[9]{n}$ where n is the number of rowers.

   a. Use a calculator to find the speed of a boat for crews of 2 people, 4 people, and 8 people.

   b. Find the time (in minutes) it takes each crew from part (a) to complete a 2000 meter race.

   c. Does doubling the number of rowers double the speed? *Explain.*

3. The table shows volume formulas for various right prisms that have length ℓ and whose bases are regular polygons with side length s.

Base	Triangle	Pentagon	Hexagon	Octagon	Decagon
Diagram					
Volume	$V = 0.433\ell s^2$	$V = 1.72\ell s^2$	$V = 2.60\ell s^2$	$V = 4.83\ell s^2$	$V = 7.69\ell s^2$

   a. Find the volume of a cube with an edge length of 4 inches.

   b. Suppose that each prism in the table has the same volume as the cube from part (a) and $\ell = s$. Find the side length s for each prism.

   c. In part (b), what happens to the side length s as the number of sides of the prism's base increases? *Explain.*

4. You have two hemispherical snow globes. One globe has twice as much surface area as the other.

   a. Solve the formula for the surface area of a hemisphere, $S = 3\pi r^2$, for r.

   b. Substitute the expression for r from part (a) into the formula for the volume of a hemisphere, $V = \frac{2}{3}\pi r^3$. Simplify the result.

   c. *Compare* the volumes of the two snow globes.

224 Chapter 3 Rational Exponents and Rational Functions

MULTIPLE CHOICE

5. What is the solution of the equation
$\sqrt{2x + 3} = 5$?

   A   −14   **B**   −4

   C   1   **D**   11

6. The graph of which function is shown?

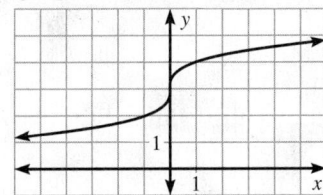

   A $y = \sqrt[3]{x} + 3$ **B** $y = \sqrt[3]{x} - 3$

   C $y = \sqrt[3]{x + 3}$ **D** $y = \sqrt[3]{x - 3}$

7. What is the inverse of $y = -2x^5 + 10$?

   A $y = \sqrt[5]{5 - \frac{1}{2}x}$ **B** $y = 20 - \sqrt[5]{2x}$

   C $y = \sqrt[5]{2x} - 20$ **D** $y = \sqrt[5]{\frac{1}{2}x - 5}$

GRIDDED RESPONSE

8. What is the solution of the equation $(8x)^{3/5} = 8$?

9. Let $f(x) = 2x^{1/2}$ and $g(x) = 3x^2$. What is the value of $g(f(9))$?

10. What is the value of $\left(\dfrac{5^5}{2^5}\right)^{-1/5}$?

11. In the equation $\sqrt[4]{16x^3y^4z} = 2x^ayz^b$, what is the sum of a and b? Assume all variables are positive.

12. What is the value of $\dfrac{1}{\left(\sqrt[4]{625}\right)^{-2}}$?

13. Let $f(x) = \dfrac{2}{5}x^{-0.25}$ and $g(x) = 5x^{3.25}$. What is the value of $f(x) \cdot g(x)$ when $x = 3$?

14. What is the y-intercept of the graph of the function $y = \sqrt[3]{x - 8} + 5$?

15. For what value of x does $f(x) = g(x)$ where $f(x) = \sqrt{x - 2} + 3$ and $g(x) = \sqrt{x + 13}$?

16. Consider the function $y = 3x + 9$. What is the slope of the graph of the inverse?

SHORT RESPONSE

17. Solve the equation $-\sqrt{x + 4} = \sqrt{x - 1} + 1$ algebraically. Then solve the equation by graphing. Are the results the same? *Explain* why or why not.

18. A function for converting x millimeters to y inches is $y = 0.03937x$. Find the inverse of the function. What information can you obtain from the inverse function? Use the inverse function to find the area (in square millimeters) of a 3 inch by 5 inch index card.

19. You have a $10 gift card to spend at a local toy store. The store has a sale offering 15% off all board games. Use composition of functions to find the final price of a board game that originally costs $27 when the $10 is subtracted before the 15% discount is applied. Then use composition of functions to find the final price of the board game when the 15% discount is applied before the $10 is subtracted. How much more money can you save if the store applies the 15% discount first?

20. The graphs of two functions f and g are shown at the right. Are f and g inverse functions? *Explain* why or why not.

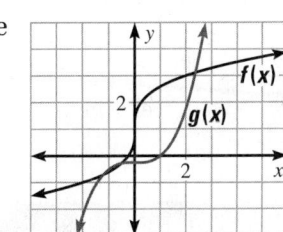

4 Exponential and Logarithmic Functions

Before

Previously, you learned the following skills, which you'll use in this chapter: finding simple interest, evaluating powers, and solving for a variable.

Prerequisite Skills

VOCABULARY CHECK

Copy and complete the statement using the graph.

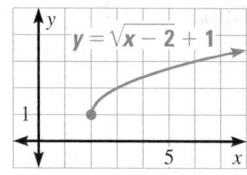

$y = \sqrt{x-2} + 1$

1. The **domain** of the function is ___?___ .

2. The **range** of the function is ___?___ .

3. The **inverse** of the function is ___?___ .

SKILLS CHECK

Use the simple interest formula $I = Prt$ where I = interest, P = principal, r = interest rate (as a decimal), and t = time (in years), to find the total amount (principal plus interest) in the account.

4. $5000 invested at 3% for 4 years   5. $2300 invested at 4% for 5 years

Evaluate the power.

6. 7^2 7. $(-4)^3$ 8. 3^4

Solve the equation for y.

9. $2x + 4y = 16$ 10. $3x + 5y = 20$ 11. $9x + 3y = 72$

In this chapter, you will apply the big ideas listed below and reviewed in the Chapter Summary. You will also use the key vocabulary listed below.

Big Ideas

① Graphing exponential and logarithmic functions
② Solving exponential and logarithmic equations
③ Writing and applying exponential and power functions

KEY VOCABULARY

- exponential function
- exponential growth function
- growth factor
- asymptote

- exponential decay function
- decay factor
- natural base e
- logarithm of y with base b

- common logarithm
- natural logarithm
- exponential equation
- logarithmic equation

Why?

You can use exponential and logarithmic functions to model many scientific relationships. For example, you can use a logarithmic function to relate the size of a telescope lens and the ability of the telescope to see certain stars.

Animated Algebra

The animation illustrated below helps you answer a question from this chapter: How is the diameter of a telescope's objective lens related to the apparent magnitude of the dimmest star that can be seen with the telescope?

The magnitude of stars is a measure of their brightness as viewed from Earth.

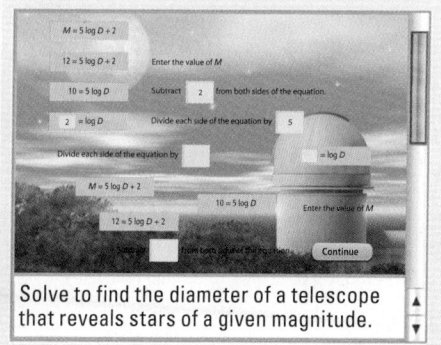

Solve to find the diameter of a telescope that reveals stars of a given magnitude.

Animated Algebra at my.hmh.com

4.1 Graph Exponential Growth Functions

Before You graphed polynomial and radical functions.

Now You will graph and use exponential growth functions.

Why? So you can model sports equipment costs, as in Ex. 40.

Key Vocabulary
• exponential function
• exponential growth function
• growth factor
• asymptote

CC.9-12.F.IF.7 Graph functions expressed symbolically and show key features of the graph, by hand in simple cases and using technology for more complicated cases.*
e. Graph exponential and logarithmic functions, showing intercepts and end behavior, and trigonometric functions, showing period, midline, and amplitude.

An **exponential function** has the form $y = ab^x$ where $a \neq 0$ and the base b is a positive number other than 1. If $a > 0$ and $b > 1$, then the function $y = ab^x$ is an **exponential growth function**, and b is called the **growth factor**. The simplest type of exponential growth function has the form $y = b^x$.

KEY CONCEPT
For Your Notebook

Parent Function for Exponential Growth Functions

The function $f(x) = b^x$, where $b > 1$, is the parent function for the family of exponential growth functions with base b. The general shape of the graph of $f(x) = b^x$ is shown below.

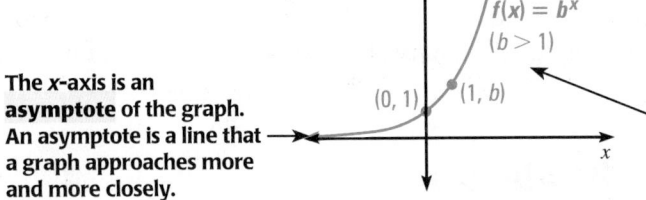

The **x-axis** is an **asymptote** of the graph. An asymptote is a line that a graph approaches more and more closely.

$f(x) = b^x$ $(b > 1)$

$(0, 1)$ $(1, b)$

The graph rises from left to right, passing through the points $(0, 1)$ and $(1, b)$.

The domain of $f(x) = b^x$ is all real numbers. The range is $y > 0$.

EXAMPLE 1 Graph $y = b^x$ for $b > 1$

Graph $y = 2^x$.

Solution

STEP 1 **Make** a table of values.

x	-2	-1	0	1	2	3
y	$\frac{1}{4}$	$\frac{1}{2}$	1	2	4	8

STEP 2 **Plot** the points from the table.

STEP 3 **Draw**, from *left* to *right*, a smooth curve that begins just above the x-axis, passes through the plotted points, and moves up to the right.

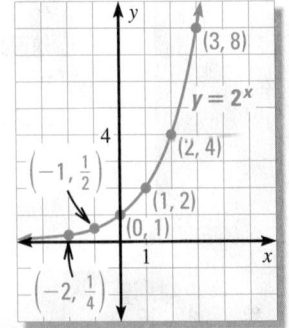

$(3, 8)$
$y = 2^x$
$(2, 4)$
$\left(-1, \frac{1}{2}\right)$
$(1, 2)$
$(0, 1)$
$\left(-2, \frac{1}{4}\right)$

The graph of a function $y = ab^x$ is a vertical stretch or shrink of the graph of $y = b^x$. The y-intercept of the graph of $y = ab^x$ occurs at $(0, a)$ rather than $(0, 1)$.

EXAMPLE 2 Graph $y = ab^x$ for $b > 1$

Graph the function.

a. $y = \dfrac{1}{2} \cdot 4^x$

b. $y = -\left(\dfrac{5}{2}\right)^x$

Solution

a. Plot $\left(0, \dfrac{1}{2}\right)$ and $(1, 2)$. Then, from *left* to *right*, draw a curve that begins just above the x-axis, passes through the two points, and moves up to the right.

b. Plot $(0, -1)$ and $\left(1, -\dfrac{5}{2}\right)$. Then, from *left* to *right*, draw a curve that begins just below the x-axis, passes through the two points, and moves down to the right.

CLASSIFY FUNCTIONS
Note that the function in part (b) of Example 2 is not an exponential growth function because $a = -1 < 0$.

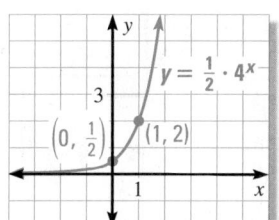

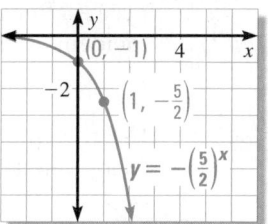

TRANSLATIONS To graph a function of the form $y = ab^{x-h} + k$, begin by sketching the graph of $y = ab^x$. Then translate the graph horizontally by h units and vertically by k units.

EXAMPLE 3 Graph $y = ab^{x-h} + k$ for $b > 1$

Graph $y = 4 \cdot 2^{x-1} - 3$. State the domain and range.

Solution

Begin by sketching the graph of $y = 4 \cdot 2^x$, which passes through $(0, 4)$ and $(1, 8)$. Then translate the graph right 1 unit and down 3 units to obtain the graph of $y = 4 \cdot 2^{x-1} - 3$.

The graph's asymptote is the line $y = -3$. The domain is all real numbers, and the range is $y > -3$.

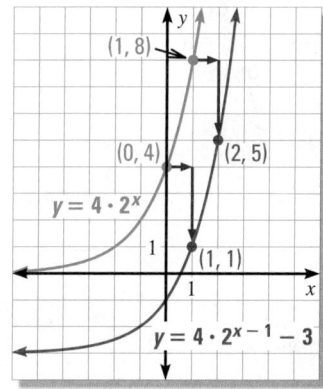

✓ **GUIDED PRACTICE** for Examples 1, 2, and 3

Graph the function. State the domain and range.

1. $y = 4^x$

2. $y = \dfrac{1}{2} \cdot 3^x$

3. $f(x) = 3^{x+1} + 2$

EXPONENTIAL GROWTH MODELS When a real-life quantity increases by a fixed percent each year (or other time period), the amount *y* of the quantity after *t* years can be modeled by the equation

$$y = a(1 + r)^t$$

where *a* is the initial amount and *r* is the percent increase expressed as a decimal. Note that the quantity $1 + r$ is the growth factor.

❖ **EXAMPLE 4** **Solve a multi-step problem**

COMPUTERS In 1996, there were 2573 computer viruses and other computer security incidents. During the next 7 years, the number of incidents increased by about 92% each year.

- Write an exponential growth model giving the number *n* of incidents *t* years after 1996. About how many incidents were there in 2003?

- Graph the model.

- Use the graph to estimate the year when there were about 125,000 computer security incidents.

Solution

STEP 1 The initial amount is $a = 2573$ and the percent increase is $r = 0.92$. So, the exponential growth model is:

$n = a(1 + r)^t$ **Write exponential growth model.**

$= 2573(1 + 0.92)^t$ **Substitute 2573 for *a* and 0.92 for *r*.**

$= 2573(1.92)^t$ **Simplify.**

AVOID ERRORS
Notice that the percent increase and the growth factor are two different values. An increase of 92% corresponds to a growth factor of 1.92.

Using this model, you can estimate the number of incidents in 2003 ($t = 7$) to be $n = 2573(1.92)^7 \approx 247{,}485$.

STEP 2 The graph passes through the points (0, 2573) and (1, 4940.16). Plot a few other points. Then draw a smooth curve through the points.

STEP 3 Using the graph, you can estimate that the number of incidents was about 125,000 during 2002 ($t \approx 6$).

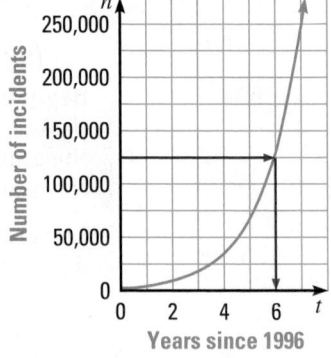

Animated Algebra   at my.hrw.com

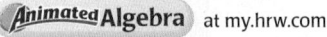

✓ **GUIDED PRACTICE** for Example 4

4. **WHAT IF?** In Example 4, estimate the year in which there were about 250,000 computer security incidents.

5. In the exponential growth model $y = 527(1.39)^x$, identify the initial amount, the growth factor, and the percent increase.

COMPOUND INTEREST Exponential growth functions are used in real-life situations involving *compound interest*. Compound interest is interest paid on the initial investment, called the *principal*, and on previously earned interest. Interest paid only on the principal is called *simple interest*.

KEY CONCEPT   *For Your Notebook*

Compound Interest

Consider an initial principal P deposited in an account that pays interest at an annual rate r (expressed as a decimal), compounded n times per year. The amount A in the account after t years is given by this equation:

$$A = P\left(1 + \frac{r}{n}\right)^{nt}$$

EXAMPLE 5   **Find the balance in an account**

FINANCE You deposit \$4000 in an account that pays 2.92% annual interest. Find the balance after 1 year if the interest is compounded with the given frequency.

a. Quarterly

b. Daily

Solution

a. With interest compounded quarterly, the balance after 1 year is:

$A = P\left(1 + \frac{r}{n}\right)^{nt}$ Write compound interest formula.

$= 4000\left(1 + \frac{0.0292}{4}\right)^{4 \cdot 1}$ $P = 4000, r = 0.0292, n = 4, t = 1$

$= 4000(1.0073)^4$ Simplify.

≈ 4118.09 Use a calculator.

▶ The balance at the end of 1 year is \$4118.09.

b. With interest compounded daily, the balance after 1 year is:

$A = P\left(1 + \frac{r}{n}\right)^{nt}$ Write compound interest formula.

$= 4000\left(1 + \frac{0.0292}{365}\right)^{365 \cdot 1}$ $P = 4000, r = 0.0292, n = 365, t = 1$

$= 4000(1.00008)^{365}$ Simplify.

≈ 4118.52 Use a calculator.

▶ The balance at the end of 1 year is \$4118.52.

✓   **GUIDED PRACTICE**   **for Example 5**

6. FINANCE You deposit \$2000 in an account that pays 4% annual interest. Find the balance after 3 years if the interest is compounded daily.

4.1 EXERCISES

HOMEWORK KEY

○ = See WORKED-OUT SOLUTIONS
Exs. 17, 29, and 37

★ = STANDARDIZED TEST PRACTICE
Exs. 2, 24, 25, 32, 40, and 41

◆ = MULTIPLE REPRESENTATIONS
Ex. 42

SKILL PRACTICE

1. **VOCABULARY** In the exponential growth model $y = 2.4(1.5)^x$, identify the initial amount, the growth factor, and the percent increase.

2. ★ **WRITING** What is an asymptote?

EXAMPLES 1 and 2
for Exs. 3–14

MATCHING GRAPHS Match the function with its graph.

3. $y = 3 \cdot 2^x$

4. $y = -3 \cdot 2^x$

5. $y = 2 \cdot 3^x$

A.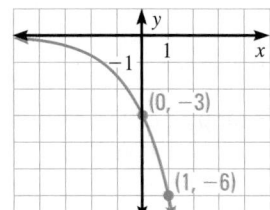

B.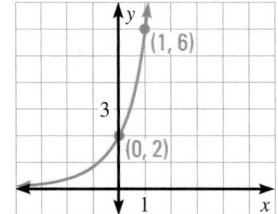

C.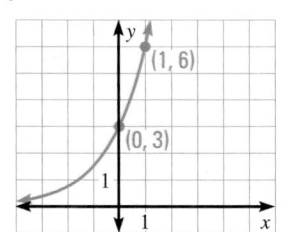

GRAPHING FUNCTIONS Graph the function.

6. $y = 3^x$

7. $y = -2^x$

8. $f(x) = 5 \cdot 2^x$

9. $y = 5^x$

10. $y = 2 \cdot 4^x$

11. $g(x) = -(1.5)^x$

12. $y = 3\left(\dfrac{4}{3}\right)^x$

13. $y = \dfrac{1}{2} \cdot 3^x$

14. $h(x) = -2(2.5)^x$

EXAMPLE 3
for Exs. 15–24

TRANSLATING GRAPHS Graph the function. State the domain and range.

15. $y = -3 \cdot 2^{x+2}$

16. $y = 5 \cdot 4^x + 2$

17. $y = 2^{x+1} + 3$

18. $y = 3^{x-2} - 1$

19. $y = 2 \cdot 3^{x-2} - 1$

20. $y = -3 \cdot 4^{x-1} - 2$

21. $f(x) = 6 \cdot 2^{x-3} + 3$

22. $g(x) = 5 \cdot 3^{x+2} - 4$

23. $h(x) = -2 \cdot 5^{x-1} + 1$

24. ★ **MULTIPLE CHOICE** The graph of which function is shown?

Ⓐ $f(x) = 2(1.5)^x - 1$

Ⓑ $f(x) = 2(1.5)^x + 1$

Ⓒ $f(x) = 3(1.5)^x - 1$

Ⓓ $f(x) = 3(1.5)^x + 1$

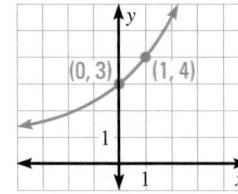

25. ★ **MULTIPLE CHOICE** The student enrollment E of a high school was 1310 in 1998 and has increased by 10% per year since then. Which exponential growth model gives the school's student enrollment in terms of t, where t is the number of years since 1998?

Ⓐ $E = 0.1(1310)^t$

Ⓑ $E = 1310(0.1)^t$

Ⓒ $E = 1.1(1310)^t$

Ⓓ $E = 1310(1.1)^t$

ERROR ANALYSIS *Describe* and correct the error in graphing the function.

26. $y = 2 \cdot 4^x$

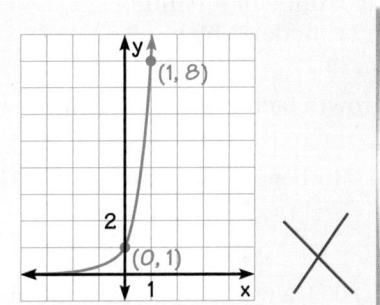

27. $y = 2^{x-3} + 3$

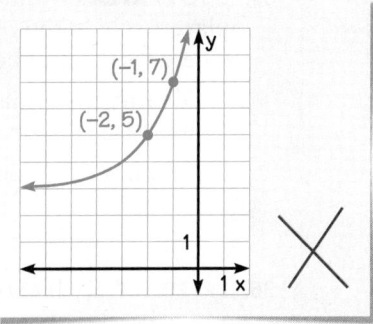

WRITING MODELS **In Exercises 28–30, write an exponential growth model that describes the situation.**

28. In 1992, 1219 monk parakeets were observed in the United States. For the next 11 years, about 12% more parakeets were observed each year.

29. You deposit $800 in an account that pays 2% annual interest compounded daily.

30. You purchase an antique table for $450. The value of the table increases by 6% per year.

31. GRAPHING CALCULATOR You deposit $1500 in a bank account that pays 3% annual interest compounded yearly.

a. Type 1500 into a graphing calculator and press **ENTER**. Then enter the formula ANS * 1.03, as shown at the right. Press **ENTER** seven times to find your balance after 7 years.

b. Find the number of years it takes for your balance to exceed $2500.

```
1500
                    1500
Ans*1.03
                    1545
              1591.35
              1639.0905
              1688.263215
```

32. ★ **OPEN-ENDED MATH** Write an exponential function of the form $y = ab^{x-h} + k$ whose graph has a *y*-intercept of 5 and an asymptote of $y = 2$.

33. GRAPHING CALCULATOR Consider the exponential growth function $y = ab^{x-h} + k$ where $a = 2$, $b = 5$, $h = -4$, and $k = 3$. Predict the effect on the function's graph of each change in *a*, *b*, *h*, or *k* described in parts (a)–(d). Use a graphing calculator to check your prediction.

a. *a* changes to 1   **b.** *b* changes to 4   **c.** *h* changes to 3   **d.** *k* changes to −1

34. CHALLENGE Consider the exponential function $f(x) = ab^x$.

a. Show that $\dfrac{f(x+1)}{f(x)} = b$.

b. Use the result from part (a) to explain why there is no exponential function of the form $f(x) = ab^x$ whose graph passes through the points in the table below.

x	0	1	2	3	4
y	4	4	8	24	72

EXAMPLE 4
for Exs. 35–36

35. DVD PLAYERS From 1997 to 2002, the number n (in millions) of DVD players sold in the United States can be modeled by $n = 0.42(2.47)^t$ where t is the number of years since 1997.

   a. Identify the initial amount, the growth factor, and the annual percent increase.

   b. Graph the function. Estimate the number of DVD players sold in 2001.

36. INTERNET Each March from 1998 to 2003, a website recorded the number y of referrals it received from Internet search engines. The results can be modeled by $y = 2500(1.50)^t$ where t is the number of years since 1998.

   a. Identify the initial amount, the growth factor, and the annual percent increase.

   b. Graph the function and state the domain and range. Estimate the number of referrals the website received from Internet search engines in March of 2002.

EXAMPLE 5
for Exs. 37–38

37. ACCOUNT BALANCE You deposit $2200 in a bank account. Find the balance after 4 years for each of the situations described below.

   a. The account pays 3% annual interest compounded quarterly.

   b. The account pays 2.25% annual interest compounded monthly.

   c. The account pays 2% annual interest compounded daily.

38. DEPOSITING FUNDS You want to have $3000 in your savings account after 3 years. Find the amount you should deposit for each of the situations described below.

   a. The account pays 2.25% annual interest compounded quarterly.

   b. The account pays 3.5% annual interest compounded monthly.

   c. The account pays 4% annual interest compounded yearly.

39. MULTI-STEP PROBLEM In 1990, the population of Austin, Texas, was 494,290. During the next 10 years, the population increased by about 3% each year.

   a. Write a model giving the population P (in thousands) of Austin t years after 1990. What was the population in 2000?

   b. Graph the model and state the domain and range.

   c. Estimate the year when the population was about 590,000.

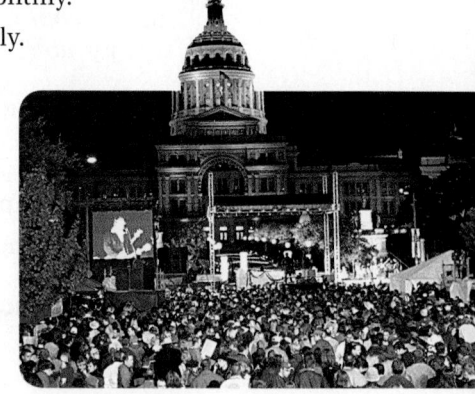

Austin, Texas

40. ★ SHORT RESPONSE At an online auction, the opening bid for a pair of in-line skates is $50. The price of the skates increases by 10.5% per bid during the next 6 bids.

   a. Write a model giving the price p (in dollars) of the skates after n bids.

   b. What was the price after 5 bids? According to the model, what will the price be after 100 bids? Is this predicted price reasonable? *Explain.*

○ = See **WORKED-OUT SOLUTIONS** in Student Resources   ★ = **STANDARDIZED TEST PRACTICE**   ◆ = **MULTIPLE REPRESENTATIONS**

41. ★ **EXTENDED RESPONSE** In 2000, the average price of a football ticket for a Minnesota Vikings game was $48.28. During the next 4 years, the price increased an average of 6% each year.

   a. Write a model giving the average price p (in dollars) of a ticket t years after 2000.

   b. Graph the model. Estimate the year when the average price of a ticket was about $60.

   c. *Explain* how you can use the graph of $p(t)$ to determine the minimum and maximum p-values over the domain for which the function gives meaningful results.

42. ◆ **MULTIPLE REPRESENTATIONS** In 1977, there were 41 breeding pairs of bald eagles in Maryland. Over the next 24 years, the number of breeding pairs increased by about 8.9% each year.

   a. **Writing an Equation** Write a model giving the number n of breeding pairs of bald eagles in Maryland t years after 1977.

   b. **Making a Table** Make a table of values for the model.

   c. **Drawing a Graph** Graph the model.

   d. **Using a Graph** About how many breeding pairs of bald eagles were in Maryland in 2001?

43. **REASONING** Is investing $3000 at 6% annual interest and $3000 at 8% annual interest equivalent to investing $6000 (the total of the two principals) at 7% annual interest (the average of the two interest rates)? *Explain.*

44. **CHALLENGE** The yearly cost for residents to attend a state university has increased exponentially from $5200 to $9000 in the last 5 years.

   a. To the nearest tenth of a percent, what has been the average annual growth rate in cost?

   b. If this growth rate continues, what will the cost be in 5 more years?

4.2 Graph Exponential Decay Functions

Before	You graphed and used exponential growth functions.
Now	You will graph and use exponential decay functions.
Why?	So you can model depreciation, as in Ex. 31.

Key Vocabulary
• exponential decay function
• decay factor

CC.9-12.F.IF.7 Graph functions expressed symbolically and show key features of the graph, by hand in simple cases and using technology for more complicated cases.*
e. Graph exponential and logarithmic functions, showing intercepts and end behavior, and trigonometric functions, showing period, midline, and amplitude.

You have studied exponential growth functions. In this lesson, you will study **exponential decay functions**, which have the form $y = ab^x$ where $a > 0$ and $0 < b < 1$. The base b of an exponential decay function is called the **decay factor**.

KEY CONCEPT   *For Your Notebook*

Parent Function for Exponential Decay Functions

The function $f(x) = b^x$, where $0 < b < 1$, is the parent function for the family of exponential decay functions with base b. The general shape of the graph of $f(x) = b^x$ is shown below.

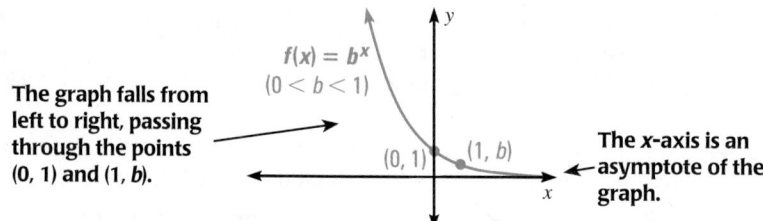

The graph falls from left to right, passing through the points (0, 1) and (1, **b**).

$f(x) = b^x$
$(0 < b < 1)$

$(0, 1)$ $(1, b)$

The *x*-axis is an asymptote of the graph.

The domain of $f(x) = b^x$ is all real numbers. The range is $y > 0$.

EXAMPLE 1   Graph $y = b^x$ for $0 < b < 1$

Graph $y = \left(\dfrac{1}{2}\right)^x$.

Solution

STEP 1 **Make** a table of values.

x	−3	−2	−1	0	1	2
y	8	4	2	1	$\dfrac{1}{2}$	$\dfrac{1}{4}$

STEP 2 **Plot** the points from the table.

STEP 3 **Draw**, from *right* to *left*, a smooth curve that begins just above the *x*-axis, passes through the plotted points, and moves up to the left.

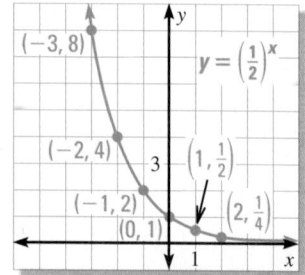

$(-3, 8)$

$y = \left(\dfrac{1}{2}\right)^x$

$(-2, 4)$ $\left(1, \dfrac{1}{2}\right)$

$(-1, 2)$ $\left(2, \dfrac{1}{4}\right)$

$(0, 1)$

TRANSFORMATIONS Recall that the graph of a function $y = ab^x$ is a vertical stretch or shrink of the graph of $y = b^x$, and the graph of $y = ab^{x-h} + k$ is a translation of the graph of $y = ab^x$.

EXAMPLE 2 Graph $y = ab^x$ for $0 < b < 1$

Graph the function.

CLASSIFY FUNCTIONS
Note that the function in part (b) of Example 2 is not an exponential decay function because $a = -3 < 0$.

a. $y = 2\left(\dfrac{1}{4}\right)^x$

b. $y = -3\left(\dfrac{2}{5}\right)^x$

Solution

a. Plot $(0, 2)$ and $\left(1, \dfrac{1}{2}\right)$. Then, from *right* to *left*, draw a curve that begins just above the x-axis, passes through the two points, and moves up to the left.

b. Plot $(0, -3)$ and $\left(1, -\dfrac{6}{5}\right)$. Then, from *right* to *left*, draw a curve that begins just below the x-axis, passes through the two points, and moves down to the left.

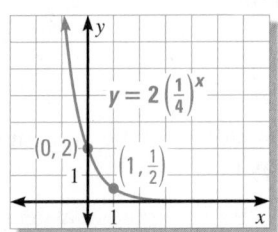

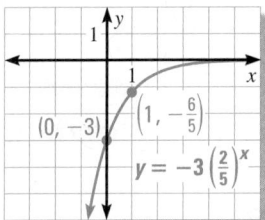

Animated Algebra at my.hrw.com

✓ **GUIDED PRACTICE** for Examples 1 and 2

Graph the function.

1. $y = \left(\dfrac{2}{3}\right)^x$

2. $y = -2\left(\dfrac{3}{4}\right)^x$

3. $f(x) = 4\left(\dfrac{1}{5}\right)^x$

EXAMPLE 3 Graph $y = ab^{x-h} + k$ for $0 < b < 1$

Graph $y = 3\left(\dfrac{1}{2}\right)^{x+1} - 2$. State the domain and range.

Solution

Begin by sketching the graph of $y = 3\left(\dfrac{1}{2}\right)^x$, which passes through $(0, 3)$ and $\left(1, \dfrac{3}{2}\right)$.

Then translate the graph left 1 unit and down 2 units. Notice that the translated graph passes through $(-1, 1)$ and $\left(0, -\dfrac{1}{2}\right)$.

The graph's asymptote is the line $y = -2$. The domain is all real numbers, and the range is $y > -2$.

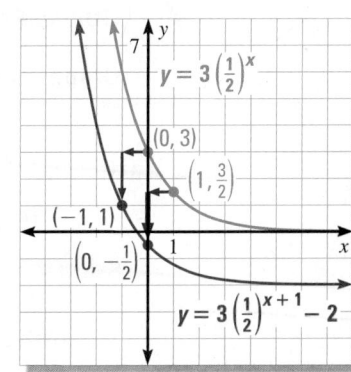

EXPONENTIAL DECAY MODELS When a real-life quantity decreases by a fixed percent each year (or other time period), the amount y of the quantity after t years can be modeled by the equation

$$y = a(1 - r)^t$$

where a is the initial amount and r is the percent decrease expressed as a decimal. Note that the quantity $1 - r$ is the decay factor.

EXAMPLE 4   Solve a multi-step problem

SNOWMOBILES A new snowmobile costs $4200. The value of the snowmobile decreases by 10% each year.

- Write an exponential decay model giving the snowmobile's value y (in dollars) after t years. Estimate the value after 3 years.

- Graph the model.

- Use the graph to estimate when the value of the snowmobile will be $2500.

Solution

STEP 1   The initial amount is $a = 4200$ and the percent decrease is $r = 0.10$. So, the exponential decay model is:

$y = a(1 - r)^t$	**Write exponential decay model.**
$= 4200(1 - 0.10)^t$	**Substitute 4200 for a and 0.10 for r.**
$= 4200(0.90)^t$	**Simplify.**

When $t = 3$, the snowmobile's value is $y = 4200(0.90)^3 = \$3061.80$.

AVOID ERRORS

Notice that the percent decrease, 10%, tells you how much value the snowmobile *loses* each year. The decay factor, 0.90, tells you what fraction of the snowmobile's value *remains* each year.

STEP 2   The graph passes through the points (0, 4200) and (1, 3780). It has the t-axis as an asymptote. Plot a few other points. Then draw a smooth curve through the points.

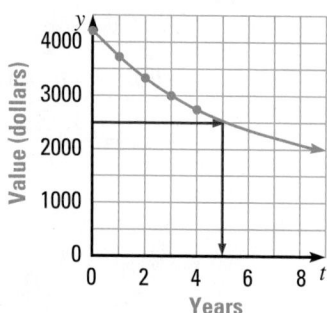

STEP 3   Using the graph, you can estimate that the value of the snowmobile will be $2500 after about 5 years.

✓ **GUIDED PRACTICE**   for Examples 3 and 4

Graph the function. State the domain and range.

4. $y = \left(\dfrac{1}{4}\right)^{x-1} + 1$ **5.** $y = 5\left(\dfrac{2}{3}\right)^{x+1} - 2$ **6.** $g(x) = -3\left(\dfrac{3}{4}\right)^{x-5} + 4$

7. WHAT IF? In Example 4, suppose the value of the snowmobile decreases by 20% each year. Write and graph an equation to model this situation. Use the graph to estimate when the value of the snowmobile will be $2500.

8. SNOWMOBILE The value of a snowmobile has been decreasing by 7% each year since it was new. After 3 years, the value is $3000. Find the original cost of the snowmobile.

4.2 EXERCISES

HOMEWORK KEY

○ = See WORKED-OUT SOLUTIONS
Exs. 9, 19, and 33

★ = STANDARDIZED TEST PRACTICE
Exs. 2, 15, 27, 28, 33, and 35

SKILL PRACTICE

1. **VOCABULARY** In the exponential decay model $y = 1250(0.85)^t$, identify the initial amount, the decay factor, and the percent decrease.

2. ★ **WRITING** *Explain* how to tell whether the function $y = b^x$ represents exponential growth or exponential decay.

CLASSIFYING FUNCTIONS **Tell whether the function represents** *exponential growth* **or** *exponential decay.*

3. $f(x) = 3\left(\dfrac{3}{4}\right)^x$

4. $f(x) = 4\left(\dfrac{5}{2}\right)^x$

5. $f(x) = \dfrac{2}{7} \cdot 4^x$

6. $f(x) = 25(0.25)^x$

EXAMPLES 1 and 2
for Exs. 7–15

GRAPHING FUNCTIONS **Graph the function.**

7. $y = \left(\dfrac{1}{4}\right)^x$

8. $y = \left(\dfrac{1}{3}\right)^x$

9. $f(x) = 2\left(\dfrac{1}{5}\right)^x$

10. $y = -(0.2)^x$

11. $y = -4\left(\dfrac{1}{3}\right)^x$

12. $g(x) = 2(0.75)^x$

13. $y = \left(\dfrac{3}{5}\right)^x$

14. $h(x) = -3\left(\dfrac{3}{8}\right)^x$

15. ★ **MULTIPLE CHOICE** The graph of which function is shown?

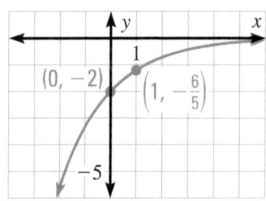

Ⓐ $y = 2\left(-\dfrac{3}{5}\right)^x$

Ⓑ $y = -2\left(\dfrac{3}{5}\right)^x$

Ⓒ $y = -2\left(\dfrac{2}{5}\right)^x$

Ⓓ $y = 2\left(-\dfrac{2}{5}\right)^x$

EXAMPLE 3
for Exs. 16–25

TRANSLATING GRAPHS **Graph the function. State the domain and range.**

16. $y = \left(\dfrac{1}{3}\right)^x + 1$

17. $y = -\left(\dfrac{1}{2}\right)^{x-1}$

18. $y = 2\left(\dfrac{1}{3}\right)^{x+1} - 3$

19. $y = \left(\dfrac{2}{3}\right)^{x-4} - 1$

20. $y = 3(0.25)^x + 3$

21. $y = \left(\dfrac{1}{3}\right)^{x-2} + 2$

22. $f(x) = -3\left(\dfrac{1}{4}\right)^{x-1}$

23. $g(x) = 6\left(\dfrac{1}{2}\right)^{x+5} - 2$

24. $h(x) = 4\left(\dfrac{1}{2}\right)^{x+1}$

25. **GRAPHING CALCULATOR** Consider the exponential decay function $y = ab^{x-h} + k$ where $a = 3$, $b = 0.4$, $h = 2$, and $k = -1$. Predict the effect on the function's graph of each change in a, b, h, or k described in parts (a)–(d). Use a graphing calculator to check your prediction.

   a. a changes to 4

   b. b changes to 0.2

   c. h changes to 5

   d. k changes to 3

26. **ERROR ANALYSIS** You invest $500 in the stock of a company. The value of the stock decreases 2% each year. *Describe* and correct the error in writing a model for the value of the stock after t years.

$$y = \left(\begin{array}{c}\text{Initial} \\ \text{amount}\end{array}\right)\left(\begin{array}{c}\text{Decay} \\ \text{factor}\end{array}\right)^t$$

$$y = 500(0.02)^t$$

27. ★ **MULTIPLE CHOICE** What is the asymptote of the graph of $y = \left(\frac{1}{2}\right)^{x-2} + 3$?

     A $y = -3$ **B** $y = -2$ **C** $y = 2$ **D** $y = 3$

28. ★ **OPEN-ENDED MATH** Write an exponential function whose graph lies between the graphs of $y = (0.5)^x$ and $y = (0.25)^x + 3$.

29. **CHALLENGE** Do $f(x) = 5(4)^{-x}$ and $g(x) = 5(0.25)^x$ represent the same function? *Justify* your answer.

PROBLEM SOLVING

EXAMPLE 4
for Exs. 30–31

30. **MEDICINE** When a person takes a dosage of I milligrams of ibuprofen, the amount A (in milligrams) of medication remaining in the person's bloodstream after t hours can be modeled by the equation $A = I(0.71)^t$.

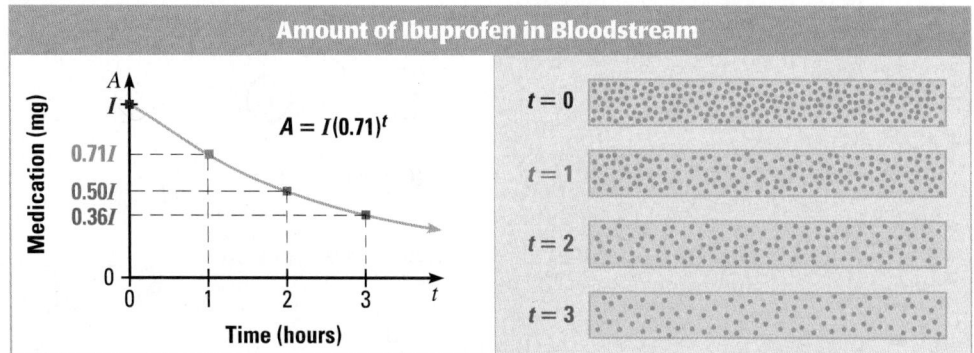

    Find the amount of ibuprofen remaining in a person's bloodstream for the given dosage and elapsed time since the medication was taken.

    a. Dosage: 200 mg   **b.** Dosage: 325 mg   **c.** Dosage: 400 mg
         Time: 1.5 hours   Time: 3.5 hours   Time: 5 hours

31. **BIKE COSTS** You buy a new mountain bike for $200. The value of the bike decreases by 25% each year.

    a. Write a model giving the mountain bike's value y (in dollars) after t years. Use the model to estimate the value of the bike after 3 years.

    b. Graph the model.

    c. Estimate when the value of the bike will be $100.

32. **DEPRECIATION** The table shows the amount d that a boat depreciates during each year t since it was new. Show that the ratio of depreciation amounts for consecutive years is constant. Then write an equation that gives d as a function of t.

Year, t	1	2	3	4	5
Depreciation, d	$1906	$1832	$1762	$1692	$1627

◯ = See **WORKED-OUT SOLUTIONS** in Student Resources   ★ = **STANDARDIZED TEST PRACTICE**

33. ★ **SHORT RESPONSE** The value of a car can be modeled by the equation $y = 24{,}000(0.845)^t$ where t is the number of years since the car was purchased.

　a. Graph the model. Estimate when the value of the car will be $10,000.

　b. Use the model to predict the value of the car after 50 years. Is this a reasonable value? *Explain.*

34. **MULTI-STEP PROBLEM** When a plant or animal dies, it stops acquiring carbon-14 from the atmosphere. Carbon-14 decays over time with a half-life of about 5730 years. The percent P of the original amount of carbon-14 that remains in a sample after t years is given by this equation:

$$P = 100\left(\frac{1}{2}\right)^{t/5730}$$

　a. What percent of the original carbon-14 remains in a sample after 2500 years? 5000 years? 10,000 years?

　b. Graph the model.

　c. An archaeologist found a bison bone that contained about 37% of the carbon-14 present when the bison died. Use the graph to estimate the age of the bone when it was found.

35. ★ **EXTENDED RESPONSE** The number E of eggs a Leghorn chicken produces per year can be modeled by the equation $E = 179.2(0.89)^{w/52}$ where w is the age (in weeks) of the chicken and $w \geq 22$.

　a. **Interpret** Identify the decay factor and the percent decrease.

　b. **Graph** Graph the model.

　c. **Estimate** Estimate the egg production of a chicken that is 2.5 years old.

　d. **Reasoning** *Explain* how you can rewrite the given equation so that time is measured in years rather than in weeks.

36. **CHALLENGE** You buy a new stereo for $1300 and are able to sell it 4 years later for $275. Assume that the resale value of the stereo decays exponentially with time. Write an equation giving the stereo's resale value V (in dollars) as a function of the time t (in years) since you bought it.

Extension

Transform Expressions of Exponential Functions

CC.9-12.A.SSE.3 Choose and produce an equivalent form of an expression to reveal and explain properties of the quantity represented by the expression.*
c. Use the properties of exponents to transform expressions for exponential functions.

By rewriting exponential growth and decay functions, you can understand more completely the real-life situations that these functions model.

EXAMPLE 1 Rewrite an exponential growth function

MUSIC SALES From 2004 to 2010, the number y (in millions) of songs sold by an online music store can be modeled by $y = 100(1.08)^t$ where t is years since 2004. Find the approximate monthly percent increase in sales.

Solution

Because t is given in years and $1.08 = 1 + 0.08$, the annual percent increase is 8%. To find the monthly percent increase that gives an 8% annual increase, use the fact that $t = \frac{1}{12}(12t)$ and the properties of exponents to rewrite the model in a form that reveals the monthly growth rate.

$$y = 100(1.08)^t \qquad \text{Write original function.}$$

$$= 100(1.08)^{(1/12)(12t)} \qquad t = \left(\frac{1}{12}\right)(12t)$$

$$= 100(1.08^{1/12})^{12t} \qquad \text{Power of a power property}$$

$$\approx 100(1.0064634)^{12t} \qquad \text{Evaluate power.}$$

> **CHECK**
> **UNDERSTANDING**
> ....
> $1.08^{1/12}$ is the 12th root of 1.08, so the 12th power of the 12th root of 1.08 is 1.08.

To check the rewritten model, notice that $t = 1$ gives $100(1.006434)^{12} \approx 108$, which is the same result as for the original model with $t = 1$. The monthly increase in sales is about 0.0064, or 0.64%.

EXAMPLE 2 Rewrite an exponential decay function

MEDICAL DIAGNOSTICS The amount A (in grams) remaining of n grams of the radioactive isotope chromium-51 after t days is given by $A = n\left(\frac{1}{2}\right)^{t/28}$. What percent of the chromium-51 decays each day?

Solution

Use the fact that $\frac{t}{28} = \left(\frac{1}{28}\right)t$ to rewrite the model in a way that reveals the daily growth rate.

$$A = n\left(\frac{1}{2}\right)^{t/28} \qquad \text{Write original function.}$$

$$= n\left[\left(\frac{1}{2}\right)^{1/28}\right]^t \qquad \text{Power of a power property}$$

$$\approx n(0.9755)^t \qquad \text{Evaluate power.w}$$

$$= n(1 - 0.0245)^t \qquad \text{Rewrite in form } y = a(1 - r)^t.$$

▶ The daily decay rate is about 0.0245, or 2.45%.

242 Chapter 4 Exponents and Exponential Functions

EXAMPLE 3 **Rewrite a doubling function**

FINANCE What annual interest rate is needed for the balance of an account to double every 15 years?

Solution

STEP 1 Write an exponential function for the amount A in the account after t years when the principal (original amount) is P. Notice the following:

When $t = 15$: $A = P \cdot 2^1 = P \cdot 2^{15/15}$

When $t = 30$: $A = P \cdot 2^2 = P \cdot 2^{30/15}$

When $t = 45$: $A = P \cdot 2^3 = P \cdot 2^{45/15}$

In general, the amount in the account after t years is $A = P(2)^{t/15}$.

STEP 2 Rewrite the function to find the annual interest rate.

$A = P(2)^{t/15}$ **Write original function.**

$ = P(2^{1/15})^t$ **Power of a power property**

$ \approx P(1.0473)^t$ **Evaluate power.**

$ = P(1 + 0.0473)^t$ **Rewrite in form $y = a(1 + r)^t$.**

▸ The annual interest rate needed is about 0.0473, or 4.73%.

PRACTICE

**EXAMPLES
1 AND 2**
for Exs. 1–4

1. **ELECTRICITY** For an 8 week period beginning June 1, the amount y (in kilowatt-hours) of electricity used by a business was approximately $y = 750(1.02)^t$ where t is the number of weeks since June 1. What daily percent increase in electricity use does this model represent?

2. **HALF-LIFE** The amount y (in grams) remaining of n grams of the radioactive isotope sodium-24 after t hours is given by $A = n\left(\dfrac{1}{2}\right)^{t/15}$. Find the hourly decay rate.

3. **TECHNOLOGY** A new computer system costs $2400. The value of the computer system decreases by 28% each year. Find the daily percent decrease in the value of the computer.

4. **REAL ESTATE** From 2000 to 2010, median home prices in Austin, Texas, rose an average of 7.2% per year. Find the monthly percent increase in the value of a home in Austin during 2000–2010.

EXAMPLE 3
for Exs. 5–6

5. **FINANCE** Find the annual interest rate needed for the balance of an account to double every 10 years.

6. **MARINE BIOLOGY** The population of a species of phytoplankton doubles every 3 days. Find the daily percent increase in the population.

7. **WRITING** Suppose you are given the number of years it takes for a quantity to double. *Describe* how to find the annual rate of increase of the quantity without writing a function that models the situation.

4.3 Use Functions Involving *e*

Before	You studied exponential growth and decay functions.
Now	You will study functions involving the natural base *e*.
Why?	So you can model visibility underwater, as in Ex. 59.

Key Vocabulary
• natural base *e*

CC.9-12.F.IF.7 Graph functions expressed symbolically and show key features of the graph, by hand in simple cases and using technology for more complicated cases.*
e. Graph exponential and logarithmic functions, showing intercepts and end behavior, and trigonometric functions, showing period, midline, and amplitude.

The history of mathematics is marked by the discovery of special numbers such as π and *i*. Another special number is denoted by the letter *e*. The number is called the **natural base *e*** or the *Euler number* after its discoverer, Leonhard Euler (1707–1783). The expression $\left(1 + \frac{1}{n}\right)^n$ approaches *e* as *n* increases.

n	10^1	10^2	10^3	10^4	10^5	10^6
$\left(1 + \frac{1}{n}\right)^n$	2.59374	2.70481	2.71692	2.71815	2.71827	2.71828

KEY CONCEPT   *For Your Notebook*

The Natural Base *e*

The natural base *e* is irrational. It is defined as follows:

As n approaches $+\infty$, $\left(1 + \frac{1}{n}\right)^n$ approaches $e \approx 2.718281828$.

EXAMPLE 1 Simplify natural base expressions

Simplify the expression.

REVIEW EXPONENTS
For help with properties of exponents, you may want to review the lesson *Use Properties of Exponents.*

a. $e^2 \cdot e^5 = e^{2+5}$

$= e^7$

b. $\dfrac{12e^4}{3e^3} = 4e^{4-3}$

$= 4e$

c. $\left(5e^{-3x}\right)^2 = 5^2\left(e^{-3x}\right)^2$

$= 25e^{-6x} = \dfrac{25}{e^{6x}}$

EXAMPLE 2 Evaluate natural base expressions

Use a calculator to evaluate the expression.

Expression	Keystrokes	Display
a. e^4	[2nd] [e^x] 4 [ )] [ENTER]	54.59815003
b. $e^{-0.09}$	[2nd] [e^x] [(−)] .09 [ )] [ENTER]	0.9139311853

Cousteau Society/Getty Images

Simplify the expression.

1. $e^7 \cdot e^4$ **2.** $2e^{-3} \cdot 6e^5$ **3.** $\dfrac{24e^8}{4e^5}$ **4.** $(10e^{-4x})^3$

5. Use a calculator to evaluate $e^{3/4}$.

KEY CONCEPT *For Your Notebook*

Natural Base Functions

A function of the form $y = ae^{rx}$ is called a *natural base exponential function*.

- If $a > 0$ and $r > 0$, the function is an exponential growth function.
- If $a > 0$ and $r < 0$, the function is an exponential decay function.

The graphs of the basic functions $y = e^x$ and $y = e^{-x}$ are shown below.

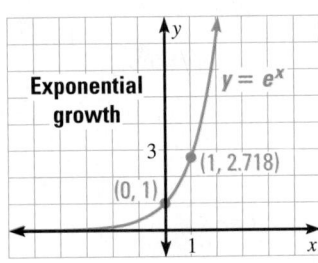 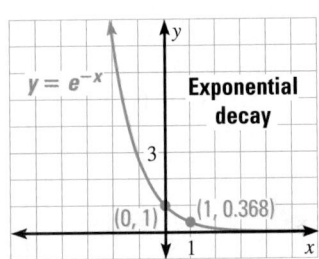

EXAMPLE 3 **Graph natural base functions**

Graph the function. State the domain and range.

a. $y = 3e^{0.25x}$

b. $y = e^{-0.75(x-2)} + 1$

Solution

ANOTHER WAY

You can also write the function from part (a) in the form $y = ab^x$ in order to graph it:

$y = 3e^{0.25x}$

$y = 3(e^{0.25})^x$

$y \approx 3(1.28)^x$

a. Because $a = 3$ is positive and $r = 0.25$ is positive, the function is an exponential growth function. Plot the points $(0, 3)$ and $(1, 3.85)$ and draw the curve.

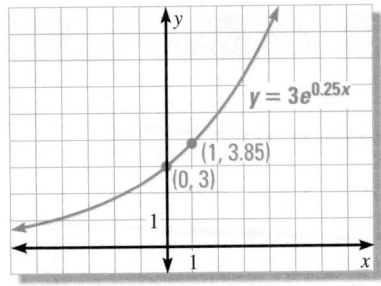

The domain is all real numbers, and the range is $y > 0$.

b. $a = 1$ is positive and $r = -0.75$ is negative, so the function is an exponential decay function. Translate the graph of $y = e^{-0.75x}$ right 2 units and up 1 unit.

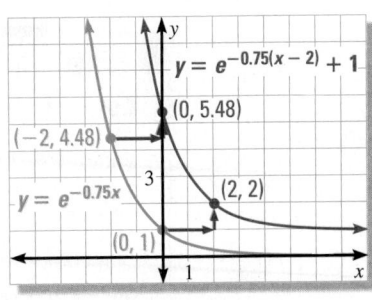

The domain is all real numbers, and the range is $y > 1$.

EXAMPLE 4 Solve a multi-step problem

BIOLOGY The length ℓ (in centimeters) of a tiger shark can be modeled by the function

$$\ell = 337 - 276e^{-0.178t}$$

where t is the shark's age (in years).

- Graph the model.
- Use the graph to estimate the length of a tiger shark that is 3 years old.

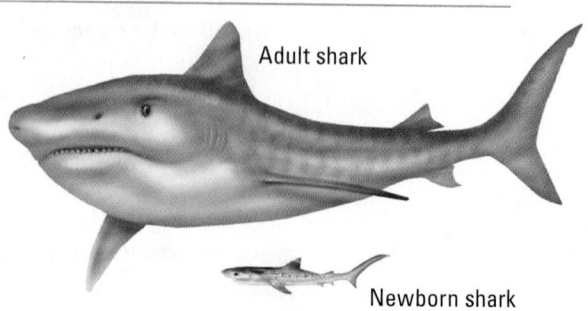

Adult shark

Newborn shark

INTERPRET VARIABLES

On a graphing calculator, enter the function $\ell = 337 - 276e^{-0.178t}$ using the variables x and y, as shown below:

$y = 337 - 276e^{-0.178x}$

Solution

STEP 1 **Graph** the model, as shown.

STEP 2 **Use** the *trace* feature to determine that $\ell \approx 175$ when $t = 3$.

▶ The length of a 3-year-old tiger shark is about 175 centimeters.

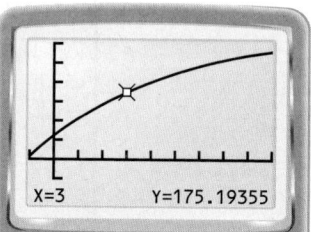

X=3   Y=175.19355

✓ **GUIDED PRACTICE** for Examples 3 and 4

Graph the function. State the domain and range.

6. $y = 2e^{0.5x}$

7. $f(x) = \dfrac{1}{2}e^{-x} + 1$

8. $y = 1.5e^{0.25(x-1)} - 2$

9. **WHAT IF?** In Example 4, use the given function to estimate the length of a tiger shark that is 5 years old.

CONTINUOUSLY COMPOUNDED INTEREST You have learned that the balance of an account earning compound interest is given by this formula:

$$A = P\left(1 + \frac{r}{n}\right)^{nt}$$

As the frequency n of compounding approaches positive infinity, the compound interest formula approximates the following formula.

KEY CONCEPT   *For Your Notebook*

Continuously Compounded Interest

When interest is compounded *continuously*, the amount A in an account after t years is given by the formula

$$A = Pe^{rt}$$

where P is the principal and r is the annual interest rate expressed as a decimal.

---

246 Chapter 4 Exponential and Logarithmic Functions

EXAMPLE 5   **Model continuously compounded interest**

FINANCE You deposit $4000 in an account that pays 6% annual interest compounded continuously. What is the balance after 1 year?

Solution

Use the formula for continuously compounded interest.

$$A = Pe^{rt}$$ **Write formula.**

$$= 4000e^{0.06(1)}$$ **Substitute 4000 for *P*, 0.06 for *r*, and 1 for *t*.**

$$\approx 4247.35$$ **Use a calculator.**

▶ The balance at the end of 1 year is $4247.35.

✓ **GUIDED PRACTICE**   **for Example 5**

10. **FINANCE** You deposit $2500 in an account that pays 5% annual interest compounded continuously. Find the balance after each amount of time.

   a. 2 years   **b.** 5 years   **c.** 7.5 years

11. **FINANCE** Find the amount of interest earned in parts (a)–(c) of Exercise 10.

4.3 EXERCISES

HOMEWORK
KEY

○ = **See WORKED-OUT SOLUTIONS**
    Exs. 5, 35, and 57

★ = **STANDARDIZED TEST PRACTICE**
    Exs. 2, 15, 16, 52, 53, and 60

SKILL PRACTICE

1. **VOCABULARY** Copy and complete: The number __?__ is an irrational number approximately equal to 2.71828.

2. ★ **WRITING** Tell whether the function $f(x) = \frac{1}{3}e^{4x}$ is an example of *exponential growth* or *exponential decay*. *Explain.*

EXAMPLE 1
for Exs. 3–18

SIMPLIFYING EXPRESSIONS **Simplify the expression.**

3. $e^3 \cdot e^4$

4. $e^{-2} \cdot e^6$

5. $(2e^{3x})^3$

6. $(2e^{-2})^{-4}$

7. $(3e^{5x})^{-1}$

8. $e^x \cdot e^{-3x} \cdot e^4$

9. $\sqrt{9e^6}$

10. $e^x \cdot 5e^{x+3}$

11. $\dfrac{3e}{e^x}$

12. $\dfrac{4e^x}{e^{4x}}$

13. $\sqrt[3]{8e^{9x}}$

14. $\dfrac{6e^{4x}}{8e}$

15. ★ **MULTIPLE CHOICE** What is the simplified form of $(4e^{2x})^3$?

   A $4e^{6x}$ **B** $4e^{8x}$ **C** $64e^{6x}$ **D** $64e^{8x}$

16. ★ **MULTIPLE CHOICE** What is the simplified form of $\sqrt{\dfrac{4(27e^{13}x)}{3e^7x^{-3}}}$?

   A $6e^{10}x$ **B** $6e^6x^4$ **C** $\dfrac{6e^3}{x^2}$ **D** $6e^3x^2$

ERROR ANALYSIS *Describe* and correct the error in simplifying the expression.

17.
$$\left(3e^{5x}\right)^2 = 3e^{(5x)(2)}$$
$$= 3e^{10x}$$

18.
$$\frac{e^{6x}}{e^{-2x}} = e^{6x-2x}$$
$$= e^{4x}$$

EXAMPLE 2
for Exs. 19–30

EVALUATING EXPRESSIONS Use a calculator to evaluate the expression.

19. e^3

20. $e^{-3/4}$

21. $e^{2.2}$

22. $e^{1/2}$

23. $e^{-2/5}$

24. $e^{4.3}$

25. e^7

26. e^{-4}

27. $2e^{-0.3}$

28. $5e^{2/3}$

29. $-6e^{2.4}$

30. $0.4e^{4.1}$

GROWTH OR DECAY Tell whether the function is an example of *exponential growth* or *exponential decay*.

31. $f(x) = 3e^{-x}$

32. $f(x) = \frac{1}{3}e^{4x}$

33. $f(x) = e^{-4x}$

34. $f(x) = \frac{3}{5}e^{x}$

35. $f(x) = \frac{1}{4}e^{-5x}$

36. $f(x) = e^{3x}$

37. $f(x) = 2e^{4x}$

38. $f(x) = 4e^{-2x}$

EXAMPLE 3
for Exs. 39–50

MATCHING GRAPHS Match the function with its graph.

39. $y = 0.5e^{0.5x}$

40. $y = 2e^{0.5x}$

41. $y = e^{0.5x} + 2$

A.
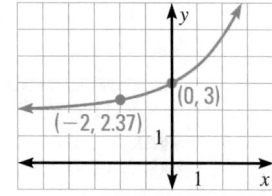

B.
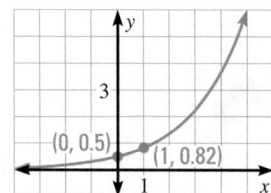

C.
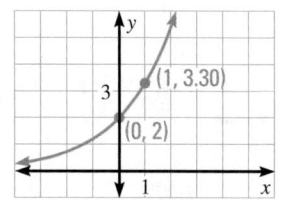

GRAPHING FUNCTIONS Graph the function. State the domain and range.

42. $y = e^{-2x}$

43. $y = 3e^{x}$

44. $y = 0.5e^{x}$

45. $y = 2e^{-3x} - 1$

46. $y = 2.5e^{-0.5x} + 2$

47. $y = 0.6e^{x-2}$

48. $f(x) = \frac{1}{2}e^{x+3} - 2$

49. $g(x) = \frac{4}{3}e^{x-1} + 1$

50. $h(x) = e^{-2(x+1)} - 3$

51. GRAPHING CALCULATOR Use the *table* feature of a graphing calculator to find the value of n for which $\left(1 + \frac{1}{n}\right)^n$ gives the value of e correct to 9 decimal places. *Explain* the process you used to find your answer.

52. ★ SHORT RESPONSE Can e be expressed as a ratio of two integers? *Explain* your reasoning.

53. ★ OPEN-ENDED MATH Find values of a, b, r, and q such that $f(x) = ae^{rx}$ and $g(x) = be^{qx}$ are exponential *decay* functions and $\frac{f(x)}{g(x)}$ is an exponential *growth* function.

54. CHALLENGE *Explain* why $A = P\left(1 + \frac{r}{n}\right)^{nt}$ approximates $A = Pe^{rt}$ as n approaches positive infinity. $\left(Hint: \text{Let } m = \frac{n}{r}.\right)$

○ = **See WORKED-OUT SOLUTIONS** in Student Resources

★ = **STANDARDIZED TEST PRACTICE**

EXAMPLE 4
for Exs. 55–56

55. CAMERA PHONES The number of camera phones shipped globally can be modeled by the function $y = 1.28e^{1.31x}$ where x is the number of years since 1997 and y is the number of camera phones shipped (in millions). How many camera phones were shipped in 2002?

56. BIOLOGY Scientists used traps to study the Formosan subterranean termite population in New Orleans. The mean number y of termites collected annually can be modeled by $y = 738e^{0.345t}$ where t is the number of years since 1989. What was the mean number of termites collected in 1999?

EXAMPLE 5
for Exs. 57–58

57. FINANCE You deposit $2000 in an account that pays 4% annual interest compounded continuously. What is the balance after 5 years?

58. FINANCE You deposit $800 in an account that pays 2.65% annual interest compounded continuously. What is the balance after 12.5 years?

59. MULTI-STEP PROBLEM The percent L of surface light that filters down through bodies of water can be modeled by the exponential function $L(x) = 100e^{kx}$ where k is a measure of the murkiness of the water and x is the depth below the surface (in meters).

   a. A recreational submersible is traveling in clear water with a k-value of about -0.02. Write and graph an equation giving the percent of surface light that filters down through clear water as a function of depth.

   b. Use your graph to estimate the percent of surface light available at a depth of 40 meters.

   c. Use your graph to estimate how deep the submersible can descend in clear water before only 50% of surface light is available.

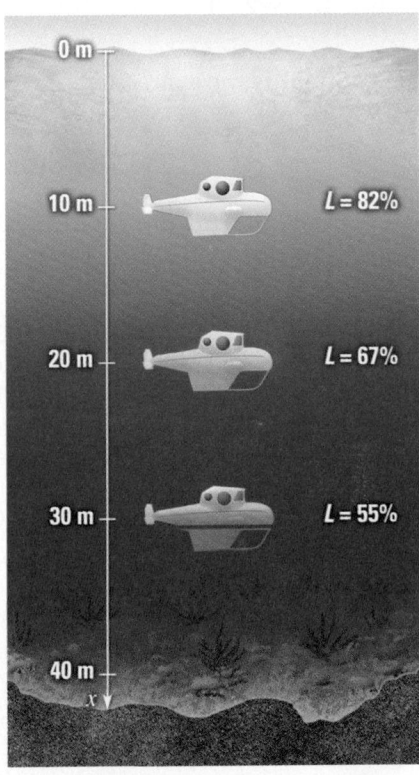

60. ★ EXTENDED RESPONSE The growth of the bacteria *mycobacterium tuberculosis* can be modeled by the function $P(t) = P_0 e^{0.116t}$ where $P(t)$ is the population after t hours and P_0 is the population when $t = 0$.

   a. Model At 1:00 P.M., there are 30 *mycobacterium tuberculosis* bacteria in a sample. Write a function for the number of bacteria after 1:00 P.M.

   b. Graph Graph the function from part (a).

   c. Estimate What is the population at 5:00 P.M.?

   d. Reasoning *Describe* how to find the population at 3:45 P.M.

61. RATE OF HEALING The area of a wound decreases exponentially with time. The area A of a wound after t days can be modeled by $A = A_0 e^{-0.05t}$ where A_0 is the initial wound area. If the initial wound area is 4 square centimeters, what is the area after 14 days?

62. CHALLENGE The height y (in feet) of the Gateway Arch in St. Louis, Missouri, can be modeled by the function $y = 757.7 - 63.85(e^{x/127.7} + e^{-x/127.7})$ where x is the horizontal distance (in feet) from the center of the arch.

    a. Use a graphing calculator to graph the function. How tall is the arch at its highest point?

    b. About how far apart are the ends of the arch?

QUIZ

Graph the function. State the domain and range.

1. $y = 2 \cdot 3^{x-2}$

2. $y = \left(\dfrac{2}{5}\right)^x$

3. $f(x) = \left(\dfrac{3}{8}\right)^x + 2$

Simplify the expression.

4. $3e^4 \cdot e^3$

5. $\left(-5e^{3x}\right)^3$

6. $\dfrac{e^{4x}}{5e}$

7. $\dfrac{8e^{5x}}{6e^{2x}}$

Graph the function. State the domain and range.

8. $y = 2e^x$

9. $y = 3e^{-2x}$

10. $y = e^{x+1} - 2$

11. $g(x) = 4e^{-3x} + 1$

12. TV SALES From 1997 to 2001, the number n (in millions) of black-and-white TVs sold in the United States can be modeled by $n = 26.8(0.85)^t$ where t is the number of years since 1997. Identify the decay factor and the percent decrease. Graph the model and state the domain and range. Estimate the number of black-and-white TVs sold in 1999.

13. FINANCE You deposit $1200 in an account that pays 4.5% annual interest compounded continuously. What is the balance after 5 years?

See **EXTRA PRACTICE** in Student Resources   🧭 **ONLINE QUIZ** at my.hrw.com

4.4 Evaluate Logarithms and Graph Logarithmic Functions

Before	You evaluated and graphed exponential functions.
Now	You will evaluate logarithms and graph logarithmic functions.
Why?	So you can model the wind speed of a tornado, as in Example 4.

Key Vocabulary
• logarithm of *y* with base *b*
• common logarithm
• natural logarithm

CC.9-12.F.IF.7 Graph functions expressed symbolically and show key features of the graph, by hand in simple cases and using technology for more complicated cases.*
e. Graph exponential and logarithmic functions, showing intercepts and end behavior, and trigonometric functions, showing period, midline, and amplitude.

You know that $2^2 = 4$ and $2^3 = 8$. However, for what value of x does $2^x = 6$? Mathematicians define this x-value using a *logarithm* and write $x = \log_2 6$. The definition of a logarithm can be generalized as follows.

KEY CONCEPT *For Your Notebook*

Definition of Logarithm with Base *b*

Let b and y be positive numbers with $b \neq 1$. The **logarithm of *y* with base *b*** is denoted by $\log_b y$ and is defined as follows:

$$\log_b y = x \quad \text{if and only if} \quad b^x = y$$

The expression $\log_b y$ is read as "log base b of y."

This definition tells you that the equations $\log_b y = x$ and $b^x = y$ are equivalent. The first is in *logarithmic form* and the second is in *exponential form*.

EXAMPLE 1 Rewrite logarithmic equations

Logarithmic Form	**Exponential Form**
a. $\log_2 8 = 3$	$2^3 = 8$
b. $\log_4 1 = 0$	$4^0 = 1$
c. $\log_{12} 12 = 1$	$12^1 = 12$
d. $\log_{1/4} 4 = -1$	$\left(\frac{1}{4}\right)^{-1} = 4$

Parts (b) and (c) of Example 1 illustrate two special logarithm values that you should learn to recognize. Let b be a positive real number such that $b \neq 1$.

Logarithm of 1

$\log_b 1 = 0$ because $b^0 = 1$.

Logarithm of *b* with Base *b*

$\log_b b = 1$ because $b^1 = b$.

 GUIDED PRACTICE for Example 1

Rewrite the equation in exponential form.

1. $\log_3 81 = 4$ **2.** $\log_7 7 = 1$ **3.** $\log_{14} 1 = 0$ **4.** $\log_{1/2} 32 = -5$

Chuck Carlton/Index Stock Imagery/photolibrary

EXAMPLE 2 **Evaluate logarithms**

Evaluate the logarithm.

  a. $\log_4 64$ **b.** $\log_5 0.2$ **c.** $\log_{1/5} 125$ **d.** $\log_{36} 6$

Solution

To help you find the value of $\log_b y$, ask yourself what power of b gives you y.

  a. 4 to what power gives 64? $4^3 = 64$, so $\log_4 64 = 3$.

  b. 5 to what power gives 0.2? $5^{-1} = 0.2$, so $\log_5 0.2 = -1$.

  c. $\frac{1}{5}$ to what power gives 125? $\left(\frac{1}{5}\right)^{-3} = 125$, so $\log_{1/5} 125 = -3$.

  d. 36 to what power gives 6? $36^{1/2} = 6$, so $\log_{36} 6 = \frac{1}{2}$.

SPECIAL LOGARITHMS A **common logarithm** is a logarithm with base 10. It is denoted by $\log_{10}$ or simply by log. A **natural logarithm** is a logarithm with base e. It can be denoted by $\log_e$, but is more often denoted by ln.

      Common Logarithm   **Natural Logarithm**

        $\log_{10} x = \log x$ $\log_e x = \ln x$

Most calculators have keys for evaluating common and natural logarithms.

EXAMPLE 3 **Evaluate common and natural logarithms**

Expression	Keystrokes	Display	Check
a. $\log 8$	`LOG` 8 `)` `ENTER`	0.903089987	$10^{0.903} \approx 8$ ✓
b. $\ln 0.3$	`LN` .3 `)` `ENTER`	−1.203972804	$e^{-1.204} \approx 0.3$ ✓

EXAMPLE 4 **Evaluate a logarithmic model**

TORNADOES The wind speed s (in miles per hour) near the center of a tornado can be modeled by

$$s = 93 \log d + 65$$

where d is the distance (in miles) that the tornado travels. In 1925, a tornado traveled 220 miles through three states. Estimate the wind speed near the tornado's center.

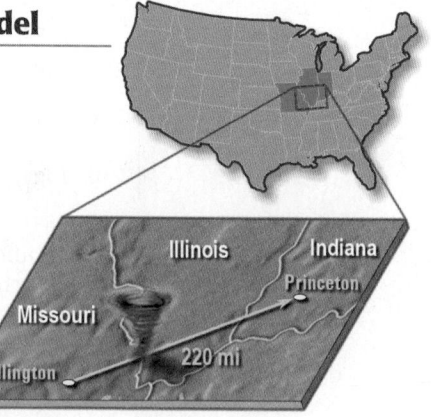

Not drawn to scale

Solution

$s = 93 \log d + 65$	Write function.
$= 93 \log 220 + 65$	Substitute 220 for d.
$\approx 93(2.342) + 65$	Use a calculator.
$= 282.806$	Simplify.

▶ The wind speed near the tornado's center was about 283 miles per hour.

Evaluate the logarithm. Use a calculator if necessary.

5. $\log_2 32$ **6.** $\log_{27} 3$ **7.** $\log 12$ **8.** $\ln 0.75$

9. WHAT IF? Use the function in Example 4 to estimate the wind speed near a tornado's center if its path is 150 miles long.

INVERSE FUNCTIONS By the definition of a logarithm, it follows that the logarithmic function $g(x) = \log_b x$ is the inverse of the exponential function $f(x) = b^x$. This means that:

$$g(f(x)) = \log_b b^x = x \quad \text{and} \quad f(g(x)) = b^{\log_b x} = x$$

EXAMPLE 5 **Use inverse properties**

Simplify the expression.

a. $10^{\log 4}$ **b.** $\log_5 25^x$

Solution

a. $10^{\log 4} = 4$ $b^{\log_b x} = x$

b. $\log_5 25^x = \log_5 \left(5^2\right)^x$ **Express 25 as a power with base 5.**

$\quad\quad\quad\quad = \log_5 5^{2x}$ **Power of a power property**

$\quad\quad\quad\quad = 2x$ $\log_b b^x = x$

EXAMPLE 6 **Find inverse functions**

Find the inverse of the function.

a. $y = 6^x$ **b.** $y = \ln(x + 3)$

Solution

a. From the definition of logarithm, the inverse of $y = 6^x$ is $y = \log_6 x$.

b. $y = \ln(x + 3)$ **Write original function.**

$\quad\quad x = \ln(y + 3)$ **Switch x and y.**

$\quad\quad e^x = y + 3$ **Write in exponential form.**

$\quad e^x - 3 = y$ **Solve for y.**

▶ The inverse of $y = \ln(x + 3)$ is $y = e^x - 3$.

 GUIDED PRACTICE for Examples 5 and 6

Simplify the expression.

10. $8^{\log_8 x}$ **11.** $\log_7 7^{-3x}$ **12.** $\log_2 64^x$ **13.** $e^{\ln 20}$

14. Find the inverse of $y = 4^x$.

15. Find the inverse of $y = \ln(x - 5)$.

GRAPHING LOGARITHMIC FUNCTIONS You can use the inverse relationship between exponential and logarithmic functions to graph logarithmic functions.

KEY CONCEPT   *For Your Notebook*

Parent Graphs for Logarithmic Functions

The graph of $f(x) = \log_b x$ is shown below for $b > 1$ and for $0 < b < 1$. Because $f(x) = \log_b x$ and $g(x) = b^x$ are inverse functions, the graph of $f(x) = \log_b x$ is the reflection of the graph of $g(x) = b^x$ in the line $y = x$.

Graph of $f(x) = \log_b x$ for $b > 1$ **Graph of $f(x) = \log_b x$ for $0 < b < 1$**

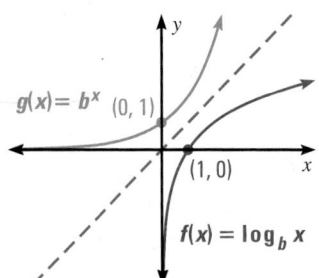   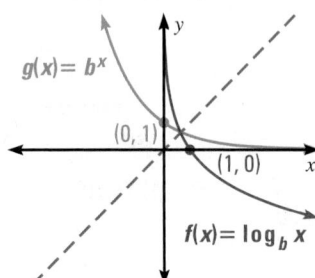

Note that the y-axis is a vertical asymptote of the graph of $f(x) = \log_b x$. The domain of $f(x) = \log_b x$ is $x > 0$, and the range is all real numbers.

EXAMPLE 7   **Graph logarithmic functions**

Graph the function.

a. $y = \log_3 x$

b. $y = \log_{1/2} x$

Solution

a. Plot several convenient points, such as (1, 0), (3, 1), and (9, 2). The y-axis is a vertical asymptote.

From *left* to *right*, draw a curve that starts just to the right of the y-axis and moves up through the plotted points, as shown below.

b. Plot several convenient points, such as (1, 0), (2, −1), (4, −2), and (8, −3). The y-axis is a vertical asymptote.

From *left* to *right*, draw a curve that starts just to the right of the y-axis and moves down through the plotted points, as shown below.

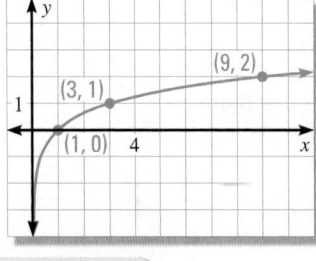   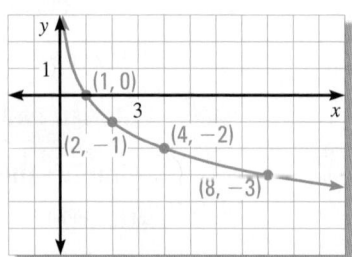

Animated Algebra   at my.hrw.com

TRANSLATIONS You can graph a logarithmic function of the form $y = \log_b (x - h) + k$ by translating the graph of the parent function $y = \log_b x$.

EXAMPLE 8 **Translate a logarithmic graph**

Graph $y = \log_2 (x + 3) + 1$. State the domain and range.

Solution

STEP 1 **Sketch** the graph of the parent function $y = \log_2 x$, which passes through $(1, 0)$, $(2, 1)$, and $(4, 2)$.

STEP 2 **Translate** the parent graph left 3 units and up 1 unit. The translated graph passes through $(-2, 1)$, $(-1, 2)$, and $(1, 3)$. The graph's asymptote is $x = -3$. The domain is $x > -3$, and the range is all real numbers.

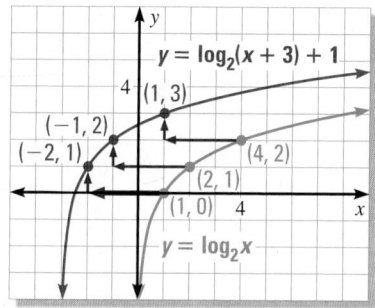

✓ **GUIDED PRACTICE** for Examples 7 and 8

Graph the function. State the domain and range.

16. $y = \log_5 x$

17. $y = \log_{1/3} (x - 3)$

18. $f(x) = \log_4 (x + 1) - 2$

4.4 EXERCISES

HOMEWORK KEY
◯ = See WORKED-OUT SOLUTIONS
Exs. 13, 33, and 61

★ = STANDARDIZED TEST PRACTICE
Exs. 2, 36, 61, and 62

SKILL PRACTICE

1. VOCABULARY Copy and complete: A logarithm with base 10 is called a(n) __?__ logarithm.

2. ★ WRITING *Describe* the relationship between $y = 5^x$ and $y = \log_5 x$.

EXAMPLE 1
for Exs. 3–7

EXPONENTIAL FORM Rewrite the equation in exponential form.

3. $\log_4 16 = 2$

4. $\log_7 343 = 3$

5. $\log_6 \frac{1}{36} = -2$

6. $\log_{64} 1 = 0$

7. ERROR ANALYSIS *Describe* and correct the error in rewriting the equation $2^{-3} = \frac{1}{8}$ in logarithmic form.

$$\log_2 -3 = \frac{1}{8}$$ ✗

EXAMPLE 2
for Exs. 8–19

EVALUATING LOGARITHMS Evaluate the logarithm without using a calculator.

8. $\log_{15} 15$

9. $\log_7 49$

10. $\log_6 216$

11. $\log_2 64$

12. $\log_9 1$

13. $\log_{1/2} 8$

14. $\log_3 \frac{1}{27}$

15. $\log_{16} \frac{1}{4}$

16. $\log_{1/4} 16$

17. $\log_8 512$

18. $\log_5 625$

19. $\log_{11} 121$

EXAMPLE 3
for Exs. 20–27

CALCULATING LOGARITHMS Use a calculator to evaluate the logarithm.

20. $\log 14$ **21.** $\ln 6$ **22.** $\ln 0.43$ **23.** $\log 6.213$

24. $\log 27$ **25.** $\ln 5.38$ **26.** $\log 0.746$ **27.** $\ln 110$

EXAMPLE 5
for Exs. 28–36

USING INVERSE PROPERTIES Simplify the expression.

28. $7^{\log_7 x}$ **29.** $\log_5 5^x$ **30.** $30^{\log_{30} 4}$ **31.** $10^{\log 8}$

32. $\log_6 36^x$ **33.** $\log_3 81^x$ **34.** $\log_5 125^x$ **35.** $\log_2 32^x$

36. ★ **MULTIPLE CHOICE** Which expression is equivalent to $\log 100^x$?

(**A**) x (**B**) $2x$ (**C**) $10x$ (**D**) $100x$

EXAMPLE 6
for Exs. 37–44

FINDING INVERSES Find the inverse of the function.

37. $y = \log_8 x$ **38.** $y = 7^x$ **39.** $y = (0.4)^x$ **40.** $y = \log_{1/2} x$

41. $y = e^{x+2}$ **42.** $y = 2^x - 3$ **43.** $y = \ln(x+1)$ **44.** $y = 6 + \log x$

GRAPHING FUNCTIONS Graph the function. State the domain and range.

45. $y = \log_4 x$ **46.** $y = \log_6 x$ **47.** $y = \log_{1/3} x$

48. $y = \log_{1/5} x$ **49.** $y = \log_2(x-3)$ **50.** $y = \log_3 x + 4$

51. $f(x) = \log_4(x+2) - 1$ **52.** $g(x) = \log_6(x-4) + 2$ **53.** $h(x) = \log_5(x+1) - 3$

CHALLENGE Evaluate the logarithm. (*Hint:* For each logarithm $\log_b x$, rewrite b and x as powers of the same number.)

54. $\log_{27} 9$ **55.** $\log_8 32$ **56.** $\log_{125} 625$ **57.** $\log_4 128$

PROBLEM SOLVING

EXAMPLE 4
for Exs. 58–59

58. ALTIMETER Skydivers use an instrument called an altimeter to track their altitude as they fall. The altimeter determines altitude by measuring air pressure. The altitude h (in meters) above sea level is related to the air pressure P (in pascals) by the function in the diagram below.

$$h = -8005 \ln \frac{P}{101,300}$$

$h = 3552$ m
$P = 65,000$ Pa

$h = ?$
$P = 57,000$ Pa

$h = 7438$ m
$P = 40,000$ Pa

Not drawn to scale

What is the altitude above sea level when the air pressure is 57,000 pascals?

59. CHEMISTRY The pH value for a substance measures how acidic or alkaline the substance is. It is given by the formula $\text{pH} = -\log[\text{H}^+]$ where H^+ is the hydrogen ion concentration (in moles per liter). Lemon juice has a hydrogen ion concentration of $10^{-2.3}$ moles per liter. What is its pH value?

60. MULTI-STEP PROBLEM Biologists have found that an alligator's length ℓ (in inches) and weight w (in pounds) are related by the function $\ell = 27.1 \ln w - 32.8$. Graph the function. Use your graph to estimate the weight of an alligator that is 10 feet long.

61. ★ **SHORT RESPONSE** The energy magnitude M of an earthquake can be modeled by

$$M = 0.29(\ln E) - 9.9$$

where E is the amount of energy released (in ergs).

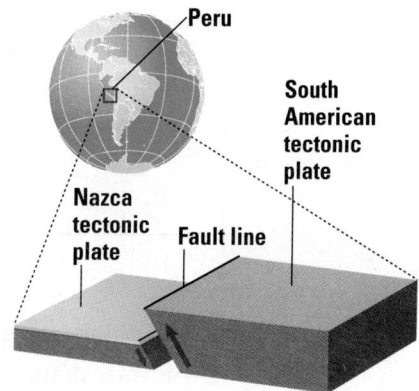

Peru

South American tectonic plate

Nazca tectonic plate

Fault line

a. In 2001, a powerful earthquake in Peru, caused by the slippage of two tectonic plates along a fault, released 2.5×10^{24} ergs. What was the energy magnitude of the earthquake?

b. Find the inverse of the given function. *Describe* what it represents.

62. ★ **EXTENDED RESPONSE** A study in Florida found that the number of fish species s in a pool or lake can be modeled by the function

$$s = 30.6 - 20.5(\log A) + 3.8(\log A)^2$$

where A is the area (in square meters) of the pool or lake.

a. Graph Use a graphing calculator to graph the function on the domain $200 \le A \le 35{,}000$.

b. Estimate Use your graph to estimate the number of fish species in a lake with an area of 30,000 square meters.

c. Estimate Use your graph to estimate the area of a lake that contains 6 species of fish.

d. Reasoning *Describe* what happens to the number of fish species as the area of a pool or lake increases. *Explain* why your answer makes sense.

63. CHALLENGE The function $s = 0.159 + 0.118(\log d)$ gives the slope s of a beach in terms of the average diameter d (in millimeters) of sand particles on the beach. Find the inverse of this function. Then use the inverse to estimate the average diameter of the sand particles on a beach with a slope of 0.2.

MIXED REVIEW *of Problem Solving*

MATHEMATICAL PRACTICES Make sense of problems and persevere in solving them.

1. **MULTI-STEP PROBLEM** The graph shown below is a translation of the graph of $y = \log_3 x$.

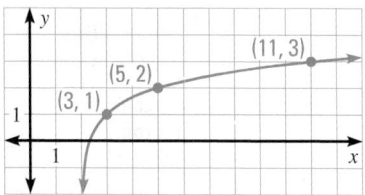

(11, 3)
(5, 2)
(3, 1)

   a. Write an equation of the graph.

   b. Graph the inverse of the function whose graph is shown above.

2. **MULTI-STEP PROBLEM** When a piece of paper is folded in half, the paper is divided into two regions, each of which has half the area of the paper. If this process is repeated, the number of regions increases while the area of each region decreases. The table below shows the number of regions and the fractional area of each region after each successive fold.

Fold number	0	1	2	3	4
Number of regions	1	2	?	?	?
Fractional area of each region	1	$\frac{1}{2}$	?	?	?

   a. Copy and complete the table.

   b. Write functions giving the number of regions $R(n)$ and the fractional area of each region $A(n)$ after n folds. Tell whether each function represents *exponential growth*, *exponential decay*, or *neither*.

3. **OPEN-ENDED** The value of one item *increases* by r% per year while the value of another item *decreases* by r% per year. After 2 years, both items are worth $100. Choose a value for r and write a function giving each item's value y after t years. Graph both functions in the same coordinate plane.

4. **SHORT RESPONSE** You deposit $2000 in an account that pays 4% annual interest compounded continuously. What is your balance after 2 years? After how many full years will your balance first exceed $2250? *Explain* how you found your answers.

5. **EXTENDED RESPONSE** A local bank offers certificate of deposit (CD) accounts that you can use to save money and earn interest. You are considering two different CDs: a three-year CD that requires a minimum balance of $1500 and pays 2% annual interest, and a five-year CD that requires a minimum balance of $2000 and pays 3% annual interest. The interest for both accounts is compounded monthly.

   a. If you deposit the minimum required amount in each CD, how much money is in each account at the end of its term? How much interest does each account earn?

   b. What is the difference in the amounts of interest?

   c. *Describe* the benefits and drawbacks of each account.

6. **GRIDDED ANSWER** Tritium is a radioactive substance used to illuminate exit signs. The amount of tritium disappears over time, a process called radioactive decay. If you start with a 10 milligram sample of tritium, the number y of milligrams left after t years is given by $y = 10e^{-0.0564t}$. How many milligrams of tritium are left after 10 years? Round your answer to the nearest hundredth.

7. **MULTI-STEP PROBLEM** The amount y of oil collected by a petroleum company drilling on the U.S. continental shelf can be modeled by $y = 12.263 \ln x - 45.381$ where y is measured in billions of barrels and x is the number of wells drilled.

   a. Graph the model.

   b. About how many barrels of oil would you expect to collect after drilling 1000 wells?

   c. About how many wells need to be drilled to collect 50 billion barrels of oil?

258 Chapter 4 Exponential and Logarithmic Functions

©Royalty-Free/Corbis

4.5 Apply Properties of Logarithms

Before	You evaluated logarithms.
Now	You will rewrite logarithmic expressions.
Why?	So you can model the loudness of sounds, as in Ex. 63.

Key Vocabulary
• base

CC.9-12.F.BF.5 (+) Understand the inverse relationship between exponents and logarithms and use this relationship to solve problems involving logarithms and exponents.

KEY CONCEPT
For Your Notebook

Properties of Logarithms

Let b, m, and n be positive numbers such that $b \neq 1$.

Product Property	$\log_b mn = \log_b m + \log_b n$
Quotient Property	$\log_b \dfrac{m}{n} = \log_b m - \log_b n$
Power Property	$\log_b m^n = n \log_b m$

EXAMPLE 1 Use properties of logarithms

Use $\log_4 3 \approx 0.792$ and $\log_4 7 \approx 1.404$ to evaluate the logarithm.

AVOID ERRORS
Note that in general
$\log_b \dfrac{m}{n} \neq \dfrac{\log_b m}{\log_b n}$ and
$\log_b mn \neq (\log_b m)(\log_b n)$.

a. $\log_4 \dfrac{3}{7} = \log_4 3 - \log_4 7$ **Quotient property**

$\approx 0.792 - 1.404$ **Use the given values of $\log_4 3$ and $\log_4 7$.**

$= -0.612$ **Simplify.**

b. $\log_4 21 = \log_4 (3 \cdot 7)$ **Write 21 as $3 \cdot 7$.**

$= \log_4 3 + \log_4 7$ **Product property**

$\approx 0.792 + 1.404$ **Use the given values of $\log_4 3$ and $\log_4 7$.**

$= 2.196$ **Simplify.**

c. $\log_4 49 = \log_4 7^2$ **Write 49 as 7^2.**

$= 2 \log_4 7$ **Power property**

$\approx 2(1.404)$ **Use the given value of $\log_4 7$.**

$= 2.808$ **Simplify.**

 GUIDED PRACTICE   for Example 1

Use $\log_6 5 \approx 0.898$ and $\log_6 8 \approx 1.161$ to evaluate the logarithm.

1. $\log_6 \dfrac{5}{8}$ **2.** $\log_6 40$ **3.** $\log_6 64$ **4.** $\log_6 125$

REWRITING EXPRESSIONS You can use the properties of logarithms to expand and condense logarithmic expressions.

EXAMPLE 2 Expand a logarithmic expression

Expand $\log_6 \dfrac{5x^3}{y}$.

$$\log_6 \frac{5x^3}{y} = \log_6 5x^3 - \log_6 y \qquad \text{Quotient property}$$

$$= \log_6 5 + \log_6 x^3 - \log_6 y \qquad \text{Product property}$$

$$= \log_6 5 + 3\log_6 x - \log_6 y \qquad \text{Power property}$$

EXAMPLE 3 Standardized Test Practice

Which of the following is equivalent to $\log 9 + 3\log 2 - \log 3$?

(A) $\log 8$ (B) $\log 14$ (C) $\log 18$ (D) $\log 24$

Solution

$$\log 9 + 3\log 2 - \log 3 = \log 9 + \log 2^3 - \log 3 \qquad \text{Power property}$$

$$= \log\left(9 \cdot 2^3\right) - \log 3 \qquad \text{Product property}$$

$$= \log \frac{9 \cdot 2^3}{3} \qquad \text{Quotient property}$$

$$= \log 24 \qquad \text{Simplify.}$$

▶ The correct answer is D. (A) (B) (C) (D)

✓ **GUIDED PRACTICE** for Examples 2 and 3

5. Expand $\log 3x^4$.

6. Condense $\ln 4 + 3\ln 3 - \ln 12$.

CHANGE-OF-BASE FORMULA Logarithms with any base other than 10 or e can be written in terms of common or natural logarithms using the *change-of-base formula*. This allows you to evaluate any logarithm using a calculator.

KEY CONCEPT   *For Your Notebook*

Change-of-Base Formula

If a, b, and c are positive numbers with $b \neq 1$ and $c \neq 1$, then:

$$\log_c a = \frac{\log_b a}{\log_b c}$$

In particular, $\log_c a = \dfrac{\log a}{\log c}$ and $\log_c a = \dfrac{\ln a}{\ln c}$.

EXAMPLE 4   **Use the change-of-base formula**

Evaluate $\log_3 8$ using common logarithms and natural logarithms.

Solution

Using common logarithms: $\log_3 8 = \dfrac{\log 8}{\log 3} \approx \dfrac{0.9031}{0.4771} \approx 1.893$

Using natural logarithms: $\log_3 8 = \dfrac{\ln 8}{\ln 3} \approx \dfrac{2.0794}{1.0986} \approx 1.893$

EXAMPLE 5   **Use properties of logarithms in real life**

SOUND INTENSITY For a sound with intensity I (in watts per square meter), the loudness $L(I)$ of the sound (in decibels) is given by the function

$$L(I) = 10 \log \frac{I}{I_0}$$

where I_0 is the intensity of a barely audible sound (about 10^{-12} watts per square meter). An artist in a recording studio turns up the volume of a track so that the sound's intensity doubles. By how many decibels does the loudness increase?

Solution

Let I be the original intensity, so that $2I$ is the doubled intensity.

Increase in loudness $= L(2I) - L(I)$ **Write an expression.**

$= 10 \log \dfrac{2I}{I_0} - 10 \log \dfrac{I}{I_0}$ **Substitute.**

$= 10\left(\log \dfrac{2I}{I_0} - \log \dfrac{I}{I_0} \right)$ **Distributive property**

$= 10\left(\log 2 + \log \dfrac{I}{I_0} - \log \dfrac{I}{I_0} \right)$ **Product property**

$= 10 \log 2$ **Simplify.**

≈ 3.01 **Use a calculator.**

▶ The loudness increases by about 3 decibels.

 GUIDED PRACTICE   for Examples 4 and 5

Use the change-of-base formula to evaluate the logarithm.

7. $\log_5 8$ **8.** $\log_8 14$ **9.** $\log_{26} 9$ **10.** $\log_{12} 30$

11. WHAT IF? In Example 5, suppose the artist turns up the volume so that the sound's intensity triples. By how many decibels does the loudness increase?

4.5 EXERCISES

HOMEWORK KEY

○ = See WORKED-OUT SOLUTIONS
Exs. 11, 17, and 71

★ = STANDARDIZED TEST PRACTICE
Exs. 2, 43, 44, 64, 71, and 73

SKILL PRACTICE

1. **VOCABULARY** Copy and complete: To condense the expression $\log_3 2x + \log_3 y$, you need to use the __?__ property of logarithms.

2. ★ **WRITING** *Describe* two ways to evaluate $\log_7 12$ using a calculator.

EXAMPLE 1
for Exs. 3–14

MATCHING EXPRESSIONS Match the expression with the logarithm that has the same value.

3. $\ln 6 - \ln 2$ 4. $2 \ln 6$ 5. $6 \ln 2$ 6. $\ln 6 + \ln 2$

A. $\ln 64$ B. $\ln 3$ C. $\ln 12$ D. $\ln 36$

APPROXIMATING EXPRESSIONS Use $\log 4 \approx 0.602$ and $\log 12 \approx 1.079$ to evaluate the logarithm.

7. $\log 3$ 8. $\log 48$ 9. $\log 16$ 10. $\log 64$

11. $\log 144$ 12. $\log \frac{1}{3}$ 13. $\log \frac{1}{4}$ 14. $\log \frac{1}{12}$

EXAMPLE 2
for Exs. 15–32

EXPANDING EXPRESSIONS Expand the expression.

15. $\log_3 4x$ 16. $\ln 15x$ 17. $\log 3x^4$ 18. $\log_5 x^5$

19. $\log_2 \frac{2}{5}$ 20. $\ln \frac{12}{5}$ 21. $\log_4 \frac{x}{3y}$ 22. $\ln 4x^2 y$

23. $\log_7 5x^3 yz^2$ 24. $\log_6 36x^2$ 25. $\ln x^2 y^{1/3}$ 26. $\log 10x^3$

27. $\log_2 \sqrt{x}$ 28. $\ln \frac{6x^2}{y^4}$ 29. $\ln \sqrt[4]{x^3}$ 30. $\log_3 \sqrt{9x}$

ERROR ANALYSIS *Describe* and correct the error in expanding the logarithmic expression.

31.
$$\log_2 5x = (\log_2 5)(\log_2 x)$$ ✗

32.
$$\ln 8x^3 = 3 \ln 8 + \ln x$$ ✗

EXAMPLE 3
for Exs. 33–43

CONDENSING EXPRESSIONS Condense the expression.

33. $\log_4 7 - \log_4 10$ 34. $\ln 12 - \ln 4$

35. $2 \log x + \log 11$ 36. $6 \ln x + 4 \ln y$

37. $5 \log x - 4 \log y$ 38. $5 \log_4 2 + 7 \log_4 x + 4 \log_4 y$

39. $\ln 40 + 2 \ln \frac{1}{2} + \ln x$ 40. $\log_5 4 + \frac{1}{3} \log_5 x$

41. $6 \ln 2 - 4 \ln y$ 42. $2(\log_3 20 - \log_3 4) + 0.5 \log_3 4$

43. ★ **MULTIPLE CHOICE** Which of the following is equivalent to $3 \log_4 6$?

 (A) $\log_4 18$ (B) $\log_4 72$ (C) $\log_4 216$ (D) $\log_4 256$

44. ★ **MULTIPLE CHOICE** Which of the following statements is *not* correct?

(A) $\log_3 48 = \log_3 16 + \log_3 3$

(B) $\log_3 48 = 3 \log_3 2 + \log_3 6$

(C) $\log_3 48 = 2 \log_3 4 + \log_3 3$

(D) $\log_3 48 = \log_3 8 + 2 \log_3 3$

EXAMPLE 4
for Exs. 45–61

CHANGE-OF-BASE FORMULA **Use the change-of-base formula to evaluate the logarithm.**

45. $\log_4 7$

46. $\log_5 13$

47. $\log_3 15$

48. $\log_8 22$

49. $\log_3 6$

50. $\log_5 14$

51. $\log_6 17$

52. $\log_2 28$

53. $\log_7 19$

54. $\log_4 48$

55. $\log_9 27$

56. $\log_8 32$

57. $\log_6 \dfrac{24}{5}$

58. $\log_2 \dfrac{15}{7}$

59. $\log_3 \dfrac{9}{40}$

60. $\log_7 \dfrac{3}{16}$

61. **ERROR ANALYSIS** *Describe* and correct the error in using the change-of-base formula.

$$\log_3 7 = \frac{\log 3}{\log 7} \qquad \times$$

EXAMPLE 5
for Exs. 62–63

SOUND INTENSITY In Exercises 62 and 63, use the function in Example 5.

62. Find the decibel level of the sound made by each object shown below.

a.
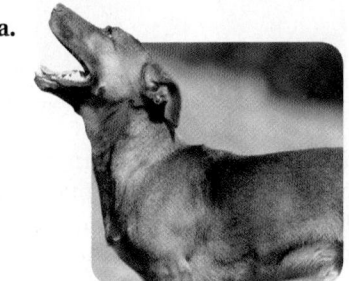

b.
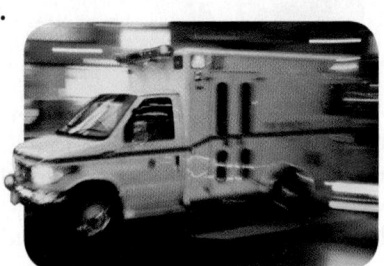

c.

Barking dog: $I = 10^{-4}$ W/m^2 Ambulance siren: $I = 10^0$ W/m^2 Bee: $I = 10^{-6.5}$ W/m^2

63. The intensity of the sound of a trumpet is 10^3 watts per square meter. Find the decibel level of a trumpet.

64. ★ **OPEN-ENDED MATH** For each statement, find positive numbers M, N, and b (with $b \neq 1$) that show the statement is false in general.

a. $\log_b (M + N) = \log_b M + \log_b N$

b. $\log_b (M - N) = \log_b M - \log_b N$

CHALLENGE In Exercises 65–68, use the given hint and properties of exponents to prove the property of logarithms.

65. **Product property** $\log_b mn = \log_b m + \log_b n$

(*Hint:* Let $x = \log_b m$ and let $y = \log_b n$. Then $m = b^x$ and $n = b^y$.)

66. **Quotient property** $\log_b \dfrac{m}{n} = \log_b m - \log_b n$

(*Hint:* Let $x = \log_b m$ and let $y = \log_b n$. Then $m = b^x$ and $n = b^y$.)

67. **Power property** $\log_b m^n = n \log_b m$

(*Hint:* Let $x = \log_b m$. Then $m = b^x$ and $m^n = b^{nx}$.)

68. **Change-of-base formula** $\log_c a = \dfrac{\log_b a}{\log_b c}$

(*Hint:* Let $x = \log_b a$, $y = \log_b c$, and $z = \log_c a$. Then $a = b^x$, $c = b^y$, and $a = c^z$, so that $b^x = c^z$.)

EXAMPLE 5
for Exs. 69–72

69. CONVERSATION Three groups of people are having separate conversations in a room. The sound of each conversation has an intensity of 1.4×10^{-5} watts per square meter. What is the decibel level of the combined conversations in the room?

70. PARKING GARAGE The sound made by each of five cars in a parking garage has an intensity of 3.2×10^{-4} watts per square meter. What is the decibel level of the sound made by all five cars in the parking garage?

71. ★ **SHORT RESPONSE** The intensity of the sound TV ads make is ten times as great as the intensity for an average TV show. How many decibels louder is a TV ad? *Justify* your answer using properties of logarithms.

Intensity of Television Sound

During show: Intensity = I

50% off all eyeglasses

During ad: Intensity = $10I$

72. BIOLOGY The loudest animal on Earth is the blue whale. It can produce a sound with an intensity of $10^{6.8}$ watts per square meter. The loudest sound a human can make has an intensity of $10^{0.8}$ watts per square meter. *Compare* the decibel levels of the sounds made by a blue whale and a human.

73. ★ **EXTENDED RESPONSE** The f-stops on a 35 millimeter camera control the amount of light that enters the camera. Let s be a measure of the amount of light that strikes the film and let f be the f-stop. Then s and f are related by the equation:

$$s = \log_2 f^2$$

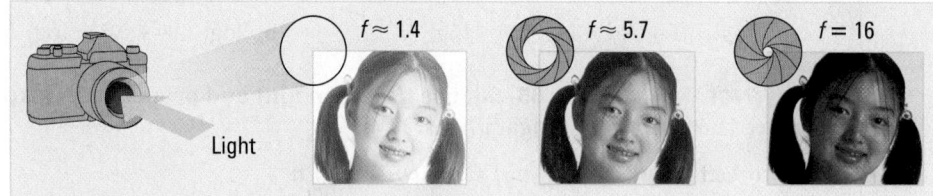

$f \approx 1.4$

$f \approx 5.7$

$f = 16$

Light

a. Use Properties Expand the expression for s.

b. Calculate The table shows the first eight f-stops on a 35 millimeter camera. Copy and complete the table. *Describe* the pattern you observe.

f	1.414	2.000	2.828	4.000	5.657	8.000	11.314	16.000
s	?	?	?	?	?	?	?	?

c. Reasoning Many 35 millimeter cameras have nine f-stops. What do you think the ninth f-stop is? *Explain* your reasoning.

○ = See WORKED-OUT SOLUTIONS in Student Resources   ★ = STANDARDIZED TEST PRACTICE

74. CHALLENGE Under certain conditions, the wind speed s (in knots) at an altitude of h meters above a grassy plain can be modeled by this function:

$$s(h) = 2 \ln (100h)$$

a. By what amount does the wind speed increase when the altitude doubles?

b. Show that the given function can be written in terms of common logarithms as $s(h) = \dfrac{2}{\log e} (\log h + 2)$.

QUIZ

Evaluate the logarithm without using a calculator.

1. $\log_4 16$ **2.** $\log_5 1$ **3.** $\log_8 8$ **4.** $\log_{1/2} 32$

Graph the function. State the domain and range.

5. $y = \log_2 x$ **6.** $y = \ln x + 2$ **7.** $y = \log_3 (x + 4) - 1$

Expand the expression.

8. $\log_2 5x$ **9.** $\log_5 x^7$ **10.** $\ln 5xy^3$ **11.** $\log_3 \dfrac{6y^4}{x^8}$

Condense the expression.

12. $\log_3 5 - \log_3 20$ **13.** $\ln 6 + \ln 4x$ **14.** $\log_6 5 + 3 \log_6 2$ **15.** $4 \ln x - 5 \ln x$

Use the change-of-base formula to evaluate the logarithm.

16. $\log_3 10$ **17.** $\log_7 14$ **18.** $\log_5 24$ **19.** $\log_8 40$

20. SOUND INTENSITY The sound of an alarm clock has an intensity of $I = 10^{-4}$ watts per square meter. Use the model $L(I) = 10 \log \dfrac{I}{I_0}$, where $I_0 = 10^{-12}$ watts per square meter, to find the alarm clock's loudness $L(I)$.

my.hrw.com
Keystrokes

Graph Logarithmic Functions

Use appropriate tools
strategically.

QUESTION How can you graph logarithmic functions on a graphing
calculator?

You can use a graphing calculator to graph logarithmic functions simply by using
the ``LOG`` or ``LN`` key. To graph a logarithmic function having a base other than 10
or *e*, you need to use the change-of-base formula to rewrite the function in terms
of common or natural logarithms.

EXAMPLE Graph logarithmic functions

Use a graphing calculator to graph $y = \log_2 x$ and $y = \log_2 (x - 3) + 1$.

STEP 1 *Rewrite functions* Use the change-of-base formula to rewrite each
function in terms of common logarithms.

$$y = \log_2 x \qquad\qquad y = \log_2 (x - 3) + 1$$

$$= \frac{\log x}{\log 2} \qquad\qquad = \frac{\log (x - 3)}{\log 2} + 1$$

STEP 2 *Enter functions*
Enter each function into a
graphing calculator.

STEP 3 *Graph functions*
Graph the functions.

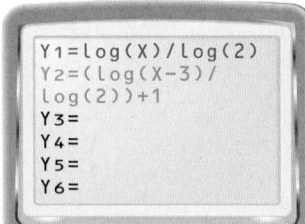

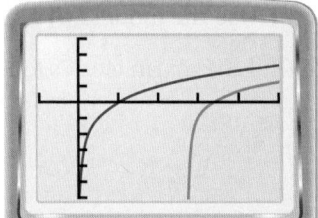

PRACTICE

Use a graphing calculator to graph the function.

1. $y = \log_4 x$
2. $y = \log_8 x$
3. $f(x) = \log_3 x$

4. $y = \log_5 x$
5. $y = \log_{12} x$
6. $g(x) = \log_9 x$

7. $y = \log_3 (x + 2)$
8. $y = \log_5 x - 1$
9. $f(x) = \log_4 (x - 5) - 2$

10. $y = \log_2 (x + 4) - 7$
11. $y = \log_7 (x - 5) + 3$
12. $g(x) = \log_3 (x + 6) - 6$

13. **REASONING** Graph $y = \ln x$. If your calculator did not have a natural
    logarithm key, explain how you could graph $y = \ln x$ using the ``LOG`` key.

4.6 Solve Exponential and Logarithmic Equations

Before	You studied exponential and logarithmic functions.
Now	You will solve exponential and logarithmic equations.
Why?	So you can solve problems about astronomy, as in Example 7.

Key Vocabulary
- exponential equation
- logarithmic equation
- extraneous solution

CC.9-12.F.LE.4 For exponential models, express as a logarithm the solution to $ab^{ct} = d$ where a, c, and d are numbers and the base b is 2, 10, or e; evaluate the logarithm using technology.*

Exponential equations are equations in which variable expressions occur as exponents. The result below is useful for solving certain exponential equations.

KEY CONCEPT   *For Your Notebook*

Property of Equality for Exponential Equations

Algebra   If b is a positive number other than 1, then $b^x = b^y$ if and only if $x = y$.

Example   If $3^x = 3^5$, then $x = 5$. If $x = 5$, then $3^x = 3^5$.

EXAMPLE 1   Solve by equating exponents

Solve $4^x = \left(\dfrac{1}{2}\right)^{x-3}$.

$4^x = \left(\dfrac{1}{2}\right)^{x-3}$ Write original equation.

$(2^2)^x = (2^{-1})^{x-3}$ Rewrite 4 and $\dfrac{1}{2}$ as powers with base 2.

$2^{2x} = 2^{-x+3}$ Power of a power property

$2x = -x + 3$ Property of equality for exponential equations

$x = 1$ Solve for x.

▶ The solution is 1.

CHECK   Check the solution by substituting it into the original equation.

$4^1 \overset{?}{=} \left(\dfrac{1}{2}\right)^{1-3}$ Substitute 1 for x.

$4 \overset{?}{=} \left(\dfrac{1}{2}\right)^{-2}$ Simplify.

$4 = 4$ ✓   Solution checks.

✓ **GUIDED PRACTICE**   for Example 1

Solve the equation.

1. $9^{2x} = 27^{x-1}$ **2.** $100^{7x+1} = 1000^{3x-2}$ **3.** $81^{3-x} = \left(\dfrac{1}{3}\right)^{5x-6}$

When it is not convenient to write each side of an exponential equation using the same base, you can solve the equation by taking a logarithm of each side.

EXAMPLE 2   **Take a logarithm of each side**

ANOTHER WAY

For an alternative method for solving the problem in Example 2, See the **Problem Solving Workshop**.

Solve $4^x = 11$.

$4^x = 11$ Write original equation.

$\log_4 4^x = \log_4 11$ Take $\log_4$ of each side.

$x = \log_4 11$ $\log_b b^x = x$

$x = \dfrac{\log 11}{\log 4}$ Change-of-base formula

$x \approx 1.73$ Use a calculator.

▶ The solution is about 1.73. Check this in the original equation.

NEWTON'S LAW OF COOLING An important application of exponential equations is *Newton's law of cooling*. This law states that for a cooling substance with initial temperature T_0, the temperature T after t minutes can be modeled by

$$T = (T_0 - T_R)e^{-rt} + T_R$$

where T_R is the surrounding temperature and r is the substance's cooling rate.

EXAMPLE 3   **Use an exponential model**

CARS You are driving on a hot day when your car overheats and stops running. It overheats at 280°F and can be driven again at 230°F. If $r = 0.0048$ and it is 80°F outside, how long (in minutes) do you have to wait until you can continue driving?

Solution

$T = (T_0 - T_R)e^{-rt} + T_R$ Newton's law of cooling

$230 = (280 - 80)e^{-0.0048t} + 80$ Substitute for T, T_0, T_R, and r.

$150 = 200e^{-0.0048t}$ Subtract 80 from each side.

$0.75 = e^{-0.0048t}$ Divide each side by 200.

$\ln 0.75 = \ln e^{-0.0048t}$ Take natural log of each side.

$-0.2877 \approx -0.0048t$ $\ln e^x = \log_e e^x = x$

$60 \approx t$ Divide each side by -0.0048.

▶ You have to wait about 60 minutes until you can continue driving.

✓   **GUIDED PRACTICE**   for Examples 2 and 3

Solve the equation.

4. $2^x = 5$ **5.** $7^{9x} = 15$ **6.** $4e^{-0.3x} - 7 = 13$

Jeff Sherman/Getty Images

SOLVING LOGARITHMIC EQUATIONS **Logarithmic equations** are equations that involve logarithms of variable expressions. You can use the following property to solve some types of logarithmic equations.

KEY CONCEPT   *For Your Notebook*

Property of Equality for Logarithmic Equations

Algebra   If b, x, and y are positive numbers with $b \neq 1$, then $\log_b x = \log_b y$ if and only if $x = y$.

Example   If $\log_2 x = \log_2 7$, then $x = 7$. If $x = 7$, then $\log_2 x = \log_2 7$.

EXAMPLE 4   **Solve a logarithmic equation**

Solve $\log_5 (4x - 7) = \log_5 (x + 5)$.

$\log_5 (4x - 7) = \log_5 (x + 5)$ **Write original equation.**

$4x - 7 = x + 5$ **Property of equality for logarithmic equations**

$3x - 7 = 5$ **Subtract x from each side.**

$3x = 12$ **Add 7 to each side.**

$x = 4$ **Divide each side by 3.**

▶ The solution is 4.

CHECK   Check the solution by substituting it into the original equation.

$\log_5 (4x - 7) = \log_5 (x + 5)$ **Write original equation.**

$\log_5 (4 \cdot 4 - 7) \overset{?}{=} \log_5 (4 + 5)$ **Substitute 4 for x.**

$\log_5 9 = \log_5 9$ ✓   **Solution checks.**

EXPONENTIATING TO SOLVE EQUATIONS The property of equality for exponential equations implies that if you are given an equation $x = y$, then you can *exponentiate* each side to obtain an equation of the form $b^x = b^y$. This technique is useful for solving some logarithmic equations.

EXAMPLE 5   **Exponentiate each side of an equation**

Solve $\log_4 (5x - 1) = 3$.

$\log_4 (5x - 1) = 3$ **Write original equation.**

$4^{\log_4 (5x - 1)} = 4^3$ **Exponentiate each side using base 4.**

$5x - 1 = 64$ $b^{\log_b x} = x$

$5x = 65$ **Add 1 to each side.**

$x = 13$ **Divide each side by 5.**

▶ The solution is 13.

CHECK $\log_4 (5x - 1) = \log_4 (5 \cdot 13 - 1) = \log_4 64$

Because $4^3 = 64$, $\log_4 64 = 3$. ✓

EXTRANEOUS SOLUTIONS Because the domain of a logarithmic function generally does not include all real numbers, be sure to check for extraneous solutions of logarithmic equations. You can do this algebraically or graphically.

  EXAMPLE 6 **Standardized Test Practice**

What is (are) the solution(s) of $\log 2x + \log (x - 5) = 2$?

(**A**) $-5, 10$ (**B**) 5 (**C**) 10 (**D**) $5, 10$

ELIMINATE CHOICES
Instead of solving the equation in Example 6 directly, you can substitute each possible answer into the equation to see whether it is a solution.

Solution

$\log 2x + \log (x - 5) = 2$	Write original equation.
$\log [2x(x - 5)] = 2$	Product property of logarithms
$10^{\log [2x(x - 5)]} = 10^2$	Exponentiate each side using base 10.
$2x(x - 5) = 100$	$b^{\log_b x} = x$
$2x^2 - 10x = 100$	Distributive property
$2x^2 - 10x - 100 = 0$	Write in standard form.
$x^2 - 5x - 50 = 0$	Divide each side by 2.
$(x - 10)(x + 5) = 0$	Factor.
$x = 10$ or $x = -5$	Zero product property

CHECK Check the apparent solutions 10 and -5 using algebra or a graph.

Algebra Substitute 10 and -5 for x in the original equation.

$\log 2x + \log (x - 5) = 2$

$\log (2 \cdot 10) + \log (10 - 5) \stackrel{?}{=} 2$

$\log 20 + \log 5 \stackrel{?}{=} 2$

$\log 100 \stackrel{?}{=} 2$

$2 = 2 \checkmark$

So, 10 is a solution.

$\log 2x + \log (x - 5) = 2$

$\log [2(-5)] + \log (-5 - 5) \stackrel{?}{=} 2$

$\log (-10) + \log (-10) \stackrel{?}{=} 2$

Because $\log (-10)$ is not defined, -5 is *not* a solution.

Graph Graph $y = \log 2x + \log (x - 5)$ and $y = 2$ in the same coordinate plane. The graphs intersect only once, when $x = 10$. So, 10 is the only solution.

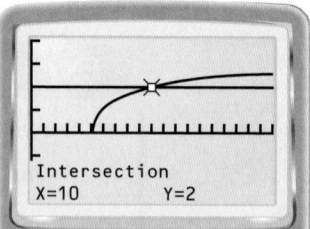

▶ The correct answer is C. (**A**) (**B**) (**C**) (**D**)

 GUIDED PRACTICE for Examples 4, 5, and 6

Solve the equation. Check for extraneous solutions.

7. $\ln (7x - 4) = \ln (2x + 11)$

8. $\log_2 (x - 6) = 5$

9. $\log 5x + \log (x - 1) = 2$

10. $\log_4 (x + 12) + \log_4 x = 3$

270 Chapter 4 Exponential and Logarithmic Functions

EXAMPLE 7 **Use a logarithmic model**

ASTRONOMY The *apparent magnitude* of a star is a measure of the brightness of the star as it appears to observers on Earth. The apparent magnitude M of the dimmest star that can be seen with a telescope is given by the function

$$M = 5 \log D + 2$$

where D is the diameter (in millimeters) of the telescope's objective lens. If a telescope can reveal stars with a magnitude of 12, what is the diameter of its objective lens?

Light ray
Eyepiece
Objective lens

ANOTHER WAY

For an alternative method for solving the problem in Example 7, See the **Problem Solving Workshop**.

Solution

$M = 5 \log D + 2$	**Write original equation.**
$12 = 5 \log D + 2$	**Substitute 12 for M.**
$10 = 5 \log D$	**Subtract 2 from each side.**
$2 = \log D$	**Divide each side by 5.**
$10^2 = 10^{\log D}$	**Exponentiate each side using base 10.**
$100 = D$	**Simplify.**

▶ The diameter is 100 millimeters.

Animated Algebra at my.hrw.com

✓ **GUIDED PRACTICE**   for Example 7

11. **WHAT IF?** Use the information from Example 7 to find the diameter of the objective lens of a telescope that can reveal stars with a magnitude of 7.

4.6 **EXERCISES**

HOMEWORK
KEY

◯ = See WORKED-OUT SOLUTIONS
Exs. 15, 35, and 57

★ = STANDARDIZED TEST PRACTICE
Exs. 2, 44, 47, 58, and 60

◆ = MULTIPLE REPRESENTATIONS
Ex. 59

SKILL PRACTICE

1. **VOCABULARY** Copy and complete: The equation $5^x = 8$ is an example of a(n) __?__ equation.

2. ★ **WRITING** When do logarithmic equations have extraneous solutions?

EXAMPLE 1
for Exs. 3–11

SOLVING EXPONENTIAL EQUATIONS **Solve the equation.**

3. $5^{x-4} = 25^{x-6}$

4. $7^{3x+4} = 49^{2x+1}$

5. $8^{x-1} = 32^{3x-2}$

6. $27^{4x-1} = 9^{3x+8}$

7. $4^{2x-5} = 64^{3x}$

8. $3^{3x-7} = 81^{12-3x}$

9. $36^{5x+2} = \left(\dfrac{1}{6}\right)^{11-x}$

10. $10^{3x-10} = \left(\dfrac{1}{100}\right)^{6x-1}$

11. $25^{10x+8} = \left(\dfrac{1}{125}\right)^{4-2x}$

EXAMPLE 2
for Exs. 12–23

SOLVING EXPONENTIAL EQUATIONS Solve the equation.

12. $8^x = 20$

13. $e^{-x} = 5$

14. $7^{3x} = 18$

15. $11^{5x} = 33$

16. $7^{6x} = 12$

17. $4e^{-2x} = 17$

18. $10^{3x} + 4 = 9$

19. $-3e^{2x} + 16 = 5$

20. $0.5^x - 0.25 = 4$

21. $\frac{1}{3}(6)^{-4x} + 1 = 6$

22. $2^{0.1x} - 5 = 7$

23. $\frac{3}{4}e^{2x} + \frac{7}{2} = 4$

EXAMPLE 4
for Exs. 24–31

SOLVING LOGARITHMIC EQUATIONS Solve the equation. Check for extraneous solutions.

24. $\log_5 (5x + 9) = \log_5 6x$

25. $\ln (4x - 7) = \ln (x + 11)$

26. $\ln (x + 19) = \ln (7x - 8)$

27. $\log_5 (2x - 7) = \log_5 (3x - 9)$

28. $\log (12x - 11) = \log (3x + 13)$

29. $\log_3 (18x + 7) = \log_3 (3x + 38)$

30. $\log_6 (3x - 10) = \log_6 (14 - 5x)$

31. $\log_8 (5 - 12x) = \log_8 (6x - 1)$

EXPONENTIATING TO SOLVE EQUATIONS Solve the equation. Check for extraneous solutions.

32. $\log_4 x = -1$

33. $5 \ln x = 35$

34. $\frac{1}{3} \log_5 12x = 2$

35. $5.2 \log_4 2x = 16$

36. $\log_2 (x - 4) = 6$

37. $\log_2 x + \log_2 (x - 2) = 3$

38. $\log_4 (-x) + \log_4 (x + 10) = 2$

39. $\ln (x + 3) + \ln x = 1$

40. $4 \ln (-x) + 3 = 21$

41. $\log_5 (x + 4) + \log_5 (x + 1) = 2$

42. $\log_6 3x + \log_6 (x - 1) = 3$

43. $\log_3 (x - 9) + \log_3 (x - 3) = 2$

44. ★ **MULTIPLE CHOICE** What is the solution of $3 \log_8 (2x + 7) + 8 = 10$?

Ⓐ -1.5 Ⓑ -1.179 Ⓒ 4 Ⓓ 4.642

ERROR ANALYSIS *Describe* and correct the error in solving the equation.

45.
$$3^{x+1} = 6^x$$
$$\log_3 3^{x+1} = \log_3 6^x$$
$$x + 1 = x \log_3 6$$
$$x + 1 = 2x$$
$$1 = x \quad \times$$

46.
$$\log_3 10x = 5$$
$$e^{\log_3 10x} = e^5$$
$$10x = e^5$$
$$x = \frac{e^5}{10} \quad \times$$

47. ★ **OPEN-ENDED MATH** Give an example of an exponential equation whose only solution is 4 and an example of a logarithmic equation whose only solution is −3.

CHALLENGE Solve the equation.

48. $3^{x+4} = 6^{2x-5}$

49. $10^{3x-8} = 2^{5-x}$

50. $\log_2 (x + 1) = \log_8 3x$

51. $\log_3 x = \log_9 6x$

52. $2^{2x} - 12 \cdot 2^x + 32 = 0$

53. $5^{2x} + 20 \cdot 5^x - 125 = 0$

◯ = **See WORKED-OUT SOLUTIONS**
in Student Resources

◆ = **MULTIPLE REPRESENTATIONS**

EXAMPLE 3
for Exs. 54–58

54. COOKING You are cooking beef stew. When you take the beef stew off the stove, it has a temperature of 200°F. The room temperature is 75°F and the cooling rate of the beef stew is $r = 0.054$. How long (in minutes) will it take to cool the beef stew to a serving temperature of 100°F?

55. THERMOMETER As you are hanging an outdoor thermometer, its reading drops from the indoor temperature of 75°F to 37°F in one minute. If the cooling rate is $r = 1.37$, what is the outdoor temperature?

56. COMPOUND INTEREST You deposit $100 in an account that pays 6% annual interest. How long will it take for the balance to reach $1000 for each given frequency of compounding?

    a. Annual   **b.** Quarterly   **c.** Daily

(57.) RADIOACTIVE DECAY One hundred grams of radium are stored in a container. The amount R (in grams) of radium present after t years can be modeled by $R = 100e^{-0.00043t}$. After how many years will only 5 grams of radium be present?

58. ★ MULTIPLE CHOICE You deposit $800 in an account that pays 2.25% annual interest compounded continuously. About how long will it take for the balance to triple?

    (A) 24 years   **(B)** 36 years

    (C) 48.8 years   **(D)** 52.6 years

EXAMPLE 7
for Ex. 59

59. ◆ MULTIPLE REPRESENTATIONS The Richter scale is used for measuring the magnitude of an earthquake. The Richter magnitude R is given by the function

$$R = 0.67 \log (0.37E) + 1.46$$

where E is the energy (in kilowatt-hours) released by the earthquake.

USA — Ocotillo Wells, CA, May 20, 2005, $R = 4.1$
GREECE — Athens, Sept. 7, 1999, $R = 5.9$
JAPAN — Fukuoka, March 20, 2005, $R = 6.6$

    a. Making a Graph Graph the function using a graphing calculator. Use your graph to approximate the amount of energy released by each earthquake indicated in the diagram above.

    b. Solving Equations Write and solve a logarithmic equation to find the amount of energy released by each earthquake in the diagram.

60. ★ **EXTENDED RESPONSE** If X-rays of a fixed wavelength strike a material x centimeters thick, then the intensity $I(x)$ of the X-rays transmitted through the material is given by $I(x) = I_0 e^{-\mu x}$, where I_0 is the initial intensity and μ is a number that depends on the type of material and the wavelength of the X-rays. The table shows the values of μ for various materials. These μ-values apply to X-rays of medium wavelength.

Material	Aluminum	Copper	Lead
Value of μ	0.43	3.2	43

a. Find the thickness of aluminum shielding that reduces the intensity of X-rays to 30% of their initial intensity. (*Hint:* Find the value of x for which $I(x) = 0.3I_0$.)

b. Repeat part (a) for copper shielding.

c. Repeat part (a) for lead shielding.

d. **Reasoning** Your dentist puts a lead apron on you before taking X-rays of your teeth to protect you from harmful radiation. Based on your results from parts (a)–(c), explain why lead is a better material to use than aluminum or copper.

61. **CHALLENGE** You plant a sunflower seedling in your garden. The seedling's height h (in centimeters) after t weeks can be modeled by the function below, which is called a *logistic function*.

$$h(t) = \frac{256}{1 + 13e^{-0.65t}}$$

Find the time it takes the sunflower seedling to reach a height of 200 centimeters.

See **EXTRA PRACTICE** in Student Resources   ✈ **ONLINE QUIZ** at my.hrw.com

AM Corporation/Alamy

PROBLEM SOLVING WORKSHOP
LESSON 4.6

Using ALTERNATIVE METHODS

Another Way to Solve Examples 2 and 7

MATHEMATICAL PRACTICES

Make sense of problems and persevere in solving them.

MULTIPLE REPRESENTATIONS In Examples 2 and 7, respectively, you solved exponential and logarithmic equations algebraically. You can also solve such equations using tables and graphs.

PROBLEM 1

Solve the following exponential equation: $4^x = 11$.

METHOD 1

Using a Table One way to solve the equation is to make a table of values.

STEP 1 **Enter** the function $y = 4^x$ into a graphing calculator.

STEP 2 **Create** a table of values for the function.

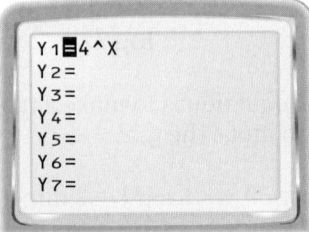

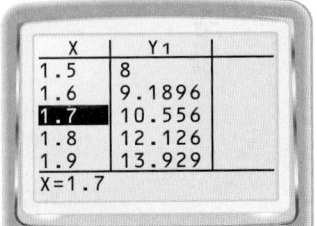

STEP 3 **Scroll** through the table to find when $y = 11$. The table in Step 2 shows that $y = 11$ between $x = 1.7$ and $x = 1.8$.

▸ The solution of $4^x = 11$ is between 1.7 and 1.8.

METHOD 2

Using a Graph You can also use a graph to solve the equation.

STEP 1 **Enter** the functions $y = 4^x$ and $y = 11$ into a graphing calculator.

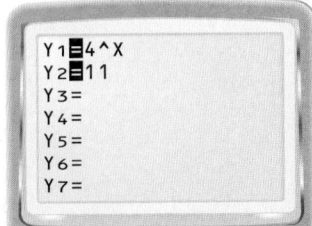

STEP 2 **Graph** the functions. Use the *intersect* feature to find the intersection point of the graphs. The graphs intersect at about (1.73, 11).

Use a viewing window of $0 \leq x \leq 5$ and $0 \leq y \leq 20$.

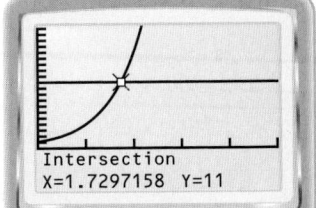

▸ The solution of $4^x = 11$ is about 1.73.

PROBLEM 2

ASTRONOMY The *apparent magnitude* of a star is a measure of the brightness of the star as it appears to observers on Earth. The apparent magnitude *M* of the dimmest star that can be seen with a telescope is given by the function

$$M = 5 \log D + 2$$

where *D* is the diameter (in millimeters) of the telescope's objective lens. If a telescope can reveal stars with a magnitude of 12, what is the diameter of its objective lens?

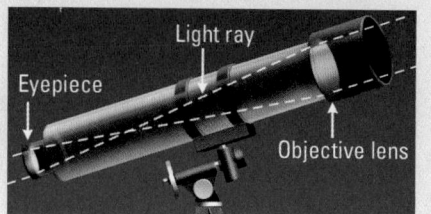

METHOD 1

Using a Table Notice that the problem requires solving the following logarithmic equation:

$$5 \log D + 2 = 12$$

One way to solve this equation is to make a table of values. You can use a graphing calculator to make the table.

STEP 1 **Enter** the function $y = 5 \log x + 2$ into a graphing calculator.

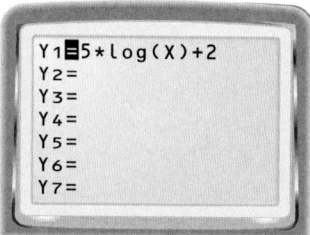

STEP 2 **Create** a table of values for the function. Make sure that the *x*-values are in the domain of the function ($x > 0$).

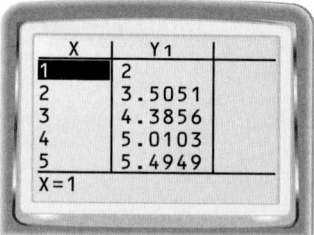

STEP 3 **Scroll** through the table of values to find when $y = 12$.

The table shows that $y = 12$ when $x = 100$.

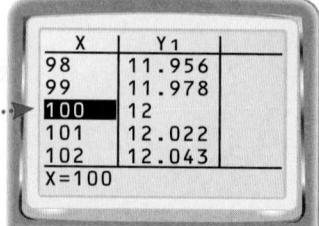

▶ To reveal stars with a magnitude of 12, a telescope must have an objective lens with a diameter of 100 millimeters.

METHOD 2   **Using a Graph** You can also use a graph to solve the equation $5 \log D + 2 = 12$.

STEP 1 **Enter** the functions $y = 5 \log x + 2$ and $y = 12$ into a graphing calculator.

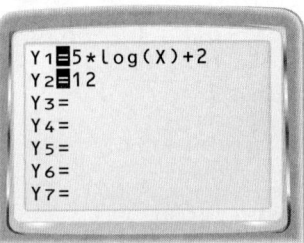

```
Y1=5*log(X)+2
Y2=12
Y3=
Y4=
Y5=
Y6=
Y7=
```

STEP 2 **Graph** the functions. Use the *intersect* feature to find the intersection point of the graphs. The graphs intersect at (100, 12).

Use a viewing window of $0 \le x \le 150$ and $0 \le y \le 20$.

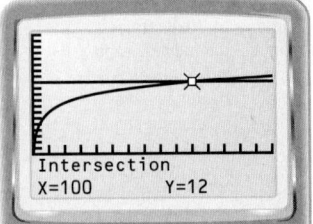

```
Intersection
X=100        Y=12
```

▶ To reveal stars with a magnitude of 12, a telescope must have an objective lens with a diameter of 100 millimeters.

PRACTICE

EXPONENTIAL EQUATIONS Solve the equation using a table and using a graph.

1. $8 - 2e^{3x} = -14$

2. $7 - 10^{5-x} = -9$

3. $e^{5x-8} + 3 = 15$

4. $1.6(3)^{-4x} + 5.6 = 6$

LOGARITHMIC EQUATIONS Solve the equation using a table and using a graph.

5. $\log_2 5x = 2$

6. $\log(-3x + 7) = 1$

7. $4 \ln x + 6 = 12$

8. $11 \log(x + 9) - 5 = 8$

9. ECONOMICS From 1998 to 2003, the United States gross national product y (in billions of dollars) can be modeled by $y = 8882(1.04)^x$ where x is the number of years since 1998. Use a table and a graph to find the year when the gross national product was $10 trillion.

10. WRITING In Method 1 of Problem 1 explain how you could use a table to find the solution of $4^x = 11$ more precisely.

11. WHAT IF? In Problem 2, suppose the telescope can reveal stars of magnitude 14. Find the diameter of the telescope's objective lens using a table and using a graph.

12. FINANCE You deposit $5000 in an account that pays 3% annual interest compounded quarterly. How long will it take for the balance to reach $6000? Solve the problem using a table and using a graph.

13. OCEANOGRAPHY The density d (in grams per cubic centimeter) of seawater with a salinity of 30 parts per thousand is related to the water temperature T (in degrees Celsius) by the following equation:

$$d = 1.0245 - e^{0.1226T - 7.828}$$

For deep water in the South Atlantic Ocean off Antarctica, $d = 1.0241$ g/cm^3. Use a table and a graph to find the water's temperature.

Extension

Solve Exponential and Logarithmic Inequalities

GOAL Solve exponential and logarithmic inequalities using tables and graphs.

In the Problem Solving Workshop, you learned how to solve exponential and logarithmic equations using tables and graphs. You can use these same methods to solve exponential and logarithmic inequalities.

CC.9-12.A.REI.11 Explain why the *x*-coordinates of the points where the graphs of the equations $y = f(x)$ and $y = g(x)$ intersect are the solutions of the equation $f(x) = g(x)$; find the solutions approximately, e.g., using technology to graph the functions, make tables of values, or find successive approximations. Include cases where $f(x)$ and/or $g(x)$ are linear, polynomial, rational, absolute value, exponential, and logarithmic functions.*

EXAMPLE 1 Solve an exponential inequality

CARS Your family purchases a new car for $20,000. Its value decreases by 15% each year. During what interval of time does the car's value exceed $10,000?

Solution

Let *y* represent the value of the car (in dollars) *x* years after it is purchased. A function relating *x* and *y* is $y = 20{,}000(1 - 0.15)^x$, or $y = 20{,}000(0.85)^x$. To find the values of *x* for which $y > 10{,}000$, solve the inequality $20{,}000(0.85)^x > 10{,}000$.

METHOD 1 Use a table

STEP 1 **Enter** the function $y = 20{,}000(0.85)^x$ into a graphing calculator. Set the starting *x*-value of the table to 0 and the step value to 0.1.

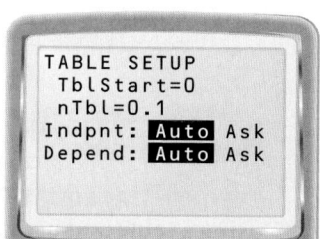

STEP 2 **Use** the *table* feature to create a table of values. Scrolling through the table shows that $y > 10{,}000$ when $0 \le x \le 4.2$.

▶ The car value exceeds $10,000 for about the first 4.2 years after it is purchased.

To check the solution's reasonableness, note that $y \approx 10{,}440$ when $x = 4$ and $y \approx 8874$ when $x = 5$. So, $4 < x < 5$, which agrees with the solution obtained above.

METHOD 2 Use a graph

Graph $y = 20{,}000(0.85)^x$ and $y = 10{,}000$ in the same viewing window. Set the viewing window to show $0 \le x \le 8$ and $0 \le y \le 25{,}000$. Using the *intersect* feature, you can determine that the graphs intersect when $x \approx 4.27$.

The graph of $y = 20{,}000(0.85)^x$ is above the graph of $y = 10{,}000$ when $0 \le x < 4.27$.

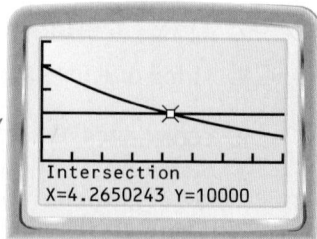

▶ The car value exceeds $10,000 for about the first 4.27 years after it is purchased.

EXAMPLE 2 Solve a logarithmic inequality

Solve $\log_2 x \le 2$.

Solution

METHOD 1 Use a table

STEP 1 **Enter** the function $y = \log_2 x$ into a graphing calculator as $y = \dfrac{\log x}{\log 2}$.

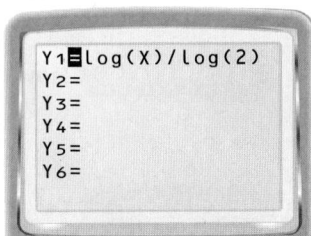

STEP 2 **Use** the *table* feature to create a table of values. Identify the x-values for which $y \le 2$. These x-values are given by $0 < x \le 4$.

> Make sure that the x-values are reasonable and in the domain of the function ($x > 0$).

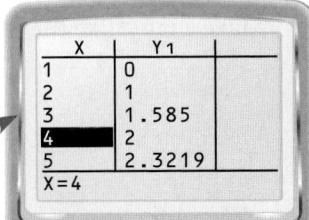

▶ The solution is $0 < x \le 4$.

METHOD 2 Use a graph

Graph $y = \log_2 x$ and $y = 2$ in the same viewing window. Using the *intersect* feature, you can determine that the graphs intersect when $x = 4$.

> The graph of $y = \log_2 x$ is on or below the graph of $y = 2$ when $0 < x \le 4$.

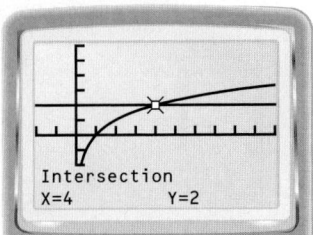

▶ The solution is $0 < x \le 4$.

PRACTICE

EXAMPLE 1
for Exs. 1–6

Solve the exponential inequality using a table and using a graph.

1. $3^x \le 20$

2. $28\left(\dfrac{2}{3}\right)^x > 9$

3. $244(0.35)^x \ge 50$

4. $-63(0.96)^x < -27$

5. $95(1.6)^x \le 1620$

6. $-284\left(\dfrac{9}{7}\right)^x > -135$

EXAMPLE 2
for Exs. 7–12

Solve the logarithmic inequality using a table and using a graph.

7. $\log_3 x \ge 3$

8. $\log_5 x < 2$

9. $\log_6 x + 9 \le 11$

10. $2 \log_4 x - 1 > 4$

11. $-4 \log_2 x > -20$

12. $0 \le \log_7 x \le 1$

13. **FINANCE** You deposit $1000 in an account that pays 3.5% annual interest compounded monthly. When is your balance at least $1200?

14. **RATES OF RETURN** An investment that earns a rate of return r doubles in value in t years, where $t = \dfrac{\ln 2}{\ln (1 + r)}$ and r is expressed as a decimal. What rates of return will double the value of an investment in less than 10 years?

Model Data with an Exponential Function

MATERIALS · 100 pennies · cup · graphing calculator

QUESTION How can you model data with an exponential function?

Model with mathematics.

EXPLORE Collect and record data

STEP 1 *Make a table*

Make a table like the one shown to record your results.

Number of toss, x	0	1	2	3	4	5	6	7
Number of pennies remaining, y	?	?	?	?	?	?	?	?

STEP 2 *Perform an experiment*

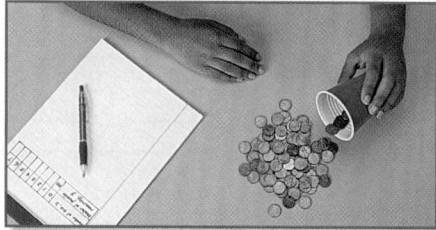

Record the initial number of pennies in the table, and place the pennies in a cup. Shake the pennies, and then spill them onto a flat surface.

Remove all of the pennies showing "heads." Count the number of pennies remaining, and record this number in the table.

STEP 3 *Continue collecting data*

Repeat Step 2 with the remaining pennies until there are no pennies left to return to the cup.

DRAW CONCLUSIONS Use your observations to complete these exercises

1. What is the initial number of pennies? By what percent would you expect the number of pennies remaining to decrease after each toss?

2. Use your answers from Exercise 1 to write an exponential function that should model the data in the table.

3. Use a graphing calculator to make a scatter plot of the data pairs (x, y). In the same viewing window, graph your function from Exercise 2. Is the function a good model for the data? *Explain.*

4. Use the calculator's *exponential regression* feature to find an exponential function that models the data. *Compare* this function with the function you wrote in Exercise 2.

Jay Penni Photography/HMH Photo

4.7 Write and Apply Exponential and Power Functions

Before	You wrote linear, quadratic, and other polynomial functions.
Now	You will write exponential and power functions.
Why?	So you can model biology problems, as in Example 5.

Key Vocabulary
- **power function**
- **exponential function**

CC.9-12.F.LE.2 Construct linear and exponential functions, including arithmetic and geometric sequences, given a graph, a description of a relationship, or two input-output pairs (include reading these from a table).*

You know that two points determine a line. Similarly, two points determine an exponential curve.

EXAMPLE 1 Write an exponential function

Write an exponential function $y = ab^x$ whose graph passes through (1, 12) and (3, 108).

Solution

STEP 1 **Substitute** the coordinates of the two given points into $y = ab^x$.

$12 = ab^1$ **Substitute 12 for *y* and 1 for *x*.**

$108 = ab^3$ **Substitute 108 for *y* and 3 for *x*.**

STEP 2 **Solve** for *a* in the first equation to obtain $a = \dfrac{12}{b}$, and substitute this expression for *a* in the second equation.

$108 = \left(\dfrac{12}{b}\right)b^3$ **Substitute $\dfrac{12}{b}$ for *a* in second equation.**

$108 = 12b^2$ **Simplify.**

$9 = b^2$ **Divide each side by 12.**

$3 = b$ **Take the positive square root because $b > 0$.**

STEP 3 **Determine** that $a = \dfrac{12}{b} = \dfrac{12}{3} = 4$. So, $y = 4 \cdot 3^x$.

TRANSFORMING EXPONENTIAL DATA A set of more than two points (x, y) fits an exponential pattern if and only if the set of transformed points $(x, \ln y)$ fits a linear pattern.

Graph of points (x, y)

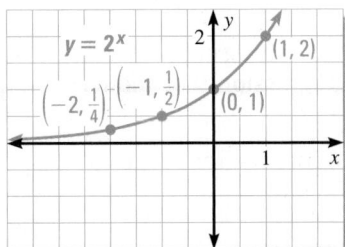

The graph is an exponential curve.

Graph of points $(x, \ln y)$

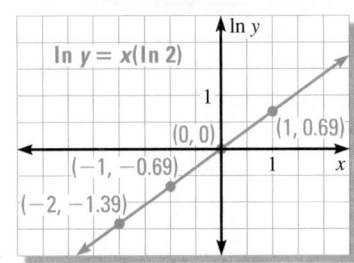

The graph is a line.

EXAMPLE 2 **Find an exponential model**

SCOOTERS A store sells motor scooters. The table shows the number y of scooters sold during the xth year that the store has been open.

Year, x	1	2	3	4	5	6	7
Number of scooters sold, y	12	16	25	36	50	67	96

- Draw a scatter plot of the data pairs $(x, \ln y)$. Is an exponential model a good fit for the original data pairs (x, y)?
- Find an exponential model for the original data.

Solution

STEP 1 **Use** a calculator to create a table of data pairs $(x, \ln y)$.

x	1	2	3	4	5	6	7
$\ln y$	2.48	2.77	3.22	3.58	3.91	4.20	4.56

STEP 2 **Plot** the new points as shown. The points lie close to a line, so an exponential model should be a good fit for the original data.

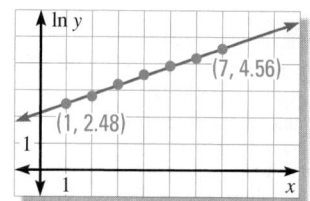

USE POINT-SLOPE FORM
Because the axes are x and $\ln y$, the point-slope form is rewritten as $\ln y - y_1 = m(x - x_1)$. The slope of the line through (1, 2.48) and (7, 4.56) is:

$$\frac{4.56 - 2.48}{7 - 1} \approx 0.35$$

STEP 3 **Find** an exponential model $y = ab^x$ by choosing two points on the line, such as (1, 2.48) and (7, 4.56). Use these points to write an equation of the line. Then solve for y.

$\ln y - 2.48 = 0.35(x - 1)$	**Equation of line**
$\ln y = 0.35x + 2.13$	**Simplify.**
$y = e^{0.35x + 2.13}$	**Exponentiate each side using base e.**
$y = e^{2.13}(e^{0.35})^x$	**Use properties of exponents.**
$y = 8.41(1.42)^x$	**Exponential model**

EXPONENTIAL REGRESSION A graphing calculator that performs exponential regression uses all of the original data to find the best-fitting model.

EXAMPLE 3 **Use exponential regression**

SCOOTERS Use a graphing calculator to find an exponential model for the data in Example 2. Predict the number of scooters sold in the eighth year.

Solution

Enter the original data into a graphing calculator and perform an exponential regression. The model is $y = 8.46(1.42)^x$.

Substituting $x = 8$ (for year 8) into the model gives $y = 8.46(1.42)^8 \approx 140$ scooters sold.

Write an exponential function $y = ab^x$ whose graph passes through the given points.

1. $(1, 6)$, $(3, 24)$ **2.** $(2, 8)$, $(3, 32)$ **3.** $(3, 8)$, $(6, 64)$

4. WHAT IF? In Examples 2 and 3, how would the exponential models change if the scooter sales were as shown in the table below?

Year, x	1	2	3	4	5	6	7
Number of scooters sold, y	15	23	40	52	80	105	140

WRITING POWER FUNCTIONS Recall that a power function has the form $y = ax^b$. Because there are only two constants (a and b), only two points are needed to determine a power curve through the points.

EXAMPLE 4 **Write a power function**

Write a power function $y = ax^b$ whose graph passes through $(3, 2)$ and $(6, 9)$.

Solution

STEP 1 **Substitute** the coordinates of the two given points into $y = ax^b$.

$2 = a \cdot 3^b$ Substitute 2 for y and 3 for x.

$9 = a \cdot 6^b$ Substitute 9 for y and 6 for x.

STEP 2 **Solve** for a in the first equation to obtain $a = \dfrac{2}{3^b}$, and substitute this expression for a in the second equation.

$9 = \left(\dfrac{2}{3^b}\right)6^b$ Substitute $\dfrac{2}{3^b}$ for a in second equation.

$9 = 2 \cdot 2^b$ Simplify.

$4.5 = 2^b$ Divide each side by 2.

$\log_2 4.5 = b$ Take $\log_2$ of each side.

$\dfrac{\log 4.5}{\log 2} = b$ Change-of-base formula

$2.17 \approx b$ Use a calculator.

STEP 3 **Determine** that $a = \dfrac{2}{3^{2.17}} \approx 0.184$. So, $y = 0.184x^{2.17}$.

Write a power function $y = ax^b$ whose graph passes through the given points.

5. $(2, 1)$, $(7, 6)$ **6.** $(3, 4)$, $(6, 15)$ **7.** $(5, 8)$, $(10, 34)$

8. REASONING Try using the method of Example 4 to find a power function whose graph passes through $(3, 5)$ and $(3, 7)$. What can you conclude?

TRANSFORMING POWER DATA A set of more than two points (x, y) fits a power pattern if and only if the set of transformed points $(\ln x, \ln y)$ fits a linear pattern.

Graph of points (x, y)

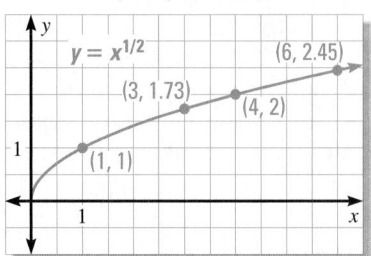

The graph is a power curve.

Graph of points $(\ln x, \ln y)$

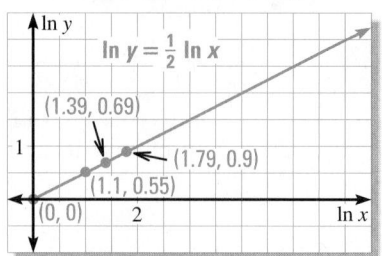

The graph is a line.

EXAMPLE 5   Find a power model

BIOLOGY The table at the right shows the typical wingspans x (in feet) and the typical weights y (in pounds) for several types of birds.

- Draw a scatter plot of the data pairs $(\ln x, \ln y)$. Is a power model a good fit for the original data pairs (x, y)?

- Find a power model for the original data.

Bird	Wingspan (ft), x	Weight (lb), y
Cuckoo	1.90	0.23
Crow	2.92	1.04
Curlew	3.41	1.69
Goose	5.35	6.76
Vulture	8.40	16.03

Solution

STEP 1 **Use** a calculator to create a table of data pairs $(\ln x, \ln y)$.

$\ln x$	0.642	1.072	1.227	1.677	2.128
$\ln y$	−1.470	0.039	0.525	1.911	2.774

STEP 2 **Plot** the new points as shown. The points lie close to a line, so a power model should be a good fit for the original data.

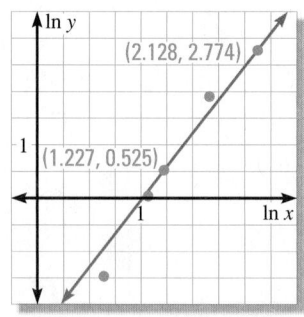

STEP 3 **Find** a power model $y = ax^b$ by choosing two points on the line, such as $(1.227, 0.525)$ and $(2.128, 2.774)$. Use these points to write an equation of the line. Then solve for y.

$\ln y - y_1 = m(\ln x - x_1)$ **Equation when axes are $\ln x$ and $\ln y$**

$\ln y - 2.774 = 2.5(\ln x - 2.128)$ **Substitute.**

$\ln y = 2.5 \ln x - 2.546$ **Simplify.**

$\ln y = \ln x^{2.5} - 2.546$ **Power property of logarithms**

$y = e^{\ln x^{2.5} - 2.546}$ **Exponentiate each side using base e.**

$y = e^{-2.546} \cdot e^{\ln x^{2.5}}$ **Product of powers property**

$y = 0.0784 x^{2.5}$ **Simplify.**

USE POINT-SLOPE FORM

The slope of the line is $\dfrac{2.774 - 0.525}{2.128 - 1.227} \approx 2.50.$

POWER REGRESSION A graphing calculator that performs power regression uses all of the original data to find the best-fitting model.

EXAMPLE 6 Use power regression

BIOLOGY Use a graphing calculator to find a power model for the data in Example 5. Estimate the weight of a bird with a wingspan of 4.5 feet.

Solution

Enter the original data into a graphing calculator and perform a power regression. The model is $y = 0.0442x^{2.87}$.

Substituting $x = 4.5$ into the model gives $y = 0.0442(4.5)^{2.87} \approx 3.31$ pounds.

```
PwrReg
 y=a*x^b
 a=.0442336613
 b=2.871717024
```

✓ **GUIDED PRACTICE** for Examples 5 and 6

9. The table below shows the atomic number x and the melting point y (in degrees Celsius) for the alkali metals. Find a power model for the data.

Alkali metal	Lithium	Sodium	Potassium	Rubidium	Cesium
Atomic number, x	3	11	19	37	55
Melting point, y	180.5	97.8	63.7	38.9	28.5

4.7 EXERCISES

HOMEWORK KEY

◯ = See WORKED-OUT SOLUTIONS
Exs. 11, 23, and 33

★ = STANDARDIZED TEST PRACTICE
Exs. 2, 27, 33, and 35

SKILL PRACTICE

1. **VOCABULARY** Copy and complete: Given a set of more than two data pairs (x, y), you can decide whether a(n) __?__ function fits the data well by making a scatter plot of the points $(x, \ln y)$.

2. ★ **WRITING** *Explain* how you can determine whether a power function is a good model for a set of data pairs (x, y).

EXAMPLE 1
for Exs. 3–10

WRITING EXPONENTIAL FUNCTIONS Write an exponential function $y = ab^x$ whose graph passes through the given points.

3. $(1, 3), (2, 12)$ 4. $(2, 24), (3, 144)$ 5. $(3, 1), (5, 4)$ 6. $(3, 27), (5, 243)$

7. $(1, 2), (3, 50)$ 8. $(1, 40), (3, 640)$ 9. $(-1, 10), (4, 0.31)$ 10. $(2, 6.4), (5, 409.6)$

EXAMPLE 2
for Exs. 11–14

FINDING EXPONENTIAL MODELS Use the points (x, y) to draw a scatter plot of the points $(x, \ln y)$. Then find an exponential model for the data.

⑪. $(1, 18), (2, 36), (3, 72), (4, 144), (5, 288)$ 12. $(1, 3.3), (2, 10.1), (3, 30.6), (4, 92.7), (5, 280.9)$

13. $(1, 9.8), (2, 12.2), (3, 15.2), (4, 19), (5, 23.8)$ 14. $(1, 1.4), (2, 6.7), (3, 32.9), (4, 161.4), (5, 790.9)$

EXAMPLE 4
for Exs. 15–22

WRITING POWER FUNCTIONS Write a power function $y = ax^b$ whose graph passes through the given points.

15. (4, 3), (8, 15) **16.** (5, 9), (8, 34) **17.** (2, 3), (6, 12) **18.** (3, 14), (9, 44)

19. (4, 8), (8, 30) **20.** (5, 10), (12, 81) **21.** (4, 6.2), (7, 23) **22.** (3.1, 5), (6.8, 9.7)

EXAMPLE 5
for Exs. 23–26

FINDING POWER MODELS Use the given points (x, y) to draw a scatter plot of the points $(\ln x, \ln y)$. Then find a power model for the data.

23. (1, 0.6), (2, 4.1), (3, 12.4), (4, 27), (5, 49.5) **24.** (1, 1.5), (2, 4.8), (3, 9.5), (4, 15.4), (5, 22.3)

25. (1, 2.5), (2, 3.7), (3, 4.7), (4, 5.5), (5, 6.2) **26.** (1, 0.81), (2, 0.99), (3, 1.11), (4, 1.21), (5, 1.29)

27. ★ **MULTIPLE CHOICE** Which equation is equivalent to $\log y = 2x + 1$?

(A) $y = 10(100)^x$ **(B)** $y = 10^x$ **(C)** $y = e^{2x + 1}$ **(D)** $y = e^2$

ERROR ANALYSIS *Describe* and correct the error in writing y as a function of x.

28.
$$\ln y = 2x + 1$$
$$y = e^{2x + 1}$$
$$y = e^{2x} + e^1$$
$$y = (e^2)^x + e$$
$$y = 7.39^x + 2.72$$

29.
$$\ln y = 3 \ln x - 2$$
$$\ln y = \ln 3x - 2$$
$$y = e^{\ln 3x - 2}$$
$$y = e^{\ln 3x} \cdot e^{-2}$$
$$y = (3x)(0.135) = 0.405x$$

30. CHALLENGE Take the natural logarithm of both sides of the equations $y = ab^x$ and $y = ax^b$. What are the slope and y-intercept of the line relating x and $\ln y$ for $y = ab^x$? of the line relating $\ln x$ and $\ln y$ for $y = ax^b$?

PROBLEM SOLVING

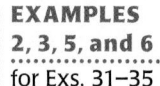 **GRAPHING CALCULATOR** You may wish to use a graphing calculator to complete the following Problem Solving exercises.

31. BIOLOGY Scientists use the circumference of an animal's femur to estimate the animal's weight. The table shows the femur circumference C (in millimeters) and the weight W (in kilograms) for several animals.

Animal	Giraffe	Polar bear	Lion	Squirrel	Otter
C (mm)	173	135	93.5	13	28
W (kg)	710	448	143	0.399	9.68

a. Draw a scatter plot of the data pairs $(\ln C, \ln W)$.

b. Find a power model for the original data.

c. Predict the weight of a cheetah if the circumference of its femur is 68.7 millimeters.

 = See WORKED-OUT SOLUTIONS in Student Resources

★ = STANDARDIZED TEST PRACTICE

32. ASTRONOMY The table shows the mean distance x from the sun (in astronomical units) and the period y (in years) of six planets. Draw a scatter plot of the data pairs (ln x, ln y). Find a power model for the original data.

Planet	Mercury	Venus	Earth	Mars	Jupiter	Saturn
x	0.387	0.723	1.000	1.524	5.203	9.539
y	0.241	0.615	1.000	1.881	11.862	29.458

33. ★ **SHORT RESPONSE** The table shows the numbers of business and non-business users of instant messaging for the years 1998–2004.

Years since 1997	1	2	3	4	5	6	7
Business users (in millions)	1	2	5	7	20	40	80
Non-business users (in millions)	55	97	140	160	195	235	260

a. Find an exponential model for the number of business users over time.

b. *Explain* how to tell whether a linear, exponential, or power function best models the number of non-business users over time. Then find the best-fitting model.

34. MULTI-STEP PROBLEM The boiling point of water increases with atmospheric pressure. At sea level, where the atmospheric pressure is about 760 millimeters of mercury, water boils at 100°C. The table shows the boiling point T of water (in degrees Celsius) for several different values of atmospheric pressure P (in millimeters of mercury).

P	T
149	60
234	70
355	80
526	90
760	100
1075	110

a. Graph Draw a scatter plot of the data pairs (ln P, ln T).

b. Model Find a power model for the original data.

c. Predict When the atmospheric pressure is 620 millimeters of mercury, at what temperature does water boil?

35. ★ **EXTENDED RESPONSE** Your visual *near point* is the closest point at which your eyes can see an object distinctly. Your near point moves farther away from you as you grow older. The diagram shows the near point y (in centimeters) at age x (in years).

a. Graph Draw a scatter plot of the data pairs (x, ln y).

b. Graph Draw a scatter plot of the data pairs (ln x, ln y).

c. Interpret Based on your scatter plots, does an exponential function or a power function best fit the original data? *Explain* your reasoning.

d. Model Based on your answer for part (c), write a model for the original data. Use your model to predict the near point for an 80-year-old person.

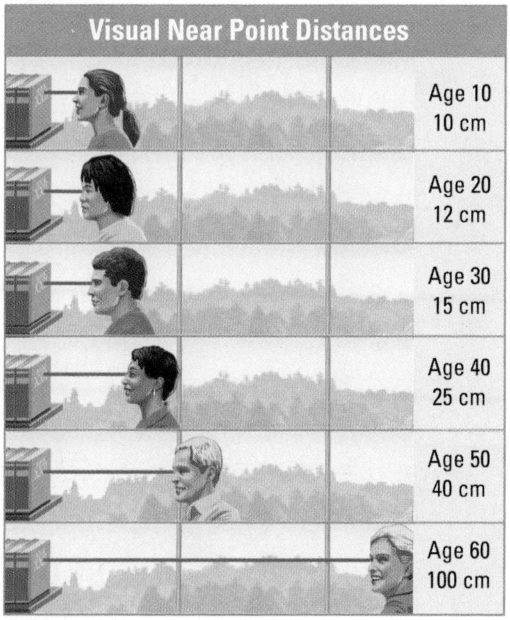

Visual Near Point Distances

Age 10
10 cm

Age 20
12 cm

Age 30
15 cm

Age 40
25 cm

Age 50
40 cm

Age 60
100 cm

36. CHALLENGE A doctor measures an astronaut's pulse rate y (in beats per minute) at various times x (in minutes) after the astronaut has finished exercising. The results are shown in the table. The astronaut's resting pulse rate is 70 beats per minute. Write an exponential model for the data.

x	0	2	4	6	8	10	12	14
y	172	132	110	92	84	78	75	72

QUIZ

Solve the equation. Check for extraneous solutions.

1. $2^{x+1} = 16^{x+2}$

2. $e^{-x} = 4$

3. $3^{2x} + 5 = 13$

4. $3^{x+1} - 5 = 10$

5. $\log_4 (4x + 7) = \log_4 11x$

6. $\ln (3x - 2) = \ln 6x$

7. $\log_3 x = -1$

8. $6 \ln x = 30$

9. $\log_2 (x + 4) = 5$

Write an exponential function $y = ab^x$ whose graph passes through the given points.

10. $(1, 5), (2, 30)$

11. $(1, 4), (2, 32)$

12. $(2, 15), (3, 45)$

Write a power function $y = ax^b$ whose graph passes through the given points.

13. $(4, 8), (9, 23)$

14. $(3, 12), (10, 36)$

15. $(5, 4), (11, 51)$

16. BIOLOGY The average weight y (in kilograms) of an Atlantic cod from the Gulf of Maine can be modeled by $y = 0.51(1.46)^x$ where x is the age of the cod (in years). Estimate the age of a cod that weighs 15 kilograms.

See **EXTRA PRACTICE** in Student Resources   🖈 **ONLINE QUIZ** at my.hrw.com

MIXED REVIEW *of Problem Solving*

MATHEMATICAL PRACTICES — Make sense of problems and persevere in solving them.

1. MULTI-STEP PROBLEM The total expenditures in the United States for elementary and secondary schools are shown below.

   a. Draw a scatter plot of the data pairs $(x, \ln y)$.

   b. Draw a scatter plot of the data pairs $(\ln x, \ln y)$.

   c. Based on your results from parts (a) and (b), find a model for the original data.

   d. Predict the total expenditures in 2005.

Years since 1997, x	Total expenditures (billions of dollars), y
1	398
2	416
3	433
4	450
5	463

2. MULTI-STEP PROBLEM In music, a *cent* is a unit that is used to express a small step up or down in pitch. The number c of cents by which two notes differ in pitch is given by

$$c = 1200 \log_2 \frac{a}{b}$$

where a and b are the frequencies of the notes a and b.

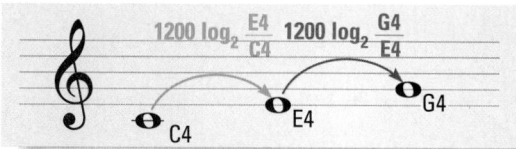

   a. Three notes on the standard scale are C4, E4, and G4. You can compare the difference in the number of cents from C4 to E4 with the difference from E4 to G4 by evaluating this expression:

   $$1200 \log_2 \frac{E4}{C4} - 1200 \log_2 \frac{G4}{E4}$$

   Write the expression as a single logarithm.

   b. C4 has a frequency of 264 hertz, E4 has a frequency of 330 hertz, and G4 has a frequency of 396 hertz. Use this information to evaluate your expression from part (a).

3. OPEN-ENDED Write an exponential function whose graph passes through the point (2, 7).

4. SHORT RESPONSE The total number of miles traveled by motor vehicles in the United States is shown below for various years. Does an exponential model or a power model best fit the data? *Explain* your reasoning.

Years since 1990, x	Miles (billions), y
7	2562
8	2632
9	2691
10	2747
11	2782

5. EXTENDED RESPONSE The *effective interest rate* is a rate associated with the formula for continuously compounded interest. The effective interest rate takes into account the effects of compounding on the *nominal interest rate* (the interest rate in the formula for continuous compounding).

The relationship between the effective interest rate E and the nominal interest rate N is given by the equation

$$N = \ln (E + 1)$$

where E and N are expressed as decimals.

   a. What is the effective interest rate for an account that has a nominal interest rate of 5%? Leave your answer in terms of e.

   b. What is the effective interest rate for an account that has a nominal interest rate of 10%? Leave your answer in terms of e.

   c. The effective interest rate from part (b) is how many times as great as the effective interest rate from part (a)? Write your answer as a ratio in terms of e.

   d. Show that the ratio from part (c) is equal to $e^{0.05} + 1$.

6. GRIDDED ANSWER You invest $4000 in an account that pays 2% annual interest compounded continuously. To the nearest year, how long will it take to earn $1000 interest?

BIG IDEAS
For Your Notebook

Big Idea 1

Graphing Exponential and Logarithmic Functions

Parent functions for exponential functions have the form $y = b^x$. Parent functions for logarithmic functions have the form $y = \log_b x$.

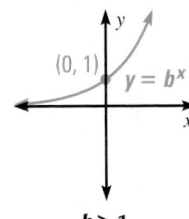
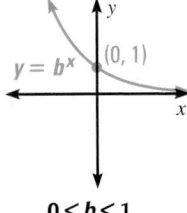
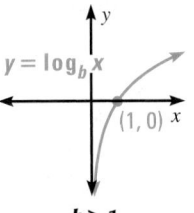
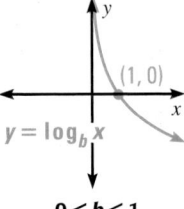

Exponential Growth   **Exponential Decay**   **Logarithmic Functions**

$b > 1$ $0 < b < 1$ $b > 1$ $0 < b < 1$

Big Idea 2

Solving Exponential and Logarithmic Equations

Solving an Exponential Equation	Solving a Logarithmic Equation
If each side can be written using the same base, equate exponents. $$3^{x+1} = 9^x$$ $$3^{x+1} = \left(3^2\right)^x$$ $$x + 1 = 2x$$ $$1 = x$$	If the equation has the form $\log_b x = \log_b y$, use the fact that $x = y$. $$\log_2 (4x - 2) = \log_2 3x$$ $$4x - 2 = 3x$$ $$x = 2$$
If each side cannot be written using the same base, take a logarithm of each side. $$6^x = 15$$ $$\log_6 6^x = \log_6 15$$ $$x = \frac{\log 15}{\log 6} \approx 1.511$$	If a logarithm is set equal to a constant, exponentiate each side. $$\log_5 (x + 1) = 2$$ $$x + 1 = 5^2$$ $$x = 24$$

Big Idea 3

Writing and Applying Exponential and Power Functions

Write an Exponential Model	Write a Power Model
An exponential model fits a set of data pairs (x, y) if a linear model fits the set of data pairs $(x, \ln y)$.	A power model fits a set of data pairs (x, y) if a linear model fits the set of data pairs $(\ln x, \ln y)$.

$y = b^x$ $\ln y = x \ln b$ $y = x^b$ $\ln y = b \ln x$

REVIEW KEY VOCABULARY

- exponential function
- exponential growth function
- growth factor
- asymptote

- exponential decay function
- decay factor
- natural base e
- logarithm of y with base b

- common logarithm
- natural logarithm
- exponential equation
- logarithmic equation

VOCABULARY EXERCISES

1. What is the asymptote of the graph of the function $y = -2\left(\dfrac{1}{4}\right)^{x+1} + 5$?

2. Identify the decay factor in the model $y = 7.2(0.89)^x$.

3. **WRITING** *Explain* the meaning of $\log_b y$.

4. Copy and complete: A logarithm with base e is called a(n) __?__ logarithm.

5. Is $y = (1.4)^x$ an *exponential function* or a *power function*? *Explain*.

REVIEW EXAMPLES AND EXERCISES

Use the review examples and exercises below to check your understanding of the concepts you have learned in each lesson of this chapter.

4.1 Graph Exponential Growth Functions

EXAMPLE

Graph $y = 2 \cdot 3^{x-2} + 3$. State the domain and range.

Begin by sketching the graph of $y = 2 \cdot 3^x$, which passes through (0, 2) and (1, 6). Then translate the graph right 2 units and up 3 units. Notice that the translated graph passes through (2, 5) and (3, 9).

The graph's asymptote is the line $y = 3$. The domain is all real numbers, and the range is $y > 3$.

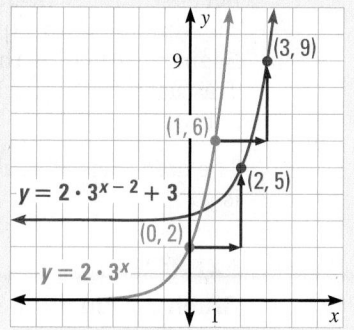

EXERCISES

EXAMPLES
1, 2, 3, and 5
for Exs. 6–9

Graph the function. State the domain and range.

6. $y = 5^x$

7. $y = 3(2.5)^x$

8. $f(x) = -3 \cdot 4^{x+1} - 2$

9. **FINANCE** You deposit $1500 in an account that pays 7% annual interest compounded daily. Find the balance after 2 years.

4.2 Graph Exponential Decay Functions

EXAMPLE

Graph $y = 2\left(\frac{1}{4}\right)^{x+2} - 2$. State the domain and range.

Begin by sketching the graph of $y = 2\left(\frac{1}{4}\right)^{x}$,

which passes through $(0, 2)$ and $\left(1, \frac{1}{2}\right)$. Then

translate the graph left 2 units and down 2 units.
Notice that the translated graph passes through

$(-2, 0)$ and $\left(-1, -\frac{3}{2}\right)$.

The graph's asymptote is the line $y = -2$.
The domain is all real numbers, and the range
is $y > -2$.

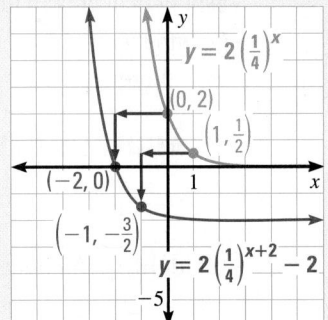

EXERCISES

Graph the function. State the domain and range.

**EXAMPLES
1, 2, and 3**
for Exs. 10–12

10. $y = \left(\frac{1}{8}\right)^{x}$

11. $y = \left(\frac{1}{3}\right)^{x} - 4$

12. $f(x) = 2(0.8)^{x-1} + 3$

4.3 Use Functions Involving e

EXAMPLE

Graph $y = e^{0.25(x-1)} - 5$. State the domain
and range.

Because $a = 1$ is positive and $r = 0.25$ is positive,
the function is an exponential growth function.
Begin by sketching the graph of $y = e^{0.25x}$.
Translate the graph right 1 unit and down
5 units.

The domain is all real numbers, and the range
is $y > -5$.

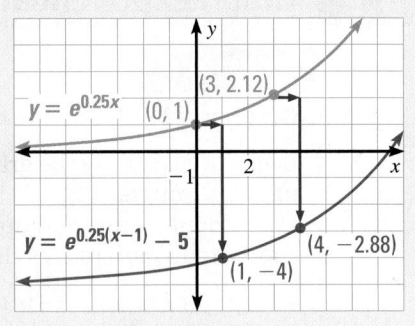

EXERCISES

Graph the function. State the domain and range.

**EXAMPLES
3 and 5**
for Exs. 13–16

13. $y = 2e^{-x}$

14. $y = e^{x-2}$

15. $f(x) = e^{-0.4(x+2)} + 6$

16. PHYSIOLOGY Nitrogen-13 is a radioactive isotope of nitrogen used in a
physiological test called positron emission tomograph (PET). A typical PET
scan begins with 6.9 picograms of nitrogen-13 (1 picogram = 10^{-12} grams).
The number N of picograms of nitrogen-13 remaining after t minutes can be
modeled by $N = 6.9e^{-0.0695t}$. How many picograms of nitrogen-13 remain after
10 minutes?

4.4 Find Logarithms and Graph Logarithmic Functions

EXAMPLE

Evaluate the logarithm.

a. $\log_5 625$ **b.** $\log 0.001$ **c.** $\log_{125} 5$ **d.** $\log_2 \frac{1}{64}$

To help you find the value of $\log_b y$, ask yourself what power of b gives you y.

a. 5 to what power gives 625?
$5^4 = 625$, so $\log_5 625 = 4$.

b. 10 to what power gives 0.001?
$10^{-3} = 0.001$, so $\log 0.001 = -3$.

c. 125 to what power gives 5?
$125^{1/3} = 5$, so $\log_{125} 5 = \frac{1}{3}$.

d. 2 to what power gives $\frac{1}{64}$?
$2^{-6} = \frac{1}{64}$, so $\log_2 \frac{1}{64} = -6$.

EXERCISES

Evaluate the logarithm without using a calculator.

EXAMPLES 2, 4, 7, and 8 for Exs. 17–24

17. $\log_3 243$ **18.** $\log_7 1$ **19.** $\log_{1/6} 216$ **20.** $\log_{125} \frac{1}{5}$

Graph the function. State the domain and range.

21. $y = \log_{1/6} x$ **22.** $y = \log_3 x - 4$ **23.** $f(x) = \ln(x - 1) + 3$

24. BIOLOGY Researchers have found that after 25 years of age, the average size of the pupil in a person's eye decreases. The relationship between pupil diameter d (in millimeters) and age a (in years) can be modeled by $d = -2.1158 \ln a + 13.669$. What is the average diameter of a pupil for a person 25 years old? 50 years old?

4.5 Apply Properties of Logarithms

EXAMPLES

Expand the expression.

$\log_5 \frac{6x}{y^3} = \log_5 6x - \log_5 y^3$
$= \log_5 6 + \log_5 x - \log_5 y^3$
$= \log_5 6 + \log_5 x - 3 \log_5 y$

Condense the expression.

$3 \log_3 8 - \log_3 16 = \log_3 8^3 - \log_3 16$
$= \log_3 \frac{8^3}{16}$
$= \log_3 32$

EXERCISES

Expand the expression.

EXAMPLES 2 and 3 for Exs. 25–31

25. $\log_8 3xy$ **26.** $\ln 10x^3 y$ **27.** $\log \frac{8}{y^4}$ **28.** $\ln \frac{3y}{x^5}$

Condense the expression.

29. $3 \log_7 4 + \log_7 6$ **30.** $\ln 12 - 2 \ln x$ **31.** $2 \ln 3 + 5 \ln 2 - \ln 8$

4.6 Solve Exponential and Logarithmic Equations

EXAMPLE

Solve the equation.

a. $7^x = 12$

$\log_7 7^x = \log_7 12$

$x = \log_7 12$

$x = \dfrac{\log 12}{\log 7} \approx 1.277$

b. $\log_2 (3x - 7) = 5$

$2^{\log_2 (3x - 7)} = 2^5$

$3x - 7 = 32$

$x = 13$

EXAMPLES
2, 5, and 6
for Exs. 32–34

EXERCISES

Solve the equation. Check for extraneous solutions.

32. $5^x = 32$

33. $\log_3 (2x - 5) = 2$

34. $\ln x + \ln (x + 2) = 3$

4.7 Write and Apply Exponential and Power Functions

EXAMPLE

Write an exponential function $y = ab^x$ whose graph passes through $(-1, 2)$ and $(3, 32)$.

Substitute the coordinates of the two given points into $y = ab^x$.

$2 = ab^{-1}$ Substitute 2 for *y* and −1 for *x*.

$32 = ab^3$ Substitute 32 for *y* and 3 for *x*.

Solve for *a* in the first equation to obtain $a = 2b$, and substitute this expression for *a* in the second equation.

$32 = (2b)b^3$ Substitute 2*b* for *a* in second equation.

$32 = 2b^4$ Product of powers property

$16 = b^4$ Divide each side by 2.

$2 = b$ Take the positive fourth root because $b > 0$.

Because $b = 2$, it follows that $a = 2(2) = 4$. So, $y = 4 \cdot 2^x$.

EXAMPLES
1 and 5
for Exs. 35–38

EXERCISES

Write an exponential function $y = ab^x$ whose graph passes through the points.

35. $(3, 8), (5, 2)$

36. $(-2, 2), (1, 0.25)$

37. $(2, 9), (4, 324)$

38. SPORTING GOODS A store begins selling a new type of basketball shoe. The table shows sales of the shoe over time. Find a power model for the data.

Week, *x*	1	2	3	4	5	6
Pairs sold, *y*	28	47	64	79	94	107

Graph the function. State the domain and range.

1. $y = 3^x$

2. $y = 2 \cdot 4^{x-2}$

3. $f(x) = -5 \cdot 2^{x+3} + 3$

4. $y = 4(0.25)^x$

5. $y = 2\left(\dfrac{1}{3}\right)^{x+2}$

6. $g(x) = \left(\dfrac{2}{3}\right)^x + 2$

7. $y = \dfrac{1}{2}e^{-x}$

8. $y = 2.5e^{-0.5x} + 1$

9. $h(x) = \dfrac{1}{3}e^{x-1} - 2$

Evaluate the logarithm without using a calculator.

10. $\log_5 25$

11. $\log_2 \dfrac{1}{32}$

12. $\log_6 1$

Graph the function. State the domain and range.

13. $y = \log_2 x$

14. $y = \ln x - 3$

15. $f(x) = \log(x + 3) + 2$

Condense the expression.

16. $2 \ln 7 - 3 \ln 4$

17. $\log_4 3 + 5 \log_4 2$

18. $\log 5 + \log x - 2 \log 3$

Use the change-of-base formula to evaluate the logarithm.

19. $\log_5 50$

20. $\log_6 23$

21. $\log_9 45$

Solve the equation. Check for extraneous solutions.

22. $7^{2x} = 30$

23. $3 \log(x - 4) = 6$

24. $\log_4 x + \log_4(x + 6) = 2$

25. Write an exponential function $y = ab^x$ whose graph passes through $(-1, 48)$ and $(2, 6)$.

26. Write a power function $y = ax^b$ whose graph passes through $(3, 8)$ and $(6, 15)$.

27. **LANDSCAPING** From 1996 to 2001, the number of households that purchased lawn and garden products at home gardening centers increased by about 4.85% per year. In 1996, about 62 million households purchased lawn and garden products. Write a function giving the number of households H (in millions) that purchased lawn and garden products t years after 1996.

28. **FINANCE** You deposit $2500 in an account that pays 3.5% annual interest compounded continuously. What is the balance after 8 years?

29. **EARTH SCIENCE** Rivers and streams carry small particles of sediment downstream. The table shows the diameter x (in millimeters) of several particles of sediment and the speed y (in meters per second) of the current needed to carry each particle downstream.

   a. Draw a scatter plot of the data pairs $(\ln x, \ln y)$.

   b. Find a power model for the original data. Estimate the speed of the current needed to carry a particle with a diameter of 120 millimeters downstream.

Type of sediment	x	y
Mud	0.2	0.10
Gravel	5	0.50
Coarse gravel	11	0.75
Pebbles	20	1.00
Small stones	45	1.50

4 ★ *Standardized* TEST PREPARATION

MULTIPLE CHOICE QUESTIONS

If you have difficulty solving a multiple choice problem directly, you may be able to use another approach to eliminate incorrect answer choices and obtain the correct answer.

PROBLEM 1

Which exponential function has a graph that passes through the points $(2, -12)$ and $(4, -48)$?

A $y = 3 \cdot 2^x$ **B** $y = -\sqrt{3} \cdot 2^x$ **C** $y = -\dfrac{4}{3} \cdot 3^x$ **D** $y = -3 \cdot 2^x$

METHOD 1

SOLVE DIRECTLY Substitute the coordinates of the two points into $y = ab^x$ and solve the resulting system.

STEP 1 **Substitute** the coordinates of the points into $y = ab^x$.

$-12 = ab^2$ **Substitute (2, −12).**

$-48 = ab^4$ **Substitute (4, −48).**

STEP 2 **Solve** the first equation for a.

$\dfrac{-12}{b^2} = a$ **Divide each side by b^2.**

STEP 3 **Substitute** $\dfrac{-12}{b^2}$ for a in the second equation and solve for b.

$-48 = \left(\dfrac{-12}{b^2}\right)b^4$ **Substitute.**

$-48 = -12b^2$ **Simplify.**

$4 = b^2$ **Divide each side by −12.**

$2 = b$ **Take the positive square root because $b > 0$.**

STEP 4 **Substitute** the value of b into $a = \dfrac{-12}{b^2}$ to find the value of a.

$a = \dfrac{-12}{b^2} = \dfrac{-12}{2^2} = \dfrac{-12}{4} = -3$

The equation is $y = -3 \cdot 2^x$.

▶ The correct answer is D.   Ⓐ Ⓑ Ⓒ **Ⓓ**

METHOD 2

ELIMINATE CHOICES Another method is to check whether both of the points are solutions of the equations given in the answer choices.

Substitute the coordinates of the points into the equation in each answer choice. You can stop as soon as you realize that one of the points is not a solution.

Choice A: $y = 3 \cdot 2^x$

$-12 \overset{?}{=} 3 \cdot 2^2$

$-12 \neq 12$

Choice B: $y = -\sqrt{3} \cdot 2^x$

$-12 \overset{?}{=} -\sqrt{3} \cdot 2^2$

$-12 \neq -4\sqrt{3}$

Choice C: $y = -\dfrac{4}{3} \cdot 3^x$ $y = -\dfrac{4}{3} \cdot 3^x$

$-12 \overset{?}{=} -\dfrac{4}{3} \cdot 3^2$ $-48 \overset{?}{=} -\dfrac{4}{3} \cdot 3^4$

$-12 = -12 \checkmark$ $-48 \neq -108$

Choice D: $y = -3 \cdot 2^x$ $y = -3 \cdot 2^x$

$-12 \overset{?}{=} -3 \cdot 2^2$ $-48 \overset{?}{=} -3 \cdot 2^4$

$-12 = -12 \checkmark$ $-48 = -48 \checkmark$

▶ The correct answer is D.   Ⓐ Ⓑ Ⓒ **Ⓓ**

PROBLEM 2

You buy a new personal computer for \$1600. It is estimated that the computer's value will decrease by 50% each year. After about how many years will the computer be worth \$250?

(A) $1\frac{1}{3}$ years   (B) 2 years   (C) $2\frac{2}{3}$ years   (D) 3 years

METHOD 1

SOLVE DIRECTLY Write and solve an equation to find the time it takes for the computer to depreciate to \$250.

Let y be the value (in dollars) of the computer t years after the purchase. An exponential decay model for the value is:

$$y = a(1 - r)^t$$

$$250 = 1600(1 - 0.5)^t$$

$$0.156 \approx (0.5)^t$$

$$\log_{0.5} 0.156 = \log_{0.5} (0.5)^t$$

$$\frac{\log 0.156}{\log 0.5} \approx 2.68 \approx t$$

The computer will be worth \$250 after about $2.68 \approx 2\frac{2}{3}$ years.

▶ The correct answer is C. (A) (B) **(C)** (D)

METHOD 2

ELIMINATE CHOICES Use estimation to find how long it will take for the computer to depreciate to \$250.

The computer depreciates by 50% each year.

After 0 years, it is worth \$1600.

After 1 year, it will be worth 0.5(\$1600) = \$800.

After 2 years, it will be worth 0.5(\$800) = \$400.

After 3 years, it will be worth 0.5(\$400) = \$200.

The computer will be worth \$250 at some time strictly between 2 and 3 years after purchase. So, you can eliminate choices A, B, and D.

▶ The correct answer is C. (A) (B) **(C)** (D)

PRACTICE

Explain why you can eliminate the highlighted answer choice.

1. Which power function has a graph that passes through the points $(-2, -16)$ and $(1, 2)$?

   (A) $y = \frac{1}{2}x^5$ (B) $y = 2x^5$ (C)✗ $y = 2x^{1/2}$ (D) $y = 2x^3$

2. For which equation is 4 a solution?

   (A)✗ $e^{2x} + 1 = 17$ (B) $\log_2 (x + 2) = \log_2 2x$

   (C) $3^{x-2} + 1 = 10$ (D) $\ln (x + 2) + \ln x = 1$

3. What is the domain of the function $y = -5 \cdot 2^{x+2}$?

   (A) All real numbers   (B)✗ All real numbers except -2

   (C) All real numbers less than 0   (D) All real numbers greater than -5

MULTIPLE CHOICE

1. In 1999, the tuition for one year at Harvard University was $22,054. During the next 4 years, the tuition increased by 4.25% each year. Which model represents the situation?

   Ⓐ $y = 22{,}054(0.0425)^t$

   Ⓑ $y = 22{,}054(0.425)^t$

   Ⓒ $y = 22{,}054(1.0425)^t$

   Ⓓ $y = 22{,}054(1.425)^t$

2. You deposit $1000 in an account that pays 3% annual interest. How much more interest is earned after 2 years if the interest is compounded daily than if the interest is compounded monthly?

   Ⓐ $.07   Ⓑ $1.27

   Ⓒ $61.76   Ⓓ $1061.76

3. The graph of which function is shown?

   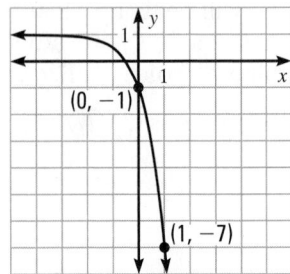

   Ⓐ $y = 2 \cdot 4^x + 1$ Ⓑ $y = -2 \cdot 4^x + 1$

   Ⓒ $y = 2 \cdot 4^x - 1$ Ⓓ $y = -2 \cdot 4^x - 1$

4. Which function can be obtained by translating the graph of $y = \log_3 (x + 2) - 4$ left 1 unit?

   Ⓐ $y = \log_3 (x + 2) - 5$

   Ⓑ $y = \log_3 (x + 2) - 3$

   Ⓒ $y = \log_3 (x + 1) - 4$

   Ⓓ $y = \log_3 (x + 3) - 4$

5. Which expression is equivalent to $3 \log x + \log 3$?

   Ⓐ $\log 9x$ Ⓑ $4 \log 3x$

   Ⓒ $\log 3x^3$ Ⓓ $\log (x^3 + 3)$

6. The population of the United States is expected to increase by 0.9% each year from 2003 to 2014. The U.S. population was about 290 million in 2003. To the nearest million, what is the projected population for 2010?

   Ⓐ 295 million

   Ⓑ 309 million

   Ⓒ 574 million

   Ⓓ 4891 million

7. Which expression is equivalent to $\sqrt{100e^{6x}}$?

   Ⓐ $10e^{3x}$ Ⓑ $7e^x + 3e^{2x}$

   Ⓒ $(2e^x)^3$ Ⓓ $10e^{\sqrt{6x}}$

8. Which function is an exponential decay function?

   Ⓐ $y = 2 \cdot 5^x$ Ⓑ $y = -2 \cdot 5^x$

   Ⓒ $y = 2e^x$ Ⓓ $y = 2(0.5)^x$

9. Which function is the inverse of $y = e^{2x} - 3$?

   Ⓐ $y = 2 \ln (x + 3)$ Ⓑ $y = 2 \ln (x - 3)$

   Ⓒ $y = \dfrac{\ln (x + 3)}{2}$ Ⓓ $y = \dfrac{\ln (x - 3)}{2}$

10. What is (are) the solution(s) of the equation $\log (x + 3) + \log x = 1$?

    Ⓐ 2, −5   Ⓑ 2

    Ⓒ 5   Ⓓ 2, 5

11. The graph of which function is shown?

    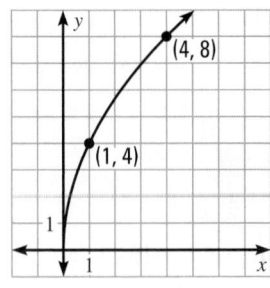

    Ⓐ $y = 4x^{0.25}$ Ⓑ $y = 4x^{0.5}$

    Ⓒ $y = \dfrac{1}{2}x^2$ Ⓓ $y = 2x^{1/3}$

GRIDDED ANSWER

12. You deposit $500 in an account that pays 3.5% annual interest compounded continuously. To the nearest dollar, how much interest have you earned after 1 year?

13. The model $y = 7.7e^{0.14x}$ gives the number y (in thousands per cubic centimeter) of bacteria in a liquid culture after x hours. After how many hours will there be 50,000 bacteria per cubic centimeter? Round your answer to the nearest tenth of an hour.

14. What is the solution of the equation $9^{2x + 1} = 3^{5x - 1}$?

15. What is the value of $\log_2 72 - 2 \log_2 3$?

16. The graph of an exponential function $f(x) = ab^x$ passes through the points $(0, 8)$ and $(2, 2)$. What is the value of $f(5)$?

17. What is the solution of the equation $\log_3 (5x + 3) = 5$?

SHORT RESPONSE

18. To make fudge, you must heat the mixture to 232°F and then let it cool at room temperature, 68°F. According to the recipe, it should take 20 minutes for the fudge to reach 110°F. To the nearest thousandth, what is the cooling rate of the fudge? If you are in a hurry, how could you increase the cooling rate? *Explain* your reasoning.

19. A movie grosses $37 million in its first week of release. The weekly gross y decreases by 30% each week. Write an exponential decay model for the weekly gross in week x. What is a reasonable domain for this situation? *Explain* your reasoning.

20. A double exponential function is a function of the form $y = a^{a^x}$. Graph the functions $y = 2^x$ and $y = 2^{2^x}$ in the same coordinate plane. Which function grows more quickly? *Explain*.

EXTENDED RESPONSE

21. The table shows the number of transistors per integrated circuit for computers introduced in various years.

  a. Let x be the number of years since 1974, and let y be the number of transistors. Draw a scatter plot of the data pairs $(x, \ln y)$.

  b. Find an exponential model for the original data.

  c. Use your model to predict the number of transistors per integrated circuit in 2008.

  d. In 1965, Gordon Moore made an observation that became known as Moore's law. Moore's law states that the number of transistors per integrated circuit would double about every 18 months. According to your model, does Moore's law hold? *Explain* your reasoning.

Year	Transistors
1974	6,000
1979	29,000
1982	134,000
1985	275,000
1989	1,200,000
1993	3,100,000
1997	7,500,000
1999	9,500,000
2000	42,000,000
2004	125,000,000

22. For a temperature of 60°F and a height of h feet above sea level, the air pressure P (in pounds per square inch) can be modeled by the equation $P = 14.7e^{-0.0004h}$, and the air density D (in pounds per cubic foot) can be modeled by the equation $D = 0.0761e^{-0.0004h}$.

  a. What is the air density at 10,000 feet above sea level?

  b. To the nearest foot, at what height is the air pressure 12 pounds per square inch?

  c. What is the relationship between air pressure and air density at 60°F? *Explain* your reasoning.

  d. One rule of thumb states that air pressure decreases by about 1% for every 80 meter increase in altitude. Do you agree with this? *Explain*.

5 Rational Functions

COMMON CORE

Lesson
5.1 CC.9-12.A.CED.2*
5.2 CC.9-12.F.IF.7d (+)*
5.3 CC.9-12.F.IF.7d (+)*
5.4 CC.9-12.A.APR.7 (+)
5.5 CC.9-12.A.APR.7 (+)
5.6 CC.9-12.A.REI.2
5.7 CC.9-12.F.IF.9

Before

Previously, you learned the following skills, which you'll use in this chapter: factoring polynomials, performing polynomial operations, and finding least common multiples.

Prerequisite Skills

VOCABULARY CHECK

1. The **asymptote** of the graph at the right is __?__.

2. Two variables x and y show **direct variation** provided __?__ where a is a nonzero constant.

3. An **extraneous solution** of a transformed equation is not an actual __?__ of the original equation.

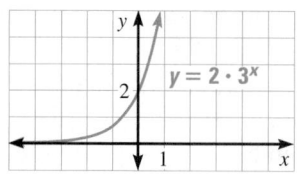

SKILLS CHECK

Factor the polynomial.

4. $x^2 - 11x - 26$ 5. $x^2 + 5x + 6$ 6. $x^2 - 13x + 40$

Perform the indicated operation.

7. $(3x^2 - 6) + (7x^2 - x)$ 8. $(-2x^2 + 6) - (x^2 - x)$ 9. $(x + 2)(x - 9)^2$

Find the least common multiple (LCM) of the numbers.

10. 14, 6   11. 8, 10   12. 4, 13

In this chapter, you will apply the big ideas listed below and reviewed in the Chapter Summary. You will also use the key vocabulary listed below.

Big Ideas

1. **Graphing rational functions**
2. **Performing operations with rational expressions**
3. **Solving rational equations**

KEY VOCABULARY

- constant of variation
- complex fraction
- cross multiplying
- decreasing

- even function
- inverse variation
- increasing
- joint variation

- odd function
- rational function
- simplified form of a rational expression

Why?

You can use rational functions to model real-life situations. For example, you can model the time it takes to travel across the United States and back in an airplane.

Animated Algebra

The animation illustrated below helps you answer a question from this chapter: How does the time required to fly from New York to Los Angeles and back depend on the speeds of the airplane and the jet stream?

The winds of the jet stream affect the overall speed of an airplane.

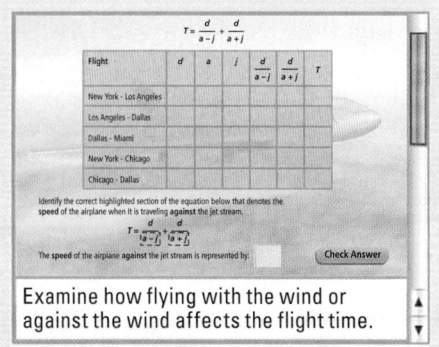

Examine how flying with the wind or against the wind affects the flight time.

Animated Algebra at my.hrw.com

Investigating Inverse Variation

MATHEMATICAL
PRACTICES

Model with mathematics.

MATERIALS • tape measure or meter stick • centimeter ruler • masking tape

QUESTION How can you model data that show inverse variation?

EXPLORE Collect and record data

STEP 1 *Mark distances*

Work with a partner. Have your partner stand against a wall. Place the end of the tape measure against the wall between your partner's feet. Use tape to mark off distances from 3 meters to 9 meters away from the wall.

STEP 2 *Measure apparent height*

Face your partner, with your toes touching the 3 meter mark. Hold a centimeter ruler at arm's length and line up the "0" end of the ruler with the top of your partner's head. Measure the apparent height of your partner to the nearest centimeter.

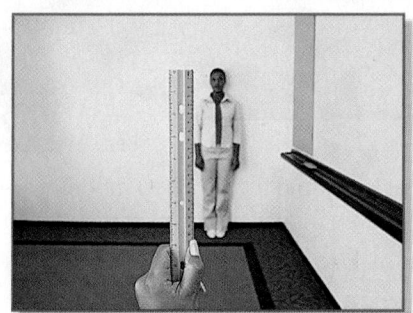

STEP 3 *Repeat for other distances*

Repeat Step 2 for each marked distance and record your results in a table like the one shown.

Distance (m), x	3	4	5	6	7	8	9
Apparent height (cm), y	?	?	?	?	?	?	?

DRAW CONCLUSIONS Use your observations to complete these exercises

1. Does apparent height vary directly with distance? *Justify* your answer mathematically.

2. Find the product $x \cdot y$ for each ordered pair in the table. What do you notice?

3. Based on your results from Exercise 2, write an equation relating distance and apparent height.

4. Use your equation to predict your partner's apparent height at an unmeasured distance. Then test your prediction by measuring your partner's apparent height at that distance. How close was your prediction?

5.1 Model Inverse and Joint Variation

Before	You wrote and used direct variation models.
Now	You will use inverse variation and joint variation models.
Why?	So you can model music frequencies, as in Ex. 40.

Key Vocabulary
• inverse variation
• constant of variation
• joint variation

CC.9-12.A.CED.2 Create equations in two or more variables to represent relationships between quantities; graph equations on coordinate axes with labels and scales.*

You have learned that two variables x and y show direct variation if $y = ax$ for some nonzero constant a. Another type of variation is called *inverse variation*.

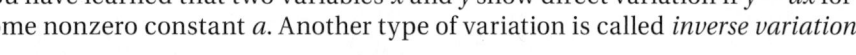

KEY CONCEPT *For Your Notebook*

Inverse Variation

Two variables x and y show **inverse variation** if they are related as follows:

$$y = \frac{a}{x}, \; a \neq 0$$

The constant a is the **constant of variation**, and y is said to *vary inversely* with x.

EXAMPLE 1 Classify direct and inverse variation

Tell whether x and y show *direct variation*, *inverse variation*, or *neither*.

	Given Equation	Rewritten Equation	Type of Variation
a.	$xy = 7$	$y = \dfrac{7}{x}$	Inverse
b.	$y = x + 3$		Neither
c.	$\dfrac{y}{4} = x$	$y = 4x$	Direct

REVIEW DIRECT VARIATION

The equation in part (b) does not show direct variation because $y = x + 3$ is not of the form $y = ax$.

EXAMPLE 2 Write an inverse variation equation

The variables x and y vary inversely, and $y = 7$ when $x = 4$. Write an equation that relates x and y. Then find y when $x = -2$.

$y = \dfrac{a}{x}$ **Write general equation for inverse variation.**

$7 = \dfrac{a}{4}$ **Substitute 7 for y and 4 for x.**

$28 = a$ **Solve for a.**

▸ The inverse variation equation is $y = \dfrac{28}{x}$. When $x = -2$, $y = \dfrac{28}{-2} = -14$.

EXAMPLE 3 **Write an inverse variation model**

MP3 PLAYERS The number of songs that can be stored on an MP3 player varies inversely with the average size of a song. A certain MP3 player can store 2500 songs when the average size of a song is 4 megabytes (MB).

- Write a model that gives the number n of songs that will fit on the MP3 player as a function of the average song size s (in megabytes).

- Make a table showing the number of songs that will fit on the MP3 player if the average size of a song is 2 MB, 2.5 MB, 3 MB, and 5 MB as shown below. What happens to the number of songs as the average song size increases?

2 MB   2.5 MB   3 MB   5 MB

Solution

STEP 1 **Write** an inverse variation model.

$$n = \frac{a}{s}$$ **Write general equation for inverse variation.**

$$2500 = \frac{a}{4}$$ **Substitute 2500 for n and 4 for s.**

$$10{,}000 = a$$ **Solve for a.**

▶ A model is $n = \dfrac{10{,}000}{s}$.

STEP 2 **Make** a table of values.

Average size of song (MB), s	2	2.5	3	5
Number of songs, n	5000	4000	3333	2000

▶ From the table, you can see that the number of songs that will fit on the MP3 player decreases as the average song size increases.

 GUIDED PRACTICE for Examples 1, 2, and 3

Tell whether x and y show *direct variation*, *inverse variation*, or *neither*.

1. $3x = y$

2. $xy = 0.75$

3. $y = x - 5$

The variables x and y vary inversely. Use the given values to write an equation relating x and y. Then find y when $x = 2$.

4. $x = 4, y = 3$

5. $x = 8, y = -1$

6. $x = \frac{1}{2}, y = 12$

7. WHAT IF? In Example 3, what is a model for the MP3 player if it stores 3000 songs when the average song size is 5 MB?

age fotostock/SuperStock

CHECKING FOR INVERSE VARIATION The general equation $y = \dfrac{a}{x}$ for inverse variation can be rewritten as $xy = a$. This tells you that a set of data pairs (x, y) shows inverse variation if the products xy are constant or approximately constant.

EXAMPLE 4 **Check data for inverse variation**

COMPUTER CHIPS The table compares the area A (in square millimeters) of a computer chip with the number c of chips that can be obtained from a silicon wafer.

- Write a model that gives c as a function of A.

- Predict the number of chips per wafer when the area of a chip is 81 square millimeters.

Area (mm²), A	58	62	66	70
Number of chips, c	448	424	392	376

Solution

AVOID ERRORS
To check data pairs (x, y) for *direct* variation, you find the *quotients* $\dfrac{y}{x}$. However, to check data pairs for *inverse* variation, you find the *products* xy.

STEP 1 **Calculate** the product $A \cdot c$ for each data pair in the table.

$$58(448) = 25{,}984$$

$$62(424) = 26{,}288$$

$$66(392) = 25{,}872$$

$$70(376) = 26{,}320$$

Each product is approximately equal to 26,000. So, the data show inverse variation. A model relating A and c is:

$$A \cdot c = 26{,}000, \text{ or } c = \dfrac{26{,}000}{A}$$

STEP 2 **Make** a prediction. The number of chips per wafer for a chip with an area of 81 square millimeters is $c = \dfrac{26{,}000}{81} \approx 321$.

✓ **GUIDED PRACTICE** for Example 4

8. **WHAT IF?** In Example 4, predict the number of chips per wafer when the area of each chip is 79 square millimeters.

KEY CONCEPT *For Your Notebook*

Joint Variation

Joint variation occurs when a quantity varies directly with *the product of two or more* other quantities. In the equations below, a is a nonzero constant.

$$z = axy \qquad z \text{ varies jointly with } x \text{ and } y.$$

$$p = aqrs \qquad p \text{ varies jointly with } q, r, \text{ and } s.$$

EXAMPLE 5 **Write a joint variation equation**

The variable z varies jointly with x and y. Also, $z = -75$ when $x = 3$ and $y = -5$. Write an equation that relates x, y, and z. Then find z when $x = 2$ and $y = 6$.

Solution

STEP 1 **Write** a general joint variation equation.

$$z = axy$$

STEP 2 **Use** the given values of z, x, and y to find the constant of variation a.

$-75 = a(3)(-5)$ **Substitute** -75 for z, 3 for x, and -5 for y.

$-75 = -15a$ **Simplify.**

$5 = a$ **Solve for** a.

STEP 3 **Rewrite** the joint variation equation with the value of a from Step 2.

$$z = 5xy$$

STEP 4 **Calculate** z when $x = 2$ and $y = 6$ using substitution.

$$z = 5xy = 5(2)(6) = 60$$

EXAMPLE 6 **Compare different types of variation**

Write an equation for the given relationship.

Relationship	Equation
a. y varies inversely with x.	$y = \dfrac{a}{x}$
b. z varies jointly with x, y, and r.	$z = axyr$
c. y varies inversely with the square of x.	$y = \dfrac{a}{x^2}$
d. z varies directly with y and inversely with x.	$z = \dfrac{ay}{x}$
e. x varies jointly with t and r and inversely with s.	$x = \dfrac{atr}{s}$

Animated Algebra   at my.hrw.com

✓ **GUIDED PRACTICE**   for Examples 5 and 6

The variable z varies jointly with x and y. Use the given values to write an equation relating x, y, and z. Then find z when $x = -2$ and $y = 5$.

9. $x = 1$, $y = 2$, $z = 7$ **10.** $x = 4$, $y = -3$, $z = 24$

11. $x = -2$, $y = 6$, $z = 18$ **12.** $x = -6$, $y = -4$, $z = 56$

Write an equation for the given relationship.

13. x varies inversely with y and directly with w.

14. p varies jointly with q and r and inversely with s.

5.1 EXERCISES

HOMEWORK
KEY

○ = See WORKED-OUT SOLUTIONS
Exs. 15, 21, and 39

★ = STANDARDIZED TEST PRACTICE
Exs. 2, 11, 30, 35, and 41

SKILL PRACTICE

1. **VOCABULARY** Copy and complete: If z varies directly with the product of x and y, then z is said to vary ___?___ with x and y.

2. ★ **WRITING** *Describe* how to tell whether a set of data pairs (x, y) shows inverse variation.

EXAMPLE 1
for Exs. 3–11

DETERMINING VARIATION Tell whether x and y show *direct variation*, *inverse variation*, or *neither*.

3. $xy = \dfrac{1}{5}$
4. $y = x + 4$
5. $\dfrac{y}{x} = 8$
6. $4x = y$

7. $y = \dfrac{2}{x}$
8. $x + y = 6$
9. $8y = x$
10. $xy = 12$

11. ★ **MULTIPLE CHOICE** Which equation represents inverse variation?

(A) $y = 4x$
(B) $y = x - 1$
(C) $xy = 5$
(D) $\dfrac{y}{7} = x$

EXAMPLE 2
for Exs. 12–19

USING INVERSE VARIATION The variables x and y vary inversely. Use the given values to write an equation relating x and y. Then find y when $x = 3$.

12. $x = 5, y = -4$
13. $x = 1, y = 9$
14. $x = -3, y = 8$
15. $x = 7, y = 2$

16. $x = \dfrac{3}{4}, y = 28$
17. $x = -4, y = -\dfrac{5}{4}$
18. $x = -12, y = -\dfrac{1}{6}$
19. $x = \dfrac{5}{3}, y = -7$

EXAMPLE 4
for Exs. 20–23

INTERPRETING DATA Determine whether x and y show *direct variation*, *inverse variation*, or *neither*.

20.

x	y
1.5	40
2.5	24
4	15
7.5	8
10	6

21.

x	y
12	132
18	198
23	253
29	319
34	374

22.

x	y
4	16
5	11
6.2	10
7	9
11	6

23.

x	y
4	21
6	14
8	10.5
8.4	10
12	7

EXAMPLE 5
for Exs. 24–30

USING JOINT VARIATION Write an equation relating x, y, and z given that z varies jointly with x and y. Then find z when $x = -4$ and $y = 5$.

24. $x = 2, y = -6, z = 24$
25. $x = 8, y = 6, z = 12$
26. $x = -\dfrac{1}{4}, y = -3, z = 15$

27. $x = 6, y = -7, z = -3$
28. $x = 9, y = -2, z = 6$
29. $x = 5, y = -3, z = 75$

30. ★ **MULTIPLE CHOICE** Suppose z varies jointly with x and y, and $z = -36$ when $x = -3$ and $y = -4$. What is the constant of variation?

(A) -3
(B) -2
(C) 3
(D) 12

EXAMPLE 6
for Exs. 31–33

WRITING EQUATIONS Write an equation for the given relationship.

31. x varies directly with y and inversely with z.

32. y varies jointly with x and the square of z.

33. w varies inversely with y and jointly with x and z.

34. ERROR ANALYSIS A variable z varies jointly with x and the cube of y and inversely with the square root of w. *Describe* and correct the error in writing an equation relating the variables.

$$z = \frac{a\sqrt{w}}{xy^3}$$ ✗

35. ★ **OPEN-ENDED MATH** Let $f(x)$ represent a direct variation function, $g(x)$ represent an inverse variation function, and $h(x)$ be the sum of $f(x)$ and $g(x)$. Write possible functions $f(x)$ and $g(x)$ so that $h(2) = 5$.

36. CHALLENGE Suppose x varies inversely with y and y varies inversely with z. How does x vary with z? *Justify* your answer algebraically.

PROBLEM SOLVING

37. DIGITAL CAMERAS The number n of photos your digital camera can store varies inversely with the average size s (in megapixels) of the photos. Your digital camera can store 54 photos when the average photo size is 1.92 megapixels. Write a model that gives n as a function of s. How many photos can your camera store when the average photo size is 3.87 megapixels?

38. ELECTRONICS The table below compares the current I (in milliamps) with the resistance R (in ohms) for several electrical circuits. Write a model that gives R as a function of I. Then predict R when $I = 34$ milliamps.

Current (milliamps), I	7.4	8.9	12.1	17.9
Resistance (ohms), R	1200	1000	750	500

39. SNOWSHOES When you stand on snow, the average pressure P (in pounds per square inch) that you exert on the snow varies inversely with the total area A (in square inches) of the soles of your footwear. Suppose the pressure is 0.43 pound per square inch when you wear the snowshoes shown. Write an equation that gives P as a function of A. Then find the pressure if you wear the boots shown.

$A = 400$ in.² $A = 60$ in.²

40. MULTI-STEP PROBLEM A piano string's frequency f (in hertz) varies directly with the square root of the string's tension T (in Newtons) and inversely with both the string's length L and diameter d (each in centimeters).

   a. The middle C note has a frequency of 262 Hz. The string producing this note has a tension of 670 N, a length of 62 cm, and a diameter of 0.1025 cm. Write an equation relating f, T, L, and d.

   b. Find the frequency of the note produced by a string with a tension of 1629 N, a length of 201.6 cm, and a diameter of 0.49 cm.

○ = See **WORKED-OUT SOLUTIONS**
 in Student Resources

★ = **STANDARDIZED
TEST PRACTICE**

41. ★ EXTENDED RESPONSE The *law of universal gravitation* states that the gravitational force F (in Newtons) between two objects varies jointly with their masses m_1 and m_2 (in kilograms) and inversely with the square of the distance d (in meters) between the two objects. The constant of variation is denoted by G and is called the *universal gravitational constant.*

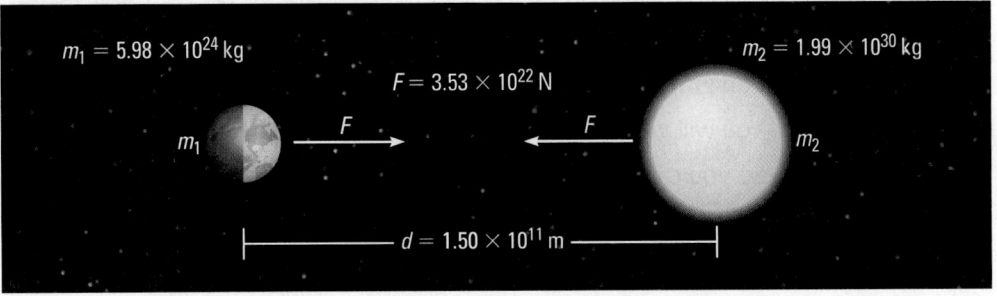

$m_1 = 5.98 \times 10^{24}$ kg
$m_2 = 1.99 \times 10^{30}$ kg
$F = 3.53 \times 10^{22}$ N
F
F
m_1
m_2
$d = 1.50 \times 10^{11}$ m

a. Model Write an equation that gives F in terms of m_1, m_2, d and G.

b. Approximate Use the information above about Earth and the Sun to approximate the universal gravitational constant G.

c. Reasoning *Explain* what happens to the gravitational force as the masses of the two objects increase and the distance between them is held constant. *Explain* what happens to the gravitational force as the masses of the two objects are held constant and the distance between them increases.

42. CHALLENGE The load P (in pounds) that can be safely supported by a horizontal beam varies jointly with the beam's width W and the square of its depth D, and inversely with its unsupported length L.

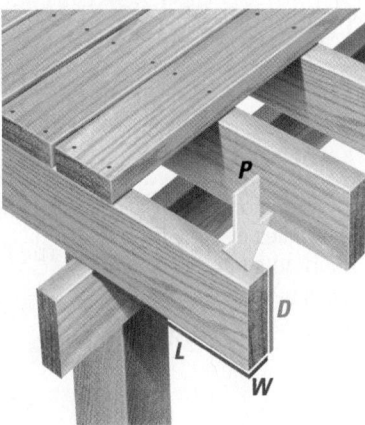

a. How does P change when the width and length of the beam are doubled?

b. How does P change when the width and depth of the beam are doubled?

c. How does P change when all three dimensions are doubled?

d. *Describe* several ways a beam can be modified if the safe load it is required to support is increased by a factor of 4.

5.2 Graph Simple Rational Functions

Before You graphed polynomial functions.

Now You will graph rational functions.

Why? So you can find average monthly costs, as in Ex. 38.

Key Vocabulary
- rational function
- domain
- range
- asymptote

CC.9-12.F.IF.7d (+) Graph rational functions, identifying zeros and asymptotes when suitable factorizations are available, and showing end behavior.*

A **rational function** has the form $f(x) = \dfrac{p(x)}{q(x)}$ where $p(x)$ and $q(x)$ are polynomials and $q(x) \neq 0$. The inverse variation function $f(x) = \dfrac{a}{x}$ is a rational function. The graph of this function when $a = 1$ is shown below.

KEY CONCEPT *For Your Notebook*

Parent Function for Simple Rational Functions

The graph of the parent function $f(x) = \dfrac{1}{x}$ is a *hyperbola*, which consists of two symmetrical parts called *branches*. The domain and range are all nonzero real numbers.

Any function of the form $g(x) = \dfrac{a}{x}$ $(a \neq 0)$ has the same asymptotes, domain, and range as the function $f(x) = \dfrac{1}{x}$.

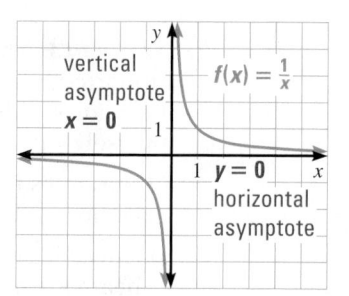

ANALYZE GRAPHS

The function $f(x) = \dfrac{a}{x}$ $(a > 0)$ lies entirely in quadrants I and III. So $f(x)$ is negative for $x < 0$ and positive for $x > 0$.

EXAMPLE 1 **Graph a rational function of the form** $y = \dfrac{a}{x}$

Graph the function $y = \dfrac{6}{x}$. Compare the graph with the graph of $y = \dfrac{1}{x}$.

Solution

INTERPRET TRANSFORMATIONS

The graph of $y = \dfrac{6}{x}$ is a vertical stretch of the graph of $y = \dfrac{1}{x}$ by a factor of 6.

STEP 1 **Draw** the asymptotes $x = 0$ and $y = 0$.

STEP 2 **Plot** points to the left and to the right of the vertical asymptote, such as $(-3, -2)$, $(-2, -3)$, $(2, 3)$, and $(3, 2)$.

STEP 3 **Draw** the branches of the hyperbola so that they pass through the plotted points and approach the asymptotes.

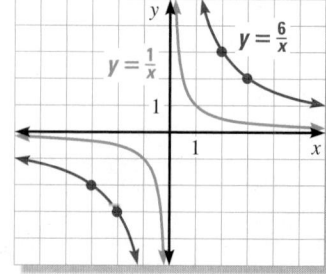

The graph of $y = \dfrac{6}{x}$ lies farther from the axes than the graph of $y = \dfrac{1}{x}$.

Both graphs lie in the first and third quadrants and have the same asymptotes, domain, and range.

Graphing Translations of Simple Rational Functions

To graph a rational function of the form $y = \dfrac{a}{x - h} + k$, follow these steps:

STEP 1   **Draw** the asymptotes $x = h$ and $y = k$.

STEP 2   **Plot** points to the left and to the right of the vertical asymptote.

STEP 3   **Draw** the two branches of the hyperbola so that they pass through the plotted points and approach the asymptotes.

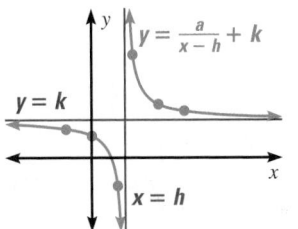

EXAMPLE 2   **Graph a rational function of the form** $y = \dfrac{a}{x - h} + k$

Graph $y = \dfrac{-4}{x + 2} - 1$. State the domain and range.

Solution

STEP 1   **Draw** the asymptotes $x = -2$ and $y = -1$.

STEP 2   **Plot** points to the left of the vertical asymptote, such as $(-3, 3)$ and $(-4, 1)$, and points to the right, such as $(-1, -5)$ and $(0, -3)$.

STEP 3   **Draw** the two branches of the hyperbola so that they pass through the plotted points and approach the asymptotes.

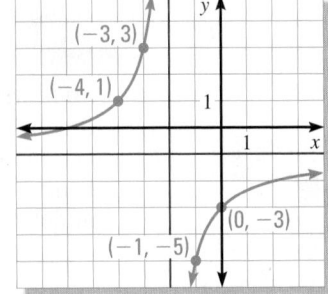

The domain is all real numbers except -2, and the range is all real numbers except -1.

INTERPRET TRANSFORMATIONS

The graph of $y = \dfrac{-4}{x + 2} - 1$ is the graph of $y = \dfrac{-4}{x}$ translated left 2 units and down 1 unit.

Animated Algebra at my.hrw.com

✓   **GUIDED PRACTICE**   for Examples 1 and 2

Graph the function. State the domain and range.

1. $f(x) = \dfrac{-4}{x}$ **2.** $y = \dfrac{8}{x} - 5$ **3.** $y = \dfrac{1}{x - 3} + 2$

OTHER RATIONAL FUNCTIONS   All rational functions of the form $y = \dfrac{ax + b}{cx + d}$ also have graphs that are hyperbolas.

- The vertical asymptote of the graph is the line $x = -\dfrac{d}{c}$, because the function is undefined when the denominator $cx + d$ is zero.

- The horizontal asymptote is the line $y = \dfrac{a}{c}$.

EXAMPLE 3 Graph a rational function of the form $y = \dfrac{ax + b}{cx + d}$

Graph $y = \dfrac{2x + 1}{x - 3}$. State the domain and range.

Solution

STEP 1 **Draw** the asymptotes. Solve $x - 3 = 0$ for x to find the vertical asymptote $x = 3$. The horizontal asymptote is the line $y = \dfrac{a}{c} = \dfrac{2}{1} = 2$.

STEP 2 **Plot** points to the left of the vertical asymptote, such as $(2, -5)$ and $\left(0, -\dfrac{1}{3}\right)$, and points to the right, such as $(4, 9)$ and $\left(6, \dfrac{13}{3}\right)$.

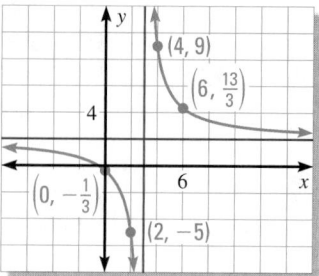

STEP 3 **Draw** the two branches of the hyperbola so that they pass through the plotted points and approach the asymptotes.

▸ The domain is all real numbers except 3. The range is all real numbers except 2.

❖ **EXAMPLE 4** Solve a multi-step problem

3-D MODELING A 3-D printer builds up layers of material to make three-dimensional models. Each deposited layer bonds to the layer below it. A company decides to make small display models of engine components using a 3-D printer. The printer costs $24,000. The material for each model costs $300.

• Write an equation that gives the average cost per model as a function of the number of models printed.

• Graph the function. Use the graph to estimate how many models must be printed for the average cost per model to fall to $700.

• What happens to the average cost as more models are printed?

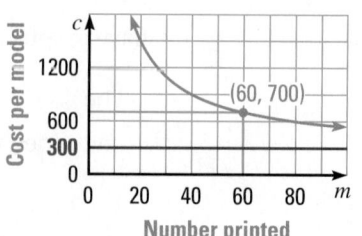

Solution

STEP 1 **Write** a function. Let c be the average cost and m be the number of models printed.

$$c = \frac{\text{Unit cost} \cdot \text{Number printed} + \text{Cost of printer}}{\text{Number printed}} = \frac{300m + 24{,}000}{m}$$

DRAW GRAPHS
....
Because the number of models and average cost cannot be negative, graph only the branch of the hyperbola that lies in the first quadrant.

STEP 2 **Graph** the function. The asymptotes are the lines $m = 0$ and $c = 300$. The average cost falls to $700 per model after 60 models are printed.

STEP 3 **Interpret** the graph. As more models are printed, the average cost per model approaches $300.

Graph the function. State the domain and range.

4. $y = \dfrac{x-1}{x+3}$

5. $y = \dfrac{2x+1}{4x-2}$

6. $f(x) = \dfrac{-3x+2}{-x-1}$

7. **WHAT IF?** In Example 4, how do the function and graph change if the cost of the 3-D printer is $21,000?

5.2 EXERCISES

HOMEWORK KEY

○ = See WORKED-OUT SOLUTIONS
Exs. 5, 21, and 39

★ = STANDARDIZED TEST PRACTICE
Exs. 2, 23, 35, 40, and 41

◆ = MULTIPLE REPRESENTATIONS
Ex. 39

SKILL PRACTICE

1. VOCABULARY Copy and complete: The function $y = \dfrac{7}{x+4} + 3$ has a(n) __?__ of all real numbers except 3 and a(n) __?__ of all real numbers except -4.

2. ★ WRITING Is $f(x) = \dfrac{-3x+5}{2^x+1}$ a rational function? *Explain* your answer.

EXAMPLE 1
for Exs. 3–10

GRAPHING FUNCTIONS Graph the function. Compare the graph with the graph of $y = \dfrac{1}{x}$.

3. $y = \dfrac{3}{x}$

4. $y = \dfrac{10}{x}$

5. $y = \dfrac{-5}{x}$

6. $y = \dfrac{-0.5}{x}$

7. $y = \dfrac{0.1}{x}$

8. $f(x) = \dfrac{15}{x}$

9. $g(x) = \dfrac{-6}{x}$

10. $h(x) = \dfrac{-3}{x}$

EXAMPLE 2
for Exs. 11–23

GRAPHING FUNCTIONS Graph the function. State the domain and range.

11. $y = \dfrac{4}{x} + 3$

12. $y = \dfrac{3}{x} - 2$

13. $y = \dfrac{6}{x-1}$

14. $f(x) = \dfrac{1}{x+2}$

15. $y = \dfrac{-5}{x} - 7$

16. $y = \dfrac{-6}{x} + 4$

17. $y = \dfrac{-3}{x+2}$

18. $g(x) = \dfrac{-2}{x-7}$

19. $y = \dfrac{-4}{x+4} + 3$

20. $y = \dfrac{10}{x+7} - 5$

21. $y = \dfrac{-3}{x-4} - 1$

22. $h(x) = \dfrac{11}{x-9} + 9$

23. ★ MULTIPLE CHOICE What are the asymptotes of the graph of $y = \dfrac{3}{x+8} - 3$?

A $x = 8, y = 3$ **B** $x = 8, y = -3$ **C** $x = -8, y = 3$ **D** $x = -8, y = -3$

24. GRAPHING CALCULATOR Consider the function $y = \dfrac{a}{x-h} + k$ where $a = 1$, $h = 3$, and $k = -2$. Predict the effect on the functions graph of each change in a, h, or k described in parts (a)–(c). Use a graphing calculator to check your prediction by graphing the original and revised functions in the same coordinate plane.

a. a changes to -3

b. h changes to -1

c. k changes to 2

ERROR ANALYSIS *Describe* and correct the error in the graph.

25. $y = \dfrac{-8}{x}$

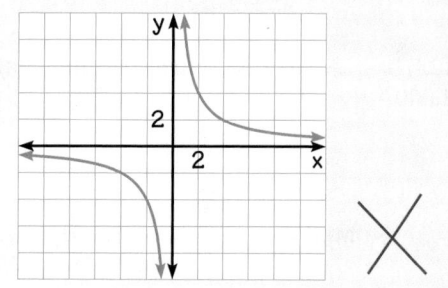

26. $y = \dfrac{2}{x-1} - 2$

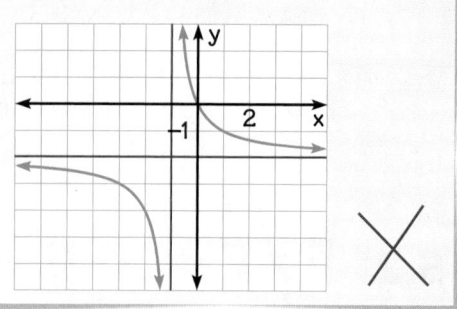

EXAMPLE 3
for Exs. 27–34

GRAPHING FUNCTIONS Graph the function. State the domain and range.

27. $y = \dfrac{x+4}{x-3}$

28. $y = \dfrac{x-1}{x+5}$

29. $y = \dfrac{x+6}{4x-8}$

30. $y = \dfrac{8x+3}{2x-6}$

31. $y = \dfrac{-5x+2}{4x+5}$

32. $f(x) = \dfrac{6x-1}{3x-1}$

33. $g(x) = \dfrac{5x}{2x+3}$

34. $h(x) = \dfrac{5x+3}{-x+10}$

35. ★ **OPEN-ENDED MATH** Write a rational function such that the domain is all real numbers except -8 and the range is all real numbers except 3.

36. **CHALLENGE** Show that the equation $f(x) = \dfrac{a}{x-h} + k$ represents a rational function by writing the right side as a quotient of polynomials.

PROBLEM SOLVING

EXAMPLE 4
for Exs. 37–38

37. **INTERNET SERVICE** An Internet service provider charges a $50 installation fee and a monthly fee of $43. Write and graph an equation that gives the average cost per month as a function of the number of months of service. After how many months will the average cost be $53?

38. **ROCK CLIMBING GYM** To join a rock climbing gym, you must pay an initial fee of $100 and a monthly fee of $59. Write and graph an equation that gives the average cost per month as a function of the number of months of membership. After how many months will the average cost be $69?

39. ◆ **MULTIPLE REPRESENTATIONS** The time t (in seconds) it takes for sound to travel 1 kilometer can be modeled by $t = \dfrac{1000}{0.6T + 331}$ where T is the air temperature (in degrees Celsius).

   a. **Evaluating a Function** How long does it take for sound to travel 5 kilometers when the air temperature is 25°C? *Explain.*

   b. **Drawing a Graph** Suppose you are 1 kilometer from a lightning strike, and it takes 3 seconds to hear the thunder. Graph the given function, and use the graph to estimate the air temperature.

○ = See WORKED-OUT SOLUTIONS in Student Resources   ★ = STANDARDIZED TEST PRACTICE   ◆ = MULTIPLE REPRESENTATIONS

40. ★ **SHORT RESPONSE** A business is studying the cost to remove a pollutant from the ground at its site. The function $y = \dfrac{15x}{1.1 - x}$ models the estimated cost y (in thousands of dollars) to remove x percent (expressed as a decimal) of the pollutant.

   a. Graph the function. *Describe* a reasonable domain and range.

   b. How much does it cost to remove 20% of the pollutant? 40% of the pollutant? 80% of the pollutant? Does doubling the percent of the pollutant removed double the cost? *Explain.*

41. ★ **EXTENDED RESPONSE** The *Doppler effect* occurs when the source of a sound is moving relative to a listener, so that the frequency f_l (in hertz) heard by the listener is different from the frequency f_s (in hertz) at the source. The frequency heard depends on whether the sound source is approaching or moving away from the listener. In both equations below, r is the speed (in miles per hour) of the sound source.

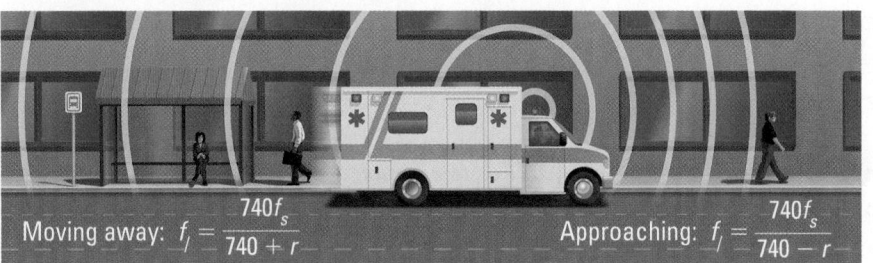

Moving away: $f_l = \dfrac{740 f_s}{740 + r}$ Approaching: $f_l = \dfrac{740 f_s}{740 - r}$

   a. An ambulance siren has a frequency of 2000 hertz. Write two equations modeling the frequencies you hear when the ambulance is approaching and when the ambulance is moving away.

   b. Graph the equations from part (a) using the domain $0 \le r \le 60$.

   c. For any speed r, how does the frequency heard for an approaching sound source compare with the frequency heard when the source moves away?

42. **CHALLENGE** A sailboat travels at a speed of 10 knots for 3 hours. It then uses a motor for power, which increases its speed to 15 knots. Write and graph an equation giving the boat's average speed s (in knots) for the entire trip as a function of the time t (in hours) that it uses the motor for power.

my.hrw.com
Keystrokes

Graph Rational Functions

MATHEMATICAL
PRACTICES

Use appropriate tools strategically.

QUESTION How can you use a graphing calculator to graph rational functions?

Most graphing calculators have two graphing modes: *connected* mode and *dot* mode. *Connected* mode displays the graph of a rational function as a smooth curve, while *dot* mode displays the graph as a series of dots.

EXAMPLE Graph a rational function

Graph $y = \dfrac{x + 3}{x - 3}$.

STEP 1 *Enter function*

Enter the rational function, using parentheses.

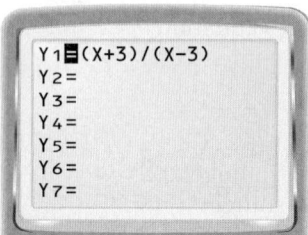

STEP 2 *Use connected mode*

Graph the function in *connected* mode.

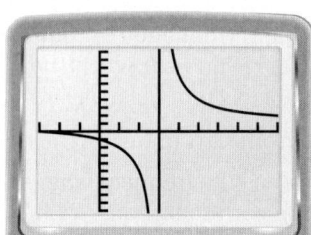

STEP 3 *Use dot mode*

Graph the function in *dot* mode.

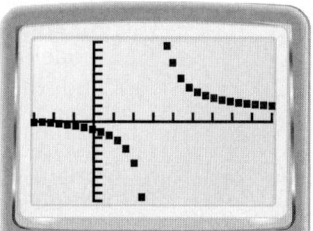

The graph in Step 2 includes a vertical line at approximately $x = 3$. This line is *not* part of the graph. It is simply the graphing calculator's attempt at connecting the two branches of the graph.

PRACTICE

Use a graphing calculator to graph the rational function. Choose a viewing window that displays the important characteristics of the graph.

1. $y = \dfrac{5}{x} + 2$

2. $y = 7 - \dfrac{3}{x}$

3. $y = 4 + \dfrac{2}{x - 5}$

4. $y = \dfrac{6}{x + 1} + 2$

5. $y = \dfrac{7}{2x + 8}$

6. $y = \dfrac{9 - 2x}{x - 3}$

7. $f(x) = \dfrac{x - 4}{x + 2}$

8. $g(x) = \dfrac{5x - 2}{3x + 9}$

9. **SKATEBOARDING** You are trying to decide whether it is worth joining a skate park. It costs $100 to join and then $4 for each visit. Write a function that gives the average cost y per visit after x visits. Graph the function. What happens to the average cost as the number of visits increases? What are a reasonable domain and range for the function?

Rewrite Rational Expressions

GOAL Use division to rewrite rational expressions in different forms.

COMMON CORE

CC.9-12.A.APR.6 Rewrite simple rational expressions in different forms; write $a(x)/b(x)$ in the form $q(x) + r(x)/b(x)$, where $a(x)$, $b(x)$, $q(x)$, and $r(x)$ are polynomials with the degree of $r(x)$ less than the degree of $b(x)$, using inspection, long division, or, for the more complicated examples, a computer algebra system.

Rewriting a rational expression may reveal properties of the related function and its graph. For example, a simple rational function that can be rewritten in the *graphing form* $y = \dfrac{a}{x-h} + k$ reveals that it is a translation of the parent function $y = \dfrac{a}{x}$ with vertical asymptote $x = h$ and horizontal asymptote $y = k$.

EXAMPLE 1 Rewrite and graph a rational function

Rewrite the function $y = \dfrac{3x+7}{x+2}$ in graphing form. Then graph it.

Solution

Method 1

By inspection: $\dfrac{3x+7}{x+2} = \dfrac{3(x+2)+1}{x+2} = 3 + \dfrac{1}{x+2}$

Method 2

By long division:
$$x+2 \overline{\big)\,\substack{\textstyle 3 \\ \textstyle 3x+7}}$$
$$\underline{3x+6}$$
$$1$$

The function in graphing form is $y = \dfrac{1}{x+2} + 3$.

The graph is the graph of $y = \dfrac{1}{x}$ translated left 2 units and up 3 units.

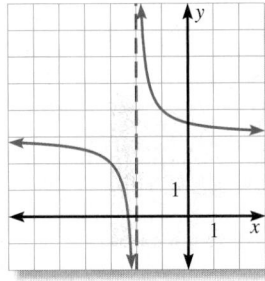

EXAMPLE 2 Write an average cost function in graphing form

GIFTS A company charges $.20 each, plus a shipping charge of $5.00, for a style of gift bag from its online store. Write an equation in graphing form for the average cost C per bag as a function of the number n of bags ordered. Then graph the function.

Solution

The average cost per bag is the total cost divided by the number of bags:

$$C = \frac{5 + 0.20n}{n} = \frac{5}{n} + \frac{0.20n}{n} = \frac{5}{n} + 0.2$$

The graph is that of $y = \dfrac{5}{n}$ translated up 0.2 unit. The cost cannot be negative, so graph only the portion in Quadrant I.

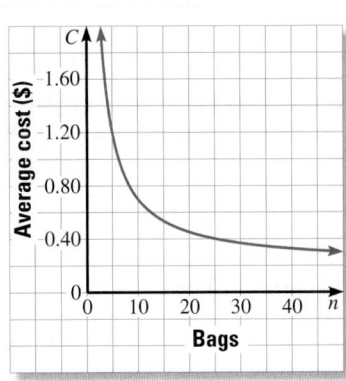

EXAMPLE 3 Use division to reveal end behavior

Write $\dfrac{2x^2 - x - 2}{x - 1}$ as the sum of a quotient and a remainder where the degree of the remainder's numerator is less than that of its denominator. What happens to the graph of the related function as $|x|$ increases without bound?

Solution

The divisor $x - 1$ is linear, so use synthetic division to evaluate when $x = 1$.

$$
\begin{array}{r|rrr}
1 & 2 & -1 & -2 \\
  &   & 2 & 1 \\
\hline
  & 2 & 1 & -1 \\
\end{array}
\qquad\qquad
\dfrac{2x^2 - x - 2}{x - 1} = 2x + 1 + \dfrac{-1}{x - 1}
$$

Because the remainder term approaches 0 as $|x|$ increases without bound, the graph gets closer and closer to the graph of $y = 2x + 1$.

PRACTICE

EXAMPLES 1 AND 3 for Exs. 1–8

Rewrite each rational function in graphing form. Then graph it.

1. $y = \dfrac{2x - 4}{x - 3}$

2. $y = \dfrac{8x + 7}{2x + 1}$

3. $y = \dfrac{3x + 4}{x + 1}$

4. $y = \dfrac{5x + 1}{x - 2}$

Rewrite each rational function as the sum of a quotient and a remainder where the degree of the remainder's numerator is less than that of its denominator.

5. $y = \dfrac{3x^2 + 2x + 1}{x - 1}$

6. $y = \dfrac{x^2 + 3x + 2}{x^2 - 4}$

7. $y = \dfrac{2x^2 - 9}{x^2 + 2x + 1}$

8. END BEHAVIOR Write $\dfrac{x^4 + 2x^2 - 1}{x^2 + 2}$ as the sum of a quotient and a remainder where the degree of the remainder's numerator is less than that of its denominator. What happens to the graph of the related function as $|x|$ increases without bound? *Explain.*

EXAMPLE 2 for Exs. 9–10

9. T-SHIRTS You are having T-shirts printed for a reunion. There is a set-up fee of \$35 and a charge of \$10 per shirt. Write an equation in graphing form that gives the average cost C per T-shirt as a function of the number n of T-shirts printed. Then graph the function.

10. BATTING AVERAGE A softball player's batting average is the ratio of hits to times at bat. So far this season, a player has 11 hits in 40 at-bats.

   a. The player wants to know what her season batting average will be if she has a .350 batting average from her next at-bat through the remainder of the season. Write a rational expression for her season batting average where n is the number of at-bats remaining in the season.

   b. Rewrite the expression in part (a) in graphing form. Can the player ever improve her batting average to .350 for the season? *Explain.*

   c. The player gets a hit the next 10 at-bats in a row, then bats .400 for the remainder of the season. Write a new expression for her season batting average.

5.3 Graph General Rational Functions

Before	You graphed rational functions involving linear polynomials.
Now	You will graph rational functions with higher-degree polynomials.
Why?	So you can solve problems about altitude, as in Ex. 35.

Key Vocabulary
- end behavior
- asymptote
- rational function

CC.9-12.F.IF.7d (+) Graph rational functions, identifying zeros and asymptotes when suitable factorizations are available, and showing end behavior.*

KEY CONCEPT   *For Your Notebook*

Graphs of Rational Functions

Let $p(x)$ and $q(x)$ be polynomials with no common factors other than ± 1. The graph of the following rational function has the characteristics listed below.

$$f(x) = \frac{p(x)}{q(x)} = \frac{a_m x^m + a_{m-1}x^{m-1} + \cdots + a_1 x + a_0}{b_n x^n + b_{n-1}x^{n-1} + \cdots + b_1 x + b_0}$$

1. The x-intercepts of the graph of f are the real zeros of $p(x)$.

2. The graph of f has a vertical asymptote at each real zero of $q(x)$.

3. The graph of f has at most one horizontal asymptote, which is determined by the degrees m and n of $p(x)$ and $q(x)$.

$m < n$	The line $y = 0$ is a horizontal asymptote.
$m = n$	The line $y = \dfrac{a_m}{b_n}$ is a horizontal asymptote.
$m > n$	The graph has no horizontal asymptote. The graph's end behavior is the same as the graph of $y = \dfrac{a_m}{b_n}x^{m-n}$.

EXAMPLE 1   Graph a rational function ($m < n$)

Graph $y = \dfrac{6}{x^2 + 1}$. State the domain and range.

Solution

The numerator has no zeros, so there is no x-intercept. The denominator has no real zeros, so there is no vertical asymptote.

The degree of the numerator, 0, is less than the degree of the denominator, 2. So, the line $y = 0$ (the x-axis) is a horizontal asymptote.

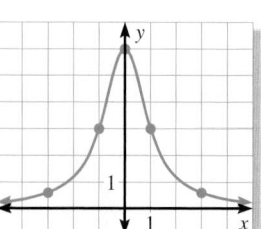

The graph passes through the points $(-3, 0.6)$, $(-1, 3)$, $(0, 6)$, $(1, 3)$, and $(3, 0.6)$. The domain is all real numbers, and the range is $0 < y \leq 6$.

EXAMPLE 2   **Graph a rational function ($m = n$)**

Graph $y = \dfrac{2x^2}{x^2 - 9}$.

Solution

The zero of the numerator $2x^2$ is 0, so 0 is an x-intercept. The zeros of the denominator $x^2 - 9$ are ± 3, so $x = 3$ and $x = -3$ are vertical asymptotes.

The numerator and denominator have the same degree, so the horizontal asymptote is $y = \dfrac{a_m}{b_n} = \dfrac{2}{1} = 2$.

Plot points between and beyond the vertical asymptotes.

	x	y
To the left of $x = -3$	−5	3.1
	−4	4.6
Between $x = -3$ and $x = 3$	−2	−1.6
	0	0
	2	−1.6
To the right of $x = 3$	4	4.6
	5	3.1

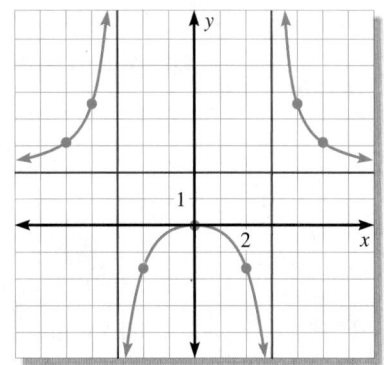

EXAMPLE 3   **Graph a rational function ($m > n$)**

Graph $y = \dfrac{x^2 + 3x - 4}{x - 2}$.

Solution

The numerator factors as $(x + 4)(x - 1)$, so the x-intercepts are -4 and 1. The zero of the denominator $x - 2$ is 2, so $x = 2$ is a vertical asymptote.

The degree of the numerator, 2, is greater than the degree of the denominator, 1, so the graph has no horizontal asymptote. The graph has the same end behavior as the graph of $y = x^{2-1} = x$. Plot points on each side of the vertical asymptote.

	x	y
To the left of $x = 2$	−8	−3.6
	−4	0
	0	2
	1	0
To the right of $x = 2$	3	14
	4	12
	8	14
	12	17.6

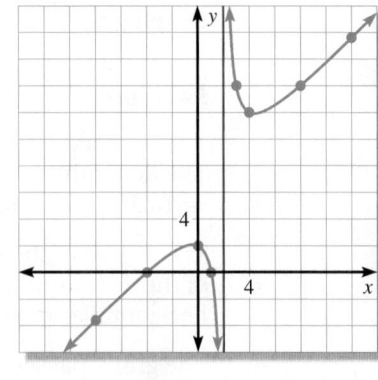

Graph the function.

1. $y = \dfrac{4}{x^2 + 2}$

2. $y = \dfrac{3x^2}{x^2 - 1}$

3. $f(x) = \dfrac{x^2 - 5}{x^2 + 1}$

4. $y = \dfrac{x^2 - 2x - 3}{x - 4}$

❖ **EXAMPLE 4** **Solve a multi-step problem**

MANUFACTURING A food manufacturer wants to find the most efficient packaging for a can of soup with a volume of 342 cubic centimeters. Find the dimensions of the can that has this volume and uses the least amount of material possible.

Solution

STEP 1 **Write** an equation that gives the height h of the soup can in terms of its radius r. Use the formula for the volume of a cylinder and the fact that the soup can's volume is 342 cubic centimeters.

$V = \pi r^2 h$ **Formula for volume of cylinder**

$342 = \pi r^2 h$ **Substitute 342 for V.**

$\dfrac{342}{\pi r^2} = h$ **Solve for h.**

STEP 2 **Write** a function that gives the surface area S of the soup can in terms of only its radius r.

$S = 2\pi r^2 + 2\pi r h$ **Formula for surface area of cylinder**

$= 2\pi r^2 + 2\pi r\left(\dfrac{342}{\pi r^2}\right)$ **Substitute $\dfrac{342}{\pi r^2}$ for h.**

$= 2\pi r^2 + \dfrac{684}{r}$ **Simplify.**

INTERPRET FUNCTIONS

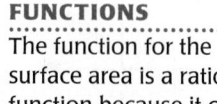

The function for the surface area is a rational function because it can be written as a quotient of polynomials:

$S = \dfrac{2\pi r^3 + 684}{r}$

STEP 3 **Graph** the function for the surface area S using a graphing calculator. Then use the *minimum* feature to find the minimum value of S.

You get a minimum value of about 271, which occurs when $r \approx 3.79$ and

$h \approx \dfrac{342}{\pi(3.79)^2} \approx 7.58$.

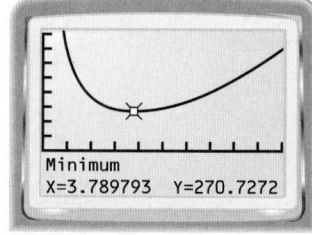

Minimum
X=3.789793 Y=270.7272

▶ So, the soup can using the least amount of material has a radius of about 3.79 centimeters and a height of about 7.58 centimeters. Notice that the height and the diameter are equal for this can.

✔ **GUIDED PRACTICE** for Example 4

5. **WHAT IF?** In Example 4, suppose the manufacturer wants to find the most efficient packaging for a soup can with a volume of 544 cubic centimeters. Find the dimensions of this can.

5.3 EXERCISES

HOMEWORK
KEY

○ = See WORKED-OUT SOLUTIONS
Exs. 7, 15, and 33

★ = STANDARDIZED TEST PRACTICE
Exs. 2, 6, 14, 24, and 35

◆ = MULTIPLE REPRESENTATIONS
Ex. 33

SKILL PRACTICE

1. **VOCABULARY** Copy and complete: The graph of a rational function f has no _?_ when the degree of the function's numerator is greater than the degree of its denominator.

2. ★ **WRITING** Let $f(x) = \dfrac{p(x)}{q(x)}$ where $p(x)$ and $q(x)$ are polynomials with no common factors other than ± 1. *Describe* how to find the x-intercepts and the vertical asymptotes of the graph of f.

EXAMPLES
1, 2, and 3
for Exs. 3–23

MATCHING GRAPHS **Match the function with its graph.**

3. $y = \dfrac{-10}{x^2 - 9}$

4. $y = \dfrac{x^2 - 10}{x^2 + 3}$

5. $y = \dfrac{x^3}{x^2 - 4}$

A.
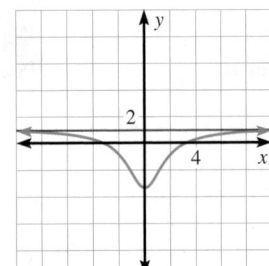

B.
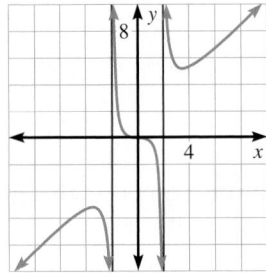

C.
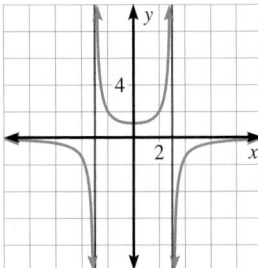

6. ★ **MULTIPLE CHOICE** The graph of which function is shown?

ⓐ $y = \dfrac{3}{x^2 - 4}$

ⓑ $y = \dfrac{3x^2}{x^2 - 4}$

ⓒ $y = \dfrac{x^2 - 4}{3x^2}$

ⓓ $y = \dfrac{x^3}{x^2 - 4}$

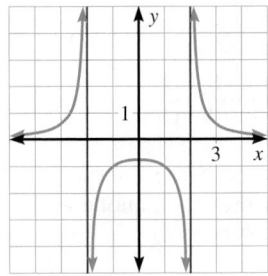

Animated Algebra at my.hrw.com

ANALYZING GRAPHS **Identify the x-intercept(s) and vertical asymptote(s) of the graph of the function.**

7. $y = \dfrac{5}{x^2 - 1}$

8. $y = \dfrac{x + 1}{x^2 + 5}$

9. $f(x) = \dfrac{x^2 + 9}{x^2 - 2x - 15}$

10. $y = \dfrac{x^2 - 7x - 60}{x + 3}$

11. $y = \dfrac{x^3 + 27}{3x^2 + x}$

12. $g(x) = \dfrac{2x^2 - 3x - 20}{x^2 + 1}$

13. **ERROR ANALYSIS** *Describe* and correct the error in finding the vertical asymptote(s) of $f(x) = \dfrac{x - 2}{x^2 - 8x + 7}$.

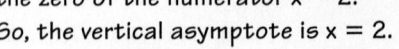

The vertical asymptote occurs at
the zero of the numerator x − 2.
So, the vertical asymptote is x = 2.

14. ★ MULTIPLE CHOICE What is the horizontal asymptote of the graph of the function $y = \dfrac{4x^2 - 21x + 5}{x^2 - 12}$?

(A) $y = 0$ **(B)** $y = \dfrac{1}{4}$ **(C)** $y = 4$ **(D)** $y = 4x$

GRAPHING FUNCTIONS Graph the function.

15. $y = \dfrac{2x}{x^2 - 1}$

16. $y = \dfrac{8}{x^2 - x - 6}$

17. $f(x) = \dfrac{x^2 - 9}{2x^2 + 1}$

18. $y = \dfrac{x - 4}{x^2 - 3x}$

19. $y = \dfrac{x^2 + 11x + 18}{2x + 1}$

20. $g(x) = \dfrac{x^3 - 8}{6 - x^2}$

21. $y = \dfrac{x^2 + 3}{2x^3}$

22. $y = \dfrac{x^2 - 5x - 36}{3x}$

23. $h(x) = \dfrac{3x^2 + 10x - 8}{x^2 + 4}$

24. ★ OPEN-ENDED MATH Write two different rational functions whose graphs have the same end behavior as the graph of $y = 3x^2$.

GRAPHING CALCULATOR Use a graphing calculator to find the range of the rational function.

25. $y = \dfrac{15}{x^2 + 2}$

26. $y = \dfrac{3x^2}{x^2 - 9}$

27. $y = \dfrac{x^2 - 2x}{2x + 3}$

CHALLENGE The graph of a function of the form $f(x) = \dfrac{a}{x^2 + b}$ is shown. Find the values of a and b.

28.
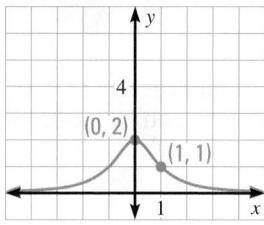

29.
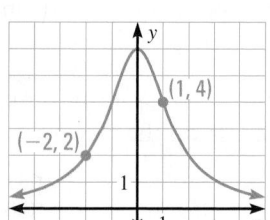

30.
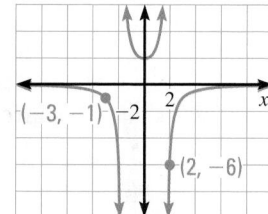

PROBLEM SOLVING

EXAMPLE 4
for Exs. 31–32

GRAPHING CALCULATOR You may wish to use a graphing calculator to complete the following Problem Solving exercises.

31. AGRICULTURE A farmer makes cylindrical bales of hay that have a volume of 100 cubic feet. Each bale is to be wrapped in plastic to keep the hay dry.

a. Using the formula for the volume of a cylinder, write an equation that gives the length ℓ of a bale in terms of the radius r.

b. Write a function that gives the surface area of a bale in terms of only the radius r.

c. Find the dimensions of a bale that has the given volume and uses the least amount of plastic possible when the bale is wrapped.

32. AQUARIUM DESIGN A manufacturer is designing an aquarium whose base is a regular hexagon. The aquarium should have a volume of 24 cubic feet and use the least amount of material possible. Let s be the length (in feet) of a side of the base, and let h be the height (in feet).

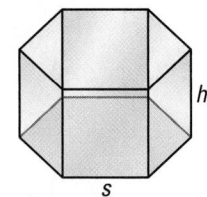

   a. Write an equation that gives h in terms of s. (*Hint:* The volume of the aquarium is given by $V = \frac{3\sqrt{3}}{2}s^2h$.)

   b. Find the dimensions s and h that minimize the amount of material used. (*Hint:* The surface area of the aquarium is given by $S = \frac{3\sqrt{3}}{2}s^2 + 6sh$.)

(33.) ◆◆ **MULTIPLE REPRESENTATIONS** The mean temperature T (in degrees Celsius) of the Atlantic Ocean between latitudes 40°N and 40°S can be modeled by

$$T = \frac{17{,}800d + 20{,}000}{3d^2 + 740d + 1000}$$

where d is the depth (in meters).

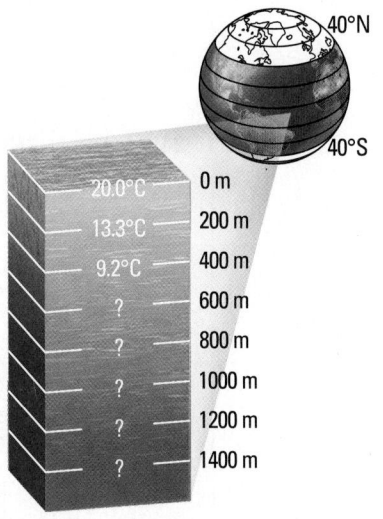

   a. Making a Table Make a table of values showing the mean temperature for depths from 1000 meters to 1300 meters in 50 meter intervals.

   b. Using a Graph Graph the model. Use your graph to estimate the depth at which the mean temperature is 4°C.

34. MULTI-STEP PROBLEM From 1993 to 2002, the number n (in billions) of shares of stock sold on the New York Stock Exchange can be modeled by

$$n = \frac{1054t + 6204}{-6.62t + 100}$$

where t is the number of years since 1993.

   a. Graph the model.

   b. *Describe* the general trends shown by the graph.

   c. Estimate the year when the number of shares of stock sold was first greater than 100 billion.

35. ★ **EXTENDED RESPONSE** The acceleration due to gravity g (in meters per second squared) changes as altitude changes and is given by the function

$$g = \frac{3.99 \times 10^{14}}{h^2 + (1.28 \times 10^7)h + (4.07 \times 10^{13})}$$

where h is the altitude (in meters) above sea level.

   a. Graph Graph the function.

   b. Apply A mountaineer is climbing to a height of 8000 meters. What is the value of g at this altitude?

   c. Apply A spacecraft reaches an altitude of 112 kilometers above Earth. What is the value of g at this altitude?

   d. Explain *Describe* what happens to the value of g as altitude increases.

This spacecraft reached an altitude of 112 km in 2004.

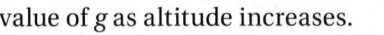

  ◯ = **See WORKED-OUT SOLUTIONS** in Student Resources   ★ = **STANDARDIZED TEST PRACTICE**   ◆ = **MULTIPLE REPRESENTATIONS**

36. CHALLENGE You need to build a cylindrical water tank using 100 cubic feet of concrete. The sides and the base of the tank must be 1 foot thick.

    a. Write an equation that gives the tank's inner height h in terms of its inner radius r.

    b. Write an equation that gives the volume V of water that the tank can hold as a function of r.

    c. Graph the equation from part (b). What values of r and h maximize the tank's capacity?

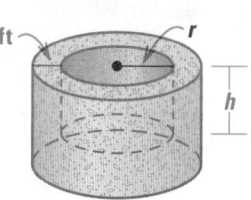

QUIZ

The variables x and y vary inversely. Use the given values to write an equation relating x and y. Then find y when $x = -4$.

  1. $x = 8, y = 3$ **2.** $x = 2, y = -9$ **3.** $x = -5, y = \dfrac{8}{3}$ **4.** $x = -\dfrac{1}{4}, y = -32$

Graph the function.

  5. $y = \dfrac{3}{2x}$ **6.** $y = \dfrac{4}{x-2} + 1$ **7.** $f(x) = \dfrac{-2x}{3x-6}$

  8. $y = \dfrac{-8}{x^2-1}$ **9.** $y = \dfrac{x^2-6}{x^2+2}$ **10.** $g(x) = \dfrac{x^3-8}{2x^2}$

11. SOFTBALL A pitcher throws 16 strikes in her first 38 pitches. The table shows how the pitcher's strike percentage changes if she throws x consecutive strikes after the first 38 pitches. Write a rational function for the strike percentage in terms of x. Graph the function. How many consecutive strikes must the pitcher throw to reach a strike percentage of 0.60?

x	Total strikes	Total pitches	Strike percentage
0	16	38	0.42
5	21	43	0.49
10	26	48	0.54
x	$x + 16$	$x + 38$	?

MATHEMATICAL PRACTICES · Make sense of problems and persevere in solving them.

1. **MULTI-STEP PROBLEM** Your family buys a photo printer to print out digital pictures. The printer costs $200. The ink and paper cost about $.60 for each photo you print.

   a. Write an equation that gives the average cost of a printed photo as a function of the number of photos printed.

   b. Graph the function from part (a). Use the graph to estimate the number of photos you have to print before the average cost drops to $10 per printed photo.

   c. What happens to the average cost as the number of photos printed increases?

2. **MULTI-STEP PROBLEM** A food manufacturer wants to find the most efficient packaging for a canister of oatmeal with a volume of 1663 cubic centimeters.

   a. Use the formula for the volume of a cylinder, $V = \pi r^2 h$, to write an equation that gives the height h of a possible canister in terms of its radius r.

   b. Write an equation that gives the canister's surface area S in terms of its radius r by substituting the expression for h from part (a) into the formula for the surface area of a cylinder, $S = 2\pi r^2 + 2\pi rh$.

   c. Graph the equation from part (b) using a graphing calculator. What are the dimensions r and h of the canister that uses the least material possible?

3. **SHORT RESPONSE** The table shows the number y of candy boxes a manufacturer sells each month at different prices x (in dollars). Do the data show inverse variation? *Explain* your reasoning.

x	5	6	7	8
y	800	667	571	500

4. **OPEN-ENDED** Write a rational function whose domain is all real numbers except $x = 2$ and $x = 3$.

5. **GRIDDED ANSWER** The variables x and y vary inversely, and $y = 4$ when $x = 5$. What is the value of y when $x = 10$?

6. **EXTENDED RESPONSE** The body mass index b of a person varies directly with the person's weight w and inversely with the square of the person's height h. A person who is 1.6 meters tall and weighs 51.2 kilograms has a body mass index of 20.

   a. Write an equation that relates b, w, and h.

   b. Use the equation from part (a) to complete the table below.

Body mass index	Height (m)	Weight (kg)
20	?	45
?	1.4	41
19	1.5	?

   c. Suppose two people weigh the same, but the height of one person is 10% greater than the height of the other person. *Compare* the body mass indices of the two people.

7. **GRIDDED ANSWER** The intensity I of a sound (in watts per square meter) varies inversely with the square of the distance d (in meters) from the source of the sound. At a distance of 1 meter from the stage, the sound intensity of a rock concert is about 10 watts per square meter. What is the intensity of the sound you hear if you are 15 meters from the stage?

8. **SHORT RESPONSE** The value M (in dollars) of a motorcycle t years after it was purchased new can be estimated using the function

$$M(t) = \frac{3500}{t} + 500 \text{ where } t \geq 1.$$

   a. Estimate the motorcycle's value 5 years after it was purchased.

   b. What does the value of the motorcycle approach as time passes? *Explain*.

5.4 Multiply and Divide Rational Expressions

Before	You graphed rational functions.
Now	You will multiply and divide rational expressions.
Why?	So you can compare the efficiencies of two designs, as in Ex. 51.

Key Vocabulary
- simplified form of a rational expression
- reciprocal

CC.9-12.A.APR.7 (+)
Understand that rational expressions form a system analogous to the rational numbers, closed under addition, subtraction, multiplication, and division by a nonzero rational expression; add, subtract, multiply, and divide rational expressions.

A rational expression is in **simplified form** if its numerator and denominator have no common factors (other than ±1). To simplify a rational expression, apply the following property.

Simplifying a rational expression usually requires two steps. First, factor the numerator and denominator. Then, divide out any factors that are common to both the numerator and denominator. Here is an example:

$$\frac{x^2 + 7x}{x^2} = \frac{\cancel{x}(x+7)}{\cancel{x} \cdot x} = \frac{x+7}{x}$$

Notice that you can divide out common factors in the second expression above. However, you cannot divide out like terms in the third expression.

EXAMPLE 1   Simplify a rational expression

Simplify: $\dfrac{x^2 - 2x - 15}{x^2 - 9}$

AVOID ERRORS
Do not divide out variable terms that are not factors.
$$\frac{x-5}{x-3} \neq \frac{-5}{-3}$$

$$\frac{x^2 - 2x - 15}{x^2 - 9} = \frac{(x+3)(x-5)}{(x+3)(x-3)}$$ Factor numerator and denominator.

$$= \frac{\cancel{(x+3)}(x-5)}{\cancel{(x+3)}(x-3)}$$ Divide out common factor.

$$= \frac{x-5}{x-3}$$ Simplified form

AP Images/Mary Ann Chastain

EFFICIENCY Manufacturers often package their products in a way that uses the least amount of packaging material. One measure of the efficiency of a package is the ratio of its surface area to its volume. The smaller the ratio, the more efficient the packaging.

EXAMPLE 2 Solve a multi-step problem

PACKAGING A company makes a tin to hold flavored popcorn. The tin is a rectangular prism with a square base. The company is designing a new tin with the same base and twice the height of the old tin.

- Find the surface area and volume of each tin.

- Calculate the ratio of surface area to volume for each tin.

- What do the ratios tell you about the efficiencies of the two tins?

Solution

	Old tin	New tin	
STEP 1	$S = 2s^2 + 4sh$	$S = 2s^2 + 4s(2h)$	Find surface area, *S*.
		$= 2s^2 + 8sh$	
	$V = s^2h$	$V = s^2(2h)$	Find volume, *V*.
		$= 2s^2h$	

STEP 2 $\dfrac{S}{V} = \dfrac{2s^2 + 4sh}{s^2h}$ $\dfrac{S}{V} = \dfrac{2s^2 + 8sh}{2s^2h}$ **Write ratio of *S* to *V*.**

$= \dfrac{\cancel{s}(2s + 4h)}{\cancel{s}(sh)}$ $= \dfrac{2\cancel{s}(s + 4h)}{2\cancel{s}(sh)}$ **Divide out common factor.**

$= \dfrac{2s + 4h}{sh}$ $= \dfrac{s + 4h}{sh}$ **Simplified form**

STEP 3 $\dfrac{2s + 4h}{sh} > \dfrac{s + 4h}{sh}$ because the left side of the inequality has a greater numerator than the right side and both have the same (positive) denominator. The ratio of surface area to volume is *greater* for the old tin than for the new tin. So, the old tin is *less* efficient than the new tin.

✓ **GUIDED PRACTICE**   for Examples 1 and 2

Simplify the expression, if possible.

1. $\dfrac{2(x + 1)}{(x + 1)(x + 3)}$

2. $\dfrac{40x + 20}{10x + 30}$

3. $\dfrac{4}{x(x + 2)}$

4. $\dfrac{x + 4}{x^2 - 16}$

5. $\dfrac{x^2 - 2x - 3}{x^2 - x - 6}$

6. $\dfrac{2x^2 + 10x}{3x^2 + 16x + 5}$

7. **WHAT IF?** In Example 2, suppose the new popcorn tin is the same height as the old tin but has a base with sides twice as long. What is the ratio of surface area to volume for this tin?

Multiplying Rational Expressions

The rule for multiplying rational expressions is the same as the rule for multiplying numerical fractions: multiply numerators, multiply denominators, and write the new fraction in simplified form.

Let a, b, c, and d be expressions with $b \neq 0$ and $d \neq 0$.

Property $\dfrac{a}{b} \cdot \dfrac{c}{d} = \dfrac{ac}{bd}$ Simplify $\dfrac{ac}{bd}$ if possible.

Example $\dfrac{5x^2}{2xy^2} \cdot \dfrac{6xy^3}{10y} = \dfrac{30x^3y^3}{20xy^3} = \dfrac{\cancel{10} \cdot 3 \cdot \cancel{x} \cdot x^2 \cdot \cancel{y^3}}{\cancel{10} \cdot 2 \cdot \cancel{x} \cdot \cancel{y^3}} = \dfrac{3x^2}{2}$

EXAMPLE 3   **Standardized Test Practice**

What is a simplified form of $\dfrac{8x^3y}{2xy^2} \cdot \dfrac{7x^4y^3}{4y}$?

(A) $\dfrac{5}{2}x^6y$ (B) $7x^6y$ (C) $7x^{11}y$ (D) $7x^7y^{4/3}$

ANOTHER WAY

In Example 3, you can also first simplify each fraction, then multiply, and finally simplify the result:

$\dfrac{8x^3y}{2xy^2} \cdot \dfrac{7x^4y^3}{4y}$

$= \dfrac{4x^2}{y} \cdot \dfrac{7x^4y^2}{4}$

$= \dfrac{\cancel{4} \cdot 7 \cdot x^6 \cdot \cancel{y} \cdot y}{\cancel{4} \cdot \cancel{y}}$

$= 7x^6y$

Solution

$\dfrac{8x^3y}{2xy^2} \cdot \dfrac{7x^4y^3}{4y} = \dfrac{56x^7y^4}{8xy^3}$ **Multiply numerators and denominators.**

$= \dfrac{\cancel{8} \cdot 7 \cdot x \cdot x^6 \cdot \cancel{y^3} \cdot y}{\cancel{8} \cdot \cancel{x} \cdot \cancel{y^3}}$ **Factor and divide out common factors.**

$= 7x^6y$ **Simplified form**

▶ The correct answer is B.   (A) (B) (C) (D)

EXAMPLE 4   **Multiply rational expressions**

Multiply: $\dfrac{3x - 3x^2}{x^2 + 4x - 5} \cdot \dfrac{x^2 + x - 20}{3x}$

$\dfrac{3x - 3x^2}{x^2 + 4x - 5} \cdot \dfrac{x^2 + x - 20}{3x} = \dfrac{3x(1 - x)}{(x - 1)(x + 5)} \cdot \dfrac{(x + 5)(x - 4)}{3x}$ **Factor numerators and denominators.**

$= \dfrac{3x(1 - x)(x + 5)(x - 4)}{(x - 1)(x + 5)(3x)}$ **Multiply numerators and denominators.**

$= \dfrac{3x(-1)(x - 1)(x + 5)(x - 4)}{(x - 1)(x + 5)(3x)}$ **Rewrite $1 - x$ as $(-1)(x - 1)$.**

$= \dfrac{\cancel{3x}(-1)\cancel{(x - 1)}\cancel{(x + 5)}(x - 4)}{\cancel{(x - 1)}\cancel{(x + 5)}\cancel{(3x)}}$ **Divide out common factors.**

$= (-1)(x - 4)$ **Simplify.**

$= -x + 4$ **Multiply.**

EXAMPLE 5 Multiply a rational expression by a polynomial

Multiply: $\dfrac{x+2}{x^3-27} \cdot (x^2+3x+9)$

$$\dfrac{x+2}{x^3-27} \cdot (x^2+3x+9) = \dfrac{x+2}{x^3-27} \cdot \dfrac{x^2+3x+9}{1}$$ Write polynomial as a rational expression.

$$= \dfrac{(x+2)(x^2+3x+9)}{(x-3)(x^2+3x+9)}$$ Factor denominator.

$$= \dfrac{(x+2)\cancel{(x^2+3x+9)}}{(x-3)\cancel{(x^2+3x+9)}}$$ Divide out common factors.

$$= \dfrac{x+2}{x-3}$$ Simplified form

✔ **GUIDED PRACTICE**   for Examples 3, 4, and 5

Multiply the expressions. Simplify the result.

8. $\dfrac{3x^5y^2}{8xy} \cdot \dfrac{6xy^2}{9x^3y}$

9. $\dfrac{2x^2-10x}{x^2-25} \cdot \dfrac{x+3}{2x^2}$

10. $\dfrac{x+5}{x^3-1} \cdot (x^2+x+1)$

KEY CONCEPT   *For Your Notebook*

Dividing Rational Expressions

To divide one rational expression by another, multiply the first rational expression by the reciprocal of the second rational expression.

Let a, b, c, and d be expressions with $b \neq 0$, $c \neq 0$ and $d \neq 0$.

Property $\dfrac{a}{b} \div \dfrac{c}{d} = \dfrac{a}{b} \cdot \dfrac{d}{c} = \dfrac{ad}{bc}$ Simplify $\dfrac{ad}{bc}$ if possible.

Examples $\dfrac{2}{5} \div \dfrac{7}{3} = \dfrac{2}{5} \cdot \dfrac{3}{7} = \dfrac{6}{35}$

$$\dfrac{7}{x+1} \div \dfrac{x+2}{2x-3} = \dfrac{7}{x+1} \cdot \dfrac{2x-3}{x+2} = \dfrac{7(2x-3)}{(x+1)(x+2)}$$

EXAMPLE 6 Divide rational expressions

Divide: $\dfrac{7x}{2x-10} \div \dfrac{x^2-6x}{x^2-11x+30}$

$$\dfrac{7x}{2x-10} \div \dfrac{x^2-6x}{x^2-11x+30} = \dfrac{7x}{2x-10} \cdot \dfrac{x^2-11x+30}{x^2-6x}$$ Multiply by reciprocal.

$$= \dfrac{7x}{2(x-5)} \cdot \dfrac{(x-5)(x-6)}{x(x-6)}$$ Factor.

$$= \dfrac{7\cancel{x}\cancel{(x-5)}\cancel{(x-6)}}{2\cancel{(x-5)}\cancel{(x)}\cancel{(x-6)}}$$ Divide out common factors.

$$= \dfrac{7}{2}$$ Simplified form

EXAMPLE 7 Divide a rational expression by a polynomial

Divide: $\dfrac{6x^2 + x - 15}{4x^2} \div (3x^2 + 5x)$

$\dfrac{6x^2 + x - 15}{4x^2} \div (3x^2 + 5x) = \dfrac{6x^2 + x - 15}{4x^2} \cdot \dfrac{1}{3x^2 + 5x}$ Multiply by reciprocal.

$= \dfrac{(3x + 5)(2x - 3)}{4x^2} \cdot \dfrac{1}{x(3x + 5)}$ Factor.

$= \dfrac{(3x + 5)(2x - 3)}{4x^2(x)(3x + 5)}$ Divide out common factors.

$= \dfrac{2x - 3}{4x^3}$ Simplified form

✔ **GUIDED PRACTICE** for Examples 6 and 7

Divide the expressions. Simplify the result.

11. $\dfrac{4x}{5x - 20} \div \dfrac{x^2 - 2x}{x^2 - 6x + 8}$

12. $\dfrac{2x^2 + 3x - 5}{6x} \div (2x^2 + 5x)$

5.4 EXERCISES

HOMEWORK KEY

◯ = See WORKED-OUT SOLUTIONS
Exs. 7, 25, and 49

★ = STANDARDIZED TEST PRACTICE
Exs. 2, 20, 23, 50, and 52

SKILL PRACTICE

1. VOCABULARY Copy and complete: To divide one rational expression by another, multiply the first rational expression by the __?__ of the second rational expression.

2. ★ WRITING How do you know when a rational expression is simplified?

EXAMPLE 1
for Exs. 3–20

REASONING Match the rational expression with its simplified form.

3. $\dfrac{x^2 - 9x + 14}{x^2 - 5x - 14}$

4. $\dfrac{x^2 - 4}{x^2 + 9x + 14}$

5. $\dfrac{x^2 + 5x - 14}{x^2 - 4x + 4}$

A. $\dfrac{x - 2}{x + 7}$

B. $\dfrac{x - 2}{x + 2}$

C. $\dfrac{x + 7}{x - 2}$

SIMPLIFYING Simplify the rational expression, if possible.

6. $\dfrac{4x^2}{20x^2 - 12x}$

7. $\dfrac{x^2 - x - 20}{x^2 + 2x - 15}$

8. $\dfrac{x^2 + 2x - 24}{x^2 + 7x + 6}$

9. $\dfrac{x^2 - 11x + 24}{x^2 - 3x - 40}$

10. $\dfrac{x^2 + 4x + 4}{x^2 - 5x + 4}$

11. $\dfrac{2x^2 + 2x - 4}{x^2 - 5x - 14}$

12. $\dfrac{x - 4}{x^3 - 64}$

13. $\dfrac{x^2 - 36}{x^2 + 12x + 36}$

14. $\dfrac{3x^3 + 6x^2 + 12x}{x^3 - 8}$

15. $\dfrac{8x^2 + 10x - 3}{6x^2 + 13x + 6}$

16. $\dfrac{5x^2 + 18x - 8}{10x^2 - x - 2}$

17. $\dfrac{x^3 - 5x^2 - 3x + 15}{x^2 - 8x + 15}$

ERROR ANALYSIS *Describe* and correct the error in simplifying the rational expression.

18.
$$\frac{\cancel{x^2} + 16x - 80}{+ 5\,\cancel{x^2} - 16} = \frac{16x - 80}{-16} = -x$$ ✗

19.
$$\frac{x^2 + \overset{2}{16}x + \overset{3}{48}}{x^2 + \underset{1}{8}x + \underset{1}{16}} = \frac{x^2 + 2x + 3}{x^2 + x + 1}$$ ✗

20. ★ **MULTIPLE CHOICE** Which rational expression is in simplified form?

Ⓐ $\dfrac{x^2 - x - 6}{x^2 + 3x + 2}$ Ⓑ $\dfrac{x^2 + 6x + 8}{x^2 + 2x - 3}$ Ⓒ $\dfrac{x^2 - 6x + 9}{x^2 - 2x - 3}$ Ⓓ $\dfrac{x^2 + 3x - 4}{x^2 + x - 2}$

EXAMPLE 2
for Exs. 21–23

GEOMETRY A farmer wants to fence in the field shown. Write a simplified rational expression for the ratio of the field's perimeter to its area.

21.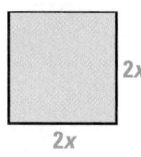
$2x$
$2x$

22.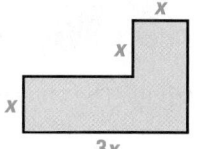
x
x
x
$3x$

23. ★ **SHORT RESPONSE** Which of the fields in Exercises 21 and 22 has the lower fencing cost per unit of area? *Explain.*

EXAMPLES 3, 4, and 5
for Exs. 24–33

MULTIPLYING Multiply the expressions. Simplify the result.

24. $\dfrac{5x^3y}{x^2y^2} \cdot \dfrac{y^3}{15x^2}$

25. $\dfrac{48x^5y^3}{y^4} \cdot \dfrac{x^2y}{6x^3y^2}$

26. $\dfrac{x(x-3)}{x-2} \cdot \dfrac{(x+3)(x-2)}{x}$

27. $\dfrac{4(x+5)}{x^2} \cdot \dfrac{x(x+1)}{2(x+5)}$

28. $\dfrac{3x-12}{x+5} \cdot \dfrac{x+6}{2x-8}$

29. $\dfrac{x+5}{4x-16} \cdot \dfrac{2x^2-32}{x^2-25}$

30. $\dfrac{x^2+3x-4}{x^2+4x+4} \cdot \dfrac{2x^2+4x}{x^2-4x+3}$

31. $\dfrac{x^2-3x-10}{x^2-2x-15} \cdot (x^2+10x+21)$

32. $\dfrac{x^2+5x-36}{x^2-49} \cdot (x^2-11x+28)$

33. $\dfrac{4x^2+20x}{x^3+4x^2} \cdot (x^2+8x+16)$

EXAMPLES 6 and 7
for Exs. 34–43

DIVIDING Divide the expressions. Simplify the result.

34. $\dfrac{5x^2y^3}{x^7} \div \dfrac{30xy^4}{y^3}$

35. $\dfrac{8x^2y^2z}{xz^3} \div \dfrac{10xy}{x^4z}$

36. $\dfrac{(x+3)(x-2)}{x(x+1)} \div \dfrac{x+3}{x}$

37. $\dfrac{8x^2}{x+4} \div \dfrac{x}{2(x-4)}$

38. $\dfrac{x^2-6x-27}{2x^2+2x} \div \dfrac{x^2-14x+45}{x^2}$

39. $\dfrac{x^2-4x-5}{x+5} \div (x^2+6x+5)$

40. $\dfrac{3x^2+13x+4}{x^2-4} \div \dfrac{4x+16}{x+2}$

41. $\dfrac{x^2-x-2}{x^2+4x-5} \div \dfrac{x-2}{5x+25}$

42. $\dfrac{x^2-8x+15}{x^2+4x} \div (x^2-x-20)$

43. $\dfrac{x^2+12x+32}{6x+42} \div \dfrac{x^2+4x}{x^2-49}$

○ = **See WORKED-OUT SOLUTIONS** in Student Resources   ★ = **STANDARDIZED TEST PRACTICE**

POINT DISCONTINUITY In Exercises 44–46, use the following information.

The graph of a rational function can have a hole in it, called a *point discontinuity*, where the function is undefined. An example is shown below.

$$y = \frac{x^2 - 16}{x + 4} = \frac{(x + 4)(x - 4)}{x + 4} = x - 4$$

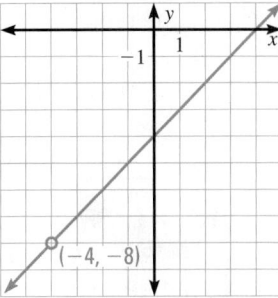

The graph of $y = \frac{x^2 - 16}{x + 4}$ is the same as the graph of $y = x - 4$ except that there is a hole at $(-4, -8)$ because the rational function is not defined when $x = -4$.

Graph the rational function. Use an open circle for a point discontinuity.

44. $y = \frac{x^2 + 10x + 21}{x + 3}$

45. $y = \frac{x^2 - 36}{x - 6}$

46. $y = \frac{2x^2 - x - 10}{x + 2}$

47. CHALLENGE Find the ratio of the perimeter to the area of the triangle shown at the right.

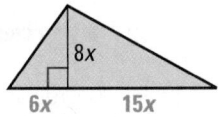

PROBLEM SOLVING

EXAMPLE 2
for Exs. 48,
50–52

48. ⬛ **GEOMETRY** Find the ratio of the volume of the square pyramid to the volume of the inscribed cone. Write your answer in simplified form.

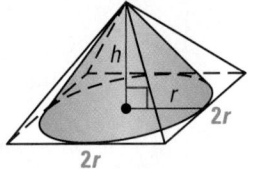

49. **ENTERTAINMENT** From 1992 to 2002, the gross ticket sales S (in millions of dollars) to Broadway shows and the total attendance A (in millions) at the shows can be modeled by

$$S = \frac{-6420t + 292,000}{6.02t^2 - 125t + 1000} \quad \text{and} \quad A = \frac{-407t + 7220}{5.92t^2 - 131t + 1000}$$

where t is the number of years since 1992. Write a model for the *average* dollar amount a person paid per ticket as a function of the year. What was the average amount a person paid per ticket in 1999?

50. ★ **SHORT RESPONSE** Almost all of the energy generated by a long-distance runner is released in the form of heat. For a runner with height H and speed V, the rate h_g of heat generated and the rate h_r of heat released can be modeled by $h_g = k_1 H^3 V^2$ and $h_r = k_2 H^2$ where k_1 and k_2 are constants.

a. Write the ratio of heat generated to heat released. Simplify the expression.

b. When the ratio of heat generated to heat released equals 1, how is speed related to height? Does a taller or shorter runner have the advantage? *Explain.*

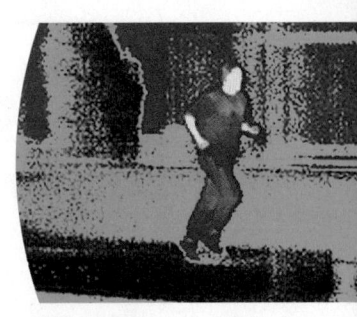

Thermogram of runner

51. MULTI-STEP PROBLEM A manufacturer is comparing two designs for a water tower: a sphere and a cylinder. Both designs have the same volume and the same radius.

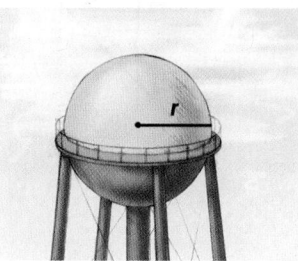 

a. Show that the height h of the cylindrical tank is $\frac{4}{3}r$.

b. Write an expression for the surface area of each tank in terms of r.

c. Find the ratio of the surface area of the spherical tank to the surface area of the cylindrical tank. *Explain* what the ratio tells you about which water tower would take less material to build.

52. ★ EXTENDED RESPONSE The surface area S and the volume V of a cylindrical can are given by $S = 2\pi r^2 + 2\pi rh$ and $V = \pi r^2 h$ where r is the radius and h is the height.

a. Model Write and simplify an expression for the efficiency ratio $\frac{S}{V}$.

b. Calculate Find the efficiency ratio for each can listed in the table.

	Soup can	Coffee can	Paint can
Height, h	10.2 cm	15.9 cm	19.4 cm
Radius, r	3.4 cm	7.8 cm	8.4 cm

c. Compare Rank the three cans in part (b) according to efficiency. *Explain* your ranking.

53. CHALLENGE A fuel storage container is shaped like a cylinder with a hemisphere on each end, as shown. The length of the cylinder is ℓ and the radius of each hemisphere is r. Show that the ratio of the surface area to the volume of the container is $\dfrac{6(2r + \ell)}{r(4r + 3\ell)}$.

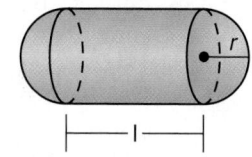

Verify Operations with Rational Expressions

MATHEMATICAL PRACTICES
Use appropriate tools strategically.

QUESTION How can you use a graphing calculator to verify the results of operations on rational expressions?

EXAMPLE Check a simplified rational expression in two ways

Simplify $\dfrac{x^2 - x - 12}{x^2 - 9x + 20}$. Then verify the result numerically and graphically.

STEP 1 *Simplify expression*

Simplify the rational expression by factoring the numerator and denominator, then dividing out common factors.

$$\frac{x^2 - x - 12}{x^2 - 9x + 20} = \frac{(x - 4)(x + 3)}{(x - 4)(x - 5)} = \frac{x + 3}{x - 5}$$

STEP 2 *Enter expressions*

Enter the original expression as y_1 and the simplified result as y_2. Use the *thick* graph style for y_2.

STEP 3 *Display table*

Use the *table* feature to examine corresponding values of the two expressions.

STEP 4 *Display graphs*

Put your calculator in *connected* mode. Display the graphs in an appropriate viewing window.

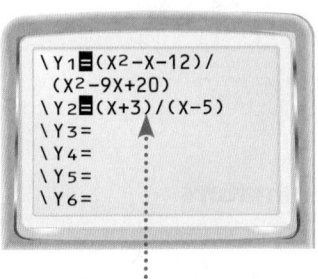

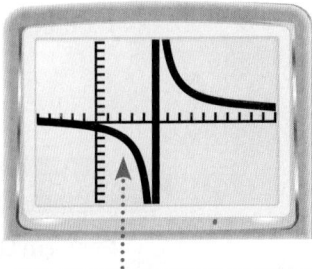

Remember to use parentheses correctly.

The values of y_1 and y_2 are the same, except that y_1 is undefined when $x = 4$ and $x = 5$, and y_2 is undefined only when $x = 5$.

By using the *thick* graph style for y_2, you can see the graph of y_2 being drawn over the graph of y_1. So, the graphs coincide.

PRACTICE

Simplify the expression. Verify your result numerically and graphically.

1. $\dfrac{x^2 - 5x}{x^2 - 7x + 10}$

2. $\dfrac{3x^2 + 6x}{x^2 - 2x - 8}$

3. $\dfrac{x^2 + 5x + 4}{x^2 + x - 12}$

Perform the indicated operation and simplify. Verify your result numerically and graphically.

4. $\dfrac{x + 3}{5x^2} \cdot \dfrac{x - 1}{x + 3}$

5. $\dfrac{4x^2 - 8x}{5x + 15} \div \dfrac{x - 2}{x + 3}$

6. $\dfrac{x^2 - 3x - 10}{x^2 + 3x + 3} \cdot \dfrac{x^2 + 2x - 3}{x^2 + x - 2}$

5.5 Add and Subtract Rational Expressions

Before	You multiplied and divided rational expressions.
Now	You will add and subtract rational expressions.
Why?	So you can determine monthly car loan payments, as in Ex. 43.

Key Vocabulary
• complex fraction

As with numerical fractions, the procedure used to add (or subtract) two rational expressions depends upon whether the expressions have *like* or *unlike* denominators.

CC.9-12.A.APR.7 (+)
Understand that rational expressions form a system analogous to the rational numbers, closed under addition, subtraction, multiplication, and division by a nonzero rational expression; add, subtract, multiply, and divide rational expressions.

KEY CONCEPT
For Your Notebook

Adding or Subtracting with Like Denominators

To add (or subtract) rational expressions with *like* denominators, simply add (or subtract) their numerators. Then place the result over the common denominator.

Let a, b, and c be expressions with $c \neq 0$.

	Addition	**Subtraction**
Properties	$\dfrac{a}{c} + \dfrac{b}{c} = \dfrac{a+b}{c}$	$\dfrac{a}{c} - \dfrac{b}{c} = \dfrac{a-b}{c}$
Examples	$\dfrac{3x}{5x^2} + \dfrac{7}{5x^2} = \dfrac{3x+7}{5x^2}$	$\dfrac{9x^3}{x+1} - \dfrac{x^2}{x+1} = \dfrac{9x^3 - x^2}{x+1}$

EXAMPLE 1 Add or subtract with like denominators

Perform the indicated operation.

a. $\dfrac{7}{4x} + \dfrac{3}{4x}$

b. $\dfrac{2x}{x+6} - \dfrac{5}{x+6}$

Solution

a. $\dfrac{7}{4x} + \dfrac{3}{4x} = \dfrac{7+3}{4x} = \dfrac{10}{4x} = \dfrac{5}{2x}$ Add numerators and simplify result.

b. $\dfrac{2x}{x+6} - \dfrac{5}{x+6} = \dfrac{2x-5}{x+6}$ Subtract numerators.

✓ **GUIDED PRACTICE** for Example 1

Perform the indicated operation and simplify.

1. $\dfrac{7}{12x} - \dfrac{5}{12x}$

2. $\dfrac{2}{3x^2} + \dfrac{1}{3x^2}$

3. $\dfrac{4x}{x-2} - \dfrac{x}{x-2}$

4. $\dfrac{2x^2}{x^2+1} + \dfrac{2}{x^2+1}$

Luca DiCecco/Alamy

Adding or Subtracting with Unlike Denominators

To add (or subtract) two rational expressions with *unlike* denominators, find a common denominator. Rewrite each rational expression using the common denominator. Then add (or subtract).

Let *a*, *b*, *c*, and *d* be expressions with $c \neq 0$ and $d \neq 0$.

Addition

$$\frac{a}{c} + \frac{b}{d} = \frac{ad}{cd} + \frac{bc}{cd} = \frac{ad + bc}{cd}$$

Subtraction

$$\frac{a}{c} - \frac{b}{d} = \frac{ad}{cd} - \frac{bc}{cd} = \frac{ad - bc}{cd}$$

You can always find a common denominator of two rational expressions by multiplying their denominators, as shown above. However, if you use the least common denominator (LCD), which is the least common multiple (LCM) of the denominators, you may have less simplifying to do.

EXAMPLE 2 **Find a least common multiple (LCM)**

Find the least common multiple of $4x^2 - 16$ and $6x^2 - 24x + 24$.

Solution

STEP 1 **Factor** each polynomial. Write numerical factors as products of primes.

$$4x^2 - 16 = 4(x^2 - 4) = (2^2)(x + 2)(x - 2)$$
$$6x^2 - 24x + 24 = 6(x^2 - 4x + 4) = (2)(3)(x - 2)^2$$

STEP 2 **Form** the LCM by writing each factor to the highest power it occurs in either polynomial.

$$\text{LCM} = (2^2)(3)(x + 2)(x - 2)^2 = 12(x + 2)(x - 2)^2$$

EXAMPLE 3 **Add with unlike denominators**

Add: $\dfrac{7}{9x^2} + \dfrac{x}{3x^2 + 3x}$

Solution

To find the LCD, factor each denominator and write each factor to the highest power it occurs. Note that $9x^2 = 3^2x^2$ and $3x^2 + 3x = 3x(x + 1)$, so the LCD is $3^2x^2(x + 1) = 9x^2(x + 1)$.

$$\frac{7}{9x^2} + \frac{x}{3x^2 + 3x} = \frac{7}{9x^2} + \frac{x}{3x(x + 1)} \qquad \text{Factor second denominator.}$$

$$= \frac{7}{9x^2} \cdot \frac{x + 1}{x + 1} + \frac{x}{3x(x + 1)} \cdot \frac{3x}{3x} \qquad \text{LCD is } 9x^2(x + 1).$$

$$= \frac{7x + 7}{9x^2(x + 1)} + \frac{3x^2}{9x^2(x + 1)} \qquad \text{Multiply.}$$

$$= \frac{3x^2 + 7x + 7}{9x^2(x + 1)} \qquad \text{Add numerators.}$$

EXAMPLE 4 **Subtract with unlike denominators**

Subtract: $\dfrac{x+2}{2x-2} - \dfrac{-2x-1}{x^2-4x+3}$

Solution

$\dfrac{x+2}{2x-2} - \dfrac{-2x-1}{x^2-4x+3}$

$= \dfrac{x+2}{2(x-1)} - \dfrac{-2x-1}{(x-1)(x-3)}$ Factor denominators.

$= \dfrac{x+2}{2(x-1)} \cdot \dfrac{x-3}{x-3} - \dfrac{-2x-1}{(x-1)(x-3)} \cdot \dfrac{2}{2}$ LCD is $2(x-1)(x-3)$.

$= \dfrac{x^2-x-6}{2(x-1)(x-3)} - \dfrac{-4x-2}{2(x-1)(x-3)}$ Multiply.

$= \dfrac{x^2-x-6-(-4x-2)}{2(x-1)(x-3)}$ Subtract numerators.

$= \dfrac{x^2+3x-4}{2(x-1)(x-3)}$ Simplify numerator.

$= \dfrac{(x-1)(x+4)}{2(x-1)(x-3)}$ Factor numerator. Divide out common factor.

$= \dfrac{x+4}{2(x-3)}$ Simplify.

AVOID ERRORS

After you simplify the numerator, check to see if the numerator has a factor in common with the denominator. If so, the expression can be simplified further.

✓ **GUIDED PRACTICE**   for Examples 2, 3, and 4

Find the least common multiple of the polynomials.

5. $5x^3$ and $10x^2 - 15x$

6. $8x - 16$ and $12x^2 + 12x - 72$

Perform the indicated operation and simplify.

7. $\dfrac{3}{4x} - \dfrac{1}{7}$

8. $\dfrac{1}{3x^2} + \dfrac{x}{9x^2 - 12x}$

9. $\dfrac{x}{x^2-x-12} + \dfrac{5}{12x-48}$

10. $\dfrac{x+1}{x^2+4x+4} - \dfrac{6}{x^2-4}$

KEY CONCEPT   *For Your Notebook*

Simplifying Complex Fractions

A **complex fraction** is a fraction that contains a fraction in its numerator or denominator. A complex fraction can be simplified using either of the methods below.

Method 1: If necessary, simplify the numerator and denominator by writing each as a single fraction. Then divide the numerator by the denominator.

Method 2: Multiply the numerator and the denominator by the least common denominator (LCD) of *every* fraction in the numerator and denominator. Then simplify.

EXAMPLE 5 **Simplify a complex fraction (Method 1)**

PHYSICS Let f be the focal length of a thin camera lens, p be the distance between an object being photographed and the lens, and q be the distance between the lens and the film. For the photograph to be in focus, the variables should satisfy the *lens equation* below. Simplify the complex fraction.

$$\text{Lens equation: } f = \cfrac{1}{\dfrac{1}{p} + \dfrac{1}{q}}$$

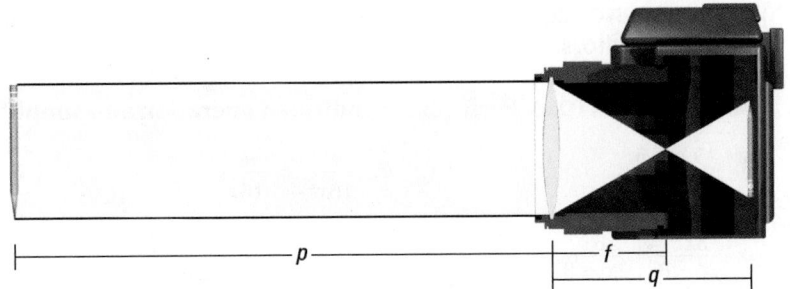

Solution

$$f = \cfrac{1}{\dfrac{1}{p} + \dfrac{1}{q}} = \cfrac{1}{\dfrac{q}{pq} + \dfrac{p}{pq}} = \cfrac{1}{\dfrac{q+p}{pq}} \qquad \text{Write denominator as a single fraction.}$$

$$= \frac{pq}{q+p} \qquad \text{Divide numerator by denominator.}$$

EXAMPLE 6 **Simplify a complex fraction (Method 2)**

Simplify: $\cfrac{\dfrac{5}{x+4}}{\dfrac{1}{x+4} + \dfrac{2}{x}}$

Solution

The LCD of all the fractions in the numerator and denominator is $x(x + 4)$.

$$\cfrac{\dfrac{5}{x+4}}{\dfrac{1}{x+4} + \dfrac{2}{x}} = \cfrac{\dfrac{5}{x+4}}{\dfrac{1}{x+4} + \dfrac{2}{x}} \cdot \frac{x(x+4)}{x(x+4)} \qquad \begin{array}{l}\text{Multiply numerator and}\\ \text{denominator by the LCD.}\end{array}$$

$$= \frac{5x}{x + 2(x+4)} \qquad \text{Simplify.}$$

$$= \frac{5x}{3x + 8} \qquad \text{Simplify.}$$

 GUIDED PRACTICE for Examples 5 and 6

Simplify the complex fraction.

11. $\cfrac{\dfrac{x}{6} - \dfrac{x}{3}}{\dfrac{x}{5} - \dfrac{7}{10}}$

12. $\cfrac{\dfrac{2}{x} - 4}{\dfrac{2}{x} + 3}$

13. $\cfrac{\dfrac{3}{x+5}}{\dfrac{2}{x-3} + \dfrac{1}{x+5}}$

5.5 EXERCISES

HOMEWORK
KEY

○ = See WORKED-OUT SOLUTIONS
Exs. 5, 17, and 43

★ = STANDARDIZED TEST PRACTICE
Exs. 2, 15, 26, 37, and 44

SKILL PRACTICE

1. **VOCABULARY** Copy and complete: A fraction that contains a fraction in its numerator or denominator is called a(n) __?__ .

2. ★ **WRITING** *Explain* how to add rational expressions with unlike denominators.

EXAMPLE 1
for Exs. 3–8

LIKE DENOMINATORS Perform the indicated operation and simplify.

3. $\dfrac{15}{4x} + \dfrac{5}{4x}$

4. $\dfrac{x}{16x^2} - \dfrac{4}{16x^2}$

5. $\dfrac{9}{x+1} - \dfrac{2x}{x+1}$

6. $\dfrac{3x^2}{x-8} + \dfrac{6x}{x-8}$

7. $\dfrac{5x}{x+3} + \dfrac{15}{x+3}$

8. $\dfrac{4x^2}{2x-1} - \dfrac{1}{2x-1}$

EXAMPLE 2
for Exs. 9–15

FINDING LCMS Find the least common multiple of the polynomials.

9. $3x$ and $3(x-2)$

10. $2x^2$ and $4x + 12$

11. $2x$ and $2x(x-5)$

12. $24x^2$ and $8x^2 - 16x$

13. $x^2 - 25$, x, and $x - 5$

14. $9x^2 - 16$ and $3x^2 - 2x - 8$

15. ★ **MULTIPLE CHOICE** What is the least common multiple of the polynomials $3x^2 - 9x$ and $6x^2$?

Ⓐ $3x(x-3)$ Ⓑ $6x^2$ Ⓒ $6x(x-3)$ Ⓓ $6x^2(x-3)$

EXAMPLES 3 and 4
for Exs. 16–26

UNLIKE DENOMINATORS Perform the indicated operation and simplify.

16. $\dfrac{12}{5x} + \dfrac{7}{6x}$

17. $\dfrac{8}{3x^2} - \dfrac{5}{4x}$

18. $\dfrac{x-4}{5x} - \dfrac{12}{5(x-4)}$

19. $\dfrac{12}{x^2 + 5x - 24} + \dfrac{3}{x-3}$

20. $\dfrac{3}{x+4} - \dfrac{1}{x+6}$

21. $\dfrac{9}{x-3} + \dfrac{2x}{x+1}$

22. $\dfrac{x+4}{x^2-4} - \dfrac{15}{x-2}$

23. $\dfrac{-15x}{x^2 - 8x + 16} + \dfrac{12}{x-4}$

24. $\dfrac{x^2 - 5}{x^2 + 5x - 14} - \dfrac{x+3}{x+7}$

25. **ERROR ANALYSIS** *Describe* and correct the error in adding the rational expressions.

$$\dfrac{x}{x+2} + \dfrac{4}{x-5} = \dfrac{x+4}{(x+2)(x-5)} \quad ✗$$

26. ★ **MULTIPLE CHOICE** Which expression is equivalent to $\dfrac{2x}{x+4} - \dfrac{x^2+4}{x^2-16}$?

Ⓐ $\dfrac{1}{x+4}$ Ⓑ $\dfrac{(x+2)(x-2)}{(x+4)(x-4)}$ Ⓒ $\dfrac{x^2 - 8x - 4}{(x+4)(x-4)}$ Ⓓ $\dfrac{3x^2 - 8x + 4}{(x+4)(x-4)}$

UNLIKE DENOMINATORS Perform the indicated operation(s) and simplify.

27. $\dfrac{x}{x^2-9} + \dfrac{x+1}{x^2 + 6x + 9}$

28. $\dfrac{x+3}{x^2 - 2x - 8} - \dfrac{x-5}{x^2 - 12x + 32}$

29. $\dfrac{x+2}{x-4} + \dfrac{2}{x} + \dfrac{5x}{3x-1}$

30. $\dfrac{x+3}{x^2 - 25} - \dfrac{x-1}{x-5} + \dfrac{3}{x+3}$

SIMPLIFYING COMPLEX FRACTIONS **Simplify the complex fraction.**

31. $\dfrac{\dfrac{x}{3} - 6}{10 + \dfrac{4}{x}}$

32. $\dfrac{15 - \dfrac{2}{x}}{\dfrac{x}{5} + 4}$

33. $\dfrac{\dfrac{16}{x - 2}}{\dfrac{4}{x + 1} + \dfrac{6}{x}}$

34. $\dfrac{\dfrac{1}{2x - 5} - \dfrac{7}{8x - 20}}{\dfrac{x}{2x - 5}}$

35. $\dfrac{\dfrac{3}{x - 2} - \dfrac{6}{x^2 - 4}}{\dfrac{3}{x + 2} + \dfrac{1}{x - 2}}$

36. $\dfrac{\dfrac{1}{3x^2 - 3}}{\dfrac{5}{x + 1} - \dfrac{x + 4}{x^2 - 3x - 4}}$

37. ★ **OPEN-ENDED MATH** Write two different complex fractions that each simplify to $\dfrac{x - 3}{x + 4}$.

CHALLENGE **Simplify the complex fraction.**

38. $\dfrac{\dfrac{1}{x} - \dfrac{x}{x^{-1} + 1}}{\dfrac{5}{x}}$

39. $\dfrac{\dfrac{3 - 2x}{x^3}}{\dfrac{2}{x^2} - \dfrac{1}{x^3 + x^2}}$

40. $\dfrac{3x^{-2} + (2x - 1)^{-1}}{\dfrac{6}{x^{-1} + 2} + 3x^{-1}}$

PROBLEM SOLVING

EXAMPLE 3
for Ex. 41

41. **JET STREAM** The total time T (in hours) needed to fly from New York to Los Angeles and back (ignoring layovers) can be modeled by the equation in the diagram, where d is the distance each way (in miles), a is the average airplane speed (in miles per hour), and j is the average speed of the jet stream (in miles per hour).

$$T = \frac{d}{a - j} + \frac{d}{a + j}$$

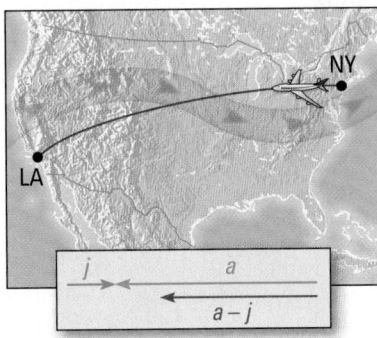

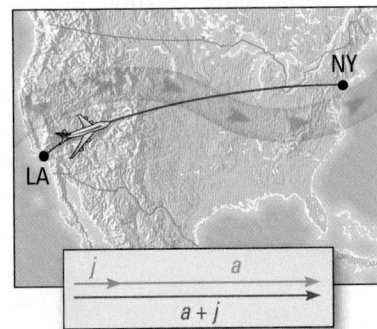

Rewrite the equation so that the right side is simplified. Then find the total time if $d = 2468$ miles, $a = 510$ mi/h, and $j = 115$ mi/h.

Animated Algebra at my.hrw.com

42. **ELECTRONICS** If two resistors in a parallel circuit have resistances R_1 and R_2 (both in ohms), then the total resistance R_t (in ohms) is given by the equation shown. Simplify the complex fraction. Then find the total resistance if $R_1 = 2000$ ohms and $R_2 = 5600$ ohms.

$$R_t = \frac{1}{\dfrac{1}{R_1} + \dfrac{1}{R_2}}$$

43. **CAR LOANS** If you borrow P dollars to buy a car and agree to repay the loan over t years at a monthly interest rate of i (expressed as a decimal), then your monthly payment M is given by either formula below.

Formula 1: $M = \dfrac{Pi}{1 - \left(\dfrac{1}{1+i}\right)^{12t}}$ **Formula 2:** $M = \dfrac{Pi(1+i)^{12t}}{(1+i)^{12t} - 1}$

  a. Show that the formulas are equivalent by simplifying the first formula.

  b. Find your monthly payment if you borrow $15,500 at a monthly interest rate of 0.5% and repay the loan over 4 years.

44. ★ **EXTENDED RESPONSE** The amount A (in milligrams) of aspirin in a person's bloodstream can be modeled by

$$A = \frac{391t^2 + 0.112}{0.218t^4 + 0.991t^2 + 1}$$

where t is the time (in hours) after one dose is taken.

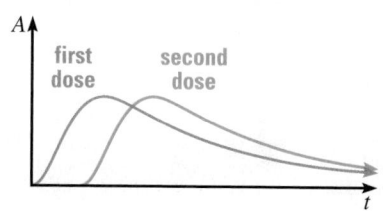
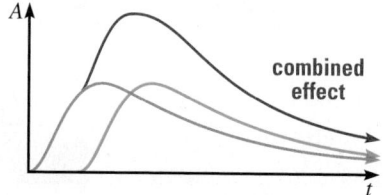

  a. Graph the equation using a graphing calculator.

  b. A second dose of the drug is taken 1 hour after the first dose. Write an equation to model the amount of the second dose in the bloodstream.

  c. Write and graph a model for the *total* amount of aspirin in the bloodstream after the second dose is taken.

  d. About how long after the second dose has been taken is the greatest amount of aspirin in the bloodstream?

45. **CHALLENGE** Find the next two expressions in the pattern shown. Then simplify all five expressions. What value do the expressions approach?

$$1 + \cfrac{1}{2 + \cfrac{1}{2}}, \quad 1 + \cfrac{1}{2 + \cfrac{1}{2 + \cfrac{1}{2}}}, \quad 1 + \cfrac{1}{2 + \cfrac{1}{2 + \cfrac{1}{2 + \cfrac{1}{2}}}}, \quad \cdots$$

 **Extension** # Investigate Polynomials, Rational Expressions, and Closure

GOAL Determine whether a set is closed under an operation.

CC.9-12.A.APR.7 (+) Understand that rational expressions form a system analogous to the rational numbers, closed under addition, subtraction, multiplication, and division by a nonzero rational expression; add, subtract, multiply, and divide rational expressions.

If an operation is performed on members of a set and the result is always a member of that set, the set is *closed* under that operation. For example, the set $\{0, 1\}$ is closed under multiplication because every possible product ($0 \cdot 0 = 0$, $0 \cdot 1 = 0$, and $1 \cdot 1 = 1$) is a member of the set. On the other hand, the set is not closed under addition because the sum $1 + 1 = 2$ is not a member of the set.

The table below lists several subsets of the set of real numbers and indicates whether they are closed under the four basic operations.

CLOSURE AND DIVISION

Exclude the undefined case of division by 0 when determining whether a set is closed under division.

Set of numbers	Closed under addition?	Closed under subtraction?	Closed under multiplication?	Closed under division?
Whole numbers	Yes	No	Yes	No
Integers	Yes	Yes	Yes	No
Rational numbers	Yes	Yes	Yes	Yes
Real numbers	Yes	Yes	Yes	Yes

Sets of algebraic expressions, like sets of numbers, can either be closed or not closed under an operation.

EXAMPLE 1 **Determine whether a set of polynomials is closed**

Tell whether the set of polynomials in a single variable with real coefficients is closed under (a) addition and (b) multiplication.

Recall that a polynomial is a monomial or a sum of monomials. Let two polynomials $p_1(x)$ and $p_2(x)$ have terms of the form $a_k x^k$ and $b_k x^k$, respectively, where the coefficients a_k and b_k are real numbers and k is a whole number.

a. Adding two polynomials involves adding like terms, so the sum $p_1(x) + p_2(x)$ has terms of the form $(a_k + b_k)x^k$. Since the set of real numbers is closed under addition, the coefficient $a_k + b_k$ is a real number. The exponent remains the whole number k. So, the sum $p_1(x) + p_2(x)$ is itself a polynomial, and the set of polynomials is closed under addition.

b. Multiplying two polynomials involves multiplying each term of one polynomial with each term of the other. Let $a_j x^j$ be a term of $p_1(x)$, and let $b_k x^k$ be a term of $p_2(x)$. Then the product $p_1(x) \cdot p_2(x)$ has terms of the form $a_j x^j \cdot b_k x^k = (a_j \cdot b_k)x^{j+k}$. Since the set of real numbers is closed under multiplication, the coefficient $a_j \cdot b_k$ is a real number. Since the set of whole numbers is closed under addition, the exponent $j + k$ is a whole number. So, the product $p_1(x) \cdot p_2(x)$ is itself a polynomial, and the set of polynomials is closed under multiplication.

EXAMPLE 2   **Determine if a set of rational expressions is closed**

Tell whether the set of rational expressions in a single variable with real coefficients is closed under (a) addition and (b) multiplication.

Recall that a rational expression is the quotient of two polynomials. Let $r_1(x) = \dfrac{p_1(x)}{p_2(x)}$ and $r_2(x) = \dfrac{p_3(x)}{p_4(x)}$ be two rational expressions with real coefficients where $p_2(x) \neq 0$ and $p_4(x) \neq 0$.

a. To add $r_1(x)$ and $r_2(x)$, you first must find a common denominator. You can use $p_2(x) \cdot p_4(x)$.

$$r_1(x) + r_2(x) = \dfrac{p_1(x)}{p_2(x)} + \dfrac{p_3(x)}{p_4(x)}$$

$$= \dfrac{p_1(x)}{p_2(x)}\left(\dfrac{p_4(x)}{p_4(x)}\right) + \dfrac{p_3(x)}{p_4(x)}\left(\dfrac{p_2(x)}{p_2(x)}\right)$$

$$= \dfrac{p_1(x) \cdot p_4(x) + p_3(x) \cdot p_2(x)}{p_2(x) \cdot p_4(x)}$$

Since the set of polynomials is closed under both addition and multiplication, both the numerator and denominator of the sum $r_1(x) + r_2(x)$ are polynomials. So, the sum $r_1(x) + r_2(x)$ is a rational expression, and the set of rational expressions is closed under addition.

b. Both the numerator and denominator of $r_1(x) \cdot r_2(x) = \dfrac{p_1(x) \cdot p_3(x)}{p_2(x) \cdot p_4(x)}$ are polynomials since the set of polynomials is closed under multiplication. So, the product $r_1(x) \cdot r_2(x)$ is a rational expression, and the set of rational expressions is closed under multiplication.

PRACTICE

1. Give an example showing that the set of integers is not closed under division.

EXAMPLE 1
for Exs. 2–3

Determine whether the given set of algebraic expressions is closed under the given operation. *Explain.*

2. the set of polynomials in one variable with real coefficients; subtraction

3. the set of polynomials in one variable with real coefficients; division

EXAMPLE 2
for Exs. 4–5

4. the set of rational expressions in one variable with real coefficients; subtraction

5. the set of rational expressions in one variable with real coefficients; division

Based on the operations under which the given set is closed, tell whether the set is most similar to *the set of whole numbers*, *the set of integers*, or *the set of rational numbers*.

6. the set of polynomials in one variable with real coefficients

7. the set of rational expressions in one variable with real coefficients

5.6 Solve Rational Equations

Before You solved polynomial equations.

Now You will solve rational equations.

Why? So you can model mobile phone costs, as in Ex. 38.

Key Vocabulary
- cross multiplying
- extraneous solution

CC.9-12.A.REI.2 Solve simple rational and radical equations in one variable, and give examples showing how extraneous solutions may arise.

You can use **cross multiplying** to solve a rational equation when each side of the equation is a single rational expression.

EXAMPLE 1 Solve a rational equation by cross multiplying

Solve: $\dfrac{3}{x+1} = \dfrac{9}{4x+5}$

$\dfrac{3}{x+1} = \dfrac{9}{4x+5}$	Write original equation.
$3(4x+5) = 9(x+1)$	Cross multiply.
$12x + 15 = 9x + 9$	Distributive property
$3x + 15 = 9$	Subtract 9x from each side.
$3x = -6$	Subtract 15 from each side.
$x = -2$	Divide each side by 3.

▶ The solution is −2. Check this in the original equation.

EXAMPLE 2 Write and use a rational model

ALLOYS An *alloy* is formed by mixing two or more metals. Sterling silver is an alloy composed of 92.5% silver and 7.5% copper by weight. Jewelry silver is composed of 80% silver and 20% copper by weight. How much pure silver should you mix with 15 ounces of jewelry silver to make sterling silver?

Solution

$$\text{Percent of copper in mixture} = \frac{\text{Weight of copper in mixture}}{\text{Total weight of mixture}}$$

$\dfrac{7.5}{100} = \dfrac{0.2(15)}{15+x}$	*x* is the amount of silver added.
$7.5(15+x) = 100(0.2)(15)$	Cross multiply.
$112.5 + 7.5x = 300$	Simplify.
$7.5x = 187.5$	Subtract 112.5 from each side.
$x = 25$	Divide each side by 7.5.

▶ You should mix 25 ounces of pure silver with the jewelry silver.

©Purestock/Getty Images

Solve the equation by cross multiplying. Check your solution(s).

1. $\dfrac{3}{5x} = \dfrac{2}{x - 7}$

2. $\dfrac{-4}{x + 3} = \dfrac{5}{x - 3}$

3. $\dfrac{1}{2x + 5} = \dfrac{x}{11x + 8}$

4. WHAT IF? In Example 2, suppose you have 10 ounces of jewelry silver. How much pure silver must be mixed with the jewelry silver to make sterling silver?

USING LCDS When a rational equation is not expressed as a proportion, you can solve it by multiplying each side of the equation by the least common denominator of each rational expression.

 EXAMPLE 3 Standardized Test Practice

What is the solution of $\dfrac{5}{x} + \dfrac{7}{4} = -\dfrac{9}{x}$?

(**A**) −10 (**B**) −8 (**C**) −4 (**D**) 6

ELIMINATE CHOICES
You can eliminate choice D because it yields a positive value on the left side of the equation and a negative value on the right side.

Solution

$\dfrac{5}{x} + \dfrac{7}{4} = -\dfrac{9}{x}$ — Write original equation.

$4x\left(\dfrac{5}{x} + \dfrac{7}{4}\right) = 4x\left(-\dfrac{9}{x}\right)$ — Multiply each side by the LCD, 4x.

$20 + 7x = -36$ — Simplify.

$7x = -56$ — Subtract 20 from each side.

$x = -8$ — Divide each side by 7.

▶ The correct answer is B. (**A**) (**B**) (**C**) (**D**)

EXAMPLE 4 Solve a rational equation with two solutions

Solve: $1 - \dfrac{8}{x - 5} = \dfrac{3}{x}$

$1 - \dfrac{8}{x - 5} = \dfrac{3}{x}$ — Write original equation.

$x(x - 5)\left(1 - \dfrac{8}{x - 5}\right) = x(x - 5) \cdot \dfrac{3}{x}$ — Multiply each side by the LCD, x(x − 5).

$x(x - 5) - 8x = 3(x - 5)$ — Simplify.

$x^2 - 5x - 8x = 3x - 15$ — Simplify.

$x^2 - 16x + 15 = 0$ — Write in standard form.

$(x - 1)(x - 15) = 0$ — Factor.

$x = 1 \quad \text{or} \quad x = 15$ — Zero product property

▶ The solutions are 1 and 15. Check these in the original equation.

EXTRANEOUS SOLUTIONS When solving a rational equation, you may obtain solutions that are extraneous. Be sure to check for extraneous solutions by substituting back into the original equation.

 EXAMPLE 5 **Check for extraneous solutions**

Solve: $\dfrac{6}{x-3} = \dfrac{8x^2}{x^2-9} - \dfrac{4x}{x+3}$

Solution

Write each denominator in factored form. The LCD is $(x+3)(x-3)$.

$$\frac{6}{x-3} = \frac{8x^2}{(x+3)(x-3)} - \frac{4x}{x+3}$$

$$(x+3)(x-3) \cdot \frac{6}{x-3} = (x+3)(x-3) \cdot \frac{8x^2}{(x+3)(x-3)} - (x+3)(x-3) \cdot \frac{4x}{x+3}$$

$$6(x+3) = 8x^2 - 4x(x-3)$$

$$6x + 18 = 8x^2 - 4x^2 + 12x$$

$$0 = 4x^2 + 6x - 18$$

$$0 = 2x^2 + 3x - 9$$

$$0 = (2x-3)(x+3)$$

$$2x - 3 = 0 \quad \text{or} \quad x + 3 = 0$$

$$x = \frac{3}{2} \quad \text{or} \quad x = -3$$

You can use algebra or a graph to check whether either of the two solutions is extraneous.

Algebra The solution $\dfrac{3}{2}$ checks, but the apparent solution -3 is extraneous, because substituting it in the equation results in division by zero, which is undefined.

$$\frac{6}{-3-3} \neq \frac{8(-3)^2}{(-3)^2-9} - \frac{4(-3)}{-3+3}$$

Division by zero is undefined

Graph Graph $y = \dfrac{6}{x-3}$ and $y = \dfrac{8x^2}{x^2-9} - \dfrac{4x}{x+3}$.

The graphs intersect when $x = \dfrac{3}{2}$, but not when $x = -3$.

▸ The solution is $\dfrac{3}{2}$.

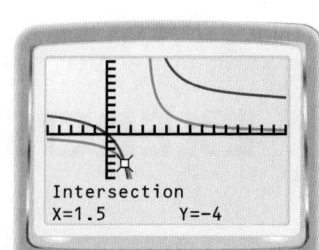

Intersection
X=1.5   Y=-4

 GUIDED PRACTICE for Examples 3, 4, and 5

Solve the equation by using the LCD. Check for extraneous solutions.

5. $\dfrac{7}{2} + \dfrac{3}{x} = 3$

6. $\dfrac{2}{x} + \dfrac{4}{3} = 2$

7. $\dfrac{3}{7} + \dfrac{8}{x} = 1$

8. $\dfrac{3}{2} + \dfrac{4}{x-1} = \dfrac{x+1}{x-1}$

9. $\dfrac{3x}{x+1} - \dfrac{5}{2x} = \dfrac{3}{2x}$

10. $\dfrac{5x}{x-2} = 7 + \dfrac{10}{x-2}$

EXAMPLE 6 **Solve a rational equation given a function**

VIDEO GAME SALES From 1995 through 2003, the annual sales S (in billions of dollars) of entertainment software can be modeled by

$$S(t) = \frac{848t^2 + 3220}{115t^2 + 1000}, \quad 0 \le t \le 8$$

where t is the number of years since 1995. For which year were the total sales of entertainment software about \$5.3 billion?

ANOTHER WAY

For alternative methods for solving the problem in Example 6, see the **Problem Solving Workshop**.

Solution

$S(t) = \dfrac{848t^2 + 3220}{115t^2 + 1000}$	**Write given function.**
$5.3 = \dfrac{848t^2 + 3220}{115t^2 + 1000}$	**Substitute 5.3 for $S(t)$.**
$5.3(115t^2 + 1000) = 848t^2 + 3220$	**Multiply each side by $115t^2 + 1000$.**
$609.5t^2 + 5300 = 848t^2 + 3220$	**Simplify.**
$5300 = 238.5t^2 + 3220$	**Subtract $609.5t^2$ from each side.**
$2080 = 238.5t^2$	**Subtract 3220 from each side.**
$8.72 \approx t^2$	**Divide each side by 238.5.**
$\pm 2.95 \approx t$	**Take square roots of each side.**

Because -2.95 is not in the domain ($0 \le t \le 8$), the only solution is 2.95.

▶ So, the total sales of entertainment software were about \$5.3 billion about 3 years after 1995, or in 1998.

✓ **GUIDED PRACTICE** for Example 6

11. WHAT IF? Use the information in Example 6 to determine in which year the total sales of entertainment software were about \$4.5 billion.

5.6 EXERCISES

HOMEWORK KEY

○ = See WORKED-OUT SOLUTIONS
Exs. 5, 15, and 35

★ = STANDARDIZED TEST PRACTICE
Exs. 2, 13, 28, 29, 34, and 36

SKILL PRACTICE

1. **VOCABULARY** Copy and complete: When you write $\frac{x}{3} = \frac{x + 2}{5}$ as $5x = 3(x + 2)$, you are __?__.

2. ★ **WRITING** A student solved the equation $\frac{5}{x - 4} = \frac{x}{x - 4}$ and got the solutions 4 and 5. Which, if either, of these is extraneous? *Explain.*

3. **REASONING** *Describe* how you can use a graph to determine if an apparent solution of a rational equation is extraneous.

Don Jon Red/Alamy

EXAMPLE 1
for Exs. 4–13

CROSS MULTIPLYING Solve the equation by cross multiplying. Check for extraneous solutions.

4. $\dfrac{4}{2x} = \dfrac{5}{x+6}$

5. $\dfrac{9}{3x} = \dfrac{4}{x+2}$

6. $\dfrac{6}{x-1} = \dfrac{9}{x+1}$

7. $\dfrac{8}{3x-2} = \dfrac{2}{x-1}$

8. $\dfrac{x}{x+1} = \dfrac{3}{x+1}$

9. $\dfrac{x-3}{x+5} = \dfrac{x}{x+2}$

10. $\dfrac{x}{x^2-2} = \dfrac{-1}{x}$

11. $\dfrac{4(x-4)}{x^2+2x-8} = \dfrac{4}{x+4}$

12. $\dfrac{9}{x^2-6x+9} = \dfrac{3x}{x^2-3x}$

13. ★ **MULTIPLE CHOICE** What is the solution of $\dfrac{3}{x+2} = \dfrac{6}{x-1}$?

  (A) -5 (B) -4 (C) -1 (D) 4

LEAST COMMON DENOMINATOR Solve the equation by using the LCD. Check for extraneous solutions.

14. $\dfrac{4}{x} + x = 5$

15. $\dfrac{2}{3x} + \dfrac{1}{6} = \dfrac{4}{3x}$

16. $\dfrac{5}{x} - 2 = \dfrac{2}{x+3}$

17. $\dfrac{1}{2x} + \dfrac{3}{x+7} = \dfrac{-1}{x}$

18. $\dfrac{1}{x-2} + 2 = \dfrac{3x}{x+2}$

19. $\dfrac{5}{x^2+x-6} = 2 + \dfrac{x-3}{x-2}$

20. $\dfrac{x+1}{x+6} + \dfrac{1}{x} = \dfrac{2x+1}{x+6}$

21. $\dfrac{2}{x-3} + \dfrac{1}{x} = \dfrac{x-1}{x-3}$

22. $\dfrac{6x}{x+4} + 4 = \dfrac{2x+2}{x-1}$

23. $\dfrac{10}{x} + 3 = \dfrac{x+9}{x-4}$

24. $\dfrac{18}{x^2-3x} - \dfrac{6}{x-3} = \dfrac{5}{x}$

25. $\dfrac{x+3}{x-3} + \dfrac{x}{x-5} = \dfrac{x+5}{x-5}$

ERROR ANALYSIS *Describe* and correct the error in the first step of solving the equation.

26.
$$\dfrac{3}{2x} + \dfrac{4}{x^2} = 1$$
$$3x^2 + 8x = 1$$
✗

27.
$$\dfrac{5}{x} + \dfrac{23}{6} = \dfrac{45}{x}$$
$$\dfrac{28}{x+6} = \dfrac{45}{x}$$
✗

28. ★ **MULTIPLE CHOICE** What is (are) the solution(s) of $\dfrac{2}{x-3} = \dfrac{1}{x^2-2x-3}$?

  (A) $-3, -\dfrac{1}{2}$ (B) $-\dfrac{1}{2}, 3$ (C) $-\dfrac{1}{2}$ (D) 3

29. ★ **OPEN-ENDED MATH** Give an example of a rational equation that you would solve using cross multiplication. Then give an example of a rational equation that you would solve by multiplying each side by the LCD of the fractions.

CHALLENGE In Exercises 30–32, *a* is a nonzero real number. Tell whether the algebraic statement is *always true*, *sometimes true*, or *never true*. *Explain* your answer.

30. For the equation $\dfrac{1}{x-a} = \dfrac{x}{x-a}$, $x = a$ is an extraneous solution.

31. The equation $\dfrac{3}{x-a} = \dfrac{x}{x-a}$ has exactly one solution.

32. The equation $\dfrac{1}{x-a} = \dfrac{2}{x+a} + \dfrac{2a}{x^2-a^2}$ has no solution.

EXAMPLE 2
for Exs. 33–34

33. VOLLEYBALL So far in your volleyball match, you have put into play 37 of the 44 serves you have attempted. Solve the equation $\frac{90}{100} = \frac{37 + x}{44 + x}$ to find the number of consecutive serves you need to put into play in order to raise your service percentage to 90%.

34. ★ **EXTENDED RESPONSE** A speed skater travels 9 kilometers in the same amount of time that it takes a second skater to travel 8 kilometers. The first skater travels 4.38 kilometers per hour faster than the second skater.

   a. Use the verbal model below to write an equation that relates the skating times of the skaters.

$$\frac{\text{Distance for skater 1}}{\text{Skater 1 speed}} = \frac{\text{Distance for skater 2}}{\text{Skater 2 speed}}$$

   b. Solve the equation in part (a) to find the speeds of both skaters.

   c. How long did the skaters skate? *Explain* your answer.

EXAMPLE 6
for Ex. 35

35. MUSIC INDUSTRY From 1994 through 2003, the number n (in millions) of CDs shipped can be modeled by

$$n = \frac{635t^2 - 7350t + 27{,}200}{t^2 - 11.5t + 39.4}, \quad 0 \le t \le 9$$

where t is the number of years since 1994. During which year was the total number of CDs shipped about 720 million?

36. ★ **EXTENDED RESPONSE** You can paint a room in 8 hours. Working together, you and your friend can paint the room in just 5 hours.

   a. Let t be the time (in hours) your friend would take to paint the room when working alone. Copy and complete the table.

	Work Rate	·	Time	=	Work Done
You	$\frac{1 \text{ room}}{8 \text{ hours}}$		5 hours		?
Friend	?		5 hours		?

   b. What is the sum of the expressions in the table's last column? *Explain*.

   c. Write and solve an equation to find how long your friend would take to paint the room when working alone. *Explain* your answer.

37. **GEOMETRY** *Golden rectangles* are rectangles for which the ratio of the width w to the length ℓ is equal to the ratio of ℓ to $\ell + w$. The ratio of the length to the width for these rectangles is called the *golden ratio*. Find the value of the golden ratio using a rectangle with a width of 1 unit.

○ = **See WORKED-OUT SOLUTIONS** in Student Resources   ★ = **STANDARDIZED TEST PRACTICE**

38. CHALLENGE Let x be the number of years since 1998, let $g(x)$ be the average monthly bill (in dollars) for mobile phone users in the United States, and let $h(x)$ be the average number of minutes used by U.S. mobile phone users. Then $g(x)$ and $h(x)$ are as given below.

$$g(x) = -0.27x^3 + 1.40x^2 + 1.05x + 39.4$$
$$h(x) = -8.25x^3 + 53.1x^2 - 7.82x + 138$$

a. Write a rational function $f(x)$ that gives the average price per minute x years after 1998.

b. Find the average price per minute in 1998.

c. In what year did the average price per minute fall to 11 cents?

Using ALTERNATIVE METHODS

Another Way to Solve Example 6

MATHEMATICAL
PRACTICES

Make sense of problems and persevere in solving them.

MULTIPLE REPRESENTATIONS In Example 6, you solved a rational equation algebraically. You can also solve rational equations using tables and graphs.

PROBLEM

VIDEO GAME SALES From 1995 through 2003, the annual sales S (in billions of dollars) of entertainment software can be modeled by

$$S(t) = \frac{848t^2 + 3220}{115t^2 + 1000}, \quad 0 \le t \le 8$$

where t is the number of years since 1995. For which year were the total sales of entertainment software about \$5.3 billion?

METHOD 1

Using a Table The problem requires solving the following rational equation:

$$5.3 = \frac{848u^2 + 3220}{115t^2 + 1000}$$

One way to solve this equation is to make a table of values. You can use a graphing calculator to make the table.

STEP 1 **Enter** the function $y = \dfrac{848x^2 + 3220}{115x^2 + 1000}$ into a graphing calculator.

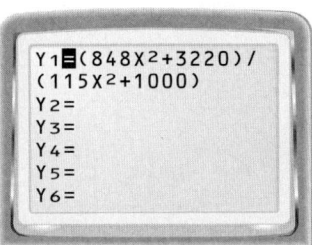

STEP 2 **Set up** a table of values for the function. Start the table at zero so that the first several x-values in the table are in the domain of the function. The step value ($\triangle$Tbl) should represent one entire year.

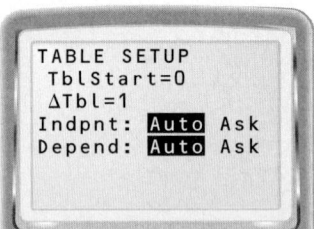

STEP 3 **Create** the table of values. You can see that $y \approx 5.3$ when $x = 3$.

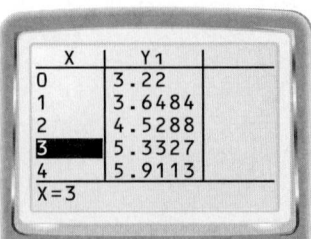

▶ Because $x = 3$ represents the number of years after 1995, total sales of entertainment software were about \$5.3 billion in 1998.

METHOD 2   **Using a Graph** You can also use a graph to solve $5.3 = \dfrac{848t^2 + 3220}{115t^2 + 1000}$.

STEP 1 **Enter** the functions $y = \dfrac{848x^2 + 3220}{115x^2 + 1000}$ and $y = 5.3$ into a graphing calculator.

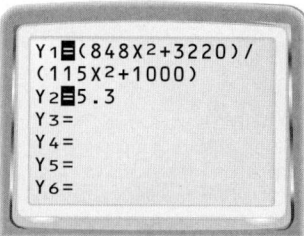

STEP 2 **Graph** the functions. Adjust the viewing window so that it shows the point in the first quadrant where the graphs intersect.

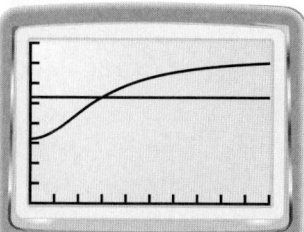

STEP 3 **Find** the intersection point of the graphs using the calculator's *intersect* feature. The graphs intersect at about (3.0, 5.3).

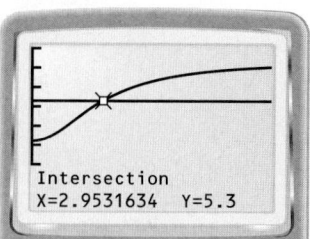

▶ Total sales of entertainment software were about $5.3 billion 3 years after 1995, or in the year 1998.

PRACTICE

RATIONAL EQUATIONS **Solve the equation using a table and using a graph.**

1. $\dfrac{80x^2 + 300}{15x^2 + 200} = 4.2$

2. $\dfrac{5x + 5}{x^2 + 4} = 2$

3. $\dfrac{9x + 2}{x - 5} = 20.75$

4. $\dfrac{6x^2}{2x - 3} = 18$

5. $\dfrac{14x^2 + 60}{5x^2 + 7} = 3.5$

6. **WHAT IF?** In Example 6, suppose you want to find the year when total sales of entertainment software were $4.5 billion. Find this year using a table and using a graph.

7. **DIVING** The recommended percent p of oxygen (by volume) in the air that a diver breathes is given by $p = \dfrac{660}{d + 33}$ where d is the depth (in feet) of the diver.

   a. At what depth is air containing 5% oxygen recommended? Use a table to find the answer.

   b. At what depth is air containing 10% oxygen recommended? Use a graph to find the answer.

Solve Rational Inequalities

GOAL Find solutions of rational inequalities.

You have solved rational equations. You can also solve rational inequalities using tables, graphs, or algebraic methods.

CC.9-12.A.REI.2 Solve simple rational and radical equations in one variable, and give examples showing how extraneous solutions may arise.

EXAMPLE 1 Solve a rational inequality using a table

Use a table to solve $\dfrac{x^2 - 2x + 1}{x - 2} > x$.

Solution

Subtract x from each side of the inequality so that 0 is on one side.

$$\dfrac{x^2 - 2x + 1}{x - 2} - x > 0 \qquad \textbf{Subtract } x \textbf{ from each side.}$$

Enter $y = \dfrac{x^2 - 2x + 1}{x - 2} - x$ into a graphing calculator.

Use the *table* feature to find values of x for which y is positive.

The value of y is undefined when $x = 2$ and appears to be positive when $x > 2$. Use a smaller step value for x to convince yourself of this.

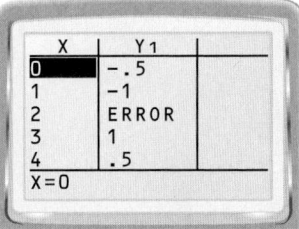

▶ The solution is $x > 2$.

EXAMPLE 2 Solve a rational inequality by graphing

From 1990 to 2001, the number d (in thousands) of doctors in the United States can be modeled by the function $d = \dfrac{966t^2 + 50{,}300}{t^2 + 79.7}$ where t is the number of years since 1990. When were there fewer than 800,000 doctors?

Solution

The problem requires solving this inequality:

$$\dfrac{966t^2 + 50{,}300}{t^2 + 79.7} < 800$$

Enter $y_1 = \dfrac{966x^2 + 50{,}300}{x^2 + 79.7}$ and $y_2 = 800$ into a graphing calculator.

Graph the functions and use the *intersect* feature. The graph of y_1 lies below the graph of y_2 when $0 \le x \le 9$.

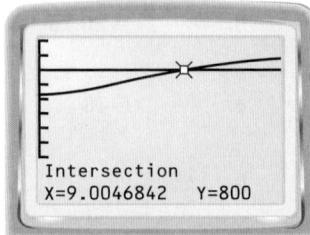

▶ In the years 1990–1999, there were fewer than 800,000 doctors.

EXAMPLE 3   **Solve a rational inequality algebraically**

Solve $\dfrac{6}{x-2} \geq -4$ algebraically.

Solution

STEP 1 **Rewrite** the inequality so that one side is 0. Then write the other side as a simplified rational expression.

$$\dfrac{6}{x-2} \geq -4 \qquad \text{Write original inequality.}$$

$$\dfrac{6}{x-2} + 4 \geq 0 \qquad \text{Add 4 to each side.}$$

$$\dfrac{6 + 4(x-2)}{x-2} \geq 0 \qquad \text{Write left side as a single fraction.}$$

$$\dfrac{4x-2}{x-2} \geq 0 \qquad \text{Simplify.}$$

AVOID ERRORS
Do not multiply each side of an inequality by an expression involving x if the expression can take on both positive and negative values.

STEP 2 **Identify** the *critical x-values*, which are the x-values that make the numerator or denominator equal to 0.

Numerator equal to 0:   Denominator equal to 0:

$4x - 2 = 0$ $x - 2 = 0$

$\qquad x = \dfrac{1}{2}$ $x = 2$

So, the critical x-values are $x = \dfrac{1}{2}$ and $x = 2$.

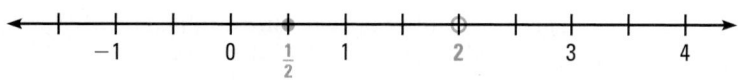

The critical x-values divide the number line into three intervals. Note that $x = \dfrac{1}{2}$ will be included in the solution, but $x = 2$ will not because it results in division by zero.

STEP 3 **Test** an x-value in each interval to see if it satisfies the original inequality. If it does, *every* x-value in the interval will satisfy the inequality. If it does not, *no* x-value in the interval will satisfy the inequality.

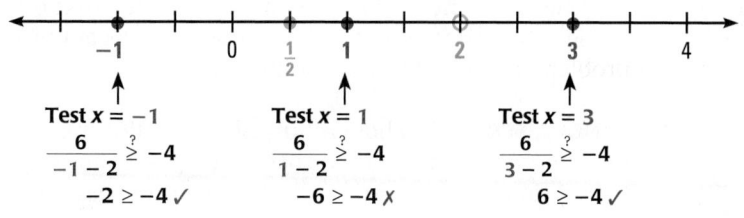

STEP 4 **Graph** the intervals where the tested x-values produce true statements.

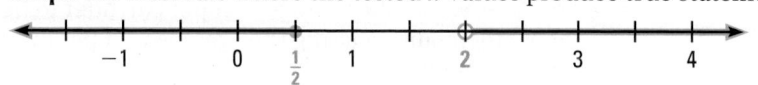

STEP 5 **Write** inequalities to describe the solution.

▶ The solution is $x \leq \dfrac{1}{2}$ or $x > 2$.

EXAMPLE 1
for Exs. 1–6

Use a table to solve the inequality.

1. $\dfrac{5}{x-2} < 0$

2. $\dfrac{x-5}{x+3} > 1$

3. $\dfrac{x^2 - 3x + 2}{x - 3} < x$

4. $\dfrac{10}{x+2} > 0$

5. $\dfrac{-2x-3}{x-4} > 0$

6. $\dfrac{x^2 - 4x + 8}{x - 1} < x$

EXAMPLE 2
for Exs. 7–12

Use a graph to solve the inequality.

7. $-\dfrac{4}{x+5} < 0$

8. $\dfrac{4}{x-3} < 0$

9. $\dfrac{8}{x^2+1} \geq 4$

10. $\dfrac{20}{x^2+1} < 2$

11. $\dfrac{3x+2}{x-1} < -2$

12. $\dfrac{3x+2}{x-1} > x$

EXAMPLE 3
for Exs. 13–18

Solve the inequality algebraically.

13. $\dfrac{3}{x+2} > 0$

14. $-\dfrac{1}{x+5} \leq -2$

15. $\dfrac{2}{x+2} > \dfrac{1}{x+3}$

16. $\dfrac{5}{x-4} < \dfrac{1}{x+4}$

17. $\dfrac{5}{x+3} \geq \dfrac{4}{x+2}$

18. $\dfrac{2}{x+6} > \dfrac{-3}{x-3}$

19. **EGG PRODUCTION** From 1994 to 2002, the total number E (in billions) of eggs produced in the United States can be modeled by

$$E = \dfrac{-3680}{t - 50}, \quad 0 \leq t \leq 8$$

where t is the number of years since 1994. For what years was the number of eggs produced greater than 80 billion?

20. **PHONE COSTS** One phone company advertises a flat rate of $.07 per minute for long-distance calls. Your long-distance plan charges $5.00 per month plus a rate of $.05 per minute. How many minutes do you have to talk each month so that your average cost is less than $.07 per minute?

21. **SATELLITE TV** You subscribe to a satellite television service. The monthly cost for programming is $43, and there is a one-time installation fee of $50. The average monthly cost c of the service is given by $c = \dfrac{43t + 50}{t}$ where t is the time (in months) that you have subscribed to the service. For what subscription times is the average monthly cost at most $47? Solve the problem using a table and using a graph.

22. **FUNDRAISER** Your school is publishing a wildlife calendar to raise money for a local charity. The total cost of using the photos in the calendar is $710. In addition to this one-time charge, the unit cost of printing each calendar is $4.50.

    a. The school wants the average cost per calendar to be below $10. Write a rational inequality relating the average cost per calendar to the desired cost per calendar.

    b. Solve the inequality from part (a) by graphing. How many calendars need to be printed to bring the average cost per calendar below $10?

    c. Suppose the school wanted to have the average cost per calendar be below $6. How many calendars would then need to be printed?

5.7 Describe and Compare Function Characteristics

Before You studied characteristics of functions and their graphs.

Now You will analyze and compare functions.

Why? So you can sketch a graph from a verbal description, as in Ex. 4.

Key Vocabulary
• **increasing**
• **decreasing**
• **odd function**
• **even function**

CC.9-12.F.IF.9 Compare properties of two functions each represented in a different way (algebraically, graphically, numerically in tables, or by verbal descriptions).

The graphs of $y = x$ and $y = 2^x$ rise from left to right for all real numbers. These functions are always **increasing**. The graphs of $y = -x$ and $y = 0.5^x$ fall from left to right for all real numbers. These functions are always **decreasing**. The function $y = x^2$ is decreasing for $x \leq 0$, but increasing for $x \geq 0$. The table shows when a function is increasing or decreasing over an interval of its domain.

	Increasing over an interval	Decreasing over an interval
Values of $f(x)$	$f(x_1) < f(x_2)$ whenever $x_1 < x_2$.	$f(x_1) > f(x_2)$ whenever $x_1 < x_2$.
Graph of $f(x)$	Rises from left to right.	Falls from left to right.

EXAMPLE 1 Sketch a graph given a verbal description

FLYING Sketch a graph of $a(t)$ where a represents altitude and t represents time for the situation below. Label key information such as local minima and maxima and intervals where $a(t)$ is increasing or decreasing.

A small plane flying at a constant cruising altitude is caught in a storm. Air currents carry the plane up before pushing it down rapidly below its original altitude. The plane exits the storm and returns gradually to its cruising altitude.

Solution

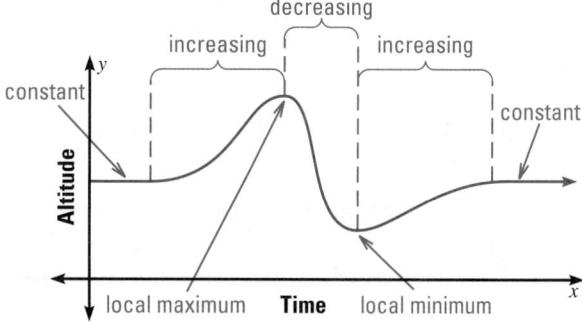

✓ **GUIDED PRACTICE** for Example 1

1. Sketch a graph for the situation described below. Label key information.

The US gross domestic product (GDP) growth rate over a 2 year period can be modeled by a polynomial that began slightly positive before dropping to significantly negative, swinging back to significantly positive, then falling to a growth rate a little higher than at the beginning of the period.

AVERAGE RATE OF CHANGE For a *linear* function, the rate of change is *constant*, and is indicated by the slope. Even for a nonlinear function, however, you can find the *average* rate of change over any interval by finding the slope of the segment that connects the points on the graph determined by the endpoints of the interval.

The graph of $f(x) = \log_3 x$ at the right shows that $f(x)$ is always increasing. You can see, however, that the slope between the labeled pairs of points decreases as x increases, that is, the average rate of change is decreasing over successive x-intervals. So, although the graph is always rising, the rise becomes slower and slower for greater and greater x-values.

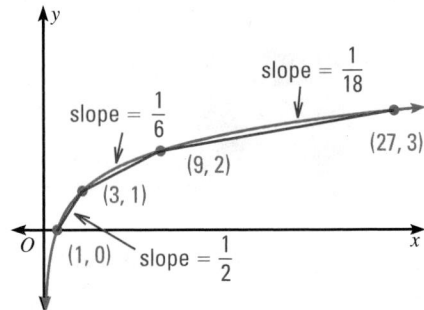

EXAMPLE 2 **Investigate average rate of change**

For the function $f(x) = 2^{x-2} + 1$, find the average rate of change over the intervals $[-2, 0]$, $[0, 2]$, $[2, 4]$, $[4, 6]$, and $[6, 8]$. What happens to the average rate of change as x increases? What does this mean for the graph of $f(x)$?

Solution

The average rate of change over an interval $[x_1, x_2]$ is $\dfrac{f(x_2) - f(x_1)}{x_2 - x_1}$.

Interval	Average rate of change
$[-2, 0]$	$\dfrac{(2^{0-2} + 1) - (2^{-2-2} + 1)}{2} = \dfrac{1.25 - 1.0625}{2} = 0.09375$
$[0, 2]$	$\dfrac{(2^{2-2} + 1) - (2^{0-2} + 1)}{2} = \dfrac{2 - 1.25}{2} = 0.375$
$[2, 4]$	$\dfrac{(2^{4-2} + 1) - (2^{2-2} + 1)}{2} = \dfrac{5 - 2}{2} = 1.5$
$[4, 6]$	$\dfrac{(2^{6-2} + 1) - (2^{4-2} + 1)}{2} = \dfrac{17 - 5}{2} = 6$
$[6, 8]$	$\dfrac{(2^{8-2} + 1) - (2^{6-2} + 1)}{2} = \dfrac{65 - 17}{2} = 24$

The average rate of change is always positive, so the graph always rises. The average rate of change increases over successive intervals of the domain (by a factor of 4 for each increase of 2 in x). Because the average rate of change over each interval is equivalent to the slope of the segment from $(x_1, f(x_1))$ to $(x_2, f(x_2))$, the graph rises more and more steeply as x increases.

✓ **GUIDED PRACTICE** for Example 2

2. For the function $f(x) = -\log_2 x$, find the average rate of change over the intervals $[0.125, 0.25]$, $[0.25, 0.5]$, $[0.5, 1]$, $[1, 2]$, and $[2, 4]$. What does this mean for the graph?

EXAMPLE 3 **Compare functions in different representations**

AREA AND VOLUME Anna and Zeke cut squares from the corners of rectangular pieces of cardboard and fold up the sides to make open boxes. Anna's cardboard is 10 inches by 12 inches. Zeke's is 8 inches by 15 inches. The volume V as a function of cut-out side length x is shown for Anna at the right and Zeke below.

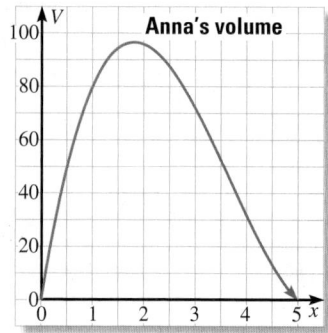

Zeke's volume: $V(x) = x(8 - 2x)(15 - 2x)$

Compare the maximums and x-intercepts of the functions. Interpret the significance of the results.

Solution

Use a graphing calculator for Zeke's function. The maximum is about 91 when x is about 1.7. The graph for Anna shows a maximum of about 97 when x is about 1.8. The pieces of cardboard have equal area, but Anna can make a box with greater volume.

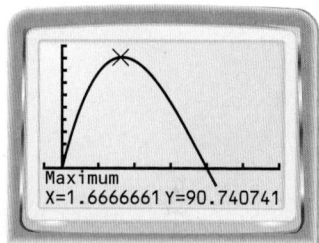

The x-intercepts, which represent cut-out sizes that correspond to volumes of 0, are 0 and 4 for Zeke, and 0 and 5 for Anna. The volume of Anna's box decreases less with increasing cut-out size.

EXAMPLE 4 **Compare functions in different representations**

FOOTBALL Fantasy football participants "draft" players for their teams. Below are models predicting fantasy points for two positions as a function of the player's rank. Compare fantasy points as a function of rank for the models.

INTERPRET THE TABLE
The table predicts the top tight end will score 175 fantasy points, but the 20th ranked tight end will score only 60 fantasy points.

Tight Ends

Rank	Fantasy points
1	175
10	90
20	60
30	45
40	35
50	25

Running Backs

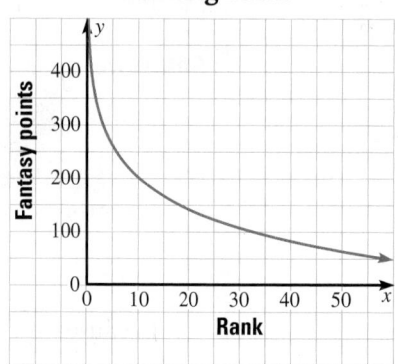

Solution

Use the graph to estimate the ordered pairs (rank, fantasy points) for running backs that correspond to the ordered pairs for tight ends from the table.

Tight ends: (1, 175)   (10, 90)   (20, 60)   (30, 45)   (40, 35)   (50, 25)

Running backs: (1, 400)   (10, 200)   (20, 140)   (30, 110)   (40, 85)   (50, 65)

Comparing ordered pairs, the points for running backs are always greater than for tight ends for each rank over the domain shown, but for running backs, the points decrease more rapidly as rank changes than for tight ends.

EVEN AND ODD FUNCTIONS A function f is an **even function** if $f(-x) = f(x)$ for all x in its domain. The graph of an even function is symmetric about the y-axis. A function f is an **odd function** if $f(-x) = -f(x)$ for all x in its domain. The graph of an odd function is *symmetric about the origin*. One way to recognize a graph that is symmetric about the origin is that it looks the same after a 180° rotation about the origin.

Even Function

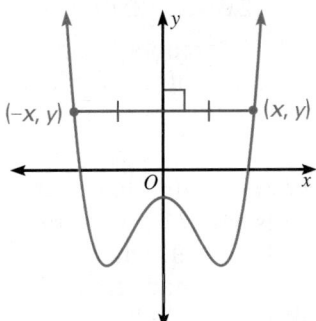

Odd Function

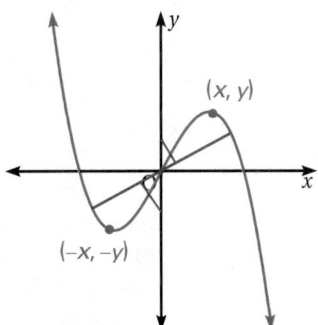

For an even function, if (x, y) is on the graph, then $(-x, y)$ is also on the graph. The y-axis is the perpendicular bisector of the segment between any pair of points (x, y) and $(-x, y)$.

For an odd function, if (x, y) is on the graph, then $(-x, -y)$ is also on the graph. The origin bisects the segment between any pair of points (x, y) and $(-x, -y)$.

EXAMPLE 5 **Identify even and odd functions**

Determine whether the function is *even*, *odd*, or *neither*.

a. $f(x) = x^3 - 7x$

b. $g(x) = \dfrac{6}{x + 1}$

Solution

a. Replace x with $-x$ in the equation for the function, and then simplify.

$$f(-x) = (-x)^3 - 7(-x) = -x^3 + 7x = -(x^3 - 7x) = -f(x)$$

Because $f(-x) = -f(x)$, the function is odd.

b. $g(-x) = \dfrac{6}{(-x) + 1} = \dfrac{6}{-x + 1}$

Because $\dfrac{6}{-x + 1} \neq \dfrac{6}{x + 1}$ and $\dfrac{6}{-x + 1} \neq -\dfrac{6}{x + 1}$, $g(x)$ is neither even nor odd.

✔ **GUIDED PRACTICE** for Examples 3–5

3. Refer to Example 4. For quarterbacks, the equation $y = 475 - 110 \ln x$ models fantasy points as a function of rank. Compare the point totals as a function of rank for quarterbacks and running backs.

4. Determine whether $f(x) = -x^6 + 3x^4 - 2x^2 - 7$ is *even*, *odd*, or *neither*.

5. Determine whether $f(x) = \dfrac{-5x}{12 - x^2 - x^4}$ is *even*, *odd*, or *neither*.

5.7 EXERCISES

HOMEWORK KEY

○ = See WORKED-OUT SOLUTIONS
Exs. 5 and 27

★ = STANDARDIZED TEST PRACTICE
Exs. 2, 11, 14, 24, 30, and 31

SKILL PRACTICE

1. **VOCABULARY** Copy and complete: A function f is a(n) __?__ function if $f(-x) = f(x)$ for all values of x in the domain of f.

2. ★ **WRITING** *Describe* how to determine when a function is increasing or decreasing over its domain or over an interval of its domain.

EXAMPLE 1
for Exs. 3–5

SKETCHING GRAPHS **Sketch a graph for each situation. Label key information, including local extremes, intercepts, and intervals of increase or decrease.**

3. The number of customers $c(t)$ in a coffee shop t hours after it opens is as follows: opens with no customers, increases until midmorning, decreases, increases at lunch to its greatest number of customers for the day, then slowly decreases until the shop closes in the late afternoon.

4. Your height $h(t)$ in feet above the ground t seconds from the beginning of an amusement park ride is as follows: starts at its highest point, quickly drops halfway to the ground, climbs back up—but not as high as before—then quickly drops to the ground, leveling out at the end.

○5. The normal fill level of a reservoir is marked as "0" on a marker pole. The water level $w(t)$ where t is in weeks drops slowly and steadily from the fill level during a summer drought, then rapidly rises well above fill level from large storms. The level is then brought back down to the fill level, where it is held constant.

EXAMPLE 2
for Exs. 6–11

INVESTIGATING RATES OF CHANGE **Find the average rate of change of the function over the given intervals. Describe what happens to the graph of the function as x increases.**

6. $f(x) = 3^{x+4} - 6$ over the intervals $[-4, -3], [-3, -2], [-2, -1], [-1, 0]$

7. $f(x) = \log_{1/2}(x - 3)$ over the intervals $[4, 5], [5, 7], [7, 11], [11, 19]$

8.
x	−1	0	1	2	3
$f(x)$	−1	−0.5	0.25	1.375	3.0625

9.
x	$\frac{7}{3}$	3	5	11	29
$f(x)$	−1	0	1	2	3

10. **ERROR ANALYSIS** *Describe* and correct the error in the statement about the function graphed at the right.

As x increases, the absolute value of the average rate of change of the function increases.

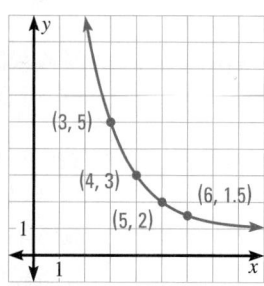

(3, 5)
(4, 3)
(6, 1.5)
(5, 2)

11. ★ **SHORT RESPONSE** You are given a function rule for a function $f(x)$ and an interval $[x_1, x_2]$ for which $x_2 > x_1$. You determine that $f(x_2) > f(x_1)$. Can you conclude that $f(x)$ is increasing over the interval $[x_1, x_2]$? *Explain.*

EXAMPLES
3 AND 4
for Exs. 12–14

COMPARING FUNCTIONS Compare the properties of the two functions and the key characteristics of their graphs. Include information such as the domain and range, asymptotes, end behavior, and general appearance of the graphs.

12. **Function 1:** an inverse variation function with constant of variation $a = 25$

    Function 2: $y = -\dfrac{1}{x}$

13. **Function 1:** a square root function whose graph passes through the points $(0, 0)$, $(1, 1)$, $(4, 2)$, $(9, 3)$

    Function 2: $y = 3\sqrt{x - 1} + 5$

14. ★ **MULTIPLE CHOICE** Which statement is true about the functions shown?

    Function 1: $y = \log(x - 4)$ **Function 2:**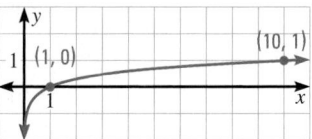

    (**A**) The graphs of the functions have the same x-intercept.

    (**B**) The functions have the same domain.

    (**C**) The functions have the same asymptote(s).

    (**D**) The functions have the same range.

EXAMPLE 5
for Exs. 15–24

IDENTIFYING EVEN AND ODD FUNCTIONS Determine whether the function is *even*, *odd*, or *neither*.

15. 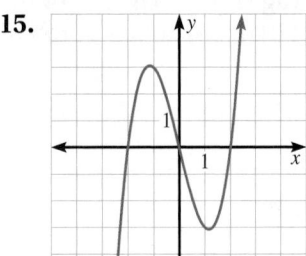   16. 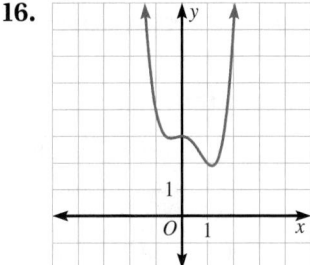   17.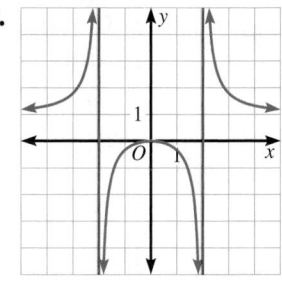

18. $f(x) = x^2 + x$ 19. $g(x) = x^5 + x^3 + x$ 20. $g(x) = x^4 + 2x^2$

21. $k(x) = 5x^6 + 9x^4 + x^2$ 22. $m(x) = \dfrac{12}{x}$ 23. $m(x) = \dfrac{3}{x} + 5$

24. ★ **MULTIPLE CHOICE** Which function is even?

    (**A**) $g(x) = 11x^6 + 7x^2$ (**B**) $k(x) = 8x^7 - x^5 + 12x^3$

    (**C**) $h(x) = \dfrac{9}{x}$ (**D**) $j(x) = \dfrac{11}{x + 2} - 4$

25. **CHALLENGE** Tell whether each statement is *always*, *sometimes*, or *never* true. *Explain.*

    a. The product of two even functions is an even function.

    b. The product of two odd functions is an odd function.

EXAMPLES
3 AND 4
for Exs. 26–28

26. PACKAGING Box 1 and Box 2 are open boxes formed by cutting squares from the corners of rectangular pieces of cardboard and folding up the sides. The cardboard for Box 1 is 8 inches by 3 inches, and the cardboard for Box 2 is 6 inches by 4 inches. The volume V (in cubic inches) for Box 1 is $V = x(8 - 2x)(3 - 2x)$, where x is the side length of the square cut-outs. The volume for Box 2 is shown in the graph. Compare the x-intercepts and the maximums of the functions. Interpret the significance of the results.

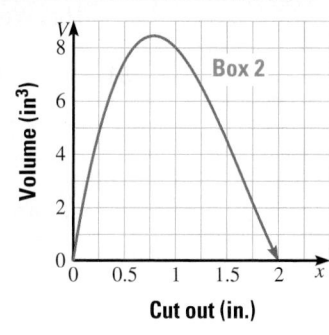

27. AUTOMOBILES The function $y = 25{,}000(0.82)^t$ gives the value y (in dollars) of one model of minivan as it depreciates over t years. The graph at the right shows the depreciating value of one model of sports utility vehicle. Compare y-intercepts and the rate of decrease in value for each vehicle. Interpret the significance of the results.

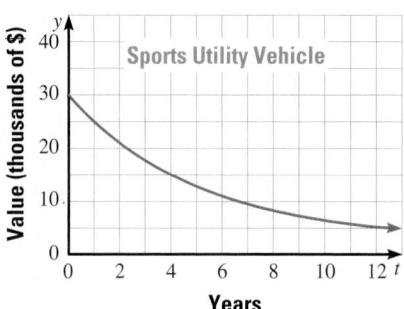

28. PACKAGING A company uses two 1200 cubic centimeter containers for powdered art supplies: a cylinder and a rectangular prism with a square base. The cylinder's diameter is the same as a side of the prism's base. The graph shows surface area S as a function of diameter d for the cylinder. The ordered pairs $(d, S(d))$ below are for the prism.

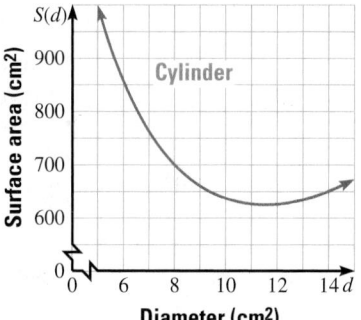

    (9.4, 687.4), (9.8, 681.9), (10.2, 678.7),

    (10.6, 677.6), (11, 678.4), (11.4, 681.0)

   a. Compare the minimum surface areas and corresponding values of d.

   b. The respective heights of the prism and cylinder are $h = \dfrac{1200}{d^2}$ and $h = \dfrac{4800}{\pi d^2}$. Compare the heights that correspond to the minimum surface areas for the containers. What do you notice?

29. FINANCE You and your sister deposit money in a savings account.

   a. You deposit $1000 into an account that pays 2.8% annual interest, compounded annually. Copy and complete the table to determine the account balance A (rounded to the nearest cent) after t years.

t (years)	1	2	3	4	5
A (dollars)	?	?	?	?	?

   b. The balance in your sister's account is given by $A = 1500(1.0175)^t$ after t years. Compare this function to the function in part (a). Interpret what your observations mean in the context of the situation.

30. ★ **OPEN-ENDED** Give a real-world example of a situation that can be modeled by a function that is decreasing, but for which the magnitude of the average rate of change is getting less and less.

31. ★ **EXTENDED RESPONSE** Observe the patterns below.

  Pattern 1: 1, 16, 81, 256, …

  Pattern 2: 4, 16, 64, 256, …

  a. Model Each pattern can be represented using ordered pairs (x, y), where x is the position of the number in the pattern and y is the number. For example, Pattern 1 can be represented as (1, 1), (2, 16), (3, 81), and so on. Write a function rule that models the ordered pairs for each pattern.

  b. Graph Graph both functions from part (a) on the same set of axes. Does the value of one function eventually exceed and increase more rapidly than the value of the other as x continues to increase? *Explain.*

  c. Interpret In general, as the value of x increases will a quantity that is increasing exponentially eventually exceed a quantity that is increasing as a polynomial function? *Explain* your reasoning and give examples to support your answer.

32. **CHALLENGE** A manufacturer produces an open box with two flaps from a square piece of cardboard by cutting congruent rectangles from each corner. The height of each of the rectangles is equal to twice its width.

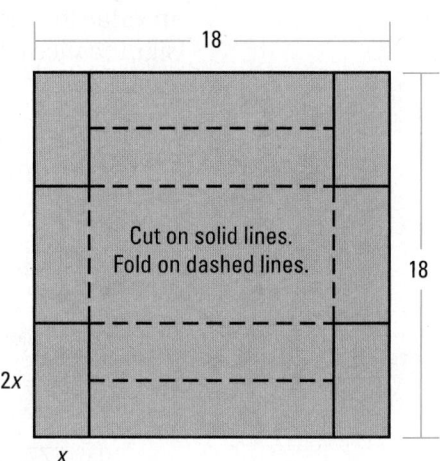

  a. A box like the one described above is made from an 18 inch square piece of cardboard. The volume V (in cubic inches) of the box is $V = x(18 - 2x)(18 - 4x)$. Find the average rate of change of the function over the intervals [0, 1], [1, 2], [2, 3], and [3, 4].

  b. Does a maximum or minimum value occur over any of the intervals in part (a)? If so, is it a maximum or a minimum? *Explain* your reasoning.

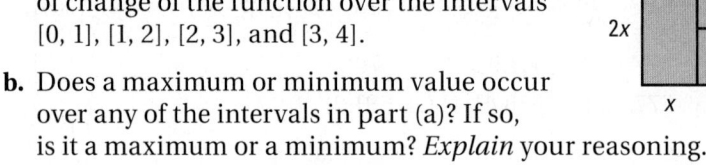

QUIZ

Solve the equation. Check for extraneous solutions.

1. $\dfrac{x-4}{x-1} = \dfrac{10}{x+7}$

2. $\dfrac{x-4}{x-2} = \dfrac{2x-1}{x-2} = 2$

3. $\dfrac{3x+1}{x^2-2} = \dfrac{x+1}{x-2}$

4. For the function $f(x) = 2^{x+1} - 2$, find the average rate of change over the intervals [–1, 0], [0, 1], [1, 2], and [2, 3]. What happens to the average rate of change as x increases? What does this mean for the graph of $f(x)$?

5. **BATTING AVERAGE** So far this baseball season, you have gotten a hit 12 times out of 60 at-bats. Solve the equation $0.360 = \dfrac{12 + x}{60 + x}$ to find the number of consecutive hits you have to get to raise your batting average to 0.360.

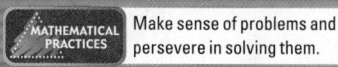
1. MULTI-STEP PROBLEM A cyclist travels 50 miles from her home to a state park at a speed of s miles per hour. On the return trip, she increases her speed by 5 miles per hour.

   a. Write an expression in terms of s for the time the cyclist takes to travel from her home to the state park.

   b. Write an expression in terms of s for the time the cyclist takes to return home from the state park.

   c. Write an expression in simplified form for the *total* time of the cyclist's round trip.

2. SHORT RESPONSE Determine whether the function $f(x) = x^2 - x^3$ is *even, odd*, or *neither*. *Explain* your reasoning.

3. SHORT RESPONSE A manufacturer of instant rice is considering two different styles of packaging. One is a rectangular container with a square base. The other is a cylinder.

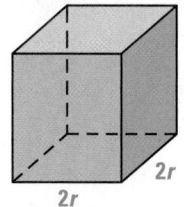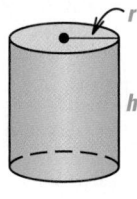

   a. Find the ratio of surface area to volume for each container.

   b. Using the ratios, what can you determine about the efficiencies of the containers?

4. OPEN-ENDED Write two rational expressions $r(x)$ and $s(x)$ such that $r(x)$ and $s(x)$ each contain a quadratic polynomial and
$$r(x) \cdot s(x) = \frac{x - 3}{x + 4}.$$

5. MULTI-STEP PROBLEM Brass is an alloy composed of 55% copper and 45% zinc by weight. You have 25 ounces of copper, and you want to determine how many ounces of zinc you need to make brass.

   a. Let x be the number of ounces of zinc you need. Write a verbal model and then a rational equation that you can use to find x.

   b. Solve the equation from part (a) to find the number of ounces of zinc you need to make brass.

   c. Consider the more general case where you have c ounces of copper. In terms of c, how many ounces of zinc must be added to make brass?

6. EXTENDED RESPONSE A car travels 120 miles in the same amount of time that it takes a truck to travel 100 miles. The car travels 10 miles per hour faster than the truck.

   a. Use the verbal model below to write an equation that relates the speeds of the vehicles.

$$\frac{\text{Distance for car}}{\text{Speed of car}} = \frac{\text{Distance for truck}}{\text{Speed of truck}}$$

   b. Solve the equation from part (a) to find the speeds of the car and the truck.

   c. How much time did the vehicles spend traveling? *Explain* your answer.

7. GRIDDED ANSWER Find the ratio of the volume of the sphere to the volume of the cube in the diagram below.

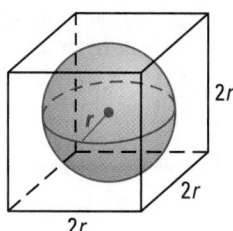

Use the formula $V = \frac{4}{3}\pi r^3$ for the volume of a sphere and the formula $V = s^3$ for the volume of a cube where r is the radius of the sphere and s is the side length of the cube. Write your answer as a decimal rounded to the nearest hundreth.

Animated Algebra
my.hrw.com
Electronic Function Library

BIG IDEAS
For Your Notebook

Big Idea 1

Graphing Rational Functions

Use the following steps to graph $f(x) = \dfrac{p(x)}{q(x)} = \dfrac{a_m x^m + a_{m-1} x^{m-1} + \cdots + a_1 x + a_0}{b_n x^n + b_{n-1} x^{n-1} + \cdots + b_1 x + b_0}$

where $p(x)$ and $q(x)$ have no common factors other than ± 1.

STEP 1 **Plot** the x-intercepts. The x-intercepts are the real zeros of $p(x)$.

STEP 2 **Draw** the vertical asymptote(s). A vertical asymptote occurs at each real zero of $q(x)$.

STEP 3 **Draw** the horizontal asymptote, if it exists.

If $m < n$, $y = 0$ is a horizontal asymptote.

If $m = n$, $y = \dfrac{a_m}{b_n}$ is a horizontal asymptote.

If $m > n$, there is no horizontal asymptote.

STEP 4 **Plot** several points on both sides of each vertical asymptote.

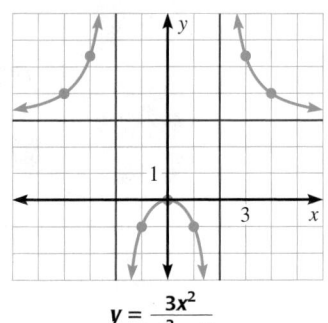

$$y = \dfrac{3x^2}{x^2 - 4}$$

Big Idea 2

Performing Operations with Rational Expressions

Operation	Example
Simplify Divide out common factors from the numerator and denominator.	$\dfrac{x^2 + 3x}{x^2 + 8x + 15} = \dfrac{x(x + 3)}{(x + 5)(x + 3)} = \dfrac{x}{x + 5}$
Multiply Multiply numerators and denominators. Then simplify.	$\dfrac{x}{15} \cdot \dfrac{3}{x^2 + 7x} = \dfrac{3x}{15x(x + 7)} = \dfrac{1}{5(x + 7)}$
Divide Multiply the first expression by the reciprocal of the second expression. Then simplify.	$\dfrac{x^2}{3x + 1} \div \dfrac{1}{6x + 2} = \dfrac{x^2}{3x + 1} \cdot \dfrac{2(3x + 1)}{1} = 2x^2$
Add or Subtract Write the expressions with like denominators. Then add or subtract the numerators over the common denominator. Lastly, simplify.	$\dfrac{5}{x} + \dfrac{x}{x + 2} = \dfrac{5(x + 2)}{x(x + 2)} + \dfrac{x^2}{x(x + 2)} = \dfrac{x^2 + 5x + 10}{x(x + 2)}$

Big Idea 3

Solving Rational Equations

Solve $\dfrac{x}{x + 1} + \dfrac{2}{x + 4} = 1$.

STEP 1 **Find** the LCD. LCD is $(x + 1)(x + 4)$.

STEP 2 **Multiply** each side of the equation by the LCD. $x(x + 4) + 2(x + 1) = (x + 1)(x + 4)$

STEP 3 **Solve** the resulting equation. $x^2 + 4x + 2x + 2 = x^2 + 5x + 4$

$$6x + 2 = 5x + 4$$

$$x = 2$$

REVIEW KEY VOCABULARY

- increasing
- decreasing
- odd function
- even function

- inverse variation
- constant of variation
- joint variation
- rational function

- simplified form of a rational expression
- complex fraction
- cross multiplying

VOCABULARY EXERCISES

1. Copy and complete: If two variables x and y are related by an equation of the form $y = \dfrac{a}{x}$ where $a \neq 0$, then x and y show __?__.

2. Suppose z varies jointly with x and y. What can you say about $\dfrac{z}{xy}$?

3. Copy and complete: A function of the form $f(x) = \dfrac{p(x)}{q(x)}$ where $p(x)$ and $q(x)$ are polynomials and $q(x) \neq 0$ is called a(n) __?__.

4. Give two examples of a complex fraction.

5. Copy and complete: When you rewrite the equation $\dfrac{3}{x} = \dfrac{2}{x-1}$ as $3(x-1) = 2x$, you are __?__.

REVIEW EXAMPLES AND EXERCISES

Use the review examples and exercises below to check your understanding of the concepts you have learned in each lesson of this chapter.

5.1 Model Inverse and Joint Variation

EXAMPLE

The variables x and y vary inversely, and $y = 12$ when $x = 3$. Write an equation that relates x and y. Then find y when $x = -4$.

$y = \dfrac{a}{x}$ Write general equation for inverse variation.

$12 = \dfrac{a}{3}$ Substitute 12 for y and 3 for x.

$36 = a$ Solve for a.

▶ The inverse variation equation is $y = \dfrac{36}{x}$. When $x = -4$, $y = \dfrac{36}{-4} = -9$.

EXERCISES

EXAMPLE 2
for Exs. 6–9

The variables x and y vary inversely. Use the given values to write an equation relating x and y. Then find y when $x = -3$.

6. $x = 1, y = 5$
7. $x = -4, y = -6$
8. $x = \dfrac{5}{2}, y = 18$
9. $x = -12, y = \dfrac{2}{3}$

5.2 Graph Simple Rational Functions

> **EXAMPLE**

Graph $y = \dfrac{2x + 5}{x - 1}$. State the domain and range.

STEP 1 **Draw** the asymptotes. Solve $x - 1 = 0$ for x to find the vertical asymptote $x = 1$. The horizontal asymptote is the line $y = \dfrac{2}{1} = 2$.

STEP 2 **Plot** points to the left and to the right of the vertical asymptote.

STEP 3 **Draw** the two branches of the hyperbola so that they pass through the plotted points and approach the asymptotes.

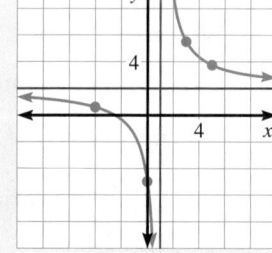

▸ The domain is all real numbers except 1. The range is all real numbers except 2.

EXAMPLES
2 and 3
for Exs. 10–12

EXERCISES

Graph the function. State the domain and range.

10. $y = \dfrac{4}{x - 3}$

11. $y = \dfrac{1}{x + 5} + 2$

12. $f(x) = \dfrac{3x - 2}{x - 4}$

5.3 Graph General Rational Functions

> **EXAMPLE**

Graph $y = \dfrac{2x^2}{x + 2}$.

- The numerator has 0 as its only zero, so the graph has an x-intercept at $(0, 0)$.

- The denominator has -2 as its only zero, so the graph has a vertical asymptote at $x = -2$.

- The degree of the numerator (2) is greater than the degree of the denominator (1). So, there is no horizontal asymptote. The graph has the same end behavior as the graph of $y = \dfrac{2}{1}x^{2-1} = 2x$.

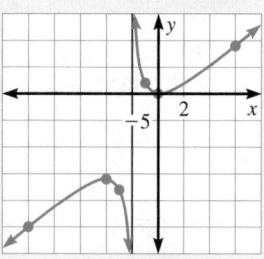

EXAMPLES
1, 2, and 3
for Exs. 13–18

EXERCISES

Graph the function.

13. $y = \dfrac{5}{x^2 + 1}$

14. $y = \dfrac{4x^2}{x - 1}$

15. $h(x) = \dfrac{6x^2}{x - 2}$

16. $y = \dfrac{-8}{x^2 + 3}$

17. $y = \dfrac{x^2 + 6}{x^2 - 3x - 40}$

18. $g(x) = \dfrac{x^2 - 1}{x + 4}$

5.4 Multiply and Divide Rational Expressions

EXAMPLE

Divide: $\dfrac{3x + 27}{6x - 48} \div \dfrac{x^2 + 9x}{x^2 - 4x - 32}$

$\dfrac{3x + 27}{6x - 48} \div \dfrac{x^2 + 9x}{x^2 - 4x - 32} = \dfrac{3x + 27}{6x - 48} \cdot \dfrac{x^2 - 4x - 32}{x^2 + 9x}$ Multiply by reciprocal.

$= \dfrac{3(x + 9)}{6(x - 8)} \cdot \dfrac{(x + 4)(x - 8)}{x(x + 9)}$ Factor.

$= \dfrac{3(x + 9)(x + 4)(x - 8)}{2(3)(x - 8)(x)(x + 9)}$ Divide out common factors.

$= \dfrac{x + 4}{2x}$ Simplified form

EXERCISES

EXAMPLES 3, 4, 6, and 7 for Exs. 19–22

Perform the indicated operation. Simplify the result.

19. $\dfrac{80x^4}{y^3} \cdot \dfrac{xy}{5x^2}$

20. $\dfrac{x - 3}{2x - 8} \cdot \dfrac{6x^2 - 96}{x^2 - 9}$

21. $\dfrac{16x^2 - 8x + 1}{x^3 - 7x^2 + 12x} \div \dfrac{20x^2 - 5x}{15x^3}$

22. $\dfrac{x^2 - 13x + 40}{x^2 - 2x - 15} \div (x^2 - 5x - 24)$

5.5 Add and Subtract Rational Expressions

EXAMPLE

Add: $\dfrac{x}{6x + 24} + \dfrac{x + 2}{x^2 + 9x + 20}$

The denominators factor as $6(x + 4)$ and $(x + 4)(x + 5)$, so the LCD is $6(x + 4)(x + 5)$. Use this result to rewrite each expression with a common denominator, and then add.

$\dfrac{x}{6x + 24} + \dfrac{x + 2}{x^2 + 9x + 20} = \dfrac{x}{6(x + 4)} + \dfrac{x + 2}{(x + 4)(x + 5)}$

$= \dfrac{x}{6(x + 4)} \cdot \dfrac{x + 5}{x + 5} + \dfrac{x + 2}{(x + 4)(x + 5)} \cdot \dfrac{6}{6}$

$= \dfrac{x^2 + 5x}{6(x + 4)(x + 5)} + \dfrac{6x + 12}{6(x + 4)(x + 5)}$

$= \dfrac{x^2 + 11x + 12}{6(x + 4)(x + 5)}$

EXERCISES

EXAMPLES 3 and 4 for Exs. 23–25

Perform the indicated operation and simplify.

23. $\dfrac{5}{6(x + 3)} + \dfrac{x + 4}{2x}$

24. $\dfrac{5x}{x + 8} + \dfrac{4x - 9}{x^2 + 5x - 24}$

25. $\dfrac{x + 2}{x^2 + 4x + 3} - \dfrac{5x}{x^2 - 9}$

5.6 Solve Rational Equations

EXAMPLE

Solve: $\dfrac{3x}{x+1} + \dfrac{6}{2x} = \dfrac{7}{x}$

The least common denominator is $2x(x+1)$.

$$\dfrac{3x}{x+1} + \dfrac{6}{2x} = \dfrac{7}{x} \qquad \text{Write original equation.}$$

$$2x(x+1)\left(\dfrac{3x}{x+1} + \dfrac{6}{2x}\right) = 2x(x+1) \cdot \dfrac{7}{x} \qquad \text{Multiply each side by the LCD, } 2x(x+1).$$

$$2x(3x) + 6(x+1) = 2(x+1)(7) \qquad \text{Simplify.}$$

$$6x^2 - 8x - 8 = 0 \qquad \text{Simplify, write in standard form.}$$

$$2(3x+2)(x-2) = 0 \qquad \text{Factor.}$$

$$3x + 2 = 0 \quad \text{or} \quad x - 2 = 0 \qquad \text{Zero product property}$$

$$x = -\dfrac{2}{3} \quad \text{or} \qquad x = 2 \qquad \text{Solve for } x.$$

▶ The solutions are $-\dfrac{2}{3}$ and 2. Check to make sure neither solution is extraneous.

EXERCISES

EXAMPLES
1, 4, and 5
for Exs. 26–36

Solve the equation by cross multiplying. Check your solution(s).

26. $\dfrac{5}{x} = \dfrac{7}{x+2}$

27. $\dfrac{x+12}{3} = \dfrac{2x+3}{x+2}$

28. $\dfrac{2x}{x+4} = \dfrac{-3x}{4x-3}$

Solve the equation by using the LCD. Check for extraneous solutions.

29. $\dfrac{8(x-1)}{x^2-4} = \dfrac{4}{x+2}$

30. $\dfrac{2(x+7)}{x+4} - 2 = \dfrac{2x+20}{2x+8}$

5.7 Describe and Compare Function Characteristics

EXAMPLE

Determine whether the function $f(x) = x^2 - x^3$ is *even*, *odd*, or *neither*.
Replace x with $\alpha-x$ in the equation for the function, then simplify.

$$f(-x) = 2(-x)^2 + (-x)^4 = 2(-1)^2\, x^2 + (-1)^2\, x^4 = 2x^2 + x^4 = f(x)$$

Because $f(x) = f(-x)$, the function is even.

EXERCISES

Determine whether the function is *even*, *odd*, or *neither*.

31. $p(x) = x^{17} + 4x^3$

32. $q(x) = \sin(x)$

33. $r(x) = \sin(x^2)$

The variables x and y vary inversely. Use the given values to write an equation relating x and y. Then find y when $x = 4$.

1. $x = 5, y = 2$

2. $x = -4, y = \dfrac{7}{2}$

3. $x = \dfrac{3}{4}, y = \dfrac{5}{8}$

Graph the function. State the domain and range.

4. $y = \dfrac{2}{x + 5} - 3$

5. $y = \dfrac{-1}{x - 4} - 1$

6. $f(x) = \dfrac{6 - x}{2x + 1}$

Graph the function.

7. $y = \dfrac{4}{x^2 + 2}$

8. $y = \dfrac{x^2 - 4}{x^2 + 8x + 15}$

9. $g(x) = \dfrac{x^2 + 3}{2x - 1}$

Find the least common multiple of the polynomials.

10. $(x - 3)(x + 5)$ and $x(x + 5)$

11. $4x^2(x - 2)$ and $8x(x + 2)$

12. $x^2 - 4x$ and $x^2 - 2x - 8$

13. $2x + 6$ and $x^3 + 10x^2 + 21x$

Perform the indicated operation and simplify.

14. $\dfrac{3x^2 y}{4x^3 y^5} \div \dfrac{6y^2}{2xy^3}$

15. $\dfrac{x^2 - 3x - 4}{x^2 - 3x - 18} \cdot \dfrac{x - 6}{x + 1}$

16. $\dfrac{x^2 - 8x + 15}{x^2 + 12x + 32} \cdot \dfrac{x + 4}{x^2 - 25}$

17. $\dfrac{x^2 - 11x + 28}{x^2 + 5x + 4} \div (x^2 - 16)$

18. $\dfrac{3x}{x^2 + x - 12} - \dfrac{6}{x + 4}$

19. $\dfrac{4}{x + 5} + \dfrac{2x}{x^2 - 25}$

Solve the equation. Check for extraneous solutions.

20. $\dfrac{3}{x + 2} = \dfrac{x - 3}{2x + 4}$

21. $\dfrac{1}{x + 6} + \dfrac{x + 1}{x} = \dfrac{13}{x + 6}$

22. $\dfrac{x - 2}{x - 1} = \dfrac{x + 2}{x + 4}$

23. For the function $f(x) = 4^{x - 3}$, find the average rate of change over the intervals [3, 4], [4, 5], [5, 6], and [6, 7]. What happens to the average rate of change as x increases? What does this mean for the graph of $f(x)$?

24. **SOUND INTENSITY** The intensity I of a sound varies inversely with the square of the distance r from the source of the sound. Write an equation relating I, r, and a constant a.

25. **CABLE TV** You have subscribed to a cable television service. The cable company charges you a one-time installation fee of $30 and a monthly fee of $50. Write and graph a model that gives the average cost per month as a function of the number of months you have subscribed to the service. After how many months will the average cost be $56?

26. **WEB HOSTING** You are building a new website for your school. A company that hosts websites offers a dedicated server for a $50 setup fee plus a monthly fee of $99. How many months would you need to use this service in order for your average monthly cost to fall to $100?

CONTEXT-BASED MULTIPLE CHOICE QUESTIONS

Some of the information you need to solve a context-based multiple choice question may appear in a table, a diagram, or a graph.

> **PROBLEM 1**
>
> Which rational expression represents the ratio of the perimeter to the area of the playground shown in the diagram?
>
> (A) $\dfrac{9}{7x}$ (B) $\dfrac{1}{x}$
>
> (C) $\dfrac{11}{14x}$ (D) $\dfrac{1}{2x}$
>
>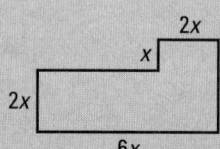

Plan

INTERPRET THE DIAGRAM Determine the missing dimensions on the diagram. Then use them to write expressions for the perimeter and area of the playground.

STEP 1
Find the missing dimensions and write an expression for the perimeter.

Solution

Copy the diagram. Then find and label the missing dimensions.

Use subtraction and addition to find the dimensions that are not labeled on the diagram. The missing dimensions are **4x** and **3x**.

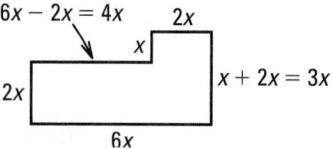

Perimeter = $\mathbf{4x} + x + 2x + \mathbf{3x} + 6x + 2x$

$= 18x$

STEP 2
Write an expression for the area.

The playground consists of two rectangles, one with dimensions x by $\mathbf{2x}$ and the other with dimensions $\mathbf{2x}$ by $6x$.

To find the area of the playground, add the areas of the two rectangles.

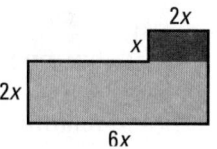

Area = $\mathbf{x}(2\mathbf{x}) + \mathbf{2x}(6\mathbf{x})$

$= 2x^2 + 12x^2$

$= 14x^2$

STEP 3
Find the ratio of the perimeter to the area.

The ratio of the perimeter to the area is:

$$\dfrac{\text{Perimeter}}{\text{Area}} = \dfrac{18x}{14x^2} = \dfrac{2x(9)}{2x(7x)} = \dfrac{9}{7x}$$

▶ The correct answer is A. (A) (B) (C) (D)

PROBLEM 2

The table shows how the force F (in pounds) needed to loosen a certain bolt with a wrench depends on the length ℓ (in inches) of the wrench's handle. Which equation relates ℓ and F?

ℓ (in.)	F (lb)
4	375
6	250
10	150
12	125

A $F = 1500\ell$

B $F = 93.75\ell$

C $F = \dfrac{1500}{\ell}$

D $F = \dfrac{93.75}{\ell}$

Plan

INTERPRET THE TABLE The table shows four data pairs (ℓ, F). To write an equation relating ℓ and F, you need to find a pattern in the data.

Solution

STEP 1

Identify a pattern in the data pairs (ℓ, F).

▶ Find the product $\ell \cdot F$ for each data pair.

$4(375) = 1500 \qquad 6(250) = 1500$

$10(150) = 1500 \qquad 12(125) = 1500$

Each product equals 1500, so the data show inverse variation.

STEP 2

Write an equation that relates ℓ and F.

▶ An equation relating ℓ and F is the following:

$\ell \cdot F = 1500$ **Use the result from Step 1.**

$F = \dfrac{1500}{\ell}$ **Solve for F.**

▶ The correct answer is C. **A B Ⓒ D**

PRACTICE

1. Which rational expression represents the ratio of the perimeter to the area of the figure shown?

   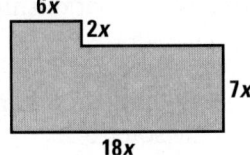

   A $\dfrac{29}{67x}$

   B $\dfrac{3}{10x^2}$

   C $\dfrac{11x}{18x^2}$

   D $\dfrac{9}{23x}$

2. Which equation represents the ordered pairs in the table?

x	2	4	6	8	10
y	180	90	60	45	36

   A $y = \dfrac{360}{x}$

   B $y = \dfrac{x}{360}$

   C $y = \dfrac{90}{x}$

   D $y = \dfrac{x}{90}$

MULTIPLE CHOICE

In Exercises 1 and 2, use the given graph of a rational function.

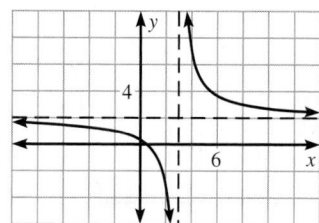

1. What is the range of the function?

    (A) All real numbers

    (B) All real numbers except 2

    (C) All real numbers except 3

    (D) All real numbers except 5

2. Which statement is false?

    (A) The line $x = 3$ is an asymptote.

    (B) The line $y = 2$ is an asymptote.

    (C) The function is undefined for $x = 2$.

    (D) The point $(-2, 1)$ lies on the graph.

In Exercises 3 and 4, use the given table.

p	−12	3	30	−1.5
q	2	1	−5	−0.5
r	−2	1	−2	1

3. What is the relationship among the variables?

    (A) The variable p varies jointly with q and r.

    (B) The variable p varies jointly with q and the square of r.

    (C) The variable r varies inversely with the sum of p and q.

    (D) The variable q varies inversely with the sum of p and r.

4. What is the value of r when $p = 20$ and $q = -4$?

    (A) -5

    (B) $-\dfrac{10}{3}$

    (C) $-\dfrac{5}{3}$

    (D) $-\dfrac{1}{5}$

In Exercises 5 and 6, use the given graph of a rational function.

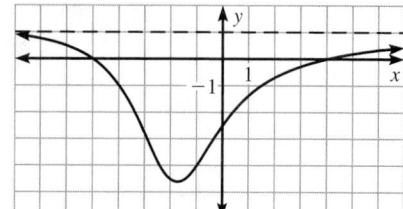

5. What are the x-intercepts of the graph?

    (A) -5 and -2.5

    (B) -2.5 and 4

    (C) -4 and 5

    (D) -5 and 4

6. What is the horizontal asymptote of the graph?

    (A) $x = -2$

    (B) $y = 0$

    (C) $x = 1$

    (D) $y = 1$

7. Consider a rectangle whose dimensions change but whose area remains constant. The rectangle's length ℓ varies inversely with its width w. The diagram below shows the rectangle at one moment in time. Which equation relates ℓ and w?

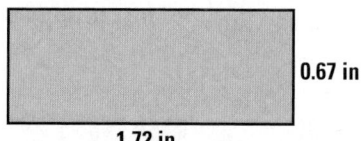

0.67 in

1.72 in.

    (A) $w = 0.67\ell$

    (B) $\ell w = 1.1524$

    (C) $w = 1.72\ell$

    (D) $\ell = 1.1524w$

8. What is the approximate radius of a cylinder that has the same volume as the rectangular prism below and has the least surface area possible?

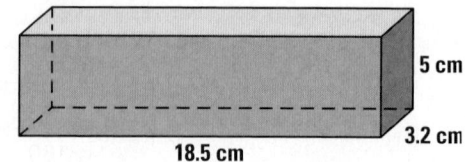

5 cm

3.2 cm

18.5 cm

    (A) 3.61 cm

    (B) 3.84 cm

    (C) 6.00 cm

    (D) 7.66 cm

GRIDDED ANSWER

9. What is the solution of the equation
$$\frac{4}{x+1} - \frac{1}{x} = 1?$$

10. The variables m and n vary inversely, and $m = -2$ when $n = -8$. What is the value of n when $m = 5$?

11. The variable q varies jointly with r and the square of s and inversely with the square root of t. Also, $q = -1.75$ when $r = -2$, $s = 1$, and $t = 16$. What is the value of q when $r = 5$, $s = -3$, and $t = 25$?

12. What number is not in the domain of the function $f(x) = \dfrac{x-3}{2x^2 - 4x + 2}$?

13. So far this quarter, a student has handed in 15 of 17 homework assignments. Solve the equation $0.95 = \dfrac{15 + x}{17 + x}$ to determine the number of consecutive assignments the student must turn in to raise her homework percentage up to 95%.

SHORT RESPONSE

14. Lisa steps onto an escalator and begins descending. After riding for 12 feet, she realized that she dropped her keys on the upper floor and walks back up the escalator to retrieve them. The total time T of her trip down and up the escalator is given by the equation
$$T = \frac{12}{s} + \frac{12}{w - s}$$
where s is the speed of the escalator and w is Lisa's walking speed. The trip took 9 seconds and Lisa walks at a speed of 6 feet per second. Find the speed of the escalator.

15. From 1960 to 1995 in the United States, the daily water consumption C (in billions of gallons) and the population P (in thousands) can be modeled by
$$C = \frac{2.89x^2 + 61.0}{0.0293x^2 + 1} \text{ and } P = 2460x + 180,000$$
where x represents the number of years since 1960. Write a model for the daily *per capita* water consumption (in gallons per person) as a function of the year. *Explain* all of your steps.

EXTENDED RESPONSE

16. From 1980 to 2001, the number n (in millions) of males enrolled in high school in the United States can be modeled by
$$n = \frac{0.0441x^2 - 1.08x + 7.25}{0.00565x^2 - 0.142x + 1.00}$$
where x is the number of years since 1980.

   a. Make a table of values showing the enrollment at 2 year intervals for the years 1980 to 2000.

   b. Graph the model.

   c. Use your graph to estimate the year in which 7.7 million males were enrolled in high school.

   d. Analyze the graph's trend. Do you think it will it continue indefinitely? *Explain* your answer.

17. A digital video recorder costs $99.99, and a programming service for the digital video recorder costs $12.95 per month.

   a. Write a model that gives the average cost per month C as a function of the number of months m you have subscribed to the service.

   b. Graph the model. Use the graph to estimate the number of months that you need to subscribe before the average cost drops to $14 per month.

   c. What is the equation of the horizontal asymptote? What does the asymptote represent?

6 Data Analysis and Statistics

Before

In previous chapters, you learned the following skills, which you'll use in this chapter: describing distributions, ordering real numbers, and finding probabilities.

Prerequisite Skills

VOCABULARY CHECK

Copy and complete the statement.

1. The **probability** of an event is a number from __?__ to __?__ that indicates the likelihood the event will occur.

2. The **binomial distribution** at the right is not skewed. Instead, it is __?__.

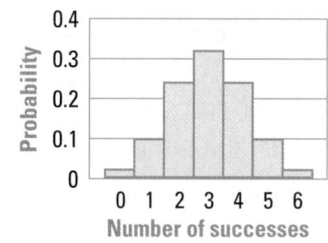

SKILLS CHECK

Graph the numbers on a number line. Then write the numbers in increasing order.

3. $-\frac{3}{4}, 0.4, \sqrt{7}, -1.3, \frac{2}{3}, -\sqrt{12}$

4. $1.5, \frac{4}{3}, -1.24, \sqrt{2}, -\sqrt{3}, \frac{6}{5}$

5. Evaluate the expression $\frac{x-68}{4}$ for the x-values 64, 72, and 76.

Find the square root of each number.

6. $\sqrt{100}$ 7. $\sqrt{49}$ 8. $\sqrt{900}$ 9. $\sqrt{10,000}$

In this chapter, you will apply the big ideas listed below and reviewed in the Chapter Summary. You will also use the key vocabulary listed below.

Big Ideas

1 **Using normal distributions**

2 **Working with samples**

KEY VOCABULARY

- combination
- Pascal's triangle
- binomial theorem
- random variable
- probability distribution
- binomial distribution
- binomial experiment
- symmetric
- skewed

- normal distribution
- normal curve
- standard normal distribution
- z-score
- sample
- unbiased sample
- biased sample
- margin of error

- biased questions
- experiment
- observational study
- controlled experiment
- control group
- treatment group
- randomized comparative experiment

Why?

You can use statistics to determine probabilities. For example, you can determine the probability of an event based on the results of a survey.

Animated Algebra

The animation illustrated below can help you answer a question from this chapter: What is the probability that at most 2 households in a randomly chosen group of 6 have a soccer ball?

According to a survey, about 41% of all U.S. households have a soccer ball.

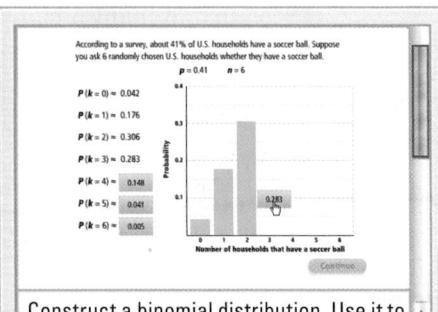

According to a survey, about 41% of U.S. households have a soccer ball. Suppose you ask 6 randomly chosen U.S. households whether they have a soccer ball.

$p = 0.41$ $n = 6$

$P(k = 0) \approx 0.042$
$P(k = 1) \approx 0.176$
$P(k = 2) \approx 0.306$
$P(k = 3) \approx 0.283$
$P(k = 4) \approx 0.148$
$P(k = 5) \approx 0.041$
$P(k = 6) \approx 0.005$

Construct a binomial distribution. Use it to determine a probability.

Animated Algebra at my.hrw.com

(Insa) Getty Images/Photodisc

6.1 Use Combinations and the Binomial Theorem

Before	You used the counting principle and permutations.
Now	You will use combinations and the binomial theorem.
Why?	So you can find ways to form a set, as in Example 2.

Key Vocabulary
- combination
- Pascal's triangle
- binomial theorem

You have learned that order is important for some counting problems. For other counting problems, order is not important. For instance, if you purchase a package of trading cards, the order of the cards inside the package is not important. A **combination** is a selection of r objects from a group of n objects where the order is not important.

CC.9-12.A.APR.5 (+) Know and apply the Binomial Theorem for the expansion of $(x + y)^n$ in powers of x and y for a positive integer n, where x and y are any numbers, with coefficients determined for example by Pascal's Triangle.

KEY CONCEPT *For Your Notebook*

Combinations of n Objects Taken r at a Time

The number of combinations of r objects taken from a group of n distinct objects is denoted by $_nC_r$ and is given by this formula:

$$_nC_r = \frac{n!}{(n - r)! \cdot r!}$$

EXAMPLE 1 **Find combinations**

CARDS A standard deck of 52 playing cards has 4 suits with 13 different cards in each suit.

a. If the order in which the cards are dealt is not important, how many different 5-card hands are possible?

b. In how many 5-card hands are all 5 cards of the same color?

Standard 52-Card Deck

K ♠	K ♥	K ♦	K ♣
Q ♠	Q ♥	Q ♦	Q ♣
J ♠	J ♥	J ♦	J ♣
10 ♠	10 ♥	10 ♦	10 ♣
9 ♠	9 ♥	9 ♦	9 ♣
8 ♠	8 ♥	8 ♦	8 ♣
7 ♠	7 ♥	7 ♦	7 ♣
6 ♠	6 ♥	6 ♦	6 ♣
5 ♠	5 ♥	5 ♦	5 ♣
4 ♠	4 ♥	4 ♦	4 ♣
3 ♠	3 ♥	3 ♦	3 ♣
2 ♠	2 ♥	2 ♦	2 ♣
A ♠	A ♥	A ♦	A ♣

Solution

a. The number of ways to choose **5** cards from a deck of **52** cards is:

$$_{52}C_5 = \frac{52!}{47! \cdot 5!} = \frac{52 \cdot 51 \cdot 50 \cdot 49 \cdot 48 \cdot \cancel{47!}}{\cancel{47!} \cdot 5!} = 2{,}598{,}960$$

b. For all 5 cards to be the same color, you need to choose **1** of the **2** colors and then **5** of the **26** cards in that color. So, the number of possible hands is:

$$_2C_1 \cdot {}_{26}C_5 = \frac{2!}{1! \cdot 1!} \cdot \frac{26!}{21! \cdot 5!} = \frac{2}{1 \cdot 1} \cdot \frac{26 \cdot 25 \cdot 24 \cdot 23 \cdot 22 \cdot \cancel{21!}}{\cancel{21!} \cdot 5!} = 131{,}560$$

MULTIPLE EVENTS When finding the number of ways both an event *A and* an event *B* can occur, you need to multiply, as in part (b) of Example 1. When finding the number of ways that event *A or* event *B* can occur, you add instead.

EXAMPLE 2 Decide to multiply or add combinations

THEATER William Shakespeare wrote 38 plays that can be divided into three genres. Of the 38 plays, 18 are comedies, 10 are histories, and 10 are tragedies.

a. How many different sets of *exactly* 2 comedies and 1 tragedy can you read?

b. How many different sets of *at most* 3 plays can you read?

AVOID ERRORS
When finding the number of ways to select *at most n* objects, be sure to include the possibility of selecting 0 objects.

Solution

a. You can choose 2 of the 18 comedies and 1 of the 10 tragedies. So, the number of possible sets of plays is:

$$_{18}C_2 \cdot {}_{10}C_1 = \frac{18!}{16! \cdot 2!} \cdot \frac{10!}{9! \cdot 1!} = \frac{18 \cdot 17 \cdot \cancel{16!}}{\cancel{16!} \cdot 2 \cdot 1} \cdot \frac{10 \cdot \cancel{9!}}{\cancel{9!} \cdot 1} = 153 \cdot 10 = 1530$$

b. You can read 0, 1, 2, or 3 plays. Because there are 38 plays that can be chosen, the number of possible sets of plays is:

$$_{38}C_0 + {}_{38}C_1 + {}_{38}C_2 + {}_{38}C_3 = 1 + 38 + 703 + 8436 = 9178$$

SUBTRACTING POSSIBILITIES Counting problems that involve phrases like "at least" or "at most" are sometimes easier to solve by subtracting possibilities you do not want from the total number of possibilities.

EXAMPLE 3 Solve a multi-step problem

BASKETBALL During the school year, the girl's basketball team is scheduled to play 12 home games. You want to attend *at least* 3 of the games. How many different combinations of games can you attend?

Solution

Of the 12 home games, you want to attend 3 games, or 4 games, or 5 games, and so on. So, the number of combinations of games you can attend is:

$$_{12}C_3 + {}_{12}C_4 + {}_{12}C_5 + \cdots + {}_{12}C_{12}$$

Instead of adding these combinations, use the following reasoning. For each of the 12 games, you can choose to attend or not attend the game, so there are 2^{12} total combinations. If you attend at least 3 games, you do not attend only a total of 0, 1, or 2 games. So, the number of ways you can attend at least 3 games is:

$$2^{12} - ({}_{12}C_0 + {}_{12}C_1 + {}_{12}C_2) = 4096 - (1 + 12 + 66) = 4017$$

✓ **GUIDED PRACTICE** for Examples 1, 2, and 3

Find the number of combinations.

1. $_8C_3$

2. $_{10}C_6$

3. $_7C_2$

4. $_{14}C_5$

5. **WHAT IF?** In Example 2, how many different sets of *exactly* 3 tragedies and 2 histories can you read?

PASCAL'S TRIANGLE If you arrange the values of $_nC_r$ in a triangular pattern in which each row corresponds to a value of n, you get what is called **Pascal's triangle**. Pascal's triangle is named after the French mathematician Blaise Pascal (1623–1662).

KEY CONCEPT

For Your Notebook

Pascal's Triangle

Pascal's triangle is shown below with its entries represented by combinations and with its entries represented by numbers. The first and last numbers in each row are 1. Every number other than 1 is the sum of the closest two numbers in the row directly above it.

	Pascal's triangle as combinations	Pascal's triangle as numbers
$n = 0$ (0th row)	$_0C_0$	1
$n = 1$ (1st row)	$_1C_0 \quad _1C_1$	1 1
$n = 2$ (2nd row)	$_2C_0 \quad _2C_1 \quad _2C_2$	1 2 1
$n = 3$ (3rd row)	$_3C_0 \quad _3C_1 \quad _3C_2 \quad _3C_3$	1 3 3 1
$n = 4$ (4th row)	$_4C_0 \quad _4C_1 \quad _4C_2 \quad _4C_3 \quad _4C_4$	1 4 6 4 1
$n = 5$ (5th row)	$_5C_0 \quad _5C_1 \quad _5C_2 \quad _5C_3 \quad _5C_4 \quad _5C_5$	1 5 10 10 5 1

EXAMPLE 4   Use Pascal's triangle

SCHOOL CLUBS The 6 members of a Model UN club must choose 2 representatives to attend a state convention. Use Pascal's triangle to find the number of combinations of 2 members that can be chosen as representatives.

Solution

Because you need to find $_6C_2$, write the 6th row of Pascal's triangle by adding numbers from the previous row.

$n = 5$ (5th row)   1   5   10   10   5   1

$n = 6$ (6th row)   1   6   15   20   15   6   1
                    $_6C_0 \quad _6C_1 \quad _6C_2 \quad _6C_3 \quad _6C_4 \quad _6C_5 \quad _6C_6$

▸ The value of $_6C_2$ is the third number in the 6th row of Pascal's triangle, as shown above. Therefore, $_6C_2 = 15$. There are 15 combinations of representatives for the convention.

✓ **GUIDED PRACTICE**   for Example 4

6. **WHAT IF?** In Example 4, use Pascal's triangle to find the number of combinations of 2 members that can be chosen if the Model UN club has 7 members.

BINOMIAL EXPANSIONS There is an important relationship between powers of binomials and combinations. The numbers in Pascal's triangle can be used to find coefficients in binomial expansions. For example, the coefficients in the expansion of $(a + b)^4$ are the numbers of combinations in the row of Pascal's triangle for $n = 4$:

$$(a + b)^4 = 1a^4 + 4a^3b + 6a^2b^2 + 4ab^3 + 1b^4$$
$$\quad\quad\quad {}_4C_0 \quad {}_4C_1 \quad {}_4C_2 \quad {}_4C_3 \quad {}_4C_4$$

This result is generalized in the **binomial theorem**.

KEY CONCEPT *For Your Notebook*

Binomial Theorem

For any positive integer n, the binomial expansion of $(a + b)^n$ is:

$$(a + b)^n = {}_nC_0 a^n b^0 + {}_nC_1 a^{n-1} b^1 + {}_nC_2 a^{n-2} b^2 + \cdots + {}_nC_n a^0 b^n$$

Notice that each term in the expansion of $(a + b)^n$ has the form ${}_nC_r a^{n-r} b^r$ where r is an integer from 0 to n.

EXAMPLE 5 **Expand a power of a binomial sum**

Use the binomial theorem to write the binomial expansion.

$$(x^2 + y)^3 = {}_3C_0 (x^2)^3 y^0 + {}_3C_1 (x^2)^2 y^1 + {}_3C_2 (x^2)^1 y^2 + {}_3C_3 (x^2)^0 y^3$$
$$= (1)(x^6)(1) + (3)(x^4)(y) + (3)(x^2)(y^2) + (1)(1)(y^3)$$
$$= x^6 + 3x^4 y + 3x^2 y^2 + y^3$$

POWERS OF BINOMIAL DIFFERENCES To expand a power of a binomial difference, you can rewrite the binomial as a sum. The resulting expansion will have terms whose signs alternate between + and −.

EXAMPLE 6 **Expand a power of a binomial difference**

AVOID ERRORS

When a binomial has a term or terms with a coefficient other than 1, the coefficients of the binomial expansion are not the same as the corresponding row of Pascal's triangle.

Use the binomial theorem to write the binomial expansion.

$$(a - 2b)^4 = [a + (-2b)]^4$$
$$= {}_4C_0 a^4 (-2b)^0 + {}_4C_1 a^3 (-2b)^1 + {}_4C_2 a^2 (-2b)^2 + {}_4C_3 a^1 (-2b)^3 + {}_4C_4 a^0 (-2b)^4$$
$$= (1)(a^4)(1) + (4)(a^3)(-2b) + (6)(a^2)(4b^2) + (4)(a)(-8b^3) + (1)(1)(16b^4)$$
$$= a^4 - 8a^3 b + 24a^2 b^2 - 32ab^3 + 16b^4$$

✓ **GUIDED PRACTICE** for Examples 5 and 6

Use the binomial theorem to write the binomial expansion.

7. $(x + 3)^5$ **8.** $(a + 2b)^4$ **9.** $(2p - q)^4$ **10.** $(5 - 2y)^3$

EXAMPLE 7 Find a coefficient in an expansion

Find the coefficient of x^4 in the expansion of $(3x + 2)^{10}$.

Solution

From the binomial theorem, you know the following:

$$(3x + 2)^{10} = {}_{10}C_0(3x)^{10}(2)^0 + {}_{10}C_1(3x)^9(2)^1 + \cdots + {}_{10}C_{10}(3x)^0(2)^{10}$$

Each term in the expansion has the form ${}_{10}C_r(3x)^{10-r}(2)^r$. The term containing x^4 occurs when $r = 6$:

$${}_{10}C_6(3x)^4(2)^6 = (210)\big(81x^4\big)(64) = 1{,}088{,}640x^4$$

▶ The coefficient of x^4 is 1,088,640.

✓ **GUIDED PRACTICE** for Example 7

11. Find the coefficient of x^5 in the expansion of $(x - 3)^7$.

12. Find the coefficient of x^3 in the expansion of $(2x + 5)^8$.

6.1 EXERCISES

HOMEWORK KEY : ◯ = See WORKED-OUT SOLUTIONS Exs. 17, 29, and 49

★ = STANDARDIZED TEST PRACTICE Exs. 2, 35, 40, 41, and 52

SKILL PRACTICE

1. **VOCABULARY** Copy and complete: The binomial expansion of $(a + b)^n$ is given by the __?__.

2. ★ **WRITING** *Explain* the difference between permutations and combinations.

EXAMPLES 1, 2, and 3 for Exs. 3–18

COMBINATIONS Find the number of combinations.

3. ${}_5C_2$ 4. ${}_{10}C_3$ 5. ${}_9C_6$ 6. ${}_8C_2$

7. ${}_{11}C_{11}$ 8. ${}_{12}C_4$ 9. ${}_7C_5$ 10. ${}_{14}C_6$

ERROR ANALYSIS *Describe* and correct the error in finding the number of combinations.

11.
$${}_6C_2 = \frac{6!}{(6-2)!} = \frac{720}{24} = 30 \quad ✗$$

12.
$${}_8C_3 = \frac{8!}{3!} = \frac{40{,}320}{6} = 6720 \quad ✗$$

CARD HANDS Find the number of possible 5-card hands that contain the cards specified. The cards are taken from a standard 52-card deck.

13. 5 face cards (kings, queens, or jacks)   14. 4 kings and 1 other card

15. 1 ace and 4 cards that are not aces   16. 5 hearts or 5 diamonds

17. At most 1 queen   18. At least 1 spade

EXAMPLE 4
for Exs. 19–23

19. USING PATTERNS Copy Pascal's triangle and add rows for $n = 6, 7, 8, 9,$ and 10.

PASCAL'S TRIANGLE Use the rows of Pascal's triangle from Exercise 19 to write the binomial expansion.

20. $(x + 3)^6$ **21.** $(y - 3z)^{10}$ **22.** $(a + b^2)^8$ **23.** $(2s - t^4)^7$

EXAMPLES 5 and 6
for Exs. 24–31

BINOMIAL THEOREM Use the binomial theorem to write the binomial expansion.

24. $(x + 2)^3$ **25.** $(c - 4)^5$ **26.** $(a + 3b)^4$ **27.** $(4p - q)^6$

28. $(w^3 - 3)^4$ **29.** $(2s^4 + 5)^5$ **30.** $(3u + v^2)^6$ **31.** $(x^3 - y^2)^4$

EXAMPLE 7
for Exs. 32–35

32. Find the coefficient of x^5 in the expansion of $(x - 2)^{10}$.

33. Find the coefficient of x^3 in the expansion of $(3x + 2)^5$.

34. Find the coefficient of x^6 in the expansion of $(x^2 - 3)^8$.

35. ★ **MULTIPLE CHOICE** Which is the coefficient of x^4 in the expansion of $(x - 3)^7$?

 (A) -945 **(B)** -35 **(C)** -27 **(D)** 2835

PASCAL'S TRIANGLE In Exercises 36 and 37, use the diagrams shown.

36. What is the sum of the numbers in each of rows 0–4 of Pascal's triangle? What is the sum in row n?

37. *Describe* the pattern formed by the sums of the numbers along the diagonal segments of Pascal's triangle.

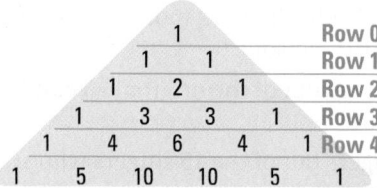

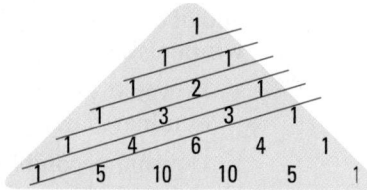

REASONING In Exercises 38 and 39, decide whether the problem requires *combinations* or *permutations* to find the answer. Then solve the problem.

38. NEWSPAPER Your school newspaper has an editor-in-chief and an assistant editor-in-chief. The staff of the newspaper has 12 students. In how many ways can students be chosen for these two positions?

39. STUDENT COUNCIL Five representatives from a senior class of 280 students are to be chosen for the student council. In how many ways can students be chosen to represent the senior class on the student council?

40. ★ **MULTIPLE CHOICE** A relay race has a team of 4 runners who run different parts of the race. There are 20 students on your track squad. In how many ways can the coach select students to compete on the relay team?

 (A) 4845 **(B)** $40,000$ **(C)** $116,280$ **(D)** $160,000$

41. ★ **SHORT RESPONSE** *Explain* how the formula for $_nC_n$ suggests the definition $0! = 1$.

CHALLENGE Verify the identity. *Justify* each of your steps.

42. $_nC_0 = 1$ **43.** $_nC_n = 1$ **44.** $_nC_r \cdot {}_rC_m = {}_nC_m \cdot {}_{n-m}C_{r-m}$

45. $_nC_1 = {}_nP_1$ **46.** $_nC_r = {}_nC_{n-r}$ **47.** $_{n+1}C_r = {}_nC_r + {}_nC_{r-1}$

EXAMPLES
1, 2, and 3
for Exs. 48–50

48. MUSIC You want to purchase 3 CDs from an online collection that contains the types of music shown at the right. You want each CD to contain a different type of music such that 2 CDs are different types of contemporary music and 1 CD is a type of classical music. How many different sets of music types can you choose?

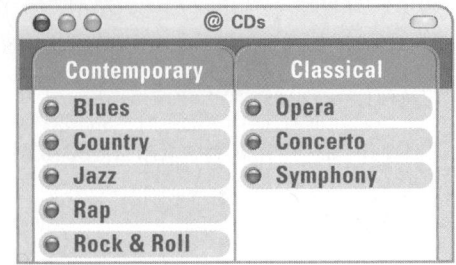

Contemporary	Classical
Blues	Opera
Country	Concerto
Jazz	Symphony
Rap	
Rock & Roll	

@ CDs

49. FLOWERS You are buying a bouquet. The florist has 18 types of flowers that you can use to make the bouquet. You want to use *exactly* 3 types of flowers. How many different combinations of flower types can you use in your bouquet?

50. ARCADE GAMES An arcade has 20 different arcade games. You want to play at least 14 of them. How many different combinations of arcade games can you play?

51. MULTI-STEP PROBLEM A televised singing competition picks a winner from 20 original contestants over the course of five episodes. During each of the first, second, and third episodes, 5 singers are eliminated by the end of the episode. The fourth episode eliminates 2 more singers, and the winner is selected at the end of the fifth episode.

a. How many combinations of 5 singers out of the original 20 can be eliminated during the first episode?

b. How many combinations of 5 singers out of the 15 singers who started the second episode can be eliminated during the second episode?

c. How many combinations of singers can be eliminated during the third episode? during the fourth episode? during the fifth episode?

d. Find the total number of ways in which the 20 original contestants can be eliminated to produce a winner.

52. ★ EXTENDED RESPONSE A group of 15 high school students is volunteering at a local fire station. Of these students, 5 will be assigned to wash fire trucks, 7 will be assigned to repaint the station's interior, and 3 will be assigned to do maintenance on the station's exterior.

a. Calculate One way to count the number of possible job assignments is to find the number of permutations of 5 W's (for "wash"), 7 R's (for "repainting"), and 3 M's (for "maintenance"). Use this method to write the number of possible job assignments first as an expression involving factorials and then as a number.

b. Calculate Another way to count the number of possible job assignments is to first choose the 5 W's, then choose the 7 R's, and then choose the 3 M's. Use this method to write the number of possible job assignments first as an expression involving factorials and then as a number.

c. Analyze *Compare* your results from parts (a) and (b). *Explain* why they make sense.

Volunteers in Aniak, Alaska

AP Images/Marc Lester

○ = **See WORKED-OUT SOLUTIONS** in Student Resources   ★ = **STANDARDIZED TEST PRACTICE**

53. **CHALLENGE** A polygon is *convex* if no line that contains a side of the polygon contains a point in the interior of the polygon. Consider a convex polygon with *n* sides.

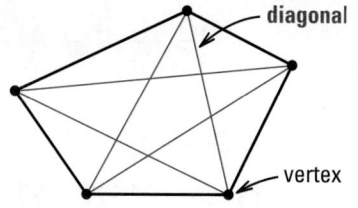

a. Use the combinations formula to write an expression for the number of line segments that join pairs of vertices on an *n*-sided polygon.

b. Use your result from part (a) to write a formula for the number of diagonals of an *n*-sided convex polygon.

Investigating Algebra **ACTIVITY** *Use before Construct and Interpret Binomial Distributions*

Use a Simulation to Test an Assumption

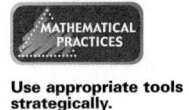

MATHEMATICAL PRACTICES

Use appropriate tools strategically.

MATERIALS • coins • graphing calculator

QUESTION How do you determine whether a coin is fair?

How do you know if a coin is "fair"? That is, when you flip it, how do you know a coin is equally likely to land heads or tails?

You can flip an actual coin many times to help you decide whether you think it's fair. But what kinds of seemingly "unusual" outcomes might occur even with a fair coin? How do you know what you can expect?

In this activity, you will perform physical experiments with a coin and also use *simulation* with a graphing calculator to model flipping a coin. The simulation lets you quickly repeat an event with two equally likely outcomes to compare with results that you might get from an actual coin.

EXPLORE 1 Perform an experiment

A friend gives you a coin. You flip it 4 times, and you get tails all 4 times. Would you feel confident in concluding that the coin is not fair?

STEP 1 *Flip coins*

Working in pairs, flip a coin 4 times. Repeat this experiment a total of 10 times, so that you have 10 trials of 4 flips. Record your results in a table like the one shown. Count the number of trials that fall into each of these categories: 4 heads, 3 heads and 1 tails, 2 heads and 2 tails, 1 heads and 3 tails, 4 tails.

	Flip 1	Flip 2	Flip 3	Flip 4
Trial 1	?	?	?	?
Trial 2	?	?	?	?

STEP 2 *Display results*

Collect all of the data generated by the pairs of students in your class. Combine the outcomes for all of the trials, and then display the class data using a bar graph set up like the one at the right.

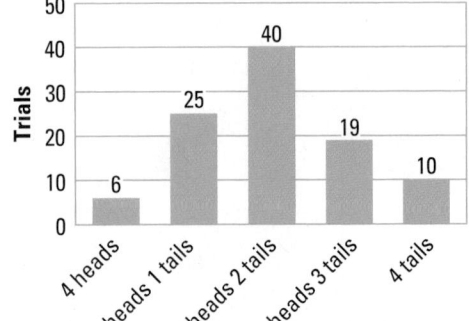

STEP 3 *Analyze results*

What outcome or outcomes occurred the most frequently? How many times did 4 heads or 4 tails occur? Would you be reasonably certain concluding that the coin your friend gave you is not fair? *Explain.*

Perform a simulation of an experiment

A friend gives you a coin. You flip it 7 times, and you get tails all 7 times. Would you feel confident in concluding that the coin is not fair?

STEP 1 *Generate data*

For the simulation, let 0 represent flipping heads and let 1 represent flipping tails. On a graphing calculator, press the
MATH key, select the "PRB" menu, and choose "randInt(."
Perform the keystrokes for "randInt(0, 1, 7)" and press ENTER .
The calculator will produce a list of seven digits (0 or 1) at random, as shown, where the outcomes 0 and 1 are equally likely to occur.

```
randInt(0,1,7)
   {0 1 1 0 0 1 0}
```

Press ENTER 20 times to obtain 20 lists of 7 "coin flips." Keep a tally to record the number of these 20 trials whose results fall into each of these categories: 7 heads, 6 heads and 1 tail, 5 heads and 2 tails, ..., 1 heads and 6 tails, 7 tails.

STEP 2 *Display results*

Collect all of the data generated by the pairs in your class. Combine the outcomes for all of the trials and display the class data using a bar graph similar to the one used in Explore 1. It will have 8 bars.

STEP 3 *Analyze results*

What outcome or outcomes occurred the most? How many times did 7 heads or 7 tails occur? Would you be reasonably certain concluding that the coin your friend gave you is not fair? *Explain.*

DRAW CONCLUSIONS Use your observations to complete these exercises

1. In Explore 1, find the theoretical probability of flipping 4 tails in a row. Does this affect your confidence in the coin's fairness or unfairness? *Explain.*

2. In Explore 2, find the theoretical probability of flipping 7 tails in a row. Does this affect your confidence in the coin's fairness or unfairness? *Explain.*

3. A simulation of flipping a coin 5 times in a row is performed 200 times. The results of the simulation are shown in the table below.

	5 heads 0 tails	4 heads 1 tails	3 heads 2 tails	2 heads 3 tails	1 heads 4 tails	0 heads 5 tails
Outcomes	1	5	27	61	72	34

a. Make a bar graph of the data.

b. Do you think that the simulation represents a coin that is fair or not fair? *Explain.*

6.2 Construct and Interpret Binomial Distributions

Before	You found probabilities of events.
Now	You will study probability distributions.
Why?	So you can describe interest in museums, as in Ex. 46.

Key Vocabulary
- random variable
- probability distribution
- binomial distribution
- binomial experiment
- symmetric
- skewed

CC.9-12.S.MD.3 (+) Develop a probability distribution for a random variable defined for a sample space in which theoretical probabilities can be calculated; find the expected value.*

A **random variable** is a variable whose value is determined by the outcomes of a random event. For example, when you roll a six-sided die, you can define a random variable X that represents the number showing on the die. So, the possible values of X are 1, 2, 3, 4, 5, and 6. For every random variable, a *probability distribution* can be defined.

KEY CONCEPT *For Your Notebook*

Probability Distributions

A **probability distribution** is a function that gives the probability of each possible value of a random variable. The sum of all the probabilities in a probability distribution must equal 1.

Probability Distribution for Rolling a Die					
X	1	2	3	4	5	6
P(X)	$\frac{1}{6}$	$\frac{1}{6}$	$\frac{1}{6}$	$\frac{1}{6}$	$\frac{1}{6}$	$\frac{1}{6}$

❖ **EXAMPLE 1** **Construct a probability distribution**

Let X be a random variable that represents the sum when two six-sided dice are rolled. Make a table and a histogram showing the probability distribution for X.

REVIEW COMPOUND EVENTS

Recall that there are 36 possible outcomes when rolling two six-sided dice. These are listed in Example 4.

Solution

The possible values of X are the integers from 2 to 12. The table shows how many outcomes of rolling two dice produce each value of X. Divide the number of outcomes for X by 36 to find $P(X)$.

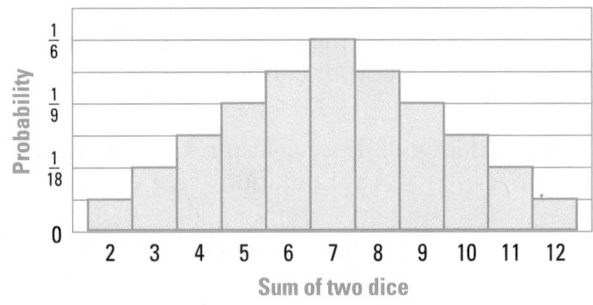

Sum of two dice

X (sum)	2	3	4	5	6	7	8	9	10	11	12
Outcomes	1	2	3	4	5	6	5	4	3	2	1
P(X)	$\frac{1}{36}$	$\frac{1}{18}$	$\frac{1}{12}$	$\frac{1}{9}$	$\frac{5}{36}$	$\frac{1}{6}$	$\frac{5}{36}$	$\frac{1}{9}$	$\frac{1}{12}$	$\frac{1}{18}$	$\frac{1}{36}$

EXAMPLE 2 **Interpret a probability distribution**

Use the probability distribution in Example 1 to answer each question.

a. What is the most likely sum when rolling two six-sided dice?

b. What is the probability that the sum of the two dice is at least 10?

Solution

a. The most likely sum when rolling two six-sided dice is the value of X for which $P(X)$ is greatest. This probability is greatest for $X = 7$. So, the most likely sum when rolling the two dice is 7.

b. The probability that the sum of the two dice is at least 10 is:

$$P(X \geq 10) = P(X = 10) + P(X = 11) + P(X = 12)$$

$$= \frac{3}{36} + \frac{2}{36} + \frac{1}{36}$$

$$= \frac{6}{36}$$

$$= \frac{1}{6}$$

$$\approx 0.167$$

 GUIDED PRACTICE   for Examples 1 and 2

A tetrahedral die has four sides numbered 1 through 4. Let X be a random variable that represents the sum when two such dice are rolled.

1. Make a table and a histogram showing the probability distribution for X.

2. What is the most likely sum when rolling the two dice? What is the probability that the sum of the two dice is at most 3?

BINOMIAL DISTRIBUTIONS One type of probability distribution is a **binomial distribution**. A binomial distribution shows the probabilities of the outcomes of a *binomial experiment*.

KEY CONCEPT   *For Your Notebook*

Binomial Experiments

A **binomial experiment** meets the following conditions:

• There are n independent trials.

• Each trial has only two possible outcomes: success and failure.

• The probability of success is the same for each trial. This probability is denoted by p. The probability of failure is given by $1 - p$.

For a binomial experiment, the probability of exactly k successes in n trials is:

$$P(k \text{ successes}) = {}_nC_k p^k (1 - p)^{n - k}$$

6.2 Construct and Interpret Binomial Distributions   **389**

EXAMPLE 3 **Construct a binomial distribution**

SPORTS SURVEYS According to a survey, about 41% of U.S. households have a soccer ball. Suppose you ask 6 randomly chosen U.S. households whether they have a soccer ball. Draw a histogram of the binomial distribution for your survey.

Solution

The probability that a randomly selected household has a soccer ball is $p = 0.41$. Because you survey 6 households, $n = 6$.

AVOID ERRORS
You can check your calculations for a binomial distribution by adding all the probabilities. The sum should always be 1.

$P(k = 0) = {}_6C_0(0.41)^0(0.59)^6 \approx 0.042$

$P(k = 1) = {}_6C_1(0.41)^1(0.59)^5 \approx 0.176$

$P(k = 2) = {}_6C_2(0.41)^2(0.59)^4 \approx 0.306$

$P(k = 3) = {}_6C_3(0.41)^3(0.59)^3 \approx 0.283$

$P(k = 4) = {}_6C_4(0.41)^4(0.59)^2 \approx 0.148$

$P(k = 5) = {}_6C_5(0.41)^5(0.59)^1 \approx 0.041$

$P(k = 6) = {}_6C_6(0.41)^6(0.59)^0 \approx 0.005$

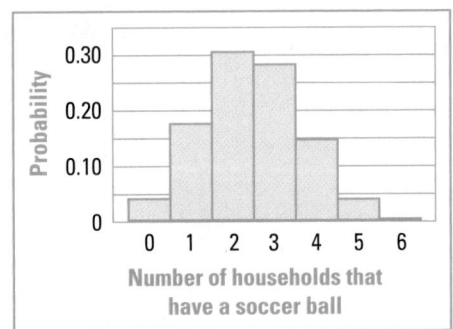

A histogram of the distribution is shown.

Animated Algebra at my.hrw.com

EXAMPLE 4 **Interpret a binomial distribution**

Use the binomial distribution in Example 3 to answer each question.

a. What is the most likely outcome of the survey?

b. What is the probability that at most 2 households have a soccer ball?

Solution

a. The most likely outcome of the survey is the value of k for which $P(k)$ is greatest. This probability is greatest for $k = 2$. So, the most likely outcome is that 2 of the 6 households have a soccer ball.

b. The probability that at most 2 households have a soccer ball is:

$P(k \leq 2) = P(k = 2) + P(k = 1) + P(k = 0)$

$\approx 0.306 + 0.176 + 0.042$

≈ 0.524

▸ So, the probability is about 52%.

✓ **GUIDED PRACTICE** for Examples 3 and 4

In Sweden, 61% of households have a soccer ball. Suppose you ask 6 randomly chosen Swedish households whether they have a soccer ball.

3. Draw a histogram showing the binomial distribution for your survey.

4. What is the most likely outcome of your survey? What is the probability that at most 2 households you survey have a soccer ball?

CLASSIFY
DISTRIBUTIONS
Note that the
distribution in
Example 1 is symmetric,
while the distribution in
Example 3 is skewed.

SYMMETRIC AND SKEWED DISTRIBUTIONS Suppose a probability distribution is represented by a histogram. The distribution is **symmetric** if you can draw a vertical line that divides the histogram into two parts that are mirror images. A distribution that is *not* symmetric is called **skewed**.

EXAMPLE 5 Classify distributions as symmetric or skewed

Describe the shape of the binomial distribution that shows the probability of exactly k successes in 8 trials if (a) $p = 0.5$ and (b) $p = 0.9$.

Solution

a.
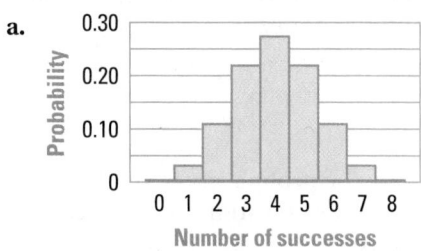

Symmetric; the left half is a mirror image of the right half.

b.
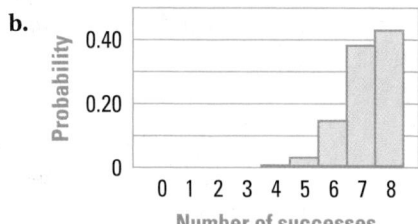

Skewed; the distribution is not symmetric about any vertical line.

✓ **GUIDED PRACTICE** for Example 5

5. A binomial experiment consists of 5 trials with probability p of success on each trial. Describe the shape of the binomial distribution that shows the probability of exactly k successes if (**a**) $p = 0.4$ and (**b**) $p = 0.5$.

6.2 EXERCISES

SKILL PRACTICE

1. **VOCABULARY** Copy and complete: A probability distribution represented by a histogram is __?__ if you can draw a vertical line dividing the histogram into two parts that are mirror images.

2. ★ **WRITING** *Explain* the difference between a binomial experiment and a binomial distribution.

EXAMPLE 1
for Exs. 3–5

CONSTRUCTING PROBABILITY DISTRIBUTIONS Make a table and a histogram showing the probability distribution for the random variable.

3. X = the number on a table tennis ball randomly chosen from a bag that contains 5 balls labeled "1," 3 balls labeled "2," and 2 balls labeled "3."

4. W = 1 if a randomly chosen letter is A, E, I, O, or U and 2 otherwise.

5. N = the number of digits in a random integer from 0 through 999.

EXAMPLE 2
for Exs. 6–9

INTERPRETING PROBABILITY DISTRIBUTIONS In Exercises 6–9, use the given histogram of a probability distribution for a random variable *X*.

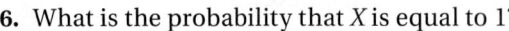

6. What is the probability that *X* is equal to 1?

7. What is the most likely value for *X*?

8. What is the probability that *X* is odd?

9. ★ **MULTIPLE CHOICE** What is the probability that *X* is at least 3?

    (A) 0.2   (B) 0.4   (C) 0.6   (D) 0.8

CALCULATING PROBABILITIES Calculate the probability of tossing a coin 20 times and getting the given number of heads.

10. 1   11. 2   12. 4   13. 6

14. 9   15. 12   16. 15   17. 18

BINOMIAL PROBABILITIES Calculate the probability of randomly guessing the given number of correct answers on a 30-question multiple choice exam that has choices A, B, C, and D for each question.

18. 0   19. 2   20. 6   (21.) 11

22. 15   23. 21   24. 26   25. 30

ERROR ANALYSIS *Describe* and correct the error in calculating the probability of rolling a 1 exactly 3 times in 5 rolls of a six-sided die.

26.
$$P(k = 3) = {}_5C_3\left(\frac{1}{6}\right)^{5-3}\left(\frac{5}{6}\right)^3$$
$$\approx 0.161$$

27.
$$P(k = 3) = \left(\frac{1}{6}\right)^3\left(\frac{5}{6}\right)^{5-3}$$
$$\approx 0.003$$

BINOMIAL DISTRIBUTIONS Calculate the probability of *k* successes for a binomial experiment consisting of *n* trials with probability *p* of success on each trial.

28. $k \le 3$, $n = 7$, $p = 0.3$ 29. $k \ge 5$, $n = 8$, $p = 0.6$

30. $k \le 2$, $n = 5$, $p = 0.12$ 31. $k \ge 10$, $n = 15$, $p = 0.75$

32. ★ **MULTIPLE CHOICE** You perform a binomial experiment consisting of 10 trials with a probability of success of 36% on each trial. What is the most likely number of successes?

    (A) 3   (B) 4   (C) 6   (D) 7

EXAMPLE 5
for Exs. 33–38

HISTOGRAMS A binomial experiment consists of *n* trials with probability *p* of success on each trial. Draw a histogram of the binomial distribution that shows the probability of exactly *k* successes. *Describe* the distribution as either *symmetric* or *skewed*. Then find the most likely number of successes.

33. $n = 3$, $p = 0.3$ 34. $n = 6$, $p = 0.5$ 35. $n = 4$, $p = 0.16$

36. $n = 7$, $p = 0.85$ 37. $n = 8$, $p = 0.025$ 38. $n = 12$, $p = 0.5$

39. ★ **OPEN-ENDED MATH** Construct a symmetric probability distribution for a random variable *X* and a skewed probability distribution for a random variable *Y*. Make a table and a histogram for each distribution.

In Exercises 40–42, you will derive the binomial probability formula. Consider a binomial experiment with *n* trials and probability *p* of success on each trial.

40. For any particular sequence of *k* successes and *n* − *k* failures, what is the probability that the sequence occurs? *Explain.*

41. How many sequences of *k* successes and *n* − *k* failures are there? *Explain.*

42. **CHALLENGE** Use your results from Exercises 40 and 41 to justify the binomial probability formula.

PROBLEM SOLVING

EXAMPLES
3 and 4
for Exs. 43–46

43. **HEALTH** About 1% of people are allergic to bee stings. What is the probability that exactly 1 person in a class of 25 is allergic to bee stings?

44. **BASKETBALL** Predrag Stojakovic of the Sacramento Kings made 92.7% of his free throw attempts in the 2003–2004 NBA regular season. What is the probability that he will make exactly 10 of his next 15 free throw attempts?

45. **BLOOD TYPE** The chart shows the distribution of blood types (O, A, B, AB) and Rh factor (⁺ or ⁻) for human blood. If, at random, 10 people donate blood to a blood bank during a certain hour, find the probability of each event.

Percent of Population by Blood Type							
O⁺	O⁻	A⁺	A⁻	B⁺	B⁻	AB⁺	AB⁻
37%	6%	34%	6%	10%	2%	4%	1%

a. Exactly 5 of the people are type A⁺. **b.** Exactly 2 of the people are Rh⁻.
c. At most 2 of the people are type O. **d.** At least 5 of the people are Rh⁺.

46. **FINE ARTS** A survey states that 35% of people in the United States visited an art museum in a certain year. You randomly select 10 U.S. citizens.

a. Draw a histogram showing the binomial distribution of the number of people who visited an art museum.

b. What is the probability that at most 4 people visited an art museum?

47. ◆ **MULTIPLE REPRESENTATIONS** An average of 7 gopher holes appear on the farm shown each week. Let *X* represent how many of the 7 gopher holes appear in the carrot patch. Assume that a gopher hole has an equal chance of appearing at any point on the farm.

a. **Calculating Probabilities** Find *P*(*X*) for *X* = 0, 1, 2, . . . , 7.

b. **Making a Table** Make a table showing the probability distribution for *X*.

c. **Making a Histogram** Make a histogram showing the probability distribution for *X*.

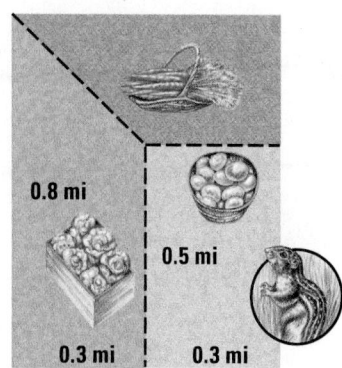
0.8 mi
0.5 mi
0.3 mi 0.3 mi

6.2 Construct and Interpret Binomial Distributions   393

48. ★ **EXTENDED RESPONSE** Assume that having a male child and having a female child are independent events and that the probability of each is 0.5.

    a. A couple has 4 male children. Evaluate the validity of this statement: "The first 4 kids were all boys, so the next one will probably be a girl."

    b. What is the probability of having 4 male children and then a female child?

    c. Let X be a random variable that represents the number of children a couple already has when they have their first female child. Draw a histogram of the distribution of $P(X)$ for $0 \leq X \leq 10$ and describe its shape.

49. **CHALLENGE** An entertainment system has n speakers. Each speaker will function properly with probability p, independent of whether the other speakers are functioning. The system will operate effectively if at least 50% of its speakers are functioning. For what values of p is a 5-speaker system more likely to operate than a 3-speaker system?

QUIZ

Find the number of combinations.

1. $_8C_6$ **2.** $_7C_4$ **3.** $_9C_0$ **4.** $_{12}C_{11}$

Use the binomial theorem to write the binomial expansion.

5. $(x + 5)^5$ **6.** $(2s - 3)^6$ **7.** $(3u + v)^4$ **8.** $(2x^3 - 3y)^5$

9. Find the coefficient of x^3 in the expansion of $(x + 2)^9$.

10. **MENU CHOICES** A pizza parlor runs a special where you can buy a large pizza with 1 cheese, 1 vegetable, and 2 meats for $12. You have a choice of 5 cheeses, 10 vegetables, and 6 meats. How many different variations of the pizza special are possible?

Calculate the probability of getting the given number of 6's when rolling a six-sided die 10 times.

11. 0   **12.** 1   **13.** 4   **14.** 8

A binomial experiment consists of n trials with probability p of success on each trial. Draw a histogram of the binomial distribution that shows the probability of exactly k successes.

15. $n = 5, p = 0.2$ **16.** $n = 8, p = 0.5$ **17.** $n = 6, p = 0.72$

Using ALTERNATIVE METHODS

Another Way to Solve Examples 3

MATHEMATICAL PRACTICES

Make sense of problems and persevere in solving them.

MULTIPLE REPRESENTATIONS In Example 3, you constructed a binomial distribution. Some calculators have a binomial probability distribution function that you can use to calculate binomial probabilities. You can then use the calculator to draw a histogram of the distribution.

PROBLEM 1

SPORTS SURVEYS According to a survey, about 41% of U.S. households have a soccer ball. Suppose you ask 6 randomly chosen U.S. households whether they have a soccer ball. Draw a histogram of the binomial distribution for your survey.

METHOD

STEP 1 **Enter** values of k. Let $p = 0.41$ be the probability that a randomly selected household has a soccer ball. Enter the k-values 0 through 6 into list L_1 on the graphing calculator.

STEP 2 **Find** values of $P(k)$. Enter the binomial probability command to generate $P(k)$ for all seven k-values. Store the results in list L_2.

STEP 3 **Draw** histogram. Set up the histogram to use the numbers in list L_1 as x-values and the numbers in list L_2 as frequencies. Draw the histogram in a suitable viewing window.

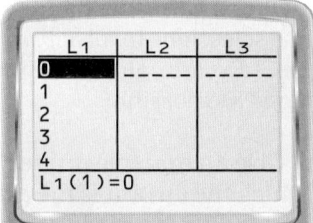

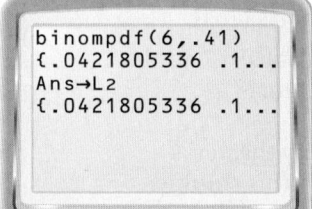

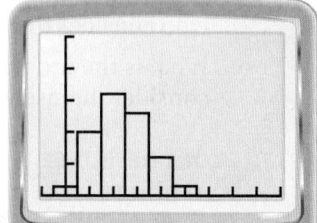

PRACTICE

A binomial experiment consists of n trials with probability p of success on each trial. Use a graphing calculator to draw a histogram of the binomial distribution that shows the probability of exactly k successes. Then find the most likely number of successes.

1. $n = 12$, $p = 0.29$ 2. $n = 14$, $p = 0.58$ 3. $n = 15$, $p = 0.805$

4. **WHAT IF?** In the example, how do your histogram and the most likely number of adults change if you survey 14 adults at random?

MATHEMATICAL PRACTICES Make sense of problems and persevere in solving them.

1. **MULTI-STEP PROBLEM** About 71% of households in Alonso's town have a pet. Alonso is tasked with finding the probability distribution for a survey of 7 random households. Part of his calculation is given:

$$P(k = 3) = {}_7C_3(0.71)^3(0.29)^4 < 0.089$$

   a. Explain what $P(k = 3)$ represents in this calculation.

   b. Explain what ${}_7C_3$ represents in this calculation.

   c. Explain what $(0.71)^3$ represents in this calculation.

   d. Explain what $(0.29)^4$ represents in this calculation.

2. **MULTI-STEP PROBLEM** According to a survey, 62% of U.S. adults consider themselves sports fans. You randomly select 14 adults to survey.

   a. Draw a histogram of the binomial distribution showing the probability that k adults consider themselves sports fans.

   b. What is the most likely number of adults who consider themselves sports fans?

   c. What is the probability that at least 7 adults consider themselves sports fans?

3. **SHORT RESPONSE** A community theater is presenting a series of 15 operas this summer. Melinda wants to attend at least 4 of them. Write a subtractive expression using notation representing the number of different combinations of operas she can attend, and then find that number.

4. **GRIDDED ANSWER** You want to make a fruit smoothie using 3 of the fruits listed. How many different fruit smoothies can you make?

- Orange
- Banana
- Strawberry
- Pineapple
- Canteloupe
- Watermelon
- Kiwi
- Peach

5. **GRIDDED ANSWER** A softball player gets a hit in about 31% of her at-bats. You randomly select 15 of the player's at-bats. What is the most likely number of hits the player will have in those at bats?

6. **SHORT RESPONSE** You must take 18 elective courses to meet your graduation requirements for college. There are 30 courses that you are interested in. Does finding the number of possible course selections involve *permutations* or *combinations*? *Explain.* How many different course selections are possible?

7. **OPEN-ENDED** Give an example of a real-life problem for which the answer is the product of two combinations. Provide a solution.

8. **GRIDDED ANSWER** An ice cream shop offers a choice of 31 flavors. How many different ice cream cones can be made with three scoops of ice cream if each scoop is a different flavor and the order of the scoops is not important?

Investigate the Shapes of Data Distributions

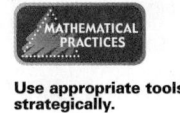

MATHEMATICAL PRACTICES

Use appropriate tools strategically.

MATERIALS • graph paper • graphing calculator

QUESTION How do you describe and interpret data distributions with various shapes?

A histogram of data can have different shapes. It may be symmetrical or not, may be bell-shaped or not, or may have a long "tail" in one direction. It may have no recognizable shape. There are recurring patterns in data distributions, however, that let you predict probabilities involving data values.

EXPLORE 1 Simulate rolling a die repeatedly until you get a 5

STEP 1 *Perform a simulation*

Press [MATH], then select "PRB," then "randInt(." The command randInt(1, 6) gives a random integer from 1 to 6 when you press [ENTER]. The screen shows 6 results.

```
randInt(1,6)
                2
                5
                6
                4
                1
                5
```

STEP 2 *Make a plot*

In Step 1, a "5" first appears in the 2nd trial. It takes 4 more trials to get the next "5." These two results are shown below. Make a similar plot for your data. Plot 40 or 50 results.

Number of trials to get a 5

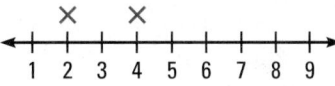

STEP 3 *Observe and compare*

Describe your plot. Include the following.

• What is the general shape?
• Is it symmetric?
• Does it have a clear "middle?"

Compare your plot with those of other groups. Were their results similar?

What was the greatest number of rolls required by any single group to get a 5?

EXPLORE 2 Simulate rolling a die 100 times

STEP 1 *Perform a simulation*

To simulate 100 rolls of a die, you can perform all 100 "rolls" at once and store the results in a list by entering the command below.

    randInt(1, 6, 100) [STO ▶]
    [2nd] [L1]

Pressing [ENTER] displays the list on the home screen and enters it in the Statistics memory.

STEP 2 *Make a histogram*

Press [2nd] [Stat Plot], turn on Plot1, and select the histogram icon. Set "Xlist" to L1 and "Freq" to 1. Enter the window below, then press [GRAPH].

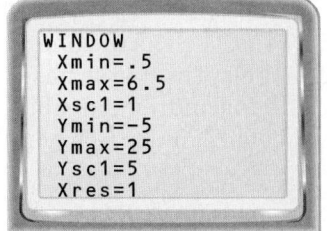

STEP 3 *Observe and compare*

Describe your plot and compare plots as you did in Step 3 above.

You can very quickly make a new plot:

Press [2nd] [QUIT] to return to the home screen. Press [ENTER] to produce a new list. Then press [GRAPH]. Do this a few times. How does the graph change?

EXPLORE 3 Simulate rolling 10 dice and counting how many display "even results"

STEP 1 *Perform a simulation*

Enter randInt(1, 6, 10) and press **ENTER** to simulate rolling 10 dice. Below you can see three "dice" that display even results. (To see the last three results in the list, scroll to the right.)

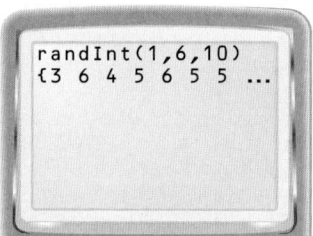

STEP 2 *Make a plot*

Press **ENTER**, count the number of even numbers in the new list, and record it in a plot like the one below, which shows results for 10 rolls of 10 dice. Repeat as many times as time allows.

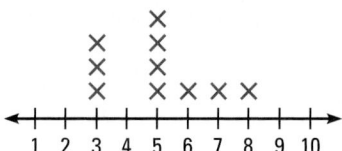

STEP 3 *Observe and compare*

Describe your plot and compare plots as you did in Explore 1 and 2.

How does the shape of this plot compare with the shapes of the plots from Explore 1 and 2?

EXPLORE 4 Combine data

STEP 1 *Combine results from Explore 1* Combine the results of all groups to make a class histogram. Compare your plot and the class histogram.

STEP 2 *Simulate combining results from Explore 2* To simulate combining results from Explore 2 for 10 groups, repeat the first two steps of Explore 2, but use the command randInt(1, 6, 999). (Note that 999 is the largest number the calculator allows.) Also, change the viewing window to Ymin = −50, Ymax = 250, and Yscl = 50. Compare your histogram and the class histogram.

STEP 3 *Combine results from Explore 3* Combine the results of all groups to make a class histogram. Compare your plot and the class histogram.

DRAW CONCLUSIONS Use your observations to complete these exercises

1. Did the graphs in each Explore have similar or very different shapes? *Explain.*

2. For each Explore, how did combining the results of the groups into one graph change the shapes? Predict what you think the shape of each histogram might be if you could repeat each simulation thousands of times.

3. Symmetric, bell-shaped data distributions, such as the one at the right, occur frequently in real world models. This curve has special properties that make it extremely useful for finding probabilities. Which of the Explore results most closely resembles a curve with this shape?

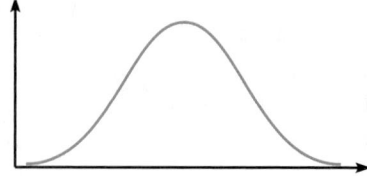

6.3 Use Normal Distributions

Before You interpreted probability distributions.

Now You will study normal distributions.

Why? So you can model animal populations, as in Example 3.

Key Vocabulary
• normal distribution
• normal curve
• standard normal distribution
• z-score

CC.9-12.S.ID.4 Use the mean and standard deviation of a data set to fit it to a normal distribution and to estimate population percentages. Recognize that there are data sets for which such a procedure is not appropriate. Use calculators, spreadsheets, and tables to estimate areas under the normal curve.*

INTERPRET GRAPHS

An area under a normal curve can be interpreted either as a percentage of the data values in the distribution or as a probability.

You have studied probability distributions. One type of probability distribution is a *normal distribution*. A **normal distribution** is modeled by a bell-shaped curve called a **normal curve** that is symmetric about the mean.

KEY CONCEPT   *For Your Notebook*

Areas Under a Normal Curve

A normal distribution with mean $\overline{x}$ and standard deviation σ has the following properties:

• The total area under the related normal curve is 1.

• About 68% of the area lies within 1 standard deviation of the mean.

• About 95% of the area lies within 2 standard deviations of the mean.

• About 99.7% of the area lies within 3 standard deviations of the mean.

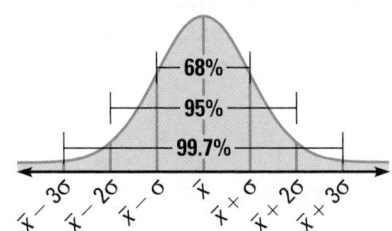
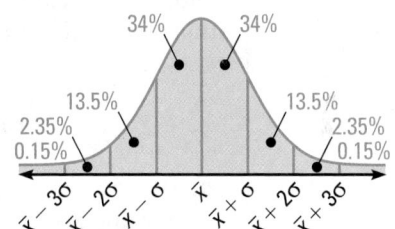

EXAMPLE 1 Find a normal probability

A normal distribution has mean $\overline{x}$ and standard deviation σ. For a randomly selected x-value from the distribution, find $P(\overline{x} - 2\sigma \leq x \leq \overline{x})$.

Solution

The probability that a randomly selected x-value lies between between $\overline{x} - 2\sigma$ and $\overline{x}$ is the shaded area under the normal curve shown.

$$P(\overline{x} - 2\sigma \leq x \leq \overline{x}) = 0.135 + 0.34 = 0.475$$

Animated Algebra at my.hrw.com

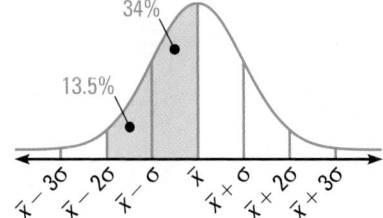

EXAMPLE 2 **Interpret normally distributed data**

HEALTH The blood cholesterol readings for a group of women are normally distributed with a mean of 172 mg/dl and a standard deviation of 14 mg/dl.

  a. About what percent of the women have readings between 158 and 186?

  b. Readings less than 158 are considered desirable. About what percent of the readings are desirable?

Solution

  a. The readings of 158 and 186 represent one standard deviation on either side of the mean, as shown below. So, 68% of the women have readings between 158 and 186.

  b. A reading of 158 is one standard deviation to the left of the mean, as shown. So, the percent of readings that are desirable is 0.15% + 2.35% + 13.5%, or 16%.

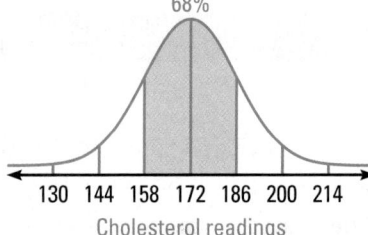

Cholesterol readings

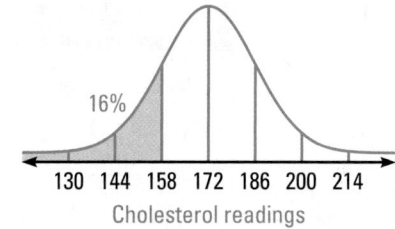

Cholesterol readings

✓ **GUIDED PRACTICE**   for Examples 1 and 2

A normal distribution has mean $\overline{x}$ and standard deviation σ. Find the indicated probability for a randomly selected *x*-value from the distribution.

  1. $P(x \le \overline{x})$

  2. $P(x \ge \overline{x})$

  3. $P(\overline{x} \le x \le \overline{x} + 2\sigma)$

  4. $P(\overline{x} - \sigma \le x \le \overline{x})$

  5. $P(x \le \overline{x} - 3\sigma)$

  6. $P(x \ge \overline{x} + \sigma)$

  7. **WHAT IF?** In Example 2, what percent of the women have readings between 172 and 200?

STANDARD NORMAL DISTRIBUTION The **standard normal distribution** is the normal distribution with mean 0 and standard deviation 1. The formula below can be used to transform *x*-values from a normal distribution with mean $\overline{x}$ and standard deviation σ into *z*-values having a standard normal distribution.

Formula: $z = \dfrac{x - \overline{x}}{\sigma}$

Subtract the mean from the given *x*-value, then divide by the standard deviation.

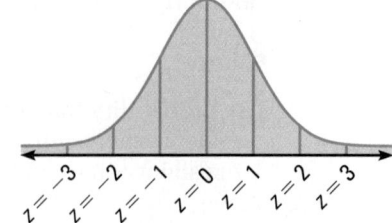

The *z*-value for a particular *x*-value is called the **z-score** for the *x*-value and is the number of standard deviations the *x*-value lies above or below the mean $\overline{x}$.

STANDARD NORMAL TABLE If z is a randomly selected value from a standard normal distribution, you can use the table below to find the probability that z is less than or equal to some given value. For example, the table shows that $P(z \le -0.4) = 0.3446$. You can find the value of $P(z \le -0.4)$ in the table by finding the value where row **−0** and column **.4** intersect.

Standard Normal Table

z	.0	.1	.2	.3	.4	.5	.6	.7	.8	.9
−3	.0013	.0010	.0007	.0005	.0003	.0002	.0002	.0001	.0001	.0000+
−2	.0228	.0179	.0139	.0107	.0082	.0062	.0047	.0035	.0026	.0019
−1	.1587	.1357	.1151	.0968	.0808	.0668	.0548	.0446	.0359	.0287
−0	.5000	.4602	.4207	.3821	.3446	.3085	.2743	.2420	.2119	.1841
0	.5000	.5398	.5793	.6179	.6554	.6915	.7257	.7580	.7881	.8159
1	.8413	.8643	.8849	.9032	.9192	.9332	.9452	.9554	.9641	.9713
2	.9772	.9821	.9861	.9893	.9918	.9938	.9953	.9965	.9974	.9981
3	.9987	.9990	.9993	.9995	.9997	.9998	.9998	.9999	.9999	1.0000−

READING

In the table, the value .0000+ means "slightly more than 0" and the value 1.0000− means "slightly less than 1."

You can also use the standard normal table to find probabilities for *any* normal distribution by first converting values from the distribution to z-scores.

EXAMPLE 3 Use a z-score and the standard normal table

BIOLOGY Scientists conducted aerial surveys of a seal sanctuary and recorded the number x of seals they observed during each survey. The numbers of seals observed were normally distributed with a mean of 73 seals and a standard deviation of 14.1 seals. Find the probability that at most 50 seals were observed during a survey.

Solution

STEP 1 Find the z-score corresponding to an x-value of 50.

$$z = \frac{x - \overline{x}}{\sigma} = \frac{50 - 73}{14.1} \approx -1.6$$

STEP 2 Use the table to find $P(x \le 50) \approx P(z \le -1.6)$.

The table shows that $P(z \le -1.6) = 0.0548$. So, the probability that at most 50 seals were observed during a survey is about 0.0548.

z	.0	.1	.2	.3	.4	.5	.6	.7	.8	.9
−3	.0013	.0010	.0007	.0005	.0003	.0002	.0002	.0001	.0001	.0000+
−2	.0228	.0179	.0139	.0107	.0082	.0062	.0047	.0035	.0026	.0019
−1	.1587	.1357	.1151	.0968	.0808	.0668	.0548	.0446	.0359	.0287
−0	.5000	.4602	.4207	.3821	.3446	.3085	.2743	.2420	.2119	.1841
0	.5000	.5398	.5793	.6179	.6554	.6915	.7257	.7580	.7881	.8159

✓ GUIDED PRACTICE for Example 3

8. **WHAT IF?** In Example 3, find the probability that at most 90 seals were observed during a survey.

9. **REASONING** *Explain* why it makes sense that $P(z \le 0) = 0.5$.

6.3 EXERCISES

HOMEWORK KEY

○ = See WORKED-OUT SOLUTIONS
Exs. 3, 11, and 33

★ = STANDARDIZED TEST PRACTICE
Exs. 2, 17, 18, 28, and 35

SKILL PRACTICE

1. **VOCABULARY** Copy and complete: A(n) __?__ is a bell-shaped curve that is symmetric about the mean.

2. ★ **WRITING** *Describe* how to use the standard normal table to find $P(z \leq 1.4)$.

EXAMPLE 1
for Exs. 3–10

FIND A NORMAL PROBABILITY A normal distribution has mean $\overline{x}$ and standard deviation σ. Find the indicated probability for a randomly selected x-value from the distribution.

3. $P(x \leq \overline{x} - \sigma)$ 4. $P(x \geq \overline{x} + 2\sigma)$ 5. $P(x \leq \overline{x} + \sigma)$

6. $P(x \geq \overline{x} - \sigma)$ 7. $P(\overline{x} - \sigma \leq x \leq \overline{x} + \sigma)$ 8. $P(\overline{x} - 3\sigma \leq x \leq \overline{x})$

USING A NORMAL CURVE Give the percent of the area under the normal curve represented by the shaded region.

9. 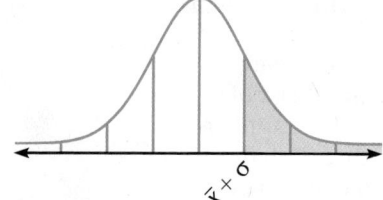   10.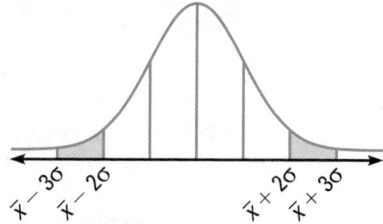

EXAMPLE 2
for Exs. 11–18

NORMAL DISTRIBUTIONS A normal distribution has a mean of 33 and a standard deviation of 4. Find the probability that a randomly selected x-value from the distribution is in the given interval.

11. Between 29 and 37   12. Between 33 and 45   13. Between 21 and 41

14. At least 25   15. At least 29   16. At most 37

17. ★ **MULTIPLE CHOICE** A normal distribution has a mean of 84 and a standard deviation of 5. What is the probability that a randomly selected x-value from the distribution is between 74 and 94?

   (A) 0.475   (B) 0.68   (C) 0.95   (D) 0.997

18. ★ **MULTIPLE CHOICE** A normal distribution has a mean of 51 and a standard deviation of 3. What is the probability that a randomly selected x-value from the distribution is at most 48?

   (A) 0.025   (B) 0.16   (C) 0.84   (D) 0.975

EXAMPLE 3
for Exs. 19–27

STANDARD NORMAL TABLE A normal distribution has a mean of 64 and a standard deviation of 7. Use the standard normal table to find the indicated probability for a randomly selected x-value from the distribution.

19. $P(x \leq 68)$ 20. $P(x \leq 80)$ 21. $P(x \leq 45)$

22. $P(x \leq 54)$ 23. $P(x \leq 64)$ 24. $P(x \geq 59)$

25. $P(x \geq 75)$ 26. $P(60 \leq x \leq 75)$ 27. $P(45 \leq x \leq 65)$

402   Chapter 6   Data Analysis and Statistics

28. ★ **WRITING** When n% of the data are less than or equal to a certain value, that value is called the nth percentile. For normally distributed data, describe the value that represents the 84th percentile in terms of the mean and standard deviation.

29. **ERROR ANALYSIS** In a study, the wheat yields (in bushels) for several plots of land were normally distributed with a mean of 4 bushels and a standard deviation of 0.25 bushel. *Describe* and correct the error in finding the probability that a plot yielded at least 3.8 bushels.

$$z = \frac{x - \bar{x}}{\sigma} = \frac{3.8 - 4}{0.25} = -0.8$$

From the standard normal table, $P(z \geq -0.8) = 0.2119$. So, the probability that a plot yielded at least 3.8 bushels is 0.2119.

30. **CHALLENGE** A normal curve is defined by an equation of this form:

$$y = \frac{1}{\sigma \sqrt{2\pi}}\, e^{-\frac{1}{2}\left(\frac{x - \bar{x}}{\sigma}\right)^2}$$

   a. **Graphing Calculator** Graph three equations of the given form. The equations should use the same mean but different standard deviations.

   b. **Reasoning** *Describe* the effect of the standard deviation on the shape of a normal curve.

PROBLEM SOLVING

EXAMPLES
2 and 3
for Exs. 31–34

31. **BIOLOGY** The illustration shows a housefly at several times its actual size and indicates the fly's wing length. A study found that the wing lengths of houseflies are normally distributed with a mean of about 4.6 millimeters and a standard deviation of about 0.4 millimeter. What is the probability that a randomly selected housefly has a wing length of at least 5 millimeters?

Wing length

32. **FIRE DEPARTMENT** The time a fire department takes to arrive at the scene of an emergency is normally distributed with a mean of 6 minutes and a standard deviation of 1 minute.

   a. What is the probability that the fire department takes at most 8 minutes to arrive at the scene of an emergency?

   b. What is the probability that the fire department takes between 4 minutes and 7 minutes to arrive at the scene of an emergency?

33. **MULTI-STEP PROBLEM** Boxes of cereal are filled by a machine. Tests of the machine's accuracy show that the amount of cereal in each box varies. The weights are normally distributed with a mean of 20 ounces and a standard deviation of 0.25 ounce.

   a. Find the z-scores for weights of 19.4 ounces and 20.4 ounces.

   b. What is the probability that a randomly selected cereal box weighs at most 19.4 ounces?

   c. What is the probability that a randomly selected cereal box weighs between 19.4 ounces and 20.4 ounces? *Explain* your reasoning.

34. **BOTANY** The guayule plant, which grows in the southwestern United States and in Mexico, is one of several plants that can be used as a source of rubber. In a large group of guayule plants, the heights of the plants are normally distributed with a mean of 12 inches and a standard deviation of 2 inches.

Guayule plants

   a. What percent of the plants are taller than 16 inches?

   b. What percent of the plants are at most 13 inches?

   c. What percent of the plants are between 7 inches and 14 inches?

   d. What percent of the plants are at least 3 inches taller than or at least 3 inches shorter than the mean height?

35. ★ **EXTENDED RESPONSE** Lisa and Ann took different college entrance tests. The scores on the test that Lisa took are normally distributed with a mean of 20 points and a standard deviation of 4.2 points. The scores on the test that Ann took are normally distributed with a mean of 500 points and a standard deviation of 90 points. Lisa scored 30 on her test, and Ann scored 610 on her test.

   a. Calculate Find the z-score for Lisa's test score.

   b. Calculate Find the z-score for Ann's test score.

   c. Interpret Which student scored better on her college entrance test? *Explain* your reasoning.

36. **CHALLENGE** According to a survey by the National Center for Health Statistics, the heights of adult men in the United States are normally distributed with a mean of 69 inches and a standard deviation of 2.75 inches.

   a. If you randomly choose 3 adult men, what is the probability that all of them are more than 6 feet tall?

   b. What is the probability that 5 randomly selected men all have heights between 65 inches and 75 inches?

Find the Area Under a Normal Curve

Use appropriate tools strategically.

QUESTION How can you use a graphing calculator to find the area under a normal curve?

EXAMPLE 1 Find a normal probability

The lengths of a group of newborn babies are normally distributed with a mean of 19.8 inches and a standard deviation of 1.6 inches. Find the probability that a randomly chosen baby in this group is at most 20.5 inches long.

STEP 1 *Clarify the problem* We want to find $P(x \leq 20.5)$ for a normal distribution with a mean of 19.8 and a standard deviation of 1.6.

STEP 2 *Enter information* Access the "Distributions" menu by pressing [2nd] [VARS]. Select "normalcdf(," then enter (lower bound, upper bound, mean, standard deviation). Use 0 as the lower bound. You can see at the right that the probability is about 66.9%.

EXAMPLE 2 Find and display an area under a normal curve

Find $P(19 \leq x \leq 22)$ for the situation in Example 1.

STEP 1 *Enter information* In the Distributions menu, select "DRAW" at the top and then "ShadeNorm(." You must enter (lower bound, upper bound, mean, standard deviation). Enter 19 for the lower bound and 22 for the upper bound. Do not yet press [ENTER].

STEP 2 *Choose a viewing window* For a window that shows about 3 standard deviations to either side of the mean, let Xmin = 15 and Xmax = 25. The area under the curve is 1, so the maximum Y-value will be well less than 1. Let Ymin = −0.075 and Ymax = 0.25. Return to the home screen and press [ENTER]. You can see at the right that the area is about 0.607, so the probability is about 60.7%.

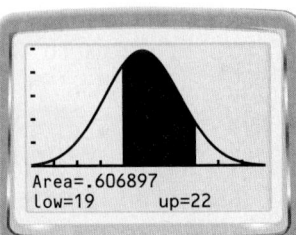

PRACTICE

1. The mean number of potatoes per 15 pound bag from a supplier is 42, with a standard deviation of 4.5. The distribution is normal. Find the probability that a randomly selected bag contains the given number of potatoes.

   a. 50 or fewer   **b.** at least 35   **c.** 37 to 47   **d.** 40 to 44

2. Scores on a qualifying exam are normally distributed with a mean score of 230 and a standard deviation of 43. A score of 250 is required to pass.

   a. Find and display the area under the normal curve for passing scores.

   b. Find and display the area under the normal curve for scores of 200−250. (*Note:* You will first need to clear the drawing from part (a).)

6.4 Select and Draw Conclusions from Samples

Before	You used statistics to describe sets of data.
Now	You will study different sampling methods for collecting data.
Why?	So you can interpret the results of a survey, as in Ex. 27.

Key Vocabulary
- population
- sample
- unbiased sample
- biased sample
- margin of error

CC.9-12.S.IC.1 Understand statistics as a process for making inferences about population parameters based on a random sample from that population.*

> **READING**
> A survey of an entire population is called a *census*.

A **population** is a group of people or objects that you want information about. When it is too difficult, time-consuming, or expensive to survey everyone in a population, information is gathered from a **sample**, or subset, of the population. Some methods for selecting a sample are described below.

In a *self-selected sample*, members of a population can volunteer to be in the sample.

In a *systematic sample*, a rule is used to select members of a population, such as selecting every other person.

In a *convenience sample*, easy-to-reach members of a population are selected, such as those in the first row.

In a *random sample*, each member of a population has an equal chance of being selected.

EXAMPLE 1 Classify samples

BASEBALL A sportswriter wants to survey college baseball coaches about whether they think wooden bats should be mandatory throughout college baseball. Identify the type of sample described.

a. The sportswriter contacts only the coaches that he has cell phone numbers for in order to get quick responses.

b. The sportswriter mails out surveys to all the coaches and uses only the surveys that are returned.

Solution

a. The sportswriter selected coaches that are easily accessible. So, the sample is a convenience sample.

b. The coaches can choose whether or not to respond. So, the sample is a self-selected sample.

BIAS IN SAMPLING In order to draw accurate conclusions about a population from a sample, you should select an *unbiased sample*. An **unbiased sample** is representative of the population you want information about. A sample that overrepresents or underrepresents part of the population is a **biased sample**.

EXAMPLE 2 Identify a biased sample

CONCERT ATTENDANCE The manager of a concert hall wants to know how often people in the community attend concerts. The manager asks 50 people standing in line for a rock concert how many concerts per year they attend. Tell whether the sample is *biased* or *unbiased*. Explain your reasoning.

Solution

The sample is biased because people standing in line for a rock concert are more likely to attend concerts than people in general.

CHOOSING UNBIASED SAMPLES Although there are many ways of sampling a population, a random sample is preferred because it is most likely to be representative of the population.

EXAMPLE 3 Choose an unbiased sample

SENIOR CLASS PROM You are a member of the prom committee. You want to poll members of the senior class to find out where they want to hold the prom. There are 324 students in the senior class. Describe a method for selecting a random sample of 40 seniors to poll.

Solution

STEP 1 **Make** a list of all 324 seniors. Assign each senior a different integer from 1 to 324.

STEP 2 **Generate** 40 unique random integers from 1 to 324 using the *randInt* feature of a graphing calculator. The screen at the right shows six such random integers.

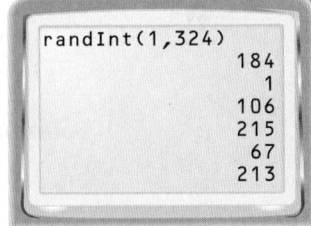

If while generating the integers you obtain a duplicate, discard it and generate a new, unique integer as a replacement.

STEP 3 **Choose** the 40 students that correspond to the 40 integers you generated in Step 2.

✓ **GUIDED PRACTICE** for Examples 1, 2, and 3

1. **SCHOOL WEBSITE** A computer science teacher wants to know if students would like the morning announcements posted on the school's website. He surveys students in one of his computer science classes. Identify the type of sample described, and tell whether the sample is biased.

2. **WHAT IF?** In Example 3, what is another method you could use to generate a random sample of 40 students?

SAMPLE SIZE When conducting a survey, you need to make the size of your sample large enough so that it accurately represents the population. As the sample size increases, the *margin of error* decreases.

The **margin of error** gives a limit on how much the responses of the sample would differ from the responses of the population. For example, if 40% of the people in a poll prefer candidate A, and the margin of error is ±4%, then it is likely that between 36% and 44% of the entire population prefer candidate A.

KEY CONCEPT   *For Your Notebook*

Margin of Error Formula

When a random sample of size n is taken from a large population, the margin of error is approximated by this formula:

$$\text{Margin of error} = \pm \frac{1}{\sqrt{n}}$$

This means that if the percent of the sample responding a certain way is p (expressed as a decimal), then the percent of the population that would respond the same way is likely to be between $p - \frac{1}{\sqrt{n}}$ and $p + \frac{1}{\sqrt{n}}$.

EXAMPLE 4   **Find a margin of error**

MEDIA SURVEY In a survey of 1011 people, 52% said that television is their main source of news.

a. What is the margin of error for the survey?

b. Give an interval that is likely to contain the exact percent of all people who use television as their main source of news.

Main Source of News

- Television 52%
- Newspaper 29%
- Radio 10%
- Internet 5%
- Other 4%

Solution

a. Use the margin of error formula.

$\text{Margin of error} = \pm \frac{1}{\sqrt{n}}$ **Write margin of error formula.**

$= \pm \frac{1}{\sqrt{1011}}$ **Substitute 1011 for n.**

$\approx \pm 0.031$ **Use a calculator.**

▶ The margin of error for the survey is about ±3.1%.

b. To find the interval, subtract and add 3.1% to the percent of people surveyed who said television is their main source of news (52%).

$52\% - 3.1\% = 48.9\%$ $52\% + 3.1\% = 55.1\%$

▶ It is likely that the exact percent of all people who use television as their main source of news is between 48.9% and 55.1%.

A polling company conducts a poll for a U.S. presidential election. How many people did the company survey if the margin of error is ±5%?

(A) 25 people   (B) 250 people   (C) 400 people   (D) 625 people

Solution

Use the margin of error formula.

$\text{Margin of error} = \pm\dfrac{1}{\sqrt{n}}$ Write margin of error formula.

$\pm 0.05 = \pm\dfrac{1}{\sqrt{n}}$ Substitute ±0.05 for margin of error.

$0.0025 = \dfrac{1}{n}$ Square each side.

$n = 400$ Solve for n.

There were 400 people surveyed.

▸ The correct answer is C. (A) (B) (C) (D)

✓ **GUIDED PRACTICE**   for Examples 4 and 5

3. **INTERNET** In a survey of 1202 people, 11% said that they use the Internet or e-mail more than 10 hours per week. What is the margin of error for the survey? How many people would need to be surveyed to reduce the margin of error to ±2%?

6.4 EXERCISES

HOMEWORK KEY

◯ = See WORKED-OUT SOLUTIONS
    Exs. 7, 19, and 29

★ = STANDARDIZED TEST PRACTICE
    Exs. 2, 14, 23, 29, and 31

SKILL PRACTICE

1. **VOCABULARY** Copy and complete: A sample for which each member of a population has an equal chance of being selected is a(n) __?__ sample.

2. ★ **WRITING** *Describe* the difference between an unbiased sample and a biased sample.

EXAMPLES
1 and 2
for Exs. 3–5

CLASSIFYING SAMPLES **Identify the type of sample described. Then tell if the sample is biased.** *Explain* **your reasoning.**

3. A taxicab company wants to know if its customers are satisfied with the service. Each driver surveys every tenth customer during the day.

4. A town council wants to know if residents support having an off-leash area for dogs in the town park. Eighty dog owners are surveyed at the park.

5. An English teacher needs to pick 5 students to present book reports to the class. The teacher writes the names of all students in the class on pieces of paper, puts the pieces in a hat, and chooses 5 names without looking.

EXAMPLE 4
for Exs. 6–14

FINDING MARGIN OF ERROR **Find the margin of error for a survey that has the given sample size. Round your answer to the nearest tenth of a percent.**

6. 260　　　　　**(7.)** 1000　　　　　**8.** 750　　　　　**9.** 6400

10. 3275　　　　**11.** 525　　　　　**12.** 2024　　　　**13.** 10,000

14. ★ **MULTIPLE CHOICE** In a survey of 2000 voters, 45% said they planned to vote for candidate A. What is the margin of error for the survey?

Ⓐ ±1.8%　　　Ⓑ ±2.2%　　　Ⓒ ±3.6%　　　Ⓓ ±4.5%

EXAMPLE 5
for Exs. 15–23

FINDING SAMPLE SIZES **Find the sample size required to achieve the given margin of error. Round your answer to the nearest whole number.**

15. ±3%　　　　**16.** ±8%　　　　**17.** ±10%　　　　**18.** ±4.2%

(19.) ±5.6%　　　**20.** ±1.5%　　　**21.** ±6.5%　　　**22.** ±2.5%

23. ★ **MULTIPLE CHOICE** The margin of error for a poll is ±2%. What is the size of the sample?

Ⓐ 200　　　　Ⓑ 400　　　　Ⓒ 1000　　　　Ⓓ 2500

24. **ERROR ANALYSIS** In a survey of high school students, 13% said that they play basketball regularly. The margin of error is ±4%. *Describe* and correct the error in calculating the sample size.

$$\pm 0.13 = \pm \frac{1}{\sqrt{n}}$$
$$0.0169 = \frac{1}{n}$$
$$n \approx 59$$

25. **REASONING** A survey claims the percent of a city's residents that favor building a new football stadium is likely between 52.3% and 61.7%. How many people were surveyed?

26. **CHALLENGE** Suppose a random sample of size n is required to produce a margin of error of $\pm E$. Write an expression in terms of n for the sample size needed to reduce the margin of error to $\pm \frac{1}{2}E$. By how many times must the sample size be increased in order to cut the margin of error in half?

PROBLEM SOLVING

27. **VACATION SURVEY** In a survey of 439 teenagers in the United States, 14% said that they worked during their summer vacation.

a. What is the margin of error for the survey?

b. Give an interval that is likely to contain the exact percent of all U.S. teenagers who worked during their summer vacation.

28. **NEWSLETTER** The staff for a student newsletter wants to conduct a survey of students' favorite TV shows. There are 1225 students in the school. The newsletter staff would like to survey 250 students. *Describe* a method for selecting an unbiased, random sample of students.

29. ★ **SHORT RESPONSE** Based on the newspaper report shown below, is it reasonable to assume that Kosta is certain to win the election? *Explain.*

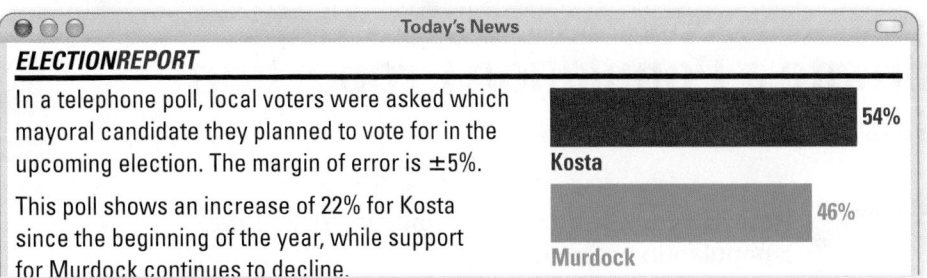

Today's News

ELECTIONREPORT

In a telephone poll, local voters were asked which mayoral candidate they planned to vote for in the upcoming election. The margin of error is ±5%.

This poll shows an increase of 22% for Kosta since the beginning of the year, while support for Murdock continues to decline.

Kosta **54%**

Murdock **46%**

30. MULTI-STEP PROBLEM A Gallup Youth Survey reported that 23% of students surveyed, or about 181 students, say that math is their favorite subject in school.

  a. How many students were surveyed?

  b. What is the margin of error for the survey?

  c. Give an interval that is likely to contain the exact percent of all students who would say that math is their favorite subject.

31. ★ **EXTENDED RESPONSE** A survey reported that 235 out of 500 voters in a sample voted for candidate A and the remainder voted for candidate B.

  a. Find Percents What percent of the voters in the sample voted for candidate A? for candidate B?

  b. Find Margin of Error What is the margin of error for the survey?

  c. Find Intervals For each candidate, find an interval that is likely to contain the exact percent of all voters who voted for the candidate.

  d. Reasoning Based on your intervals, can you be confident that candidate B won? If not, how many people in the sample would need to vote for candidate B for you to be confident of her victory? (*Hint:* Find the least number of voters for candidate B such that the intervals do not overlap.)

32. CHALLENGE In a survey, 52% of the respondents said they prefer cola X and 48% said they prefer cola Y. How many people would have to be surveyed for you to be confident that cola X is truly preferred by more than half the population? *Explain* your reasoning.

Estimate a Population Proportion

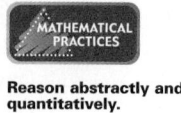

MATERIALS • graphing calculator

Reason abstractly and quantitatively.

QUESTION How can you use a sample proportion to estimate a population proportion?

You can use statistics to make reasonable predictions, or *inferences*, about an entire population from a sample of the population. A *population proportion* is the ratio of members of a population with a particular characteristic to total members of the population. A *sample proportion* is the ratio of members of a sample of the population with a particular characteristic to total members of the sample.

EXPLORE 1 Compare sample proportions from a population with known proportion

In the "population" of randomly-generated decimals between 0 and 1, the proportion of decimals less than 0.6 is 0.6. Simulate random samples of decimals from this population, and compare the sample proportions with the population proportion.

STEP 1 *Perform a simulation*

Use a graphing calculator to generate 40 random decimals between 0 and 1. Press **MATH**, choose the "PRB" menu, select "rand," and press **ENTER**. The display will be similar to the one at the right.

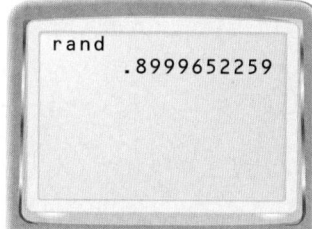

Press **ENTER** 40 times to generate 40 random numbers. Keep a tally of the number of decimals below 0.6. Then find your sample proportion by dividing the number of decimals below 0.6—the "successes"—by the number of trials, which is 40.

Repeat the simulation to find another sample proportion. Each group will need to do enough simulations so that there are 40 in all for the class.

STEP 2 *Display sample proportions*

Collect all 40 sample proportions. Make a histogram of the sample proportions using intervals of 0.05, for example, [0.55, 0.6). The histogram for one set of 40 sample proportions is shown at the right.

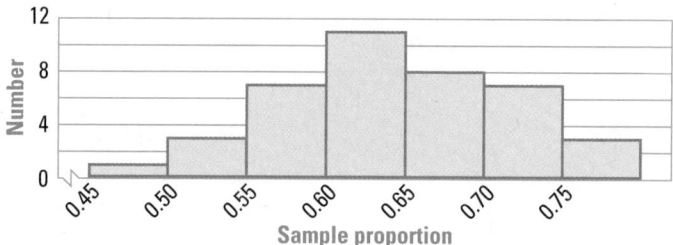

STEP 3 *Investigate sample proportions*

Exclude the single smallest and single greatest of the 40 sample proportions. Then find the interval that contains the remaining 38 sample proportions.

Plot the interval containing the middle 38 sample proportions as shown. The blue horizontal segment represents the middle 38 of 40, or 95%, of the sample proportions. So, 95% of the time, the sample proportion from the simulation fell within the interval graphed.

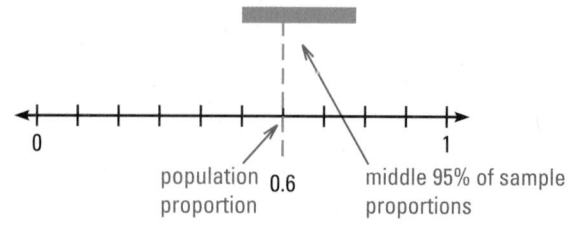

EXPLORE 2 Estimate a population proportion from a sample proportion

Sample Proportions, n = 40

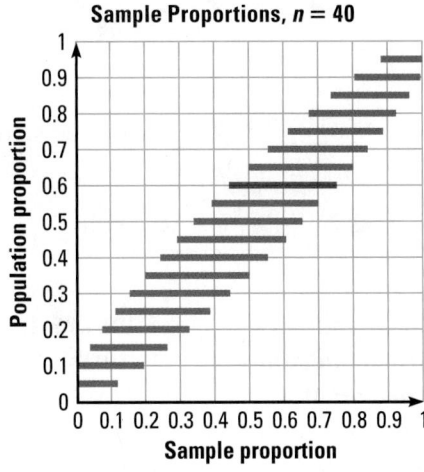

STEP 1 *Investigate sample proportions*

There are formulas for calculating intervals expected to contain 95% of the sample proportions given any population proportion and sample size. The chart at the right shows the 95% sample proportion intervals for population proportions of 0.05, 0.1, 0.15, ..., 0.9, 0.95 where the sample size is $n = 40$.

The interval in red is the calculated 95% sample proportion interval for a population proportion of 0.6. Compare this interval with the 95% interval your class created for the simulation in Explore 1.

STEP 2 *Use a sample proportion*

It's not usually possible to collect data for entire populations. So, data from samples are used to estimate unknown population proportions. Suppose you want to estimate a population proportion using a sample of size 40, and your sample has a sample proportion of 0.6. Which populations are most likely to have produced a sample like yours?

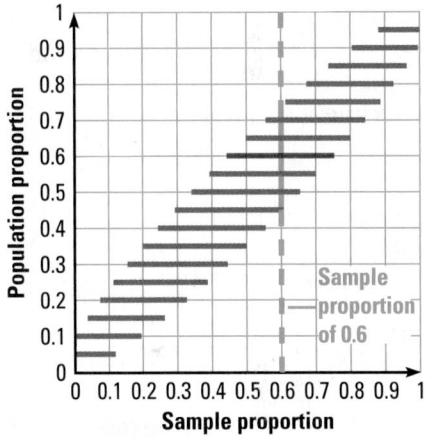

The green vertical line shown at right highlights a sample proportion of 0.6. Any horizontal bar that this line touches corresponds to a population that will produce a sample whose sample proportion lies within that bar 95% of the time. The green line touches the bars for population proportions of 0.45 up to 0.75. So, *if we have a sample of size 40 with a sample proportion of 0.6, then, 95% of the time, the population proportion should lie in the interval from 0.45 to 0.75.*

STEP 3 *Estimate a population proportion*

For a sample of size 40 with sample proportion 0.3, use the chart to estimate the interval that contains the corresponding population proportion 95% of the time.

DRAW CONCLUSIONS **Use your observations to complete these exercises**

1. As a class, repeat Steps 1 and 2 of Explore 1, but with each trial count the number of decimals less than 0.6 out of *80* random decimals. *Describe* how increasing the sample size in each trial affects the shape of the histogram.

2. You have used the *margin of error* $\pm \frac{1}{\sqrt{n}}$ for a sample of size n to estimate an interval containing a population proportion. More precisely, this expression is $\pm 2\sqrt{\frac{\hat{p}(1-\hat{p})}{n}}$, where the symbol $\hat{p}$ (read as "*p*-hat") is the sample proportion. Then $\hat{p} - 2\sqrt{\frac{\hat{p}(1-\hat{p})}{n}} < p < \hat{p} + 2\sqrt{\frac{\hat{p}(1-\hat{p})}{n}}$ is a 95% *confidence interval* for the population proportion p. We can expect the population proportion to be in this interval 95% of the time. Find a 95% confidence interval for the population proportion for a sample of size 150 with a sample proportion of 0.8.

6.5 Compare Surveys, Experiments, and Observational Studies

Before You studied sampling methods for collecting data using a survey.

Now You will learn how studies are used to collect data.

Why So you can design a study to collect data, as in Ex. 16.

Key Vocabulary
- **biased questions**
- **experiment**
- **observational study**
- **controlled experiment**
- **control group**
- **treatment group**
- **randomized comparative experiment**

CC.9-12.S.IC.3 Recognize the purposes of and differences among sample surveys, experiments, and observational studies; explain how randomization relates to each.*

SURVEYS Previously, you learned that in choosing a sample of a population to survey, you should do your best to select an unbiased sample to help ensure that the survey data represent the population. Random samples are preferred since they are less likely to be biased.

In designing a survey, it is also very important to word survey questions carefully. Answers to poorly worded questions may not accurately reflect the opinions or actions of those being surveyed. Questions that are flawed in a way that leads to inaccurate results are called **biased questions**. Questions may be biased in several ways:

- The wording of the question may encourage or pressure the respondent to answer in a particular way.
- The question may be perceived as too sensitive to answer truthfully.
- The question may not provide the respondent with enough information to give an accurate opinion.

Bias may also be introduced in survey questioning in other ways, such as by the order in which questions are asked or by respondents giving answers they believe will please the questioner.

EXAMPLE 1   Identify and correct bias in survey questioning

Tell why the question may be biased or otherwise introduce bias into the survey. Describe a way to correct the flaw.

a.

A reporter asks parents:

Do you agree with the school board's proposal for new technology in our schools?

b.

A dentist asks patients:

Do you brush your teeth at least twice per day and floss every day?

Solution

a. This question assumes that the respondent is familiar with the proposal. To get accurate results that lead to valid conclusions, state the proposal clearly using neutral language before asking the question.

b. Patients who brush less than twice per day or do not floss daily may be afraid to admit this since the dentist is asking the question. One improvement would be to have patients answer questions about dental hygiene on paper and put the paper anonymously into a box.

EXPERIMENTS AND OBSERVATIONAL STUDIES You have seen that surveys are one way to collect data, but different situations and purposes require different data gathering techniques. For example, many studies are designed to try to determine whether a quantity that varies can be associated with measured differences in two different groups of individuals.

An **experiment** imposes a treatment on individuals in order to collect data on their response to the treatment. The treatment may be a medical treatment, or it can be any action that might affect a variable in the experiment, such as adding methanol to gasoline and then measuring its effect on fuel efficiency.

In some cases, it may be difficult to control or isolate the variable being studied, or it may be unethical to subject people to a certain treatment or to withhold it from them. In this case, an *observational study* is used. An **observational study** observes individuals and measures variables without controlling the individuals or their environment.

EXAMPLE 2 Identify experiments and observational studies

Determine whether each situation is an example of an experiment or an observational study. Explain.

a. A researcher asks college students how many hours of sleep they get on an average night and examines whether the number of hours of sleep affects students' grades.

b. A Parks Department employee wants to know if latex paint is more durable than non-latex paint. She has 50 park benches painted with latex paint and has 50 park benches painted with non-latex paint.

Solution

a. The researcher gathers data without controlling the individuals or applying a treatment. The situation is an observational study.

b. A treatment (painting benches with latex paint) is applied to some of the individuals (benches) in the study. The situation is an experiment.

✓ **GUIDED PRACTICE** for Examples 1 and 2

1. Tell whether the survey question below may be biased or otherwise introduce bias into the survey. *Explain.*

"Do you, like most people your age, enjoy watching the latest music videos?"

2. Determine whether the situation described in the research summary shown at the right is an example of an experiment or an observational study. *Explain.*

> **...TECH NOTES...**
>
> **A Faster Web Site**
>
> To test the redesign of its Web site, an online bookseller assembled 96 users of the site and randomly divided them into two groups. One group used the new Web site to make an online purchase and one group used the old Web site to do the same transaction. Users of the new site were able to complete the purchase 22% faster.

CONTROLLED EXPERIMENTS In a **controlled experiment**, two groups are studied under identical conditions with the exception of one variable. The group under ordinary conditions is the **control group**. The group that is subjected to the treatment is the **treatment group**.

In a **randomized comparative experiment**, individuals are randomly assigned to the control group or the treatment group. The comparison of the control group and the treatment group makes it possible to determine any effects of the treatment.

Randomization minimizes bias and produces groups of individuals that are theoretically similar in all ways before the treatment is applied. Conclusions drawn from an experiment that is not a randomized comparative experiment may not be valid.

EXAMPLE 3 Evaluate a published report

Determine whether the study described in the health bulletin below is a randomized comparative experiment. If it is, describe the treatment, the treatment group, and the control group. If it is not, explain why not and discuss whether the conclusions drawn from the study are valid.

Health Watch!

Milk Fights Cavities

At Ashland Middle School, students were given the choice of drinking milk or other beverages at lunch. Fifty students who chose milk were monitored for one year, as were 50 students who chose other beverages. At the end of the year, students in the "milk" group had 15% fewer cavities than students in the other group.

Solution

The study is not a randomized comparative experiment because the individuals were not randomly assigned to a control group and a treatment group. (In fact, the study is an observational study, not an experiment, since no treatment is imposed.)

The study's conclusion that milk fights cavities may or may not be valid. There may be other reasons why students who chose milk had fewer cavities. For example, students who voluntarily choose milk at lunch may be more likely to have other healthy eating or dental care habits that could affect the number of cavities they have.

✓ **GUIDED PRACTICE** for Example 3

3. Determine whether the study described in the research summary for Guided Practice Exercise 2 is a randomized comparative experiment. If it is, describe the treatment, the treatment group, and the control group. If it is not, explain why not and discuss whether the conclusions drawn from the study are valid.

WELL-DESIGNED STUDIES Randomization is a key element of well-designed studies. How randomization applies to different kinds of studies varies, as shown below.

Sample survey	Observational study	Experiment
A random sample is selected to be surveyed from the population studied.	As possible, random samples can be selected for the groups being studied.	Individuals are assigned at random to the treatment group or the control group.

Surveys do not compare groups, and so do not address cause and effect. Good observational studies and experiments are designed to be comparative—to compare data from two or more groups looking for a relationship between variables. But only a well-designed experiment can determine a cause-and-effect relationship.

KEY CONCEPT *For Your Notebook*

Comparative Studies and Causality

- An observational study can identify *correlation* between variables, but not *causality*. Variables other than what is being measured may be affecting the results. For example, vigorous exercise in older people correlates with longer life, but comparing groups only on exercise and lifespan ignores other factors, such as that people who are unhealthy to begin with may not be able to exercise vigorously.

- A rigorous randomized comparative experiment, by eliminating sources of variation other than the controlled variable, can make valid cause-and-effect conclusions possible.

EXAMPLE 4 **Design an experiment or observational study**

Explain whether the following research topic is best investigated through an experiment or an observational study. Then explain how you would design the experiment or observational study.

You want to know if listening to music using earphones for more than one hour per day affects a person's hearing.

Solution

The treatment (listening to music using earphones for more than one hour a day) may affect an individual's hearing, so it is not ethical to assign individuals to a control or treatment group. Use an observational study.

Randomly choose one group of individuals who already listen to music using earphones for more than one hour per day.

Randomly choose one group of individuals who do not listen to music using earphones for more than one hour per day.

Monitor the hearing of the individuals in both groups at regular intervals.

6.5 EXERCISES

SKILL PRACTICE

1. **VOCABULARY** Copy and complete: An __?__ observes individuals and measures variables without controlling the individuals or their environment.

2. ★ **WRITING** *Describe* the difference between an experiment and an observational study.

EXAMPLE 1
for Exs. 3–6

IDENTIFYING BIASED SURVEY QUESTIONS **Tell why the question may be biased or otherwise introduce bias into the survey. Describe a way to correct the flaw.**

3. "Do you agree with all of the budget cuts proposed by the mayor?"

4. "Would you rather watch the latest award-winning movie or just read some book?

5. "The tap water coming from our western water supply contains twice the level of arsenic of water from our eastern supply. Do you think the government should address this health problem?"

6. A child with an adult asks, "Will you vote for our school bond issue?"

EXAMPLE 2
for Exs. 7–9

CLASSIFYING STUDIES **Determine whether each situation is an example of an *experiment* or an *observational study*. Explain.**

7. A researcher compares incomes of people who live in rural areas with incomes of people who live in large cities.

8. A farmer wants to know if a new fertilizer affects the weight of the fruit produced by strawberry plants. She applies the fertilizer to 10 rows of plants and does not apply the fertilizer to 10 other rows of plants.

9. ★ **MULTIPLE CHOICE** A doctor studies the effects of nicotine on a person's health by monitoring the health of 100 randomly selected smokers and 100 randomly selected nonsmokers. This is an example of what type of study?

(A) experiment   (B) observational study
(C) sample survey   (D) none of the above

EXAMPLE 3
for Exs. 10, 11

ERROR ANALYSIS *Describe* and correct the error in describing the study given below.

A company's researchers want to study the effects of adding shea butter to their existing hair conditioner. They monitor the hair quality of 50 randomly selected volunteers using the old conditioner and 50 randomly selected volunteers using the new shea butter conditioner.

10.
> The control group Is volunteers who do not use either of the conditioners. ✗

11.
> The study is a comparative observational study. ✗

12. **CHALLENGE** *Explain* why observational studies, rather than experiments, are usually used in astronomy.

○ = See WORKED-OUT SOLUTIONS in Student Resources   ★ = STANDARDIZED TEST PRACTICE

PROBLEM SOLVING

EXAMPLE 4
for Exs. 13–15

Explain whether the research topic is best addressed through an *experiment* or an *observational study*. Then explain how you would design the experiment or the observational study.

13. You want to know if homes that are close to parks or schools have higher property values than other homes.

14. You want to know if flowers sprayed twice a day with a mist of water stay fresh longer than flowers that are not sprayed.

15. Determine whether the study described in the report is a randomized comparative experiment. If it is, describe the treatment, the treatment group, and the control group. If it is not, explain why not and discuss whether the conclusions drawn from the study are valid.

> **Early Birds Make Better Drivers**
> A recent study shows that adults who rise before 6:30 A.M. are better drivers than other adults. The study monitored the driving records of 140 volunteers who always wake up before 6:30 and 140 volunteers who never wake up before 6:30. The early risers had 12% fewer accidents.

16. Describe how you would set up a randomized, controlled experiment to investigate the hypothesis below. Include any precautions you would take to ensure that your conclusions are valid.

   Dog food with added Omega-3 fatty acids will give dogs a shiny coat.

17. **MEDICINE** A researcher studied the effect of fiber supplements on heart disease. She identified 175 people who take fiber supplements and 175 people who do not take fiber supplements. She found that those who took the supplements had 19% fewer heart attacks those who did not. She concluded that taking fiber supplements reduces the incidence of heart attacks.

   a. *Explain* why the researcher's conclusion may not be valid.

   b. *Describe* how the researcher could have conducted the study differently to produce valid results.

18. **CHALLENGE** Will replicating an experiment on many individuals produce data that is more likely to accurately represent a population than performing the experiment only once? *Explain.*

QUIZ

A normal distribution has a mean of 47 and a standard deviation of 6. Find the probability that a randomly selected *x*-value is in the given interval.

1. Between 35 and 65
2. At least 41
3. At most 29

Find the sample size required to achieve the given margin of error. Round your answer to the nearest whole number.

4. ±3%
5. ±7%
6. ±4.5%
7. ±0.8%

8. ★ **WRITING** *Explain* why a randomized comparative experiment should be used to collect data whenever possible.

Simulate an Experimental Difference

MATHEMATICAL PRACTICES

MATERIALS • index cards • scissors • small paper bag • graphing calculator

Use appropriate tools strategically.

QUESTION How can you test a hypothesis about an experiment?

When you perform a randomized comparative experiment and measure a difference between the control and treatment groups, how do you know if the difference is from the treatment or if it's just a chance result of the choice of the groups? One way is to *resample*: combine all the measurements from both groups, and repeatedly create new "control" and "treatment" groups at random from the measurements. Then see how often you get chance differences between the new groups that are at least as large as the one you measured.

EXPLORE 1 Resample data

A randomized experiment tests whether a soil supplement affects the total yield (in kilograms) of cherry tomato plants. The table below shows the results. How does the difference in the means of the control and treatment groups compare with differences resulting from chance?

Total Yield of Tomato Plants (kilograms)									
Control group	1.4	0.9	1.2	1.3	2.0	1.2	0.7	1.9	1.4	1.7
Treatment group	1.4	0.9	1.5	1.8	1.6	1.8	2.4	1.9	1.9	1.7

STEP 1 *Calculate means* Find the mean yield of the control group, $\bar{x}_{control}$, and the mean yield of the treatment group, $\bar{x}_{treatment}$. Then find the difference $\bar{x}_{treatment} - \bar{x}_{control}$. Note that the difference can be positive or negative, and is 0 when $\bar{x}_{treatment} = \bar{x}_{control}$.

STEP 2 *Combine measurements and resample* Working in pairs, cut index cards to make 20 equal-sized pieces, and write one yield measurement on each. Place the pieces in a bag, shake, and randomly choose 10. Call this the "treatment" group, and call the 10 pieces in the bag the "control" group. Find the mean for each group, record $\bar{x}_{treatment} - \bar{x}_{control}$, and return the pieces to the bag.

Perform the resampling experiment 5 times, each time finding the difference of means. Sample results for 5 resamplings made by each of two pairs of students are shown at the right.

$\bar{x}_{treatment} - \bar{x}_{control}$:

Pair 1: $-0.28, -0.24, -0.18, -0.12, 0.30$

Pair 2: $-0.26, 0.00, 0.12, 0.18, 0.28$

STEP 3 *State the null hypothesis* The *null hypothesis* is the assumption that measured differences between a treatment group and a control group are a result of chance. The null hypothesis for this activity is the following:

The soil nutrient has no effect on the yield of the cherry tomato plants.

© Image Source/Corbis

EXPLORE 2 Evaluate the null hypothesis

To conclude that the treatment *is* responsible for the difference in yield, you need strong evidence to *reject* the null hypothesis. To evaluate the null hypothesis, compare the experimental difference of means with the resampling differences.

STEP 1 *Collect and display results* Collect all the differences $\overline{x}_{treatment} - \overline{x}_{control}$ calculated by pairs of students in the class in Explore 1. Display the differences in a histogram. A sample histogram for 50 resamplings made using a graphing calculator and an interval for the difference of means of 0.05 is shown at the right.

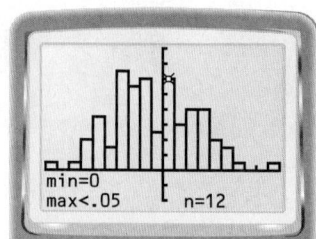

STEP 2 *Analyze resampling data* In Step 1 of Explore 1, you calculated the experimental difference of means. Draw a vertical line on your class histogram to represent this difference.

If the experimental difference of means lies in one of the tails of the resampling distribution, then resampling gave a difference of means at least as large as the experimental difference only rarely. This gives evidence for rejecting the null hypothesis. More specifically, the following are true:

- If the experimental difference of means falls outside of the middle 90% of the resampling differences of means, you can reject the null hypothesis at the 90% confidence level.

- If the experimental difference of means falls outside of the middle 95% of the resampling differences of means, you can reject the null hypothesis at the 95% confidence level.

STEP 3 *Evaluate results* Is your class able to reject the null hypothesis? *Explain*. What does this mean regarding the original experiment?

DRAW CONCLUSIONS Use your observations to complete these exercises

1. Find the mean of all of the resampling differences of means collected by all pairs of students in Step 1 of Explore 2. This mean should approximate the most likely result when the null hypothesis is true. Is the mean of the resampling differences of means for your class close to this value?

2. In Explore 1, how many resampling choices for the treatment and control groups are theoretically possible? Suppose that a computer is programmed to generate all possible control and treatment group assignments, to find the differences of means, and then to draw a histogram of the results. Would you prefer to make conclusions about the experiment using the histogram from the computer or the histogram for your class? *Explain*.

3. Suppose the company that produces the soil nutrient featured in the experiment described in Explore 1 advertises that growing tomato plants in soil enriched with the nutrient will increase the yield of the tomato plants. Is this an accurate statement? *Explain*.

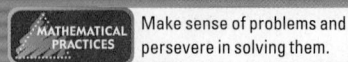

MIXED REVIEW *of Problem Solving*

1. **MULTI-STEP PROBLEM** A fly fisher records in a table the weight of 20 Maine landlocked salmon he caught and finds they are normally distributed.

Fly fishing for salmon

1.9, 1.5, 2.0, 2.0, 2.1, 2.0, 1.8, 1.5, 2.2, 1.9, 1.8, 1.7, 2.1, 2.2, 1.7, 2.1, 2.0, 1.5, 1.8, 2.1

 a. Find the mean of the data set.

 b. Find the standard deviation of the data set.

 c. If all the fly fishers that come to the river in a year collectively catch 3000 fish, how many of the salmon caught do you expect weigh less than 1.443 lb?

2. **MULTI-STEP PROBLEM** In a survey of 1022 people who shop online, 73% said that they do so because of the convenience.

 a. What is the margin of error for the survey?

 b. Give an interval that is likely to contain the exact percent of all online shoppers who shop because of the convenience.

3. **GRIDDED ANSWER** At a tree nursery, the heights of scotch pine trees are normally distributed with a mean of 200 centimeters and a standard deviation of 20 centimeters. Find the percent of scotch pine trees that have a height of at least 220 centimeters. Round your answer to the nearest whole number.

4. **EXTENDED RESPONSE** Explain whether the following research topic is best investigated through an experiment or an observational study. Then explain how you would design the experiment or observational study.

 Jody wants to know whether water that has high levels of dissolved calcium will inhibit or promote orchid growth.

5. **SHORT RESPONSE** The amount of juice dispensed from a machine is normally distributed with a mean of 10.5 ounces and a standard deviation of 0.75 ounce. Within what range do about 68% of the amounts dispensed fall? *Explain* your reasoning.

6. **SHORT RESPONSE** A survey shows that the time spent by shoppers in a supermarket is normally distributed with a mean of 45 minutes and a standard deviation of 12 minutes. What is the probability that a randomly chosen shopper will spend between 45 and 69 minutes in the supermarket? *Explain* your reasoning.

7. **MULTI-STEP PROBLEM** A survey of students shows that 15% of respondents, or 315 students, prefer having gym class during the last period of the day.

 a. How many students were surveyed?

 b. What is the margin of error for the survey?

 c. Give an interval that is likely to contain the exact percent of all students who would prefer to have gym class during the last period of the day.

8. **SHORT RESPONSE** A local sports TV station wants to find the number of hours per week people in the viewing area watch sporting events on television. The station surveys people at a nearby sports stadium. What type of sample is described? Is this sample biased? *Explain* your reasoning.

BIG IDEAS

Big Idea ①

Using Normal Distributions

A normal distribution is modeled by a symmetric, bell-shaped curve. The area under a normal curve is distributed as shown below. A *z*-score is the number of standard deviations a data value lies above or below the mean. You can use *z*-scores and the standard normal table to find probabilities related to any normal distribution.

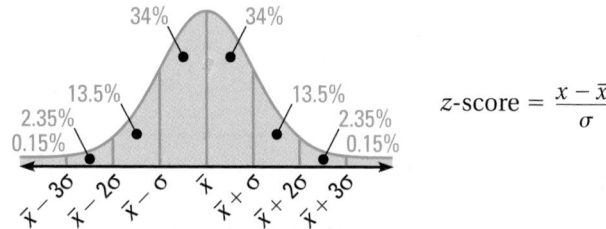

$$z\text{-score} = \frac{x - \bar{x}}{\sigma}$$

Big Idea ②

Working with Samples

You can use several different methods to choose a sample from a population. Random sampling is most likely to produce an unbiased sample.

Self-selected sample	Members volunteer.	Often biased
Systematic sample	A rule is used to select members.	Sometimes biased
Convenience sample	Easy-to-reach members are selected.	Often biased
Random sample	Every member has an equal chance of being selected.	Unbiased

6 CHAPTER REVIEW

@HomeTutor

my.hrw.com
• Multi-Language Glossary
• Vocabulary practice

REVIEW KEY VOCABULARY

- combination
- Pascal's triangle
- binomial theorem
- random variable
- probability distribution
- binomial distribution
- binomial experiment
- symmetric
- skewed

- normal distribution
- normal curve
- standard normal distribution
- *z*-score
- population
- sample
- unbiased sample
- biased sample
- margin of error

- biased questions
- experiment
- observational study
- controlled experiment
- control group
- treatment group
- randomized comparative experiment

VOCABULARY EXERCISES

1. Copy and complete: A(n) __?__ is a selection of *r* objects from a group of *n* objects where the order of the objects selected is not important.

2. In a controlled experiment, two groups are studied under identical conditions with the exception of one variable. The group under ordinary conditions is the __?__ .

3. Copy and complete: The __?__ for an *x*-value from a normal distribution represents the number of standard deviations the *x*-value lies above or below the mean.

REVIEW EXAMPLES AND EXERCISES

Use the review examples and exercises below to check your understanding of the concepts you have learned in each lesson of this chapter.

6.1 Use Combinations and the Binomial Theorem

EXAMPLE

Use the binomial theorem to expand $(x + 5y)^4$.

$$(x + 5y)^4 = {}_4C_0 x^4 (5y)^0 + {}_4C_1 x^3 (5y)^1 + {}_4C_2 x^2 (5y)^2 + {}_4C_3 x^1 (5y)^3 + {}_4C_4 x^0 (5y)^4$$

$$= (1)(x^4)(1) + (4)(x^3)(5y) + (6)(x^2)(25y^2) + (4)(x)(125y^3) + (1)(1)(625y^4)$$

$$= x^4 + 20x^3 y + 150x^2 y^2 + 500xy^3 + 625y^4$$

EXERCISES

EXAMPLES 3, 5, and 6
for Exs. 10–14

Use the binomial theorem to write the binomial expansion.

1. $(t + 3)^6$

2. $(2a + b^2)^4$

3. $(w - 8v)^4$

4. $(r^3 - 4s)^5$

5. **ICE CREAM** An ice cream vendor sells 15 flavors of ice cream. You want to sample *at least* 4 of the flavors. How many different combinations of ice cream flavors can you sample?

6.2 Construct and Interpret Binomial Distributions

EXAMPLE

Find the probability of tossing a coin 12 times and getting exactly 4 heads.

$$P(k = 4) = {}_nC_k \, p^k(1 - p)^{n-k} = {}_{12}C_4(0.5)^4(1 - 0.5)^8 = 495(0.5)^4(0.5)^8 \approx 0.121$$

EXERCISES

EXAMPLE 3
for Exs. 26–29

Find the probability of tossing a coin 8 times and getting the given number of heads.

6. 6   **7.** 4   **8.** 7   **9.** 0

6.3 Use Normal Distributions

EXAMPLE

A normal distribution has a mean of 76 and a standard deviation of 9. Use the standard normal table in the lesson to find the probability that a randomly selected x-value from the distribution is at most 64.

$$z = \frac{x - \bar{x}}{\sigma} = \frac{64 - 76}{9} \approx -1.3 \qquad \text{Find } z\text{-score for } x = 64.$$

$$P(x \le 64) \approx P(z \le -1.3) = 0.0968 \qquad \text{Use the standard normal table.}$$

EXERCISES

EXAMPLE 3
for Exs. 12–17

A normal distribution has a mean of 95 and a standard deviation of 7. Use the standard normal table in the lesson to find the indicated probability for a randomly selected x-value from the distribution.

10. $P(x \le 89)$ **11.** $P(x \le 84)$ **12.** $P(91 < x \le 100)$

13. $P(x \le 50)$ **14.** $P(x > 100)$ **15.** $P(50 < x \le 80)$

6.4 Select and Draw Conclusions from Samples

EXAMPLE

In a survey of 582 people, 57% said that summer is their favorite season. What is the margin of error for the survey?

$$\text{Margin of error} = \pm\frac{1}{\sqrt{n}} = \pm\frac{1}{\sqrt{582}} \approx \pm 0.041 = \pm 4.1\%$$

EXERCISES

EXAMPLE 4
for Exs. 18–22

Find the margin of error for a survey that has the given sample size. Round your answer to the nearest tenth of a percent.

16. 300   **17.** 2500   **18.** 800   **19.** 4900

20. **SURVEYS** In a Gallup Youth Survey of 517 teenagers, 34% said that their favorite way to spend an evening was to hang out with family or friends. What is the margin of error for the survey?

EXAMPLE

Determine whether the study described in the news bulletin below is a randomized comparative experiment. If it is, describe the treatment, the treatment group, and the control group. If it is not, explain why not and discuss whether the conclusions drawn from the study are valid.

Aural Anomaly! Headphones Hurt Hearing

A study of 100 college and high school students compared their time spent listening to music using headphones with hearing loss. Twelve percent of people who listened to headphones more than 1 hour per day were found to have measurable hearing loss over the course of the three-year study. The study is not a randomized comparative experiment because the individuals were not randomly assigned to a control group and a treatment group. The study is an observational study, because no treatment was imposed. The study's conclusion that headphone use impairs hearing ability may or may not be valid. People who listen to over an hour of music per day may be more likely to attend loud concerts that are known to affect hearing.

EXERCISES

EXAMPLE 2
for Exs. 21–23

Decide whether the following are examples of observational studies, surveys, or randomized controlled experiments.

21. Preparing for an employee appreciation dinner, a human resources representative asks people to name their favorite type of sandwich bread.

22. A market researcher tracks customer data to find out which type of sandwich bread attracts the most repeat customers.

23. Various types of batteries each run a flashlight constantly until the light goes off.

24. An apple grower concerned about the of effect the orchard's new canning plant may have on the business compares the number of apples produced in each tree with the tree's distance from the canning plant.

Find the number of permutations or combinations.

1. $_4C_3$ 2. $_7C_7$ 3. $_{18}C_4$ 4. $_9C_5$

Use the binomial theorem to write the binomial expansion.

5. $(x + 5)^3$ 6. $(3a - 3)^5$ 7. $(s + t^2)^4$ 8. $(c^3 - 2d^2)^6$

Calculate the probability of k successes for a binomial experiment consisting of n trials with probability p of success on each trial.

9. $k = 4, n = 11, p = 0.4$ 10. $k \leq 2, n = 5, p = 0.7$ 11. $k \geq 8, n = 9, p = 0.9$

12. **TRUE-OR-FALSE QUIZ** Calculate the probability of randomly guessing at least 8 correct answers on a 10 question true-or-false quiz.

13. **GOVERNMENT** There are 15 members on a city council. On a recent agenda item, 8 of the council members voted in favor of a budget increase for city park improvements. How many combinations of council members could have voted in favor of the budget increase?

A normal distribution has a mean of 72 and a standard deviation of 5. Find the probability that a randomly selected x-value from the distribution is in the given interval.

14. Between 67 and 77 15. Between 57 and 72 16. At least 62

Find the margin of error for a survey that has the given sample size. Round your answer to the nearest tenth of a percent.

17. 340 18. 8125 19. 931 20. 1560

21. **TEST SCORES** The scores on a standardized test administered to 10,000 students have a mean of 50 and a standard deviation of 10. Find the z-score for each student whose score is given.

    a. Kevin: 55 b. Manuel: 70 c. Colby: 40 d. Neal: 47

22. **SHOPPING SURVEY** In a survey of 1600 U.S. adults, 61% said that they have purchased a product online. Find the margin of error for the survey. Then give an interval that is likely to contain the exact percent of all U.S. adults who have purchased a product online.

23. **FISHING** A study found that 9% of people cite fishing as their favorite leisure-time activity. Suppose you randomly survey 8 people about their leisure-time activities. What is the probability that at least 2 of the people cite fishing as their favorite?

MULTIPLE CHOICE QUESTIONS

If you have difficulty solving a multiple choice problem directly, you may be able to use another approach to eliminate incorrect answer choices and obtain the correct answer.

PROBLEM 1

The Nielsen ratings measure how many viewers watch different TV programs. There are 5000 Nielsen households, which are chosen randomly from U.S. households with televisions. Suppose the Nielsen ratings report that 9.2% of Neilson households watched a certain program. What interval is likely to contain the exact percent of all U.S. households with televisions that watched the program?

(A) 4.0% to 14.0%

(B) 7.8% to 10.6%

(C) 8.3% to 10.3%

(D) 9.2% to 9.6%

METHOD 1

SOLVE DIRECTLY Calculate the margin of error. Then use the margin of error and the percent given in the problem to find the interval.

STEP 1 **Calculate** the margin of error.

$$\text{Margin of error} = \pm \frac{1}{\sqrt{n}}$$

$$= \pm \frac{1}{\sqrt{5000}}$$

$$\approx \pm 0.014$$

$$= \pm 1.4\%$$

STEP 2 **Find** the lower bound for the interval.

$$\text{Lower bound} = 9.2\% - 1.4\%$$

$$= 7.8\%$$

STEP 3 **Find** the upper bound for the interval.

$$\text{Upper bound} = 9.2\% + 1.4\%$$

$$= 10.6\%$$

STEP 4 **Write** the interval.

The interval is 7.8% to 10.6%.

▶ The correct answer is B. (A) (B) (C) (D)

METHOD 2

ELIMINATE CHOICES Another method is to check the intervals given in the answer choices.

You know that 9.2% must fall exactly in the middle of the interval.

Choice A: $\frac{4.0 + 14.0}{2} = \frac{18.0}{2} = 9.0$, so 9.2% does not fall exactly in the middle of the interval. You can eliminate choice A. ✗

Choice B: $\frac{7.8 + 10.6}{2} = \frac{18.4}{2} = 9.2$, so 9.2% falls exactly in the middle of the interval.

Choice C: $\frac{8.3 + 10.3}{2} = \frac{18.6}{2} = 9.3$, so 9.2% does not fall exactly in the middle of the interval. You can eliminate choice C. ✗

Choice D: $\frac{9.2 + 9.6}{2} = \frac{18.8}{2} = 9.4$, so 9.2% does not fall exactly in the middle of the interval. You can eliminate choice D. ✗

▶ The correct answer is B. (A) (B) (C) (D)

PROBLEM 2

At a local bank, the waiting times for an available teller are normally distributed with a mean of 10 minutes and a standard deviation of 2 minutes. What is the approximate probability that a randomly selected customer at the bank waits no more than 13 minutes for a teller?

(A) 60.7% **(B)** 82.0% **(C)** 93.3% **(D)** 98.5%

METHOD 1

SOLVE DIRECTLY Use a z-score and a standard normal table to find the desired probability.

STEP 1 **Find** the z-score for a waiting time of 13 minutes.

$$z = \frac{x - \bar{x}}{\sigma}$$

$$= \frac{13 - 10}{2}$$

$$= 1.5$$

STEP 2 **Use** the standard normal table to find $P(z \le 1.5)$.

$$P(z \le 1.5) = 0.9332 \approx 93.3\%$$

The probability of waiting no more than 13 minutes is about 93.3%.

▸ The correct answer is C. (A) (B) **(C)** (D)

METHOD 2

ELIMINATE CHOICES Use facts about normal distributions to eliminate incorrect answer choices.

For a randomly selected customer with a waiting time of x minutes, you know the following:

$$P(x \le 12) = P(x \le \bar{x} + \sigma)$$

$$= 50\% + 34\%$$

$$= 84\%$$

$$P(x \le 14) = P(x \le \bar{x} + 2\sigma)$$

$$= 50\% + 34\% + 13.5\%$$

$$= 97.5\%$$

It follows that $P(x \le 13)$ is between 84% and 97.5%. Only the probability of 93.3% in answer choice C satisfies this condition.

▸ The correct answer is C. (A) (B) **(C)** (D)

PRACTICE

Explain why you can eliminate the highlighted answer choice.

1. A normal distribution has a mean of 4.06 and a standard deviation of 0.04. What is the probability that a randomly selected value from the distribution is between 4.06 and 4.14?

   (A) 0.01 **(B)** 0.475 **(C)** 0.68 **(D)** ✗ 0.99

2. If you add the same nonzero constant to each value in a data set, which statistic does not change?

   (A) Mean **(B)** Median **(C)** ✗ Mode **(D)** Range

3. Which type of function best models the data represented by the scatter plot at the right?

   (A) Linear **(B)** Quadratic

   (C) Cubic **(D)** ✗ Exponential

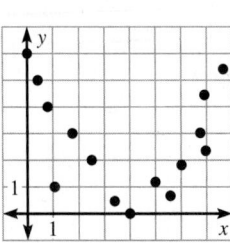

MULTIPLE CHOICE

1. Which binomial expansion includes the term $40x^2$?

   (A) $(x + 1)^5$ (B) $(x + 5)^5$

   (C) $(2x + 1)^5$ (D) $(2x + 5)^5$

2. What is the fourth term of the expansion of $(x - 2)^6$?

   (A) $60x^4$ (B) $-60x^4$

   (C) $-96x^3$ (D) $96x^3$

3. According to a survey from the National Center for Health Statistics, the heights of adult women in the United States are normally distributed with a mean of 64 inches and a standard deviation of 2.7 inches. What is the approximate probability that 4 randomly selected women are all between 58.6 inches and 66.7 inches tall?

   (A) 34%   (B) 44%

   (C) 68%   (D) 81.5%

4. What is the percent of the area under a normal curve that is represented by the shaded region?

   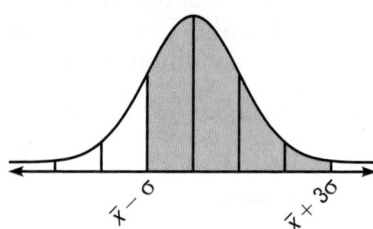

   (A) 50%   (B) 81.5%

   (C) 83.85%   (D) 84%

5. Rachel scored an 88 on her physics test. The class average was 79.3, and the standard deviation was 7.5. What is the z-score for Rachel's test score?

   (A) 1.16   (B) 1.30

   (C) 1.45   (D) 1.60

6. You perform a binomial experiment consisting of 20 trials with a probability of success of 41%. What is the most likely number of successes?

   (A) 8   (B) 5

   (C) 4   (D) 16

7. In a nationwide poll of 1015 U.S. adults, Tom Hanks was voted America's favorite movie star. What is the approximate margin of error for the survey?

   (A) ±0.031%   (B) ±0.31%

   (C) ±3.1%   (D) ±31%

8. A normal distribution has a mean of 165 and a standard deviation of 6.7. What is the z-score of a data point measuring 192?

   (A) 53.28   (B) 10.43

   (C) 0.78   (D) 4.02

9. Complete the sentence: A(n) _____?_____ observes individuals and measures variables without controlling the individuals or their environment.

   (A) controlled experiment   (B) control group

   (C) observational study   (D) treatment group

10. A survey claims the percent of customers who favor brand X cereal over brand Y is likely between 78.01% and 45.99%. How many people were surveyed?

    (A) 62   (B) 10

    (C) 39   (D) 32

GRIDDED ANSWER

11. A normal distribution has a mean of 77 and a standard deviation of 4. What is the z-score corresponding to an x-value of 80?

12. What is the coefficient of x^3 in the expansion of $(4x - 1)^9$?

13. What is the value of the expression $_5C_3 - {_5C_2}$?

14. In a normal distribution, about what percent of the area under the related normal curve lies within 2 standard deviations of the mean?

15. What is the probability rounded to the nearest thousandth of tossing a coin 50 times and getting exactly 15 heads?

16. In a survey of adults who follow more than one sport, 30% listed football as their favorite sport. You survey 15 adults who follow more than one sport. What is the probability rounded to the nearest thousandth that fewer than 4 of them will say that football is their favorite sport?

SHORT RESPONSE

17. According to a certain poll, 51% of adults in the United States follow professional football. The margin of error is ±2%. About how many people were surveyed? *Explain* whether you know for certain that football is followed by the majority of adults in the United States.

18. A student is conducting a survey about the Internet usage of high school students. He sends the survey by e-mail to each person in his address book, and uses only the surveys that are returned. What type of sample is this? Is the sample biased or unbiased? *Explain.*

EXTENDED RESPONSE

19. The results of a survey of the newsgathering habits of adults age 18–29 are displayed in the table.

  a. How many people were surveyed?

  b. Why might the conclusion, "Young adults generally don't get news from TV" be inaccurate to draw from this data?

  c. Aleida decides to test the results of the poll. She decides to survey people at random from that age group. What is the probability, to the nearest tenth of a percent, that the Internet is the primary source of news for at least 3 out of the 6 people she will choose to survey?

What is your primary source of news?	
TV	32%
Internet	41%
Newspaper	12%
Radio	15%
(*margin of error* ±4.47%)	

  d. Aleida finds that 4 of 6 respondents (or 66.7%) to her poll said that the Internet was their primary source of news. She concludes that the poll was inaccurate. Why might she be wrong?

  e. To the nearest tenth of a percent, what is the margin of error in Aleida's survey?

7 Sequences and Series

Before

Previously, you learned the following skills, which you'll use in this chapter: solving equations and performing function composition.

Prerequisite Skills

VOCABULARY CHECK

Copy and complete the statement using $f(x) = \frac{1}{x}$ and $g(x) = 4x + 2$.

1. The **domain** of $f(x)$ is ___?___.

2. The **range** of $g(x)$ is ___?___.

3. The **composition** $f(g(x))$ is equal to ___?___.

SKILLS CHECK

Solve the equation. Check your solution.

4. $7x + 3 = 31$
5. $9 = 2x - 7$
6. $14 = -3x + 8$

7. $10 - 3x = 28$
8. $11x + 9 = 3x + 17$
9. $2x + 3 = -6 - x$

Copy and complete the table for the linear function.

10. $y = 3 - 2x$

x	y
1	
2	
3	

11. $y = 5x + 1$

x	y
2	
3	
4	

12. $y = -x + 24$

x	y
5	
10	
15	

In this chapter, you will apply the big ideas listed below and reviewed in the Chapter Summary. You will also use the key vocabulary listed below.

Big Ideas

1. **Analyze sequences**
2. **Find sums of series**
3. **Use recursive rules**

KEY VOCABULARY

- sequence
- terms of a sequence
- series
- summation notation
- sigma notation

- arithmetic sequence
- common difference
- arithmetic series
- geometric sequence
- common ratio

- geometric series
- partial sum
- explicit rule
- recursive rule
- iteration

Why?

You can use sequences to describe patterns in the real world. For example, you can use the Fibonacci sequence to describe patterns in nature.

Animated Algebra

The animation illustrated below helps you answer a question from this chapter: How can you generate Fibonacci numbers?

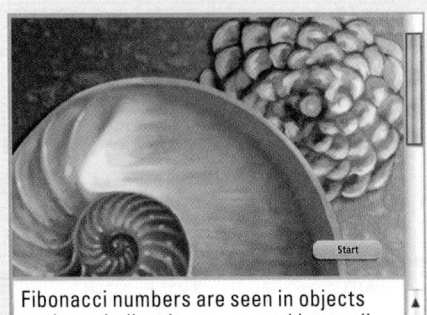

Fibonacci numbers are seen in objects such as shells, pinecones, and broccoli.

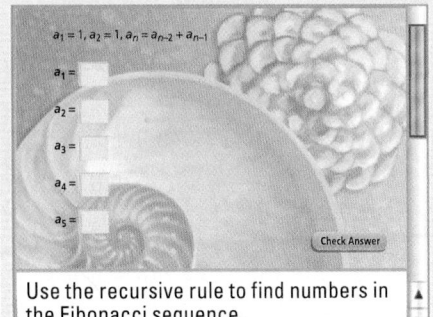

$a_1 = 1, a_2 = 1, a_n = a_{n-2} + a_{n-1}$

$a_1 =$
$a_2 =$
$a_3 =$
$a_4 =$
$a_5 =$

Use the recursive rule to find numbers in the Fibonacci sequence.

Animated Algebra at my.hrw.com

7.1 Define and Use Sequences and Series

Before	You identified and wrote functions.
Now	You will recognize and write rules for number patterns.
Why?	So you can find angle measures, as in Ex. 63.

Key Vocabulary
- sequence
- terms of a sequence
- series
- summation notation
- sigma notation

CC.9-12.F.IF.3 Recognize that sequences are functions, sometimes defined recursively, whose domain is a subset of the integers.

KEY CONCEPT
For Your Notebook

Sequences

A **sequence** is a function whose domain is a set of consecutive integers. If a domain is not specified, it is understood that the domain starts with 1. The values in the range are called the **terms** of the sequence.

Domain: 1   2   3   4 . . . n The relative position of each term

Range: a_1 a_2 a_3 a_4 . . . a_n Terms of the sequence

A *finite sequence* has a limited number of terms. An *infinite sequence* continues without stopping.

Finite sequence: 2, 4, 6, 8   **Infinite sequence:** 2, 4, 6, 8, . . .

A sequence can be specified by an equation, or *rule*. For example, both sequences above can be described by the rule $a_n = 2n$ or $f(n) = 2n$.

EXAMPLE 1 Write terms of sequences

Write the first six terms of (a) $a_n = 2n + 5$ and (b) $f(n) = (-3)^{n-1}$.

Solution

a. $a_1 = 2(1) + 5 = 7$ 1st term   b. $f(1) = (-3)^{1-1} = 1$ 1st term

$a_2 = 2(2) + 5 = 9$ 2nd term $f(2) = (-3)^{2-1} = -3$ 2nd term

$a_3 = 2(3) + 5 = 11$ 3rd term $f(3) = (-3)^{3-1} = 9$ 3rd term

$a_4 = 2(4) + 5 = 13$ 4th term $f(4) = (-3)^{4-1} = -27$ 4th term

$a_5 = 2(5) + 5 = 15$ 5th term $f(5) = (-3)^{5-1} = 81$ 5th term

$a_6 = 2(6) + 5 = 17$ 6th term $f(6) = (-3)^{6-1} = -243$ 6th term

---

 GUIDED PRACTICE   for Example 1

Write the first six terms of the sequence.

1. $a_n = n + 4$ **2.** $f(n) = (-2)^{n-1}$ **3.** $a_n = \dfrac{n}{n+1}$

Roger Wood/Corbis

WRITING RULES If the terms of a sequence have a recognizable pattern, then you may be able to write a rule for the nth term of the sequence.

EXAMPLE 2 **Write rules for sequences**

Describe the pattern, write the next term, and write a rule for the nth term of the sequence (a) $-1, -8, -27, -64, \ldots$ and (b) $0, 2, 6, 12, \ldots$.

Solution

a. You can write the terms as $(-1)^3, (-2)^3, (-3)^3, (-4)^3, \ldots$. The next term is $a_5 = (-5)^3 = -125$. A rule for the nth term is $a_n = (-n)^3$.

b. You can write the terms as $0(1), 1(2), 2(3), 3(4), \ldots$. The next term is $f(5) = 4(5) = 20$. A rule for the nth term is $f(n) = (n - 1)n$.

GRAPHING SEQUENCES To graph a sequence, let the horizontal axis represent the position numbers (the domain) and the vertical axis represent the terms (the range).

EXAMPLE 3 **Solve a multi-step problem**

RETAIL DISPLAYS You work in a grocery store and are stacking apples in the shape of a square pyramid with 7 layers. Write a rule for the number of apples in each layer. Then graph the sequence.

← First layer

Solution

STEP 1 **Make** a table showing the number of fruit in the first three layers. Let a_n represent the number of apples in layer n.

Layer, n	1	2	3
Number of apples, a_n	$1 = 1^2$	$4 = 2^2$	$9 = 3^2$

STEP 2 **Write** a rule for the number of apples in each layer. From the table, you can see that $a_n = n^2$.

STEP 3 **Plot** the points $(1, 1), (2, 4), (3, 9), \ldots,$ $(7, 49)$. The graph is shown at the right.

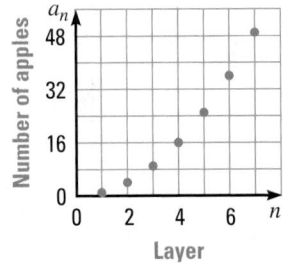

✓ **GUIDED PRACTICE** for Examples 2 and 3

4. For the sequence 3, 8, 15, 24, . . . , describe the pattern, write the next term, graph the first five terms, and write a rule for the nth term.

5. **WHAT IF?** In Example 3, suppose there are 9 layers of apples. How many apples are in the 9th layer?

Series and Summation Notation

When the terms of a sequence are added together, the resulting expression is a **series**. A series can be finite or infinite.

Finite series: $2 + 4 + 6 + 8$ **Infinite series:** $2 + 4 + 6 + 8 + \cdots$

You can use **summation notation** to write a series. For example, the two series above can be written in summation notation as follows:

> **READING**
> When written in summation notation, this series is read as "the sum of 2*i* for values of *i* from 1 to 4."

$$2 + 4 + 6 + 8 = \sum_{i=1}^{4} 2i \qquad\qquad 2 + 4 + 6 + 8 + \cdots = \sum_{i=1}^{\infty} 2i$$

For both series, the *index of summation* is *i* and the *lower limit of summation* is 1. The *upper limit of summation* is 4 for the finite series and ∞ (infinity) for the infinite series. Summation notation is also called **sigma notation** because it uses the uppercase Greek letter *sigma*, written Σ.

EXAMPLE 4   **Write series using summation notation**

Write the series using summation notation.

   a. $25 + 50 + 75 + \cdots + 250$ **b.** $\dfrac{1}{2} + \dfrac{2}{3} + \dfrac{3}{4} + \dfrac{4}{5} + \cdots$

Solution

  a. Notice that the first term is 25(1), the second is 25(2), the third is 25(3), and the last is 25(10). So, the terms of the series can be written as:

$$a_i = 25i \text{ where } i = 1, 2, 3, \ldots, 10$$

The lower limit of summation is 1 and the upper limit of summation is 10.

   ▸ The summation notation for the series is $\displaystyle\sum_{i=1}^{10} 25i$.

  b. Notice that for each term the denominator of the fraction is 1 more than the numerator. So, the terms of the series can be written as:

$$a_i = \frac{i}{i+1} \text{ where } i = 1, 2, 3, 4, \ldots$$

The lower limit of summation is 1 and the upper limit of summation is infinity.

   ▸ The summation notation for the series is $\displaystyle\sum_{i=1}^{\infty} \frac{i}{i+1}$.

 GUIDED PRACTICE   for Example 4

Write the series using summation notation.

  6. $5 + 10 + 15 + \cdots + 100$ **7.** $\dfrac{1}{2} + \dfrac{4}{5} + \dfrac{9}{10} + \dfrac{16}{17} + \cdots$

  8. $6 + 36 + 216 + 1296 + \cdots$ **9.** $5 + 6 + 7 + \cdots + 12$

INDEX OF SUMMATION The index of summation for a series does not have to be i—any letter can be used. Also, the index does not have to begin at 1. For instance, the index begins at 4 in the next example.

EXAMPLE 5 Find the sum of a series

Find the sum of the series.

$$\sum_{k=4}^{8} (3 + k^2) = (3 + 4^2) + (3 + 5^2) + (3 + 6^2) + (3 + 7^2) + (3 + 8^2)$$

$$= 19 + 28 + 39 + 52 + 67$$

$$= 205$$

SPECIAL FORMULAS For series with many terms, finding the sum by adding the terms can be tedious. Below are formulas you can use to find the sums of three special types of series.

KEY CONCEPT *For Your Notebook*

Formulas for Special Series

Sum of n terms of 1	Sum of first n positive integers	Sum of squares of first n positive integers
$\displaystyle\sum_{i=1}^{n} 1 = n$	$\displaystyle\sum_{i=1}^{n} i = \frac{n(n+1)}{2}$	$\displaystyle\sum_{i=1}^{n} i^2 = \frac{n(n+1)(2n+1)}{6}$

EXAMPLE 6 Use a formula for a sum

RETAIL DISPLAYS How many apples are in the stack in Example 3?

Solution

From Example 3 you know that the ith term of the series is given by $a_i = i^2$ where $i = 1, 2, 3, \ldots, 7$. Using summation notation and the third formula listed above, you can find the total number of apples as follows:

$$1^2 + 2^2 + \cdots + 7^2 = \sum_{i=1}^{7} i^2 = \frac{7(7+1)(2 \cdot 7 + 1)}{6} = \frac{7(8)(15)}{6} = 140$$

▶ There are 140 apples in the stack. Check this by actually adding the number of apples in each of the seven layers.

✓ **GUIDED PRACTICE** for Examples 5 and 6

Find the sum of the series.

10. $\displaystyle\sum_{i=1}^{5} 8i$ **11.** $\displaystyle\sum_{k=3}^{7} (k^2 - 1)$ **12.** $\displaystyle\sum_{i=1}^{34} 1$ **13.** $\displaystyle\sum_{n=1}^{6} n$

14. WHAT IF? Suppose there are 9 layers in the apple stack in Example 3. How many apples are in the stack?

7.1 EXERCISES

HOMEWORK KEY
○ = See **WORKED-OUT SOLUTIONS**
Exs. 19, 47, and 65

★ = **STANDARDIZED TEST PRACTICE**
Exs. 2, 27, 58, 64, and 67

SKILL PRACTICE

1. **VOCABULARY** Copy and complete: Another name for summation notation is ___?___ .

2. ★ **WRITING** *Explain* the difference between a sequence and a series.

EXAMPLE 1
for Exs. 3–14

WRITING TERMS Write the first six terms of the sequence.

3. $a_n = n + 2$
4. $a_n = 6 - n$
5. $a_n = n^2$
6. $f(n) = n^3 + 2$

7. $a_n = 4^{n-1}$
8. $a_n = -n^2$
9. $f(n) = n^2 - 5$
10. $a_n = (n + 3)^2$

11. $f(n) = -\dfrac{4}{n}$
12. $a_n = \dfrac{3}{n}$
13. $a_n = \dfrac{2n}{n + 2}$
14. $f(n) = \dfrac{n}{2n - 1}$

EXAMPLE 2
for Exs. 15–27

WRITING RULES For the sequence, describe the pattern, write the next term, and write a rule for the nth term.

15. $1, 6, 11, 16, \ldots$
16. $1, 2, 4, 8, \ldots$
17. $-4, 8, -12, 16, \ldots$

19. $\dfrac{2}{3}, \dfrac{2}{6}, \dfrac{2}{9}, \dfrac{2}{12}, \ldots$
18. $2, 9, 28, 65, \ldots$
20. $\dfrac{2}{3}, \dfrac{4}{4}, \dfrac{6}{5}, \dfrac{8}{6}, \ldots$

21. $\dfrac{1}{4}, \dfrac{2}{4}, \dfrac{3}{4}, \dfrac{4}{4}, \dfrac{5}{4}, \ldots$
22. $\dfrac{1}{10}, \dfrac{3}{20}, \dfrac{5}{30}, \dfrac{7}{40}, \ldots$
23. $3.1, 3.8, 4.5, 5.2, \ldots$

24. $4.2, 2.6, 1, -0.6, -2.2, \ldots$
25. $1.2, 4.2, 9.2, 16.2, \ldots$
26. $9, 16.8, 24.6, 32.4, \ldots$

27. ★ **MULTIPLE CHOICE** Which rule gives the total number of squares in the nth figure of the pattern shown?

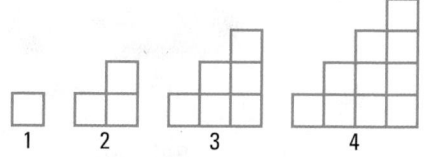

Ⓐ $a_n = 3n - 3$ Ⓑ $a_n = 4n - 5$ Ⓒ $a_n = n$ Ⓓ $a_n = \dfrac{n(n + 1)}{2}$

EXAMPLE 3
for Exs. 28–36

GRAPHING SEQUENCES Graph the sequence.

28. $-2, -5, -8, -11, -14$
29. $2, 4, 8, 16, 32, 64$
30. $1, 5, 9, 13, \ldots, 29$

31. $-2, 4, -6, 8, \ldots, -22$
32. $0, 3, 8, 15, 24, 35$
33. $-1, 0, 1, 8, 27$

34. $4, -9, 14, -19, 24$
35. $\dfrac{1}{2}, \dfrac{3}{2}, \dfrac{5}{2}, \ldots, \dfrac{13}{2}$
36. $\dfrac{1}{9}, \dfrac{2}{8}, \dfrac{3}{7}, \dfrac{4}{6}, \ldots, \dfrac{9}{1}$

EXAMPLE 4
for Exs. 37–44

WRITING SUMMATION NOTATION Write the series using summation notation.

37. $7 + 10 + 13 + 16 + 19$
38. $5 + 11 + 17 + 23 + 29$

39. $-1 + 1 + 3 + 5 + 7 + \cdots$
40. $-2 + 4 - 8 + 16 - 32 + \cdots$

41. $3 + 10 + 17 + 24 + 31 + \cdots$
42. $\dfrac{1}{3} + \dfrac{1}{9} + \dfrac{1}{27} + \dfrac{1}{81}$

43. $\dfrac{1}{4} + \dfrac{2}{5} + \dfrac{3}{6} + \dfrac{4}{7} + \dfrac{5}{8} + \dfrac{6}{9} + \dfrac{7}{10}$
44. $-1 + 2 + 7 + 14 + 23 + \cdots$

USING SUMMATION NOTATION Find the sum of the series.

45. $\displaystyle\sum_{i=1}^{6} 2i$

46. $\displaystyle\sum_{i=1}^{5} 7i$

47. $\displaystyle\sum_{n=0}^{4} n^3$

48. $\displaystyle\sum_{k=1}^{4} 3k^2$

49. $\displaystyle\sum_{k=3}^{6} (5k-2)$

50. $\displaystyle\sum_{n=1}^{5} (n^2-1)$

51. $\displaystyle\sum_{i=1}^{8} \frac{2}{i}$

52. $\displaystyle\sum_{k=1}^{6} \frac{k}{k+1}$

53. $\displaystyle\sum_{i=1}^{35} 1$

54. $\displaystyle\sum_{n=1}^{16} n$

55. $\displaystyle\sum_{i=1}^{25} i$

56. $\displaystyle\sum_{n=1}^{18} n^2$

57. ERROR ANALYSIS *Describe* and correct the error in finding the sum of the series.

$$\sum_{i=0}^{5} (2i+3) = 5 + 7 + 9 + 11 + 13 = 45 \quad \times$$

58. PI NOTATION You use sigma notation for writing a sum. You can use *pi notation* for writing a product. For example, $\displaystyle\prod_{i=2}^{4} \frac{2}{i} = \frac{2}{2} \cdot \frac{2}{3} \cdot \frac{2}{4} = \frac{1}{3}$.

   a. Write the factors for the product $\displaystyle\prod_{i=2}^{8} \left(1 - \frac{1}{i}\right)$ as fractions. Then find the product.

   b. Use the pattern from part (a) to write an expression for $\displaystyle\prod_{i=2}^{n} \left(1 - \frac{1}{i}\right)$.

CHALLENGE Tell whether the statement is *true* or *false*. **If the statement is true, prove it. If the statement is false, give a counterexample.**

59. $\displaystyle\sum_{i=1}^{n} ka_i = k\sum_{i=1}^{n} a_i$

60. $\displaystyle\sum_{i=1}^{n} (a_i + b_i) = \sum_{i=1}^{n} a_i + \sum_{i=1}^{n} b_i$

61. $\displaystyle\sum_{i=1}^{n} a_i b_i = \left(\sum_{i=1}^{n} a_i\right)\left(\sum_{i=1}^{n} b_i\right)$

62. $\displaystyle\sum_{i=1}^{n} (a_i)^k = \left(\sum_{i=1}^{n} a_i\right)^k$

PROBLEM SOLVING

63. GEOMETRY For a regular n-sided polygon ($n \geq 3$), the measure a_n of an interior angle is given by this formula:

$$a_n = \frac{180(n-2)}{n}$$

Write the first five terms of the sequence. Write a rule for the sequence giving the total measure T_n of the interior angles in each regular n-sided polygon. Use the rule to find the total measure of the angles in the Guggenheim Museum skylight, which is a regular dodecagon.

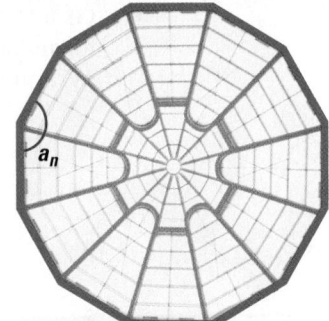

Guggenheim Museum Skylight

64. ★ SHORT RESPONSE You want to save $500 for a school trip. You begin by saving a penny on the first day. You plan to save an additional penny each day after that. For example, you will save 2 pennies on the second day, 3 pennies on the third day, and so on. How much money will you have saved after 100 days? How many days must you save to have saved $500? *Explain* how you used a series to find your answer.

65. **TOWER OF HANOI** In the puzzle called the Tower of Hanoi, the object is to use a series of moves to take the rings from one peg and stack them in order on another peg. A move consists of moving exactly one ring, and no ring may be placed on top of a smaller ring. The minimum number a_n of moves required to move n rings is 1 for 1 ring, 3 for 2 rings, 7 for 3 rings, 15 for 4 rings, and 31 for 5 rings. Find a formula for the sequence. What is the minimum number of moves required to move 6 rings? 7 rings? 8 rings?

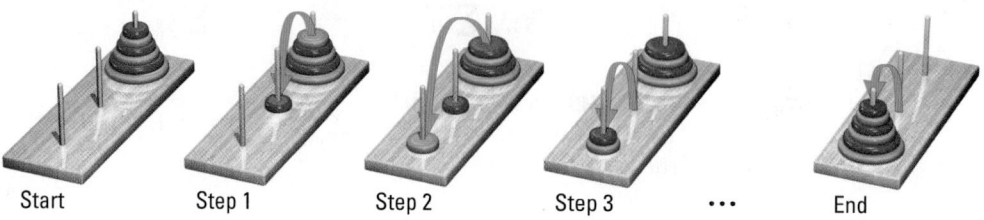

Start   Step 1   Step 2   Step 3   • • •   End

66. **MULTI-STEP PROBLEM** The mean distance d_n (in astronomical units) of each planet (except Neptune) from the sun is approximated by the Titius-Bode rule, $d_n = 0.3(2)^{n-2} + 0.4$, where n is a positive integer representing the position of the planet from the sun.

   a. **Evaluate** The value of n is 4 for Mars. Use the Titius-Bode rule to approximate the distance of Mars from the sun.

   b. **Convert** One astronomical unit is equal to about 149,600,000 kilometers. How far is Mars from the sun in kilometers?

   c. **Graph** Graph the sequence given by the Titius-Bode rule.

67. ★ **EXTENDED RESPONSE** For a display at a sports store, you are stacking soccer balls in a pyramid whose base is an equilateral triangle. The number a_n of balls per layer is given by $a_n = \dfrac{n(n+1)}{2}$ where $n = 1$ represents the top layer.

   a. How many balls are in the fifth layer?

   b. How many balls are in a stack with five layers?

   c. *Compare* the number of balls in a layer of a triangular pyramid with the number of balls in the same layer of a square pyramid.

68. **CHALLENGE** Using the true statements from Exercises 59–62 and the special formulas, find a formula for the number of balls in the top n layers of the pyramid from Exercise 67.

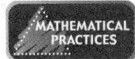
Work with Sequences

MATHEMATICAL PRACTICES

Use appropriate tools strategically.

QUESTION How can you use a graphing calculator to perform operations with sequences?

EXAMPLE Find, graph, and sum terms of a sequence

Use a graphing calculator to find the first eight terms of $a_n = 5n - 3$. Graph the sequence. Then find the sum of the first eight terms of the sequence.

STEP 1 *Enter sequence*

Put the graphing calculator in *sequence* mode and *dot* mode. Enter the sequence. Note that the calculator uses $u(n)$ rather than a_n.

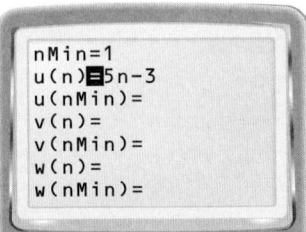

STEP 2 *Calculate terms*

Use the *table* feature to view the terms of the sequence. The first eight terms are 2, 7, 12, 17, 22, 27, 32, and 37.

STEP 3 *Graph sequence*

Set the viewing window so that $1 \le n \le 8$, $0 \le x \le 9$, and $0 \le y \le 40$. Graph the sequence. Use the *trace* feature to view the terms of the sequence.

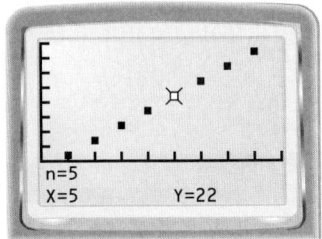

STEP 4 *Find sum of terms*

Use the *summation* feature to find the sum of the first eight terms of the sequence. The screen shows that the sum is 156.

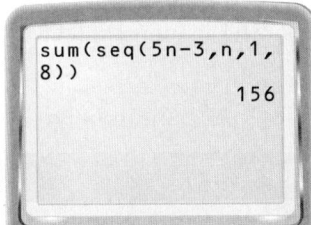

PRACTICE

Use a graphing calculator to (a) find the first ten terms of the sequence, (b) graph the sequence, and (c) find the sum of the first ten terms of the sequence.

1. $a_n = 4n + 1$

2. $a_n = 3(n + 2)$

3. $a_n = 35 - 3n$

4. $a_n = 15 + 2n$

5. $a_n = 3 + n^2$

6. $a_n = 2^{n-1}$

7.2 Analyze Arithmetic Sequences and Series

Before You worked with general sequences and series.

Now You will study arithmetic sequences and series.

Why? So you can arrange a marching band, as in Ex. 64.

Key Vocabulary
- arithmetic sequence
- common difference
- arithmetic series

CC.9-12.F.BF.2 Write arithmetic and geometric sequences both recursively and with an explicit formula, use them to model situations, and translate between the two forms.*

In an **arithmetic sequence**, the difference of consecutive terms is constant. This constant difference is called the **common difference** and is denoted by d.

EXAMPLE 1 Identify arithmetic sequences

Tell whether the sequence is arithmetic.

a. $-4, 1, 6, 11, 16, \ldots$

b. $3, 5, 9, 15, 23, \ldots$

Solution

Find the differences of consecutive terms.

a. $a_2 - a_1 = 1 - (-4) = 5$
$a_3 - a_2 = 6 - 1 = 5$
$a_4 - a_3 = 11 - 6 = 5$
$a_5 - a_4 = 16 - 11 = 5$

▶ Each difference is 5, so the sequence is arithmetic.

b. $a_2 - a_1 = 5 - 3 = 2$
$a_3 - a_2 = 9 - 5 = 4$
$a_4 - a_3 = 15 - 9 = 6$
$a_5 - a_4 = 23 - 15 = 8$

▶ The differences are not constant, so the sequence is not arithmetic.

✓ **GUIDED PRACTICE** for Example 1

1. Tell whether the sequence $17, 14, 11, 8, 5, \ldots$ is arithmetic. *Explain* why or why not.

KEY CONCEPT *For Your Notebook*

Rule for an Arithmetic Sequence

Algebra The nth term of an arithmetic sequence with first term a_1 and common difference d is given by:

$$a_n = a_1 + (n - 1)d$$

Example The nth term of an arithmetic sequence with a first term of 2 and common difference 3 is given by:

$$a_n = 2 + (n - 1)3, \text{ or } a_n = -1 + 3n$$

EXAMPLE 2 Write a rule for the *n*th term

Write a rule for the *n*th term of the sequence. Then find a_{15}.

a. 4, 9, 14, 19, . . . **b.** 60, 52, 44, 36, . . .

Solution

a. The sequence is arithmetic with first term $a_1 = 4$ and common difference $d = 9 - 4 = 5$. So, a rule for the *n*th term is:

$$a_n = a_1 + (n - 1)d \qquad \text{Write general rule.}$$
$$= 4 + (n - 1)5 \qquad \text{Substitute 4 for } a_1 \text{ and 5 for } d.$$
$$= -1 + 5n \qquad \text{Simplify.}$$

The 15th term is $a_{15} = -1 + 5(15) = 74$.

b. The sequence is arithmetic with first term $a_1 = 60$ and common difference $d = 52 - 60 = -8$. So, a rule for the *n*th term is:

$$a_n = a_1 + (n - 1)d \qquad \text{Write general rule.}$$
$$= 60 + (n - 1)(-8) \qquad \text{Substitute 60 for } a_1 \text{ and } -8 \text{ for } d.$$
$$= 68 - 8n \qquad \text{Simplify.}$$

The 15th term is $a_{15} = 68 - 8(15) = -52$.

AVOID ERRORS

In the general rule for an arithmetic sequence, note that the common difference *d* is multiplied by $n - 1$, not *n*.

EXAMPLE 3 Write a rule given a term and common difference

One term of an arithmetic sequence is $a_{19} = 48$. The common difference is $d = 3$.

a. Write a rule for the *n*th term. **b.** Graph the sequence.

Solution

a. Use the general rule to find the first term.

$$a_n = a_1 + (n - 1)d \qquad \text{Write general rule.}$$
$$a_{19} = a_1 + (19 - 1)d \qquad \text{Substitute 19 for } n.$$
$$48 = a_1 + 18(3) \qquad \text{Substitute 48 for } a_{19} \text{ and 3 for } d.$$
$$-6 = a_1 \qquad \text{Solve for } a_1.$$

So, a rule for the *n*th term is:

$$a_n = a_1 + (n - 1)d \qquad \text{Write general rule.}$$
$$= -6 + (n - 1)3 \qquad \text{Substitute } -6 \text{ for } a_1 \text{ and 3 for } d.$$
$$= -9 + 3n \qquad \text{Simplify.}$$

b. Create a table of values for the sequence. The graph of the first 6 terms of the sequence is shown. Notice that the points lie on a line. This is true for *any* arithmetic sequence.

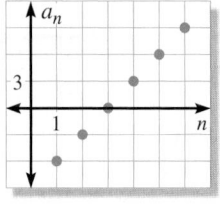

n	1	2	3	4	5	6
a_n	−6	−3	0	3	6	9

EXAMPLE 4 **Write a rule given two terms**

Two terms of an arithmetic sequence are $a_8 = 21$ and $a_{27} = 97$. Find a rule for the nth term.

Solution

STEP 1 **Write** a system of equations using $a_n = a_1 + (n - 1)d$ and substituting 27 for n (Equation 1) and then 8 for n (Equation 2).

$$a_{27} = a_1 + (27 - 1)d \implies 97 = a_1 + 26d \quad \text{Equation 1}$$

$$a_8 = a_1 + (8 - 1)d \implies 21 = a_1 + 7d \quad \text{Equation 2}$$

STEP 2 **Solve** the system.

$$76 = 19d \quad \text{Subtract.}$$

$$4 = d \quad \text{Solve for } d.$$

$$97 = a_1 + 26(4) \quad \text{Substitute for } d \text{ in Equation 1.}$$

$$-7 = a_1 \quad \text{Solve for } a_1.$$

STEP 3 **Find** a rule for a_n.

$$a_n = a_1 + (n - 1)d \quad \text{Write general rule.}$$

$$= -7 + (n - 1)4 \quad \text{Substitute for } a_1 \text{ and } d.$$

$$= -11 + 4n \quad \text{Simplify.}$$

✓ **GUIDED PRACTICE** for Examples 2, 3, and 4

Write a rule for the nth term of the arithmetic sequence. Then find a_{20}.

2. 17, 14, 11, 8, . . .   **3.** $a_{11} = -57, d = -7$ **4.** $a_7 = 26, a_{16} = 71$

ARITHMETIC SERIES The expression formed by adding the terms of an arithmetic sequence is called an **arithmetic series**. The sum of the first n terms of an arithmetic series is denoted by S_n. To find a rule for S_n, you can write S_n in two different ways and add the results.

$$S_n = a_1 \qquad + (a_1 + d) + (a_1 + 2d) + \cdots + a_n$$

$$S_n = a_n \qquad + (a_n - d) + (a_n - 2d) + \cdots + a_1$$

$$2S_n = (a_1 + a_n) + (a_1 + a_n) + (a_1 + a_n) + \cdots + (a_1 + a_n)$$

You can conclude that $2S_n = n(a_1 + a_n)$, which leads to the following result.

KEY CONCEPT *For Your Notebook*

The Sum of a Finite Arithmetic Series

The sum of the first n terms of an arithmetic series is:

$$S_n = n\left(\frac{a_1 + a_n}{2}\right)$$

In words, S_n is the mean of the first and nth terms, multiplied by the number of terms.

EXAMPLE 5 **Standardized Test Practice**

> What is the sum of the arithmetic series $\displaystyle\sum_{i=1}^{20}(3+5i)$?
>
> **(A)** 103 **(B)** 111 **(C)** 1110 **(D)** 2220

CLASSIFY SERIES

You can verify that the series in Example 5 is arithmetic by evaluating $3 + 5i$ for the first few values of the index i. The resulting terms are 8, 13, 18, 23, . . . , which have a common difference of 5.

Solution

$a_1 = 3 + 5(1) = 8$ **Identify first term.**

$a_{20} = 3 + 5(20) = 103$ **Identify last term.**

$S_{20} = 20\left(\dfrac{8 + 103}{2}\right)$ **Write rule for S_{20}, substituting 8 for a_1 and 103 for a_{20}.**

$= 1110$ **Simplify.**

▶ The correct answer is C. **(A) (B) (C) (D)**

EXAMPLE 6 **Use an arithmetic sequence and series in real life**

HOUSE OF CARDS You are making a house of cards similar to the one shown.

a. Write a rule for the number of cards in the nth row if the top row is row 1.

b. What is the total number of cards if the house of cards has 14 rows?

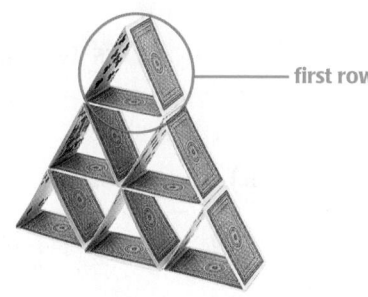

first row

Solution

a. Starting with the top row, the numbers of cards in the rows are 3, 6, 9, 12, ... These numbers form an arithmetic sequence with a first term of 3 and a common difference of 3. So, a rule for the sequence is:

$a_n = a_1 + (n - 1)d$ **Write general rule.**

$= 3 + (n - 1)3$ **Substitute 3 for a_1 and 3 for d.**

$= 3n$ **Simplify.**

b. Find the sum of an arithmetic series with first term $a_1 = 3$ and last term $a_{14} = 3(14) = 42$.

Total number of cards $= S_{14} = 14\left(\dfrac{a_1 + a_{14}}{2}\right) = 14\left(\dfrac{3 + 42}{2}\right) = 315$

Animated Algebra at my.hrw.com

 GUIDED PRACTICE for Examples 5 and 6

5. Find the sum of the arithmetic series $\displaystyle\sum_{i=1}^{12}(2 + 7i)$.

6. **WHAT IF?** In Example 6, what is the total number of cards if the house of cards has 8 rows?

7.2 EXERCISES

HOMEWORK KEY
○ = See WORKED-OUT SOLUTIONS
    Exs. 15, 41, and 65
★ = STANDARDIZED TEST PRACTICE
    Exs. 2, 29, 39, 52, and 68
◆ = MULTIPLE REPRESENTATIONS
    Ex. 66

SKILL PRACTICE

1. **VOCABULARY** Copy and complete: The constant difference between consecutive terms of an arithmetic sequence is called the __?__.

2. ★ **WRITING** *Explain* the difference between an arithmetic sequence and an arithmetic series.

EXAMPLE 1
for Exs. 3–11

IDENTIFYING ARITHMETIC SEQUENCES **Tell whether the sequence is arithmetic.** *Explain* **why or why not.**

3. $1, -2, -5, -8, -11, \ldots$

4. $16, 14, 11, 6, 3, \ldots$

5. $5, 14, 23, 32, 41, \ldots$

6. $-10, -7, -5, -2, 0, \ldots$

7. $0.5, 1, 1.5, 2, 2.5, \ldots$

8. $20, 10, 5, 2.5, 1.25, \ldots$

9. $\frac{7}{4}, \frac{5}{4}, \frac{3}{4}, -\frac{3}{4}, -\frac{5}{4}, \ldots$

10. $\frac{1}{7}, \frac{2}{7}, \frac{4}{7}, \frac{8}{7}, \frac{16}{7}, \ldots$

11. $-\frac{5}{2}, -1, \frac{1}{2}, 2, \frac{7}{2}, \ldots$

EXAMPLE 2
for Exs. 12–22

WRITING RULES **Write a rule for the *n*th term of the arithmetic sequence. Then find a_{20}.**

12. $1, 4, 7, 10, 13, \ldots$

13. $5, 11, 17, 23, 29, \ldots$

14. $8, 21, 34, 47, 60, \ldots$

15. $-3, -1, 1, 3, 5, \ldots$

16. $6, 2, -2, -6, -10, \ldots$

17. $25, 14, 3, -8, -19, \ldots$

18. $0, \frac{2}{3}, \frac{4}{3}, 2, \frac{8}{3}, \ldots$

19. $2, \frac{5}{3}, \frac{4}{3}, 1, \frac{2}{3}, \ldots$

20. $1.5, 3.6, 5.7, 7.8, 9.9, \ldots$

ERROR ANALYSIS *Describe* **and correct the error in writing the rule for the *n*th term of the arithmetic sequence** $37, 24, 11, -2, -15, \ldots$.

21.
Use $a_1 = 37$ and $d = -13$.

$a_n = a_1 + nd$

$a_n = 37 + n(-13)$

$a_n = 37 - 13n$ ✗

22.
The first term is 37 and the common difference is −13.

$a_n = -13 + (n - 1)(37)$

$a_n = -50 + 37n$ ✗

EXAMPLE 3
for Exs. 23–29

WRITING RULES **Write a rule for the *n*th term of the arithmetic sequence. Then graph the first six terms of the sequence.**

23. $a_{16} = 52, d = 5$

24. $a_6 = -16, d = 9$

25. $a_4 = 96, d = -14$

26. $a_{12} = -3, d = -7$

27. $a_{10} = 30, d = \frac{7}{2}$

28. $a_{11} = \frac{1}{2}, d = -\frac{1}{2}$

29. ★ **MULTIPLE CHOICE** For a certain arithmetic sequence, $a_{30} = 57$ and $d = 4$. What is a rule for the *n*th term of the sequence?

Ⓐ $a_n = -63 - 4n$

Ⓑ $a_n = -59 - 4n$

Ⓒ $a_n = -63 + 4n$

Ⓓ $a_n = -59 + 4n$

EXAMPLE 4
for Exs. 30–39

WRITING RULES Write a rule for the *n*th term of the arithmetic sequence that has the two given terms.

30. $a_4 = 31$, $a_{10} = 85$ **31.** $a_6 = 39$, $a_{14} = 79$ **32.** $a_3 = -2$, $a_{17} = 40$

33. $a_8 = -10$, $a_{20} = -58$ **34.** $a_9 = 89$, $a_{15} = 137$ **35.** $a_2 = 17$, $a_{11} = 35$

36. $a_7 = 4$, $a_{12} = -9$ **37.** $a_5 = 15$, $a_9 = 24$ **38.** $a_6 = 0$, $a_{11} = -2$

39. ★ **MULTIPLE CHOICE** For a certain arithmetic sequence, $a_6 = -6$ and $a_{13} = -48$. What is a rule for the *n*th term of the sequence?

(A) $a_n = 18 + 6n$ (B) $a_n = 30 - 6n$

(C) $a_n = -6 + 24n$ (D) $a_n = -36 - 6n$

EXAMPLE 5
for Exs. 40–48

FINDING SUMS Find the sum of the arithmetic series.

40. $\sum_{i=1}^{10} (1 + 3i)$ **41.** $\sum_{i=1}^{8} (-3 - 2i)$ **42.** $\sum_{i=1}^{18} (14 - 6i)$

43. $\sum_{i=1}^{22} (-9 + 11i)$ **44.** $\sum_{i=3}^{9} (72 - 6i)$ **45.** $\sum_{i=5}^{14} (-54 + 9i)$

46. $2 + 6 + 10 + \cdots + 58$ **47.** $-1 + 4 + 9 + \cdots + 34$ **48.** $44 + 37 + 30 + \cdots + 2$

USING GRAPHS Write a rule for the sequence whose graph is shown.

49. 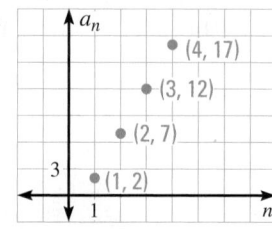   **50.** 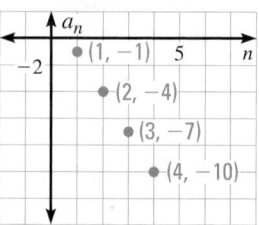   **51.**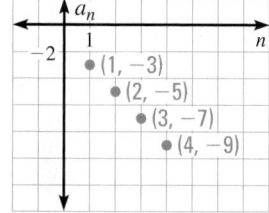

52. ★ **WRITING** *Compare* the graph of $a_n = 3n + 2$, where *n* is a positive integer, with the graph of $f(x) = 3x + 2$, where *x* is a real number. Discuss how the graph of an arithmetic sequence is similar to and different from the graph of a linear function.

REASONING Tell whether the statement is *true* or *false*. *Explain* your answer.

53. If the common difference of an arithmetic series is doubled while the first term and number of terms in the series remain unchanged, then the sum of the series is doubled.

54. If the numbers *a*, *b*, and *c* are the first three terms of an arithmetic sequence, then *b* is half the sum of *a* and *c*.

SOLVING EQUATIONS Find the value of *n*.

55. $\sum_{i=1}^{n} (-5 + 7i) = 486$ **56.** $\sum_{i=1}^{n} (10 - 3i) = -28$ **57.** $\sum_{i=1}^{n} (58 - 8i) = -1150$

58. $\sum_{i=1}^{n} (5 - 5i) = -50$ **59.** $\sum_{i=3}^{n} (-3 - 4i) = -507$ **60.** $\sum_{i=5}^{n} (7 + 12i) = 455$

61. **REASONING** Find the sum of all positive odd integers less than 300.

62. **CHALLENGE** The numbers $3 - x$, x, and $1 - 3x$ are the first three terms in an arithmetic sequence. Find the value of *x* and the next term in the sequence.

63. HONEYCOMBS Domestic bees make their honeycomb by starting with a single hexagonal cell, then forming ring after ring of hexagonal cells around the initial cell, as shown. The numbers of cells in successive rings form an arithmetic sequence.

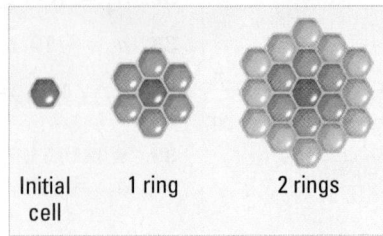

Initial cell   1 ring   2 rings

  a. Write a rule for the number of cells in the nth ring.

  b. What is the total number of cells in the honeycomb after the 9th ring is formed? (*Hint:* Do not forget to count the initial cell.)

64. MARCHING BAND A marching band is arranged in 7 rows. The first row has 3 band members, and each row after the first has 2 more band members than the row before it. Write a rule for the number of band members in the nth row. Then find the total number of band members.

65. SCULPTURE Sol LeWitt's sculpture *Four-Sided Pyramid* in the National Gallery of Art Sculpture Garden is made of concrete blocks. As shown in the diagram, each layer has 8 more visible blocks than the layer in front of it.

  a. Write a rule for the number of visible blocks in the nth layer where $n = 1$ represents the front layer.

  b. When you view the pyramid from one corner, a total of 12 layers are visible. How many of the pyramid's blocks are visible?

66. ◆ **MULTIPLE REPRESENTATIONS** The distance D (in feet) that an object falls in t seconds can be modeled by $D(t) = 16t^2$.

  a. Making a Table Let $d(n)$ represent the distance the object falls in the nth second. Make a table of values showing $d(1)$, $d(2)$, $d(3)$, and $d(4)$. (*Hint:* The distance $d(1)$ that the object falls in the first second is $D(1) - D(0)$.)

  b. Writing a Rule Write a rule for the sequence of distances given by $d(n)$.

  c. Drawing a Graph Graph the sequence from part (b).

67. ENTERTAINMENT During a high school spirit week, students dress up in costumes. A cash prize is given each day to the student with the best costume. The organizing committee has $1000 to give away over five days. The committee wants to increase the amount of the prize by $50 each day. How much should the committee give away on the first day?

68. ★ **EXTENDED RESPONSE** A paper towel manufacturer sells paper towels rolled onto cardboard dowels. The thickness of the paper is 0.004 inch. The diameter of a dowel is 2 inches, and the total diameter of a roll is 5 inches.

n	d_n (in.)	ℓ_n (in.)
1	2	2π
2	?	?
3	?	?
4	?	?

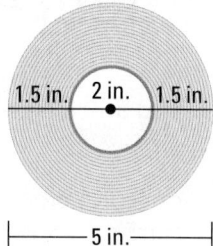

a. **Calculate** Let n be the number of times the paper towel is wrapped around the dowel, let d_n be the diameter of the roll just before the nth wrap, and let ℓ_n be the length of paper added in the nth wrap. Copy and complete the table.

b. **Model** What kind of sequence is $\ell_1, \ell_2, \ell_3, \ell_4, \ldots$? Write a rule for the nth term of the sequence.

c. **Apply** Find the number of times the paper must be wrapped around the dowel to create a roll with a 5 inch diameter. Use your answer and the rule from part (b) to find the length of paper in a roll with a 5 inch diameter.

d. **Interpret** Suppose a roll with a 5 inch diameter costs $1.50. How much would you expect to pay for a roll with a 7 inch diameter whose dowel also has a diameter of 2 inches? *Explain* your reasoning and any assumptions you make.

69. CHALLENGE A theater has n rows of seats, and each row has d more seats than the row in front of it. There are x seats in the last (nth) row and a total of y seats in the entire theater. How many seats are in the front row of the theater? Write your answer in terms of n, x, and y.

7.3 Analyze Geometric Sequences and Series

Before	You studied arithmetic sequences and series.
Now	You will study geometric sequences and series.
Why?	So you can solve problems about sports tournaments, as in Ex. 58.

Key Vocabulary
- geometric sequence
- common ratio
- geometric series

CC.9-12.A.SSE.4 Derive the formula for the sum of a finite geometric series (when the common ratio is not 1), and use the formula to solve problems.*

In a **geometric sequence**, the ratio of any term to the previous term is constant. This constant ratio is called the **common ratio** and is denoted by r.

EXAMPLE 1 Identify geometric sequences

Tell whether the sequence is geometric.

   a. 4, 10, 18, 28, 40, . . .
                                       b. 625, 125, 25, 5, 1, . . .

Solution

To decide whether a sequence is geometric, find the ratios of consecutive terms.

  a. $\dfrac{a_2}{a_1} = \dfrac{10}{4} = \dfrac{5}{2}$ $\dfrac{a_3}{a_2} = \dfrac{18}{10} = \dfrac{9}{5}$ $\dfrac{a_4}{a_3} = \dfrac{28}{18} = \dfrac{14}{9}$ $\dfrac{a_5}{a_4} = \dfrac{40}{28} = \dfrac{10}{7}$

    ▸ The ratios are different, so the sequence is not geometric.

  b. $\dfrac{a_2}{a_1} = \dfrac{125}{625} = \dfrac{1}{5}$ $\dfrac{a_3}{a_2} = \dfrac{25}{125} = \dfrac{1}{5}$ $\dfrac{a_4}{a_3} = \dfrac{5}{25} = \dfrac{1}{5}$ $\dfrac{a_5}{a_4} = \dfrac{1}{5}$

    ▸ Each ratio is $\dfrac{1}{5}$, so the sequence is geometric.

✓ **GUIDED PRACTICE**   for Example 1

Tell whether the sequence is geometric. *Explain* why or why not.

  1. 81, 27, 9, 3, 1, . . .   **2.** 1, 2, 6, 24, 120, . . .   **3.** −4, 8, −16, 32, −64, . . .

KEY CONCEPT   *For Your Notebook*

Rule for a Geometric Sequence

Algebra   The nth term of a geometric sequence with first term a_1 and common ratio r is given by:

$$a_n = a_1 r^{n-1}$$

Example   The nth term of a geometric sequence with a first term of 3 and common ratio 2 is given by:

$$a_n = 3(2)^{n-1}$$

PhotoStockFile/Alamy

EXAMPLE 2 Write a rule for the *n*th term

Write a rule for the *n*th term of the sequence. Then find a_7.

a. 4, 20, 100, 500, . . . **b.** 152, −76, 38, −19, . . .

Solution

a. The sequence is geometric with first term $a_1 = 4$ and common ratio
$r = \dfrac{20}{4} = 5$. So, a rule for the *n*th term is:

$$a_n = a_1 r^{n-1} \qquad \text{Write general rule.}$$

$$ = 4(5)^{n-1} \qquad \text{Substitute 4 for } a_1 \text{ and 5 for } r.$$

The 7th term is $a_7 = 4(5)^{7-1} = 62{,}500$.

> **AVOID ERRORS**
> In the general rule for a geometric sequence, note that the exponent is $n-1$, not n.

b. The sequence is geometric with first term $a_1 = 152$ and common ratio
$r = \dfrac{-76}{152} = -\dfrac{1}{2}$. So, a rule for the *n*th term is:

$$a_n = a_1 r^{n-1} \qquad \text{Write general rule.}$$

$$ = 152\left(-\frac{1}{2}\right)^{n-1} \qquad \text{Substitute 152 for } a_1 \text{ and } -\frac{1}{2} \text{ for } r.$$

The 7th term is $a_7 = 152\left(-\dfrac{1}{2}\right)^{7-1} = \dfrac{19}{8}$.

EXAMPLE 3 Write a rule given a term and common ratio

One term of a geometric sequence is $a_4 = 12$. The common ratio is $r = 2$.

a. Write a rule for the *n*th term. **b.** Graph the sequence.

Solution

a. Use the general rule to find the first term.

$$a_n = a_1 r^{n-1} \qquad \text{Write general rule.}$$

$$a_4 = a_1 r^{4-1} \qquad \text{Substitute 4 for } n.$$

$$12 = a_1 (2)^3 \qquad \text{Substitute 12 for } a_4 \text{ and 2 for } r.$$

$$1.5 = a_1 \qquad \text{Solve for } a_1.$$

So, a rule for the *n*th term is:

$$a_n = a_1 r^{n-1} \qquad \text{Write general rule.}$$

$$ = 1.5(2)^{n-1} \qquad \text{Substitute 1.5 for } a_1 \text{ and 2 for } r.$$

b. Create a table of values for the sequence. The graph of the first 6 terms of the sequence is shown. Notice that the points lie on an exponential curve. This is true for *any* geometric sequence with $r > 0$.

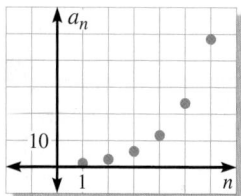

n	1	2	3	4	5	6
a_n	1.5	3	6	12	24	48

Animated Algebra at my.hrw.com

EXAMPLE 4 **Write a rule given two terms**

Two terms of a geometric sequence are $a_3 = -48$ and $a_6 = 3072$. Find a rule for the nth term.

Solution

STEP 1 **Write** a system of equations using $a_n = a_1 r^{n-1}$ and substituting 3 for n (Equation 1) and then **6** for n (Equation 2).

$$a_3 = a_1 r^{3-1} \longrightarrow -48 = a_1 r^2 \qquad \text{Equation 1}$$
$$a_6 = a_1 r^{6-1} \longrightarrow 3072 = a_1 r^5 \qquad \text{Equation 2}$$

STEP 2 **Solve** the system.

$$\frac{-48}{r^2} = a_1 \qquad \text{Solve Equation 1 for } a_1.$$

$$3072 = \frac{-48}{r^2}\left(r^5\right) \qquad \text{Substitute for } a_1 \text{ in Equation 2.}$$

$$3072 = -48r^3 \qquad \text{Simplify.}$$

$$-4 = r \qquad \text{Solve for } r.$$

$$-48 = a_1(-4)^2 \qquad \text{Substitute for } r \text{ in Equation 1.}$$

$$-3 = a_1 \qquad \text{Solve for } a_1.$$

STEP 3 **Find** a rule for a_n. $\qquad a_n = a_1 r^{n-1} \qquad$ Write general rule.

$$a_n = -3(-4)^{n-1} \qquad \text{Substitute for } a_1 \text{ and } r.$$

 GUIDED PRACTICE for Examples 2, 3, and 4

Write a rule for the nth term of the geometric sequence. Then find a_8.

4. $3, 15, 75, 375, \ldots$ **5.** $a_6 = -96, r = 2$ **6.** $a_2 = -12, a_4 = -3$

GEOMETRIC SERIES The expression formed by adding the terms of a geometric sequence is called a **geometric series**. The sum of the first n terms of a geometric series is denoted by S_n. You can develop a rule for S_n as follows.

$$S_n = a_1 + a_1 r + a_1 r^2 + a_1 r^3 + \cdots + a_1 r^{n-1}$$
$$-rS_n = \qquad - a_1 r - a_1 r^2 - a_1 r^3 - \cdots - a_1 r^{n-1} - a_1 r^n$$
$$\overline{S_n(1-r) = a_1 + 0 + 0 + 0 + \cdots + 0 - a_1 r^n}$$

So, $S_n(1 - r) = a_1\left(1 - r^n\right)$. If $r \neq 1$, you can divide each side of this equation by $1 - r$ to obtain the following rule for S_n.

KEY CONCEPT *For Your Notebook*

The Sum of a Finite Geometric Series

The sum of the first n terms of a geometric series with common ratio $r \neq 1$ is:

$$S_n = a_1\left(\frac{1 - r^n}{1 - r}\right)$$

EXAMPLE 5 **Find the sum of a geometric series**

Find the sum of the geometric series $\displaystyle\sum_{i=1}^{16} 4(3)^{i-1}$.

$a_1 = 4(3)^{1-1} = 4$ **Identify first term.**

$r = 3$ **Identify common ratio.**

$S_{16} = a_1\left(\dfrac{1 - r^{16}}{1 - r}\right)$ **Write rule for S_{16}.**

$\quad = 4\left(\dfrac{1 - 3^{16}}{1 - 3}\right)$ **Substitute 4 for a_1 and 3 for r.**

$\quad = 86{,}093{,}440$ **Simplify.**

▸ The sum of the series is 86,093,440.

EXAMPLE 6 **Use a geometric sequence and series in real life**

MOVIE REVENUE In 1990, the total box office revenue at U.S. movie theaters was about $5.02 billion. From 1990 through 2003, the total box office revenue increased by about 5.9% per year.

a. Write a rule for the total box office revenue a_n (in billions of dollars) in terms of the year. Let $n = 1$ represent 1990.

b. What was the total box office revenue at U.S. movie theaters for the entire period 1990–2003?

Solution

a. Because the total box office revenue increased by the same percent each year, the total revenues from year to year form a geometric sequence. Use $a_1 = 5.02$ and $r = 1 + 0.059 = 1.059$ to write a rule for the sequence.

$\quad a_n = 5.02(1.059)^{n-1}$ **Write a rule for a_n.**

b. There are **14** years in the period 1990–2003, so find S_{14}.

$$S_{14} = a_1\left(\frac{1 - r^{14}}{1 - r}\right) = 5.02\left(\frac{1 - (1.059)^{14}}{1 - 1.059}\right) \approx 105$$

▸ The total movie box office revenue for the period 1990–2003 was about $105 billion.

✓ **GUIDED PRACTICE**   **for Examples 5 and 6**

7. Find the sum of the geometric series $\displaystyle\sum_{i=1}^{8} 6(-2)^{i-1}$.

8. **MOVIE REVENUE** Use the rule in part (a) of Example 6 to estimate the total box office revenue at U.S. movie theaters in 2000.

7.3 EXERCISES

HOMEWORK KEY

○ = See WORKED-OUT SOLUTIONS
Exs. 19, 49, and 59

★ = STANDARDIZED TEST PRACTICE
Exs. 2, 27, 54, 55, and 59

◆ = MULTIPLE REPRESENTATIONS
Ex. 61

SKILL PRACTICE

1. **VOCABULARY** Copy and complete: The constant ratio of consecutive terms in a geometric sequence is called the __?__.

2. ★ **WRITING** How can you determine whether a sequence is geometric?

EXAMPLE 1
for Exs. 3–14

IDENTIFYING GEOMETRIC SEQUENCES Tell whether the sequence is geometric. *Explain* why or why not.

3. $1, 4, 8, 16, 32, \ldots$

4. $4, 16, 64, 256, 1024, \ldots$

5. $216, 36, 6, 1, \frac{1}{6}, \ldots$

6. $\frac{1}{3}, \frac{2}{3}, \frac{4}{3}, \frac{8}{3}, \frac{16}{3}, \ldots$

7. $\frac{1}{2}, 1, \frac{3}{2}, 2, \frac{5}{2}, \ldots$

8. $-\frac{1}{4}, \frac{3}{8}, -\frac{3}{16}, \frac{1}{32}, -\frac{3}{64}, \ldots$

9. $10, 5, 2.5, 1.25, 0.625, \ldots$

10. $-3, -6, 12, 24, -48, \ldots$

11. $-4, 12, -36, 108, -324, \ldots$

12. $0.2, 0.6, 1.8, 5.4, 16.2, \ldots$

13. $-5, 10, 20, 40, 80, \ldots$

14. $0.75, 1.5, 2.25, 3, 3.75, \ldots$

EXAMPLE 2
for Exs. 15–27

WRITING RULES Write a rule for the nth term of the geometric sequence. Then find a_7.

15. $1, -4, 16, -64, \ldots$

16. $6, 18, 54, 162, \ldots$

17. $4, 24, 144, 864, \ldots$

18. $7, -35, 175, -875, \ldots$

19. $2, \frac{3}{2}, \frac{9}{8}, \frac{27}{32}, \ldots$

20. $3, -\frac{6}{5}, \frac{12}{25}, -\frac{24}{125}, \ldots$

21. $4, 2, 1, 0.5, \ldots$

22. $-0.3, 0.6, -1.2, 2.4, \ldots$

23. $-2, -0.8, -0.32, -0.128, \ldots$

24. $7, -4.2, 2.52, -1.512, \ldots$

25. $5, -14, 39.2, -109.76, \ldots$

26. $120, 180, 270, 405, \ldots$

27. ★ **MULTIPLE CHOICE** What is a rule for the nth term of the geometric sequence $5, 20, 80, 320, \ldots$?

Ⓐ $a_n = 5(2)^{n-1}$

Ⓑ $a_n = 5(4)^{n-1}$

Ⓒ $a_n = 5(-4)^{n-1}$

Ⓓ $a_n = 5(-2)^{n-1}$

EXAMPLE 3
for Exs. 28–38

WRITING RULES Write a rule for the nth term of the geometric sequence. Then graph the first six terms of the sequence.

28. $a_1 = 5, r = 3$

29. $a_1 = -2, r = 6$

30. $a_2 = 6, r = 2$

31. $a_2 = 15, r = \frac{1}{2}$

32. $a_5 = 1, r = \frac{1}{8}$

33. $a_4 = -12, r = -\frac{1}{4}$

34. $a_3 = 75, r = 5$

35. $a_2 = 8, r = 4$

36. $a_4 = 500, r = 5$

ERROR ANALYSIS *Describe* and correct the error in writing the rule for the nth term of the geometric sequence for which $a_1 = 3$ and $r = 2$.

37.
$$a_n = a_1 r^n$$
$$a_n = 3(2)^n$$

38.
$$a_n = r a_1^{n-1}$$
$$a_n = 2(3)^{n-1}$$

EXAMPLE 4
for Exs. 39–47

WRITING RULES Write a rule for the nth term of the geometric sequence that has the two given terms.

39. $a_1 = 3$, $a_3 = 12$

40. $a_1 = 1$, $a_5 = 625$

41. $a_1 = -\dfrac{1}{4}$, $a_4 = -16$

42. $a_3 = 10$, $a_6 = 270$

43. $a_2 = -40$, $a_4 = -10$

44. $a_2 = -24$, $a_5 = 1536$

45. $a_4 = 162$, $a_7 = 4374$

46. $a_3 = \dfrac{7}{4}$, $a_5 = \dfrac{7}{16}$

47. $a_4 = 6$, $a_7 = \dfrac{243}{8}$

EXAMPLE 5
for Exs. 48–54

FINDING SUMS Find the sum of the geometric series.

48. $\displaystyle\sum_{i=1}^{10} 5(2)^{i-1}$

49. $\displaystyle\sum_{i=1}^{8} 6(4)^{i-1}$

50. $\displaystyle\sum_{i=0}^{7} 12\left(-\dfrac{1}{2}\right)^{i}$

51. $\displaystyle\sum_{i=1}^{6} 4\left(\dfrac{1}{4}\right)^{i-1}$

52. $\displaystyle\sum_{i=1}^{12} 8\left(\dfrac{3}{2}\right)^{i-1}$

53. $\displaystyle\sum_{i=0}^{10} (-4)^{i}$

54. ★ **MULTIPLE CHOICE** What is the sum of the geometric series $\displaystyle\sum_{i=1}^{9} 2(3)^{i-1}$?

(A) 19,680

(B) 19,681

(C) 19,682

(D) 19,683

55. ★ **WRITING** Compare the graph of $a_n = 5(3)^{n-1}$, where n is a positive integer, with the graph of $f(x) = 5 \cdot 3^{x-1}$, where x is a real number.

56. **CHALLENGE** Using the rule for the sum of a finite geometric series, write each polynomial as a rational expression.

    a. $1 + x + x^2 + x^3 + x^4$

    b. $3x + 6x^3 + 12x^5 + 24x^7$

PROBLEM SOLVING

EXAMPLE 6
for Exs. 57–59

57. **SKYDIVING** In a skydiving formation with R rings, each ring after the first has twice as many skydivers as the preceding ring. The formation for $R = 2$ is shown.

    a. Let a_n be the number of skydivers in the nth ring. Find a rule for a_n.

    b. Find the total number of skydivers if there are $R = 4$ rings.

First ring

Second ring

58. **SOCCER** A regional soccer tournament has 64 participating teams. In the first round of the tournament, 32 games are played. In each successive round, the number of games played decreases by a factor of one half.

    a. Find a rule for the number of games played in the nth round. For what values of n does your rule make sense?

    b. Find the total number of games played in the regional soccer tournament.

59. ★ **SHORT RESPONSE** A *binary search* technique used on a computer involves jumping to the middle of an ordered list of data (such as an alphabetical list of names) and deciding whether the item being searched for is there. If not, the computer decides whether the item comes before or after the middle. Half of the list is ignored on the next pass, and the computer jumps to the middle of the remaining list. This is repeated until the item is found.

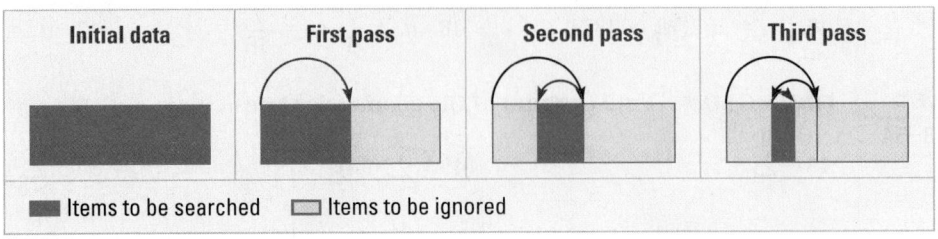

| ■ Items to be searched | □ Items to be ignored |

a. Find a rule for the number of items remaining after the nth pass through an ordered list of 1024 items.

b. In the worst case, the item to be found is the only one left in the list after n passes through the list. What is the worst-case value of n for a binary search of a list with 1024 items? *Explain.*

60. FRACTALS The *Sierpinski carpet* is a fractal created using squares. The process involves removing smaller squares from larger squares. First, divide a large square into nine congruent squares. Remove the center square. Repeat these steps for each smaller square, as shown below. Assume that each side of the initial square is one unit long.

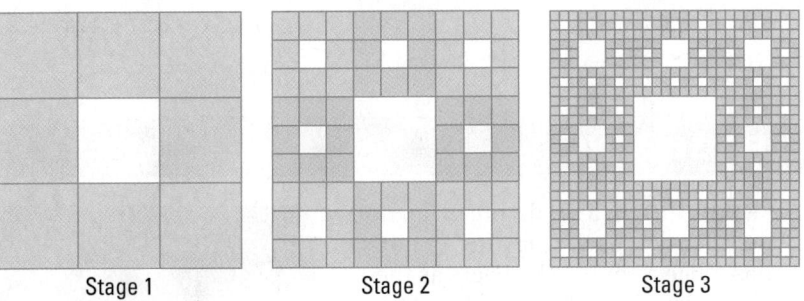

Stage 1   Stage 2   Stage 3

a. Let a_n be the number of squares removed at the nth stage. Find a rule for a_n. Then find the total number of squares removed through stage 8.

b. Let b_n be the remaining area of the original square after the nth stage. Find a rule for b_n. Then find the remaining area of the original square after stage 12.

61. ◆ **MULTIPLE REPRESENTATIONS** Two companies, company A and company B, offer the same starting salary of $20,000 per year. Company A gives a raise of $1000 each year. Company B gives a raise of 4% each year.

a. Writing Rules Write rules giving the salaries a_n and b_n in the nth year at companies A and B, respectively. Tell whether the sequence represented by each rule is *arithmetic*, *geometric*, or *neither*.

b. Drawing Graphs Graph each sequence in the same coordinate plane.

c. Finding Sums For each company, find the sum of wages earned during the first 20 years of employment.

d. Using Technology Use a graphing calculator or spreadsheet to find after how many years the total amount earned at company B is greater than the total amount earned at company A.

○ = See **WORKED-OUT SOLUTIONS** in Student Resources
★ = **STANDARDIZED TEST PRACTICE**
◆ = **MULTIPLE REPRESENTATIONS**

62. CHALLENGE On January 1 of each year, you deposit $2000 in an individual retirement account (IRA) that pays 5% annual interest. You make a total of 30 deposits. How much money do you have in your IRA immediately after you make your last deposit?

QUIZ

Write the next term in the sequence. Then write a rule for the nth term.

1. 1, 3, 5, 7, . . .

2. −5, 10, −15, 20, . . .

3. $\dfrac{1}{20}, \dfrac{2}{30}, \dfrac{3}{40}, \dfrac{4}{50}, \cdots$

4. 4, 16, 64, 256, . . .

5. 2, 6, 12, 20, . . .

6. 9, 36, 81, 144, . . .

Find the sum of the series.

7. $\displaystyle\sum_{i=1}^{4} 2i^3$

8. $\displaystyle\sum_{k=1}^{5} (k^2 + 3)$

9. $\displaystyle\sum_{n=2}^{6} \dfrac{1}{n-1}$

Write a rule for the nth term a_n of the arithmetic or geometric sequence. Find a_{15}, then find the sum of the first 15 terms of the sequence.

10. 1, 7, 13, 19, . . .

11. $\dfrac{1}{2}, 2, \dfrac{7}{2}, 5, \ldots$

12. 5, 2, −1, −4, −7, . . .

13. 2, 8, 32, 128, . . .

14. $2, \dfrac{4}{3}, \dfrac{8}{9}, \dfrac{16}{27}, \ldots$

15. −3, 15, −75, 375, . . .

16. COLLEGE TUITION In 1995, the average tuition at a public college in the United States was $2057. From 1995 through 2002, the average tuition at public colleges increased by about 6% per year. Write a rule for the average tuition a_n in terms of the year. Let $n = 1$ represent 1995. What was the average tuition at a public college in 2002?

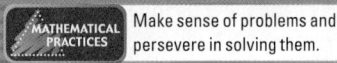
1. **MULTI-STEP PROBLEM** You accept a job as an environmental engineer that pays a salary of $45,000 in the first year. After the first year, your salary increases by 3.5% per year.

   a. Write a rule giving your salary a_n for your nth year of employment.

   b. What will your salary be during your 5th year of employment?

   c. What is the total amount you will earn if you work for the company for 30 years?

2. **EXTENDED RESPONSE** A target has rings that are each 1 foot wide.

   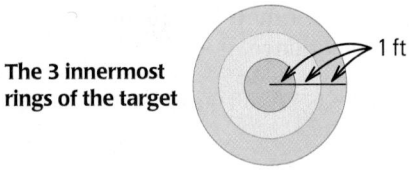

   The 3 innermost rings of the target   1 ft

   a. Write a rule for the area of the nth ring.

   b. Use summation notation to write a series that gives the total area of a target with n rings.

   c. Evaluate your expression from part (b) when $n = 1, 2, 4,$ and 8. What effect does doubling the number of rings have on the area of the target?

3. **SHORT RESPONSE** Rectangular tables are placed together along their short edges, as shown in the diagram. Write a rule for the number of people that can be seated around n tables. *Compare* the number of people that can be seated around n tables in this arrangement with the number that can be seated around n tables if the same tables are placed together along their long edges.

4. **OPEN-ENDED** Write an arithmetic series with eight terms such that the sum of the series is 70.

5. **GRIDDED ANSWER** Pieces of chalk are stacked in a pile. Part of the pile is shown below.

   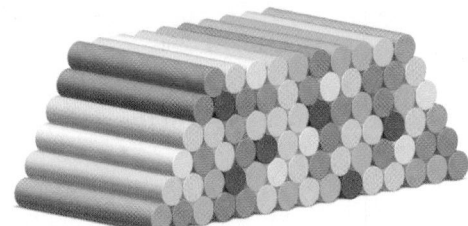

   The bottom row has 15 pieces of chalk and the top row has 6 pieces of chalk. Each row has one less piece of chalk than the row below it. How many pieces of chalk are in the pile?

6. **SHORT RESPONSE** A builder is constructing a staircase for a deck. At the foot of the staircase, there is a concrete slab that is 2 inches tall. Each stair is 7 inches tall. Write a rule for the height of the top of the nth stair. Find the height of the top of the 10th stair. *Explain* how you could modify the rule so that it gives the height of the bottom of the nth stair.

7. **EXTENDED RESPONSE** A scientist is studying the radioactive decay of Platinum-197. The scientist starts with a 66 gram sample of Platinum-197 and measures the amount remaining every two hours. The amounts (in grams) recorded are 66, 33, 16.5, 8.25, ...

   a. Is this sequence *arithmetic, geometric,* or *neither*? *Explain* how you know.

   b. Write a rule for the nth term of the sequence.

   c. Graph the sequence. *Describe* the curve on which the points lie.

   d. After how many hours will the scientist first measure an amount of Platinum-197 that is less than 1 gram?

8. **OPEN-ENDED** Write an arithmetic series and a geometric series such that both series have five terms and the same sum.

Investigating an Infinite Geometric Series

MATHEMATICAL PRACTICES

Reason abstractly and quantitatively.

MATERIALS · scissors · paper

QUESTION What is the sum of an infinite geometric series?

You can illustrate an infinite geometric series by cutting a piece of paper into smaller and smaller pieces.

EXPLORE Model an infinite geometric series

Start with a rectangular piece of paper. Define its area to be 1 square unit.

STEP 1 *Cut paper in half*

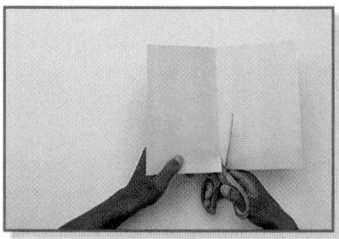

Fold the paper in half and cut along the fold. Place one half on a desktop and hold the remaining half.

STEP 2 *Cut paper again*

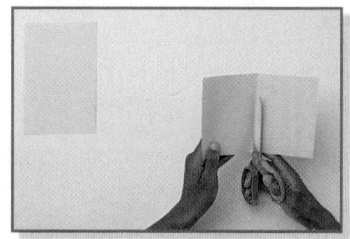

Fold the piece of paper you are holding in half and cut along the fold. Place one half on the desktop and hold the remaining half.

STEP 3 *Repeat steps*

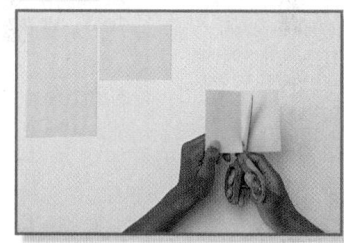

Repeat Steps 1 and 2 until you find it too difficult to fold and cut the piece of paper you are holding.

STEP 4 *Find areas* The first piece of paper on the desktop has an area of $\frac{1}{2}$ square unit. The second piece has an area of $\frac{1}{4}$ square unit. Write the areas of the next three pieces of paper. Explain why these areas form a geometric sequence.

STEP 5 *Make a table*
Copy and complete the table by recording the number of pieces of paper on the desktop and the combined area of the pieces at each step.

Number of pieces	1	2	3	4	. . .
Combined area	$\frac{1}{2}$	$\frac{1}{2} + \frac{1}{4} = ?$	?	?	. . .

DRAW CONCLUSIONS Use your observations to complete these exercises

1. Based on your table, what number does the combined area of the pieces of paper appear to be approaching?

2. Using the formula for the sum of a finite geometric series, write and simplify a rule for the combined area A_n of the pieces of paper after n cuts. What happens to A_n as $n \to \infty$? Justify your answer mathematically.

7.4 Find Sums of Infinite Geometric Series

Before	You found the sums of finite geometric series.
Now	You will find the sums of infinite geometric series.
Why?	So you can analyze a fractal, as in Ex. 42.

Key Vocabulary
• partial sum

COMMON CORE

CC.9-12.A.SSE.3 Choose and produce an equivalent form of an expression to reveal and explain properties of the quantity represented by the expression.*

The sum S_n of the first n terms of an infinite series is called a **partial sum**. The partial sums of an infinite geometric series may approach a limiting value.

EXAMPLE 1 Find partial sums

Consider the infinite geometric series $\frac{1}{2} + \frac{1}{4} + \frac{1}{8} + \frac{1}{16} + \frac{1}{32} + \cdots$. Find and graph the partial sums S_n for $n = 1, 2, 3, 4,$ and 5. Then describe what happens to S_n as n increases.

Solution

$$S_1 = \frac{1}{2} = 0.5$$

$$S_2 = \frac{1}{2} + \frac{1}{4} = 0.75$$

$$S_3 = \frac{1}{2} + \frac{1}{4} + \frac{1}{8} \approx 0.88$$

$$S_4 = \frac{1}{2} + \frac{1}{4} + \frac{1}{8} + \frac{1}{16} \approx 0.94$$

$$S_5 = \frac{1}{2} + \frac{1}{4} + \frac{1}{8} + \frac{1}{16} + \frac{1}{32} \approx 0.97$$

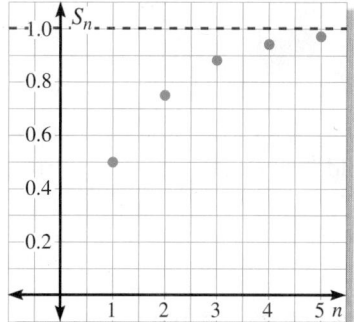

From the graph, S_n appears to approach 1 as n increases.

Animated Algebra at my.hrw.com

SUMS OF INFINITE SERIES In Example 1, you can understand why S_n approaches 1 as n increases by considering the rule for S_n:

$$S_n = a_1\left(\frac{1 - r^n}{1 - r}\right) = \frac{1}{2}\left(\frac{1 - \left(\frac{1}{2}\right)^n}{1 - \frac{1}{2}}\right) = 1 - \left(\frac{1}{2}\right)^n$$

As n increases, $\left(\frac{1}{2}\right)^n$ approaches 0, so S_n approaches 1. Therefore, 1 is defined to be the sum of the infinite geometric series in Example 1. More generally, as n increases for *any* infinite geometric series with common ratio r between -1 and 1, the value of $S_n = a_1\left(\frac{1 - r^n}{1 - r}\right) \approx a_1\left(\frac{1 - 0}{1 - r}\right) = \frac{a_1}{1 - r}$.

Courtesy of Gayla Chandler

The Sum of an Infinite Geometric Series

The sum of an infinite geometric series with first term a_1 and common ratio r is given by

$$S = \frac{a_1}{1 - r}$$

provided $|r| < 1$. If $|r| \geq 1$, the series has no sum.

EXAMPLE 2 **Find sums of infinite geometric series**

Find the sum of the infinite geometric series.

a. $\displaystyle\sum_{i=1}^{\infty} 5(0.8)^{i-1}$

b. $1 - \dfrac{3}{4} + \dfrac{9}{16} - \dfrac{27}{64} + \cdots$

Solution

a. For this series, $a_1 = 5$ and $r = 0.8$.

$$S = \frac{a_1}{1 - r} = \frac{5}{1 - 0.8} = 25$$

b. For this series, $a_1 = 1$ and $r = -\dfrac{3}{4}$.

$$S = \frac{a_1}{1 - r} = \frac{1}{1 - \left(-\dfrac{3}{4}\right)} = \frac{4}{7}$$

EXAMPLE 3 **Standardized Test Practice**

AVOID ERRORS

If you substitute 1 for a_1 and -3 for r in the formula $S = \dfrac{a_1}{1 - r}$, you get an answer of $S = \dfrac{1}{4}$ for the sum. However, this answer is not correct because the sum formula does not apply when $|r| \geq 1$.

What is the sum of the infinite geometric series $1 - 3 + 9 - 27 + \cdots$?

Ⓐ $\dfrac{1}{4}$ Ⓑ $\dfrac{4}{3}$ Ⓒ 3 Ⓓ Does not exist

Solution

You know that $a_1 = 1$ and $a_2 = -3$. So, $r = \dfrac{-3}{1} = -3$.

Because $|-3| \geq 1$, the sum does not exist.

▸ The correct answer is D. Ⓐ Ⓑ Ⓒ **Ⓓ**

✓ **GUIDED PRACTICE** for Examples 1, 2, and 3

1. Consider the series $\dfrac{2}{5} + \dfrac{4}{25} + \dfrac{8}{125} + \dfrac{16}{625} + \dfrac{32}{3125} + \cdots$. Find and graph the partial sums S_n for $n = 1, 2, 3, 4,$ and 5. Then describe what happens to S_n as n increases.

Find the sum of the infinite geometric series, if it exists.

2. $\displaystyle\sum_{n=1}^{\infty} \left(-\frac{1}{2}\right)^{n-1}$

3. $\displaystyle\sum_{n=1}^{\infty} 3\left(\frac{5}{4}\right)^{n-1}$

4. $3 + \dfrac{3}{4} + \dfrac{3}{16} + \dfrac{3}{64} + \cdots$

EXAMPLE 4 Use an infinite series as a model

PENDULUMS A pendulum that is released to swing freely travels 18 inches on the first swing. On each successive swing, the pendulum travels 80% of the distance of the previous swing. What is the total distance the pendulum swings?

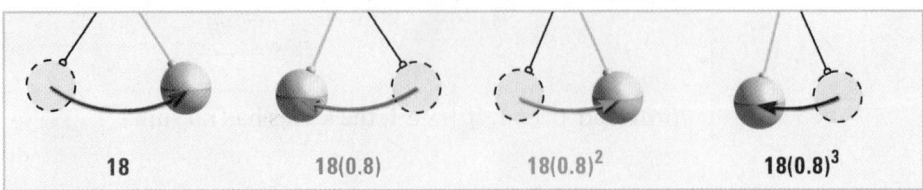

18   18(0.8) $18(0.8)^2$ $18(0.8)^3$

Solution

The total distance traveled by the pendulum is:

$$d = 18 + 18(0.8) + 18(0.8)^2 + 18(0.8)^3 + \cdots$$

$$= \frac{a_1}{1 - r} \qquad \textbf{Write formula for sum.}$$

$$= \frac{18}{1 - 0.8} \qquad \textbf{Substitute 18 for } a_1 \textbf{ and 0.8 for } r.$$

$$= 90 \qquad \textbf{Simplify.}$$

▶ The pendulum travels a total distance of 90 inches, or 7.5 feet.

EXAMPLE 5 Write a repeating decimal as a fraction

Write 0.242424... as a fraction in lowest terms.

$$0.242424\ldots = 24(0.01) + 24(0.01)^2 + 24(0.01)^3 + \cdots$$

$$= \frac{a_1}{1 - r} \qquad \textbf{Write formula for sum.}$$

$$= \frac{24(0.01)}{1 - 0.01} \qquad \textbf{Substitute 24(0.01) for } a_1 \textbf{ and 0.01 for } r.$$

$$= \frac{0.24}{0.99} \qquad \textbf{Simplify.}$$

$$= \frac{24}{99} \qquad \textbf{Write as a quotient of integers.}$$

$$= \frac{8}{33} \qquad \textbf{Reduce fraction to lowest terms.}$$

▶ The repeating decimal 0.242424... is $\frac{8}{33}$ as a fraction.

✓ **GUIDED PRACTICE**   for Examples 4 and 5

5. WHAT IF? In Example 4, suppose the pendulum travels 10 inches on its first swing. What is the total distance the pendulum swings?

Write the repeating decimal as a fraction in lowest terms.

6. 0.555...   **7.** 0.727272...   **8.** 0.131313...

7.4 EXERCISES

HOMEWORK KEY

○ = See WORKED-OUT SOLUTIONS
Exs. 13, 27, and 39

★ = STANDARDIZED TEST PRACTICE
Exs. 2, 32, 34, 39, 40, and 41

SKILL PRACTICE

1. **VOCABULARY** Copy and complete: The sum S_n of the first n terms of an infinite series is called a(n)   ? .

2. ★ **WRITING** *Explain* how to tell whether the series $\sum_{i=1}^{\infty} a_1 r^{i-1}$ has a sum.

EXAMPLE 1
for Exs. 3–6

PARTIAL SUMS For the given series, find and graph the partial sums S_n for $n = 1, 2, 3, 4,$ and 5. *Describe* what happens to S_n as n increases.

3. $\dfrac{1}{2} + \dfrac{1}{6} + \dfrac{1}{18} + \dfrac{1}{54} + \dfrac{1}{162} + \cdots$

4. $\dfrac{2}{3} + \dfrac{1}{3} + \dfrac{1}{6} + \dfrac{1}{12} + \dfrac{1}{24} + \cdots$

5. $4 + \dfrac{12}{5} + \dfrac{36}{25} + \dfrac{108}{125} + \dfrac{324}{625} + \cdots$

6. $\dfrac{1}{4} + \dfrac{5}{4} + \dfrac{25}{4} + \dfrac{125}{4} + \dfrac{625}{4} + \cdots$

EXAMPLES 2 and 3
for Exs. 7–23

FINDING SUMS Find the sum of the infinite geometric series, if it exists.

7. $\sum_{n=1}^{\infty} 8\left(\dfrac{1}{5}\right)^{n-1}$

8. $\sum_{k=1}^{\infty} -6\left(\dfrac{3}{2}\right)^{k-1}$

9. $\sum_{i=1}^{\infty} \dfrac{2}{5}\left(\dfrac{5}{3}\right)^{i-1}$

10. $\sum_{k=1}^{\infty} \dfrac{11}{3}\left(\dfrac{3}{8}\right)^{k-1}$

11. $\sum_{i=1}^{\infty} 2\left(\dfrac{1}{6}\right)^{i-1}$

12. $\sum_{n=1}^{\infty} -5\left(\dfrac{2}{5}\right)^{n-1}$

13. $\sum_{k=1}^{\infty} 7\left(-\dfrac{8}{9}\right)^{k-1}$

14. $\sum_{n=1}^{\infty} \dfrac{1}{2}\left(-\dfrac{10}{3}\right)^{n-1}$

15. $\sum_{k=1}^{\infty} 9(4)^{k-1}$

16. $\sum_{i=1}^{\infty} -2\left(-\dfrac{1}{4}\right)^{i-1}$

17. $\sum_{i=0}^{\infty} \left(-\dfrac{3}{7}\right)^{i}$

18. $\sum_{n=0}^{\infty} \dfrac{5}{6}(3)^{n}$

19. **ERROR ANALYSIS** *Describe* and correct the error in finding the sum of the infinite geometric series $\sum_{n=1}^{\infty} \left(\dfrac{7}{2}\right)^{n-1}$.

For this series, $a_1 = 1$ and $r = \dfrac{7}{2}$.

$$S = \dfrac{a_1}{1-r} = \dfrac{1}{1 - \dfrac{7}{2}} = \dfrac{1}{-\dfrac{5}{2}} = -\dfrac{2}{5}$$ ✗

FINDING SUMS Find the sum of the infinite geometric series, if it exists.

20. $-\dfrac{1}{8} - \dfrac{1}{12} - \dfrac{1}{18} - \dfrac{1}{27} + \cdots$

21. $\dfrac{2}{3} - \dfrac{2}{9} + \dfrac{2}{27} - \dfrac{2}{81} + \cdots$

22. $\dfrac{4}{15} + \dfrac{4}{9} + \dfrac{20}{27} + \dfrac{100}{81} + \cdots$

23. $3 + \dfrac{5}{2} + \dfrac{25}{12} + \dfrac{125}{72} + \cdots$

EXAMPLE 5
for Exs. 24–32

REWRITING DECIMALS Write the repeating decimal as a fraction in lowest terms.

24. $0.222\ldots$

25. $0.444\ldots$

26. $0.161616\ldots$

27. $0.625625625\ldots$

28. $32.3232\ldots$

29. $130.130130\ldots$

30. $0.090909\ldots$

31. $0.2777\ldots$

32. ★ **MULTIPLE CHOICE** Which fraction is equal to the repeating decimal $18.1818\ldots$?

Ⓐ $\dfrac{2}{11}$

Ⓑ $\dfrac{1836}{101}$

Ⓒ $\dfrac{200}{11}$

Ⓓ $\dfrac{181}{9}$

33. **REASONING** Show that $0.999\ldots$ is equal to 1.

34. ★ **OPEN-ENDED MATH** Find two infinite geometric series whose sums are each 5.

CHALLENGE Specify the values of x for which the given infinite geometric series has a sum. Then find the sum in terms of x.

35. $1 + 4x + 16x^2 + 64x^3 + \cdots$

36. $6 + \dfrac{3}{2}x + \dfrac{3}{8}x^2 + \dfrac{3}{32}x^3 + \cdots$

PROBLEM SOLVING

EXAMPLE 4
for Exs. 37–39

37. TIRE SWING A person is given one push on a tire swing and then allowed to swing freely. On the first swing, the person travels a distance of 14 feet. On each successive swing, the person travels 80% of the distance of the previous swing. What is the total distance the person swings?

38. BUSINESS A company had a profit of $350,000 in its first year. Since then, the company's profit has decreased by 12% per year. If this trend continues, what is an upper limit on the total profit the company can make over the course of its lifetime? *Justify* your answer using an infinite geometric series.

39. ★ **MULTIPLE CHOICE** In 1994, the number of cassette tapes shipped in the United States was 345 million. In each successive year, the number decreased by about 21.7%. What is the total number of cassettes that will ship in 1994 and after if this trend continues?

A 420 million   **B** 440 million   **C** 615 million   **D** 1.59 billion

40. ★ **SHORT RESPONSE** Can the Greek hero Achilles, running at 20 feet per second, ever catch up to a tortoise that runs 10 feet per second if the tortoise has a 20 foot head start? The Greek mathematician Zeno said no. He reasoned as follows:

 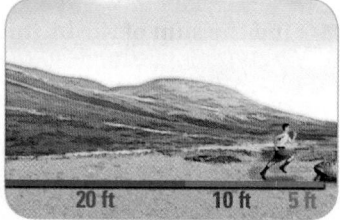 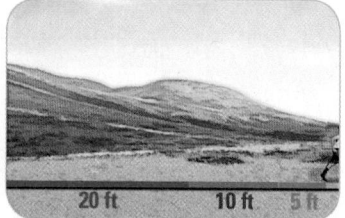

When Achilles runs 20 feet, the tortoise will be in a new spot, 10 feet away.

Then, when Achilles gets to that spot, the tortoise will be 5 feet away.

Achilles will keep halving the distance but will never catch up to the tortoise.

In actuality, looking at the race as Zeno did, you can see that both the distances and the times Achilles required to traverse them form infinite geometric series. Using the table, show that both series have finite sums. Does Achilles catch up to the tortoise? *Explain.*

Distance (ft)	20	10	5	2.5	1.25	0.625	. . .
Time (sec)	1	0.5	0.25	0.125	0.0625	0.03125	. . .

◯ = **See WORKED-OUT SOLUTIONS** in Student Resources   ★ = **STANDARDIZED TEST PRACTICE**

41. ★ **EXTENDED RESPONSE** A student drops a rubber ball from a height of 8 feet. Each time the ball hits the ground, it bounces to 75% of its previous height.

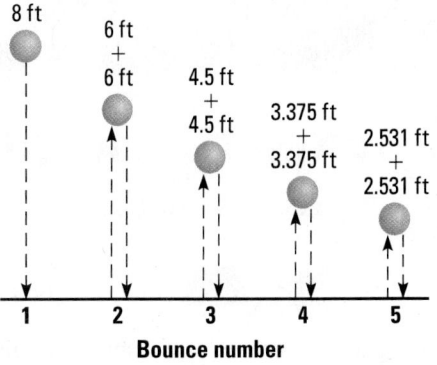

8 ft

6 ft
+
6 ft

4.5 ft
+
4.5 ft

3.375 ft
+
3.375 ft

2.531 ft
+
2.531 ft

1   2   3   4   5
Bounce number

a. How far does the ball travel between the first and second bounces? between the second and third bounces?

b. Write an infinite series to model the total distance traveled by the ball, excluding the distance traveled before the first bounce.

c. Find the total distance traveled by the ball, including the distance traveled before the first bounce.

d. Show that if the ball is dropped from a height of h feet, then the total distance traveled by the ball (including the distance traveled before the first bounce) is $7h$ feet.

42. **CHALLENGE** The *Sierpinski triangle* is a fractal created using equilateral triangles. The process involves removing smaller triangles from larger triangles by joining the midpoints of the sides of the larger triangles as shown below. Assume that the initial triangle has an area of 1 square unit.

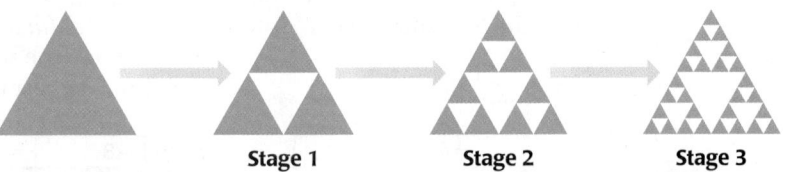

Stage 1   Stage 2   Stage 3

a. Let a_n be the total area of all the triangles that are removed at stage n. Write a rule for a_n.

b. Find $\sum_{n=1}^{\infty} a_n$. What does your answer mean in the context of this problem?

Exploring Recursive Rules

MATERIALS • computer with spreadsheet program

MATHEMATICAL PRACTICES

Use appropriate tools strategically.

QUESTION How can you evaluate a recursive rule for a sequence?

A *recursive rule* for a sequence gives the beginning term or terms of the sequence and then an equation relating the nth term a_n to one or more preceding terms. For example, the rule $a_1 = 4$, $a_n = a_{n-1} + 7$ defines a sequence recursively.

EXPLORE Find terms of a sequence given by a recursive rule

Find the first eight terms of the sequence defined by $a_1 = 4$, $a_n = a_{n-1} + 7$. What type of sequence does this rule represent?

STEP 1 *Enter first term*

Enter the value of a_1 into cell A1.

A1	4		
	A	**B**	**C**
1	4		
2			
3			
4			
5			
6			
7			
8			

STEP 2 *Enter recursive equation*

Enter the formula "=A1+7" into cell A2.

A2	=A1+7		
	A	**B**	**C**
1	4		
2	11		
3			
4			
5			
6			
7			
8			

STEP 3 *Fill cells*

Use the *fill down* command to copy the recursive equation into the rest of column A.

A8	=A7+7		
	A	**B**	**C**
1	4		
2	11		
3	18		
4	25		
5	32		
6	39		
7	46		
8	53		

STEP 4 *Identify terms and type of sequence*

The first eight terms of the sequence are 4, 11, 18, 25, 32, 39, 46, and 53. This sequence is an arithmetic sequence because the difference of consecutive terms is always 7.

DRAW CONCLUSIONS Use your observations to complete these exercises

1. Find the first eight terms of the sequence defined by $a_1 = 4$, $a_n = 7a_{n-1}$. What type of sequence does this rule represent?

2. Write a recursive rule for the sequence 15, 11, 7, 3, −1, −5, ...

3. Write a recursive rule for the sequence 81, 27, 9, 3, 1, $\frac{1}{3}$, ...

4. What equation relates the nth term a_n to the preceding term a_{n-1} for an arithmetic sequence with common difference d? for a geometric sequence with common ratio r?

7.5 Use Recursive Rules with Sequences and Functions

Before   You used explicit rules for sequences.

Now   You will use recursive rules for sequences.

Why?   So you can model evaporation from a pool, as in Ex. 44.

Key Vocabulary
- explicit rule
- recursive rule
- iteration

CC.9-12.F.BF.2 Write arithmetic and geometric sequences both recursively and with an explicit formula, use them to model situations, and translate between the two forms.*

So far in this chapter you have worked with *explicit rules* for the nth term of a sequence, such as $a_n = 3n - 2$ and $a_n = 3(2)^n$. An **explicit rule** gives a_n as a function of the term's position number n in the sequence.

In this lesson you will learn another way to define a sequence—by a *recursive rule*. A **recursive rule** gives the beginning term or terms of a sequence and then a *recursive equation* that tells how a_n is related to one or more preceding terms.

EXAMPLE 1   Evaluate recursive rules

Write the first six terms of the sequence.

a. $a_0 = 1, a_n = a_{n-1} + 4$ **b.** $a_1 = 1, a_n = 3a_{n-1}$

Solution

a. $a_0 = 1$

$a_1 = a_0 + 4 = 1 + 4 = 5$

$a_2 = a_1 + 4 = 5 + 4 = 9$

$a_3 = a_2 + 4 = 9 + 4 = 13$

$a_4 = a_3 + 4 = 13 + 4 = 17$

$a_5 = a_4 + 4 = 17 + 4 = 21$

b. $a_1 = 1$

$a_2 = 3a_1 = 3(1) = 3$

$a_3 = 3a_2 = 3(3) = 9$

$a_4 = 3a_3 = 3(9) = 27$

$a_5 = 3a_4 = 3(27) = 81$

$a_6 = 3a_5 = 3(81) = 243$

ARITHMETIC AND GEOMETRIC SEQUENCES In part (a) of Example 1, observe that the *differences* of consecutive terms of the sequence are constant, so the sequence is arithmetic. In part (b), the *ratios* of consecutive terms are constant, so the sequence is geometric. In general, rules for arithmetic and geometric sequences can be written recursively as follows.

KEY CONCEPT   *For Your Notebook*

Recursive Equations for Arithmetic and Geometric Sequences

Arithmetic Sequence

$a_n = a_{n-1} + d$ where d is the common difference

Geometric Sequence

$a_n = r \cdot a_{n-1}$ where r is the common ratio

EXAMPLE 2 · Write recursive rules

Write a recursive rule for the sequence.

a. 3, 13, 23, 33, 43, . . .

b. 16, 40, 100, 250, 625, . . .

Solution

a. The sequence is arithmetic with first term $a_1 = 3$ and common difference $d = 13 - 3 = 10$.

$a_n = a_{n-1} + d$ **General recursive equation for a_n**

$ = a_{n-1} + 10$ **Substitute 10 for d.**

▶ So, a recursive rule for the sequence is $a_1 = 3$, $a_n = a_{n-1} + 10$.

b. The sequence is geometric with first term $a_1 = 16$ and common ratio $r = \frac{40}{16} = 2.5$.

$a_n = r \cdot a_{n-1}$ **General recursive equation for a_n**

$ = 2.5a_{n-1}$ **Substitute 2.5 for r.**

▶ So, a recursive rule for the sequence is $a_1 = 16$, $a_n = 2.5a_{n-1}$.

✓ **GUIDED PRACTICE**   for Examples 1 and 2

Write the first five terms of the sequence.

1. $a_1 = 3$, $a_n = a_{n-1} - 7$

2. $a_0 = 162$, $a_n = 0.5a_{n-1}$

3. $a_0 = 1$, $a_n = a_{n-1} + n$

4. $a_1 = 4$, $a_n = 2a_{n-1} - 1$

Write a recursive rule for the sequence.

5. 2, 14, 98, 686, 4802, . . .

6. 19, 13, 7, 1, −5, . . .

7. 11, 22, 33, 44, 55, . . .

8. 324, 108, 36, 12, 4, . . .

RECURSIVE RULES FOR SPECIAL SEQUENCES For some sequences, it is difficult to write an explicit rule but relatively easy to write a recursive rule.

EXAMPLE 3 · Write recursive rules for special sequences

Write a recursive rule for the sequence.

a. 1, 1, 2, 3, 5, . . .

b. 1, 1, 2, 6, 24, . . .

Solution

a. Beginning with the third term in the sequence, each term is the sum of the two previous terms.

▶ So, a recursive rule is $a_1 = 1$, $a_2 = 1$, $a_n = a_{n-2} + a_{n-1}$.

b. Denote the first term by $a_0 = 1$. Then note that $a_1 = 1 = 1 \cdot a_0$, $a_2 = 2 = 2 \cdot a_1$, $a_3 = 6 = 3 \cdot a_2$, and so on.

▶ So, a recursive rule is $a_0 = 1$, $a_n = n \cdot a_{n-1}$.

EXAMPLE 4 **Solve a multi-step problem**

MUSIC SERVICE An online music service initially has 50,000 annual members. Each year it loses 20% of its current members and adds 5000 new members.

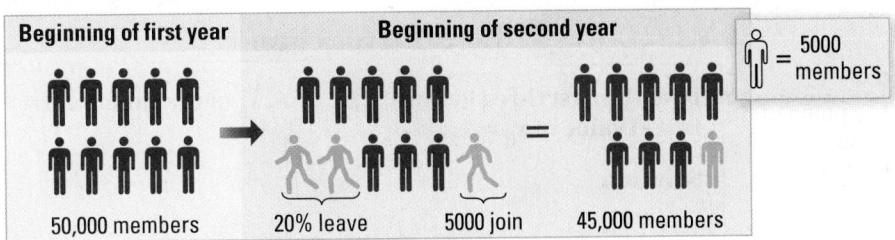

- Write a recursive rule for the number a_n of members at the start of the nth year.

- Find the number of members at the start of the 5th year.

- Describe what happens to the number of members over time.

ANOTHER WAY

For alternative methods for solving the problem in Example 4, see the **Problem Solving Workshop**.

Solution

STEP 1 **Write** a recursive rule. Because the number of members declines 20% each year, 80% of the members are retained from one year to the next. Also, 5000 new members are added each year.

Members at start of year n	= 0.8 ·	Members at start of year $(n - 1)$	+	New members added
a_n	= 0.8 ·	a_{n-1}	+	5000

▸ A recursive rule is $a_1 = 50{,}000$, $a_n = 0.8a_{n-1} + 5000$.

STEP 2 **Find** the number of members at the start of the 5th year. Enter 50,000 (the value of a_1) into a graphing calculator. Then enter the rule $0.8 \times \text{Ans} + 5000$ to find a_2. Press [ENTER] three more times to find a_5.

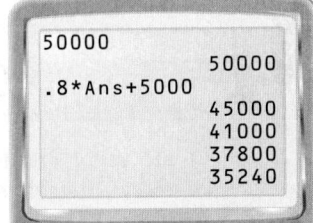

▸ There are about 35,240 members at the start of the 5th year.

STEP 3 **Describe** what happens to the number of members over time. Continue pressing [ENTER] on the calculator. As shown at the right, after many years the number of members approaches 25,000.

▸ The number of members stabilizes at about 25,000 members.

✓ **GUIDED PRACTICE** for Examples 3 and 4

9. Write a recursive rule for the sequence 1, 2, 2, 4, 8, 32, ...

10. **WHAT IF?** In Example 4, suppose 70% of the members are retained each year. What happens to the number of members over time?

ITERATING FUNCTIONS **Iteration** involves the repeated composition of a function f with itself. The result of one iteration is $f(f(x))$. The result of two iterations is $f(f(f(x)))$. You can use iteration to generate a sequence recursively. Begin with an initial value x_0, and let $x_1 = f(x_0)$, $x_2 = f(x_1) = f(f(x_0))$, and so on.

EXAMPLE 5 Iterate a function

READING
An *iterate* is a number that is the result of iterating a function.

Find the first three iterates x_1, x_2, and x_3 of the function $f(x) = -3x + 1$ for an initial value of $x_0 = 2$.

Solution

$$
\begin{array}{lll}
x_1 = f(x_0) & x_2 = f(x_1) & x_3 = f(x_2) \\
\quad = f(2) & \quad = f(-5) & \quad = f(16) \\
\quad = -3(2) + 1 & \quad = -3(-5) + 1 & \quad = -3(16) + 1 \\
\quad = -5 & \quad = 16 & \quad = -47
\end{array}
$$

▶ The first three iterates are -5, 16, and -47.

 GUIDED PRACTICE for Example 5

Find the first three iterates of the function for the given initial value.

11. $f(x) = 4x - 3$, $x_0 = 2$

12. $f(x) = x^2 - 5$, $x_0 = -1$

7.5 EXERCISES

HOMEWORK KEY

○ = See WORKED-OUT SOLUTIONS
 Exs. 15, 27, and 45

★ = STANDARDIZED TEST PRACTICE
 Exs. 2, 12, 33, 40, 45, and 47

SKILL PRACTICE

1. **VOCABULARY** Copy and complete: The repeated composition of a function with itself is called   ? .

2. ★ **WRITING** *Explain* the difference between an explicit rule for a sequence and a recursive rule for a sequence.

EXAMPLE 1
for Exs. 3–12

WRITING TERMS **Write the first five terms of the sequence.**

3. $a_1 = 1$
 $a_n = a_{n-1} + 3$

4. $a_0 = 4$
 $a_n = 2a_{n-1}$

5. $a_1 = -1$
 $a_n = a_{n-1} - 5$

6. $a_0 = 3$
 $a_n = a_{n-1} - n^2$

7. $a_1 = 2$
 $a_n = (a_{n-1})^2 + 1$

8. $a_0 = 4$
 $a_n = (a_{n-1})^2 - 10$

9. $a_1 = 2$
 $a_n = n^2 + 3n - a_{n-1}$

10. $a_0 = 2$, $a_1 = 4$
 $a_n = a_{n-1} - a_{n-2}$

11. $a_1 = 2$, $a_2 = 3$
 $a_n = a_{n-1} \cdot a_{n-2}$

12. ★ **MULTIPLE CHOICE** What are the first four terms of the sequence for which $a_1 = 1$, $a_2 = 4$, and $a_n = a_{n-1} \cdot a_{n-2}$?

Ⓐ 1, 4, 4, 16
Ⓑ 1, 4, 16, 64
Ⓒ 1, 4, 8, 16
Ⓓ 1, 4, 4, 8

WRITING RULES Write a recursive rule for the sequence. The sequence may be arithmetic, geometric, or neither.

13. $21, 14, 7, 0, -7, \ldots$

14. $3, 12, 48, 192, 768, \ldots$

15. $4, -12, 36, -108, 324, \ldots$

16. $1, 8, 15, 22, 29, \ldots$

17. $44, 11, \frac{11}{4}, \frac{11}{16}, \frac{11}{64}, \ldots$

18. $1, 4, 5, 9, 14, \ldots$

19. $54, 43, 32, 21, 10, \ldots$

20. $3, 5, 15, 75, 1125, \ldots$

21. $16, 9, 7, 2, 5, \ldots$

ERROR ANALYSIS *Describe* and correct the error in writing a recursive rule for the sequence $5, 2, 3, -1, 4, \ldots$.

22.

> Beginning with the third term in the sequence, each term a_n equals $a_{n-2} - a_{n-1}$. So a recursive rule is given by:
>
> $a_n = a_{n-2} - a_{n-1}$

23.

> Beginning with the second term in the sequence, each term a_n is $a_{n-1} - 3$. So a recursive rule is given by:
>
> $a_1 = 5, a_n = a_{n-1} - 3$

EXAMPLE 5
for Exs. 24–33

ITERATING FUNCTIONS Find the first three iterates of the function for the given initial value.

24. $f(x) = 3x - 2, x_0 = 2$

25. $f(x) = 5x + 6, x_0 = -2$

26. $g(x) = -4x + 7, x_0 = 1$

27. $f(x) = \frac{1}{2}x - 3, x_0 = 2$

28. $f(x) = \frac{2}{3}x + 5, x_0 = 6$

29. $h(x) = x^2 - 4, x_0 = -3$

30. $f(x) = 2x^2 + 1, x_0 = -1$

31. $f(x) = x^2 - x + 2, x_0 = 1$

32. $g(x) = -3x^2 + 2x, x_0 = 2$

33. ★ **MULTIPLE CHOICE** What are the first three iterates x_1, x_2, and x_3 of the function $f(x) = -2x + 3$ for an initial value of $x_0 = 2$?

A $-1, 1, 3$
B $1, -5, 7$
C $-1, 5, -7$
D $1, -1, -3$

WRITING RULES Write a recursive rule for the sequence.

34. $3, 8, 17, 81, 370, \ldots$

35. $1, 2, 12, 56, 272, \ldots$

36. $5, 5\sqrt{3}, 15, 15\sqrt{3}, 45, \ldots$

37. $2, 5, 11, 26, 59, \ldots$

38. $8, 4, 2, 2, 1, \ldots$

39. $-3, -2, 5, -3, -2, \ldots$

40. ★ **OPEN-ENDED MATH** Give an example of a sequence in which each term after the third term is a function of the three terms preceding it. Write a recursive rule for the sequence and find its first eight terms.

41. **REASONING** *Explain* why there are not a function f and an initial value x_0 such that the function's first three iterates are $x_1 = 2$, $x_2 = 2$, and $x_3 = 8$.

42. **CHALLENGE** The rule for a recursive sequence is as follows:

$$a_1 = 3, a_2 = 10$$

$$a_n = 4 + 2a_{n-1} - a_{n-2}$$

a. Write the first five terms of the sequence.

b. Use finite differences to find a pattern. What type of relationship do the terms of the sequence show?

c. Find an explicit rule for the sequence.

EXAMPLE 4
for Exs. 43–45

43. FISH POPULATION A lake initially contains 5000 fish. Each year the population declines 20% due to fishing and other causes, and the lake is restocked with 500 fish.

   a. Write a recursive rule for the number a_n of fish at the beginning of the nth year. How many fish are there at the beginning of the 5th year?

   b. What happens to the population of fish in the lake over time?

44. POOL CARE You are adding chlorine to a swimming pool. You add 34 ounces of chlorine the first week and 16 ounces every week thereafter. Each week 40% of the chlorine in the pool evaporates. Write a recursive rule for the amount of chlorine in the pool each week. What happens to the amount of chlorine in the pool over time?

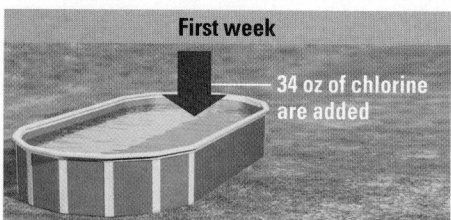
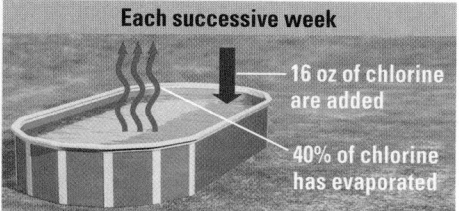

45. ★ **SHORT RESPONSE** Gladys owes $2000 to a credit card company that charges interest at a rate of 1.4% per month. At the end of each month she makes a payment of $100. Write a recursive rule for the balance a_n of the account at the beginning of the nth month. How long will it take to pay off the account? *Explain* your reasoning.

46. FIBONACCI SEQUENCE The Fibonacci sequence, which is defined recursively in Example 3, occurs many places in nature. This sequence can also be defined explicitly as follows:

$$f_n = \frac{1}{\sqrt{5}}\left(\frac{1+\sqrt{5}}{2}\right)^n - \frac{1}{\sqrt{5}}\left(\frac{1-\sqrt{5}}{2}\right)^n, \, n \geq 1$$

Use the explicit rule to find the first five terms of the Fibonacci sequence.

Animated Algebra   at my.hrw.com

47. ★ **EXTENDED RESPONSE** A person repeatedly takes 20 milligrams of a prescribed drug every 4 hours. Thirty percent of the drug is removed from the bloodstream every 4 hours.

   a. Write a recursive rule for the amount of the drug in the bloodstream after n doses.

   b. The value that a drug level in a person's body approaches after an extended period of time is called the *maintenance level*. What is the maintenance level of this drug, given a dosage of 20 milligrams?

   c. How does doubling the dosage affect the maintenance level of the drug? *Justify* your answer mathematically.

○ = See **WORKED-OUT SOLUTIONS** in Student Resources   ★ = **STANDARDIZED TEST PRACTICE**

48. CHALLENGE You are saving money for retirement. You plan to withdraw $30,000 at the beginning of each year for 20 years after you retire. Based on the type of investment you are making, you can expect to earn an annual return of 8% on your savings after you retire.

   a. Let a_n be your balance n years after retiring. Write a recursive equation that shows how a_n is related to a_{n-1}.

   b. Solve the equation from part (a) for a_{n-1}. Find a_0, the minimum amount of money you should have in your account when you retire. (*Hint:* Let $a_{20} = 0$.)

QUIZ

Find the sum of the infinite geometric series, if it exists.

1. $\displaystyle\sum_{n=1}^{\infty} 2\left(\frac{3}{7}\right)^{n-1}$

2. $\displaystyle\sum_{n=0}^{\infty} 4\left(-\frac{5}{6}\right)^{n}$

3. $\dfrac{3}{4} + \dfrac{15}{8} + \dfrac{75}{16} + \dfrac{375}{32} + \cdots$

Write the repeating decimal as a fraction in lowest terms.

4. $0.777\ldots$

5. $0.393939\ldots$

6. $123.123123\ldots$

Write the first five terms of the sequence.

7. $a_1 = 2$
$a_n = a_{n-1} + 4$

8. $a_0 = 3$
$a_n = (a_{n-1})^2 - 5$

9. $a_1 = 1, a_2 = 4$
$a_n = a_{n-1} - a_{n-2}$

Write a recursive rule for the sequence. The sequence may be arithmetic, geometric, or neither.

10. $5, \dfrac{17}{4}, \dfrac{7}{2}, \dfrac{11}{4}, 2, \ldots$

11. $2, 6, 12, 72, 864, \ldots$

12. $8, 24, 72, 216, 648, \ldots$

Find the first three iterates of the function for the given initial value.

13. $f(x) = -3x - 2, x_0 = 1$

14. $g(x) = 4x + 1, x_0 = 2$

15. $f(x) = -2x + 3, x_0 = -2$

16. $f(x) = 5x - 7, x_0 = -3$

17. $h(x) = x^2 - 6, x_0 = -1$

18. $f(x) = 3x^2 + 2, x_0 = 0$

19. PENDULUMS A pendulum that is released to swing freely travels 25 inches on the first swing. On each successive swing, the pendulum travels 85% as far as the previous swing. What is the total distance the pendulum swings?

Using ALTERNATIVE METHODS

Another Way to Solve Example 4

Make sense of problems and persevere in solving them.

MULTIPLE REPRESENTATIONS In Example 4, you found the number that a real-life sequence approaches over time by using a calculator to evaluate the rule for the sequence. You can also solve this problem using a graph or an algebraic method.

PROBLEM

MUSIC SERVICE An online music service initially has 50,000 annual members. Each year the music service loses 20% of its current members and adds 5000 new members. What happens to the number of members over time?

METHOD 1

Using a Graph A recursive rule for the number a_n of members at the beginning of the nth year is $a_1 = 50,000$, $a_n = 0.8a_{n-1} + 5000$. One alternative method for finding the number this sequence approaches is to graph the sequence on a graphing calculator.

STEP 1 **Set** the calculator to *sequence* mode and *dot* mode.

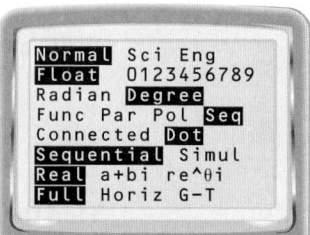

STEP 2 **Press** Y= and enter the equations nMin = 1, $u(n) = 0.8u(n-1) + 5000$, and $u(n$Min$) = 50,000$. Press WINDOW and enter the following parameters:

nMin = 1	Xmin = 0	Ymin = 15,000
nMax = 100	Xmax = 100	Ymax = 35,000
PlotStart = 1	Xscl = 10	Yscl = 5000
PlotStep = 1		

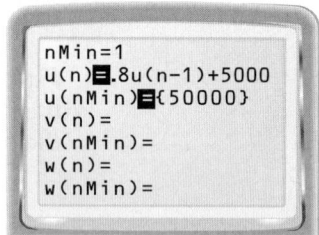

STEP 3 **Graph** the sequence. Use the *trace* feature to find the value that the sequence approaches as n becomes large. From the graph, you can see that the sequence approaches 25,000.

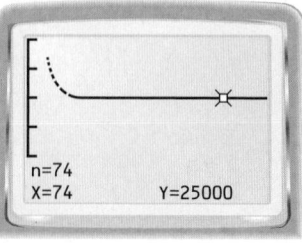

▶ Over time, the number of members of the music service approaches 25,000.

METHOD 2 **Using Algebra** Another approach is to use an algebraic method to determine what happens to the number of members over time.

> *STEP 1* **Write** the recursive rule.
>
> $$a_1 = 50{,}000, \ a_n = 0.8a_{n-1} + 5000.$$
>
> *STEP 2* **Assume** that the sequence has a limit L, which is the value that the sequence approaches as n becomes large.
>
> *STEP 3* **Consider** what happens to the equation $a_n = 0.8a_{n-1} + 5000$ as n becomes large. The value of a_n (the left-hand side) approaches L while the value of $0.8a_{n-1} + 5000$ (the right-hand side) approaches $0.8L + 5000$. So, you can conclude that $L = 0.8L + 5000$.
>
> *STEP 4* **Solve** the equation $L = 0.8L + 5000$ for L.
>
> | | |
> |---|---|
> | $L = 0.8L + 5000$ | **Write equation.** |
> | $0.2L = 5000$ | **Subtract 0.8L from each side.** |
> | $L = 25{,}000$ | **Divide each side by 0.2.** |
>
> ▶ The sequence approaches the limit $L = 25{,}000$ as n becomes large. So, over time the number of members of the music service approaches 25,000.

PRACTICE

Describe what happens to the terms of the sequence as n becomes large.

1. $a_1 = 3000, \ a_n = 0.25a_{n-1} + 300$

2. $a_1 = 1700, \ a_n = 0.38a_{n-1} + 512$

3. **WHAT IF?** Suppose the online music service in the problem loses 8% of its current members and adds 1200 new members each year. Use the graphing method and the algebraic method to determine what happens to the number of members over time.

4. **TOWN LIBRARY** A town library initially has 54,000 books in its collection. Each year 2% of the books are lost or discarded. The library can afford to purchase 1150 new books each year. Write a recursive rule for the number a_n of books in the library at the beginning of the nth year. Use the graphing method and the algebraic method to determine what happens to the number of books in the library over time.

5. **ERROR ANALYSIS** A student attempted to solve the problem in Exercise 4 as shown below. *Describe* and correct the error in the student's work.

> $a_1 = 54{,}000, \ a_n = 0.02a_{n-1} + 1150$
> Let L be the limit of the sequence. Then:
>
> $$L = 0.02L + 1150$$
>
> $$0.98L = 1150$$
>
> $$L \approx 1173$$
>
> So, over time the number of books in the library approaches about 1173.

6. **REASONING** Give an example of a real-life situation which you can represent with a recursive rule that does not approach a limit. Write a recursive rule that represents the situation.

Translate Between Recursive and Explicit Rules for Sequences

GOAL Translate between recursive and explicit rules for arithmetic and geometric sequences.

CC.9-12.F.BF.2 Write arithmetic and geometric sequences both recursively and with an explicit formula, use them to model situations, and translate between the two forms.*

The box below summarizes the recursive and explicit rules for arithmetic sequences with common difference d, and for geometric sequences with common ratio r.

KEY CONCEPT   *For Your Notebook*

Sequence Formulas

Recursive Formulas

    Arithmetic sequence: $a_n = a_{n-1} + d$

    Geometric sequence: $a_n = r \cdot a_{n-1}$

Explicit Formulas

    Arithmetic sequence: $a_n = a_1 + (n-1)d$

    Geometric sequence: $a_n = a_1 r^{n-1}$

To translate from an explicit rule to a recursive rule for an arithmetic sequence, find the first term a_1 and the common difference d. To translate from an explicit rule to a recursive rule for a geometric sequence, find a_1 and the common ratio r.

EXAMPLE 1   **Translate from an explicit rule to a recursive rule**

Write a recursive rule for the sequence.

   a. $a_n = -6 + 8n$ **b.** $a_n = -3\left(\dfrac{1}{2}\right)^{n-1}$

Solution

  a. $a_n = -6 + 8n$ Write explicit rule.

     $a_1 = -6 + 8(1) = 2$ Substitute 1 for n.

     $d = 8$ The coefficient of n is d.

     $a_1 = 2, \; a_n = a_{n-1} + 8$ Write recursive rule.

  b. $a_n = -3\left(\dfrac{1}{2}\right)^{n-1}$ Write explicit rule.

     $a_1 = -3\left(\dfrac{1}{2}\right)^0 = -3$ Substitute 1 for n.

     $r = \dfrac{1}{2}$ The common ratio is $\dfrac{1}{2}$.

     $a_1 = -3, \; a_n = \dfrac{1}{2} a_{n-1}$ Write recursive rule.

To translate from a recursive rule to an explicit rule for an arithmetic sequence, find the common difference d. To translate from a recursive rule to an explicit rule for a geometric sequence, find the common ratio r.

EXAMPLE 2 **Translate from a recursive rule to an explicit rule**

Write an explicit rule for the sequence.

a. $a_1 = -5, a_n = a_{n-1} - 2$ **b.** $a_1 = 10, a_n = 2a_{n-1}$

Solution

a. $a_1 = -5, a_n = a_{n-1} - 2$ Write recursive rule.

$d = -2$ The number added or subtracted is d.

$a_n = -5 + (n-1)(-2)$ Substitute -5 for a_1 and -2 for d.

$a_n = -3 - 2n$ Write explicit rule.

b. $a_1 = 10, a_n = 2a_{n-1}$ Write recursive rule.

$r = 2$ The coefficient of a_{n-1} is r.

$a_n = 10(2)^{n-1}$ Substitute 10 for a_1 and 2 for r to write explicit rule.

PRACTICE

EXAMPLE 1
for Exs. 1–4

Write a recursive rule for the sequence.

1. $a_n = 17 - 4n$

2. $a_n = 126 + 12.5n$

3. $a_n = 16(3)^{n-1}$

4. $a_n = 100{,}000(1.02)^{n-1}$

EXAMPLE 2
for Exs. 5–8

Write an explicit rule for the sequence.

5. $a_1 = -12, a_n = a_{n-1} + 16$

6. $a_1 = 158, a_n = a_{n-1} - 7$

7. $a_1 = 2, a_n = -6a_{n-1}$

8. $a_1 = -\frac{1}{2}, a_n = 100a_{n-1}$

9. SAVINGS Juliana has saved \$82 so far to buy a bicycle. She saves an additional \$30 each month. The explicit rule $a_n = 30n + 82$ gives the amount saved after n months. Write a recursive rule for the amount Juliana has saved n months from now.

10. SOUP CANS A grocery store arranges cans in a pyramid-shaped display with 20 cans in the bottom row and 2 fewer cans in each subsequent row going up. The number of cans in each row is represented by the recursive rule $a_1 = 20, a_n = a_{n-1} - 2$. Write an explicit rule for the number of cans in row n.

11. SALARY Linda's salary is given by the explicit rule $a_n = 35{,}000(1.04)^{n-1}$, where n is the number of years she has worked. Write a recursive rule for her salary.

12. DEPRECIATION The value of Tim's car is given by the recursive rule $a_1 = 25{,}600$, $a_n = 0.86a_{n-1}$, where n is the number of years since Tim bought the car. Write an explicit rule for the value of Tim's car after n years.

1. **MULTI-STEP PROBLEM** A ball is dropped from a height of 12 feet. Each time the ball hits the ground, it bounces to 70% of its previous height.

   a. Write an infinite series to model the total distance traveled by the ball, excluding the distance traveled before the first bounce.

   b. Find the total distance traveled by the ball, including the distance traveled before the first bounce.

2. **MULTI-STEP PROBLEM** A fractal tree starts with a single branch (the trunk). At each stage, the new branches from the previous stage each grow two more branches as shown.

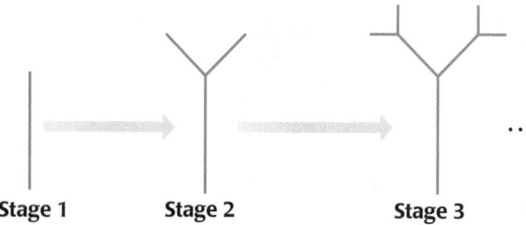

Stage 1   Stage 2   Stage 3

   a. List the number of *new* branches in each of the first six stages.

   b. Is the sequence of numbers from part (a) *arithmetic*, *geometric*, or *neither*?

   c. Write an explicit rule and a recursive rule for the sequence from part (a).

3. **GRIDDED ANSWER** What is the sum of the first three iterates of the function $f(x) = x^2 - 8$ when the initial value is $x_0 = 2$?

4. **OPEN-ENDED** Give an example of an explicit rule for a sequence and a recursive rule for the same sequence.

5. **SHORT RESPONSE** Why does the sum of an infinite geometric series not exist if $|r| \geq 1$ where r is the common ratio?

6. **SHORT RESPONSE** The length ℓ_1 of the first loop of a spring is 16 inches. The length ℓ_2 of the second loop is 0.9 times the length of the first loop. The length ℓ_3 of the third loop is 0.9 times the length of the second loop, and so on. If the spring could have infinitely many loops, would its length be *finite* or *infinite*? *Explain*. If its length is finite, find the length.

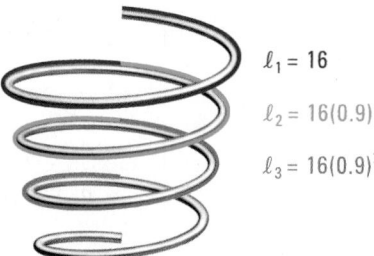

$\ell_1 = 16$

$\ell_2 = 16(0.9)$

$\ell_3 = 16(0.9)^2$

7. **EXTENDED RESPONSE** You take out a five year loan of $10,000 to buy a car. The loan has an annual interest rate of 6.5% compounded monthly. Each month you make a monthly payment of $196 (except the last month when you make a payment of only $165).

   a. Find the monthly interest rate. Then write a recursive rule for the amount of money you owe after n months.

   b. How much money do you owe after 12 months?

   c. Suppose you had decided to pay an additional $50 with each monthly payment. Use a graphing calculator to find the number of months you would have needed to repay the loan.

   d. In your opinion, is it beneficial to pay the additional $50 with each payment? *Explain* your reasoning.

8. **GRIDDED ANSWER** A tree farm initially has 8000 trees. Each year 10% of the trees are harvested and 500 seedlings are planted. What number of trees eventually exists on the farm after an extended period of time?

9. **OPEN-ENDED** Write an infinite geometric series that has a sum of 4.

BIG IDEAS
For Your Notebook

Big Idea 1

Analyze Sequences

The information below highlights the similarities and differences between arithmetic and geometric sequences.

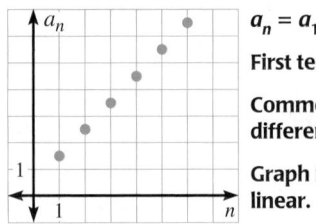

Arithmetic Sequence

$a_n = a_1 + (n - 1)d$

First term: a_1

Common difference: d

Graph is linear.

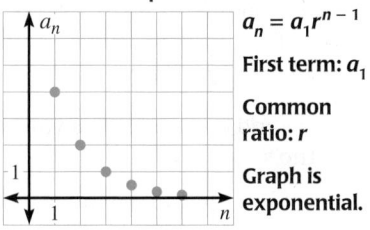

Geometric Sequence

$a_n = a_1 r^{n - 1}$

First term: a_1

Common ratio: r

Graph is exponential.

Big Idea 2

Find Sums of Series

The most common formulas for sums of series are shown below.

Arithmetic Series	Geometric Series	Infinite Geometric Series
Sum of the first n terms:	Sum of the first n terms:	Sum of the series:
$S_n = n\left(\dfrac{a_1 + a_n}{2}\right)$	$S_n = a_1\left(\dfrac{1 - r^n}{1 - r}\right), r \neq 1$	$S = \dfrac{a_1}{1 - r}, \ |r| < 1$
Example:	Example:	Example:
$4 + 9 + 14 + 19 + 24$	$3 + 6 + 12 + 24$	$5 + 1 + 0.2 + 0.04 + \cdots$
$S_5 = 5\left(\dfrac{4 + 24}{2}\right) = 70$	$S_4 = 3\left(\dfrac{1 - 2^4}{1 - 2}\right) = 45$	$S = \dfrac{5}{1 - 0.2} = 6.25$

Other common sum formulas:

$$\sum_{i=1}^{n} 1 = n \qquad \sum_{i=1}^{n} i = \frac{n(n + 1)}{2} \qquad \sum_{i=1}^{n} i^2 = \frac{n(n + 1)(2n + 1)}{6}$$

Big Idea 3

Use Recursive Rules

The table shows explicit and recursive rules for arithmetic and geometric sequences.

	Explicit Rule	Recursive Rule
Arithmetic Sequence Example: 3, 5, 7, 9, 11, . . .	$a_n = a_1 + (n - 1)d$ $a_n = 1 + 2n$	$a_n = a_{n-1} + d$ $a_1 = 3, a_n = a_{n-1} + 2$
Geometric Sequence Example: 8, 4, 2, 1, 0.5, . . .	$a_n = a_1 r^{n-1}$ $a_n = 8(0.5)^{n-1}$	$a_n = r \cdot a_{n-1}$ $a_1 = 8, a_n = 0.5a_{n-1}$

REVIEW KEY VOCABULARY

• sequence	• arithmetic sequence	• geometric series
• terms of a sequence	• common difference	• partial sum
• series	• arithmetic series	• explicit rule
• summation notation	• geometric sequence	• recursive rule
• sigma notation	• common ratio	• iteration

VOCABULARY EXERCISES

1. Copy and complete: The values in the range of a sequence are called the __?__ of the sequence.

2. **WRITING** How can you determine whether a sequence is arithmetic?

3. Copy and complete: A(n) __?__ rule gives a_n as a function of the term's position number n in the sequence.

4. Copy and complete: In a(n) __?__ sequence, the ratio of any term to the previous term is constant.

REVIEW EXAMPLES AND EXERCISES

Use the review examples and exercises below to check your understanding of the concepts you have learned in each lesson of this chapter.

7.1 Define and Use Sequences and Series

EXAMPLE

Find the sum of the series $\displaystyle\sum_{i=1}^{4} (i^2 - 4)$.

$a_1 = 1^2 - 4 = -3$	First term
$a_2 = 2^2 - 4 = 0$	Second term
$a_3 = 3^2 - 4 = 5$	Third term
$a_4 = 4^2 - 4 = 12$	Fourth term

The sum of the series is $\displaystyle\sum_{i=1}^{4} (i^2 - 4) = -3 + 0 + 5 + 12 = 14$.

EXERCISES

EXAMPLES
5 and 6
for Exs. 5–8

Find the sum of the series.

5. $\displaystyle\sum_{n=1}^{6} (n^2 + 7)$ 6. $\displaystyle\sum_{i=2}^{6} (10 - 4i)$ 7. $\displaystyle\sum_{i=1}^{17} i$ 8. $\displaystyle\sum_{k=1}^{25} k^2$

7.2 Analyze Arithmetic Sequences and Series

EXAMPLE

Write a rule for the nth term of the sequence 9, 13, 17, 21, 25, ...

The sequence is arithmetic with first term $a_1 = 9$ and common difference $d = 4$. So, a rule for the nth term is:

$$a_n = a_1 + (n - 1)d \qquad \text{Write general rule.}$$

$$= 9 + (n - 1)(4) \qquad \text{Substitute 9 for } a_1 \text{ and 4 for } d.$$

$$= 5 + 4n \qquad \text{Simplify.}$$

EXERCISES

**EXAMPLES
2, 3, 4, and 5
for Exs. 9–16**

Write a rule for the nth term of the arithmetic sequence.

9. $8, 5, 2, -1, -4, \ldots$ **10.** $d = 7, a_8 = 54$ **11.** $a_4 = 27, a_{11} = 69$

Find the sum of the series.

12. $\displaystyle\sum_{i=1}^{15} (3 + 2i)$ **13.** $\displaystyle\sum_{i=1}^{26} (25 - 3i)$ **14.** $\displaystyle\sum_{i=1}^{22} (6i - 5)$ **15.** $\displaystyle\sum_{i=1}^{30} (-84 + 8i)$

16. COMPUTER Joe buys a \$600 computer on layaway by making a \$200 down payment and then paying \$25 per month. Write a rule for the total amount of money paid on the computer after n months.

7.3 Analyze Geometric Sequences and Series

EXAMPLE

Find the sum of the series $\displaystyle\sum_{i=1}^{7} 5(3)^{i-1}$.

The series is geometric with first term $a_1 = 5$ and common ratio $r = 3$.

$$S_7 = a_1\left(\frac{1 - r^7}{1 - r}\right) \qquad \text{Write rule for } S_7.$$

$$= 5\left(\frac{1 - 3^7}{1 - 3}\right) \qquad \text{Substitute 5 for } a_1 \text{ and 3 for } r.$$

$$= 5465 \qquad \text{Simplify.}$$

EXERCISES

**EXAMPLES
2, 3, 4, and 5
for Exs. 17–23**

Write a rule for the nth term of the geometric sequence.

17. $256, 64, 16, 4, 1, \ldots$ **18.** $r = 5, a_2 = 200$ **19.** $a_1 = 144, a_3 = 16$

Find the sum of the series.

20. $\displaystyle\sum_{i=1}^{6} 3(5)^{i-1}$ **21.** $\displaystyle\sum_{i=1}^{9} 8(2)^{i-1}$ **22.** $\displaystyle\sum_{i=1}^{5} 15\left(\frac{2}{3}\right)^{i-1}$ **23.** $\displaystyle\sum_{i=1}^{7} 40\left(\frac{1}{2}\right)^{i-1}$

7.4 Find Sums of Infinite Geometric Series

EXAMPLE

Find the sum of the series $\sum_{i=1}^{\infty}\left(\frac{4}{5}\right)^{i-1}$, if it exists.

For this series, $a_1 = 1$ and $r = \frac{4}{5}$. Because $|r| < 1$, the sum of this series exists.

The sum is $S = \dfrac{a_1}{1-r} = \dfrac{1}{1-\frac{4}{5}} = 5$.

EXERCISES

**EXAMPLES
2 and 5**
for Exs. 24–31

Find the sum of the infinite geometric series, if it exists.

24. $\sum_{i=1}^{\infty} 3\left(\frac{5}{8}\right)^{i-1}$ **25.** $\sum_{i=1}^{\infty} 7\left(-\frac{3}{4}\right)^{i-1}$ **26.** $\sum_{i=1}^{\infty} 4(1.3)^{i-1}$ **27.** $\sum_{i=1}^{\infty} -0.2(0.5)^{i-1}$

Write the repeating decimal as a fraction in lowest terms.

28. $0.888\ldots$ **29.** $0.546546546\ldots$ **30.** $0.3787878\ldots$ **31.** $0.7838383\ldots$

7.5 Use Recursive Rules with Sequences and Functions

EXAMPLE

Write a recursive rule for the sequence 6, 10, 14, 18, 22, ...

The sequence is arithmetic with first term $a_1 = 6$ and common difference $d = 10 - 6 = 4$.

$a_n = a_{n-1} + d$ **General recursive rule for a_n**

$\quad = a_{n-1} + 4$ **Substitute 4 for d.**

So, a recursive rule for the sequence is $a_1 = 6$, $a_n = a_{n-1} + 4$.

EXERCISES

**EXAMPLES
1, 2, and 3**
for Exs. 32–38

Write the first five terms of the sequence.

32. $a_1 = 4$, $a_n = a_{n-1} + 9$ **33.** $a_1 = 8$, $a_n = 5a_{n-1}$ **34.** $a_1 = 2$, $a_n = n \cdot a_{n-1}$

Write a recursive rule for the sequence.

35. 6, 18, 54, 162, 486, . . .   **36.** 4, 6, 9, 13, 18, . . .   **37.** 7, 13, 19, 25, 31, . . .

38. POPULATION A town's population increases at a rate of about 1% per year. In 2000, the town had a population of 26,000. Write a recursive rule for the town's population P_n in year n. Let $n = 1$ represent 2000.

Tell whether the sequence is *arithmetic*, *geometric*, or *neither*. Explain.

1. $5, 9, 13, 17, \ldots$ **2.** $3, 6, 12, 24, \ldots$ **3.** $40, 10, \dfrac{5}{2}, \dfrac{5}{8}, \ldots$ **4.** $4, 7, 12, 19, \ldots$

Write the first six terms of the sequence.

5. $a_n = 6 - n^2$ **6.** $a_n = 7n^3$ **7.** $a_1 = 4$
$a_n = 5a_{n-1}$ **8.** $a_1 = -1$
$a_n = a_{n-1} + 6$

Write the next term of the sequence, and then write a rule for the *n*th term.

9. $5, 11, 17, 23, \ldots$ **10.** $3, 15, 75, 375, \ldots$ **11.** $\dfrac{6}{5}, \dfrac{7}{10}, \dfrac{8}{15}, \dfrac{9}{20}, \ldots$ **12.** $1.6, 3.2, 4.8, 6.4, \ldots$

Find the sum of the series.

13. $\displaystyle\sum_{i=1}^{48} i$ **14.** $\displaystyle\sum_{n=1}^{28} n^2$ **15.** $\displaystyle\sum_{i=1}^{10} (4i - 9)$ **16.** $\displaystyle\sum_{i=1}^{19} (2i + 5)$

17. $\displaystyle\sum_{i=1}^{5} 9(2)^{i-1}$ **18.** $\displaystyle\sum_{i=1}^{6} 12\left(\dfrac{1}{3}\right)^{i-1}$ **19.** $\displaystyle\sum_{i=1}^{\infty} 8\left(\dfrac{3}{4}\right)^{i-1}$ **20.** $\displaystyle\sum_{i=1}^{\infty} 20\left(\dfrac{3}{10}\right)^{i-1}$

Write the repeating decimal as a fraction in lowest terms.

21. $0.111\ldots$ **22.** $0.464646\ldots$ **23.** $0.187187187\ldots$ **24.** $0.3252525\ldots$

Write a recursive rule for the sequence.

25. $2, 12, 72, 432, \ldots$ **26.** $3, 10, 17, 24, \ldots$ **27.** $135, 45, 15, 5, \ldots$ **28.** $1, -3, 9, -27, \ldots$

Find the first three iterates of the function for the given initial value.

29. $f(x) = 3x - 7,\ x_0 = 4$ **30.** $f(x) = 8 - 5x,\ x_0 = 1$ **31.** $f(x) = x^2 + 2,\ x_0 = -1$

32. QUILTS Use the pattern of checkerboard quilts shown.

$n = 1, a_n = 1$ $n = 2, a_n = 2$ $n = 3, a_n = 5$ $n = 4, a_n = 8$

a. What does n represent for each quilt? What does a_n represent?

b. Make a table that shows n and a_n for $n = 1, 2, 3, 4, 5, 6, 7$, and 8.

c. Use the rule $a_n = \dfrac{n^2}{2} + \dfrac{1}{4}[1 - (-1)^n]$ to find a_n for $n = 1, 2, 3, 4, 5, 6, 7$, and 8. *Compare* these values with the results in your table. What can you conclude about the sequence defined by this rule?

33. AUDITIONS Several rounds of auditions are being held to cast the three main parts in a play. There are 3072 actors at the first round of auditions. In each successive round of auditions, one fourth of the actors from the previous round remain. Find a rule for the number a_n of actors in the nth round of auditions. For what values of n does your rule make sense?

CONTEXT-BASED MULTIPLE CHOICE QUESTIONS

Some of the information you need to solve a context-based multiple choice question may appear in a table, a diagram, or a graph.

PROBLEM 1

The frequencies (in hertz) of the notes on a piano form a geometric sequence. The frequencies of G (labeled "8") and A (labeled "10") are shown in the diagram. What is the approximate frequency of E flat (labeled "4")?

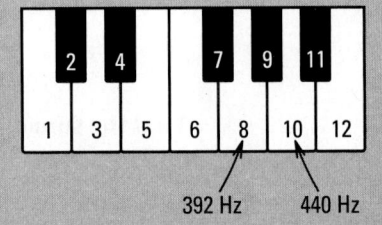

A 247 Hz   **B** 311 Hz

C 330 Hz   **D** 554 Hz

Plan

INTERPRET THE DIAGRAM The diagram gives you the frequencies of the 8th and 10th notes. Use these frequencies to find the frequency of the 4th note.

Solution

STEP 1
Write a system of equations.

Let a_n be the frequency (in hertz) of the nth note. Because the frequencies form a geometric sequence, a rule for a_n has the form $a_n = a_1 r^{n-1}$. From the diagram, $a_8 = 392$ and $a_{10} = 440$. Use these values to write a system of equations.

$a_8 = a_1 r^{8-1}$ ⟹ $392 = a_1 r^7$ **Equation 1**

$a_{10} = a_1 r^{10-1}$ ⟹ $440 = a_1 r^9$ **Equation 2**

STEP 2
Solve the system of equations to find the values of r and a_1.

$a_1 = \dfrac{392}{r^7}$ **Solve Equation 1 for a_1.**

$440 = \dfrac{392}{r^7} \cdot r^9$ **Substitute $\dfrac{392}{r^7}$ for a_1 in Equation 2.**

$440 = 392r^2$ **Simplify.**

$1.12 \approx r^2$ **Divide each side by 392.**

$1.06 \approx r$ **Take positive square root of each side.**

Find a_1 by substituting the value of r into revised Equation 1.

$a_1 = \dfrac{392}{r^7} = \dfrac{392}{(1.06)^7} \approx 261$

STEP 3
Write a rule for the nth term and find a_4.

A rule for the sequence is $a_n = a_1 r^{n-1} = 261(1.06)^{n-1}$.

So, $a_4 = 261(1.06)^3 \approx 311$.

▶ The correct answer is B.   **A** **B** **C** **D**

> **PROBLEM 2**

> The first 4 terms of an infinite arithmetic sequence
> are shown in the graph. Which rule describes
> the nth term in the sequence?
>
> **Ⓐ** $a_n = 2n - 5$ **Ⓑ** $a_n = 2n + 5$
>
> **Ⓒ** $a_n = 5n - 2$ **Ⓓ** $a_n = n + 5$

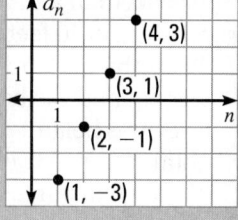

Plan

INTERPRET THE GRAPH In order to find a rule for the sequence, you must first use the graph to write the terms of the sequence.

Solution

STEP 1
......................➤ The points shown in the graph are:
Write the terms of the
sequence.
$(1, -3), (2, -1), (3, 1), (4, 3)$

Therefore, the sequence is $-3, -1, 1, 3, \ldots$.

STEP 2
......................➤ The first term a_1 of the sequence is -3.
Find the first term and
the common difference.
Because each term after the first is 2 more than the previous term, the common difference d is 2.

STEP 3
......................➤ $a_n = a_1 + (n - 1)d$ **Write general rule for an arithmetic sequence.**
Write a rule for the nth
term.
$\quad = -3 + (n - 1)2$ **Substitute −3 for a_1 and 2 for d.**

$\quad = -3 + 2n - 2$ **Distributive property**

$\quad = 2n - 5$ **Simplify.**

▸ The correct answer is A. **Ⓐ** **Ⓑ** **Ⓒ** **Ⓓ**

PRACTICE

In Exercises 1 and 2, use the graph in Problem 2.

1. What is the value of a_{15}?

    Ⓐ -35 **Ⓑ** 25

    Ⓒ 30   **Ⓓ** 165

2. Which statement is true about the sequence that is graphed?

    Ⓐ The sum of the first 14 terms is 140.

    Ⓑ The value of a_{20} is 40.

    Ⓒ A recursive rule for the sequence is $a_1 = 2, a_n = a_{n-1} - 5$.

    Ⓓ The ratio of any term to the previous term is constant.

7 ★ *Standardized* TEST PRACTICE

MULTIPLE CHOICE

1. The diagram shows the bounce heights of a basketball and a baseball dropped from a height of 10 feet. On each bounce, the basketball bounces to 36% of its previous height, and the baseball bounces to 30% of its previous height. About how much greater is the total distance traveled by the basketball than the total distance traveled by the baseball?

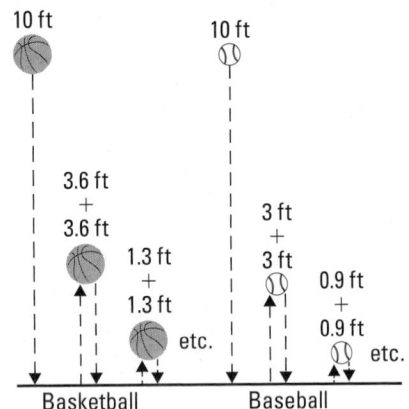

10 ft   10 ft

3.6 ft + 3.6 ft
1.3 ft + 1.3 ft
etc.

3 ft + 3 ft
0.9 ft + 0.9 ft
etc.

Basketball   Baseball

Ⓐ 1.34 feet Ⓑ 2.00 feet

Ⓒ 2.62 feet Ⓓ 5.63 feet

2. The table shows the domain and range of a sequence. Which recursive rule describes the sequence?

Domain	1	2	3	4	5
Range	20	10	5	2.5	1.25

Ⓐ $a_1 = 20, a_n = a_{n-1} + 10$

Ⓑ $a_1 = 20, a_n = a_{n-1} - 10$

Ⓒ $a_1 = 20, a_n = 0.5a_{n-1}$

Ⓓ $a_1 = 20, a_n = 2a_{n-1}$

3. What type of sequence is graphed at the right?

Ⓐ Arithmetic

Ⓑ Geometric with $0 < r < 1$

Ⓒ Geometric with $r > 1$

Ⓓ Neither arithmetic nor geometric

In Exercises 4 and 5, use the information below. Cheryl is researching her lineage for a history project. So far, she has created a family tree for three generations, as shown below. Cheryl is only including relatives from whom she is directly descended. Siblings are not included.

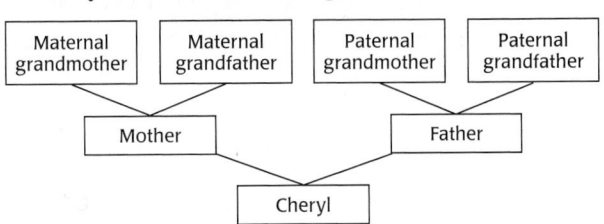

Maternal grandmother | Maternal grandfather | Paternal grandmother | Paternal grandfather

Mother   Father

Cheryl

4. Assume that Cheryl is in generation 1, her parents are in generation 2, and so on. Let a_n be the number of relatives in generation n. What is a rule for a_n?

Ⓐ $a_n = n + 2$ Ⓑ $a_n = 2^{n-1}$

Ⓒ $a_n = 2^n$ Ⓓ $a_n = 2^{n+1}$

5. Cheryl creates a family tree with 8 generations of her family. How many people are in her family tree?

Ⓐ 8 Ⓑ 64

Ⓒ 128 Ⓓ 255

In Exercises 6 and 7, use the diagram of a stack of blocks.

6. Which rule describes the number of blocks in the *n*th layer, where $n = 1$ represents the top layer?

Ⓐ $a_n = n + 1$ Ⓑ $a_n = n(n + 1)$

Ⓒ $a_n = 2n^2$ Ⓓ $a_n = n^2 + 1$

7. Which sum gives the number of blocks shown?

Ⓐ $\sum_{i=2}^{20} (i + 1)$ Ⓑ $\sum_{i=1}^{4} (i + 1)$

Ⓒ $\sum_{i=2}^{20} i(i + 1)$ Ⓓ $\sum_{i=1}^{4} i(i + 1)$

GRIDDED ANSWER

8. Two terms of a geometric sequence are $a_3 = 12$ and $a_5 = 48$. What is the value of a_1?

9. What is the eighth term of this sequence?

$$-4, 12, -36, 108, \ldots$$

10. What is the sum of the following series?

$$\sum_{i=1}^{5} 0.5(2)^{i-1}$$

11. Write the repeating decimal 0.151515... as a fraction in lowest terms.

12. What is the sum of the first three iterates of the function $f(x) = 2x - 1$ for an initial value of $x_0 = 2$?

13. What is the eighth term of the sequence given by the recursive rule $a_1 = 0.5$, $a_n = 2a_{n-1} + 5$?

14. What is the sum of the first 15 terms of the sequence $a_n = 6n + 3$?

15. What is the common difference d of the sequence 3, 6, 9, 12, ...?

SHORT RESPONSE

16. You receive an e-mail that you are to forward to 10 of your friends. There were 10 recipients in the first round, 100 recipients in the second round, and so on. By the time you receive the e-mail, it has already been sent to just over 100 million people. What round of recipients must you be in? *Explain* your reasoning.

17. The number of diagonals in a convex polygon is given by the formula $d_n = \frac{1}{2}n(n - 3)$ where n is the number of sides of the polygon ($n \geq 3$). Write the first six terms of the sequence given by the formula. Then tell whether the sequence is *arithmetic, geometric,* or *neither. Explain.*

18. During a baseball season, a company pledges a donation to a charity of $5000 plus $100 for every home run hit by the local team. Does it make more sense to represent this situation using a sequence or a series? *Explain* your reasoning.

EXTENDED RESPONSE

19. A running track is shaped like a rectangle with two semicircular ends, as shown. The track has 8 lanes that are each 1.22 meters wide. The lanes are numbered from 1 to 8 starting from the inside lane. The length of each line segment that extends from the center of the left semicircle to the inside of a lane is called the lane's curve radius.

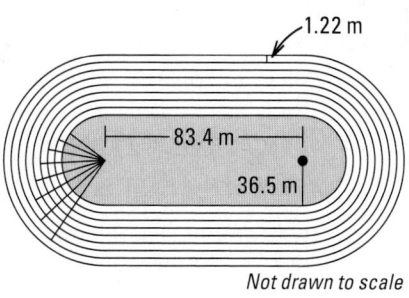

Not drawn to scale

a. Is the sequence formed by the curve radii *arithmetic, geometric,* or *neither*? *Explain.*

b. Write a formula for the sequence from part (a).

c. World records must be set on tracks that have a curve radius of at most 50 meters in the outside lane. Does the track shown meet the requirement? *Explain.*

20. Mark takes out a loan for $16,000 with an interest rate of 0.75% per month. At the end of each month he makes a payment of $300.

a. Write a recursive rule for the balance a_n of the loan at the beginning of the nth month.

b. How much will Mark owe at the beginning of the 18th month?

c. How long will it take Mark to pay off the loan?

d. If Mark pays $350 instead of $300 each month, how long will it take him to pay off the loan? Will he end up paying less overall? *Explain.*

8 Quadratic Relations and Conic Sections

Lesson
8.1 CC.9-12.G.GPE.4
8.2 CC.9-12.G.GPE.2
8.3 CC.9-12.G.GPE.1
8.4 CC.9-12.G.GPE.3 (+)
8.5 CC.9-12.G.GPE.3 (+)
8.6 CC.9-12.G.GPE.3 (+)
8.7 CC.9-12.A.REI.7

Before

Previously, you learned the following skills, which you'll use in this chapter: simplifying radical expressions, rewriting equations, and completing the square.

Are You Ready?

VOCABULARY CHECK

Copy and complete the statement.

1. The graph of a(n) __?__ function is a **parabola**.

2. The graph of the **rational function** $y = \dfrac{2}{x}$, shown at the right, is a __?__.

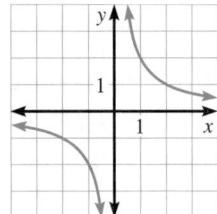

3. Two equations of the form $Ax + By = C$ and $Dx + Ey = F$ form a __?__ **system of equations**.

SKILLS CHECK

Simplify the expression.

4. $\sqrt{25} \cdot \sqrt{144}$

5. $\sqrt{3(12)}$

6. $\sqrt{\dfrac{9}{16}}$

Solve the equation for y.

7. $6x - 3y = 12$

8. $4y + 8x = 14$

9. $3x + 7y = 42$

Find the value of c that makes the expression a perfect square trinomial, and write the expression as the square of a binomial.

10. $x^2 - 4x + c$

11. $x^2 - 8x + c$

12. $x^2 + 3x + c$

In this chapter, you will apply the big ideas listed below and reviewed in the Chapter Summary. You will also use the key vocabulary listed below.

Big Ideas

1 Writing equations of conic sections

2 Graphing equations of conic sections

3 Solving quadratic systems

KEY VOCABULARY

- distance formula
- focus, foci
- directrix
- circle
- ellipse

- vertices
- major axis
- co-vertices
- minor axis
- hyperbola

- transverse axis
- conic sections
- general second-degree equation
- quadratic system

Why?

You can use conic sections to describe the shapes of real-world objects. For example, you can use a parabola to model the cross section of a radio telescope.

Animated Algebra

The animation illustrated below helps you answer a question from this chapter: How do the dimensions of a radio telescope determine the equation that models its cross section?

Radio telescopes have a parabolic cross section that concentrates radio waves.

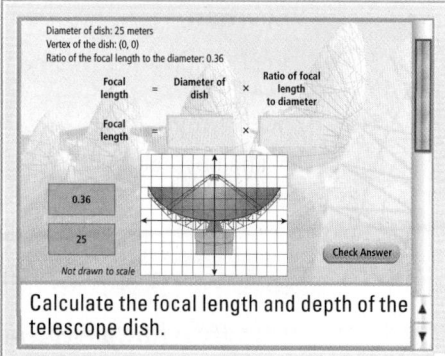

Calculate the focal length and depth of the telescope dish.

Animated Algebra at my.hrw.com

8.1 Apply the Distance and Midpoint Formulas

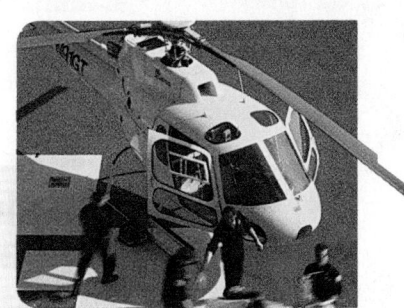

Before	You found the slope of a line passing through two points.
Now	You will find the length and midpoint of a line segment.
Why?	So you can find real-world distances, as in Exs. 48–51.

Key Vocabulary
• distance formula
• midpoint formula

CC.9-12.G.GPE.4 Use coordinates to prove simple geometric theorems algebraically.

To find the distance d between $A(x_1, y_1)$ and $B(x_2, y_2)$, apply the Pythagorean theorem to right triangle ABC.

$$(AB)^2 = (AC)^2 + (BC)^2$$
$$d^2 = (x_2 - x_1)^2 + (y_2 - y_1)^2$$
$$d = \sqrt{(x_2 - x_1)^2 + (y_2 - y_1)^2}$$

The final equation is the **distance formula**.

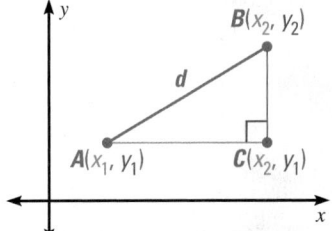

KEY CONCEPT · *For Your Notebook*

The Distance Formula

The distance d between (x_1, y_1) and (x_2, y_2) is $d = \sqrt{(x_2 - x_1)^2 + (y_2 - y_1)^2}$.

EXAMPLE 1   **Standardized Test Practice**

> **What is the distance between (−3, 5) and (4, −1)?**
>
> **(A)** $\sqrt{13}$ **(B)** $\sqrt{65}$ **(C)** $\sqrt{85}$ **(D)** 13

Solution

Let $(x_1, y_1) = (-3, 5)$ and $(x_2, y_2) = (4, -1)$.

$$d = \sqrt{(x_2 - x_1)^2 + (y_2 - y_1)^2} = \sqrt{(4 - (-3))^2 + (-1 - 5)^2} = \sqrt{49 + 36} = \sqrt{85}$$

▶ The correct answer is C. **(A) (B) (C) (D)**

EXAMPLE 2   **Classify a triangle using the distance formula**

Classify △ABC as *scalene*, *isosceles*, or *equilateral*.

$$AB = \sqrt{(7 - 4)^2 + (3 - 6)^2} = \sqrt{18} = 3\sqrt{2}$$

$$BC = \sqrt{(2 - 7)^2 + (1 - 3)^2} = \sqrt{29}$$

$$AC = \sqrt{(2 - 4)^2 + (1 - 6)^2} = \sqrt{29}$$

▶ Because $BC = AC$, △ABC is isosceles.

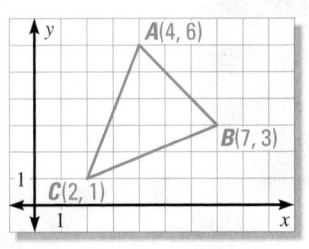

Nick Vedros & Assoc./Getty Images

1. What is the distance between $(3, -3)$ and $(-1, 5)$?

2. The vertices of a triangle are $R(-1, 3)$, $S(5, 2)$, and $T(3, 6)$. Classify $\triangle RST$ as *scalene*, *isosceles*, or *equilateral*.

KEY CONCEPT   *For Your Notebook*

The Midpoint Formula

A line segment's *midpoint* is equidistant from the segment's endpoints. The **midpoint formula**, shown below, gives the midpoint of the line segment joining $A(x_1, y_1)$ and $B(x_2, y_2)$.

$$M\left(\frac{x_1 + x_2}{2}, \frac{y_1 + y_2}{2}\right)$$

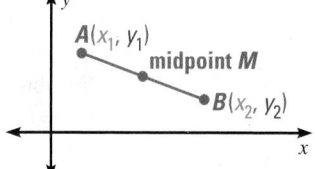

In words, each coordinate of M is the mean of the corresponding coordinates of A and B.

EXAMPLE 3   **Find the midpoint of a line segment**

Find the midpoint of the line segment joining $(-5, 1)$ and $(-1, 6)$.

Solution

Let $(x_1, y_1) = (-5, 1)$ and $(x_2, y_2) = (-1, 6)$.

$$\left(\frac{x_1 + x_2}{2}, \frac{y_1 + y_2}{2}\right) = \left(\frac{-5 + (-1)}{2}, \frac{1 + 6}{2}\right) = \left(-3, \frac{7}{2}\right)$$

Animated **Algebra**   at my.hrw.com

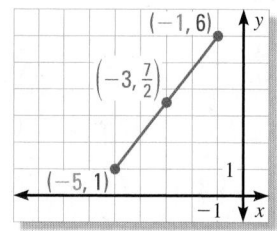

EXAMPLE 4   **Find a perpendicular bisector**

REVIEW EQUATIONS
For help with writing equations of perpendicular lines, you may want to review writing equations of lines.

Write an equation for the perpendicular bisector of the line segment joining $A(-3, 4)$ and $B(5, 6)$.

Solution

STEP 1 **Find** the midpoint of the line segment.

$$\left(\frac{x_1 + x_2}{2}, \frac{y_1 + y_2}{2}\right) = \left(\frac{-3 + 5}{2}, \frac{4 + 6}{2}\right) = (1, 5)$$

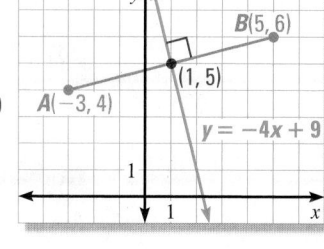

STEP 2 **Calculate** the slope of $\overline{AB}$.

$$m = \frac{y_2 - y_1}{x_2 - x_1} = \frac{6 - 4}{5 - (-3)} = \frac{2}{8} = \frac{1}{4}$$

STEP 3 **Find** the slope of the perpendicular bisector: $-\dfrac{1}{m} = -\dfrac{1}{1/4} = -4$.

STEP 4 **Use** point-slope form: $y - 5 = -4(x - 1)$, or $y = -4x + 9$.

▶ An equation for the perpendicular bisector of $\overline{AB}$ is $y = -4x + 9$.

FINDING A CIRCLE'S CENTER Recall from geometry that the perpendicular bisector of any chord of a circle passes through the circle's center. You can use this theorem to find the center of a circle given three points on the circle.

EXAMPLE 5 **Solve a multi-step problem**

ASTEROID CRATER Many scientists believe that an asteroid slammed into Earth about 65 million years ago on what is now Mexico's Yucatan peninsula, creating an enormous crater that is now deeply buried by sediment. Use the labeled points on the outline of the circular crater to estimate its diameter. (Each unit in the coordinate plane represents 1 mile.)

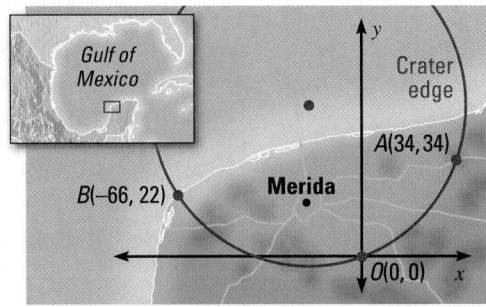

Solution

STEP 1 **Write** equations for the perpendicular bisectors of $\overline{AO}$ and $\overline{OB}$ using the method of Example 4.

$y = -x + 34$ Perpendicular bisector of $\overline{AO}$

$y = 3x + 110$ Perpendicular bisector of $\overline{OB}$

STEP 2 **Find** the coordinates of the center of the circle, where $\overline{AO}$ and $\overline{OB}$ intersect, by solving the system formed by the two equations in Step 1.

> **REVIEW SYSTEMS**
> You may want to review solving linear systems algebraically.

$y = -x + 34$ **Write first equation.**

$3x + 110 = -x + 34$ **Substitute for y.**

$4x = -76$ **Simplify.**

$x = -19$ **Solve for x.**

$y = -(-19) + 34$ **Substitute the x-value into the first equation.**

$y = 53$ **Solve for y.**

The center of the circle is $C(-19, 53)$.

STEP 3 **Calculate** the radius of the circle using the distance formula. The radius is the distance between C and any of the three given points.

$$OC = \sqrt{(-19 - 0)^2 + (53 - 0)^2} = \sqrt{3170} \approx 56.3$$

Use $(x_1, y_1) = (0, 0)$ and $(x_2, y_2) = (-19, 53)$.

▶ The crater has a diameter of about $2(56.3) = 112.6$ miles.

 GUIDED PRACTICE for Examples 3, 4, and 5

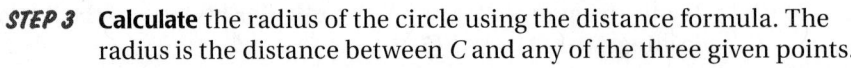

For the line segment joining the two given points, (a) find the midpoint and (b) write an equation for the perpendicular bisector.

3. $(0, 0)$, $(-4, 12)$ **4.** $(-2, 1)$, $(4, -7)$ **5.** $(3, 8)$, $(-5, -10)$

6. The points $(0, 0)$, $(6, -2)$, and $(16, 8)$ lie on a circle. Use the method given in Example 5 to find the diameter of the circle.

8.1 EXERCISES

SKILL PRACTICE

1. VOCABULARY State the distance and midpoint formulas.

2. ★ WRITING When finding the midpoint of a line segment joining two points, does it matter which point you choose as (x_1, y_1)? *Explain.*

EXAMPLES 1 and 3
for Exs. 3–21

USING THE FORMULAS Find the distance between the two points. Then find the midpoint of the line segment joining the two points.

3. $(0, 0), (8, 15)$ **4.** $(0, 0), (4, 2)$ **5.** $(0, 6), (5, -4)$

6. $(-7, 0), (5, 3)$ **7.** $(2, -1), (6, -5)$ **8.** $(-1, -2), (8, 4)$

9. $(-4, 8), (8, -4)$ **10.** $(6, -3), (10, -9)$ **11.** $(-4, 4), (5, -4)$

12. $(11, -12), (18, 12)$ **13.** $(-5, 1), (15, 8)$ **14.** $(9, 9), (-16, -16)$

15. $(-3.8, 15), (6.2, -11)$ **16.** $(1.5, 4), (2.3, 9)$ **17.** $(-2.4, -6.7), (3.1, -5.3)$

18. ★ MULTIPLE CHOICE What is the distance between $(-4, 3)$ and $(6, 6)$?

Ⓐ $\sqrt{13}$ Ⓑ $\sqrt{85}$ Ⓒ $\sqrt{109}$ Ⓓ $\sqrt{181}$

19. ★ MULTIPLE CHOICE What is the midpoint of the line segment joining $(-3, 7)$ and $(5, -2)$?

Ⓐ $\left(1, \frac{5}{2}\right)$ Ⓑ $\left(-4, \frac{5}{2}\right)$ Ⓒ $\left(1, \frac{9}{2}\right)$ Ⓓ $\left(-4, \frac{9}{2}\right)$

ERROR ANALYSIS *Describe* and correct the error in finding the distance between the two points.

20. $(5, -1), (2, 6)$

21. $(-4, 3), (2, 8)$

$$d = \sqrt{(2-5)^2 + (6-1)^2}$$
$$= \sqrt{9 + 25} = \sqrt{34}$$ ✗

$$d = \sqrt{(2-(-4))^2 - (8-3)^2}$$
$$= \sqrt{36 - 25} = \sqrt{11}$$ ✗

EXAMPLE 2
for Exs. 22–30

CLASSIFYING TRIANGLES The vertices of a triangle are given. Classify the triangle as *scalene, isosceles,* or *equilateral.*

22. $(-5, 0), (0, 6), (5, 0)$ **23.** $(0, -3), (0, 3), (3, 0)$ **24.** $(3, 5), (5, -3), (7, -3)$

25. $(-2, 5), (1, -1), (4, 6)$ **26.** $(1, 4), (4, 1), (7, 4)$ **27.** $(-4, 1), (-2, 6), (0, -1)$

28. $(-1, -6), (1, 1), (4, -5)$ **29.** $(-4, 3), (2, -1), (8, -1)$ **30.** $(3, 5), (6, 9), (11, 9)$

EXAMPLE 4
for Exs. 31–36

WRITING EQUATIONS Write an equation for the perpendicular bisector of the line segment joining the two points.

31. $(3, 8), (7, 14)$ **32.** $(-5, 6), (1, 8)$ **33.** $(-3, -6), (-1, 2)$

34. $(1, 4), (6, -6)$ **35.** $(-3, -5), (9, -2)$ **36.** $(5, 10), (10, 7)$

37. ★ OPEN-ENDED MATH Find two points not on the lines $x = 4$ or $y = 2$ such that the midpoint of the line segment joining the points is $(4, 2)$.

GEOMETRY A *median* of a triangle is a line segment joining a vertex and the midpoint of the opposite side. The ordered pairs represent vertices of a triangle. Write an equation of the line containing the median that joins the first vertex to the side opposite it.

38. $(8, 4), (0, 0), (10, 0)$ **39.** $(3, 10), (4, 2), (10, 8)$ **40.** $(2, 6), (3, 1), (7, 5)$

FINDING A COORDINATE Use the given distance d between the two points to find the value of x or y.

41. $(0, 3), (x, 5); d = 2\sqrt{10}$ **42.** $(-3, -1), (2, y); d = \sqrt{41}$

43. $(x, 7), (-4, 1); d = 6\sqrt{2}$ **44.** $(1, y), (8, 13); d = \sqrt{74}$

45. REASONING Let (x, y) be any point on the line $y = 2x$. Write and simplify an equation that gives the distance d between (x, y) and $(2, 3)$ as a function of x alone. Then find the coordinates of two points on the line $y = 2x$ that are each $\sqrt{10}$ units from $(2, 3)$.

46. CHALLENGE Show that $M\left(\dfrac{x_1 + x_2}{2}, \dfrac{y_1 + y_2}{2}\right)$ is the midpoint of the line segment with endpoints (x_1, y_1) and (x_2, y_2). To do this, show that M is equidistant from each endpoint and that M lies on the line containing (x_1, y_1) and (x_2, y_2).

PROBLEM SOLVING

EXAMPLE 1
for Exs. 47–52

47. ROBOTS A remote-controlled robot can be instructed to move by entering coordinates on a control panel. If the robot is instructed to move from $(6, 11)$ straight to $(-2, 26)$, how far does the robot move? Assume the coordinates are in meters.

HELICOPTER RESCUE In Exercises 48–51, use the information given to find the distance a medical evacuation ("medevac") helicopter would have to fly to Memorial Medical Center from each location.

The Highway Department in Sangamon County, Illinois, uses a map that has its origin in central Springfield. Each unit on the map represents 1 mile, and the letters N, S, E, and W indicate direction. For example, 4W 5.6N is 4 miles west and 5.6 miles north of the origin. On a coordinate plane, 4W 5.6N corresponds to the point $(-4, 5.6)$. Memorial Medical is at 0 0.5N, or $(0, 0.5)$.

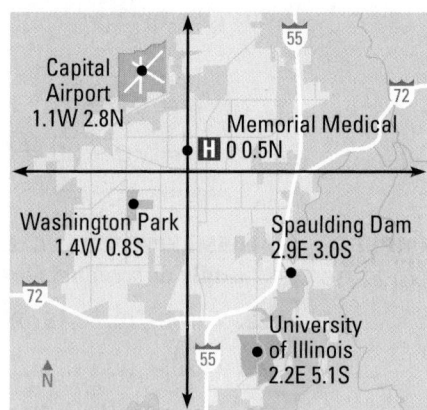

48. Capital Airport   **49.** University of Illinois

50. Washington Park   **51.** Spaulding Dam

52. COMMUTING To get from her home to her office, Li must drive around a lake. If she drives 2 miles north, then 5 miles east, and then 4 miles south, what is the straight-line distance between Li's home and her office?

○ = **See WORKED-OUT SOLUTIONS** in Student Resources   ★ = **STANDARDIZED TEST PRACTICE**

494

Reuters/Corbis

EXAMPLE 3
for Ex. 53

53. **MULTI-STEP PROBLEM** The diagram shows part of a trail system at a nature preserve. Each unit represents 0.1 mile. Suppose that you go from the visitor center *V* to the observation stand *S*, and then take a break at *M*, halfway between the observation stand and the picnic area *P*.

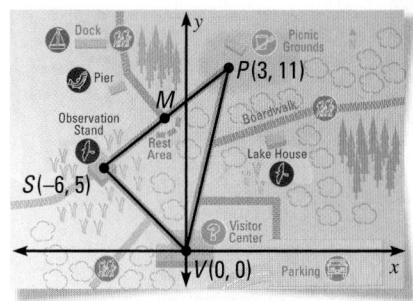

a. What are the coordinates of *M*?

b. What is the total distance traveled from *V* to *M*?

c. What is the distance from *M* back to *V* through *P*?

EXAMPLE 5
for Exs. 54–55

54. **ARCHAEOLOGY** While on an archaeological dig, you uncover a piece of a circular dish. You lay the piece on a coordinate plane and mark three points on the dish's edge at $(-4, 2)$, $(0, 0)$, and $(6, 4)$ where each unit represents 1 inch. What was the original diameter of the dish?

55. **METEOR CRATERS** Five meteor craters are clustered together near Odessa, Texas. Three points on the edge of the circular main crater can be represented by $(-220, 220)$, $(0, 0)$, and $(200, 40)$ where each unit represents 1 foot. What is the diameter of the crater to the nearest 10 feet?

56. ★ **EXTENDED RESPONSE** You are ordering a triangular sail for your sailboat. When you get the sail, you plan to sew a thin decorative strip connecting the midpoints M_1 and M_2 of two sides of the sail, as shown in the diagram.

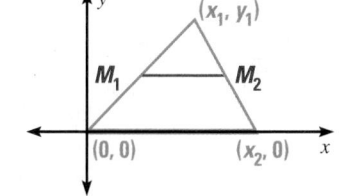

a. Write expressions for the coordinates of M_1 and M_2.

b. Write a simplified expression for the length of the strip. *Compare* this length with the length of the sail's base.

c. Do your results from part (b) depend upon the shape of the triangular sail? *Explain.*

57. **CHALLENGE** At time $t = 0$, a car begins traveling east at 60 miles per hour from a point 100 miles west and 40 miles north of a radio tower. The tower has a transmission range of 50 miles. Use the distance formula to find the times t during which the car is in range of the tower.

8.2 Graph and Write Equations of Parabolas

Before	You graphed and wrote equations of parabolas that open up or down.
Now	You will graph and write equations of parabolas that open left or right.
Why?	So you can model sound projection, as in Ex. 56.

Key Vocabulary
- focus
- directrix
- parabola
- vertex

CC.9-12.G.GPE.2 Derive the equation of a parabola given a focus and directrix.

You know that the graph of $y = ax^2$ is a parabola that opens up or down with vertex (0, 0) and axis of symmetry $x = 0$. On any parabola, each point is equidistant from a point called the **focus** and a line called the **directrix**.

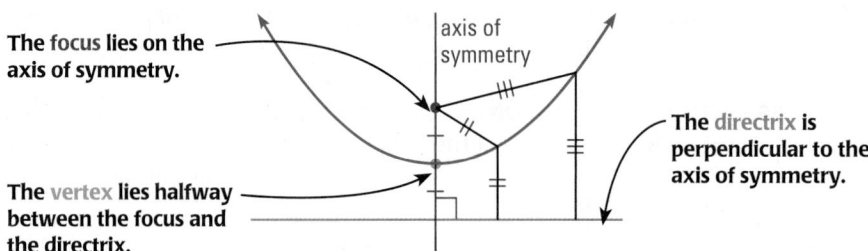

The focus lies on the axis of symmetry.

The vertex lies halfway between the focus and the directrix.

The directrix is perpendicular to the axis of symmetry.

The equation of a parabola that opens up or down and has vertex (0, 0) can also be written in the form $x^2 = 4py$. Parabolas can open left or right as well, in which case the equation has the form $y^2 = 4px$ when the vertex is (0, 0). Note below that for any parabola, the focus and directrix each lie $|p|$ units from the vertex.

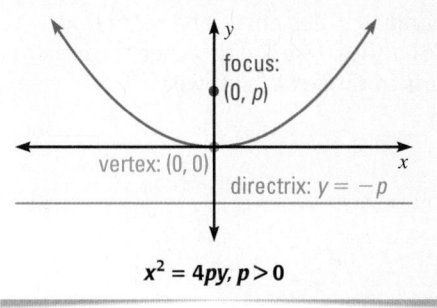

$x^2 = 4py, p > 0$

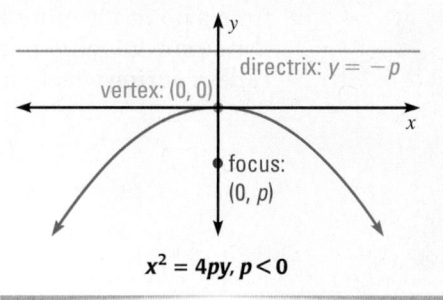

$x^2 = 4py, p < 0$

IDENTIFY FUNCTIONS
Notice that parabolas that open left or right do *not* represent functions.

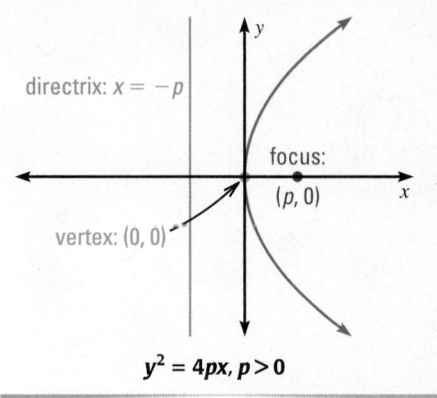

$y^2 = 4px, p > 0$

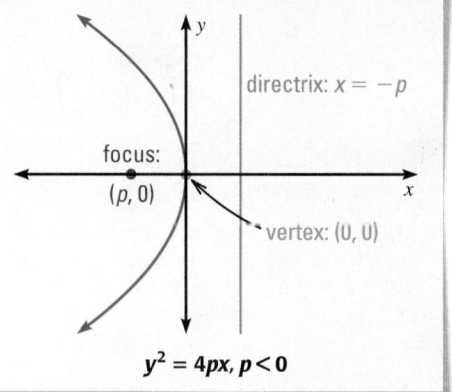

$y^2 = 4px, p < 0$

Standard Equation of a Parabola with Vertex at the Origin

The standard form of the equation of a parabola with vertex at $(0, 0)$ is as follows:

Equation	Focus	Directrix	Axis of Symmetry
$x^2 = 4py$	$(0, p)$	$y = -p$	Vertical ($x = 0$)
$y^2 = 4px$	$(p, 0)$	$x = -p$	Horizontal ($y = 0$)

EXAMPLE 1   Graph an equation of a parabola

Graph $x = -\frac{1}{8}y^2$. Identify the focus, directrix, and axis of symmetry.

Solution

STEP 1   **Rewrite** the equation in standard form.

$$x = -\frac{1}{8}y^2 \qquad \text{Write original equation.}$$

$$-8x = y^2 \qquad \text{Multiply each side by } -8.$$

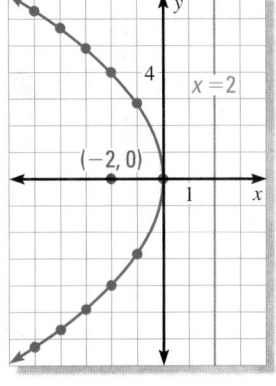

STEP 2   **Identify** the focus, directrix, and axis of symmetry. The equation has the form $y^2 = 4px$ where $p = -2$. The focus is $(p, 0)$, or $(-2, 0)$. The directrix is $x = -p$, or $x = 2$. Because y is squared, the axis of symmetry is the x-axis.

STEP 3   **Draw** the parabola by making a table of values and plotting points. Because $p < 0$, the parabola opens to the left. So, use only negative x-values.

SOLVE FOR Y

To fill in the table, note that because $-8x = y^2$, $y = \pm\sqrt{-8x}$. The value of y will be a real number only when $x \le 0$.

x	-1	-2	-3	-4	-5
y	± 2.83	± 4	± 4.90	± 5.66	± 6.32

Animated Algebra   at my.hrw.com

EXAMPLE 2   Write an equation of a parabola

Write an equation of the parabola shown.

Solution

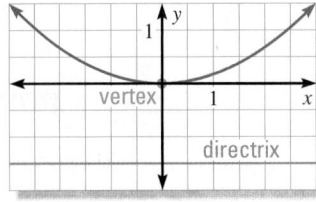

The graph shows that the vertex is $(0, 0)$ and the directrix is $y = -p = -\frac{3}{2}$. Substitute $\frac{3}{2}$ for p in the standard form of the equation of a parabola.

$$x^2 = 4py \qquad \text{Standard form, vertical axis of symmetry}$$

$$x^2 = 4\left(\frac{3}{2}\right)y \qquad \text{Substitute } \frac{3}{2} \text{ for } p.$$

$$x^2 = 6y \qquad \text{Simplify.}$$

Graph the equation. Identify the focus, directrix, and axis of symmetry of the parabola.

1. $y^2 = -6x$ **2.** $x^2 = 2y$ **3.** $y = -\frac{1}{4}x^2$ **4.** $x = \frac{1}{3}y^2$

Write the standard form of the equation of the parabola with vertex at (0, 0) and the given directrix or focus.

5. Directrix: $y = 2$ **6.** Directrix: $x = 4$ **7.** Focus: $(-2, 0)$ **8.** Focus: $(0, 3)$

PARABOLIC REFLECTORS *Parabolic reflectors* have cross sections that are parabolas. Incoming sound, light, or other energy that arrives at a parabolic reflector parallel to the axis of symmetry is directed to the focus (Diagram 1). Similarly, energy that is emitted from the focus of a parabolic reflector and then strikes the reflector is directed parallel to the axis of symmetry (Diagram 2).

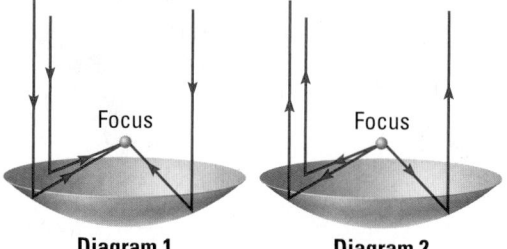

Diagram 1   **Diagram 2**

EXAMPLE 3 **Solve a multi-step problem**

SOLAR ENERGY The EuroDish, developed to provide electricity in remote areas, uses a parabolic reflector to concentrate sunlight onto a high-efficiency engine located at the reflector's focus. The sunlight heats helium to 650°C to power the engine.

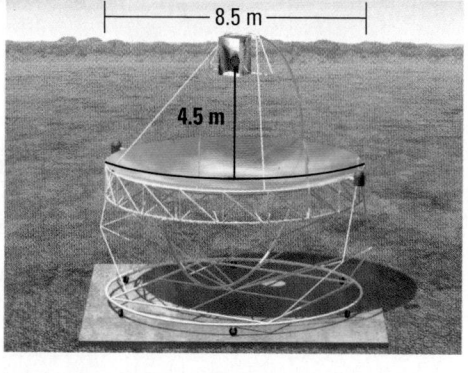

- Write an equation for the EuroDish's cross section with its vertex at (0, 0).

- How deep is the dish?

Solution

STEP 1 **Write** an equation for the cross section. The engine is at the focus, which is $|p| = 4.5$ meters from the vertex. Because the focus is above the vertex, p is positive, so $p = 4.5$. An equation for the cross section of the EuroDish with its vertex at the origin is as follows:

$x^2 = 4py$ **Standard form, vertical axis of symmetry**

$x^2 = 4(\mathbf{4.5})y$ **Substitute 4.5 for *p*.**

$x^2 = 18y$ **Simplify.**

STEP 2 **Find** the depth of the EuroDish. The depth is the y-value at the dish's outside edge. The dish extends $\frac{8.5}{2} = 4.25$ meters to either side of the vertex (0, 0), so substitute 4.25 for x in the equation from Step 1.

$x^2 = 18y$ **Equation for the cross section**

$(4.25)^2 = 18y$ **Substitute 4.25 for *x*.**

$1.0 \approx y$ **Solve for *y*.**

▶ The dish is about 1 meter deep.

9. **MICROWAVES** A parabolic microwave antenna is 16 feet in diameter. Find an equation for the cross section of the antenna with its vertex at the origin and its focus 10 feet to the right of its vertex. Then find the antenna's depth.

8.2 EXERCISES

HOMEWORK KEY

◯ = See **WORKED-OUT SOLUTIONS**
Exs. 15, 27, and 57

★ = **STANDARDIZED TEST PRACTICE**
Exs. 2, 25, 38, 51, 52, and 59

SKILL PRACTICE

1. **VOCABULARY** Copy and complete: A parabola is the set of all points in a plane equidistant from a point called the __?__ and a line called the __?__ .

2. ★ **WRITING** *Compare* the graphs of $x^2 = 4py$ and $y^2 = 4px$.

EXAMPLE 1
for Exs. 3–25

GRAPHING **Graph the equation. Identify the focus, directrix, and axis of symmetry of the parabola.**

3. $y^2 = 16x$
4. $x^2 = -6y$
5. $x^2 = 20y$
6. $y^2 = 28x$

7. $y^2 = -10x$
8. $x^2 = 30y$
9. $y^2 = -2x$
10. $x^2 = -36y$

11. $x^2 = 12y$
12. $-2y = x^2$
13. $x = 4y^2$
14. $-x^2 = 48y$

15. $5x^2 = -15y$
16. $-y^2 = 18x$
17. $-24x = 3y^2$
18. $14x = 6y^2$

19. $\frac{1}{8}x^2 - y = 0$
20. $4x - 11y^2 = 0$
21. $5x^2 + 12y = 0$
22. $-5x + \frac{1}{3}y^2 = 0$

ERROR ANALYSIS *Describe* and correct the error in graphing the parabola.

23.

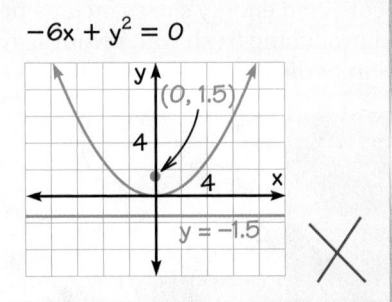

$-6x + y^2 = 0$

(0, 1.5)

$y = -1.5$

24.

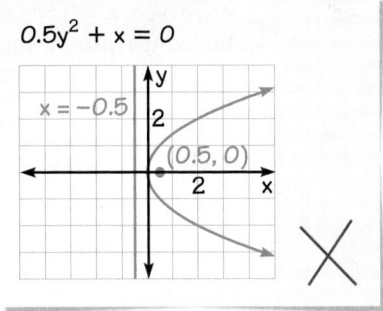

$0.5y^2 + x = 0$

$x = -0.5$

(0.5, 0)

25. ★ **MULTIPLE CHOICE** What is the directrix of the parabola $15y + 3x^2 = 0$?

Ⓐ $x = -5$
Ⓑ $x = -1.25$
Ⓒ $y = -1.25$
Ⓓ $y = 1.25$

EXAMPLE 2
for Exs. 26–50

WRITING EQUATIONS **Write the standard form of the equation of the parabola with the given focus and vertex at (0, 0).**

26. $(2, 0)$
27. $(-5, 0)$
28. $(3, 0)$
29. $(0, -4)$

30. $(0, 8)$
31. $(0, -10)$
32. $(0, -6)$
33. $(-9, 0)$

34. $\left(0, \frac{7}{4}\right)$
35. $\left(0, -\frac{3}{8}\right)$
36. $\left(\frac{5}{2}, 0\right)$
37. $\left(-\frac{9}{16}, 0\right)$

38. ★ **MULTIPLE CHOICE** What is an equation of the parabola with focus at $(-8, 0)$ and vertex at $(0, 0)$?

  A $y^2 = -32x$ **B** $y^2 = -0.5x$ **C** $x^2 = -8y$ **D** $x^2 = -32y$

WRITING EQUATIONS Write the standard form of the equation of the parabola with the given directrix and vertex at **(0, 0).**

39. $x = 3$ **40.** $y = -7$ **41.** $x = -5$ **42.** $y = 12$

43. $y = -4$ **44.** $x = -2$ **45.** $y = 6$ **46.** $x = 11$

47. $x = -\dfrac{3}{2}$ **48.** $y = \dfrac{5}{12}$ **49.** $y = -\dfrac{11}{6}$ **50.** $x = -\dfrac{1}{18}$

51. ★ **SHORT RESPONSE** Predict how the indicated change in a will affect the focus, directrix, and shape of the given equation's graph. Then graph both the original and revised equations in the same coordinate plane.

  a. $x^2 = ay$; a changes from 1 to 4   **b.** $y^2 = ax$; a changes from 6 to $-\dfrac{1}{2}$

52. ★ **WRITING** Suppose that $x^2 = 4py$ and $y = ax^2$ represent the same parabola. *Explain* how a and p are related.

53. **VISUAL THINKING** As $|p|$ increases, how does the width of the graph of $x^2 = 4py$ change? *Explain.*

54. **CHALLENGE** Consider the parabola with focus $(0, p)$ and directrix $y = -p$. Let (x, y) be any point on the parabola. Use the fact that (x, y) is equidistant from the focus and directrix to show that $x^2 = 4py$.

PROBLEM SOLVING

EXAMPLE 3
for Exs. 55–59

55. **SOLAR ENERGY** Solar energy can be concentrated using long troughs that have a parabolic cross section. The collected energy's uses include heating buildings, producing electricity, and producing fresh water from seawater. Write an equation for the cross section of the trough shown. How deep is it?

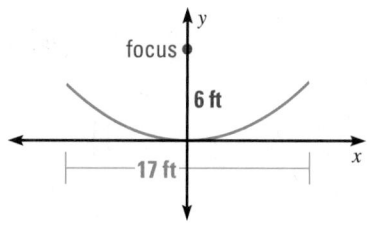

56. **BIOLOGY** Scientists studying dolphin *echolocation* can simulate the projection of a dolphin's clicking sounds using computer models. The models originate the sounds at the focus of a parabolic reflector. The parabola in the graph models the cross section (with units in inches) of the reflector used to simulate sound projection for a bottlenose dolphin. What is the *focal length* (the distance from the vertex to the focus)?

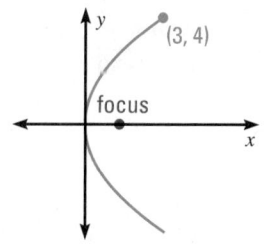

○ = See **WORKED-OUT SOLUTIONS**
   in Student Resources

★ = **STANDARDIZED TEST PRACTICE**

Hank Morgan/Time Life Pictures/Getty Images

57. **MULTI-STEP PROBLEM** The parabolic antenna used by a television station to transmit is 146 inches in diameter. Its focus is 48 inches from the vertex.

    a. Sketch the antenna twice: once opening upward and once opening left.

    b. Use your sketches from part (a) to write two equations for the antenna's cross section: one of the form $x^2 = 4py$ and one of the form $y^2 = 4px$.

    c. How deep is the antenna's dish? Does it matter which equation from part (b) you use to find your answer? *Explain*.

58. **RADIO TELESCOPES** The Very Large Array in New Mexico consists of 27 radio telescopes. For each parabolic telescope dish, the diameter is 25 meters and the distance between the vertex and focus is 0.36 times the diameter. Write an equation for the cross section of a dish opening upward with its vertex at the origin. How deep is each dish?

Animated **Algebra** at my.hrw.com

59. ★ **EXTENDED RESPONSE** Searchlights use parabolic reflectors to project their beams. The cross section of a 9.5-inch-deep searchlight reflector has equation $x^2 = 10.5y$.

    a. How wide is the beam of light projected from the searchlight's reflector?

    b. Write an equation for the cross section of a reflector that has the same depth as the original reflector, but which projects a wider beam. *Explain* how you found your answer. How wide is the new reflector's beam?

    c. Repeat part (b) for a beam narrower than the original.

60. **CHALLENGE** The *latus rectum* of a parabola is the line segment that is parallel to the directrix, passes through the focus, and has endpoints that lie on the parabola. Find the length in terms of p of the latus rectum of a parabola with equation $x^2 = 4py$.

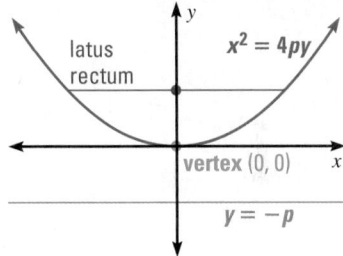

8.3 Graph and Write Equations of Circles

Before	You graphed and wrote equations of parabolas.
Now	You will graph and write equations of circles.
Why?	So you can model transmission ranges, as in Ex. 62.

Key Vocabulary
• circle
• center
• radius

CC.9-12.G.GPE.1 Derive the equation of a circle of given center and radius using the Pythagorean Theorem; complete the square to find the center and radius of a circle given by an equation.

A **circle** is the set of all points (x, y) in a plane that are equidistant from a fixed point, called the **center** of the circle. The distance r between the center and any point (x, y) on the circle is the **radius**.

For a circle with center at the origin and radius r, the distance between any point (x, y) on the circle and the center $(0, 0)$ is r, so the following is true:

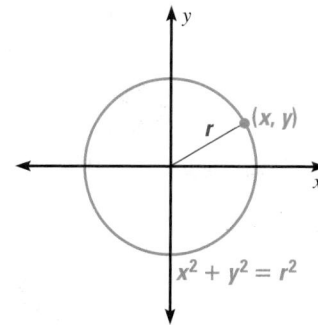

$\sqrt{(x - 0)^2 + (y - 0)^2} = r$ **Distance formula**

$(x - 0)^2 + (y - 0)^2 = r^2$ **Square each side.**

$x^2 + y^2 = r^2$ **Simplify.**

KEY CONCEPT   *For Your Notebook*

Standard Equation of a Circle with Center at the Origin

The standard form of the equation of a circle with center at $(0, 0)$ and radius r is as follows:

$$x^2 + y^2 = r^2$$

EXAMPLE 1   Graph an equation of a circle

Graph $y^2 = -x^2 + 36$. Identify the radius of the circle.

Solution

STEP 1 **Rewrite** the equation $y^2 = -x^2 + 36$ in standard form as $x^2 + y^2 = 36$.

STEP 2 **Identify** the center and radius. From the equation, the graph is a circle centered at the origin with radius $r = \sqrt{36} = 6$.

STEP 3 **Draw** the circle. First plot several convenient points that are 6 units from the origin, such as $(0, 6)$, $(6, 0)$, $(0, -6)$, and $(-6, 0)$. Then draw the circle that passes through the points.

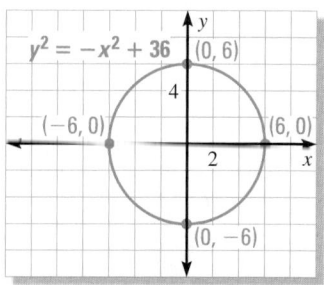

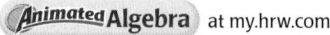 **Algebra** at my.hrw.com

Royalty-Free/Corbis

EXAMPLE 2 **Write an equation of a circle**

The point $(2, -5)$ lies on a circle whose center is the origin. Write the standard form of the equation of the circle.

Solution

Because the point $(2, -5)$ lies on the circle, the circle's radius r must be the distance between the center $(0, 0)$ and $(2, -5)$. Use the distance formula.

$$r = \sqrt{(2-0)^2 + (-5-0)^2} = \sqrt{4+25} = \sqrt{29} \quad \text{The radius is } \sqrt{29}.$$

Use the standard form with $r = \sqrt{29}$ to write an equation of the circle.

$x^2 + y^2 = r^2$ **Standard form**

$x^2 + y^2 = \left(\sqrt{29}\right)^2$ **Substitute $\sqrt{29}$ for r.**

$x^2 + y^2 = 29$ **Simplify.**

 EXAMPLE 3 **Standardized Test Practice**

What is an equation of the line tangent to the circle $x^2 + y^2 = 13$ at $(-3, 2)$?

A $y = \frac{2}{3}x + 4$ **B** $y = \frac{3}{2}x - \frac{5}{2}$ **C** $y = \frac{3}{2}x + \frac{13}{2}$ **D** $y = -\frac{3}{2}x + \frac{13}{3}$

ELIMINATE CHOICES

In Example 3, you can eliminate choice D because a quick sketch of the circle shows that the slope of the tangent line at $(-3, 2)$ must be positive.

Solution

A line tangent to a circle is perpendicular to the radius at the point of tangency. Because the radius to the point $(-3, 2)$ has slope $m = \frac{2-0}{-3-0} = -\frac{2}{3}$, the slope of the tangent line at $(-3, 2)$ is the negative reciprocal of $-\frac{2}{3}$, or $\frac{3}{2}$. An equation of the tangent line is as follows:

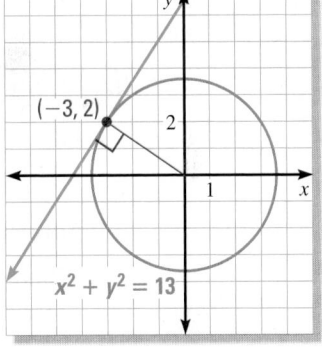

$y - 2 = \frac{3}{2}(x - (-3))$ **Point-slope form**

$y - 2 = \frac{3}{2}x + \frac{9}{2}$ **Distributive property**

$y = \frac{3}{2}x + \frac{13}{2}$ **Solve for y.**

▶ The correct answer is C.   Ⓐ Ⓑ ⓒ Ⓓ

✓ **GUIDED PRACTICE**   for Examples 1, 2, and 3

Graph the equation. Identify the radius of the circle.

1. $x^2 + y^2 = 9$ **2.** $y^2 = -x^2 + 49$ **3.** $x^2 - 18 = -y^2$

4. Write the standard form of the equation of the circle that passes through $(5, -1)$ and whose center is the origin.

5. Write an equation of the line tangent to the circle $x^2 + y^2 = 37$ at $(6, 1)$.

CIRCLES AND INEQUALITIES The regions inside and outside the circle $x^2 + y^2 = r^2$ can be described by inequalities, with $x^2 + y^2 < r^2$ representing the region inside the circle and $x^2 + y^2 > r^2$ representing the region outside the circle.

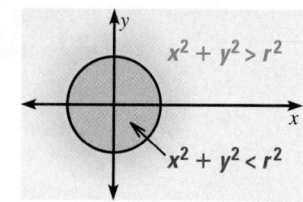

EXAMPLE 4 Write a circular model

CELL PHONES A cellular phone tower services a 10 mile radius. You get a flat tire 4 miles east and 9 miles north of the tower. Are you in the tower's range?

Solution

STEP 1 **Write** an inequality for the region covered by the tower. From the diagram, this region is all points that satisfy the following inequality:

$$x^2 + y^2 < 10^2$$

STEP 2 **Substitute** the coordinates $(4, 9)$ into the inequality from Step 1.

$x^2 + y^2 < 10^2$ **Inequality from Step 1**

$4^2 + 9^2 \overset{?}{<} 10^2$ **Substitute for x and y.**

$97 < 100$ ✓   **The inequality is true.**

▶ So, you are in the tower's range.

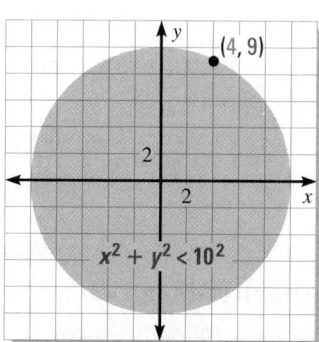

In the diagram above, the origin represents the tower and the positive y-axis represents north.

EXAMPLE 5 Apply a circular model

CELL PHONES In Example 4, suppose that you fix your tire and then drive south. For how many more miles will you be in range of the tower?

Solution

When you leave the tower's range, you will be at a point on the circle $x^2 + y^2 = 10^2$ whose x-coordinate is 4 and whose y-coordinate is negative. Find the point $(4, y)$ where $y < 0$ on the circle $x^2 + y^2 = 10^2$.

$x^2 + y^2 = 10^2$ **Equation of the circle**

$4^2 + y^2 = 10^2$ **Substitute 4 for x.**

$y = \pm\sqrt{84}$ **Solve for y.**

$y \approx \pm 9.2$ **Use a calculator.**

▶ Because $y < 0$, $y \approx -9.2$. You will be in the tower's range from $(4, 9)$ to $(4, -9.2)$, a distance of $|9 - (-9.2)| = 18.2$ miles.

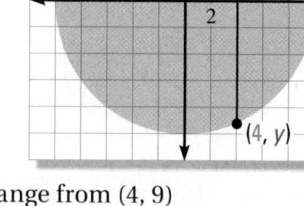

✓ **GUIDED PRACTICE**   for Examples 4 and 5

6. **WHAT IF?** In Examples 4 and 5, suppose you drive west after fixing your tire. For how many more miles will you be in range of the tower?

8.3 EXERCISES

HOMEWORK
KEY

◯ = See WORKED-OUT SOLUTIONS
Exs. 17, 39, and 65

★ = STANDARDIZED TEST PRACTICE
Exs. 2, 21, 43, 59, 64, and 66

◆ = MULTIPLE REPRESENTATIONS
Ex. 68

SKILL PRACTICE

1. **VOCABULARY** The radius of a circle is the distance from any point on the circle to a fixed point called the circle's __?__ .

2. ★ **WRITING** How are the slope of a line tangent to a circle and the slope of the radius at the point of tangency related?

EXAMPLE 1
for Exs. 3–21

MATCHING GRAPHS Match the equation with its graph.

3. $x^2 + y^2 = 9$ 4. $x^2 + y^2 = 36$ 5. $x^2 + y^2 = 4$

6. $x^2 + y^2 = 6$ 7. $x^2 + y^2 = 16$ 8. $x^2 + y^2 = 3$

A. 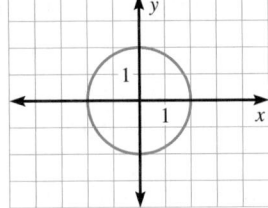   B. 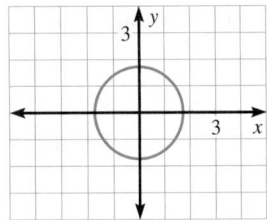   C.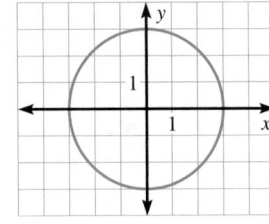

D. 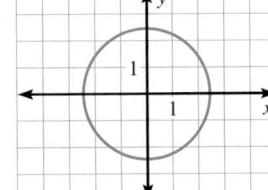   E. 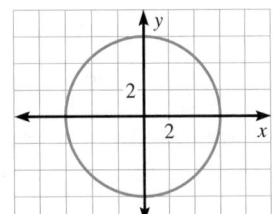   F.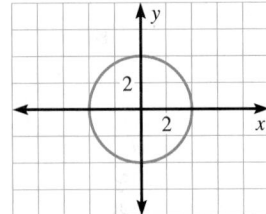

GRAPHING Graph the equation. Identify the radius of the circle.

9. $x^2 + y^2 = 1$ 10. $x^2 + y^2 = 81$ 11. $x^2 + y^2 = 25$

12. $x^2 + y^2 = 12$ 13. $y^2 = 27 - x^2$ 14. $x^2 = -y^2 + 40$

15. $x^2 = 15 - y^2$ 16. $y^2 = -x^2 + 9$ (17.) $15x^2 + 15y^2 = 60$

18. $7x^2 + 7y^2 = 112$ 19. $4x^2 + 4y^2 = 128$ 20. $8x^2 + 8y^2 = 192$

21. ★ **MULTIPLE CHOICE** What is the radius of the circle $3x^2 + 3y^2 = 54$?

   A $3\sqrt{2}$ **B** $3\sqrt{6}$ **C** 18   **D** 54

EXAMPLE 2
for Exs. 22–43

WRITING EQUATIONS Write the standard form of the equation of the circle with the given radius and whose center is the origin.

22. 12   23. 8   24. 2   25. 16

26. $\sqrt{2}$ 27. $\sqrt{15}$ 28. $5\sqrt{2}$ 29. $4\sqrt{6}$

30. **ERROR ANALYSIS** *Describe* and correct the error in writing an equation of the circle with the given center and radius.

Center: (0, 0); Radius: 12
Equation: $x^2 + y^2 = 12$ ╳

WRITING EQUATIONS Write the standard form of the equation of the circle that passes through the given point and whose center is the origin.

31. $(-6, 0)$ **32.** $(0, 5)$ **33.** $(-4, 3)$ **34.** $(2, -4)$

35. $(-6, 8)$ **36.** $(-9, 2)$ **37.** $(4, -10)$ **38.** $(-8, -5)$

39. $(-8, 14)$ **40.** $(5, -12)$ **41.** $(-11, -11)$ **42.** $(9, 40)$

43. ★ **MULTIPLE CHOICE** What is the equation in standard form of the circle that passes through the point $(4, -6)$ and whose center is the origin?

     (A) $x^2 + y^2 = 5$ **(B)** $x^2 + y^2 = 10$ **(C)** $x^2 + y^2 = 52$ **(D)** $x^2 + y^2 = 2\sqrt{13}$

GRAPHING In Exercises 44–52, equations of both circles and parabolas are given. Graph the equation.

44. $y^2 + x^2 = 49$ **45.** $4x^2 + y = 0$ **46.** $7x^2 + 7y^2 = 63$

47. $y^2 - 121 = -x^2$ **48.** $x^2 + 16y = 0$ **49.** $3x = -y^2$

50. $12x^2 + 12y^2 = 192$ **51.** $2x^2 + 2y^2 = 16$ **52.** $6x + 6y^2 = 0$

EXAMPLE 3
for Exs. 53–58

TANGENT LINES Write an equation of the line tangent to the given circle at the given point.

53. $x^2 + y^2 = 17$; $(1, 4)$ **54.** $x^2 + y^2 = 13$; $(2, -3)$ **55.** $x^2 + y^2 = 34$; $(-5, 3)$

56. $x^2 + y^2 = 40$; $(-6, -2)$ **57.** $x^2 + y^2 = 106$; $(-5, 9)$ **58.** $x^2 + y^2 = 250$; $(15, 5)$

59. ★ **OPEN-ENDED MATH** Write equations in standard form for three circles centered at the origin so that each circle passes between $(-3, 5)$ and $(-6, 2)$.

60. **REASONING** Use the diagram to show that an angle inscribed in a semicircle is a right angle. (*Hint:* Show that the segments meeting at (x, y) have slopes that are negative reciprocals.)

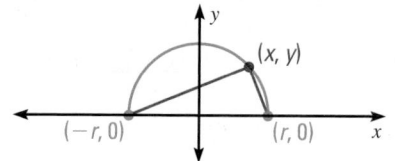

61. **CHALLENGE** Suppose two congruent circles intersect so that each passes through the other's center, as shown. Write an equation that gives the length ℓ of the chord formed by joining the intersection points in terms of the radius r of each circle.

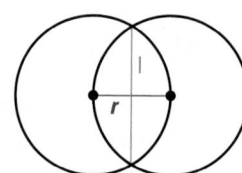

PROBLEM SOLVING

EXAMPLE 4
for Exs. 62–64

62. **CELL PHONES** A cellular phone tower services a 15 mile radius. On a hiking trip, you are 9 miles east and 11 miles north of the cell tower. Are you in the region served by the tower?

63. **BATS** During the warmer months, more than 1 million Mexican free-tailed bats live under the Congress Avenue Bridge in Austin, Texas. The bats have an estimated feeding range of 50 miles. Is a location 40 miles north and 25 miles west of the bridge located within this range?

○ = See **WORKED-OUT SOLUTIONS** in Student Resources   ★ = **STANDARDIZED TEST PRACTICE**   ◆ = **MULTIPLE REPRESENTATIONS**

64. ★ **MULTIPLE CHOICE** An appliance store claims to provide free delivery up to 100 miles from the store. The following points represent the locations of houses, with the origin representing the store. (All coordinates are in miles.) Which house is located outside the free delivery area?

  (A) (95, 30)   **(B)** (90, 35)   **(C)** (80, 55)   **(D)** (75, 70)

EXAMPLE 5
for Exs. 65–67

65. **MULTI-STEP PROBLEM** "Class B" airspace sometimes consists of a stack of cylindrical layers as shown. Seen from above, the airspace forms circles whose origin is the control tower. A plane in straight and level flight flies through the top layer along the line $y = -4$, as shown.

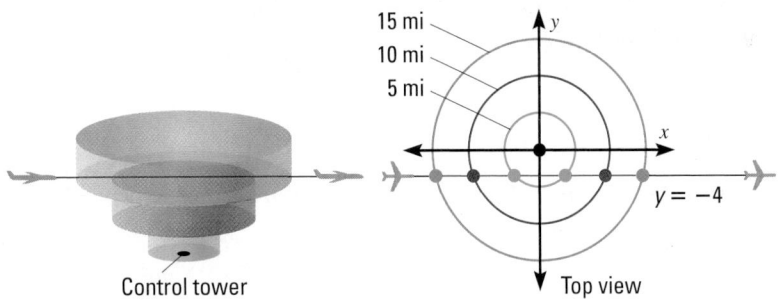

Control tower   Top view

   a. For how many miles will the plane be in the top-most layer of Class B airspace?

   b. For how many miles will the plane be above the middle layer of Class B airspace?

   c. For how many miles will the plane be above the lowest layer of Class B airspace?

66. ★ **SHORT RESPONSE** A circular utility tunnel 8 feet in diameter has a 6-foot-wide walkway across its bottom. Could a worker who is 6 feet 2 inches tall walk down the center of the walkway without ducking? *Explain.* (*Hint:* Write an equation of the tunnel's cross section. Find the x-coordinate of an endpoint of the walkway and substitute to find the y-coordinate.)

67. **GROUNDSKEEPING** A row of sprinklers is to be installed parallel to and 4.5 feet away from the back edge of a flower bed. Each sprinkler waters a region with a 6 foot radius. How far apart should the sprinklers be placed to water the entire flower bed with the least possible overlap in coverage, as shown?

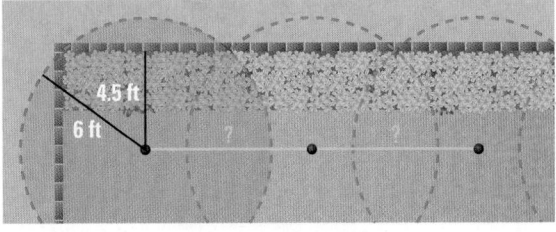

68. ◆ **MULTIPLE REPRESENTATIONS** The Modified Mercalli Intensity Scale rates an earthquake's "shaking strength." In general, the rating decreases as distance from the earthquake's epicenter increases. Suppose an earthquake has a Mercalli rating of 6.0 at its epicenter, a 5.7 rating 15 miles away from the epicenter, a 5.4 rating 25 miles away, and a 5.1 rating 35 miles away.

   a. **Drawing Graphs** Represent the situation described above using circles in a coordinate plane.

   b. **Writing Inequalities** For each circle from part (a), write an inequality describing the coordinates of locations with a Mercalli rating *at least* as great as the Mercalli rating represented by the circle.

   c. **Making a Prediction** What can you predict about the Mercalli rating 12 miles west and 16 miles south of the epicenter? *Explain.*

69. CHALLENGE Two radio transmitters, one with a 40 mile range and one with a 60 mile range, stand 80 miles apart. You are driving 60 miles per hour on a highway parallel to the line segment connecting the two towers. How long will you be within range of *both* transmitters simultaneously?

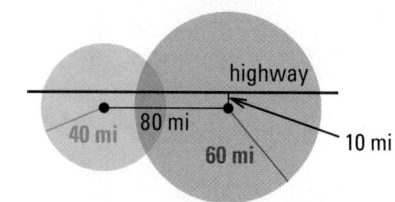

QUIZ

Find the distance between the two points. Then find the midpoint of the line segment joining the two points.

1. $(4, -3), (8, -7)$ 　　　　**2.** $(-2, 5), (4, 9)$ 　　　　**3.** $(-5, 1), (-4, 8)$

4. $(1, 2), (7, 1)$ 　　　　　**5.** $(-6, -5), (-1, 8)$ 　　　**6.** $(3, -2), (6, 5)$

Write the standard form of the equation of the parabola with the given focus and vertex at (0, 0).

7. $(0, 3)$ 　　　　　　　**8.** $(-2, 0)$ 　　　　　　**9.** $(6, 0)$

10. $(0, -4)$ 　　　　　　**11.** $(0, 5)$ 　　　　　　**12.** $(-1, 0)$

Graph the equation. Identify the radius of the circle.

13. $x^2 + y^2 = 4$ 　　　　**14.** $x^2 + y^2 = 64$ 　　　**15.** $x^2 + y^2 = 20$

16. $x^2 + y^2 = 75$ 　　　**17.** $3x^2 + 3y^2 = 48$ 　　**18.** $6x^2 + 6y^2 = 108$

19. ASTRONOMY If the plane in which Jupiter orbits the sun is a coordinate plane with its origin at the sun and coordinates in millions of miles, then a circle through the point (350, 370) just encloses Jupiter's orbit. Imagine replacing the sun with the star KY Cygni, whose radius is about 650 million miles. Would KY Cygni contain Jupiter's orbit? *Explain.*

See **EXTRA PRACTICE** in Student Resources 　　🧭 **ONLINE QUIZ** at my.hrw.com

my.hrw.com
Keystrokes

Graph Equations of Circles

MATHEMATICAL PRACTICES

Use appropriate tools strategically.

QUESTION How can you use a graphing calculator to graph a circle?

To graph a circle on most graphing calculators, you must first rewrite the circle's equation as two functions that taken together represent the circle.

EXAMPLE Graph a circle

Use a graphing calculator to graph $x^2 + y^2 = 25$.

STEP 1 *Solve for y*

Begin by solving the equation for y.

$$x^2 + y^2 = 25$$
$$y^2 = 25 - x^2$$
$$y = \pm\sqrt{25 - x^2}$$

Together, the functions $y = \sqrt{25 - x^2}$ and $y = -\sqrt{25 - x^2}$ represent the circle.

STEP 2 *Enter functions*

Enter the two functions as y_1 and y_2. You can enter y_2 as $-y_1$.

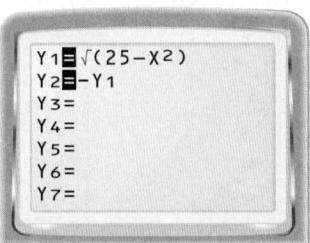

```
Y1=√(25-X²)
Y2=-Y1
Y3=
Y4=
Y5=
Y6=
Y7=
```

STEP 3 *Graph functions*

The graphs are shown in the standard window ($-10 \le x \le 10$ and $-10 \le y \le 10$). Because the calculator screen is not square, a horizontal distance of 1 unit is longer than a vertical distance of 1 unit, and the circle is stretched into an oval.

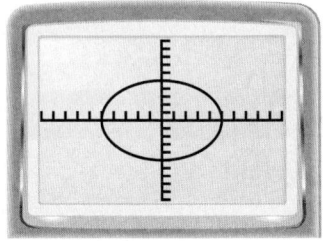

STEP 4 *Adjust graph*

To show the circle in true proportion, set a window so that the ratio of (Xmax − Xmin) to (Ymax − Ymin) is 3:2. Such a "square window" can also be obtained by pressing ZOOM and selecting ZSquare.

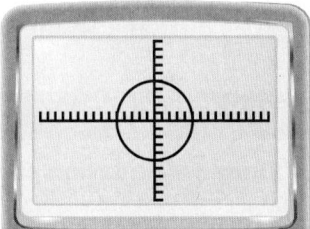

PRACTICE

Use a graphing calculator to graph the equation. Give the viewing window that you used and verify that it is a "square window."

1. $x^2 + y^2 = 144$ 2. $x^2 + y^2 = 80$ 3. $x^2 + y^2 = 576$

4. $0.5x^2 + 0.5y^2 = 12$ 5. $7x^2 + 7y^2 = 105$ 6. $16x^2 + 16y^2 = 9$

8.4 Graph and Write Equations of Ellipses

Before	You graphed and wrote equations of parabolas and circles.
Now	You will graph and write equations of ellipses.
Why?	So you can model an elliptical region, as in Example 3.

Key Vocabulary
- ellipse
- foci
- vertices
- major axis
- center
- co-vertices
- minor axis

An **ellipse** is the set of all points P in a plane such that the sum of the distances between P and two fixed points, called the **foci**, is a constant.

The line through the foci intersects the ellipse at the two **vertices**. The **major axis** joins the vertices. Its midpoint is the ellipse's **center**.

The line perpendicular to the major axis at the center intersects the ellipse at the two **co-vertices**, which are joined by the **minor axis**. In this chapter, ellipses have a horizontal or a vertical major axis.

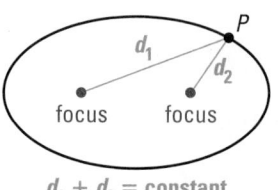

$d_1 + d_2 = \text{constant}$

CC.9-12.G.GPE.3 (+) Derive the equations of ellipses and hyperbolas given the foci, using the fact that the sum or difference of distances from the foci is constant.

IDENTIFY AXES
Observe that the major axis of an ellipse contains the foci and is always longer than the minor axis.

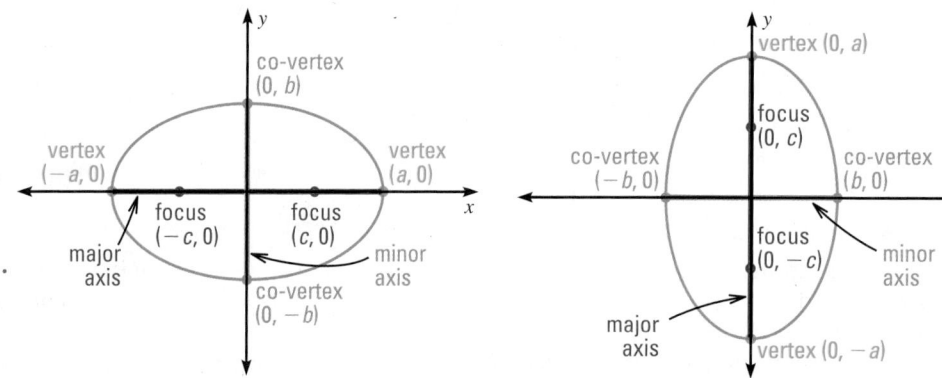

Ellipse with horizontal major axis

$$\frac{x^2}{a^2} + \frac{y^2}{b^2} = 1$$

Ellipse with vertical major axis

$$\frac{x^2}{b^2} + \frac{y^2}{a^2} = 1$$

KEY CONCEPT   *For Your Notebook*

Standard Equation of an Ellipse with Center at the Origin

Equation	Major Axis	Vertices	Co-Vertices
$\dfrac{x^2}{a^2} + \dfrac{y^2}{b^2} = 1$	Horizontal	$(\pm a, 0)$	$(0, \pm b)$
$\dfrac{x^2}{b^2} + \dfrac{y^2}{a^2} = 1$	Vertical	$(0, \pm a)$	$(\pm b, 0)$

The major and minor axes are of lengths $2a$ and $2b$, respectively, where $a > b > 0$. The foci of the ellipse lie on the major axis at a distance of c units from the center, where $c^2 = a^2 - b^2$.

EXAMPLE 1 **Graph an equation of an ellipse**

Graph the equation $4x^2 + 25y^2 = 100$. Identify the vertices, co-vertices, and foci of the ellipse.

Solution

STEP 1 **Rewrite** the equation in standard form.

$$4x^2 + 25y^2 = 100 \qquad \text{Write original equation.}$$

$$\frac{4x^2}{100} + \frac{25y^2}{100} = \frac{100}{100} \qquad \text{Divide each side by 100.}$$

$$\frac{x^2}{25} + \frac{y^2}{4} = 1 \qquad \text{Simplify.}$$

STEP 2 **Identify** the vertices, co-vertices, and foci. Note that $a^2 = 25$ and $b^2 = 4$, so $a = 5$ and $b = 2$. The denominator of the x^2-term is greater than that of the y^2-term, so the major axis is horizontal.

The vertices of the ellipse are at $(\pm a, 0) = (\pm 5, 0)$. The co-vertices are at $(0, \pm b) = (0, \pm 2)$. Find the foci.

$$c^2 = a^2 - b^2 = 5^2 - 2^2 = 21, \text{ so } c = \sqrt{21}$$

The foci are at $(\pm\sqrt{21}, 0)$, or about $(\pm 4.6, 0)$.

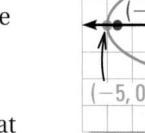

STEP 3 **Draw** the ellipse that passes through each vertex and co-vertex.

ANOTHER WAY

You can graph the ellipse using a graphing calculator by solving for y to obtain

$$y = \pm 2\sqrt{1 - \frac{x^2}{25}}$$

and then entering this equation as two separate functions.

✓ **GUIDED PRACTICE** for Example 1

Graph the equation. Identify the vertices, co-vertices, and foci of the ellipse.

1. $\dfrac{x^2}{16} + \dfrac{y^2}{9} = 1$ **2.** $\dfrac{x^2}{36} + \dfrac{y^2}{49} = 1$ **3.** $25x^2 + 9y^2 = 225$

 EXAMPLE 2 **Write an equation given a vertex and a co-vertex**

Write an equation of the ellipse that has a vertex at $(0, 4)$, a co-vertex at $(-3, 0)$, and center at $(0, 0)$.

Solution

Sketch the ellipse as a check for your final equation. By symmetry, the ellipse must also have a vertex at $(0, -4)$ and a co-vertex at $(3, 0)$.

Because the vertex is on the y-axis and the co-vertex is on the x-axis, the major axis is vertical with $a = 4$, and the minor axis is horizontal with $b = 3$.

▶ An equation is $\dfrac{x^2}{3^2} + \dfrac{y^2}{4^2} = 1$, or $\dfrac{x^2}{9} + \dfrac{y^2}{16} = 1$.

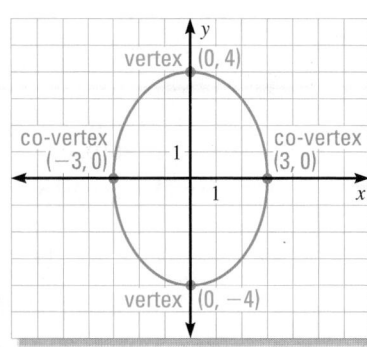

EXAMPLE 3 **Solve a multi-step problem**

LIGHTNING When lightning strikes, an elliptical region where the strike most likely hit can often be identified. Suppose it is determined that there is a 50% chance that a lightning strike hit within the elliptical region shown in the diagram.

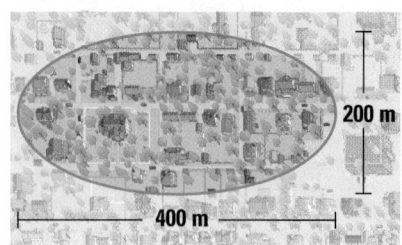

200 m

400 m

• Write an equation of the ellipse.

• The area A of an ellipse is $A = \pi ab$. Find the area of the elliptical region.

ANOTHER WAY

For an alternative method for solving the problem in Example 3, see the **Problem Solving Workshop**.

Solution

STEP 1 The major axis is horizontal, with $a = \dfrac{400}{2} = 200$ and $b = \dfrac{200}{2} = 100$.

An equation is $\dfrac{x^2}{200^2} + \dfrac{y^2}{100^2} = 1$, or $\dfrac{x^2}{40{,}000} + \dfrac{y^2}{10{,}000} = 1$.

STEP 2 The area is $A = \pi(200)(100) \approx 62{,}800$ square meters.

EXAMPLE 4 **Write an equation given a vertex and a focus**

Write an equation of the ellipse that has a vertex at $(-8, 0)$, a focus at $(4, 0)$, and center at $(0, 0)$.

Solution

Make a sketch of the ellipse. Because the given vertex and focus lie on the x-axis, the major axis is horizontal, with $a = 8$ and $c = 4$. To find b, use the equation $c^2 = a^2 - b^2$.

$$4^2 = 8^2 - b^2$$

$$b^2 = 8^2 - 4^2 = 48$$

$$b = \sqrt{48}, \text{ or } 4\sqrt{3}$$

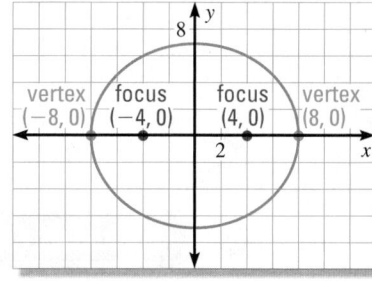

▶ An equation is $\dfrac{x^2}{8^2} + \dfrac{y^2}{(4\sqrt{3})^2} = 1$, or $\dfrac{x^2}{64} + \dfrac{y^2}{48} = 1$.

✓ **GUIDED PRACTICE** for Examples 2, 3, and 4

Write an equation of the ellipse with the given characteristics and center at $(0, 0)$.

4. Vertex: $(7, 0)$; co-vertex: $(0, 2)$

5. Vertex: $(0, 6)$; co-vertex: $(-5, 0)$

6. Vertex: $(0, 8)$; focus: $(0, -3)$

7. Vertex: $(-5, 0)$; focus: $(3, 0)$

8. **WHAT IF?** In Example 3, suppose that the elliptical region is 250 meters from east to west and 350 meters from north to south. Write an equation of the elliptical boundary and find the area of the region.

8.4 EXERCISES

SKILL PRACTICE

1. **VOCABULARY** Copy and complete: An ellipse is the set of all points P such that the sum of the distances between P and two fixed points, called the __?__, is a constant.

2. ★ **WRITING** *Describe* how to find the foci of an ellipse given the coordinates of its vertices and co-vertices.

EXAMPLE 1
for Exs. 3–16

GRAPHING Graph the equation. Identify the vertices, co-vertices, and foci of the ellipse.

3. $\dfrac{x^2}{16} + \dfrac{y^2}{4} = 1$

4. $\dfrac{x^2}{4} + y^2 = 25$

5. $\dfrac{x^2}{9} + \dfrac{y^2}{49} = 1$

6. $\dfrac{x^2}{144} + \dfrac{y^2}{64} = 1$

7. $\dfrac{x^2}{400} + \dfrac{y^2}{81} = 1$

8. $\dfrac{x^2}{36} + \dfrac{y^2}{225} = 1$

9. $4x^2 + y^2 = 36$

10. $9x^2 + y^2 = 9$

⑪ $16x^2 + 9y^2 = 144$

12. $25x^2 + 49y^2 = 1225$

13. $16x^2 + 25y^2 = 1600$

14. $72x^2 + 8y^2 = 648$

ERROR ANALYSIS *Describe* and correct the error in graphing the ellipse.

15.

$\dfrac{x^2}{4} + \dfrac{y^2}{16} = 1$

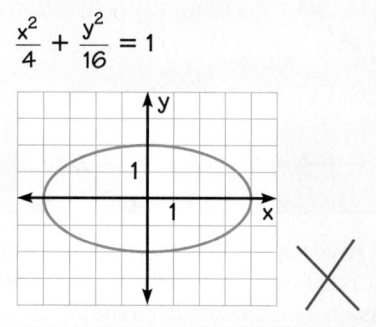

16.

$\dfrac{x^2}{2} + \dfrac{y^2}{3} = 1$

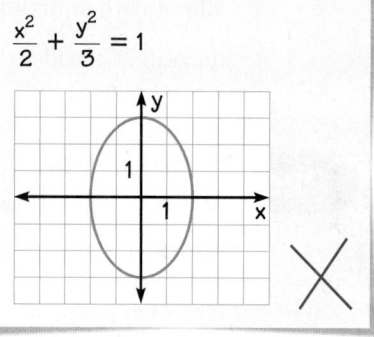

EXAMPLES 2 and 4
for Exs. 17–35

WRITING EQUATIONS Write an equation of the ellipse with the given characteristics and center at (0, 0).

17. Vertex: (5, 0)
Co-vertex: (0, −3)

18. Vertex: (0, −10)
Co-vertex: (6, 0)

19. Vertex: (14, 0)
Co-vertex: (0, −9)

20. Vertex: (0, −6)
Co-vertex: (4, 0)

21. Vertex: (0, 12)
Co-vertex: (11, 0)

22. Vertex: (20, 0)
Co-vertex: (0, −16)

23. Vertex: (0, 8)
Focus: (0, 6)

24. Vertex: (4, 0)
Focus: $(\sqrt{7}, 0)$

25. Vertex: (0, 9)
Focus: $(0, -4\sqrt{2})$

26. Vertex: (−5, 0)
Focus: (3, 0)

27. Vertex: (0, −4)
Focus: $(0, -2\sqrt{3})$

28. Vertex: (13, 0)
Focus: $(-4\sqrt{3}, 0)$

㉙ Co-vertex: $(0, \sqrt{7})$
Focus: (−3, 0)

30. Co-vertex: $(-3\sqrt{5}, 0)$
Focus: (0, 6)

31. Co-vertex: $(0, -5\sqrt{7})$
Focus: (−15, 0)

32. Co-vertex: (0, 15)
Focus: (−8, 0)

33. Co-vertex: $(2\sqrt{15}, 0)$
Focus: (0, 14)

34. Co-vertex: (−32, 0)
Focus: (0, 24)

35. ★ **MULTIPLE CHOICE** What is an equation of the ellipse with center at the origin, a vertex at (0, −12), and a co-vertex at (−8, 0)?

A $\dfrac{x^2}{144} + \dfrac{y^2}{64} = 1$ **B** $\dfrac{x^2}{64} + \dfrac{y^2}{144} = 1$ **C** $\dfrac{x^2}{12} + \dfrac{y^2}{8} = 1$ **D** $\dfrac{x^2}{8} + \dfrac{y^2}{12} = 1$

GRAPHING In Exercises 36–44, the equations of parabolas, circles, and ellipses are given. Graph the equation.

36. $x^2 + y^2 = 64$

37. $25x^2 + 81y^2 = 2025$

38. $36y + x^2 = 0$

39. $65y^2 = 130x$

40. $30x^2 + 30y^2 = 480$

41. $\dfrac{x^2}{75} + \dfrac{4y}{25} = 0$

42. $\dfrac{3x^2}{48} + \dfrac{4y^2}{400} = 1$

43. $\dfrac{x^2}{64} + \dfrac{y^2}{64} = 4$

44. $16x^2 + 10y^2 = 160$

45. ★ **SHORT RESPONSE** Consider the graph of $\dfrac{x^2}{9} + \dfrac{y^2}{25} = 1$. *Describe* the effects on the graph of changing the denominator of the y^2-term first from 25 to 9 and then from 9 to 4. Graph the original equation and the two revised equations in the same coordinate plane.

46. ★ **OPEN-ENDED MATH** Write an equation of an ellipse in standard form. Graph the equation on a graphing calculator by rewriting it as two functions. Give a viewing window that does not distort the shape of the ellipse, and explain how you found your viewing window.

47. **CHALLENGE** Use the definition of an ellipse to show that $c^2 = a^2 - b^2$ for any ellipse with equation $\dfrac{x^2}{a^2} + \dfrac{y^2}{b^2} = 1$ and foci at $(c, 0)$ and $(-c, 0)$. (*Hint:* Draw a diagram. Consider the point $P(a, 0)$ on the ellipse.)

PROBLEM SOLVING

EXAMPLE 3
for Exs. 48–50

48. **MARS** On January 3, 2004, the Mars rover Spirit bounced on its airbags to a landing within Gusev crater. Scientists had estimated that there was a 99% chance the rover would land inside an ellipse with a major axis 81 kilometers long and a minor axis 12 kilometers long. Write an equation of the ellipse. Then find its area.

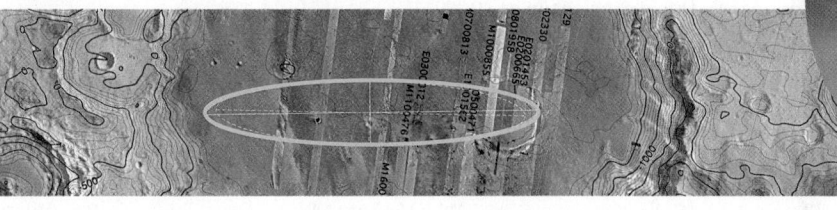

Artist's rendering of landing

49. **AUSTRALIAN FOOTBALL** The playing field for Australian football is an ellipse that is between 135 and 185 meters long and between 110 and 155 meters wide. Write equations of ellipses with vertical major axes that model the largest and smallest fields described. Then write an inequality that describes the possible areas of these fields.

center right Detlev Van Ravenswaay/SPL/Photo Researchers, Inc.; center left NASA/ARC

50. HEALTH CARE A *lithotripter* uses shock waves to break apart kidney stones or gallstones inside the body. Shock waves generated at one focus of an *ellipsoid* (a three-dimensional shape with an elliptical cross section) reflect to the stone positioned at the second focus. Write an equation for the cross section of the ellipsoid with the dimensions shown. How far apart are the foci?

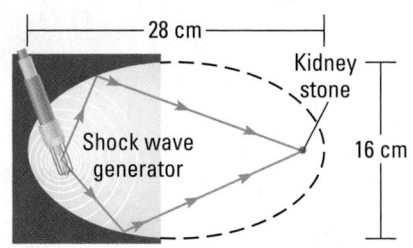

51. ★ **SHORT RESPONSE** Halley's comet ranges from 0.59 to 35.3 astronomical units from the sun, which is at one focus of the comet's elliptical orbit. (An *astronomical unit* is Earth's mean distance from the sun.) *Explain* using a sketch how to find *a* and *c*. Then write an equation for the orbit.

52. ★ **EXTENDED RESPONSE** A small airplane with enough fuel to fly 600 miles safely will take off from airport A and land at airport B, 450 miles away.

   a. Reason The region in which the airplane can fly is bounded by an ellipse. *Explain* why this is so.

   b. Calculate Let (0, 0) represent the center of the ellipse. Find the coordinates of each airport.

   c. Apply Suppose the plane flies from airport A straight past airport B to a vertex of the ellipse and then straight back to airport B. How far does the plane fly? Use your answer to find the coordinates of the vertex.

   d. Model Write an equation of the ellipse.

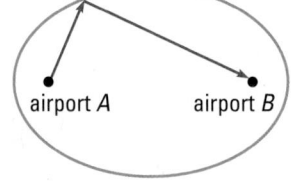

53. CHALLENGE An art museum worker leaves an 8-foot-tall painting leaning against a wall. Later, the top of the painting slides down the wall, and the painting falls to the floor. Use the diagram to find an equation of the path of the point (*x*, *y*) as the painting falls.

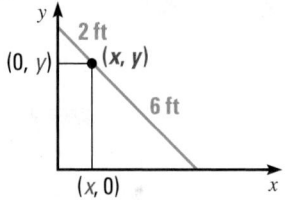

Using ALTERNATIVE METHODS

Another Way to Solve Example 3

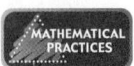

Make sense of problems and persevere in solving them.

MULTIPLE REPRESENTATIONS In the second part of Example 3, you found the area of an ellipse using a formula. You can also approximate the area of an ellipse by summing the areas of rectangles.

PROBLEM

LIGHTNING When lightning strikes, an elliptical region where the strike most likely hit can often be identified. Suppose it is determined that there is a 50% chance that a lightning strike hit within the elliptical region shown in the diagram.

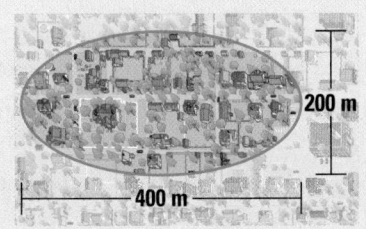

- Write an equation of the ellipse.

- Find the area of the elliptical region.

METHOD

Summing Rectangles As you saw in Example 3, the ellipse has the equation $\frac{x^2}{200^2} + \frac{y^2}{100^2} = 1$. Approximate the area of the ellipse as follows.

STEP 1 **Graph** the first-quadrant portion of the ellipse. Then draw rectangles of width 40 and height equal to the *y*-value of the ellipse at the rectangle's left edge. The first rectangle's height is $y_1 = 100$. To find the other *y*-values, solve for *y* to obtain $y = \sqrt{100^2 - \frac{x^2}{4}}$. Use a calculator to get $y_2 \approx 98.0$, $y_3 \approx 91.7$, $y_4 = 80$, and $y_5 = 60$.

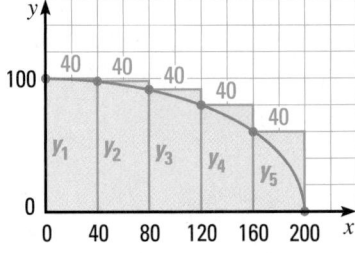

STEP 2 **Calculate** the total area *A* of the rectangles.

$$A \approx 40(100) + 40(98.0) + 40(91.7) + 40(80) + 40(60) = 17{,}188 \text{ m}^2$$

STEP 3 **Multiply** the total area of the rectangles by 4 to obtain an estimate of $4(17{,}188) \approx 68{,}800$ square meters for the area of the ellipse.

PRACTICE

1. Solve the problem above using rectangles of width 20. Is this estimate better or worse than the estimate above? *Explain.*

2. **REASONING** *Explain* using your results from Exercise 1 how to obtain a closer and closer approximation of the ellipse's area.

3. **WHAT IF?** Suppose that the ellipse in the problem had a horizontal major axis of 250 meters and a minor axis of 200 meters.

   a. Write an equation of the ellipse.

   b. Use the method above to approximate the area of the ellipse.

1. **MULTI-STEP PROBLEM** Parabolic reflectors with a microphone at the focus allow you to listen to sounds from far away. A parabolic microphone has a reflector that is 22.4 inches in diameter and 8 inches deep.

   a. How far is the focus from the vertex?

   b. Write an equation for the cross section of the reflector such that the vertex is at (0, 0) and the reflector opens to the right.

   c. Graph the equation from part (b).

2. **MULTI-STEP PROBLEM** A fishing boat's radar has a range of 16 miles. A second boat is 12 miles west and 12 miles south of the fishing boat.

   a. Write an inequality describing the region covered by the radar if the fishing boat is anchored at the origin.

   b. Is the second boat in range of the radar?

   c. A third boat 6 miles north and 4 miles east of the fishing boat begins moving westward. For what distance will the third boat be in radar range of the fishing boat?

3. **MULTI-STEP PROBLEM** In its elliptical orbit, Mercury ranges from 29 million miles to 44 million miles from the sun, which is at one focus of the orbit.

   a. Draw a sketch of the situation.

   b. Find the values of a and c.

   c. Write an equation for Mercury's orbit.

4. **OPEN-ENDED** Write an equation of an ellipse that has its center at the origin, a horizontal minor axis, and lies completely between the circles $x^2 + y^2 = 25$ and $x^2 + y^2 = 64$.

5. **EXTENDED RESPONSE** A car skids while turning to avoid an accident. The car's speed v (in meters per second) can be estimated using $v = \sqrt{9.8\mu r}$ where r is the radius (in meters) of the circular skid mark and μ is a constant that depends on the road surface and weather conditions ($0 \le \mu \le 1$).

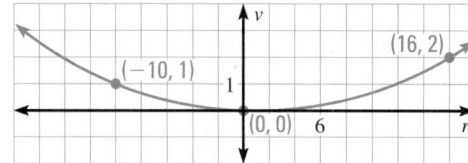

   a. Find the radius of the skid mark shown.

   b. Estimate how fast the car was traveling if it is determined that $\mu = 0.7$.

   c. How does the car's speed while skidding affect the radius of the circle? *Explain.*

6. **SHORT RESPONSE** Two lines are tangent to the circle $x^2 + y^2 = 13$, one at (−2, −3) and one at (3, −2). What is the relationship between the two lines? *Explain.*

7. **OPEN-ENDED** Write an equation of a parabola that has its vertex at the origin and passes between (−2, 4) and (−3, 9).

8. **GRIDDED ANSWER** To get from your home to the beach, you drive 8 miles south, then 16 miles east, and then 4 miles south. What is the straight-line distance from your home to the beach?

9. **GRIDDED ANSWER** You can make a solar hot dog cooker by shaping foil-lined cardboard into a parabolic trough and passing a wire through the focus of each end piece. For the trough shown, how far from the bottom, to the nearest tenth of an inch, should the wire be placed?

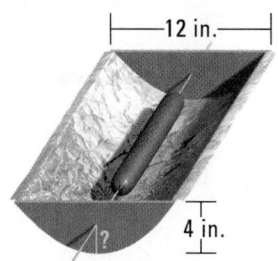

8.5 Graph and Write Equations of Hyperbolas

Before	You graphed and wrote equations of parabolas, circles, and ellipses.
Now	You will graph and write equations of hyperbolas.
Why?	So you can model curved mirrors, as in Example 3.

Key Vocabulary
- **hyperbola**
- **foci**
- **vertices**
- **transverse axis**
- **center**

CC.9-12.G.GPE.3 (+) Derive the equations of ellipses and hyperbolas given the foci, using the fact that the sum or difference of distances from the foci is constant.

IDENTIFY AXES

If the x^2-term in the equation of a hyperbola is positive, the transverse axis lies on the x-axis. If the y^2-term is positive, the transverse axis lies on the y-axis.

Recall that an ellipse is the set of all points P in a plane such that the *sum* of the distances between P and two fixed points (the foci) is a constant.

A **hyperbola** is the set of all points P such that the *difference* of the distances between P and two fixed points, again called the **foci**, is a constant.

The line through the foci intersects the hyperbola at the two **vertices**. The **transverse axis** joins the vertices. Its midpoint is the hyperbola's **center**. A hyperbola has two *branches*, and has two asymptotes that contain the diagonals of a rectangle centered at the hyperbola's center, as shown.

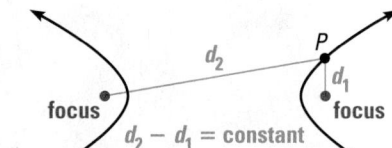

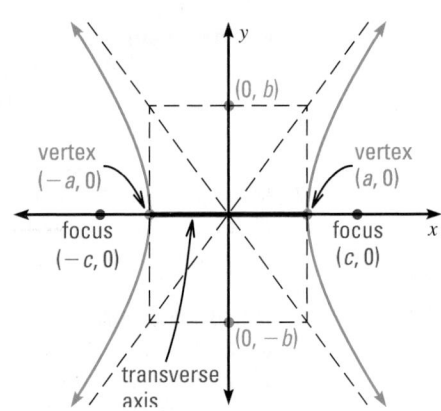

Hyperbola with horizontal transverse axis
$$\frac{x^2}{a^2} - \frac{y^2}{b^2} = 1$$

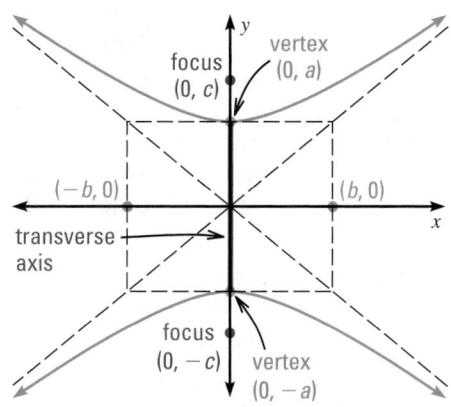

Hyperbola with vertical transverse axis
$$\frac{y^2}{a^2} - \frac{x^2}{b^2} = 1$$

KEY CONCEPT *For Your Notebook*

Standard Equation of a Hyperbola with Center at the Origin

Equation	Transverse Axis	Asymptotes	Vertices
$\dfrac{x^2}{a^2} - \dfrac{y^2}{b^2} = 1$	Horizontal	$y = \pm\dfrac{b}{a}x$	$(\pm a, 0)$
$\dfrac{y^2}{a^2} - \dfrac{x^2}{b^2} = 1$	Vertical	$y = \pm\dfrac{a}{b}x$	$(0, \pm a)$

The foci lie on the transverse axis, c units from the center, where $c^2 = a^2 + b^2$.

EXAMPLE 1   Graph an equation of a hyperbola

Graph $25y^2 - 4x^2 = 100$. Identify the vertices, foci, and asymptotes of the hyperbola.

Solution

STEP 1   **Rewrite** the equation in standard form.

$$25y^2 - 4x^2 = 100 \qquad \text{Write original equation.}$$

$$\frac{25y^2}{100} - \frac{4x^2}{100} = \frac{100}{100} \qquad \text{Divide each side by 100.}$$

$$\frac{y^2}{4} - \frac{x^2}{25} = 1 \qquad \text{Simplify.}$$

STEP 2   **Identify** the vertices, foci, and asymptotes. Note that $a^2 = 4$ and $b^2 = 25$, so $a = 2$ and $b = 5$. The y^2-term is positive, so the transverse axis is vertical and the vertices are at $(0, \pm 2)$. Find the foci.

$$c^2 = a^2 + b^2 = 2^2 + 5^2 = 29, \text{ so } c = \sqrt{29}$$

The foci are at $\left(0, \pm\sqrt{29}\right) \approx (0, \pm 5.4)$.

The asymptotes are $y = \pm\dfrac{a}{b}x$, or $y = \pm\dfrac{2}{5}x$.

SOLVE FOR Y

To plot points on the hyperbola, solve its equation for *y* to obtain $y = \pm 2\sqrt{1 + \dfrac{x^2}{25}}$. Then make a table of values.

STEP 3   **Draw** the hyperbola. First draw a rectangle centered at the origin that is $2a = 4$ units high and $2b = 10$ units wide. The asymptotes pass through opposite corners of the rectangle. Then, draw the hyperbola passing through the vertices and approaching the asymptotes.

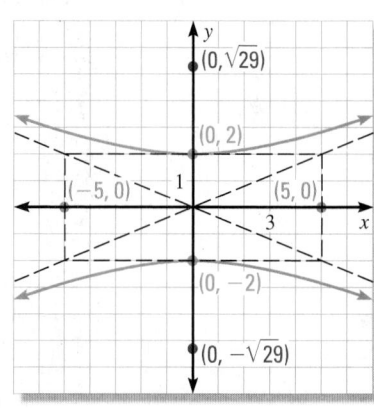

Animated Algebra   at my.hrw.com

EXAMPLE 2   Write an equation of a hyperbola

Write an equation of the hyperbola with foci at $(-4, 0)$ and $(4, 0)$ and vertices at $(-3, 0)$ and $(3, 0)$.

Solution

The foci and vertices lie on the *x*-axis equidistant from the origin, so the transverse axis is horizontal and the center is the origin. The foci are each 4 units from the center, so $c = 4$. The vertices are each 3 units from the center, so $a = 3$.

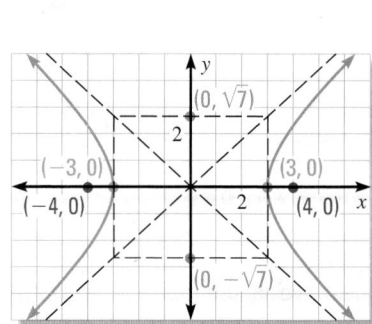

Because $c^2 = a^2 + b^2$, you have $b^2 = c^2 - a^2$. Find b^2.

$$b^2 = c^2 - a^2 = 4^2 - 3^2 = 7$$

Because the transverse axis is horizontal, the standard form of the equation is as follows:

$$\frac{x^2}{3^2} - \frac{y^2}{7} = 1 \qquad \text{Substitute 3 for } a \text{ and 7 for } b^2.$$

$$\frac{x^2}{9} - \frac{y^2}{7} = 1 \qquad \text{Simplify.}$$

Graph the equation. Identify the vertices, foci, and asymptotes of the hyperbola.

1. $\dfrac{x^2}{16} - \dfrac{y^2}{49} = 1$ **2.** $\dfrac{y^2}{36} - x^2 = 1$ **3.** $4y^2 - 9x^2 = 36$

Write an equation of the hyperbola with the given foci and vertices.

4. Foci: $(-3, 0)$, $(3, 0)$
   Vertices: $(-1, 0)$, $(1, 0)$

5. Foci: $(0, -10)$, $(0, 10)$
   Vertices: $(0, -6)$, $(0, 6)$

EXAMPLE 3 Solve a multi-step problem

PHOTOGRAPHY You can take panoramic photographs using a hyperbolic mirror. Light rays heading toward the focus behind the mirror are reflected to a camera positioned at the other focus as shown. After a photograph is taken, computers can "unwarp" the distorted image into a 360° view.

- Write an equation for the cross section of the mirror.

- The mirror is 6 centimeters wide. How tall is it?

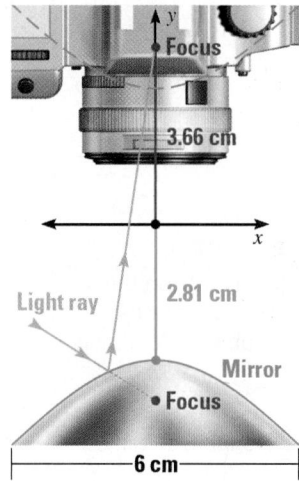

Solution

STEP 1 From the diagram, $a = 2.81$ and $c = 3.66$.

To write an equation, find b^2.

$$b^2 = c^2 - a^2 = 3.66^2 - 2.81^2 \approx 5.50$$

▶ Because the transverse axis is vertical, the standard form of the equation for the cross section of the mirror is as follows:

$$\dfrac{y^2}{2.81^2} - \dfrac{x^2}{5.50} = 1, \quad \text{or} \quad \dfrac{y^2}{7.90} - \dfrac{x^2}{5.50} = 1$$

STEP 2 Find the y-coordinate at the mirror's bottom edge. Because the mirror is 6 centimeters wide, substitute $x = 3$ into the equation and solve.

$$\dfrac{y^2}{7.90} - \dfrac{3^2}{5.50} = 1 \qquad \text{Substitute 3 for } x.$$

$$y^2 \approx 20.83 \qquad \text{Solve for } y^2.$$

$$y \approx -4.56 \qquad \text{Solve for } y.$$

AVOID ERRORS
The mirror is below the x-axis, so choose the negative square root.

▶ So, the mirror has a height of $-2.81 - (-4.56) = 1.75$ centimeters.

6. WHAT IF? In Example 3, suppose that the mirror remains 6 centimeters wide, but that $a = 3$ centimeters and $c = 5$ centimeters. How tall is the mirror?

8.5 EXERCISES

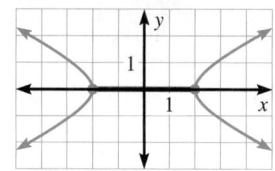

○ = See WORKED-OUT SOLUTIONS
Exs. 13, 23, and 41

★ = STANDARDIZED TEST PRACTICE
Exs. 2, 15, 26, 33, 35, and 43

◆ = MULTIPLE REPRESENTATIONS
Ex. 42

SKILL PRACTICE

1. **VOCABULARY** Copy and complete: The points $(-2, 0)$ and $(2, 0)$ in the graph at the right are the __?__ of the hyperbola. The line segment joining these two points is the __?__.

2. ★ **WRITING** *Compare* the definitions of an ellipse and a hyperbola.

EXAMPLE 1
for Exs. 3–17

GRAPHING **Graph the equation. Identify the vertices, foci, and asymptotes of the hyperbola.**

3. $\dfrac{x^2}{25} - \dfrac{y^2}{4} = 1$

4. $\dfrac{x^2}{9} - \dfrac{y^2}{36} = 1$

5. $\dfrac{y^2}{81} - \dfrac{x^2}{25} = 1$

6. $\dfrac{x^2}{144} - \dfrac{y^2}{36} = 1$

7. $\dfrac{y^2}{196} - \dfrac{x^2}{100} = 1$

8. $\dfrac{y^2}{49} - \dfrac{x^2}{121} = 1$

9. $4x^2 - y^2 = 256$

10. $49x^2 - 4y^2 = 196$

11. $9y^2 - 25x^2 = 225$

12. $25y^2 - 64x^2 = 1600$

13. $81x^2 - 16y^2 = 1296$

14. $49y^2 - 100x^2 = 4900$

15. ★ **MULTIPLE CHOICE** What are the foci of the hyperbola with equation $45y^2 - 200x^2 = 1800$?

Ⓐ $(\pm 2\sqrt{10}, 0)$ Ⓑ $(0, \pm 2\sqrt{10})$ Ⓒ $(\pm 7, 0)$ Ⓓ $(0, \pm 7)$

ERROR ANALYSIS *Describe* and correct the error in graphing the equation.

16.
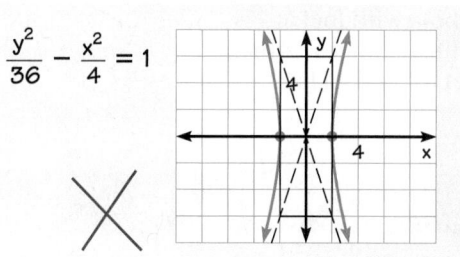
$\dfrac{y^2}{36} - \dfrac{x^2}{4} = 1$

17.
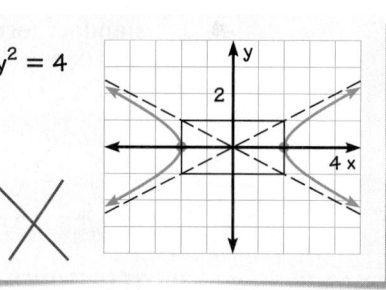
$\dfrac{x^2}{4} - y^2 = 4$

EXAMPLE 2
for Exs. 18–26

WRITING EQUATIONS **Write an equation of the hyperbola with the given foci and vertices.**

18. Foci: $(0, -4), (0, 4)$
Vertices: $(0, -2), (0, 2)$

19. Foci: $(-6, 0), (6, 0)$
Vertices: $(-2, 0), (2, 0)$

20. Foci: $(-5, 0), (5, 0)$
Vertices: $(-1, 0), (1, 0)$

21. Foci: $(0, -12), (0, 12)$
Vertices: $(0, -7), (0, 7)$

22. Foci: $(-10, 0), (10, 0)$
Vertices: $(-5\sqrt{3}, 0), (5\sqrt{3}, 0)$

23. Foci: $(0, -4\sqrt{5}), (0, 4\sqrt{5})$
Vertices: $(0, -4), (0, 4)$

24. Foci: $(0, -3), (0, 3)$
Vertices: $(0, -2\sqrt{2}), (0, 2\sqrt{2})$

25. Foci: $(-3\sqrt{6}, 0), (3\sqrt{6}, 0)$
Vertices: $(-2, 0), (2, 0)$

8.5 Graph and Write Equations of Hyperbolas **521**

26. ★ **MULTIPLE CHOICE** What is an equation of the hyperbola with foci at $\left(0, -6\sqrt{3}\right)$ and $\left(0, 6\sqrt{3}\right)$ and with vertices at $(0, -8)$ and $(0, 8)$?

(A) $\dfrac{x^2}{64} - \dfrac{y^2}{108} = 1$ (B) $\dfrac{x^2}{44} - \dfrac{y^2}{68} = 1$ (C) $\dfrac{y^2}{64} - \dfrac{x^2}{44} = 1$ (D) $\dfrac{y^2}{108} - \dfrac{x^2}{64} = 1$

GRAPHING In Exercises 27–32, the equations of parabolas, circles, ellipses, and hyperbolas are given. Graph the equation.

27. $\dfrac{x^2}{25} - \dfrac{y^2}{49} = 1$

28. $y^2 = 18x$

29. $48x^2 + 12y^2 = 48$

30. $\dfrac{x^2}{144} + \dfrac{y^2}{256} = 1$

31. $\dfrac{y^2}{25} - \dfrac{x^2}{121} = 1$

32. $18x^2 + 18y^2 = 288$

33. ★ **SHORT RESPONSE** *Describe* the effects of the indicated change on the shape of the hyperbola and on the locations of the vertices and foci.

a. $\dfrac{x^2}{9} - \dfrac{y^2}{36} = 1$; change 36 to 4

b. $\dfrac{y^2}{16} - \dfrac{x^2}{4} = 1$; change 4 to 25

34. **GRAPHING CALCULATOR** Graph each hyperbola using a graphing calculator. Tell what two functions you entered into the calculator.

a. $\dfrac{y^2}{15} - \dfrac{x^2}{30} = 1$

b. $\dfrac{x^2}{8.4} - \dfrac{y^2}{5.5} = 1$

c. $5x^2 - 7.5y^2 = 12$

35. ★ **OPEN-ENDED MATH** Give equations of three hyperbolas with horizontal transverse axes and asymptotes $y = \pm 2x$. *Compare* the hyperbolas.

36. **REASONING** Use the diagram at the right to show that $|d_2 - d_1| = 2a$. (*Hint:* $|d_2 - d_1|$ is constant, so choose a convenient location for (x, y).)

37. **CHALLENGE** Using the distance formula and the definition of a hyperbola, write an equation in standard form of the hyperbola with foci at $(\pm 2, 0)$ if the difference in the distances from a point (x, y) on the hyperbola to the foci is 2.

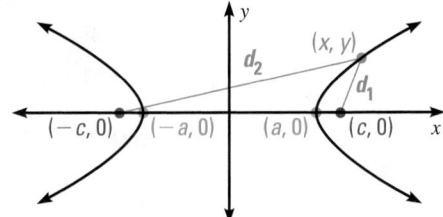

PROBLEM SOLVING

EXAMPLE 3
for Exs. 38–40

38. **TELESCOPES** A satellite is carrying a telescope that has a hyperbolic mirror for which $a = 33$ and $c = 56$ (in centimeters). Write an equation for the cross section of the mirror if the transverse axis is horizontal.

39. **SPINNING CUBE** The outline of a cube spinning around an axis through a pair of opposite corners contains a portion of a hyperbola, as shown. The coordinates given represent a vertex and a focus of the hyperbola for a cube that measures 1 unit on each edge. Write an equation that models this hyperbola.

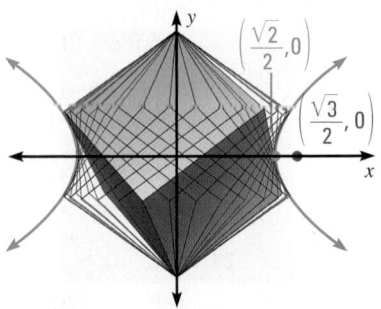

○ = See **WORKED-OUT SOLUTIONS** in Student Resources   ★ = **STANDARDIZED TEST PRACTICE**   ◆ = **MULTIPLE REPRESENTATIONS**

40. SUN'S SHADOW Each day, except at the fall and spring equinoxes, the tip of the shadow of a vertical pole traces a branch of a hyperbola across the ground. The diagram shows shadow paths for a 20 meter tall flagpole in Dallas, Texas.

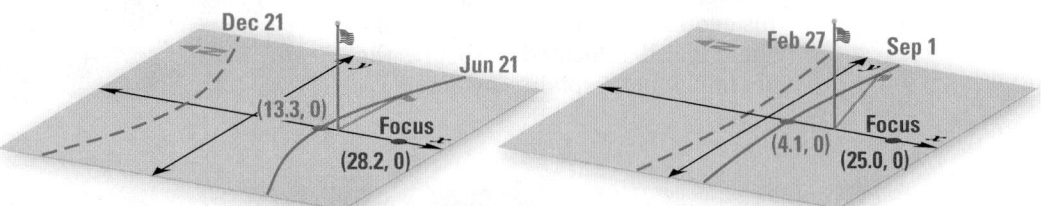

a. Write an equation of the hyperbola with center at the origin that models the June 21 path, given that $a = 13.3$ meters and $c = 28.2$ meters.

b. Write an equation of the hyperbola with center at the origin that models the September 1 path, given that $a = 4.1$ meters and $c = 25.0$ meters.

41. MULTI-STEP PROBLEM The roof of the St. Louis Science Center has a hyperbolic cross section with the dimensions shown.

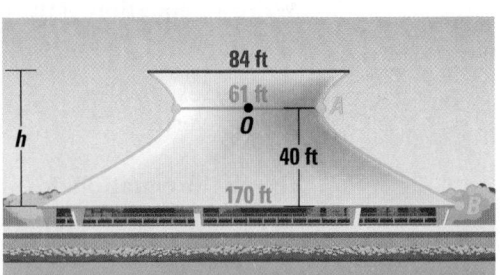

a. Suppose a coordinate grid is overlaid on the diagram with its origin at O, the center of the narrowest part of the roof. What are the coordinates of the points at A and B?

b. Use your answers from part (a) to write an equation that models the cross section.

c. Find the total height h of the roof.

42. ◆ MULTIPLE REPRESENTATIONS A circular walkway is to be built around a statue in a park. There is enough concrete available for the walkway to have an area of 600 square feet.

a. Writing an Equation Let the inside and outside radii of the walkway be x feet and y feet, respectively. Draw a diagram of the situation. Then write an equation relating x and y.

b. Making a Table Give four possible pairs of dimensions x and y that satisfy the equation from part (a).

c. Drawing a Graph Graph the equation from part (a). What portion of the graph represents solutions that make sense in this situation?

d. Reasoning How does the width of the walkway, $y - x$, change as both x and y increase? *Explain* why this makes sense.

43. ★ SHORT RESPONSE Two stones dropped at the same time into still water produce circular ripples whose intersection points form hyperbolas with foci where the stones hit the water. The graph shows one hyperbola formed by stones dropped 12 feet apart with ripples at 1 foot intervals.

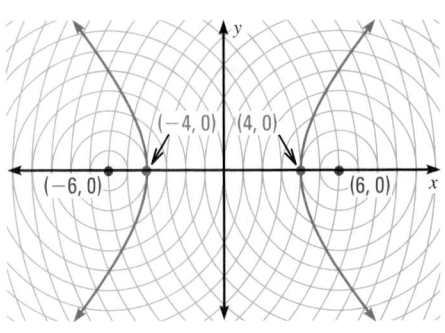

a. Write an equation of this hyperbola.

b. Use the definition of a hyperbola to explain why the graph shown is a hyperbola. (*Hint:* Examine the distances from each intersection point to the foci.)

44. CHALLENGE Two microphones placed 1 mile apart record the bugling of a bull elk. Microphone A receives the sound 2 seconds after microphone B. Sound travels at 1100 feet per second. Is this enough information to determine where the elk is located? If so, give the location. If not, explain why not.

QUIZ

Graph the equation. Identify the vertices, co-vertices, and foci of the ellipse.

1. $\dfrac{x^2}{25} + \dfrac{y^2}{4} = 1$

2. $\dfrac{x^2}{16} + \dfrac{y^2}{49} = 1$

3. $36x^2 + 9y^2 = 324$

Write an equation of the ellipse with the given characteristics and center at (0, 0).

4. Vertex: (0, 5)
Co-vertex: (−4, 0)

5. Vertex: (10, 0)
Focus: (−8, 0)

6. Co-vertex: $(-\sqrt{15}, 0)$
Focus: (0, −5)

Graph the equation. Identify the vertices, foci, and asymptotes of the hyperbola.

7. $\dfrac{y^2}{25} - \dfrac{x^2}{64} = 1$

8. $4x^2 - 16y^2 = 64$

9. $12y^2 - 20x^2 = 240$

Write an equation of the hyperbola with the given foci and vertices.

10. Foci: (−5, 0), (5, 0)
Vertices: (−2, 0), (2, 0)

11. Foci: (0, −3), (0, 3)
Vertices: (0, −1), (0, 1)

12. Foci: $(-3\sqrt{6}, 0), (3\sqrt{6}, 0)$
Vertices: (−3, 0), (3, 0)

13. ASTEROIDS The largest asteroid, 1 Ceres, ranges from 2.55 astronomical units to 2.98 astronomical units from the sun, which is located at one focus of the asteroid's elliptical orbit. Find a and c. Then write an equation of the orbit of 1 Ceres.

See **EXTRA PRACTICE** in Student Resources   ✎ **ONLINE QUIZ** at my.hrw.com

my.hrw.com
Keystrokes

Exploring Intersections of Planes and Cones

MATHEMATICAL PRACTICES

Reason abstractly and quantitatively.

MATERIALS · flashlight · graph paper

QUESTION How do a plane and a double-napped cone intersect to form different conic sections?

The reason that parabolas, circles, ellipses, and hyperbolas are called *conics* or *conic sections* is that each can be formed by the intersection of a plane and a double-napped cone, as shown below.

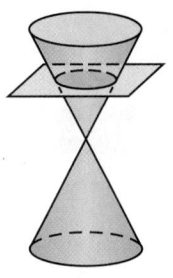
Circle

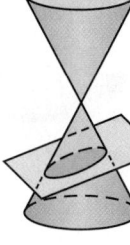
Ellipse

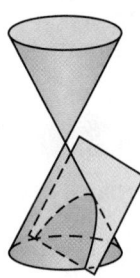
Parabola

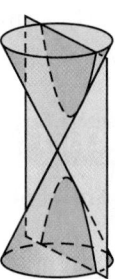
Hyperbola

EXPLORE Find an equation of a conic

STEP 1 *Draw axes*

Work in a group. On a piece of graph paper, draw *x*- and *y*-axes to make a coordinate plane. Then tape the paper to a wall.

STEP 2 *Model a circle*

Aim a flashlight perpendicular to the paper so that the light forms a circle centered on the origin of the coordinate plane. Trace the circle on the graph paper. Find the circle's radius, and use it to write the standard form of the circle's equation.

STEP 3 *Model an ellipse*

Tilt the flashlight, and aim it at the paper to form an ellipse with a vertical major axis and center at the origin. Trace the ellipse and write the standard form of its equation.

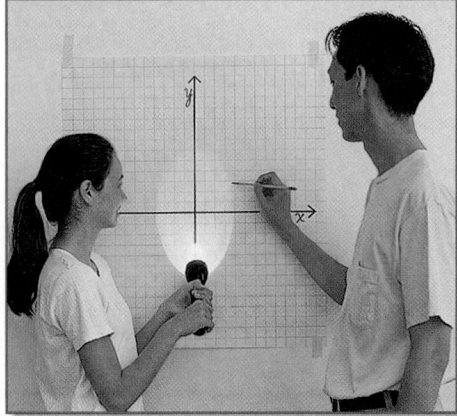

DRAW CONCLUSIONS Use your observations to complete these exercises

1. *Compare* the equations for your circle and for your ellipse with the equations of other groups. Are your equations all the same? Why or why not?

2. Refer to the diagram of a hyperbola to explain how you can orient the flashlight beam to form a branch of a hyperbola on the wall.

8.6 Translate and Classify Conic Sections

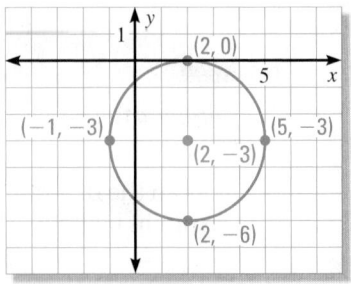

Before You graphed and wrote equations of conic sections.

Now You will translate conic sections.

Why? So you can model motion, as in Ex. 49.

Key Vocabulary
- conic sections (conics)
- general second-degree equation
- discriminant

CC.9-12.G.GPE.3 (+) Derive the equations of ellipses and hyperbolas given the foci, using the fact that the sum or difference of distances from the foci is constant.

Because parabolas, circles, ellipses, and hyperbolas are formed when a plane intersects a double-napped cone, they are called **conic sections** or **conics**.

Previously, you studied equations of parabolas with vertices at the origin and equations of circles, ellipses, and hyperbolas with centers at the origin. Now you will study how translating conics in the coordinate plane affects their equations.

KEY CONCEPT *For Your Notebook*

Standard Form of Equations of Translated Conics

In the following equations, the point (h, k) is the *vertex* of the parabola and the *center* of the other conics.

Circle $\qquad (x - h)^2 + (y - k)^2 = r^2$

	Horizontal axis	**Vertical axis**
Parabola	$(y - k)^2 = 4p(x - h)$	$(x - h)^2 = 4p(y - k)$
Ellipse	$\dfrac{(x - h)^2}{a^2} + \dfrac{(y - k)^2}{b^2} = 1$	$\dfrac{(x - h)^2}{b^2} + \dfrac{(y - k)^2}{a^2} = 1$
Hyperbola	$\dfrac{(x - h)^2}{a^2} - \dfrac{(y - k)^2}{b^2} = 1$	$\dfrac{(y - k)^2}{a^2} - \dfrac{(x - h)^2}{b^2} = 1$

EXAMPLE 1 Graph the equation of a translated circle

Graph $(x - 2)^2 + (y + 3)^2 = 9.$

Solution

STEP 1 **Compare** the given equation to the standard form of an equation of a circle. You can see that the graph is a circle with center at $(h, k) = (2, -3)$ and radius $r = \sqrt{9} = 3$.

STEP 2 **Plot** the center. Then plot several points that are each 3 units from the center:

$(2 + 3, -3) = (5, -3) \qquad (2 - 3, -3) = (-1, -3)$

$(2, -3 + 3) = (2, 0) \qquad (2, -3 - 3) = (2, -6)$

STEP 3 **Draw** a circle through the points.

Courtesy of Superdairyboy

EXAMPLE 2 Graph the equation of a translated hyperbola

Graph $\dfrac{(y-3)^2}{4} - \dfrac{(x+1)^2}{9} = 1$.

Solution

STEP 1 **Compare** the given equation to the standard forms of equations of hyperbolas. The equation's form tells you that the graph is a hyperbola with a vertical transverse axis. The center is at $(h, k) = (-1, 3)$. Because $a^2 = 4$ and $b^2 = 9$, you know that $a = 2$ and $b = 3$.

STEP 2 **Plot** the center, vertices, and foci. The vertices lie $a = 2$ units above and below the center, at $(-1, 5)$ and $(-1, 1)$. Because $c^2 = a^2 + b^2 = 13$, the foci lie $c = \sqrt{13} \approx 3.6$ units above and below the center, at $(-1, 6.6)$ and $(-1, -0.6)$.

SOLVE FOR Y

To plot additional points on the hyperbola, solve for y to obtain

$$y = 3 \pm 2\sqrt{1 + \dfrac{(x+1)^2}{9}}.$$

Then make a table of values.

STEP 3 **Draw** the hyperbola. Draw a rectangle centered at $(-1, 3)$ that is $2a = 4$ units high and $2b = 6$ units wide. Draw the asymptotes through the opposite corners of the rectangle. Then draw the hyperbola passing through the vertices and approaching the asymptotes.

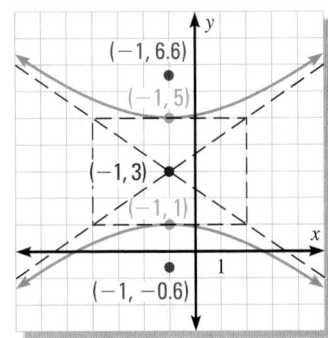

Animated Algebra at my.hrw.com

✓ **GUIDED PRACTICE** for Examples 1 and 2

Graph the equation. Identify the important characteristics of the graph.

1. $(x+1)^2 + (y-3)^2 = 4$

2. $(x-2)^2 = 8(y+3)$

3. $(x+3)^2 - \dfrac{(y-4)^2}{4} = 1$

4. $\dfrac{(x-2)^2}{16} + \dfrac{(y-1)^2}{9} = 1$

❖ EXAMPLE 3 Write an equation of a translated parabola

Write an equation of the parabola whose vertex is at $(-2, 3)$ and whose focus is at $(-4, 3)$.

Solution

STEP 1 **Determine** the form of the equation. Begin by making a rough sketch of the parabola. Because the focus is to the left of the vertex, the parabola opens to the left, and its equation has the form $(y - k)^2 = 4p(x - h)$ where $p < 0$.

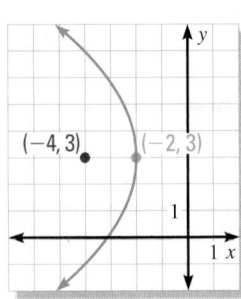

STEP 2 **Identify** h and k. The vertex is at $(-2, 3)$, so $h = -2$ and $k = 3$.

STEP 3 **Find** p. The vertex $(-2, 3)$ and focus $(-4, 3)$ both lie on the line $y = 3$, so the distance between them is $|p| = |-4 - (-2)| = 2$, and thus $p = \pm 2$. Because $p < 0$, it follows that $p = -2$, so $4p = -8$.

▶ The standard form of the equation is $(y - 3)^2 = -8(x + 2)$.

EXAMPLE 4 **Write an equation of a translated ellipse**

Write an equation of the ellipse with foci at (1, 2) and (7, 2) and co-vertices at (4, 0) and (4, 4).

Solution

STEP 1 **Determine** the form of the equation. First sketch the ellipse. The foci lie on the major axis, so the axis is horizontal. The equation has this form:

$$\frac{(x-h)^2}{a^2} + \frac{(y-k)^2}{b^2} = 1$$

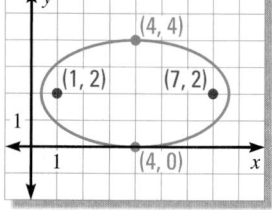

STEP 2 **Identify** h and k by finding the center, which is halfway between the foci (or the co-vertices).

$$(h, k) = \left(\frac{1+7}{2}, \frac{2+2}{2} \right) = (4, 2)$$

FIND DISTANCE
The co-vertices lie on a vertical line through the center and the foci lie on a horizontal line through the center, so you do not have to use the distance formula.

STEP 3 **Find** b, the distance between a co-vertex and the center (4, 2), and c, the distance between a focus and the center. Choose the co-vertex (4, 4) and the focus (1, 2): $b = |4 - 2| = 2$ and $c = |1 - 4| = 3$.

STEP 4 **Find** a. For an ellipse, $a^2 = b^2 + c^2 = 2^2 + 3^2 = 13$, so $a = \sqrt{13}$.

▶ The standard form of the equation is $\frac{(x-4)^2}{13} + \frac{(y-2)^2}{4} = 1$.

EXAMPLE 5 **Identify symmetries of conic sections**

Identify the line(s) of symmetry for each conic section in Examples 1–4.

Solution

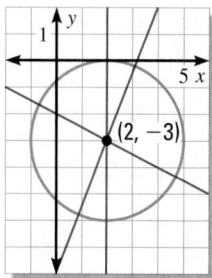

For the circle in Example 1, any line through the center (2, −3) is a line of symmetry.

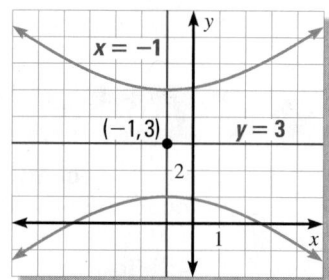

For the hyperbola in Example 2, $x = -1$ and $y = 3$ are lines of symmetry.

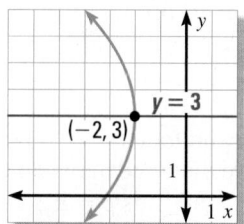

For the parabola in Example 3, $y = 3$ is a line of symmetry.

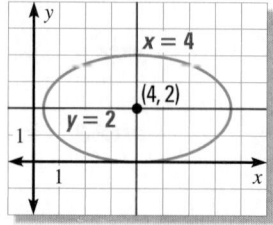

For the ellipse in Example 4, $x = 4$ and $y = 2$ are lines of symmetry.

Write an equation of the conic section.

5. Parabola with vertex at $(3, -1)$ and focus at $(3, 2)$

6. Hyperbola with vertices at $(-7, 3)$ and $(-1, 3)$ and foci at $(-9, 3)$ and $(1, 3)$

Identify the line(s) of symmetry for the conic section.

7. $\dfrac{(x-5)^2}{64} + \dfrac{y^2}{16} = 1$ 8. $(x+5)^2 = 8(y-2)$ 9. $\dfrac{(x-1)^2}{49} - \dfrac{(y-2)^2}{121} = 1$

KEY CONCEPT *For Your Notebook*

Classifying Conics Using Their Equations

Any conic can be described by a **general second-degree equation** in x and y: $Ax^2 + Bxy + Cy^2 + Dx + Ey + F = 0$. The expression $B^2 - 4AC$ is the **discriminant** of the equation and can be used to identify the type of conic.

Discriminant	Type of Conic
$B^2 - 4AC < 0$, $B = 0$, and $A = C$	Circle
$B^2 - 4AC < 0$ and either $B \neq 0$ or $A \neq C$	Ellipse
$B^2 - 4AC = 0$	Parabola
$B^2 - 4AC > 0$	Hyperbola

If $B = 0$, each axis of the conic is horizontal or vertical.

EXAMPLE 6 **Classify a conic**

Classify the conic given by $4x^2 + y^2 - 8x - 8 = 0$. Then graph the equation.

Solution

Note that $A = 4$, $B = 0$, and $C = 1$, so the value of the discriminant is:

$B^2 - 4AC = 0^2 - 4(4)(1) = -16$

Because $B^2 - 4AC < 0$ and $A \neq C$, the conic is an ellipse.

COMPLETE THE SQUARE
For help with completing the square you may want to review the lesson *Complete the Square*.

To graph the ellipse, first complete the square in x.

$4x^2 + y^2 - 8x - 8 = 0$

$(4x^2 - 8x) + y^2 = 8$

$4(x^2 - 2x) + y^2 = 8$

$4(x^2 - 2x + \mathbf{?}) + y^2 = 8 + 4(\mathbf{?})$

$4(x^2 - 2x + \mathbf{1}) + y^2 = 8 + 4(\mathbf{1})$

$4(x - 1)^2 + y^2 = 12$

$\dfrac{(x-1)^2}{3} + \dfrac{y^2}{12} = 1$

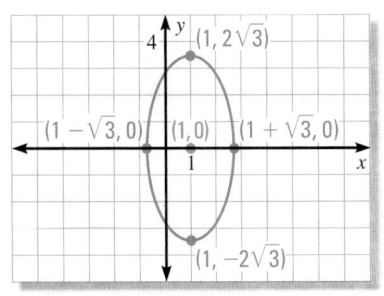

From the equation, you can see that $(h, k) = (1, 0)$, $a = \sqrt{12} = 2\sqrt{3}$, and $b = \sqrt{3}$. Use these facts to draw the ellipse.

EXAMPLE 7 **Solve a multi-step problem**

PHYSICAL SCIENCE In a lab experiment, you record images of a steel ball rolling past a magnet. The equation $16x^2 - 9y^2 - 96x + 36y - 36 = 0$ models the ball's path.

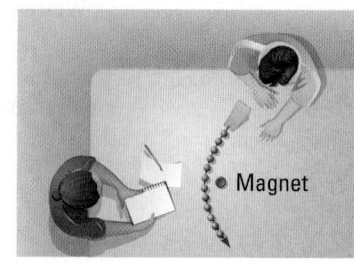
• Magnet

• What is the shape of the path?

• Write an equation for the path in standard form.

• Graph the equation of the path.

Solution

STEP 1 **Identify** the shape. The equation is a general second-degree equation with $A = 16$, $B = 0$, and $C = -9$. Find the value of the discriminant.

$$B^2 - 4AC = 0^2 - 4(16)(-9) = 576$$

Because $B^2 - 4AC > 0$, the shape of the path is a hyperbola.

STEP 2 **Write** an equation. To write an equation of the hyperbola, complete the square in both x and y simultaneously.

$$16x^2 - 9y^2 - 96x + 36y - 36 = 0$$

$$(16x^2 - 96x) - (9y^2 - 36y) = 36$$

$$16(x^2 - 6x + \boxed{?}) - 9(y^2 - 4y + \boxed{?}) = 36 + 16(\boxed{?}) - 9(\boxed{?})$$

$$16(x^2 - 6x + \mathbf{9}) - 9(y^2 - 4y + \mathbf{4}) = 36 + 16(\mathbf{9}) - 9(\mathbf{4})$$

$$16(x - 3)^2 - 9(y - 2)^2 = 144$$

$$\frac{(x - 3)^2}{9} - \frac{(y - 2)^2}{16} = 1$$

> **AVOID ERRORS**
> To complete the square in two variables, you must add a quantity to or subtract a quantity from each side for *each* variable.

STEP 3 **Graph** the equation. From the equation, the transverse axis is horizontal, $(h, k) = (3, 2)$, $a = \sqrt{9} = 3$, and $b = \sqrt{16} = 4$. The vertices are at $(3 \pm a, 2)$, or $(6, 2)$ and $(0, 2)$.

Plot the center and vertices. Then draw a rectangle $2a = 6$ units wide and $2b = 8$ units high centered at $(3, 2)$, draw the asymptotes, and draw the hyperbola.

Notice that the path of the ball is modeled by just the right-hand branch of the hyperbola.

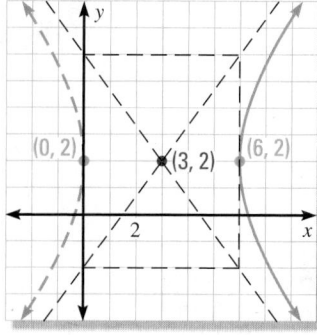

✓ **GUIDED PRACTICE** for Examples 6 and 7

Classify the conic section and write its equation in standard form. Then graph the equation.

10. $x^2 + y^2 - 2x + 4y + 1 = 0$

11. $2x^2 + y^2 - 4x \ 4 = 0$

12. $y^2 - 4y - 2x + 6 = 0$

13. $4x^2 - y^2 - 16x - 4y - 4 = 0$

14. **ASTRONOMY** An asteroid's path is modeled by $4x^2 + 6.25y^2 - 12x - 16 = 0$ where x and y are in astronomical units from the sun. Classify the path and write its equation in standard form. Then graph the equation.

8.6 EXERCISES

HOMEWORK KEY

○ = See WORKED-OUT SOLUTIONS
Exs. 3, 19, and 49

★ = STANDARDIZED TEST PRACTICE
Exs. 2, 12, 36, 45, 51, and 52

SKILL PRACTICE

1. **VOCABULARY** *Explain* why circles, ellipses, parabolas, and hyperbolas are called conic sections.

2. ★ **WRITING** *Explain* how the discriminant of a general second-degree equation can be used to identify what conic the equation represents.

EXAMPLES 1 and 2
for Exs. 3–12

GRAPHING Graph the equation. Identify the important characteristics of the graph.

3. $(x + 4)^2 = -8(y - 2)$

4. $(x - 2)^2 + (y - 7)^2 = 9$

5. $\dfrac{(x - 6)^2}{25} - (y + 1)^2 = 1$

6. $\dfrac{(y + 4)^2}{49} - \dfrac{(x + 8)^2}{9} = 1$

7. $\dfrac{(x + 2)^2}{16} + \dfrac{(y - 2)^2}{36} = 1$

8. $(x - 5)^2 + (y + 1)^2 = 64$

9. $(y - 1)^2 = 4(x + 6)$

10. $\dfrac{x^2}{25} + \dfrac{(y - 2)^2}{4} = 1$

11. $\dfrac{(x + 3)^2}{9} - \dfrac{(y - 4)^2}{16} = 1$

12. ★ **MULTIPLE CHOICE** What are the coordinates of the co-vertices of the ellipse with equation $\dfrac{(x - 4)^2}{16} + \dfrac{(y - 1)^2}{4} = 1$?

Ⓐ $(0, 1), (8, 1)$ Ⓑ $(-8, 1), (0, 1)$ Ⓒ $(4, 3), (4, -1)$ Ⓓ $(-4, 3), (-4, -1)$

EXAMPLES 3 and 4
for Exs. 13–21

WRITING EQUATIONS Write an equation of the conic section.

13. Circle with center at $(-5, 1)$ and radius 6

14. Circle with center at $(9, -1)$ and radius 2

15. Parabola with vertex at $(-4, -3)$ and focus at $(1, -3)$

16. Parabola with vertex at $(5, 3)$ and directrix $y = 6$

17. Ellipse with vertices at $(-3, 4)$ and $(5, 4)$ and foci at $(-1, 4)$ and $(3, 4)$

18. Ellipse with vertices at $(-2, 1)$ and $(-2, 9)$ and co-vertices at $(-4, 5)$ and $(0, 5)$

19. Hyperbola with vertices at $(6, -3)$ and $(6, 1)$ and foci at $(6, -6)$ and $(6, 4)$

20. Hyperbola with vertices at $(1, 7)$ and $(7, 7)$ and foci at $(-1, 7)$ and $(9, 7)$

21. **ERROR ANALYSIS** *Describe* and correct the error in writing an equation of the ellipse with vertices at $(-7, 3)$ and $(3, 3)$ and co-vertices at $(-2, 6)$ and $(-2, 0)$.

> Axis is horizontal; $(h, k) = (-2, 3)$;
> $a = \left|-7 - (-2)\right| = 5; b = \left|6 - 3\right| = 3;$
> Equation: $\dfrac{(x - 2)^2}{25} + \dfrac{(y + 3)^2}{9} = 1$

EXAMPLE 5
for Exs. 22–27

LINES OF SYMMETRY Identify the line(s) of symmetry for the conic section.

22. $\dfrac{(x + 5)^2}{49} + \dfrac{(y - 2)^2}{16} = 1$

23. $(y - 4)^2 = 6(x + 6)$

24. $\dfrac{(x - 1)^2}{36} - \dfrac{(y - 2)^2}{9} = 1$

25. $(y - 5)^2 - \dfrac{(x - 3)^2}{9} = 1$

26. $(x + 3)^2 = 10(y - 1)$

27. $(x + 2)^2 + (y + 1)^2 = 121$

EXAMPLE 6
for Exs. 28–36

CLASSIFYING CONICS Use the discriminant to classify the conic section.

28. $6x^2 - 2y^2 + 24x + 2y - 1 = 0$

29. $x^2 + y^2 - 10x - 6y + 18 = 0$

30. $y^2 - 10y - 5x + 57 = 0$

31. $4x^2 + y^2 - 48x - 14y + 189 = 0$

32. $9x^2 + 4y^2 + 8y + 18x - 41 = 0$

33. $x^2 - 18x + 6y + 99 = 0$

34. $x^2 + y^2 - 6x + 8y - 24 = 0$

35. $8x^2 - 9y^2 - 40x + 4y + 145 = 0$

36. ★ **MULTIPLE CHOICE** The equation $4x^2 + y^2 + 32x - 10y + 85 = 0$ represents what conic section?

(**A**) Circle   (**B**) Ellipse   (**C**) Hyperbola   (**D**) Parabola

CLASSIFYING AND GRAPHING Classify the conic section and write its equation in standard form. Then graph the equation.

37. $x^2 + y^2 - 14x + 4y - 11 = 0$

38. $x^2 + 4y^2 - 10x + 16y + 37 = 0$

39. $x^2 - 16x - 8y + 80 = 0$

40. $9y^2 - x^2 - 54y + 8x + 56 = 0$

41. $9x^2 + 4y^2 - 36x - 24y + 36 = 0$

42. $y^2 + 14y + 16x + 33 = 0$

43. $x^2 + y^2 + 16x - 8y + 16 = 0$

44. $x^2 - 4y^2 + 8x - 24y - 24 = 0$

45. ★ **SHORT RESPONSE** Consider a general second-degree equation where $B = 0$. *Explain* how you can classify the equation's graph without graphing or using the discriminant.

46. **REASONING** In Chapter 8, you graphed hyperbolas with equations of the form $y = \dfrac{a}{x}$. Write $y = \dfrac{a}{x}$ as a general second-degree equation, and use the discriminant to show that the graph is a hyperbola.

47. **CHALLENGE** Find expressions in terms of c, h, and k for the coordinates of the foci of a hyperbola with a vertical transverse axis and center (h, k). Then find equations of the asymptotes in terms of a, b, h, and k.

PROBLEM SOLVING

48. **ICE SKATING** A figure skater practices skating figure eights, which are formed by etching two externally tangent circles in the ice. Write equations for the circles in a figure eight if each is 8 feet in diameter, the circles intersect at the origin, and the centers of the circles are on the y-axis.

49. **JUMPING STILTS** The leap of a person wearing "jumping stilts" is modeled by $x^2 - 10x + 4y = 0$ where x and y are in feet and the origin marks the start of the leap. Write an equation in standard form for the path of the leap. How high and how far does the person jump?

50. **SPACECRAFT** A spacecraft uses Saturn's gravitational force to "slingshot" around the planet on the path $21y^2 - 210y - 4x^2 = -441$, where the origin represents Saturn's center and x and y are in hundreds of thousands of kilometers. What is the shape of the path? Write an equation in standard form for the path. Then graph the equation.

◯ = See **WORKED-OUT SOLUTIONS** in Student Resources   ★ = **STANDARDIZED TEST PRACTICE**

AP Images/Erik S. Lesser

51. ★ **EXTENDED RESPONSE** You are in a park surfing the Internet on a wireless connection. A hotel's wireless transmitter is located 100 yards east and 60 yards south of you. It has a range of 150 yards. A café's transmitter is located 80 yards west and 70 yards south of you. It has a range of 100 yards.

   a. With your location as the origin, write inequalities for circular regions around the hotel and café in which you can get wireless Internet access.

   b. Graph the inequalities. Are you in only one region or in both? *Explain*.

   c. *Explain* how to determine whether the regions overlap without graphing.

52. ★ **SHORT RESPONSE** Tell what conic section is formed in the situation described. *Explain* your reasoning.

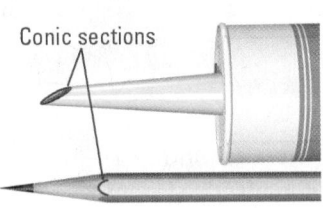
Conic sections

   a. To use a new tube of caulk for the first time, you cut the cone-shaped tip diagonally as shown.

   b. When you sharpen a pencil with flat sides, each side intersects the cone-shaped tip as shown.

53. **CHALLENGE** A *degenerate* conic results when the intersection of a plane with a double-napped cone is not a parabola, circle, ellipse, or hyperbola.

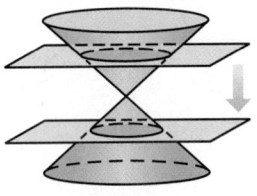

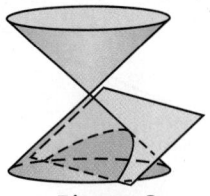

Diagram 1   **Diagram 2**   **Diagram 3**

   a. In Diagram 1, a plane perpendicular to the cone's axis passes through the cone, intersecting it in a circle whose radius decreases and then increases. When is the intersection not a circle? What is it?

   b. In Diagram 2, a plane parallel to the cone's axis passes through the cone, intersecting it in a hyperbola whose vertices get closer together and then farther apart. When is the intersection not a hyperbola? What is it?

   c. In Diagram 3, a plane parallel to the cone's nappe passes through the cone, intersecting it in a parabola that first gets narrower, then flips and gets wider. When is the intersection not a parabola? What is it?

8.7 Solve Quadratic Systems

Before	You solved linear systems.
Now	You will solve quadratic systems.
Why?	So you can find intersections involving conics, as in Ex. 40.

Key Vocabulary
• **quadratic system**

CC.9-12.A.REI.7 Solve a simple system consisting of a linear equation and a quadratic equation in two variables algebraically and graphically.

Previously, you solved systems of linear equations by graphing, substitution, and elimination. You can use the same techniques to solve systems that include one or more equations of conics. These systems are called **quadratic systems**.

If the graphs of the equations in a system are a line and a conic section, the graphs can intersect in zero, one, or two points, and so the system can have zero, one, or two solutions. Three possible scenarios are shown below.

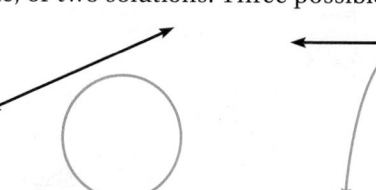

No solution   **One solution**   **Two solutions**

EXAMPLE 1 Solve a linear-quadratic system by graphing

Solve the system using a graphing calculator.

$$y^2 - 7x + 3 = 0 \qquad \text{Equation 1}$$
$$2x - y = 3 \qquad \text{Equation 2}$$

Solution

STEP 1 **Solve** each equation for y.

$$y^2 - 7x + 3 = 0 \qquad\qquad 2x - y = 3$$
$$y^2 = 7x - 3 \qquad\qquad\qquad -y = -2x + 3$$
$$y = \pm\sqrt{7x - 3} \quad \text{Equation 1} \qquad y = 2x - 3 \quad \text{Equation 2}$$

AVOID ERRORS
To graph Equation 1, be sure to enter both $y = \sqrt{7x - 3}$ and $y = -\sqrt{7x - 3}$ into the graphing calculator.

STEP 2 **Graph** the equations $y = \sqrt{7x - 3}$, $y = -\sqrt{7x - 3}$, and $y = 2x - 3$.

Use the calculator's *intersect* feature to find the coordinates of the intersection points. The graphs of $y = -\sqrt{7x - 3}$ and $y = 2x - 3$ intersect at $(0.75, -1.5)$. The graphs of $y = \sqrt{7x - 3}$ and $y = 2x - 3$ intersect at $(4, 5)$.

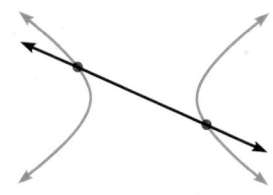

Intersection
X=.75   Y=-1.5

▶ The solutions are $(0.75, -1.5)$ and $(4, 5)$. Check the solutions by substituting the coordinates of the points into each of the original equations.

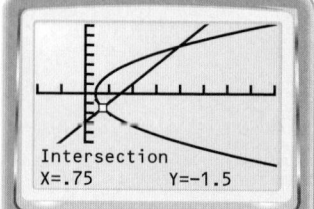

Yellow Dog Productions/Image Bank/Getty Images

EXAMPLE 2 Solve a linear-quadratic system by substitution

Solve the system using substitution.

$x^2 + y^2 = 10$ **Equation 1**
$y = -3x + 10$ **Equation 2**

Solution

Substitute $-3x + 10$ for y in Equation 1 and solve for x.

$$x^2 + y^2 = 10 \qquad \text{Equation 1}$$
$$x^2 + (-3x + 10)^2 = 10 \qquad \text{Substitute for } y.$$
$$x^2 + 9x^2 - 60x + 100 = 10 \qquad \text{Expand the power.}$$
$$10x^2 - 60x + 90 = 0 \qquad \text{Combine like terms.}$$
$$x^2 - 6x + 9 = 0 \qquad \text{Divide each side by 10.}$$
$$(x - 3)^2 = 0 \qquad \text{Perfect square trinomial}$$
$$x = 3 \qquad \text{Zero product property}$$

AVOID ERRORS

You can also substitute $x = 3$ in Equation 1 to find y. This yields *two* apparent solutions, (3, 1) and (3, −1). However, (3, −1) is extraneous because it does not satisfy Equation 2.

To find the y-coordinate of the solution, substitute $x = 3$ in Equation 2.

$$y = -3(3) + 10 = 1$$

▶ The solution is (3, 1).

CHECK You can check the solution by graphing the equations in the system. You can see from the graph shown that the line and the circle intersect only at the point (3, 1).

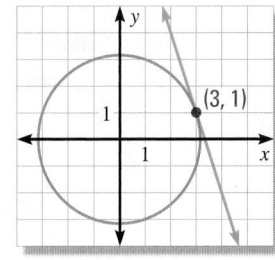

✔ **GUIDED PRACTICE**   for Examples 1 and 2

Solve the system using a graphing calculator.

1. $x^2 + y^2 = 13$
$y = x - 1$

2. $x^2 + 8y^2 - 4 = 0$
$y = 2x + 7$

3. $y^2 + 6x - 1 = 0$
$y = -0.4x + 2.6$

Solve the system using substitution.

4. $y = 0.5x - 3$
$x^2 + 4y^2 - 4 = 0$

5. $y^2 - 2x - 10 = 0$
$y = -x - 1$

6. $y = 4x - 8$
$9x^2 - y^2 - 36 = 0$

QUADRATIC SYSTEMS Two distinct conic sections can have from zero to four points of intersection. Several possible scenarios are shown below.

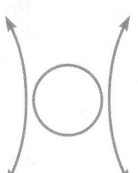   

    No solution   **One solution**   **Two solutions**   **Three solutions**   **Four solutions**

In the examples on the next page, you will use elimination to solve systems of two second-degree equations.

EXAMPLE 3 Solve a quadratic system by elimination

Solve the system by elimination.

$$9x^2 + y^2 - 90x + 216 = 0 \qquad \text{Equation 1}$$
$$x^2 - y^2 - 16 = 0 \qquad \text{Equation 2}$$

Solution

ANOTHER WAY
You can also solve by substitution: Solve Equation 2 for y^2, then substitute the result in Equation 1.

Add the equations to eliminate the y^2-term and obtain a quadratic equation in x.

$$9x^2 + y^2 - 90x + 216 = 0$$
$$\underline{\quad x^2 - y^2 \qquad\quad - \ 16 = 0 \quad}$$

$10x^2 \qquad - 90x + 200 = 0$	**Add.**
$x^2 - 9x + 20 = 0$	**Divide each side by 10.**
$(x - 4)(x - 5) = 0$	**Factor.**
$x = 4 \text{ or } x = 5$	**Zero product property**

When $x = 4$, $y = 0$. When $x = 5$, $y = \pm 3$.

▶ The solutions are $(4, 0)$, $(5, 3)$, and $(5, -3)$, as shown.

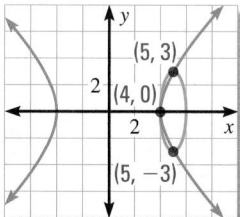

EXAMPLE 4 Solve a real-life quadratic system

NAVIGATION A ship uses LORAN (long-distance radio navigation) to find its position. Radio signals from stations A and B locate the ship on the blue hyperbola, and signals from stations B and C locate the ship on the red hyperbola. The equations of the hyperbolas are given below. Find the ship's position if it is east of the y-axis.

$$x^2 - y^2 - 16x + 32 = 0 \qquad \text{Equation 1}$$
$$-x^2 + y^2 - 8y + 8 = 0 \qquad \text{Equation 2}$$

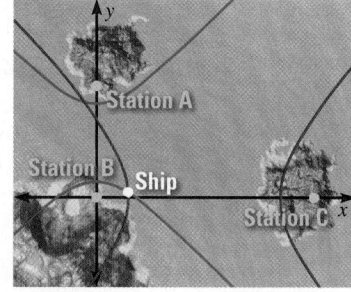

Solution

STEP 1   **Add** the equations to eliminate the x^2- and y^2-terms.

$$x^2 - y^2 - 16x \qquad\quad + 32 = 0$$
$$\underline{-x^2 + y^2 \qquad\quad - 8y + \ 8 = 0 \quad}$$

$-16x - 8y + 40 = 0$	**Add.**
$y = -2x + 5$	**Solve for y.**

STEP 2   **Substitute** $-2x + 5$ for y in Equation 1 and solve for x.

$x^2 - y^2 - 16x + 32 = 0$	**Equation 1**
$x^2 - (-2x + 5)^2 - 16x + 32 = 0$	**Substitute for y.**
$3x^2 - 4x - 7 = 0$	**Simplify.**
$(x + 1)(3x - 7) = 0$	**Factor.**
$x = -1 \text{ or } x = \dfrac{7}{3}$	**Zero product property**

STEP 3   **Substitute** for x in $y = -2x + 5$ to find the solutions $(-1, 7)$ and $\left(\dfrac{7}{3}, \dfrac{1}{3}\right)$.

▶ Because the ship is east of the y-axis, it is at $\left(\dfrac{7}{3}, \dfrac{1}{3}\right)$.

Solve the system.

7. $-2y^2 + x + 2 = 0$
$x^2 + y^2 - 1 = 0$

8. $x^2 + y^2 - 16x + 39 = 0$
$x^2 - y^2 - 9 = 0$

9. $x^2 + 4y^2 + 4x + 8y = 8$
$y^2 - x + 2y = 5$

10. WHAT IF? In Example 4, suppose that a ship's LORAN system locates the ship on the two hyperbolas whose equations are given below. Find the ship's location if it is south of the x-axis.

$x^2 - y^2 - 12x + 18 = 0$ **Equation 1**
$y^2 - x^2 - 4y + 2 = 0$ **Equation 2**

8.7 EXERCISES

HOMEWORK KEY

◯ = See WORKED-OUT SOLUTIONS
Exs. 5, 15, and 41

★ = STANDARDIZED TEST PRACTICE
Exs. 2, 21, 34, 42, and 44

SKILL PRACTICE

1. VOCABULARY Copy and complete: The equations $x^2 + 5x + 3y^2 = 9$ and $4x^2 - 12y + 16 = 0$ form a(n) __?__ system of equations.

2. ★ **WRITING** *Explain* what method you would use to solve the following system. Do not solve the system.

$3x^2 + y^2 - 5x = 0$ **Equation 1**
$2x^2 + y^2 - 15 = 0$ **Equation 2**

EXAMPLE 1
for Exs. 3–8

SOLVING BY GRAPHING Solve the system using a graphing calculator.

3. $x^2 + y^2 - 32 = 0$
$y - x = 0$

4. $y + 2x^2 - 9 = 0$
$y + 4x + 1 = 0$

5. $y - 3x + 4 = 0$
$-3x^2 + y^2 - 6 = 0$

6. $y + 2x = 6$
$3x^2 + y^2 = 12$

7. $x^2 + y^2 = 16$
$y - 2x = 1$

8. $3(y + 3)^2 + 4x = 0$
$y - 2x = 11$

EXAMPLE 2
for Exs. 9–21

SOLVING BY SUBSTITUTION Solve the system using substitution.

9. $y^2 - x - 6 = 0$
$y + x = 0$

10. $x^2 + y^2 - 25 = 0$
$y = 2x - 10$

11. $-2x + y - 8 = 0$
$x^2 + 4y^2 - 40 = 0$

12. $-x^2 + 2y^2 = 8$
$-x + y = -2$

13. $6x^2 + 3y^2 = 12$
$y = -x + 2$

14. $-3x + y = 6$
$8x + y^2 + 24 = 0$

15. $4x^2 - 5y^2 = -76$
$2x + y = -6$

16. $x^2 + y^2 = 20$
$y = x - 4$

17. $9x^2 + 4y^2 = 36$
$-x + y = -4$

18. $x^2 + 6x + 4y - 3 = 0$
$y + 3x + 1 = 0$

19. $4x^2 + 2y^2 - x - y = 6$
$3x - y = 2$

20. $4x^2 - y^2 - 32x - 2y = -59$
$2x + y - 7 = 0$

21. ★ **MULTIPLE CHOICE** Which ordered pair is a solution of the linear-quadratic system below?

$6x^2 - 5x + 8y^2 + y = 23$
$-x + y = -1$

(A) $(-1, -2)$ **(B)** $(2, 1)$ **(C)** $(3, 2)$ **(D)** $(-2, -3)$

EXAMPLES
3 and 4
for Exs. 22–35

SOLVING QUADRATIC SYSTEMS **Solve the system.**

22. $6x^2 - y^2 - 15 = 0$
$x^2 + y^2 - 13 = 0$

23. $5x^2 + 25y^2 - 125 = 0$
$-x + y^2 - 5 = 0$

24. $10y = x^2$
$x^2 - 6 = -2$

25. $x^2 - y^2 - 4x + 2 = 0$
$-x^2 + y^2 - 4y + 2 = 0$

26. $x^2 - 2y = 6$
$x^2 - y^2 = -27$

27. $x^2 + 2y^2 - 10 = 0$
$4y^2 + x + 4 = 0$

28. $x^2 + y^2 - 16x + 39 = 0$
$x^2 - y^2 - 9 = 0$

29. $x^2 - y^2 - 8x + 8y = 24$
$x^2 + y^2 - 8x - 8y = -24$

30. $16x^2 - y^2 + 16y - 128 = 0$
$y^2 - 48x - 16y - 32 = 0$

31. $4x^2 - 56x + 9y^2 = -160$
$4x^2 + y^2 - 64 = 0$

32. $x^2 - y^2 - 32x + 128 = 0$
$y^2 - x^2 - 8y + 8 = 0$

33. $y^2 + x - 3 = 0$
$x^2 - 4x + 3y + 1 = 0$

34. ★ **MULTIPLE CHOICE** How many solutions does the system consisting of the equations $x^2 + y^2 + 6x = 0$ and $y^2 + x - 6 = 0$ have?

(A) 0   (B) 1   (C) 2   (D) 4

35. **ERROR ANALYSIS** *Describe* and correct the error in using substitution to begin solving the system below. Then solve the system.

$x^2 + y^2 - 2x - 2y = -1$ **Equation 1**
$y^2 + x = 1$ **Equation 2**

Solve Equation 2 for x: $x = 1 - y^2$

Substitute for x in Equation 1:

$(1 - y^2)^2 + y^2 - 2(1 - y^2) - 2y = -1$
$1 - 2y^2 + y^2 + y^2 - 2 + 2y^2 - 2y = -1$
$2y^2 - 2y = 0$ ✗

36. **REASONING** Solve the system consisting of the equations $\frac{x^2}{2} + \frac{y^2}{4} = 1$ and $4y^2 = 16 - 8x^2$. What do you notice?

37. **GRAPHING CALCULATOR** Consider the system consisting of the equations $3y^2 + x^2 + 4x + 18y = -28$ and $9y^2 - 4x^2 + 8x + 90y = -185$. Solve each equation for *y*. Then use a graphing calculator to solve the system.

38. **CHALLENGE** Solve the system of three equations shown.

$x^2 + y^2 = 1$ **Equation 1**
$x^2 + y^2 + 4x + 4y - 5 = 0$ **Equation 2**
$x + y - 1 = 0$ **Equation 3**

PROBLEM SOLVING

EXAMPLE 2
for Exs. 39–41

39. **TRAFFIC SAFETY** A car passes a parked police car and continues at a constant speed *r*. The police car begins accelerating at a constant rate when it is passed. The diagram indicates the distance *d* (in miles) the police car travels as a function of time *t* (in minutes) after being passed. Write and solve a system of equations to find how long it takes the police car to catch up to the other car.

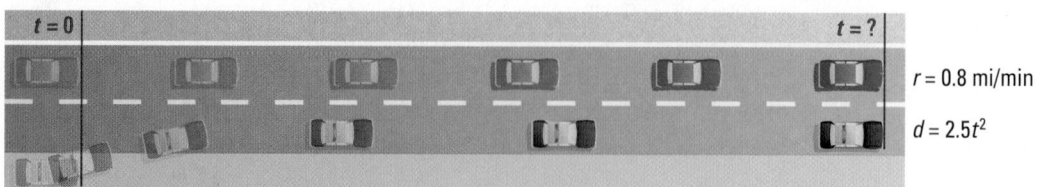

$t = 0$ $t = ?$
$r = 0.8$ mi/min
$d = 2.5t^2$

○ = See WORKED-OUT SOLUTIONS in Student Resources   ★ = STANDARDIZED TEST PRACTICE

40. BASEBALL The path of a baseball hit for a home run can be modeled by $y = -\dfrac{x^2}{484} + x + 3$ where x and y are in feet and home plate is the origin. The ball lands in the stands, which are modeled by $4y - x = -352$ for $x \geq 400$. How far horizontally and vertically from home plate does the ball land?

41. **MULTI-STEP PROBLEM** To be eligible for a parking pass on a college campus, a student must live at least 1 mile from the campus center.

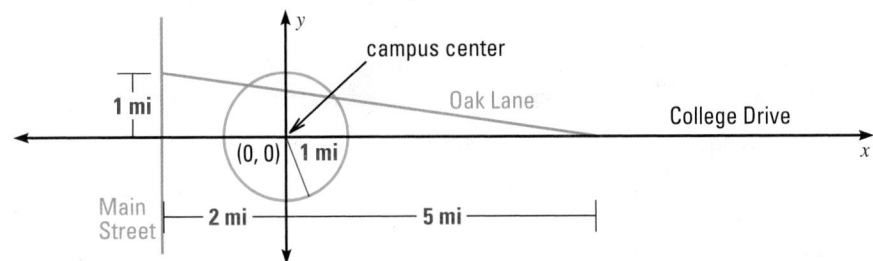

a. Write equations that represent the circle and Oak Lane.

b. Solve the system that consists of the equations from part (a).

c. For what length of Oak Lane are students *not* eligible for a parking pass?

EXAMPLES 3 and 4
for Exs. 42–43

42. ★ SHORT RESPONSE A high school gym has a dome-shaped ceiling modeled by $x^2 + y^2 + 60y - 3456 = 0$ where x and y are in feet. A tennis player in the gym hits a shot modeled by $x^2 + y = 36$ where the origin is located at the base of the net. Solve the system of equations by both elimination and substitution. Do any solutions represent the ball hitting the ceiling? *Explain.*

43. NAVIGATION A ship's LORAN system locates the ship on hyperbolas with the given equations. Find the ship's location for each pair of hyperbolas. In part (b), assume the ship is west of the y-axis.

a. $x^2 - y^2 - 8x + 8 = 0$
   $y^2 - x^2 - 8y + 8 = 0$

b. $xy - 24 = 0$
   $x^2 - 25y^2 + 100 = 0$

44. ★ EXTENDED RESPONSE A *seismograph* measures the intensity of an earthquake. A seismograph can determine distance to an earthquake's epicenter, but not direction. On January 22, 2003, a powerful earthquake struck Mexico's state of Colima. The diagram shows approximate distances from three seismic stations to the epicenter. The relative positions of the seismic stations are described below.

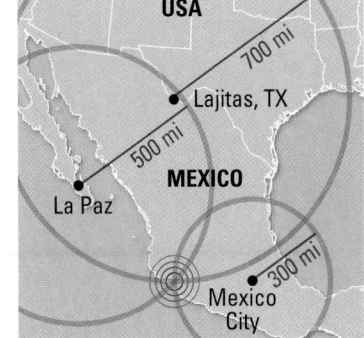

Mexico City: 700 miles south and 300 miles east of Lajitas

La Paz: 400 miles south and 400 miles west of Lajitas

a. **Model** Using Lajitas as the origin, write an equation of each circle. Let each unit represent 100 miles.

b. **Eliminate** Use the equation for the circle centered at Lajitas with each of the other two equations from part (a) to eliminate the x^2- and y^2-terms and find two new equations.

c. **Solve** Solve the system of linear equations that results from part (b) to find the coordinates of the epicenter.

d. **Reasoning** *Explain* why three stations are required to locate the epicenter.

45. CHALLENGE What is the width w of the thickest box that will fit in a mailbox with the dimensions shown? (*Hint:* Use the Pythagorean theorem and the fact that $\triangle ABC \sim \triangle CDE$ to write a system of two second-degree equations.)

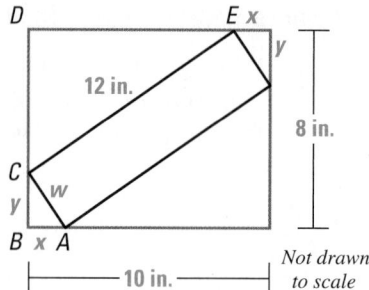

Not drawn to scale

QUIZ

Write an equation of the conic section.

1. Ellipse with vertices at $(3, -10)$ and $(3, 6)$ and foci at $(3, -7)$ and $(3, 3)$

2. Parabola with vertex at $(-5, 2)$ and focus at $(-5, -1)$

3. Hyperbola with foci at $(-3, 1)$ and $(6, 1)$ and vertices at $(0, 1)$ and $(3, 1)$

Classify the conic section and write its equation in standard form. Then graph the equation.

4. $9x^2 - 4y^2 - 36x - 32y - 64 = 0$
         5. $-x^2 - y^2 - 4x + 12y + 129 = 0$

6. $x^2 + 6x - y + 16 = 0$
         7. $12x^2 + 45y^2 + 120x + 90y - 150 = 0$

Solve the system.

8. $x + 2y^2 = -6$
$x + 8y = 0$

9. $x^2 + 4x + y^2 + 6y = 12$
$2x - y = 4$

10. $x^2 - y - 4 = 0$
$x^2 + 3y^2 - 4y - 10 = 0$

11. $y^2 - 6x - 2y - 3 = 0$
$2y^2 - 4y + x + 6 = 0$

12. $y^2 - 4x^2 - 4y = 0$
$2x^2 + y^2 - 8x - 4y = -8$

13. $16x^2 + 9y^2 + 32x - 18y = 119$
$x^2 + y^2 + 2x + 6y = 15$

14. **RADAR** A radar station reports that a ship is 10 miles away. At the same time, a second station 20 miles east and 15 miles north of the first one reports that the ship is 15 miles away. Write and solve a system of equations to locate the ship relative to the first station. Is only one location possible? *Explain.*

Extension

Determine Eccentricity of Conic Sections

GOAL Find and apply the eccentricity of a conic section.

Key Vocabulary
• eccentricity

CC.9-12.G.GPE.3 (+) Derive the equations of ellipses and hyperbolas given the foci, using the fact that the sum or difference of distances from the foci is constant.

In an ellipse that is nearly circular, the ratio $c:a$ is close to 0. In a more oval ellipse, $c:a$ is close to 1. This ratio is the **eccentricity** of the ellipse. Every conic has an eccentricity e associated with it.

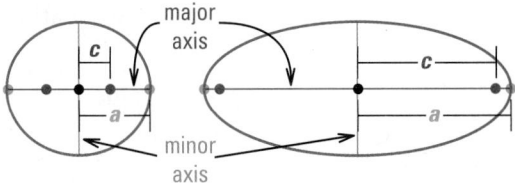

KEY CONCEPT *For Your Notebook*

Eccentricity of Conic Sections

The eccentricity of each conic section is defined below. For an ellipse or hyperbola, c is the distance from each focus to the center, and a is the distance from each vertex to the center.

Circle: $e = 0$ **Parabola:** $e = 1$

Ellipse: $e = \dfrac{c}{a}$, and $0 < e < 1$ **Hyperbola:** $e = \dfrac{c}{a}$, and $e > 1$

EXAMPLE 1 **Find eccentricity**

Find the eccentricity of the conic section represented by the equation.

  a. $(x + 3)^2 + (y - 1)^2 = 25$ **b.** $\dfrac{(x + 4)^2}{36} + \dfrac{(y - 2)^2}{16} = 1$

Solution

  a. Because this equation represents a circle, the eccentricity is $e = 0$.

  b. This equation represents an ellipse with $a = \sqrt{36} = 6$, $b = \sqrt{16} = 4$, and $c = \sqrt{a^2 - b^2} = 2\sqrt{5}$. The eccentricity is $e = \dfrac{c}{a} = \dfrac{2\sqrt{5}}{6} \approx 0.745$.

EXAMPLE 2 **Use eccentricity to write an equation**

Write an equation of a hyperbola with center $(-2, 6)$, vertex $(6, 6)$, and $e = 2$.

Solution

Use the form $\dfrac{(x - h)^2}{a^2} - \dfrac{(y - k)^2}{b^2} = 1$. The vertex lies $6 - (-2) = 8$ units from the center, so $a = 8$. Because $e = \dfrac{c}{a} = 2$, you know that $\dfrac{c}{8} = 2$, or $c = 16$.

So, $b^2 = c^2 - a^2 = 256 - 64 = 192$. The equation is $\dfrac{(x + 2)^2}{64} - \dfrac{(y - 6)^2}{192} = 1$.

EXAMPLE 3 **Use eccentricity to write a model**

ASTRONOMY Pluto orbits the sun in an elliptical path with the center of the sun at one focus. The eccentricity of the orbit is $e = 0.249$ and the length of the major axis is about 79.0 astronomical units. Find an equation of Pluto's orbit. (Assume that the major axis is horizontal.)

Solution

The equation of the orbit has the form $\dfrac{x^2}{a^2} + \dfrac{y^2}{b^2} = 1$. Using the length of the major axis, you know that $2a = 79.0$, or $a = 39.5$. You can use the eccentricity and the value of a to find the value of c, and then use the values of a and c to find b.

$$e = \frac{c}{a}, \text{ so } 0.249 = \frac{c}{39.5}, \text{ or } c \approx 9.84$$

$$c^2 = a^2 - b^2, \text{ so } b = \sqrt{a^2 - c^2} = \sqrt{(39.5)^2 - (9.84)^2} \approx 38.3$$

So, an equation for Pluto's orbit is $\dfrac{x^2}{(39.5)^2} + \dfrac{y^2}{(38.3)^2} = 1$, or $\dfrac{x^2}{1560} + \dfrac{y^2}{1470} = 1$,

where x and y are measured in astronomical units.

PRACTICE

EXAMPLE 1
for Exs. 1–6

Find the eccentricity of the conic section.

1. $7(x - 3)^2 + 7(y + 7)^2 = 56$

2. $16(x + 1)^2 - 9(y - 5)^2 = 144$

3. $\dfrac{(x - 6)^2}{49} + \dfrac{(y - 5)^2}{64} = 1$

4. $\dfrac{(y - 4)^2}{100} - \dfrac{(x + 2)^2}{9} = 1$

5. $(x - 5)^2 = 10y$

6. $81(x + 4)^2 + (y - 9)^2 = 81$

EXAMPLE 2
for Exs. 7–12

Write an equation of the conic section.

7. Ellipse with vertices at $(-6, 4)$ and $(6, 4)$, and $e = 0.4$

8. Ellipse with foci at $(-4, 2)$ and $(-4, -2)$, and $e = 0.5$

9. Ellipse with center at $(0, 5)$, vertex at $(7, 5)$, and $e = 0.2$

10. Hyperbola with foci at $(4, -5)$ and $(4, 3)$, and $e = 2.5$

11. Hyperbola with vertices at $(1, -4)$ and $(7, -4)$, and $e = 1.8$

12. Hyperbola with center at $(-2, 3)$, focus at $(-5, 3)$, and $e = 4$

EXAMPLE 3
for Exs. 13–14

13. **ASTRONOMY** Nereid, a moon of Neptune, has the most eccentric orbit of any moon in the solar system. The eccentricity of the orbit is $e = 0.751$ and the length of the major axis is about 11.0 million kilometers. Find an equation of Nereid's orbit.

14. **SATELLITES** A communications satellite is in an elliptical orbit around Earth, whose center is one focus of the orbit. The eccentricity of the orbit is $e = 0.394$, and the satellite is 14,300 kilometers from Earth's center at the closest point in its orbit. What is the satellite's distance from Earth's center at the farthest point in its orbit?

15. **REASONING** *Explain* why the definition of eccentricity for ellipses and hyperbolas implies that $0 < e < 1$ for an ellipse and $e > 1$ for a hyperbola.

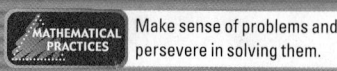
1. **MULTI-STEP PROBLEM** A person at the focus of one of two facing parabolic dishes can hear even a very soft sound made at the focus of the other dish. Two such "whisper dishes" are positioned with their vertices 47 feet apart. Each dish's focus is 1.5 feet from its vertex.

a. Write an equation in standard form for the cross section of each dish if the vertex of one dish is at the origin and the vertex of the other dish is on the positive x-axis.

b. The diameter of each dish is 67 inches. How deep is each dish?

c. How far apart are the focus and vertex for a dish 8 feet in diameter and 1.25 feet deep?

2. **MULTI-STEP PROBLEM** A hyperbolic mirror reflects light directed toward one focus to the other focus. The hyperbolic mirror shown has foci at $(\pm 12, 0)$ and vertices at $(\pm 8, 0)$.

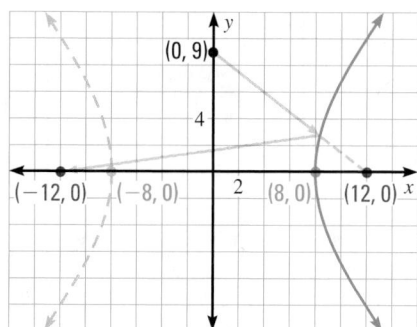

a. Write an equation for the mirror.

b. Write an equation for the path of the light beam originating at the point $(0, 9)$ before the beam reflects off the mirror.

c. At what point does the light beam in part (b) reflect off the mirror?

3. **OPEN-ENDED** Sketch five different examples of two conics that intersect in exactly four points.

4. **EXTENDED RESPONSE** When a jet breaks the sound barrier, sound waves form a "Mach cone" behind the jet, and a sonic boom is heard as the cone passes. The Mach cone for a jet in level flight meets the ground in a hyperbola with the jet directly above the center. Suppose a jet makes a sonic boom heard along $\frac{x^2}{36} - \frac{y^2}{100} = 1$ where x and y are in miles.

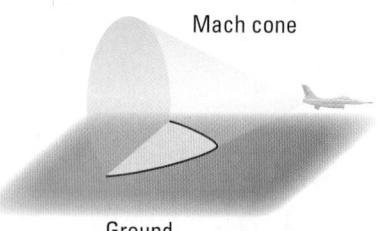

Mach cone

Ground

a. What is the shortest possible horizontal distance you could be from the jet when you first hear the sonic boom? *Explain.*

b. The jet passes a second time, creating a sonic boom heard along $\frac{x^2}{9} - \frac{y^2}{25} = 1$. Answer the question from part (a) for this sonic boom.

c. *Describe* the relationship between the two hyperbolas.

5. **SHORT RESPONSE** The diagram shows the mirrors in a Cassegrain telescope. The equations of the mirrors are given below. Classify each mirror as *parabolic, elliptical,* or *hyperbolic. Explain* your reasoning.

a. Mirror A: $y^2 - 72x - 450 = 0$

b. Mirror B: $88.4x^2 - 49.7y^2 - 4390 = 0$

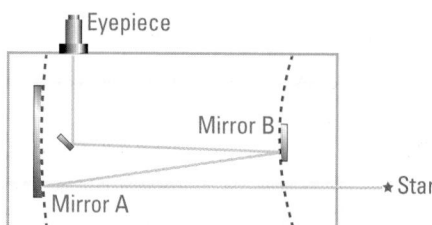

6. **GRIDDED ANSWER** A logo has intersecting ellipses modeled by $9x^2 + y^2 + 8y = 20$ and $x^2 + 4y^2 = 16$. What is the y-coordinate of the uppermost point of intersection?

BIG IDEAS
For Your Notebook

Big Idea 1

Writing Equations of Conic Sections

Conic	Equation	Key facts		
Circle	$x^2 + y^2 = r^2$	radius r		
Parabola	$x^2 = 4py$	*Axis of symmetry* vertical	*Focus* $(0, p)$	*Directrix* $y = -p$
	$y^2 = 4px$	*Axis of symmetry* horizontal	*Focus* $(p, 0)$	*Directrix* $x = -p$
Ellipse	$\dfrac{x^2}{a^2} + \dfrac{y^2}{b^2} = 1$	*Major axis* horizontal	*Vertices* $(\pm a, 0)$	*Co-vertices* $(0, \pm b)$
	$\dfrac{x^2}{b^2} + \dfrac{y^2}{a^2} = 1$	*Major axis* vertical	*Vertices* $(0, \pm a)$	*Co-vertices* $(\pm b, 0)$
Hyperbola	$\dfrac{x^2}{a^2} - \dfrac{y^2}{b^2} = 1$	*Transverse axis* horizontal	*Asymptotes* $y = \pm\dfrac{b}{a}x$	*Vertices* $(\pm a, 0)$
	$\dfrac{y^2}{a^2} - \dfrac{x^2}{b^2} = 1$	*Transverse axis* vertical	*Asymptotes* $y = \pm\dfrac{a}{b}x$	*Vertices* $(0, \pm a)$

Big Idea 2

Graphing Equations of Conic Sections

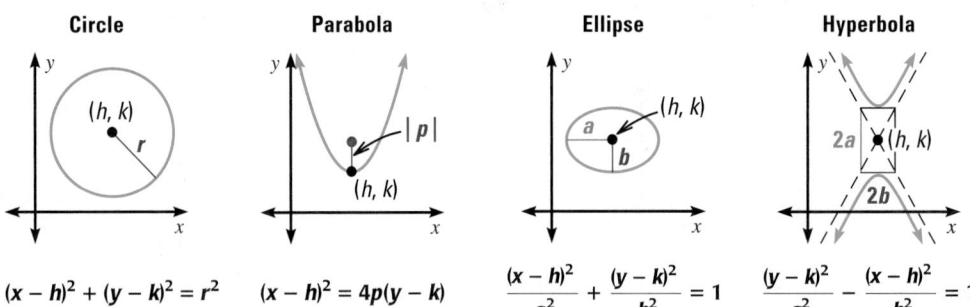

Circle

$(x - h)^2 + (y - k)^2 = r^2$

Parabola

$(x - h)^2 = 4p(y - k)$

Ellipse

$\dfrac{(x - h)^2}{a^2} + \dfrac{(y - k)^2}{b^2} = 1$

Hyperbola

$\dfrac{(y - k)^2}{a^2} - \dfrac{(x - h)^2}{b^2} = 1$

Big Idea 3

Solving Quadratic Systems

Method	Description	When to use
Graphing	Graph the equations. Identify any points of intersection.	When graphing is easy or when using a graphing calculator
Substitution	Solve one equation for one of the variables and substitute it into the other equation.	When you can easily solve for one variable (or its square) in terms of the other variable
Elimination	Multiply one or both equations by a constant as needed, and add.	When you can eliminate one or more of the variable terms

REVIEW KEY VOCABULARY

- distance formula
- midpoint formula
- focus, foci
- directrix
- circle
- center
- radius

- ellipse
- vertices
- major axis
- co-vertices
- minor axis
- hyperbola

- transverse axis
- conic sections
- general second-degree equation
- discriminant
- quadratic system

VOCABULARY EXERCISES

1. Copy and complete: A(n) __?__ is the set of all points in a plane equidistant from a point called the focus and a line called the directrix.

2. Copy and complete: The line segment joining the two co-vertices of an ellipse is the __?__ .

3. Copy and complete: The line segment joining the two vertices of a hyperbola is the __?__ .

4. **WRITING** *Describe* how the asymptotes of a hyperbola help you draw the hyperbola.

REVIEW EXAMPLES AND EXERCISES

Use the review examples and exercises below to check your understanding of the concepts you have learned in each lesson of this chapter.

8.1 Apply the Distance and Midpoint Formulas

EXAMPLE

Find the distance between $(-5, 3)$ and $(1, -3)$. Then find the midpoint of the line segment joining the two points.

$$d = \sqrt{(x_2 - x_1)^2 + (y_2 - y_1)^2} = \sqrt{(1 - (-5))^2 + (-3 - 3)^2} = \sqrt{72} = 6\sqrt{2} \approx 8.49$$

$$M\left(\frac{x_1 + x_2}{2}, \frac{y_1 + y_2}{2}\right) = \left(\frac{-5 + 1}{2}, \frac{3 + (-3)}{2}\right) = (-2, 0)$$

EXERCISES

EXAMPLES
1 and 3
for Exs. 5–8

Find the distance between the two points. Then find the midpoint of the line segment joining the two points.

5. $(-6, -5), (2, -3)$ 6. $(-2, 5), (1, 9)$ 7. $(-3, -4), (2, 5)$

8. **SKYDIVING** A skydiver lands 200 yards west and 40 yards north of a target. A second skydiver lands 30 yards east and 140 yards south of the same target. How far from each other do the two skydivers land?

8.2 Graph and Write Equations of Parabolas

EXAMPLE

Graph $x = \frac{1}{12}y^2$. Identify the focus, directrix, and axis of symmetry.

STEP 1 **Rewrite** $x = \frac{1}{12}y^2$ in standard form as $y^2 = 12x$.

STEP 2 **Identify** the focus, directrix, and axis of symmetry. The equation has the form $y^2 = 4px$ with $4p = 12$, so $p = 3$. The focus is $(p, 0)$, or **(3, 0)**, and the directrix is $x = -p$, or $x = -3$. Because y is squared, the axis of symmetry is the x-axis.

STEP 3 **Draw** the parabola. Because $p > 0$, the parabola opens to the right. Some points on the parabola are $(0, 0)$, $(1, \pm3.46)$, and $(2, \pm4.90)$.

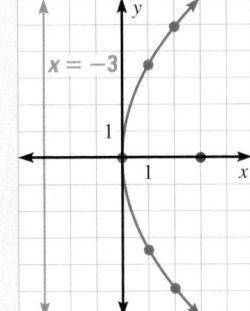

EXERCISES

Graph the equation. Identify the focus, directrix, and axis of symmetry of the parabola.

EXAMPLES 1 and 2 for Exs. 9–14

9. $x^2 = 16y$

10. $y^2 = -6x$

11. $x^2 + 4y = 0$

Write the standard form of the equation of the parabola with the given focus or directrix and vertex at (0, 0).

12. Focus: $(-5, 0)$

13. Focus: $(0, 3)$

14. Directrix: $x = -6$

8.3 Graph and Write Equations of Circles

EXAMPLE

Graph $x^2 = 64 - y^2$. Identify the radius of the circle.

STEP 1 **Rewrite** $x^2 = 64 - y^2$ in standard form as $x^2 + y^2 = 64$.

STEP 2 **Identify** the radius. The graph is a circle with center at the origin and radius $r = \sqrt{64} = 8$.

STEP 3 **Draw** a circle passing through points that are 8 units from the origin, such as $(8, 0)$, $(0, 8)$, $(-8, 0)$, and $(0, -8)$.

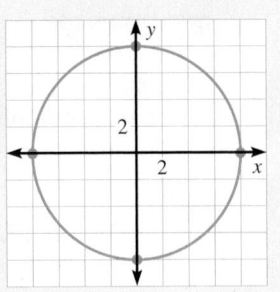

EXERCISES

Graph the equation. Identify the radius of the circle.

EXAMPLES 1 and 2 for Exs. 15–20

15. $x^2 + y^2 = 81$

16. $x^2 = 40 - y^2$

17. $3x^2 + 3y^2 = 147$

Write the standard form of the equation of the circle that passes through the given point and whose center is the origin.

18. $(5, 9)$

19. $(-8, 2)$

20. $(-7, -4)$

8.4 Graph and Write Equations of Ellipses

EXAMPLE

Graph $4x^2 + y^2 = 16$. Identify the vertices, co-vertices, and foci.

STEP 1   **Rewrite** $4x^2 + y^2 = 16$ in standard form as $\dfrac{x^2}{4} + \dfrac{y^2}{16} = 1$.

STEP 2   **Identify** the vertices, co-vertices, and foci. Note that $a^2 = 16$ and $b^2 = 4$, so $a = 4$, $b = 2$, and $c^2 = a^2 - b^2 = 12$, or $c \approx 3.5$. The major axis is vertical. The vertices are at $(0, \pm 4)$. The co-vertices are at $(\pm 2, 0)$. The foci are at $(0, \pm 3.5)$.

STEP 3   **Draw** the ellipse.

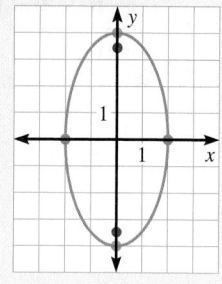

EXERCISES

EXAMPLES 1, 2, and 4 for Exs. 21–25

Graph the equation. Identify the vertices, co-vertices, and foci of the ellipse.

21. $16x^2 + 25y^2 = 400$ **22.** $81x^2 + 9y^2 = 729$ **23.** $64x^2 + 36y^2 = 2304$

Write an equation of the ellipse with the given characteristics and center at $(0, 0)$.

24. Vertex: $(-6, 0)$; co-vertex: $(0, -3)$ **25.** Vertex: $(0, -8)$; focus: $(0, 5)$

8.5 Graph and Write Equations of Hyperbolas

EXAMPLE

Graph $4x^2 - 9y^2 = 36$. Identify the vertices, foci, and asymptotes.

STEP 1   **Rewrite** $4x^2 - 9y^2 = 36$ in standard form as $\dfrac{x^2}{9} - \dfrac{y^2}{4} = 1$.

STEP 2   **Identify** the vertices, foci, and asymptotes. Note that $a^2 = 9$ and $b^2 = 4$, so $a = 3$, $b = 2$, and $c^2 = a^2 + b^2 = 13$, or $c \approx 3.6$. The transverse axis is horizontal. The vertices are at $(\pm 3, 0)$. The foci are at $(\pm 3.6, 0)$. The asymptotes are $y = \pm \dfrac{b}{a} x = \pm \dfrac{2}{3} x$.

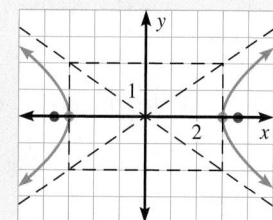

STEP 3   **Draw** asymptotes through opposite corners of a rectangle centered at $(0, 0)$ that is $2a = 6$ units wide and $2b = 4$ units high. Draw the hyperbola.

EXERCISES

EXAMPLES 1 and 2 for Exs. 26–30

Graph the equation. Identify the vertices, foci, and asymptotes.

26. $9x^2 - y^2 = 9$ **27.** $4x^2 - 16y^2 = 64$ **28.** $100y^2 - 36x^2 = 3600$

Write an equation of the hyperbola with the given foci and vertices.

29. Foci: $(0, \pm 5)$; vertices: $(0, \pm 2)$ **30.** Foci: $(\pm 9, 0)$; vertices: $(\pm 4, 0)$

8.6 Translate and Classify Conic Sections

EXAMPLE

Classify the conic section $-4x^2 + y^2 + 32x - 12y - 32 = 0$ and write its equation in standard form. Then graph the equation.

Because $A = -4$, $B = 0$, and $C = 1$, the discriminant is $B^2 - 4AC = 16 > 0$, so the conic is a hyperbola. Complete the square to write the equation in standard form.

$$-4x^2 + y^2 + 32x - 12y - 32 = 0$$
$$(y^2 - 12y) - 4(x^2 - 8x) = 32$$
$$(y^2 - 12y + 36) - 4(x^2 - 8x + 16) = 32 + 36 - 4(16)$$
$$(y - 6)^2 - 4(x - 4)^2 = 4$$
$$\frac{(y - 6)^2}{4} - (x - 4)^2 = 1$$

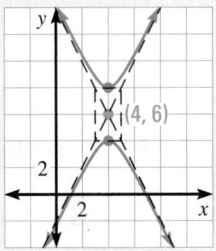

From the equation, $(h, k) = (4, 6)$, $a = \sqrt{4} = 2$, and $b = 1$. The vertices are $(4, 6 + 2) = (4, 8)$ and $(4, 6 - 2) = (4, 4)$. The graph is shown above.

EXERCISES

EXAMPLE 6
for Exs. 31–34

Classify the conic section and write its equation in standard form. Then graph the equation.

31. $4x^2 + 9y^2 + 40x + 72y + 208 = 0$ **32.** $y^2 - 10y - 8x + 1 = 0$

33. $9x^2 - y^2 - 18x - 4y - 5 = 0$ **34.** $x^2 + y^2 + 4x - 14y + 17 = 0$

8.7 Solve Quadratic Systems

EXAMPLE

Solve the system. $12x^2 - 81y^2 + 16 = 0$
$2x^2 + 9y = 0$

Write the second equation as $y = -\frac{2}{9}x^2$. Then substitute in the first equation.

$12x^2 - 81\left(-\frac{2}{9}x^2\right)^2 + 16 = 0$ Substitute for y in first equation.

$12x^2 - 4x^4 + 16 = 0$ Simplify.

$x^4 - 3x^2 - 4 = 0$ Divide each side by -4.

$(x^2 - 4)(x^2 + 1) = 0$ Factor.

By the zero product property, $x = \pm 2$. The solutions are $\left(2, -\frac{8}{9}\right)$ and $\left(-2, -\frac{8}{9}\right)$.

EXERCISES

EXAMPLES 2 and 3
for Exs. 35–37

Solve the system.

35. $y^2 = 4x$
$2x - 5y = -8$

36. $x^2 + y^2 - 100 = 0$
$x + y - 14 = 0$

37. $16x^2 - 4y^2 = 64$
$4x^2 + 9y^2 - 40x = -64$

Find the distance between the two points. Then find the midpoint of the line segment joining the two points.

1. $(-1, 5)$, $(7, 3)$

2. $(4, 2)$, $(8, 8)$

3. $(-1, -6)$, $(1, 5)$

4. $(2, -5)$, $(3, 1)$

5. $(-6, -2)$, $(-3, 5)$

6. $(1, 9)$, $(10, -2)$

Graph the equation.

7. $y^2 - 24x = 0$

8. $x^2 + y^2 = 16$

9. $64y^2 - x^2 = 64$

10. $18x^2 + 2y^2 = 18$

11. $(x - 6)^2 + (y + 1)^2 = 36$

12. $(x + 4)^2 = 6(y - 2)$

13. $\dfrac{(x + 4)^2}{9} - \dfrac{(y - 7)^2}{49} = 1$

14. $\dfrac{(x - 8)^2}{81} + \dfrac{(y - 2)^2}{100} = 1$

15. $\dfrac{(y - 5)^2}{9} - (x + 3)^2 = 1$

Write the standard form of the equation of the conic section with the given characteristics.

16. Parabola with vertex at $(0, 0)$ and directrix at $x = -6$

17. Parabola with vertex at $(-2, -1)$ and focus at $(-2, 5)$

18. Circle with center at $(0, 0)$ and passing through $(-5, 2)$

19. Circle with center at $(1, -4)$ and radius 6

20. Ellipse with center at $(0, 0)$, vertex at $(0, 6)$, and co-vertex at $(-3, 0)$

21. Ellipse with vertices at $(-1, 4)$ and $(7, 4)$ and foci at $(1, 4)$ and $(5, 4)$

22. Hyperbola with vertices at $(0, -6)$ and $(0, 6)$ and foci at $(0, -9)$ and $(0, 9)$

23. Hyperbola with vertex at $(2, -5)$, focus at $(-1, -5)$, and center at $(5, -5)$

Classify the conic section and write its equation in standard form.

24. $x^2 + 4y^2 - 6x - 16y + 21 = 0$

25. $x^2 + y^2 + 8x + 12y + 3 = 0$

26. $4x^2 - 9y^2 - 40x + 64 = 0$

27. $y^2 - 16y - 12x + 40 = 0$

28. $25x^2 + 4y^2 + 50x - 24y - 39 = 0$

29. $y^2 - 16x^2 + 14y + 64x - 31 = 0$

Solve the system.

30. $4x^2 + y^2 = 16$
$x + y = 2$

31. $x^2 + 4y^2 - 8y = 4$
$y^2 - 2y - 8x - 16 = 0$

32. $y^2 - x^2 + 2x - 5 = 0$
$x^2 + y^2 - 2x - 3 = 0$

33. WATER SURFACE A cylindrical glass of water has a 1.5 inch radius. If the glass is tilted 60°, the water's surface meets the glass in an ellipse with minor axis 3 inches long and major axis 6 inches long. Write equations that model the water's surface with the glass upright and after the glass is tilted. Use the center of the water's surface as the origin.

34. ASTRONOMY The Green Bank Telescope in West Virginia has a main reflector whose cross section is a portion of a "parent" parabola. A diagram of the reflector's cross section and the parent parabola is shown. Write an equation that models the parent parabola if its vertex is at $(0, 0)$. What is the distance from the vertex to the focus?

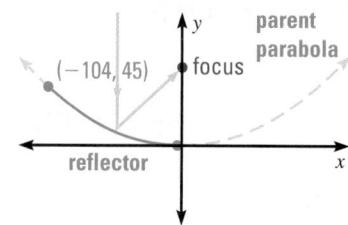

SHORT RESPONSE QUESTIONS

> **PROBLEM**
>
> Two vertices of an equilateral triangle are $A(0, 0)$ and $B(6, 0)$. Write and solve a system of equations to find the coordinates of the third vertex C of $\triangle ABC$. Is there only one possible position for the third vertex? *Explain.*

Below are sample solutions to the problem. Read each solution and the comments on the left to see why the sample represents full credit, partial credit, or no credit.

SAMPLE 1: Full credit solution

The solution is set up logically and thoroughly.

Because $AB = 6 - 0 = 6$ and $\triangle ABC$ is equilateral, $AC = BC = 6$. Let (x, y) represent the coordinates of vertex C. Use the distance formula.

For AC: $\sqrt{(x - 0)^2 + (y - 0)^2} = 6$ For BC: $\sqrt{(x - 6)^2 + (y - 0)^2} = 6$

$\qquad\qquad\qquad\qquad x^2 + y^2 = 36$ $\qquad\qquad\qquad\qquad (x - 6)^2 + y^2 = 36$

$\qquad\qquad\qquad\qquad\qquad\qquad\qquad\qquad\qquad\qquad x^2 - 12x + 36 + y^2 = 36$

$\qquad\qquad\qquad\qquad\qquad\qquad\qquad\qquad\qquad\qquad x^2 + y^2 - 12x = 0$

The correct equations are obtained, and a valid method is used to solve the system.

Solve the system by adding -1 times the second equation to the first.

$$x^2 + y^2 \qquad\quad = 36$$
$$\underline{-x^2 - y^2 + 12x = 0}$$
$$\qquad\quad 12x = 36 \quad \blacksquare\!\!\longrightarrow \quad x = 3$$

Substitute **3** for x in the first equation: $3^2 + y^2 = 36$, so $y^2 = 27$, or $y = \pm 3\sqrt{3}$.

The system is solved correctly. A correct conclusion is drawn.

The solutions of the system are $(3, \pm 3\sqrt{3})$. So, the third vertex is at $C(3, 3\sqrt{3})$ or $C(3, -3\sqrt{3})$. There are two solutions, because C can be above or below $\overline{AB}$.

SAMPLE 2: Partial credit solution

The distance between A and B is 6.

$\qquad AC = 6 \quad \blacksquare\!\!\longrightarrow \quad x^2 + y^2 = 36 \qquad\qquad BC = 6 \quad \blacksquare\!\!\longrightarrow \quad x^2 + y^2 - 12x = 0$

The system is correct, but steps are omitted in writing and solving it.

Solve the system by substituting **36** for $x^2 + y^2$ in the second equation.

$$x^2 + y^2 - 12x = 0$$
$$36 - 12x = 0$$
$$x = 3$$

The additional vertex is omitted. An incorrect conclusion is drawn.

Find y when $x = 3$: $x^2 + y^2 = 36$, so $y^2 = 27$, and $y = \pm 3\sqrt{3}$. The coordinates of the third vertex are $C(3, 3\sqrt{3})$. This is the only possible position of the vertex, because the dimensions of a triangle must be positive.

SAMPLE 3: Partial credit solution

A valid approach is used, and the solution is set up logically and thoroughly.

The equations of the circles are correct.

The answer is correct, but work is not shown.

The distance between A and B is 6. So, the other two sides of $\triangle ABC$ have lengths of 6. Draw circles with radii of 6 centered at A and B. The points of intersection of the circles will be the possible positions of the third vertex.

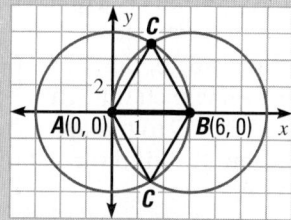

Equation of circle A: $x^2 + y^2 = 36$

Equation of circle B: $(x - 6)^2 + y^2 = 36$

The solutions of the system are $(3, 3\sqrt{3})$ and $(3, -3\sqrt{3})$, so the possible coordinates of the third vertex are $C(3, 3\sqrt{3})$ or $C(3, -3\sqrt{3})$.

SAMPLE 4: No credit solution

The answer shows a basic misunderstanding.

Because $AB = 6$ and $\overline{AB}$ is horizontal, the vertex at C is 6 units above or below either A or B. The possible coordinates of C are $(0, 6)$, $(0, -6)$, $(6, 6)$, or $(6, -6)$.

PRACTICE Apply the Scoring Rubric

Use the rubric on the previous page to score the solution to the problem below as *full credit*, *partial credit*, or *no credit*. *Explain* your reasoning.

> **PROBLEM** $\triangle RST$ is isosceles with $RT = ST$ and has vertices at $R(-2, 2)$, $S(4, -1)$, and $T(2, y)$. Find y. Is there only one possible value of y? *Explain*.

1.
$$\sqrt{[2 - (-2)]^2 + (y - 2)^2} = \sqrt{(2 - 4)^2 + [y - (-1)]^2}$$
$$\sqrt{16 + y^2 - 4y + 4} = \sqrt{4 + y^2 + 2y + 1}$$
$$y^2 - 4y + 20 = y^2 + 2y + 5$$
$$15 = 6y, \text{ so } 2.5 = y$$

2. If $\triangle RST$ is isosceles with $RT = ST$, then T lies on the perpendicular bisector of $\overline{RS}$.

$$\text{Midpoint of } \overline{RS} = \left(\frac{-2 + 4}{2}, \frac{2 + (-1)}{2}\right) = (1, 0.5)$$

$$\text{Slope of } \overline{RS} = \frac{-1 - 2}{4 - (-2)} = \frac{-3}{6} = -0.5$$

The perpendicular bisector of $\overline{RS}$ has a slope of 2, the negative reciprocal of -0.5. Its equation is $y - 0.5 = 2(x - 1)$, or $y = 2x - 1.5$. Substituting 2 for x gives $y = 2.5$. Since $y = 2x - 1.5$ is a function, this is the only value of y for $x = 2$.

SHORT RESPONSE

1. A rhombus is a quadrilateral with four congruent sides. The vertices of figure *ABCD* are $A(6, 3)$, $B(-3, 5)$, $C(-5, -4)$, and $D(4, -5)$. Can you change the coordinates of one vertex of *ABCD* to make it a rhombus? If so, explain how and find the coordinates. If not, explain why not.

2. A lamp for indoor gardening uses a parabolic reflector with the height and width shown to concentrate light on plants. Is the focus of the reflector above or below the reflector's bottom edge? *Explain* your reasoning.

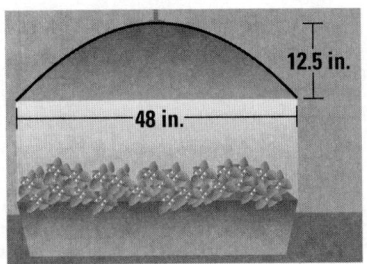

12.5 in.

48 in.

3. Three points on the edge of the circular Copernicus crater on the moon can be represented by the coordinates $(-35, 35)$, $(0, 0)$, and $(40, 80)$ where each unit represents one kilometer. Is the point located at $(55, 25)$ inside the crater or outside the crater? *Explain* your reasoning.

4. For each set of concentric circles shown below, the measures of the radii are the consecutive integers from 1 to 9. *Explain* how you can use this information to demonstrate that the points of intersection shown below lie on an ellipse whose foci are the centers of the circles. Then write an equation of the ellipse.

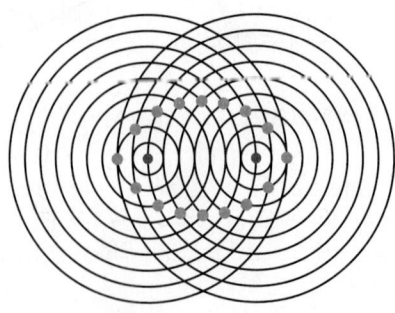

5. A soccer field has a penalty-kick mark 12 yards from the goal. From the mark's center, an arc with a radius of 10 yards is drawn outside the penalty area as shown in the diagram. *Explain* how to use an equation of a circle to find the distance *d* along the edge of the penalty area between the endpoints of the arc.

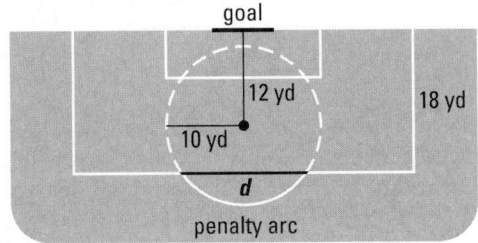

goal

12 yd

18 yd

10 yd

d

penalty arc

6. A coordinate grid contains two hyperbolas centered at the origin, one with a vertical transverse axis and one with a horizontal transverse axis. What are the possible numbers of solutions of the system that the hyperbolas represent? Use sketches to justify your answer.

7. The *Tractricious* sculpture at the Fermi National Accelerator Laboratory in Batavia, Illinois, has a hyperbolic cross section as shown below.

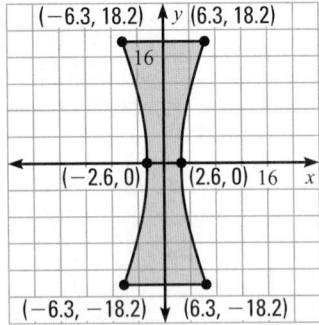

$(-6.3, 18.2)$ y $(6.3, 18.2)$

16

$(-2.6, 0)$ $(2.6, 0)$ 16 x

$(-6.3, -18.2)$ $(6.3, -18.2)$

Use the graph to write an equation of the hyperbola that models the cross section of the sculpture. (Each unit represents 1 foot.) Then explain how to modify your equation so the origin is at the bottom left of the sculpture.

8. Without applying area formulas, compare the areas of the ellipses represented by $4x^2 + 6y^2 = 48$ and $\dfrac{(x-5)^2}{12} + \dfrac{(y+7)^2}{8} = 1$. *Explain* how you made your comparison.

MULTIPLE CHOICE

9. Which equation represents a hyperbola?

A $x^2 - 3y + 4x - 15 = 0$

B $x^2 + y^2 + 4x - 18y - 15 = 0$

C $x^2 - y^2 + 4x - 18y - 15 = 0$

D $-2x^2 - y^2 + 4x - 18y - 15 = 0$

10. At what point(s) do the graphs represented by $x^2 + y^2 = 36$ and $-y^2 + x = 6$ intersect?

A $(6, 0)$

B $(-6, 0)$

C $(-7, -\sqrt{13})$

D $(6, 0)$ and $(-6, 0)$

11. Which statement about the graph of the equation $12(x - 6) = -(y + 4)^2$ is *not* true?

A The vertex is at $(6, -4)$.

B The axis of symmetry is $y = -4$.

C The focus is at $(6, -7)$.

D The graph represents a function.

GRIDDED ANSWER

12. The conic section represented by the equation $\dfrac{(x-2)^2}{81} - \dfrac{(y-5)^2}{4} = 1$ has the line of symmetry $x = s$. What is the value of s?

13. To the nearest tenth, what is the distance between $(-10, 2)$ and $(7, 7)$?

14. What is the length of the transverse axis of the hyperbola represented by the equation $9x^2 - 4y^2 = 324$?

15. What is the radius of the circle represented by the equation $8x^2 + 8y^2 = 720$? Round your answer to the nearest tenth.

16. Evaluating $\pi\left[3a + 3b - \sqrt{(a + 3b)(b + 3a)}\,\right]$ approximates the circumference of an ellipse with major axis of length $2a$ and minor axis of length $2b$. Approximate the circumference of an ellipse with center $(0, 0)$, vertex $(0, -5)$, and focus $(0, 3)$. Round your answer to the nearest unit.

EXTENDED RESPONSE

17. A satellite in a *geostationary* orbit appears to stay above a single place on Earth's surface. A satellite originally in a low orbit can be boosted using an elliptical *Hohmann transfer orbit* to a higher geostationary orbit. A satellite originally in a circular orbit 4200 miles from Earth's center is boosted to a circular geostationary orbit 22,240 miles from Earth's center.

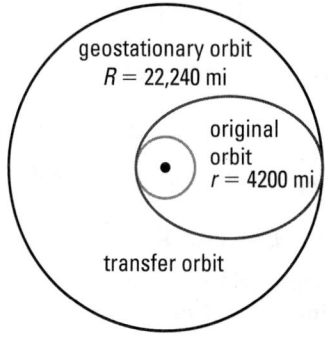

a. Write equations that model the original and geostationary orbits. Use Earth's center as the origin.

b. Earth's center is at one focus of the transfer orbit. *Explain* how you can find the values of a and c for the transfer orbit.

c. Write an equation that models the transfer orbit. Use Earth's center as the origin, and choose a horizontal major axis as shown in the diagram.

18. Points one quarter of the way along the sides of the large square are connected to form an inscribed square. The pattern continues.

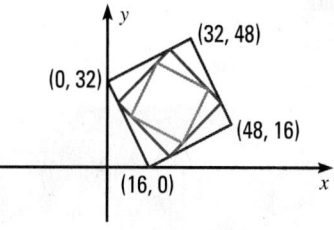

a. *Explain* how to use the midpoint formula to find the coordinates of the vertices for each new square in the pattern.

b. Find the missing coordinates of the vertices of the squares shown.

c. *Compare* the areas of the squares. What do you notice?

9 Trigonometric Ratios and Functions

Before

In previous courses and in previous chapters, you learned the following skills, which you'll use in this chapter: using the Pythagorean theorem, solving equations using inverse functions, and finding angle measures in triangles.

Prerequisite Skills

VOCABULARY CHECK

Copy and complete the statement.

1. The **reciprocal** of $\frac{4}{5}$ is ___?___.

2. Functions f and g are **inverses** of each other if ___?___ and ___?___.

3. An equation of the **circle** with center $(0, 0)$ and a radius of 1 unit is ___?___.

SKILLS CHECK

A right triangle has legs with lengths a and b and a hypotenuse with length c. Find the unknown side length.

4. $a = 8, b = 10$ 5. $a = 2.5, c = 6.5$ 6. $b = 9, c = 11$

Solve each proportion.

7. $\frac{x}{10} = \frac{4}{15}$ 8. $\frac{40}{21} = \frac{5}{x}$ 9. $\frac{98}{21} = \frac{x}{3}$

The measures of the angles of a triangle are given. Find the value of x.

10. $x°, 65°, 55°$ 11. $90°, x°, x°$ 12. $41°, 107°, x°$

In this chapter, you will apply the big ideas listed below and reviewed in the Chapter Summary. You will also use the key vocabulary listed below.

Big Ideas

① Using trigonometric functions

② Using inverse trigonometric functions

③ Applying the law of sines and law of cosines

KEY VOCABULARY

- sine
- cosine
- tangent
- cosecant
- secant

- cotangent
- radian
- central angle
- unit circle
- reference angle

- inverse sine
- inverse cosine
- inverse tangent
- law of sines
- law of cosines

Why?

You can use angle measures and trigonometry to find lengths and areas in real life. For example, you can use an angle measure to find the area of each step in a spiral staircase.

Animated Algebra

The animation illustrated below helps you answer a question from this chapter: How does the central angle of a step in a spiral staircase affect the step's area?

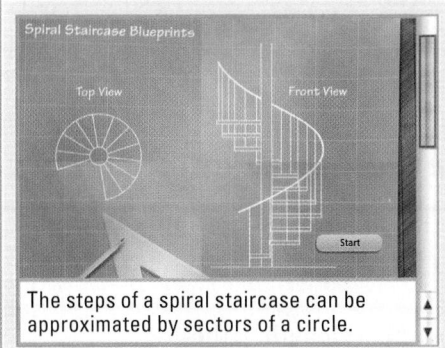

The steps of a spiral staircase can be approximated by sectors of a circle.

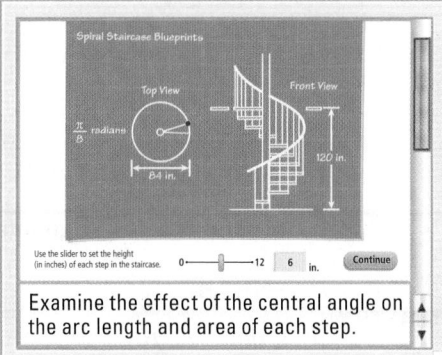

Examine the effect of the central angle on the arc length and area of each step.

Animated Algebra at my.hrw.com

9.1 Use Trigonometry with Right Triangles

Before	You used the Pythagorean theorem to find lengths.
Now	You will use trigonometric functions to find lengths.
Why?	So you can measure distances indirectly, as in Example 5.

Key Vocabulary
- **sine**
- **cosine**
- **tangent**
- **cosecant**
- **secant**
- **cotangent**

CC.9-12.G.SRT.6 Understand that by similarity, side ratios in right triangles are properties of the angles in the triangle, leading to definitions of trigonometric ratios for acute angles.

Consider a right triangle that has an acute angle θ (the Greek letter *theta*). The three sides of the triangle are the *hypotenuse*, the side *opposite* θ, and the side *adjacent* to θ.

Ratios of a right triangle's side lengths are used to define the six trigonometric functions: **sine**, **cosine**, **tangent**, **cosecant**, **secant**, and **cotangent**. These six functions are abbreviated sin, cos, tan, csc, sec, and cot, respectively.

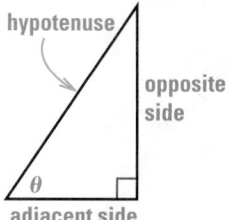

KEY CONCEPT
For Your Notebook

Right Triangle Definitions of Trigonometric Functions

Let θ be an acute angle of a right triangle. The six trigonometric functions of θ are defined as follows:

$$\sin \theta = \frac{\text{opposite}}{\text{hypotenuse}} \qquad \cos \theta = \frac{\text{adjacent}}{\text{hypotenuse}} \qquad \tan \theta = \frac{\text{opposite}}{\text{adjacent}}$$

$$\csc \theta = \frac{\text{hypotenuse}}{\text{opposite}} \qquad \sec \theta = \frac{\text{hypotenuse}}{\text{adjacent}} \qquad \cot \theta = \frac{\text{adjacent}}{\text{opposite}}$$

The abbreviations *opp*, *adj*, and *hyp* are often used to represent the side lengths of the right triangle. Note that the ratios in the second row are reciprocals of the ratios in the first row:

$$\csc \theta = \frac{1}{\sin \theta} \qquad \sec \theta = \frac{1}{\cos \theta} \qquad \cot \theta = \frac{1}{\tan \theta}$$

EXAMPLE 1 Evaluate trigonometric functions

Evaluate the six trigonometric functions of the angle θ.

Solution

REVIEW GEOMETRY
For help with the Pythagorean theorem, see p. SR21.

From the Pythagorean theorem, the length of the hypotenuse is $\sqrt{5^2 + 12^2} = \sqrt{169} = 13$.

$$\sin \theta = \frac{\text{opp}}{\text{hyp}} \quad \frac{12}{13} \qquad \cos \theta = \frac{\text{adj}}{\text{hyp}} \quad \frac{5}{13} \qquad \tan \theta = \frac{\text{opp}}{\text{adj}} \quad \frac{12}{5}$$

$$\csc \theta = \frac{\text{hyp}}{\text{opp}} \quad \frac{13}{12} \qquad \sec \theta = \frac{\text{hyp}}{\text{adj}} \quad \frac{13}{5} \qquad \cot \theta = \frac{\text{adj}}{\text{opp}} \quad \frac{5}{12}$$

National Park Service

EXAMPLE 2 **Standardized Test Practice**

If θ is an acute angle of a right triangle and $\sin \theta = \dfrac{4}{7}$, what is $\tan \theta$?

(A) $\dfrac{3}{7}$ (B) $\dfrac{4\sqrt{33}}{33}$ (C) $\dfrac{\sqrt{33}}{7}$ (D) $\dfrac{4}{3}$

Solution

STEP 1 **Draw** a right triangle with acute angle θ such that the leg opposite θ has length 4 and the hypotenuse has length 7. By the Pythagorean theorem, the length x of the other leg is $x = \sqrt{7^2 - 4^2} = \sqrt{33}$.

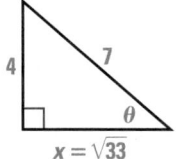

STEP 2 **Find** the value of $\tan \theta$.

$$\tan \theta = \frac{\text{opp}}{\text{adj}} = \frac{4}{\sqrt{33}} = \frac{4\sqrt{33}}{33}$$

▶ The correct answer is B. (A) (B) (C) (D)

 GUIDED PRACTICE for Examples 1 and 2

Evaluate the six trigonometric functions of the angle θ.

1. 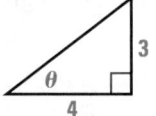   2. 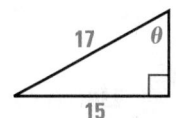   3.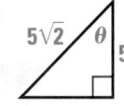

4. In a right triangle, θ is an acute angle and $\cos \theta = \dfrac{7}{10}$. What is $\sin \theta$?

SPECIAL ANGLES The angles 30°, 45°, and 60° occur frequently in trigonometry. You can use the trigonometric values for these angles to find unknown side lengths in special right triangles.

KEY CONCEPT *For Your Notebook*

Trigonometric Values for Special Angles

The table below gives the values of the six trigonometric functions for the angles 30°, 45°, and 60°. You can obtain these values from the triangles shown.

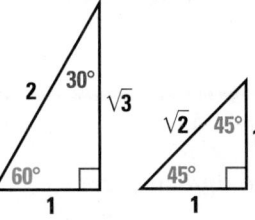

θ	$\sin \theta$	$\cos \theta$	$\tan \theta$	$\csc \theta$	$\sec \theta$	$\cot \theta$
30°	$\dfrac{1}{2}$	$\dfrac{\sqrt{3}}{2}$	$\dfrac{\sqrt{3}}{3}$	2	$\dfrac{2\sqrt{3}}{3}$	$\sqrt{3}$
45°	$\dfrac{\sqrt{2}}{2}$	$\dfrac{\sqrt{2}}{2}$	1	$\sqrt{2}$	$\sqrt{2}$	1
60°	$\dfrac{\sqrt{3}}{2}$	$\dfrac{1}{2}$	$\sqrt{3}$	$\dfrac{2\sqrt{3}}{3}$	2	$\dfrac{\sqrt{3}}{3}$

EXAMPLE 3 **Find an unknown side length of a right triangle**

Find the value of x for the right triangle shown.

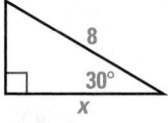

Solution

Write an equation using a trigonometric function that involves the ratio of x and 8. Solve the equation for x.

$\cos 30° = \dfrac{adj}{hyp}$ **Write trigonometric equation.**

$\dfrac{\sqrt{3}}{2} = \dfrac{x}{8}$ **Substitute.**

$4\sqrt{3} = x$ **Multiply each side by 8.**

▸ The length of the side is $x = 4\sqrt{3} \approx 6.93$.

Animated Algebra at my.hrw.com

SOLVING A TRIANGLE Finding *all* unknown side lengths and angle measures of a triangle is called *solving* the triangle. Solving right triangles that have acute angles other than 30°, 45°, and 60° may require the use of a calculator.

To find values of the sine, cosine, and tangent functions on a calculator, use the keys **SIN**, **COS**, and **TAN**. Use these keys and the reciprocal key for cosecant, secant, and cotangent. Be sure the calculator is set in degree mode.

EXAMPLE 4 **Use a calculator to solve a right triangle**

Solve $\triangle ABC$.

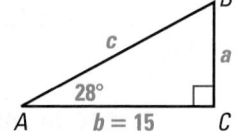

Solution

READING
Throughout this chapter, a capital letter is used to denote both an angle of a triangle and its measure. The same letter in lowercase is used to denote the length of the side opposite that angle.

A and B are complementary angles, so $B = 90° - 28° = 62°$.

$\tan 28° = \dfrac{opp}{adj}$ $\sec 28° = \dfrac{hyp}{adj}$ **Write trigonometric equation.**

$\tan 28° = \dfrac{a}{15}$ $\sec 28° = \dfrac{c}{15}$ **Substitute.**

$15(\tan 28°) = a$ $15\left(\dfrac{1}{\cos 28°}\right) = c$ **Solve for the variable.**

$7.98 \approx a$ $17.0 \approx c$ **Use a calculator.**

▸ So, $B = 62°$, $a \approx 7.98$, and $c \approx 17.0$.

✓ **GUIDED PRACTICE**   for Examples 3 and 4

Solve $\triangle ABC$ using the diagram at the right and the given measurements.

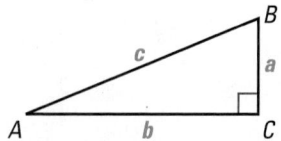

5. $B = 45°$, $c = 5$ **6.** $A = 32°$, $b = 10$

7. $A = 71°$, $c = 20$ **8.** $B = 60°$, $a = 7$

EXAMPLE 5 Use indirect measurement

GRAND CANYON While standing at Yavapai Point near the Grand Canyon, you measure an angle of 90° between Powell Point and Widforss Point, as shown. You then walk to Powell Point and measure an angle of 76° between Yavapai Point and Widforss Point. The distance between Yavapai Point and Powell Point is about 2 miles. How wide is the Grand Canyon between Yavapai Point and Widforss Point?

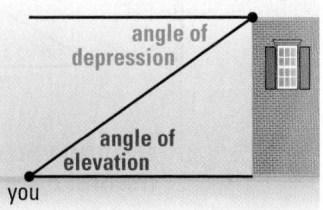

Solution

CHOOSE FUNCTIONS
The tangent function is used to find the unknown distance because it involves the ratio of *x* and 2.

$$\tan 76° = \frac{x}{2} \qquad \text{Write trigonometric equation.}$$

$$2(\tan 76°) = x \qquad \text{Multiply each side by 2.}$$

$$8.0 \approx x \qquad \text{Use a calculator.}$$

▶ The width is about 8.0 miles.

ANGLES OF SIGHT If you look at a point above you, such as the top of a building, the angle that your line of sight makes with a line parallel to the ground is called the **angle of elevation**. At the top of the building, the angle between a line parallel to the ground and your line of sight is called the **angle of depression**. These two angles have the same measure.

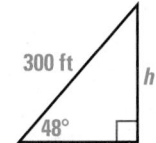

EXAMPLE 6 Use an angle of elevation

PARASAILING A parasailer is attached to a boat with a rope 300 feet long. The angle of elevation from the boat to the parasailer is 48°. Estimate the parasailer's height above the boat.

Solution

STEP 1 **Draw** a diagram that represents the situation.

STEP 2 **Write** and solve an equation to find the height *h*.

$$\sin 48° = \frac{h}{300} \qquad \text{Write trigonometric equation.}$$

$$300(\sin 48°) = h \qquad \text{Multiply each side by 300.}$$

$$223 \approx h \qquad \text{Use a calculator.}$$

▶ The height of the parasailer above the boat is about 223 feet.

✓ GUIDED PRACTICE for Examples 5 and 6

9. **GRAND CANYON** In Example 5, find the distance between Powell Point and Widforss Point.

10. **WHAT IF?** In Example 6, estimate the height of the parasailer above the boat if the angle of elevation is 38°.

9.1 EXERCISES

HOMEWORK
KEY

○ = See WORKED-OUT SOLUTIONS
 Exs. 5, 11, and 33

★ = STANDARDIZED TEST PRACTICE
 Exs. 2, 15, 20, 33, and 36

◆ = MULTIPLE REPRESENTATIONS
 Ex. 34

SKILL PRACTICE

1. **VOCABULARY** What is an angle of elevation?

2. ★ **WRITING** *Explain* what it means to solve a right triangle.

EXAMPLE 1
for Exs. 3–8

EVALUATING FUNCTIONS Evaluate the six trigonometric functions of the angle θ.

3.
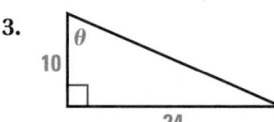

4.
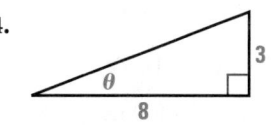

5.
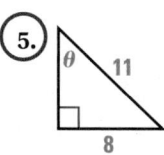

6.
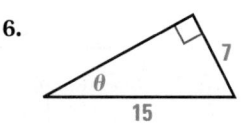

7.
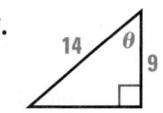

8.
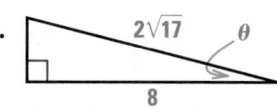

EXAMPLE 2
for Exs. 9–16

FINDING VALUES Let θ be an acute angle of a right triangle. Find the values of the other five trigonometric functions of θ.

9. $\sin \theta = \dfrac{5}{6}$

10. $\cos \theta = \dfrac{5}{8}$

11. $\tan \theta = \dfrac{7}{3}$

12. $\csc \theta = \dfrac{10}{7}$

13. $\sec \theta = \dfrac{12}{5}$

14. $\cot \theta = \dfrac{6}{11}$

15. ★ **MULTIPLE CHOICE** In a right triangle, θ is an acute angle and $\cos \theta = \dfrac{4}{9}$. What is the value of $\tan \theta$?

(A) $\dfrac{4\sqrt{65}}{65}$

(B) $\dfrac{\sqrt{65}}{9}$

(C) $\dfrac{\sqrt{65}}{4}$

(D) $\dfrac{9}{4}$

16. **ERROR ANALYSIS** *Describe* and correct the error in finding $\csc \theta$, given that θ is an acute angle of a right triangle and $\cos \theta = \dfrac{7}{11}$.

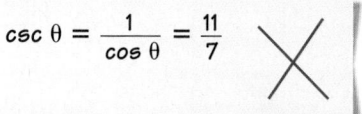

EXAMPLE 3
for Exs. 17–20

FINDING SIDE LENGTHS Find the exact values of x and y.

17.
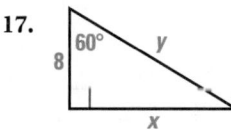

18.
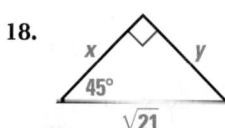

19.
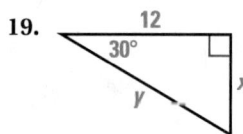

20. ★ **MULTIPLE CHOICE** In a 30°-60°-90° triangle, the longer leg has a length of 5. What is the length of the shorter leg?

(A) $\dfrac{5\sqrt{3}}{3}$

(B) $\dfrac{5\sqrt{3}}{2}$

(C) $\dfrac{10\sqrt{3}}{3}$

(D) $5\sqrt{3}$

EXAMPLE 4
for Exs. 21–28

SOLVING TRIANGLES Solve △*ABC* using the diagram and the given measurements.

21. $A = 35°, c = 16$ **22.** $B = 53°, a = 12$

23. $B = 18°, c = 24$ **24.** $A = 67°, b = 7$

25. $B = 75°, a = 15$ **26.** $A = 49°, c = 27$

27. $A = 64°, b = 32$ **28.** $B = 24°, c = 10.8$

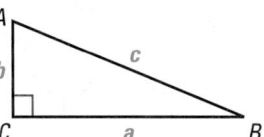

29. CHALLENGE A procedure for approximating π based on the work of Archimedes is to inscribe a regular hexagon in a circle.

a. Use the diagram at the right to solve for *x*. What is the perimeter of the hexagon?

b. Show that a regular *n*-sided polygon inscribed in a circle of radius 1 has a perimeter of $2n \cdot \sin\left(\dfrac{180}{n}\right)°$.

c. Use the result from part (b) to find an expression in terms of *n* that approximates π. Then evaluate the expression when $n = 50$.

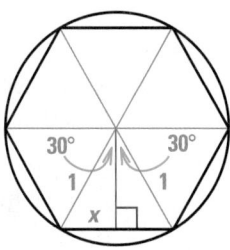

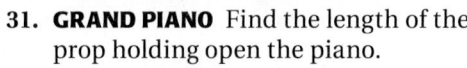

PROBLEM SOLVING

In Exercises 30 and 31, use the information in the diagram to solve the problem.

30. TREE HEIGHT A tree casts the shadow shown. What is the height of the tree?

31. GRAND PIANO Find the length of the prop holding open the piano.

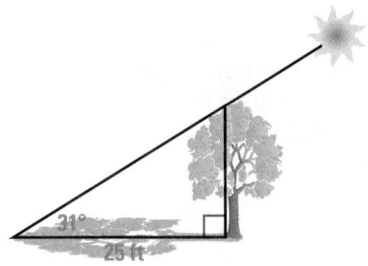

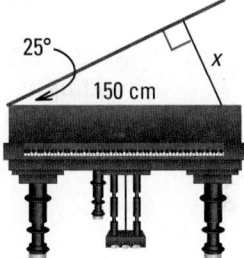

32. RAILWAY The Falls Incline Railway at Niagara Falls has an angle of elevation of 36°. The railway extends a horizontal distance of about 138 feet. Find the height and length of the railway.

33. ★ **SHORT RESPONSE** A submersible traveling at a depth of 250 feet dives at an angle of 15° with respect to a line parallel to the water's surface. It travels a horizontal distance of 1500 feet during the dive. What is the depth of the submersible after the dive? *Explain* how the angle of the dive affects the final depth.

34. ◆ **MULTIPLE REPRESENTATIONS** You are climbing Mount Massive in Colorado. You are at an altitude of 11,200 feet. You measure the angle of elevation to a ridge above you to be 29.4°. The distance (along the face of the mountain) between you and the ridge is 6315 feet.

a. Drawing a Diagram Draw a diagram that represents this situation.

b. Writing an Equation Write and solve an equation to find the altitude of the ridge.

35. TROPIC OF CANCER The Tropic of Cancer is the circle of latitude farthest north of the equator where the sun can appear directly overhead. It lies 23.5° north of the equator, as shown.

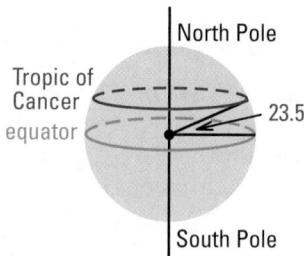

    a. Find the circumference of the Tropic of Cancer using 3960 miles as Earth's approximate radius.

    b. What is the distance between two points on the Tropic of Cancer that lie directly across from each other?

36. ★ EXTENDED RESPONSE A passenger in an airplane sees two towns directly to the left of the plane.

    a. What is the distance *d* from the airplane to the first town?

    b. What is the horizontal distance *x* from the airplane to the first town?

    c. What is the distance *y* between the two towns? *Explain* the process you used to find your answer.

37. CHALLENGE You measure the angle of elevation from the ground to the top of a building as 32°. When you move 50 meters closer to the building, the angle of elevation is 53°. How high is the building?

9.2 Define General Angles and Use Radian Measure

Before	You used acute angles measured in degrees.
Now	You will use general angles that may be measured in radians.
Why?	So you can find the area of a curved playing field, as in Example 4.

Key Vocabulary
• initial side
• terminal side
• standard position
• coterminal
• radian
• sector
• central angle

CC.9-12.F.TF.1 Understand radian measure of an angle as the length of the arc on the unit circle subtended by the angle.

In this lesson, you will expand your study of angles to include angles with measures that can be any real numbers.

KEY CONCEPT   *For Your Notebook*

Angles in Standard Position

In a coordinate plane, an angle can be formed by fixing one ray, called the **initial side**, and rotating the other ray, called the **terminal side**, about the vertex.

An angle is in **standard position** if its vertex is at the origin and its initial side lies on the positive *x*-axis.

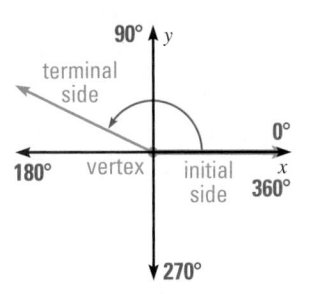

The measure of an angle is positive if the rotation of its terminal side is counterclockwise, and negative if the rotation is clockwise. The terminal side of an angle can make more than one complete rotation.

EXAMPLE 1 **Draw angles in standard position**

Draw an angle with the given measure in standard position.

 a. 240°   **b.** 500°   **c.** −50°

Solution

a. Because 240° is 60° more than 180°, the terminal side is 60° counterclockwise past the negative *x*-axis.

b. Because 500° is 140° more than 360°, the terminal side makes one whole revolution counterclockwise plus 140° more.

c. Because −50° is negative, the terminal side is 50° clockwise from the positive *x*-axis.

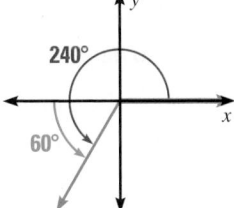

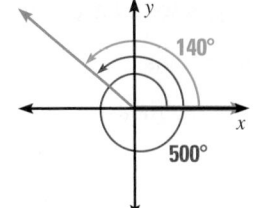

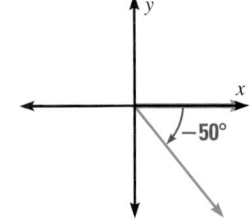

COTERMINAL ANGLES In Example 1, the angles 500° and 140° are **coterminal** because their terminal sides coincide. An angle coterminal with a given angle can be found by adding or subtracting multiples of 360°.

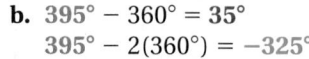

Find coterminal angles

Find one positive angle and one negative angle that are coterminal with **(a) −45° and (b) 395°.**

Solution

There are many such angles, depending on what multiple of 360° is added or subtracted.

a. $-45° + 360° = 315°$
$-45° - 360° = -405°$

b. $395° - 360° = 35°$
$395° - 2(360°) = -325°$

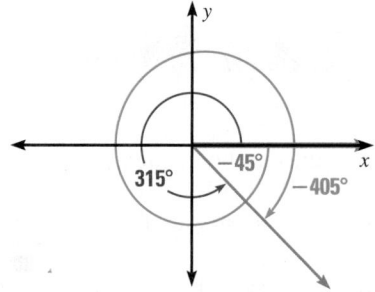

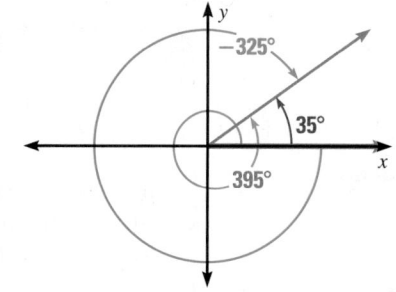

 GUIDED PRACTICE for Examples 1 and 2

Draw an angle with the given measure in standard position. Then find one positive coterminal angle and one negative coterminal angle.

1. 65°   **2.** 230°   **3.** 300°   **4.** 740°

RADIAN MEASURE Angles can also be measured in *radians*. To define a radian, consider a circle with radius *r* centered at the origin as shown. One **radian** is the measure of an angle in standard position whose terminal side intercepts an arc of length *r*.

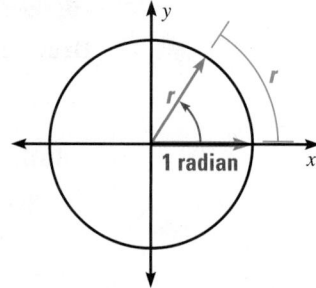

Because the circumference of a circle is $2\pi r$, there are 2π radians in a full circle. Degree measure and radian measure are therefore related by the equation $360° = 2\pi$ radians, or $180° = \pi$ radians.

KEY CONCEPT *For Your Notebook*

Converting Between Degrees and Radians

Degrees to radians

Multiply degree measure by $\dfrac{\pi \text{ radians}}{180°}$.

Radians to degrees

Multiply radian measure by $\dfrac{180°}{\pi \text{ radians}}$.

EXAMPLE 3 **Convert between degrees and radians**

READING

The unit "radians" is often omitted. For instance, the measure $-\frac{\pi}{12}$ radians may be written simply as $-\frac{\pi}{12}$.

Convert (a) $125°$ to radians and (b) $-\frac{\pi}{12}$ radians to degrees.

a. $125° = 125°\left(\dfrac{\pi\,\text{radians}}{180°}\right)$

$\quad = \dfrac{25\pi}{36}$ radians

b. $-\dfrac{\pi}{12} = \left(-\dfrac{\pi}{12}\text{ radians}\right)\left(\dfrac{180°}{\pi\,\text{radians}}\right)$

$\quad = -15°$

CONCEPT SUMMARY *For Your Notebook*

Degree and Radian Measures of Special Angles

The diagram shows equivalent degree and radian measures for special angles from $0°$ to $360°$ (0 radians to 2π radians).

You may find it helpful to memorize the equivalent degree and radian measures of special angles in the first quadrant and for $90° = \frac{\pi}{2}$ radians. All other special angles are just multiples of these angles.

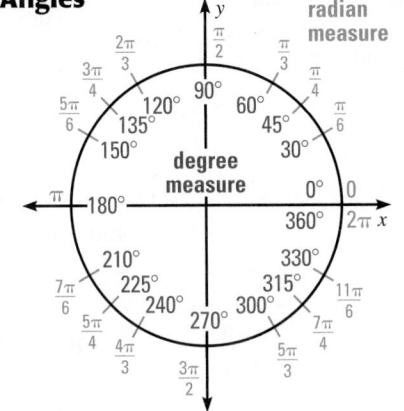

✔ **GUIDED PRACTICE** for Example 3

Convert the degree measure to radians or the radian measure to degrees.

5. $135°$ **6.** $-50°$ **7.** $\dfrac{5\pi}{4}$ **8.** $\dfrac{\pi}{10}$

SECTORS OF CIRCLES A **sector** is a region of a circle that is bounded by two radii and an arc of the circle. The **central angle** θ of a sector is the angle formed by the two radii. There are simple formulas for the arc length and area of a sector when the central angle is measured in radians.

KEY CONCEPT *For Your Notebook*

Arc Length and Area of a Sector

The arc length s and area A of a sector with radius r and central angle θ (measured in radians) are as follows.

Arc length: $s = r\theta$

Area: $A = \dfrac{1}{2}r^2\theta$

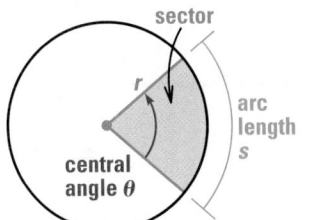

EXAMPLE 4 Solve a multi-step problem

SOFTBALL A softball field forms a sector with the dimensions shown. Find the length of the outfield fence and the area of the field.

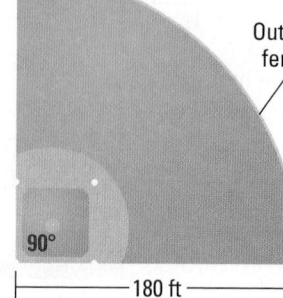

Outfield fence

90°

180 ft

Solution

STEP 1 **Convert** the measure of the central angle to radians.

AVOID ERRORS
You must write the measure of an angle in radians when using the formulas for the arc length and area of a sector.

$$90° = 90°\left(\frac{\pi \text{ radians}}{180°}\right) = \frac{\pi}{2} \text{ radians}$$

STEP 2 **Find** the arc length and the area of the sector.

Arc length: $s = r\theta = 180\left(\frac{\pi}{2}\right) = 90\pi \approx 283$ feet

Area: $A = \frac{1}{2}r^2\theta = \frac{1}{2}(180)^2\left(\frac{\pi}{2}\right) = 8100\pi \approx 25,400 \text{ ft}^2$

▶ The length of the outfield fence is about 283 feet. The area of the field is about 25,400 square feet.

✓ **GUIDED PRACTICE** for Example 4

9. **WHAT IF?** In Example 4, estimate the length of the outfield fence and the area of the field if the outfield fence is 220 feet from home plate.

9.2 EXERCISES

HOMEWORK KEY

○ = See WORKED-OUT SOLUTIONS
Exs. 11, 23, and 51

★ = STANDARDIZED TEST PRACTICE
Exs. 2, 14, 31, 50, and 53

SKILL PRACTICE

1. **VOCABULARY** Copy and complete: An angle is in standard position if its vertex is at the __?__ and its __?__ lies on the positive x-axis.

2. ★ **WRITING** How does the sign of an angle's measure determine its direction of rotation?

EXAMPLES 1 and 3
for Exs. 3–14

VISUAL THINKING Match the angle measure with the angle.

3. −240°

4. 600°

5. $-\frac{9\pi}{4}$

A.
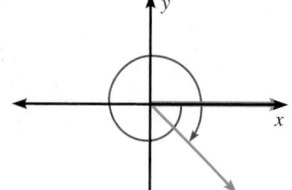

B.
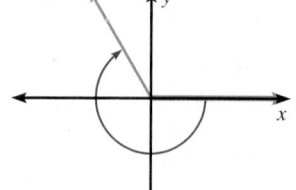

C.
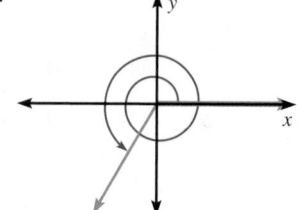

DRAWING ANGLES Draw an angle with the given measure in standard position.

6. 110° **7.** −10° **8.** 450° **9.** −900°

10. 6π **11.** $\frac{5\pi}{18}$ **12.** $-\frac{5\pi}{3}$ **13.** $\frac{26\pi}{9}$

14. ★ **MULTIPLE CHOICE** Which angle measure is shown in the diagram?

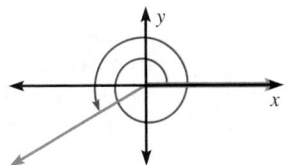

(**A**) −150°   (**B**) 210°

(**C**) 570°   (**D**) 930°

EXAMPLES
2 and 3
for Exs. 15–22

FINDING COTERMINAL ANGLES Find one positive angle and one negative angle that are coterminal with the given angle.

15. 70° **16.** 255° **17.** −125° **18.** 820°

19. $\frac{9\pi}{2}$ **20.** $-\frac{7\pi}{6}$ **21.** $\frac{28\pi}{9}$ **22.** $\frac{20\pi}{3}$

EXAMPLE 3
for Exs. 23–31

CONVERTING MEASURES Convert the degree measure to radians or the radian measure to degrees.

23. 40° **24.** 315° **25.** −260° **26.** 500°

27. $\frac{\pi}{9}$ **28.** $-\frac{\pi}{4}$ **29.** 5π **30.** $\frac{14\pi}{15}$

31. ★ **MULTIPLE CHOICE** Which angle measure is equivalent to $\frac{13\pi}{6}$ radians?

(**A**) 30°   (**B**) 390°   (**C**) 750°   (**D**) 1110°

EXAMPLE 4
for Exs. 32–38

FINDING ARC LENGTH AND AREA Find the arc length and area of a sector with the given radius r and central angle θ.

32. $r = 4$ in., $\theta = \frac{\pi}{6}$ **33.** $r = 3$ m, $\theta = \frac{5\pi}{12}$ **34.** $r = 15$ cm, $\theta = 45°$

35. $r = 12$ ft, $\theta = 150°$ **36.** $r = 18$ m, $\theta = 25°$ **37.** $r = 25$ in., $\theta = 270°$

38. **ERROR ANALYSIS** *Describe* and correct the error in finding the area of a sector with a radius of 6 centimeters and a central angle of 40°.

$$A = \frac{1}{2}(6)^2(40) = 720 \text{ cm}^2 \qquad \times$$

HINT
For Exs. 39–46, set your calculator in radian mode.

EVALUATING FUNCTIONS Evaluate the trigonometric function using a calculator if necessary. If possible, give an exact answer.

39. $\cos \frac{\pi}{3}$ **40.** $\sin \frac{\pi}{4}$ **41.** $\tan \frac{\pi}{6}$ **42.** $\sec \frac{\pi}{9}$

43. $\cot \frac{\pi}{8}$ **44.** $\cos \frac{\pi}{6}$ **45.** $\sin \frac{3\pi}{7}$ **46.** $\csc \frac{4\pi}{15}$

47. **CHALLENGE** There are 60 *minutes* in 1 degree of arc, and 60 *seconds* in 1 minute of arc. The notation 50° 30' 10" represents an angle with a measure of 50 degrees, 30 minutes, and 10 seconds.

a. Write the angle measure 70.55° using the notation above.

b. Write the angle measure 110° 45' 30" to the nearest thousandth of a degree.

EXAMPLES
1 and 3
for Exs. 48–50

48. ASTRONOMY In astronomy, the *terminator* is the day-night line on a planet that divides the planet into daytime and nighttime regions. The terminator moves across the planet's surface as the planet rotates. It takes about 4 hours for Earth's terminator to move across the continental United States. Through what angle has Earth rotated during this time? Give the answer in both degrees and radians.

49. CD PLAYER When a CD player reads information from the outer edge of a CD, the CD spins about 200 revolutions per minute. At that speed, through what angle does a point on the CD spin in one minute? Give the answer in both degrees and radians.

50. ★ SHORT RESPONSE You work every Saturday from 9:00 A.M. to 5:00 P.M. Draw a diagram that shows the rotation completed by the hour hand of a clock during this time. Find the measure of the angle generated by the hour hand in both degrees and radians. *Compare* this angle with the angle generated by the minute hand from 9:00 A.M. to 5:00 P.M.

EXAMPLE 4
for Exs. 51–53

51. MULTI-STEP PROBLEM A scientist performed an experiment to study the effects of gravitational force on humans. In order for humans to experience twice Earth's gravity, they were placed in a centrifuge 58 feet long and spun at a rate of about 15 revolutions per minute.

a. Through how many radians did the people rotate each second?

b. Find the length of the arc through which the people rotated each second.

52. MULTI-STEP PROBLEM In the shot put event at the 2004 Summer Olympic Games, the winning shot was 21.16 meters. For a shot put to be fair, it must land within a sector having a central angle of 34.92°.

a. If the officials drew an arc across the fair landing area marking the farthest throw, how long would the arc be?

b. All fair shot puts in the 2004 Olympics landed within a sector bounded by the arc from part (a). What is the area of this sector?

53. ★ EXTENDED RESPONSE A spiral staircase has 15 steps. Each step is a sector with a radius of 42 inches and a central angle of $\frac{\pi}{8}$.

a. What is the length of the arc formed by the outer edge of a step?

b. Through what angle would you rotate by climbing the stairs? Include a sixteenth turn for stepping up on the landing. *Explain* your reasoning.

c. How many square inches of carpeting would you need to cover the 15 steps?

Animated Algebra at my.hrw.com

568

○ = See **WORKED-OUT SOLUTIONS** in Student Resources

★ = **STANDARDIZED TEST PRACTICE**

54. CHALLENGE A dartboard is divided into 20 sectors. Each sector is worth a point value from 1 to 20 and has shaded regions that double or triple this value. A sector is shown below.

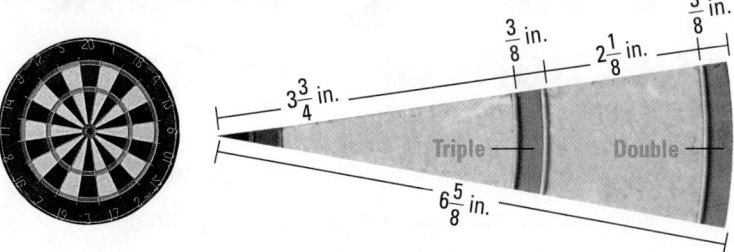

$\frac{3}{8}$ in. $\frac{3}{8}$ in. $2\frac{1}{8}$ in. $\frac{3}{8}$ in.

$3\frac{3}{4}$ in.

Triple   Double

$6\frac{5}{8}$ in.

a. Find the areas of the entire sector, the double region, and the triple region.

b. A dart you throw randomly lands somewhere inside the sector. What is the probability that it lands in the double region? in the triple region?

QUIZ

Solve $\triangle ABC$ using the diagram and the given measurements.

1. $A = 50°$, $a = 14$
2. $A = 25°$, $b = 10$
3. $B = 70°$, $a = 5$
4. $B = 42°$, $c = 18$
5. $A = 15°$, $a = 9$
6. $B = 37°$, $c = 12$

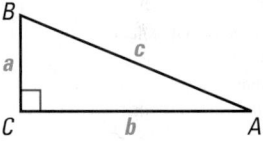

Find one positive angle and one negative angle that are coterminal with the given angle.

7. $115°$
8. $290°$
9. $\frac{4\pi}{9}$
10. $\frac{7\pi}{5}$

11. Find the arc length and area of a sector with a radius of 8 inches and a central angle of $\theta = 115°$.

12. **ESCALATOR** The escalator at the Wilshire/Vermont Metro Rail Station in Los Angeles has an angle of elevation of $30°$. The length of the escalator is 152 feet. What is the height of the escalator?

9.3 Evaluate Trigonometric Functions of Any Angle

Before	You evaluated trigonometric functions of an acute angle.
Now	You will evaluate trigonometric functions of any angle.
Why?	So you can calculate distances involving rotating objects, as in Ex. 37.

Key Vocabulary
• unit circle
• quadrantal angle
• reference angle

CC.9-12.F.TF.2 Explain how the unit circle in the coordinate plane enables the extension of trigonometric functions to all real numbers, interpreted as radian measures of angles traversed counterclockwise around the unit circle.

You can generalize the right-triangle definitions of trigonometric functions so that they apply to *any* angle in standard position.

KEY CONCEPT

For Your Notebook

General Definitions of Trigonometric Functions

Let θ be an angle in standard position, and let (x, y) be the point where the terminal side of θ intersects the circle $x^2 + y^2 = r^2$. The six trigonometric functions of θ are defined as follows:

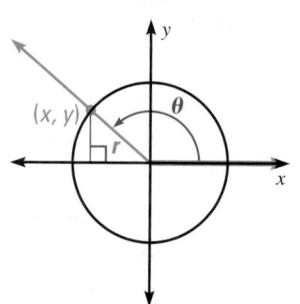

$$\sin \theta = \frac{y}{r} \qquad\qquad \csc \theta = \frac{r}{y},\ y \neq 0$$

$$\cos \theta = \frac{x}{r} \qquad\qquad \sec \theta = \frac{r}{x},\ x \neq 0$$

$$\tan \theta = \frac{y}{x},\ x \neq 0 \qquad \cot \theta = \frac{x}{y},\ y \neq 0$$

These functions are sometimes called *circular functions*.

EXAMPLE 1 Evaluate trigonometric functions given a point

Let $(-4, 3)$ be a point on the terminal side of an angle θ in standard position. Evaluate the six trigonometric functions of θ.

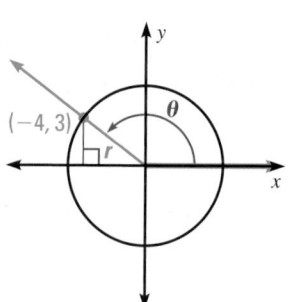

Solution

Use the Pythagorean theorem to find the value of r.

$$r = \sqrt{x^2 + y^2} = \sqrt{(-4)^2 + 3^2} = \sqrt{25} = 5$$

Using $x = -4$, $y = 3$, and $r = 5$, you can write the following:

$$\sin \theta = \frac{y}{r} = \frac{3}{5} \qquad \cos \theta = \frac{x}{r} = -\frac{4}{5} \qquad \tan \theta = \frac{y}{x} = -\frac{3}{4}$$

$$\csc \theta = \frac{r}{y} = \frac{5}{3} \qquad \sec \theta = \frac{r}{x} = -\frac{5}{4} \qquad \cot \theta = \frac{x}{y} = -\frac{4}{3}$$

The Unit Circle

The circle $x^2 + y^2 = 1$, which has center $(0, 0)$ and radius 1, is called the **unit circle**. The values of $\sin \theta$ and $\cos \theta$ are simply the y-coordinate and x-coordinate, respectively, of the point where the terminal side of θ intersects the unit circle.

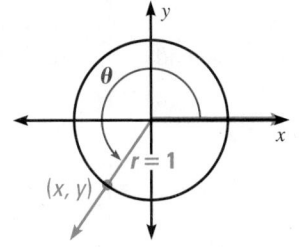

$$\sin \theta = \frac{y}{r} = \frac{y}{1} = y \qquad \cos \theta = \frac{x}{r} = \frac{x}{1} = x$$

It is convenient to use the unit circle to find trigonometric functions of *quadrantal angles*. A **quadrantal angle** is an angle in standard position whose terminal side lies on an axis. The measure of a quadrantal angle is always a multiple of 90°, or $\frac{\pi}{2}$ radians.

EXAMPLE 2 Use the unit circle

Use the unit circle to evaluate the six trigonometric functions of $\theta = 270°$.

ANOTHER WAY

The general circle $x^2 + y^2 = r^2$ can also be used to find the trigonometric functions of $\theta = 270°$. The terminal side of θ intersects the circle at $(0, -r)$. Therefore:

$$\sin \theta = \frac{y}{r} = \frac{-r}{r} = -1$$

The other functions can be evaluated similarly.

Solution

Draw the unit circle, then draw the angle $\theta = 270°$ in standard position. The terminal side of θ intersects the unit circle at $(0, -1)$, so use $x = 0$ and $y = -1$ to evaluate the trigonometric functions.

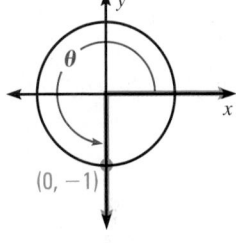

$$\sin \theta = \frac{y}{r} = \frac{-1}{1} = -1 \qquad \csc \theta = \frac{r}{y} = \frac{1}{-1} = -1$$

$$\cos \theta = \frac{x}{r} = \frac{0}{1} = 0 \qquad \sec \theta = \frac{r}{x} = \frac{1}{0} \text{ undefined}$$

$$\tan \theta = \frac{y}{x} = \frac{-1}{0} \text{ undefined} \qquad \cot \theta = \frac{x}{y} = \frac{0}{-1} = 0$$

Animated **Algebra** at my.hrw.com

✓ **GUIDED PRACTICE** for Examples 1 and 2

Evaluate the six trigonometric functions of θ.

1.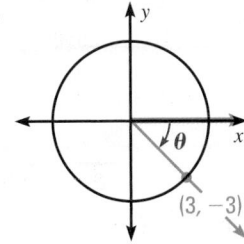

$(3, -3)$

2.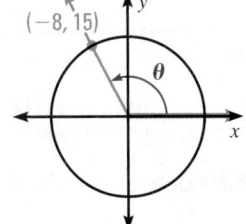

$(-8, 15)$

3.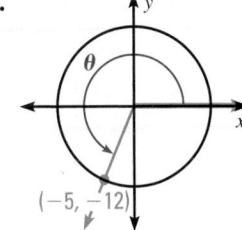

$(-5, -12)$

4. Use the unit circle to evaluate the six trigonometric functions of $\theta = 180°$.

KEY CONCEPT   *For Your Notebook*

Reference Angle Relationships

Let θ be an angle in standard position. The **reference angle** for θ is the acute angle θ' formed by the terminal side of θ and the x-axis. The relationship between θ and θ' is shown below for nonquadrantal angles θ such that $90° < \theta < 360°$ $\left(\dfrac{\pi}{2} < \theta < 2\pi\right)$.

Quadrant II	**Quadrant III**	**Quadrant IV**
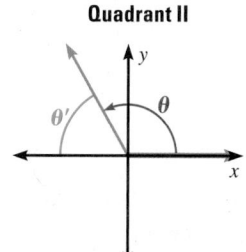	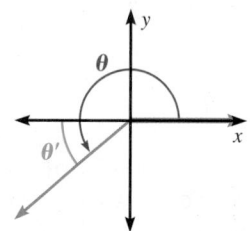	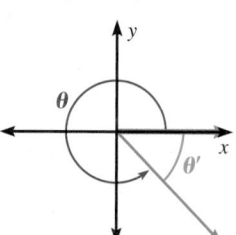
Degrees: $\theta' = 180° - \theta$	**Degrees:** $\theta' = \theta - 180°$	**Degrees:** $\theta' = 360° - \theta$
Radians: $\theta' = \pi - \theta$	**Radians:** $\theta' = \theta - \pi$	**Radians:** $\theta' = 2\pi - \theta$

EXAMPLE 3   **Find reference angles**

Find the reference angle θ' for (a) $\theta = \dfrac{5\pi}{3}$ and (b) $\theta = -130°$.

Solution

  a. The terminal side of θ lies in Quadrant IV. So, $\theta' = 2\pi - \dfrac{5\pi}{3} = \dfrac{\pi}{3}$.

  b. Note that θ is coterminal with 230°, whose terminal side lies in Quadrant III. So, $\theta' = 230° - 180° = 50°$.

EVALUATING TRIGONOMETRIC FUNCTIONS Reference angles allow you to evaluate a trigonometric function for any angle θ. The sign of the trigonometric function value depends on the quadrant in which θ lies.

KEY CONCEPT   *For Your Notebook*

Evaluating Trigonometric Functions

Use these steps to evaluate a trigonometric function for any angle θ:

    STEP 1   **Find** the reference angle θ'.

    STEP 2   **Evaluate** the trigonometric function for θ'.

    STEP 3   **Determine** the sign of the trigonometric function value from the quadrant in which θ lies.

Signs of Function Values

Quadrant II	Quadrant I
$\sin\theta$, $\csc\theta$: $+$	$\sin\theta$, $\csc\theta$: $+$
$\cos\theta$, $\sec\theta$: $-$	$\cos\theta$, $\sec\theta$: $+$
$\tan\theta$, $\cot\theta$: $-$	$\tan\theta$, $\cot\theta$: $+$
Quadrant III	Quadrant IV
$\sin\theta$, $\csc\theta$: $-$	$\sin\theta$, $\csc\theta$: $-$
$\cos\theta$, $\sec\theta$: $-$	$\cos\theta$, $\sec\theta$: $+$
$\tan\theta$, $\cot\theta$: $+$	$\tan\theta$, $\cot\theta$: $-$

Use reference angles to evaluate functions

Evaluate (a) tan (−240°) and (b) csc $\frac{17\pi}{6}$.

Solution

a. The angle −240° is coterminal with 120°. The reference angle is $\theta' = 180° − 120° = 60°$. The tangent function is negative in Quadrant II, so you can write:

$$\tan (−240°) = −\tan 60° = −\sqrt{3}$$

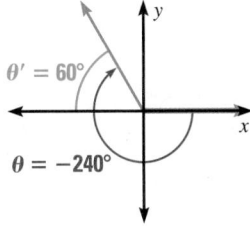

b. The angle $\frac{17\pi}{6}$ is coterminal with $\frac{5\pi}{6}$. The reference angle is $\theta' = \pi − \frac{5\pi}{6} = \frac{\pi}{6}$. The cosecant function is positive in Quadrant II, so you can write:

$$\csc \frac{17\pi}{6} = \csc \frac{\pi}{6} = 2$$

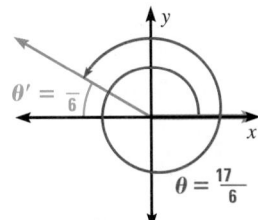

✓ **GUIDED PRACTICE** for Examples 3 and 4

Sketch the angle. Then find its reference angle.

5. 210°   **6.** −260°   **7.** $-\frac{7\pi}{9}$ **8.** $\frac{15\pi}{4}$

9. Evaluate cos (−210°) without using a calculator.

Calculate horizontal distance traveled

ROBOTICS The "frogbot" is a robot designed for exploring rough terrain on other planets. It can jump at a 45° angle and with an initial speed of 16 feet per second. On Earth, the horizontal distance d (in feet) traveled by a projectile launched at an angle θ and with an initial speed v (in feet per second) is given by:

Frogbot

INTERPRET MODELS
This model neglects air resistance and assumes that the projectile's starting and ending heights are the same.

$$d = \frac{v^2}{32} \sin 2\theta$$

How far can the frogbot jump on Earth?

Solution

$d = \frac{v^2}{32} \sin 2\theta$ **Write model for horizontal distance.**

$= \frac{16^2}{32} \sin (2 \cdot 45°)$ **Substitute 16 for v and 45° for θ.**

$= 8$ **Simplify.**

▶ The frogbot can jump a horizontal distance of 8 feet on Earth.

Courtesy NASA/JPL–Caltech

EXAMPLE 6 **Model with a trigonometric function**

ROCK CLIMBING A rock climber is using a rock climbing treadmill that is 10.5 feet long. The climber begins by lying horizontally on the treadmill, which is then rotated about its midpoint by 110° so that the rock climber is climbing towards the top. If the midpoint of the treadmill is 6 feet above the ground, how high above the ground is the top of the treadmill?

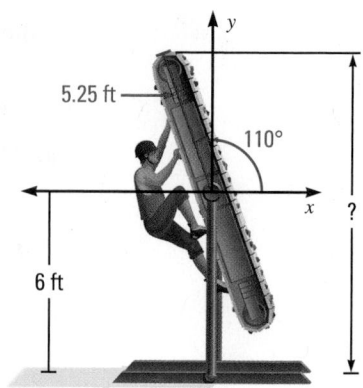

Solution

$$\sin\theta = \frac{y}{r} \qquad \text{Use definition of sine.}$$

$$\sin 110° = \frac{y}{5.25} \qquad \text{Substitute 110° for } \theta \text{ and } \frac{10.5}{2} = 5.25 \text{ for } r.$$

$$4.9 \approx y \qquad \text{Solve for } y.$$

▶ The top of the treadmill is about 6 + 4.9 = 10.9 feet above the ground.

✔ **GUIDED PRACTICE**   for Examples 5 and 6

10. **TRACK AND FIELD** Estimate the horizontal distance traveled by a track and field long jumper who jumps at an angle of 20° and with an initial speed of 27 feet per second.

11. **WHAT IF?** In Example 6, how high is the top of the rock climbing treadmill if it is rotated 100° about its midpoint?

9.3 EXERCISES

HOMEWORK KEY

◯ = See WORKED-OUT SOLUTIONS
Exs. 5, 17, and 37

★ = STANDARDIZED TEST PRACTICE
Exs. 2, 11, 33, 37, and 39

SKILL PRACTICE

1. **VOCABULARY** Copy and complete: A(n) __?__ is an angle in standard position whose terminal side lies on an axis.

2. ★ **WRITING** Given an angle θ in Quadrant III, explain how you can use a reference angle to find $\cos\theta$.

EXAMPLE 1
for Exs. 3–11

USING A POINT Use the given point on the terminal side of an angle θ in standard position to evaluate the six trigonometric functions of θ.

3. $(8, 15)$ 4. $(-9, 12)$ 5. $(-7, -24)$ 6. $(5, -12)$

7. $(2, -2)$ 8. $(-6, 9)$ 9. $(-3, -5)$ 10. $\left(5, -\sqrt{11}\right)$

11. ★ **MULTIPLE CHOICE** Let $(-7, -4)$ be a point on the terminal side of an angle θ in standard position. What is the value of $\tan\theta$?

  Ⓐ $-\dfrac{7}{4}$ Ⓑ $-\dfrac{4}{7}$ Ⓒ $\dfrac{4}{7}$ Ⓓ $\dfrac{7}{4}$

EXAMPLE 2
for Exs. 12–15

QUADRANTAL ANGLES Evaluate the six trigonometric functions of θ.

12. $\theta = 0°$

13. $\theta = \dfrac{\pi}{2}$

14. $\theta = 540°$

15. $\theta = \dfrac{7\pi}{2}$

EXAMPLE 3
for Exs. 16–23

FINDING REFERENCE ANGLES Sketch the angle. Then find its reference angle.

16. $-100°$

17. $150°$

18. $320°$

19. $-370°$

20. $-\dfrac{5\pi}{6}$

21. $\dfrac{8\pi}{3}$

22. $\dfrac{15\pi}{4}$

23. $-\dfrac{13\pi}{6}$

EXAMPLE 4
for Exs. 24–31

EVALUATING FUNCTIONS Evaluate the function without using a calculator.

24. $\sec 135°$

25. $\tan 240°$

26. $\sin (-150°)$

27. $\csc (-420°)$

28. $\cos \dfrac{7\pi}{4}$

29. $\cot \left(-\dfrac{8\pi}{3}\right)$

30. $\tan \left(-\dfrac{3\pi}{4}\right)$

31. $\sec \dfrac{11\pi}{6}$

32. ERROR ANALYSIS Let $(4, 3)$ be a point on the terminal side of an angle θ in standard position. *Describe* and correct the error in finding $\tan \theta$.

$$\tan \theta = \frac{x}{y} = \frac{4}{3} \qquad \times$$

33. ★ **SHORT RESPONSE** Write $\tan \theta$ as the ratio of two other trigonometric functions. Use this ratio to explain why $\tan 90°$ is undefined but $\cot 90° = 0$.

34. CHALLENGE A line with slope m passes through the origin. An angle θ in standard position has a terminal side that coincides with the line. Use a trigonometric function to relate the slope of the line to the angle.

PROBLEM SOLVING

EXAMPLE 5
for Exs. 35–36

In Exercises 35 and 36, use the formula in Example 5.

35. FOOTBALL You and a friend each kick a football with an initial speed of 49 feet per second. Your kick is projected at an angle of 45° and your friend's kick is projected at an angle of 60°. About how much farther will your football travel than your friend's football?

36. IN-LINE SKATING At what speed must the in-line skater launch himself off the ramp in order to land on the other side of the ramp?

18°   5 ft

EXAMPLE 6
for Exs. 37–38

37. ★ **SHORT RESPONSE** A Ferris wheel has a radius of 75 feet. You board a car at the bottom of the Ferris wheel, which is 10 feet above the ground, and rotate 255° counterclockwise before the ride temporarily stops. How high above the ground are you when the ride stops? If the radius of the Ferris wheel is doubled, is your height above the ground doubled? *Explain.*

38. MULTI-STEP PROBLEM When two atoms in a molecule are bonded to a common atom, chemists are interested in both the bond angle and the lengths of the bonds. An ozone molecule (O_3) is made up of two oxygen atoms bonded to a third oxygen atom, as shown.

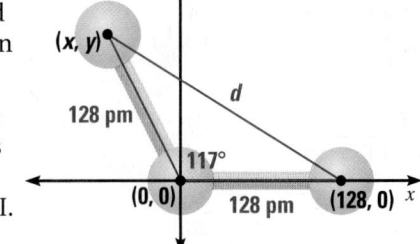

a. In the diagram, coordinates are given in picometers (pm). (*Note:* 1 pm = 10^{-12} m.) Find the coordinates (x, y) of the center of the oxygen atom in Quadrant II.

b. Find the distance d (in picometers) between the centers of the two unbonded oxygen atoms.

39. ★ EXTENDED RESPONSE A sprinkler at ground level is used to water a garden. The water leaving the sprinkler has an initial speed of 25 feet per second.

a. Calculate Copy the table below. Use the formula in Example 5 to complete the table.

Angle of sprinkler, θ	25°	30°	35°	40°	45°	50°	55°	60°	65°
Horizontal distance water travels, d	?	?	?	?	?	?	?	?	?

b. Interpret What value of θ appears to maximize the horizontal distance traveled by the water? Use the formula for horizontal distance traveled and the unit circle to explain why your answer makes sense.

c. Compare *Compare* the horizontal distance traveled by the water when $\theta = (45 - k)°$ with the distance when $\theta = (45 + k)°$.

40. CHALLENGE The latitude of a point on Earth is the degree measure of the shortest arc from that point to the equator. For example, the latitude of point P in the diagram equals the degree measure of arc PE. At what latitude θ is the circumference of the circle of latitude at P half the distance around the equator?

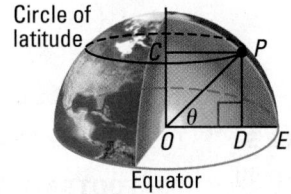

MIXED REVIEW *of Problem Solving*

MATHEMATICAL PRACTICES — Make sense of problems and persevere in solving them.

1. MULTI-STEP PROBLEM Your school's marching band is performing at halftime during a football game. In the last formation, the band members form a circle 100 feet wide in the center of the field. You start at a point on the circle 100 feet from the goal line, march 300° around the circle, and then walk toward the goal line to exit the field.

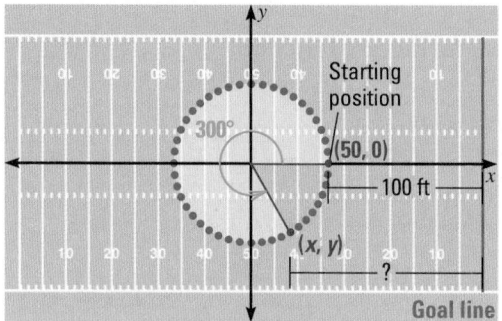

a. How far from the goal line are you at the point where you leave the circle?

b. How far do you march around the circle?

2. MULTI-STEP PROBLEM You are flying a kite at an angle of 70°. You have let out a total of 400 feet of string and are holding the reel steady 4 feet above the ground.

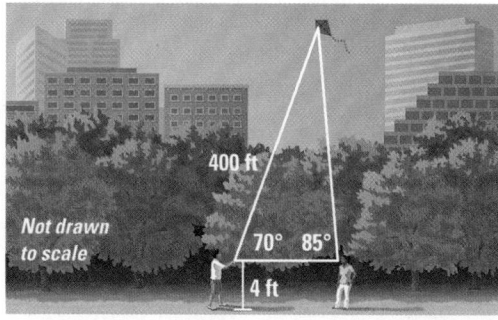

a. How high above the ground is the kite?

b. A friend watching the kite estimates that the angle of elevation to the kite is 85°. How far from your friend are you standing?

3. GRIDDED ANSWER What is the reference angle, in degrees, for the angle $\theta = 560°$?

4. OPEN-ENDED What is the measure, in degrees, of an angle for which the secant is positive and the cotangent is negative?

5. SHORT RESPONSE The top of the Space Needle in Seattle, Washington, is a revolving, circular restaurant. The restaurant has a radius of 47.25 feet and makes one complete revolution in about an hour. You have dinner at a window table from 7:00 P.M. to 8:55 P.M.

a. How many feet do you revolve?

b. Do diners seated 5 feet away from the windows revolve the same distance? *Explain.*

6. MULTI-STEP PROBLEM You are standing 100 meters from the main entrance of the Sears Tower in Chicago, Illinois. You estimate that the angle of elevation to the top of the skyscraper is 77°.

a. What is the approximate height h of the Sears Tower?

b. Suppose one of your friends is at the top of the Sears Tower. What is the straight-line distance d between you and your friend?

7. EXTENDED RESPONSE A pizza shop offers two choices for individual pizza slices, as shown.

a. Find the area of each slice of pizza.

b. Which slice is the better deal? *Explain* your reasoning.

c. How could you change the price of the 7 inch slice so that neither slice offers a better deal than the other?

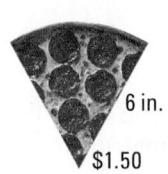

6 in.

$1.50

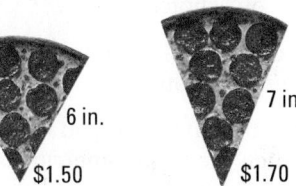

7 in.

$1.70

Investigating Inverse Trigonometric Functions

MATHEMATICAL PRACTICES

Reason abstractly and quantitatively.

MATERIALS · paper and pencil

QUESTION Do the sine and cosine functions have inverse functions?

EXPLORE Determine if a trigonometric function has an inverse function

STEP 1 *Make a table* Copy and complete the table to find the values of $f(\theta) = \sin \theta$ and $g(\theta) = \cos \theta$ for each of the given values of θ.

θ	$-\pi$	$-\dfrac{3\pi}{4}$	$-\dfrac{\pi}{2}$	$-\dfrac{\pi}{4}$	0	$\dfrac{\pi}{4}$	$\dfrac{\pi}{2}$	$\dfrac{3\pi}{4}$	π
$f(\theta) = \sin \theta$	?	?	?	?	?	?	?	?	?
$g(\theta) = \cos \theta$	?	?	?	?	?	?	?	?	?

STEP 2 *Analyze sine* Use the table to explain why $f(\theta) = \sin \theta$ does not have an inverse function on the domain $-\pi \le \theta \le \pi$.

STEP 3 *Analyze cosine* Does $g(\theta) = \cos \theta$ have an inverse function on the domain $-\pi \le \theta \le \pi$? Explain why or why not.

STEP 4 *Use graphs* The graphs of $f(\theta) = \sin \theta$ and $g(\theta) = \cos \theta$ are shown for the domain $-\pi \le \theta \le \pi$. Explain how the graphs justify your answers in Steps 2 and 3.

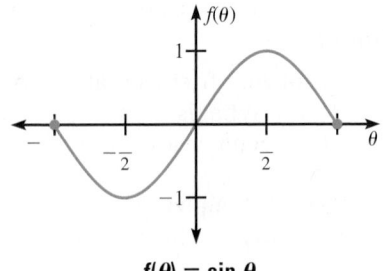

$f(\theta) = \sin \theta$

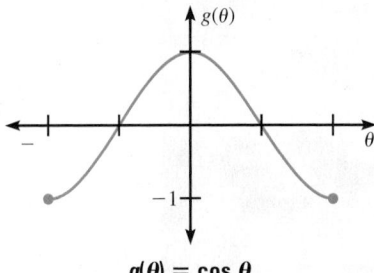

$g(\theta) = \cos \theta$

DRAW CONCLUSIONS Use your observations to complete these exercises

1. Use the graph of $f(\theta) = \sin \theta$ in Step 4 to choose a restricted domain for which the sine function does have an inverse function. *Explain* how you made your choice.

2. Give a restricted domain for which $g(\theta) = \cos \theta$ has an inverse function. *Explain* how you chose the domain.

3. Are the domains that you wrote in Exercises 1 and 2 the *only* domains for which the trigonometric functions have inverse functions? *Explain*.

9.4 Evaluate Inverse Trigonometric Functions

Before You found values of trigonometric functions given angles.

Now You will find angles given values of trigonometric functions.

Why? So you can find launch angles, as in Example 4.

Key Vocabulary
- inverse sine
- inverse cosine
- inverse tangent

COMMON CORE

CC.9-12.F.TF.6 (+) Understand that restricting a trigonometric function to a domain on which it is always increasing or always decreasing allows its inverse to be constructed.

So far in this chapter, you have learned to evaluate trigonometric functions of a given angle. In this lesson, you will study the reverse problem—finding an angle that corresponds to a given value of a trigonometric function.

Suppose you were asked to find an angle θ whose sine is 0.5. After considering the problem, you would realize *many* such angles exist. For instance, the angles

$$\frac{\pi}{6}, \frac{5\pi}{6}, \frac{13\pi}{6}, \frac{17\pi}{6}, \text{ and } -\frac{7\pi}{6}$$

all have a sine value of 0.5. To obtain a unique angle θ such that $\sin \theta = 0.5$, you must restrict the domain of the sine function. Domain restrictions allow the *inverse sine*, *inverse cosine*, and *inverse tangent* functions to be defined.

KEY CONCEPT
For Your Notebook

Inverse Trigonometric Functions

If $-1 \le a \le 1$, then the **inverse sine** of a is an angle θ, written $\theta = \sin^{-1} a$, where:

(1) $\sin \theta = a$

(2) $-\frac{\pi}{2} \le \theta \le \frac{\pi}{2}$ (or $-90° \le \theta \le 90°$)

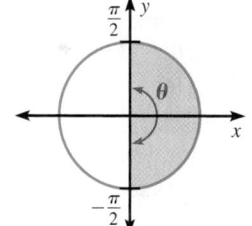

If $-1 \le a \le 1$, then the **inverse cosine** of a is an angle θ, written $\theta = \cos^{-1} a$, where:

(1) $\cos \theta = a$

(2) $0 \le \theta \le \pi$ (or $0° \le \theta \le 180°$)

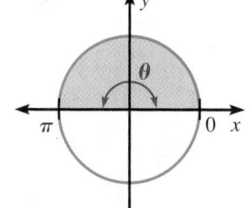

If a is any real number, then the **inverse tangent** of a is an angle θ, written $\theta = \tan^{-1} a$, where:

(1) $\tan \theta = a$

(2) $-\frac{\pi}{2} < \theta < \frac{\pi}{2}$ (or $-90° < \theta < 90°$)

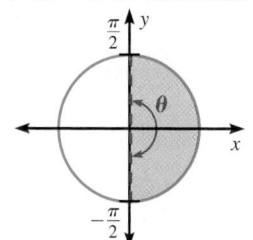

EXAMPLE 1 Evaluate inverse trigonometric functions

Evaluate the expression in both radians and degrees.

a. $\cos^{-1} \dfrac{\sqrt{3}}{2}$ **b.** $\sin^{-1} 2$ **c.** $\tan^{-1}\left(-\sqrt{3}\right)$

Solution

a. When $0 \le \theta \le \pi$, or $0° \le \theta \le 180°$, the angle whose cosine is $\dfrac{\sqrt{3}}{2}$ is:

$$\theta = \cos^{-1} \dfrac{\sqrt{3}}{2} = \dfrac{\pi}{6} \quad \text{or} \quad \theta = \cos^{-1} \dfrac{\sqrt{3}}{2} = 30°$$

b. There is no angle whose sine is 2. So, $\sin^{-1} 2$ is undefined.

c. When $-\dfrac{\pi}{2} < \theta < \dfrac{\pi}{2}$, or $-90° < \theta < 90°$, the angle whose tangent is $-\sqrt{3}$ is:

$$\theta = \tan^{-1}\left(-\sqrt{3}\right) = -\dfrac{\pi}{3} \quad \text{or} \quad \theta = \tan^{-1}\left(-\sqrt{3}\right) = -60°$$

EXAMPLE 2 Solve a trigonometric equation

Solve the equation $\sin \theta = -\dfrac{5}{8}$ where $180° < \theta < 270°$.

Solution

USE A CALCULATOR
On most calculators, you can evaluate inverse trigonometric functions using the keys **2nd** **SIN** for inverse sine, **2nd** **COS** for inverse cosine, and **2nd** **TAN** for inverse tangent.

STEP 1 **Use** a calculator to determine that in the interval $-90° \le \theta \le 90°$, the angle whose sine is $-\dfrac{5}{8}$ is $\sin^{-1}\left(-\dfrac{5}{8}\right) \approx -38.7°$. This angle is in Quadrant IV, as shown.

STEP 2 **Find** the angle in Quadrant III (where $180° < \theta < 270°$) that has the same sine value as the angle in Step 1. The angle is:

$$\theta \approx 180° + 38.7° = 218.7°$$

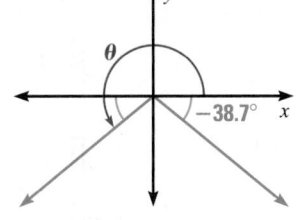

CHECK Use a calculator to check the answer.

$$\sin 218.7° \approx -0.625 = -\dfrac{5}{8} \checkmark$$

 GUIDED PRACTICE for Examples 1 and 2

Evaluate the expression in both radians and degrees.

1. $\sin^{-1} \dfrac{\sqrt{2}}{2}$ **2.** $\cos^{-1} \dfrac{1}{2}$ **3.** $\tan^{-1}(-1)$ **4.** $\sin^{-1}\left(-\dfrac{1}{2}\right)$

Solve the equation for θ.

5. $\cos \theta = 0.4;\ 270° < \theta < 360°$ **6.** $\tan \theta = 2.1;\ 180° < \theta < 270°$

7. $\sin \theta = -0.23;\ 270° < \theta < 360°$ **8.** $\tan \theta = 4.7;\ 180° < \theta < 270°$

9. $\sin \theta = 0.62;\ 90° < \theta < 180°$ **10.** $\cos \theta = -0.39;\ 180° < \theta < 270°$

EXAMPLE 3 **Standardized Test Practice**

What is the measure of the angle θ in the triangle shown?

Ⓐ 28.6° Ⓑ 33.1°

Ⓒ 56.9° Ⓓ 61.4°

AVOID ERRORS
All the answer choices are in degrees. Therefore, check that your calculator is set in degree mode, not radian mode.

Solution

In the right triangle, you are given the lengths of the side adjacent to θ and the hypotenuse, so use the inverse cosine function to solve for θ.

$$\cos \theta = \frac{\text{adj}}{\text{hyp}} = \frac{6}{11} \qquad\longrightarrow\qquad \theta = \cos^{-1} \frac{6}{11} \approx 56.9°$$

▶ The correct answer is C. Ⓐ Ⓑ Ⓒ Ⓓ

EXAMPLE 4 **Write and solve a trigonometric equation**

MONSTER TRUCKS A monster truck drives off a ramp in order to jump onto a row of cars. The ramp has a height of 8 feet and a horizontal length of 20 feet. What is the angle θ of the ramp?

Solution

STEP 1 **Draw** a triangle that represents the ramp.

STEP 2 **Write** a trigonometric equation that involves the ratio of the ramp's height and horizontal length.

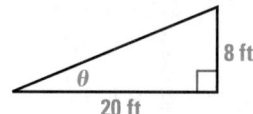

$$\tan \theta = \frac{\text{opp}}{\text{adj}} = \frac{8}{20}$$

STEP 3 **Use** a calculator to find the measure of θ.

$$\theta = \tan^{-1} \frac{8}{20} \approx 21.8°$$

▶ The angle of the ramp is about 22°.

✓ **GUIDED PRACTICE** for Examples 3 and 4

Find the measure of the angle θ.

11.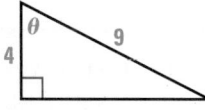

12.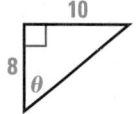

13.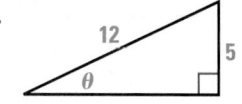

14. **WHAT IF?** In Example 4, suppose a monster truck drives 26 feet on a ramp before jumping onto a row of cars. If the ramp is 10 feet high, what is the angle θ of the ramp?

9.4 EXERCISES

HOMEWORK KEY
○ = See WORKED-OUT SOLUTIONS
Exs. 7, 23, and 37

★ = STANDARDIZED TEST PRACTICE
Exs. 2, 11, 30, 31, 37, and 38

SKILL PRACTICE

1. **VOCABULARY** Copy and complete: The __?__ sine of $\frac{1}{2}$ is $\frac{\pi}{6}$, or 30°.

2. ★ **WRITING** *Explain* why $\tan^{-1} 3$ is defined, but $\cos^{-1} 3$ is undefined.

EXAMPLE 1
for Exs. 3–11

EVALUATING EXPRESSIONS Evaluate the expression without using a calculator. Give your answer in both radians and degrees.

3. $\sin^{-1} 1$ 4. $\tan^{-1} (-1)$ 5. $\cos^{-1} 0$ 6. $\cos^{-1} (-2)$

7. $\sin^{-1} \frac{\sqrt{3}}{2}$ 8. $\sin^{-1} \frac{1}{2}$ 9. $\tan^{-1} \left(-\frac{\sqrt{3}}{3}\right)$ 10. $\cos^{-1} \left(-\frac{1}{2}\right)$

11. ★ **MULTIPLE CHOICE** What is the value of the expression $\cos^{-1} \frac{\sqrt{2}}{2}$?

(A) 0°   (B) 30°   (C) 45°   (D) 60°

USING A CALCULATOR Use a calculator to evaluate the expression in both radians and degrees.

12. $\sin^{-1} 0.18$ 13. $\tan^{-1} 2.6$ 14. $\cos^{-1} 0.36$ 15. $\cos^{-1} (-0.4)$

16. $\tan^{-1} (-0.75)$ 17. $\sin^{-1} (-0.2)$ 18. $\sin^{-1} 0.8$ 19. $\cos^{-1} 0.99$

EXAMPLE 2
for Exs. 20–26

SOLVING EQUATIONS Solve the equation for θ.

20. $\cos \theta = -0.82; 180° < \theta < 270°$ 21. $\sin \theta = -0.45; 180° < \theta < 270°$

22. $\sin \theta = 0.15; 90° < \theta < 180°$ 23. $\tan \theta = 3.2; 180° < \theta < 270°$

24. $\tan \theta = -5.3; 90° < \theta < 180°$ 25. $\cos \theta = 0.25; 270° < \theta < 360°$

26. **ERROR ANALYSIS** *Describe* and correct the error in solving the equation $\sin \theta = 0.7$ where $90° < \theta < 180°$.

> The angle whose sine is 0.7 is $\sin^{-1} 0.7 \approx 44.4°$, so $\theta \approx 44.4°$.

EXAMPLE 3
for Exs. 27–29

FINDING ANGLES Find the measure of the angle θ.

27. 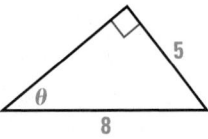   28.    29.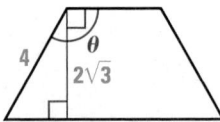

30. ★ **OPEN-ENDED MATH** Suppose $\cos \theta > 0$ and $\sin \theta < 0$. Give a possible value of θ such that $-360° \le \theta \le 0°$.

31. ★ **OPEN-ENDED MATH** Suppose $\sin \theta < 0$ and $\tan \theta > 0$. Give a possible value of θ such that $360° \le \theta \le 720°$.

CHALLENGE Rewrite the expression so that it does not involve trigonometric functions or inverse trigonometric functions.

32. $\csc (\sin^{-1} x)$ 33. $\cot (\tan^{-1} x)$ 34. $\sec (\cos^{-1} x)$

35. LADDER ANGLE A fire truck has a 100 foot ladder whose base is 10 feet above the ground. A firefighter extends a ladder toward a burning building to reach a window 90 feet above the ground. Draw a diagram to represent this situation. At what angle should the firefighter set the ladder?

36. ANGLE OF DESCENT An airplane is flying at an altitude of 31,000 feet when it begins its descent for landing. If the runway is 104 miles away, at what angle does the airplane descend?

37. ★ **SHORT RESPONSE** Different types of granular substances naturally settle at different angles when stored in cone-shaped piles. The angle θ is called the *angle of repose*. When rock salt is stored in a cone-shaped pile 11 feet high, the diameter of the pile's base is about 34 feet. Find the angle of repose for rock salt. If another pile of rock salt is 15 feet high, what is the diameter of its base? *Explain.*

38. ★ **EXTENDED RESPONSE** If you are in shallow water and look at an object below the surface of the water, the object will look farther away from you than it really is. This is because when light rays pass between air and water, the water *refracts*, or bends, the light rays. The *index of refraction* for water is 1.333. This is the ratio of the sine of θ_1 to the sine of θ_2 for the angles θ_1 and θ_2 shown below.

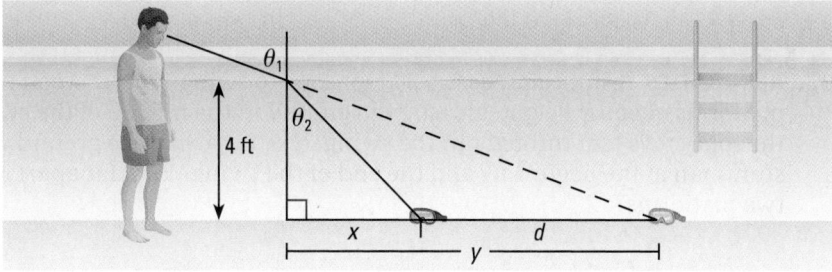

a. You are in 4 feet of water in the shallow end of a pool. You look down at some goggles at angle $\theta_1 = 70°$ (measured from a line perpendicular to the surface of the water). Find θ_2.

b. Find the distances x and y.

c. Find the distance d between where the goggles are and where they appear to be.

d. *Explain* what happens to d as you move closer to the goggles.

39. CYCLING As a spectator at a cycling road race, you are sitting 100 feet from the center of a straightaway. A cyclist traveling 30 miles per hour passes in front of you. At what angle do you have to turn your head to see the cyclist t seconds later? Assume the cyclist is still on the straightaway and is traveling at a constant speed. (*Hint:* First convert 30 miles per hour to a speed v in feet per second. The expression vt represents the distance, in feet, traveled by the cyclist.)

40. CHALLENGE You want to photograph a painting with a camera mounted on a tripod. The painting is 3 feet tall, and the bottom of the painting is 1 foot above the camera lens, as shown. How far should the camera be positioned from the wall in order to have the largest possible viewing angle θ when you take the photograph? (*Hint:* Write an equation for θ in terms of x only, and then use a graphing calculator to find the value of x that maximizes θ.)

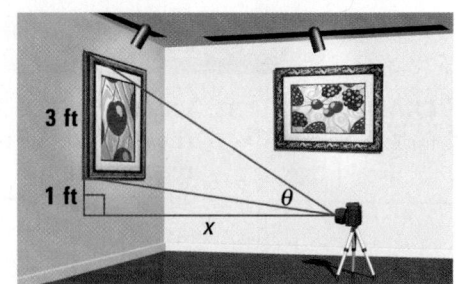

QUIZ

Use the given point on the terminal side of an angle θ in standard position to evaluate the six trigonometric functions of θ.

1. $(6, -2)$ **2.** $(-7, 5)$ **3.** $(4, 8)$ **4.** $(-12, -3)$

Evaluate the expression without using a calculator.

5. $\cos 150°$ **6.** $\tan \dfrac{8\pi}{3}$ **7.** $\sin(-840°)$ **8.** $\sec\left(-\dfrac{15\pi}{4}\right)$

Evaluate the expression without using a calculator. Give your answer in both radians and degrees.

9. $\cos^{-1}\left(-\dfrac{\sqrt{2}}{2}\right)$ **10.** $\sin^{-1}(-1)$ **11.** $\tan^{-1}\dfrac{\sqrt{3}}{3}$ **12.** $\cos^{-1}\dfrac{1}{2}$

Solve the equation for θ.

13. $\sin \theta = 0.3;\ 90° < \theta < 180°$ **14.** $\tan \theta = 6;\ 180° < \theta < 270°$

15. $\cos \theta = -0.72;\ 90° < \theta < 180°$ **16.** $\sin \theta = -0.55;\ 270° < \theta < 360°$

17. ACROBATICS A stuntman uses a 30 foot rope to swing 136° between two platforms of equal height, grazing the ground in the middle of the swing. If the rope stays taut throughout the swing, how far above the ground was the stuntman at the beginning and the end of the swing? How far apart are the two platforms?

Explore the Law of Sines

MATHEMATICAL PRACTICES
Use appropriate tools strategically.

QUESTION How can you use geometry software to explore the law of sines?

EXPLORE Investigate a relationship between the angles and sides of a triangle

STEP 1 *Draw a triangle*
Draw △ABC. Label the vertices and sides as shown.

STEP 2 *Measure parts of triangle*
Find the side lengths *a*, *b*, and *c*. Also find the measures of angles *A*, *B*, and *C*.

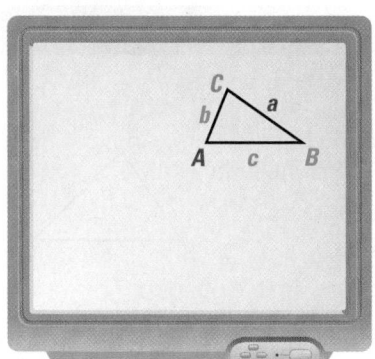

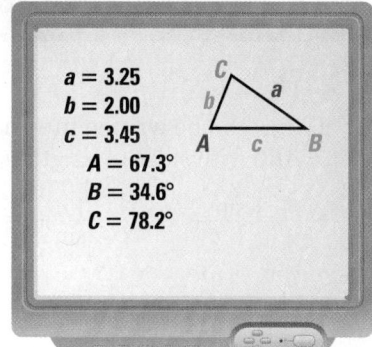

$a = 3.25$
$b = 2.00$
$c = 3.45$
$A = 67.3°$
$B = 34.6°$
$C = 78.2°$

STEP 3 *Calculate ratios*
Find the ratios $\frac{\sin A}{a}$, $\frac{\sin B}{b}$, and $\frac{\sin C}{c}$.

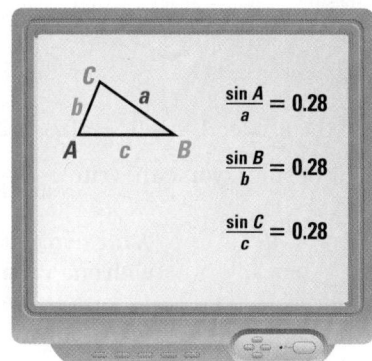

$\frac{\sin A}{a} = 0.28$

$\frac{\sin B}{b} = 0.28$

$\frac{\sin C}{c} = 0.28$

DRAW CONCLUSIONS Use your observations to complete these exercises

1. What are the values of the ratios $\frac{\sin A}{a}$, $\frac{\sin B}{b}$, and $\frac{\sin C}{c}$ for your triangle? What do you notice about these values?

2. Change the shape of your triangle by dragging its vertices, and observe how the ratios you found in Step 3 change. Make a conjecture about how these ratios are related for *any* triangle.

9.5 Apply the Law of Sines

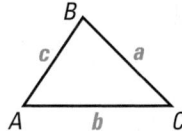

Before	You solved right triangles.
Now	You will solve triangles that have no right angle.
Why?	So you can find the distance between faraway objects, as in Ex. 44.

Key Vocabulary
• law of sines

Previously, you solved right triangles. To solve a triangle with no right angle, you need to know the length of at least one side and any two other parts of the triangle. The **law of sines** can be used to solve triangles when two angles and the length of any side are known (AAS or ASA cases), or when the lengths of two sides and an angle opposite one of the two sides are known (SSA case).

CC.9-12.G.SRT.11 (+)
Understand and apply the Law of Sines and the Law of Cosines to find unknown measurements in right and non-right triangles (e.g., surveying problems, resultant forces).

KEY CONCEPT   *For Your Notebook*

Law of Sines

The law of sines can be written in either of the following forms for $\triangle ABC$ with sides of length a, b, and c.

$$\frac{\sin A}{a} = \frac{\sin B}{b} = \frac{\sin C}{c} \qquad \frac{a}{\sin A} = \frac{b}{\sin B} = \frac{c}{\sin C}$$

EXAMPLE 1   Solve a triangle for the AAS or ASA case

Solve $\triangle ABC$ with $C = 107°$, $B = 25°$, and $b = 15$.

Solution

First find the angle: $A = 180° - 107° - 25° = 48°$.

By the law of sines, you can write $\dfrac{a}{\sin 48°} = \dfrac{15}{\sin 25°} = \dfrac{c}{\sin 107°}$.

$$\frac{a}{\sin 48°} = \frac{15}{\sin 25°} \qquad \text{Write two equations, each} \qquad \frac{c}{\sin 107°} = \frac{15}{\sin 25°}$$

with one variable.

$$a = \frac{15 \sin 48°}{\sin 25°} \qquad \text{Solve for each variable.} \qquad c = \frac{15 \sin 107°}{\sin 25°}$$

$$a \approx 26.4 \qquad \text{Use a calculator.} \qquad c \approx 33.9$$

▶ In $\triangle ABC$, $A = 48°$, $a \approx 26.4$, and $c \approx 33.9$.

 GUIDED PRACTICE   for Example 1

Solve $\triangle ABC$.

  1. $B = 34°$, $C = 100°$, $b = 8$ **2.** $A = 51°$, $B = 44°$, $c = 11$

DESCRIBE CASES
Because the SSA case can result in 0, 1, or 2 triangles, it is called the *ambiguous case*.

SSA CASE Two angles and one side (AAS or ASA) determine exactly one triangle. Two sides and an angle opposite one of the sides (SSA) may determine no triangle, one triangle, or two triangles.

KEY CONCEPT *For Your Notebook*

Possible Triangles in the SSA Case

Consider a triangle in which you are given a, b, and A. By fixing side b and angle A, you can sketch the possible positions of side a to figure out how many triangles can be formed. In the diagrams below, note that $h = b \sin A$.

A is obtuse. | **A is acute.**

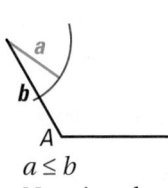

$a \le b$
No triangle

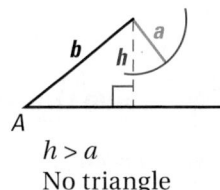

$h > a$
No triangle

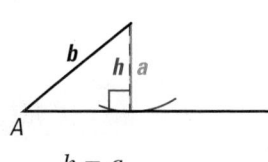

$h = a$
One triangle

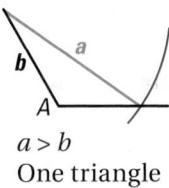

$a > b$
One triangle

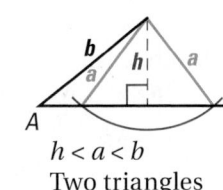

$h < a < b$
Two triangles

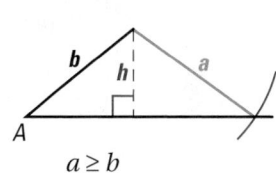

$a \ge b$
One triangle

EXAMPLE 2 **Solve the SSA case with one solution**

Solve $\triangle ABC$ **with** $A = 115°$, $a = 20$, **and** $b = 11$.

Solution

First make a sketch. Because A is obtuse and the side opposite A is longer than the given adjacent side, you know that only one triangle can be formed. Use the law of sines to find B.

$$\frac{\sin B}{11} = \frac{\sin 115°}{20} \qquad \text{Law of sines}$$

$$\sin B = \frac{11 \sin 115°}{20} \approx 0.4985 \qquad \text{Multiply each side by 11.}$$

$$B \approx 29.9° \qquad \text{Use inverse sine function.}$$

You then know that $C \approx 180° - 115° - 29.9° = 35.1°$. Use the law of sines again to find the remaining side length c of the triangle.

$$\frac{c}{\sin 35.1°} = \frac{20}{\sin 115°} \qquad \text{Law of sines}$$

$$c = \frac{20 \sin 35.1°}{\sin 115°} \qquad \text{Multiply each side by } \sin 35.1°.$$

$$c \approx 12.7 \qquad \text{Use a calculator.}$$

▶ In $\triangle ABC$, $B \approx 29.9°$, $C \approx 35.1°$, and $c \approx 12.7$.

EXAMPLE 3 Examine the SSA case with no solution

Solve $\triangle ABC$ with $A = 51°$, $a = 3.5$, and $b = 5$.

Solution

Begin by drawing a horizontal line. On one end form a 51° angle (A) and draw a segment 5 units long ($\overline{AC}$, or b). At vertex C, draw a segment 3.5 units long (a). You can see that a needs to be at least $5 \sin 51° \approx 3.9$ units long to reach the horizontal side and form a triangle. So, it is not possible to draw the indicated triangle.

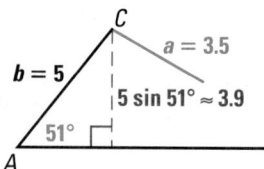

EXAMPLE 4 Solve the SSA case with two solutions

Solve $\triangle ABC$ with $A = 40°$, $a = 13$, and $b = 16$.

Solution

First make a sketch. Because $b \sin A = 16 \sin 40° \approx 10.3$, and $10.3 < 13 < 16$ ($h < a < b$), two triangles can be formed.

Triangle 1

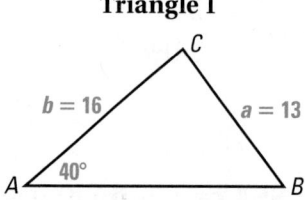

Triangle 2

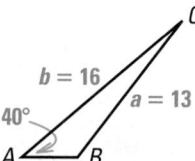

Use the law of sines to find the possible measures of B.

$$\frac{\sin B}{16} = \frac{\sin 40°}{13} \qquad \textbf{Law of sines}$$

$$\sin B = \frac{16 \sin 40°}{13} \approx 0.7911 \qquad \textbf{Use a calculator.}$$

There are two angles B between 0° and 180° for which $\sin B \approx 0.7911$. One is acute and the other is obtuse. Use your calculator to find the acute angle: $\sin^{-1} 0.7911 \approx 52.3°$.

The obtuse angle has 52.3° as a reference angle, so its measure is $180° - 52.3° = 127.7°$. Therefore, $B \approx 52.3°$ or $B \approx 127.7°$.

Now find the remaining angle C and side length c for each triangle.

Triangle 1

$C \approx 180° - 40° - 52.3° = 87.7°$

$$\frac{c}{\sin 87.7°} = \frac{13}{\sin 40°}$$

$$c = \frac{13 \sin 87.7°}{\sin 40°} \approx 20.2$$

▶ In Triangle 1, $B \approx 52.3°$, $C \approx 87.7°$, and $c \approx 20.2$.

Triangle 2

$C \approx 180° - 40° - 127.7° = 12.3°$

$$\frac{c}{\sin 12.3°} = \frac{13}{\sin 40°}$$

$$c = \frac{13 \sin 12.3°}{\sin 40°} \approx 4.3$$

▶ In Triangle 2, $B \approx 127.7°$, $C \approx 12.3°$, and $c \approx 4.3$.

Animated Algebra at my.hrw.com

Solve △ABC.

3. $A = 122°$, $a = 18$, $b = 12$ **4.** $A = 36°$, $a = 9$, $b = 12$

5. $A = 50°$, $a = 2.8$, $b = 4$ **6.** $B = 105°$, $b = 13$, $a = 6$

AREA OF A TRIANGLE You can use the following result to find the area of a triangle when you know the lengths of two sides and the measure of the included angle. This result can also be used to derive the law of sines (see Exercise 42).

KEY CONCEPT   *For Your Notebook*

Area of a Triangle

The area of any triangle is given by one half the product of the lengths of two sides times the sine of their included angle. For △ABC shown, there are three ways to calculate the area:

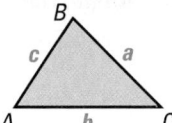

$$\text{Area} = \frac{1}{2}bc \sin A \qquad \text{Area} = \frac{1}{2}ac \sin B \qquad \text{Area} = \frac{1}{2}ab \sin C$$

EXAMPLE 5 **Find the area of a triangle**

BIOLOGY Black-necked stilts are birds that live throughout Florida and surrounding areas but breed mostly in the triangular region shown on the map. Find the area of this region.

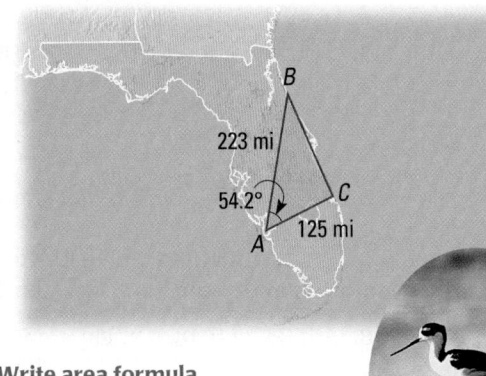

Solution

The area of the region is:

$\text{Area} = \frac{1}{2}bc \sin A$ **Write area formula.**

$= \frac{1}{2}(125)(223) \sin 54.2°$ **Substitute.**

$\approx 11{,}300$ **Use a calculator.**

▶ The area of the region is about 11,300 square miles.

 GUIDED PRACTICE for Example 5

Find the area of △ABC with the given side lengths and included angle.

7. $a = 10$, $b = 14$, $C = 46°$ **8.** $a = 19$, $c = 8$, $B = 75°$

9. $b = 11$, $c = 7$, $A = 120°$ **10.** $a = 20$, $b = 24$, $C = 87°$

©Steve Bein

9.5 EXERCISES

HOMEWORK
KEY

○ = See WORKED-OUT SOLUTIONS
Exs. 13, 31, and 45

★ = STANDARDIZED TEST PRACTICE
Exs. 2, 28, 41, 47, and 48

◆ = MULTIPLE REPRESENTATIONS
Ex. 45

SKILL PRACTICE

1. **VOCABULARY** What information do you need to use the law of sines?

2. ★ **WRITING** Suppose a, b, and A are given for $\triangle ABC$ where $A < 90°$. Under what conditions would you have no triangle? one triangle? two triangles?

EXAMPLES
1, 2, 3, and 4
for Exs. 3–28

IDENTIFYING CASES State the case (AAS, ASA, or SSA) applicable to the given measurements. Then decide whether the measurements determine *one triangle, two triangles,* or *no triangle.*

3. $A = 112°$, $a = 9$, $b = 4$

4. $A = 40°$, $C = 75°$, $c = 20$

5. $A = 52°$, $a = 32$, $b = 42$

6. $A = 37°$, $a = 8$, $b = 14$

7. $A = 28°$, $B = 64°$, $c = 55$

8. $A = 149°$, $a = 7$, $b = 10$

9. $B = 34°$, $b = 5$, $a = 16$

10. $B = 70°$, $b = 85$, $c = 88$

11. $C = 48°$, $c = 28$, $b = 20$

SOLVING TRIANGLES Solve $\triangle ABC$.

12.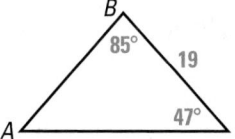

(13.)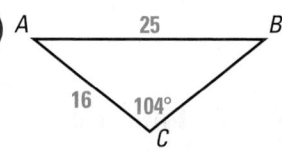

14.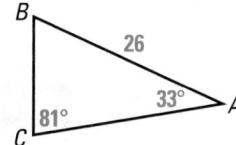

15.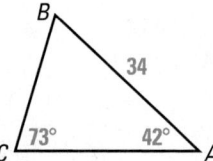

16.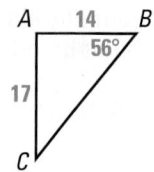

17.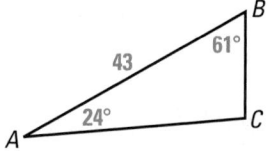

SOLVING TRIANGLES Solve $\triangle ABC$. (*Hint:* Some of the "triangles" have no solution and some have two solutions.)

18. $A = 73°$, $a = 18$, $b = 11$

19. $A = 26°$, $C = 35°$, $b = 13$

20. $B = 102°$, $C = 43°$, $b = 21$

21. $A = 38°$, $a = 19$, $b = 25$

22. $A = 55°$, $B = 64°$, $c = 34$

23. $A = 114°$, $a = 15$, $b = 10$

24. $C = 98°$, $c = 29$, $a = 33$

25. $A = 49°$, $B = 32°$, $b = 44$

26. $B = 21°$, $b = 17$, $c = 32$

27. **ERROR ANALYSIS** *Describe* and correct the error in finding the measure of angle C in the triangle below.

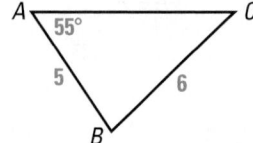

$$\frac{\sin C}{6} = \frac{\sin 55°}{5}$$

$$\sin C = \frac{6 \sin 55°}{5} \approx 0.9830$$

$$C \approx 79.4°$$

28. ★ **MULTIPLE CHOICE** What is the side length c in $\triangle ABC$ if $A = 32°$, $C = 67°$, and $b = 31$ ft?

Ⓐ 16.6 ft   Ⓑ 28.9 ft   Ⓒ 33.3 ft   Ⓓ 57.8 ft

EXAMPLE 5
for Exs. 29–41

FINDING AREA Find the area of △ABC with the given side lengths and included angle.

29. $B = 124°$, $a = 9$, $c = 11$ 30. $A = 68°$, $b = 13$, $c = 7$ (31.) $A = 34°$, $b = 29$, $c = 36$

32. $C = 79°$, $a = 25$, $b = 17$ 33. $B = 57°$, $a = 9$, $c = 5$ 34. $C = 96°$, $a = 7$, $b = 15$

35. $A = 130°$, $b = 23$, $c = 20$ 36. $B = 60°$, $a = 19$, $c = 14$ 37. $C = 29°$, $a = 38$, $b = 31$

FINDING AREA Find the area of △ABC.

38.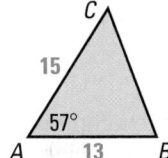

39.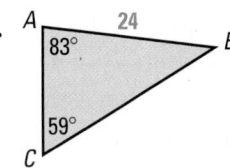

40.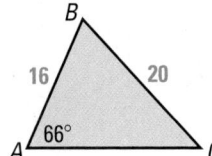

41. ★ **MULTIPLE CHOICE** What is the area of △ABC if $B = 52°$, $a = 29$, and $c = 24$?

   Ⓐ 274 units^2 Ⓑ 348 units^2 Ⓒ 548 units^2 Ⓓ 696 units^2

42. **CHALLENGE** Using the triangle shown at the right as a reference, derive the formulas for the area of a triangle given in *For Your Notebook*. Then use the area formulas to derive the law of sines.

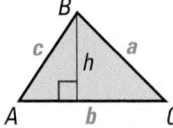

PROBLEM SOLVING

EXAMPLE 1
for Ex. 43

43. **LIFEGUARDS** Two lifeguards are watching a windsurfer. Use the information in the diagram to find the distance from each lifeguard to the windsurfer.

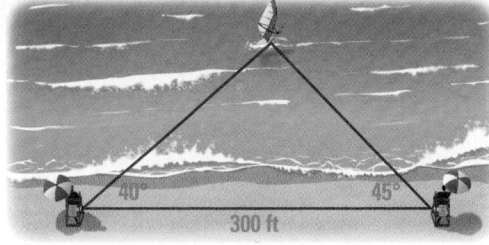

EXAMPLE 2
for Ex. 44

44. **NEW YORK CITY** You are on the observation deck of the Empire State Building looking at the Chrysler Building. When you turn 145° clockwise, you see the Statue of Liberty. You know that the Chrysler Building and the Empire State Building are about 0.6 mile apart and that the Chrysler Building and the Statue of Liberty are about 5.7 miles apart. Estimate the distance between the Empire State Building and the Statue of Liberty.

EXAMPLE 5
for Exs. 45–46

(45.) ◈ **MULTIPLE REPRESENTATIONS** You are fertilizing a triangular garden. One side of the garden is 62 feet long and another side is 54 feet long. The angle opposite the 62 foot side is 58°.

  a. **Drawing a Diagram** Draw a diagram to represent this situation.

  b. **Solving a Triangle** Use the law of sines to solve the triangle you drew in part (a).

  c. **Applying a Formula** One bag of fertilizer covers an area of 200 square feet. How many bags of fertilizer will you need to cover the entire garden?

46. MULTI-STEP PROBLEM Quadrilateral *ABCD* shown at the right is a kite.

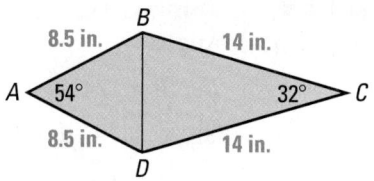

　a. Find the area of △*ABD*.

　b. Find the area of △*BCD*.

　c. What is the area of the kite?

47. ★ **SHORT RESPONSE** A building is constructed on top of a cliff that is 300 meters high. A person standing on level ground below the cliff observes that the angle of elevation to the top of the building is 72°, and the angle of elevation to the top of the cliff is 63°.

　a. How far away is the person from the base of the cliff?

　b. *Describe* two different methods you can use to find the height of the building. Use one of these methods to find the building's height.

48. ★ **EXTENDED RESPONSE** Use a graphing calculator to explore how the included angle in the formulas in *For Your Notebook* affects a triangle's area.

　a. **Model** Choose lengths for two sides of the triangle. Let *x* represent the measure (in degrees) of the included angle. Write an equation that gives the triangle's area *y* as a function of *x*.

　b. **Graphing Calculator** Enter the equation from part (a) into a graphing calculator. Use the *table* feature to examine values of the area for $0° < x° < 180°$. Does the area always increase as *x* increases? *Explain*.

　c. **Interpret** What value of *x* maximizes the triangle's area? What is the maximum area, and how is it related to the side lengths you chose in part (a)?

49. CHALLENGE The distance between Mercury and the sun is approximately 36 million miles. The distance between Earth and the sun is approximately 93 million miles. If on a certain day the angle (measured from Earth) between the sun and Mercury is 22°, what are the possible distances between Mercury and Earth?

9.6 Apply the Law of Cosines

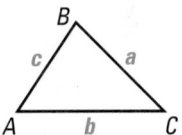

Before	You solved triangles using the law of sines.
Now	You will solve triangles using the law of cosines.
Why?	So you can find angles formed by trapeze artists, as in Ex. 43.

Key Vocabulary
• law of cosines

Previously, you solved triangles for the AAS, ASA, and SSA cases. In this lesson, you will use the **law of cosines** to solve triangles when two sides and the included angle are known (SAS), or when all three sides are known (SSS).

CC.9-12.G.SRT.11 (+)
Understand and apply the Law of Sines and the Law of Cosines to find unknown measurements in right and non-right triangles (e.g., surveying problems, resultant forces).

KEY CONCEPT
For Your Notebook

Law of Cosines

If $\triangle ABC$ has sides of length a, b, and c as shown, then:

$$a^2 = b^2 + c^2 - 2bc \cos A$$

$$b^2 = a^2 + c^2 - 2ac \cos B$$

$$c^2 = a^2 + b^2 - 2ab \cos C$$

EXAMPLE 1   Solve a triangle for the SAS case

Solve $\triangle ABC$ with $a = 11$, $c = 14$, and $B = 34°$.

Solution

Use the law of cosines to find side length b.

$b^2 = a^2 + c^2 - 2ac \cos B$	Law of cosines
$b^2 = 11^2 + 14^2 - 2(11)(14) \cos 34°$	Substitute for *a*, *c*, and *B*.
$b^2 \approx 61.7$	Simplify.
$b \approx \sqrt{61.7} \approx 7.85$	Take positive square root.

ANOTHER WAY
When you know all three sides and one angle, you can use the law of cosines *or* the law of sines to find the measure of a second angle.

Use the law of sines to find the measure of angle A.

$\dfrac{\sin A}{a} = \dfrac{\sin B}{b}$	Law of sines
$\dfrac{\sin A}{11} = \dfrac{\sin 34°}{7.85}$	Substitute for *a*, *b*, and *B*.
$\sin A = \dfrac{11 \sin 34°}{7.85} \approx 0.7836$	Multiply each side by 11 and simplify.
$A \approx \sin^{-1} 0.7836 \approx 51.6°$	Use inverse sine.

The third angle C of the triangle is $C \approx 180° - 34° - 51.6° = 94.4°$.

▶ In $\triangle ABC$, $b \approx 7.85$, $A \approx 51.6°$, and $C \approx 94.4°$.

EXAMPLE 2 Solve a triangle for the SSS case

Solve $\triangle ABC$ with $a = 12$, $b = 27$, and $c = 20$.

AVOID ERRORS
In Example 2, the largest angle is found first to make sure that the other two angles are acute. This way, when you use the law of sines to find another angle measure, you will know that it is between 0° and 90°.

Solution

First find the angle opposite the longest side, $\overline{AC}$. Use the law of cosines to solve for B.

$$b^2 = a^2 + c^2 - 2ac \cos B$$ **Law of cosines**

$$27^2 = 12^2 + 20^2 - 2(12)(20) \cos B$$ **Substitute.**

$$\frac{27^2 - 12^2 - 20^2}{-2(12)(20)} = \cos B$$ **Solve for cos B.**

$$-0.3854 \approx \cos B$$ **Simplify.**

$$B \approx \cos^{-1}(-0.3854) \approx 112.7°$$ **Use inverse cosine.**

Now use the law of sines to find A.

$$\frac{\sin A}{a} = \frac{\sin B}{b}$$ **Law of sines**

$$\frac{\sin A}{12} = \frac{\sin 112.7°}{27}$$ **Substitute for a, b, and B.**

$$\sin A = \frac{12 \sin 112.7°}{27} \approx 0.4100$$ **Multiply each side by 12 and simplify.**

$$A \approx \sin^{-1} 0.4100 \approx 24.2°$$ **Use inverse sine.**

The third angle C of the triangle is $C \approx 180° - 24.2° - 112.7° = 43.1°$.

▶ In $\triangle ABC$, $A \approx 24.2°$, $B \approx 112.7°$, and $C \approx 43.1°$.

EXAMPLE 3 Use the law of cosines in real life

SCIENCE Scientists can use a set of footprints to calculate an organism's *step angle*, which is a measure of walking efficiency. The closer the step angle is to 180°, the more efficiently the organism walked.

The diagram at the right shows a set of footprints for a dinosaur. Find the step angle B.

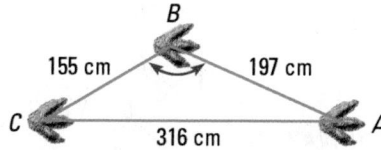

Solution

$$b^2 = a^2 + c^2 - 2ac \cos B$$ **Law of cosines**

$$316^2 = 155^2 + 197^2 - 2(155)(197) \cos B$$ **Substitute.**

$$\frac{316^2 - 155^2 - 197^2}{-2(155)(197)} = \cos B$$ **Solve for cos B.**

$$-0.6062 \approx \cos B$$ **Simplify.**

$$B \approx \cos^{-1}(-0.6062) \approx 127.3°$$ **Use inverse cosine.**

▶ The step angle B is about 127.3°.

Solve △ABC.

1. $a = 8$, $c = 10$, $B = 48°$

2. $a = 14$, $b = 16$, $c = 9$

3. **WHAT IF?** In Example 3, suppose that $a = 193$ cm, $b = 335$ cm, and $c = 186$ cm. Find the step angle θ.

HERON'S AREA FORMULA The law of cosines can be used to establish the following formula for the area of a triangle. The formula is credited to the Greek mathematician Heron (circa A.D. 100).

KEY CONCEPT *For Your Notebook*

Heron's Area Formula

The area of the triangle with sides of length a, b, and c is

$$\text{Area} = \sqrt{s(s - a)(s - b)(s - c)}$$

where $s = \frac{1}{2}(a + b + c)$. The variable s is called the *semiperimeter*, or half-perimeter, of the triangle.

EXAMPLE 4 **Solve a multi-step problem**

URBAN PLANNING The intersection of three streets forms a piece of land called a traffic triangle. Find the area of the traffic triangle shown.

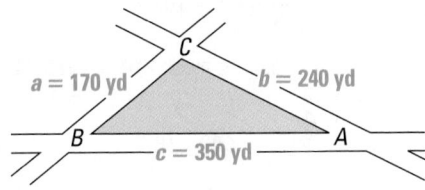

Solution

> **ANOTHER WAY**
> For an alternative method for solving the problem in Example 4, see the **Problem Solving Workshop**.

STEP 1 **Find** the semiperimeter s.

$$s = \frac{1}{2}(a + b + c) = \frac{1}{2}(170 + 240 + 350) = 380$$

STEP 2 **Use** Heron's formula to find the area of △ABC.

$$\text{Area} = \sqrt{s(s - a)(s - b)(s - c)}$$
$$= \sqrt{380(380 - 170)(380 - 240)(380 - 350)} \approx 18{,}300$$

▶ The area of the traffic triangle is about 18,300 square yards.

Find the area of △ABC.

4.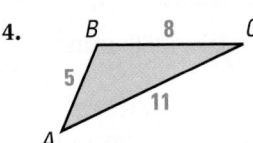

5.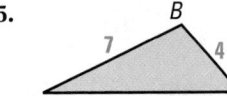

6.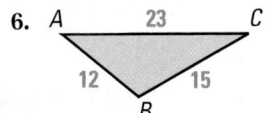

HOMEWORK
KEY

◯ = See WORKED-OUT SOLUTIONS
Exs. 17, 25, and 45

★ = STANDARDIZED TEST PRACTICE
Exs. 2, 20, 33, 34, 45, and 47

SKILL PRACTICE

1. **VOCABULARY** Copy and complete: In a triangle with sides of length a, b, and c, $\frac{1}{2}(a + b + c)$ is called the ___?___.

2. ★ **WRITING** Express Heron's formula in words.

EXAMPLES
1 and 2
for Exs. 3–20

CHOOSING A METHOD For the given case, tell whether you would use the *law of sines* or the *law of cosines* to solve the triangle.

3. SSS   4. ASA   5. SSA   6. SAS   7. AAS

SOLVING TRIANGLES Solve △ABC.

8. 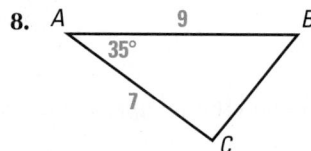   9. 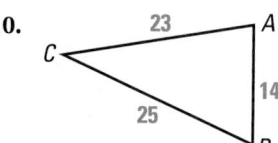   10.

SOLVING TRIANGLES Solve △ABC.

11. $B = 25°$, $a = 8$, $c = 6$
12. $A = 103°$, $b = 15$, $c = 24$
13. $a = 18$, $b = 28$, $c = 13$
14. $a = 38$, $b = 31$, $c = 35$
15. $C = 48°$, $a = 17$, $b = 20$
16. $B = 63°$, $a = 29$, $c = 38$
17. $a = 10$, $b = 3$, $c = 12$
18. $a = 23$, $b = 24$, $c = 20$
19. $C = 96°$, $a = 35$, $b = 43$

20. ★ **MULTIPLE CHOICE** What is the measure of angle B in △ABC if $a = 17$, $b = 29$, and $c = 14$?

   A 18.7°   **B** 22.9°   **C** 111.2°   **D** 138.4°

EXAMPLE 4
for Exs. 21–33

FINDING AREA Find the area of △ABC.

21. 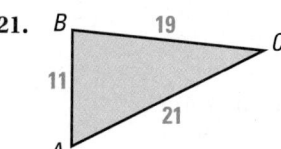   22. 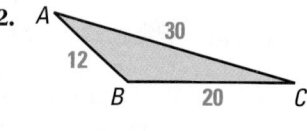   23.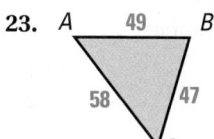

FINDING AREA Find the area of △ABC with the given side lengths.

24. $a = 12$, $b = 7$, $c = 8$
25. $a = 5$, $b = 11$, $c = 10$
26. $a = 25$, $b = 24$, $c = 19$
27. $a = 14$, $b = 20$, $c = 28$
28. $a = 31$, $b = 23$, $c = 17$
29. $a = 81$, $b = 67$, $c = 71$
30. $a = 43$, $b = 59$, $c = 48$
31. $a = 51$, $b = 51$, $c = 43$
32. $a = 38$, $b = 25$, $c = 61$

33. ★ **MULTIPLE CHOICE** What is the area of △ABC if $a = 21$, $b = 16$, and $c = 13$?

   A 66 units^2 **B** 104 units^2 **C** 1350 units^2 **D** 4368 units^2

34. ★ **SHORT RESPONSE** Use the law of cosines to show that the measure of each angle of an equilateral triangle is 60°. *Explain* your reasoning.

35. ERROR ANALYSIS *Describe* and correct the error in finding the measure of angle A in $\triangle ABC$ if $a = 18$, $b = 15$, and $c = 10$.

$$\cos A = \frac{15^2 + 10^2 - 18^2}{2(18)(15)} \approx 0.0019$$

$$A \approx \cos^{-1} 0.0019 \approx 89.9°$$

CHOOSING A METHOD Use the law of sines, the law of cosines, or the Pythagorean theorem to solve $\triangle ABC$.

36. $A = 72°$, $B = 44°$, $b = 14$ **37.** $B = 98°$, $C = 37°$, $a = 18$ **38.** $C = 65°$, $a = 12$, $b = 21$

39. $B = 90°$, $a = 15$, $c = 6$ **40.** $C = 40°$, $b = 36$, $c = 27$ **41.** $a = 34$, $b = 19$, $c = 27$

42. CHALLENGE Given $\triangle ABC$ with height h, derive the law of cosines. *Explain* how the Pythagorean theorem is related to the law of cosines.

PROBLEM SOLVING

EXAMPLE 3
for Ex. 43

43. TRAPEZE ARTISTS The diagram shows the paths of two trapeze artists who are both 5 feet long when hanging by their knees. The "flyer" on the left bar is preparing to make hand-to-hand contact with the "catcher" on the right bar. At what angle θ will the two meet?

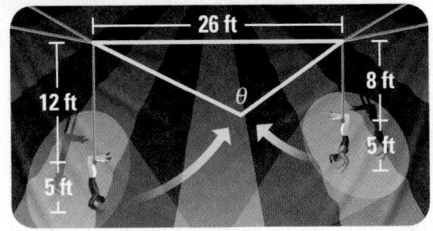

EXAMPLE 4
for Exs. 44–45

44. RESEARCH TRIANGLE Raleigh, Durham, and Chapel Hill are three cities in North Carolina that form what is known as the Research Triangle. It is about 18 miles from Raleigh to Durham, 23 miles from Raleigh to Chapel Hill, and 8 miles from Chapel Hill to Durham. Find the area of the Research Triangle.

45. ★ **SHORT RESPONSE** The diagram shows the dimensions of a plot of land. What is the area of the land in acres? (Use the fact that 1 acre = 43,560 square feet.) *Explain* how you could also determine the area by first finding the length of $\overline{AC}$.

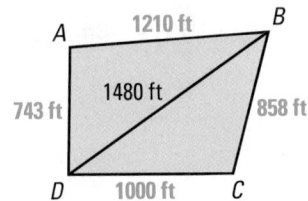

46. MULTI-STEP PROBLEM A golfer hits a drive 260 yards on a hole that is 400 yards long. The shot is 15° off target.

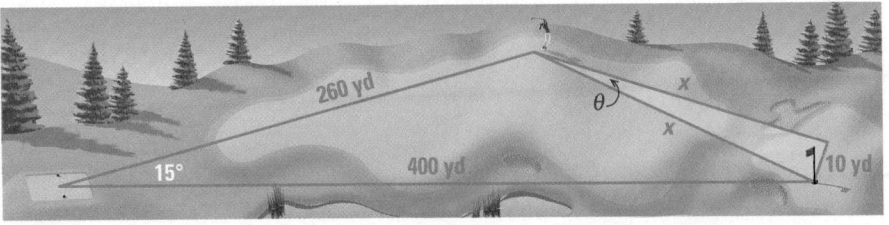

a. What is the distance x from the golfer's ball to the hole?

b. Assume the golfer is able to hit the ball precisely the distance found in part (a). What is the maximum angle θ by which the ball can be off target in order to land no more than 10 yards from the hole?

47. ★ **EXTENDED RESPONSE** Starting at the same point in a forest, two hikers take different paths. The first hiker walks due north at a speed of 2 miles per hour. The second hiker walks 60° east of north at a speed of 3 miles per hour.

    a. How far apart are the hikers after 1 hour?

    b. The two hikers carry walkie-talkies with a range of 10 miles. After how much time are the hikers out of range of each other?

    c. Suppose after two hours the first hiker stops and tells the second hiker to meet her. How long will it take the second hiker to meet the first hiker? In what direction should the second hiker walk? *Explain* your reasoning.

48. **CHALLENGE** An airplane flies 55° east of north from city A to city B, a distance of 470 miles. Another airplane flies 7° north of east from city A to city C, a distance of 890 miles. What is the distance between cities B and C?

QUIZ

Solve $\triangle ABC$.

1. $A = 50°$, $B = 74°$, $c = 12$
2. $C = 66°$, $a = 18$, $c = 17$
3. $a = 20$, $b = 14$, $c = 23$
4. $C = 118°$, $a = 26$, $b = 34$
5. $A = 102°$, $C = 25°$, $a = 31$
6. $a = 49$, $b = 52$, $c = 38$
7. $B = 53°$, $a = 41$, $c = 29$
8. $A = 112°$, $B = 48°$, $c = 5$

Find the area of $\triangle ABC$.

9. $B = 94°$, $a = 13$, $c = 15$
10. $C = 18°$, $a = 16$, $b = 11$
11. $a = 18$, $b = 25$, $c = 19$
12. $a = 27$, $b = 21$, $c = 37$
13. $a = 62$, $b = 47$, $c = 53$
14. $A = 70°$, $b = 44$, $c = 36$

15. **GEOMETRY** The base of a right triangular prism has sides of length 8 centimeters, 10 centimeters, and 13 centimeters. The height of the prism is 5 centimeters. What is the volume of the prism?

Using ALTERNATIVE METHODS

Another Way to Solve Example 4

Make sense of problems and persevere in solving them.

MULTIPLE REPRESENTATIONS In Example 4, you found the area of a triangle given the lengths of its sides by using Heron's formula. You can also find the area of the triangle by writing and solving a system of equations.

PROBLEM

URBAN PLANNING The intersection of three streets forms a piece of land called a traffic triangle. Find the area of the traffic triangle shown.

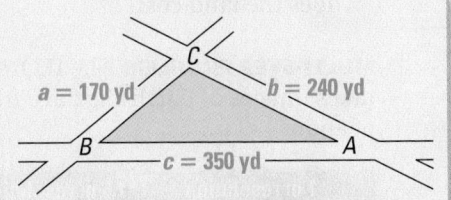

METHOD

Using a System of Equations Use a system of quadratic equations to find the triangle's height h. Then find the area of the triangle using the formula $A = \frac{1}{2}bh$.

STEP 1 **Draw** a new diagram of the triangle as shown. Let h be the height of the triangle. The altitude labeled by h divides $\overline{AB}$ into two segments of length x and $350 - x$.

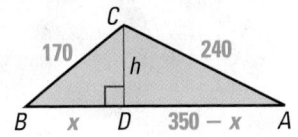

STEP 2 **Use** the Pythagorean theorem to write a system of quadratic equations.

$$h^2 + x^2 = 170^2$$
$$h^2 + (350 - x)^2 = 240^2$$

STEP 3 **Solve** the first equation for h^2 to get $h^2 = 170^2 - x^2$. Substitute this expression for h^2 in the second equation, and solve for x.

$$170^2 - x^2 + (350 - x)^2 = 240^2$$
$$28{,}900 - x^2 + 122{,}500 - 700x + x^2 = 57{,}600$$
$$-700x = -93{,}800$$
$$x = 134$$

STEP 4 **Use** the Pythagorean theorem to find that $h = \sqrt{170^2 - 134^2} \approx 104.6$.

So the area of the triangle is $A = \frac{1}{2}bh \approx \frac{1}{2}(350)(104.6) \approx 18{,}300$.

▶ The area of the triangle is about 18,300 square yards.

PRACTICE

FINDING AREAS Use the method above to find the area of $\triangle ABC$ with the given side lengths.

1. $a = 12$, $b = 17$, $c = 26$

2. $a = 63$, $b = 92$, $c = 87$

3. $a = 101$, $b = 94$, $c = 153$

4. **WHAT IF?** Suppose $a = 200$ yd in the problem above. Find the area of the triangle.

5. **GARDEN AREA** A triangular garden has sides with lengths 50 feet, 38 feet, and 43 feet. Use the method above to find the area of the garden.

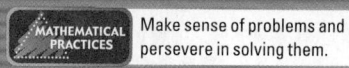
1. **MULTI-STEP PROBLEM** You are buying a triangular piece of property. Two sides of the triangle are 540 yards and 330 yards long and have an included angle of 100°.

   a. How long is the third side of the property?

   b. The price of the land is $2500 per acre (1 acre = 4840 square yards). How much does the land cost?

2. **MULTI-STEP PROBLEM** The IKONOS satellite takes images of Earth's surface from a height of about 423 miles.

   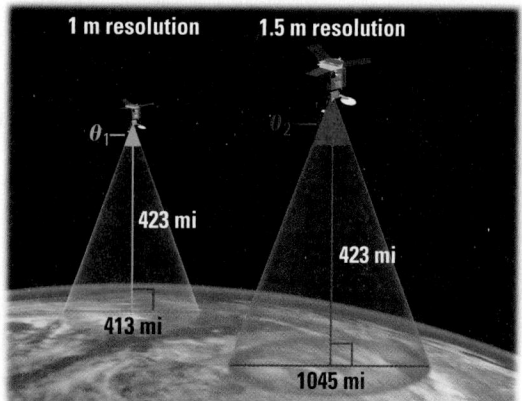

   Not drawn to scale

   a. IKONOS can take photographs that show objects 1 meter across provided the objects lie within a region about 413 miles across, as shown above. Find the value of θ_1.

   b. The largest region IKONOS can view is about 1045 miles across, as shown above. What is the maximum angle θ_2 through which IKONOS can rotate?

3. **OPEN-ENDED** A triangle has a 30° angle. Give the lengths of two sides that include the angle and produce a triangle with an area of 40 square inches.

4. **GRIDDED ANSWER** After walking 20 feet into the water at a beach, you notice that the depth of the water is 3 feet. Find the angle θ at which the beach slopes. Round your answer to the nearest tenth of a degree.

   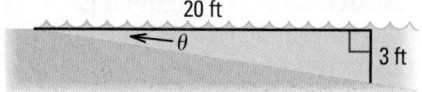

5. **SHORT RESPONSE** On a baseball field, the pitcher's mound at P is 60.5 feet from home plate at H and 95 feet from an arc where the outfield grass begins.

   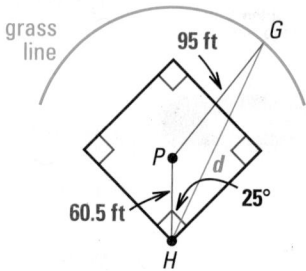

   A ball is hit 25° to the right of the pitcher's mound and travels to the edge of the grass. What distance d must an outfielder at G throw the ball to make an out at home plate? *Explain.*

6. **EXTENDED RESPONSE** A trough can be made by folding a rectangular piece of metal in half and then enclosing the ends. The volume of water the trough can hold depends on how far you bend the metal.

   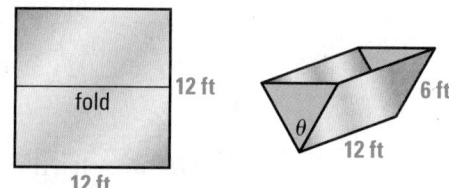

   a. Predict the value of θ that will maximize the volume of the trough shown.

   b. Find the volume of the trough as a function of θ. (*Hint:* You will need to find the area of one of the triangular faces.)

   c. *Describe* how the volume changes as θ increases from 0° to 180°.

   d. What value of θ maximizes the volume? *Compare* this value with your prediction.

7. **SHORT RESPONSE** You are building a triangular concrete patio that has sides of length 8 feet, 11 feet, and 15 feet, and a thickness of 0.5 foot. If one bag of cement makes 0.33 cubic foot of concrete, how many bags of cement do you need to build the patio? *Explain* your reasoning.

Animated Algebra
my.hrw.com
Electronic Function Library

BIG IDEAS
For Your Notebook

Big Idea 1

Using Trigonometric Functions

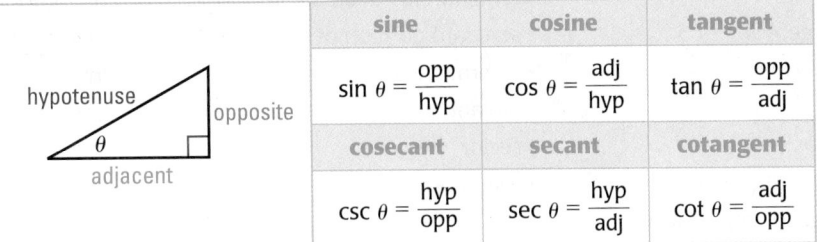

	sine	cosine	tangent
hypotenuse / opposite / θ / adjacent	$\sin \theta = \dfrac{opp}{hyp}$	$\cos \theta = \dfrac{adj}{hyp}$	$\tan \theta = \dfrac{opp}{adj}$
	cosecant	**secant**	**cotangent**
	$\csc \theta = \dfrac{hyp}{opp}$	$\sec \theta = \dfrac{hyp}{adj}$	$\cot \theta = \dfrac{adj}{opp}$

Big Idea 2

Using Inverse Trigonometric Functions

Inverse trigonometric functions can be used to solve trigonometric equations.

If $-1 \le a \le 1$, then the inverse sine of a is an angle θ, written $\sin^{-1} a = \theta$, where $\sin \theta = a$ and $-\dfrac{\pi}{2} \le \theta \le \dfrac{\pi}{2}$.

If $-1 \le a \le 1$, then the inverse cosine of a is an angle θ, written $\cos^{-1} a = \theta$, where $\cos \theta = a$ and $0 \le \theta \le \pi$.

If a is any real number, then the inverse tangent of a is an angle θ, written $\tan^{-1} a = \theta$, where $\tan \theta = a$ and $-\dfrac{\pi}{2} < \theta < \dfrac{\pi}{2}$.

2 / 1 / 30°

$$\sin^{-1} \frac{1}{2} = 30°$$

2 / 45° / $\sqrt{2}$

$$\cos^{-1} \frac{\sqrt{2}}{2} = 45°$$

60° / 1 / $\sqrt{3}$

$$\tan^{-1} \sqrt{3} = 60°$$

Big Idea 3

Applying the Law of Sines and Law of Cosines

Use the table below to help you remember when to apply each law.

If you know this information . . .		use this law . . .	to find this information.
angle-angle-side	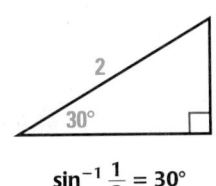	Law of sines	remaining sides*
angle-side-angle		Law of sines	remaining sides*
side-side-angle		Law of sines	remaining side and one angle*
side-angle-side		Law of cosines	remaining side and one angle*
side-side-side		Law of cosines	two angles*

* Find the remaining angle by using the triangle sum theorem.

9 CHAPTER REVIEW

@HomeTutor

my.hrw.com
• Multi-Language Glossary
• Vocabulary practice

REVIEW KEY VOCABULARY

- sine
- cosine
- tangent
- cosecant
- secant
- cotangent
- angle of elevation
- angle of depression

- initial side of an angle
- terminal side of an angle
- standard position of an angle
- coterminal angles
- radian
- sector
- central angle
- unit circle

- quadrantal angle
- reference angle
- inverse sine
- inverse cosine
- inverse tangent
- law of sines
- law of cosines

VOCABULARY EXERCISES

1. **WRITING** *Describe* an angle in standard position.

2. Identify the relationship between the angles $-225°$ and $135°$.

3. What is the name of a circle with center at the origin and radius 1 unit?

4. Copy and complete: If $\cos\theta = a$ and $0 \le \theta \le \pi$, then the __?__ of a equals θ.

5. **WRITING** State the law of sines in words.

REVIEW EXAMPLES AND EXERCISES

Use the review examples and exercises below to check your understanding of the concepts you have learned in each lesson of this chapter.

9.1 Use Trigonometry with Right Triangles

EXAMPLE

Evaluate the six trigonometric functions of the angle θ.

From the Pythagorean theorem, the length of the hypotenuse is $\sqrt{6^2 + 8^2} = \sqrt{100} = 10$.

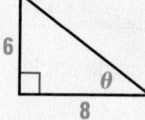

$$\sin\theta = \frac{\text{opp}}{\text{hyp}} = \frac{6}{10} = \frac{3}{5} \qquad \cos\theta = \frac{\text{adj}}{\text{hyp}} = \frac{8}{10} = \frac{4}{5} \qquad \tan\theta = \frac{\text{opp}}{\text{adj}} = \frac{6}{8} = \frac{3}{4}$$

$$\csc\theta = \frac{\text{hyp}}{\text{opp}} = \frac{10}{6} = \frac{5}{3} \qquad \sec\theta = \frac{\text{hyp}}{\text{adj}} = \frac{10}{8} = \frac{5}{4} \qquad \cot\theta = \frac{\text{adj}}{\text{opp}} = \frac{8}{6} = \frac{4}{3}$$

EXERCISES

**EXAMPLES
1 and 3**
for Exs. 6–7

6. In $\triangle ABC$, $a = 4$, $b = 5$, and $C = 90°$. Evaluate the six trigonometric functions of angle B.

7. **HOT AIR BALLOON** You are standing 50 meters from a hot air balloon that is preparing to take off. The angle of elevation to the top of the balloon is $28°$. Find the height of the balloon.

9.2 Define General Angles and Use Radian Measure

EXAMPLE

Convert 110° to radians and $\frac{7\pi}{12}$ radians to degrees.

$$110° = 110°\left(\frac{\pi \text{ radians}}{180°}\right) \qquad \frac{7\pi}{12} \text{ radians} = \left(\frac{7\pi}{12} \text{ radians}\right)\left(\frac{180°}{\pi \text{ radians}}\right)$$

$$= \frac{11\pi}{18} \text{ radians} \qquad\qquad\qquad = 105°$$

EXERCISES

EXAMPLE 3
for Exs. 8–11

Convert the degree measure to radians or the radian measure to degrees.

8. 145° **9.** −80° **10.** $\frac{4\pi}{3}$ **11.** $\frac{11\pi}{6}$

9.3 Evaluate Trigonometric Functions of Any Angle

EXAMPLE

Evaluate sec 120°.

The reference angle is $\theta' = 180° - 120° = 60°$. The secant function is negative in Quadrant II, so you can write:

$$\sec 120° = -\sec 60° = -2$$

EXERCISES

EXAMPLE 4
for Exs. 12–15

Evaluate the function without using a calculator.

12. tan 330° **13.** csc (−405°) **14.** $\sin \frac{13\pi}{6}$ **15.** $\sec \frac{11\pi}{3}$

9.4 Evaluate Inverse Trigonometric Functions

EXAMPLE

Evaluate $\tan^{-1} 1$ in both radians and degrees.

When $-\frac{\pi}{2} < \theta < \frac{\pi}{2}$, or $-90° < \theta < 90°$, the angle θ whose tangent is 1 is:

$$\theta = \tan^{-1} 1 = \frac{\pi}{4} \quad \text{or} \quad \theta = \tan^{-1} 1 = 45°$$

EXERCISES

EXAMPLES
1 and 4
for Exs. 16–17

16. Evaluate $\sin^{-1} (-0.5)$ in both radians and degrees.

17. RAMP You use a 12 foot ramp to load items into a van. If the floor of the van is 4 feet off the ground, what is the angle of elevation of the ramp?

9.5 Apply the Law of Sines

EXAMPLE

Solve $\triangle ABC$ with $A = 28°$, $C = 74°$, and $b = 22$.

Find angle B: $B = 180° - 28° - 74° = 78°$.

Use the law of sines to solve for a and c.

$$\frac{a}{\sin 28°} = \frac{22}{\sin 78°} \qquad\qquad \frac{c}{\sin 74°} = \frac{22}{\sin 78°}$$

$$a = \frac{22 \sin 28°}{\sin 78°} \approx 10.6 \qquad\qquad c = \frac{22 \sin 74°}{\sin 78°} \approx 21.6$$

▶ For $\triangle ABC$, $B = 78°$, $a \approx 10.6$, and $c \approx 21.6$.

EXERCISES

EXAMPLES
1, 2, 3 and 4
for Exs. 18–21

Solve $\triangle ABC$. (*Hint:* Some of the "triangles" may have no solution and some may have two solutions.)

18. $A = 43°$, $C = 83°$, $b = 12$
19. $B = 104°$, $b = 25$, $c = 18$
20. $C = 55°$, $a = 17$, $c = 15$
21. $B = 60°$, $C = 73°$, $b = 20$

9.6 Apply the Law of Cosines

EXAMPLE

Solve $\triangle ABC$ with $A = 66°$, $b = 16$, and $c = 21$.

Use the law of cosines to find the length a.

$$a^2 = b^2 + c^2 - 2bc \cos A$$

$$a^2 = 16^2 + 21^2 - 2(16)(21) \cos 66°$$

$$a^2 \approx 423.7$$

$$a \approx 20.6$$

Now find angle B and angle C.

$$\frac{\sin B}{16} = \frac{\sin 66°}{20.6}$$

$$\sin B = \frac{16 \sin 66°}{20.6} \approx 0.7095$$

$$B = \sin^{-1} 0.7095 \approx 45.2°$$

$$C \approx 180° - 66° - 45.2° \approx 68.8°$$

▶ For $\triangle ABC$, $B \approx 45.2°$, $C \approx 68.8°$, and $a \approx 20.6$.

EXERCISES

EXAMPLES
1 and 2
for Exs. 22–24

Solve $\triangle ABC$.

22. $a = 19$, $b = 11$, $c = 14$
23. $B = 75°$, $a = 20$, $c = 17$
24. $a = 30$, $b = 35$, $c = 39$

Evaluate the six trigonometric functions of the angle θ.

1.
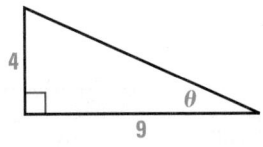

2.
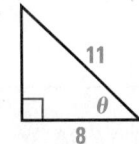

3.
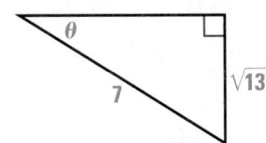

Convert the degree measure to radians or the radian measure to degrees.

4. 260°

5. −50°

6. $\dfrac{4\pi}{5}$

7. $\dfrac{8\pi}{3}$

Evaluate the function without using a calculator.

8. tan 150°

9. sec (−480°)

10. $\sin\left(-\dfrac{5\pi}{3}\right)$

11. $\cos\dfrac{11\pi}{6}$

Evaluate the expression in both radians and degrees without using a calculator.

12. $\cos^{-1} 1$

13. $\tan^{-1}\sqrt{3}$

14. $\sin^{-1}\left(-\dfrac{\sqrt{2}}{2}\right)$

15. $\cos^{-1}\left(-\dfrac{\sqrt{3}}{2}\right)$

Solve △ABC. (*Hint:* Some of the "triangles" may have no solution and some may have two solutions.)

16. $A = 47°, C = 32°, c = 12$

17. $a = 24, b = 12, c = 17$

18. $B = 63°, a = 11, b = 8$

19. $C = 101°, a = 23, b = 19$

20. $a = 24, b = 30, c = 21$

21. $A = 26°, B = 77°, c = 50$

Find the area of △ABC.

22. $A = 81°, b = 16, c = 18$

23. $a = 8, b = 6, c = 7$

24. $a = 25, b = 24, c = 38$

25. $C = 111°, a = 7, b = 13$

26. $a = 16, b = 33, c = 24$

27. $B = 61°, a = 12, c = 18$

28. SURVEYING To measure the width of a river, you plant a stake at point A on one side of the riverbank, directly across from a tree stump at point B on the other side of the riverbank. From point A, you walk 80 meters along the riverbank to point C. You find the measure of angle C to be 39°. What is the width w of the river?

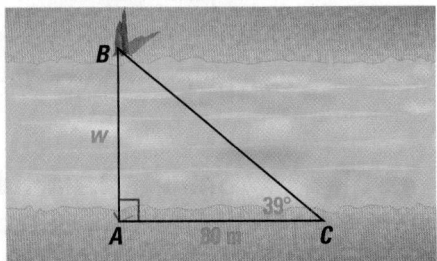

29. CONSTRUCTION A crane has a 200 foot arm with a lower end that is 5 feet off the ground. The arm has to reach to the top of a building that is 160 feet high. At what angle θ should the arm be set?

30. NAVIGATION A boat travels 40 miles due west before turning 20° and traveling an additional 25 miles. How far is the boat from its point of departure?

SHORT RESPONSE QUESTIONS

PROBLEM

According to the ADA Accessibility Guidelines, the maximum slope of a wheelchair ramp is 1:12. What is the maximum angle of elevation of an acceptable ramp? What is the angle of elevation of the ramp shown? Does the ramp shown meet the guidelines? *Explain* your reasoning.

30 ft

5 ft

5 ft

18 in.

Not drawn to scale

Below are sample solutions to the problem. Read each solution and the comments on the left to see why the sample represents full credit, partial credit, or no credit.

SAMPLE 1: Full credit solution

⋯⋯⋯⋯⋯⋯▶ The diagram, calculations, and reasoning are correct.

A ramp with the maximum acceptable slope is shown.

From the diagram, $\tan \theta = \frac{1}{12}$, so $\theta = \tan^{-1} \frac{1}{12} \approx 4.76°$.

The maximum angle of elevation is about 4.76°.

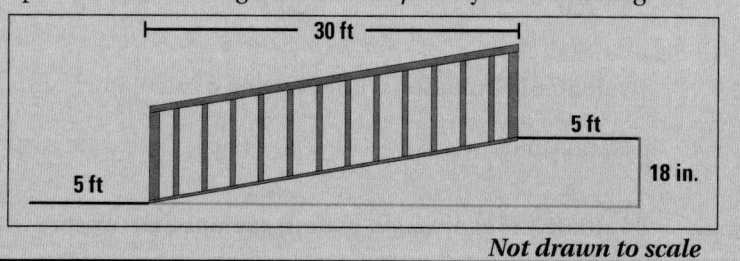

θ
12
1
Ramp meeting ADA guidelines

⋯⋯⋯⋯⋯⋯▶ The diagram and calculations are correct and clearly explained.

The length of the ramp given in the problem is 30 feet.

The rise of this ramp is 18 inches, or $\frac{18}{12} = 1.5$ feet.

So, $\tan \theta = \frac{1.5}{30}$ and $\theta = \tan^{-1} \frac{1.5}{30} \approx 2.86°$.

The ramp's angle of elevation is about 2.86°.

θ
30 ft
1.5 ft

⋯⋯⋯⋯⋯⋯▶ The answer is correct.

The ramp given in the problem has an angle of elevation less than the maximum acceptable angle, so the ramp meets the ADA guidelines.

SAMPLE 2: Partial credit solution

⋯⋯⋯⋯⋯⋯▶ The maximum acceptable angle is correctly calculated.

The slope of an acceptable ramp can be at most 1:12, so $\tan \theta = \frac{1}{12}$ where θ is the maximum angle. Therefore, $\theta = \tan^{-1} \frac{1}{12} \approx 4.76°$. The maximum angle of elevation for a wheelchair ramp is about 4.76°.

⋯⋯⋯⋯⋯⋯▶ The student forgot to use the same units when calculating slope, so the rest of the answers are incorrect.

The slope of the ramp given in the problem is $\frac{18}{30}$, so $\tan \theta = \frac{18}{30}$. Therefore, $\theta = \tan^{-1} \frac{18}{30} \approx 30.96°$. The ramp's angle of elevation is about 31°.

The angle of elevation exceeds the maximum acceptable angle of elevation, so the ramp does not meet the guidelines.

SAMPLE 3: Partial credit solution

The rise is 18 inches. The run is 30 feet,

or 30 ft · $\dfrac{12 \text{ in.}}{1 \text{ ft}}$ = 360 inches.

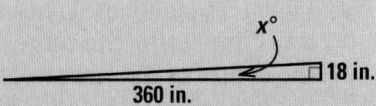

You know the lengths of the sides opposite and adjacent to the angle, so use the tangent ratio.

$$\tan x = \frac{\text{opp}}{\text{adj}} = \frac{18}{360} \qquad x = \tan^{-1} \frac{18}{360} \approx 2.86°$$

The angle of elevation of the ramp given in the problem is about 2.86°.

SAMPLE 4: No credit solution

The maximum slope of an acceptable wheelchair ramp is 1:12, so the maximum angle of elevation is $\dfrac{1}{12} \approx 0.083°$. The slope of the ramp shown in the problem is 18 in.:30 ft, or 1:20, so the angle of elevation is $\dfrac{1}{20} = 0.05°$.

PRACTICE   Apply the Scoring Rubric

Use the rubric on the previous page to score the solution to the problem below as *full credit*, *partial credit*, or *no credit*. *Explain* your reasoning.

PROBLEM Find the volume of the right triangular prism shown.

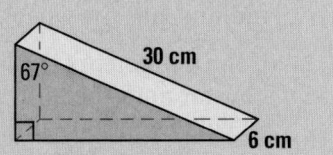

1. To find the prism's volume, multiply the three given measures:
   30(6)(67) = 12,060 cm³

2. To find the area of the base of the prism, first find the side lengths b and h shown in the diagram.

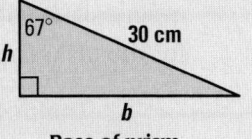

   $$\sin 67° = \frac{b}{30} \qquad\qquad \cos 67° = \frac{h}{30}$$

   $$30(\sin 67°) = b \qquad\qquad 30(\cos 67°) = h$$

   $$27.62 \approx b \qquad\qquad\qquad 11.72 \approx h$$

   The area of the base is $\frac{1}{2}bh = \frac{1}{2}(27.62)(11.72) \approx 161.9$ cm².

   The volume of the prism is (area of base)(height) = 161.9(6) = 971.4 cm³.

SHORT RESPONSE

1. Kepler's second law states that an imaginary line connecting the center of a planet and the center of the sun sweeps out equal areas in equal time intervals. The diagram below shows the location of Mars in orbit over a ten day period.

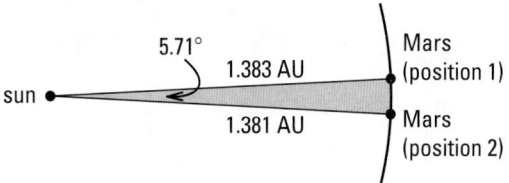

   a. Approximate the area Mars swept out during this time by finding the area of the triangle formed by the sun and the starting and ending positions of Mars. Give the answer in square miles. (*Hint:* 1 AU is 1 astronomical unit, which is equal to about 93 million miles.)

   b. As a planet moves closer to the sun along its orbit, what does Kepler's law imply about the planet's speed? *Explain.*

2. The wheel of a unicycle completes 6 full revolutions.

   a. Through what angle, in degrees and radians, has the wheel rotated?

   b. If the diameter of the wheel is 24 inches, how far does the unicycle travel in 6 wheel revolutions? *Explain.*

3. The table lists several tools used to make vertical transitions from one point to a higher point. It also lists the recommended range of angles of elevation for each tool. If a certain task requires making a vertical transition with a slope of $\frac{3}{5}$, which tool would be appropriate for the task? *Explain* your reasoning.

Tool	Range of angles
Ramp	0°–30°
Fixed steps	30°–35°
Ladder stairs	35°–75°
Portable stairs	68°–80°
Fixed ladder	75°–90°

4. A tennis player is practicing her serve. She aims for a can placed 57 feet from her in the service box. If she hits the ball when it is 9 feet in the air, what angle must the path of the ball make with the ground in order for the ball to hit the can's base? Assume the ball travels along a straight line. *Explain* your answer.

5. The diagrams below show the distances between atoms in a water molecule in liquid and ice forms. The measurements are given in picometers (pm), where 1 pm = 10^{-12} m. Are the obtuse angles in the diagrams the same? *Explain.*

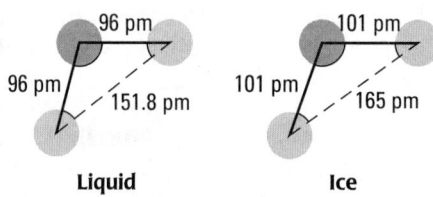

6. You are standing 30 feet from the base of a tree. The angle of elevation from your eyes to the top of the tree is 70°. If the height at eye level is 5 feet, what is the height of the tree to the nearest foot? *Explain* all of your steps.

7. You kick a soccer ball with an initial velocity of 40 feet per second at an angle of 45°. Your teammate kicks a soccer ball at an angle of 25°. With what initial velocity does your teammate have to kick the ball in order for both of the soccer balls to travel the same horizontal distance? *Explain* your reasoning.

8. Find the radius r (in inches) and the central angle θ (in radians) of a sector with an arc length of $\frac{10\pi}{3}$ inches and an area of $\frac{25\pi}{3}$ square inches. *Explain* your reasoning.

MULTIPLE CHOICE

9. Which angle measure is shown in the diagram?

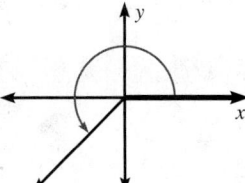

Ⓐ $\frac{\pi}{4}$ radians   Ⓑ $\frac{3\pi}{4}$ radians

Ⓒ $\frac{5\pi}{4}$ radians   Ⓓ $\frac{3\pi}{2}$ radians

10. What is the approximate value of a in $\triangle ABC$ if $A = 85°$, $B = 27°$, and $c = 5.0$ cm?

Ⓐ 1.0 cm   Ⓑ 5.4 cm

Ⓒ 5.9 cm   Ⓓ 11.0 cm

11. What is the reference angle for 300°?

Ⓐ 30°   Ⓑ 60°

Ⓒ 120°   Ⓓ 240°

GRIDDED ANSWER

12. If θ is an acute angle of a right triangle and $\sin \theta = \frac{3}{5}$, what is the value of $\cos \theta$?

13. What angle, in degrees, is equivalent to $\frac{5\pi}{6}$ radians?

14. What is the value of $\sin^{-1} 0.5$ in degrees?

15. What is the area of the triangle, to the nearest tenth of a square unit?

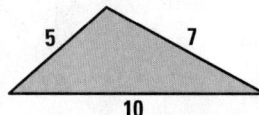

16. Let (10, 24) be a point on the terminal side of an angle θ in standard position. What is the value of sec θ?

17. What is the degree measure of angle A in $\triangle ABC$ if $a = 13$, $b = 9$, and $c = 7$? Round your answer to the nearest degree.

EXTENDED RESPONSE

18. A boat uses 50 feet of rope to drop anchor in a lake. The angle θ that the rope makes with the bottom of the lake is 20°.

a. Find the depth of the water.

b. The boat moves to deeper water but still lets out the same amount of rope when dropping anchor. If the horizontal distance from the boat to the anchor is 37 feet, what angle θ does the rope make with the lake bottom?

c. *Describe* how θ changes as the boat travels to deeper water with a constant length of anchor rope let out. Assume the rope is always taut.

19. You are making a lampshade out of fabric for the lamp shown. The pattern for the lampshade is shown in the diagram on the left.

a. Use the smaller sector to write an equation that relates θ and x.

b. Use the larger sector to write an equation that relates θ and $x + 10$.

c. Solve the system of equations from parts (a) and (b) to find x and θ.

d. Use the formula for the area of a sector to find the amount of fabric (in square inches) that you will use.

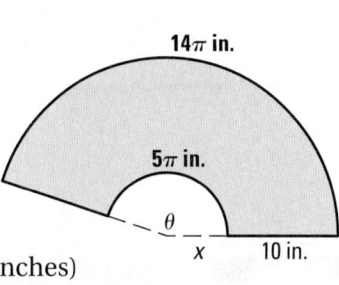

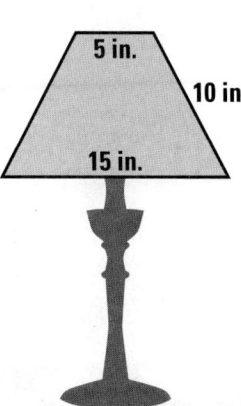

10 Trigonometric Graphs, Identities, and Equations

COMMON CORE

Lesson
10.1 C.9-12.F.IF.7e*
10.2 CC.9-12.F.TF.5*
10.3 CC.9-12.F.TF.8
10.4 CC.9-12.F.TF.7 (+)*
10.5 CC.9-12.F.TF.5*
10.6 CC.9-12.F.TF.9 (+)
10.7 CC.9-12.F.TF.9 (+)

Before

Previously, you learned the following skills, which you'll use in this chapter: evaluating trigonometric functions, finding reference angles, and evaluating inverse trigonometric functions.

Prerequisite Skills

VOCABULARY CHECK

Copy and complete the statement.

1. The **sine** of θ is __?__ .

2. The **cosine** of θ is __?__ .

3. The **tangent** of θ is __?__ .

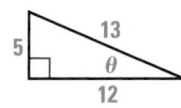

SKILLS CHECK

Simplify the expression.

4. $|10 - 6|$ 5. $\dfrac{4}{|-8|}$ 6. $\dfrac{-12}{|-4|}$ 7. $|-3|$

Solve the equation.

8. $5x^2 = 3x^2 + 50$ 9. $144 = x^2 + 23$ 10. $x^2 + 4 = 40 - 3x^2$

Simplify the square root.

11. $-\sqrt{\dfrac{1 - \dfrac{1}{2}}{2}}$ 12. $\sqrt{\dfrac{1 + 8}{16}}$ 13. $-\sqrt{\dfrac{1 + \dfrac{1}{3}}{3}}$

In this chapter, you will apply the big ideas listed below and reviewed in the Chapter Summary. You will also use the key vocabulary listed below.

Big Ideas

① **Graphing trigonometric functions**
② **Solving trigonometric equations**
③ **Applying trigonometric formulas**

KEY VOCABULARY

- amplitude
- periodic function
- cycle

- period
- frequency

- trigonometric identity
- sinusoid

Why?

You can use trigonometric functions to model characteristics of a projectile's path. For example, you can find the horizontal distance traveled by a soccer ball using trigonometric functions.

Animated Algebra

The animation illustrated below helps you answer a question from this chapter: How does changing the initial speed and angle of a soccer ball kicked from ground level affect the horizontal distance the ball travels?

The angle and speed at which a ball is kicked influence the distance it travels.

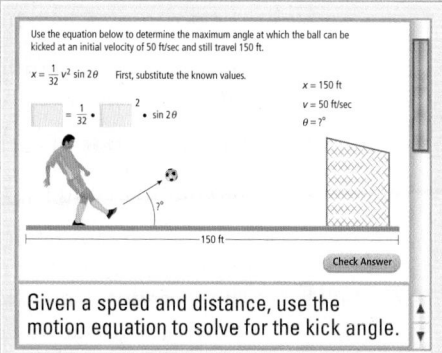

Use the equation below to determine the maximum angle at which the ball can be kicked at an initial velocity of 50 ft/sec and still travel 150 ft.

$x = \frac{1}{32} v^2 \sin 2\theta$ First, substitute the known values.

$\boxed{} = \frac{1}{32} \cdot \boxed{}^2 \cdot \sin 2\theta$

$x = 150$ ft
$v = 50$ ft/sec
$\theta = ?°$

150 ft

Given a speed and distance, use the motion equation to solve for the kick angle.

Animated Algebra at my.hrw.com

10.1 Graph Sine, Cosine, and Tangent Functions

Before You evaluated sine, cosine, and tangent functions.

Now You will graph sine, cosine, and tangent functions.

Why? So you can model oscillating motion, as in Ex. 31.

Key Vocabulary
- **amplitude**
- **periodic function**
- **cycle**
- **period**
- **frequency**

CC.9-12.F.IF.7e Graph exponential and logarithmic functions, showing intercepts and end behavior, and trigonometric functions, showing period, midline, and amplitude.*

In this lesson, you will learn to graph functions of the form $y = a \sin bx$ and $y = a \cos bx$ where a and b are positive constants and x is in radian measure. The graphs of all sine and cosine functions are related to the graphs of the parent functions $y = \sin x$ and $y = \cos x$, which are shown below.

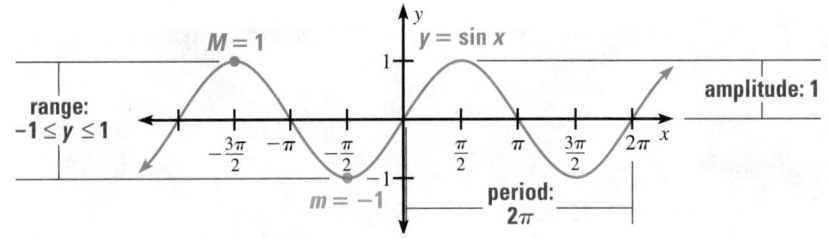

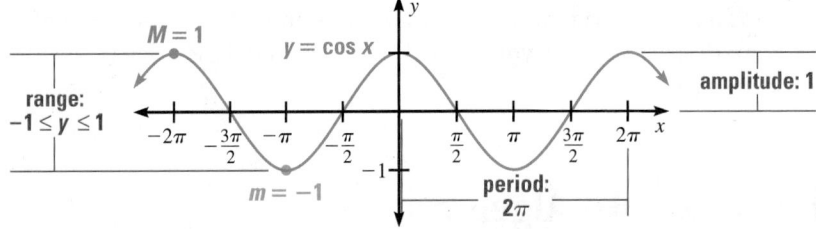

KEY CONCEPT *For Your Notebook*

Characteristics of $y = \sin x$ and $y = \cos x$

- The domain of each function is all real numbers.

- The range of each function is $-1 \le y \le 1$. Therefore, the minimum value of each function is $m = -1$ and the maximum value is $M = 1$.

- The **amplitude** of each function's graph is half the difference of the maximum M and the minimum m, or $\frac{1}{2}(M - m) = \frac{1}{2}[1 - (-1)] = 1$.

- Each function is **periodic**, which means that its graph has a repeating pattern. The shortest repeating portion of the graph is called a **cycle**. The horizontal length of each cycle is called the **period**. Each graph shown above has a period of 2π.

- The x-intercepts for $y = \sin x$ occur when $x = 0, \pm\pi, \pm 2\pi, \pm 3\pi, \ldots$.

- The x-intercepts for $y = \cos x$ occur when $x = \pm\frac{\pi}{2}, \pm\frac{3\pi}{2}, \pm\frac{5\pi}{2}, \pm\frac{7\pi}{2}, \ldots$.

Amplitude and Period

The amplitude and period of the graphs of $y = a \sin bx$ and $y = a \cos bx$, where a and b are nonzero real numbers, are as follows:

$$\text{Amplitude} = |a| \qquad \text{Period} = \frac{2\pi}{|b|}$$

GRAPHING KEY POINTS Each graph below shows five key x-values on the interval $0 \le x \le \frac{2\pi}{b}$ that you can use to sketch the graphs of $y = a \sin bx$ and $y = a \cos bx$ for $a > 0$ and $b > 0$. These are the x-values where the maximum and minimum values occur and the x-intercepts.

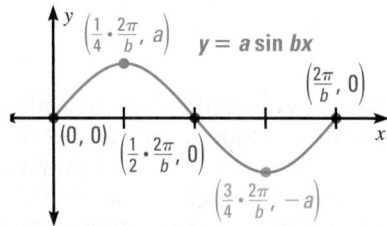
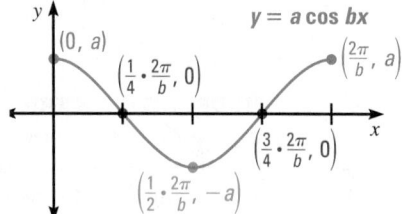

EXAMPLE 1 **Graph sine and cosine functions**

Graph (a) $y = 4 \sin x$ and (b) $y = \cos 4x$.

VARY CONSTANTS

Notice how changes in a and b affect the graphs of $y = a \sin bx$ and $y = a \cos bx$. When the value of a increases, the amplitude increases. When the value of b increases, the period decreases.

Solution

a. The amplitude is $a = 4$ and the period is $\frac{2\pi}{b} = \frac{2\pi}{1} = 2\pi$.

Intercepts: $(0, 0); \left(\frac{1}{2} \cdot 2\pi, 0\right) = (\pi, 0); (2\pi, 0)$

Maximum: $\left(\frac{1}{4} \cdot 2\pi, 4\right) = \left(\frac{\pi}{2}, 4\right)$

Minimum: $\left(\frac{3}{4} \cdot 2\pi, -4\right) = \left(\frac{3\pi}{2}, -4\right)$

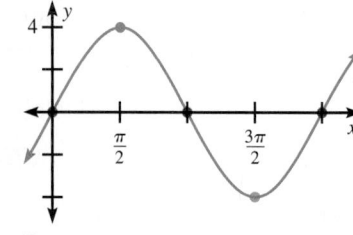

b. The amplitude is $a = 1$ and the period is $\frac{2\pi}{b} = \frac{2\pi}{4} = \frac{\pi}{2}$.

Intercepts: $\left(\frac{1}{4} \cdot \frac{\pi}{2}, 0\right) = \left(\frac{\pi}{8}, 0\right); \left(\frac{3}{4} \cdot \frac{\pi}{2}, 0\right) = \left(\frac{3\pi}{8}, 0\right)$

Maximums: $(0, 1); \left(\frac{\pi}{2}, 1\right)$

Minimum: $\left(\frac{1}{2} \cdot \frac{\pi}{2}, -1\right) = \left(\frac{\pi}{4}, -1\right)$

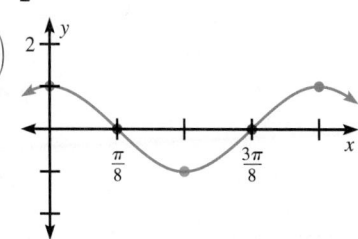

✓ **GUIDED PRACTICE** for Example 1

Graph the function.

1. $y = 2 \cos x$ **2.** $y = 5 \sin x$ **3.** $f(x) = \sin \pi x$ **4.** $g(x) = \cos 4\pi x$

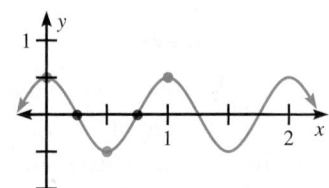

EXAMPLE 2 Graph a cosine function

Graph $y = \frac{1}{2} \cos 2\pi x$.

Solution

The amplitude is $a = \frac{1}{2}$ and the period is $\frac{2\pi}{b} = \frac{2\pi}{2\pi} = 1$.

Intercepts: $\left(\frac{1}{4} \cdot 1, 0\right) = \left(\frac{1}{4}, 0\right)$;

$\left(\frac{3}{4} \cdot 1, 0\right) = \left(\frac{3}{4}, 0\right)$

Maximums: $\left(0, \frac{1}{2}\right); \left(1, \frac{1}{2}\right)$

Minimum: $\left(\frac{1}{2} \cdot 1, -\frac{1}{2}\right) = \left(\frac{1}{2}, -\frac{1}{2}\right)$

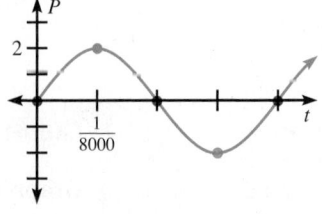

SKETCH A GRAPH

After you have drawn one complete cycle of the graph in Example 2 on the interval $0 \leq x \leq 1$, you can extend the graph by copying the cycle as many times as desired to the left and right of $0 \leq x \leq 1$.

MODELING WITH TRIGONOMETRIC FUNCTIONS The periodic nature of trigonometric functions is useful for modeling *oscillating* motions or repeating patterns that occur in real life. Some examples are sound waves, the motion of a pendulum, and seasons of the year. In such applications, the reciprocal of the period is called the **frequency**, which gives the number of cycles per unit of time.

❖ **EXAMPLE 3** Model with a sine function

AUDIO TEST A sound consisting of a single frequency is called a pure tone. An *audiometer* produces pure tones to test a person's auditory functions. Suppose an audiometer produces a pure tone with a frequency f of 2000 hertz (cycles per second). The maximum pressure P produced from the pure tone is 2 millipascals. Write and graph a sine model that gives the pressure P as a function of the time t (in seconds).

Solution

STEP 1 **Find** the values of a and b in the model $P = a \sin bt$. The maximum pressure is 2, so $a = 2$. You can use the frequency f to find b.

$$\text{frequency} = \frac{1}{\text{period}} \implies 2000 = \frac{b}{2\pi} \implies 4000\pi = b$$

The pressure P as a function of time t is given by $P = 2 \sin 4000\pi t$.

STEP 2 **Graph** the model. The amplitude is $a = 2$ and the period is $\frac{1}{f} = \frac{1}{2000}$.

Intercepts: $(0, 0)$;

$\left(\frac{1}{2} \cdot \frac{1}{2000}, 0\right) = \left(\frac{1}{4000}, 0\right); \left(\frac{1}{2000}, 0\right)$

Maximum: $\left(\frac{1}{4} \cdot \frac{1}{2000}, 2\right) = \left(\frac{1}{8000}, 2\right)$

Minimum: $\left(\frac{3}{4} \cdot \frac{1}{2000}, -2\right) = \left(\frac{3}{8000}, -2\right)$

Graph the function.

5. $y = \frac{1}{4} \sin \pi x$ **6.** $y = \frac{1}{3} \cos \pi x$ **7.** $f(x) = 2 \sin 3x$ **8.** $g(x) = 3 \cos 4x$

9. WHAT IF? In Example 3, how would the function change if the audiometer produced a pure tone with a frequency of 1000 hertz?

GRAPH OF $Y = $ TAN X The graphs of all tangent functions are related to the graph of the parent function $y = \tan x$, which is shown below.

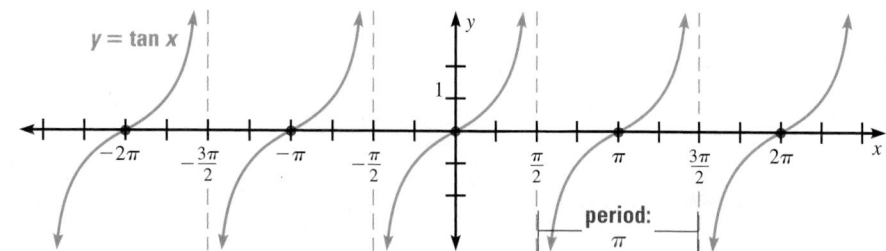

FIND ODD MULTIPLES

Odd multiples of $\frac{\pi}{2}$ are values such as these:

$\pm 1 \cdot \frac{\pi}{2} = \pm\frac{\pi}{2}$

$\pm 3 \cdot \frac{\pi}{2} = \pm\frac{3\pi}{2}$

$\pm 5 \cdot \frac{\pi}{2} = \pm\frac{5\pi}{2}$

The function $y = \tan x$ has the following characteristics:

1. The domain is all real numbers except odd multiples of $\frac{\pi}{2}$. At these x-values, the graph has vertical asymptotes.

2. The range is all real numbers. So, the function $y = \tan x$ does not have a maximum or minimum value, and therefore the graph of $y = \tan x$ does not have an amplitude.

3. The graph has a period of π.

4. The x-intercepts of the graph occur when $x = 0, \pm\pi, \pm 2\pi, \pm 3\pi, \ldots$.

KEY CONCEPT   *For Your Notebook*

Characteristics of $y = a \tan bx$

The period and vertical asymptotes of the graph of $y = a \tan bx$, where a and b are nonzero real numbers, are as follows:

• The period is $\dfrac{\pi}{|b|}$.

• The vertical asymptotes are at odd multiples of $\dfrac{\pi}{2|b|}$.

GRAPHING KEY POINTS The graph at the right shows five key x-values that can help you sketch the graph of $y = a \tan bx$ for $a > 0$ and $b > 0$. These are the **x-intercept**, the x-values where the **asymptotes** occur, and the x-values halfway between the x-intercept and the asymptotes. At each halfway point, the function's value is either a or $-a$.

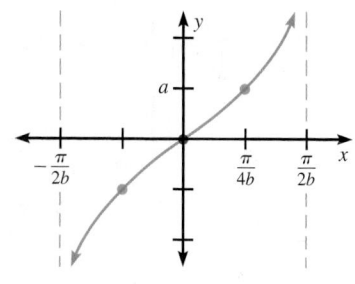

EXAMPLE 4 **Graph a tangent function**

Graph one period of the function $y = 2 \tan 3x$.

Solution

The period is $\dfrac{\pi}{b} = \dfrac{\pi}{3}$.

Intercept: $(0, 0)$

Asymptotes: $x = \dfrac{\pi}{2b} = \dfrac{\pi}{2 \cdot 3}$, or $x = \dfrac{\pi}{6}$;

$$x = -\dfrac{\pi}{2b} = -\dfrac{\pi}{2 \cdot 3}, \text{ or } x = -\dfrac{\pi}{6}$$

Halfway points: $\left(\dfrac{\pi}{4b}, a \right) = \left(\dfrac{\pi}{4 \cdot 3}, 2 \right) = \left(\dfrac{\pi}{12}, 2 \right)$;

$$\left(-\dfrac{\pi}{4b}, -a \right) = \left(-\dfrac{\pi}{4 \cdot 3}, -2 \right) = \left(-\dfrac{\pi}{12}, -2 \right)$$

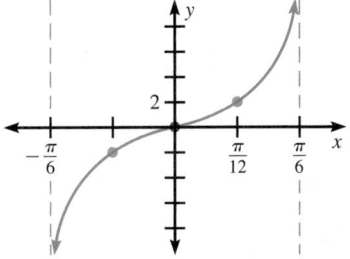

Animated Algebra at my.hrw.com

✓ **GUIDED PRACTICE** for Example 4

Graph one period of the function.

10. $y = 3 \tan x$ **11.** $y = \tan 2x$ **12.** $f(x) = 2 \tan 4x$ **13.** $g(x) = 5 \tan \pi x$

10.1 EXERCISES

SKILL PRACTICE

1. VOCABULARY Copy and complete: The graphs of the functions $y = \sin x$ and $y = \cos x$ both have a(n) __?__ of 2π.

2. ★ WRITING *Compare* the domains and ranges of the functions $y = a \sin bx$, $y = a \cos bx$, and $y = a \tan bx$ where a and b are positive constants.

EXAMPLE 1
for Exs. 3–14

ANALYZING FUNCTIONS Identify the amplitude and the period of the graph of the function.

3.

4.

5.
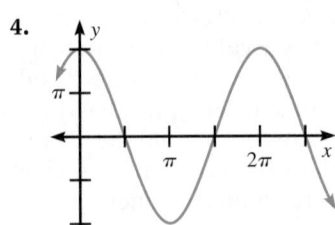
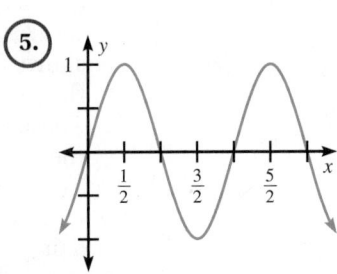

GRAPHING **Graph the function.**

6. $y = \sin \frac{1}{5}x$ **7.** $y = 4 \cos x$ **8.** $f(x) = \cos \frac{2}{5}x$ **9.** $y = \sin \pi x$

10. $f(x) = \frac{2}{3} \sin x$ **11.** $f(x) = \sin \frac{\pi}{2}x$ **12.** $y = \frac{\pi}{4} \cos x$ **13.** $f(x) = \cos 24x$

14. ERROR ANALYSIS *Describe* and correct the error in finding the period of the function $y = \sin \frac{2}{3}x$.

$$\text{Period} = \frac{|b|}{2\pi} = \frac{\left|\frac{2}{3}\right|}{2\pi} = \frac{1}{3\pi} \quad \diagdown$$

15. ★ **MULTIPLE CHOICE** The graph of which function has an amplitude of 4 and a period of 2?

(A) $y = 4 \cos 2x$ **(B)** $y = 2 \sin 4x$ **(C)** $y = 4 \sin \pi x$ **(D)** $y = 2 \cos \frac{1}{2}\pi x$

EXAMPLES
2, 3, and 4
for Exs. 16–24

GRAPHING **Graph the function.**

16. $y = 2 \sin 8x$ **17.** $f(x) = 4 \tan x$ **18.** $y = 3 \cos \pi x$ **19.** $y = 5 \sin 2x$

20. $f(x) = 2 \tan 4x$ **21.** $y = 2 \cos \frac{1}{4}\pi x$ **22.** $f(x) = 4 \tan \pi x$ **23.** $y = \pi \cos 4\pi x$

24. ★ **MULTIPLE CHOICE** Which of the following is an asymptote of the graph of $y = 2 \tan 3x$?

(A) $x = \frac{\pi}{6}$ **(B)** $x = -\pi$ **(C)** $x = \frac{1}{6}$ **(D)** $x = -\frac{\pi}{12}$

25. ★ **OPEN-ENDED MATH** *Describe* a real-life situation that can be modeled by a periodic function.

CHALLENGE **Sketch the graph of the function by plotting points. Then state the function's domain, range, and period.**

26. $y = \csc x$ **27.** $y = \sec x$ **28.** $y = \cot x$

PROBLEM SOLVING

EXAMPLE 3
for Exs. 29–30

29. **PENDULUMS** The motion of a certain pendulum can be modeled by the function $d = 4 \cos \pi t$ where d is the pendulum's horizontal displacement (in inches) relative to its position at rest and t is the time (in seconds). Graph the function. What is the greatest horizontal distance the pendulum will travel from its position at rest?

30. **TUNING FORKS** A tuning fork produces a sound pressure wave that can be modeled by

$$P = 0.001 \sin 880t$$

where P is the pressure (in pascals) and t is the time (in seconds). Find the period and frequency of this function. Then graph the function.

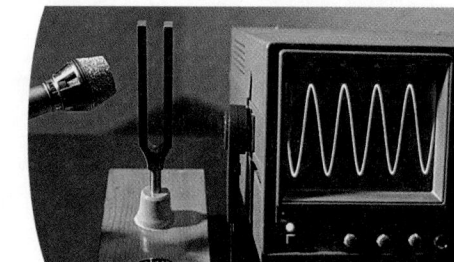

31. ★ **SHORT RESPONSE** A buoy oscillates up and down as waves go past. The buoy moves a total of 3.5 feet from its low point to its high point, and then returns to its high point every 6 seconds.

  a. Write an equation that gives the buoy's vertical position y at time t if the buoy is at its highest point when $t = 0$.

  b. *Explain* why you chose $y = a \sin bt$ or $y = a \cos bt$ for part (a).

32. ◆ **MULTIPLE REPRESENTATIONS** You are standing on a bridge, 140 feet above the ground. You look down at a car traveling away from the underpass.

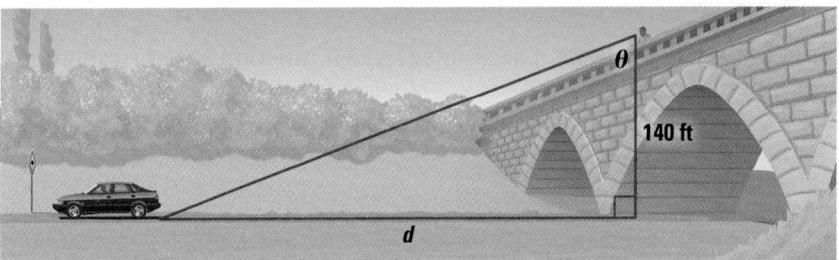

  a. **Writing an Equation** Write an equation that gives the car's distance d from the base of the bridge as a function of the angle θ.

  b. **Drawing a Graph** Graph the function found in part (a). *Explain* how the graph relates to the given situation.

  c. **Making a Table** Make a table of values for the function. Use the table to find the car's distance from the bridge when $\theta = 20°$, $40°$, and $60°$.

33. **CHALLENGE** The motion of a spring can be modeled by $y = A \cos kt$ where y is the spring's vertical displacement (in feet) relative to its position at rest, A is the initial displacement (in feet), k is a constant that measures the elasticity of the spring, and t is the time (in seconds).

  a. Suppose you have a spring whose motion can be modeled by the function $y = 0.2 \cos 6t$. Find the initial displacement and the period of the spring. Then graph the given function.

  b. **Graphing Calculator** If a damping force is applied to the spring, the motion of the spring can be modeled by the function $y = 0.2e^{-4.5t} \cos 4t$. Graph this function. What effect does damping have on the motion?

See **EXTRA PRACTICE** in Student Resources   ⟋ **ONLINE QUIZ** at my.hrw.com

10.2 Translate and Reflect Trigonometric Graphs

Before	You graphed sine, cosine, and tangent functions.
Now	You will translate and reflect trigonometric graphs.
Why?	So you can model predator-prey populations, as in Ex. 54.

Key Vocabulary
- translation
- reflection
- amplitude
- period

CC.9-12.F.TF.5 Choose trigonometric functions to model periodic phenomena with specified amplitude, frequency, and midline.*

KEY CONCEPT *For Your Notebook*

Translations of Sine and Cosine Graphs

To graph $y = a \sin b(x - h) + k$ or $y = a \cos b(x - h) + k$ where $a > 0$ and $b > 0$, follow these steps:

STEP 1 **Identify** the amplitude a, the period $\frac{2\pi}{b}$, the horizontal shift h, and the vertical shift k of the graph.

STEP 2 **Draw** the horizontal line $y = k$, called the *midline* of the graph.

STEP 3 **Find** the five key points by translating the key points of $y = a \sin bx$ or $y = a \cos bx$ horizontally h units and vertically k units.

STEP 4 **Draw** the graph through the five translated key points.

EXAMPLE 1 Graph a vertical translation

Graph $y = 2 \sin 4x + 3$.

Solution

STEP 1 **Identify** the amplitude, period, horizontal shift, and vertical shift.

Amplitude: $a = 2$ Horizontal shift: $h = 0$

Period: $\frac{2\pi}{b} = \frac{2\pi}{4} = \frac{\pi}{2}$ Vertical shift: $k = 3$

STEP 2 **Draw** the midline of the graph, $y = 3$.

FIND KEY POINTS
Because the graph is shifted up 3 units, the y-coordinates of the five key points will be increased by 3.

STEP 3 **Find** the five key points.

On $y = k$: $(0, 0 + 3) = (0, 3)$;

$$\left(\frac{\pi}{4}, 0 + 3\right) = \left(\frac{\pi}{4}, 3\right); \left(\frac{\pi}{2}, 0 + 3\right) = \left(\frac{\pi}{2}, 3\right)$$

Maximum: $\left(\frac{\pi}{8}, 2 + 3\right) = \left(\frac{\pi}{8}, 5\right)$

Minimum: $\left(\frac{3\pi}{8}, -2 + 3\right) = \left(\frac{3\pi}{8}, 1\right)$

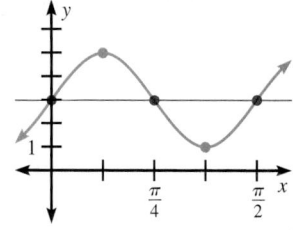

STEP 4 **Draw** the graph through the key points.

(tl), Courtesy of Texas Department of Transportation; (tr), Photo 24/Brand X Pictures/Getty Images

EXAMPLE 2 **Graph a horizontal translation**

Graph $y = 5 \cos 2(x - 3\pi)$.

Solution

STEP 1 **Identify** the amplitude, period, horizontal shift, and vertical shift.

Amplitude: $a = 5$ Horizontal shift: $h = 3\pi$

Period: $\dfrac{2\pi}{b} = \dfrac{2\pi}{2} = \pi$ Vertical shift: $k = 0$

STEP 2 **Draw** the midline of the graph. Because $k = 0$, the midline is the x-axis.

FIND KEY POINTS
Because the graph is shifted to the right 3π units, the x-coordinates of the five key points will be increased by 3π.

STEP 3 **Find** the five key points.

On $y = k$: $\left(\dfrac{\pi}{4} + 3\pi, 0 \right) = \left(\dfrac{13\pi}{4}, 0 \right);$

$\left(\dfrac{3\pi}{4} + 3\pi, 0 \right) = \left(\dfrac{15\pi}{4}, 0 \right)$

Maximums: $(0 + 3\pi, 5) = (3\pi, 5);$
$(\pi + 3\pi, 5) = (4\pi, 5)$

Minimum: $\left(\dfrac{\pi}{2} + 3\pi, -5 \right) = \left(\dfrac{7\pi}{2}, -5 \right)$

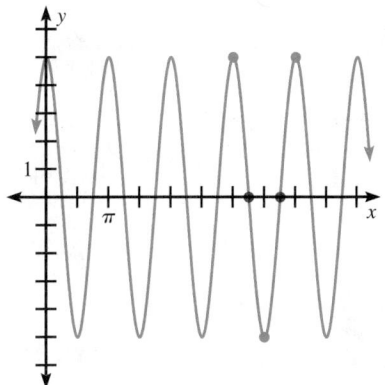

STEP 4 **Draw** the graph through the key points.

EXAMPLE 3 **Graph a model for circular motion**

FERRIS WHEEL Suppose you are riding a Ferris wheel that turns for 180 seconds. Your height h (in feet) above the ground at any time t (in seconds) can be modeled by the equation $h = 85 \sin \dfrac{\pi}{20}(t - 10) + 90$.

a. Graph your height above the ground as a function of time.

b. What are your maximum and minimum heights?

Solution

a. The amplitude is 85 and the period is $\dfrac{2\pi}{\frac{\pi}{20}} = 40$. The wheel turns

$\dfrac{180}{40} = 4.5$ times in 180 seconds, so the graph below shows 4.5 cycles.

The five key points are $(10, 90)$, $(20, 175)$, $(30, 90)$, $(40, 5)$, and $(50, 90)$.

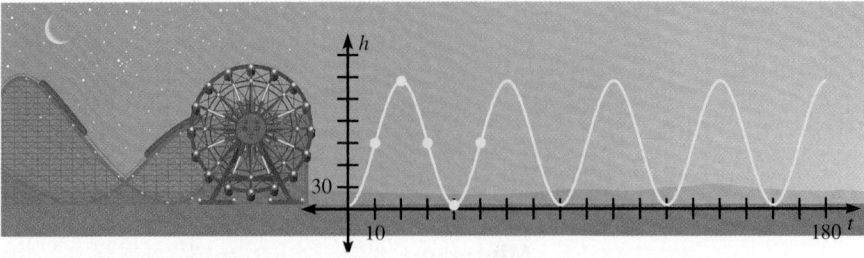

b. Your maximum height is $90 + 85 = 175$ feet and your minimum height is $90 - 85 = 5$ feet.

Graph the function.

1. $y = \cos x + 4$ **2.** $y = 3 \sin\left(x - \dfrac{\pi}{2}\right)$ **3.** $f(x) = \sin(x + \pi) - 1$

REFLECTIONS You have graphed functions of the form $y = a \sin b(x - h) + k$ and $y = a \cos b(x - h) + k$ where $a > 0$. To see what happens when $a < 0$, consider the graphs of $y = -\sin x$ and $y = -\cos x$.

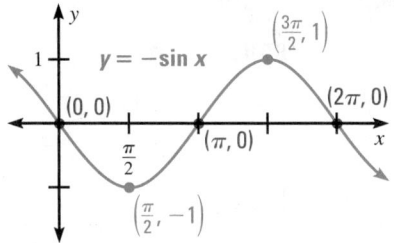 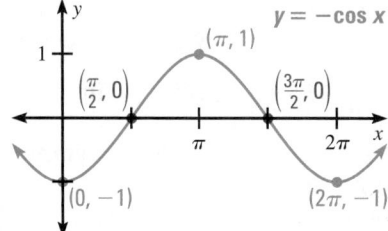

Notice that the graphs are reflections of the graphs of $y = \sin x$ and $y = \cos x$ in the x-axis. In general, when $a < 0$ the graphs of $y = a \sin b(x - h) + k$ and $y = a \cos b(x - h) + k$ are reflections of the graphs of $y = |a| \sin b(x - h) + k$ and $y = |a| \cos b(x - h) + k$, respectively, in the midline $y = k$.

EXAMPLE 4 **Combine a translation and a reflection**

Graph $y = -2 \sin \dfrac{2}{3}\left(x - \dfrac{\pi}{2}\right)$.

Solution

STEP 1 **Identify** the amplitude, period, horizontal shift, and vertical shift.

Amplitude: $|a| = |-2| = 2$ Horizontal shift: $h = \dfrac{\pi}{2}$

Period: $\dfrac{2\pi}{b} = \dfrac{2\pi}{\frac{2}{3}} = 3\pi$ Vertical shift: $k = 0$

STEP 2 **Draw** the midline of the graph. Because $k = 0$, the midline is the x-axis.

STEP 3 **Find** the five key points of $y = |-2| \sin \dfrac{2}{3}\left(x - \dfrac{\pi}{2}\right)$.

On $y = k$: $\left(0 + \dfrac{\pi}{2}, 0\right) = \left(\dfrac{\pi}{2}, 0\right); \left(\dfrac{3\pi}{2} + \dfrac{\pi}{2}, 0\right) = (2\pi, 0); \left(3\pi + \dfrac{\pi}{2}, 0\right) = \left(\dfrac{7\pi}{2}, 0\right)$

Maximum: $\left(\dfrac{3\pi}{4} + \dfrac{\pi}{2}, 2\right) = \left(\dfrac{5\pi}{4}, 2\right)$ **Minimum:** $\left(\dfrac{9\pi}{4} + \dfrac{\pi}{2}, -2\right) = \left(\dfrac{11\pi}{4}, -2\right)$

GRAPH REFLECTIONS
....
The maximum and minimum of the original graph become the minimum and maximum, respectively, of the reflected graph.

STEP 4 **Reflect** the graph. Because $a < 0$, the graph is reflected in the midline $y = 0$. So, $\left(\dfrac{5\pi}{4}, 2\right)$ becomes $\left(\dfrac{5\pi}{4}, -2\right)$ and $\left(\dfrac{11\pi}{4}, -2\right)$ becomes $\left(\dfrac{11\pi}{4}, 2\right)$.

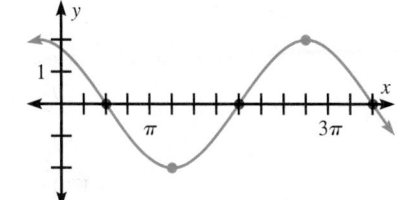

STEP 5 **Draw** the graph through the key points.

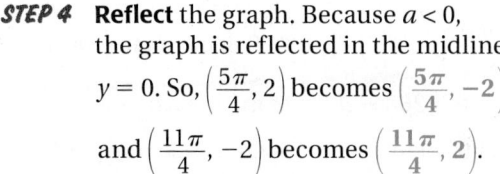 at my.hrw.com

TANGENT FUNCTIONS Graphing tangent functions using translations and reflections is similar to graphing sine and cosine functions.

EXAMPLE 5 **Combine a translation and a reflection**

Graph $y = -3 \tan x + 5$.

Solution

STEP 1 **Identify** the period, horizontal shift, and vertical shift.

Period: π Horizontal shift: $h = 0$ Vertical shift: $k = 5$

STEP 2 **Draw** the midline of the graph, $y = 5$.

STEP 3 **Find** the asymptotes and key points of $y = |-3| \tan x + 5$.

Asymptotes: $x = -\dfrac{\pi}{2 \cdot 1} = -\dfrac{\pi}{2}$; $x = \dfrac{\pi}{2 \cdot 1} = \dfrac{\pi}{2}$

On $y = k$: $(0, 0 + 5) = (0, 5)$

Halfway points: $\left(-\dfrac{\pi}{4}, -3 + 5\right) = \left(-\dfrac{\pi}{4}, 2\right)$; $\left(\dfrac{\pi}{4}, 3 + 5\right) = \left(\dfrac{\pi}{4}, 8\right)$

FIND ASYMPTOTES
Notice that the asymptotes are not shifted. This is because there is no horizontal shift.

STEP 4 **Reflect** the graph. Because $a < 0$, the graph is reflected in the midline $y = 5$. So, $\left(-\dfrac{\pi}{4}, 2\right)$ becomes $\left(-\dfrac{\pi}{4}, 8\right)$ and $\left(\dfrac{\pi}{4}, 8\right)$ becomes $\left(\dfrac{\pi}{4}, 2\right)$.

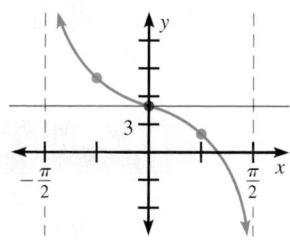

STEP 5 **Draw** the graph through the key points.

EXAMPLE 6 **Model with a tangent function**

GLASS ELEVATOR You are standing 120 feet from the base of a 260 foot building. You watch your friend go down the side of the building in a glass elevator. Write and graph a model that gives your friend's distance d (in feet) from the top of the building as a function of the angle of elevation θ.

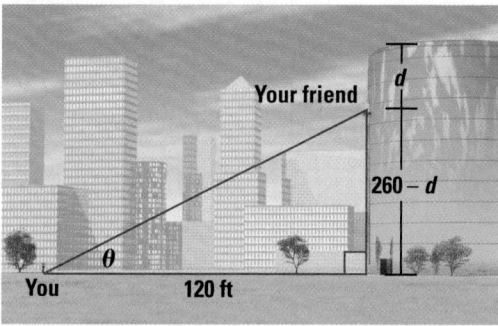

Solution

Use a tangent function to write an equation relating d and θ.

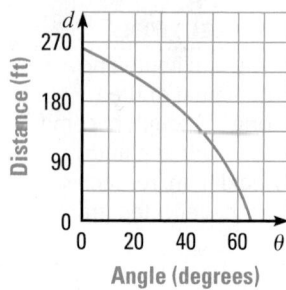

$\tan \theta = \dfrac{\text{opp}}{\text{adj}} = \dfrac{260 - d}{120}$ **Definition of tangent**

$120 \tan \theta = 260 - d$ **Multiply each side by 120.**

$120 \tan \theta - 260 = -d$ **Subtract 260 from each side.**

$-120 \tan \theta + 260 = d$ **Solve for d.**

The graph of $d = -120 \tan \theta + 260$ is shown at the right.

Graph the function.

4. $y = -\cos\left(x + \dfrac{\pi}{2}\right)$ **5.** $y = -3\sin\dfrac{1}{2}x + 2$ **6.** $f(x) = -\tan 2x - 1$

7. WHAT IF? In Example 6, how does the model change if you are standing 150 feet from a building that is 400 feet tall?

10.2 EXERCISES

SKILL PRACTICE

1. **VOCABULARY** Copy and complete: The graph of $y = \cos 2(x - 3)$ is the graph of $y = \cos 2x$ translated __?__ units to the right.

2. ★ **WRITING** *Describe* the difference between the graphs of $y = \tan x$ and $y = -\tan x$. How are the graphs related?

EXAMPLES 1 and 2
for Exs. 3–21

MATCHING Match the function with its graph.

3. $y = \sin 2\left(x + \dfrac{\pi}{2}\right)$ **4.** $f(x) = \cos(x + \pi)$ **5.** $y = \cos x - 2$

6. $y = \sin\left(x + \dfrac{\pi}{4}\right)$ **7.** $y = \cos\dfrac{1}{2}x + 1$ **8.** $f(x) = \sin\dfrac{1}{2}(x - \pi)$

A. 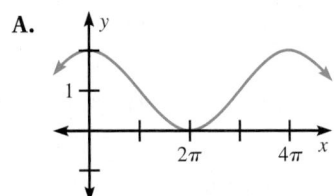   **B.** 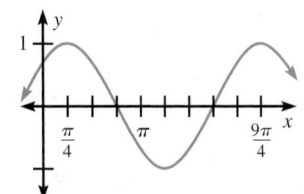   **C.**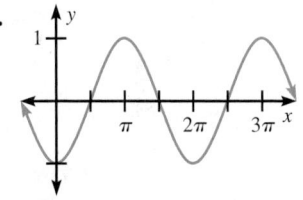

D. 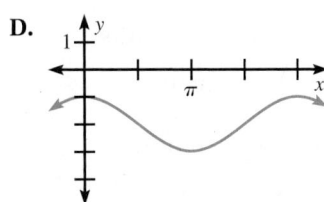   **E.** 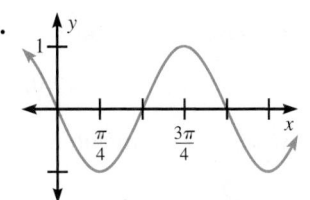   **F.**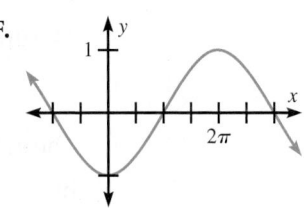

GRAPHING Graph the sine or cosine function.

9. $y = \sin x + 3$ **10.** $y = \cos x - 5$ **11.** $y = 2\cos x + 1$

12. $y = \sin 3x - 4$ **13.** $f(x) = \sin\left(x + \dfrac{\pi}{4}\right)$ **14.** $y = \cos\left(x - \dfrac{\pi}{2}\right)$

15. $y = \cos 2(x + \pi)$ **16.** $f(x) = \dfrac{1}{2}\sin\left(x - \dfrac{3\pi}{2}\right)$ **17.** $y = 4\sin\dfrac{1}{3}\left(x + \dfrac{\pi}{2}\right)$

18. $f(x) = \cos\left(x - \dfrac{\pi}{8}\right) + 2$ **19.** $y = 3\cos\left(x + \dfrac{3\pi}{4}\right) - 1$ **20.** $y = \sin 2(x + 2\pi) - 3$

21. ★ **MULTIPLE CHOICE** The graph of which function is shown?

    Ⓐ $y = \cos \frac{1}{2}x + 3$ Ⓑ $y = \cos x + 3$

    Ⓒ $y = \cos 2x + 3$ Ⓓ $y = \cos (x + \pi) + 3$

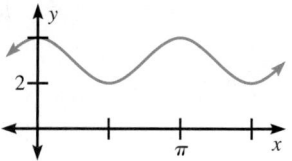

EXAMPLE 4
for Exs. 22–33

GRAPHING Graph the sine or cosine function.

22. $f(x) = -\sin x + 2$ ㉓ $y = -\sin \frac{1}{2}x + 3$ 24. $y = -\cos 2x - 2$

25. $y = -\sin\left(x - \frac{\pi}{4}\right)$ 26. $f(x) = -\sin (x - \pi)$ 27. $y = -2 \cos \frac{1}{4}x$

28. $y = -3 \cos (x - \pi) + 4$ 29. $y = -\cos (x + \pi) + 1$ 30. $f(x) = 1 - 3 \sin (x + \pi)$

31. $y = -\sin\left(x - \frac{3\pi}{2}\right) + 2$ 32. $f(x) = -\cos\left(x + \frac{\pi}{2}\right) - 2$ 33. $y = -4 \cos 2\left(x - \frac{\pi}{4}\right)$

34. **ERROR ANALYSIS** *Describe* and correct the error in determining the maximum point of the function $y = 2 \sin\left(x - \frac{\pi}{2}\right)$.

    Maximum: $\left(\left(\frac{1}{4} \cdot 2\pi\right) - \frac{\pi}{2}, 2\right) = \left(\frac{\pi}{2} - \frac{\pi}{2}, 2\right) = (0, 2)$ ✕

35. ★ **MULTIPLE CHOICE** Which of the following is a maximum point of the graph of $y = -4 \cos\left(x - \frac{\pi}{2}\right)$?

    Ⓐ $\left(-\frac{\pi}{2}, 4\right)$ Ⓑ $(0, 4)$ Ⓒ $\left(\frac{\pi}{2}, 4\right)$ Ⓓ $(\pi, 4)$

EXAMPLE 5
for Exs. 36–41

GRAPHING Graph the tangent function.

36. $y = -\frac{1}{2} \tan x$ 37. $y = \tan 2x - 3$ 38. $y = -\tan 4x + 2$

39. $y = 2 \tan\left(x + \frac{\pi}{2}\right)$ 40. $y = -\tan 2\left(x - \frac{\pi}{2}\right)$ 41. $y = -\frac{1}{2} \tan\left(x - \frac{\pi}{4}\right)$

WRITING EQUATIONS In Exercises 42–46, write an equation of the graph described.

42. The graph of $y = \cos 2\pi x$ translated down 4 units and left 3 units

43. The graph of $y = 3 \sin x$ translated up 2 units and right π units

44. The graph of $y = 5 \tan x$ translated right $\frac{\pi}{4}$ unit and then reflected in the x-axis

45. The graph of $y = \frac{1}{3} \cos \pi x$ translated down 1 unit and then reflected in the line $y = -1$

46. The graph of $y = \frac{1}{2} \sin 6x$ translated down $\frac{3}{2}$ units and right 1 unit, and then reflected in the line $y = -\frac{3}{2}$

47. **REASONING** *Explain* how you can obtain the graph of $y = \cos x$ by translating the graph of $y = \sin x$.

◯ = See **WORKED-OUT SOLUTIONS** in Student Resources   ★ = **STANDARDIZED TEST PRACTICE**

48. ★ SHORT RESPONSE *Explain* why there is more than one tangent function whose graph passes through the origin and has asymptotes at $x = -\pi$ and $x = \pi$.

49. CHALLENGE Find a tangent function whose graph intersects the graph of $y = 2 + 2 \sin x$ only at minimum points of the sine graph.

PROBLEM SOLVING

EXAMPLE 3
for Exs. 50–51

50. WATER WHEEL The Great Laxey wheel, located on the Isle of Man, is one of the largest working water wheels in the world. The wheel was built in 1854 to pump water from the mines underneath it. The height h (in feet) above the viewing platform of a bucket on the wheel can be approximated by the function

$$h = 36.25 \sin \frac{\pi}{12} t + 34.25$$

where t is time (in seconds). Graph the function. Find the diameter of the wheel if the lowest point on the wheel is 2 feet below the viewing platform.

51. AUTOMOTIVE MECHANICS The pistons in an engine force the crank pins to rotate in a circle around the center of the crankshaft. The graph shows the height h (in inches) of a crank pin relative to the axle as a function of time t (in seconds). Write a cosine function for the height of the crank pin.

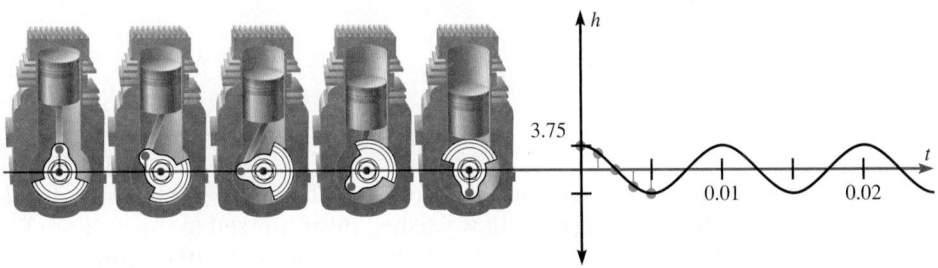

52. BLOOD PRESSURE For a certain person at rest, the blood pressure P (in millimeters of mercury) at time t (in seconds) is given by this function:

$$P = 100 - 20 \cos \frac{8\pi}{3} t$$

Graph the function. If one cycle is equivalent to one heartbeat, what is the person's pulse rate in heartbeats per minute?

EXAMPLE 6
for Ex. 53

53. MULTI-STEP PROBLEM You are standing 300 feet from the base of a 200 foot cliff. Your friend is rappelling down the cliff.

a. Write a model that gives your friend's distance d (in feet) from the top of the cliff as a function of the angle of elevation θ.

b. Graph the function from part (a).

c. Determine the angle of elevation if your friend has rappelled halfway down the cliff.

54. ★ **EXTENDED RESPONSE** In a particular region, the population C of coyotes (the predator) and the population R of rabbits (the prey) can be modeled by

$$C = 9000 + 3000 \sin \frac{\pi}{12}t \quad \text{and} \quad R = 20{,}000 + 8000 \cos \frac{\pi}{12}t$$

where t is the time in months.

   a. Determine the ratio of rabbits to coyotes when $t = 0$, 6, 12, and 18 months.

   b. Graph both functions in the same coordinate plane.

   c. Use the graphs to explain how the changes in the two populations appear to be related.

55. **CHALLENGE** Suppose a Ferris wheel has a radius of 25 feet and operates at a speed of 2 revolutions per minute. The bottom car is 5 feet above the ground. Write a model for a person's height h (in feet) above the ground if the value of h is 44 feet when $t = 0$.

QUIZ

Find the amplitude and the period of the graph of the function.

   1. $y = \cos 4x$

   2. $y = \frac{3}{2} \sin 5x$

   3. $f(x) = \frac{1}{4} \sin x$

   4. $y = \frac{1}{2} \cos 2\pi x$

   5. $y = \sin \pi x$

   6. $g(x) = 3 \cos \frac{\pi}{2}x$

Graph the function.

   7. $y = 4 \sin \pi x$

   8. $y = \frac{1}{2} \cos \frac{3}{2}\pi x$

   9. $g(x) = 2 \tan \frac{1}{4}x$

   10. $f(x) = -2 \sin 3x + 4$

   11. $y = \cos (x + \pi) + 2$

   12. $y = -\tan 2\left(x + \frac{\pi}{2}\right)$

13. **WINDOW WASHERS** You are standing 70 feet from the base of a 250 foot building watching a window washer lower himself to the ground. Write and graph a model that gives the window washer's distance d (in feet) from the top of the building as a function of the angle of elevation θ.

Investigating Trigonometric Identities

MATHEMATICAL
PRACTICES

Use appropriate tools strategically.

MATERIALS · graphing calculator

QUESTION How can you use a graphing calculator to verify trigonometric identities?

EXPLORE Investigate a trigonometric identity

Determine whether the equation $\sin^2 x + \cos^2 x = 1$ is true for *no x-values*, *some x-values*, or *all x-values*.

STEP 1 *Enter equations*	**STEP 2** *Set viewing window*	**STEP 3** *Graph equations*
Enter the left side of the equation as y_1 and the right side as y_2. Use the "thick" graph style for y_2 to distinguish the graphs.	Set your calculator in radian mode. Adjust the viewing window so that the x-axis shows $-2\pi \le x \le 2\pi$ and the y-axis shows $-2 \le y \le 2$.	Graph the equations. The calculator first graphs $y_1 = \sin^2 x + \cos^2 x$ and then $y_2 = 1$ as a thicker line over the graph of y_1.

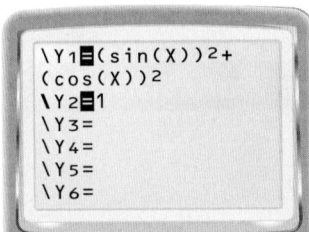

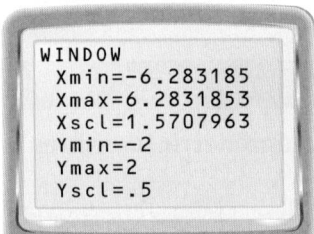

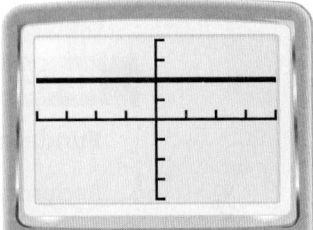

▸ The graphs of each side of the equation $\sin^2 x + \cos^2 x = 1$ are the same. So, the equation is true for all x-values.

DRAW CONCLUSIONS Use your observations to complete these exercises

Use a graphing calculator to determine whether the equation is true for *no x-values*, *some x-values*, or *all x-values*. (Set your calculator in radian mode and use $-2\pi \le x \le 2\pi$ and $-2 \le y \le 2$ for the viewing window.)

1. $\tan x = \dfrac{\sin x}{\cos x}$ 2. $\sin x = -\cos x$ 3. $\tan x = \dfrac{1}{x}$

4. $\cos(-3x) = \cos 3x$ 5. $\cos x = 1.5$ 6. $\sin(x - \pi) = \cos x$

7. $\sin(-x) = -\sin x$ 8. $\cos \dfrac{x}{2} = \dfrac{1}{2}\cos x$ 9. $\cos\left(x - \dfrac{\pi}{2}\right) = \sin x$

10. **REASONING** Trigonometric equations that are true for *all* values of x (in their domain) are called trigonometric identities. Which trigonometric equations in Exercises 1–9 are trigonometric identities?

10.3 Verify Trigonometric Identities

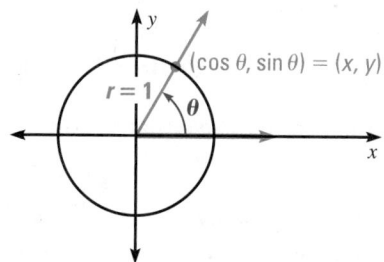

Before	You graphed trigonometric functions.
Now	You will verify trigonometric identities.
Why?	So you can model the path of Halley's comet, as in Ex. 41.

Key Vocabulary
• trigonometric identity

CC.9-12.F.TF.8 Prove the Pythagorean identity $\sin^2(\theta) + \cos^2(\theta) = 1$ and use it to find $\sin(\theta)$, $\cos(\theta)$, or $\tan(\theta)$ given $\sin(\theta)$, $\cos(\theta)$, or $\tan(\theta)$ and the quadrant of the angle.

Recall that if an angle θ is in standard position with its terminal side intersecting the unit circle at (x, y), then $x = \cos \theta$ and $y = \sin \theta$. Because (x, y) is on a circle centered at the origin with radius 1, it follows that:

$$x^2 + y^2 = 1$$
$$\cos^2 \theta + \sin^2 \theta = 1$$

The equation $\cos^2 \theta + \sin^2 \theta = 1$ is true for any value of θ. A trigonometric equation that is true for all values of the variable for which both sides of the equation are defined is called a **trigonometric identity**. Several fundamental trigonometric identities are listed below, some of which you have already learned.

KEY CONCEPT *For Your Notebook*

Fundamental Trigonometric Identities

Reciprocal Identities

$$\csc \theta = \frac{1}{\sin \theta} \qquad \sec \theta = \frac{1}{\cos \theta} \qquad \cot \theta = \frac{1}{\tan \theta}$$

Tangent and Cotangent Identities

$$\tan \theta = \frac{\sin \theta}{\cos \theta} \qquad \cot \theta = \frac{\cos \theta}{\sin \theta}$$

Pythagorean Identities

$$\sin^2 \theta + \cos^2 \theta = 1 \qquad 1 + \tan^2 \theta = \sec^2 \theta \qquad 1 + \cot^2 \theta = \csc^2 \theta$$

Cofunction Identities

$$\sin\left(\frac{\pi}{2} - \theta\right) = \cos \theta \qquad \cos\left(\frac{\pi}{2} - \theta\right) = \sin \theta \qquad \tan\left(\frac{\pi}{2} - \theta\right) = \cot \theta$$

Negative Angle Identities

$$\sin(-\theta) = -\sin \theta \qquad \cos(-\theta) = \cos \theta \qquad \tan(-\theta) = -\tan \theta$$

You can use trigonometric identities to evaluate trigonometric functions, simplify trigonometric expressions, and verify other identities.

EXAMPLE 1 Find trigonometric values

Given that $\sin \theta = \dfrac{4}{5}$ and $\dfrac{\pi}{2} < \theta < \pi$, find the values of the other five trigonometric functions of θ.

Solution

STEP 1 Find $\cos \theta$.

$$\sin^2 \theta + \cos^2 \theta = 1 \qquad \text{Write Pythagorean identity.}$$

$$\left(\frac{4}{5}\right)^2 + \cos^2 \theta = 1 \qquad \text{Substitute } \frac{4}{5} \text{ for } \sin \theta.$$

$$\cos^2 \theta = 1 - \left(\frac{4}{5}\right)^2 \qquad \text{Subtract } \left(\frac{4}{5}\right)^2 \text{ from each side.}$$

$$\cos^2 \theta = \frac{9}{25} \qquad \text{Simplify.}$$

$$\cos \theta = \pm \frac{3}{5} \qquad \text{Take square roots of each side.}$$

REVIEW TRIGONOMETRY
For help with finding the sign of a trigonometric function value, review the lesson *Evaluate Trigonometric Functions of Any Angle.*

$$\cos \theta = -\frac{3}{5} \qquad \text{Because } \theta \text{ is in Quadrant II, } \cos \theta \text{ is negative.}$$

STEP 2 Find the values of the other four trigonometric functions of θ using the known values of $\sin \theta$ and $\cos \theta$.

$$\tan \theta = \frac{\sin \theta}{\cos \theta} = \frac{\frac{4}{5}}{-\frac{3}{5}} = -\frac{4}{3} \qquad \cot \theta = \frac{\cos \theta}{\sin \theta} = \frac{-\frac{3}{5}}{\frac{4}{5}} = -\frac{3}{4}$$

$$\csc \theta = \frac{1}{\sin \theta} = \frac{1}{\frac{4}{5}} = \frac{5}{4} \qquad \sec \theta = \frac{1}{\cos \theta} = \frac{1}{-\frac{3}{5}} = -\frac{5}{3}$$

EXAMPLE 2 Simplify a trigonometric expression

Simplify the expression $\tan\left(\dfrac{\pi}{2} - \theta\right) \sin \theta$.

$$\tan\left(\frac{\pi}{2} - \theta\right) \sin \theta = \cot \theta \sin \theta \qquad \text{Cofunction identity}$$

$$= \left(\frac{\cos \theta}{\sin \theta}\right)(\sin \theta) \qquad \text{Cotangent identity}$$

$$= \cos \theta \qquad \text{Simplify.}$$

EXAMPLE 3 Simplify a trigonometric expression

Simplify the expression $\csc \theta \cot^2 \theta + \dfrac{1}{\sin \theta}$.

$$\csc \theta \cot^2 \theta + \frac{1}{\sin \theta} = \csc \theta \cot^2 \theta + \csc \theta \qquad \text{Reciprocal identity}$$

$$= \csc \theta \left(\csc^2 \theta - 1\right) + \csc \theta \qquad \text{Pythagorean identity}$$

$$= \csc^3 \theta - \csc \theta + \csc \theta \qquad \text{Distributive property}$$

$$= \csc^3 \theta \qquad \text{Simplify.}$$

Find the values of the other five trigonometric functions of θ.

1. $\cos \theta = \dfrac{1}{6}, 0 < \theta < \dfrac{\pi}{2}$

2. $\sin \theta = -\dfrac{3}{7}, \pi < \theta < \dfrac{3\pi}{2}$

Simplify the expression.

3. $\sin x \cot x \sec x$

4. $\dfrac{\tan x \csc x}{\sec x}$

5. $\dfrac{\cos\left(\dfrac{\pi}{2} - \theta\right) - 1}{1 + \sin\left(-\theta\right)}$

VERIFYING IDENTITIES You can use the fundamental identities from this chapter to verify new trigonometric identities. When verifying an identity, begin with the expression on one side. Use algebra and trigonometric properties to manipulate the expression until it is identical to the other side.

EXAMPLE 4 Verify a trigonometric identity

Verify the identity $\dfrac{\sec^2 \theta - 1}{\sec^2 \theta} = \sin^2 \theta.$

$\dfrac{\sec^2 \theta - 1}{\sec^2 \theta} = \dfrac{\sec^2 \theta}{\sec^2 \theta} - \dfrac{1}{\sec^2 \theta}$ **Write as separate fractions.**

$= 1 - \left(\dfrac{1}{\sec \theta}\right)^2$ **Simplify.**

$= 1 - \cos^2 \theta$ **Reciprocal identity**

$= \sin^2 \theta$ **Pythagorean identity**

EXAMPLE 5 Verify a trigonometric identity

Verify the identity $\sec x + \tan x = \dfrac{\cos x}{1 - \sin x}.$

$\sec x + \tan x = \dfrac{1}{\cos x} + \tan x$ **Reciprocal identity**

$= \dfrac{1}{\cos x} + \dfrac{\sin x}{\cos x}$ **Tangent identity**

$= \dfrac{1 + \sin x}{\cos x}$ **Add fractions.**

VERIFY IDENTITIES
To verify the identity, you must introduce $1 - \sin x$ into the denominator. Multiply the numerator and the denominator by $1 - \sin x$ so you get an equivalent expression.

$= \dfrac{1 + \sin x}{\cos x} \cdot \dfrac{1 - \sin x}{1 - \sin x}$ **Multiply by** $\dfrac{1 - \sin x}{1 - \sin x}.$

$= \dfrac{1 - \sin^2 x}{\cos x \left(1 - \sin x\right)}$ **Simplify numerator.**

$= \dfrac{\cos^2 x}{\cos x \left(1 - \sin x\right)}$ **Pythagorean identity**

$= \dfrac{\cos x}{1 - \sin x}$ **Simplify.**

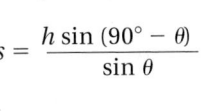 **EXAMPLE 6** Verify a real-life trigonometric identity

SHADOW LENGTH A vertical *gnomon* (the part of a sundial that projects a shadow) has height h. The length s of the shadow cast by the gnomon when the angle of the sun above the horizon is θ can be modeled by the equation below. Show that the equation is equivalent to $s = h \cot \theta$.

$$s = \frac{h \sin (90° - \theta)}{\sin \theta}$$

Solution

Simplify the equation.

$s = \dfrac{h \sin (90° - \theta)}{\sin \theta}$ **Write original equation.**

$= \dfrac{h \sin \left(\frac{\pi}{2} - \theta\right)}{\sin \theta}$ **Convert 90° to radians.**

$= \dfrac{h \cos \theta}{\sin \theta}$ **Cofunction identity**

$= h \cot \theta$ **Cotangent identity**

✓  **GUIDED PRACTICE**   **for Examples 4, 5, and 6**

Verify the identity.

   6. $\cot (-\theta) = -\cot \theta$ **7.** $\csc^2 x\,(1 - \sin^2 x) = \cot^2 x$

   8. $\cos x \csc x \tan x = 1$ **9.** $(\tan^2 x + 1)(\cos^2 x - 1) = -\tan^2 x$

10.3 EXERCISES

HOMEWORK KEY

   ◯ = **See WORKED-OUT SOLUTIONS**
      Exs. 5, 11, and 41

   ★ = **STANDARDIZED TEST PRACTICE**
      Exs. 2, 9, 24, 42, 43, and 44

   ◆ = **MULTIPLE REPRESENTATIONS**
      Ex. 41

SKILL PRACTICE

   1. VOCABULARY What is a trigonometric identity?

   2. ★ WRITING What does the cofunction identity $\sin\left(\frac{\pi}{2} - \theta\right) = \cos \theta$ tell you about the graphs of $y = \sin x$ and $y = \cos x$?

EXAMPLE 1
for Exs. 3–9

FINDING VALUES **Find the values of the other five trigonometric functions of θ.**

   3. $\sin \theta = \dfrac{1}{3}, 0 < \theta < \dfrac{\pi}{2}$ **4.** $\tan \theta = \dfrac{3}{7}, 0 < \theta < \dfrac{\pi}{2}$ **⑤** $\cos \theta = \dfrac{5}{6}, \dfrac{3\pi}{2} < \theta < 2\pi$

   6. $\sin \theta = -\dfrac{7}{10}, \pi < \theta < \dfrac{3\pi}{2}$ **7.** $\cot \theta = -\dfrac{2}{5}, \dfrac{\pi}{2} < \theta < \pi$ **8.** $\sec \theta = -\dfrac{9}{4}, \dfrac{\pi}{2} < \theta < \pi$

9. ★ **MULTIPLE CHOICE** If $\csc \theta = \frac{3}{2}$ and $\frac{\pi}{2} < \theta < \pi$, what is the value of $\tan \theta$?

(A) $-\frac{2\sqrt{5}}{5}$ (B) $-\frac{2\sqrt{13}}{13}$ (C) $\frac{2\sqrt{13}}{13}$ (D) $\frac{2\sqrt{5}}{5}$

EXAMPLES
2 and 3
for Exs. 10–24

SIMPLIFYING EXPRESSIONS Simplify the expression.

10. $\sin x \cot x$

11. $\dfrac{\sin (-\theta)}{\cos (-\theta)}$

12. $\csc \theta \sin \theta + \cot^2 \theta$

13. $\cos \theta (1 + \tan^2 \theta)$

14. $1 + \tan^2 \left(\dfrac{\pi}{2} - x\right)$

15. $\dfrac{\cos \left(\dfrac{\pi}{2} - x\right)}{\csc x}$

16. $\dfrac{\cos \left(\dfrac{\pi}{2} -, \theta\right)}{\csc \theta} + \cos^2 \theta$

17. $\sin \left(\dfrac{\pi}{2} - \theta\right) \sec \theta$

18. $\dfrac{\cos^2 x}{\cot^2 x}$

19. $\dfrac{\sec x \sin x + \cos \left(\dfrac{\pi}{2} - x\right)}{1 + \sec x}$

20. $\dfrac{\csc^2 x - \cot^2 x}{\sin (-x) \cot x}$

21. $\dfrac{\cos^2 x \tan^2 (-x) - 1}{\cos^2 x}$

ERROR ANALYSIS *Describe* and correct the error in simplifying the expression.

22.
$$1 - \sin^2 \theta = 1 - (1 - \cos^2 \theta)$$
$$= 1 - 1 - \cos^2 \theta$$
$$= -\cos^2 \theta$$
✕

23.
$$\tan (-x) \csc x = \frac{\sin x}{\cos x} \cdot \frac{1}{\sin x}$$
$$= \frac{1}{\cos x}$$
$$= \sec x$$
✕

24. ★ **MULTIPLE CHOICE** Which of the following is the simplified form of the expression $\cos \theta \sec \theta$?

(A) $\tan \theta$ (B) 1 (C) 2 (D) $1 - \sin^2 \theta$

EXAMPLES
4 and 5
for Exs. 25–34

VERIFYING IDENTITIES Verify the identity.

25. $\sin x \csc x = 1$

26. $\tan \theta \csc \theta \cos \theta = 1$

27. $\dfrac{\cos \left(\dfrac{\pi}{2} - \theta\right) + 1}{1 - \sin (-\theta)} = 1$

28. $\sin \left(\dfrac{\pi}{2} - x\right) \tan x = \sin x$

29. $\dfrac{\csc^2 \theta - \cot^2 \theta}{1 - \sin^2 \theta} = \sec^2 \theta$

30. $2 - \cos^2 \theta = 1 + \sin^2 \theta$

31. $\sin x + \cos x \cot x = \csc x$

32. $\dfrac{\sin^2 (-x)}{\tan^2 x} = \cos^2 x$

33. $\dfrac{1 + \cos x}{\sin x} + \dfrac{\sin x}{1 + \cos x} = 2 \csc x$

34. $\dfrac{\sin x}{1 - \cos (-x)} = \csc x + \cot x$

35. **ODD AND EVEN FUNCTIONS** A function f is *odd* if $f(-x) = -f(x)$. A function f is *even* if $f(-x) = f(x)$. Which of the six trigonometric functions are odd? Which are even?

VERIFYING IDENTITIES Verify the identity.

36. $\ln |\sec \theta| = -\ln |\cos \theta|$

37. $\ln |\tan \theta| = \ln |\sin \theta| - \ln |\cos \theta|$

38. **CHALLENGE** Use the Pythagorean identity $\sin^2 \theta + \cos^2 \theta = 1$ to derive the other Pythagorean identities, $1 + \tan^2 \theta = \sec^2 \theta$ and $1 + \cot^2 \theta = \csc^2 \theta$.

EXAMPLE 6
....
for Exs. 39–41

39. RATE OF CHANGE In calculus, it can be shown that the rate of change of the function $f(x) = \sec x + \cos x$ is given by this expression:

$$\sec x \tan x - \sin x$$

Show that the expression for the rate of change can be written as $\sin x \tan^2 x$.

40. PHYSICAL SCIENCE Static friction is the amount of force necessary to keep a stationary object on a flat surface from moving. Suppose a book weighing W pounds is lying on a ramp inclined at an angle θ. The coefficient of static friction u for the book can be found using this equation:

$$uW \cos \theta = W \sin \theta$$

   a. Solve the equation for u and simplify the result.

   b. Use the equation from part (a) to determine what happens to the value of u as the angle θ increases from 0° to 90°.

41. ◆ **MULTIPLE REPRESENTATIONS** The path of Halley's comet is an ellipse with the sun as a focus. The equation below gives the comet's distance r from the sun (in astronomical units) as a function of the angle θ (in radians) between the major axis and the comet.

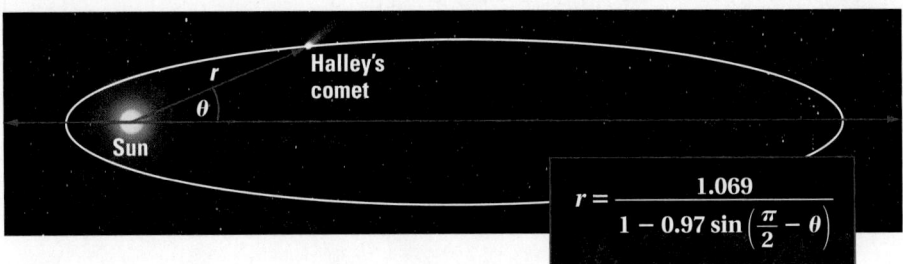

$$r = \frac{1.069}{1 - 0.97 \sin\left(\frac{\pi}{2} - \theta\right)}$$

   a. Writing an Equation Simplify the equation given above.

   b. Drawing a Graph Use a graphing calculator to graph the equation from part (a).

   c. Making a Table Make a table of values for the equation from part (a) in which θ starts at 0 and increases in increments of $\frac{\pi}{4}$. Use the table to approximate the closest and farthest distance, in miles, that Halley's comet is from the sun. (*Note:* 1 astronomical unit ≈ 93 million miles.)

42. ★ **SHORT RESPONSE** Use a reciprocal identity to describe what happens to the value of $\sec \theta$ as the value of $\cos \theta$ increases. On what intervals does this happen?

43. ★ **EXTENDED RESPONSE** Find the intervals on which $\sin \theta$ and $\cos \theta$ are both positive. Then tell whether $\sin \theta$ and $\cos \theta$ are increasing or decreasing on those intervals. Finally, use the tangent identity to describe what happens to the value of $\tan \theta$ on these intervals.

44. ★ **EXTENDED RESPONSE** When light traveling in a medium (such as air) strikes the surface of a second medium (such as water) at an angle θ_1, the light begins to travel at a different angle θ_2. This change of direction is defined by Snell's law, $n_1 \sin \theta_1 = n_2 \sin \theta_2$, where n_1 and n_2 are the *indices of refraction* for the two mediums. Snell's law can be derived from the equation:

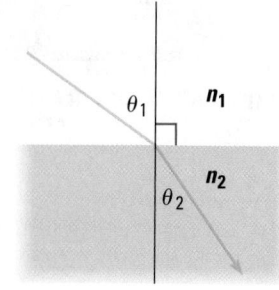

$$\frac{n_1}{\sqrt{\cot^2 \theta_1 + 1}} = \frac{n_2}{\sqrt{\cot^2 \theta_2 + 1}}$$

a. Derive Simplify the equation to derive Snell's law: $n_1 \sin \theta_1 = n_2 \sin \theta_2$.

b. Solve If $\theta_1 = 55°$, $\theta_2 = 35°$, and $n_2 = 2$, what is the value of n_1?

c. Interpret If $\theta_1 = \theta_2$, what must be true about the values of n_1 and n_2? *Explain* when this situation would occur.

45. CHALLENGE Brewster's angle is the angle θ_1, at which light reflected off water is completely polarized, so that glare is minimized when you look at the water with polarized sunglasses. Brewster's angle can be found using Snell's law (see Exercise 44).

a. Let $\sin^2 \theta_2 = \left(\dfrac{n_1}{n_2} \sin \theta_1\right)^2$ and $\cos^2 \theta_2 = \left(\dfrac{n_2}{n_1} \cos \theta_1\right)^2$.

Add the two equations to show that

$$\frac{n_1^{\ 2}}{n_2^{\ 2}} \sin^2 \theta_1 + \frac{n_2^{\ 2}}{n_1^{\ 2}} \cos^2 \theta_1 = 1.$$

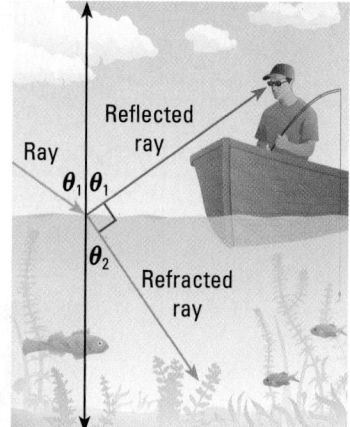

b. Show that the equation from part (a) can be simplified

to $\dfrac{n_2^{\ 2} - n_1^{\ 2}}{n_2^{\ 2}} \sin^2 \theta_1 = \dfrac{n_2^{\ 2} - n_1^{\ 2}}{n_1^{\ 2}} \cos^2 \theta_1$.

c. Solve the equation from part (b) to find Brewster's angle:

$$\theta_1 = \tan^{-1}\left(\frac{n_2}{n_1}\right)$$

10.4 Solve Trigonometric Equations

Before You verified trigonometric identities.

Now You will solve trigonometric equations.

Why? So you can solve surface area problems, as in Ex. 43.

Key Vocabulary
• extraneous solution

You have verified trigonometric identities. In this lesson, you will solve trigonometric equations. To see the difference, consider the following:

$$\sin^2 x + \cos^2 x = 1 \qquad \textbf{Equation 1}$$

$$\sin x = 1 \qquad \textbf{Equation 2}$$

Equation 1 is an identity because it is true for all real values of x. Equation 2, however, is true only for some values of x. When you find these values, you are solving the equation.

EXAMPLE 1 Solve a trigonometric equation

CC.9-12.F.TF.7 (+) Use inverse functions to solve trigonometric equations that arise in modeling contexts; evaluate the solutions using technology, and interpret them in terms of the context.

Solve $2 \sin x - \sqrt{3} = 0$.

Solution

First isolate $\sin x$ on one side of the equation.

$$2 \sin x - \sqrt{3} = 0 \qquad \textbf{Write original equation.}$$

$$2 \sin x = \sqrt{3} \qquad \textbf{Add } \sqrt{3} \textbf{ to each side.}$$

$$\sin x = \frac{\sqrt{3}}{2} \qquad \textbf{Divide each side by 2.}$$

One solution of $\sin x = \frac{\sqrt{3}}{2}$ in the interval $0 \le x < 2\pi$ is $x = \sin^{-1} \frac{\sqrt{3}}{2} = \frac{\pi}{3}$.
The other solution in the interval is $x = \pi - \frac{\pi}{3} = \frac{2\pi}{3}$. Moreover, because $y = \sin x$ is periodic, there will be infinitely many solutions.

You can use the two solutions found above to write the general solution:

WRITE GENERAL SOLUTION
To write the general solution of a trigonometric equation, you can add multiples of the period to all the solutions from one cycle.

$$x = \frac{\pi}{3} + 2n\pi \qquad \text{or} \qquad x = \frac{2\pi}{3} + 2n\pi \qquad \text{(where } n \text{ is any integer)}$$

CHECK You can check the answer by graphing $y = \sin x$ and $y = \frac{\sqrt{3}}{2}$ in the same coordinate plane. Then find the points where the graphs intersect. You can see that there are infinitely many such points.

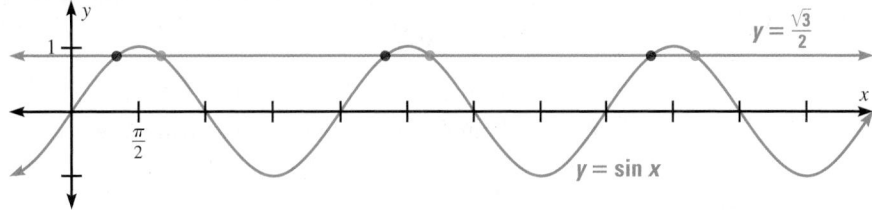

Digital Vision/Getty Images

EXAMPLE 2   Solve a trigonometric equation in an interval

Solve $9 \tan^2 x + 2 = 3$ in the interval $0 \le x < 2\pi$.

$9 \tan^2 x + 2 = 3$ Write original equation.

$9 \tan^2 x = 1$ Subtract 2 from each side.

$\tan^2 x = \dfrac{1}{9}$ Divide each side by 9.

$\tan x = \pm\dfrac{1}{3}$ Take square roots of each side.

REVIEW INVERSE FUNCTIONS

For help with inverse trigonometric functions, review the lesson *Evaluate Inverse Trigonometric Functions*.

Using a calculator, you find that $\tan^{-1} \dfrac{1}{3} \approx 0.322$ and $\tan^{-1}\left(-\dfrac{1}{3}\right) \approx -0.322$. Therefore, the general solution of the equation is:

$x \approx 0.322 + n\pi$ or $x \approx -0.322 + n\pi$ (where n is any integer)

▶ The specific solutions in the interval $0 \le x < 2\pi$ are:

$x \approx 0.322$ $x \approx -0.322 + \pi \approx 2.820$

$x \approx 0.322 + \pi \approx 3.464$ $x \approx -0.322 + 2\pi \approx 5.961$

EXAMPLE 3   Solve a real-life trigonometric equation

OCEANOGRAPHY The water depth d for the Bay of Fundy can be modeled by

$$d = 35 - 28 \cos \frac{\pi}{6.2}t$$

where d is measured in feet and t is the time in hours. If $t = 0$ represents midnight, at what time(s) is the water depth 7 feet?

High tide

Low tide

ANOTHER WAY

For alternative methods for solving the problem in Example 3, see the **Problem Solving Workshop**.

Solution

Substitute 7 for d in the model and solve for t.

$35 - 28 \cos \dfrac{\pi}{6.2}t = 7$ Substitute 7 for d.

$-28 \cos \dfrac{\pi}{6.2}t = -28$ Subtract 35 from each side.

$\cos \dfrac{\pi}{6.2}t = 1$ Divide each side by -28.

$\dfrac{\pi}{6.2}t = 2n\pi$ $\cos \theta = 1$ when $\theta = 2n\pi$.

$t = 12.4n$ Solve for t.

▶ On the interval $0 \le t \le 24$ (representing one full day), the water depth is 7 feet when $t = 12.4(0) = 0$ (that is, at midnight) and when $t = 12.4(1) = 12.4$ (that is, at 12:24 P.M.).

Christopher Mackay/Tantramar Interactive

✔ **GUIDED PRACTICE** for Examples 1, 2, and 3

1. Find the general solution of the equation $2 \sin x + 4 = 5$.

2. Solve the equation $3 \csc^2 x = 4$ in the interval $0 \leq x < 2\pi$.

3. **OCEANOGRAPHY** In Example 3, at what time(s) is the water depth 63 feet?

EXAMPLE 4 **Standardized Test Practice**

What is the general solution of $\sin^3 x - 4 \sin x = 0$?

(A) $x = \dfrac{\pi}{2} + 2n\pi$ or $x = \dfrac{3\pi}{2} + 2n\pi$ (B) $x = \dfrac{\pi}{2} + 2n\pi$ or $x = \pi + 2n\pi$

(C) $x = \pi + 2n\pi$ (D) $x = 2n\pi$ or $x = \pi + 2n\pi$

Solution

$$\sin^3 x - 4 \sin x = 0 \quad \text{Write original equation.}$$

$$\sin x (\sin^2 x - 4) = 0 \quad \text{Factor out sin x.}$$

$$\sin x (\sin x + 2)(\sin x - 2) = 0 \quad \text{Factor difference of squares.}$$

Set each factor equal to 0 and solve for x, if possible.

$\sin x = 0$	$\sin x + 2 = 0$	$\sin x - 2 = 0$
$x = 0$ or $x = \pi$	$\sin x = -2$	$\sin x = 2$

ELIMINATE SOLUTIONS Because sin x is never less than −1 or greater than 1, there are no solutions of sin x = −2 and sin x = 2.

The only solutions in the interval $0 \leq x < 2\pi$ are $x = 0$ and $x = \pi$.

The general solution is $x = 2n\pi$ or $x = \pi + 2n\pi$ where n is any integer.

▸ The correct answer is D. Ⓐ Ⓑ Ⓒ ●

EXAMPLE 5 **Use the quadratic formula**

Solve $\cos^2 x - 5 \cos x + 2 = 0$ in the interval $0 \leq x \leq \pi$.

Solution

Because the equation is in the form $au^2 + bu + c = 0$ where $u = \cos x$, you can use the quadratic formula to solve for $\cos x$.

$$\cos^2 x - 5 \cos x + 2 = 0 \quad \text{Write original equation.}$$

$$\cos x = \dfrac{-(-5) \pm \sqrt{(-5)^2 - 4(1)(2)}}{2(1)} \quad \text{Quadratic formula}$$

$$= \dfrac{5 \pm \sqrt{17}}{2} \quad \text{Simplify.}$$

$$\approx 4.56 \text{ or } 0.44 \quad \text{Use a calculator.}$$

$x = \cos^{-1} 4.56$	$x = \cos^{-1} 0.44$	Use inverse cosine.
No solution	≈ 1.12	Use a calculator, if possible.

▸ In the interval $0 \leq x \leq \pi$, the only solution is $x \approx 1.12$.

EXTRANEOUS SOLUTIONS When solving a trigonometric equation, it is possible to obtain extraneous solutions. So, you should always check your solutions in the original equation.

 EXAMPLE 6 **Solve an equation with an extraneous solution**

Solve $1 + \cos x = \sin x$ in the interval $0 \le x < 2\pi$.

REVIEW
FOIL METHOD
For help multiplying binomials, review the FOIL method in the lesson *Graph Quadratic Functions in Vertex Form.*

$1 + \cos x = \sin x$	Write original equation.
$(1 + \cos x)^2 = (\sin x)^2$	Square both sides.
$1 + 2\cos x + \cos^2 x = \sin^2 x$	Multiply.
$1 + 2\cos x + \cos^2 x = 1 - \cos^2 x$	Pythagorean identity
$2\cos^2 x + 2\cos x = 0$	Quadratic form
$2\cos x (\cos x + 1) = 0$	Factor out $2\cos x$.
$2\cos x = 0$ or $\cos x + 1 = 0$	Zero product property
$\cos x = 0$ or $\cos x = -1$	Solve for cos x.

On the interval $0 \le x < 2\pi$, $\cos x = 0$ has two solutions: $x = \frac{\pi}{2}$ or $x = \frac{3\pi}{2}$.

On the interval $0 \le x < 2\pi$, $\cos x = -1$ has one solution: $x = \pi$.

Therefore, $1 + \cos x = \sin x$ has three possible solutions: $x = \frac{\pi}{2}$, π, and $\frac{3\pi}{2}$.

CHECK To check the solutions, substitute them into the original equation and simplify.

$1 + \cos x = \sin x$	$1 + \cos x = \sin x$	$1 + \cos x = \sin x$
$1 + \cos \frac{\pi}{2} \overset{?}{=} \sin \frac{\pi}{2}$	$1 + \cos \pi \overset{?}{=} \sin \pi$	$1 + \cos \frac{3\pi}{2} \overset{?}{=} \sin \frac{3\pi}{2}$
$1 + 0 \overset{?}{=} 1$	$1 + (-1) \overset{?}{=} 0$	$1 + 0 \overset{?}{=} -1$
$1 = 1 \checkmark$	$0 = 0 \checkmark$	$1 \ne -1$

▶ The apparent solution $x = \frac{3\pi}{2}$ is extraneous because it does not check in the original equation. The only solutions in the interval $0 \le x < 2\pi$ are $x = \frac{\pi}{2}$ and $x = \pi$. Graphs of each side of the original equation confirm the solutions.

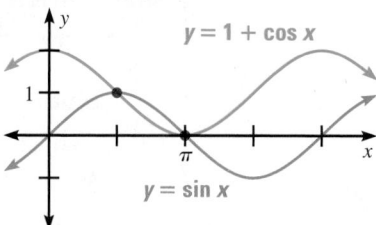

 GUIDED PRACTICE for Examples 4, 5, and 6

Find the general solution of the equation.

4. $\sin^3 x - \sin x = 0$

5. $1 - \cos x = \sqrt{3} \sin x$

Solve the equation in the interval $0 \le x \le \pi$.

6. $2 \sin x = \csc x$

7. $\tan^2 x - \sin x \tan^2 x = 0$

10.4 EXERCISES

HOMEWORK KEY

○ = See WORKED-OUT SOLUTIONS
Exs. 5, 13, and 43

★ = STANDARDIZED TEST PRACTICE
Exs. 2, 15, 36, 42, and 44

◆ = MULTIPLE REPRESENTATIONS
Ex. 43

SKILL PRACTICE

1. **VOCABULARY** What is the difference between a trigonometric equation and a trigonometric identity?

2. ★ **WRITING** *Describe* several techniques for solving trigonometric equations.

EXAMPLE 1
for Exs. 3–15

CHECKING SOLUTIONS Verify that the given *x*-value is a solution of the equation.

3. $2 + 3 \cos x - 5 = 0$, $x = 4\pi$

4. $\pi \sec x + \pi = 0$, $x = \pi$

5. $12 \sin^2 x - 3 = 0$, $x = \dfrac{\pi}{6}$

6. $5 \tan^3 x - 5 = 0$, $x = \dfrac{\pi}{4}$

7. $2 \cos^4 x - \cos^2 x = 0$, $x = \dfrac{\pi}{2}$

8. $3 \cot^4 x - \cot^2 x - 24 = 0$, $x = \dfrac{7\pi}{6}$

GENERAL SOLUTIONS Find the general solution of the equation.

9. $2 \sin x - 1 = 0$

10. $\sqrt{3} \csc x + 2 = 0$

11. $3 \tan x - \sqrt{3} = 0$

12. $\sin x + \sqrt{2} = -\sin x$

13. $4 \cos^2 x - 3 = 0$

14. $3 \tan^2 x - 9 = 0$

15. ★ **MULTIPLE CHOICE** What is the general solution of the equation $4 \sin x = 2 \sin x + 1$?

Ⓐ $x = \dfrac{\pi}{6} + 2n\pi$ or $x = \dfrac{7\pi}{6} + 2n\pi$

Ⓑ $x = \dfrac{\pi}{6} + n\pi$ or $x = \dfrac{5\pi}{6} + n\pi$

Ⓒ $x = \dfrac{\pi}{6} + 2n\pi$ or $x = \dfrac{5\pi}{6} + 2n\pi$

Ⓓ $x = \dfrac{\pi}{6} + n\pi$ or $x = \dfrac{7\pi}{6} + n\pi$

EXAMPLE 2
for Exs. 16–23

SOLVING EQUATIONS Solve the equation in the interval $0 \le x < 2\pi$.

16. $5 + 2 \sin x - 7 = 0$

17. $3 \tan x - \sqrt{3} = 0$

18. $3 \cos x = \cos x - 1$

19. $2 \sin^2 x - 1 = 0$

20. $5 \tan^2 x - 15 = 0$

21. $4 \cos^2 x - 1 = 0$

ERROR ANALYSIS *Describe* and correct the error in solving the equation in the interval $0 \le x \le \dfrac{\pi}{2}$.

22.
$\sin^2 x = \dfrac{1}{2} \sin x$

$\sin x = \dfrac{1}{2}$

$x = \dfrac{\pi}{6}$

23.
$-2 \cos x = -1$

$\cos x = -\dfrac{1}{2}$

$x = \dfrac{2\pi}{3}$

EXAMPLE 4
for Exs. 24–29

GENERAL SOLUTIONS Find the general solution of the equation.

24. $\sin x \cos x - 3 \cos x = 0$

25. $\sqrt{3} \cos x \tan x - \cos x = 0$

26. $2 \sin^3 x = \sin x$

27. $2 \tan^4 x - \tan^2 x - 15 = 0$

28. $\sqrt{\cos x} = 2 \cos x - 1$

29. $1 + \cos x = \sqrt{3} \sin x$

SOLVING Solve the equation in the given interval. Check your solutions.

30. $\sec x \csc^2 x = 2 \sec x; 0 \le x < 2\pi$

31. $\sqrt{3} \cos^2 x = \cos^2 x \tan x; 0 \le x \le \pi$

32. $2 \sin^2 x - \cos x - 1 = 0; 0 \le x < 2\pi$

33. $\sin^2 x + 5 \sin x - 3 = 0; -\frac{\pi}{2} \le x < \frac{\pi}{2}$

34. $\tan^2 x - 3 \tan x + 2 = 0; 0 \le x \le \pi$

35. $\cos x + \sin x \tan x = 2; \pi \le x < 2\pi$

36. ★ **MULTIPLE CHOICE** What are the points of intersection of the graphs of $y = 4 \sin x + 1$ and $y = 2 \sin x + 2$ on the interval $0 \le x < 2\pi$?

Ⓐ $\left(\frac{\pi}{6}, -3\right), \left(\frac{\pi}{2}, -3\right)$

Ⓑ $\left(\frac{\pi}{6}, 3\right), \left(\frac{5\pi}{6}, 3\right)$

Ⓒ $\left(\frac{\pi}{2}, 3\right), \left(\frac{7\pi}{6}, 3\right)$

Ⓓ $\left(\frac{\pi}{6}, 3\right), \left(\frac{11\pi}{6}, 3\right)$

INTERSECTION POINTS Find the points of intersection of the graphs of the given functions in the interval $0 \le x < 2\pi$.

37. $y = \cos^2 x$
$y = 2 \cos x - 1$

38. $y = 9 \sin^2 x$
$y = \sin^2 x + 8 \sin x - 2$

39. $y = \sqrt{3} \tan^2 x$
$y = \sqrt{3} - 2 \tan x$

40. **CHALLENGE** A number c is a *fixed point* of a function f if $f(c) = c$. For example, 0 is a fixed point of $f(x) = \sin x$ because $f(0) = \sin 0 = 0$.

   a. Reasoning Use graphs to explain why the function $g(x) = \cos x$ has only one fixed point.

   b. Graphing Calculator Find the fixed point of $g(x) = \cos x$.

PROBLEM SOLVING

EXAMPLE 3
for Exs. 41–42

41. WIND SPEED The average wind speed s (in miles per hour) in the Boston Harbor can be approximated by $s = 3.38 \sin \frac{\pi}{180}(t + 3) + 11.6$ where t is the time in days, with $t = 0$ representing January 1. On which days of the year is the average wind speed 10 miles per hour?

42. ★ **SHORT RESPONSE** The number of degrees θ north of due east ($\theta > 0$) or south of due east ($\theta < 0$) that the sun rises in Cheyenne, Wyoming, can be modeled by

$$\theta(t) = 31 \sin\left(\frac{2\pi}{365}t - 1.4\right)$$

where t is the time in days, with $t = 1$ representing January 1. Use an algebraic method to find at what day(s) the sun is 20° north of due east at sunrise. *Explain* how you can use the graph of $\theta(t)$ to check your answer.

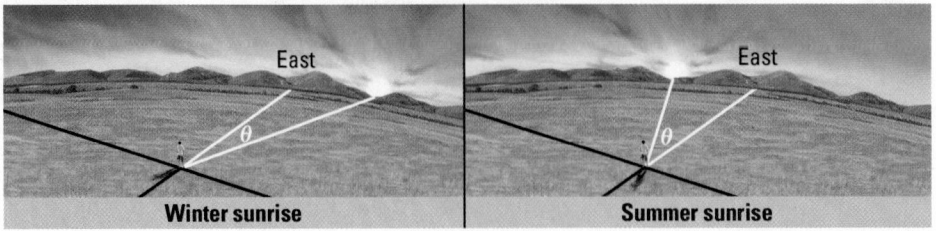

Winter sunrise   Summer sunrise

640

◯ = See WORKED-OUT SOLUTIONS
    in Student Resources

★ = STANDARDIZED
    TEST PRACTICE

◆ = MULTIPLE
    REPRESENTATIONS

43. 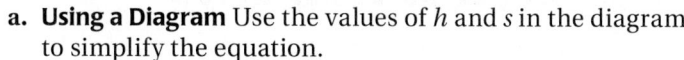 **MULTIPLE REPRESENTATIONS** The surface area *S* of a honeycomb cell can be estimated by the equation shown at the right. In the equation, *h* is the height (in inches), *s* is the width of a side (in inches), and θ is the angle (in degrees) indicated in the diagram.

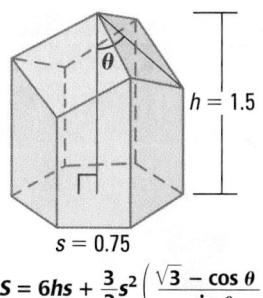

$h = 1.5$

$s = 0.75$

$$S = 6hs + \frac{3}{2}s^2 \left(\frac{\sqrt{3} - \cos\theta}{\sin\theta} \right)$$

a. **Using a Diagram** Use the values of *h* and *s* in the diagram to simplify the equation.

b. **Making a Table** Use a graphing calculator to make a table for the function from part (a). For what value(s) of θ does $S = 9$ square inches?

c. **Drawing a Graph** Use a graphing calculator to graph the function from part (a). What value of θ minimizes the surface area?

44. ★ **EXTENDED RESPONSE** The power *P* (in watts) used by a microwave oven is the product of the voltage *V* (in volts) and the current *I* (in amperes). Suppose the voltage and current can be modeled by

$$V = 170 \cos 120\pi t \quad \text{and} \quad I = 11.3 \cos 120\pi t$$

where *t* is the time (in seconds).

a. **Model** Write the function *P*(*t*) for the power used by the microwave.

b. **Solve** At what times does the microwave use 375 watts of power?

c. **Graphing Calculator** Graph the function *P*(*t*). *Describe* how the graph differs from that of a cosine function of the form $y = a \cos bt$.

45. **CHALLENGE** Matrix multiplication can be used to rotate a point (*x*, *y*) counterclockwise about the origin through an angle θ. The coordinates of the resulting point (*x'*, *y'*) are determined by the matrix equation shown at the right.

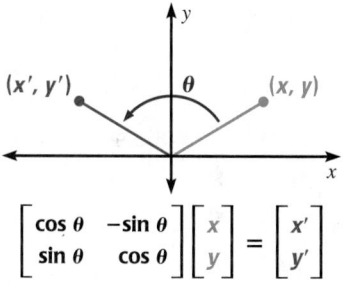

$$\begin{bmatrix} \cos\theta & -\sin\theta \\ \sin\theta & \cos\theta \end{bmatrix} \begin{bmatrix} x \\ y \end{bmatrix} = \begin{bmatrix} x' \\ y' \end{bmatrix}$$

a. The point (2, 3) is rotated counterclockwise about the origin through an angle of $\frac{\pi}{3}$. What are the coordinates of the resulting point?

b. Through what angle θ must the point (6, 2) be rotated to produce $(x', y') = (3\sqrt{3} - 1, \sqrt{3} + 3)$?

Using ALTERNATIVE METHODS

Another Way to Solve Example 3

MATHEMATICAL PRACTICES

Make sense of problems and persevere in solving them.

MULTIPLE REPRESENTATIONS In Example 3, you solved a trigonometric equation algebraically. You can also solve a trigonometric equation using a table or using a graph.

PROBLEM

OCEANOGRAPHY The water depth d for the Bay of Fundy can be modeled by

$$d = 35 - 28 \cos \frac{\pi}{6.2} t$$

where d is measured in feet and t is the time in hours. If $t = 0$ represents midnight, at what time(s) is the water depth 7 feet?

METHOD 1

Using a Table The problem requires solving the equation $35 - 28 \cos \frac{\pi}{6.2} t = 7$.

One way to solve this equation is to make a table of values. You can use a graphing calculator to make the table.

STEP 1 **Enter** the function $y = 35 - 28 \cos \frac{\pi}{6.2} x$
into a graphing calculator. Note that time is now represented by x and water depth is now represented by y.

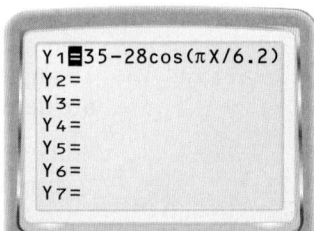

```
Y1▪35-28cos(πX/6.2)
Y2=
Y3=
Y4=
Y5=
Y6=
Y7=
```

STEP 2 **Make** a table of values for the function. Set the table so that the x-values start at 0 and increase in increments of 0.1. (Be sure that the calculator is set in radian mode.)

```
  X    │  Y1
 0     │ 7
 .1    │ 7.0359
 .2    │ 7.1437
 .3    │ 7.3229
 .4    │ 7.5732
X=0
```

STEP 3 **Scroll** through the table to find all the times x at which the water depth y is 7 feet. On the interval $0 \le x \le 24$ (which represents one full day), you can see that the function equals 7 when x is 0 and 12.4.

```
  X    │  Y1
12.1   │ 7.3229
12.2   │ 7.1437
12.3   │ 7.0359
12.4   │ 7
12.5   │ 7.0359
X=12.4
```

▶ The water depth is 7 feet when $x = 0$ (that is, at midnight) and when $x = 12.4$ (that is, at 12:24 P.M.).

METHOD 2

Using a Graph Another approach is to use a graph to solve the equation $35 - 28 \cos \frac{\pi}{6.2} t = 7$. You can use a graphing calculator to make the graph.

STEP 1 **Enter** the functions $y = 35 - 28 \cos \frac{\pi}{6.2}x$ and $y = 7$ into a graphing calculator. Again, note that time is now represented by x and water depth is now represented by y.

STEP 2 **Graph** the functions. Set your calculator in radian mode. Adjust the viewing window so that you can see where the graphs intersect on the interval $0 \le x \le 24$.

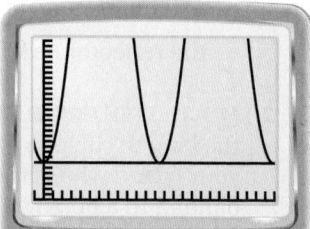

STEP 3 **Find** the intersection points of the two graphs using the *intersect* feature of the graphing calculator. On the interval $0 \le x \le 24$, the graphs intersect at $(0, 7)$ and $(12.4, 7)$. Because x represents the number of hours since midnight, you know that the water depth is 7 feet at midnight and 12:24 P.M.

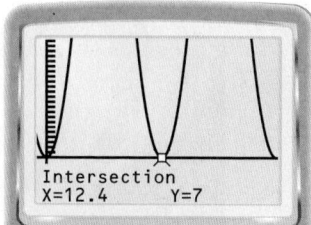

PRACTICE

SOLVING EQUATIONS Solve the equation using a table and using a graph.

1. $20 \sin \frac{\pi}{4}x - 6 = 8$

2. $5 \cos \frac{\pi}{6}x + 6 = 2$

3. $-10 \cos 2\pi x = 3$

4. $3 + 4 \sin \frac{\pi}{2}x = 2$

5. $-15 - 10 \sin \frac{\pi}{20}x = -11$

6. $-34 \cos \frac{\pi}{5}\left(x - \frac{\pi}{10}\right) + 22 = 17$

7. **WHAT IF?** In the problem on the facing page, suppose you want to find the time(s) when the depth of the water in the Bay of Fundy is 15 feet. Find the time(s) using a table and using a graph.

8. **WRITING** *Explain* why the equation $2 \sin x + 3 = 0$ has no solution. How does a graph show this?

9. **BUOY** An ocean buoy bobs up and down as waves travel past it. The buoy's displacement d (in feet) with respect to sea level can be modeled by $d = 3 \sin \pi t$ where t is the time (in seconds). During the one second interval $0 \le t \le 1$, when is the buoy 1.5 feet above sea level? Solve the problem using a table and using a graph.

MIXED REVIEW *of Problem Solving*

MATHEMATICAL PRACTICES Make sense of problems and persevere in solving them.

1. **MULTI-STEP PROBLEM** You put a reflector on a spoke of your bicycle wheel. As you ride your bicycle, the reflector's height h (in inches) above the ground is modeled by

$$h = 13.5 + 11.5 \cos 2\pi t$$

where t is the time (in seconds).

   a. Graph the given function.

   b. What is the frequency of the function? What does the frequency represent in this situation?

   c. At what time(s) on the interval $0 \le t \le \frac{\pi}{2}$ will the reflector be 8 inches above the ground?

2. **MULTI-STEP PROBLEM** You stand 80 feet from the launch site of a hot air balloon. You look at your friend who is traveling straight up in the balloon to a height of 150 feet.

   a. Write and graph an equation that gives your friend's distance d (in feet) above the ground as a function of the angle of elevation θ from you to your friend.

   b. What is the angle of elevation when your friend is at a height of 120 feet?

3. **GRIDDED ANSWER** What is the amplitude of the graph below?

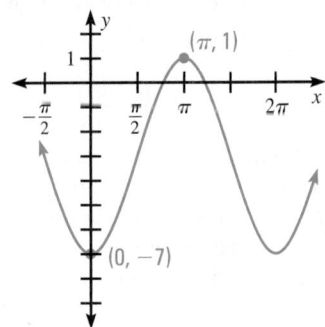

4. **EXTENDED RESPONSE** At an amusement park you watch your friend go on a ride that simulates a free-fall. You are standing 200 feet from the base of the ride as it slowly begins to pull your friend up to the top. The ride is 120 feet tall.

   a. Write an equation that gives the distance d (in feet) your friend is from the top as a function of the angle of elevation θ.

   b. What is the domain of the function?

   c. Graph the function. *Explain* how the graph relates to the given situation.

5. **OPEN-ENDED** Find two different cosine functions that have $(0, 6)$ as a maximum and $(\pi, -4)$ as a minimum.

6. **GRIDDED ANSWER** The number n (in millions) of gallons of ice cream produced in the United States can be approximated by

$$n = 24.5 \sin\left(\frac{\pi}{210}t - 1.09\right) + 113$$

where t is the time (in days) with $t = 1$ representing January 1. What value of t corresponds to the first day that 125 million gallons of ice cream will be produced? Round your answer to the nearest integer.

7. **SHORT RESPONSE** In calculus, it can be shown that the rate of change of the function $f(x) = -\csc x - \sin x$ is given by this expression:

$$\csc x \cot x - \cos x$$

   a. Show that the expression for the rate of change can be written as $\cos x \cot^2 x$.

   b. List the identities used to solve part (a).

10.5 Write Trigonometric Functions and Models

Before You graphed sine and cosine functions.

Now You will model data using sine and cosine functions.

Why? So you can model the number of bicyclists, as in Ex. 26.

Key Vocabulary
• sinusoid

CC.9-12.F.TF.5 Choose trigonometric functions to model periodic phenomena with specified amplitude, frequency, and midline.*

Graphs of sine and cosine functions are called **sinusoids**. One method to write a sine or cosine function that models a sinusoid is to find the values of a, b, h, and k for

$$y = a \sin b(x - h) + k \quad \text{or} \quad y = a \cos b(x - h) + k$$

where $|a|$ is the amplitude, $\frac{2\pi}{b}$ is the period $(b > 0)$, h is the horizontal shift, and k is the vertical shift.

EXAMPLE 1 Solve a multi-step problem

Write a function for the sinusoid shown below.

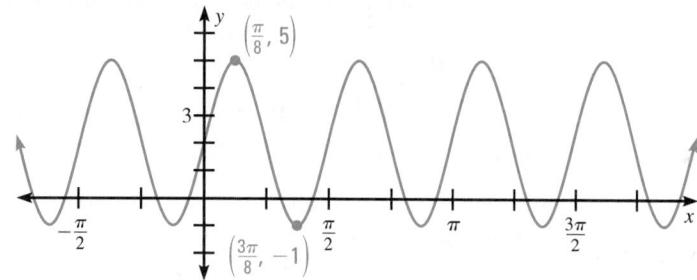

Solution

STEP 1 **Find** the maximum value M and minimum value m. From the graph, $M = 5$ and $m = -1$.

STEP 2 **Identify** the vertical shift, k. The value of k is the mean of the maximum and minimum values. The vertical shift is $k = \dfrac{M + m}{2} = \dfrac{5 + (-1)}{2} = \dfrac{4}{2} = 2$. So, $k = 2$.

STEP 3 **Decide** whether the graph should be modeled by a sine or cosine function. Because the graph crosses the midline $y = 2$ on the y-axis, the graph is a sine curve with no horizontal shift. So, $h = 0$.

FIND PERIOD
Because the graph repeats every $\frac{\pi}{2}$ units, the period is $\frac{\pi}{2}$.

STEP 4 **Find** the amplitude and period. The period is $\dfrac{\pi}{2} = \dfrac{2\pi}{b}$. So, $b = 4$.

The amplitude is $|a| = \dfrac{M - m}{2} = \dfrac{5 - (-1)}{2} = \dfrac{6}{2} = 3$. The graph is not a reflection, so $a > 0$. Therefore, $a = 3$.

▶ The function is $y = 3 \sin 4x + 2$.

EXAMPLE 2 **Model circular motion**

JUMP ROPE At a Double Dutch competition, two people swing jump ropes as shown in the diagram below. The highest point of the middle of each rope is 75 inches above the ground, and the lowest point is 3 inches. The rope makes 2 revolutions per second. Write a model for the height h (in feet) of a rope as a function of the time t (in seconds) if the rope is at its lowest point when $t = 0$.

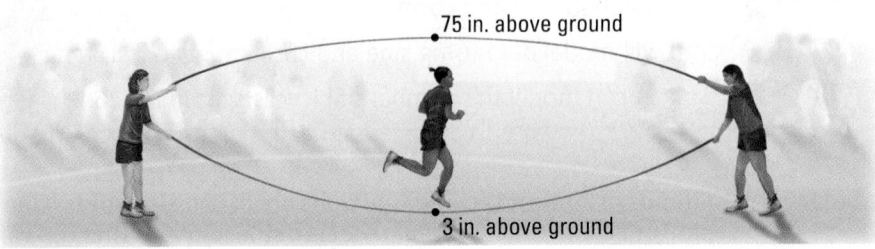

75 in. above ground

3 in. above ground

Solution

STEP 1 **Find** the maximum and minimum values of the function. A rope's maximum height is 75 inches, so $M = 75$. A rope's minimum height is 3 inches, so $m = 3$.

STEP 2 **Identify** the vertical shift. The vertical shift for the model is:

$$k = \frac{M + m}{2} = \frac{75 + 3}{2} = \frac{78}{2} = 39$$

STEP 3 **Decide** whether the height should be modeled by a sine or cosine function. When $t = 0$, the height is at its minimum. So, use a cosine function whose graph is a reflection in the x-axis with no horizontal shift ($h = 0$).

STEP 4 **Find** the amplitude and period.

The amplitude is $|a| = \frac{M - m}{2} = \frac{75 - 3}{2} = 36$.

Because the graph is a reflection, $a < 0$. So, $a = -36$. Because a rope is rotating at a rate of 2 revolutions per second, one revolution is completed in 0.5 second. So, the period is $\frac{2\pi}{b} = 0.5$, and $b = 4\pi$.

▶ A model for the height of a rope is $h = -36 \cos 4\pi t + 39$.

 GUIDED PRACTICE for Examples 1 and 2

Write a function for the sinusoid.

1.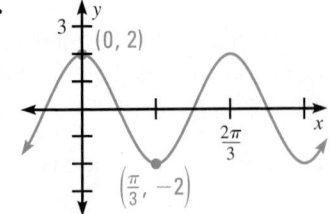

2.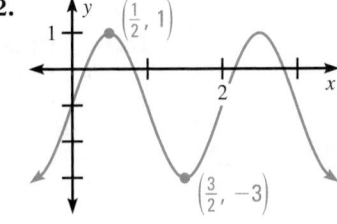

3. **WHAT IF?** *Describe* how the model in Example 2 would change if the lowest point of a rope is 5 inches above the ground and the highest point is 70 inches above the ground.

SINUSOIDAL REGRESSION Another way to model sinusoids is to use a graphing calculator that has a sinusoidal regression feature. The advantage of this method is that it uses all of the data points to find the model.

EXAMPLE 3 Use sinusoidal regression

ENERGY The table below shows the number of kilowatt hours K (in thousands) used each month for a given year by a hangar at the Cape Canaveral Air Station in Florida. The time t is measured in months, with $t = 1$ representing January. Write a trigonometric model that gives K as a function of t.

t	1	2	3	4	5	6	7	8	9	10	11	12
K	61.9	59	62	70.1	81.4	93.1	102.3	106.8	105.4	92.9	81.2	69.9

Solution

STEP 1 **Enter** the data in a graphing calculator.

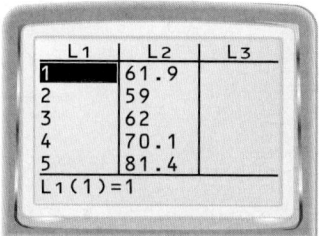

STEP 2 **Make** a scatter plot.

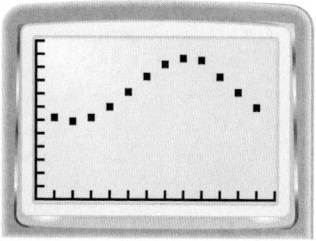

STEP 3 **Perform** a sinusoidal regression, because the scatter plot appears sinusoidal.

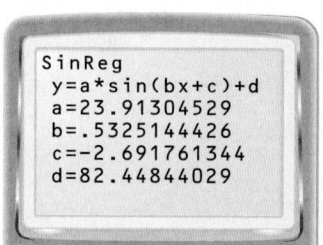

STEP 4 **Graph** the model and the data in the same viewing window.

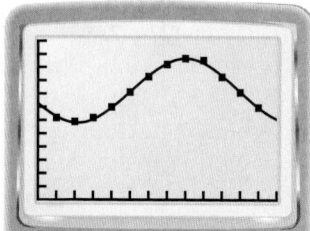

▶ The model appears to be a good fit. So, a model for the data is
$K = 23.9 \sin (0.533t - 2.69) + 82.4$.

✓ **GUIDED PRACTICE** for Example 3

4. **METEOROLOGY** Use a graphing calculator to write a sine model that gives the average daily temperature T (in degrees Fahrenheit) for Boston, Massachusetts, as a function of the time t (in months), where $t = 1$ represents January.

t	1	2	3	4	5	6	7	8	9	10	11	12
T	29	32	39	48	59	68	74	72	65	54	45	35

10.5 EXERCISES

HOMEWORK KEY
◯ = See WORKED-OUT SOLUTIONS
Exs. 5, 9, and 25

★ = STANDARDIZED TEST PRACTICE
Exs. 2, 18, 19, 20, and 28

SKILL PRACTICE

1. **VOCABULARY** What is a sinusoid?

2. ★ **WRITING** *Describe* two methods you can use to model a sinusoid.

EXAMPLE 1
for Exs. 3–19

WRITING FUNCTIONS Write a function for the sinusoid.

3.
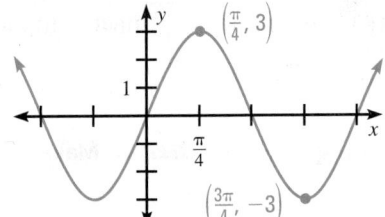

4.
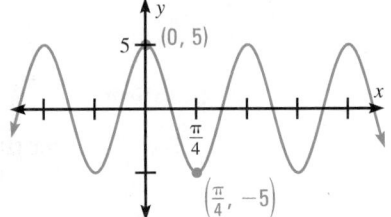

5.
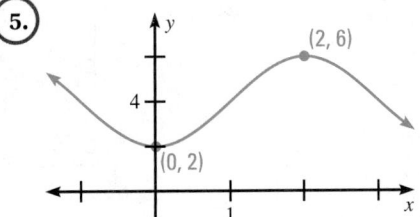

6.
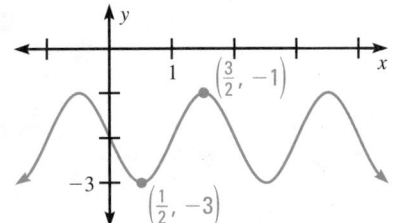

ERROR ANALYSIS *Describe* and correct the error in finding the amplitude and vertical shift for a sinusoid with a maximum point at (2, 10) and a minimum point at (4, −6).

7.
$$|a| = \frac{M - m}{2}$$
$$= \frac{10 - 6}{2}$$
$$= 2$$ ✗

8.
$$k = \frac{M + m}{2}$$
$$= \frac{2 + 4}{2}$$
$$= 3$$ ✗

WRITING FUNCTIONS Write a function for the sinusoid with maximum at point *A* and minimum at point *B*.

9. $A(\pi, 6)$, $B(3\pi, -6)$

10. $A(0, 4)$, $B(\pi, -4)$

11. $A\left(\frac{\pi}{3}, 5\right)$, $B(0, 3)$

12. $A\left(\frac{\pi}{6}, 8\right)$, $B(0, -6)$

13. $A\left(\frac{3\pi}{4}, 9\right)$, $B(2\pi, 5)$

14. $A(0, 5)$, $B(6, -11)$

15. $A(0, 0)$, $B(4\pi, -4)$

16. $A\left(\frac{\pi}{3}, -3\right)$, $B\left(\frac{\pi}{12}, -7\right)$

17. $A\left(\frac{2\pi}{3}, 0\right)$, $B(0, -12)$

18. ★ **MULTIPLE CHOICE** During one cycle, a sinusoid has a minimum at (16, 38) and a maximum at (24, 60). What is the amplitude of this sinusoid?

(A) 8   (B) 11   (C) 22   (D) 49

19. ★ **MULTIPLE CHOICE** What is an equation of the graph shown at the right?

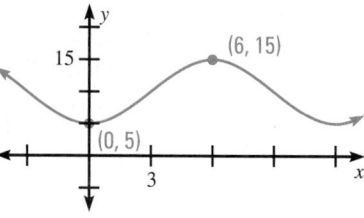

Ⓐ $y = -3 \cos \frac{\pi}{6}x + 12$ **Ⓑ** $y = -5 \cos \frac{\pi}{6}x + 10$

Ⓒ $y = 3 \sin \frac{\pi}{6}x + 12$ **Ⓓ** $y = -5 \sin \frac{\pi}{6}x + 10$

20. ★ **WRITING** Any sinusoid can be modeled by both a sine function and a cosine function. Therefore, you can choose the type of function that is more convenient. *Explain* which type of function you would choose to model a sinusoid whose *y*-intercept occurs at the minimum value of the function.

21. **REASONING** Model the sinusoid in Example 1 in this lesson with a cosine function of the form $y = a \cos b(x - h) + k$. Use identities to show that the model you found is equivalent to the sine model in Example 1.

22. **CHALLENGE** Write a sine function for the sinusoid with a minimum at $\left(\frac{\pi}{2}, 3\right)$ and a maximum at $\left(\frac{\pi}{4}, 8\right)$.

PROBLEM SOLVING

EXAMPLE 1
for Exs. 23–24

23. **CIRCUITS** A circuit has an alternating voltage of 100 volts that peaks every 0.5 second. Use the graph shown at the right to write a sinusoidal model for the voltage *V* as a function of the time *t* (in seconds).

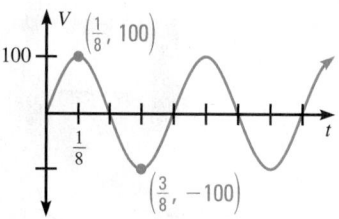

24. **CLIMATOLOGY** The graph below shows the average daily temperature of Houston, Texas. Write a sinusoidal model for the average daily temperature *T* (in degrees Fahrenheit) as a function of time *t* (in months).

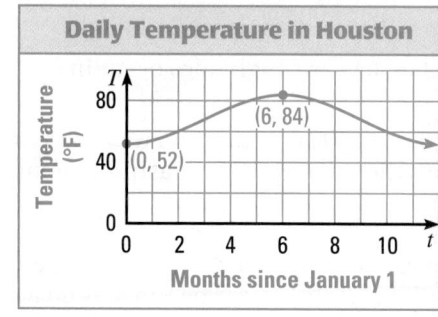

EXAMPLE 2
for Ex. 25

25. **CIRCULAR MOTION** One of the largest sewing machines in the world has a *flywheel* (which turns as the machine sews) that is 5 feet in diameter. Write a model for the height *h* (in feet) of the handle at the edge of the flywheel as a function of the time *t* (in seconds). Assume that the wheel makes a complete turn every 2 seconds and the handle is at its minimum height of 4 feet above the ground when *t* = 0.

10.5 Write Trigonometric Functions and Models **649**

EXAMPLE 3
....
for Exs. 26–27

26. **BICYCLISTS** The table below shows the number of adult residents R (in millions) in the United States who rode a bicycle during the months of October 2001 through September 2002. The time t is measured in months, with $t = 1$ representing October 2001. Use a graphing calculator to write a sinusoidal model that gives R as a function of t.

t	1	2	3	4	5	6	7	8	9	10	11	12
R	35	30	24	24	26	29	35	34	39	43	44	37

27. **MULTI-STEP PROBLEM** The table below shows the number of employees N (in thousands) at a sporting goods company each year for eleven years. The time t is measured in years, with $t = 1$ representing the first year.

t	1	2	3	4	5	6	7	8	9	10	11
N	20.8	22.7	24.6	23.2	20	17.5	16.7	17.8	21	22	24.1

a. **Model** Use a graphing calculator to write a sinusoidal model that gives N as a function of t.

b. **Calculate** Predict the number of employees in the twelfth year.

28. ★ **EXTENDED RESPONSE** The low tide at Eastport, Maine, is 3.5 feet and occurs at midnight. After 6 hours, Eastport is at high tide, which is 16.5 feet.

High tide: 16.5 ft

Low tide: 3.5 ft

a. **Model** Write a sinusoidal model that gives the tide depth d (in feet) as a function of the time t (in hours). Let $t = 0$ represent midnight.

b. **Calculate** Find all the times when low and high tides occur in a 24 hour period.

c. **Reasoning** *Explain* how the graph of the function you wrote in part (a) is related to a graph that shows the tide depth d at Eastport t hours after 3:00 A.M.

29. **CHALLENGE** The table below shows the average monthly sea temperatures T (in degrees Celsius) for Santa Barbara, California. The time t is measured in months, with $t = 1$ representing January.

t	1	2	3	4	5	6	7	8	9	10	11	12
T	14	13.6	13.4	12.5	13.9	15.6	16.8	17.2	17.7	17.1	15.5	14.1

a. Use a graphing calculator to write a sine model that gives T as a function of t.

b. Find a cosine model for the data.

○ = **See WORKED-OUT SOLUTIONS** in Student Resources

★ = **STANDARDIZED TEST PRACTICE**

QUIZ

Simplify the expression.

1. $\sin x \sec x$

2. $\sin \theta (1 + \cot^2 \theta)$

3. $\tan\left(\dfrac{\pi}{2} - \theta\right) \cot \theta - \csc^2 \theta$

4. $\cos^2 \theta + \sin^2 \theta + \tan^2 \theta$

5. $\dfrac{\tan\left(\dfrac{\pi}{2} - x\right) \sec x}{1 - \csc^2 x}$

6. $\dfrac{\sin(-x)}{\csc x} + \dfrac{\cos(-x)}{\sec x}$

Find the general solution of the equation.

7. $\cos x + \cos(-x) = 1$

8. $\sqrt{2} \cos x \sin x - \cos x = 0$

9. $2 \sin^2 x - \sin x = 1$

Write a function for the sinusoid.

10.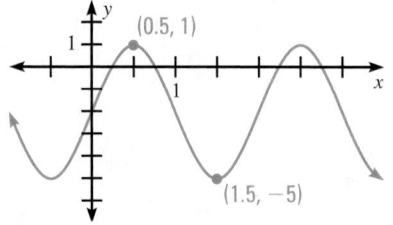

11.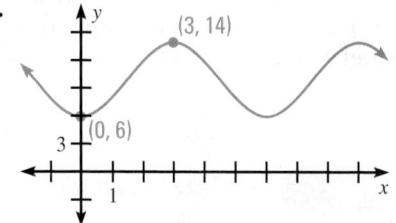

12. DAILY TEMPERATURES The table below shows the average daily temperature D (in degrees Fahrenheit) in Detroit, Michigan. The time t is measured in months, with $t = 1$ representing January. Use a graphing calculator to write a sinusoidal model that gives D as a function of t.

t	1	2	3	4	5	6	7	8	9	10	11	12
D	24.5	27.2	36.9	48.1	59.8	69	73.5	71.8	63.9	51.9	40.7	29.6

CBL ACTIVITY

Use before Write Trigonometric Functions and Models

my.hrw.com
Keystrokes

Collect and Model Trigonometric Data

MATHEMATICAL PRACTICES

Use appropriate tools strategically.

MATERIALS • musical instrument • Calculator Based Laboratory (CBL)
• CBL microphone • graphing calculator

QUESTION How is music related to trigonometry?

Sound is a variation in pressure transmitted through air, water, or other matter. Sound travels as a wave. The sound of a pure note can be represented using a sine (or cosine) wave. More complicated sounds can be modeled by the sum of several sine waves.

EXPLORE Analyze the sound of a musical instrument

Play a note on a musical instrument. Write a sine function to describe the note.

STEP 1 *Play note*

Play a pure note on a musical instrument. Use the CBL and the CBL microphone to collect the sound data and store it in a graphing calculator.

STEP 2 *Graph function*

Use the graphing calculator to graph the pressure of the sound as a function of time.

STEP 3 *Find characteristics of graph*

Use the graph of the sound data to calculate the note's amplitude and frequency (the number of cycles in one second).

STEP 4 *Write function*

Write a sine function for the note.

DRAW CONCLUSIONS Use your observations to complete these exercises

1. Choose a note to play and have a classmate also choose a note. Find two sine functions $y = f(x)$ and $y = g(x)$ that model the two notes. Then play the notes simultaneously and use the CBL and a graphing calculator to graph the resulting sound wave. *Compare* this graph with the graph of $y = f(x) + g(x)$. What do you notice?

2. The pitch of a sound wave is determined by the wave's frequency. The greater the frequency, the higher the pitch. Which of the notes in Exercise 1 had a higher pitch?

3. When you change the volume of a note, what happens to the graph of the sound wave?

4. *Compare* the sine waves for different instruments playing the same note.

RMIP/Richard Haynes/HMH Photo

10.6 Apply Sum and Difference Formulas

Before You found trigonometric functions of a given angle.

Now You will use trigonometric sum and difference formulas.

Why? So you can simplify a ratio used for aerial photography, as in Ex. 43.

Key Vocabulary
• trigonometric identity

CC.9-12.F.TF.9 (+) Prove the addition and subtraction formulas for sine, cosine, and tangent and use them to solve problems.

In this lesson, you will study formulas that allow you to evaluate trigonometric functions of the sum or difference of two angles.

KEY CONCEPT   *For Your Notebook*

Sum and Difference Formulas

Sum Formulas	**Difference Formulas**
$\sin(a + b) = \sin a \cos b + \cos a \sin b$	$\sin(a - b) = \sin a \cos b - \cos a \sin b$
$\cos(a + b) = \cos a \cos b - \sin a \sin b$	$\cos(a - b) = \cos a \cos b + \sin a \sin b$
$\tan(a + b) = \dfrac{\tan a + \tan b}{1 - \tan a \tan b}$	$\tan(a - b) = \dfrac{\tan a - \tan b}{1 + \tan a \tan b}$

In general, $\sin(a + b) \neq \sin a + \sin b$. Similar statements can be made for the other trigonometric functions of sums and differences.

EXAMPLE 1   Evaluate a trigonometric expression

Find the exact value of (a) $\sin 15°$ and (b) $\tan \dfrac{7\pi}{12}$.

a. $\sin 15° = \sin(60° - 45°)$ Substitute $60° - 45°$ for $15°$.

$\qquad = \sin 60° \cos 45° - \cos 60° \sin 45°$ Difference formula for sine

$\qquad = \dfrac{\sqrt{3}}{2}\left(\dfrac{\sqrt{2}}{2}\right) - \dfrac{1}{2}\left(\dfrac{\sqrt{2}}{2}\right)$ Evaluate.

$\qquad = \dfrac{\sqrt{6} - \sqrt{2}}{4}$ Simplify.

b. $\tan \dfrac{7\pi}{12} = \tan\left(\dfrac{\pi}{3} + \dfrac{\pi}{4}\right)$ Substitute $\dfrac{\pi}{3} + \dfrac{\pi}{4}$ for $\dfrac{7\pi}{12}$.

$\qquad = \dfrac{\tan \dfrac{\pi}{3} + \tan \dfrac{\pi}{4}}{1 - \tan \dfrac{\pi}{3} \tan \dfrac{\pi}{4}}$ Sum formula for tangent

$\qquad = \dfrac{\sqrt{3} + 1}{1 - \sqrt{3} \cdot 1}$ Evaluate.

$\qquad = -2 - \sqrt{3}$ Simplify.

Howard Kingsnorth/Getty Images

EXAMPLE 2 **Use a difference formula**

Find $\cos (a - b)$ given that $\cos a = -\frac{4}{5}$ with $\pi < a < \frac{3\pi}{2}$ and $\sin b = \frac{5}{13}$ with $0 < b < \frac{\pi}{2}$.

Solution

Using a Pythagorean identity and quadrant signs gives $\sin a = -\frac{3}{5}$ and $\cos b = \frac{12}{13}$.

$\cos (a - b) = \cos a \cos b + \sin a \sin b$ **Difference formula for cosine**

$\qquad\qquad = -\frac{4}{5}\left(\frac{12}{13}\right) + \left(-\frac{3}{5}\right)\left(\frac{5}{13}\right)$ **Substitute.**

$\qquad\qquad = -\frac{63}{65}$ **Simplify.**

✔ **GUIDED PRACTICE**   for Examples 1 and 2

Find the exact value of the expression.

1. $\sin 105°$ **2.** $\cos 75°$ **3.** $\tan \frac{5\pi}{12}$ **4.** $\cos \frac{\pi}{12}$

5. Find $\sin (a - b)$ given that $\sin a = \frac{8}{17}$ with $0 < a < \frac{\pi}{2}$ and $\cos b = -\frac{24}{25}$ with $\pi < b < \frac{3\pi}{2}$.

EXAMPLE 3 **Simplify an expression**

Simplify the expression $\cos (x + \pi)$.

$\cos (x + \pi) = \cos x \cos \pi - \sin x \sin \pi$ **Sum formula for cosine**

$\qquad\qquad = (\cos x)(-1) - (\sin x)(0)$ **Evaluate.**

$\qquad\qquad = -\cos x$ **Simplify.**

EXAMPLE 4 **Solve a trigonometric equation**

Solve $\sin \left(x + \frac{\pi}{3}\right) + \sin \left(x - \frac{\pi}{3}\right) = 1$ for $0 \leq x < 2\pi$.

ANOTHER WAY

You can also solve by using a graphing calculator. First graph each side of the original equation and then use the *intersect* feature to find the *x*-value(s) where the expressions are equal.

$\sin \left(x + \frac{\pi}{3}\right) + \sin \left(x - \frac{\pi}{3}\right) = 1$ **Write equation.**

$\sin x \cos \frac{\pi}{3} + \cos x \sin \frac{\pi}{3} + \sin x \cos \frac{\pi}{3} - \cos x \sin \frac{\pi}{3} = 1$ **Use formulas.**

$\frac{1}{2} \sin x + \frac{\sqrt{3}}{2} \cos x + \frac{1}{2} \sin x - \frac{\sqrt{3}}{2} \cos x = 1$ **Evaluate.**

$\sin x = 1$ **Simplify.**

▶ In the interval $0 \leq x < 2\pi$, the only solution is $x = \frac{\pi}{2}$.

EXAMPLE 5 **Solve a multi-step problem**

DAYLIGHT HOURS The number h of hours of daylight for Dallas, Texas, and Anchorage, Alaska, can be approximated by the equations below, where t is the time in days and $t = 0$ represents January 1. On which days of the year will the two cities have the same amount of daylight?

Dallas: $h_1 = 2 \sin \left(\dfrac{\pi t}{182} - 1.35 \right) + 12.1$ **Anchorage:** $h_2 = -6 \cos \left(\dfrac{\pi t}{182} \right) + 12.1$

Solution

STEP 1 **Solve** the equation $h_1 = h_2$ for t.

$$2 \sin \left(\dfrac{\pi t}{182} - 1.35 \right) + 12.1 = -6 \cos \left(\dfrac{\pi t}{182} \right) + 12.1$$

$$\sin \left(\dfrac{\pi t}{182} - 1.35 \right) = -3 \cos \left(\dfrac{\pi t}{182} \right)$$

$$\sin \left(\dfrac{\pi t}{182} \right) \mathbf{\cos 1.35} - \cos \left(\dfrac{\pi t}{182} \right) \mathbf{\sin 1.35} = -3 \cos \left(\dfrac{\pi t}{182} \right)$$

$$\sin \left(\dfrac{\pi t}{182} \right) \mathbf{(0.219)} - \cos \left(\dfrac{\pi t}{182} \right) \mathbf{(0.976)} = -3 \cos \left(\dfrac{\pi t}{182} \right)$$

$$0.219 \sin \left(\dfrac{\pi t}{182} \right) = -2.024 \cos \left(\dfrac{\pi t}{182} \right)$$

$$\tan \left(\dfrac{\pi t}{182} \right) = -9.242$$

$$\dfrac{\pi t}{182} = \tan^{-1} (-9.242) + n\pi$$

$$\dfrac{\pi t}{182} \approx -1.463 + n\pi$$

$$t \approx -84.76 + 182n$$

STEP 2 **Find** the days within one year (365 days) for which Dallas and Anchorage will have the same amount of daylight.

$t \approx -84.76 + 182(\mathbf{1}) \approx 97$, or on April 8

$t \approx -84.76 + 182(\mathbf{2}) \approx 279$, or on October 7

✓ **GUIDED PRACTICE**   for Examples 3, 4, and 5

Simplify the expression.

6. $\sin (x + 2\pi)$ **7.** $\cos (x - 2\pi)$ **8.** $\tan (x - \pi)$

9. Solve $6 \cos \left(\dfrac{\pi t}{75} \right) + 5 = -24 \sin \left(\dfrac{\pi t}{75} + 22 \right) + 5$ for $0 \le t < 2\pi$.

10.6 EXERCISES

SKILL PRACTICE

1. **VOCABULARY** Give the sum and difference formulas for sine, cosine, and tangent.

2. ★ **WRITING** *Explain* how you can evaluate tan 75° using either the sum or difference formula for tangent.

EXAMPLE 1
for Exs. 3–10

FINDING VALUES Find the exact value of the expression.

3. $\tan(-15°)$

4. $\sin(-165°)$

5. $\tan 195°$

6. $\cos 15°$

7. $\sin \frac{23\pi}{12}$

8. $\tan \frac{17\pi}{12}$

9. $\cos\left(-\frac{5\pi}{12}\right)$

10. $\sin\left(-\frac{7\pi}{12}\right)$

11. ★ **SHORT RESPONSE** Derive the cofunction identity $\sin\left(\frac{\pi}{2} - \theta\right) = \cos\theta$ using the difference formula for sine.

EXAMPLE 2
for Exs. 12–18

EVALUATING EXPRESSIONS Evaluate the expression given that $\cos a = \frac{4}{5}$ with $0 < a < \frac{\pi}{2}$ and $\sin b = -\frac{15}{17}$ with $\frac{3\pi}{2} < b < 2\pi$.

12. $\sin(a + b)$

13. $\cos(a + b)$

14. $\tan(a + b)$

15. $\sin(a - b)$

16. $\cos(a - b)$

17. $\tan(a - b)$

18. ★ **MULTIPLE CHOICE** What is the value of $\sin(a - b)$ given that $\sin a = -\frac{3}{5}$ with $\pi < a < \frac{3\pi}{2}$ and $\cos b = \frac{12}{13}$ with $0 < b < \frac{\pi}{2}$?

(A) $-\frac{18}{55}$

(B) $-\frac{16}{65}$

(C) $\frac{14}{45}$

(D) $\frac{20}{43}$

EXAMPLE 3
for Exs. 19–31

SIMPLIFYING EXPRESSIONS Simplify the expression.

19. $\tan(x + \pi)$

20. $\sin(x + \pi)$

21. $\cos(x + 2\pi)$

22. $\tan(x - 2\pi)$

23. $\sin\left(x - \frac{3\pi}{2}\right)$

24. $\tan\left(x + \frac{\pi}{2}\right)$

25. $\sin\left(x + \frac{3\pi}{2}\right)$

26. $\cos\left(x - \frac{3\pi}{2}\right)$

27. $\tan\left(x + \frac{3\pi}{2}\right)$

28. $\cos\left(x - \frac{\pi}{2}\right)$

29. $\tan\left(x + \frac{5\pi}{2}\right)$

30. $\cos\left(x + \frac{5\pi}{2}\right)$

31. **ERROR ANALYSIS** *Describe* and correct the error in simplifying the expression.

$$\tan\left(x + \frac{\pi}{4}\right) = \frac{\tan x + \tan \frac{\pi}{4}}{1 + \tan x \tan \frac{\pi}{4}} = \frac{\tan x + 1}{1 + \tan x} = 1 \quad \times$$

EXAMPLE 4
for Exs. 32–38

32. ★ **MULTIPLE CHOICE** What is a solution of the equation $\sin(x - 2\pi) + \tan(x - 2\pi) = 0$ on the interval $\pi < x < 3\pi$?

(A) $\frac{\pi}{2}$

(B) $\frac{3\pi}{2}$

(C) 2π

(D) 3π

SOLVING TRIGONOMETRIC EQUATIONS Solve the equation for $0 \leq x < 2\pi$.

33. $\cos\left(x + \dfrac{\pi}{6}\right) - 1 = \cos\left(x - \dfrac{\pi}{6}\right)$

34. $\sin\left(x + \dfrac{\pi}{4}\right) + \sin\left(x - \dfrac{\pi}{4}\right) = 0$

35. $\sin\left(x + \dfrac{5\pi}{6}\right) + \sin\left(x - \dfrac{5\pi}{6}\right) = 1$

36. $\tan\left(x + \pi\right) + \cos\left(x + \dfrac{\pi}{2}\right) = 0$

37. $\tan\left(x + \pi\right) + 2\sin\left(x + \pi\right) = 0$

38. $\sin\left(x + \pi\right) + \cos\left(x + \pi\right) = 0$

39. CHALLENGE Consider a complex number $z = a + bi$ in the complex plane shown. Let r be the length of the line segment joining z and the origin, and let θ be the angle that this segment makes with the positive real axis, as shown.

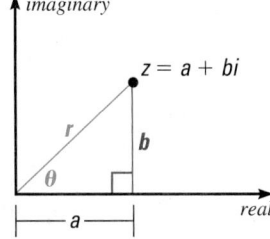

a. *Explain* why $a = r\cos\theta$ and $b = r\sin\theta$, so that $z = (r\cos\theta) + i(r\sin\theta)$.

b. Use the result from part (a) to show the following:
$z^2 = r^2[(\cos\theta\cos\theta - \sin\theta\sin\theta) + i(\sin\theta\cos\theta + \cos\theta\sin\theta)]$

c. Use the sum and difference formulas to show that the equation in part (b) can be written as $z^2 = r^2(\cos 2\theta + i\sin 2\theta)$.

PROBLEM SOLVING

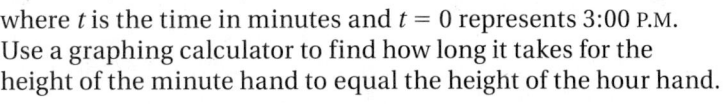

EXAMPLE 5
for Exs. 40–41

40. METEOROLOGY The number h of hours of daylight for Rome, Italy, and Miami, Florida, can be approximated by the equations below, where t is the time in days and $t = 0$ represents January 1.

Rome: $h_1 = 2.7\sin\left(\dfrac{\pi t}{182} - 4.94\right) + 12.1$ **Miami:** $h_2 = -1.6\cos\dfrac{\pi t}{182} + 12.1$

On which days of the year will the cities have the same amount of daylight?

41. CLOCK TOWER The heights m and h (in feet) of a clock tower's minute hand and hour hand, respectively, can be approximated by

$m = 182.5 - 11.5\sin\left(\dfrac{\pi t}{30} - \dfrac{\pi}{2}\right)$ and $h = 182.5 - 7\sin\left(\dfrac{\pi t}{360}\right)$

where t is the time in minutes and $t = 0$ represents 3:00 P.M. Use a graphing calculator to find how long it takes for the height of the minute hand to equal the height of the hour hand.

42. PHYSICAL SCIENCE When a wave travels through a taut string, the displacement y of each point on the string depends on the time t and the point's position x. The equation of a *standing wave* can be obtained by adding the displacements of two waves traveling in opposite directions. Suppose two waves can be modeled by these equations:

$y_1 = A\cos\left(\dfrac{2\pi t}{3} - \dfrac{2\pi x}{5}\right)$ $y_2 = A\cos\left(\dfrac{2\pi t}{3} + \dfrac{2\pi x}{5}\right)$

Show that $y_1 + y_2 = 2A\cos\left(\dfrac{2\pi t}{3}\right)\cos\left(\dfrac{2\pi x}{5}\right)$.

43. **MULTI-STEP PROBLEM** A photographer is at a height h taking aerial photographs. The ratio of the image length WQ to the length NA of the actual object is

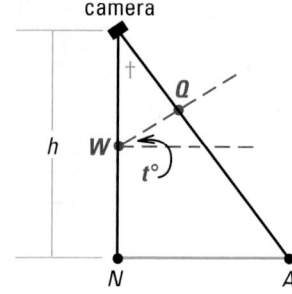
camera

$$\frac{WQ}{NA} = \frac{f \tan(\theta - t) + f \tan t}{h \tan \theta}$$

where f is the focal length of the camera, θ is the angle between the vertical line perpendicular to the ground and the line from the camera to point A, and t is the tilt angle of the film.

a. Use the difference formula for tangent to simplify the ratio.

b. Show that $\dfrac{WQ}{NA} = \dfrac{f}{h}$ when $t = 0$.

44. ★ **EXTENDED RESPONSE** Your friend pulls on a weight attached to a spring and then releases it. A split second later, you begin filming the spring to analyze its motion. You find that the spring's distance y (in inches) from its equilibrium point can be modeled by $y = 5 \sin(2t + C)$ where $C = \tan^{-1} \dfrac{3}{4}$ and t is the elapsed time (in seconds) since you began filming.

a. Find the values of $\sin C$ and $\cos C$.

b. Use a sum formula to show that $y = 5 \sin(2t + C)$ can be written as $y = 4 \sin 2t + 3 \cos 2t$.

c. Graph the function found in part (b) and find its maximum value. *Explain* what this value represents.

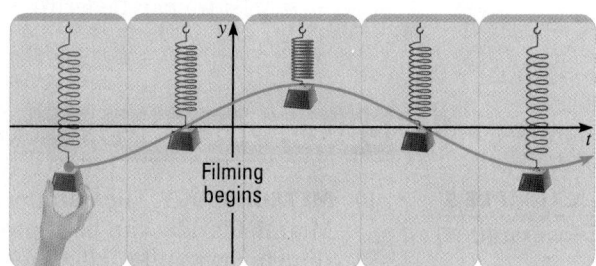
Filming begins

45. **CHALLENGE** The busy signal on a touch-tone phone is a combination of two tones with frequencies of 480 hertz and 620 hertz. The individual tones can be modeled by the following equations:

480 hertz: $y_1 = \cos 960\pi t$ **620 hertz:** $y_2 = \cos 1240\pi t$

The sound of the busy signal can be modeled by $y_1 + y_2$. Show that:

$$y_1 + y_2 = 2 \cos 1100\pi t \cos 140\pi t$$

10.7 Apply Double-Angle and Half-Angle Formulas

Before	You evaluated expressions using sum and difference formulas.
Now	You will use double-angle and half-angle formulas.
Why?	So you can find the distance an object travels, as in Example 4.

Key Vocabulary

- sine
- cosine
- tangent

In this lesson, you will use formulas for double angles (angles of measure $2a$) and half angles $\left(\text{angles of measure } \dfrac{a}{2}\right)$.

CC.9-12.F.TF.9 (+) Prove the addition and subtraction formulas for sine, cosine, and tangent and use them to solve problems.

KEY CONCEPT *For Your Notebook*

Double-Angle and Half-Angle Formulas

Double-Angle Formulas

$$\sin 2a = 2 \sin a \cos a \qquad \cos 2a = 1 - 2\sin^2 a \qquad \tan 2a = \frac{2 \tan a}{1 - \tan^2 a}$$

$$\cos 2a = 2\cos^2 a - 1$$

$$\cos 2a = \cos^2 a - \sin^2 a$$

Half-Angle Formulas

$$\sin \frac{a}{2} = \pm\sqrt{\frac{1 - \cos a}{2}} \qquad \cos \frac{a}{2} = \pm\sqrt{\frac{1 + \cos a}{2}} \qquad \tan \frac{a}{2} = \frac{1 - \cos a}{\sin a}$$

The signs of $\sin \dfrac{a}{2}$ and $\cos \dfrac{a}{2}$ depend on the quadrant in which $\dfrac{a}{2}$ lies.

$$\tan \frac{a}{2} = \frac{\sin a}{1 + \cos a}$$

EXAMPLE 1 | Evaluate trigonometric expressions

Find the exact value of (a) cos 165° and (b) tan $\dfrac{\pi}{12}$.

a. $\cos 165° = \cos \dfrac{1}{2}(330°)$

CHOOSE SIGNS
Because 165° is in Quadrant II and the value of cosine is negative in Quadrant II, the following formula is used:
$$\cos \frac{a}{2} = -\sqrt{\frac{1 + \cos a}{2}}$$

$$= -\sqrt{\frac{1 + \cos 330°}{2}}$$

$$= -\sqrt{\frac{1 + \dfrac{\sqrt{3}}{2}}{2}}$$

$$= -\frac{\sqrt{2 + \sqrt{3}}}{2}$$

b. $\tan \dfrac{\pi}{12} = \tan \dfrac{1}{2}\left(\dfrac{\pi}{6}\right)$

$$= \frac{1 - \cos \dfrac{\pi}{6}}{\sin \dfrac{\pi}{6}}$$

$$= \frac{1 - \dfrac{\sqrt{3}}{2}}{\dfrac{1}{2}}$$

$$= 2 - \sqrt{3}$$

EXAMPLE 2 Evaluate trigonometric expressions

Given $\cos a = \dfrac{5}{13}$ with $\dfrac{3\pi}{2} < a < 2\pi$, find (a) $\sin 2a$ and (b) $\sin \dfrac{a}{2}$.

Solution

MULTIPLY AN INEQUALITY

In part (b), you can multiply through the inequality $\dfrac{3\pi}{2} < a < 2\pi$ by $\dfrac{1}{2}$ to get $\dfrac{3\pi}{4} < \dfrac{a}{2} < \pi$. So, $\dfrac{a}{2}$ is in Quadrant II.

a. Using a Pythagorean identity gives $\sin a = -\dfrac{12}{13}$.

$$\sin 2a = 2 \sin a \cos a = 2\left(-\dfrac{12}{13}\right)\left(\dfrac{5}{13}\right) = -\dfrac{120}{169}$$

b. Because $\dfrac{a}{2}$ is in Quadrant II, $\sin \dfrac{a}{2}$ is positive.

$$\sin \dfrac{a}{2} = \sqrt{\dfrac{1 - \cos a}{2}} = \sqrt{\dfrac{1 - \dfrac{5}{13}}{2}} = \sqrt{\dfrac{4}{13}} = \dfrac{2\sqrt{13}}{13}$$

★ EXAMPLE 3 Standardized Test Practice

Which expression is equivalent to $\dfrac{\sin 2\theta}{1 - \cos 2\theta}$?

Ⓐ $\sin \theta$ Ⓑ $\cot \theta$ Ⓒ $\csc \theta$ Ⓓ $\cos \theta$

Solution

$$\dfrac{\sin 2\theta}{1 - \cos 2\theta} = \dfrac{2 \sin \theta \cos \theta}{1 - (1 - 2\sin^2\theta)} \qquad \text{Use double-angle formulas.}$$

$$= \dfrac{2 \sin \theta \cos \theta}{2 \sin^2\theta} \qquad \text{Simplify denominator.}$$

$$= \dfrac{\cos \theta}{\sin \theta} \qquad \text{Divide out common factor } 2 \sin \theta.$$

$$= \cot \theta \qquad \text{Use cotangent identity.}$$

▸ The correct answer is B. Ⓐ Ⓑ Ⓒ Ⓓ

✓ GUIDED PRACTICE for Examples 1, 2, and 3

Find the exact value of the expression.

1. $\tan \dfrac{\pi}{8}$ **2.** $\sin \dfrac{5\pi}{8}$ **3.** $\cos 15°$

4. Given $\sin a = \dfrac{\sqrt{2}}{2}$ with $0 < a < \dfrac{\pi}{2}$, find $\cos 2a$ and $\tan \dfrac{a}{2}$.

5. Given $\cos a = -\dfrac{3}{5}$ with $\pi < a < \dfrac{3\pi}{2}$, find $\sin 2a$ and $\sin \dfrac{a}{2}$.

Simplify the expression.

6. $\dfrac{\cos 2\theta}{\sin \theta + \cos \theta}$ **7.** $\dfrac{\tan 2x}{\tan x}$ **8.** $\sin 2x \tan \dfrac{x}{2}$

PATH OF A PROJECTILE The path traveled by an object that is projected at an initial height of h_0 feet, an initial speed of v feet per second, and an initial angle θ is given by

$$y = -\frac{16}{v^2 \cos^2 \theta}x^2 + (\tan \theta)x + h_0$$

where x is the horizontal distance (in feet) and y is the vertical distance (in feet). (This model neglects air resistance.)

EXAMPLE 4   **Derive a trigonometric model**

SOCCER Write an equation for the horizontal distance traveled by a soccer ball kicked from ground level ($h_0 = 0$) at speed v and angle θ.

Solution

$-\dfrac{16}{v^2 \cos^2 \theta}x^2 + (\tan \theta)x + 0 = 0$	Let $h_0 = 0$.
$-x\left(\dfrac{16}{v^2 \cos^2 \theta}x - \tan \theta\right) = 0$	Factor.
$\dfrac{16}{v^2 \cos^2 \theta}x - \tan \theta = 0$	Zero product property
$\dfrac{16}{v^2 \cos^2 \theta}x = \tan \theta$	Add $\tan \theta$ to each side.
$x = \dfrac{1}{16}v^2 \cos^2 \theta \tan \theta$	Multiply each side by $\frac{1}{16}v^2 \cos^2 \theta$.
$x = \dfrac{1}{16}v^2 \cos \theta \sin \theta$	Use $\cos \theta \tan \theta = \sin \theta$.
$x = \dfrac{1}{32}v^2 (2 \cos \theta \sin \theta)$	Rewrite $\frac{1}{16}$ as $\frac{1}{32} \cdot 2$.
$x = \dfrac{1}{32}v^2 \sin 2\theta$	Use a double-angle formula.

USE ZERO PRODUCT PROPERTY

One solution of this equation is $x = 0$, which corresponds to the point where the ball leaves the ground. This solution is ignored in later steps, because the problem requires finding where the ball *lands*.

✓   **GUIDED PRACTICE**   **for Example 4**

9. **WHAT IF?** Suppose you kick a soccer ball from ground level with an initial speed of 70 feet per second. Can you make the ball travel 200 feet?

10. **REASONING** Use the equation $x = \frac{1}{32}v^2 \sin 2\theta$ to explain why the projection angle that maximizes the distance a soccer ball travels is $\theta = 45°$.

EXAMPLE 5 Verify a trigonometric identity

Verify the identity $\cos 3x = 4 \cos^3 x - 3 \cos x$.

$$\cos 3x = \cos (2x + x)$$ Rewrite $\cos 3x$ as $\cos (2x + x)$.

$$= \cos 2x \cos x - \sin 2x \sin x$$ Use a sum formula.

$$= (2 \cos^2 x - 1) \cos x - (2 \sin x \cos x) \sin x$$ Use double-angle formulas.

$$= 2 \cos^3 x - \cos x - 2 \sin^2 x \cos x$$ Multiply.

$$= 2 \cos^3 x - \cos x - 2(1 - \cos^2 x) \cos x$$ Use a Pythagorean identity.

$$= 2 \cos^3 x - \cos x - 2 \cos x + 2 \cos^3 x$$ Distributive property

$$= 4 \cos^3 x - 3 \cos x$$ Combine like terms.

EXAMPLE 6 Solve a trigonometric equation

Solve $\sin 2x + 2 \cos x = 0$ for $0 \le x < 2\pi$.

Solution

$$\sin 2x + 2 \cos x = 0$$ Write original equation.

$$2 \sin x \cos x + 2 \cos x = 0$$ Use a double-angle formula.

$$2 \cos x (\sin x + 1) = 0$$ Factor.

Set each factor equal to 0 and solve for x.

$2 \cos x = 0$	$\sin x + 1 = 0$
$\cos x = 0$	$\sin x = -1$
$x = \dfrac{\pi}{2}, \dfrac{3\pi}{2}$	$x = \dfrac{3\pi}{2}$

CHECK Graph the function $y = \sin 2x + 2 \cos x$ on a graphing calculator. Then use the *zero* feature to find the x-values on the interval $0 \le x < 2\pi$ for which $y = 0$. The two x-values are:

$$x = \frac{\pi}{2} \approx 1.57 \quad \text{and} \quad x = \frac{3\pi}{2} \approx 4.71$$

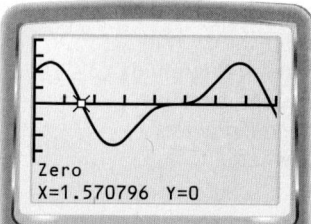

Zero
X=1.570796 Y=0

EXAMPLE 7 Find a general solution

Find the general solution of $2 \sin \frac{x}{2} = 1$.

CHECK SOLUTIONS

You can check the particular solutions in Example 7 by graphing $y = 2 \sin \frac{x}{2} - 1$ on the interval $0 \le x < 4\pi$ (because the period of the function is 4π) and finding the function's zeros on this interval.

$$2 \sin \frac{x}{2} = 1$$ Write original equation.

$$\sin \frac{x}{2} = \frac{1}{2}$$ Divide each side by 2.

$$\frac{x}{2} = \frac{\pi}{6} + 2n\pi \quad \text{or} \quad \frac{5\pi}{6} + 2n\pi$$ General solution for $\frac{x}{2}$

$$x = \frac{\pi}{3} + 4n\pi \quad \text{or} \quad \frac{5\pi}{3} + 4n\pi$$ General solution for x

GUIDED PRACTICE for Examples 5, 6, and 7

Verify the identity.

11. $\sin 3x = 3 \sin x - 4 \sin^3 x$

12. $1 + \cos 10x = 2 \cos^2 5x$

Solve the equation.

13. $\tan 2x + \tan x = 0$ for $0 \le x < 2\pi$

14. $2 \cos \frac{x}{2} + 1 = 0$

10.7 **EXERCISES**

HOMEWORK KEY

◯ = See WORKED-OUT SOLUTIONS
Exs. 7, 13, and 53

★ = STANDARDIZED TEST PRACTICE
Exs. 2, 11, 27, 54, and 55

SKILL PRACTICE

1. VOCABULARY Copy and complete: $\sin 2a = 2 \sin a \cos a$ is called the ___?___ formula for sine.

2. ★ WRITING *Explain* how to determine the sign of the answer when evaluating a half-angle formula for sine or cosine.

EXAMPLE 1
for Exs. 3–11

EVALUATING EXPRESSIONS Find the exact value of the expression.

3. $\sin 105°$

4. $\tan 112.5°$

5. $\tan (-165°)$

6. $\cos (-75°)$

7. $\cos \frac{\pi}{8}$

8. $\sin \frac{5\pi}{12}$

9. $\tan \left(-\frac{5\pi}{8}\right)$

10. $\sin \left(-\frac{11\pi}{12}\right)$

11. ★ MULTIPLE CHOICE What is the exact value of $\tan 15°$?

A $-\sqrt{3}$

B $2 - \sqrt{3}$

C $\sqrt{3}$

D $2 + \sqrt{3}$

EXAMPLE 2
for Exs. 12–20

HALF-ANGLE FORMULAS Find the exact values of $\sin \frac{a}{2}$, $\cos \frac{a}{2}$, and $\tan \frac{a}{2}$.

12. $\cos a = \frac{4}{5}, 0 < a < \frac{\pi}{2}$

13. $\cos a = \frac{1}{3}, \frac{3\pi}{2} < a < 2\pi$

14. $\sin a = \frac{12}{13}, \frac{\pi}{2} < a < \pi$

15. $\sin a = -\frac{3}{5}, \pi < a < \frac{3\pi}{2}$

16. ERROR ANALYSIS *Describe* and correct the error in finding the exact value of $\sin \frac{a}{2}$ given that $\cos a = -\frac{3}{5}$ with $\frac{\pi}{2} < a < \pi$.

$$\sin \frac{a}{2} = -\sqrt{\frac{1 - \cos a}{2}} = -\sqrt{\frac{1 + \frac{3}{5}}{2}} = -\sqrt{\frac{4}{5}} = -\frac{2\sqrt{5}}{5} \quad \times$$

DOUBLE-ANGLE FORMULAS Find the exact values of $\sin 2a$, $\cos 2a$, and $\tan 2a$.

17. $\tan a = 2, \pi < a < \frac{3\pi}{2}$

18. $\tan a = -\sqrt{3}, \frac{\pi}{2} < a < \pi$

19. $\sin a = -\frac{2}{3}, \pi < a < \frac{3\pi}{2}$

20. $\cos a = \frac{2}{5}, -\frac{\pi}{2} < a < 0$

EXAMPLE 3
for Exs. 21–29

SIMPLIFYING EXPRESSIONS Rewrite the expression without double angles or half angles, given that $0 < \theta < \frac{\pi}{2}$. Then simplify the expression.

21. $\dfrac{\cos 2\theta}{1 - 2 \sin^2 \theta}$

22. $\dfrac{\sin 2\theta}{2 \cos \theta}$

23. $(1 - \tan \theta) \tan 2\theta$

24. $\dfrac{\cos 2\theta}{\sin \theta - \cos \theta}$

25. $\dfrac{-\tan \frac{\theta}{2}}{\csc \theta}$

26. $2 \sin \frac{\theta}{2} \cos \frac{\theta}{2}$

27. ★ **MULTIPLE CHOICE** Which expression is equivalent to $\cot \theta + \tan \theta$?

(A) $\csc 2\theta$

(B) $2 \csc 2\theta$

(C) $\sec 2\theta$

(D) $2 \sec 2\theta$

ERROR ANALYSIS *Describe* and correct the error in simplifying the expression.

28.

$$\dfrac{\cos 2x}{\cos^2 x} = \dfrac{\cos^2 x - \sin^2 x}{\cos^2 x}$$

$$= \dfrac{1}{\cos^2 x}$$

$$= \sec^2 x \quad \times$$

29.

$$\sin 22.5° = \sin \frac{1}{2}(45°)$$

$$= 2 \sin 45° \cos 45°$$

$$= 2 \left(\dfrac{\sqrt{2}}{2} \right) \left(\dfrac{\sqrt{2}}{2} \right)$$

$$= 1 \quad \times$$

EXAMPLE 5
for Exs. 30–35

VERIFYING IDENTITIES Verify the identity.

30. $2 \cos^2 \theta = 1 + \cos 2\theta$

31. $\sin 3\theta = \sin \theta (4 \cos^2 \theta - 1)$

32. $\dfrac{1}{2} \sin \frac{2x}{3} = \sin \frac{x}{3} \cos \frac{x}{3}$

33. $2 \sin^2 x \tan \frac{x}{2} = 2 \sin x - \sin 2x$

34. $-\dfrac{\cos 2\theta}{\sin \theta} = 2 \sin \theta - \csc \theta$

35. $\cos 4\theta = \cos^4 \theta - 6 \sin^2 \theta \cos^2 \theta + \sin^4 \theta$

EXAMPLE 6
for Exs. 36–41

SOLVING EQUATIONS Solve the equation for $0 \le x < 2\pi$.

36. $\sin \frac{x}{2} = 1$

37. $2 \cos \frac{x}{2} + 1 = 0$

38. $\tan x - \tan 2x = 0$

39. $\tan \frac{x}{2} = \dfrac{2 - \sqrt{2}}{2 \sin x}$

40. $\cos 2x = -2 \cos^2 x$

41. $2 \sin 2x \sin x = 3 \cos x$

EXAMPLE 7
for Exs. 42–47

FINDING GENERAL SOLUTIONS Find the general solution of the equation.

42. $\cos \frac{x}{2} = 1$

43. $\tan \frac{x}{2} = \sin x$

44. $\sin 2x = \sin x$

45. $\cos 2x + \cos x = 0$

46. $\cos \frac{x}{2} + \sin x = 0$

47. $\sin \frac{x}{2} + \cos x = 0$

48. REASONING Show that the three double-angle formulas for cosine are equivalent.

49. CHALLENGE Use the diagram shown at the right to derive the formulas for $\sin \frac{\theta}{2}$, $\cos \frac{\theta}{2}$, and $\tan \frac{\theta}{2}$ when θ is an acute angle.

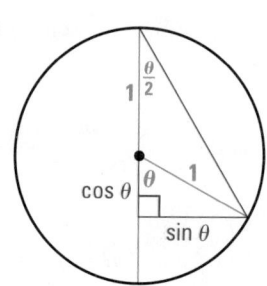

○ = See **WORKED-OUT SOLUTIONS**
    in Student Resources

★ = **STANDARDIZED TEST PRACTICE**

EXAMPLE 4
for Exs. 50–51

50. GOLF Use the equation $x = \frac{1}{32}v^2 \sin 2\theta$ from Example 4 in this lesson to find the horizontal distance a golf ball will travel if it is hit at an initial speed of 50 feet per second and at an initial angle of 40°.

51. SOCCER Suppose you are attempting to kick a soccer ball from ground level. Through what range of angles can you kick the soccer ball with an initial speed of 80 feet per second to make it travel at least 150 feet?

Animated **Algebra** at my.hrw.com

52. MULTI-STEP PROBLEM At latitude L, the acceleration due to gravity g (in centimeters per second squared) at sea level can be approximated by:

$$g = 978 + 5.17 \sin^2 L - 0.014 \sin L \cos L$$

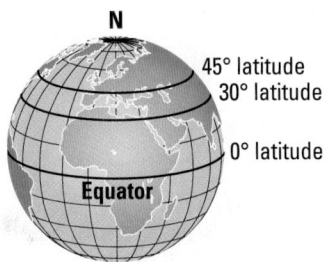

a. Simplify the equation above to show that $g = 978 + 5.17 \sin^2 L - 0.007 \sin 2L$.

b. Graph the function from part (a).

c. Use the graph to approximate the acceleration due to gravity when the latitude is 45°, 30°, and 0°.

53. MACH NUMBER An airplane's Mach number M is the ratio of its speed to the speed of sound. When an airplane travels faster than the speed of sound, the sound waves form a cone behind the airplane. The Mach number is related to the apex angle θ of the cone by the equation $\sin \frac{\theta}{2} = \frac{1}{M}$. Find the angle θ that corresponds to a Mach number of 2.5.

54. ★ SHORT RESPONSE A *Mercator projection* is a map projection of the globe onto a plane that preserves angles. On a globe with radius r, consider a point P that has latitude L and longitude T. The coordinates (x, y) of the corresponding point P' on the plane can be found using these equations:

$$x = rT \qquad y = r \ln\left[\tan\left(\frac{\frac{\pi}{2} + L}{2}\right)\right]$$

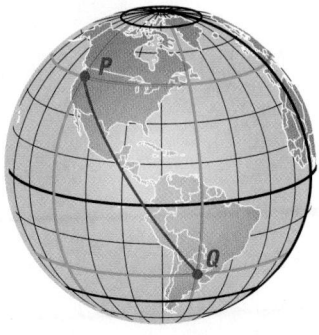 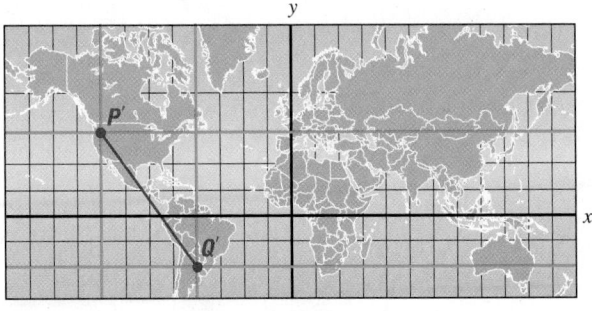

a. Use half-angle and sum formulas to show that the equation for the y-coordinate can be written as $y = r \ln\left(\frac{1 + \sin L}{\cos L}\right)$.

b. What is a reasonable domain for the equation in part (a)? *Explain.*

55. ★ **EXTENDED RESPONSE** At a basketball game, a person has a chance to win 1 million dollars by making a half court shot. The distance from half court to the point below the 10-foot-high basketball rim is 41.75 feet.

    a. Write an equation that models the path of the basketball if the person releases the ball 6 feet high with an initial speed of 40 feet per second.

    b. Simplify the equation. Use a calculator to find the angles at which the person can make the half court shot.

    c. Assume the person releases the ball at one of the angles found in part (b). What other assumption(s) must you make to say that the shot is made?

56. **CHALLENGE** A rectangle is inscribed in a semicircle with radius 1, as shown. What value of θ creates the rectangle with the largest area?

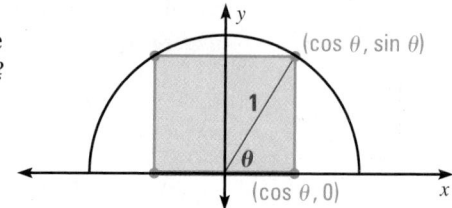

QUIZ

Find the exact value of the expression.

    1. $\sin \dfrac{\pi}{12}$
    2. $\sin(-22.5°)$
    3. $\tan(-345°)$
    4. $\cos \dfrac{\pi}{8}$

Solve the equation for $0 \le x < 2\pi$.

    5. $\sin\left(x + \dfrac{\pi}{2}\right) - \sin\left(x - \dfrac{\pi}{2}\right) = 0$
    6. $\cos 2x = 3 \sin x + 2$

Find the exact values of $\sin \dfrac{a}{2}$, $\cos \dfrac{a}{2}$, and $\tan 2a$.

    7. $\tan a = \dfrac{3}{5}$, $0 < a < \dfrac{\pi}{2}$
    8. $\cos a = -\dfrac{4}{7}$, $\pi < a < \dfrac{3\pi}{2}$

    9. **FOOTBALL** Use the formula $x = \dfrac{1}{32} v^2 \sin 2\theta$ to find the horizontal distance x (in feet) that a football travels if it is kicked from ground level with an initial speed of 25 feet per second at an angle of 30°.

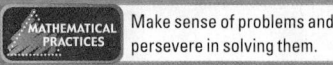
1. **MULTI-STEP PROBLEM** Suppose two middle-A tuning forks are struck at different times so that their vibrations are slightly out of phase. The combined pressure change P (in pascals) caused by the tuning forks at time t (in seconds) is given by:

$$P = 3 \sin 880\pi t + 4 \cos 880\pi t$$

   a. Graph the equation on a graphing calculator. Use a viewing window of $0 \le t \le 0.005$ and $-6 \le P \le 6$. What do you observe about the graph?

   b. Write the given model in the form $y = a \cos b(x - h)$.

   c. Graph the model from part (b) to confirm that the graphs are the same.

2. **OPEN-ENDED** Recall that a special angle is one that is a multiple of 30° or 45°. Find an angle that is not a special angle but that can be written as the sum or difference of two special angles. Then use a sum or difference formula to find the cosine of the angle.

3. **SHORT RESPONSE** The formula for the index of refraction n of a transparent material is the ratio of the speed of light in a vacuum to the speed of light in the material. Some common materials and their indices are air (1.00), water (1.33), and glass (1.5). Triangular prisms are often used to measure the index of refraction based on the formula shown below.

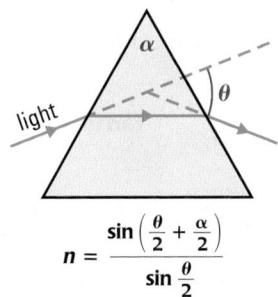

$$n = \frac{\sin\left(\frac{\theta}{2} + \frac{\alpha}{2}\right)}{\sin\frac{\theta}{2}}$$

   a. Show that the index of refraction can be simplified as shown:

   $$n = \cos\frac{\alpha}{2} + \sin\frac{\alpha}{2} \cot\frac{\theta}{2}$$

   b. Use a graphing calculator to find the value of θ when $\alpha = 60°$ and the prism is made of glass.

4. **GRIDDED ANSWER** In the figure shown below, the acute angle of intersection, $\theta_2 - \theta_1$, of two lines with slopes m_1 and m_2 is given by this equation:

$$\tan(\theta_2 - \theta_1) = \frac{m_2 - m_1}{1 + m_1 m_2}$$

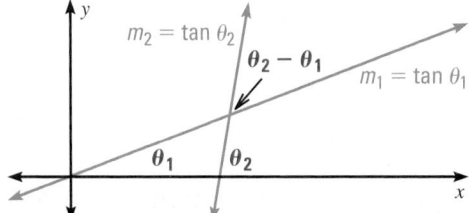

Find the acute angle of intersection of the lines $y = \frac{1}{2}x$ and $y = 2x - 4$. Round your answer to the nearest tenth of a degree.

5. **EXTENDED RESPONSE** The graph below shows the average daily temperature T (in degrees Fahrenheit) in Denver, Colorado. The time t is measured in months, with $t = 0$ representing January 1.

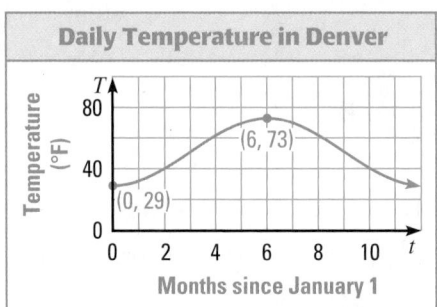

Daily Temperature in Denver

   a. Tell whether the graph should be modeled by a sine or cosine function. *Explain* your reasoning.

   b. Write a trigonometric model for the average daily temperature in Denver, Colorado.

   c. On which days of the year is the average daily temperature in Denver, Colorado, 70°F?

Mixed Review of Problem Solving   **667**

BIG IDEAS   *For Your Notebook*

Big Idea 1

Graphing Trigonometric Functions

The graphs of $y = a \sin bx$ and $y = a \cos bx$ are shown below for $a > 0$ and $b > 0$.

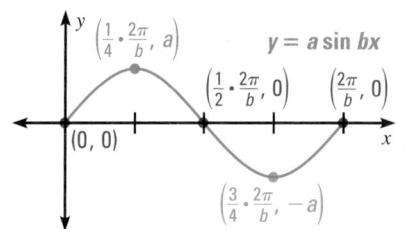 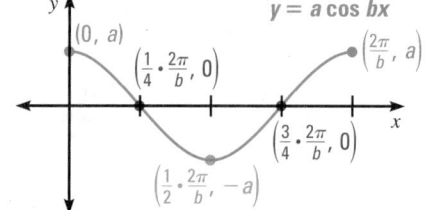

To graph a function of the form $y = a \sin b(x - h) + k$ or $y = a \cos b(x - h) + k$, shift the graph of $y = a \sin bx$ or $y = a \cos bx$, respectively, horizontally h units and vertically k units. Then, if $a < 0$, reflect the graph in the midline $y = k$.

Big Idea 2

Solving Trigonometric Equations

The table below shows strategies that may help you solve trigonometric equations. Only the first few steps are shown.

Factor	Use the quadratic formula	Use an identity
$x \sin^2 x - x = 0$	$\cos^2 x - 6 \cos x + 1 = 0$	$\cos^2 x - 1 = 9 \sin^2 x$
$x(\sin^2 x - 1) = 0$	$\cos x = \dfrac{6 \pm \sqrt{36 - 4(1)(1)}}{2(1)}$	$\cos^2 x - 1 = 9(1 - \cos^2 x)$
$x(\sin x + 1)(\sin x - 1) = 0$	$\cos x = 3 \pm 2\sqrt{2}$	$10 \cos^2 x = 10$
		$\cos^2 x = 1$

Big Idea 3

Applying Trigonometric Formulas

Use the formulas below to evaluate trigonometric functions of certain angles.

Sum formulas	$\sin(a + b) = \sin a \cos b + \cos a \sin b$ $\cos(a + b) = \cos a \cos b - \sin a \sin b$	$\tan(a + b) = \dfrac{\tan a + \tan b}{1 - \tan a \tan b}$
Difference formulas	$\sin(a - b) = \sin a \cos b - \cos a \sin b$ $\cos(a - b) = \cos a \cos b + \sin a \sin b$	$\tan(a - b) = \dfrac{\tan a - \tan b}{1 + \tan a \tan b}$
Double-angle formulas	$\cos 2a = \cos^2 a - \sin^2 a$ $\cos 2a = 2 \cos^2 a - 1$ $\cos 2a = 1 - 2 \sin^2 a$ $\sin 2a = 2 \sin a \cos a$	$\tan 2a = \dfrac{2 \tan a}{1 - \tan^2 a}$
Half-angle formulas	$\sin \dfrac{a}{2} = \pm\sqrt{\dfrac{1 - \cos a}{2}}$ $\cos \dfrac{a}{2} = \pm\sqrt{\dfrac{1 + \cos a}{2}}$	$\tan \dfrac{a}{2} = \dfrac{1 - \cos a}{\sin a}$ $\tan \dfrac{a}{2} = \dfrac{\sin a}{1 + \cos a}$

REVIEW KEY VOCABULARY

- amplitude
- periodic function
- cycle
- period
- frequency
- trigonometric identity
- sinusoid

VOCABULARY EXERCISES

1. Copy and complete: Frequency gives the number of __?__ per unit of time.

2. **WRITING** *Explain* how to find the period of $y = a \sin b(x - h) + k$.

Determine whether the given number is the *amplitude*, *period*, or *frequency* of the graph of $y = \pi \cos \dfrac{\pi x}{2}$.

3. 4   4. π 5. 0.25

REVIEW EXAMPLES AND EXERCISES

Use the review examples and exercises below to check your understanding of the concepts you have learned in each lesson of this chapter.

10.1 Graph Sine, Cosine, and Tangent Functions

EXAMPLE

Graph (a) $y = \dfrac{1}{2} \cos 2x$ and (b) $y = 3 \tan \dfrac{x}{2}$.

a. **Amplitude:** $a = \dfrac{1}{2}$ **Period:** $\dfrac{2\pi}{2} = \pi$

   Intercepts: $(0, 0); \left(\dfrac{\pi}{2}, 0\right); (\pi, 0)$

   Maximum: $\left(\dfrac{\pi}{4}, \dfrac{1}{2}\right)$ **Minimum:** $\left(\dfrac{3\pi}{4}, -\dfrac{1}{2}\right)$

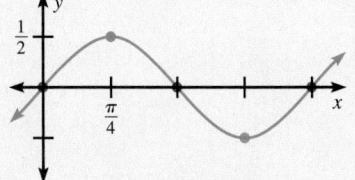

b. **Period:** $\dfrac{\pi}{\frac{1}{2}} = 2\pi$ **Intercept:** $(0, 0)$

   Asymptotes: $x = -\pi; x = \pi$

   Halfway points: $\left(-\dfrac{\pi}{2}, -3\right); \left(\dfrac{\pi}{2}, 3\right)$

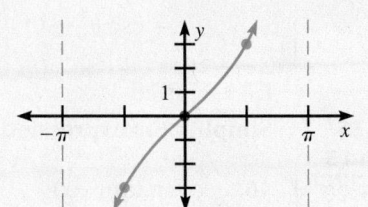

EXAMPLES 1, 2, and 4 for Exs. 6–9

EXERCISES

Graph the function.

6. $y = \sin 2x$

7. $f(x) = \dfrac{1}{2} \cos \dfrac{x}{2}$

8. $g(x) = 5 \sin \pi x$

9. $y = 2 \tan \dfrac{1}{3}x$

EXAMPLE

Graph $y = 3 \cos (x - \pi) - 1$.

To graph $y = 3 \cos (x - \pi) - 1$, start with the graph of $y = 3 \cos x$. Then, translate the graph right π units and down 1 unit.

Amplitude: $|3| = 3$ **Period:** 2π

Horizontal shift: π **Vertical shift:** -1

On $y = k$: $\left(\dfrac{3\pi}{2}, -1 \right); \left(\dfrac{5\pi}{2}, -1 \right)$

Minimum: $(2\pi, -4)$

Maximums: $(\pi, 2); (3\pi, 2)$

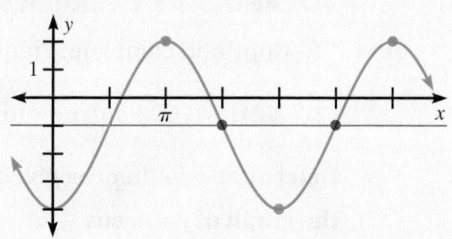

EXERCISES

Graph the function.

EXAMPLES
1, 2, and 4
for Exs. 10–15

10. $f(x) = \cos 2x + 4$

11. $y = \dfrac{1}{2} \sin 5(x - \pi)$

12. $y = 2 \sin \left(x - \dfrac{\pi}{2} \right) + 3$

13. $y = 2 \cos \dfrac{1}{3}x + 3$

14. $g(x) = -1 - 3 \cos 4x$

15. $y = 4 - \sin 3\left(x - \dfrac{\pi}{3} \right)$

EXAMPLE

Verify the identity $\dfrac{\cot^2 \theta}{\csc \theta} = \csc \theta - \sin \theta$.

$\dfrac{\cot^2 \theta}{\csc \theta} = \dfrac{\csc^2 \theta - 1}{\csc \theta}$ **Pythagorean identity**

$= \dfrac{\csc^2 \theta}{\csc \theta} - \dfrac{1}{\csc \theta}$ **Write as separate fractions.**

$= \csc \theta - \dfrac{1}{\csc \theta}$ **Simplify.**

$= \csc \theta - \sin \theta$ **Reciprocal identity**

EXERCISES

Simplify the expression.

EXAMPLES
2, 3, 4, and 5
for Exs. 16–20

16. $-\cos x \tan (-x)$

17. $\sec x \tan^2 x + \sec x$

18. $\sin \left(\dfrac{\pi}{2} - x \right) \tan x$

Verify the identity.

19. $\dfrac{\sin^2 (-x) - 1}{\cot^2 x} = -\sin^2 x$

20. $\tan \left(\dfrac{\pi}{2} - x \right) \cot x = \csc^2 x - 1$

10.4 Solve Trigonometric Equations

EXAMPLE

Solve $2\cos^2 x = 1$ in the interval $0 \le x < 2\pi$.

$2\cos^2 x = 1$ Write original equation.

$\cos^2 x = \dfrac{1}{2}$ Divide each side by 2.

$\cos x = \pm\dfrac{\sqrt{2}}{2}$ Take square roots of each side.

▶ In the interval $0 \le x < 2\pi$, the solutions are $x = \dfrac{\pi}{4}, \dfrac{3\pi}{4}, \dfrac{5\pi}{4}$, and $\dfrac{7\pi}{4}$.

EXAMPLES
1 and 4
for Exs. 21–23

EXERCISES

Solve the equation in the interval $0 \le x < 2\pi$.

21. $-4\sin^2 x = -3$ **22.** $\cos^2 x = \cos x$ **23.** $\tan^2 4x = 3$

10.5 Write Trigonometric Functions and Models

EXAMPLE

Write a function for the sinusoid.

STEP 1 **Find** the maximum value M and minimum value m. From the graph, $M = 3$ and $m = -1$.

STEP 2 **Identify** the vertical shift, k.

$k = \dfrac{M + m}{2} = \dfrac{3 + (-1)}{2} = \dfrac{2}{2} = 1$

STEP 3 **Decide** whether the graph should be modeled by a sine or cosine function. Because the graph crosses the midline, $y = 1$, on the y-axis and then decreases to its minimum value, the graph is a sine curve with a reflection but no horizontal shift. So, $a < 0$ and $h = 0$.

STEP 4 **Find** the amplitude and period. The period is $\dfrac{2\pi}{3} = \dfrac{2\pi}{b}$. So, $b = 3$.

The amplitude is $|a| = \dfrac{M - m}{2} = \dfrac{3 - (-1)}{2} = \dfrac{4}{2} = 2$. So, $a = -2$.

A function for the sinusoid is $y = -2\sin 3x + 1$.

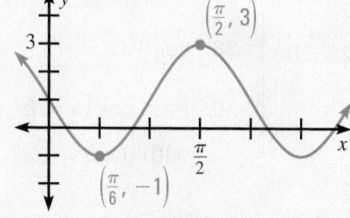

EXERCISES

EXAMPLE 1
for Exs. 24–25

Write a function for the sinusoid.

24.

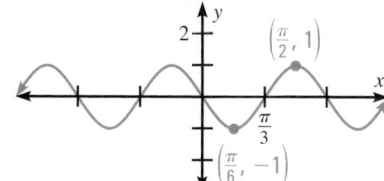

25.

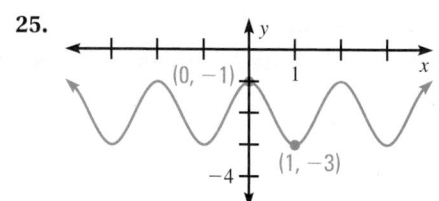

10.6 Apply Sum and Difference Formulas

EXAMPLE

Find the exact value of the expression.

a. $\cos 225° = \cos (270° - 45°)$ Substitute $270° - 45°$ for $225°$.

$\qquad = \cos 270° \cos 45° + \sin 270° \sin 45°$ Difference formula for cosine

$\qquad = 0\left(\dfrac{\sqrt{2}}{2}\right) - 1\left(\dfrac{\sqrt{2}}{2}\right)$ Evaluate.

$\qquad = -\dfrac{\sqrt{2}}{2}$ Simplify.

b. $\sin \dfrac{7\pi}{12} = \sin \left(\dfrac{\pi}{3} + \dfrac{\pi}{4}\right)$ Substitute $\dfrac{\pi}{3} + \dfrac{\pi}{4}$ for $\dfrac{7\pi}{12}$.

$\qquad = \sin \dfrac{\pi}{3} \cos \dfrac{\pi}{4} + \cos \dfrac{\pi}{3} \sin \dfrac{\pi}{4}$ Sum formula for sine

$\qquad = \dfrac{\sqrt{3}}{2}\left(\dfrac{\sqrt{2}}{2}\right) + \dfrac{1}{2}\left(\dfrac{\sqrt{2}}{2}\right)$ Evaluate.

$\qquad = \dfrac{\sqrt{6} + \sqrt{2}}{4}$ Simplify.

EXERCISES

EXAMPLES 1 and 2 for Exs. 26–30

Find the exact value of the expression.

26. $\cos 195°$ **27.** $\tan 75°$ **28.** $\sin \dfrac{13\pi}{12}$ **29.** $\cos \dfrac{5\pi}{6}$

30. Find $\cos (a - b)$, given that $\sin a = \dfrac{8}{17}$ with $\dfrac{\pi}{2} < a < \pi$ and $\cos b = \dfrac{1}{2}$ with $0 < b < \dfrac{\pi}{2}$.

10.7 Apply Double-Angle and Half-Angle Formulas

EXAMPLE

Find the exact value of the expression.

a. $\tan 135° = \tan \dfrac{1}{2}(270°) = \dfrac{1 - \cos 270°}{\sin 270°} = \dfrac{1 - 0}{-1} = -1$

b. $\sin \dfrac{\pi}{12} = \sin \dfrac{1}{2}\left(\dfrac{\pi}{6}\right) = \sqrt{\dfrac{1 - \cos \dfrac{\pi}{6}}{2}} = \sqrt{\dfrac{1 - \dfrac{\sqrt{3}}{2}}{2}} = \dfrac{1}{2}\sqrt{2 - \sqrt{3}}$

EXERCISES

EXAMPLES 1 and 2 for Exs. 31–35

Find the exact value of the expression.

31. $\sin 75°$ **32.** $\tan (-15°)$ **33.** $\cos \dfrac{\pi}{12}$ **34.** $\cos \dfrac{3\pi}{4}$

35. Given $\cos a = \dfrac{1}{2}$ with $0 < a < \dfrac{\pi}{2}$, find $\sin 2a$ and $\tan \dfrac{a}{2}$.

10 CHAPTER TEST

Graph the function.

1. $f(x) = 4 \cos 2x$

2. $y = \dfrac{3}{2} \sin \pi x$

3. $f(x) = -4 \tan \dfrac{\pi}{2} x$

4. $y = \sin(x - \pi) - 2$

5. $f(x) = 3 \tan\left(x - \dfrac{\pi}{2}\right)$

6. $y = -2 \cos \dfrac{1}{3} x + 3$

Simplify the expression.

7. $\dfrac{\sin(-\theta)}{\tan(-\theta)}$

8. $\cos^2 x + \sin^2 x - \csc^2 x$

9. $\dfrac{\sin\left(\dfrac{\pi}{2} - x\right)}{\sec x}$

Write a function for the sinusoid.

10.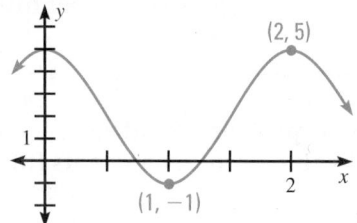

11.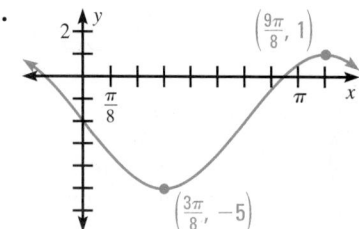

12. Verify the identity $\cos 3x = 4 \cos^3 x - 3 \cos x$.

Solve the equation in the interval $0 \le x < 2\pi$.

13. $9 \sin^2 x \tan x = 16 \tan x$

14. $(1 - \tan^2 x) \tan 2x = 2\sqrt{3}$

15. $\sin \dfrac{x}{2} = \dfrac{\sqrt{2}}{2}$

Find the general solution of the equation.

16. $6 \tan^2 x - 2 = 0$

17. $\cos x = \sin 2x \sin x$

18. $\sin \dfrac{x}{2} = 1 - \cos x$

Find the exact value of the expression.

19. $\sin 255°$

20. $\cos\left(-\dfrac{\pi}{8}\right)$

21. $\tan \dfrac{5\pi}{12}$

22. $\sin \dfrac{10\pi}{3}$

23. **BOATING** The paddle wheel of a ship is 11 feet in diameter, revolves 15 times per minute when moving at top speed, and is 2 feet below the water's surface at its lowest point. Using this speed and starting from a point at the very top of the wheel, write a model for the height h (in feet) of the end of the paddle relative to the water's surface as a function of time t (in minutes).

24. **PRECIPITATION** The table below shows the monthly precipitation P (in inches) in Bismarck, North Dakota. The time t is measured in months, with $t = 1$ representing January. Use a graphing calculator to write a sinusoidal model that gives P as a function of t.

t	1	2	3	4	5	6	7	8	9	10	11	12
P	0.5	0.5	0.9	1.5	2.2	2.6	2.6	2.2	1.6	1.3	0.7	0.4

EXTENDED RESPONSE QUESTIONS

Scoring Rubric

Full Credit
- solution is complete and correct

Partial Credit
- solution is complete but has errors, or
- solution is without error but incomplete

No Credit
- no solution is given, or
- solution makes no sense

> **PROBLEM**
>
> The horizontal distance x (in feet) traveled by a football kicked from ground level at speed v and angle θ can be modeled by $x = \frac{1}{32}v^2 \sin 2\theta$.
>
> **a.** Write an expression for half of the horizontal distance. How is this expression related to the football's maximum height?
>
> **b.** Write a simplified expression for the football's maximum height.
>
> **c.** What is the maximum height of a football kicked from ground level with a speed of 80 feet per second and an angle of 35°?

Below are sample solutions to the problem. Read each solution and the comments on the left to see why the sample represents full credit, partial credit, or no credit.

SAMPLE 1: Full credit solution

The expression is correct, and its significance is fully explained.

a. Half of the horizontal distance $= \frac{1}{2} \cdot \frac{1}{32}v^2 \sin 2\theta = \frac{1}{64}v^2 \sin 2\theta$

Because the ball travels in a parabolic path, the maximum height occurs at half the horizontal distance.

b. Substitute the expression from part (a) for x in the equation for the path of a projectile. Note that the initial height h_0 is 0.

The correct formula is used for the path of a projectile.

$$y = -\frac{16}{v^2 \cos^2 \theta}x^2 + (\tan \theta)x + h_0$$

$$y = -\frac{16}{v^2 \cos^2 \theta}\left(\frac{1}{64}v^2 \sin 2\theta\right)^2 + (\tan \theta)\left(\frac{1}{64}v^2 \sin 2\theta\right) + 0$$

$$= -\frac{v^2 (\sin 2\theta)(\sin 2\theta)}{256 \cos^2 \theta} + \frac{(v^2 \sin 2\theta)\tan \theta}{64}$$

A double-angle formula is used correctly, and the resulting expression is correctly simplified.

$$= -\frac{v^2(2 \sin \theta \cos \theta)(2 \sin \theta \cos \theta)}{256 \cos \theta \cos \theta} + \frac{v^2(2 \sin \theta)(\cos \theta \tan \theta)}{64}$$

$$= -\frac{v^2 (2 \sin \theta \cos \theta)(2 \sin \theta \cos \theta)}{\underset{\mathbf{64}}{256} \cos \theta \cos \theta} + \frac{v^2 (2 \sin \theta)(\sin \theta)}{64}$$

$$= -\frac{v^2 \sin^2 \theta}{64} + \frac{2v^2 \sin^2 \theta}{64}$$

$$= \frac{1}{64}v^2 \sin^2 \theta$$

c. To find the maximum height of the ball, substitute 80 for v and 35° for θ.

The answer is correct.

Maximum height $= \frac{1}{64}v^2 \sin^2 \theta = \frac{1}{64} \cdot 80^2 \sin^2 35° \approx 33$ feet

SAMPLE 2: Partial credit solution

a. $\frac{1}{64}v^2 \sin 2\theta$

The answer is correct, but work is not shown and no explanation is given.

b. $y = -\dfrac{16}{v^2 \cos^2 \theta}x^2 + (\tan \theta)x + h_0$

$= -\dfrac{16}{v^2 \cos^2 \theta}\left(\dfrac{1}{64}v^2 \sin 2\theta\right)^2 + (\tan \theta)\left(\dfrac{1}{64}v^2 \sin 2\theta\right) + 0$

$= -\dfrac{16}{v^2 \cos^2 \theta}\left(\dfrac{1}{4096}v^4 \sin^2 2\theta\right) + (\tan \theta)\left(\dfrac{1}{64}v^2 \sin 2\theta\right)$

$= -\dfrac{v^2 \sin^2 2\theta}{256 \cos^2 \theta} + \dfrac{v^2 \tan \theta \sin 2\theta}{64}$

The expression is not fully simplified.

c. The maximum height of the football is:

$-\dfrac{v^2 \sin^2 2\theta}{256 \cos^2 \theta} + \dfrac{v^2 \tan \theta \sin 2\theta}{64} = -\dfrac{80^2 \sin^2 70°}{256 \cos^2 35°} + \dfrac{80^2 \tan 35° \sin 70°}{64} \approx 33 \text{ ft}$

The answer is correct.

SAMPLE 3: No credit solution

a. $x = \dfrac{1}{64}v^2 \sin \theta$

The expressions in parts (a) and (b) are incorrect, and no work is shown.

b. The maximum height is given by $\dfrac{1}{64}v^2 \sin \theta$.

c. $x = \dfrac{1}{64}v^2 \sin \theta = \dfrac{1}{64} \cdot 35^2 \sin 80° \approx 19 \text{ feet}$

The values are substituted incorrectly. The answer is wrong.

The maximum height is about 19 feet.

PRACTICE   Apply the Scoring Rubric

Score the following solution to the problem on the previous page as *full credit*, *partial credit*, or *no credit*. *Explain* your reasoning. If you choose *partial credit* or *no credit*, explain how you would change the solution so that it earns a score of full credit.

a. Half of the total horizontal distance is $\dfrac{1}{64}v^2 \sin 2\theta$. This is the horizontal distance when the ball is at its maximum height.

b. A simplified expression for the maximum height of the ball is $\dfrac{1}{64}v^2 \sin^2 \theta$.

c. Substitute 80 for v and 35° for θ in the expression from part (b) to find the maximum height of the football.

$\dfrac{1}{64}v^2 \sin^2 \theta = \dfrac{1}{64} \cdot 80^2 \sin^2 35° \approx \dfrac{1}{64} \cdot 6400(0.574)^2 \approx 33 \text{ feet}$

EXTENDED RESPONSE

1. Sound travels in waves that can be represented using sine functions. When two notes are played at the same time on a musical instrument, the resulting sound wave can be modeled by the sum of two sound waves.

   a. Playing C and G together creates harmony and produces a pleasant sound. Use a graphing calculator to graph the sound wave that results from playing C and G at the same time.

Note	Sound wave
C	$y = \sin 523.26t$
G	$y = \sin 784t$
B	$y = \sin 987.76t$

   b. Playing C and B together creates dissonance and produces an unpleasant sound. Use a graphing calculator to graph the sound wave that results from playing B and C at the same time.

   c. Make a conjecture about the relationship between how the notes sound when played together and the resulting sound wave. *Explain* your reasoning.

2. The blades of a fan rotate counterclockwise at 800 rotations per minute. The length of each blade is 9 inches. The maximum height of the tip of a fan blade above the ground is 48 inches.

   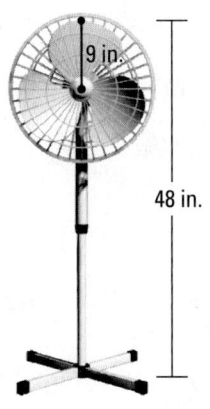

   a. What is the minimum height of the tip of the labeled fan blade above the ground?

   b. Write a function that models the height of the tip of the labeled fan blade as a function of time. Assume that the blade starts in the position shown in the diagram.

   c. Do your answers to parts (a) and (b) change if the fan rotates clockwise? *Explain* why or why not.

3. The chart shows the average monthly temperature (in degrees Fahrenheit) and a household's gas usage (in cubic feet) for 12 months.

   a. Use the chart to make a table of values giving the month t (with January corresponding to $t = 0$), the average monthly temperature y_1, and the gas usage y_2 (in thousands of cubic feet).

January	February	March	April
32°F	21°F	15°F	22°F
20,000 ft³	27,000 ft³	23,000 ft³	22,000 ft³

May	June	July	August
35°F	49°F	62°F	78°F
21,000 ft³	14,000 ft³	8,000 ft³	9,000 ft³

September	October	November	December
71°F	63°F	55°F	40°F
13,000 ft³	15,000 ft³	19,000 ft³	23,000 ft³

   b. Use the table from part (a) and a graphing calculator to find trigonometric models for the average monthly temperature y_1 as a function of time and the gas usage y_2 as a function of time.

   c. Graph the two regression equations in the same coordinate plane on your graphing calculator. *Describe* the relationship between the graphs.

MULTIPLE CHOICE

4. The graph of which function is shown?

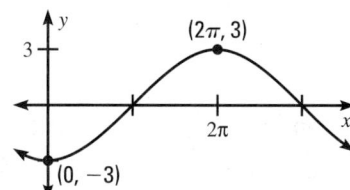

(2π, 3)

3

2π

x

(0, −3)

Ⓐ $y = -3 \cos 2x$ **Ⓑ** $y = -2 \cos 3x$

Ⓒ $y = -\frac{1}{2} \cos 3x$ **Ⓓ** $y = -3 \cos \frac{1}{2}x$

5. Which expression is *not* equivalent to 1?

Ⓐ $\tan x \sec x \cos x$ **Ⓑ** $\sin^2 x + \cos^2 x$

Ⓒ $\dfrac{\cos^2 (-x) \tan^2 x}{\sin^2 (-x)}$ **Ⓓ** $\cos\left(\dfrac{\pi}{2} - x\right) \csc x$

6. What is the general solution of the equation $\cos^3 x = 25 \cos x$?

Ⓐ $\dfrac{\pi}{2} + 2n\pi$ **Ⓑ** $\dfrac{\pi}{2} + n\pi$

Ⓒ $\dfrac{3\pi}{2} + 2n\pi$ **Ⓓ** $\dfrac{\pi}{4} + 2n\pi$

GRIDDED ANSWER

7. What is the *x*-intercept of the graph of $y = \sin \frac{1}{2}\pi x$ on the interval $0 < x < 3$?

8. Find the value of $\tan (a + b)$ given that the following are true:

$\sin a = \dfrac{3}{5}$ with $0 < a < \dfrac{\pi}{2}$ and

$\cos b = \dfrac{\sqrt{2}}{2}$ with $0 < b < \dfrac{\pi}{2}$

9. Find the *y*-coordinate of the point of intersection of the graphs of $y = 2 + \sin x$ and $y = 3 - \sin x$ in the interval $0 < x < \dfrac{\pi}{2}$.

10. Find the amplitude of the sinusoid shown below.

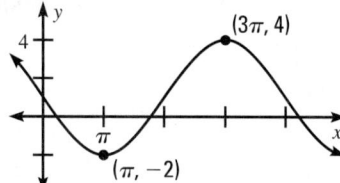

4

(3π, 4)

π

x

(π, −2)

SHORT RESPONSE

11. Use the fact that the frequency of a periodic function's graph is the reciprocal of the period to show that an oscillating motion with maximum displacement *a* and frequency *f* can be modeled by $y = a \sin 2\pi ft$ or $y = a \cos 2\pi ft$.

12. A basketball is dropped from a height of 15 feet. Can the height of the basketball over time be modeled by a trigonometric function? If so, write the function. If not, explain why not.

13. Consider the following function:

$$f(x) = \sin x \cos x$$

Without graphing the function, what would you expect the graph to look like? *Explain* your reasoning. Copy and complete the table below and determine whether your prediction was correct.

x	$-\pi$	$-\dfrac{3\pi}{4}$	$-\dfrac{\pi}{2}$	$-\dfrac{\pi}{4}$	0	$\dfrac{\pi}{4}$	$\dfrac{\pi}{2}$	$\dfrac{3\pi}{4}$	π
$f(x)$	?	?	?	?	?	?	?	?	?

Contents
of Student Resources

Skills Review Handbook

Operations with Positive and Negative Numbers

To add positive and negative numbers, you can use a number line.

To subtract any number, add its opposite.

To add a positive number, move to the right.

To add a negative number, move to the left.

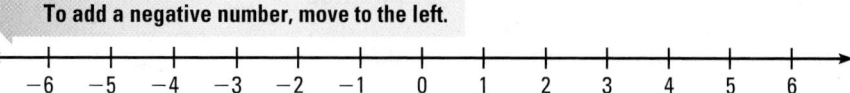

EXAMPLE **Add or subtract.**

a. $1 + (-5)$

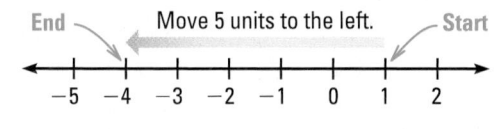

End   Move 5 units to the left.   Start

▶ $1 + (-5) = -4$

b. $-2 - (-5) = -2 + 5$ The opposite of −5 is 5.

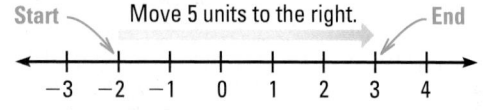

Start   Move 5 units to the right.   End

▶ $-2 - (-5) = 3$

To multiply or divide positive and negative numbers, use the following rules.

• The product or quotient of two numbers with the *same* sign is *positive*.

• The product or quotient of two numbers with *different* signs is *negative*.

EXAMPLE **Multiply or divide.**

a. $3 \cdot 7 = 21$

b. $-3(-7) = 21$

c. $18 \div 2 = 9$

d. $-18 \div (-2) = 9$

e. $-3(7) = -21$

f. $3(-7) = -21$

g. $-18 \div 2 = -9$

h. $18 \div (-2) = -9$

PRACTICE

Perform the indicated operation.

1. $2 + (-8)$ **2.** $5 - 12$ **3.** $-6(10)$ **4.** $-30 \div (-2)$ **5.** $-4 + 6$

6. $7(-5)$ **7.** $18 - 10$ **8.** $-7 + (-12)$ **9.** $11(4)$ **10.** $81 \div (-9)$

11. $-12 \div 3$ **12.** $-9(-8)$ **13.** $-1 + 13$ **14.** $45 \div (-9)$ **15.** $-6(12)$

16. $14 - (-9)$ **17.** $-32 \div 16$ **18.** $-23 + (-5)$ **19.** $-8 - (-5)$ **20.** $17 - (-18)$

21. $-9(-1)$ **22.** $-3 - (-11)$ **23.** $-18 \div (-3)$ **24.** $14 + (-7)$ **25.** $5(-3)$

26. $21 + (-8)$ **27.** $-2 - 10$ **28.** $-9 + 26$ **29.** $-20 \div (-4)$ **30.** $22 \div (-2)$

31. $-7(-6)$ **32.** $1 - 24$ **33.** $-15 - 2$ **34.** $0 + (-4)$ **35.** $16 \div 8$

Fractions, Decimals, and Percents

A **percent** is a ratio with a denominator of 100. The word *percent* means "per hundred," or "out of one hundred." The symbol for percent is %.

In the model at the right, 71 of the 100 squares are shaded. You can write the shaded part of the model as a fraction, a decimal, or a percent.

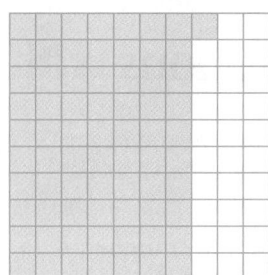

Fraction: seventy-one divided by one hundred, or $\frac{71}{100}$

Decimal: seventy-one hundredths, or 0.71

Percent: seventy-one percent, or 71%

EXAMPLE   **Write as a fraction.**

a. $94\% = \frac{94}{100} = \frac{47}{50}$ **b.** $20\% = \frac{20}{100} = \frac{1}{5}$ **c.** $0.3 = \text{three tenths} = \frac{3}{10}$

EXAMPLE   **Write as a decimal.**

a. $15\% = \frac{15}{100} = 0.15$ **b.** $106\% = \frac{106}{100} = 1.06$ **c.** $\frac{5}{8} = 5 \div 8 = 0.625$

EXAMPLE   **Write as a percent.**

a. $0.41 = \frac{41}{100} = 41\%$ **b.** $0.8 = \frac{8}{10} = \frac{80}{100} = 80\%$ **c.** $\frac{5}{4} = \frac{5 \cdot 25}{4 \cdot 25} = \frac{125}{100} = 125\%$

PRACTICE

Write as a fraction.

1. 0.65   **2.** 0.08   **3.** 1.5   **4.** 0.13   **5.** 0.7

6. 50%   **7.** 26%   **8.** 3%   **9.** 95%   **10.** 110%

Write as a decimal.

11. $\frac{1}{4}$ **12.** $\frac{9}{10}$ **13.** $\frac{30}{25}$ **14.** $\frac{2}{5}$ **15.** $\frac{3}{8}$

16. 16%   **17.** 142%   **18.** 1%   **19.** 30%   **20.** 6.5%

Write as a percent.

21. 0.6   **22.** 0.24   **23.** 1.3   **24.** 0.07   **25.** 0.45

26. $\frac{1}{10}$ **27.** $\frac{4}{5}$ **28.** $\frac{17}{20}$ **29.** $\frac{5}{2}$ **30.** $\frac{3}{16}$

Calculating with Percents

You can use equations to calculate with percents. Replace words with symbols as shown in the table at the right. Below are three types of questions you can answer with percents.

Word	what	of	is
Symbol	n	$\times$	$=$

EXAMPLE Answer the question.

a. What is 15% of 20?

$n = 0.15 \times 20$

$n = 3$

3 is 15% of 20.

b. What percent of 8 is 6?

$n \times 8 = 6$

$n = 6 \div 8 = 0.75 = 75\%$

75% of 8 is 6.

c. 80% of what number is 4?

$0.8 \times n = 4$

$n = 4 \div 0.8 = 5$

80% of 5 is 4.

To find a percent of change, calculate $\dfrac{\text{Amount of increase or decrease}}{\text{Original amount}}$.

EXAMPLE Find the percent of change.

a. A class increases from 21 students to 25 students.

$\dfrac{25 - 21}{21} = \dfrac{4}{21} \approx 0.19 = 19\%$ increase

b. A price decreases from $12 to $9.

$\dfrac{12 - 9}{12} = \dfrac{3}{12} = 0.25 = 25\%$ decrease

PRACTICE

Answer the question.

1. What is 98% of 200?
2. What is 25% of 8?
3. What is 30% of 128?
4. What is 5% of 700?
5. What is 100% of 17?
6. What is 150% of 14?
7. What is 0.2% of 500?
8. What is 6.5% of 3000?
9. What percent of 100 is 54?
10. What percent of 18 is 9?
11. What percent of 80 is 8?
12. What percent of 15 is 20?
13. What percent of 30 is 6?
14. What percent of 5 is 8?
15. What percent of 50 is 1?
16. 50% of what number is 6?
17. 55% of what number is 44?
18. 10% of what number is 6?
19. 75% of what number is 45?
20. 1% of what number is 2?
21. 90% of what number is 63?
22. 12% of what number is 60?
23. 200% of what number is 16?

Find the percent of change. Round to the nearest percent if necessary.

24. A class increases from 20 to 28 students.
25. Time decreases from 60 to 45 minutes.
26. A price is reduced from $200 to $180.
27. Votes increase from 200 to 300.
28. A test is shortened from 40 to 32 items.
29. Membership increases from 820 to 1605.
30. A wage rises from $8.75 to $10.00.
31. The temperature drops from 24°F to 5°F.

Factors and Multiples

Factors are numbers or expressions that are multiplied together. A **prime number** is a whole number greater than 1 that has exactly two whole number factors, 1 and itself. The table shows all the prime numbers less than 100. A **composite number** is a whole number greater than 1 that has more than two whole number factors.

Prime Numbers Less Than 100
2, 3, 5, 7, 11, 13, 17, 19, 23, 29, 31, 37, 41, 43, 47, 53, 59, 61, 67, 71, 73, 79, 83, 89, 97

When you write a composite number as a product of prime numbers, you are writing its **prime factorization**.

EXAMPLE Write the prime factorization of 60.

Use a *factor tree*. Write 60 at the top. Then draw two branches and write 60 as the product of two factors. Continue to draw branches until all the factors are prime numbers. Two factor trees for 60 are given at the right. Both show $60 = 2 \cdot 2 \cdot 3 \cdot 5$.

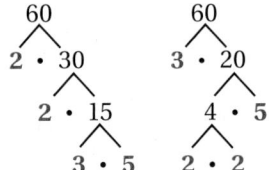

▶ The prime factorization of 60 is $2^2 \cdot 3 \cdot 5$.

A whole number that is a factor of two or more nonzero whole numbers is a **common factor** of the numbers. The largest of the common factors is the **greatest common factor (GCF)**.

EXAMPLE Find the greatest common factor (GCF) of 18 and 45.

Method 1 List factors.

Factors of 18: 1, 2, 3, 6, **9**, 18

Factors of 45: 1, 3, 5, **9**, 15, 45

The GCF is 9, the greatest of the common factors.

Method 2 Use prime factorization.

Prime factorization of 18: $2 \cdot 3 \cdot 3$

Prime factorization of 45: $3 \cdot 3 \cdot 5$

The GCF is the product of the common prime factors: $3 \cdot 3 = 9$.

A **multiple** of a whole number is the product of the number and any nonzero whole number. A **common multiple** of two or more numbers is a multiple of all of the numbers. The **least common multiple (LCM)** is the smallest of the common multiples.

EXAMPLE Find the least common multiple (LCM) of 12 and 15.

Method 1 List multiples.

Multiples of 12: 12, 24, 36, 48, **60**, . . .

Multiples of 15: 15, 30, 45, **60**, . . .

The LCM is 60, the least of the common multiples.

Method 2 Use prime factorization.

Prime factorization of 12: $2^2 \cdot 3$

Prime factorization of 15: $3 \cdot 5$

Form the LCM of the numbers by writing each prime factor to the highest power it occurs in either number: $2^2 \cdot 3 \cdot 5 = 60$.

The **least common denominator (LCD)** of two fractions is the least common multiple of the denominators. Use the LCD to add or subtract fractions with different denominators.

EXAMPLE Add: $\dfrac{3}{10} + \dfrac{5}{8}$

The least common multiple of the denominators, 10 and 8, is 40.
So, the least common denominator (LCD) of the fractions is 40.

Rewrite the fractions using the LCD of 40: $\dfrac{3}{10} = \dfrac{3 \cdot 4}{10 \cdot 4} = \dfrac{12}{40}$ and $\dfrac{5}{8} = \dfrac{5 \cdot 5}{8 \cdot 5} = \dfrac{25}{40}$

Add the numerators and keep the same denominator: $\dfrac{3}{10} + \dfrac{5}{8} = \dfrac{12}{40} + \dfrac{25}{40} = \dfrac{37}{40}$

PRACTICE

Write the prime factorization of the number. If the number is prime, write *prime*.

1. 42	**2.** 104	**3.** 75	**4.** 23	**5.** 70
6. 27	**7.** 72	**8.** 180	**9.** 47	**10.** 100
11. 88	**12.** 49	**13.** 83	**14.** 142	**15.** 32

Find the greatest common factor (GCF) of the numbers.

16. 4, 6	**17.** 24, 40	**18.** 10, 25	**19.** 55, 44	**20.** 28, 35
21. 8, 20	**22.** 5, 8	**23.** 15, 12	**24.** 16, 32	**25.** 70, 90
26. 2, 18	**27.** 9, 21	**28.** 36, 42, 54	**29.** 7, 12, 17	**30.** 45, 63, 81

Find the least common multiple (LCM) of the numbers.

31. 4, 16	**32.** 2, 14	**33.** 5, 6	**34.** 16, 24	**35.** 6, 8
36. 12, 20	**37.** 3, 6	**38.** 18, 8	**39.** 9, 12	**40.** 9, 5
41. 10, 15	**42.** 7, 9	**43.** 40, 4, 5	**44.** 25, 30, 3	**45.** 27, 81, 33

Perform the indicated operation(s). Simplify the result.

46. $\dfrac{1}{2} + \dfrac{3}{8}$ **47.** $\dfrac{3}{4} - \dfrac{5}{16}$ **48.** $\dfrac{7}{10} - \dfrac{3}{5}$ **49.** $\dfrac{1}{2} + \dfrac{1}{3}$

50. $\dfrac{5}{12} + \dfrac{1}{3}$ **51.** $\dfrac{4}{5} + \dfrac{1}{8}$ **52.** $\dfrac{1}{10} + \dfrac{3}{4}$ **53.** $\dfrac{5}{6} - \dfrac{1}{2}$

54. $\dfrac{7}{8} - \dfrac{11}{16}$ **55.** $\dfrac{9}{10} - \dfrac{1}{3}$ **56.** $\dfrac{2}{3} - \dfrac{1}{6}$ **57.** $\dfrac{1}{4} + \dfrac{2}{5}$

58. $\dfrac{4}{5} + \dfrac{1}{12} - \dfrac{5}{6}$ **59.** $\dfrac{3}{2} - \dfrac{3}{10} - \dfrac{3}{4}$ **60.** $\dfrac{9}{10} - \dfrac{1}{5} - \dfrac{1}{2}$ **61.** $\dfrac{7}{8} + \dfrac{3}{16} - \dfrac{1}{4}$

62. $\dfrac{8}{9} + \dfrac{2}{3} - \dfrac{7}{12}$ **63.** $\dfrac{1}{6} + \dfrac{4}{15} + \dfrac{1}{3}$ **64.** $\dfrac{1}{2} + \dfrac{2}{3} + \dfrac{1}{4}$ **65.** $\dfrac{15}{16} - \dfrac{7}{10} + \dfrac{1}{2}$

66. $\dfrac{5}{24} - \dfrac{1}{6} + \dfrac{7}{12}$ **67.** $\dfrac{1}{2} + \dfrac{3}{5} - \dfrac{1}{4}$ **68.** $\dfrac{5}{6} - \dfrac{3}{5} - \dfrac{2}{15}$ **69.** $\dfrac{4}{9} + \dfrac{3}{4} - \dfrac{7}{12}$

Ratios and Proportions

A **ratio** uses division to compare two quantities.

You can write a ratio of two quantities a and b, where b is not equal to 0, in three ways.

You should write ratios in simplest form.

Three Ways to Write the Ratio of a to b		
a to b	$a:b$	$\dfrac{a}{b}$

EXAMPLE **Write the ratio of 12 boys to 16 girls in three ways.**

First write the ratio as a fraction in simplest form: $\dfrac{\text{Boys}}{\text{Girls}} = \dfrac{12}{16} = \dfrac{12 \div 4}{16 \div 4} = \dfrac{3}{4}$

▶ Three ways to write the ratio of boys to girls are 3 to 4, 3 : 4, and $\dfrac{3}{4}$.

A **proportion** is an equation stating that two ratios are equal.

You can use cross multiplication to solve a proportion.

Using Cross Multiplication to Solve Proportions
If $\dfrac{a}{b} = \dfrac{c}{d}$, where $b \neq 0$ and $d \neq 0$, then $ad = bc$.

EXAMPLE **Solve the proportion.**

a. $\dfrac{5}{9} = \dfrac{n}{54}$

$5 \cdot 54 = 9 \cdot n$ Cross multiply.

$270 = 9n$ Simplify.

$30 = n$ Solve for n.

b. $\dfrac{x}{40} = \dfrac{3}{8}$

$x \cdot 8 = 40 \cdot 3$ Cross multiply.

$8x = 120$ Simplify.

$x = 15$ Solve for x.

PRACTICE

Write the ratio in simplest form. Express the answer in three ways.

1. 3 to 9
2. 16 to 24
3. 10 to 8
4. 6 to 2
5. 25 to 30
6. 60 to 10
7. 4 to 4
8. 8 to 20
9. 32 to 72
10. 42 to 15
11. 14 to 2
12. 12 to 15

Solve the proportion.

13. $\dfrac{x}{14} = \dfrac{12}{24}$
14. $\dfrac{8}{24} = \dfrac{d}{36}$
15. $\dfrac{15}{n} = \dfrac{3}{4}$
16. $\dfrac{9}{45} = \dfrac{5}{h}$
17. $\dfrac{a}{6} = \dfrac{4}{12}$
18. $\dfrac{13}{t} = \dfrac{91}{7}$
19. $\dfrac{75}{120} = \dfrac{r}{8}$
20. $\dfrac{b}{90} = \dfrac{2}{3}$
21. $\dfrac{4}{11} = \dfrac{n}{110}$
22. $\dfrac{5}{z} = \dfrac{150}{90}$
23. $\dfrac{9}{8} = \dfrac{x}{6}$
24. $\dfrac{72}{105} = \dfrac{24}{m}$
25. $\dfrac{17}{33} = \dfrac{51}{a}$
26. $\dfrac{20}{125} = \dfrac{24}{n}$
27. $\dfrac{16}{144} = \dfrac{8}{x}$
28. $\dfrac{96}{6} = \dfrac{t}{3}$

Converting Units of Measurement

The table of measures on page T3 gives many statements of equivalent measures. Using each statement, you can write two different conversion factors.

Statement of Equivalent Measures	Conversion Factors
100 cm = 1 m	$\dfrac{100\text{ cm}}{1\text{ m}} = 1$ and $\dfrac{1\text{ m}}{100\text{ cm}} = 1$

To convert from one unit of measurement to another, multiply by a conversion factor. Use the one that will eliminate the starting unit and keep the desired unit.

EXAMPLE Copy and complete.

a. 3.5 m = __?__ cm

$$3.5\ \cancel{m} \times \frac{100\text{ cm}}{1\ \cancel{m}} = (3.5 \times 100)\text{ cm} = 350\text{ cm}$$

▸ So, 3.5 m = 350 cm.

b. 620 cm = __?__ m

$$620\ \cancel{cm} \times \frac{1\text{ m}}{100\ \cancel{cm}} = \frac{620}{100}\text{ m} = 6.2\text{ m}$$

▸ So, 620 cm = 6.2 m.

Sometimes you need to use more than one conversion factor.

EXAMPLE Copy and complete: 7 days = __?__ sec

Find the appropriate statements of equivalent measures.

24 h = 1 day, 60 min = 1 h, and 60 sec = 1 min

Write conversion factors: $\dfrac{24\text{ h}}{1\text{ day}}$, $\dfrac{60\text{ min}}{1\text{ h}}$, and $\dfrac{60\text{ sec}}{1\text{ min}}$

Multiply by conversion factors to eliminate days and keep seconds.

$$7\ \cancel{days} \times \frac{24\ \cancel{h}}{1\ \cancel{day}} \times \frac{60\ \cancel{min}}{1\ \cancel{h}} \times \frac{60\text{ sec}}{1\ \cancel{min}} = (7 \times 24 \times 60 \times 60)\text{ sec} = 604{,}800\text{ sec}$$

▸ So, 7 days = 604,800 sec.

PRACTICE

Copy and complete.

1. 6 L = __?__ mL
2. 2 mi = __?__ ft
3. 80 oz = __?__ lb
4. 4 days = __?__ h
5. 77 mm = __?__ cm
6. 5 gal = __?__ qt
7. 48 ft = __?__ yd
8. 1500 mL = __?__ L
9. 40 m = __?__ cm
10. 125 lb = __?__ oz
11. 800 g = __?__ kg
12. 900 sec = __?__ min
13. 72 in. = __?__ ft
14. 2.5 ton = __?__ lb
15. 90 min = __?__ h
16. 65,000 mg = __?__ g
17. 100 yd = __?__ in.
18. 3.5 kg = __?__ g
19. 6 pt = __?__ qt
20. 1 week = __?__ min
21. 2 oz = __?__ lb
22. 1 km = __?__ mm
23. 1 mi = __?__ in.
24. 5 gal = __?__ c
25. 288 in.^{2} = __?__ ft^2
26. 24 pt = __?__ gal
27. 4 kg = __?__ g
28. 7 hr = __?__ sec

Scientific Notation

Scientific notation is a way to write numbers using powers of 10. A number is written in **scientific notation** if it has the form $c \times 10^n$ where $1 \le c < 10$ and n is an integer. The table shows some powers of ten in order from least to greatest.

Power of Ten	10^{-3}	10^{-2}	10^{-1}	10^0	10^1	10^2	10^3
Value	0.001	0.01	0.1	1	10	100	1000

EXAMPLE Write the number in scientific notation.

a. 12,800,000 — Standard form

12,800,000 — Move the decimal point 7 places to the left.

1.28×10^7 — Use 7 as an exponent of 10.

b. 0.0000039 — Standard form

0.0000039 — Move the decimal point 6 places to the right.

3.9×10^{-6} — Use -6 as an exponent of 10.

EXAMPLE Write the number in standard form.

a. 6.1×10^4 — Scientific notation

6.1×10^4 — The exponent of 10 is 4.

61,000 — Move the decimal point 4 places to the right.

61,000 — Standard form

b. 5.74×10^{-5} — Scientific notation

5.74×10^{-5} — The exponent of 10 is -5.

0.0000574 — Move the decimal point 5 places to the left.

0.0000574 — Standard form

PRACTICE

Write the number in scientific notation.

1. 0.6
2. 25,000,000
3. 0.08
4. 0.00542
5. 40.8
6. 7
7. 0.000385
8. 8,145,000
9. 41,236
10. 0.0000016
11. 486,000
12. 0.000000009
13. 0.01002
14. 1,000,000,000
15. 7050.5
16. 0.37
17. 9850
18. 0.0000206
19. 805
20. 0.0005

Write the number in standard form.

21. 5×10^3
22. 4×10^{-2}
23. 8.2×10^{-1}
24. 6.93×10^2
25. 3.2×10^{-3}
26. 9.01×10^{-5}
27. 7.345×10^5
28. 2.38×10^{-2}
29. 1.814×10^0
30. 2.7×10^8
31. 1×10^6
32. 4.9×10^{-4}
33. 8×10^{-6}
34. 5.6×10^4
35. 1.87×10^9
36. 7×10^{-4}
37. 6.08×10^6
38. 9.009×10^{-3}
39. 3.401×10^7
40. 5.32×10^1

Significant Digits

Significant digits indicate how precisely a number is known. Use the following guidelines to determine the number of significant digits.

- All nonzero digits are significant.

- All zeros that appear between two nonzero digits are significant.

- For a decimal, all zeros that appear after the last nonzero digit are significant. For a whole number, you cannot tell whether any zeros after the last nonzero digit are significant, so you should assume that they are not significant.

Sometimes calculations involve measurements that have various numbers of significant digits. In this case, a general rule is to carry all digits through the calculation and then round the result to the same number of significant digits as the measurement with the *fewest* significant digits. When you calculate with units that cannot be divided into fractional parts, such as number of people, consider only the significant digits of the other number(s).

EXAMPLE Perform the calculation. Write your answer with the appropriate number of significant digits.

a.

12.6	3 significant digits
$\times\ 0.05$	1 significant digit
0.63	The product has 2 significant digits.
0.6	Round to 1 significant digit.

b.

840	2 significant digits
$+\ 702$	3 significant digits
1542	The sum has 4 significant digits.
1500	Round to 2 significant digits.

c. $61.20 restaurant bill $\div$ 6 people

The number of people is exact, so consider only the 4 significant digits of the bill, $61.20. The answer should have 4 significant digits.

$61.20 \div 6 = \textbf{\$10.20}$

▶ Each person pays $10.20.

PRACTICE

Perform the calculation. Write your answer with the appropriate number of significant digits.

1. $600 + 30$

2. $5 - 2.6$

3. $12 \cdot 6.75$

4. $0.098 + 0.14 + 0.369$

5. $3.6053 - 1.720$

6. $40 \div 3.5$

7. $8.0 - 3.1$

8. $31.7 \cdot 6.8 \cdot 0.435$

9. $30.5 \cdot 6.40$

10. $3.18 + 2.0005$

11. $0.088 \div 2.44$

12. $8650 + 380 - 49$

13. $4016 - 3007$

14. $1.35 + 14.8$

15. $320 \div 18$

16. $38.1 \cdot 3.04 \div 0.024$

17. $1.45 per notebook $\cdot$ 12 notebooks

18. 10.0 liters of water $-$ 4.5 liters of water

19. 260 pints of milk $\div$ 106 students

20. 0.5 yard of fabric $+$ 0.87 yard of fabric

21. 27,973 books $\div$ 11 libraries

22. 12.76 gallons of gas $+$ 6.08 gallons of gas

23. $6.95 per ticket $\cdot$ 180 tickets

24. 1540 pounds $-$ 160 pounds $-$ 85 pounds

Writing Algebraic Expressions

To solve a problem using algebra, you often need to write a phrase as an algebraic expression.

EXAMPLE Write the phrase as an algebraic expression.

a. 6 less than a number

"Less than" indicates subtraction.

▸ $n - 6$

b. The cube of a number

"Cube" indicates raising to the third power.

▸ n^3

c. Double a number

"Double" indicates multiplication by 2.

▸ $2n$

EXAMPLE Write an algebraic expression to answer the question.

a. Rebecca walks three times as far to school as Meghan does. If Meghan walks m blocks to school, how many blocks to school does Rebecca walk?

▸ $3m$

b. Kate is 8 inches taller than Noah. If Noah is n inches tall, how tall is Kate?

▸ $n + 8$

PRACTICE

Write the phrase as an algebraic expression.

1. 8 more than a number
2. 10 times a number
3. Twice a number
4. 6 less than a number
5. One fifth of a number
6. 4 greater than a number
7. 5 times a number
8. A number squared
9. 25% of a number
10. Half a number
11. 2 less than a number
12. The square root of a number

Write an algebraic expression to answer the question.

13. Allison is 4 years younger than her sister Camille. If Camille is c years old, how old is Allison?

14. Ryan bought a movie ticket for x dollars. He paid with a $20 bill. How much change should Ryan get?

15. Bridget spent $5 more than Tom spent at the mall. If Tom spent x dollars, how much did Bridget spend?

16. Marc has twice as many baseball cards as hockey cards. If Marc has h hockey cards, how many baseball cards does he have?

17. Elizabeth's ballet class is 45 minutes long. If Elizabeth is m minutes late for ballet class, how many minutes will she spend in class?

18. Steve drove x miles per hour for 5 hours. How many miles did Steve drive?

19. Wendy bought 10 pens priced at x dollars each. How much did she spend?

Binomial Products

A **monomial** is a number, a variable, or the product of a number and one or more variables. A **binomial** is the sum of two monomials. In other words, a binomial is a polynomial with two terms. You can use a geometric model to find the product of two binomials.

EXAMPLE Simplify $(2x + 1)(x + 3)$.

Draw a rectangle with dimensions $2x + 1$ and $x + 3$. Use the dimensions to divide the rectangle into parts. Then find the area of each part. The binomial product $(2x + 1)(x + 3)$ is the sum of the areas of all the parts.

There are 2 blue parts with area x^2, 7 green parts with area x, and 3 yellow parts with area 1.

$$(2x + 1)(x + 3) = 2x^2 + 7x + 3$$

Another way to find the product of two binomials is to use the distributive property systematically. Multiply the *first* terms, the *outer* terms, the *inner* terms, and the *last* terms of the binomials. This is called **FOIL** for the words **F**irst, **O**uter, **I**nner, and **L**ast.

EXAMPLE Simplify $(x + 2)(4x - 5)$.

$$\overset{\text{First}}{} \quad \overset{\text{Outer}}{} \quad \overset{\text{Inner}}{} \quad \overset{\text{Last}}{}$$

$$(x + 2)(4x - 5) = x(4x) + x(-5) + 2(4x) + 2(-5) \qquad \text{Use FOIL.}$$

$$= 4x^2 - 5x + 8x - 10 \qquad \text{Multiply.}$$

$$= 4x^2 + 3x - 10 \qquad \text{Combine like terms.}$$

PRACTICE

Simplify.

1. $(a + 5)(a + 3)$
2. $(m + 4)(m + 11)$
3. $(t + 8)(t + 7)$
4. $(z + 1)(z + 6)$
5. $(y + 4)(y + 2)$
6. $(x + 9)(x + 9)$
7. $(y - 2)^2$
8. $(n + 6)^2$
9. $(4 - z)^2$
10. $(a + 10)(a - 10)$
11. $(y + 3)(y - 7)$
12. $(k + 1)^2$
13. $(5x - 4)(5x + 4)$
14. $(3 + n)^2$
15. $(c + 5)(2c - 7)$
16. $(a + 5)(a + 5)$
17. $(7 - z)(7 + z)$
18. $(3x - 8)(x - 6)$
19. $(4a + 3)^2$
20. $(3 - g)(2g + 3)$
21. $(4 - x)(8 + x)$
22. $(3n - 1)(n - 4)$
23. $(-a + 9)(a - 9)$
24. $(8x + 1)(x + 1)$
25. $(5x + 2)(2x - 5)$
26. $(2d - 5)(3d - 1)$
27. $(-4z + 3)(6z - 1)$

LCDs of Rational Expressions

A **rational expression** is a fraction whose numerator and denominator are nonzero polynomials. The **least common denominator (LCD)** of two rational expressions is the least common multiple of the denominators. To find the LCD, follow these three steps:

STEP 1 **Write** each denominator as the product of its factors.

STEP 2 **Write** the product consisting of the highest power of each factor that appears in either denominator.

STEP 3 **Simplify** the product from Step 2 to write the LCD.

EXAMPLE **Find the least common denominator of the rational expressions.**

a. $\dfrac{2}{5xy}$ and $\dfrac{2}{y^3}$

b. $\dfrac{3}{8x^2}$ and $\dfrac{1}{12x}$

c. $\dfrac{-1}{3x+6}$ and $\dfrac{x}{x^2-3x-10}$

STEP 1 **Factors:**
$$5xy = 5 \cdot x \cdot y$$
$$y^3 = y^3$$

Factors:
$$8x^2 = 2^3 \cdot x^2$$
$$12x = 2^2 \cdot 3 \cdot x$$

Factors:
$$3x + 6 = 3 \cdot (x+2)$$
$$x^2 - 3x - 10 = (x+2) \cdot (x-5)$$

STEP 2 **Product:** $5 \cdot x \cdot y^3$

Product: $2^3 \cdot 3 \cdot x^2$

Product: $3 \cdot (x+2) \cdot (x-5)$

STEP 3 **LCD:** $5xy^3$

LCD: $24x^2$

LCD: $3(x+2)(x-5)$

PRACTICE

Find the least common denominator of the rational expressions.

1. $\dfrac{1}{2ab}$ and $\dfrac{4}{a^2}$

2. $\dfrac{5}{6k^2}$ and $\dfrac{6}{7k^2}$

3. $\dfrac{2}{z^3}$ and $\dfrac{2}{z^2}$

4. $\dfrac{4}{5x}$ and $\dfrac{-3}{10x}$

5. $\dfrac{m}{14}$ and $\dfrac{1}{18m}$

6. $\dfrac{19}{20xy}$ and $\dfrac{3}{16xy}$

7. $\dfrac{1}{3y^2}$ and $\dfrac{1}{3y}$

8. $\dfrac{-4}{9ab^2}$ and $\dfrac{2}{21a^2b}$

9. $\dfrac{n}{n+2}$ and $\dfrac{n^2}{n-2}$

10. $\dfrac{-1}{x-1}$ and $\dfrac{3}{x+3}$

11. $\dfrac{-8}{5n+5}$ and $\dfrac{4}{n+1}$

12. $\dfrac{y}{8}$ and $\dfrac{1}{2y+8}$

13. $\dfrac{1}{2m-6}$ and $\dfrac{2}{3m-9}$

14. $\dfrac{a}{n^2}$ and $\dfrac{-a}{n^2-6n}$

15. $\dfrac{1}{x-4}$ and $\dfrac{1}{(x-4)^2}$

16. $\dfrac{3}{4x+12}$ and $\dfrac{4}{6x+18}$

17. $\dfrac{1}{2n^3}$ and $\dfrac{-9}{10n^2+8n}$

18. $\dfrac{10}{15b-30}$ and $\dfrac{17b}{9b-18}$

19. $\dfrac{-5}{(k+3)^4}$ and $\dfrac{3}{(k+3)^2}$

20. $\dfrac{1}{y-5}$ and $\dfrac{8}{3y-15}$

21. $\dfrac{n^2}{10n+20}$ and $\dfrac{n}{7n+14}$

22. $\dfrac{20}{5z-40}$ and $\dfrac{1}{9z-56}$

23. $\dfrac{2a}{a^2+4a+4}$ and $\dfrac{2}{a+2}$

24. $\dfrac{1}{2z-6}$ and $\dfrac{-1}{z^2-z-6}$

25. $\dfrac{3k}{k-3}$ and $\dfrac{-k}{k^2-5k+6}$

26. $\dfrac{x}{x^2-9}$ and $\dfrac{-x}{x^2+3x-18}$

27. $\dfrac{m^2}{m^2-11m+28}$ and $\dfrac{-5}{m^2+5m-45}$

SR12 Student Resources

The Coordinate Plane

A **coordinate plane** is formed by the intersection of a horizontal number line called the **x-axis** and a vertical number line called the **y-axis**. The axes meet at a point called the **origin** and divide the coordinate plane into four **quadrants**, numbered I, II, III, and IV.

Each point in a coordinate plane is represented by an **ordered pair**. The first number is the **x-coordinate**, and the second number is the **y-coordinate**.

The ordered pair (3, 1) is graphed at the right. The x-coordinate is 3, and the y-coordinate is 1. So, the point is right 3 units and up 1 unit from the origin.

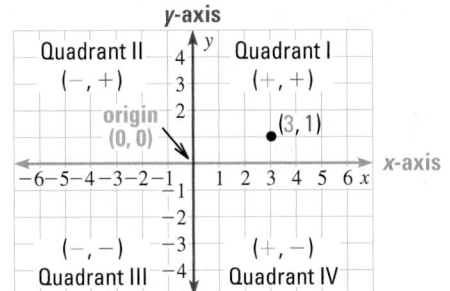

EXAMPLE Graph the points A(2, −1) and B(−4, 0) in a coordinate plane.

A(2, −1) Start at the origin.
The x-coordinate is 2, so move right 2 units.
The y-coordinate is −1, so move down 1 unit.
Draw a point at (2, −1) and label it A.

B(−4, 0) Start at the origin.
The x-coordinate is −4, so move left 4 units.
The y-coordinate is 0, so move up 0 units.
Draw a point at (−4, 0) and label it B.

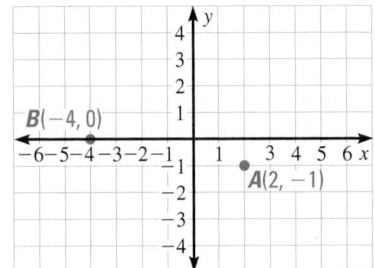

PRACTICE

Graph the points in a coordinate plane.

1. $A(7, 2)$	**2.** $B(6, -7)$	**3.** $C(2, -3)$	**4.** $D(-8, 0)$	**5.** $E(-4, -8)$
6. $F(1, 3)$	**7.** $G(3, 0)$	**8.** $H(1, -5)$	**9.** $I(0, -2)$	**10.** $J(-6, 5)$
11. $K(5, 8)$	**12.** $L(8, -2)$	**13.** $M(-3, -4)$	**14.** $N(-7, 8)$	**15.** $P(-5, 1)$
16. $Q(-2, -6)$	**17.** $R(0, 6)$	**18.** $S(-4, -1)$	**19.** $T(4, 4)$	**20.** $V(-3, 7)$

Give the coordinates and the quadrant or axis of the point.

21. A	**22.** B	**23.** C
24. D	**25.** E	**26.** F
27. G	**28.** H	**29.** J
30. K	**31.** L	**32.** M
33. N	**34.** O	**35.** P
36. Q	**37.** R	**38.** S
39. T	**40.** U	**41.** V
42. W	**43.** X	**44.** Y

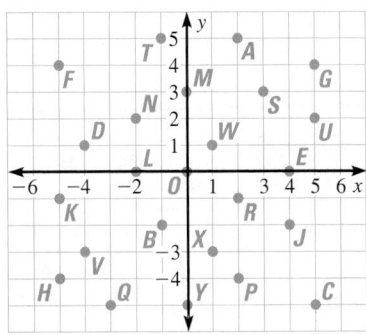

Transformations

A **transformation** is a change made to the position or to the size of a figure. Each point (x, y) of the figure is mapped to a new point, and the new figure is called an **image**.

A **translation** is a transformation in which each point of a figure moves the same distance in the same direction. A figure and its translated image are congruent.

Translation a Units Horizontally and b Units Vertically
$(x, y) \rightarrow (x + a, y + b)$

EXAMPLE Translate $\overline{FG}$ right 3 units and down 1 unit.

To move right 3 units, use $a = 3$. To move down 1 unit, use $b = -1$. So, use $(x, y) \rightarrow (x + 3, y + (-1))$ with each endpoint.

$F(2, 4) \rightarrow F'(2 + 3, 4 + (-1)) = F'(5, 3)$
$G(1, 1) \rightarrow G'(1 + 3, 1 + (-1)) = G'(4, 0)$

Graph the endpoints (5, 3) and (4, 0). Then draw the image.

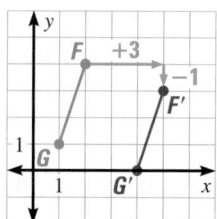

A **reflection** is a transformation in which a figure is reflected, or flipped, in a line, called the **line of reflection**. A figure and its reflected image are congruent.

Reflection in x-axis	Reflection in y-axis
$(x, y) \rightarrow (x, -y)$	$(x, y) \rightarrow (-x, y)$

EXAMPLE Reflect $\triangle ABC$ in the y-axis.

Use $(x, y) \rightarrow (-x, y)$ with each vertex.

$A(4, 3) \rightarrow A'(-4, 3)$ Change each
$B(1, 2) \rightarrow B'(-1, 2)$ x-coordinate
$C(3, 1) \rightarrow C'(-3, 1)$ to its opposite.

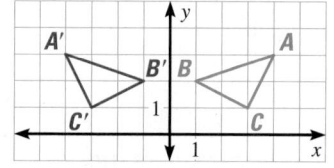

Graph the new vertices. Then draw the image.

A **rotation** is a transformation in which a figure is turned about a fixed point, called the **center of rotation**. The direction can be clockwise or counterclockwise. A figure and its rotated image are congruent.

Rotation About the Origin	
180° either direction	$(x, y) \rightarrow (-x, -y)$
90° clockwise	$(x, y) \rightarrow (y, -x)$
90° counterclockwise	$(x, y) \rightarrow (-y, x)$

EXAMPLE Rotate $RSTV$ 180° about the origin.

Use $(x, y) \rightarrow (-x, -y)$ with each vertex.

$R(2, 2) \rightarrow R'(-2, -2)$ Change every
$S(4, 2) \rightarrow S'(-4, -2)$ coordinate
$T(4, 1) \rightarrow T'(-4, -1)$ to its opposite.
$V(1, 0) \rightarrow V'(-1, 0)$

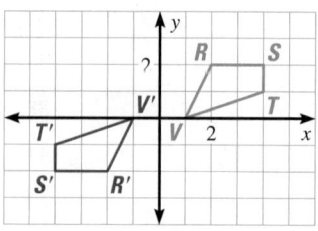

Graph the new vertices. Then draw the image.

A **dilation** is a transformation in which a figure stretches or shrinks depending on the dilation's **scale factor**. A figure *stretches* if $k > 1$ and *shrinks* if $0 < k < 1$. A figure and its dilated image are similar.

Dilation with Scale Factor k with Respect to the Origin
$(x, y) \rightarrow (kx, ky)$

EXAMPLE   Dilate *JKLM* using a scale factor of 0.5.

The scale factor is $k = 0.5$, so multiply every coordinate by 0.5. Use $(x, y) \rightarrow (0.5x, 0.5y)$ with each vertex.

$J(4, 4) \rightarrow J'(0.5 \cdot 4, 0.5 \cdot 4) = J'(2, 2)$
$K(6, 4) \rightarrow K'(0.5 \cdot 6, 0.5 \cdot 4) = K'(3, 2)$
$L(6, -1) \rightarrow L'(0.5 \cdot 6, 0.5 \cdot (-1)) = L'(3, -0.5)$
$M(4, -1) \rightarrow M'(0.5 \cdot 4, 0.5 \cdot (-1)) = M'(2, -0.5)$

Graph the new vertices. Then draw the image.

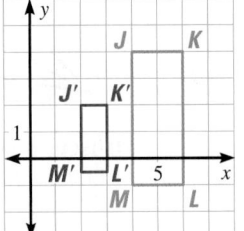

PRACTICE

Find the coordinates of $N(-3, 8)$ after the given transformation. For rotations, rotate about the origin.

1. Rotate 180°.
2. Reflect in *x*-axis.
3. Translate up 3 units.
4. Reflect in *y*-axis.
5. Rotate 90° clockwise.
6. Translate left 5 units.
7. Rotate 90° counterclockwise.
8. Translate right 2 units and down 9 units.

Transform △*PST*. Graph the result. For rotations, rotate about the origin.

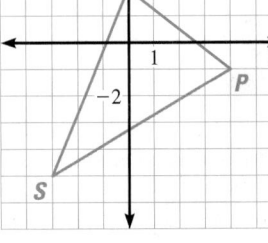

9. Reflect in *x*-axis.
10. Rotate 90° counterclockwise.
11. Rotate 90° clockwise.
12. Translate down 7 units.
13. Reflect in *y*-axis.
14. Translate left 4 units.
15. Rotate 180°.
16. Translate right 2 units.
17. Translate right 1 unit and up 4 units.
18. Translate left 6 units and up 2 units.

The coordinates of the vertices of a polygon are given. Draw the polygon. Then find the coordinates of the vertices of the image after the specified dilation, and draw the image.

19. (1, 3), (3, 2), (2, 5); dilate using a scale factor of 3

20. (2, 8), (2, 4), (6, 8), (6, 4); dilate using a scale factor of $\frac{3}{2}$

21. (3, 3), (6, 3), (3, -3), (6, -3); dilate using a scale factor of $\frac{1}{3}$

22. (2, 2), (2, 7), (5, 7); dilate using a scale factor of 2

23. (2, -2), (6, -2), (4, -6), (0, -6); dilate using a scale factor of $\frac{1}{2}$

Line Symmetry

A figure has **line symmetry** if a line, called a **line of symmetry**, divides the figure into two parts that are mirror images of each other. Below are four figures with their lines of symmetry shown in red.

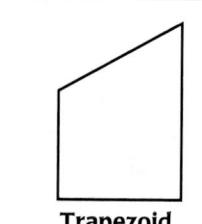	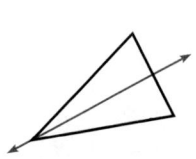	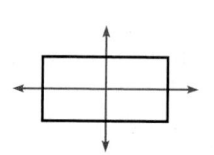	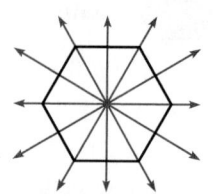
Trapezoid No lines of symmetry	**Isosceles Triangle** 1 line of symmetry	**Rectangle** 2 lines of symmetry	**Regular Hexagon** 6 lines of symmetry

EXAMPLE A line of symmetry for the figure is shown in red. Find the coordinates of point A.

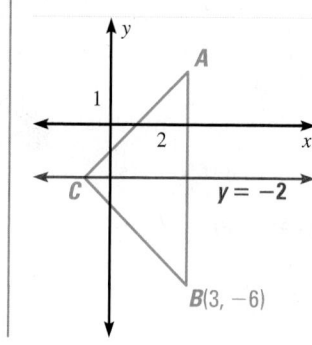

Point A is the mirror image of the point (3, −6) with respect to the line of symmetry $y = -2$. The x-coordinate of A is 3, the same as the x-coordinate of (3, −6). Because −6 is the y-coordinate of (3, −6), and −2 − (−6) = 4, the point (3, −6) is *down* 4 units from the line of symmetry. Therefore, point A must be *up* 4 units from the line of symmetry. So, the y-coordinate of A is −2 + 4 = 2. The coordinates of point A are (3, 2).

PRACTICE

Tell how many lines of symmetry the figure has.

1.    **2.** 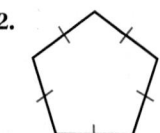   **3.** 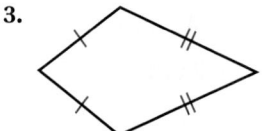   **4.**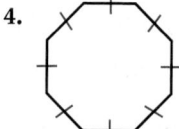

5. A parallelogram   **6.** A square   **7.** A rhombus   **8.** An equilateral triangle

A line of symmetry for the figure is shown in red. Find the coordinates of point A.

9.   **10.** 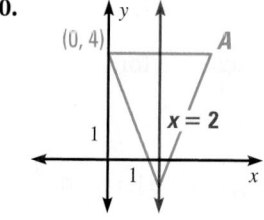   **11.**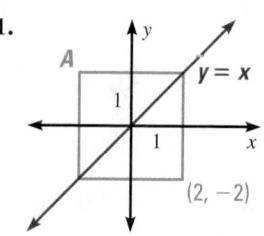

Perimeter and Area

The **perimeter** P of a figure is the distance around it. To find the perimeter of a figure, add the side lengths.

EXAMPLE Find the perimeter of the figure.

a.

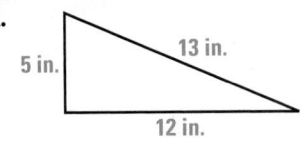

b.

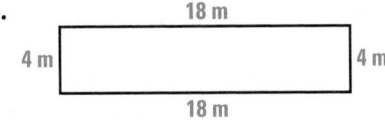

$P = 5 + 12 + 13 = 30$ in. $\qquad\qquad P = 2(4) + 2(18) = 8 + 36 = 44$ m

The **area** A of a figure is the number of square units enclosed by the figure.

Area of a Triangle	Area of a Rectangle	Area of a Parallelogram	Area of a Trapezoid
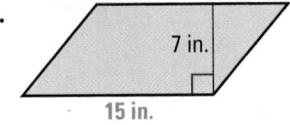	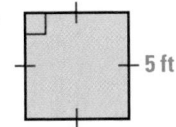	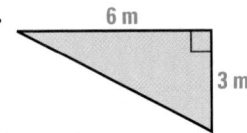	(diagram)
$A = \frac{1}{2}bh$	$A = \ell w$	$A = bh$	$A = \frac{1}{2}(b_1 + b_2)h$

EXAMPLE Find the area of the figure.

a.
(parallelogram: 7 in., 15 in.)

b.
(square: 5 ft)

c.
(triangle: 6 m, 3 m)

$A = (15)(7) = 105$ in.^{2} $\qquad A = (5)(5) = 25$ ft^2 $\qquad A = \frac{1}{2}(6)(3) = 9$ m^2

PRACTICE

Find the perimeter and area of the figure.

1.

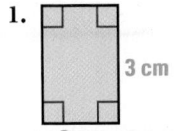

2.

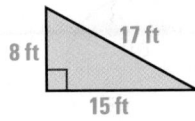

3.

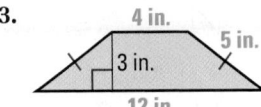

4.

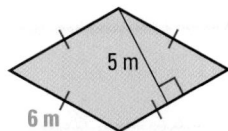

5.

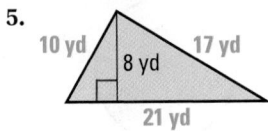

6.

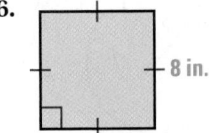

7.

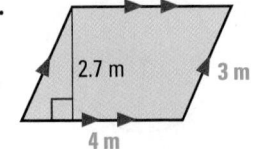

8.

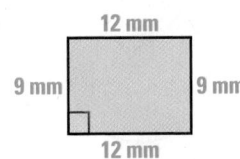

Circumference and Area of a Circle

A **circle** consists of all points in a plane that are the same distance from a fixed point called the **center**.

The distance between the center and any point on the circle is the **radius**. The distance across the circle through the center is the **diameter**. The diameter is twice the radius.

The **circumference** of a circle is the distance around the circle. For any circle, the ratio of the circumference to the diameter is π (pi), an irrational number that is approximately 3.14 or $\frac{22}{7}$.

To find the circumference C of a circle with radius r, use the formula $C = 2\pi r$.

To find the area A of a circle with radius r, use the formula $A = \pi r^2$.

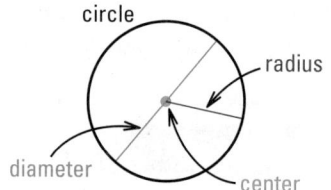

EXAMPLE Find the circumference and area of a circle with radius 6 cm. Give an exact answer and an approximate answer for each.

Circumference

$C = 2\pi r$

$\quad = 2\pi(6)$

$\quad = 12\pi$

$\quad \approx 12(3.14)$

$\quad \approx 37.7$

▸ The circumference is 12π centimeters, or about 37.7 centimeters.

Area

$A = \pi r^2$

$\quad = \pi(6)^2$

$\quad = 36\pi$

$\quad \approx 36(3.14)$

$\quad \approx 113$

▸ The area is 36π square centimeters, or about 113 square centimeters.

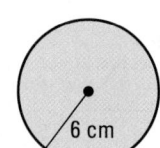

PRACTICE

Find the circumference and area of the circle. Give an exact answer and an approximate answer for each.

1.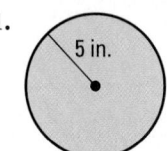
5 in.

2.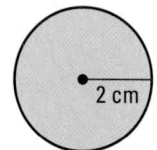
2 cm

3.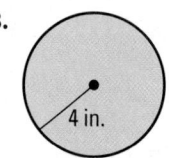
4 in.

4.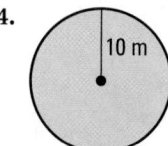
10 m

5.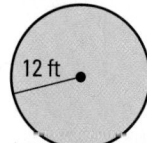
12 ft

6.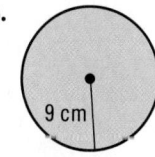
9 cm

7.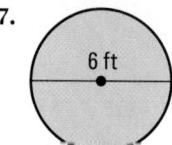
6 ft

8.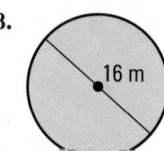
16 m

9.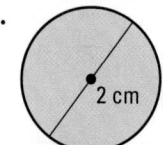
2 cm

10.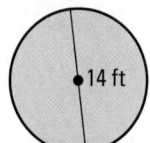
14 ft

11.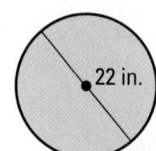
22 in.

12.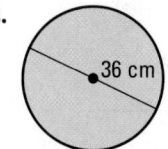
36 cm

Surface Area and Volume

A **solid** is a three-dimensional figure that encloses part of space.

The **surface area** S of a solid is the area of the solid's outer surface(s).

The **volume** V of a solid is the amount of space that the solid occupies.

Rectangular Prism	Cylinder
$S = 2\ell w + 2\ell h + 2wh$ $V = \ell wh$ 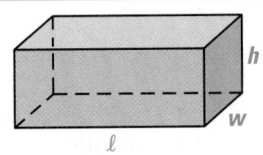	$S = 2\pi r^2 + 2\pi rh$ $V = \pi r^2 h$ 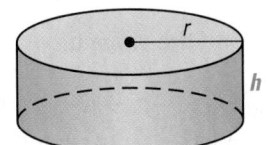

EXAMPLE Find the surface area and volume of the rectangular prism.

Surface area

$S = 2\ell w + 2\ell h + 2wh$

$\quad = 2(5)(3) + 2(5)(7) + 2(3)(7)$

$\quad = 30 + 70 + 42$

$\quad = 142 \text{ ft}^2$

Volume

$V = \ell wh$

$\quad = (5)(3)(7)$

$\quad = 105 \text{ ft}^3$

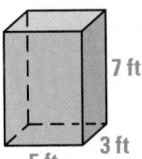

EXAMPLE Find the surface area and volume of the cylinder.

Surface area

$S = 2\pi r^2 + 2\pi rh$

$\quad = 2\pi(3)^2 + 2\pi(3)(12)$

$\quad = 90\pi \text{ m}^2$ **Exact answer**

$\quad \approx 283 \text{ m}^2$ **Approximate answer**

Volume

$V = \pi r^2 h$

$\quad = \pi(3)^2(12)$

$\quad = 108\pi \text{ m}^3$ **Exact answer**

$\quad \approx 339 \text{ m}^3$ **Approximate answer**

PRACTICE

Find the surface area and volume of the solid.

1.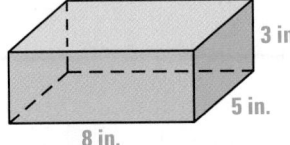
   3 in.
   5 in.
   8 in.

2.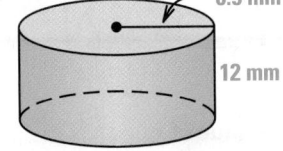
   6.5 mm
   12 mm

3.
   3 cm
   3 cm
   3 cm

4.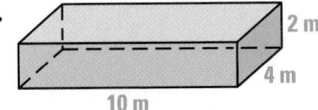
   2 m
   4 m
   10 m

5.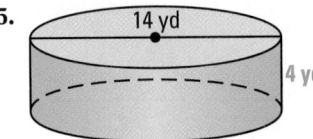
   14 yd
   4 yd

6.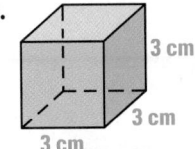
   10 ft
   15 ft

Angle Relationships

An **angle bisector** is a ray that divides an angle into two congruent angles.
Two angles are **complementary angles** if the sum of their measures is 90°.
Two angles are **supplementary angles** if the sum of their measures is 180°.

EXAMPLE Find the value of *x*.

a. $\overrightarrow{BD}$ bisects ∠ABC and m∠ABC = 64°.

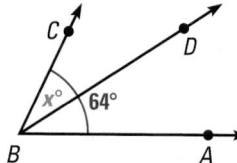

Because $\overrightarrow{BD}$ bisects ∠ABC, the value of *x* is half m∠ABC.

$x = \dfrac{64}{2} = 32$

b. ∠GFJ and ∠HFJ are complementary.

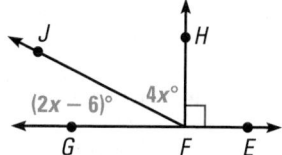

Because ∠GFJ and ∠HFJ are complementary angles, their sum is 90°.

$(2x - 6) + 4x = 90$

$6x - 6 = 90$

$x = 16$

c. ∠CBD and ∠ABD are supplementary.

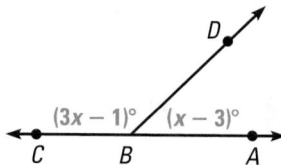

Because ∠CBD and ∠ABD are supplementary angles, their sum is 180°.

$(3x - 1) + (x - 3) = 180$

$4x - 4 = 180$

$x = 46$

PRACTICE

$\overrightarrow{BD}$ is the angle bisector of ∠ABC. Find the value of *x*.

1.
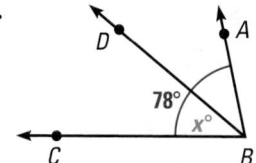

2.
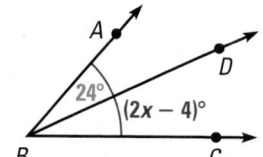

3.
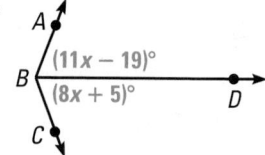

∠ABD and ∠DBC are complementary. Find the value of *x*.

4.
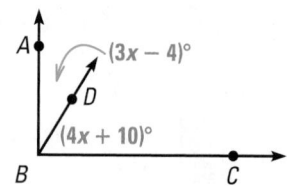

5.
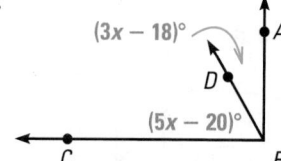

6.
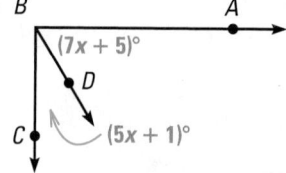

∠ABD and ∠DBC are supplementary. Find the value of *x*.

7.
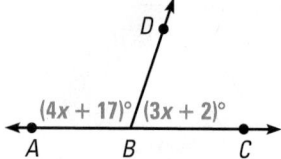

8.
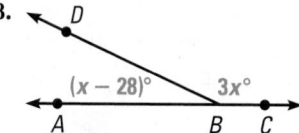

9.
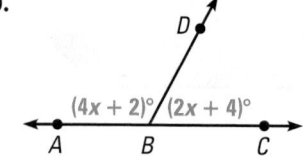

Triangle Relationships

The sum of the angle measures of any triangle is 180°.

EXAMPLE Find the value of *x*.

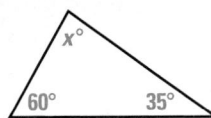

$60 + 35 + x = 180$ **The sum of the angle measures is 180°.**

$95 + x = 180$ **Simplify.**

$x = 85$ **Solve for *x*.**

In a right triangle, the **hypotenuse** is the side opposite the right angle. The **legs** are the sides that form the right angle. The **Pythagorean theorem** states that the sum of the squares of the lengths of the legs equals the square of the length of the hypotenuse.

Pythagorean Theorem
$a^2 + b^2 = c^2$ 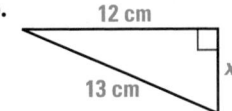

EXAMPLE Find the value of *x*.

a.

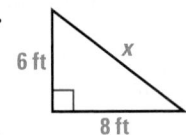

$6^2 + 8^2 = x^2$ **Pythagorean theorem**

$36 + 64 = x^2$ **Simplify.**

$100 = x^2$ **Simplify.**

$x = 10$ ft   **Solve for *x*.**

b.

$x^2 + 12^2 = 13^2$ **Pythagorean theorem**

$x^2 + 144 = 169$ **Simplify.**

$x^2 = 25$ **Solve for x^2.**

$x = 5$ cm   **Solve for *x*.**

PRACTICE

Find the value of *x*.

1.

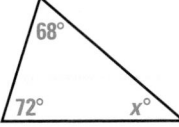

2.

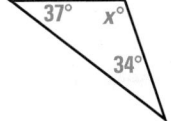

3.

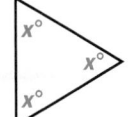

4.

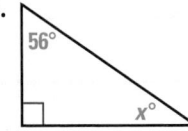

5.

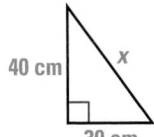

6.

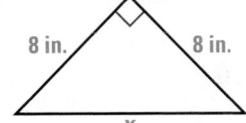

7.

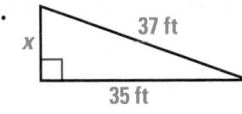

8.

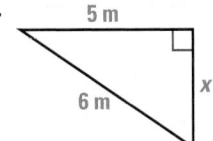

9. A triangle with angles that measure $x°$, $x°$, and 70°

Congruent and Similar Figures

Two figures are **congruent** if they have the same shape and the same size. If two figures are congruent, then corresponding angles are congruent and corresponding sides are congruent. The triangles at the right are congruent. Matching arcs show congruent angles, and matching tick marks show congruent sides.

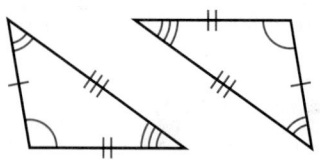

Two figures are **similar** if they have the same shape but not necessarily the same size. If two figures are similar, then corresponding angles are congruent and the ratios of the lengths of corresponding sides are equal.

EXAMPLE   Tell whether the figures are *congruent, similar,* or *neither.*

a.

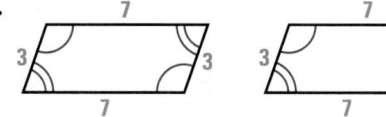

As shown, corresponding angles are congruent and corresponding sides are congruent. So, the figures are congruent.

b.

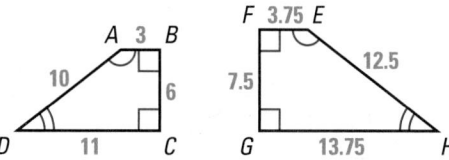

As shown, corresponding angles are congruent, but corresponding sides have different lengths. So, the figures are not congruent, but they may be similar.

The figures are similar if the ratios of the lengths of corresponding sides are equal.

$$\frac{AB}{EF} = \frac{3}{3.75} = 0.8 \qquad \frac{BC}{FG} = \frac{6}{7.5} = 0.8 \qquad \frac{CD}{GH} = \frac{11}{13.75} = 0.8 \qquad \frac{AD}{EH} = \frac{10}{12.5} = 0.8$$

▸ Because corresponding angles are congruent and the ratios of the lengths of corresponding sides are equal, *ABCD* is similar to *EFGH*.

EXAMPLE   The two polygons are similar. Find the value of *x*.

a.

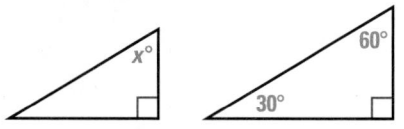

The angle with measure $x°$ corresponds to the angle with measure 60°, so $x = 60$.

b.

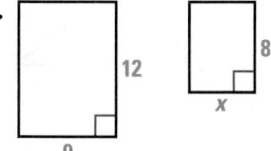

The side with length 12 corresponds to the side with length 8, and the side with length 9 corresponds to the side with length x.

$$\frac{12}{8} = \frac{9}{x} \qquad \text{Write a proportion.}$$

$$12x = 72 \qquad \text{Cross multiply.}$$

$$x = 6 \qquad \text{Solve for } x.$$

PRACTICE

Tell whether the figures are *congruent*, *similar*, or *neither*. Explain.

1.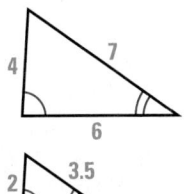

2.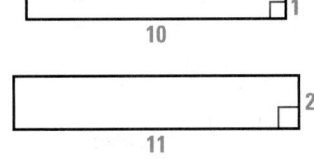

3.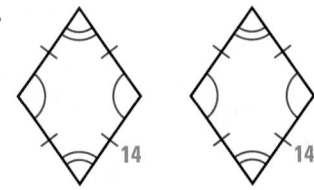

4.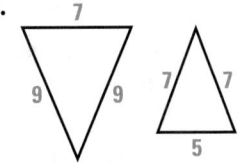

5.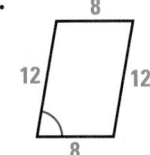

6.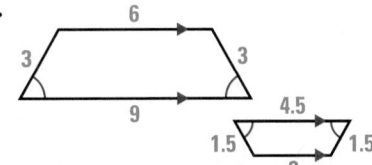

7.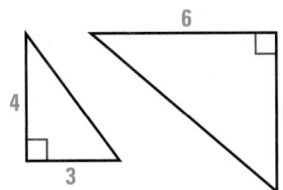

8.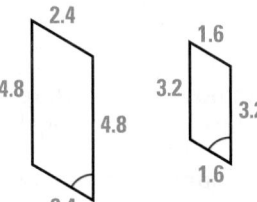

9.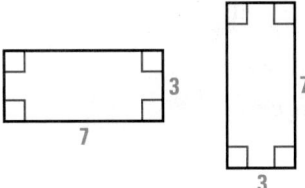

The two polygons are similar. Find the value of x.

10.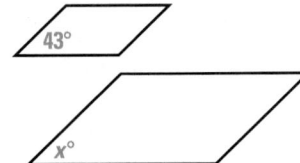

11.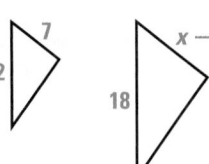

12.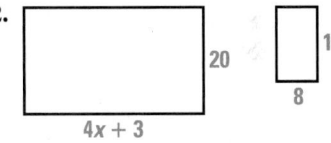

13.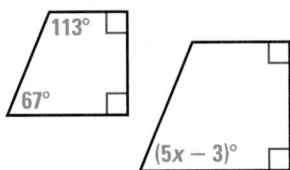

14.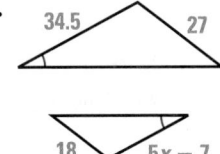

15.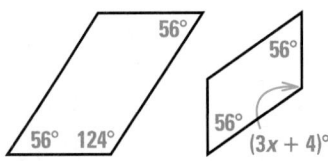

16.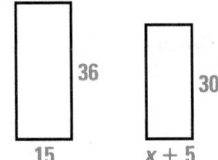

17.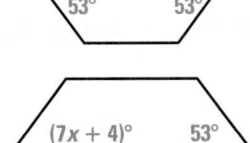

18.

More Problem Solving Strategies

Problem solving strategies can help you solve mathematical and real-life problems. You have learned how to apply the strategies *use a formula, look for a pattern, draw a diagram*, and *use a verbal model*. Below are four more strategies.

Strategy	When to Use	How to Use
Make a list or table	Make a list or table when a problem requires you to record, generate, or organize information.	Make a table with columns, rows, and any given information. Generate a systematic list that can help you solve the problem.
Work backward	Work backward when a problem gives you an end result and you need to find beginning conditions.	Work backward from the given information until you solve the problem. Work forward through the problem to check your answer.
Guess, check, and revise	Guess, check, and revise when you need a place to start or you want to see how the problem works.	Make a reasonable guess. Check to see if your guess solves the problem. If it does not, revise your guess and check again.
Solve a simpler problem	Solve a simpler problem when a problem can be made easier by using simpler numbers.	Think of a way to make the problem simpler. Solve the simpler problem, then use what you learned to solve the original problem.

EXAMPLE **Lee works as a cashier. In how many different ways can Lee make $.50 in change using quarters, dimes, and nickels?**

Use the strategy *make a list or table*. Then count the number of different ways.

Quarters	Dimes	Nickels
2	0	0
1	2	1
1	1	3
1	0	5
0	5	0
0	4	2
0	3	4
0	2	6
0	1	8
0	0	10

← Start with the greatest number of quarters.

Then list all the possibilities with 1 quarter, starting with the greatest number of dimes.

Then list all the possibilities with 0 quarters, starting with the greatest number of dimes.

▶ Lee can make $.50 in quarters, dimes, and nickels in 10 different ways.

EXAMPLE **In a cafeteria, 3 cookies cost $.50 less than a sandwich. If a sandwich costs $4.25, how much does one cookie cost?**

Use the strategy *work backward*.

$4.25 - 0.50 = 3.75$	Cost of 3 cookies		***CHECK*** $1.25 \times 3 = 3.75$	Cost of 3 cookies
$3.75 \div 3 = 1.25$	Cost of 1 cookie		$3.75 + 0.50 = 4.25$	Cost of sandwich

▶ One cookie costs $1.25.

EXAMPLE Nolan's class has 6 more boys than girls. There are 28 students altogether. How many girls are in Nolan's class?

Use the strategy *guess, check, and revise.* Guess a number of girls that is less than half of 28.

First guess:	12 girls, 12 + 6 = 18 boys, 12 + 18 = 30 students	Too high ✗
Second guess:	10 girls, 10 + 6 = 16 boys, 10 + 16 = 26 students	Too low ✗
Third guess:	11 girls, 11 + 6 = 17 boys, 11 + 17 = 28 students	Correct ✓

▸ There are 11 girls in Nolan's class.

EXAMPLE How many diagonals does a regular decagon have?

Use the strategy *solve a simpler problem.* A decagon has 10 sides, so find the number of diagonals of polygons with fewer sides and look for a pattern.

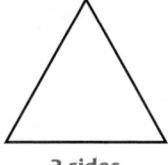  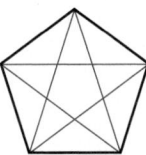 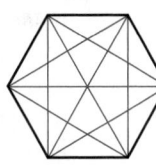 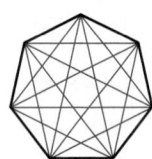

| 3 sides | 4 sides | 5 sides | 6 sides | 7 sides |
| 0 diagonals | 2 diagonals | 5 diagonals | 9 diagonals | 14 diagonals |

Notice that the difference of the numbers of diagonals for consecutive figures keeps increasing by 1:

$$2 - 0 = 2 \qquad 5 - 2 = 3 \qquad 9 - 5 = 4 \qquad 14 - 9 = 5$$

So, an 8-sided polygon has 14 + 6 = 20 diagonals, a 9-sided polygon has 20 + 7 = 27 diagonals, and a 10-sided polygon has 27 + 8 = 35 diagonals.

▸ A regular decagon (a 10-sided polygon) has 35 diagonals.

PRACTICE

1. Ben has a concert at 7:30 P.M. First he must do 2 hours of homework. Then, dinner and a shower will take about 45 minutes. Ben wants to allow a half hour to get to the concert. What time should Ben start his homework?

2. Quinn and Kyle collected 87 aluminum cans to recycle. Quinn collected twice as many cans as Kyle. How many cans did each person collect?

3. In how many different ways can three sisters form a line at a ticket booth?

4. The 8 × 8 grid at the right has some 1 × 1 squares, some 2 × 2 squares, some 3 × 3 squares, and so on. How many total squares does the grid have?

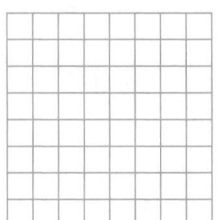

5. If Kaleigh draws 20 different diameters in a circle, into how many parts will the circle be divided?

6. Six friends form a tennis league. Each friend will play a match with every other friend. How many matches will be played?

7. Susan has 13 coins in her pocket with a total value of $1.05. She has only dimes and nickels. How many of each type of coin does Susan have?

Logical Argument

A logical argument has two given statements, called **premises**, and a statement, called a **conclusion**, that follows from the premises. Below is an example.

Premise 1	If a triangle has a right angle, then it is a right triangle.
Premise 2	In $\triangle ABC$, $\angle B$ is a right angle.
Conclusion	$\triangle ABC$ is a right triangle.

Letters are often used to represent the statements of a logical argument and to write a pattern for the argument. The table below gives five types of logical arguments. In the examples, p, q, and r represent the following statements.

p: a figure is a square q: a figure is a rectangle r: a figure is a parallelogram

Type of Argument	Pattern	Example
Direct Argument	If p is true, then q is true. p is true. Therefore, q is true.	If *ABCD* is a square, then it is a rectangle. *ABCD* is a square. Therefore, *ABCD* is a rectangle.
Indirect Argument	If p is true, then q is true. q is not true. Therefore, p is not true.	If *ABCD* is a square, then it is a rectangle. *ABCD* is not a rectangle. Therefore, *ABCD* is not a square.
Chain Rule	If p is true, then q is true. If q is true, then r is true. Therefore, if p, then r.	If *ABCD* is a square, then it is a rectangle. If *ABCD* is a rectangle, then it is a parallelogram. Therefore, if *ABCD* is a square, then it is a parallelogram.
Or Rule	p is true or q is true. p is not true. Therefore, q is true.	*ABCD* is a square or a rectangle. *ABCD* is not a square. Therefore, *ABCD* is a rectangle.
And Rule	p and q are not both true. q is true. Therefore, p is not true.	*ABCD* is not both a square and a rectangle. *ABCD* is a rectangle. Therefore, *ABCD* is not a square.

An argument that follows one of these patterns correctly has a **valid conclusion**.

EXAMPLE   State whether the conclusion is *valid* or *invalid*. If the conclusion is valid, name the type of logical argument used.

a. If it is raining at noon, Peter's family will not have a picnic lunch. Peter's family had a picnic lunch. Therefore, it was not raining at noon.

▶ The conclusion is valid. This is an example of indirect argument.

b. If a triangle is equilateral, then it is an acute triangle. Triangle *XYZ* is an acute triangle. Therefore, triangle *XYZ* is equilateral.

▶ The conclusion is invalid.

c. If $x = 4$, then $2x - 7 = 1$. If $2x - 7 = 1$, then $2x = 8$. Therefore, if $x = 4$, then $2x = 8$.

▶ The conclusion is valid. This is an example of the chain rule.

d. If it is at least 80°F outside today, you will go swimming. It is 85°F outside today. Therefore, you will go swimming.

▶ The conclusion is valid. This is an example of direct argument.

A **compound statement** has two or more parts joined by *or* or *and*.

- For an *and* compound statement to be true, each part must be true.
- For an *or* compound statement to be true, at least one part must be true.

EXAMPLE State whether the compound statement is *true* or *false*.

a. $12 < 20$ and $-12 > -20$
     True   True
  ▸ True, because each part is true.

b. $2 < 4$ and $4 < 3$
     True   False
  ▸ False, because one part is false.

c. $10 > 0$ or $-10 > 0$
     True   False
  ▸ True, because at least one part is true.

d. $-8 > -7$ or $-7 > -6$ or $-6 > -5$
     False   False   False
  ▸ False, because every part is false.

PRACTICE

State whether the conclusion is *valid* or *invalid*. If the conclusion is valid, name the type of logical argument used.

1. If Scott goes to the store, then he will buy sugar. If he buys sugar, then he will bake cookies. Scott goes to the store. Therefore, he will bake cookies.

2. If a triangle has at least two congruent sides, then it is isosceles. Triangle *MNP* has sides 5 in., 6 in., and 5 in. long. Therefore, triangle *MNP* is isosceles.

3. If a horse is an Arabian, then it is less than 16 hands tall. Andrea's horse is 13 hands tall. Therefore, Andrea's horse is an Arabian.

4. If a figure is a rhombus, then it has four sides. Figure *WXYZ* has four sides. Therefore, *WXYZ* is a rhombus.

5. Jeff cannot buy both a new coat and new boots. Jeff decides to buy new boots. Therefore, Jeff cannot buy a new coat.

6. If $x = 0$, then $y = 4$. If $y = 4$, then $z = 7$. Therefore, if $z = 7$, then $x = 0$.

7. Kate will order either tacos or burritos for lunch. Kate does not order tacos for lunch. Therefore, Kate orders burritos for lunch.

8. If a triangle is equilateral, then it is equiangular. Triangle *ABC* is not equiangular. Therefore, triangle *ABC* is not equilateral.

9. An animal cannot be both a fish and a bird. Courtney's pet is not a fish. Therefore, Courtney's pet must be a bird.

State whether the compound statement is *true* or *false*.

10. $-7 < -5$ and $-5 < -6$

11. $6 > 2$ or $8 < 4$

12. $0 \leq -1$ or $5 \geq 5$

13. $4 \leq 3$ or $12 \geq 13$

14. $3 < 5$ and $-3 < -5$

15. $1 = -1$ or $1 = 1$ or $1 = 0$

16. $7 < 8$ and $8 < 12$

17. $-2 < 2$ and $3 \geq 2$

18. $3(-4) = 12$ or $-3(4) = 12$

19. $-8 > 8$ or $-8 = 8$ or $-8 \geq 0$

20. $140 \neq 145$ or $140 > -145$ or $-140 < -145$

21. $-8(9) = -72$ and $8(-9) = -72$

22. $22 \leq 23$ and $-22 < -23$ and $23 > 22$

Conditional Statements and Counterexamples

A **conditional statement** has two parts, a hypothesis and a conclusion. When a conditional statement is written in **if-then form**, the "if" part contains the **hypothesis** and the "then" part contains the **conclusion**. An example of a conditional statement is shown below.

If **a triangle is equiangular**, then each angle of the triangle measures 60°.

$$\underbrace{\hspace{2.5cm}}_{\text{Hypothesis}} \qquad \underbrace{\hspace{5cm}}_{\text{Conclusion}}$$

The **converse** of a conditional statement is formed by switching the hypothesis and the conclusion. The converse of the statement above is as follows:

If each angle of a triangle measures 60°, then **the triangle is equiangular**.

EXAMPLE Rewrite the conditional statement in if-then form. Then write its converse and tell whether the converse is *true* or *false*.

a. Bob will earn $20 by mowing the lawn.

If-then form: If Bob mows the lawn, then he will earn $20.

Converse: If Bob earns $20, then he mowed the lawn. False

b. $x = 8$ when $5x + 1 = 41$.

If-then form: If $5x + 1 = 41$, then $x = 8$.

Converse: If $x = 8$, then $5x + 1 = 41$. True

A **biconditional statement** is a statement that has the words "if and only if." You can write a conditional statement and its converse together as a biconditional statement.

A triangle is equiangular if and only if each angle of the triangle measures 60°.

A biconditional statement is true only when the conditional statement and its converse are both true.

EXAMPLE Tell whether the biconditional statement is *true* or *false*. Explain.

a. An angle measures 90° if and only if it is a right angle.

Conditional: If an angle is a right angle, then it measures 90°. True
Converse: If an angle measures 90°, then it is a right angle. True

▸ The biconditional statement is true because the conditional and its converse are both true.

b. Bonnie has $.50 if and only if she has two quarters.

Conditional: If Bonnie has two quarters, then she has $.50. True
Converse: If Bonnie has $.50, then she has two quarters. False

▸ The biconditional statement is false because the converse is not true.

A **counterexample** is an example that shows that a statement is false.

EXAMPLE Tell whether the statement is *true* or *false*. If false, give a counterexample.

a. If a polygon has four sides and opposite sides are parallel, then it is a rectangle.

> ▸ False. A counterexample is the parallelogram shown.

b. If $x^2 = 49$, then $x = 7$.

> ▸ False. A counterexample is $x = -7$, because $(-7)^2 = 49$.

PRACTICE

Rewrite the conditional statement in if-then form. Then write its converse and tell whether the converse is *true* or *false*.

1. The graph of the equation $y = mx + b$ is a line.

2. You will earn $35 for working 5 hours.

3. Abby can go swimming if she finishes her homework.

4. In a right triangle, the sum of the squares of the lengths of the legs equals the square of the length of the hypotenuse.

5. $x = 5$ when $4x + 8 = 28$.

6. The sum of two even numbers is an even number.

Tell whether the biconditional statement is *true* or *false*. *Explain.*

7. Two lines are perpendicular if and only if they intersect to form a right angle.

8. $x^3 = 27$ if and only if $x = 3$.

9. A vegetable is a carrot if and only if it is orange.

10. A rhombus is a square if and only if it has four right angles.

11. The graph of a function is a parabola if and only if the function is $y = x^2$.

12. An integer is odd if and only if it is not even.

Tell whether the statement is *true* or *false*. If false, give a counterexample.

13. If an integer is not negative, then it is positive.

14. If you were born in the summer, then you were born in July.

15. If a polygon has exactly 5 congruent sides, then the polygon is a pentagon.

16. If $x = -6$, then $x^2 = 36$.

17. If B is 6 inches from A and 8 inches from C, then A is 14 inches from C.

18. If a triangle is isosceles, then it is obtuse.

19. If Charlie has $1.00 in coins, then he has four quarters.

20. If you are in Montana, then you are in the United States.

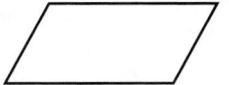

Venn Diagrams

A **Venn diagram** uses shapes to show how sets are related.

EXAMPLE   **Draw a Venn diagram of the positive integers less than 13 where set *A* consists of factors of 12 and set *B* consists of even numbers.**

Positive integers less than 13:
1, 2, 3, 4, 5, 6, 7, 8, 9, 10, 11, 12

Set *A* (factors of 12): 1, 2, 3, 4, 6, 12

Set *B* (even numbers): 2, 4, 6, 8, 10, 12

Both set *A* and set *B*: **2, 4, 6, 12**

Neither set *A* nor set *B*: 5, 7, 9, 11

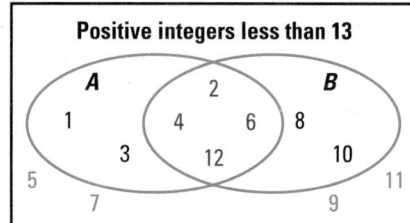

Positive integers less than 13

EXAMPLE   **Use the Venn diagram above to decide if the statement is *true* or *false*. Explain your reasoning.**

a. If a positive integer less than 13 is not even, then it is not a factor of 12.

▶ False. 1 and 3 are not even, but they are factors of 12.

b. All positive integers less than 13 that are even are factors of 12.

▶ False. 8 and 10 are even, but they are not factors of 12.

PRACTICE

Draw a Venn diagram of the sets described.

1. Of the positive integers less than 11, set *A* consists of factors of 10 and set *B* consists of odd numbers.

2. Of the positive integers less than 10, set *A* consists of prime numbers and set *B* consists of even numbers.

3. Of the positive integers less than 25, set *A* consists of multiples of 3 and set *B* consists of multiples of 4.

Use the Venn diagrams you drew in Exercises 1–3 to decide if the statement is *true* or *false*. *Explain* your reasoning.

4. The only factors of 10 less than 11 that are not odd are 2 and 10.

5. If a number is neither a multiple of 3 nor a multiple of 4, then it is odd.

6. All prime numbers less than 10 are not even.

7. If a positive odd integer less than 11 is a factor of 10, then it is 5.

8. There are 2 positive integers less than 25 that are both a multiple of 3 and a multiple of 4.

9. If a positive even integer less than 10 is prime, then it is 2.

Mean, Median, Mode, and Range

Mean, median, and mode are measures of central tendency; they measure the center of data. Range is a measure of dispersion; it measures the spread of data.

The **mean** of a data set is the sum of the values divided by the number of values. The mean is also called the *average*.	The **median** of a data set is the middle value when the values are written in numerical order. If a data set has an even number of values, the median is the mean of the two middle values.	The **mode** of a data set is the value that occurs most often. A data set can have no mode, one mode, or more than one mode.	The **range** of a data set is the difference between the greatest value and the least value.

EXAMPLE Find the mean, median, mode(s), and range of the data.

Daily High Temperatures, Week of June 21–27							
Day	Sunday	Monday	Tuesday	Wednesday	Thursday	Friday	Saturday
Temperature (°F)	76	74	70	69	70	75	78

Mean   Add the values. Then divide by the number of values.

$$76 + 74 + 70 + 69 + 70 + 75 + 78 = 512$$

mean $= 512 \div 7 \approx 73$ The **mean** of the data is about 73°F.

Median Write the values in order from least to greatest. Find the middle value(s).

69, 70, 70, <u>74</u>, 75, 76, 78

median $= 74$ The **median** of the data is 74°F.

Mode   Find the value that occurs most often.

mode $= 70$ The **mode** of the data is 70°F.

Range Subtract the least value from the greatest value.

range $= 78 - 69 = 9$ The **range** of the data is 9°F.

PRACTICE

Find the mean, median, mode(s), and range of the data.

1. Apartment rents: $650, $800, $700, $525, $675, $750, $500, $650, $725

2. Ages of new drivers: 15, 15, 15, 15, 16, 16, 16, 16, 16, 17, 17, 17, 18, 18

3. Monthly cell-phone minutes: 581, 713, 423, 852, 948, 337, 810, 604, 897

4. Prices of a CD: $12.98, $14.99, $13.49, $12.98, $13.89, $16.98, $11.98

5. Cookies in a batch: 36, 60, 52, 44, 48, 45, 48, 41, 60, 45, 38, 55, 60, 48, 40

6. Ages of family members: 41, 45, 8, 10, 40, 44, 3, 5, 42, 42, 13, 14, 67, 70

7. Hourly rates of pay: $8.80, $6.50, $10.85, $7.90, $9.50, $9, $8.70, $12.35

8. Weekly quiz scores: 8, 9, 8, 10, 10, 7, 9, 8, 9, 9, 10, 7, 8, 6, 10, 9, 9, 8, 8, 10

9. People on a bus: 9, 14, 5, 22, 18, 30, 6, 25, 18, 12, 15, 10, 8, 22, 10, 11, 20

Graphing Statistical Data

There are many ways to display data. An appropriate graph can help you analyze data. The table at the right summarizes how data are shown in some statistical graphs.

Bar Graph	Compares data in categories.
Circle Graph	Compares data as parts of a whole.
Line Graph	Shows data change over time.

EXAMPLE Use the bar graph to answer the questions.

a. On which day of the week were the greatest number of cars parked in the student lot?

▸ The tallest bar on the graph is for Friday. So, the answer is Friday.

b. How many cars were parked in the student lot on Monday?

▸ The bar for Monday shows that about 70 cars were parked in the student lot.

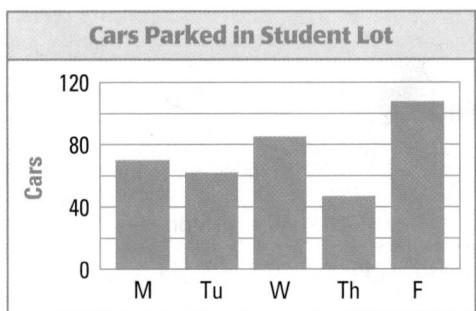

EXAMPLE Use the circle graph to answer the questions.

a. Which type of transportation is used almost half the time?

▸ Almost half of the total area of the circle is labeled "Car 45%." So, a car is used almost half the time.

b. Which type of transportation is used the least often?

▸ The smallest part of the circle is labeled "Bus 20%." So, a bus is used the least often.

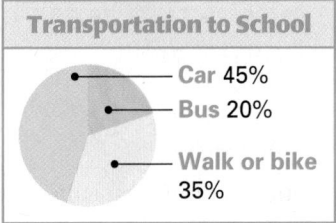

EXAMPLE Use the line graph to answer the questions.

a. In which month(s) was Jamie's balance $250?

▸ The points on the graph to the right of $250 show that Jamie's balance was $250 in May and December.

b. Between which two consecutive months did Jamie's balance increase the most?

▸ Of the graph's line segments that have positive slope, the graph is steepest from June to July. So, Jamie's balance increased the most between June and July.

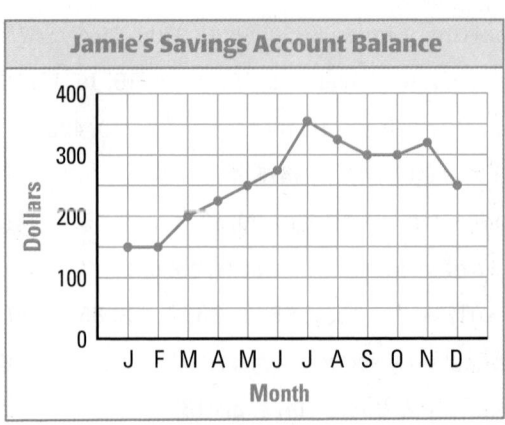

Use the line graph to answer Exercises 1–5.

1. At which hour did Ferraro's have 22 diners?

2. At which hour did Ferraro's have the most diners?

3. How many diners were at Ferraro's at 11 P.M.? Were they gone by midnight?

4. Between which two consecutive hours did the number of diners at Ferraro's change the most?

5. How many fewer diners were at Ferraro's at 10 P.M. than at 6 P.M.?

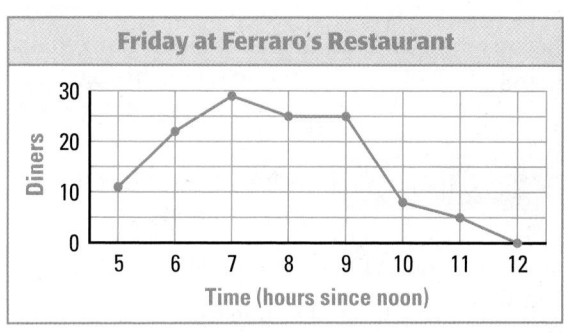

Use the bar graph to answer Exercises 6–8.

6. In which season were the fewest students born?

7. In which season(s) were 7 students born?

8. How many more students were born in spring than in summer?

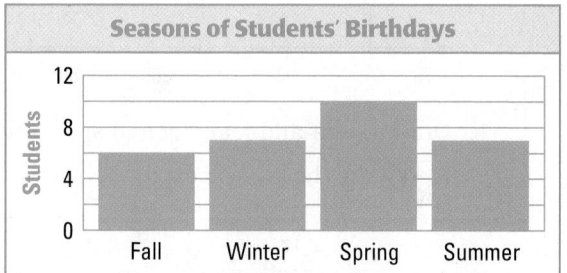

Use the circle graph to answer Exercises 9–11.

9. What is the heat source of more than half the homes in the United States?

10. What percent of homes in the United States are heated with electricity?

11. If you randomly selected 500 U.S. homes, about how many would be heated with fuel oil?

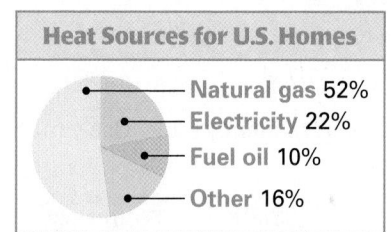

Heat Sources for U.S. Homes

Natural gas 52%
Electricity 22%
Fuel oil 10%
Other 16%

12. The table below shows the high temperatures in degrees Fahrenheit for one week. Display the data in a line graph.

Mon.	Tues.	Wed.	Thurs.	Fri.	Sat.	Sun.
83	89	79	73	69	67	71

13. A high school conducted a survey to determine the numbers of students involved in various school activities. Display the survey results in a bar graph.

Computer club	Music club	Yearbook club	Drama club	Student council	Chess club
34	75	16	57	28	12

14. The table below shows the items sold at a café in one day. Display the data in a circle graph.

Juice	Soda	Water	Muffin	Cookie
95	180	100	55	40

Organizing Statistical Data

Because it is difficult to analyze unorganized data, it is helpful to organize data using a line plot, stem-and-leaf plot, histogram, or box-and-whisker plot.

EXAMPLE **Sydney's math test scores are 90, 85, 88, 95, 100, 77, 85, 100, 80, 77, and 90.**

a. Draw a line plot to display the data.

Make a number line from 75 to 100. Each time a value is listed in the data set, draw an X above the value on the number line.

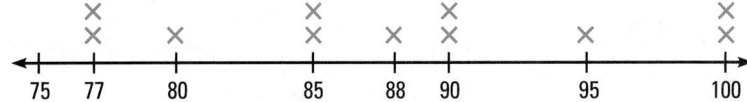

b. Draw a stem-and-leaf plot to display the data.

First write the leaves next to their stems.

```
 7 | 7  7
 8 | 5  8  5  0
 9 | 0  5  0
10 | 0  0      Key: 7|7 = 77
```

Then order the leaves from least to greatest.

```
 7 | 7  7
 8 | 0  5  5  8
 9 | 0  0  5
10 | 0  0      Key: 7|7 = 77
```

c. Draw a histogram to display the data.

First make a frequency table. Use equal intervals.

Score	Tally	Frequency
71–80	III	3
81–90	IIII	5
91–100	III	3

Then make a histogram.

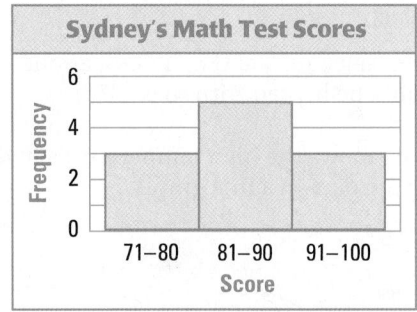

d. Draw a box-and-whisker plot to display the data.

Write the data in order from least to greatest. Ordered data are divided into a lower half and an upper half by the median. The median of the lower half is the **lower quartile**, and the median of the upper half is the **upper quartile**.

77　77　**80**　85　85　**88**　90　90　**95**　100　**100**

Low value　　Lower quartile　　Median　　Upper quartile　　High value

Plot the median, quartiles, and low and high values below a number line. Draw a box between quartiles with a vertical line through the median as shown. Draw whiskers to the low and high values.

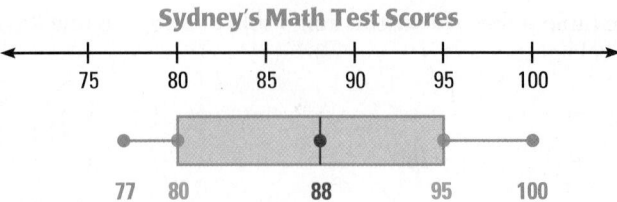

PRACTICE

Use the following list of ticket prices to answer Exercises 1–4: $50, $42, $65, $54, $70, $65, $59, $30, $67, $49, $54, $30, $73, $47, and $54.

1. Draw a line plot to display the data.
2. How many ticket prices are $50 or less?
3. Draw a stem-and-leaf plot to display the data.
4. What is the range of ticket prices costs?

Use the following list of hourly wages of employees to answer Exercises 5–8: $8.50, $6, $10, $14.25, $5.75, $7, $6.50, $14, $10, $9, $6.50, $8.25, $8.50, $11.25, $7, $16, $12, $6, $6.75.

5. Draw a histogram to display the data. Begin with the interval $5.00 to $6.99.

6. Copy and complete: The greatest number of employees earn from _?_ to _?_ per hour.

7. Draw a box-and-whisker plot to display the data.

8. Copy and complete: About half of the employees have an hourly wage of _?_ or less.

Use the line plot, which shows the results of a survey asking people the average number of e-mails they receive daily, to answer Exercises 9 and 10.

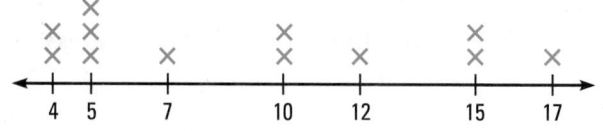

9. Copy and complete: Most people surveyed receive an average of _?_ e-mails per day.

10. How many people receive an average of more than 10 e-mails per day?

Use the stem-and-leaf plot, which shows the weights (in pounds) of dogs at an animal shelter, to answer Exercises 11–13.

2	2 5 5 9
3	1 3 5 8
4	0 0 1 2 2 5 6 7
5	0 3 5 8 9
6	4 5

Key: 2|2 = 22

11. How many dogs were at the shelter?

12. Find the median of the data.

13. Find the range of the data.

Use the histogram to answer Exercises 14–16.

14. Which age group had the greatest attendance at the baseball game? Which had the least?

15. How many children up to the age of 9 years attended the baseball game?

16. Which age group had the same attendance as the oldest group?

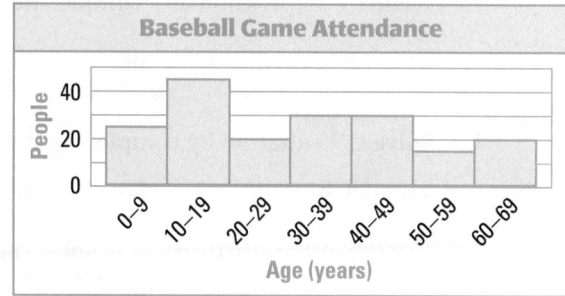

Use the box-and-whisker plot to answer Exercises 17–19.

17. What is the median number of songs on Sam's CDs?

18. What is the upper quartile of songs on Sam's CDs?

19. What is the least number of songs on one of Sam's CDs? What is the greatest number?

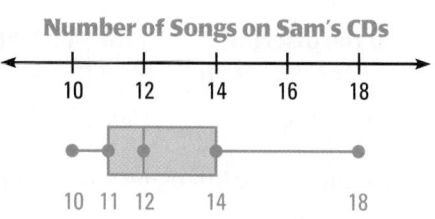

Chapter 1

1.1 Graph the function. Label the vertex and axis of symmetry.

   1. $y = 3x^2 + 5$ **2.** $y = -x^2 - 4x - 4$ **3.** $y = -2x^2 + 4x + 1$ **4.** $y = 2x^2 + 5x + 6$

1.2 Graph the function. Label the vertex and axis of symmetry.

   5. $y = 4(x - 2)^2 + 1$ **6.** $y = -(x + 3)^2 - 2$ **7.** $y = 3(x - 1)(x - 5)$ **8.** $y = \frac{1}{2}(x + 3)(x + 2)$

1.2 Write the quadratic function in standard form.

   9. $y = 7(x + 2)(x + 4)$ **10.** $y = 2(x + 5)(x - 3)$ **11.** $y = (x - 7)^2 + 7$ **12.** $y = -(x + 1)^2 - 4$

1.3 Factor the expression. If the expression cannot be factored, say so.

   13. $x^2 - 4x + 4$ **14.** $t^2 - 11t - 26$ **15.** $x^2 + 21x + 108$ **16.** $b^2 - 400$

1.3 Solve the equation.

   17. $x^2 + 5x - 14 = 0$ **18.** $x^2 - 11x + 24 = 0$ **19.** $c^2 + 6c = 55$ **20.** $n^2 = 5n$

1.4 Factor the expression. If the expression cannot be factored, say so.

   21. $2x^2 + x - 15$ **22.** $10a^2 - 19a + 7$ **23.** $3r^2 + 9r - 4$ **24.** $4t^2 + 8t + 3$

1.4 Find the zeros of the function by rewriting the function in intercept form.

   25. $y = 81x^2 - 16$ **26.** $y = 2x^2 - 9x - 5$ **27.** $y = 4x^2 + 18x + 18$ **28.** $y = -3x^2 - 30x - 27$

1.5 Simplify the expression.

   29. $\sqrt{56}$ **30.** $3\sqrt{2} \cdot \sqrt{50}$ **31.** $\sqrt{\frac{4}{7}}$ **32.** $\frac{6}{1 + \sqrt{2}}$

1.5 Solve the equation.

   33. $b^2 = 8$ **34.** $p^2 + 6 = 127$ **35.** $(x - 5)^2 = 10$ **36.** $3(x + 2)^2 - 4 = 11$

1.6 Write the expression as a complex number in standard form.

   37. $(5 + 2i) + (6 - 5i)$ **38.** $-3i(7 + i)$ **39.** $\frac{1 + 2i}{3 - 8i}$ **40.** $\frac{(3 - 2i) + 2i}{(-1 + 7i) - (2 + 3i)}$

1.7 Solve the equation by completing the square.

   41. $x^2 + 6x = 10$ **42.** $x^2 - 9x - 2 = 0$ **43.** $2c^2 - 12c + 6 = 0$ **44.** $3z^2 - 3z + 9 = 0$

1.8 Use the quadratic formula to solve the equation.

   45. $x^2 + 10x - 10 = 0$ **46.** $x^2 - x - 1 = 0$ **47.** $4s^2 + 3s = 12$ **48.** $-2r^2 = r + 17$

1.8 Find the discriminant of the quadratic equation and give the number and type of the solutions of the equation.

   49. $x^2 - 11x + 31 = 0$ **50.** $s^2 + 3s + 2.25 = 0$ **51.** $5p^2 - 10p = 5$ **52.** $3z^2 + 4z = -3z - 6$

1.9 Solve the inequality using any method.

   53. $x^2 - 10x \geq 0$ **54.** $x^2 - 8x + 12 < 0$ **55.** $-x^2 + 7x + 6 > 1$ **56.** $3x^2 + 16x + 2 \leq 3x$

Extra Practice

Chapter 2

2.1 Write the answer in scientific notation.

1. $(3.4 \times 10^3)(2.8 \times 10^8)$ **2.** $(\quad \times 10^{-6})^4$ **3.** $\dfrac{4.6 \times 10^{-7}}{9.2 \times 10^{-9}}$

2.1 Simplify the expression. Tell which properties of exponents you used.

4. $\dfrac{-14x^{-3}y^5}{35xy^3}$ **5.** $(4a^5b^{-2})^{-3}$ **6.** $(2r^3s^3)(r^{-7}s^5)$ **7.** $\dfrac{xy^{-1}}{x^2y} \cdot \dfrac{7x^3}{y^{-4}}$

2.2 Graph the polynomial function.

8. $f(x) = x^4$ **9.** $f(x) = x^3 + x + 4$ **10.** $f(x) = -x^3 + 3x$ **11.** $f(x) = x^5 + 2x^3$

2.3 Perform the indicated operation.

12. $(4z^3 + 9) + (3z^2 - 4z - 2)$ **13.** $(x^2 + 3x - 1) - (4x^2 + 7)$ **14.** $(3x - 4)^3$

2.4 Factor the polynomial completely using any method.

15. $3x^4 + 18x^3 + 27x^2$ **16.** $343x^3 + 1000$ **17.** $2x^3 + x^2 - 8x - 4$

2.4 Find the real-number solutions of the equation.

18. $3x^3 + 18x^2 = 48x$ **19.** $x^4 - 32 = 14x^2$ **20.** $2x^3 + 48 = 3x^2 + 32x$

2.5 Divide using polynomial long division or synthetic division.

21. $(2x^3 + 4x^2 - 5x + 16) \div (x - 3)$ **22.** $(x^4 + 2x^3 - 7x^2 - 14) \div (x + 2)$

2.6 Find all real zeros of the function.

23. $f(x) = 2x^3 + 3x^2 - 8x + 3$ **24.** $f(x) = 4x^4 - 4x^3 - 9x^2 + x + 2$

25. $f(x) = 2x^4 + x^3 - 53x^2 - 14x + 20$ **26.** $f(x) = x^5 - x^4 - 12x^3 + 12x^2 + 27x - 27$

2.7 Find all zeros of the polynomial function.

27. $f(x) = x^4 + 4x^3 + 7x^2 + 16x + 12$ **28.** $f(x) = 6x^4 + x^3 + 2x^2 - 4x + 1$

2.7 Determine the possible numbers of positive real zeros, negative real zeros, and imaginary zeros of the function.

29. $f(x) = -x^3 + 2x^2 - 11x - 1$ **30.** $f(x) = 4x^5 + 3x^2 - 8x - 10$ **31.** $f(x) = x^4 - 3x^3 - 7x - 13$

2.8 Estimate the coordinates of each turning point and state whether each corresponds to a local maximum or a local minimum. Then estimate all real zeros and determine the least degree the function can have.

32. 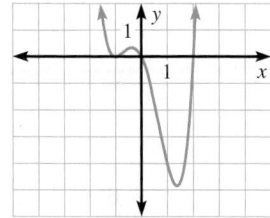   **33.** 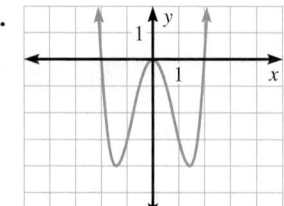   **34.**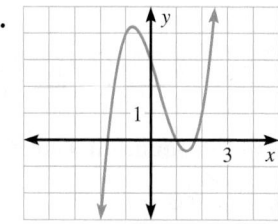

Chapter 3

3.1 **Find the indicated real nth root(s) of a.**

1. $n = 4$, $a = 81$ 2. $n = 3$, $a = 512$ 3. $n = 5$, $a = -243$

3.1 **Evaluate the expression without using a calculator.**

4. $36^{-1/2}$ 5. $64^{5/6}$ 6. $\left(\sqrt[3]{216}\right)^{-2}$ 7. $\left(\sqrt[5]{-32}\right)^4$

3.1 **Solve the equation. Round the result to two decimal places when appropriate.**

8. $x^3 = -8$ 9. $x^4 + 9 = 90$ 10. $(x - 3)^5 = 60$ 11. $-4x^6 = -400$

3.2 **Simplify the expression.**

12. $4^{5/2} \cdot 4^{-1/2}$ 13. $\dfrac{17^{3/7}}{17^{4/7}}$ 14. $\left(\sqrt[4]{5} \cdot \sqrt{5}\right)^4$ 15. $\dfrac{\sqrt[3]{135}}{\sqrt[3]{5}}$

16. $5\sqrt[5]{7} - 7\sqrt[5]{7}$ 17. $\sqrt[3]{2} + 2\sqrt[3]{128}$ 18. $\dfrac{324^{1/4}}{4^{-1/4}}$ 19. $4\sqrt[3]{108} \cdot 2\sqrt[3]{4}$

3.2 **Write the expression in simplest form. Assume all variables are positive.**

20. $\sqrt{20x^6y^7}$ 21. $\sqrt[5]{18x^3y^{14}z^{20}}$ 22. $\sqrt[4]{\dfrac{x^5}{y^{16}}}$ 23. $\sqrt[3]{16x^7y^2} \cdot \sqrt[3]{6xy^5}$

3.3 **Let $f(x) = -x + 4$, $g(x) = x^3$, and $h(x) = \dfrac{x}{4}$. Perform the indicated operation and state the domain.**

24. $f(x) + g(x)$ 25. $g(x) - f(x)$ 26. $g(x) \cdot h(x)$ 27. $\dfrac{f(x)}{g(x)}$

28. $f(g(x))$ 29. $g(h(x))$ 30. $h(f(x))$ 31. $f(f(x))$

3.4 **Verify that f and g are inverse functions.**

32. $f(x) = 2x - 4$, $g(x) = \dfrac{1}{2}x + 2$ 33. $f(x) = 3x^2 + 1$, $x \geq 0$; $g(x) = \left(\dfrac{x - 1}{3}\right)^{1/2}$

3.4 **Find the inverse of the function.**

34. $f(x) = 5x - 3$ 35. $f(x) = \dfrac{4}{3}x + 2$ 36. $f(x) = \dfrac{1}{2}x^2$, $x \geq 0$

37. $f(x) = -x^6 + 2$, $x \leq 0$ 38. $f(x) = \dfrac{4x^4 - 1}{18}$, $x \geq 0$ 39. $f(x) = 32x^5 + 4$

3.5 **Graph the function. Then state the domain and range.**

40. $y = -\dfrac{1}{3}\sqrt{x}$ 41. $y = \dfrac{2}{5}\sqrt[3]{x}$ 42. $y = \dfrac{5}{6}\sqrt{x}$ 43. $y = \sqrt{x + 2} - 3$

44. $y = -2\sqrt[3]{x - 1} + 2$ 45. $f(x) = 3\sqrt[3]{x}$ 46. $g(x) = -\dfrac{1}{2}\sqrt{x - 2}$ 47. $h(x) = -\sqrt{x + 3} + 4$

3.6 **Solve the equation. Check your solution.**

48. $\sqrt{2x + 3} = 7$ 49. $-5\sqrt{x + 1} + 12 = 2$ 50. $\sqrt[3]{5x - 1} + 6 = 10$

51. $2\sqrt[3]{8x} + 9 = 5$ 52. $7x^{4/3} = 175$ 53. $(x - 2)^{3/4} = 1$

54. $x - 8 = \sqrt{18x}$ 55. $x = \sqrt{4x - 3}$ 56. $\sqrt{2x + 1} + 5 = \sqrt{x + 12} - 8$

Extra Practice

Chapter 4

4.1 Graph the function. State the domain and range.

1. $y = \left(\dfrac{4}{3}\right)^x$

2. $y = -2 \cdot 2^x$

3. $y = 3^{x-3} - 2$

4. $y = \dfrac{1}{4} \cdot 3^{x+1} + 2$ *how wide* ⟳ *up or down*

4.2 Graph the function. State the domain and range.

5. $y = \left(\dfrac{3}{5}\right)^x$

6. $y = -2\left(\dfrac{1}{4}\right)^x + 0$

7. $y = (0.8)^{x-3} - 2$

8. $y = 2\left(\dfrac{2}{3}\right)^x + 1$

4.3 Simplify the expression.

9. $e^{-3} \cdot e^{-8}$

10. $\left(2e^{2x}\right)^{-5}$

11. $\sqrt{81e^{8x}}$

12. $\dfrac{28e^{3x}}{21e^{-x}}$

4.3 Graph the function. State the domain and range.

13. $y = 0.5e^{3x}$

14. $y = 2e^{-x} - 2$

15. $y = 1.5e^{x+1} + 3$

16. $y = e^{3(x-2)} + 1$

4.4 Evaluate the logarithm without using a calculator.

17. $\log_4 \dfrac{1}{16}$

18. $\log_6 6 = 1$ *same*

19. $\log_5 125$

20. $\log_{3/4} \dfrac{64}{27}$

4.4 Simplify the expression.

21. $5^{\log_5 x}$

22. $10^{\log 9}$

23. $\log_4 16^x$

24. $e^{\ln 5}$

4.4 Graph the function. State the domain and range.

25. $y = \log_7 x$

26. $y = \log_{1/2}(x - 4)$

27. $y = \log_5 x + 3$

28. $y = \log_3(x - 2) + 1$

4.5 Expand the expression.

29. $\log_5 \dfrac{2x}{5}$

30. $\log \dfrac{100x^2}{y}$

31. $\ln 20x^3 y^2$

32. $\log_2 \sqrt[3]{8x^4}$

4.5 Condense the expression.

33. $\log_4 20 + 4\log_4 x$

34. $\log 7 + 2\log x - 5\log y$

35. $0.5\ln 100 - 2\ln x + 8\ln y$

4.5 Use the change-of-base formula to evaluate the logarithm.

36. $\log_2 5$

37. $\log_4 80$

38. $\log_5 100$

39. $\log_7 27$

4.6 Solve the equation. Check for extraneous solutions.

40. $2^{4x+2} = 8^{x+2}$

41. $\left(\dfrac{1}{9}\right)^{x-3} = 3^{3x+1}$

42. $7^{9x} = 18$

43. $\ln(3x + 7) = \ln(x - 1)$

44. $\log_5(3x + 2) = 3$

45. $\log_6(x + 9) + \log_6 x = 2$

4.7 Write an exponential function $y = ab^x$ whose graph passes through the given points.

46. $(1, 8), (2, 32)$

47. $(1, 3), (3, 12)$

48. $(2, -9), (5, -243)$

49. $(1, 4), (2, 4)$

4.7 Write a power function $y = ax^b$ whose graph passes through the given points.

50. $(2, 2), (5, 16)$

51. $(3, 27), (6, 432)$

52. $(1, 4), (8, 17)$

53. $(5, 36), (10, 220)$

Extra Practice

Chapter 5

5.1 Determine whether x and y show *direct variation*, *inverse variation*, or *neither*.

1.

x	y
2.5	32
4	20
5	16
6.4	12.5
8	10

2.

x	y
1	2.5
3.5	8.75
5	12.5
8	20
9	22.5

3.

x	y
11	30
14	61
16	85
24	92
27	105

4.

x	y
1	12
3	4
8	1.5
12	1
15	0.8

5.2 Graph the function. State the domain and range.

5. $y = \dfrac{6}{x}$

6. $y = \dfrac{-2}{x} + 3$

7. $y = \dfrac{5}{x-1} - 2$

8. $y = \dfrac{4x+19}{x+3}$

5.3 Graph the function.

9. $y = \dfrac{x}{x^2-4}$

10. $y = \dfrac{x^2+1}{x^2+4x+3}$

11. $y = \dfrac{x^2+2x-3}{x+2}$

12. $f(x) = \dfrac{2x^2-8}{x^2-2x}$

5.4 Simplify the rational expression, if possible.

13. $\dfrac{x^2+x-6}{x^2+9x+18}$

14. $\dfrac{x^3-100x}{x^4+20x^3+100x^2}$

15. $\dfrac{x^2-5x-84}{2x^2-98}$

16. $\dfrac{x^2+7x+10}{x^2-7x+10}$

5.4 Multiply or divide the expressions. Simplify the result.

17. $\dfrac{3x^2+15x}{x^2-12x+36} \cdot (x^2-x-30)$

18. $\dfrac{6x^2+x-1}{4x^3+4x^2} \div \dfrac{6x^2-2x}{x^2-4x-5}$

19. $\dfrac{x^2-4x-32}{2x^2-13x-24} \div \dfrac{x}{4x^2-9}$

5.5 Add or subtract the expressions. Simplify the result.

20. $\dfrac{x^2}{x+1} - \dfrac{1}{x+1}$

21. $\dfrac{x+5}{x+6} + \dfrac{1}{x-2}$

22. $\dfrac{5}{x+2} + \dfrac{35}{x^2-3x-10}$

5.5 Simplify the complex fraction.

23. $\dfrac{\dfrac{x}{2x+1}}{5+\dfrac{3}{x}}$

24. $\dfrac{\dfrac{x}{3}+2}{\dfrac{1}{x}+3}$

25. $\dfrac{\dfrac{3}{x^2-4}}{\dfrac{2}{x+2}-\dfrac{x+1}{x^2-x-6}}$

5.6 Solve the equation. Check for extraneous solutions.

26. $\dfrac{7}{3x-7} = \dfrac{14}{x+1}$

27. $\dfrac{1}{3} + \dfrac{2}{x} = -\dfrac{3}{x^2}$

28. $2 - \dfrac{4}{x+2} = \dfrac{2}{x}$

29. $\dfrac{4}{x-2} + \dfrac{6x^2}{x^2-4} = \dfrac{3x}{x+2}$

5.7 Find the average rate of change of the function over the domain intervals [1, 3], [3, 5], [5, 7], [7, 9].

30. $f(x) = x^2 - 10x + 30$

31. $f(x) = 4 - \dfrac{6}{x}$

32. $f(x) = \dfrac{x^2-2x+3}{x+1}$

5.7 Determine whether the function is *even*, *odd*, or *neither*.

33. $f(x) = \dfrac{4x^2}{3x^2-5}$

34. $f(x) = (x-3)^2$

35. $f(x) = \dfrac{-2x^3}{8-x^2}$

36. $f(x) = x - 3x^3 + 5x^5$

Chapter 6

6.1 Find the number of combinations.

1. $_7C_3$ 2. $_4C_1$ 3. $_{10}C_9$ 4. $_{15}C_6$

6.1 Use the binomial theorem to write the binomial expansion.

5. $(x - 3)^3$ 6. $(2x + 3y)^4$ 7. $(p^2 + 4)^5$ 8. $\left(x^3 + y^2\right)^6$

6.2 Calculate the probability of tossing a coin 15 times and getting the given number of heads.

9. 1   10. 4   11. 7   12. 15

6.3 A normal distribution has mean $\bar{x}$ and standard deviation σ. Find the indicated probability for a randomly selected x-value from the distribution.

13. $P(x \geq \bar{x} - \sigma)$ 14. $P(-\sigma \leq x \leq \bar{x} + 2\sigma)$ 15. $P(x \leq \bar{x} - 2\sigma \text{ or } x \geq \bar{x} + 2\sigma)$

6.3 A normal distribution has a mean of 2.7 and a standard deviation of 0.3. Find the probability that a randomly selected x-value from the distribution is in the given interval.

16. Between 2.4 and 2.7   17. At least 3.0   18. At most 2.1

6.4 Identify the type of sample described. Then tell if the sample is biased. *Explain your reasoning.*

19. The owner of a movie rental store wants to know how often her customers rent movies. She asks every tenth customer how many movies the customer rents each month.

20. A school wants to consult parents about updating its attendance policy. Each student is sent home with a survey for a parent to complete. The school uses only surveys that are returned within one week.

6.4 Find the margin of error for a survey that has the given sample size. Round your answer to the nearest tenth of a percent.

21. 100   22. 600   23. 2900   24. 5000

6.4 Find the sample size required to achieve the given margin of error. Round your answer to the nearest whole number.

25. $\pm 1\%$ 26. $\pm 2\%$ 27. $\pm 5.5\%$ 28. $\pm 6.2\%$

6.5 Tell why the survey question may be biased or otherwise introduce bias into the survey. Describe a way to correct the flaw.

29. "Are you for or against passing Referendum 3 to keep more of the money you pay for state taxes in your own pocket?"

30. A nurse asks students, "How many servings of vegetables do you eat daily?"

6.5 Describe whether each situation is an example of an *experiment* or an *observational study. Explain.*

31. Yearly test scores of a randomly-selected group of students taking the same math course sequence are tracked throughout high school and compared to state averages.

32. A psychology student compares scores on a measure from a personality test for randomly-chosen groups who take the test in different rooms, one decorated to be very industrial in setting, and another decorated to be very home-like.

Extra Practice

Chapter 7

7.1 For the sequence, describe the pattern, write the next term, and write a rule for the nth term.

1. $9, 16, 25, 36, \ldots$

2. $\frac{1}{3}, \frac{2}{3}, 1, \frac{4}{3}, \ldots$

3. $12.5, 7, 1.5, -4, \ldots$

7.1 Write the series using summation notation.

4. $16 + 32 + 48 + 64 + \cdots + 144$

5. $\frac{1}{6} + \frac{2}{7} + \frac{3}{8} + \frac{4}{9} + \frac{1}{2} + \cdots$

7.1 Find the sum of the series.

6. $\sum_{i=1}^{5} (3i + 2)$

7. $\sum_{i=0}^{5} 4i^2$

8. $\sum_{n=4}^{6} \frac{n}{n+3}$

9. $\sum_{k=6}^{8} k^3$

7.2 Write a rule for the nth term of the arithmetic sequence. Then graph the first six terms of the sequence.

10. $a_5 = 15, d = 6$

11. $a_{10} = -78, d = -10$

12. $a_6 = -\frac{11}{5}, d = -\frac{2}{5}$

7.2 Write a rule for the nth term of the arithmetic sequence. Then find a_{15}.

13. $11, 20, 29, 38, \ldots$

14. $-8, -15, -22, -29, \ldots$

15. $3, \frac{7}{3}, \frac{5}{3}, 1, \ldots$

7.2 Write a rule for the nth term of the arithmetic sequence that has the two given terms.

16. $a_2 = 9, a_7 = 37$

17. $a_8 = 10.5, a_{16} = 18.5$

18. $a_3 = -\frac{14}{5}, a_{10} = -\frac{42}{5}$

7.3 Write a rule for the nth term of the geometric sequence. Then find a_{10}.

19. $\frac{1}{27}, \frac{1}{9}, \frac{1}{3}, 1, \ldots$

20. $5, 4, 3.2, 2.56, \ldots$

21. $4, \frac{16}{3}, \frac{64}{9}, \frac{256}{27}, \ldots$

7.3 Find the sum of the geometric series.

22. $\sum_{i=1}^{4} 3(4)^{i-1}$

23. $\sum_{i=1}^{7} 0.5(-3)^{i-1}$

24. $\sum_{i=1}^{5} 10\left(\frac{3}{5}\right)^{i-1}$

25. $\sum_{i=1}^{7} 2(1.2)^{i-1}$

7.4 Find the sum of the infinite geometric series, if it exists.

26. $8 + 4 + 2 + 1 + \cdots$

27. $2 - 4 + 8 - 16 + \cdots$

28. $-6.75 + 4.5 - 3 + 2 - \cdots$

7.4 Write the repeating decimal as a fraction in lowest terms.

29. $0.333\ldots$

30. $0.898989\ldots$

31. $0.212121\ldots$

32. $1.50150150\ldots$

7.5 Write a recursive rule for the sequence. The sequence may be arithmetic, geometric, or neither.

33. $2.5, 5, 10, 20, \ldots$

34. $2, -2, -6, -10, \ldots$

35. $1, 2, 2, 4, 8, 32, \ldots$

7.5 Find the first three iterates of the function for the given initial value.

36. $f(x) = 2x - 5, x_0 = 3$

37. $f(x) = \frac{4}{5}x - 2, x_0 = -10$

38. $f(x) = 3x^2 + x, x_0 = -1$

Extra Practice

Chapter 8

8.1 **Find the distance between the two points. Then find the midpoint of the line segment joining the two points.**

1. $(-5, 0), (5, 4)$ **2.** $(2, 1), (3, 7)$ **3.** $(-12, 12), (14, -4)$ **4.** $(12, -1), (18, -9)$

8.2 **Graph the equation. Identify the focus, directrix, and axis of symmetry of the parabola.**

5. $y^2 = 2x$ **6.** $x^2 = -4y$ **7.** $14x^2 = -21y$ **8.** $12y^2 + 3x = 0$

8.3 **Graph the equation. Identify the radius of the circle.**

9. $x^2 + y^2 = 4$ **10.** $x^2 + y^2 = 14$ **11.** $3x^2 + 3y^2 = 75$ **12.** $16x^2 + 16y^2 = 4$

8.3 **Write the standard form of the equation of the circle that passes through the given point and whose center is at the origin.**

13. $(8, 0)$ **14.** $(0, -9)$ **15.** $(7, -1)$ **16.** $(-5, -11)$

8.4 **Graph the equation. Identify the vertices, co-vertices, and foci of the ellipse.**

17. $\dfrac{x^2}{81} + \dfrac{y^2}{16} = 1$ **18.** $x^2 + \dfrac{y^2}{9} = 1$ **19.** $9x^2 + 4y^2 = 576$ **20.** $49x^2 + 64y^2 = 12{,}544$

8.4 **Write an equation of the ellipse with the given characteristics and center at (0, 0).**

21. Vertex: $(4, 0)$
Co-vertex: $(0, 2)$

22. Vertex: $(0, -5)$
Co-vertex: $(4, 0)$

23. Vertex: $(9, 0)$
Focus: $(-3, 0)$

24. Co-vertex: $(0, 10)$
Focus: $(8, 0)$

8.5 **Graph the equation. Identify the vertices, foci, and asymptotes of the hyperbola.**

25. $\dfrac{x^2}{36} - \dfrac{y^2}{16} = 1$ **26.** $x^2 - y^2 = 4$ **27.** $49y^2 - 81x^2 = 3969$

8.5 **Write an equation of the hyperbola with the given foci and vertices.**

28. Foci: $(0, -8), (0, 8)$
Vertices: $(0, -6), (0, 6)$

29. Foci: $(-2, 0), (2, 0)$
Vertices: $(-1, 0), (1, 0)$

30. Foci: $(0, -5), (0, 5)$
Vertices: $\left(0, -3\sqrt{2}\right), \left(0, 3\sqrt{2}\right)$

8.6 **Graph the equation. Identify the important characteristics of the graph.**

31. $\dfrac{(x - 3)^2}{25} + \dfrac{y^2}{9} = 1$ **32.** $(x + 2)^2 + (y - 1)^2 = 4$ **33.** $(y - 4)^2 - \dfrac{(x + 1)^2}{16} = 1$

8.6 **Classify the conic section and write its equation in standard form. Then graph the equation.**

34. $x^2 + y^2 + 2x + 2y - 7 = 0$ **35.** $9x^2 + 4y^2 - 72x + 16y + 16 = 0$

36. $9x^2 - 4y^2 + 16y - 52 = 0$ **37.** $x^2 - 6x - 4y + 17 = 0$

8.7 **Solve the system.**

38. $x^2 + y^2 = 4$
   $9x^2 - 4y^2 = 36$

39. $y = x - 2$
   $x^2 + y^2 - 6x - 4y - 12 = 0$

40. $y^2 = x - 5$
   $9x^2 - 25y^2 = 225$

Chapter 9

9.1 **Let θ be an acute angle of a right triangle. Find the values of the other five trigonometric functions of θ.**

   1. $\sin \theta = \dfrac{3}{5}$ **2.** $\tan \theta = \dfrac{8}{15}$ **3.** $\sec \theta = 2$ **4.** $\cos \theta = \dfrac{\sqrt{7}}{4}$

9.1 **Solve $\triangle ABC$ using the diagram and the given measurements.**

   5. $A = 21°, c = 8$ **6.** $B = 66°, a = 14$

   7. $B = 60°, c = 20$ **8.** $A = 29°, b = 6$

   9. $A = 18°, c = 18$ **10.** $B = 56°, c = 7$

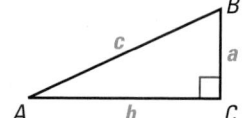

9.2 **Convert the degree measure to radians or the radian measure to degrees.**

   11. $100°$ **12.** $-6°$ **13.** $\dfrac{3\pi}{4}$ **14.** $-\dfrac{\pi}{6}$

9.2 **Find the arc length and area of a sector with the given radius r and central angle θ.**

   15. $r = 5$ ft, $\theta = 90°$ **16.** $r = 2$ in., $\theta = 300°$ **17.** $r = 12$ cm, $\theta = \pi$

9.3 **Sketch the angle. Then find its reference angle.**

   18. $250°$ **19.** $-30°$ **20.** $\dfrac{8\pi}{3}$ **21.** $-\dfrac{11\pi}{6}$

9.3 **Evaluate the function without using a calculator.**

   22. $\sin(-60°)$ **23.** $\csc 240°$ **24.** $\tan \dfrac{7\pi}{4}$ **25.** $\cos\left(-\dfrac{5\pi}{4}\right)$

9.4 **Evaluate the expression without using a calculator. Give your answer in both radians and degrees.**

   26. $\sin^{-1} 0$ **27.** $\cos^{-1}\left(-\dfrac{\sqrt{3}}{2}\right)$ **28.** $\cos^{-1} 3$ **29.** $\tan^{-1} 1$

9.4 **Solve the equation for θ.**

   30. $\sin \theta = 0.25; 90° < \theta < 180°$ **31.** $\cos \theta = 0.9; 270° < \theta < 360°$ **32.** $\tan \theta = 2; 180° < \theta < 270°$

9.5 **Solve $\triangle ABC$. (*Hint:* Some of the "triangles" may have no solution and some may have two solutions.)**

   33. $A = 34°, a = 6, b = 7$ **34.** $A = 50°, C = 65°, b = 60$ **35.** $B = 86°, b = 13, c = 11$

9.5 **Find the area of $\triangle ABC$ with the given side lengths and included angle.**

   36. $A = 35°, b = 50, c = 120$ **37.** $B = 35°, a = 7, c = 12$ **38.** $C = 20°, a = 10, b = 16$

9.6 **Solve $\triangle ABC$.**

   39. $a = 16, b = 23, c = 17$ **40.** $C = 50°, a = 12, b = 14$ **41.** $A = 80°, b = 7, c = 5$

9.6 **Find the area of $\triangle ABC$ with the given side lengths.**

   42. $a = 6, b = 3, c = 4$ **43.** $a = 14, b = 30, c = 27$ **44.** $a = 16, b = 16, c = 20$

Chapter 10

Extra Practice

10.1 Graph the function.

1. $y = \cos \frac{1}{4}x$ **2.** $y = 3 \sin x$ **3.** $y = \sin 2\pi x$ **4.** $y = 2 \tan 2x$

10.2 Graph the sine or cosine function.

5. $y = \sin 2\left(x - \frac{\pi}{4}\right) + 1$ **6.** $y = -\sin\left(x + \frac{\pi}{4}\right)$ **7.** $y = 2 \cos x + 3$

10.2 Graph the tangent function.

8. $y = 2 \tan x + 2$ **9.** $y = -\frac{1}{4} \tan 2x$ **10.** $y = \tan\left(x - \frac{\pi}{2}\right) - 1$

10.3 Simplify the expression.

11. $\cos^2\left(\frac{\pi}{2} - x\right) + \cos^2(-x)$ **12.** $\dfrac{(\sec x - 1)(\sec x + 1)}{\tan x}$ **13.** $\tan\left(\frac{\pi}{2} - x\right)\cot x - \csc^2 x$

10.3 Verify the identity.

14. $\dfrac{\cos(-x)}{1 + \sin(-x)} = \sec x + \tan x$ **15.** $\dfrac{\cos^2 x + \sin^2 x}{\tan^2 x + 1} = \cos^2 x$ **16.** $2 - \sec^2 x = 1 - \tan^2 x$

10.4 Find the general solution of the equation.

17. $12 \tan^2 x - 4 = 0$ **18.** $3 \sin x = -2 \sin x + 3$ **19.** $\tan^2 x - 2 \tan x = -1$

10.4 Solve the equation in the given interval. Check your solutions.

20. $\cos^2 x \sin x = 5 \sin x; \ 0 \le x < 2\pi$ **21.** $2 - 2 \cos^2 x = 3 + 5 \sin x; \ 0 \le x < 2\pi$

22. $8 \cos x = 4 \sec x; \ 0 \le x < \pi$ **23.** $\cos^2 x - 4 \cos x + 1 = 0; \ 0 \le x < \pi$

10.5 Write a function for the sinusoid.

24.

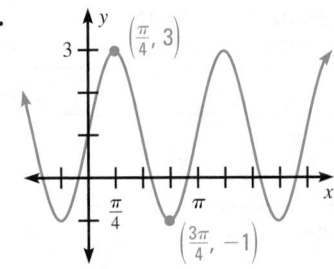

25.

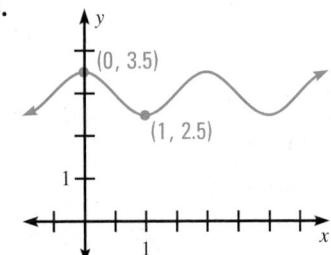

10.6 Find the exact value of the expression.

26. $\sin(-15°)$ **27.** $\cos 165°$ **28.** $\tan \dfrac{11\pi}{12}$ **29.** $\cos \dfrac{\pi}{12}$

10.7 Find the exact values of sin 2a, cos 2a, and tan 2a.

30. $\tan a = \dfrac{2}{3}, \ \pi < a < \dfrac{3\pi}{2}$ **31.** $\cos a = \dfrac{9}{10}, \ 0 < a < \dfrac{\pi}{2}$ **32.** $\sin a = -\dfrac{3}{5}, \ \dfrac{3\pi}{2} < a < 2\pi$

10.7 Find the general solution of the equation.

33. $\cos 2x - \cos x = 0$ **34.** $\cos \dfrac{x}{2} = \sin x$ **35.** $\sin 2x = -1$

Tables

Symbols

Symbol	Meaning
. . .	and so on
$\approx$	is approximately equal to
$\cdot$	multiplication, times
$-a$	opposite of a
$\dfrac{1}{a}$	reciprocal of a, $a \neq 0$
b_1	b sub 1
π	pi; irrational number ≈ 3.14
$<$	is less than
$>$	is greater than
$\leq$	is less than or equal to
$\geq$	is greater than or equal to
$|x|$	absolute value of x
$\neq$	is not equal to
(x, y)	ordered pair
$f(x)$	f of x, or the value of f at x
m	slope
$\parallel$	is parallel to
$\perp$	is perpendicular to
(x, y, z)	ordered triple
$\begin{bmatrix} 1 & 0 \\ 0 & 1 \end{bmatrix}$	matrix
$|A|$	determinant of matrix A
A^{-1}	inverse of matrix A
$\sqrt{a}$	the nonnegative square root of a
i	imaginary unit equal to $\sqrt{-1}$
$|z|$	absolute value of complex number z
$x \to +\infty$	x approaches positive infinity
$\sqrt[n]{a}$	nth root of a
f^{-1}	inverse of function f

Symbol	Meaning
e	irrational number ≈ 2.718
$\log_b y$	log base b of y
$\log x$	log base 10 of x
$\ln x$	log base e of x
$n!$	n factorial; number of permutations of n objects
$_nP_r$	number of permutations of r objects from n distinct objects
$_nC_r$	number of combinations of r objects from n distinct objects
$P(A)$	probability of event A
$P(\overline{A})$	probability of the complement of event A
$\cup$	union of two sets
$\cap$	intersection of two sets
$\emptyset$	empty set
$\subseteq$	is a subset of
$P(B|A)$	probability of event B given that event A has occurred
$\overline{x}$	x-bar; the mean of a data set
σ	sigma; the standard deviation of a data set
Σ	summation
θ	theta
sin	sine
cos	cosine
tan	tangent
csc	cosecant
sec	secant
cot	cotangent
$\sin^{-1}$	inverse sine
$\cos^{-1}$	inverse cosine
$\tan^{-1}$	inverse tangent

Measures

Time

60 seconds (sec) = 1 minute (min) 60 minutes = 1 hour (h) 24 hours = 1 day 7 days = 1 week 4 weeks (approx.) = 1 month	$\left.\begin{array}{l}\text{365 days}\\\text{52 weeks (approx.)}\\\text{12 months}\end{array}\right\}$ = 1 year 10 years = 1 decade 100 years = 1 century

Metric	United States Customary
Length 10 millimeters (mm) = 1 centimeter (cm) $\left.\begin{array}{l}\text{100 cm}\\\text{1000 mm}\end{array}\right\}$ = 1 meter (m) 1000 m = 1 kilometer (km)	**Length** 12 inches (in.) = 1 foot (ft) $\left.\begin{array}{l}\text{36 in.}\\\text{3 ft}\end{array}\right\}$ = 1 yard (yd) $\left.\begin{array}{l}\text{5280 ft}\\\text{1760 yd}\end{array}\right\}$ = 1 mile (mi)
Area 100 square millimeters = 1 square centimeter (mm^2) $\quad$ (cm^2) $10{,}000\ cm^2$ = 1 square meter (m^2) $10{,}000\ m^2$ = 1 hectare (ha)	**Area** 144 square inches $(in.^2)$ = 1 square foot (ft^2) $9\ ft^2$ = 1 square yard (yd^2) $\left.\begin{array}{l}43{,}560\ ft^2\\4840\ yd^2\end{array}\right\}$ = 1 acre (A)
Volume 1000 cubic millimeters = 1 cubic centimeter (mm^3) $\quad$ (cm^3) $1{,}000{,}000\ cm^3$ = 1 cubic meter (m^3)	**Volume** 1728 cubic inches $(in.^3)$ = 1 cubic foot (ft^3) $27\ ft^3$ = 1 cubic yard (yd^3)
Liquid Capacity $\left.\begin{array}{l}\text{1000 milliliters (mL)}\\\text{1000 cubic centimeters }(cm^3)\end{array}\right\}$ = 1 liter (L) 1000 L = 1 kiloliter (kL)	**Liquid Capacity** 8 fluid ounces (fl oz) = 1 cup (c) 2 c = 1 pint (pt) 2 pt = 1 quart (qt) 4 qt = 1 gallon (gal)
Mass 1000 milligrams (mg) = 1 gram (g) 1000 g = 1 kilogram (kg) 1000 kg = 1 metric ton (t)	**Weight** 16 ounces (oz) = 1 pound (lb) 2000 lb = 1 ton
Temperature Degrees Celsius (°C) 0°C = freezing point of water 37°C = normal body temperature 100°C = boiling point of water	**Temperature Degrees Fahrenheit (°F)** 32°F = freezing point of water 98.6°F = normal body temperature 212°F = boiling point of water

TABLES

Formulas

Formulas from Coordinate Geometry

Slope of a line	$m = \dfrac{y_2 - y_1}{x_2 - x_1}$ where m is the slope of the nonvertical line through points (x_1, y_1) and (x_2, y_2)
Parallel and perpendicular lines	If line l_1 has slope m_1 and line l_2 has slope m_2, then: $l_1 \parallel l_2$ if and only if $m_1 = m_2$ $l_1 \perp l_2$ if and only if $m_1 = -\dfrac{1}{m_2}$, or $m_1 m_2 = -1$
Distance formula	$d = \sqrt{(x_2 - x_1)^2 + (y_2 - y_1)^2}$ where d is the distance between points (x_1, y_1) and (x_2, y_2)
Midpoint formula	$M\left(\dfrac{x_1 + x_2}{2}, \dfrac{y_1 + y_2}{2}\right)$ is the midpoint of the line segment joining points (x_1, y_1) and (x_2, y_2).

Formulas from Matrix Algebra

Determinant of a 2 × 2 matrix	$\det\begin{bmatrix} a & b \\ c & d \end{bmatrix} = \begin{vmatrix} a & b \\ c & d \end{vmatrix} = ad - cb$
Determinant of a 3 × 3 matrix	$\det\begin{bmatrix} a & b & c \\ d & e & f \\ g & h & i \end{bmatrix} = \begin{vmatrix} a & b & c \\ d & e & f \\ g & h & i \end{vmatrix} = (aei + bfg + cdh) - (gec + hfa + idb)$
Area of a triangle	The area of a triangle with vertices (x_1, y_1), (x_2, y_2), and (x_3, y_3) is given by $$\text{Area} = \pm\frac{1}{2}\begin{vmatrix} x_1 & y_1 & 1 \\ x_2 & y_2 & 1 \\ x_3 & y_3 & 1 \end{vmatrix}$$ where the appropriate sign ($\pm$) should be chosen to yield a positive value.
Cramer's rule	Let $A = \begin{bmatrix} a & b \\ c & d \end{bmatrix}$ be the coefficient matrix of this linear system: $$\begin{aligned} ax + by &= e \\ cx + dy &= f \end{aligned}$$ If $\det A \neq 0$, then the system has exactly one solution. The solution is $x = \dfrac{\begin{vmatrix} e & b \\ f & d \end{vmatrix}}{\det A}$ and $y = \dfrac{\begin{vmatrix} a & e \\ c & f \end{vmatrix}}{\det A}$.
Inverse of a 2 × 2 matrix	The inverse of the matrix $A = \begin{bmatrix} a & b \\ c & d \end{bmatrix}$ is $$A^{-1} = \frac{1}{|A|}\begin{bmatrix} d & -b \\ -c & a \end{bmatrix} = \frac{1}{ad - cb}\begin{bmatrix} d & -b \\ -c & a \end{bmatrix}$$ provided $ad - cb \neq 0$.

Formulas and Theorems from Algebra

Quadratic formula	The solutions of $ax^2 + bx + c = 0$ are $$x = \frac{-b \pm \sqrt{b^2 - 4ac}}{2a}$$ where a, b, and c are real numbers such that $a \neq 0$.
Discriminant of a quadratic equation	The expression $b^2 - 4ac$ is called the discriminant of the associated equation $ax^2 + bx + c = 0$. The value of the discriminant can be positive, zero, or negative, which corresponds to an equation having two real solutions, one real solution, or two imaginary solutions, respectively.
Special product patterns	**Sum and difference:** $(a + b)(a - b) = a^2 - b^2$ **Square of a binomial:** $(a + b)^2 = a^2 + 2ab + b^2$ $(a - b)^2 = a^2 - 2ab + b^2$ **Cube of a binomial:** $(a + b)^3 = a^3 + 3a^2b + 3ab^2 + b^3$ $(a - b)^3 = a^3 - 3a^2b + 3ab^2 - b^3$
Special factoring patterns	**Sum of two cubes:** $a^3 + b^3 = (a + b)(a^2 - ab + b^2)$ **Difference of two cubes:** $a^3 - b^3 = (a - b)(a^2 + ab + b^2)$
Remainder theorem	If a polynomial $f(x)$ is divided by $x - k$, then the remainder is $r = f(k)$.
Factor theorem	A polynomial $f(x)$ has a factor $x - k$ if and only if $f(k) = 0$.
Rational zero theorem	If $f(x) = a_nx^n + \cdots + a_1x + a_0$ has *integer* coefficients, then every rational zero of f has this form: $$\frac{p}{q} = \frac{\text{factor of constant term } a_0}{\text{factor of leading coefficient } a_n}$$
Fundamental theorem of algebra	If $f(x)$ is a polynomial of degree n where $n > 0$, then the equation $f(x) = 0$ has at least one solution in the set of complex numbers.
Corollary to the fundamental theorem of algebra	If $f(x)$ is a polynomial of degree n where $n > 0$, then the equation $f(x) = 0$ has exactly n solutions provided each solution repeated twice is counted as 2 solutions, each solution repeated three times is counted as 3 solutions, and so on.
Complex conjugates theorem	If f is a polynomial function with real coefficients, and $a + bi$ is an imaginary zero of f, then $a - bi$ is also a zero of f.
Irrational conjugates theorem	Suppose f is a polynomial function with rational coefficients, and a and b are rational numbers such that $\sqrt{b}$ is irrational. If $a + \sqrt{b}$ is a zero of f, then $a - \sqrt{b}$ is also a zero of f.
Descartes' rule of signs	Let $f(x) = a_nx^n + a_{n-1}x^{n-1} + \cdots + a_2x^2 + a_1x + a_0$ be a polynomial function with real coefficients. • The number of *positive real zeros* of f is equal to the number of changes in sign of the coefficients of $f(x)$ or is less than this by an even number. • The number of *negative real zeros* of f is equal to the number of changes in sign of the coefficients of $f(-x)$ or is less than this by an even number.

Formulas and Theorems from Algebra *(continued)*

Discriminant of a general second-degree equation	Any conic can be described by a general second-degree equation in x and y: $Ax^2 + Bxy + Cy^2 + Dx + Ey + F = 0$. The expression $B^2 - 4AC$ is the discriminant of the conic equation and can be used to identify it.
	Discriminant **Type of Conic**
	$B^2 - 4AC < 0$, $B = 0$, and $A = C$ Circle
	$B^2 - 4AC < 0$, and either $B \neq 0$ or $A \neq C$ Ellipse
	$B^2 - 4AC = 0$ Parabola
	$B^2 - 4AC > 0$ Hyperbola
	If $B = 0$, each axis of the conic is horizontal or vertical.

Formulas from Combinatorics

Fundamental counting principle	If one event can occur in m ways and another event can occur in n ways, then the number of ways that both events can occur is $m \cdot n$.
Permutations of n objects taken r at a time	The number of permutations of r objects taken from a group of n distinct objects is denoted by ${}_nP_r$ and is given by: $$_nP_r = \frac{n!}{(n-r)!}$$
Permutations with repetition	The number of distinguishable permutations of n objects where one object is repeated s_1 times, another is repeated s_2 times, and so on is: $$\frac{n!}{s_1! \cdot s_2! \cdot \ldots \cdot s_k!}$$
Combinations of n objects taken r at a time	The number of combinations of r objects taken from a group of n distinct objects is denoted by ${}_nC_r$ and is given by: $$_nC_r = \frac{n!}{(n-r)! \cdot r!}$$
Pascal's triangle	If you arrange the values of ${}_nC_r$ in a triangular pattern in which each row corresponds to a value of n, you get what is called Pascal's triangle.
	$\qquad\qquad {}_0C_0 \qquad\qquad\qquad\qquad\qquad 1$
	$\qquad {}_1C_0 \quad {}_1C_1 \qquad\qquad\qquad\qquad 1 \quad 1$
	$\quad {}_2C_0 \quad {}_2C_1 \quad {}_2C_2 \qquad\qquad\qquad 1 \quad 2 \quad 1$
	${}_3C_0 \quad {}_3C_1 \quad {}_3C_2 \quad {}_3C_3 \qquad\qquad 1 \quad 3 \quad 3 \quad 1$
	${}_4C_0 \quad {}_4C_1 \quad {}_4C_2 \quad {}_4C_3 \quad {}_4C_4 \qquad 1 \quad 4 \quad 6 \quad 4 \quad 1$
	The first and last numbers in each row are 1. Every number other than 1 is the sum of the closest two numbers in the row directly above it.
Binomial theorem	The binomial expansion of $(a + b)^n$ for any positive integer n is: $$(a + b)^n = {}_nC_0 a^n b^0 + {}_nC_1 a^{n-1} b^1 + {}_nC_2 a^{n-2} b^2 + \cdots + {}_nC_n a^0 b^n$$ $$= \sum_{r=0}^{n} {}_nC_r a^{n-r} b^r$$

Formulas from Probability

Theoretical probability of an event	When all outcomes are equally likely, the theoretical probability that an event A will occur is: $$P(A) = \frac{\text{Number of outcomes in } A}{\text{Total number of outcomes}}$$
Odds in favor of an event	When all outcomes are equally likely, the odds in favor of an event A are: $$\frac{\text{Number of outcomes in } A}{\text{Number of outcomes not in } A}$$
Odds against an event	When all outcomes are equally likely, the odds against an event A are: $$\frac{\text{Number of outcomes not in } A}{\text{Number of outcomes in } A}$$
Experimental probability of an event	When an experiment is performed that consists of a certain number of trials, the experimental probability of an event A is given by: $$P(A) = \frac{\text{Number of trials where } A \text{ occurs}}{\text{Total number of trials}}$$
Probability of compound events	If A and B are any two events, then the probability of A or B is: $$P(A \text{ or } B) = P(A) + P(B) - P(A \text{ and } B)$$ If A and B are disjoint events, then the probability of A or B is: $$P(A \text{ or } B) = P(A) + P(B)$$
Probability of the complement of an event	The probability of the complement of event A, denoted $\overline{A}$, is: $$P(\overline{A}) = 1 - P(A)$$
Probability of independent events	If A and B are independent, the probability that both A and B occur is: $$P(A \text{ and } B) = P(A) \cdot P(B)$$
Probability of dependent events	If A and B are dependent, the probability that both A and B occur is: $$P(A \text{ and } B) = P(A) \cdot P(B \mid A)$$
Binomial probabilities	For a binomial experiment consisting of n trials where the probability of success on each trial is p, the probability of exactly k successes is: $$P(k \text{ successes}) = {_nC_k}p^k(1 - p)^{n-k}$$

Formulas from Statistics

Mean of a data set	$\overline{x} = \dfrac{x_1 + x_2 + \cdots + x_n}{n}$ where $\overline{x}$ (read "x-bar") is the mean of the data $x_1, x_2, \ldots, x_n$
Standard deviation of a data set	$\sigma = \sqrt{\dfrac{(x_1 - \overline{x})^2 + (x_2 - \overline{x})^2 + \ldots + (x_n - \overline{x})^2}{n}}$ where σ (read "sigma") is the standard deviation of the data $x_1, x_2, \ldots, x_n$
Areas under a normal curve	A normal distribution with mean $\overline{x}$ and standard deviation σ has these properties: • The total area under the related normal curve is 1. • About 68% of the area lies within 1 standard deviation of the mean. • About 95% of the area lies within 2 standard deviations of the mean. • About 99.7% of the area lies within 3 standard deviations of the mean.
z-score	$z = \dfrac{x - \overline{x}}{\sigma}$ where x is a data value, $\overline{x}$ is the mean, and σ is the standard deviation

Formulas for Sequences and Series

Formulas for sums of special series	$\sum_{i=1}^{n} 1 = n$ $\sum_{i=1}^{n} i = \dfrac{n(n+1)}{2}$ $\sum_{i=1}^{n} i^2 = \dfrac{n(n+1)(2n+1)}{6}$
Explicit rule for an arithmetic sequence	The nth term of an arithmetic sequence with first term a_1 and common difference d is: $$a_n = a_1 + (n-1)d$$
Sum of a finite arithmetic series	The sum of the first n terms of an arithmetic series is: $$S_n = n\left(\dfrac{a_1 + a_n}{2}\right)$$
Explicit rule for a geometric sequence	The nth term of a geometric sequence with first term a_1 and common ratio r is: $$a_n = a_1 r^{n-1}$$
Sum of a finite geometric series	The sum of the first n terms of a geometric series with common ratio $r \neq 1$ is: $$S_n = a_1\left(\dfrac{1-r^n}{1-r}\right)$$
Sum of an infinite geometric series	The sum of an infinite geometric series with first term a_1 and common ratio r is $$S = \dfrac{a_1}{1-r}$$ provided $|r| < 1$. If $|r| \geq 1$, the series has no sum.
Recursive equation for an arithmetic sequence	$a_n = a_{n-1} + d$ where d is the common difference
Recursive equation for a geometric sequence	$a_n = r \cdot a_{n-1}$ where r is the common ratio

Formulas and Identities from Trigonometry

Conversion between degrees and radians	To rewrite a degree measure in radians, multiply by $\dfrac{\pi \text{ radians}}{180°}$. To rewrite a radian measure in degrees, multiply by $\dfrac{180°}{\pi \text{ radians}}$.
Definition of trigonometric functions	Let θ be an angle in standard position and (x, y) be any point (except the origin) on the terminal side of θ. Let $r = \sqrt{x^2 + y^2}$. $\sin \theta = \dfrac{y}{r}$ $\cos \theta = \dfrac{x}{r}$ $\tan \theta = \dfrac{y}{x}, x \neq 0$ $\csc \theta = \dfrac{r}{y}, y \neq 0$ $\sec \theta = \dfrac{r}{x}, x \neq 0$ $\cot \theta = \dfrac{x}{y}, y \neq 0$
Law of sines	If $\triangle ABC$ has sides of length a, b, and c, then: $$\dfrac{\sin A}{a} = \dfrac{\sin B}{b} = \dfrac{\sin C}{c}$$
Area of a triangle (given two sides and the included angle)	If $\triangle ABC$ has sides of length a, b, and c, then its area is: $$\text{Area} = \tfrac{1}{2}bc \sin A \qquad \text{Area} = \tfrac{1}{2}ac \sin B \qquad \text{Area} = \tfrac{1}{2}ab \sin C$$

TABLES

Formulas and Identities from Trigonometry *(continued)*

Law of cosines	If $\triangle ABC$ has sides of length a, b, and c, then: $$a^2 = b^2 + c^2 - 2bc \cos A$$ $$b^2 = a^2 + c^2 - 2ac \cos B$$ $$c^2 = a^2 + b^2 - 2ab \cos C$$
Heron's area formula	The area of the triangle with sides of length a, b, and c is $$\text{Area} = \sqrt{s(s - a)(s - b)(s - c)}$$ where $s = \frac{1}{2}(a + b + c)$.
Reciprocal identities	$\csc \theta = \dfrac{1}{\sin \theta}$ $\qquad$ $\sec \theta = \dfrac{1}{\cos \theta}$ $\qquad$ $\cot \theta = \dfrac{1}{\tan \theta}$
Tangent and cotangent identities	$\tan \theta = \dfrac{\sin \theta}{\cos \theta}$ $\qquad$ $\cot \theta = \dfrac{\cos \theta}{\sin \theta}$
Pythagorean identities	$\sin^2 \theta + \cos^2 \theta = 1$ $\qquad$ $1 + \tan^2 \theta = \sec^2 \theta$ $\qquad$ $1 + \cot^2 \theta = \csc^2 \theta$
Cofunction identities	$\sin\left(\dfrac{\pi}{2} - \theta\right) = \cos \theta$ $\qquad$ $\cos\left(\dfrac{\pi}{2} - \theta\right) = \sin \theta$ $\qquad$ $\tan\left(\dfrac{\pi}{2} - \theta\right) = \cot \theta$
Negative angle identities	$\sin(-\theta) = -\sin \theta$ $\qquad$ $\cos(-\theta) = \cos \theta$ $\qquad$ $\tan(-\theta) = -\tan \theta$
Sum formulas	$$\sin(a + b) = \sin a \cos b + \cos a \sin b$$ $$\cos(a + b) = \cos a \cos b - \sin a \sin b$$ $$\tan(a + b) = \frac{\tan a + \tan b}{1 - \tan a \tan b}$$
Difference formulas	$$\sin(a - b) = \sin a \cos b - \cos a \sin b$$ $$\cos(a - b) = \cos a \cos b + \sin a \sin b$$ $$\tan(a - b) = \frac{\tan a - \tan b}{1 + \tan a \tan b}$$
Double-angle formulas	$\cos 2a = \cos^2 a - \sin^2 a$ $\qquad$ $\sin 2a = 2 \sin a \cos a$ $\cos 2a = 2 \cos^2 a - 1$ $\qquad$ $\tan 2a = \dfrac{2 \tan a}{1 - \tan^2 a}$ $\cos 2a = 1 - 2 \sin^2 a$
Half-angle formulas	$\sin \dfrac{a}{2} = \pm\sqrt{\dfrac{1 - \cos a}{2}}$ $\qquad$ $\tan \dfrac{a}{2} = \dfrac{1 - \cos a}{\sin a}$ $\cos \dfrac{a}{2} = \pm\sqrt{\dfrac{1 + \cos a}{2}}$ $\qquad$ $\tan \dfrac{a}{2} = \dfrac{\sin a}{1 + \cos a}$ The signs of $\sin \dfrac{a}{2}$ and $\cos \dfrac{a}{2}$ depend on the quadrant in which $\dfrac{a}{2}$ lies.

TABLES

Formulas from Geometry

Basic geometric figures	See pages SR17–SR19 for area formulas for basic two-dimensional geometric figures.
Area of an equilateral triangle	Area = $\frac{\sqrt{3}}{4}s^2$ where s is the length of a side
Arc length and area of a sector	Arc length = $r\theta$ where r is the radius and θ is the radian measure of the central angle that intercepts the arc Area = $\frac{1}{2}r^2\theta$
Area of an ellipse	Area = πab where a and b are half the lengths of the major and minor axes of the ellipse
Volume and surface area of a right rectangular prism	Volume = ℓwh where ℓ is the length, w is the width, and h is the height Surface area = $2(\ell w + wh + \ell h)$
Volume and surface area of a right cylinder	Volume = $\pi r^2 h$ where r is the base radius and h is the height Lateral surface area = $2\pi rh$ Surface area = $2\pi r^2 + 2\pi rh$
Volume and surface area of a right regular pyramid	Volume = $\frac{1}{3}Bh$ where B is the area of the base and h is the height Lateral surface area = $\frac{1}{2}ns\ell$ where n is the number of sides of the base, s is the length of a side of the base, and ℓ is the slant height Surface area = $B + \frac{1}{2}ns\ell$
Volume and surface area of a right circular cone	Volume = $\frac{1}{3}\pi r^2 h$ where r is the base radius and h is the height Lateral surface area = $\pi r\ell$ where ℓ is the slant height Surface area = $\pi r^2 + \pi r\ell$
Volume and surface area of a sphere	Volume = $\frac{4}{3}\pi r^3$ where r is the radius Surface area = $4\pi r^2$

Properties

Properties of Real Numbers

Let a, b, and c be real numbers.

	Addition	**Multiplication**
Closure Property	$a + b$ is a real number.	ab is a real number.
Commutative Property	$a + b = b + a$	$ab = ba$
Associative Property	$(a + b) + c = a + (b + c)$	$(ab)c = a(bc)$
Identity Property	$a + 0 = a, 0 + a = a$	$a \cdot 1 = a, 1 \cdot a = a$
Inverse Property	$a + (-a) = 0$	$a \cdot \dfrac{1}{a} = 1, a \neq 0$

Distributive Property The distributive property involves both addition and multiplication: $a(b + c) = ab + ac$

Zero Product Property Let A and B be real numbers or algebraic expressions. If $AB = 0$, then $A = 0$ or $B = 0$.

Properties of Matrices

Let A, B, and C be matrices, and let k be a scalar.

Associative Property of Addition	$(A + B) + C = A + (B + C)$
Commutative Property of Addition	$A + B = B + A$
Distributive Property of Addition	$k(A + B) = kA + kB$
Distributive Property of Subtraction	$k(A - B) = kA - kB$
Associative Property of Matrix Multiplication	$(AB)C = A(BC)$
Left Distributive Property of Matrix Multiplication	$A(B + C) = AB + AC$
Right Distributive Property of Matrix Multiplication	$(A + B)C = AC + BC$
Associative Property of Scalar Multiplication	$k(AB) = (kA)B = A(kB)$

Multiplicative Identity An $n \times n$ matrix with 1's on the main diagonal and 0's elsewhere is an identity matrix, denoted I. For any $n \times n$ matrix A, $AI = IA = A$.

Inverse Matrices If the determinant of an $n \times n$ matrix A is nonzero, then A has an inverse, denoted A^{-1}, such that $AA^{-1} = A^{-1}A = I$.

Properties of Exponents

Let a and b be real numbers, and let m and n be integers.

Product of Powers Property	$a^m \cdot a^n = a^{m+n}$
Power of a Power Property	$(a^m)^n = a^{mn}$
Power of a Product Property	$(ab)^m = a^m b^m$
Negative Exponent Property	$a^{-m} = \dfrac{1}{a^m}, a \neq 0$
Zero Exponent Property	$a^0 = 1, a \neq 0$
Quotient of Powers Property	$\dfrac{a^m}{a^n} = a^{m-n}, a \neq 0$
Power of a Quotient Property	$\left(\dfrac{a}{b}\right)^m = \dfrac{a^m}{b^m}, b \neq 0$

Properties of Radicals and Rational Exponents

Number of Real *n*th Roots	Let n be an integer greater than 1, and let a be a real number. • If n is odd, then a has one real nth root: $\sqrt[n]{a} = a^{1/n}$ • If n is even and $a > 0$, then a has two real nth roots: $\pm\sqrt[n]{a} = \pm a^{1/n}$ • If n is even and $a = 0$, then a has one nth root: $\sqrt[n]{0} = 0^{1/n} = 0$ • If n is even and $a < 0$, then a has no real nth roots.
Radicals and Rational Exponents	Let $a^{1/n}$ be an nth root of a, and let m be a positive integer. • $a^{m/n} = (a^{1/n})^m = \left(\sqrt[n]{a}\right)^m$ • $a^{-m/n} = \dfrac{1}{a^{m/n}} = \dfrac{1}{(a^{1/n})^m} = \dfrac{1}{\left(\sqrt[n]{a}\right)^m},\ a \neq 0$
Properties of Rational Exponents	All of the properties of exponents listed on the previous page apply to rational exponents as well as integer exponents.
Product and Quotient Properties of Radicals	Let n be an integer greater than 1, and let a and b be positive real numbers. Then $\sqrt[n]{a \cdot b} = \sqrt[n]{a} \cdot \sqrt[n]{b}$ and $\sqrt[n]{\dfrac{a}{b}} = \dfrac{\sqrt[n]{a}}{\sqrt[n]{b}}$.

Properties of Logarithms

	Let a, b, c, m, n, x, and y be positive real numbers such that $b \neq 1$ and $c \neq 1$.
Logarithms and Exponents	$\log_b y = x$ if and only if $b^x = y$
Special Logarithm Values	$\log_b 1 = 0$ because $b^0 = 1$ and $\log_b b = 1$ because $b^1 = b$
Common and Natural Logarithms	$\log_{10} x = \log x$ and $\log_e x = \ln x$
Product Property of Logarithms	$\log_b mn = \log_b m + \log_b n$
Quotient Property of Logarithms	$\log_b \dfrac{m}{n} = \log_b m - \log_b n$
Power Property of Logarithms	$\log_b m^n = n \log_b m$
Change of Base	$\log_c a = \dfrac{\log_b a}{\log_b c}$

Properties of Functions

Operations on Functions	Let f and g be any two functions. A new function h can be defined using any of the following operations. **Addition:** $h(x) = f(x) + g(x)$ **Subtraction:** $h(x) = f(x) - g(x)$ **Multiplication:** $h(x) = f(x) \cdot g(x)$ **Division:** $h(x) = \dfrac{f(x)}{g(x)}$ **Composition:** $h(x) = g(f(x))$ For addition, subtraction, multiplication, and division, the domain of h consists of the x-values that are in the domains of both f and g. Additionally, the domain of the quotient does not include x-values for which $g(x) = 0$. For composition, the domain of h is the set of all x-values such that x is in the domain of f and $f(x)$ is in the domain of g.
Inverse Functions	Functions f and g are inverses of each other provided: $f(g(x)) = x$ and $g(f(x)) = x$

English–Spanish Glossary

A

absolute value The absolute value of a number x, represented by the symbol $|x|$, is the distance the number is from 0 on a number line.	$\left|\frac{2}{3}\right| = \frac{2}{3}$, $|-4.3| = 4.3$, and $|0| = 0$.
valor absoluto El valor absoluto de un número x, representado por el símbolo $|x|$, es la distancia a la que está el número de 0 en una recta numérica.	$\left|\frac{2}{3}\right| = \frac{2}{3}$, $|-4.3| = 4.3$ y $|0| = 0$.
absolute value function A function that contains an absolute value expression.	$y = |x|$, $y = |x - 3|$, and $y = 4|x + 8| - 9$ are absolute value functions.
función de valor absoluto Función que contiene una expresión de valor absoluto.	$y = |x|$, $y = |x - 3|$ e $y = 4|x + 8| - 9$ son funciones de valor absoluto.
absolute value of a complex number If $z = a + bi$, then the absolute value of z, denoted $|z|$, is a nonnegative real number defined as $|z| = \sqrt{a^2 + b^2}$.	
valor absoluto de un número complejo Si $z = a + bi$, entonces el valor absoluto de z, denotado por $|z|$, es un número real no negativo definido como $|z| = \sqrt{a^2 + b^2}$.	$|-4 + 3i| = \sqrt{(-4)^2 + 3^2} = \sqrt{25} = 5$
algebraic expression An expression that consists of numbers, variables, operations, and grouping symbols. Also called variable expression.	$\frac{2}{3}p$, $\frac{8}{7 - r}$, $k - 5$, and $n^2 + 2n$ are algebraic expressions.
expresión algebraica Expresión formada por números, variables, operaciones y signos de agrupación.	$\frac{2}{3}p$, $\frac{8}{7 - r}$, $k - 5$ y $n^2 + 2n$ son expresiones algebraicas.
amplitude The amplitude of the graph of a sine or cosine function is $\frac{1}{2}(M - m)$, where M is the maximum value of the function and m is the minimum value of the function. **amplitud** La amplitud de la grafica de una función seno o coseno es $\frac{1}{2}(M - m)$, donde M es el valor máximo de la función y m es el valor mínimo de la función.	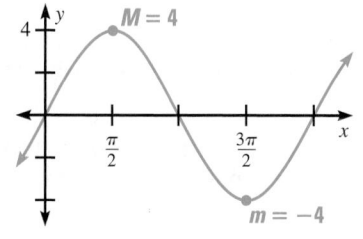 The graph of $y = 4 \sin x$ has an amplitude of $\frac{1}{2}(4 - (-4)) = 4$. La gráfica de $y = 4$ sen x tiene una amplitud de $\frac{1}{2}(4 - (-4)) = 4$.
angle of depression The angle by which an observer's line of sight must be depressed from the horizontal to the point observed.	*See* angle of elevation.
ángulo de depresión El ángulo con el que se debe bajar la línea de visión de un observador desde la horizontal hasta el punto observado.	*Ver* ángulo de elevación.

angle of elevation The angle by which an observer's line of sight must be elevated from the horizontal to the point observed. **ángulo de elevación** El ángulo con el que se debe elevar la línea de visión de un observador desde la horizontal hasta el punto observado.	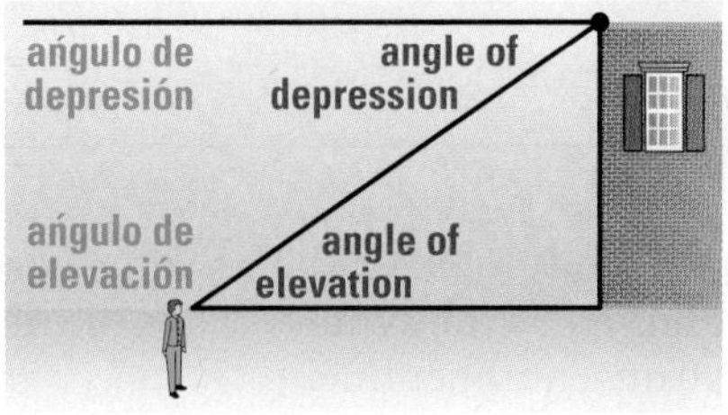
arithmetic sequence A sequence in which the difference of consecutive terms is constant. **progresión aritmética** Progresión en la que la diferencia entre los términos consecutivos es constante.	$-4, 1, 6, 11, 16, \ldots$ is an arithmetic sequence with common difference 5. $-4, 1, 6, 11, 16, \ldots$ es una progresión aritmética con una diferencia común de 5.
arithmetic series The expression formed by adding the terms of an arithmetic sequence. **serie aritmética** La expresión formada al sumar los términos de una progresión aritmética.	$$\sum_{i=1}^{5} 2i = 2 + 4 + 6 + 8 + 10$$
asymptote A line that a graph approaches more and more closely. **asíntota** Recta a la que se aproxima una gráfica cada vez más.	 The asymptote for the graph shown is the line $y = 3$. La asíntota para la gráfica que se muestra es la recta $y = 3$.
axis of symmetry of a parabola The line perpendicular to the parabola's directrix and passing through its focus and vertex. **eje de simetría de una parábola** La recta perpendicular a la directriz de la parábola y que pasa por su foco y su vértice.	*See* parabola. *Ver* parábola.

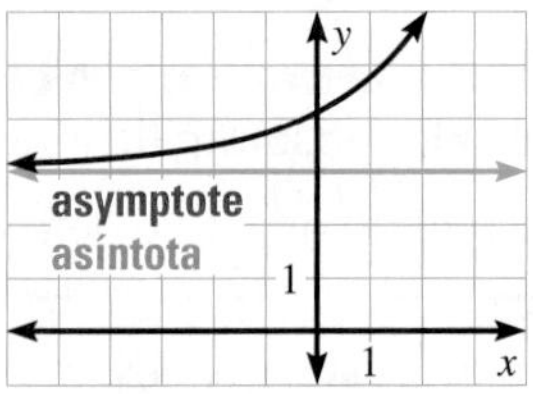

B

base of a power The number or expression that is used as a factor in a repeated multiplication. **base de una potencia** El número o la expresión que se usa como factor en la multiplicación repetida.	In the power 2^5, the base is 2. En la potencia 2^5, la base es 2.

best-fitting line The line that lies as close as possible to all the data points in a scatter plot.

mejor recta de regresión La recta que se ajusta lo más posible a todos los puntos de datos de un diagrama de dispersión.

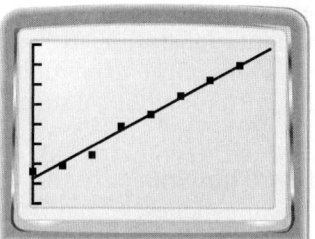

best-fitting quadratic model The model given by using quadratic regression on a set of paired data.

modelo cuadrático con mejor ajuste El modelo dado al realizar una regresión cuadrática sobre un conjunto de pares de datos.

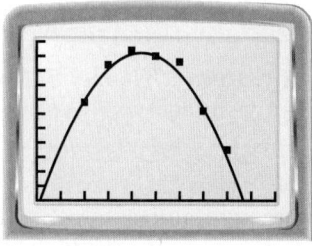

biased question A question that elicits responses that do not accurately reflect the opinions or actions of the people surveyed.

pregunta capciosa Pregunta que induce a respuestas que no reflejan con exactitud las opiniones o acciones de los encuestados.

"Would you rather see an exciting laser show or a boring movie?" is a biased question.

"¿Preferirías ver un emocionante espectáculo de láser o una película aburrida?" es una pregunta capciosa.

biased sample A sample that overrepresents or underrepresents part of a population.

muestra sesgada Muestra que representa de forma excesiva o insuficiente a parte de una población.

The members of a school's basketball team would form a biased sample for a survey about whether to build a new gym.

Los miembros del equipo de baloncesto de una escuela formarían una muestra sesgada si participaran en una encuesta sobre si quieren que se construya un nuevo gimnasio.

binomial The sum of two monomials.

binomio La suma de dos monomios.

$3x - 1$ and $t^3 - 4t$ are binomials.

$3x - 1$ y $t^3 - 4t$ son binomios.

binomial distribution The probability distribution associated with a binomial experiment.

distribución binomial La distribución de probabilidades asociada a un experimento binomial.

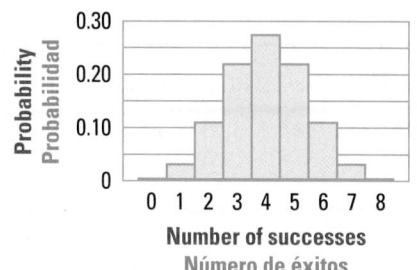

Binomial distribution for 8 trials with $p = 0.5$.

Distribución binomial de 8 pruebas con $p = 0.5$.

binomial experiment An experiment that meets the following conditions. (1) There are n independent trials. (2) Each trial has only two possible outcomes: success and failure. (3) The probability of success is the same for each trial.

experimento binomial Experimento que satisface las siguientes condiciones. (1) Hay n pruebas independientes. (2) Cada prueba tiene sólo dos resultados posibles: éxito y fracaso. (3) La probabilidad de éxito es igual para cada prueba.

A fair coin is tossed 12 times. The probability of getting exactly 4 heads is as follows:

Una moneda normal se lanza 12 veces. La probabilidad de sacar exactamente 4 caras es la siguiente:

$$P(k = 4) = {}_nC_k p^k (1-p)^{n-k}$$
$$= {}_{12}C_4 (0.5)^4 (1-0.5)^8$$
$$= 495(0.5)^4(0.5)^8$$
$$\approx 0.121$$

---

binomial theorem The binomial expansion of $(a + b)^n$ for any positive integer n:
$$(a + b)^n = {}_nC_0 a^n b^0 + {}_nC_1 a^{n-1}b^1 + {}_nC_2 a^{n-2}b^2 + \cdots + {}_nC_n a^0 b^n.$$

teorema binomial La expansión binomial de $(a + b)^n$ para cualquier número entero positivo n:
$$(a + b)^n = {}_nC_0 a^n b^0 + {}_nC_1 a^{n-1}b^1 + {}_nC_2 a^{n-2}b^2 + \cdots + {}_nC_n a^0 b^n.$$

$(x^2 + y)^3$

$$= {}_3C_0(x^2)^3 y^0 + {}_3C_1(x^2)^2 y^1 + {}_3C_2(x^2)^1 y^2 + {}_3C_3(x^2)^0 y^3$$

$$= (1)(x^6)(1) + (3)(x^4)(y) + (3)(x^2)(y^2) + (1)(1)(y^3)$$

$$= x^6 + 3x^4 y + 3x^2 y^2 + y^3$$

---

center of a circle *See* circle.

centro de un círculo *Ver* círculo.

The circle with equation $(x-3)^2 + (y + 5)^2 = 36$ has its center at $(3, -5)$. *See also* circle.

El círculo con la ecuación $(x-3)^2 + (y + 5)^2 = 36$ tiene el centro en $(3, -5)$. *Ver también* círculo.

---

center of a hyperbola The midpoint of the transverse axis of a hyperbola.

centro de una hipérbola El punto medio del eje transverso de una hipérbola.

See hyperbola.

Ver hipérbola.

---

center of an ellipse The midpoint of the major axis of an ellipse.

centro de una elipse El punto medio del eje mayor de una elipse.

See ellipse.

Ver elipse.

---

central angle An angle formed by two radii of a circle.

ángulo central Ángulo formado por dos radios de un círculo.

See sector.

Ver sector.

circle The set of all points (x, y) in a plane that are of distance r from a fixed point, called the center of the circle.

círculo El conjunto de todos los puntos (x, y) de un plano que están a una distancia r de un punto fijo, llamado centro del círculo.

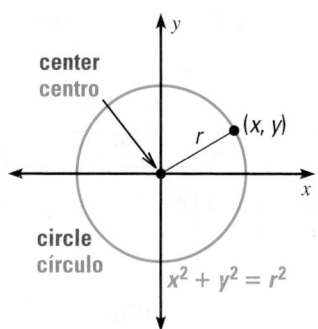

coefficient When a term is the product of a number and a power of a variable, the number is the coefficient of the power.

coeficiente Cuando un término es el producto de un número y una potencia de una variable, el número es el coeficiente de la potencia.

In the algebraic expression $2x^2 + (-4x) + (-1)$, the coefficient of $2x^2$ is 2 and the coefficient of $-4x$ is -4.

En la expresión algebraica $2x^2 + (-4x) + (-1)$, el coeficiente de $2x^2$ es 2 y el coeficiente de $-4x$ es -4.

coefficient matrix The coefficient matrix of the linear system $ax + by = e, cx + dy = f$ is $\begin{bmatrix} a & b \\ c & d \end{bmatrix}$.

matriz coeficiente La matriz coeficiente del sistema lineal $ax + by = e, cx + dy = f$ es $\begin{bmatrix} a & b \\ c & d \end{bmatrix}$.

$$9x + 4y = -6$$
$$3x - 5y = -21$$

coefficient matrix:
matriz coeficiente: $\begin{bmatrix} 9 & 4 \\ 3 & -5 \end{bmatrix}$

matrix of constants:
matriz de constantes: $\begin{bmatrix} -6 \\ -21 \end{bmatrix}$

matrix of variables:
matriz de variables: $\begin{bmatrix} x \\ y \end{bmatrix}$

combination A selection of r objects from a group of n objects where the order is not important, denoted $_nC_r$ where $_nC_r = \frac{n!}{(n-r)! \cdot r!}$.

combinación Selección de r objetos de un grupo de n objetos en el que el orden no importa, denotado $_nC_r$, donde $_nC_r = \frac{n!}{(n-r)! \cdot r!}$.

There are 6 combinations of the $n = 4$ letters A, B, C, and D selected $r = 2$ at a time: AB, AC, AD, BC, BD, and CD.

Hay 6 combinaciones de las letras $n = 4$ A, B, C y D seleccionadas $r = 2$ cada vez: AB, AC, AD, BC, BD y CD.

common difference The constant difference of consecutive terms of an arithmetic sequence.

diferencia común La diferencia constante entre los términos consecutivos de una progresión aritmética.

See arithmetic sequence.

Ver progresión aritmética.

common logarithm A logarithm with base 10. It is denoted by $\log_{10}$ or simply by log.

logaritmo común Logaritmo con base 10. Se denota por $\log_{10}$ ó simplemente por log.

$\log_{10} 100 = \log 100 = 2$ because $10^2 = 100$.

$\log_{10} 100 = \log 100 = 2$ ya que $10^2 = 100$.

common ratio The constant ratio of consecutive terms of a geometric sequence.	*See* geometric sequence.
razón común La razón constante entre los términos consecutivos de una progresión geométrica.	*Ver* progresión geométrica.
complement of a set The complement of a set A, written $\overline{A}$, is the set of all elements in the universal set U that are *not* in A.	Let U be the set of all integers from 1 to 10 and let $A = \{1, 2, 4, 8\}$. Then $\overline{A} = \{3, 5, 6, 7, 9, 10\}$.
complemento de un conjunto El complemento de un conjunto A, escrito $\overline{A}$, es el conjunto de todos los elementos del conjunto universal U que *no* están en A.	Sea U el conjunto de todos los números enteros entre 1 y 10 y sea $A = \{1, 2, 4, 8\}$. Por lo tanto, $\overline{A} = \{3, 5, 6, 7, 9, 10\}$.
completing the square The process of adding a term to a quadratic expression of the form $x^2 + bx$ to make it a perfect square trinomial.	To complete the square for $x^2 + 16x$, add $\left(\frac{16}{2}\right)^2 = 64: x^2 + 16x + 64 = (x + 8)^2$.
completar el cuadrado El proceso de sumar un término a una expresión cuadrática de la forma $x^2 + bx$, de modo que sea un trinomio cuadrado perfecto.	Para completar el cuadrado para $x^2 + 16x$, suma $\left(\frac{16}{2}\right)^2 = 64: x^2 + 16x + 64 = (x + 8)^2$.
complex conjugates Two complex numbers of the form $a + bi$ and $a - bi$.	**$2 + 4i, 2 - 4i$**
números complejos conjugados Dos números complejos de la forma $a + bi$ y $a - bi$.	
complex fraction A fraction that contains a fraction in its numerator or denominator.	$\dfrac{\frac{5}{x+4}}{\frac{6x}{3x^2}}, \dfrac{1}{\frac{1}{p}+\frac{1}{q}}$
fracción compleja Fracción que tiene una fracción en su numerador o en su denominador.	
complex number A number $a + bi$ where a and b are real numbers and i is the imaginary unit.	**$0, 2.5, \sqrt{3}, \pi, 5i, 2 - i$**
número complejo Un número $a + bi$, donde a y b son números reales e i es la unidad imaginaria.	
complex plane A coordinate plane in which each point (a, b) represents a complex number $a + bi$. The horizontal axis is the real axis and the vertical axis is the imaginary axis.	
plano complejo Plano de coordenadas en el que cada punto (a, b) representa un número complejo $a + bi$. El eje horizontal es el eje real, y el eje vertical es el eje imaginario.	
composition of functions The composition of a function g with a function f is $h(x) = g(f(x))$.	$f(x) = 5x - 2, \ g(x) = 4x^{-1}$
composición de funciones La composición de una función g con una función f es $h(x) = g(f(x))$.	$g(f(x)) = g(5x - 2) = 4(5x - 2)^{-1} = \dfrac{4}{5x - 2}, x \neq \dfrac{2}{5}$

compound event The union or intersection of two events. **suceso compuesto** La unión o la intersección de dos sucesos.	When you roll a six-sided die, the event "roll a 2 or an odd number" is a compound event. Cuando lanzas un cubo numerado de seis lados, el suceso "salir el 2 ó un número impar" es un suceso compuesto.
compound inequality Two simple inequalities joined by "and" or "or." **desigualdad compuesta** Dos desigualdades simples unidas por "y" u "o".	$2x > 0$ or $x + 4 < -1$ is a compound inequality. $2x > 0$ ó $x + 4 < -1$ es una desigualdad compuesta.
conditional probability The conditional probability of B given A, written $P(B \mid A)$, is the probability that event B will occur given that event A has occurred. **probabilidad condicional** La probabilidad condicional de B dado A, escrito $P(B \mid A)$, es la probabilidad de que ocurra el suceso B dado que ha ocurrido el suceso A.	Two cards are randomly selected from a standard deck of 52 cards. Let event A be "the first card is a club" and let event B be "the second card is a club." Then $P(B \mid A) = \frac{12}{51} = \frac{4}{17}$ because there are 12 (out of 13) clubs left among the remaining 51 cards. Dos cartas se seleccionan al azar de una baraja normal de 52 cartas. Sea el suceso A "la primera carta es de tréboles" y sea el suceso B "la segunda carta es de tréboles". Entonces $P(B \mid A) = \frac{12}{51} = \frac{4}{17}$ ya que quedan 12 (del total de 13) cartas de tréboles entre las 51 cartas restantes.
conic *See* conic section. **cónica** *Ver* sección cónica.	*See* conic section. *Ver* sección cónica.
conic section A curve formed by the intersection of a plane and a double-napped cone. Conic sections are also called conics. **sección cónica** Una curva formada por la intersección de un plano y un cono doble. Las secciones cónicas también se llaman cónicas.	*See* circle, ellipse, hyperbola, *and* parabola. *Ver* círculo, elipse, hipérbola y parábola.
conjugates The expressions $a + \sqrt{b}$ and $a - \sqrt{b}$ where a and b are rational numbers. **conjugados** Las expresiones $a + \sqrt{b}$ y $a - \sqrt{b}$ cuando a y b son números racionales.	The conjugate of $7 + \sqrt{2}$ is $7 - \sqrt{2}$. El conjugado de $7 + \sqrt{2}$ es $7 - \sqrt{2}$.

constant of variation The nonzero constant a in a direct variation equation $y = ax$, an inverse variation equation $y = \frac{a}{x}$, or a joint variation equation $z = axy$.	In the direct variation equation $y = -\frac{5}{2}x$, the constant of variation is $-\frac{5}{2}$.
constante de variación La constante distinta de cero a de una ecuación de variación directa $y = ax$, de una ecuación de variación inversa $y = \frac{a}{x}$ o de una ecuación de variación conjunta $z = axy$.	En la ecuación de variación directa $y = -\frac{5}{2}x$, la constante de variación es $-\frac{5}{2}$.
constant term A term that has a number part but no variable part.	The constant term of the algebraic expression $3x^2 + 5x + (-7)$ is -7.
término constante Término que tiene una parte numérica pero sin variable.	El término constante de la expresión algebraica $3x^2 + 5x + (-7)$ es -7.
constraints In linear programming, the linear inequalities that form a system.	*See* linear programming.
restricciones En la programación lineal, las desigualdades lineales que forman un sistema.	*Ver* programación lineal.
control group A group that does not undergo a procedure or treatment when an experiment is conducted. *See also* experimental group.	*See* experimental group.
grupo de control Grupo que no se somete a ningún procedimiento o tratamiento durante la realización de un experimento. *Ver también* grupo experimental.	*Ver* grupo experimental.
controlled experiment An experiment in which two groups are studied under conditions that are identical except for one variable.	
experimento controlado Experimento en el que se estudia a dos grupos bajo condiciones que son idénticas, excepto por una variable.	
cosecant function If θ is an acute angle of a right triangle, the cosecant of θ is the length of the hypotenuse divided by the length of the side opposite θ.	*See* sine function.
función cosecante Si θ es un ángulo agudo de un triángulo rectángulo, la cosecante de θ es la longitud de la hipotenusa dividida por la longitud del lado opuesto a θ.	*Ver* función seno.

cosine function If θ is an acute angle of a right triangle, the cosine of θ is the length of the side adjacent to θ divided by the length of the hypotenuse.

See **sine function.**

función coseno Si θ es un ángulo agudo de un triángulo rectángulo, el coseno de θ es la longitud del lado adyacente a θ dividida por la longitud de la hipotenusa.

Ver **función seno.**

---

cotangent function If θ is an acute angle of a right triangle, the cotangent of θ is the length of the side adjacent to θ divided by the length of the side opposite θ.

See **sine function.**

función cotangente Si θ es un ángulo agudo de un triángulo rectángulo, la cotangente de θ es la longitud del lado adyacente a θ dividida por la longitud del lado opuesto a θ.

Ver **función seno.**

---

coterminal angles Angles in standard position with terminal sides that coincide.

ángulos coterminales Ángulos en posición normal cuyos lados terminales coinciden.

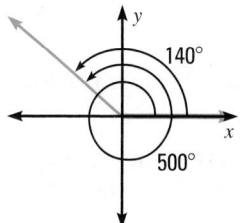

The angles with measures 500° and 140° are coterminal.

Los ángulos que miden 500° y 140° son coterminales.

---

co-vertices of an ellipse The points of intersection of an ellipse and the line perpendicular to the major axis at the center.

See **ellipse.**

puntos extremos del eje menor de una elipse Los puntos de intersección de una elipse y la recta perpendicular al eje mayor en el centro.

Ver **elipse.**

Cramer's rule A method for solving a system of linear equations using determinants: For the linear system $ax + by = e$, $cx + dy = f$, let A be the coefficient matrix. If $\det A \neq 0$, the solution of the system is as follows:

$$x = \frac{\begin{vmatrix} e & b \\ f & d \end{vmatrix}}{\det A}, \ y = \frac{\begin{vmatrix} a & e \\ c & f \end{vmatrix}}{\det A}$$

regla de Cramer Método para resolver un sistema de ecuaciones lineales usando determinantes: Para el sistema lineal $ax + by = e$, $cx + dy = f$, sea A la matriz coeficiente. Si $\det A \neq 0$, la solución del sistema es la siguiente:

$$x = \frac{\begin{vmatrix} e & b \\ f & d \end{vmatrix}}{\det A}, \ y = \frac{\begin{vmatrix} a & e \\ c & f \end{vmatrix}}{\det A}$$

$$9x + 4y = -6$$
$$3x - 5y = -21; \quad \begin{vmatrix} 9 & 4 \\ 3 & -5 \end{vmatrix} = -57$$

Applying Cramer's rule gives the following:

Al aplicar la regla de Cramer se obtiene lo siguiente:

$$x = \frac{\begin{vmatrix} -6 & 4 \\ -21 & -5 \end{vmatrix}}{-57} = \frac{114}{-57} = -2$$

$$y = \frac{\begin{vmatrix} 9 & -6 \\ 3 & -21 \end{vmatrix}}{-57} = \frac{-171}{-57} = 3$$

cross multiplying A method for solving a simple rational equation for which each side of the equation is a single rational expression.

multiplicar en cruz Método para resolver una ecuación racional simple en la que cada lado es una sola expresión racional.

To solve $\dfrac{3}{x+1} = \dfrac{9}{4x+5}$, cross multiply.

Para resolver $\dfrac{3}{x+1} = \dfrac{9}{4x+5}$, multiplica en cruz.

$$3(4x+5) = 9(x+1)$$
$$12x + 15 = 9x + 9$$
$$3x = -6$$
$$x = -2$$

---

cycle The shortest repeating portion of the graph of a periodic function.

ciclo En una función periódica, la parte más corta de la gráfica que se repite.

See periodic function.

Ver función periódica.

D

decay factor The quantity b in the exponential decay function $y = ab^x$ with $a > 0$ and $0 < b < 1$.

factor de decrecimiento La cantidad b de la función de decrecimiento exponencial $y = ab^x$, con $a > 0$ y $0 < b < 1$.

The decay factor for the function $y = 3(0.5)^x$ is 0.5.

El factor de decrecimiento de la función $y = 3(0.5)^x$ es 0.5.

---

decreasing The graph falls from left to right for all real numbers.

decreciente La gráfica desciende de izquierda a derecha para todos los números reales.

---

degree of a polynomial function The exponent in the term of a polynomial function where the variable is raised to the greatest power.

grado de una función polinómica En una función polinómica, el exponente del término donde la variable se eleva a la mayor potencia.

See polynomial function.

Ver función polinómica.

---

dependent events Two events such that the occurrence of one event affects the occurrence of the other event.

sucesos dependientes Dos sucesos tales que la ocurrencia de uno de ellos afecta a la ocurrencia del otro.

Two cards are drawn from a deck without replacement. The events "the first is a 3" and "the second is a 3" are dependent.

Se sacan dos cartas de una baraja y no se reemplazan. Los sucesos "la primera es un 3" y "la segunda es un 3" son dependientes.

dependent variable The output variable in an equation in two variables.	*See* independent variable.
variable dependiente La variable de salida de una ecuación con dos variables.	*Ver* variable independiente.
determinant A real number associated with any square matrix A, denoted by det A or $\lvert A \rvert$.	$\det \begin{bmatrix} 5 & 4 \\ 3 & 1 \end{bmatrix} = 5(1) - 3(4) = -7$
determinante Número real asociado a toda matriz cuadrada A, denotada por det A o $\lvert A \rvert$.	$\det \begin{bmatrix} a & b \\ c & d \end{bmatrix} = ad - cb$
dimensions of a matrix The dimensions of a matrix with m rows and n columns are $m \times n$.	A matrix with 2 rows and 3 columns has the dimensions 2×3 (read "2 by 3").
dimensiones de una matriz Las dimensiones de una matriz con m filas y n columnas son $m \times n$.	Una matriz con 2 filas y 3 columnas tiene por dimensiones 2×3 (leído "2 por 3").
direct variation Two variables x and y show direct variation provided that $y = ax$ where a is a nonzero constant.	The equation $5x + 2y = 0$ represents direct variation because it is equivalent to the equation $y = -\frac{5}{2}x$.
variación directa Dos variables x e y indican una variación directa siempre que $y = ax$, donde a es una constante distinta de cero.	La ecuación $5x + 2y = 0$ representa una variación directa ya que es equivalente a la ecuación $y = -\frac{5}{2}x$.
directrix of a parabola *See* parabola.	*See* parabola.
directriz de una parábola *Ver* parábola.	*Ver* parábola.
discrete function A function whose graph consists of separate points.	
función discreta Función cuya gráfica consiste en puntos aislados.	
discriminant of a general second-degree equation The expression $B^2 - 4AC$ for the equation $Ax^2 + Bxy + Cy^2 + Dx + Ey + F = 0$. Used to identify which type of conic the equation represents.	For the equation $4x^2 + y^2 - 8x - 8 = 0$, $A = 4$, $B = 0$, and $C = 1$. $$B^2 - 4AC = 0^2 - 4(4)(1) = -16$$ Because $B^2 - 4AC < 0$, $B = 0$, and $A \neq C$, the conic is an ellipse.
discriminante de una ecuación general de segundo grado La expresión $B^2 - 4AC$ para la ecuación $Ax^2 + Bxy + Cy^2 + Dx + Ey + F = 0$. Se usa para identificar qué tipo de cónica representa la ecuación.	Para la ecuación $4x^2 + y^2 - 8x - 8 = 0$, $A = 4$, $B = 0$ y $C = 1$. $$B^2 - 4AC = 0^2 - 4(4)(1) = -16$$ Debido a que $B^2 - 4AC < 0$, $B = 0$ y $A \neq C$, la cónica es un elipse.

discriminant of a quadratic equation The expression $b^2 - 4ac$ for the quadratic equation $ax^2 + bx + c = 0$; also the expression under the radical sign in the quadratic formula.	The value of the discriminant of $2x^2 - 3x - 7 = 0$ is $b^2 - 4ac = (-3)^2 - 4(2)(-7) = 65$.
discriminante de una ecuación cuadrática La expresión $b^2 - 4ac$ para la ecuación cuadrática $ax^2 + bx + c = 0$; es también la expresión situada bajo el signo radical de la fórmula cuadrática.	El valor del discriminante de $2x^2 - 3x - 7 = 0$ es $b^2 - 4ac = (-3)^2 - 4(2)(-7) = 65$.
disjoint events Events A and B are disjoint if they have no outcomes in common; also called mutually exclusive events.	When you randomly select a card from a standard deck of 52 cards, selecting a club and selecting a heart are disjoint events.
sucesos disjuntos Los sucesos A y B son disjuntos si no tienen casos en común; también se llaman sucesos mutuamente excluyentes.	Al seleccionar al azar una carta de una baraja normal de 52 cartas, sacar una de tréboles y sacar una de corazones son sucesos disjuntos.
distance formula The distance d between any two points (x_1, y_1) and (x_2, y_2) is $d = \sqrt{(x_2 - x_1)^2 + (y_2 - y_1)^2}$.	The distance between $(-3, 5)$ and $(4, -1)$ is $\sqrt{(4 - (-3))^2 + (-1 - 5)^2} = \sqrt{49 + 36} = \sqrt{85}$.
fórmula de la distancia La distancia d entre dos puntos cualesquiera (x_1, y_1) y (x_2, y_2) es $d = \sqrt{(x_2 - x_1)^2 + (y_2 - y_1)^2}$.	La distancia entre $(-3, 5)$ y $(4, -1)$ es $\sqrt{(4 - (-3))^2 + (-1 - 5)^2} = \sqrt{49 + 36} = \sqrt{85}$.
domain The set of input values of a relation.	*See* relation.
dominio El conjunto de los valores de entrada de una relación.	*Ver* relación.

E

eccentricity of a conic section The eccentricity e of a hyperbola or an ellipse is $\frac{c}{a}$ where c is the distance from each focus to the center and a is the distance from each vertex to the center. The eccentricity of a circle is $e = 0$. The eccentricity of a parabola is $e = 1$.	For the ellipse $\frac{(x + 4)^2}{36} + \frac{(y - 2)^2}{16} = 1$, $c = \sqrt{36 - 16} = 2\sqrt{5}$, so the eccentricity is $e = \frac{c}{a} = \frac{2\sqrt{5}}{\sqrt{36}} = \frac{\sqrt{5}}{3} \approx 0.745$.
excentricidad de una sección cónica La excentricidad e de una hipérbola o de una elipse es $\frac{c}{a}$, donde c es la distancia entre cada foco y el centro y a es la distancia entre cada vértice y el centro. La excentricidad de un círculo es $e = 0$. La excentricidad de una parábola es $e = 1$.	Para la elipse $\frac{(x + 4)^2}{36} + \frac{(y - 2)^2}{16} = 1$, $c = \sqrt{36 - 16} = 2\sqrt{5}$, por lo tanto la excentricidad es $e = \frac{c}{a} = \frac{2\sqrt{5}}{\sqrt{36}} = \frac{\sqrt{5}}{3} \approx 0.745$.
element of a matrix Each number in a matrix.	*See* matrix.
elemento de una matriz Cada número de una matriz.	*Ver* matriz.

element of a set Each object in a set; also called a member of the set.	The elements of the set $A = \{1, 2, 3, 4\}$ are 1, 2, 3, and 4.
elemento de un conjunto Cada objeto de un conjunto; también se llama miembro del conjunto.	Los elementos del conjunto $A = \{1, 2, 3, 4\}$ son 1, 2, 3 y 4.
elimination method A method of solving a system of equations by multiplying equations by constants, then adding the revised equations to eliminate a variable.	To use the elimination method to solve the system with equations $3x - 7y = 10$ and $6x - 8y = 8$, multiply the first equation by -2 and add the equations to eliminate x.
método de eliminación Método para resolver un sistema de ecuaciones en el que se multiplican ecuaciones por constantes y se agregan luego las ecuaciones revisadas para eliminar una variable.	Para usar el método de eliminación a fin de resolver el sistema con las ecuaciones $3x - 7y = 10$ y $6x - 8y = 8$, multiplica la primera ecuación por -2 y suma las ecuaciones para eliminar x.
ellipse The set of all points P in a plane such that the sum of the distances between P and two fixed points, called the foci, is a constant.	
elipse El conjunto de todos los puntos P de un plano tales que la suma de las distancias entre P y dos puntos fijos, llamados focos, es una constante.	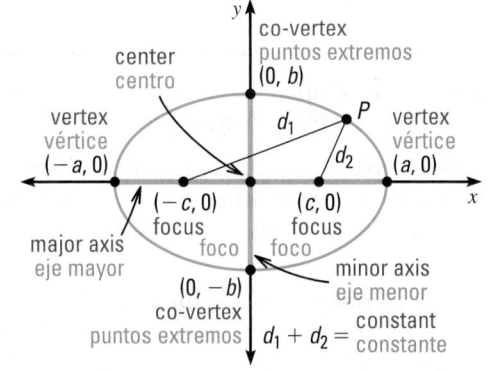
empty set The set with no elements, denoted Ø.	The set of positive integers less than 0 is the empty set, Ø.
conjunto vacío El conjunto que no tiene elementos, indicado Ø.	El conjunto de los números enteros positivos menores que 0 es el conjunto vacío, Ø.
end behavior The behavior of the graph of a function as x approaches positive infinity $(+\infty)$ or negative infinity $(-\infty)$.	
comportamiento El comportamiento de la gráfica de una función al aproximarse x a infinito positivo $(+\infty)$ o a infinito negativo $(-\infty)$.	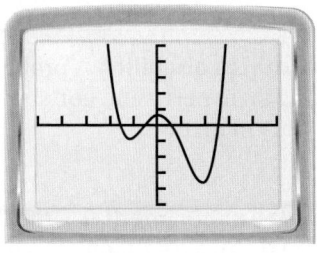 $f(x) \rightarrow +\infty$ as $x \rightarrow -\infty$ or as $x \rightarrow +\infty$. $f(x) \rightarrow +\infty$ según $x \rightarrow -\infty$ o según $x \rightarrow +\infty$.
equal matrices Matrices that have the same dimensions and equal elements in corresponding positions.	
matrices iguales Matrices que tienen las mismas dimensiones y elementos iguales en posiciones correspondientes.	$\begin{bmatrix} 6 & 0 \\ -\frac{4}{4} & \frac{3}{4} \end{bmatrix} = \begin{bmatrix} 3 \cdot 2 & -1+1 \\ -1 & 0.75 \end{bmatrix}$

equation in two variables An equation that contains two variables. **ecuación con dos variables** Ecuación que tiene dos variables.	$y = 3x - 5, d = -16t^2 + 64$
even function If $f(-x) = f(x)$ for all x in its domain. The graph is symmetric about the y-axis. **función par** Si $f(-x) = f(x)$ para toda x en su dominio. La gráfica es simétrica con respecto al eje de las y.	**Even Function**
experiment Imposes a treatment on individuals in order to collect data on their response to the treatment. **experimento** Se expone a un grupo de individuos a una manipulación determinada para que se recopilen datos sobre su respuesta a la manipulación.	
experimental group A group that undergoes some procedure or treatment when an experiment is conducted. *See also* control group. **grupo experimental** Grupo que se somete a algún procedimiento o tratamiento durante la realización de un experimento. *Ver también* grupo de control.	One group of headache sufferers, the experimental group, is given pills containing medication. Another group, the control group, is given pills containing no medication. Un grupo de personas que sufren de dolores de cabeza, el grupo experimental, recibe píldoras que contienen el medicamento. Otro grupo, el grupo de control, recibe píldoras sin el medicamento.
experimental probability A probability based on performing an experiment, conducting a survey, or looking at the history of an event. **probabilidad experimental** Probabilidad basada en la realización de un experimento o una encuesta o en el estudio de la historia de un suceso.	You roll a six-sided die 100 times and get a 4 nineteen times. The experimental probability of rolling a 4 with the die is $\frac{19}{100} = 0.19$. Lanzas 100 veces un dado de seis caras y sale diecinueve veces el 4. La probabilidad experimental de que salga el 4 al lanzar el dado es $\frac{19}{100} = 0.19$.

explicit rule A rule for a sequence that gives the nth term a_n as a function of the term's position number n in the sequence.	The rules $a_n = -11 + 4n$ and $a_n = 3(2)^{n-1}$ are explicit rules for sequences.
regla explícita Regla de una progresión que expresa el término enésimo a_n en función del número de posición n del término en la progresión.	Las reglas $a_n = -11 + 4n$ y $a_n = 3(2)^{n-1}$ son reglas explícitas de progresiones.
exponent The number or variable that represents the number of times the base of a power is used as a factor.	In the power 2^5, the exponent is 5.
exponente El número o la variable que representa la cantidad de veces que la base de una potencia se usa como factor.	En la potencia 2^5, el exponente es 5.
exponential decay function If $a > 0$ and $0 < b < 1$, then the function $y = ab^x$ is an exponential decay function with decay factor b.	
función de decrecimiento exponencial Si $a > 0$ y $0 < b < 1$, entonces la función $y = ab^x$ es una función de decrecimiento exponencial con factor de decrecimiento b.	$y = 2\left(\frac{1}{4}\right)^x$
exponential equation An equation in which a variable expression occurs as an exponent.	$4^x = \left(\frac{1}{2}\right)^{x-3}$ is an exponential equation.
ecuación exponencial Ecuación que tiene como exponente una expresión algebraica.	$4^x = \left(\frac{1}{2}\right)^{x-3}$ es una ecuación exponencial.
exponential function A function of the form $y = ab^x$, where $a \neq 0$, $b > 0$, and $b \neq 1$.	*See* exponential growth function *and* exponential decay function.
función exponencial Función de la forma $y = ab^x$, donde $a \neq 0$, $b > 0$ y $b \neq 1$.	*Ver* función de crecimiento exponencial y función de decrecimiento exponencial.
exponential growth function If $a > 0$ and $b > 1$, then the function $y = ab^x$ is an exponential growth function with growth factor b.	
función de crecimiento exponencial Si $a > 0$ y $b > 1$, entonces la función $y = ab^x$ es una función de crecimiento exponencial con factor de crecimiento b.	$y = \frac{1}{2} \cdot 4^x$
extraneous solution An apparent solution that must be rejected because it does not satisfy the original equation.	Solving $\lvert 2x + 12 \rvert = 4x$ gives the apparent solutions $x = 6$ and $x = -2$. The apparent solution -2 is extraneous because it does not satisfy the original equation.
solución extraña Solución aparente que debe rechazarse ya que no satisface la ecuación original.	Al resolver $\lvert 2x + 12 \rvert = 4x$ se obtienen las soluciones aparentes $x = 6$ y $x = -2$. La solución aparente -2 es extraña ya no satisface la ecuación original.

factor by grouping To factor a polynomial with four terms by grouping, factor common monomials from pairs of terms, and then look for a common binomial factor.

factorizar por grupos Para factorizar por grupos un polinomio con cuatro términos, factoriza unos monomios comunes a partir de los pares de términos y luego busca un factor binómico común.

$$x^3 - 3x^2 - 16x + 48$$
$$= x^2(x - 3) - 16(x - 3)$$
$$= (x^2 - 16)(x - 3)$$
$$= (x + 4)(x - 4)(x - 3)$$

---

factored completely A factorable polynomial with integer coefficients is factored completely if it is written as a product of unfactorable polynomials with integer coefficients.

completamente factorizado Un polinomio que puede factorizarse y que tiene coeficientes enteros está completamente factorizado si está escrito como producto de polinomios que no pueden factorizarse y que tienen coeficientes enteros.

$3x(x - 5)$ is factored completely.

$(x + 2)(x^2 - 6x + 8)$ is *not* factored completely because $x^2 - 6x + 8$ can be factored as $(x - 2)(x - 4)$.

$3x(x - 5)$ está completamente factorizado.

$(x + 2)(x^2 - 6x + 8)$ *no* está completamente factorizado ya que $x^2 - 6x + 8$ puede factorizarse como $(x - 2)(x - 4)$.

---

factorial For any positive integer n, the expression $n!$, read "n factorial," is the product of all the integers from 1 to n. Also, 0! is defined to be 1.

factorial Para cualquier número entero positivo n, la expresión $n!$, leída "factorial de n", es el producto de todos los números enteros entre 1 y n. También, 0! se define como 1.

$$6! = 6 \cdot 5 \cdot 4 \cdot 3 \cdot 2 \cdot 1 = 720$$

---

feasible region In linear programming, the graph of the system of constraints.

región factible En la programación lineal, la gráfica del sistema de restricciones.

See **linear programming.**

Ver **programación lineal.**

---

finite differences When the x-values in a data set are equally spaced, the differences of consecutive y-values are called finite differences.

diferencias finitas Cuando los valores de x de un conjunto de datos están a igual distancia entre sí, las diferencias entre los valores de y consecutivos se llaman diferencias finitas.

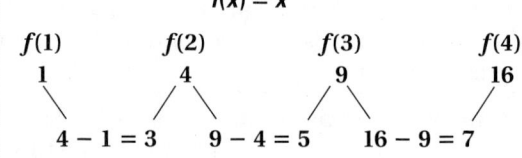

The first-order finite differences are 3, 5, and 7.

Las diferencias finitas de primer orden son 3, 5 y 7.

---

foci of a hyperbola *See* hyperbola.

focos de una hipérbola *Ver* hipérbola.

See hyperbola.

Ver hipérbola.

---

foci of an ellipse *See* ellipse.

focos de una elipse *Ver* elipse.

See ellipse.

Ver elipse.

---

focus of a parabola *See* parabola.	*See* parabola.
foco de una parábola *Ver* parábola.	*Ver* parábola.
formula An equation that relates two or more quantities, usually represented by variables.	The formula $P = 2\ell + 2w$ relates the length and width of a rectangle to its perimeter.
fórmula Ecuación que relaciona dos o más cantidades que generalmente se representan por variables.	La fórmula $P = 2\ell + 2w$ relaciona el largo y el ancho de un rectángulo con su perímetro.
frequency of a periodic function The reciprocal of the period. Frequency is the number of cycles per unit of time.	$P = 2\sin 4000\pi t$ has period $\frac{2\pi}{4000\pi} = \frac{1}{2000}$, so its frequency is 2000 cycles per second (hertz) when t represents time in seconds.
frecuencia de una función periódica El recíproco del período. La frecuencia es el número de ciclos por unidad de tiempo.	$P = 2\operatorname{sen} 4000\pi t$ tiene período $\frac{2\pi}{4000\pi} = \frac{1}{2000}$, por lo que su frecuencia es de 2000 ciclos por segundo (hertzios) cuando t representa el tiempo en segundos.
function A relation for which each input has exactly one output.	The relation $(-4, 6)$, $(3, -9)$, and $(7, -9)$ is a function. The relation $(0, 3)$, $(0, 6)$, and $(10, 8)$ is not a function because the input 0 is mapped onto both 3 and 6.
función Relación para la que cada entrada tiene exactamente una salida.	La relación $(-4, 6)$, $(3, -9)$ y $(7, -9)$ es una función. La relación $(0, 3)$, $(0, 6)$ y $(10, 8)$ no es una función ya que la entrada 0 se hace corresponder tanto con 3 como con 6.
function notation Using $f(x)$ (or a similar symbol such as $g(x)$ or $h(x)$) to represent the dependent variable of a function.	The linear function $y = mx + b$ can be written using function notation as $f(x) = mx + b$.
notación de función Usar $f(x)$ (o un símbolo semejante como $g(x)$ o $h(x)$) para representar la variable dependiente de una función.	La función lineal $y = mx + b$ escrita en notación de función es $f(x) = mx + b$.

G

general second-degree equation in x and y The form $Ax^2 + Bxy + Cy^2 + Dx + Ey + F = 0$.	$16x^2 - 9y^2 - 96x + 36y - 36 = 0$ and $4x^2 + y^2 - 8x - 8 = 0$ are second-degree equations in x and y.
ecuación general de segundo grado en x e y La forma $Ax^2 + Bxy + Cy^2 + Dx + Ey + F = 0$.	$16x^2 - 9y^2 - 96x + 36y - 36 = 0$ y $4x^2 + y^2 - 8x - 8 = 0$ son ecuaciones de segundo grado en x e y.

geometric probability A probability found by calculating a ratio of two lengths, areas, or volumes. **probabilidad geométrica** Probabilidad hallada al calcular una razón entre dos longitudes, áreas o volúmenes.	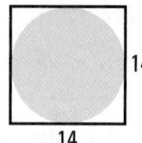 The probability that a dart that hits the square at random lands inside the circle is $\frac{\pi \cdot 7^2}{14^2} \approx 0.785$. La probabilidad de que un dardo que da con el blanco cuadrado, dé al azar en el interior del círculo es $\frac{\pi \cdot 7^2}{14^2} \approx 0.785$.
geometric sequence A sequence in which the ratio of any term to the previous term is constant. **progresión geométrica** Progresión en la que la razón entre cualquier término y el término precedente es constante.	$-19, 38, -76, 152$ is a geometric sequence with common ratio -2. $-19, 38, -76, 152$ es una progresión geométrica con una razón común de -2.
geometric series The expression formed by adding the terms of a geometric sequence. **serie geométrica** La expresión formada al sumar los términos de una progresión geométrica.	$$\sum_{i=1}^{5} 4(3)^{i-1} = 4 + 12 + 36 + 108 + 324$$
graph of a linear inequality in two variables The set of all points in a coordinate plane that represent solutions of the inequality. **gráfica de una desigualdad lineal con dos variables** El conjunto de todos los puntos de un plano de coordenadas que representan las soluciones de la desigualdad.	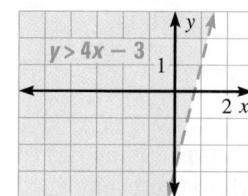
graph of a system of linear inequalities The graph of all solutions of the system. **gráfica de un sistema de desigualdades lineales** La gráfica de todas las soluciones del sistema.	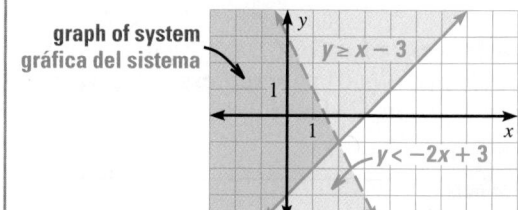
graph of an equation in two variables The set of all points (x, y) that represent solutions of the equation. **gráfica de una ecuación con dos variables** El conjunto de todos los puntos (x, y) que representan soluciones de la ecuación.	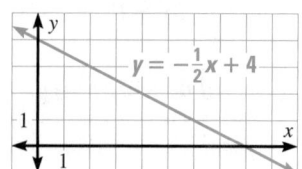

graph of an inequality in one variable All points on a number line that represent solutions of the inequality.

gráfica de una desigualdad con una variable Todos los puntos de una recta numérica que representan soluciones de la desigualdad.

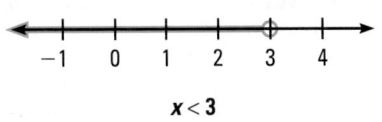

$x < 3$

---

growth factor The quantity b in the exponential growth function $y = ab^x$ with $a > 0$ and $b > 1$.

factor de crecimiento La cantidad b de la función de crecimiento exponencial $y = ab^x$, con $a > 0$ y $b > 1$.

The growth factor for the function $y = 8(3.4)^x$ is 3.4.

El factor de crecimiento de la función $y = 8(3.4)^x$ es 3.4.

---

half-planes The two regions into which the boundary line of a linear inequality divides the coordinate plane.

semiplanos Las dos regiones en que la recta límite de una desigualdad lineal divide al plano de coordenadas.

The solution of $y < 3$ is the half-plane consisting of all the points below the line $y = 3$.

La solución de $y < 3$ es el semi-plano que consta de todos los puntos que se encuentran debajo de la recta $y = 3$.

---

hyperbola The set of all points P in a plane such that the difference of the distances from P to two fixed points, called the foci, is constant.

hipérbola El conjunto de todos los puntos P de un plano tales que la diferencia de distancias entre P y dos puntos fijos, llamados focos, es constante.

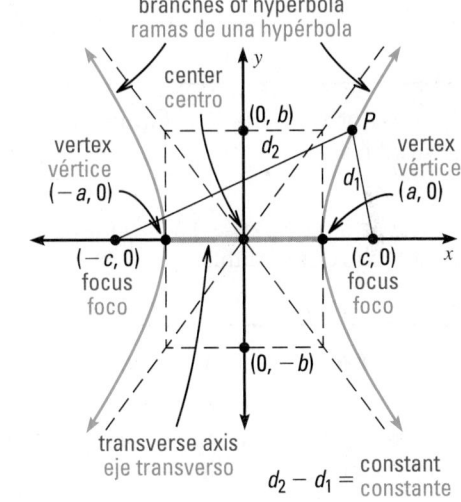

---

identity A statement that equates two equivalent expressions.

identidad Enunciado que hace iguales a dos expresiones equivalentes.

$8x + 3x = 11x$ and $2(x - 3) = 2x - 6$ are identities.

$8x + 3x = 11x$ y $2(x - 3) = 2x - 6$ son identidades.

---

identity matrix The $n \times n$ matrix that has 1's on the main diagonal and 0's elsewhere.

matriz identidad La matriz $n \times n$ que tiene los 1 en la diagonal principal y los 0 en las otras posiciones.

The 2×2 identity matrix is $\begin{bmatrix} 1 & 0 \\ 0 & 1 \end{bmatrix}$.

La matriz identidad 2×2 es $\begin{bmatrix} 1 & 0 \\ 0 & 1 \end{bmatrix}$.

imaginary number A complex number $a + bi$ where $b \neq 0$.	$5i$ and $2 - i$ are imaginary numbers.
número imaginario Un número complejo $a + bi$, donde $b \neq 0$.	$5i$ y $2 - i$ son números imaginarios.
imaginary unit i $i = \sqrt{-1}$, so $i^2 = -1$.	$\sqrt{-3} = i\sqrt{3}$
unidad imaginaria i $i = \sqrt{-1}$, por lo que $i^2 = -1$.	
increasing The graph rises from left to right for all real numbers.	
creciente La gráfica asciende de izquierda a derecha para todos los números reales.	
independent events Two events such that the occurrence of one event has no effect on the occurrence of the other event.	If a coin is tossed twice, the outcome of the first toss (heads or tails) and the outcome of the second toss are independent events.
sucesos independientes Dos sucesos tales que la ocurrencia de uno de ellos no afecta a la ocurrencia del otro.	Al lanzar una moneda dos veces, el resultado del primer lanzamiento (cara o cruz) y el resultado del segundo lanzamiento son sucesos independientes.
independent variable The input variable in an equation in two variables.	In $y = 3x - 5$, the independent variable is x. The dependent variable is y because the value of y depends on the value of x.
variable independiente La variable de entrada de una ecuación con dos variables.	En $y = 3x - 5$, la variable independiente es x. La variable dependiente es y ya que el valor de y depende del valor de x.
index of a radical The integer n, greater than 1, in the expression $\sqrt[n]{a}$.	The index of $\sqrt[3]{-216}$ is 3.
índice de un radical El número entero n, que es mayor que 1 y aparece en la expresión $\sqrt[n]{a}$.	El índice de $\sqrt[3]{-216}$ es 3.
initial side of an angle *See* terminal side of an angle.	*See* **standard position of an angle.**
lado inicial de un ángulo *Ver* lado terminal de un ángulo.	*Ver* **posición normal de un ángulo.**

intercept form of a quadratic function The form $y = a(x - p)(x - q)$, where the x-intercepts of the graph are p and q.	The function $y = 2(x + 3)(x - 1)$ is in intercept form.
forma de intercepto de una función cuadrática La forma $y = a(x - p)(x - q)$, donde los interceptos en x de la gráfica son p y q.	La función $y = 2(x + 3)(x - 1)$ está en la forma de intercepto.
intersection of sets The intersection of two sets A and B, written $A \cap B$, is the set of all elements in *both* A and B.	If $A = \{1, 2, 4, 8\}$ and $B = \{2, 4, 6, 8, 10\}$, then $A \cap B = \{2, 4, 8\}$.
intersección de conjuntos La intersección de dos conjuntos A y B, escrita $A \cap B$, es el conjunto de todos los elementos que están *tanto* en A *como* en B.	Si $A = \{1, 2, 4, 8\}$ y $B = \{2, 4, 6, 8, 10\}$, entonces $A \cap B = \{2, 4, 8\}$.
inverse cosine function If $-1 \leq a \leq 1$, then the inverse cosine of a is an angle θ, written $\theta = \cos^{-1} a$, where $\cos \theta = a$ and $0 \leq \theta \leq \pi$ (or $0° \leq \theta \leq 180°$).	When $0° \leq \theta \leq 180°$, the angle θ whose cosine is $\frac{1}{2}$ is $60°$, so $\theta = \cos^{-1} \frac{1}{2} = 60°$ (or $\theta = \cos^{-1} \frac{1}{2} = \frac{\pi}{3}$).
función inversa del coseno Si $-1 \leq a \leq 1$, entonces el coseno inverso de a es un ángulo θ; escrito $\theta = \cos^{-1} a$, donde $\cos \theta = a$ y $0 \leq \theta \leq \pi$ (ó $0° \leq \theta \leq 180°$).	Cuando $0° \leq \theta \leq 180°$, el ángulo θ cuyo coseno es $\frac{1}{2}$ es de $60°$, por lo que $\theta = \cos^{-1} \frac{1}{2} = 60°$ (ó $\theta = \cos^{-1} \frac{1}{2} = \frac{\pi}{3}$).
inverse function An inverse relation that is a function. Functions f and g are inverses provided that $f(g(x)) = x$ and $g(f(x)) = x$.	$$f(x) = x + 5;\ g(x) = x - 5$$ $$f(g(x)) = (x - 5) + 5 = x$$ $$g(f(x)) = (x + 5) - 5 = x$$ So, f and g are inverse functions.
función inversa Relación inversa que es una función. Las funciones f y g son inversas siempre que $f(g(x)) = x$ y $g(f(x)) = x$.	Entonces, f y g son funciones inversas.
inverse matrices Two $n \times n$ matrices are inverses of each other if their product (in both orders) is the $n \times n$ identity matrix. *See also* identity matrix.	$\begin{bmatrix} -5 & 8 \\ 2 & -3 \end{bmatrix}^{-1} = \begin{bmatrix} 3 & 8 \\ 2 & 5 \end{bmatrix}$ because ya que $\begin{bmatrix} 3 & 8 \\ 2 & 5 \end{bmatrix}\begin{bmatrix} -5 & 8 \\ 2 & -3 \end{bmatrix} = \begin{bmatrix} 1 & 0 \\ 0 & 1 \end{bmatrix}$ and y
matrices inversas Dos matrices $n \times n$ son inversas entre sí si su producto (de ambos órdenes) es la matriz identidad $n \times n$. *Ver también* matriz identidad.	$\begin{bmatrix} -5 & 8 \\ 2 & -3 \end{bmatrix}\begin{bmatrix} 3 & 8 \\ 2 & 5 \end{bmatrix} = \begin{bmatrix} 1 & 0 \\ 0 & 1 \end{bmatrix}$.
inverse relation A relation that interchanges the input and output values of the original relation. The graph of an inverse relation is a reflection of the graph of the original relation, with $y = x$ as the line of reflection.	To find the inverse of $y = 3x - 5$, switch x and y to obtain $x = 3y - 5$. Then solve for y to obtain the inverse relation $y = \frac{1}{3}x + \frac{5}{3}$.
relación inversa Relación en la que se intercambian los valores de entrada y de salida de la relación original. La gráfica de una relación inversa es una reflexión de la gráfica de la relación original, con $y = x$ como eje de reflexión.	Para hallar la inversa de $y = 3x - 5$, intercambia x e y para obtener $x = 3y - 5$. Luego resuelve para y para obtener la relación inversa $y = \frac{1}{3}x + \frac{5}{3}$.

inverse sine function If $-1 \leq a \leq 1$, then the inverse sine of a is an angle θ, written $\theta = \sin^{-1} a$, where $\sin \theta = a$ and $-\dfrac{\pi}{2} \leq \theta \leq \dfrac{\pi}{2}$ (or $-90° \leq \theta \leq 90°$).

función inversa del seno Si $-1 \leq a \leq 1$, entonces el seno inverso de a es un ángulo θ, escrito $\theta = \text{sen}^{-1} a$, donde $\text{sen } \theta = a$ y $-\dfrac{\pi}{2} \leq \theta \leq \dfrac{\pi}{2}$ (ó $-90° \leq \theta \leq 90°$).

When $-90° \leq \theta \leq 90°$, the angle θ whose sine is $\dfrac{1}{2}$ is 30°, so $\theta = \sin^{-1} \dfrac{1}{2} = 30°$ (or $\theta = \sin^{-1} \dfrac{1}{2} = \dfrac{\pi}{6}$).

Cuando $-90° \leq \theta \leq 90°$, el ángulo θ cuyo seno es $\dfrac{1}{2}$ es de 30°, por lo que $\theta = \text{sen}^{-1} \dfrac{1}{2} = 30°$ (ó $\theta = \text{sen}^{-1} \dfrac{1}{2} = \dfrac{\pi}{6}$).

---

inverse tangent function If a is any real number, then the inverse tangent of a is an angle θ, written $\theta = \tan^{-1} a$, where $\tan \theta = a$ and $-\dfrac{\pi}{2} < \theta < \dfrac{\pi}{2}$ (or $-90° < \theta < 90°$).

función inversa de la tangente Si a es un número real cualquiera, entonces la tangente inversa de a es un ángulo θ, escrito $\theta = \tan^{-1} a$, donde $\tan \theta = a$ y $-\dfrac{\pi}{2} < \theta < \dfrac{\pi}{2}$ (ó $-90° < \theta < 90°$).

When $-90° < \theta < 90°$, the angle θ whose tangent is $-\sqrt{3}$ is $-60°$, so $\theta = \tan^{-1}(-\sqrt{3}) = -60°$ (or $\theta = \tan^{-1}(-\sqrt{3}) = -\dfrac{\pi}{3}$).

Cuando $-90° < \theta < 90°$, el ángulo θ cuya tangente es $-\sqrt{3}$ es de $-60°$, por lo que $\theta = \tan^{-1}(-\sqrt{3}) = -60°$ (ó $\theta = \tan^{-1}(-\sqrt{3}) = -\dfrac{\pi}{3}$).

---

inverse variation The relationship of two variables x and y if there is a nonzero number a such that $y = \dfrac{a}{x}$.

variación inversa La relación entre dos variables x e y si hay un número a distinto de cero tal que $y = \dfrac{a}{x}$.

The equations $xy = 7$ and $y = -\dfrac{3}{x}$ represent inverse variation.

Las ecuaciones $xy = 7$ e $y = -\dfrac{3}{x}$ representan la variación inversa.

---

iteration The repeated composition of a function with itself. The result of one iteration is $f(f(x))$, and of two iterations is $f(f(f(x)))$.

iteración La composición repetida de una función usando la función misma. El resultado de una iteración es $f(f(x))$, y el de dos iteraciones es $f(f(f(x)))$.

$$f(x) = -3x + 1; x_0 = 2$$
$$x_1 = f(x_0) = f(2) = -3(2) + 1 = -5$$
$$x_2 = f(x_1) = f(-5) = -3(-5) + 1 = 16$$
$$x_3 = f(x_2) = f(16) = -3(16) + 1 = -47$$

---

joint variation A relationship that occurs when a quantity varies directly with the product of two or more other quantities.

variación conjunta Relación producida cuando una cantidad varía directamente con el producto de dos o más otras cantidades.

The equation $z = 5xy$ represents joint variation.

La ecuación $z = 5xy$ representa la variación conjunta.

law of cosines If $\triangle ABC$ has sides of length a, b, and c as shown, then $a^2 = b^2 + c^2 - 2bc \cos A$, $b^2 = a^2 + c^2 - 2ac \cos B$, and $c^2 = a^2 + b^2 - 2ab \cos C$.

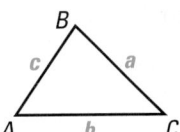

ley de los cosenos Si $\triangle ABC$ tiene lados de longitud a, b y c como se indica, entonces $a^2 = b^2 + c^2 - 2bc \cos A$, $b^2 = a^2 + c^2 - 2ac \cos B$ y $c^2 = a^2 + b^2 - 2ab \cos C$.

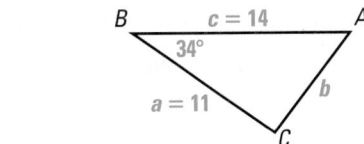

$$b^2 = a^2 + c^2 - 2ac \cos B$$
$$b^2 = 11^2 + 14^2 - 2(11)(14) \cos 34°$$
$$b^2 \approx 61.7$$
$$b \approx 7.85$$

---

law of sines If $\triangle ABC$ has sides of length a, b, and c as shown, then $\dfrac{\sin A}{a} = \dfrac{\sin B}{b} = \dfrac{\sin C}{c}$.

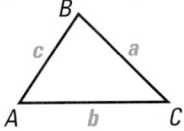

ley de los senos Si $\triangle ABC$ tiene lados de longitud a, b y c como se indica, entonces $\dfrac{\operatorname{sen} A}{a} = \dfrac{\operatorname{sen} B}{b} = \dfrac{\operatorname{sen} C}{c}$.

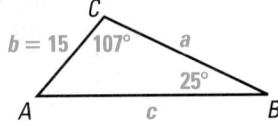

$$\frac{\sin 25°}{15} = \frac{\sin 107°}{c} \rightarrow c \approx 33.9$$
$$\frac{\operatorname{sen} 25°}{15} = \frac{\operatorname{sen} 107°}{c} \rightarrow c \approx 33.9$$

---

leading coefficient The coefficient in the term of a polynomial function that has the greatest exponent.

coeficiente inicial En una función polinómica, el coeficiente del término con el mayor exponente.

See **polynomial function.**

Ver **función polinómica.**

---

like radicals Radical expressions with the same index and radicand.

radicales semejantes Expresiones radicales con el mismo índice y el mismo radicando.

$\sqrt[4]{10}$ and $7\sqrt[4]{10}$ are like radicals.

$\sqrt[4]{10}$ y $7\sqrt[4]{10}$ son radicales semejantes.

---

like terms Terms that have the same variable parts. Constant terms are also like terms.

In the algebraic expression
$$5x^2 + (-3x) + 7 + 4x + (-2),$$
$-3x$ and $4x$ are like terms, and 7 and -2 are like terms.

términos semejantes Términos que tienen las mismas variables. Los términos constantes también son términos semejantes.

En la expresión algebraica
$$5x^2 + (-3x) + 7 + 4x + (-2),$$
$-3x$ y $4x$ son términos semejantes, y 7 y -2 también lo son.

---

linear equation in one variable An equation that can be written in the form $ax + b = 0$ where a and b are constants and $a \neq 0$.

ecuación lineal con una variable Ecuación que puede escribirse en la forma $ax + b = 0$, donde a y b son constantes y $a \neq 0$.

The equation $\frac{4}{5}x + 8 = 0$ is a linear equation in one variable.

La ecuación $\frac{4}{5}x + 8 = 0$ es una ecuación lineal con una variable.

linear equation in three variables An equation of the form $ax + by + cz = d$ where a, b, and c are not all zero.	$2x + y - z = 5$ is a linear equation in three variables.
ecuación lineal con tres variables Ecuación de la forma $ax + by + cz = d$, donde a, b y c no son todos cero.	$2x + y - z = 5$ es una ecuación lineal con tres variables.
linear function A function that can be written in the form $y = mx + b$ where m and b are constants.	The function $y = -2x - 1$ is a linear function with $m = -2$ and $b = -1$.
función lineal Función que puede escribirse en la forma $y = mx + b$, donde m y b son constantes.	La función $y = -2x - 1$ es una función lineal con $m = -2$ y $b = -1$.
linear inequality in one variable An inequality that can be written in one of the following forms, where a and b are real numbers and $a \neq 0$: $ax + b < 0$, $ax + b \leq 0$, $ax + b > 0$, or $ax + b \geq 0$.	$5x + 2 > 0$ is a linear inequality in one variable.
desigualdad lineal con una variable Desigualdad que puede escribirse de una de las siguientes formas, donde a y b son números reales y $a \neq 0$: $ax + b < 0$, $ax + b \leq 0$, $ax + b > 0$ ó $ax + b \geq 0$.	$5x + 2 > 0$ es una desigualdad lineal con una variable.
linear inequality in two variables An inequality that can be written in one of the following forms: $Ax + By < C$, $Ax + By \leq C$, $Ax + By > C$, or $Ax + By \geq C$.	$5x - 2y \geq -4$ is a linear inequality in two variables.
desigualdad lineal con dos variables Desigualdad que puede escribirse de una de las siguientes formas: $Ax + By < C$, $Ax + By \leq C$, $Ax + By > C$ o $Ax + By \geq C$.	$5x - 2y \geq -4$ es una desigualdad lineal con dos variables.
linear programming The process of maximizing or minimizing a linear objective function subject to a system of linear inequalities called constraints. The graph of the system of constraints is called the feasible region. **programación lineal** El proceso de maximizar o minimizar una función objetivo lineal sujeta a un sistema de desigualdades lineales llamadas restricciones. La gráfica del sistema de restricciones se llama región factible.	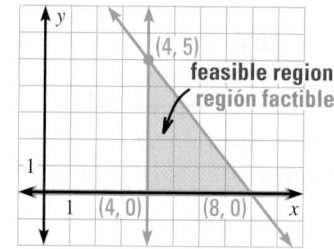 To maximize the objective function $P = 35x + 30y$ subject to the constraints $x \geq 4$, $y \geq 0$, and $5x + 4y \leq 40$, evaluate P at each vertex. The maximum value of 290 occurs at $(4, 5)$. Para maximizar la función objetivo $P = 35x + 30y$ sujeta a las restricciones $x \geq 4$, $y \geq 0$ y $5x + 4y \leq 40$, evalúa P en cada vértice. El valor máximo de 290 ocurre en $(4, 5)$.

local maximum The y-coordinate of a turning point of a function if the point is higher than all nearby points.

máximo local La coordenada y de un punto crítico de una función si el punto está situado más alto que todos los puntos cercanos.

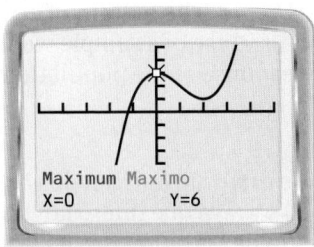

The function $f(x) = x^3 - 3x^2 + 6$ has a local maximum of $y = 6$ when $x = 0$.

La función $f(x) = x^3 - 3x^2 + 6$ tiene un máximo local de $y = 6$ cuando $x = 0$.

local minimum The y-coordinate of a turning point of a function if the point is lower than all nearby points.

mínimo local La coordenada y de un punto crítico de una función si el punto está situado más bajo que todos los puntos cercanos.

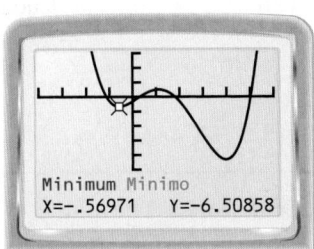

The function $f(x) = x^4 - 6x^3 + 3x^2 + 10x - 3$ has a local minimum of $y \approx -6.51$ when $x \approx -0.57$.

La función $f(x) = x^4 - 6x^3 + 3x^2 + 10x - 3$ tiene un mínimo local de $y \approx -6.51$ cuando $x \approx -0.57$.

logarithm of y with base b Let b and y be positive numbers with $b \neq 1$. The logarithm of y with base b, denoted $\log_b y$ and read "log base b of y," is defined as follows: $\log_b y = x$ if and only if $b^x = y$.

logaritmo de y con base b Sean b e y números positivos, con $b \neq 1$. El logaritmo de y con base b, denotado por $\log_b y$ y leído "log base b de y", se define de esta manera: $\log_b y = x$ si y sólo si $b^x = y$.

$\log_2 8 = 3$ because $2^3 = 8$.

$\log_{1/4} 4 = -1$ because $\left(\frac{1}{4}\right)^{-1} = 4$.

$\log_2 8 = 3$ ya que $2^3 = 8$.

$\log_{1/4} 4 = -1$ ya que $\left(\frac{1}{4}\right)^{-1} = 4$.

logarithmic equation An equation that involves a logarithm of a variable expression.

ecuación logarítmica Ecuación en la que aparece el logaritmo de una expresión algebraica.

$\log_5 (4x - 7) = \log_5 (x + 5)$ is a logarithmic equation.

$\log_5 (4x - 7) = \log_5 (x + 5)$ es una ecuación logarítmica.

major axis of an ellipse The line segment joining the vertices of an ellipse.

eje mayor de una elipse El segmento de recta que une los vértices de una elipse.

See ellipse.

Ver elipse.

margin of error The margin of error gives a limit on how much the response of a sample would be expected to differ from the response of the population.	If 40% of the people in a poll prefer candidate A, and the margin of error is ±4%, then it is expected that between 36% and 44% of the entire population prefer candidate A.
margen de error El margen de error indica un límite acerca de cuánto se prevé que diferirían las respuestas obtenidas en una muestra de las obtenidas en la población.	Si el 40% de los encuestados prefiere al candidato A y el margen de error es ±4%, entonces se prevé que entre el 36% y el 44% de la población total prefiere al candidato A.
matrix, matrices A rectangular arrangement of numbers in rows and columns. Each number in a matrix is an element. **matriz, matrices** Disposición rectangular de números colocados en filas y columnas. Cada numero de la matriz es un elemento.	$$A = \begin{bmatrix} 4 & -1 & 5 \\ 0 & 6 & 3 \end{bmatrix}$$ Matrix A has 2 rows and 3 columns. The element in the second row and first column is 0. La matriz A tiene 2 filas y 3 columnas. El elemento en la segunda fila y en la primera columna es 0.
matrix of constants The matrix of constants of the linear system $ax + by = e, cx + dy = f$ is $\begin{bmatrix} e \\ f \end{bmatrix}$. **matriz de constantes** La matriz de constantes del sistema lineal $ax + by = e, cx + dy = f$ es $\begin{bmatrix} e \\ f \end{bmatrix}$.	*See* **coefficient matrix.** *Ver* **matriz coeficiente.**
matrix of variables The matrix of variables of the linear system $ax + by = e, cx + dy = f$ is $\begin{bmatrix} x \\ y \end{bmatrix}$. **matriz de variables** La matriz de variables del sistema lineal $ax + by = e, cx + dy = f$ es $\begin{bmatrix} x \\ y \end{bmatrix}$.	*See* **coefficient matrix.** *Ver* **matriz coeficiente.**
maximum value of a quadratic function The y-coordinate of the vertex for $y = ax^2 + bx + c$ when $a < 0$. **valor máximo de una función cuadrática** La coordenada y del vértice para $y = ax^2 + bx + c$ cuando $a < 0$.	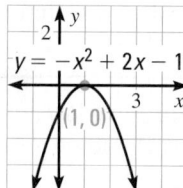 The maximum value of $y = -x^2 + 2x - 1$ is 0. El valor máximo de $y = -x^2 + 2x - 1$ es 0.
mean For the data set $x_1, x_2, \ldots, x_n$, the mean is $\bar{x} = \dfrac{x_1 + x_2 + \ldots + x_n}{n}$. Also called average. **media** Para el conjunto de datos $x_1, x_2, \ldots, x_n$, la media es $\bar{x} = \dfrac{x_1 + x_2 + \ldots + x_n}{n}$. También se llama promedio.	*See* **measure of central tendency.** *Ver* **medida de tendencia central.**

measure of central tendency A number used to represent the center or middle of a set of data values. Mean, median, and mode are three measures of central tendency.	**14, 17, 18, 19, 20, 24, 24, 30, 32**

The mean is $\dfrac{14 + 17 + 18 + \ldots + 32}{9} = \dfrac{198}{9} = 22$.

The median is the middle number, 20.
The mode is 24 because 24 occurs the most frequently. |
| **medida de tendencia central** Número usado para representar el centro o la posición central de un conjunto de valores de datos. La media, la mediana y la moda son tres medidas de tendencia central. | La media es $\dfrac{14 + 17 + 18 + \ldots + 32}{9} = \dfrac{198}{9} = 22$.

La mediana es el número central, 20.
La moda es 24 ya que 24 ocurre más veces. |
measure of dispersion A statistic that tells you how dispersed, or spread out, data values are. Range and standard deviation are measures of dispersion.	*See* range *and* standard deviation.
medida de dispersión Estadística que te indica cómo se dispersan, o distribuyen, los valores de datos. El rango y la desviación típica son medidas de dispersión.	*Ver* rango *y* desviación típica.
median The median of n numbers is the middle number when the numbers are written in numerical order. If n is even, the median is the mean of the two middle numbers.	*See* measure of central tendency.
mediana La mediana de n números es el número central cuando los números se escriben en orden numérico. Si n es par, la mediana es la media de los dos números centrales.	*Ver* medida de tendencia central.
midpoint formula The midpoint M of the line segment joining $A(x_1, y_1)$ and $B(x_2, y_2)$ is $M\left(\dfrac{x_1 + x_2}{2}, \dfrac{y_1 + y_2}{2}\right)$.	The midpoint of the line segment joining $(-2, 3)$ and $(8, 6)$ is $\left(\dfrac{-2 + 8}{2}, \dfrac{3 + 6}{2}\right) = \left(3, \dfrac{9}{2}\right)$.
fórmula del punto medio El punto medio M del segmento de recta que une $A(x_1, y_1)$ y $B(x_2, y_2)$ es $M\left(\dfrac{x_1 + x_2}{2}, \dfrac{y_1 + y_2}{2}\right)$.	El punto medio del segmento de recta que une $(-2, 3)$ y $(8, 6)$ es $\left(\dfrac{-2 + 8}{2}, \dfrac{3 + 6}{2}\right) = \left(3, \dfrac{9}{2}\right)$.
minimum value of a quadratic function The y-coordinate of the vertex for $y = ax^2 + bx + c$ when $a > 0$.	
valor mínimo de una función cuadrática La coordenada y del vértice para $y = ax^2 + bx + c$ cuando $a > 0$.

The minimum value of $y = x^2 - 6x + 5$ is -4.

El valor mínimo de $y = x^2 - 6x + 5$ es -4. |
| **minor axis of an ellipse** The line segment joining the co-vertices of an ellipse. | *See* ellipse. |
| **eje menor de una elipse** El segmento de recta que une los puntos extremos de una elipse. | *Ver* elipse. |

mode The mode of n numbers is the number or numbers that occur most frequently.	*See* **measure of central tendency.**
moda La moda de n números es el número o números que ocurren más veces.	*Ver* **medida de tendencia central.**
monomial An expression that is either a number, a variable, or the product of a number and one or more variables with whole number exponents.	$6, 0.2x, \frac{1}{2}ab$, and $-5.7n^4$ are monomials.
monomio Expresión que es un número, una variable o el producto de un número y una o más variables con exponentes naturales.	$6, 0.2x, \frac{1}{2}ab$ y $-5.7n^4$ son monomios.
mutually exclusive events *See* disjoint events.	*See* **disjoint events.**
sucesos mutuamente excluyentes *Ver* sucesos disjuntos.	*Ver* **sucesos disjuntos.**

N

natural base e An irrational number defined as follows: As n approaches $+\infty$, $\left(1 + \frac{1}{n}\right)^n$ approaches $e \approx 2.718281828$.	*See* **natural logarithm.**
base natural e Número irracional definido de esta manera: Al aproximarse n a $+\infty$, $\left(1 + \frac{1}{n}\right)^n$ se aproxima a $e \approx 2.718281828$.	*Ver* **logaritmo natural.**
natural logarithm A logarithm with base e. It can be denoted $\log_e$, but is more often denoted by ln.	$\ln 0.3 \approx -1.204$ because $e^{-1.204} \approx (2.7183)^{-1.204} \approx 0.3$.
logaritmo natural Logaritmo con base e. Puede denotarse $\log_e$, pero es más frecuente que se denote ln.	$\ln 0.3 \approx -1.204$ ya que $e^{-1.204} \approx (2.7183)^{-1.204} \approx 0.3$.
negative correlation The paired data (x, y) have a negative correlation if y tends to decrease as x increases. **correlación negativa** Los pares de datos (x, y) presentan una correlación negativa si y tiende a disminuir al aumentar x.	
normal curve A smooth, symmetrical, bell-shaped curve that can model normal distributions and approximate some binomial distributions.	*See* **normal distribution.**
curva normal Curva lisa, simétrica y con forma de campana que puede representar distribuciones normales y aproximar a algunas distribuciones binomiales.	*Ver* **distribución normal.**

normal distribution A probability distribution with mean $\bar{x}$ and standard deviation σ modeled by a bell-shaped curve with the area properties shown at the right.

distribución normal Una distribución de probabilidad con media $\bar{x}$ y desviación normal σ representada por una curva en forma de campana y que tiene las propiedades vistas a la derecha.

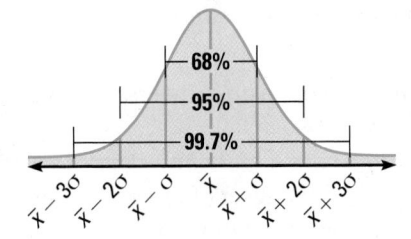

---

n*th root of *a For an integer n greater than 1, if $b^n = a$, then b is an nth root of a. Written as $\sqrt[n]{a}$.

$\sqrt[3]{-216} = -6$ because $(-6)^3 = -216$.

raíz enésima de *a* Para un número entero n mayor que 1, si $b^n = a$, entonces b es una raíz enésima de a. Se escribe $\sqrt[n]{a}$.

$\sqrt[3]{-216} = -6$ ya que $(-6)^3 = -216$.

---

objective function In linear programming, the linear function that is maximized or minimized.

See **linear programming.**

función objetivo En la programación lineal, la función lineal que se maximiza o minimiza.

Ver **programación lineal.**

---

observational study A study that observes individuals and measures variables without controlling the individuals or their environment in any way.

estudio de observación Estudio que permite observar a individuos y medir variables sin controlar a los individuos ni su ambiente.

---

odd function If $f(-x) = -f(x)$ for all x in its domain. The graph is *symmetric about the origin.*

función impar Si $f(-x) = -f(x)$ para toda x en su dominio. La gráfica es *simétrica con respecto al origen.*

Odd Function

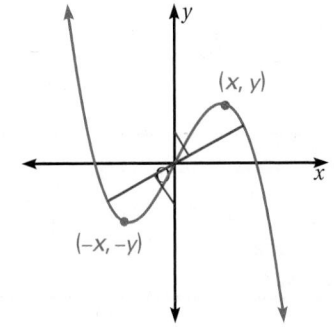

opposite The opposite, or additive inverse, of any number b is $-b$.	**6.2 and -6.2 are opposites.**
opuesto El opuesto, o inverso aditivo, de cualquier número b es $-b$.	**6.2 y -6.2 son opuestos.**
ordered triple A set of three numbers of the form (x, y, z) that represents a point in space.	**The ordered triple $(2, 1, -3)$ is a solution of the equation $4x + 2y + 3z = 1$.**
terna ordenada Un conjunto de tres números de la forma (x, y, z) que representa un punto en el espacio.	**La terna ordenada $(2, 1, -3)$ es una solución de la ecuación $4x + 2y + 3z = 1$.**
outlier A value that is much greater than or much less than most of the other values in a data set.	**3 is an outlier in the data set 3, 11, 12, 13, 13, 14, 15, 15, 15, 15, 17.**
valor extremo Valor que es mucho mayor o mucho menor que la mayoría de los otros valores de un conjunto de datos.	**3 es un valor extremo del conjunto de datos 3, 11, 12, 13, 13, 14, 15, 15, 15, 15, 17.**

P

parabola The set of all points equidistant from a point called the focus and a line called the directrix. The graph of a quadratic function $y = ax^2 + bx + c$ is a parabola.	
parábola El conjunto de todos los puntos equidistantes de un punto, llamado foco, y de una recta, llamada directriz. La gráfica de una función cuadrática $y = ax^2 + bx + c$ es una parábola.	
parallel lines Two lines in the same plane that do not intersect.	
rectas paralelas Dos rectas del mismo plano que no se cortan.	
parent function The most basic function in a family of functions.	**The parent function for the family of all linear functions is $y = x$.**
función básica La función más fundamental de una familia de funciones.	**La función básica de la familia de todas las funciones lineales es $y = x$.**
partial sum The sum S_n of the first n terms of an infinite series.	$$\frac{1}{2} + \frac{1}{4} + \frac{1}{8} + \frac{1}{16} + \frac{1}{32} + \dots$$ **The series above has the partial sums $S_1 = 0.5$, $S_2 = 0.75$, $S_3 \approx 0.88$, $S_4 \approx 0.94$, ...**
suma parcial La suma S_n de los n primeros términos de una serie infinita.	**La serie de arriba tiene las sumas parciales $S_1 = 0.5$, $S_2 = 0.75$, $S_3 \approx 0.88$, $S_4 \approx 0.94$, ...**

Pascal's triangle An arrangement of the values of $_nC_r$ in a triangular pattern in which each row corresponds to a value of n.

triángulo de Pascal Disposición de los valores de $_nC_r$ en un patrón triangular en el que cada fila corresponde a un valor de n.

$$_0C_0$$
$$_1C_0 \quad _1C_1$$
$$_2C_0 \quad _2C_1 \quad _2C_2$$
$$_3C_0 \quad _3C_1 \quad _3C_2 \quad _3C_3$$
$$_4C_0 \quad _4C_1 \quad _4C_2 \quad _4C_3 \quad _4C_4$$
$$_5C_0 \quad _5C_1 \quad _5C_2 \quad _5C_3 \quad _5C_4 \quad _5C_5$$

---

period The horizontal length of each cycle of a periodic function.

período La longitud horizontal de cada ciclo de una función periódica.

See periodic function.

Ver función periódica.

---

periodic function A function whose graph has a repeating pattern.

función periódica Función cuya gráfica tiene un patrón que se repite.

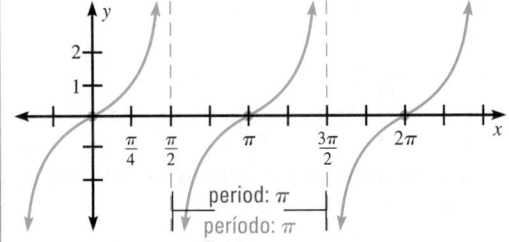

The graph shows 3 cycles of $y = \tan x$, a periodic function with a period of π.

La gráfica muestra 3 ciclos de $y = \tan x$, función periódica con período π.

---

permutation An ordering of objects. The number of permutations of r objects taken from a group of n distinct objects is denoted $_nP_r$ where $_nP_r = \dfrac{n!}{(n-r)!}$.

permutación Ordenación de objetos. El número de permutaciones de r objetos tomados de un grupo de n objetos diferenciados se indica $_nP_r$, donde $_nP_r = \dfrac{n!}{(n-r)!}$.

There are 6 permutations of the $n = 3$ letters A, B, and C taken $r = 3$ at a time: ABC, ACB, BAC, BCA, CAB, and CBA.

Hay 6 permutaciones de las letras $n = 3$ A, B y C tomadas $r = 3$ cada vez: ABC, ACB, BAC, BCA, CAB y CBA.

---

perpendicular lines Two lines in the same plane that intersect to form a right angle.

rectas perpendiculares Dos rectas del mismo plano que al cortarse forman un ángulo recto.

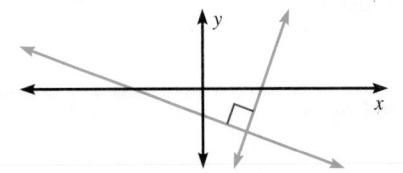

---

piecewise function A function defined by at least two equations, each of which applies to a different part of the function's domain.

función definida a trozos Función definida por al menos dos ecuaciones, cada una de las cuales se aplica a una parte diferente del dominio de la función.

$$g(x) = \begin{cases} 3x - 1, & \text{if } x < 1 \\ 0, & \text{if } x = 1 \\ -x + 4, & \text{if } x > 1 \end{cases} \quad g(x) = \begin{cases} 3x - 1, & \text{si } x < 1 \\ 0, & \text{si } x = 1 \\ -x + 4, & \text{si } x > 1 \end{cases}$$

point-slope form An equation of a line written in the form $y - y_1 = m(x - x_1)$ where the line passes through the point (x_1, y_1) and has a slope of m.	The equation $y + 2 = -4(x - 5)$ is in point-slope form.
forma punto-pendiente Ecuación de una recta escrita en la forma $y - y_1 = m(x - x_1)$, donde la recta pasa por el punto (x_1, y_1) y tiene pendiente m.	La ecuación $y + 2 = -4(x - 5)$ está en la forma punto-pendiente.
polynomial A monomial or a sum of monomials, each of which is called a term of the polynomial. *See also* monomial.	-14, $x^4 - \frac{1}{4}x^2 + 3$, and $7b - \sqrt{3} + \pi b^2$ are polynomials.
polinomio Monomio o suma de monomios, cada uno de los cuales se llama término del polinomio. *Ver también* monomio.	-14, $x^4 - \frac{1}{4}x^2 + 3$ y $7b - \sqrt{3} + \pi b^2$ son polinomios.
polynomial function A function of the form $f(x) = a_n x^n + a_{n-1} x^{n-1} + \cdots + a_1 x + a_0$ where $a_n \neq 0$, the exponents are all whole numbers, and the coefficients are all real numbers.	$f(x) = 11x^5 - 0.4x^2 + 16x - 7$ is a polynomial function. The degree of $f(x)$ is 5, the leading coefficient is 11, and the constant term is -7.
función polinómica Función de la forma $f(x) = a_n x^n + a_{n-1} x^{n-1} + \cdots + a_1 x + a_0$ donde $a_n \neq 0$, los exponentes son todos números enteros y los coeficientes son todos números reales.	$f(x) = 11x^5 - 0.4x^2 + 16x - 7$ es una función polinómica. El grado de $f(x)$ es 5, el coeficiente inicial es 11 y el término constante es -7.
polynomial long division A method used to divide polynomials similar to the way you divide numbers. **división desarrollada polinómica** Método utilizado para dividir polinomios semejante a la manera en que divides números.	$$\begin{array}{r} x^2 + 7x + 7 \\ x - 2 \overline{\smash{\big)}\ x^3 + 5x^2 - 7x + 2} \\ \underline{x^3 - 2x^2} \\ 7x^2 - 7x \\ \underline{7x^2 - 14x} \\ 7x + 2 \\ \underline{7x - 14} \\ 16 \end{array}$$ $$\frac{x^3 + 5x^2 - 7x + 2}{x - 2} = x^2 + 7x + 7 + \frac{16}{x - 2}$$
population A group of people or objects that you want information about.	A sportswriter randomly selects 5% of college baseball coaches for a survey. The population is all college baseball coaches. The 5% of coaches selected is the sample.
población Grupo de personas u objetos acerca del cual deseas informarte.	Un periodista deportiva selecciona al azar al 5% de los entrenadores universitarios de béisbol para que participe en una encuesta. La población son todos los entrenadores universitarios de béisbol. El 5% de los entrenadores que resultó seleccionado es la muestra.

positive correlation The paired data (x, y) have a positive correlation if y tends to increase as x increases. **correlacion positiva** Los pares de datos (x, y) presentan una correlación positiva si y tiende a aumentar al aumentar x.	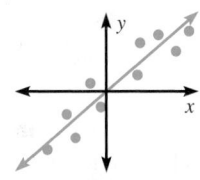
power An expression that represents repeated multiplication of the same factor. **potencia** Expresión que representa la multiplicación repetida del mismo factor.	32 is the fifth power of 2 because $32 = 2 \cdot 2 \cdot 2 \cdot 2 \cdot 2 = 2^5$. 32 es la quinta potencia de 2 ya que $32 = 2 \cdot 2 \cdot 2 \cdot 2 \cdot 2 = 2^5$.
power function A function of the form $y = ax^b$, where a is a real number and b is a rational number. **función potencial** Función de la forma $y = ax^b$, donde a es un número real y b es un número racional.	$f(x) = 4x^{3/2}$ is a power function. $f(x) = 4x^{3/2}$ es una función potencial.
probability distribution A function that gives the probability of each possible value of a random variable. The sum of all the probabilities in a probability distribution must equal 1. **distribución de probabilidades** Función que indica la probabilidad de cada valor posible de una variable aleatoria. La suma de todas las probabilidades de una distribución de probabilidades debe ser igual a 1.	Let the random variable X represent the number showing after rolling a standard six-sided die. Sea la variable aleatoria X el número que salga al lanzar un dado normal de seis caras.

Probability Distribution for Rolling a Die
Distribución de probabilidad al lanzar un dado

X	1	2	3	4	5	6
$P(X)$	$\frac{1}{6}$	$\frac{1}{6}$	$\frac{1}{6}$	$\frac{1}{6}$	$\frac{1}{6}$	$\frac{1}{6}$

probability of an event A number from 0 to 1 that indicates the likelihood that the event will occur. **probabilidad de un suceso** Número entre 0 y 1 que indica la probabilidad de que ocurra el suceso.	*See* experimental probability, geometric probability, *and* theoretical probability. *Ver* probabilidad experimental, probabilidad geométrica *y* probabilidad teórica.
pure imaginary number A complex number $a + bi$ where $a = 0$ and $b \neq 0$. **número imaginario puro** Número complejo $a + bi$, donde $a = 0$ y $b \neq 0$.	$-4i$ and $1.2i$ are pure imaginary numbers. $-4i$ y $1.2i$ son números imaginarios puros.

quadrantal angle An angle in standard position whose terminal side lies on an axis. **ángulo cuadrantal** Ángulo en posición normal cuyo lado terminal se encuentra en un eje.	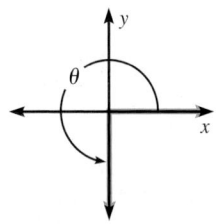

quadratic equation in one variable An equation that can be written in the form $ax^2 + bx + c = 0$ where $a \neq 0$.	The equation $x^2 - 5x = 36$ is a quadratic equation in one variable because it can be written in the form $x^2 - 5x - 36 = 0$.
ecuación cuadrática con una variable Ecuación que puede escribirse en la forma $ax^2 + bx + c = 0$, donde $a \neq 0$.	La ecuación $x^2 - 5x = 36$ es una ecuación cuadrática con una variable ya que puede escribirse en la forma $x^2 - 5x - 36 = 0$.
quadratic form The form $au^2 + bu + c$, where u is any expression in x.	The expression $16x^4 - 8x^2 - 8$ is in quadratic form because it can be written as $u^2 - 2u - 8$ where $u = 4x^2$.
forma cuadrática La forma $au^2 + bu + c$, donde u es cualquier expresión en x.	La expresión $16x^4 - 8x^2 - 8$ está en la forma cuadrática ya que puede escribirse $u^2 - 2u - 8$, donde $u = 4x^2$.
quadratic formula The formula $x = \dfrac{-b \pm \sqrt{b^2 - 4ac}}{2a}$ used to find the solutions of the quadratic equation $ax^2 + bx + c = 0$ when a, b, and c are real numbers and $a \neq 0$.	To solve $3x^2 + 6x + 2 = 0$, substitute 3 for a, 6 for b, and 2 for c in the quadratic formula.
fórmula cuadrática La fórmula $x = \dfrac{-b \pm \sqrt{b^2 - 4ac}}{2a}$ que se usa para hallar las soluciones de la ecuación cuadrática $ax^2 + bx + c = 0$ cuando a, b y c son números reales y $a \neq 0$.	Para resolver $3x^2 + 6x + 2 = 0$, sustituye a por 3, b por 6 y c por 2 en la fórmula cuadrática. $$x = \frac{-6 \pm \sqrt{6^2 - 4(3)(2)}}{2(3)} = \frac{-3 \pm \sqrt{3}}{3}$$
quadratic function A function that can be written in the form $y = ax^2 + bx + c$ where $a \neq 0$.	The functions $y = 3x^2 - 5$ and $y = x^2 - 4x + 6$ are quadratic functions.
función cuadrática Función que puede escribirse en la forma $y = ax^2 + bx + c$, donde $a \neq 0$.	Las funciones $y = 3x^2 - 5$ e $y = x^2 - 4x + 6$ son funciones cuadráticas.
quadratic inequality in one variable An inequality that can be written in the form $ax^2 + bx + c < 0$, $ax^2 + bx + c \leq 0$, $ax^2 + bx + c > 0$, or $ax^2 + bx + c \geq 0$.	$x^2 + x \leq 0$ and $2x^2 + x - 4 > 0$ are quadratic inequalities in one variable.
desigualdad cuadrática con una variable Desigualdad que se puede escribir en la forma $ax^2 + bx + c < 0$, $ax^2 + bx + c \leq 0$, $ax^2 + bx + c > 0$ ó $ax^2 + bx + c \geq 0$.	$x^2 + x \leq 0$ y $2x^2 + x - 4 > 0$ son desigualdades cuadráticas con una variable.
quadratic inequality in two variables An inequality that can be written in the form $y < ax^2 + bx + c$, $y \leq ax^2 + bx + c$, $y > ax^2 + bx + c$, or $y \geq ax^2 + bx + c$.	$y > x^2 + 3x - 4$ is a quadratic inequality in two variables.
desigualdad cuadrática con dos variables Desigualdad que se puede escribir en la forma $y < ax^2 + bx + c$, $y \leq ax^2 + bx + c$, $y > ax^2 + bx + c$ ó $y > ax^2 + bx + c$.	$y > x^2 + 3x - 4$ es una desigualdad cuadrática con dos variables.

quadratic system A system of equations that includes one or more equations of conics.	$$y^2 - 7x + 3 = 0 \qquad x^2 + 4y^2 + 8y = 16$$ $$2x - y = 3 \qquad 2x^2 - y^2 - 6x - 4 = 0$$
sistema cuadrático Sistema de ecuaciones que incluye una o más ecuaciones de cónicas.	The systems above are quadratic systems.

Los sistemas de arriba son sistemas cuadráticos. |

R

radian In a circle with radius r and center at the origin, one radian is the measure of an angle in standard position whose terminal side intercepts an arc of length r.	
radián En un círculo con radio r y cuyo centro está en el origen, un radián es la medida de un ángulo en posición normal cuyo lado terminal intercepta un arco de longitud r.	
radical An expression of the form $\sqrt{s}$ or $\sqrt[n]{s}$ where s is a number or an expression.	$$\sqrt{5}, \sqrt[3]{2x + 1}$$
radical Expresión de la forma $\sqrt{s}$ o $\sqrt[n]{s}$, donde s es un número o una expresión.	
radical equation An equation with one or more radicals that have variables in their radicands.	$$\sqrt[3]{2x + 7} = 3$$
ecuación radical Ecuación con uno o más radicales en cuyo radicando aparecen variables.	
radical function A function that contains a radical with a variable in its radicand.	$$f(x) = \frac{1}{2}\sqrt{x}, g(x) = -3\sqrt[3]{x + 5}$$
función radical Función que tiene un radical con una variable en su radicando.	
radicand The number or expression beneath a radical sign.	The radicand of $\sqrt{5}$ is 5, and the radicand of $\sqrt{8y^2}$ is $8y^2$.
radicando El número o la expresión que aparece bajo el signo radical.	El radicando de $\sqrt{5}$ es 5, y el radicando de $\sqrt{8y^2}$ es $8y^2$.
radius of a circle The distance from the center of a circle to a point on the circle. Also, a line segment that connects the center of a circle to a point on the circle. *See also* circle.	The circle with equation $(x - 3)^2 + (y + 5)^2 = 36$ has radius $\sqrt{36} = 6$. *See also* circle.
radio de un círculo La distancia desde el centro de un círculo hasta un punto del círculo. También, es un segmento de recta que une el centro de un círculo con un punto del círculo. *Ver también* círculo.	El círculo con la ecuación $(x - 3)^2 + (y + 5)^2 = 36$ tiene el radio $\sqrt{36} = 6$. *Ver también* círculo.

ENGLISH-SPANISH GLOSSARY

random variable A variable whose value is determined by the outcomes of a random event. **variable aleatoria** Variable cuyo valor viene determinado por los resultados de un suceso aleatorio.	**The random variable** X **representing the number showing after rolling a six-sided die has possible values of 1, 2, 3, 4, 5, and 6.** **La variable aleatoria** X **que representa el número que sale al lanzar un dado de seis caras tiene como valores posibles 1, 2, 3, 4, 5 y 6.**
randomized comparative experiment An experiment in which the individuals are assigned to the control group or the treatment group at random, in order to minimize bias. **experimento comparativo aleatorizado** Experimento en el que se elige al azar a los individuos para el grupo de control o para el grupo experimental, a fin de minimizar el sesgo.	
rational function A function of the form $f(x) = \dfrac{p(x)}{q(x)}$, where $p(x)$ and $q(x)$ are polynomials and $q(x) \neq 0$. **función racional** Función de la forma $f(x) = \dfrac{p(x)}{q(x)}$, donde $p(x)$ y $q(x)$ son polinomios y $q(x) \neq 0$.	**The functions** $y = \dfrac{6}{x}$ **and** $y = \dfrac{2x+1}{x-3}$ **are rational functions.** **Las funciones** $y = \dfrac{6}{x}$ **e** $y = \dfrac{2x+1}{x-3}$ **son funciones racionales.**
rationalizing the denominator The process of eliminating a radical expression in the denominator of a fraction by multiplying both the numerator and denominator by an appropriate radical expression. **racionalizar el denominador** El proceso de eliminar una expresión radical del denominador de una fracción al multiplicar tanto el numerador como el denominador por una expresión radical adecuada.	**To rationalize the denominator of** $\dfrac{\sqrt{5}}{\sqrt{2}}$, **multiply the numerator and denominator by** $\sqrt{2}$. **Para racionalizar el denominador de** $\dfrac{\sqrt{5}}{\sqrt{2}}$, **multiplica el numerador y el denominador por** $\sqrt{2}$.

ENGLISH-SPANISH GLOSSARY

recursive rule A rule for a sequence that gives the beginning term or terms of the sequence and then a recursive equation that tells how the nth term a_n is related to one or more preceding terms.

regla recursiva Regla de una progresión que da el primer término o términos de la progresión y luego una ecuación recursiva que indica qué relación hay entre el término enésimo a_n y uno o más de los términos precedentes.

The recursive rule $a_0 = 1$, $a_n = a_{n-1} + 4$ gives the arithmetic sequence 1, 5, 9, 13, … .

La regla recursiva $a_0 = 1$, $a_n = a_{n-1} + 4$ da la progresión aritmética 1, 5, 9, 13, … .

---

reference angle If θ is an angle in standard position, its reference angle is the acute angle θ' formed by the terminal side of θ and the x-axis.

ángulo de referencia Si θ es un ángulo en posición normal, su ángulo de referencia es el ángulo agudo θ' formado por el lado terminal de θ y el eje de x.

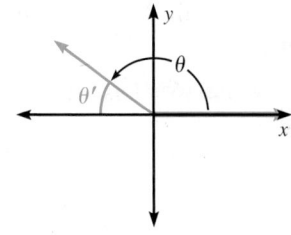

The acute angle θ' is the reference angle for angle θ.

El ángulo agudo θ' es el ángulo de referencia para el ángulo θ.

---

reflection A transformation that flips a graph or figure in a line.

reflexión Transformación que vuelca una gráfica o una figura en una recta.

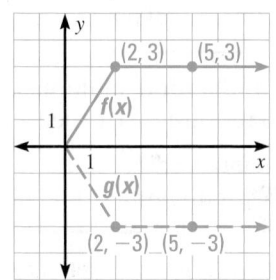

The graph of $g(x)$ is the reflection of the graph of $f(x)$ in the x-axis.

La gráfica de $g(x)$ es la reflexión de la gráfica de $f(x)$ en el eje de x.

---

relation A mapping, or pairing, of input values with output values.

relación Correspondencia entre los valores de entrada y los valores de salida.

The ordered pairs $(-2, -2)$, $(-2, 2)$, $(0, 1)$, and $(3, 1)$ represent the relation with inputs (domain) of -2, 0, and 3 and outputs (range) of -2, 1, and 2.

Los pares ordenados $(-2, -2)$, $(-2, 2)$, $(0, 1)$ y $(3, 1)$ representan la relación con entradas (dominio) de -2, 0 y 3 y salidas (rango) de -2, 1 y 2.

repeated solution For the polynomial equation $f(x) = 0$, k is a repeated solution if and only if the factor $x - k$ has an exponent greater than 1 when $f(x)$ is factored completely.

-1 is a repeated solution of the equation $(x + 1)^2 (x - 2) = 0$.

solución repetida Para la ecuación polinómica $f(x) = 0$, k es una solución repetida si y sólo si el factor $x - k$ tiene un exponente mayor que 1 cuando $f(x)$ está completamente factorizado.

-1 es una solución repetida de la ecuación $(x + 1)^2 (x - 2) = 0$.

root of an equation The solutions of a quadratic equation are its roots.

The roots of the quadratic equation $x^2 - 5x - 36 = 0$ are 9 and -4.

raíz de una ecuación Las soluciones de una ecuación cuadrática son sus raíces.

Las raíces de la ecuación cuadrática $x^2 - 5x - 36 = 0$ son 9 y -4.

S

sample A subset of a population.

See population.

muestra Subconjunto de una población.

Ver población.

scalar A real number by which you multiply a matrix.

See scalar multiplication.

escalar Número real por el que se multiplica una matriz.

Ver multiplicación escalar.

scalar multiplication Multiplication of each element of a matrix by a real number, called a scalar.

multiplicación escalar Multiplicación de cada elemento de una matriz por un número real llamado escalar.

$$-2\begin{bmatrix} 4 & -1 \\ 1 & 0 \\ 2 & 7 \end{bmatrix} = \begin{bmatrix} -8 & 2 \\ -2 & 0 \\ -4 & -14 \end{bmatrix}$$

scatter plot A graph of a set of data pairs (x, y) used to determine whether there is a relationship between the variables x and y.

diagrama de dispersión Gráfica de un conjunto de pares de datos (x, y) que sirve para determinar si hay una relación entre las variables x e y.

Test scores / Resultados de las pruebas

Hours of studying
Horas de estudio

scientific notation The representation of a number in the form $c \times 10^n$ where $1 \le c < 10$ and n is an integer.

0.693 is written in scientific notation as 6.93×10^{-1}.

notación científica La representación de un número de la forma $c \times 10^n$, donde $1 \le c < 10$ y n es un número entero.

0.693 escrito en notación científica es 6.93×10^{-1}.

secant function If θ is an acute angle of a right triangle, the secant of θ is the length of the hypotenuse divided by the length of the side adjacent to θ.	*See* sine function.
función secante Si θ es un ángulo agudo de un triángulo rectángulo, la secante de θ es la longitud de la hipotenusa dividida por la longitud del lado adyacente a θ.	*Ver* función seno.
sector A region of a circle that is bounded by two radii and an arc of the circle. The central angle θ of a sector is the angle formed by the two radii. **sector** Región de un círculo delimitada por dos radios y un arco del círculo. El ángulo central θ de un sector es el ángulo formado por dos radios.	
sequence A function whose domain is a set of consecutive integers. The domain gives the relative position of each term of the sequence. The range gives the terms of the sequence.	For the domain $n = 1, 2, 3$, and 4, the sequence defined by $a_n = 2n$ has the terms 2, 4, 6, and 8.
progresión Función cuyo dominio es un conjunto de números enteros consecutivos. El dominio da la posición relativa de cada término de la secuencia. El rango da los términos de la secuencia.	Para el dominio $n = 1, 2, 3$ y 4, la secuencia definida por $a_n = 2n$ tiene los términos 2, 4, 6 y 8.
series The expression formed by adding the terms of a sequence. A series can be finite or infinite.	Finite series: $2 + 4 + 6 + 8$ Infinite series: $2 + 4 + 6 + 8 + \cdots$
serie La expresión formada al sumar los términos de una progresión. La serie puede ser finita o infinita.	Serie finita: $2 + 4 + 6 + 8$ Serie infinita: $2 + 4 + 6 + 8 + \cdots$
set A collection of distinct objects.	If A is the set of positive integers less than 5, then $A = \{1, 2, 3, 4\}$.
conjunto Colección de objetos diferenciados.	Si A es el conjunto de números enteros positivos menores que 5, entonces $A = \{1, 2, 3, 4\}$.
sigma notation *See* summation notation.	*See* summation notation.
notación sigma *Ver* notación de sumatoria.	*Ver* notación de sumatoria.
simplest form of a radical A radical with index n is in simplest form if the radicand has no perfect nth powers as factors and any denominator has been rationalized.	$\sqrt[3]{135}$ in simplest form is $3\sqrt[3]{5}$. $\dfrac{\sqrt[5]{7}}{\sqrt[5]{8}}$ in simplest form is $\dfrac{\sqrt[5]{28}}{2}$.
forma más simple de un radical Un radical con índice n está escrito en la forma más simple si el radicando no tiene como factor ninguna potencia enésima perfecta y el denominador ha sido racionalizado.	$\sqrt[3]{135}$ en la forma más simple es $3\sqrt[3]{5}$. $\dfrac{\sqrt[5]{7}}{\sqrt[5]{8}}$ en la forma más simple es $\dfrac{\sqrt[5]{28}}{2}$.

simplified form of a rational expression A rational expression in which the numerator and denominator have no common factors other than ±1.

forma simplificada de una expresión racional Expresión racional en la que el numerador y el denominador no tienen factores comunes además de ±1.

$$\frac{x^2 - 2x - 15}{x^2 - 9} = \frac{(x+3)(x-5)}{(x+3)(x-3)} = \frac{x-5}{x-3}$$

$\uparrow$

Simplified form
Forma simplificada

---

sine function If θ is an acute angle of a right triangle, the sine of θ is the length of the side opposite θ divided by the length of the hypotenuse.

función seno Si θ es un ángulo agudo de un triángulo rectángulo, el seno de θ es la longitud del lado opuesto a θ dividida por la longitud de la hipotenusa.

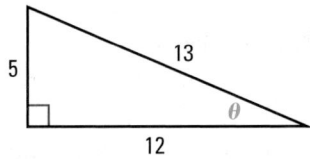

$$\sin \theta = \frac{\text{opp}}{\text{hyp}} = \frac{5}{13} \qquad \csc \theta = \frac{\text{hyp}}{\text{opp}} = \frac{13}{5}$$

$$\cos \theta = \frac{\text{adj}}{\text{hyp}} = \frac{12}{13} \qquad \sec \theta = \frac{\text{hyp}}{\text{adj}} = \frac{13}{12}$$

$$\tan \theta = \frac{\text{opp}}{\text{adj}} = \frac{5}{12} \qquad \cot \theta = \frac{\text{adj}}{\text{opp}} = \frac{12}{5}$$

$$\operatorname{sen} \theta = \frac{\text{op}}{\text{hip}} = \frac{5}{13} \qquad \operatorname{cosec} \theta = \frac{\text{hip}}{\text{op}} = \frac{13}{5}$$

$$\cos \theta = \frac{\text{ady}}{\text{hip}} = \frac{12}{13} \qquad \sec \theta = \frac{\text{hip}}{\text{ady}} = \frac{13}{12}$$

$$\tan \theta = \frac{\text{op}}{\text{ady}} = \frac{5}{12} \qquad \cot \theta = \frac{\text{ady}}{\text{op}} = \frac{12}{5}$$

---

sinusoids Graphs of sine and cosine functions.

sinusoides Gráficas de funciones seno y coseno.

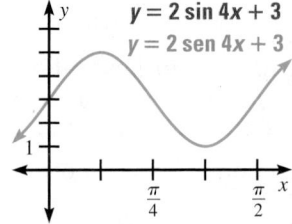

$y = 2 \sin 4x + 3$
$y = 2 \operatorname{sen} 4x + 3$

---

skewed distribution A probability distribution that is not symmetric. *See also* symmetric distribution.

distribución asimétrica Distribución de probabilidades que no es simétrica. *Ver también* distribución simétrica.

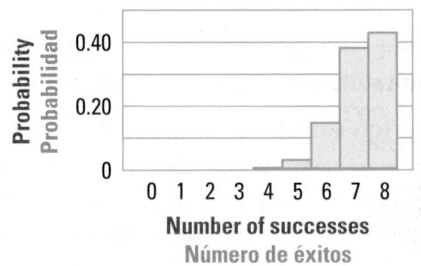

---

slope The ratio of vertical change (the rise) to horizontal change (the run) for a nonvertical line. For a nonvertical line passing through the points (x_1, y_1) and (x_2, y_2), the slope is $m = \dfrac{y_2 - y_1}{x_2 - x_1}$.

pendiente Para una recta no vertical, la razón entre el cambio vertical (distancia vertical) y el cambio horizontal (distancia horizontal). Para una recta no vertical que pasa por los puntos (x_1, y_1) y (x_2, y_2), la pendiente es $m = \dfrac{y_2 - y_1}{x_2 - x_1}$.

The slope of the line that passes through the points $(-3, 0)$ and $(3, 4)$ is:

La pendiente de la recta que pasa por los puntos $(-3, 0)$ y $(3, 4)$ es:

$$m = \frac{y_2 - y_1}{x_2 - x_1} = \frac{4 - 0}{3 - (-3)} = \frac{4}{6} = \frac{2}{3}$$

---

slope-intercept form A linear equation written in the form $y = mx + b$ where m is the slope and b is the y-intercept of the equation's graph.

forma pendiente-intercepto Ecuación lineal escrita en la forma $y = mx + b$, donde m es la pendiente y b es el intercepto en y de la gráfica de la ecuación.

The equation $y = -\dfrac{2}{3}x - 1$ is in slope-intercept form.

La ecuación $y = -\dfrac{2}{3}x - 1$ está en la forma pendiente-intercepto.

---

solution of a linear inequality in two variables An ordered pair (x, y) that produces a true statement when the values of x and y are substituted into the inequality.

solución de una desigualdad lineal con dos variables Par ordenado (x, y) que produce un enunciado verdadero cuando x e y se sustituyen por sus valores en la desigualdad.

The ordered pair $(1, 2)$ is a solution of $3x + 4y > 8$ because $3(1) + 4(2) = 11$, and $11 > 8$.

El par ordenado $(1, 2)$ es una solución de $3x + 4y > 8$ ya que $3(1) + 4(2) = 11$, y $11 > 8$.

---

solution of a system of linear equations in three variables An ordered triple (x, y, z) whose coordinates make each equation in the system true.

solución de un sistema de ecuaciones lineales en tres variables Terna ordenada (x, y, z) cuyas coordenadas hacen que cada ecuación del sistema sea verdadera.

$$4x + 2y + 3z = 1$$
$$2x - 3y + 5z = -14$$
$$6x - y + 4z = -1$$

$(2, 1, -3)$ is the solution of the system above.

$(2, 1, -3)$ es la solución del sistema de arriba.

---

solution of a system of linear equations in two variables An ordered pair (x, y) that satisfies each equation of the system.

solución de un sistema de ecuaciones lineales en dos variables Par ordenado (x, y) que satisface cada ecuación del sistema.

$$4x + y = 8$$
$$2x - 3y = 18$$

$(3, -4)$ is the solution of the system above.

$(3, -4)$ es la solución del sistema de arriba.

---

solution of a system of linear inequalities in two variables An ordered pair (x, y) that is a solution of each inequality in the system.

solución de un sistema de desigualdades lineales en dos variables Par ordenado (x, y) que es una solución de cada desigualdad del sistema.

$$y > -2x - 5$$
$$y \leq x + 3$$

$(-1, 1)$ is a solution of the system above.

$(-1, 1)$ es una solución del sistema de arriba.

solution of an equation in one variable A number that produces a true statement when substituted for the variable in the equation.	The solution of the equation $\frac{4}{5}x + 8 = 20$ is 15.
solución de una ecuación con una variable Número que produce un enunciado verdadero al sustituir la variable por él en la ecuación.	La solución de la ecuación $\frac{4}{5}x + 8 = 20$ es 15.
solution of an equation in two variables An ordered pair (x, y) that produces a true statement when the values of x and y are substituted in the equation.	$(-2, 3)$ is a solution of $y = -2x - 1$.
solución de una ecuación con dos variables Par ordenado (x, y) que produce un enunciado verdadero al sustituir x e y por sus valores en la ecuación.	$(-2, 3)$ es una solución de $y = -2x - 1$.
solution of an inequality in one variable A number that produces a true statement when substituted for the variable in the inequality.	-1 is a solution of the inequality $5x + 2 > 7x - 4$.
solución de una desigualdad con una variable Número que produce un enunciado verdadero al sustituir la variable por él en la desigualdad.	-1 es una solución de la desigualdad $5x + 2 > 7x - 4$.
solve for a variable Rewrite an equation as an equivalent equation in which the variable is on one side and does not appear on the other side.	When you solve the circumference formula $C = 2\pi r$ for r, the result is $r = \frac{C}{2\pi}$.
resolver para una variable Escribir una ecuación como ecuación equivalente que tenga la variable en uno de sus lados pero no en el otro.	Al resolver para r la fórmula de circunferencia $C = 2\pi r$, el resultado es $r = \frac{C}{2\pi}$.
square root If $b^2 = a$, then b is a square root of a. The radical symbol $\sqrt{}$ represents a nonnegative square root.	The square roots of 9 are 3 and -3 because $3^2 = 9$ and $(-3)^2 = 9$. So, $\sqrt{9} = 3$ and $-\sqrt{9} = -3$.
raíz cuadrada Si $b^2 = a$, entonces b es una raíz cuadrada de a. El signo radical $\sqrt{}$ representa una raíz cuadrada no negativa.	Las raíces cuadradas de 9 son 3 y -3 ya que $3^2 = 9$ y $(-3)^2 = 9$. Así pues, $\sqrt{9} = 3$ y $-\sqrt{9} = -3$.
standard deviation The typical difference (or deviation) between a data value and the mean. The standard deviation σ of a numerical data set $x_1, x_2, \ldots, x_n$ is given by the following formula: $$\sigma = \sqrt{\frac{(x_1 - \overline{x})^2 + (x_2 - \overline{x})^2 + \cdots + (x_n - \overline{x})^2}{n}}$$ **desviación típica** La diferencia (o desviación) más común entre un valor de los datos y la media. La desviación típica σ de un conjunto de datos numéricos $x_1, x_2, \ldots, x_n$ viene dada por la siguiente fórmula: $$\sigma = \sqrt{\frac{(x_1 - \overline{x})^2 + (x_2 - \overline{x})^2 + \cdots + (x_n - \overline{x})^2}{n}}$$	**14, 17, 18, 19, 20, 24, 24, 30, 32** Because the mean of the data set is 22, the standard deviation is: Como la media del conjunto de datos es 22, la desviación típica es: $$\sigma = \sqrt{\frac{(14 - 22)^2 + (17 - 22)^2 + \cdots + (32 - 22)^2}{9}}$$ $$= \sqrt{\frac{290}{9}} \approx 5.7$$

standard form of a complex number The form $a + bi$ where a and b are real numbers and i is the imaginary unit.	The standard form of the complex number $i(1 + i)$ is $-1 + i$.
forma general de un número complejo La forma $a + bi$, donde a y b son números reales e i es la unidad imaginaria.	La forma general del número complejo $i(1 + i)$ es $-1 + i$.
standard form of a linear equation A linear equation written in the form $Ax + By = C$ where A and B are not both zero.	The linear equation $y = -3x + 4$ can be written in standard form as $3x + y = 4$.
forma general de una ecuación lineal Ecuación lineal escrita en la forma $Ax + By = C$, donde A y B no son ambos cero.	La ecuación lineal $y = -3x + 4$ escrita en la forma general es $3x + y = 4$.
standard form of a polynomial function The form of a polynomial function that has terms written in descending order of exponents from left to right.	The function $g(x) = 7x - \sqrt{3} + \pi x^2$ can be written in standard form as $g(x) = \pi x^2 + 7x - \sqrt{3}$.
forma general de una función polinómica La forma de una función polinómica en la que los términos se ordenan de tal modo que los exponentes disminuyen de izquierda a derecha.	La función $g(x) = 7x - \sqrt{3} + \pi x^2$ escrita en la forma general es $g(x) = \pi x^2 + 7x - \sqrt{3}$.
standard form of a quadratic equation in one variable The form $ax^2 + bx + c = 0$ where $a \neq 0$.	The quadratic equation $x^2 - 5x = 36$ can be written in standard form as $x^2 - 5x - 36 = 0$.
forma general de una ecuación cuadrática con una variable La forma $ax^2 + bx + c = 0$, donde $a \neq 0$.	La ecuación cuadrática $x^2 - 5x = 36$ escrita en la forma general es $x^2 - 5x - 36 = 0$.
standard form of a quadratic function The form $y = ax^2 + bx + c$ where $a \neq 0$.	The quadratic function $y = 2(x + 3)(x - 1)$ can be written in standard form as $y = 2x^2 + 4x - 6$.
forma general de una función cuadrática La forma $y = ax^2 + bx + c$, donde $a \neq 0$.	La función cuadrática $y = 2(x + 3)(x - 1)$ escrita en la forma general es $y = 2x^2 + 4x - 6$.
standard normal distribution The normal distribution with mean 0 and standard deviation 1. *See also* z-score. **distribución normal típica** La distribución normal con media 0 y desviación típica 1. *Ver también* puntuación z.	 $z = -3$ $z = -2$ $z = -1$ $z = 0$ $z = 1$ $z = 2$ $z = 3$

standard position of an angle In a coordinate plane, the position of an angle whose vertex is at the origin and whose initial side lies on the positive x-axis.

posición normal de un ángulo En un plano de coordenadas, la posición de un ángulo cuyo vértice está en el origen y cuyo lado inicial se sitúa en el eje de x positivo.

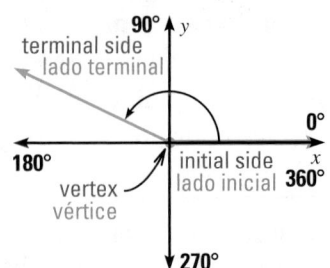

statistics Numerical values used to summarize and compare sets of data.

estadística Valores numéricos utilizados para resumir y comparar conjuntos de datos.

See mean, median, mode, range, *and* standard deviation.

Ver media, mediana, moda, rango *y* desviación típica.

step function A piecewise function defined by a constant value over each part of its domain. Its graph resembles a series of stair steps.

función escalonada Función definida a trozos y por un valor constante en cada parte de su dominio. Su gráfica parece un grupo de escalones.

$$f(x) = \begin{cases} 1, & \text{if } 0 \leq x < 1 \\ 2, & \text{if } 1 \leq x < 2 \\ 3, & \text{if } 2 \leq x < 3 \end{cases} \qquad f(x) = \begin{cases} 1, & \text{si } 0 \leq x < 1 \\ 2, & \text{si } 1 \leq x < 2 \\ 3, & \text{si } 2 \leq x < 3 \end{cases}$$

subset If every element of a set A is also an element of a set B, then A is a subset of B. This is written as $A \subseteq B$. For any set A, $\emptyset \subseteq A$ and $A \subseteq A$.

subconjunto Si cada elemento de un conjunto A es también un elemento de un conjunto B, entonces A es un subconjunto de B. Esto se escribe $A \subseteq B$. Para cualquier conjunto A, $\emptyset \subseteq A$ y $A \subseteq A$.

If $A = \{1, 2, 4, 8\}$ and B is the set of all positive integers, then A is a subset of B, or $A \subseteq B$.

Si $A = \{1, 2, 4, 8\}$ y B es el conjunto de todos los números enteros positivos, entonces A es un subconjunto de B, o $A \subseteq B$.

substitution method A method of solving a system of equations by solving one of the equations for one of the variables and then substituting the resulting expression in the other equation(s).

método de sustitución Método para resolver un sistema de ecuaciones mediante la resolución de una de las ecuaciones para una de las variables seguida de la sustitución de la expresión resultante en la(s) otra(s) ecuación (ecuaciones).

$$2x + 5y = -5$$
$$x + 3y = 3$$

Solve equation 2 for x: $x = -3y + 3$. Substitute the expression for x in equation 1 and solve for y: $y = 11$. Use the value of y to find the value of x: $x = -30$.

Resuelve la ecuación 2 para x: $x = -3y + 3$. Sustituye la expresión para x en la ecuación 1 y resuelve para y: $y = 11$. Usa el valor de y para hallar el valor de x: $x = -30$.

summation notation Notation for a series that uses the uppercase Greek letter sigma, Σ. Also called sigma notation.

notación de sumatoria Notación de una serie que usa la letra griega mayúscula sigma, Σ. También se llama notación sigma.

$$\sum_{i=1}^{5} 7i = 7(1) + 7(2) + 7(3) + 7(4) + 7(5)$$
$$= 7 + 14 + 21 + 28 + 35$$

ENGLISH-SPANISH GLOSSARY

symmetric distribution A probability distribution, represented by a histogram, in which you can draw a vertical line that divides the histogram into two parts that are mirror images.

distribución simétrica Distribución de probabilidad representada por un histograma en la que se puede trazar una recta vertical que divida al histograma en dos partes; éstas son imágenes especulares entre sí.

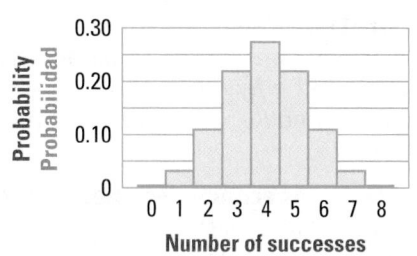

synthetic division A method used to divide a polynomial by a divisor of the form $x - k$.

división sintética Método utilizado para dividir un polinomio por un divisor en la forma $x - k$.

$$\begin{array}{r|rrrr} -3 & 2 & 1 & -8 & 5 \\ & & -6 & 15 & -21 \\ \hline & 2 & -5 & 7 & -16 \end{array}$$

$$\frac{2x^3 + x^2 - 8x + 5}{x + 3} = 2x^2 - 5x + 7 - \frac{16}{x + 3}$$

synthetic substitution A method used to evaluate a polynomial function.

sustitución sintética Método utilizado para evaluar una función polinómica.

$$\begin{array}{r|rrrrr} 3 & 2 & -5 & 0 & -4 & 8 \\ & & 6 & 3 & 9 & 15 \\ \hline & 2 & 1 & 3 & 5 & \mathbf{23} \end{array}$$

The synthetic substitution above indicates that for $f(x) = 2x^4 - 5x^3 - 4x + 8, f(3) = 23$.

La sustitución sintética de arriba indica que para $f(x) = 2x^4 - 5x^3 - 4x + 8, f(3) = 23$.

system of linear inequalities in two variables A system consisting of two or more linear inequalities in two variables. *See also* linear inequality in two variables.

sistema de desigualdades lineales con dos variables Sistema que consiste de dos o más desigualdades lineales con dos variables. *Ver también* desigualdad lineal con dos variables.

$$x + y \le 8$$
$$4x - y > 6$$

system of three linear equations in three variables A system consisting of three linear equations in three variables. *See also* linear equation in three variables.

sistema de tres ecuaciones lineales en tres variables Sistema formado por tres ecuaciones lineales con tres variables. *Ver también* ecuación lineal con tres variables.

$$2x + y - z = 5$$
$$3x - 2y + z = 16$$
$$4x + 3y - 5z = 3$$

system of two linear equations in two variables
A system consisting of two equations that can be written in the form $Ax + By = C$ and $Dx + Ey = F$ where x and y are variables, A and B are not both zero, and D and E are not both zero.

sistema de dos ecuaciones lineales con dos variables
Un sistema que consiste en dos ecuaciones que se pueden escribir de la forma $Ax + By = C$ y $Dx + Ey = F$, donde x e y son variables, A y B no son ambos cero, y D y E tampoco son ambos cero.

$$4x + y = 8$$
$$2x - 3y = 18$$

T

tangent function If θ is an acute angle of a right triangle, the tangent of θ is the length of the side opposite θ divided by the length of the side adjacent to θ.

función tangente Si θ es un ángulo agudo de un triángulo rectángulo, la tangente de θ es la longitud del lado opuesto a θ dividida por la longitud del lado adyacente a θ.

See sine function.

Ver función seno.

terminal side of an angle In a coordinate plane, an angle can be formed by fixing one ray, called the initial side, and rotating the other ray, called the terminal side, about the vertex.

lado terminal de un ángulo En un plano de coordenadas, un ángulo puede formarse al fijar un rayo, llamado lado inicial, y al girar el otro rayo, llamado lado terminal, en torno al vértice.

See standard position of an angle.

Ver posición normal de un ángulo.

terms of a sequence The values in the range of a sequence.

términos de una progresión Los valores del rango de una progresión.

The first 4 terms of the sequence 1, −3, 9, −27, 81, −243, . . . are 1, −3, 9, and −27.

Los 4 primeros términos de la progresión 1, −3, 9, −27, 81, −243, . . . son 1, −3, 9 y −27.

terms of an expression The parts of an expression that are added together.

términos de una expresión Las partes de una expresión que se suman.

The terms of the algebraic expression $3x^2 + 5x + (-7)$ are $3x^2$, $5x$, and -7.

Los términos de la expresión algebraica $3x^2 + 5x + (-7)$ son $3x^2$, $5x$ y -7.

transverse axis of a hyperbola The line segment joining the vertices of a hyperbola.	*See* hyperbola.
eje transverso de una hipérbola El segmento de recta que une los vértices de una hipérbola.	*Ver* hipérbola.
treatment group In a controlled experiment, the group that receives treatment.	
grupo experimental En un experimento controlado, el grupo que está expuesto a la manipulación.	
trigonometric identity A trigonometric equation that is true for all domain values.	$\sin(-\theta) = -\sin\theta \qquad \sin^2\theta + \cos^2\theta = 1$
identidad trigonométrica Ecuación trigonométrica que es verdadera para todos los valores del dominio.	$\text{sen}(-\theta) = -\text{sen}\,\theta \qquad \text{sen}^2\theta + \cos^2\theta = 1$
trinomial The sum of three monomials.	$4x^2 + 3x - 1$ is a trinomial.
trinomio La suma de tres monomios.	$4x^2 + 3x - 1$ es un trinomio.

unbiased sample A sample that is representative of the population you want information about.

muestra no sesgada Muestra que es representativa de la población acerca de la cual deseas informarte.

You want to poll members of the senior class about where to hold the prom. If every senior has an equal chance of being polled, then the sample is unbiased.

Quieres encuestar a algunos estudiantes de último curso sobre el lugar donde organizar el baile de fin de año. Si cada estudiante de último curso tiene iguales posibilidades de ser encuestado, entonces es una muestra no sesgada.

unit circle The circle $x^2 + y^2 = 1$, which has center $(0, 0)$ and radius 1. For an angle θ in standard position, the terminal side of θ intersects the unit circle at the point $(\cos \theta, \sin \theta)$.

círculo unidad El círculo $x^2 + y^2 = 1$, que tiene centro $(0, 0)$ y radio 1. Para un ángulo θ en posición normal, el lado terminal de θ corta al círculo unidad en el punto $(\cos \theta, \text{sen } \theta)$.

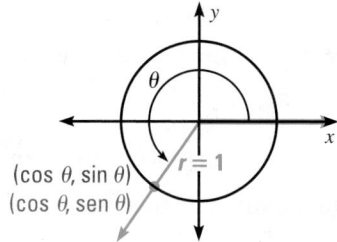

V

variable A letter that is used to represent one or more numbers.

variable Letra utilizada para representar uno o más números.

In the expressions $6x$, $3x^2 + 1$, and $12 - 5x$, the letter x is the variable.

En las expresiones $6x$, $3x^2 + 1$ y $12 - 5x$, la letra x es la variable.

variable term A term that has a variable part.

término algebraico Término que tiene variable.

The variable terms of the algebraic expression $3x^2 + 5x + (-7)$ are $3x^2$ and $5x$.

Los términos algebraicos de la expresión algebraica $3x^2 + 5x + (-7)$ son $3x^2$ y $5x$.

verbal model A word equation that represents a real-life problem.

modelo verbal Ecuación expresada mediante palabras que representa un problema de la vida real.

Distance (miles)	=	Rate (miles/hour)	⋅	Time (hours)
Distancia (millas)	=	Velocidad (millas/hora)	⋅	Tiempo (horas)

vertex form of a quadratic function The form $y = a(x - h)^2 + k$, where the vertex of the graph is (h, k) and the axis of symmetry is $x = h$.

forma de vértice de una función cuadrática La forma $y = a(x - h)^2 + k$, donde el vértice de la gráfica es (h, k) y el eje de simetría es $x = h$.

The quadratic function $y = -\frac{1}{4}(x + 2)^2 + 5$ is in vertex form.

La función cuadrática $y = -\frac{1}{4}(x + 2)^2 + 5$ está en la forma de vértice.

---

vertex of a parabola The point on a parabola that lies on the axis of symmetry.

vértice de una parábola El punto de una parábola que se encuentra en el eje de simetría.

See **parabola.**

Ver **parábola.**

---

vertex of an absolute value graph The highest or lowest point on the graph of an absolute value function.

vértice de una gráfica de valor absoluto El punto más alto o más bajo de la gráfica de una función de valor absoluto.

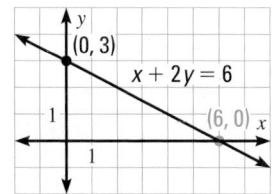

The vertex of the graph of $y = |x - 4| + 3$ is the point **(4, 3)**.

El vértice de la gráfica de $y = |x - 4| + 3$ es el punto **(4, 3)**.

---

vertices of a hyperbola The points of intersection of a hyperbola and the line through the foci of the hyperbola.

vértices de una hipérbola Los puntos de intersección de una hipérbola y la recta que pasa por los focos de la hipérbola.

See **hyperbola.**

Ver **hipérbola.**

---

vertices of an ellipse The points of intersection of an ellipse and the line through the foci of the ellipse.

vértices de una elipse Los puntos de intersección de una elipse y la recta que pasa por los focos de la elipse.

See **ellipse.**

Ver **elipse.**

X

x-intercept The x-coordinate of a point where a graph intersects the x-axis.

intercepto en x La coordenada x de un punto donde una gráfica corta al eje de x.

The x-intercept is **6**.

El intercepto en x es **6**.

Y

y-intercept The y-coordinate of a point where a graph intersects the y-axis.

intercepto en y La coordenada y de un punto donde una gráfica corta al eje de y.

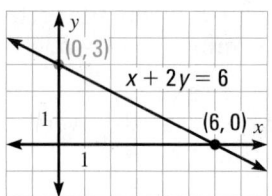

The y-intercept is 3.

El intercepto en y es 3.

Z

zero of a function A number k is a zero of a function f if $f(k) = 0$.

cero de una función Un número k es un cero de una función f si $f(k) = 0$.

The zeros of the function $f(x) = 2(x + 3)(x - 1)$ are -3 and 1.

Los ceros de la función $f(x) = 2(x + 3)(x - 1)$ son -3 y 1.

z-score The number z of standard deviations that a data value lies above or below the mean of the data set:

$z = \dfrac{x - \bar{x}}{\sigma}$.

puntuación z El número z de desviaciones típicas que un valor se encuentra por encima o por debajo de la media del conjunto de datos: $z = \dfrac{x - \bar{x}}{\sigma}$.

A normal distribution has a mean of 76 and a standard deviation of 9. The z-score for

$x = 64$ is $z = \dfrac{x - \bar{x}}{\sigma} = \dfrac{64 - 76}{9} \approx -1.3$.

Una distribución normal tiene una media de 76 y una desviación típica de 9. La puntuación z para $x = 64$ es

$z = \dfrac{x - \bar{x}}{\sigma} = \dfrac{64 - 76}{9} \approx -1.3$.

ENGLISH-SPANISH GLOSSARY

Index

earth science, 649

education, 109, 150, 235, 289, 298, 375, 380, 383, 396, 457, AL10, AL11

electricity, 43, 47, 48, 243, 308, 341, 649

employment, 188, 410, 419, 458, 568, 626

engineering, 12, 16

entertainment, 109, 333, 448, 483

equipment, 234, 256, 304, 308, 326

exercising and running, 191, 333

fairs, 24, 449

farming, AL11

finance, 110, 144, 159, 170, 231, 233, 234, 235, 238, 239, 240, 241, 243, 247, 249, 250, 258, 273, 277, 278, 289, 295, 299, 324, 342, 363, 457, 472, 478, 487

food, 17, 109, 119, 155, 273, 299, 326, 385, 396, 424, 577, 644

football, 13, 16, 64, 193, 235, 359, 431, 514, 575, 666, 674

fundraising, 356

games, 56, 74, 84, 348, 352, 384, 440, 569

gardening, 24, 30, 40, 274, 295, 507, 552, 576, 591, 599

geography, 78, 562, 576, 655, 665

geology, 92, 93, 171, 257, 273, 295, 492, 495, 507, 539

golf, 597, 665

government, 110, 159, 162, 409, 411, 427

history, 117, 143, 162, 356, 375, 486

hockey, AL11

manufacturing, 116, 125, 126, 127, 134, 185, 321, 326, 328, 365, 403

measurement, 23, 31, 101, 141, 147, 149, 152, 160, 163, 188, 196, 202, 203, 323, 365, 375, 523, 540, 559, 561, 605, 631

medicine, 240, 242, 250, 393, 419, 515

movies, 37, 101, 185, 299, 384, 430, 453

music, 8, 74, 125, 242, 289, 304, 308, 350, 407, 448, 469, 484, 568, 617, 652, 667, 676

oceanography, 636, 637, 642, 643

Olympics, 568

parabolic reflectors, 498–501, 517

photography, 8, 178, 264, 339, 520, 584, 600, 658

physics, 38, 39, 72, 98, 170, 196, 199, 202, 203, 205, 209, 210, 216, 221, 249, 261, 263, 264, 265, 271, 274, 276, 287, 299, 339, 530, 549, 568, 617, 633, 657, 661, 676

physiology, 72, 143, 196, 288, 292, 326, 430, 472, 614, 625

population, 143, 162, 234, 298, 482

racing, 203, 215

radioactive isotopes, 243

real estate, 243

recreation, 5, 65, 308, 314, 455, 532, 545, 559, 574, 575, 577, 598, 620, 625, 626, 644

safety, 538

skateboarding, 56, 101, 316

soccer, 73, 390, 455, 552, 608, 661, 665

softball, 56

space travel, 9, 324, 532

structures, 8, 12, 16, 23, 24, 55, 65, 114, 116, 117, 144, 171, 250, 448, 487, 507, 568, 577, 591, 592, 622, 625, 657

swimming, 9, 150

telephone, 64, 127, 249, 351, 356, 504, 506, 658

television, 81, 356, 371, 395, 408, 410, 428

temperature, 196, 273, 287, 314, 324, 647, 650, 651, 667, 676, SR31

tennis, 83, 93, 608

track and field, 170, 383, 568

travel, 9, 365, 517, 561

vehicles, 64, 73, 162, 196, 197, 221, 224, 282, 289, 315, 326, 363, 494, 495, 517, 522, 536, 538, 543, 561, 573, 581, 583, 602, 605, 608, 609, 625, 673

volleyball, 56, 79, 85, 350

volunteering, 384

weather, 210, 212, 252, 265, 314, 512, 640, 647, 657, 673

wildlife, 8, 17, 39, 72, 89, 102, 143, 181, 235, 393, 506, 524, 540, 626

winter sports, 101, 308

approximation. *See also* **estimation; prediction**

of the area of an ellipse, 516

exercises, 93, 309, 608

of real zeros of a function, 140–141, 142

of roots, 167, 169

Archimedes, 561

arc length, of a sector, 565–569

area, SR17. *See also* **formulas**

of circle, SR18

comparing functions, 359

of ellipse, 512, 514, 516

Heron's area formula, 595

under normal curve, 405

of parallelogram, SR17

of rectangle, SR17

of sector, 565–569

of trapezoid, SR17

of triangle, 589, 591, 592, 595, SR17

area model

for completing the square, 49

for a quadratic equation, 20, 23, 24, 27

arithmetic sequence, 442–449, 479, 481

recursive rules and, 467–473, 476, 479, 482

arithmetic series, 444–449, 479, 481

assessment. *See* **Chapter Test; Quiz; Standardized Test Practice**

assumptions, testing with simulation, 386–387

asymptote

for exponential decay functions, 236, 237

for exponential growth functions, 228, 229

horizontal, 310

of a hyperbola, 518

for logarithmic functions, 254

for rational functions, 310, 319

vertical, 310

average. *See* **mean**

average rate of change, 358, 361

Avoid Errors, 4, 13, 18, 26, 33, 43, 53, 58, 88, 96, 105, 112, 113, 120, 128, 129, 167, 168, 175, 182, 193, 230, 238, 259, 305, 327, 338, 355, 379, 381, 390, 435, 437, 443, 451, 461, 468, 520, 530, 534, 566, 581, 594, AL3

axis (axes)

of an ellipse, 510

coordinate, SR13

of symmetry for a conic section, 528, 531

of symmetry for a parabola, 2, 496

B

bar graph, SR32–SR33

base, of a logarithm, 251

biased questions, 414

biased sample, 407

bias in sampling, 407, 409, 410

bias in survey questioning, 414

biconditional statement, SR28–SR29

Big Ideas, 1, 75, 87, 153, 165, 217, 227, 290, 301, 366, 377, 423, 433, 479, 489, 544, 555, 668

binomial(s), 18. *See also* **polynomial(s)**

cube of, 105

multiplying, 105–109, SR11

square of, 105

INDEX

composition, of a function, 182–187, 217, 219
compound interest, 231, 233–235
compound statement, SR27
Concepts. *See also* **Big Ideas; Key Concept**
Concept Summary, 145, 565
condensing a logarithmic expression, 260, 262, 293
cone. *See* **conics**
confidence interval, 413
congruent figures, SR22–SR23
conics, 525–533. *See also* **circle; ellipse; hyperbola; parabola**
classifying, 529, 532
degenerate, 533
discriminant of, 529, 532
eccentricity of, 541–542
lines of symmetry of, 528, 531
translated, equations of, 526–533, 548
conjugates, 33
complex, 44, 138
Connections. *See* **Applications**
constant, common difference, 442
constant of variation, 303
constant ratio, 450
continuously compounded interest, 246–247, 249
contradiction, proof by, AL6
control group, 416, 420
controlled experiments, 416
convenience sample, 406
converse, of a conditional statement, SR28–SR29
convex polygon, 385
coordinate geometry, formulas from, T4
coordinate plane, SR13
corollary to the fundamental theorem of algebra, 137
correlation, 417
cosecant function. *See also* **trigonometric functions**
evaluating for any angle, 570–576
evaluating for right triangles, 556–562
cosine function. *See also* **trigonometric equations; trigonometric functions**
difference formula for, 653–658
double-angle formula for, 659–666
evaluating for any angle, 570–576
evaluating for right triangles, 556–562
graphing, 578, 612–618, 668, 669
reflections, 621, 624
translations, 619–621, 623–626, 670

half-angle formula for, 659–666
inverse of, 578–583, 601
sinusoids, and, 645–652
sum formula for, 653–658
cosines, law of, 593–599, 601, 604
cotangent function. *See also* **trigonometric functions**
evaluating for any angle, 570–576
evaluating for right triangles, 556–562
cotangent identities, 628, 670
coterminal angle, 564, 567
Countdown to Mastery, CC36–CC59
counterexample, SR29
co-vertices, of an ellipse, 510
critical *x*-values, 69, 355
cross multiplication, to solve rational equations, 345–346
cube root function, 199–203, 217, 220
parent, 198, 217
cubes
difference of, 112
sum of, 112
cubic function, 95. *See also* **polynomial function(s)**
inverse of, 193
cycle, of a function, 612
cylinder
surface area of, 321, 326, 334, SR19
volume of, 92, 108, 321, 326, 334, SR19

D

data. *See also* **graphs; modeling; statistics**
analyzing
margin of error, 408–411
measures of central tendency, SR31
measures of dispersion, SR31
normal distribution, 399–404, 423
quartiles, SR34–SR35
collecting, 302
from an experiment, 280
biased sample, 407
convenience sample, 406
population, 406
random sample, 406
sampling, 406–411, 423, 425
self-selected sample, 406
from a survey, 406–411, 425
systematic sample, 406
unbiased sample, 407
displaying
in a bar graph, SR32–SR33
in a circle graph, SR32–SR33
in a line graph, SR32–SR33
distribution shapes, 397–398

organizing
in a box-and-whisker plot, SR34–SR35
in a histogram, 388, 390–395, SR34–SR35
in a line plot, SR34–SR35
in a stem-and-leaf plot, SR34–SR35
in a table, 280
decay factor, 236
decay function
exponential, 236–241, 242, 290, 292
involving *e*, 245–250
decimal exponents, 177
decimals, fractions, percents, and, SR2
degree
converting between radians and, 564–568, 603
measure of a circle, 564
minutes, 567
of a polynomial function, 95, 97
seconds, 567
depression, angle of, 559
derivation
of Snell's law, 634
of a trigonometric model, 661
Descartes, René, 139
Descartes' Rule of Signs, 139–140, 142, 143
diagram
interpreting, 82, 84, 372, 373, 374, 484, 486, 487, 641
Pascal's triangle, 380, 383
tree, SR4
Venn, 182, SR30
diameter, of a circle, SR18
difference
of two cubes, 112
of two squares, 19, 111
difference formulas, 653, 668
using, 653–658, 672
dilation, on the coordinate plane, SR15
direct argument, SR26–SR27
directrix, of a parabola, 496
direct substitution, for evaluating polynomial functions, 96
discrete mathematics
greatest common factor (GCF), SR4–SR5
least common denominator (LCD), SR5
least common multiple (LCM), SR4–SR5
Pascal's triangle, 380, 383
sequences, 434–456
tree diagram, SR4
discriminant, 60, 62
of a conic equation, 529, 532

extraneous solutions
 for logarithmic equations, 270
 for radical equations, 206
 for rational equations, 347
 for trigonometric equations, 638
Extra Practice, EP2

F

factor(s), SR4
 common, 111, SR4
 conversion, SR7
 decay, 236
 growth, 228
 scale, SR15
factoring
 completely, 111
 difference of two squares, 19
 patterns, 112
 perfect square trinomials, 19
 polynomials, 111–117, 122–126,
  156
  by grouping, 112, 115
 quadratic equations, 18–31, 75,
  77–78
 quadratic expressions, 18–19,
  21–22, 25–26, 29
 with special patterns, 19, 22,
  26, 29
 the sum or difference of cubes, 112
 trinomials, 18–31
 zeros and, 28–31
factorization, prime, SR4–SR5
factor theorem, 122, 156
factor tree, SR4
Fibonacci sequence, 468, 472
Find the error. *See* **Avoid Errors**
finite sequence, 434
focal length, 339, 500
focus (foci)
 of an ellipse, 510
 of a hyperbola, 518
 of a parabola, 496
FOIL method, 14, SR11
formulas
 area
  of circle, SR18
  of ellipse, 512, 514, 516
  Heron's area formula, 595
  under normal curve, 405
  of parallelogram, SR17
  of rectangle, SR17
  of sector, 565–569
  of trapezoid, SR17
  of triangle, 589, 591, 592, 595,
   SR17
 Beaufort number, 210
 change-of-base, 260
 circumference, SR18
 combinations, 378

degrees/radians, 564
distance
 to the horizon, 202
 between points, 490, 495, 545
double angle, 659
half angle, 659
interest
 compound, 231
 continuously compounded, 246
interior angle of a regular polygon,
 439
Kelvin/Celsius, 202
margin of error, 408
midpoint, 491
Newton's law of cooling, 268
perimeter, of a rectangle, SR17
slant height, of a truncated
 pyramid, 211
standard normal distribution, 400
sum of first n positive integers,
 437
sum of squares of first n positive
 integers, 437
surface area
 of cone, 203
 of cylinder, 321, 326, 334, SR19
 of hemisphere, 224
 of rectangular prism, SR19
 of sphere, 179
table of, T4–T10
trigonometric difference, 653
trigonometric sum, 653
volume
 of cube, 108, 365
 of cylinder, 92, 108, 321, 326,
  334, SR19
 of dodecahedron, 171
 of icosahedron, 171
 of octahedron, 171
 of pyramid, 108, 131
 of rectangular prism, 92, 108,
  SR19
 of sphere, 90, 161, 179, 188, 365
 of tetrahedron, 171
forty-five degree angle,
 trigonometric values for, 557
fractal geometry
 fractal tree, 478
 Julia set, 48
 Mandelbrot set, 47
 Sierpinski carpet, 456
 Sierpinski triangle, 465
fractions
 adding, SR5
 complex, 338
 decimals, percents, and, SR2
 subtracting, SR5
 writing repeating decimals as, 462
frequency, of a periodic function,
 614

function(s). *See also* **graphs;**
  parent function; quadratic
  function(s)
 characteristics of, describing and
  comparing, 357–364
 classifying, 229, 237, 239
 composition of, 182–187, 217, 219
 cosine, 556–562, 570–576, 653–666
  (*see also* cosine function)
 cube root, 198–203, 217, 220
 domain of, 180–182
 even, 360, 362, 632
 exponential growth and decay,
  228–241, 280–283, 285–288
 inverse, 190–197, 217, 219, 253
  horizontal line test for, 192
 inverse linear, 190–191, 194–196
 iterating, 470, 471, 473
 linear, 190–191, 194–196
 logarithmic, 254–257
 logistic, 274
 natural base, 245–250
 odd, 360, 362, 632
 operations on, 180–187, 217, 219
 power, 180–187, 283–287
 properties of, T12
 quadratic, 2–17, 80 (*see also*
  quadratic function(s))
 radical, 198–203, 217, 220
 rational (*see* rational function(s))
 recursive rules and, 467–475
 sine, 556–562, 570–576, 653–666
  (*see also* sine function)
 square root, 198–203, 217, 220
 tangent, 556–562, 570–576,
  615–618, 653–666
fundamental theorem of algebra,
 137
 applying, 137–144, 157
 corollary to, 137

G

Gauss, Karl Friedrich, 137
GCF (greatest common factor),
 SR4–SR5
general rational functions, 319–325,
 366, 368
general second-degree equation, 529
geometric sequence, 450–456, 479,
 481
 recursive rules and, 467–475, 476,
  479, 482
geometric series, 452–456, 479, 481
 infinite, 459–465, 479, 482
geometry. *See also* **angle(s); circle;**
  formulas; triangle(s);
  trigonometric functions
 congruent figures, SR22–SR23
 conics, 525–533, 541–542

guess, check, and revise, problem
solving strategy, SR24–SR25

half-angle formulas, 659–666, 668,
672
Heron's area formula, 595
histogram, SR34–SR35
on a graphing calculator, 395
probability distribution, 388,
390–395
of sample proportions, 412
shapes of data distributions,
397–398
Hooke's law, 196
horizontal asymptote, 310
horizontal line test, 192, 195
horizontal translation, graphing, 620
hyperbola, 310, 518
asymptotes of, 518
branches of, 518
center of, 518
eccentricity of, 541–542
equation of
graphing, 518–524, 544, 547
translated, 526, 527, 528–533, 548
writing, 519–524, 544, 547
foci of, 518
transverse axis of, 518
vertices of, 518
hypotenuse, SR21
hypothesis, 420–421, SR28–SR29

if-then form, of a conditional
statement, SR28–SR29
imaginary number, 42
imaginary unit i, 41
index of a radical, 166
index of refraction, 583, 634, 667
index of summation, 436, 437
indirect argument, SR26–SR27
indirect measurement, 559, 561–562
induction, mathematical, AL7
inequalities
exponential, 278, 279
logarithmic, 279
quadratic, 66–73, 80
systems of, 67, 70, 71
radical, 214–215
rational, 354–356
inferences, 412
infinite geometric series, 459–465,
479, 482
infinite sequence, 434
infinite series, 436
infinity, positive and negative, 94, 97

initial side, of an angle, 563
integers
closure of set of, 343–344
operations with, SR1
intercept form, of a quadratic
function, 12–17, 75, 77
interest
compound, 231, 233–235
continuously compounded,
246–247, 249
interpret
examples, 181, 246, 312, 573
exercises, 72, 73, 93, 210, 287, 307,
404, 449, 576, 592, 634
probability distributions, 389, 390
intersection of graphs
of linear-quadratic systems, 534
of quadratic systems, 535
interval notation, 16, 149
inverse cosine, 578–583
inverse functions, 189–197, 217,
219
logarithmic and exponential, 253
trigonometric, 578–584, 601, 603
inverse property, 253
inverse relations, 190, 194
inverse sine, 578–583
inverse tangent, 578–583
inverse variation, 302–309, 367
equations, 303–309
modeling with, 302, 304, 308–309
Investigating Algebra. See Activities
irrational conjugates theorem, 138
irrational exponent, 177
iteration, 470, 471, 473

joint variation, 305–309, 367
Julia set, 48
Justify results, Throughout. See for
example, 37, 47, 149, 170, 240,
264, 302, 308, 459, 472

Kepler's second law, 608
Key Concept, 2, 3, 11, 12, 14, 19, 32,
41, 42, 45, 50, 58, 60, 88, 97,
111, 112, 121, 122, 128, 137,
138, 139, 146, 166, 167, 172,
173, 180, 190, 192, 198, 204,
228, 231, 236, 244, 245, 246,
251, 254, 259, 260, 267, 269,
303, 305, 310, 311, 319, 327,
329, 330, 336, 337, 338, 378,
380, 381, 388, 389, 399, 408,
417, 434, 436, 437, 442, 444,
450, 452, 461, 467, 476, 490,

491, 497, 502, 510, 518, 526,
529, 531, 556, 557, 563, 564,
565, 570, 571, 572, 579, 586,
587, 589, 593, 595, 612, 613,
615, 619, 628, 653, 659, AL6,
AL7

Law of Cosines, 593–599, 601, 604
Law of Sines, 585–592, 601, 604
Law of Universal Gravitation, 309
leading coefficient, of a polynomial
function, 95
least common denominator (LCD),
SR5
of a rational expression, 337,
SR12
for solving a rational equation, 346
least common multiple (LCM),
SR4–SR5
for a rational expression, 337
legs, of a triangle, SR21
like radicals, 174
adding and subtracting, 174–179
linear function(s), inverse, 190–191,
194–196
linear-quadratic systems, 534–540
line graph, SR32–SR33
line of reflection, SR14–SR15
line of symmetry
for a conic section, 528, 531
for even function, 360
for a plane figure, SR16
line plot, SR34–SR35
line(s)
horizontal line test, 192, 195
of reflection, SR14–SR15
of symmetry, 360, 528, 531, SR16
line symmetry, SR16
list, making to solve problems,
SR24–SR25
local maximum, of a polynomial
function, 146
local minimum, of a polynomial
function, 146
Location Principle, 136
logarithm(s), 251
change-of-base formula and,
260–261, 263
common, 252
natural, 252
properties of, 259–265, 293, 712
logarithmic equation(s), 269
evaluating, 251–253, 255–257, 293
modeling with, 271, 273–274,
276–277
property of equality for, 269
solving, 269–277, 290, 294

Power of a Power Property, 88, 166, 172

Power of a Product Property, 88, 172

Power of Quotients Property, 88, 172

Power Property of Logarithms, 259

power regression, 285, 287

powers. *See also* **exponent(s); exponential function(s)**
- of a binomial difference, 381, 383
- of a binomial sum, 381–383

Practice. *See* **Big Ideas; Chapter Review; Chapter Summary; Mixed Review of Problem Solving; Prerequisite Skills; Skills Review Handbook**

precision, significant digits and, SR9

prediction
- exercises, 102, 189, 287, 302, 507, 600, 677
- using exponential decay models, 238–241
- using exponential growth models, 230, 233–235
- using exponential regression, 282
  - using an inverse function, 194

premise, SR26–SR27

Prerequisite Skills, 1, 86, 164, 226, 300, 376, 432, 488, 554, 610

prime factorization, SR4–SR5

prime number, SR4–SR5

probability
- area under normal curve, 405
- binomial distribution and, 388–395
- formulas, T6–T7
- normal distribution and, 399–404
- standard normal table and, 401–404
- using to make and analyze decisions, AL10–AL11

probability distribution, 388
- binomial, 389–395
- skewed, 391, 392
- symmetric, 391, 392

problem solving strategies. *See also* **eliminate choices; Problem Solving Workshop**
- draw a graph, 39
- guess, check, and revise, SR24–SR25
- interpret a diagram, 372, 373, 374
- make a list, SR24–SR25
- make a table, 38–39, SR24–SR25
- solve a simpler problem, SR24–SR25

Problem Solving Workshop, 38–39, 118–119, 212–213, 275–277, 352–353, 395, 474–475, 516, 599, 642–643

Product of Powers Property, 88, 172

Product Property
- of Logarithms, 259

of Square Roots, 32

proof(s). *See also* **reasoning**
- by contradiction, AL6
- of properties of logarithms, 263

properties
- of complex numbers, 46–47
- for exponential equations, 267
- of exponents, 88, 172, T11–T12
- of functions, T12
- inverse, 253
- for logarithmic equations, 269
- of logarithms, 259, T12
  - proofs of, 263
- of matrix operations, T11
- of radicals, T12
- of rational exponents, 172, 217, T12
- of real numbers, 47, T11
- of square roots, 32
- zero product, 19

proportion, SR6
- population, 412–413

pure imaginary number, 42

Pythagorean identities, 628

Pythagorean theorem, SR21
- using, 556–562, 570, 599, 602

Pythagorean triple, AL4

Q

quadrantal angle, 571

quadrants, of a coordinate plane, SR13

quadratic equation(s). *See also* **polynomial(s)**
- with complex solutions, 42–48
- discriminant in, 60
- to model dropped objects, 34–36, 38–39
- to model launched objects, 61, 64
- to model vertical motion, 61, 64
- roots of, 19
- solving, 75
  - by completing the square, 50–57, 75, 79
  - by factoring, 18–31, 75, 77, 78
  - by finding square roots, 32–37, 50, 75, 78
  - using the quadratic formula, 58–65, 75, 79
- standard form of, 19
- systems of, 534–540

quadratic expression(s)
- completing the square for, 49
- factoring, 18–19, 21–22, 25–26, 29

quadratic form, of a polynomial, 113, 115

quadratic formula, 58–65, 75, 79, 637

quadratic function(s)
- graphing

in intercept form, 12–17, 75, 77

in standard form, 2–9, 75, 76

in vertex form, 11–12, 14–17, 53, 75, 77

maximum value, 4–5, 7, 10, 53

minimum value, 4–5, 7, 10

parent function, 2

zeros of, 20–22

quadratic inequality (inequalities)
- critical x-values of, 69
- graphing, 66–73, 80
- in one variable, forms, 68–71
- solving, 68–73, 80
- system of, 67, 70, 71

quadratic system, 534–540, 544, 548

quartic function, 95

quartile, SR34–SR35

Quiz, *Throughout. See for example,* 31, 57, 73, 110, 135, 150, 179, 197, 211

Quotient of Powers Property, 88, 172, 247–252, 294, 296

Quotient Property
- of Logarithms, 259
- of Square Roots, 32

quotient rule, for fractions, 619

R

radian, 564
- converting between degrees and, 564–568, 603

radian measure, 564–569

radical(s), 32
- index of, 166
- like, 174
- nth root, 166–171
- properties of, 173–179, 259, T12
- simplest form, 174

radical equation
- solving, 204–213, 217, 220
- with two radicals, 207, 209

radical function, graphing, 198–203, 217, 220

radical inequalities, 214–215

radical sign, 32

radicand, 32

radius, of a circle, 502, SR18

randomized comparative experiment, 416, 417, 420

random sample, 406

random variable, 388

range
- data, SR31
- of a function, 198–199, 229, 237
- of a sequence, 434

rate of change, average, 358, 361

ratio(s)
- golden, 350
- percent as, SR2

half-angle formulas for, 659–666
inverse, 578–584, 601, 603
modeling with, 574, 575–576, 645–652, 671
right angle, 556–562, 602
sum formulas for, 653–658
trigonometric identities, 627–634, 670
verifying, 627, 630–634, 662, 670
trigonometric ratios, 556–562
trigonometry, formulas and identities, T8–T9
trinomials, 18–31
turning points, of a polynomial function, 146, 148

unbiased sample, 407
unit circle, 571
universal gravitational constant, 309
upper limit of summation, 436
upper quartile, SR34–SR35

variable, random, 388
variation
constant of, 303
inverse, 302–309, 367
joint, 305–309, 367
Venn diagram, SR30
to show composition of functions, 182
verbal model
examples, 5, 20, 27, 28, 114, 131, 147, 312, 345, 469
exercises, 8, 23, 350, 365
verification, of trigonometric identities, 627, 630–634, 662, 670
vertex (vertices)
of an angle, 563
of an ellipse, 510, 526
of a hyperbola, 518, 526
of a parabola, 2, 496, 526

vertex form, of quadratic function, 11–12, 14–17, 53, 75, 77
vertical asymptote, 310
vertical motion problem, 61, 64
vertical shrinking, of a graph, 229, 237
vertical stretching, of a graph, 229, 237
vertical translation, graphing, 620
visual thinking. *See also* **graphs; manipulatives; modeling; multiple representations; transformation**
exercises, 47, 63, 100, 500, 566
Vocabulary
overview, 1, 87, 165, 227, 301, 377, 433, 489, 555, 611
prerequisite, 86, 164, 226, 300, 376, 432, 488, 554, 610
review, 76, 154, 218, 291, 367, 424, 480, 545, 602, 669
volume. *See also* **formulas**
of cube, 108, 365
of cylinder, 92, 108, 321, 326, 334, SR19
of dodecahedron, 171
of icosahedron, 171
of octahedron, 171
of pyramid, 108, 131
of rectangular prism, 92, 108, SR19
of sphere, 90, 161, 179, 188, 365
of tetrahedron, 171

well-designed studies, 417
Writing. *See also* **communication; verbal model**
algebraic expressions, SR10
equations of circles, 503–508
equations of ellipses, 511–515
equations of hyperbolas, 519–524
equations of parabolas, 497–501
exponential functions, 281–283, 285–288, 294
polynomial functions, 139, 142, 144

power functions, 283–287
rational equations, 345, 350–351
rules for nth term of a sequence, 443–449, 450–456
rules for sequences, 435, 438, 439–440
trigonometric equations, 581, 583–584
trigonometric functions, 645–652

x-**axis,** SR13
x-**coordinate,** SR13
x-**intercept,** of the graph of a polynomial function, 145
x-**values,** critical, 69, 355

y-**axis,** SR13
symmetry of even function, 360
y-**coordinate,** SR13
as local maximum or minimum of a function, 146

zero exponent property, 88
zero product property, 19
zeros
of a polynomial function, 122, 123, 124, 125, 128–136, 145, 157
approximating real, 140–141, 142
Descartes' Rule of Signs and, 139–140, 142, 143
fundamental theorem of algebra and, 137–144, 157
of a quadratic function, 20–22
average of, 28
of a rational function, 320
zero theorem, rational, 128–129
z-**score,** 400
standard normal table and, 401–404

Worked-Out Solutions

This section of the book provides step-by-step solutions to exercises with circled exercise numbers. These solutions provide models that can help guide your work with the homework exercises.

The separate **Selected Answers** section follows this section. It provides numerous answers that you can use to check your own answers.

Chapter 1

Lesson 1.1

15. 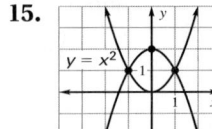 Both graphs have the same axis of symmetry. The graph of $f(x) = -x^2 + 2$ opens down, and its vertex is 2 units higher than that of $y = x^2$.

37. $f(x) = \dfrac{3}{2}x^2 + 6x + 4$

$a > 0$; the function has a minimum value.

$x = \dfrac{-b}{2a} = \dfrac{-(6)}{2\left(\frac{3}{2}\right)} = -2$

Minimum: $f(-2) = \dfrac{3}{2}(-2)^2 + 6(-2) + 4 = -2$

57. $y = \dfrac{1}{9000}x^2 - \dfrac{7}{15}x + 500$

$x = \dfrac{-b}{2a} = \dfrac{-\left(\frac{-7}{15}\right)}{2\left(\frac{1}{9000}\right)} = 2100$

$y = \dfrac{1}{9000}(2100)^2 - \dfrac{7}{15}(2100) + 500 = 10$

The cable is 10 feet above the road.

Lesson 1.2

19. 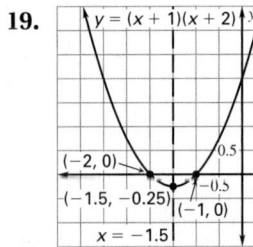 $a = 1, p = -1$, and $q = -2$

x-int.: $x = -2$ and $x = -1$

Axis of sym.:

$x = \dfrac{-2 + (-1)}{2} = -1.5$

Vertex: $(-1.5, -0.25)$

29. $y = (x - 3)^2 + 6 = (x - 3)(x - 3) + 6$

$= \left(x^2 - 3x - 3x + 9\right) + 6 = x^2 - 6x + 15$

53. a. $y = -0.000234x(x - 160)$

$= -0.000234(x - 0)(x - 160)$

$p = 0, q = 160$; the field is 160 feet wide.

b. $x = \dfrac{p + q}{2} = \dfrac{0 + 160}{2} = 80$

$y = -0.000234(80)(80 - 160) \approx 1.5$

The maximum height is about 1.5 feet.

Lesson 1.3

33. $z^2 - 3z - 54 = 0 \rightarrow (z - 9)(z + 6) = 0$

$z - 9 = 0 \rightarrow z = 9$ or $z + 6 = 0 \rightarrow z = -6$

47. $y = x^2 + 7x - 30 = (x + 10)(x - 3)$

The zeros are -10 and 3.

67. a. $A = (30)(20) = 600 \text{ ft}^2$

b.

New area (feet)	=	New length (feet)	·	New width (feet)

$1064 = (x + 30)(x + 20)$

c. $x^2 + 50x + 600 = 1064$

$(x - 58)(x - 8) = 0 \rightarrow x = -58$ or $x = 8$

Expand the length and width by 8 feet.

Lesson 1.4

27. $20x^2 + 124x + 24 = 4(5x^2 + 31x + 6)$

$= 4(5x + 1)(x + 6)$

39. $6r^2 - 7r - 5 = 0 \rightarrow (3r - 5)(2r + 1) = 0$

$r = \dfrac{5}{3} = 1\dfrac{2}{3}$ or $r = -\dfrac{1}{2}$

Worked-Out Solutions

63. $96 = (2x + 8)(2x + 12) - 96$

$0 = 4x^2 + 40x - 96$

$0 = (4x - 8)(x + 12)$

$x = 2$ or $x = -12$

The border's width should be 2 feet.

Lesson 1.5

17. $\dfrac{\sqrt{2}}{4 + \sqrt{5}} = \dfrac{\sqrt{2}}{4 + \sqrt{5}} \cdot \dfrac{4 - \sqrt{5}}{4 - \sqrt{5}} = \dfrac{4\sqrt{2} - \sqrt{10}}{11}$

27. $-3w^2 = -213 \rightarrow w^2 = 71 \rightarrow w = \pm\sqrt{71}$

41. a. $\pi r^2 = 10^2 = 100$

   b. $\pi r^2 = 100 \rightarrow r^2 = \dfrac{100}{\pi} \rightarrow r \approx 5.6$ feet

   c. $\pi r^2 = s^2 \rightarrow r^2 = \dfrac{s^2}{\pi}$

   $r = \sqrt{\dfrac{s^2}{\pi}} = \dfrac{s}{\sqrt{\pi}} \cdot \dfrac{\sqrt{\pi}}{\sqrt{\pi}} = \dfrac{s\sqrt{\pi}}{\pi}$

Lesson 1.6

11. $-5(n - 3)^2 = 10 \rightarrow (n - 3)^2 = -2$

$n - 3 = \pm\sqrt{-2} \rightarrow n = 3 \pm i\sqrt{2}$

29. $\dfrac{6i}{3 - i} = \dfrac{6i}{3 - i} \cdot \dfrac{3 + i}{3 + i} = \dfrac{18i + 6i^2}{9 + 3i - 3i - i^2}$

$= \dfrac{-6 + 18i}{10} = -\dfrac{6}{10} + \dfrac{18}{10}i = -\dfrac{3}{5} + \dfrac{9}{5}i$

67. Impedance: $12 + 8i - 6i - 10i = 12 - 8i$ ohms

Lesson 1.7

27. $x^2 - 2x = -25$

$x^2 - 2x + 1 = -25 + 1$

$(x - 1)^2 = -24$

$x - 1 = \pm\sqrt{-24} \rightarrow x = 1 \pm 2i\sqrt{6}$

45. $y = x^2 - 3x + 4$

$y + \dfrac{9}{4} = \left(x^2 - 3x + \dfrac{9}{4}\right) + 4$

$y = \left(x - \dfrac{3}{2}\right)^2 + \dfrac{7}{4}$

The vertex is $\left(\dfrac{3}{2}, \dfrac{7}{4}\right)$.

65.

$y = (200 + 10x)(40 - x)$

$y = 8000 + 200x - 10x^2$

$y - 8000 = -10(x^2 - 20x)$

$y - 8000 + (-10)(100) = -10(x^2 - 20x + 100)$

$y - 9000 = -10(x - 10)^2$

$y = -10(x - 10)^2 + 9000$

The revenue is maximized when the price is increased 10 times; 10($10) = $100. Systems should be sold for $200 + $100 = $300 to maximize revenue.

Lesson 1.8

19. $4x^2 + 3 = x^2 - 7x \rightarrow 3x^2 + 7x + 3 = 0$

$x = \dfrac{-7 \pm \sqrt{7^2 - 4(3)(3)}}{2(3)} = \dfrac{-7 \pm \sqrt{13}}{6}$

39. $7r^2 - s = 2r + 9r^2 \rightarrow -2r^2 - 2r - 5 = 0$

$b^2 - 4ac = (-2)^2 - 4(-2)(-5) = -36 < 0$

Two imaginary: $\dfrac{-(-2) \pm \sqrt{-36}}{2(-2)} = -\dfrac{1}{2} \pm \dfrac{3}{2}i$

71. $S = -0.000013E^2 + 0.042E - 21$

$10 = -0.000013E^2 + 0.042E - 21$

$0 = -0.000013E^2 + 0.042E - 31$

$E = \dfrac{-0.042 \pm \sqrt{(0.042)^2 - 4(-0.000013)(-31)}}{2(-0.000013)}$

$E = \dfrac{-0.042 \pm \sqrt{0.000152}}{-0.000026}$

$E \approx 1141$ meters or $E \approx 2090$ meters

Lesson 1.9

17. $y \leq -\dfrac{2}{3}x^2 + 3x + 1$

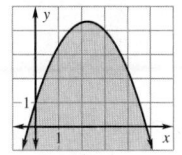

39. $3x^2 + 2x - 8 \leq 0$

$(3x - 4)(x + 2) = 0$

$x = \dfrac{4}{3}$ or $x = -2$

The solution is

$-2 \leq x \leq \dfrac{4}{3}$.

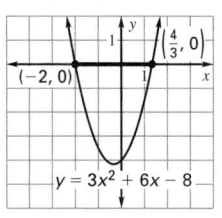

73. $0.0017x^2 + 0.145x + 2.35 > 10$

$0.0017x^2 + 0.145x - 7.65 > 0$

$x = \dfrac{-0.145 \pm \sqrt{0.073045}}{0.0034} \approx 36.84, \ -122.13$

Test values $x = 0$ and $x = 37$ to determine that $x \geq 36.84$. The domain is $0 \leq x \leq 40$. So, the larvae's length tends to be greater than 10 mm between around 37 to 40 days.

Mastering the Standards

for Mathematical Practice

The topics described in the Standards for Mathematical Content will vary from year to year. However, the *way* in which you learn, study, and think about mathematics will not. The Standards for Mathematical Practice describe skills that you will use in all of your math courses.

Mathematical Practices

1. *Make sense of problems and persevere in solving them.*
2. *Reason abstractly and quantitatively.*
3. *Construct viable arguments and critique the reasoning of others.*
4. *Model with mathematics.*
5. *Use appropriate tools strategically.*
6. *Attend to precision.*
7. *Look for and make use of structure.*
8. *Look for and express regularity in repeated reasoning.*

④ Model with mathematics.

Mathematically proficient students can apply... mathematics... to... problems... in everyday life, society, and the workplace...

In your book

Application exercises and **Mixed Reviews of Problem Solving** apply mathematics to other disciplines and in real-world scenarios.

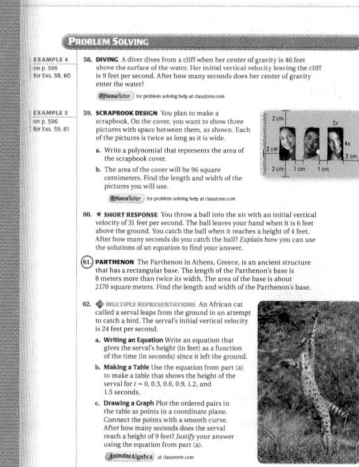

Worked-Out Solutions

This section of the book provides step-by-step solutions to exercises with circled exercise numbers. These solutions provide models that can help guide your work with the homework exercises.

The separate **Selected Answers** section follows this section. It provides numerous answers that you can use to check your own answers.

Chapter 2

Lesson 2.1

17. $(6.3 \times 10^5)(8.9 \times 10^{-12}) = 56.07 \times 10^{-7}$

$= 5.607 \times 10^1 \times 10^{-7} = 5.607 \times 10^{-6}$

31. $\dfrac{3c^3d}{9cd^{-1}} = \dfrac{3}{9}c^{3-1}d^{1-(-1)} = \dfrac{1}{3}c^2d^2$

Quotient of powers property

51. Bead: $d = 6$ mm, $r = 3$ mm

$v = \dfrac{4}{3}\pi r^3 = \dfrac{4}{3}\pi(3)^3 = 36\pi$

Pearl: $d = 9$ mm, $r = \dfrac{9}{2}$ mm

$v = \dfrac{4}{3}\pi r^3 = \dfrac{4}{3}\pi\left(\dfrac{9}{2}\right)^3 = \dfrac{243\pi}{2}$

$\dfrac{\text{Volume of pearl}}{\text{Volume of bead}} = \dfrac{\frac{243\pi}{2}}{36\pi} = \dfrac{243}{72} = 3.375$

About 3.4 times greater

Lesson 2.2

21.
```
3 | −7    11     4     0
  |      −21   −30   −78
  ─────────────────────────
    −7   −10   −26   −78
```

$f(3) = -78$

27. The degree is even and the leading coefficient is negative.

57.

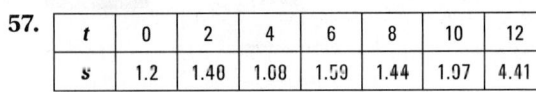

t	0	2	4	6	8	10	12
s	1.2	1.40	1.08	1.59	1.44	1.97	4.41

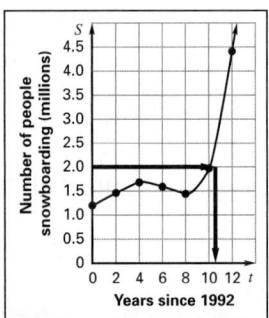

The number of snowboarders was greater than 2 million in 2002 (when $t \approx 10$).

Lesson 2.3

11. $(5b - 6b^3 + 2b^4) - (9b^3 + 4b^4 - 7)$

$= 2b^4 - 4b^4 - 6b^3 - 9b^3 + 5b + 7$

$= -2b^4 - 15b^3 + 5b + 7$

21. $(2a - 3)(a^2 - 10a - 2)$

$= (2a - 3)(a^2) - (2a - 3)(10a) - (2a - 3)(2)$

$= 2a^3 - 23a^2 + 26a + 6$

61. $P = 0.00267sF = 0.00267s(0.0116s^2 + 0.789)$

$= 0.000030972s^3 + 0.00210663s$

When $s = 10$, $P(10) = 0.0520383$.

About 0.052 horsepower is needed.

Lesson 2.4

7. $3y^5 - 48y^3 = 3y^3(y^2 - 16) = 3y^3(y + 4)(y - 4)$

23. $4c^3 + 8c^2 - 9c - 18 = 4c^2(c + 2) - 9(c + 2)$

$= (c + 2)(2c + 3)(2c - 3)$

Worked-Out Solutions

61. $\ell = x;\ h = x - 5;\ w = x - 5$

$v = \ell wh \rightarrow 250 = (x)(x - 5)(x - 5)$

$250 = x(x^2 - 10x + 25)$

$0 = x^3 - 10x^2 + 25x - 250$

$0 = x^2(x - 10) + 25(x - 10)$

$0 = (x^2 + 25)(x - 10) \rightarrow x = 10$

$\ell = 10$ in., $h = 5$ in., $w = 5$ in.

Lesson 2.5

17.
$$\begin{array}{r|rrrrr}
6 & 1 & -5 & -8 & 13 & -12 \\
& & 6 & 6 & -12 & 6 \\
\hline
& 1 & 1 & -2 & 1 & -6
\end{array}$$

$x^3 + x^2 - 2x + 1 - \dfrac{6}{x - 6}$

25.
$$\begin{array}{r|rrrr}
-9 & 1 & 2 & -51 & 108 \\
& & -9 & 63 & -108 \\
\hline
& 1 & -7 & 12 & 0
\end{array}$$

$f(x) = (x + 9)(x^2 - 7x + 12)$

$\quad = (x + 9)(x - 4)(x - 3)$

43.

$$\begin{array}{r}
-0.13x^2 + 11.2x - 560.9 \\
14.8x + 725\overline{\smash{\big)}\,-1.95x^3 + 70.1x^2 - 188x + 2150} \\
\underline{-1.95x^3 - 95.5x^2} \\
165.6x^2 - 188x \\
\underline{165.6x^2 + 8113.3x} \\
-8301.3x + 2150 \\
\underline{-8301.3x - 406{,}652.5} \\
408{,}802.5
\end{array}$$

$f(x) = -0.13x^2 + 11.2x - 560.9 + \dfrac{408{,}802.5}{14.8x + 725}$

Lesson 2.6

7. $g(x) = 4x^5 + 3x^3 - 2x - 14$

Factors of the constant term: $\pm 1, \pm 2, \pm 7, \pm 14$

Factors of the leading coefficient: $\pm 1, \pm 2, \pm 4$

Possible rational zeros: $\pm\dfrac{1}{1}, \pm\dfrac{2}{1}, \pm\dfrac{7}{1}, \pm\dfrac{14}{1}, \pm\dfrac{1}{2},$

$\pm\dfrac{2}{2}, \pm\dfrac{7}{2}, \pm\dfrac{14}{2}, \pm\dfrac{1}{4}, \pm\dfrac{2}{4}, \pm\dfrac{7}{4}, \pm\dfrac{14}{4}$

$= \pm 1, \pm 2, \pm 7, \pm 14, \pm\dfrac{1}{2}, \pm\dfrac{7}{2}, \pm\dfrac{1}{4}, \pm\dfrac{7}{4}$

21. Possible rational zeros: $\pm 1, \pm 3, \pm 5, \pm 15, \pm\dfrac{1}{2},$

$\pm\dfrac{3}{2}, \pm\dfrac{5}{2}, \pm\dfrac{15}{2}, \pm\dfrac{1}{3}, \pm\dfrac{5}{3}, \pm\dfrac{1}{6}, \pm\dfrac{5}{6}$

Reasonable zeros: $x = -3,\ x = -\dfrac{5}{3},\ x = \dfrac{1}{2}$

Test $x = -3$:
$$\begin{array}{r|rrrr}
-3 & 6 & 25 & 16 & -15 \\
& & -18 & -21 & 15 \\
\hline
& 6 & 7 & -5 & 0
\end{array}$$

$f(x) = (x + 3)(6x^2 + 7x - 5)$

$\quad = (x + 3)(2x - 1)(3x + 5)$

Real zeros are $-3, \dfrac{1}{2}, -\dfrac{5}{3}$.

47. $V = x(x - 1)(x - 2) \rightarrow 24 = x(x^2 - 3x + 2)$

$0 = x^3 - 3x^2 + 2x - 24$

Possible rational zeros: $\pm 1, \pm 2, \pm 3, \pm 4, \pm 6,$
$\pm 8, \pm 12, \pm 24$

Lesson 2.7

15. Possible rational zeros: $\pm 1, \pm 2, \pm 4, \pm 8$

$f(x) = x^4 + x^3 + 2x^2 + 4x - 8$

$\quad = (x + 2)(x^3 - x^2 + 4x - 4)$

$\quad = (x + 2)(x - 1)(x^2 + 4)$

$\quad = (x + 2)(x - 1)(x - 2i)(x + 2i)$

The zeros are $-2, 1, 2i,$ and $-2i$.

37. $h(x) = x^5 - 2x^3 - x^2 + 6x + 5$

2 sign changes; 2 or 0 positive real zeros

$h(-x) = (-x)^5 - 2(-x)^3 - (-x)^2 + 6(-x) + 5$

$\quad = -x^5 + 2x^3 - x^2 - 6x + 5$

3 sign changes; 3 or 1 positive real zeros.

Possible numbers of zeros:

Positive	Negative	Imaginary	Total
2	3	0	5
0	3	2	5
2	1	2	5
0	1	4	5

61. $S = -0.015x^3 + 0.6x^2 - 2.4x + 19$

$0 = -0.015x^3 + 0.6x^2 - 2.4x - 56$

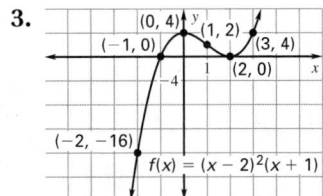

There are two positive zeros of this function, $x \approx 16.4$ and $x \approx 30.9$, but $x \approx 16.4$ is the most likely amount.

Lesson 2.8

3.

f(x) = (x − 2)²(x + 1), with points (0, 4), (−1, 0), (1, 2), (3, 4), (2, 0), (−2, −16)

19. Turning pts: $(-2.2, -38)$, local minimum; $(-1.1, 0.8)$, local maximum; $(0.3, -40)$, local minimum; $(1.9, 8)$, local maximum; $(2.8, -13)$, local minimum

Zeros: $x \approx -2.6$, $x \approx -1.2$, $x \approx -1$, $x \approx 1.5$, $x \approx 2.2$, $x \approx 3$

It must be at least a degree 6 function.

41.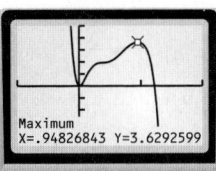

At about 0.95 seconds into the stroke the swimmer is going the fastest.

Mastering *the* Standards

for Mathematical Practice

The topics described in the Standards for Mathematical Content will vary from year to year. However, the *way* in which you learn, study, and think about mathematics will not. The Standards for Mathematical Practice describe skills that you will use in all of your math courses.

Mathematical Practices

1. *Make sense of problems and persevere in solving them.*
2. *Reason abstractly and quantitatively.*
3. *Construct viable arguments and critique the reasoning of others.*
4. *Model with mathematics.*
5. *Use appropriate tools strategically.*
6. *Attend to precision.*
7. *Look for and make use of structure.*
8. *Look for and express regularity in repeated reasoning.*

⑤ Use appropriate tools strategically.

Mathematically proficient students consider the available tools when solving a... problem... [and] are... able to use technological tools to explore and deepen their understanding...

In your book

Problem Solving Workshops explore alternative methods as tools for problem solving. A variety of **Activities** use concrete and technological tools to explore mathematical concepts.

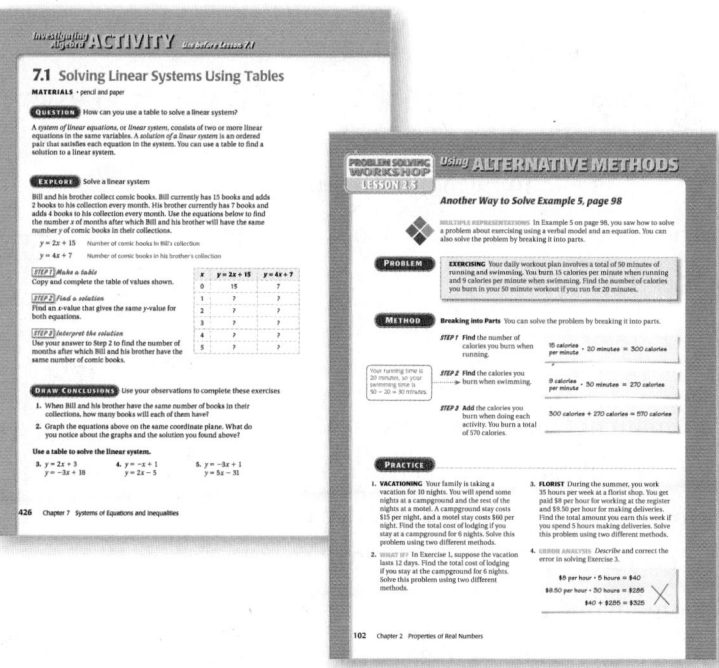

Getty Images/Image Source

This section of the book provides step-by-step solutions to exercises with circled exercise numbers. These solutions provide models that can help guide your work with the homework exercises.

The separate **Selected Answers** section follows this section. It provides numerous answers that you can use to check your own answers.

Chapter 3

Lesson 3.1

9. $\left(\sqrt[n]{a}\right)^m = a^{m/n} \rightarrow \sqrt{x^5} = x^{5/2}$

25. $27^{2/3} = \left(27^{1/3}\right)^2 = (3)^2 = 9$

63. $p = ks^3 \rightarrow 1.2 = k(1700)^3 \rightarrow k = \dfrac{3}{12,282,500,000}$

$p = \dfrac{3}{12,282,500,000}s^3 \rightarrow 1.5 = \dfrac{3}{12,282,500,000}s^3$

$\rightarrow 6,141,250,000 = s^3 \rightarrow s \approx 1831$

About 1800 revolutions per minute

Lesson 3.2

5. $3^{1/4} \cdot 27^{1/4} = 3^{1/4} \cdot 3^{1/4} \cdot 3^{1/4} \cdot 3^{1/4}$

$= 3^{(1/4 + 1/4 + 1/4 + 1/4)} = 3^1 = 3$

27. $5\sqrt[4]{64} \cdot 2\sqrt[4]{8} = 10\sqrt[4]{512} = 40\sqrt[4]{2}$

85. $d = 1.9\left[\left(5.5 \times 10^{-4}\right)\ell\right]^{1/2}$

$\ell = 10 \text{ cm} = 100 \text{ mm}$

$d = 1.9\left[\left(5.5 \times 10^{-4}\right)(100)\right]^{1/2} \approx 0.4456$

The optimum diameter is about 0.45 mm.

Lesson 3.3

3. $f(x) + g(x) = -3x^{1/3} + 4x^{1/2} + 5x^{1/3} + 4x^{1/2}$

$= 2x^{1/3} + 8x^{1/2}$

Domain of f: all nonnegative reals

Domain of g: all nonnegative reals

Domain of $f + g$: all nonnegative reals

13. $g(x) \cdot f(x) = \left(5x^{1/2}\right)\left(4x^{2/3}\right) = 20x^{7/6}$

Domain of f: all reals

Domain of g: all nonnegative reals

Domain of $g \cdot f$: all nonnegative reals

45. For \$15 discount: $f(x) = x - 15$

For 10% discount: $g(x) = x - 0.1x = 0.9x$

a. $g(f(x)) = g(x - 15) = 0.9(x - 15)$

$x = 85$: $0.9(85 - 15) = 0.9(70) = \$63.00$

b. $f(g(x)) = f(0.9x) = 0.9x - 15$

$x = 85$: $0.9(85) - 15 = 76.5 - 15 = \$61.50$

c. The 10% discount before the \$15 discount.

Lesson 3.4

7. $y = 12x + 7 \rightarrow x = 12y + 7 \rightarrow \dfrac{x}{12} - \dfrac{7}{12} = y$

15. $f(g(x)) = f(x - 4) = (x - 4) + 4 = x$ ✓

$g(f(x)) = g(x + 4) = (x + 4) - 4 = x$ ✓

49. $v = 1.34\sqrt{\ell}$ The waterline length should be

$\left(\dfrac{v}{1.34}\right)^2 = \ell$ $\ell = \left(\dfrac{7.5}{1.34}\right)^2 \approx 31.3$ feet.

Lesson 3.5

11. 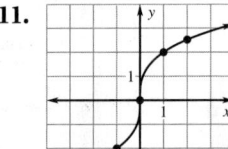 The domain and range are all real numbers.

17. 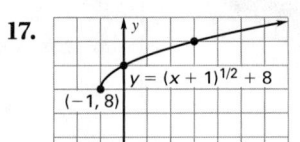 Domain: $x \geq -1$

Range: $y \geq 8$

37. a. $v = 331.5\sqrt{\dfrac{(273.15 + C)}{273.15}} = 331.5\sqrt{1 + \dfrac{C}{273.15}}$

   b. Domain: $C \geq -273.15$; range: $v \geq 0$

Lesson 3.6

5. $\sqrt{9x} + 11 = 14$ Check: $\sqrt{9(1)} + 11 \overset{?}{=} 14$

   $\qquad \sqrt{9x} = 3$ $\qquad\qquad \sqrt{9} + 11 \overset{?}{=} 14$

   $\qquad\quad 9x = 9 \rightarrow x = 1$ $\qquad\qquad\quad 14 = 14 \checkmark$

13. $\sqrt[3]{x} - 10 = -3$ Check: $\sqrt[3]{343} - 10 \overset{?}{=} -3$

   $\qquad\quad \sqrt[3]{x} = 7$ $\qquad\qquad\quad 7 - 10 \overset{?}{=} -3$

   $\qquad \left(\sqrt[3]{x}\right)^3 = (7)^3 \rightarrow x = 343$ $\qquad -3 = -3 \checkmark$

59. $h = 150$: $150 = 62.5\sqrt[3]{t} + 75.8$

   $\qquad\qquad\qquad 1.7 \approx t$

   $h = 250$: $250 = 625\sqrt[3]{t} + 75.8$

   $\qquad\qquad\qquad 21.7 \approx t$

The elephant with a shoulder height of 250 cm is about 20 years older than the elephant with the shoulder height of 150 cm.

Worked-Out Solutions

This section of the book provides step-by-step solutions to exercises with circled exercise numbers. These solutions provide models that can help guide your work with the homework exercises.

The separate **Selected Answers** section follows this section. It provides numerous answers that you can use to check your own answers.

Chapter 4

Lesson 4.1

17. 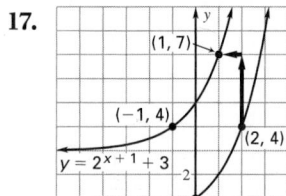 The domain is all real numbers and the range is $y > 3$.

29. $A = P\left(1 + \dfrac{r}{n}\right)^{nt} = 800\left(1 + \dfrac{0.02}{365}\right)^{365t}$

37. a. $P = 2200$; $r = 0.03$; $n = 4$; $t = 4$

$A = 2200\left(1 + \dfrac{0.03}{4}\right)^{4 \cdot 4} \approx 2479.38$

The balance is $2479.38.

b. $P = 2200$; $r = 0.0225$; $n = 12$; $t = 4$

$A = 2200\left(1 + \dfrac{0.0225}{12}\right)^{12 \cdot 4} \approx 2406.98$

The balance is $2406.98.

c. $P = 2200$; $r = 0.02$; $n = 365$; $t = 4$

$A = 2200\left(1 + \dfrac{0.02}{365}\right)^{365 \cdot 4} \approx 2383.23$

The balance is $2383.23.

Lesson 4.2

9.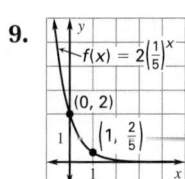

19.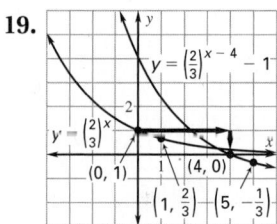

Domain: all real numbers
Range: $y > -1$

33. a.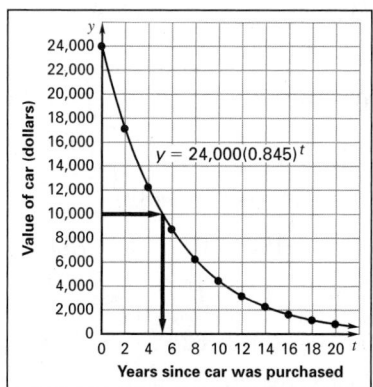

About 5 years after it was purchased

b. $y = 24{,}000(0.845)^{50} \approx \$5.29$; too low

Lesson 4.3

5. $(2e^{3x})^3 = 2^3(e^{3x})^3 = 8e^{9x}$

35. $f(x) = \dfrac{1}{4}e^{-5x}$; exponential decay

57. $P = 2000$; $r = 0.04$; $t = 5$

$A = Pe^{rt} = 2000e^{(0.04)(5)} \approx \$2442.81$

Lesson 4.4

13. $\left(\dfrac{1}{2}\right)^{-3} = 8$, so $\log_{1/2} 8 = -3$.

33. $\log_3 81^x = \log_3 (3^4)^x = \log_3 3^{4x} = 4x$

61. a. $E = 2.5 \times 10^{24}$

$M = 0.29(\ln(2.5 \times 10^{24})) - 9.9 \approx 6.39$

b. $M = 0.29(\ln E) - 9.9$

$\dfrac{M + 9.9}{0.29} = \ln E \to e^{(M + 9.9)/0.29} = E$

This represents the amount of energy released as a function of the energy magnitude.

Worked-Out Solutions

Lesson 4.5

11. $\log 144 = \log 12^2 = 2 \log 12 = 2.158$

17. $\log 3x^4 = \log 3 + \log x^4 = \log 3 + 4 \log x$

71. $L(10I) - L(I) = 10 \log \dfrac{10I}{I_0} - 10 \log \dfrac{I}{I_0}$

$= 10\left(\log \dfrac{10I}{I_0} - \log \dfrac{I}{I_0}\right)$

$= 10\left(\log 10 + \log \dfrac{I}{I_0} - \log \dfrac{I}{I_0}\right)$

$= 10 \log 10 = 10 \text{ decibels}$

Lesson 4.6

15. $11^{5x} = 33$

$\log_{11} 11^{5x} = \log_{11} 33$

$5x = \log_{11} 33 = \dfrac{\log 33}{\log 11} \to x \approx 0.2916$

35. $5.2 \log_4 2x = 16$ Check:

$\log_4 2x \approx 3.0769$

$4^{(\log_4 2x)} \approx 4^{3.0769}$

$2x \approx 71.2020$

$x \approx 35.6010$

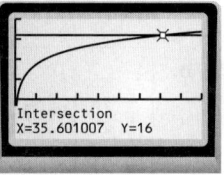

Intersection
X=35.601007 Y=16

57. $R = 100e^{-0.00043t} \to 5 = 100e^{-0.00043t}$

$0.05 = e^{-0.00043t}$

$\ln 0.05 = \ln e^{-0.00043t}$

$-2.9957 \approx -0.00043t$

$t \approx 6967 \text{ years}$

Lesson 4.7

11. $m = \dfrac{5.66 - 2.89}{5 - 1} \approx 0.69$

$\ln y - 2.89 = 0.69(x - 1)$

$\ln y = 0.69x + 2.2$

$y = e^{0.69x + 2.2}$

$y = e^{2.2}(e^{0.69})^x \approx 9(2)^x$

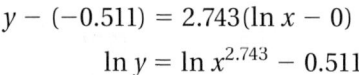

23.

ln x	0	0.693	1.099	1.386	1.609
ln y	−0.511	1.411	2.518	3.296	3.902

$m = \dfrac{3.902 - (-0.511)}{1.609 - 0} \approx 2.743$

$\ln y - (-0.511) = 2.743(\ln x - 0)$

$\ln y = \ln x^{2.743} - 0.511$

$y = e^{\ln x^{2.743} - 0.511}$

$y = e^{-0.511} \cdot e^{\ln x^{2.743}} \approx 0.6x^{2.743}$

33. a. A model is $y = 0.48(2.08)^x$.

b. Graph the transformed data pairs (x, y), $(x, \ln y)$, and $(\ln x, \ln y)$. If the graph of (x, y) is most linear, then a linear function is best. If the graph of $(x, \ln y)$ is most linear, then an exponential function is best. If the graph of $(\ln x, \ln y)$ is most linear, then a power function is best. If the graphs seem equally linear, use a graphing calculator to perform a linear regression on each set of transformed data pairs. Choose the type of model whose correlation coefficient is closest to 1. Then perform this type of regression on the original data; the best-fitting model is the power function $y = 55.7x^{0.793}$.

Worked-Out Solutions

This section of the book provides step-by-step solutions to exercises with circled exercise numbers. These solutions provide models that can help guide your work with the homework exercises.

The separate **Selected Answers** section follows this section. It provides numerous answers that you can use to check your own answers.

Chapter 5

Lesson 5.1

15. $y = \dfrac{a}{x} \rightarrow 2 = \dfrac{a}{7} \rightarrow 14 = a$

$y = \dfrac{14}{x} \rightarrow y = \dfrac{14}{3}$

21. $x \cdot y$: $12(132) = 1584$ y/x: $132/12 = 11$

$18(198) = 3564$ $198/18 = 11$

$23(253) = 5819$ $253/23 = 11$

$29(319) = 9251$ $319/29 = 11$

$34(374) = 12{,}716$ $374/34 = 11$

x and y show direct variation because the ratios y/x are equal.

39. Snow shoes: $P = \dfrac{a}{A} \rightarrow 0.43 = \dfrac{a}{400} \rightarrow 172 = a$

An equation is $P = \dfrac{172}{A}$.

Boots: $P = \dfrac{172}{60} \rightarrow P \approx 2.87$ lb/in.^{2}

Lesson 5.2

5.

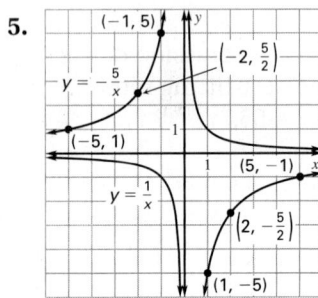

The graph of $y = \dfrac{-5}{x}$ lies farther from the axes than the graph of $y = \dfrac{1}{x}$, and it lies in Quadrants II and IV instead of Quadrants I and III.

21.

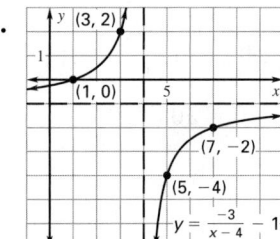

The domain is all real numbers except 4, and the range is all real numbers except -1.

39. a. $t = \dfrac{1000}{0.6T + 331} = \dfrac{1000}{0.6(25) + 331} \approx 2.89$

2.89 seconds to travel 1 kilometer;
$2.89(5) = 14.45$ seconds to travel 5 kilometers

39. b.

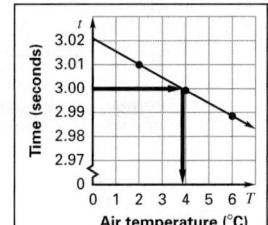

From the graph, you can estimate the temperature to be 3.9°C.

Lesson 5.3

7. $y = \dfrac{5}{x^2 - 1} \rightarrow y = \dfrac{5}{(x + 1)(x - 1)}$

No x-intercept; $x = -1$ and $x = 1$ are vertical asymptotes.

15.

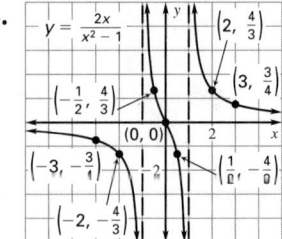

Worked-Out Solutions

33. a.

Depth	Temp.
1000	4.7634
1050	4.5796
1100	4.4094
1150	4.2515
1200	4.1044
1250	3.9672
1300	3.8389

b.

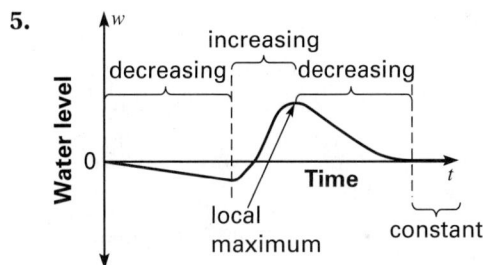

The mean temperature is 4°C at about 1238 meters.

Lesson 5.4

7. $\dfrac{(x-5)(x+4)}{(x+5)(x-3)}$ Cannot be simplified

25. $\dfrac{48x^7y^4}{6x^3y^6} = \dfrac{\cancel{6} \cdot 8 \cdot \cancel{x^3} \cdot x^4 \cdot \cancel{y^4}}{\cancel{6} \cdot \cancel{x^3} \cdot \cancel{y^4} \cdot y^2} = \dfrac{8x^4}{y^2}$

49.

$S \div A = \dfrac{-6420t + 292{,}000}{6.02t^2 - 125t + 1000} \div \dfrac{-407t + 7220}{5.92t^2 - 131t + 1000}$

$= \dfrac{-6420t + 292{,}000}{6.02t^2 - 125t + 1000} \cdot \dfrac{5.92t^2 - 131t + 1000}{-407t + 7220}$

For 1999, $t = 7$: $S \div A = \dfrac{247{,}060}{419.98} \cdot \dfrac{373.08}{4371} \approx \$50.21$

Lesson 5.5

5. $\dfrac{9}{x+1} - \dfrac{2x}{x+1} = \dfrac{9-2x}{x+1}$

17. $\dfrac{8}{3x^2} - \dfrac{5}{4x} = \dfrac{32}{12x^2} - \dfrac{15x}{12x^2} = \dfrac{32-15x}{12x^2}$

43. a. $M = \dfrac{Pi}{1 - \left(\dfrac{1}{1+i}\right)^{12t}} = \dfrac{Pi}{1 - \dfrac{1}{(1+i)^{12t}}}$

$= \dfrac{Pi}{\dfrac{(1+i)^{12t} - 1}{(1+i)^{12t}}} = \dfrac{Pi(1+i)^{12t}}{(1+i)^{12t} - 1}$

b. $P = 15{,}500;\ i = 0.005;\ t = 4$

$m = \dfrac{15{,}500(0.005)(1 + 0.005)^{48}}{(1 + 0.005)^{48} - 1} \approx \$364.02$

Lesson 5.6

5. $\dfrac{9}{3x} = \dfrac{4}{x+2}$ 　　Check: $\dfrac{9}{3(6)} \overset{?}{=} \dfrac{4}{(6)+2}$

$4(3x) = 9(x+2)$ 　　　　　$\dfrac{9}{18} \overset{?}{=} \dfrac{4}{8}$

$x = 6$ 　　　　　　　　$\dfrac{1}{2} = \dfrac{1}{2}$ ✓

15. $\dfrac{2}{3x} + \dfrac{1}{6} = \dfrac{4}{3x}$ 　　Check: $\dfrac{2}{3(4)} + \dfrac{1}{6} \overset{?}{=} \dfrac{4}{3(4)}$

$6x\left(\dfrac{2}{3x} + \dfrac{1}{6}\right) = 6x\left(\dfrac{4}{3x}\right)$ 　　$\dfrac{2}{12} + \dfrac{1}{6} \overset{?}{=} \dfrac{4}{12}$

$2(2) + 1(x) = 4(2) \rightarrow x = 4$ 　　$\dfrac{4}{12} = \dfrac{4}{12}$ ✓

35. $n = \dfrac{635t^2 - 7350t + 27{,}200}{t^2 - 11.5t + 39.4}$

$720 = \dfrac{635t^2 - 7350t + 27{,}200}{t^2 - 11.5t + 39.4}$

$720t^2 - 8280t + 28{,}368 = 635t^2 - 7350t + 27{,}200$

$85t^2 - 930 + 1168 = 0$

$t = \dfrac{930 \pm \sqrt{(930)^2 - 4(1168)(85)}}{2(85)} \approx 1.45,\ 9.45$

Because 9.45 is not in the domain ($0 \le t \le 9$), $t \approx 1.45 \rightarrow 1995$.

Lesson 5.7

5.

27. *Sample answer:* The y-intercept for the sports utility vehicle (from the graph), is 30,000, while it is 25,000 for the minivan, since when $t = 0$, $y = 25{,}000(0.82)^0 = 25{,}000$. This means that the initial value is higher for the sports utility vehicle.

After 15 years, the SUV's value is about \$3000, which is about 10% of the initial value. After 15 years, the value of the minivan is $(0.82)^{15}$, or about 5% of the initial value. So, not only does the minivan start with a lesser value, but it loses its value at a faster rate than does the SUV.

This section of the book provides step-by-step solutions to exercises with circled exercise numbers. These solutions provide models that can help guide your work with the homework exercises.

The separate **Selected Answers** section follows this section. It provides numerous answers that you can use to check your own answers.

Chapter 6

Lesson 6.1

17. *Exactly one queen*: Choose 1 of the 4 queens and 4 of the 48 that are not queens.

$$_4C_1 \cdot {}_{48}C_4 = \frac{4!}{3!1!} \cdot \frac{48!}{44!4!} = 778{,}320$$

No queen: Choose 5 cards from the 48 in a deck that are not queens.

$$_{48}C_5 = \frac{48!}{43!5!} = 1{,}712{,}304$$

The total number of possible hands is $778{,}320 + 1{,}712{,}304 = 2{,}490{,}624$.

29. $(2s^4 + 5)^5 = {}_5C_0(2s^4)^5 5^0 + {}_5C_1(2s^4)^4 5^1$

$$+ {}_5C_2(2s^4)^3 5^2 + {}_5C_3(2s^4)^2 5^3 + {}_5C_4(2s^4)^1 5^4$$

$$+ {}_5C_5(2s^4)^0 5^5 = 1(32s^{20}) + 5(16s^{16})(5)$$

$$+ 10(8s^{12})(25) + 10(4s^8)(125) + 5(2s^4)(625)$$

$$+ 1(1)(3125) = 32s^{20} + 400s^{16} + 2000s^{12}$$

$$+ 5000s^8 + 6250s^4 + 3125$$

49. You can choose 3 of the 18 types of flowers.

$$_{18}C_3 = \frac{18!}{15!3!} = \frac{18 \cdot 17 \cdot 16 \cdot \cancel{15!}}{\cancel{15!} \cdot 3!} = 816$$

Lesson 6.2

5.

N	Outcomes	P(N)
1	10	$\frac{10}{100} = \frac{1}{100}$
2	90	$\frac{90}{1000} = \frac{9}{100}$
3	900	$\frac{900}{1000} = \frac{9}{10}$

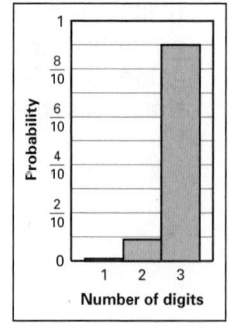

21. Each question has 4 possible answers, so the probability of guessing a correct answer is $p = 0.25$. There are 30 questions, so $n = 30$. The probability of randomly guessing 11 correct answers is $P(k = 11) =$ $_{30}C_{11}(0.25)^{11}(1 - 0.25)^{30 - 11} \approx 0.055$.

45. a. $p = 0.34$;

$$P(k = 5) = {}_{10}C_5(0.34)^5(1 - 0.34)^{10 - 5} \approx 0.14$$

b. $p = P(\text{Rh}^-) = P(\text{O}^-) + P(\text{A}^-) + P(\text{B}^-) + P(\text{AB}^-)$

$$= 0.15$$

$$P(k = 2) = {}_{10}C_2(0.15)^2(1 - 0.15)^{10 - 2} \approx 0.28$$

c. $p = P(\text{O}) = P(\text{O}^+) + P(\text{O}^-) = 0.43$

$$P(k = 0) = {}_{10}C_0(0.43)^0(1 - 0.43)^{10 - 0} \approx 0.004$$

$$P(k = 1) = {}_{10}C_1(0.43)^1(1 - 0.43)^{10 - 1} \approx 0.027$$

$$P(k = 2) = {}_{10}C_2(0.43)^2(1 - 0.43)^{10 - 2} \approx 0.093$$

$$P(k \le 2) = P(k = 0) + P(k = 1) + P(k = 2)$$

$$\approx 0.124$$

d. $p = P(\text{Rh}^+) = P(\text{O}^+) + P(\text{A}^+) + P(\text{B}^+)$

$$+ P(\text{AB}^+) = 0.85$$

$$P(k = 5) = {}_{10}C_5(0.85)^5(1 - 0.85)^{10 - 5} \approx 0.008$$

$$P(k = 6) = {}_{10}C_6(0.85)^6(1 - 0.85)^{10 - 6} \approx 0.040$$

$$P(k = 7) = {}_{10}C_7(0.85)^7(1 - 0.85)^{10 - 7} \approx 0.130$$

$$P(k = 8) = {}_{10}C_8(0.85)^8(1 - 0.85)^{10 - 8} \approx 0.276$$

$$P(k = 9) = {}_{10}C_9(0.85)^9(1 - 0.85)^{10 - 9} \approx 0.347$$

$$P(k = 10) = {}_{10}C_{10}(0.85)^{10}(1 - 0.85)^{10 - 10} \approx 0.197$$

$$P(k \ge 5) = P(k = 5) + P(k = 6) + P(k = 7)$$

$$+ P(k = 8) + P(k = 9) + P(k = 10) \approx 0.998$$

Worked-Out Solutions

Lesson 6.3

3. $P(x \leq \bar{x} - \sigma) = 0.0015 + 0.0235 + 0.135 = 0.16$

11. 29 and 37 are one standard deviation on either side of the mean, which accounts for 68% of the data. So, the probability is 0.68.

33. a. 19.4 ounces: $z = \dfrac{19.4 - 20}{0.25} = -2.4$

20.4 ounces: $z = \dfrac{20.4 - 20}{0.25} = 1.6$

b. The table shows that $P(x \leq -2.4) = 0.0082$. So, the probability is 0.0082.

c. $P(x \leq 20.4) = 0.9452$; $P(x \leq 19.4) = 0.0082$

$P(x \leq 20.4) - P(x \leq 19.4) = 0.937$

Lesson 6.4

7. Margin of error $= \pm \dfrac{1}{\sqrt{n}} = \pm \dfrac{1}{\sqrt{1000}} \approx \pm 0.032$

The margin of error is about $\pm 3.2\%$.

19. Margin of error $= \pm \dfrac{1}{\sqrt{n}}$

$\pm 0.056 = \pm \dfrac{1}{\sqrt{n}}$

$0.003136 = \dfrac{1}{n} \rightarrow n \approx 319$

29. *Sample answer*: It is not reasonable to assume that Kosta is going to win the election, because the margin of error is $\pm 5\%$. If the margin of error works in favor of Murdock, Kosta will have 49% (54% $-$ 5%) and Murdock will have 51% (46% $+$ 5%).

Lesson 6.5

5. *Sample answer:* Arsenic is poisonous, so saying that water from one supply has twice as much as water from another and stating that this is a "health problem" both bias the answer toward "Yes, the government should do something." But because arsenic is also an element that occurs naturally in tiny quantities virtually everywhere, more information must be given to obtain less biased answers. For example, you could tell those questioned the actual levels of arsenic in the water supplies, the level that various health authorities consider safe, and the levels in water supplies for other areas.

15. Because the study only examines driving records, no treatment is being imposed, so it is an observational study, not an experiment. Furthermore, it does not even mention whether drivers are chosen at random. The conclusions may not be valid, since controls are not imposed. Other variables might play a role. For example, the early risers might tend to drive to work when there is less traffic, before the main rush hour.

Worked-Out Solutions

This section of the book provides step-by-step solutions to exercises with circled exercise numbers. These solutions provide models that can help guide your work with the homework exercises.

The separate **Selected Answers** section follows this section. It provides numerous answers that you can use to check your own answers.

Chapter 7

Lesson 7.1

19. $\dfrac{2}{3 \cdot 1}, \dfrac{2}{3 \cdot 2}, \dfrac{2}{3 \cdot 3}, \dfrac{2}{3 \cdot 4}, \ldots$

Next term: $\dfrac{2}{3 \cdot 5} = \dfrac{2}{15}$; A rule is $a_n = \dfrac{2}{3n}$.

47. $\displaystyle\sum_{n=0}^{4} n^3 = 0^3 + 1^3 + 2^3 + 3^3 + 4^3$

$\qquad = 0 + 1 + 8 + 27 + 64 = 100$

65.

n	1	2	3	4	5
a_n	1	3	7	15	31

A formula for the sequence is $a_n = 2^n - 1$.

$a_6 = 2^6 - 1 = 63$ moves for 6 rings

$a_7 = 2^7 - 1 = 127$ moves for 7 rings

$a_8 = 2^8 - 1 = 255$ moves for 8 rings

Lesson 7.2

15. Arithmetic sequence

$a_1 = -3; d = -1 - (-3) = 2$

A rule for the nth term is

$a_n = a_1 + (n - 1)d = -3 + (n - 1)2 = 2n - 5$

$a_{20} = 2(20) - 5 = 35$

41. $\displaystyle\sum_{i=1}^{8} (-3 - 2i)$

$a_1 = -3 - 2(1) = -5; a_8 = -3 - 2(8) = -19$

$s_8 = 8\left(\dfrac{-5 + (-19)}{2}\right) = -96$

65. a. $a_1 = 4; d = 8$

$a_n = a_1 + (n - 1)d = 4 + (n - 1)8 = -4 + 8n$

b. $a_{12} + a_{11} + \cdots + a_2 + a_1 = 576$ blocks

Lesson 7.3

19. Geometric sequence; $a_1 = 2; r = \dfrac{\frac{3}{2}}{2} = \dfrac{3}{4}$

$a_n = a_1 r^{n-1} = 2\left(\dfrac{3}{4}\right)^{n-1}$

$a_7 = 2\left(\dfrac{3}{4}\right)^{7-1} = \dfrac{1458}{4096} = \dfrac{729}{2048}$

49. $\displaystyle\sum_{i=1}^{8} 6(4)^{i-1}$

$a_1 = 6(4)^{1-1} = 6; r = 4$

$s_8 = a_1\left(\dfrac{1 - r^8}{1 - r}\right) = 6\left(\dfrac{1 - 4^8}{1 - 4}\right) = 131{,}070$

59. a. $a_1 = 1024 \div 2 = 512; r = \dfrac{1}{2}$

$a_n = a_1(r)^{n-1} = 512\left(\dfrac{1}{2}\right)^{n-1}$

b. $n = 10$; after 10 passes, the number of items remaining is $a_{10} = 512\left(\dfrac{1}{2}\right)^{10-1} = 1$.

Lesson 7.4

13. $\displaystyle\sum_{k=1}^{\infty} 7\left(-\dfrac{8}{9}\right)^{k-1}$

$a_1 = 7; r = -\dfrac{8}{9}; s = \dfrac{a_1}{1 - r} = \dfrac{7}{1 - \left(-\frac{8}{9}\right)} = \dfrac{63}{17}$

27. $625(0.001) + 625(0.001)^2 + 625(0.001)^3 + \cdots$

$= \dfrac{a_1}{1 - r} - \dfrac{625(0.001)}{1 - 0.001} = \dfrac{0.625}{0.999} = \dfrac{625}{999}$

39. D;

$$n = 345 + 345(0.783) + 345(0.783)^2$$
$$+ 345(0.783)^3 + \cdots$$

$$= \frac{a_1}{1 - r} = \frac{345}{1 - 0.783} \approx 1.59 \text{ billion}$$

Lesson 7.5

15. Geometric sequence; $a_1 = 4$; $r = -3$

$a_n = r \cdot a_{n-1} = -3a_{n-1}$

A recursive rule is $a_1 = 4$, $a_n = -3a_{n-1}$.

27. $f(x) = \frac{1}{2}x - 3$, $x_0 = 2$

$x_1 = f(x_0)$	$x_2 = f(x_1)$	$x_3 = f(x_2)$
$= f(2)$	$= f(-2)$	$= f(-4)$
$= \frac{1}{2}(2) - 3$	$= \frac{1}{2}(-2) - 3$	$= \frac{1}{2}(-4) - 3$
$= -2$	$= -4$	$= -5$

45. Recursive rule:

$a_1 = 2000$, $a_n = 1.014a_{n-1} - 100$.

Because $a_{24} = 62.14$, the balance at the beginning of the 24th month is $62.14. So, she will be able to pay off the balance at the end of the 24th month.

This section of the book provides step-by-step solutions to exercises with circled exercise numbers. These solutions provide models that can help guide your work with the homework exercises.

The separate **Selected Answers** section follows this section. It provides numerous answers that you can use to check your own answers.

Chapter 8

Lesson 8.1

7. $d = \sqrt{(6-2)^2 + (-5-(-1))^2} = 4\sqrt{2}$

Midpoint $= \left(\dfrac{2+6}{2}, \dfrac{-1+(-5)}{2}\right) = (4, -3)$

27. $A(-4, 1)$, $B(-2, 6)$, $C(0, -1)$

$AB = \sqrt{(-2-(-4))^2 + (6-1)^2} = \sqrt{29}$

$BC = \sqrt{(0-(-2))^2 + (-1-6)^2} = \sqrt{53}$

$AC = \sqrt{(0-(-4))^2 + (-1-1)^2} = \sqrt{20} = 2\sqrt{5}$

$AB \neq BC \neq AC$, so $\triangle ABC$ is scalene.

53. a. $M = \left(\dfrac{-6+3}{2}, \dfrac{5+11}{2}\right) = \left(-\dfrac{3}{2}, 8\right)$

b. $VS = \sqrt{(-6-0)^2 + (5-0)^2} = \sqrt{61}$

$SM = \sqrt{\left(-\dfrac{3}{2}-(-6)\right)^2 + (8-5)^2} = \dfrac{\sqrt{117}}{2}$

$VS + SM = \sqrt{61} + \dfrac{\sqrt{117}}{2}$

$\approx 13.2 \; \text{units} \cdot \dfrac{0.1\,\text{mi}}{1\,\text{unit}} = 1.32\,\text{mi}$

c. $MP = \dfrac{\sqrt{117}}{2}$

$PV = \sqrt{(0-3)^2 + (0-11)^2} = \sqrt{130}$

$MP + PV = \dfrac{\sqrt{117}}{2} + \sqrt{130}$

$\approx 16.8 \; \text{units} \cdot \dfrac{0.1\,\text{mi}}{1\,\text{unit}} = 1.68\,\text{mi}$

Lesson 8.2

15. $5x^2 = -15y \rightarrow x^2 = -3y$

$4p = -3 \rightarrow p = -\dfrac{3}{4}$

Focus: $\left(0, -\dfrac{3}{4}\right)$

Directrix: $y = \dfrac{3}{4}$ Axis of symmetry: $x = 0$

27. Focus: $(-5, 0) \rightarrow p = -5 \rightarrow y^2 = -20x$

57. a.

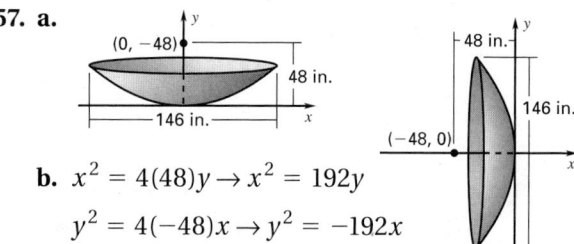

b. $x^2 = 4(48)y \rightarrow x^2 = 192y$

$y^2 = 4(-48)x \rightarrow y^2 = -192x$

c. Using $x^2 = 192y$ and $x = 73$, $y \approx 27.8$

Using $y^2 = -192x$ and $y = 73$, $x \approx -27.8$.

The dish is about 27.8 inches deep.

Lesson 8.3

17. $15x^2 + 15y^2 = 60$

$x^2 + y^2 = 4$

$r = \sqrt{4} = 2$

39. $r = \sqrt{(-8-0)^2 + (14-0)^2} = \sqrt{260}$

$x^2 + y^2 = (\sqrt{260})^2 \rightarrow x^2 + y^2 = 260$

65.

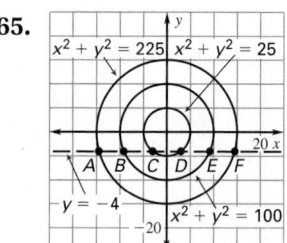

$A: x^2 + (-4)^2 = 225 \rightarrow x \approx \pm14.5 \rightarrow (-14.5, -4)$

$B: x^2 + (-4)^2 = 100 \rightarrow x \approx \pm9.2 \rightarrow (-9.2, -4)$

$C: x^2 + (-4)^2 = 25 \rightarrow x = \pm3 \rightarrow (-3, -4)$

$D: x^2 + (-4)^2 = 25 \rightarrow x = \pm3 \rightarrow (3, -4)$

$E: x^2 + (-4)^2 = 100 \rightarrow x \approx \pm9.2 \rightarrow (9.2, -4)$

$F: x^2 + (-4)^2 = 225 \rightarrow x \approx \pm14.5 \rightarrow (14.5, -4)$

a. $AF \approx \left|14.5 - (-14.5)\right| = 29$ mi

b. $BE \approx \left|9.2 - (-9.2)\right| = 18.4$ mi

c. $CD \approx \left|3 - (-3)\right| = 6$ mi

Lesson 8.4

11. $16x^2 + 9y^2 = 144$

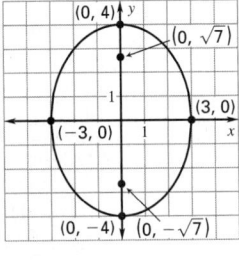

$\dfrac{x^2}{9} + \dfrac{y^2}{16} = 1$; $a = 4$, $b = 3$

Vertices: $(0, \pm 4)$;

Co-vertices: $(\pm 3, 0)$;

Foci: $\left(0, \pm\sqrt{7}\right)$

29. $b = \sqrt{7}$; $c = 3$; $a^2 = b^2 + c^2 \to a = 4$

$\dfrac{x^2}{4^2} + \dfrac{y^2}{(\sqrt{7})^2} = 1$, or $\dfrac{x^2}{16} + \dfrac{y^2}{7} = 1$

49. Largest field:

$2a = 185 \to a = 92.5$; $2b = 155 \to b = 77.5$

$\dfrac{x^2}{77.5^2} + \dfrac{y^2}{92.5^2} = 1$, or $\dfrac{x^2}{6006.25} + \dfrac{y^2}{8556.25} = 1$

$A = \pi(92.5)(77.5) \approx 22{,}521$ square meters

Smallest field:

$2a = 135 \to a = 67.5$; $2b = 110 \to b = 55$

$\dfrac{x^2}{55^2} + \dfrac{y^2}{67.5^2} = 1$, or $\dfrac{x^2}{3025} + \dfrac{y^2}{4556.25} = 1$

$A = \pi(67.5)(55) \approx 11{,}663$ square meters

$11{,}663 \le A \le 22{,}521$

Lesson 8.5

13. $81x^2 - 16y^2 = 1296$

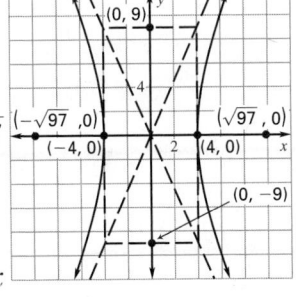

$\dfrac{x^2}{16} - \dfrac{y^2}{81} = 1$

$a = 4$; $b = 9$; $c = \sqrt{97}$

Vertices: $(\pm 4, 0)$

Foci: $\left(\pm\sqrt{97}, 0\right)$

Asymptotes: $y = \pm\dfrac{9}{4}x$

23. $c = 4\sqrt{5}$; $a = 4$; $b^2 = c^2 - a^2 = 64$; $b = 8$

$\dfrac{y^2}{4^2} - \dfrac{x^2}{8^2} = 1$, or $\dfrac{y^2}{16} - \dfrac{x^2}{64} = 1$

41. a. $A(30.5, 0)$; $B(85, -40)$

b. Vertices: $(\pm 30.5, 0)$; horizontal trans. axis

$\dfrac{x^2}{a^2} - \dfrac{y^2}{b^2} = 1 \to \dfrac{x^2}{30.5^2} - \dfrac{y^2}{b^2} = 1$

$\dfrac{85^2}{30.5^2} - \dfrac{(-40)^2}{b^2} = 1 \to b^2 \approx 236.5$

So, an equation is $\dfrac{x^2}{930.25} - \dfrac{y^2}{236.5} = 1$.

c. $x = 42$: $\dfrac{42^2}{930.25} - \dfrac{y^2}{236.5} = 1 \to y \approx 14.6$

$h = 40 + 14.6 = 54.6$ feet

Lesson 8.6

3. $(x + 4)^2 = -8(y - 2)$

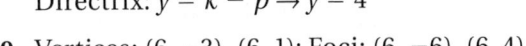

Parabola; vertical axis; vertex at $(h, k) = (-4, 2)$.

$4p = -8 \to p = -2$

Focus: $(h, k + p) = (-4, 0)$

Directrix: $y = k - p \to y = 4$

19. Vertices: $(6, -3)$, $(6, 1)$; Foci: $(6, -6)$, $(6, 4)$

Vertical transverse axis; $\dfrac{(y - k)^2}{a^2} - \dfrac{(x - h)^2}{b^2} = 1$

Center: $(h, k) = \left(\dfrac{6 + 6}{2}, \dfrac{-3 + 1}{2}\right)$

Distance between vertex $(6, -3)$ and (h, k):

$a = \left|-3 - k\right| = \left|-3 - (-1)\right| = 2$

Distance between focus $(6, -6)$ and (h, k):

$c = \left|-6 - k\right| = \left|-6 - (-1)\right| = 5$

$b^2 = c^2 - a^2 = 25 - 4 = 21 \to b = \sqrt{21}$

An equation is $\dfrac{(y + 1)^2}{4} - \dfrac{(x - 6)^2}{21} = 1$.

49. $x^2 - 10x + 4y = 0$; $A = 1$, $B = 0$, $C = 0$

$B^2 - 4AC = 0 - 4(1)(0) = 0 \to$ Parabola

$x^2 - 10x + 4y = 0$

$\left(x^2 - 10x + 25\right) = -4y + 25$

$(x - 5)^2 = -4\left(y - \dfrac{25}{4}\right)$

$(h, k) = \left(5, \dfrac{25}{4}\right)$; height $= \dfrac{25}{4} = 6.25$ feet

When $y = 0$, the x-intercepts are 0 and 10, so the distance of the jump is 10 feet.

Worked-Out Solutions

Lesson 8.7

5.

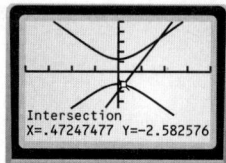 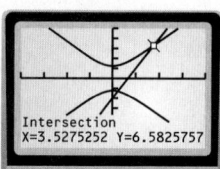

The solutions are approximately $(0.5, -2.6)$ and $(3.5, 6.6)$.

15. $4x^2 - 5y^2 = -76$

$2x + y = -6 \rightarrow y = -2x - 6$

Substitute $-2x - 6$ for y in Equation 1.

$$4x^2 - 5(-2x - 6)^2 = -76$$

$$4x^2 - 20x^2 - 120x - 180 = -76$$

$$-16x^2 - 120x - 104 = 0$$

$$2x^2 + 15x + 13 = 0$$

$$(2x + 2)\left(x + \frac{13}{2}\right) = 0 \rightarrow x = -1, x = -\frac{13}{2}$$

When $x = -1$: $y = -2(-1) - 6 = -4$

When $x = -\frac{13}{2}$: $y = -2\left(-\frac{13}{2}\right) - 6 = 7$

The solutions are $(-1, -4)$ and $\left(-\frac{13}{2}, 7\right)$.

41. a. Oak Lane: $m = -\frac{1}{7}$, $(x_1, y_1) = (-2, 1)$

$$y - 1 = -\frac{1}{7}(x + 2) \rightarrow y = -\frac{1}{7}x + \frac{5}{7}$$

Circle: $x^2 + y^2 = 1$

b. $x^2 + \left(-\frac{1}{7}x + \frac{5}{7}\right)^2 = 1$

$$x^2 + \frac{1}{49}x^2 - \frac{10}{49}x + \frac{25}{49} = 1$$

$$49x^2 + x^2 - 10x + 25 = 49$$

$$50x^2 - 10x - 24 = 0$$

$$(5x - 4)(10x + 6) = 0 \rightarrow x = \frac{4}{5}, x = -\frac{3}{5}$$

$$y = -\frac{1}{7}\left(\frac{4}{5}\right) + \frac{5}{7} = \frac{3}{5}; \; y = -\frac{1}{7}\left(-\frac{3}{5}\right) + \frac{5}{7} = \frac{4}{5}$$

The solutions are $\left(\frac{4}{5}, \frac{3}{5}\right)$ and $\left(-\frac{3}{5}, \frac{4}{5}\right)$.

c. $d = \sqrt{\left(-\frac{3}{5} - \frac{4}{5}\right)^2 + \left(\frac{4}{5} - \frac{3}{5}\right)^2} = \sqrt{2} \approx 1.4$ mi

Mastering the Standards

for Mathematical Practice

The topics described in the Standards for Mathematical Content will vary from year to year. However, the *way* in which you learn, study, and think about mathematics will not. The Standards for Mathematical Practice describe skills that you will use in all of your math courses.

Mathematical Practices

1. *Make sense of problems and persevere in solving them.*
2. *Reason abstractly and quantitatively.*
3. *Construct viable arguments and critique the reasoning of others.*
4. *Model with mathematics.*
5. *Use appropriate tools strategically.*
6. *Attend to precision.*
7. *Look for and make use of structure.*
8. *Look for and express regularity in repeated reasoning.*

---

① Make sense of problems and persevere in solving them.

Mathematically proficient students start by explaining to themselves the meaning of a problem... They analyze givens, constraints, relationships, and goals. They make conjectures about the form... of the solution and plan a solution pathway...

In your book

Verbal Models and the **Problem Solving Plan** help you translate the information in a problem into a model and then analyze your solution.

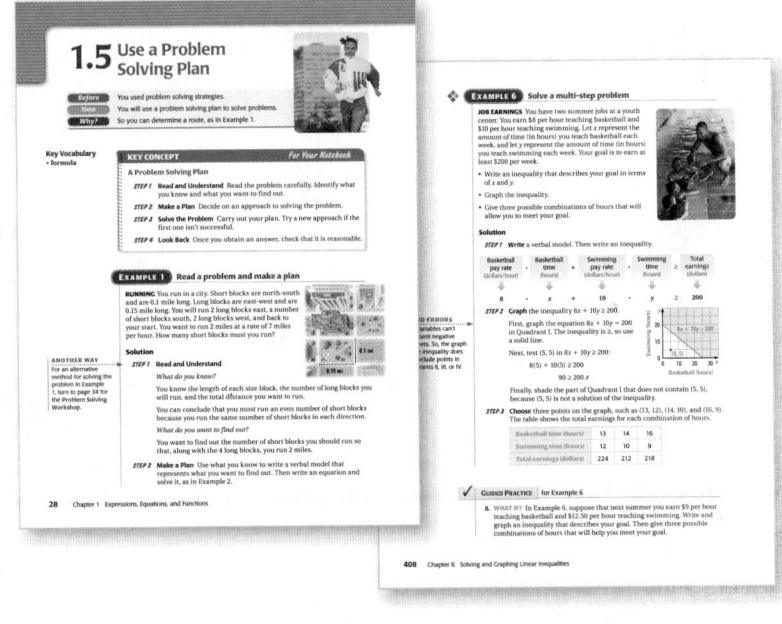

This section of the book provides step-by-step solutions to exercises with circled exercise numbers. These solutions provide models that can help guide your work with the homework exercises.

The separate **Selected Answers** section follows this section. It provides numerous answers that you can use to check your own answers.

Chapter 9

Lesson 9.1

5. 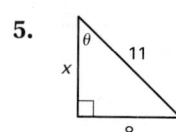 Using the Pythagorean theorem:
$$x = \sqrt{11^2 - 8^2} = \sqrt{57}$$

$$\sin \theta = \frac{8}{11} \qquad \cos \theta = \frac{\sqrt{57}}{11} \qquad \tan \theta = \frac{8\sqrt{57}}{57}$$

$$\csc \theta = \frac{11}{8} \qquad \sec \theta = \frac{11\sqrt{57}}{57} \qquad \cot \theta = \frac{\sqrt{57}}{8}$$

11. $\tan \theta = \frac{\text{opp}}{\text{adj}} = \frac{7}{3}$

$$x = \sqrt{7^2 + 3^2} = \sqrt{58}$$

$$\sin \theta = \frac{7\sqrt{58}}{58} \qquad \cos \theta = \frac{3\sqrt{58}}{58} \qquad \tan \theta = \frac{7}{3}$$

$$\csc \theta = \frac{\sqrt{58}}{7} \qquad \sec \theta = \frac{\sqrt{58}}{3} \qquad \cot \theta = \frac{3}{7}$$

33. 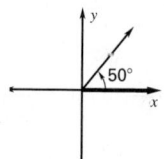 $\tan 15° = \dfrac{d}{1500}$

$$d \approx 402$$

The total depth is $402 + 250 = 652$ feet.

As the angle of the dive increases, the depth increases.

Lesson 9.2

11. $\dfrac{5\pi}{18} = \dfrac{5\,\pi\,\text{radians}}{18} \left(\dfrac{180°}{\pi\,\text{radians}} \right) = 50°$

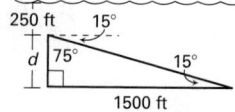

23. $40° = 40° \left(\dfrac{\pi \text{ radians}}{180°} \right) = \dfrac{2\pi}{9}$ radians

51. a. $\dfrac{15 \text{ rev}}{1 \text{ min}} \left(\dfrac{1 \text{ min}}{60 \text{ sec}} \right) \left(\dfrac{2\pi \text{ rad}}{1 \text{ rev}} \right) = \dfrac{\pi}{2}$ rad/sec

b. Arc length: $s = r\theta = 29\left(\dfrac{\pi}{2} \right) \approx 45.6$ feet

Lesson 9.3

5. $r = \sqrt{x^2 + y^2} = \sqrt{(-7)^2 + (-24)^2} = \sqrt{625} = 25$

$$\sin \theta = \frac{y}{r} = \frac{-24}{25} \qquad\qquad \cos \theta = \frac{x}{f} = \frac{-7}{25}$$

$$\tan \theta = \frac{y}{x} = \frac{-24}{-7} = \frac{24}{7} \quad \csc \theta = \frac{r}{y} = \frac{-25}{24}$$

$$\sec \theta = \frac{r}{x} = \frac{-25}{7} \qquad\qquad \cot \theta = \frac{x}{y} = \frac{7}{24}$$

17. 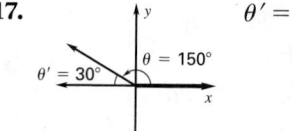 $\theta' = 180° - 150° = 30°$

37.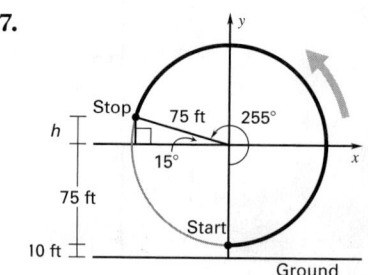

$$\theta' = 270° - 255° = 15°$$

$$\sin 15° = \frac{h}{75}$$

$$19.4 \approx h$$

When the ride stops, you are about $10 + 75 + 19.4 = 104.4$ feet above the ground. If the radius is doubled, your height above the ground is doubled only if your starting height above the ground is also doubled.

Lesson 9.4

7. When $-\dfrac{\pi}{2} \le \theta \le \dfrac{\pi}{2}$, or $-90° \le \theta \le 90°$, the

angle whose sine is $\dfrac{\sqrt{3}}{2}$ is $\theta = \sin^{-1} \dfrac{\sqrt{3}}{2} = \dfrac{\pi}{3}$,

or $\theta = \sin^{-1} \dfrac{\sqrt{3}}{2} = 60°$.

23.

$\tan \theta = 3.2$; $180° < \theta < 270°$

$\tan^{-1}(3.2) \approx 72.6°$, which is in Quadrant I. To find the angle in Quadrant III ($180° < \theta < 270°$): $\theta \approx 180 + 72.6 = 252.6°$

37.

$\tan \theta = \dfrac{11}{17}$

$\theta = \tan^{-1}\left(\dfrac{11}{17}\right) \approx 33°$

Because the angle of repose remains the same, you can use $\theta = 33°$ to find the radius of the 15 foot high pile:

$\tan 33° = \dfrac{15}{r} \rightarrow r = \dfrac{15}{\tan 33°}$

≈ 23

The diameter is about $d = 2r = 2(23) = 46$ ft.

Lesson 9.5

13. $\dfrac{\sin B}{16} = \dfrac{\sin 104°}{25}$

$\sin B = \dfrac{16 \sin 104°}{25} \approx 0.6210 \rightarrow B \approx 38.4°$

$A \approx 180° - 104° - 38.4° = 37.6°$

$\dfrac{a}{\sin 37.6°} = \dfrac{25}{\sin 104°} \rightarrow a = \dfrac{25 \sin 37.6°}{\sin 104°} \approx 15.7$

31. Area $= \dfrac{1}{2} bc \sin A$

$= \dfrac{1}{2}(29)(36)(\sin 34°)$

≈ 292 units^2

45. a.

b. $\dfrac{\sin C}{54} = \dfrac{\sin 58°}{62}$

$\sin C = \dfrac{54 \sin 58°}{62} \approx 0.7386 \rightarrow C \approx 47.6°$

$A \approx 180° - 58° - 47.6° = 74.4°$

$\dfrac{a}{\sin 74.4°} = \dfrac{62}{\sin 58°} \rightarrow a = \dfrac{62 \sin 74.4°}{\sin 58°} \approx 70.4$

c. Area $= \dfrac{1}{2} bc \sin A = \dfrac{1}{2}(62)(54)(\sin 74.4°)$

≈ 1612

$1612 \text{ ft}^2 \div 200 \text{ ft}^2/\text{bag} \approx 8.1$ bags

You will need 9 bags of fertilizer.

Lesson 9.6

17. $a^2 = b^2 + c^2 - 2bc \cos A$

$10^2 = 3^2 + 12^2 - 2(3)(12)\cos A$

$\dfrac{53}{72} = \cos A \rightarrow A \approx 43°$

$\dfrac{10}{\sin 43°} = \dfrac{3}{\sin B} \rightarrow \dfrac{3(\sin 43°)}{10} = \sin B$

$B \approx 12°$; $C \approx 180 - 43° - 12° = 125°$

In $\triangle ABC$, $A \approx 43°$, $B \approx 12°$, and $C \approx 125°$.

25. $s = \dfrac{1}{2}(a + b + c) = \dfrac{1}{2}(5 + 11 + 10) = 13$

Area $= \sqrt{s(s - a)(s - b)(s - c)}$

$= \sqrt{13(13 - 5)(13 - 11)(13 - 10)} = \sqrt{624}$

≈ 25 square units

45. $\triangle ADB$: $s = \dfrac{1}{2}(743 + 1210 + 1480) = 1716.5$

Area $=$

$\sqrt{1716.5(1716.5 - 743)(1716.5 - 1210)(1716.5 - 1480)}$

$\approx 447{,}399$

$\triangle CDB$: $s = \dfrac{1}{2}(1000 + 858 + 1480) = 1669$

Area =

$$\sqrt{1669(1669 - 1000)(1669 - 858)(1669 - 1480)}$$

$$\approx 413{,}697$$

Area $= (447{,}399 + 413{,}697)\ \text{ft}^2 \left(\dfrac{1\ \text{acre}}{43{,}560\ \text{ft}^2} \right)$

$$\approx 20\ \text{acres}$$

If you first found the length of $\overline{AC}$, you could repeat the same process using $\triangle ABC$ and $\triangle ADC$.

Mastering the Standards

for Mathematical Practice

The topics described in the Standards for Mathematical Content will vary from year to year. However, the *way* in which you learn, study, and think about mathematics will not. The Standards for Mathematical Practice describe skills that you will use in all of your math courses.

> ### Mathematical Practices
>
> 1. *Make sense of problems and persevere in solving them.*
> 2. *Reason abstractly and quantitatively.*
> 3. *Construct viable arguments and critique the reasoning of others.*
> 4. *Model with mathematics.*
> 5. *Use appropriate tools strategically.*
> 6. *Attend to precision.*
> 7. *Look for and make use of structure.*
> 8. *Look for and express regularity in repeated reasoning.*

④ Model with mathematics.

Mathematically proficient students can apply... mathematics... to... problems... in everyday life, society, and the workplace...

In your book

Application exercises and **Mixed Reviews of Problem Solving** apply mathematics to other disciplines and in real-world scenarios.

Worked-Out Solutions

This section of the book provides step-by-step solutions to exercises with circled exercise numbers. These solutions provide models that can help guide your work with the homework exercises.

The separate **Selected Answers** section follows this section. It provides numerous answers that you can use to check your own answers.

Chapter 10

Lesson 10.1

5. Amplitude: 1; period: 2

17. $f(x) = 4 \tan x$

Period: π; intercept: $(0, 0)$

Asymptotes: $x = \pm\dfrac{\pi}{2}$

Halfway points: $\left(\dfrac{\pi}{4}, 4\right)\left(-\dfrac{\pi}{4}, -4\right)$

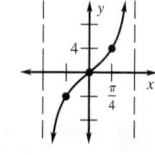

31. a. Equation has the form $y = a \cos bt$.

$a = \dfrac{1}{2}(3.5) = 1.75$

Period is 6, so $6 = \dfrac{2\pi}{b} \rightarrow b = \dfrac{\pi}{3}$.

Equation is $y = 1.75 \cos \dfrac{\pi}{3} t$.

b. Choose $y = a \cos bt$ because at $t = 0$, the buoy is at its highest point.

Lesson 10.2

11. $y = 2 \cos x + 1$

Amplitude: $a = 2$

Period: $\dfrac{2\pi}{b} = 2\pi$

Horizontal shift: $h = 0$; Vertical shift: $k = 1$

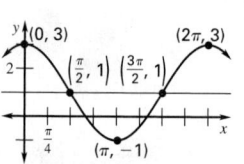

23. $y = -\sin \dfrac{1}{2} x + 3$

Amplitude: $|a| = 1$

Period: $\dfrac{2\pi}{b} = \dfrac{2\pi}{\frac{1}{2}} = 4\pi$

$h = 0$; $k = 3$; $a < 0$, so graph is reflected.

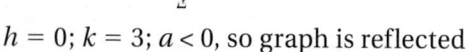

53. a. $\dfrac{200 - d}{300} = \tan \theta$

$d = -300 \tan \theta + 200$

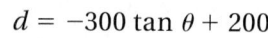
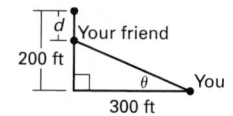

b.

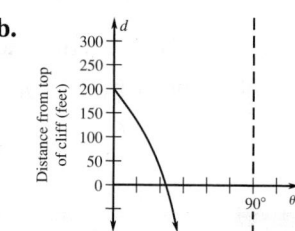

c. $100 = -300 \tan \theta + 200 \rightarrow \theta \approx 18.4°$

Lesson 10.3

5. $\cos \theta = \dfrac{5}{6}, \, 3\pi < \theta < 2\pi$

$\sin^2 \theta + \cos^2 \theta = 1$

$\sin^2 \theta + \left(\dfrac{5}{6}\right)^2 = 1$

$\sin \theta = -\dfrac{\sqrt{11}}{6} \leftarrow$ Negative because θ is in Quadrant III

$\tan \theta = \dfrac{\sin \theta}{\cos \theta} = -\dfrac{\sqrt{11}}{5}$ $\cot \theta = \dfrac{\cos \theta}{\sin \theta} = -\dfrac{5}{\sqrt{11}}$

$\csc \theta = \dfrac{1}{\sin \theta} = \dfrac{-6}{\sqrt{11}}$ $\sec \theta = \dfrac{1}{\cos \theta} = \dfrac{6}{5}$

11. $\dfrac{\sin(-\theta)}{\cos(-\theta)} = \dfrac{-\sin \theta}{\cos \theta} = -\tan \theta$

41. a. $r = \dfrac{1.069}{1 - 0.97 \sin\left(\frac{\pi}{2} - \theta\right)} = \dfrac{1.069}{1 - 0.97 \cos \theta}$

b.

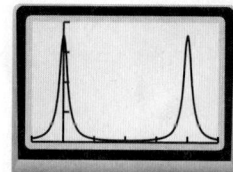

c.

θ	0	$\frac{\pi}{4}$	$\frac{\pi}{2}$	$\frac{3\pi}{4}$	π
r	35.6	3.4	1.1	0.6	0.5

θ	$\frac{5\pi}{4}$	$\frac{3\pi}{2}$	$\frac{7\pi}{4}$	2π
r	0.6	1.1	3.4	35.6

Closest distance:

0.543 a.u. $\cdot \dfrac{93{,}000{,}000 \text{ mi}}{1 \text{ a.u.}} \approx 50.5$ million mi

Farthest distance:

35.6 a.u. $\cdot \dfrac{93{,}000{,}000 \text{ mi}}{1 \text{ a.u.}} \approx 3.31$ billion mi

Lesson 10.4

5. $12\sin^2\left(\frac{\pi}{6}\right) - 3 \stackrel{?}{=} 0$

$12\left(\frac{1}{2}\right)^2 - 3 \stackrel{?}{=} 0 \rightarrow 3 - 3 = 0$ ✓

13. $4\cos^2 x - 3 = 0 \rightarrow \cos^2 x = \frac{3}{4} \rightarrow \cos x = \pm\frac{\sqrt{3}}{2}$

On $0 \leq x < 2\pi$, $x = \frac{\pi}{6}, \frac{5\pi}{6}, \frac{7\pi}{6},$ or $\frac{11\pi}{6}$.

$x = \frac{\pi}{6} + n\pi$ or $x = \frac{5\pi}{6} + n\pi$

43. a. $S = 6(1.5)(0.75) + \frac{3}{2}(0.75)^2\left(\dfrac{\sqrt{3} - \cos\theta}{\sin\theta}\right)$

$= 6.75 + 0.84375\left(\dfrac{\sqrt{3} - \cos\theta}{\sin\theta}\right)$

b.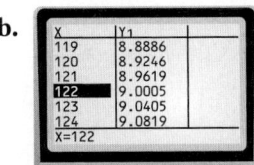

When $\theta \approx 122°$,
$S = 9$ in.^{2}

c.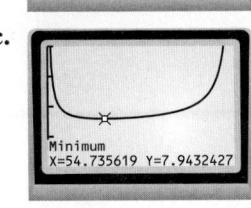

A value of $\theta \approx 54.7°$ minimizes the surface area.

Lesson 10.5

5. $M = 6,\ m = 2$

Vertical shift: $k = \dfrac{M+m}{2} = \dfrac{6+2}{2} = 4$

The graph is a cosine curve with $h = 0$.

Period $= 4 = \dfrac{2\pi}{b} \rightarrow b = \dfrac{\pi}{2}$

$|a| = \dfrac{M-m}{2} = \dfrac{6-2}{2} = 2$

The graph is a reflection, so $a = -2$.

The function is $y = -2\cos\frac{\pi}{2}x + 4$.

9. $M = 6,\ m = -6$

Vertical shift: $k = \dfrac{M+m}{2} = \dfrac{6+(-6)}{2} = 0$

The graph is a sine curve with $h = 0$.

Period $= 2(3\pi - \pi) = 4\pi = \dfrac{2\pi}{b} \rightarrow b = \dfrac{1}{2}$

$|a| = \dfrac{M-m}{2} = \dfrac{6-(-6)}{2} = 6$

The graph is not a reflection, so $a = 6$.

The function is $y = 6\sin\frac{1}{2}x$.

25. When $t = 0$, $m = 4$; when $t = 1$, $M = 9$.

$k = \dfrac{M+m}{2} = \dfrac{9+4}{2} = \dfrac{13}{2}$

The graph is a cosine curve with $h = 0$.

Period $= 2 = \dfrac{2\pi}{b} \rightarrow b = \pi$

$|a| = \dfrac{M-m}{2} = \dfrac{9-4}{2} = \dfrac{5}{2}$

The graph is a reflection, so $a = -\dfrac{5}{2}$.

A model is $y = -\dfrac{5}{2}\cos\pi x + \dfrac{13}{2}$.

Lesson 10.6

9. $\cos\left(-\dfrac{5\pi}{12}\right) = \cos\left(\dfrac{\pi}{3} - \dfrac{3\pi}{4}\right)$

$= \cos\frac{\pi}{3}\cos\frac{3\pi}{4} + \sin\frac{\pi}{3}\sin\frac{3\pi}{4}$

$= \frac{1}{2}\left(-\dfrac{\sqrt{2}}{2}\right) + \dfrac{\sqrt{3}}{2}\left(\dfrac{\sqrt{2}}{2}\right)$

$= \dfrac{\sqrt{6} - \sqrt{2}}{4}$

23. $\sin\left(x - \dfrac{3\pi}{2}\right) = \sin x\cos\frac{3\pi}{2} - \cos x\sin\frac{3\pi}{2}$

$= (\sin x)(0) - (\cos x)(-1) = \cos x$

43. a.

$$\frac{WQ}{NA} = \frac{f\tan(\theta - t) + f\tan t}{h\tan\theta}$$

$$= \frac{f}{h}\left(\tan(\theta - t) + \tan t\right)\left(\frac{1}{\tan\theta}\right)$$

$$= \frac{f}{h}\left(\frac{\tan\theta - \tan t}{1 + \tan\theta\tan t} + \frac{\tan t(1 + \tan\theta\tan t)}{1 + \tan\theta\tan t}\right)\left(\frac{1}{\tan\theta}\right)$$

$$= \frac{f}{h}\left(\frac{\tan\theta + \tan\theta\tan^2 t}{1 + \tan\theta\tan t}\right)\left(\frac{1}{\tan\theta}\right)$$

$$= \frac{f}{h}\left(\frac{\tan\theta(1 + \tan^2 t)}{1 + \tan\theta\tan t}\right)\left(\frac{1}{\tan\theta}\right)$$

$$= \frac{f}{h}\left(\frac{\sec^2 t}{1 + \tan\theta\tan t}\right)$$

b. When $t = 0$:

$$\frac{WQ}{NA} = \frac{f}{h}\left(\frac{\sec^2(0)}{1 + \tan\theta\tan(0)}\right) = \frac{f}{h}\left(\frac{1}{1 + 0}\right) = \frac{f}{h}$$

Lesson 10.7

7. $\cos\dfrac{\pi}{8} = \cos\dfrac{1}{2}\left(\dfrac{\pi}{4}\right) = \sqrt{\dfrac{1 + \cos\dfrac{\pi}{4}}{2}}$

$$= \sqrt{\dfrac{1 + \dfrac{\sqrt{2}}{2}}{2}} = \sqrt{\dfrac{2 + \sqrt{2}}{4}} = \dfrac{\sqrt{2 + \sqrt{2}}}{2}$$

13. $\cos a = \dfrac{1}{3}, \dfrac{3\pi}{2} < a < 2\pi$

$\dfrac{3\pi}{4} < \dfrac{a}{2} < \pi \rightarrow \dfrac{a}{2}$ is in Quadrant II.

$$\sin\frac{a}{2} = \sqrt{\frac{1 - \cos a}{2}} = \sqrt{\frac{1 - \frac{1}{3}}{2}} = \sqrt{\frac{1}{3}} = \frac{\sqrt{3}}{3}$$

$$\cos\frac{a}{2} = -\sqrt{\frac{1 + \cos a}{2}} = -\sqrt{\frac{1 + \frac{1}{3}}{2}} = -\sqrt{\frac{2}{3}} = -\frac{\sqrt{6}}{3}$$

$$\tan\frac{a}{2} = \frac{\sin\frac{a}{2}}{\cos\frac{a}{2}} = \frac{\frac{\sqrt{3}}{3}}{-\frac{\sqrt{6}}{3}} = \frac{\sqrt{3}}{3} \cdot \frac{-3}{\sqrt{6}} = \frac{-\sqrt{3}}{\sqrt{6}} = \frac{-\sqrt{2}}{2}$$

53. When $M = 2.5$: $\sin\dfrac{\theta}{2} = \dfrac{1}{M} = \dfrac{1}{2.5}$

Using the Pythagorean Theorem:

$$\cos\frac{\theta}{2} = \frac{\sqrt{5.25}}{2.5}$$

$$\sin\theta = 2\sin\frac{\theta}{2}\cos\frac{\theta}{2} = 2\left(\frac{1}{2.5}\right)\left(\frac{\sqrt{5.25}}{2.5}\right) \approx 0.7332$$

$$\theta \approx 47°$$

Mastering the Standards

for **Mathematical Practice**

The topics described in the Standards for Mathematical Content will vary from year to year. However, the *way* in which you learn, study, and think about mathematics will not. The Standards for Mathematical Practice describe skills that you will use in all of your math courses.

Mathematical Practices

1. *Make sense of problems and persevere in solving them.*
2. *Reason abstractly and quantitatively.*
3. *Construct viable arguments and critique the reasoning of others.*
4. *Model with mathematics.*
5. *Use appropriate tools strategically.*
6. *Attend to precision.*
7. *Look for and make use of structure.*
8. *Look for and express regularity in repeated reasoning.*

---

⑤ Use appropriate tools strategically.

Mathematically proficient students consider the available tools when solving a... problem... [and] are... able to use technological tools to explore and deepen their understanding...

In your book

Problem Solving Workshops explore alternative methods as tools for problem solving. A variety of **Activities** use concrete and technological tools to explore mathematical concepts.

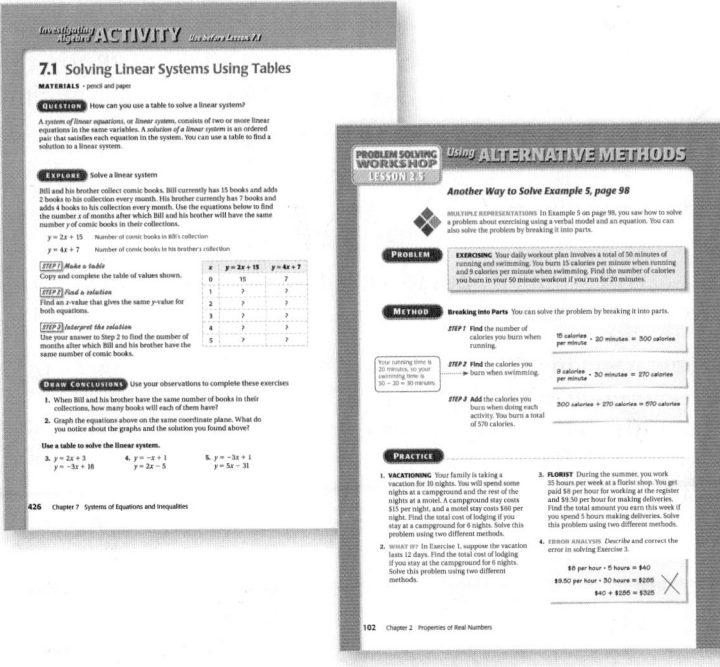

Getty Images/Image Source

Chapter 1

1.1 Skill Practice 1. parabola **3.** 16, 4, 0, 4, 16
5. 8, 2, 0, 2, 8

7. 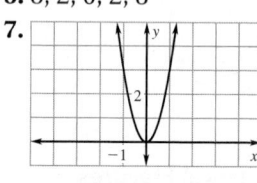 same axis of symmetry and vertex, opens up, and is narrower

9. 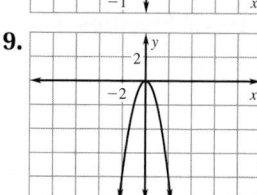 same axis of symmetry and vertex, opens down, and is narrower

19. The formula for the x-coordinate of the vertex is $-\dfrac{b}{2a}$: $-\dfrac{24}{2(4)} = -3$.

21. 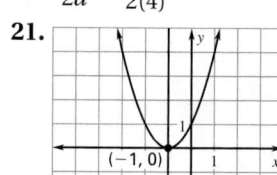 **23.**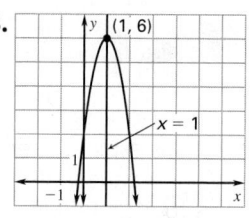

33. maximum value; -1 **35.** minimum value; -1
37. minimum value; -2 **41.** $a = -0.02$, $b = 1$, $c = 6$
43. *Sample answer:* $y = -x^2 + 8x + 3$,
$y = 2x^2 - 16x - 1$, $y = x^2 - 8x - 6$

47. 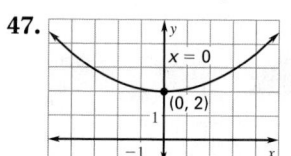 **49.**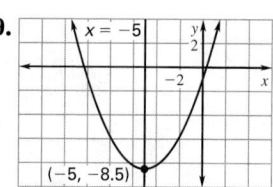

53. The axis of symmetry has to lie half way between the two x-coordinates; $x = -1$.

1.1 Problem Solving 55. Raise the price by $0.75 to increase revenue to $4900 per day.
57. about 10 ft **59. a.** profit = price • sales − expenses;
$P(x) = (20 - x)(150 + 10x) - 1500$

b.

x	P(x)
0	1500
1	1540
2	1560
3	1560
4	1540
5	1500

c. 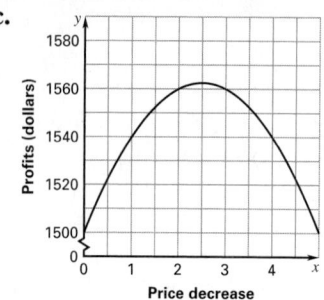 Reduce the price by $2.50 to increase profits to $1562.50 per week.

1.2 Skill Practice 1. vertex

3. 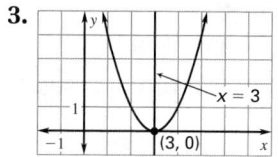 **5.**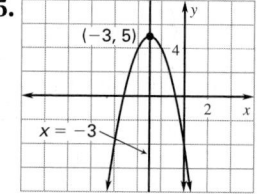

13. 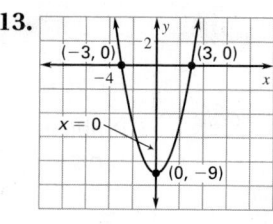 **15.**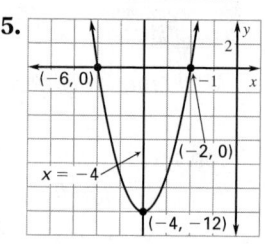

23. $p = 2$ and $q = -3$; the x-intercepts are 2 and -3. **25.** $y = x^2 - 2x - 15$ **27.** $y = -3x^2 + 18x - 24$
29. $y = x^2 - 6x + 15$ **31.** $y = 5x^2 + 30x + 41$
33. minimum: -4 **35.** minimum: 130 **37.** maximum: 729 **39.** minimum: -450 **41.** maximum: 211.25

43. 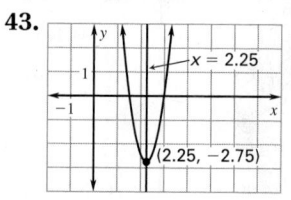 **45.**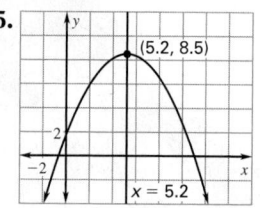

49. $(-1, 5)$; $(-\infty, -1)$ and $(5, +\infty)$

1.2 Problem Solving 51. 6 ft; about 28 ft
53. a. 160 ft **b.** about 1.5 ft **55. a.** about 14%; about 55.5 cm^3 **b.** about 13.6%; about 44.1 cm^3 **c.** hot-air: domain: $5.52 < x < 22.6$, range: $0 < y < 55.5$; hot oil: domain: $5.35 < x < 21.8$, range: $0 < y < 44.1$; since moisture content and popping volume cannot be negative, the domain and range must each be positive numbers. A positive domain occurs between the x-intercepts and the greatest number in the range occurs at the maximum point, which is the vertex.

1.3 Skill Practice 1. an x value that makes the function equal to zero **3.** $(x + 1)(x + 5)$
5. $(a - 11)(a - 2)$ **7.** cannot be factored

Selected Answers

9. $(b + 8)(b - 5)$ **11.** $(x - 9)(x + 2)$ **13.** $(x + 12)(x - 3)$ **15.** $(x + 6)(x - 6)$ **17.** $(x - 12)^2$ **19.** $(x + 4)^2$ **21.** $(n + 7)^2$ **23.** $(z - 11)(z + 11)$ **25.** 5, 6 **27.** $-7, 7$ **29.** $-4, -1$ **31.** -5 **33.** $-6, 9$ **35.** $0, -9$ **37.** 7 **39.** The equation was not factored correctly; $x^2 - x - 6 = 0$, $(x - 3)(x + 2) = 0$, $x = 3$ or $x = -2$. **43.** $3(10)(12) = (10 + x)(12 + x)$ **45.** 4 **47.** $-10, 3$ **49.** 0, 8 **51.** -5, 5 **53.** $-12, -7$ **55.** -1 **57.** $x^2 - 19x + 88 = 0$ **59.** 4 **61.** 3 **63.** *Sample answer:* $x^2 - 20x + 91 = 0$

1.3 Problem Solving 65. $3(50)(100) = (50 + x)(100 + x), -200, 50$; 100 ft by 150 ft **67. a.** 600 ft^2 **b.** area of new patio = area of existing patio + area of expansion, $(30 + x)(20 + x) = 600 + 464$ **c.** $-58, 8$; 8 ft **69.** $3(18)(15) = (18 + x)(15 + x)$, $-45, 12$; 114 ft **71.** $2(100) = (10 + x)(10 + x)$; no; there are no real numbers a and b such that $ab = -100$ and $a + b = 20$.

1.4 Skill Practice 1. 4 **3.** $(2x + 3)(x + 1)$ **5.** $(4r + 1)(r + 1)$ **7.** $(11z - 9)(z + 1)$ **9.** cannot be factored **11.** $(9d + 5)(d - 2)$ **13.** $(3x + 1)(3x - 1)$ **15.** $(7n - 4)(7n + 4)$ **17.** $(7x + 5)^2$ **19.** $(3p - 2)^2$ **21.** $(6x - 7)^2$ **23.** $2(3z + 4)(3z + 2)$ **25.** $6u(u - 4)$ **27.** $4(5x + 1)(x + 6)$ **29.** $-3(6n - 5)(2n - 1)$ **31.** 4 should be factored out of each term in the binomial; $4x^2 - 36 = 4(x^2 - 9) = 4(x + 3)(x - 3)$. **33.** $-2, 2$ **35.** $0, -\frac{2}{9}$ **37.** $-1\frac{1}{2}$ **39.** $-\frac{1}{2}, 1\frac{2}{3}$ **41.** $-\frac{1}{4}, 5$ **43.** $-\frac{3}{5}, 6$ **45.** $-\frac{3}{11}, 2$ **47.** $-1, 1\frac{1}{3}$ **49.** $-1, \frac{7}{12}$ **51.** 3 **53.** $-1, 2\frac{2}{3}$ **55.** $-\frac{7}{9}, 2$ **57.** 0, 4

1.4 Problem Solving 63. 2 ft **65.** \$5.75; letting x represent the number of \$.25 decreases in the sandwich price, the revenue R is given by the function $R = (330 + 15x)(6 - 0.25x)$. The zeros of this function are -22 and 24, and their average is 1. So, to maximize the daily revenue, each sandwich should be sold for $6 - 0.25(1)$, or \$5.75. The maximum daily revenue is then $(330 + 15(1))(5.75) = (345)(5.75) = \$1983.75$. **67. a.** 72 in. **b.** $w = 32 - h$; $V = 36(36 - h)(h)$ **c.** 18 in., 18 in., 11,664 in.^{3}; find the roots of the equation in part (b) to be 0 and 36, so the line of symmetry is at $x = \frac{36 + 0}{2} = 18$. To find the maximum volume, substitute 18 for h into the equation from part (b).

1.5 Skill Practice 1. radicand **3.** $2\sqrt{7}$ **5.** $5\sqrt{6}$ **7.** 24 **9.** $\frac{\sqrt{5}}{4}$ **11.** $\frac{8\sqrt{3}}{3}$ **13.** $\frac{3\sqrt{22}}{11}$ **15.** $-\sqrt{3} - 1$ **17.** $\frac{4\sqrt{2} - \sqrt{10}}{11}$ **21.** The equation has two solutions;

$x^2 = 81, x = \pm 9$. **23.** $\pm 5\sqrt{2}$ **25.** ± 5 **27.** $\pm\sqrt{71}$ **29.** ± 10 **31.** $1 \pm \sqrt{2}$ **33.** $-2 \pm \frac{\sqrt{26}}{2}$ **35.** Factor: $x^2 - 4 = 0$, $(x + 2)(x - 2) = 0$, $x = -2$ or $x = 2$; Solve the equation $x^2 - 4 = 0$, $x^2 = 4$, $x = \pm 2$.

1.5 Problem Solving 39. Earth: about 3.1 sec, Mars: 5 sec, Jupiter: about 2.0 sec, Saturn: about 3.2 sec, Pluto: about 12.2 sec **41. a.** $\pi r^2 = 100$ **b.** about 5.6 ft **c.** $\sqrt{\frac{s^2}{\pi}}$; $s^2 = \pi r^2, \frac{s^2}{\pi} = r^2, \sqrt{\frac{s^2}{\pi}} = r$

1.5 Problem Solving Workshop 1. 1, 5 **3.** $1\frac{2}{3}$ **5.** about -4.4, about 1.4 **7.** about 108 mph **9.** 1.25 sec

1.6 Skill Practice 1. $a + bi$ **3.** $\pm 2i\sqrt{7}$ **5.** $\pm 2i$ **7.** $\pm i\sqrt{11}$ **9.** $\pm i$ **11.** $3 \pm i\sqrt{2}$ **13.** $17 - i$ **15.** $-8 + 6i$ **17.** $19 - 9i$ **19.** $21 + 9i$ **23.** $-8 - 4i$ **25.** $-18 - 13i$ **27.** 73 **29.** $-\frac{3}{5} + \frac{9}{5}i$ **31.** $\frac{3}{4} - \frac{1}{3}i$ **33.** $-\frac{59}{106} - \frac{21}{106}i$ **43.** $\sqrt{109}$ **45.** $\sqrt{37}$ **47.** 4 **49.** $7\sqrt{2}$ **51.** $-20 + 2i$ **53.** $-125 + 90i$ **55.** $-\frac{5}{26} - \frac{51}{26}i$ **57.** $i^2 = -1$, so $-2i^2 = 2$; $4 - i + 8i - 2i^2 = 6 + 7i$. **59. a.** additive: $-2 - i$, multiplicative: $\frac{2}{5} - \frac{1}{5}i$ **b.** additive: $-5 + i$, multiplicative: $\frac{5}{26} + \frac{1}{26}i$ **c.** additive: $1 - 3i$, multiplicative: $-\frac{1}{10} - \frac{3}{10}i$

1.6 Problem Solving 65. $4 - 3i$ ohms **67.** $12 - 8i$ ohms **69.**

Powers of i	i	i^2	i^3	i^4	i^5	i^6	i^7	i^8
Simplified	i	-1	$-i$	1	i	-1	$-i$	1

The pattern repeats every four powers of i; $i^9 = i, i^{10} = -1, i^{11} = -i, i^{12} = 1$. **71.** $[(7 - 2i)(i)](-1 + i) = (2 + 7i)(-1 + i) = -9 - 5i$ $(7 - 2i)[(i)(-1 + i)] = (7 - 2i)(-1 - i) = -9 - 5i$ **75. a.** $\frac{519}{125} + \frac{167}{125}i$ **b.** $\frac{2326}{265} + \frac{668}{265}i$ **c.** $\frac{98}{37} - \frac{4}{37}i$

1.7 Skill Practice 1. A binomial is the sum of two monomials and a trinomial is the sum of three monomials. **3.** $-5, 1$ **5.** $-14, -2$ **7.** $11 \pm \sqrt{13}$ **9.** $-4 \pm 3\sqrt{5}$ **11.** $\frac{2 \pm i\sqrt{3}}{3}$ **13.** 9; $(x + 3)^2$ **15.** 144; $(x - 12)^2$ **17.** 1; $(x - 1)^2$ **19.** $\frac{49}{4}; \left(x + \frac{7}{2}\right)^2$ **21.** $\frac{1}{4}; \left(x - \frac{1}{2}\right)^2$ **23.** $-4 \pm \sqrt{15}$ **25.** $-6 \pm 3\sqrt{2}$ **27.** $1 \pm 2i\sqrt{6}$ **29.** $-7 \pm \sqrt{41}$ **31.** $-1 \pm i\sqrt{2}$ **33.** $-\frac{1}{2} \pm \frac{i\sqrt{7}}{2}$ **35.** $-5 + 5\sqrt{3}$ **37.** $-2 + 2\sqrt{21}$ **39.** (2.8, 125.44); at 2.8 seconds the water will reach a maximum height

Selected Answers

of 125.44 feet. **41.** $y = (x - 4)^2 + 3$; (4, 3)

43. $y = (x + 6)^2 + 1$; (−6, 1) **45.** $y = \left(x - \frac{3}{2}\right)^2 + \frac{7}{4}$;

$\left(\frac{3}{2}, \frac{7}{4}\right)$ **47.** $y = 2(x + 6)^2 - 47$; (−6, −47)

49. $y = 2(x - 7)^2 + 1$; (7, 1) **51.** 36 should be added to each side instead of 9; $4(x^2 + 6x + 9) = 11 + 36$;

$4(x + 3)^2 = 47$; $(x + 3)^2 = \frac{47}{4}$; $x + 3 = \pm\frac{\sqrt{47}}{2}$;

$x = -3 \pm \frac{\sqrt{47}}{2}$. **53.** $-\frac{3}{2} \pm i\frac{\sqrt{47}}{2}$ **55.** $\frac{1}{6} \pm i\frac{\sqrt{71}}{6}$

57. $-0.5 \pm 0.5i\sqrt{19}$

1.7 Problem Solving 63. 40 ft **65.** Selling systems for $300 would maximize monthly revenue at $9000. **67. a.** $1500 = (120 - 2x)(x)$ **b.** about 17.75, about 42.25; reject 17.75 because it gives a length for the eating section that is greater than the length of the side of the school. **c.** about 42.25 ft by 35.5 ft

1.8 Skill Practice 1. discriminant **3.** −1, 5

5. $-4 \pm i\sqrt{3}$ **7.** $\frac{1}{2}$ **9.** $\frac{2 \pm \sqrt{3}}{2}$ **11.** $\frac{4 \pm \sqrt{43}}{3}$ **13.** 2

15. $\frac{-3 \pm i\sqrt{47}}{2}$ **17.** $-\frac{5 \pm 2\sqrt{10}}{5}$ **19.** $\frac{-7 \pm \sqrt{13}}{6}$

21. $\frac{5 \pm \sqrt{31}}{3}$ **23.** 2, 3 **25.** −1, 3 **27.** −2, 4 **29.** −5, −3

31. 0; one real solution **33.** −32; two imaginary solutions **35.** −20; two imaginary solutions **37.** −335; two imaginary solutions **39.** −36; two imaginary solutions **41.** $\frac{1 \pm i\sqrt{67}}{2}$ **43.** $-2\frac{1}{2}, \frac{5}{14}$

45. $\frac{1 \pm \sqrt{229}}{12}$ **47.** $0.875 \pm 0.752i$ **49.** $\sqrt{-144} = 12i$;

$x = \frac{-6 \pm \sqrt{-144}}{6}$; $x = \frac{-6 \pm 12i}{6}$; $x = -1 \pm 2i$

51. $\frac{\frac{-b + \sqrt{b^2 - 4ac}}{2a} + \frac{-b - \sqrt{b^2 - 4ac}}{2a}}{2} = \frac{\frac{-2b}{2a}}{2} = \frac{-b}{2a}$,

which is the formula for the axis of symmetry.
53. negative **57. a.** $c < 16$ **b.** $c = 16$ **c.** $c > 16$
59. a. $c < 48$ **b.** $c = 48$ **c.** $c > 48$ **61. a.** $c < 0.25$
b. $c = 0.25$ **c.** $c > 0.25$ **63.** $-\frac{1}{3}x^2 - \frac{1}{3}x + 4 = 0$
65. $2x^2 + 4x + 4 = 0$ **67. a.** −3, −2, 5, 6 **b.** −3, 3

1.8 Problem Solving 71. 1141 m, 2090 m

73. a.

t	0	0.25	0.5	0.75	1
(x, y)	(0, 6)	(5, 10.25)	(10, 12.5)	(15, 12.75)	(20, 11)

b.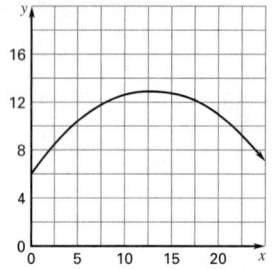

c. No; the height of the ball when $x = 15$ is 12.75 feet, which is above the backboard, so the free throw would not be made.

1.9 Skill Practice
1. *Sample answer:* $3x^2 - 2x + 5 > 0$, $y \geq x^2 + 4x - 8$

7. 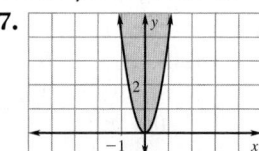 **9.**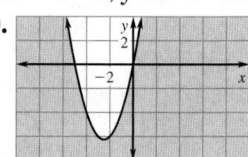

19. 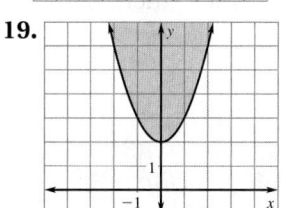 The inside of the parabola should be shaded.

21. 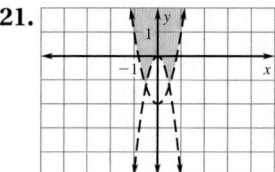 **23.**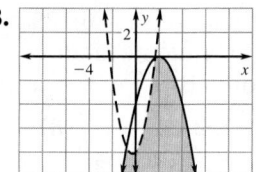

27. $x < -3$ or $x > 1$ **29.** $x \leq -2$ or $x \geq 4$ **31.** $2 < x < 8$
33. $-1 \leq x \leq 3$ **35.** $0 < x < 6$ **37.** $x < 0.59$ or $x > 3.4$
39. $-2 \leq x \leq 1.3$ **41.** $0.67 \leq x \leq 2.5$ **43.** $-1.2 < x < 3.7$
47. $-9 < x < -1$ **49.** $x < -\frac{2}{3}$ or $x > 5$ **51.** $x \leq -3.5$ or
$x \geq 1.5$ **53.** $-0.27 \leq x \leq 1.5$ **55.** $-2.8 \leq x \leq -0.72$
57. $x < -0.46$ or $x > 1.8$ **59.** $-0.89 < x < 1.3$ **61.** no
solution **63.** $x < 0.52$ or $x > 11.5$ **65.** $0 \leq x \leq 0.5$
67. no solution

1.9 Problem Solving
71.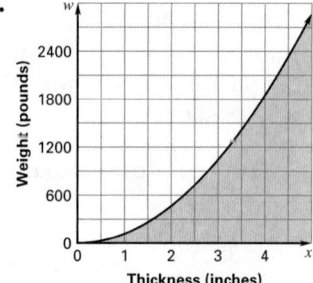

73. $37 \leq x \leq 40$; the domain restricts the number of days to less than or equal to 40. **75. a.** $-0.054x^2 + 1.43x - 8 < 0$; $x \leq 8.0$ or $x \geq 18.5$ **b.** No; the ball will go over the goal by 1.3 feet.

Chapter Review 1. If $a < 0$, the function has a maximum value and if $a > 0$, then the function has a minimum value. **3.** vertex form

5.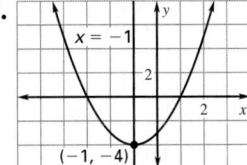

7.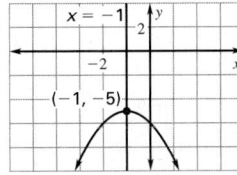

9.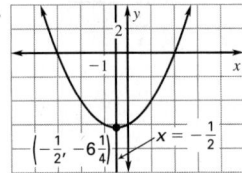

11.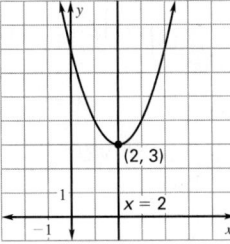

13.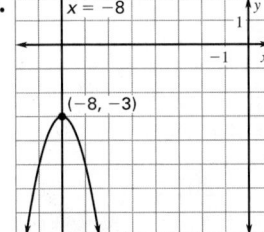

15. $-5, 0$ **17.** $-3, 9$ **19.** -9 **21.** $(72 + x)(48 + x) = 2(72)(48)$; 24 ft **23.** $4 \pm 4\sqrt{2}$ **25.** ± 6 **27.** $-1 \pm 3\sqrt{3}$

29. $-9 - 18i$ **31.** 29 **33.** $-4 + 2i$ **35.** $3 \pm 2\sqrt{6}$

37. $\dfrac{-3 \pm \sqrt{13}}{2}$ **39.** $-\dfrac{1}{3}$ **41.** about 0.2 sec

43. $-0.65 \le x \le 4.6$

Chapter 1
Extra Practice

1.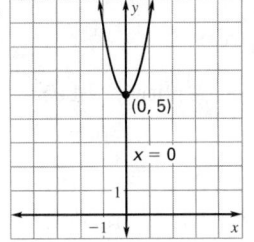

3.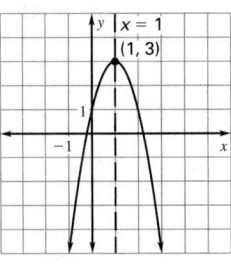

5.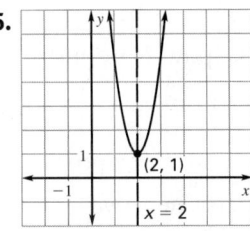

7.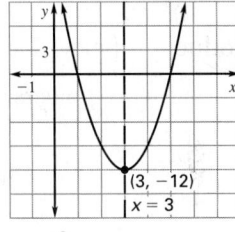

9. $y = 7x^2 + 42x + 56$ **11.** $y = x^2 - 14x + 56$
13. $(x - 2)^2$ **15.** $(x + 9)(x + 12)$ **17.** $-7, 2$ **19.** $-11, 5$
21. $(2x - 5)(x + 3)$ **23.** not factorable **25.** $-\dfrac{4}{9}, \dfrac{4}{9}$

27. $-3, -\dfrac{3}{2}$ **29.** $2\sqrt{14}$ **31.** $\dfrac{2\sqrt{7}}{7}$ **33.** $\pm 2\sqrt{2}$ **35.** $5 \pm \sqrt{10}$

37. $11 - 3i$ **39.** $-\dfrac{13}{73} + \dfrac{14}{73}i$ **41.** $-3 \pm \sqrt{19}$ **43.** $3 \pm \sqrt{6}$

45. $-5 \pm \sqrt{35}$ **47.** $-\dfrac{3}{8} \pm \dfrac{\sqrt{201}}{8}$ **49.** -3; two imaginary

solutions **51.** 200; two real solutions

53. $x \le 0$ or $x \ge 10$ **55.** $-0.653 < x < 7.65$

r 2

Practice 1. a. Product of powers property
negative exponent property **c.** Power of a product
property **3.** 243; product of powers property

5. -3125; product of powers property **7.** $\frac{1}{125}$;

quotient of powers property **9.** $\frac{343}{8}$; power of a

quotient property, negative exponent property

11. 729; quotient of powers property **13.** $\frac{1}{36}$; product

of powers property, negative exponent property
15. 6.3×10^9 **17.** 5.607×10^{-6} **19.** 9.261×10^{-12}
21. 1.5×10^3 **23.** 2.25×10^{-2} **25.** $1024y^{15}$; power
of a product property, power of a power property

27. $\frac{w^9}{x^3}$; product of powers property, negative

exponent property **29.** $\frac{1}{27a^9b^{15}}$; power of a product

property, power of a power property, negative

exponent property **31.** $\frac{c^2d^2}{3}$; quotient of powers

property **33.** $\frac{2}{3a^2b^2}$; quotient of powers property,

negative exponent property **35.** $\frac{x^6}{3y^3}$; product of

powers property, quotient of powers property,
negative exponent property **37.** The exponents
should be subtracted, not divided; x^8. **39.** The base

should not change; $(-3)^6$. **41.** $\frac{\pi x^3}{2}$ **43.** $x^{11}y^5z^{-3}$

45. $a^{-4}b^9$

2.1 Problem Solving 49. Pacific: 6.2868×10^{17} m³,
Atlantic: 3.01824×10^{17} m³, Indian: 2.71656×10^{17}
m³, Arctic: 1.7061×10^{16} m³

51. *Sample a* r: The volume of the pearl is $\frac{27}{8}$ times

as large   me of the bead. **53. a.** about
4.42

                    : 4, type: quartic, leading
               m: 6
                 $= -x^2 + 8$, degree: 2,
                  ent: -1
                    $^4 + \sqrt{6}$, degree: 4,
                      7. polynomial

                        ee: 3,

                         11. 378

27. degree: even, leading coefficient: negative
29. $-\infty, -\infty$ **31.** $-\infty, +\infty$ **33.** $+\infty, -\infty$ **35.** $+\infty, +\infty$
37. *Sample answer:* $f(x) = -x^5 - 2x^4 + 1$

39. 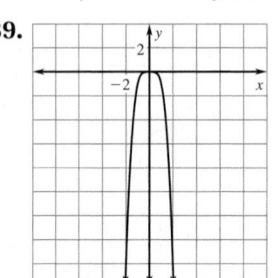 **41.**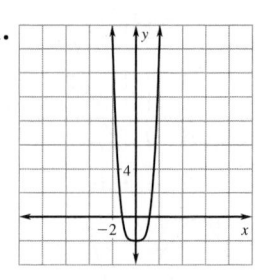

51. $g(x) \to -\infty$ as $x \to -\infty$ and $g(x) \to +\infty$ as $x \to +\infty$

2.2 Problem Solving

55.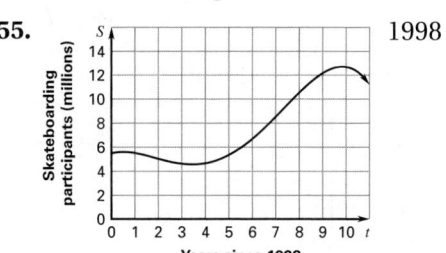

1998

57.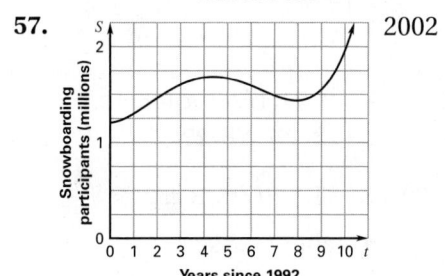

2002

59. a. 35.625 g

b.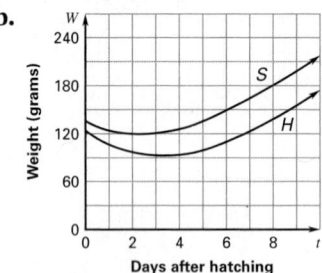

c. Sarus. *Sample answer:* Substituting 3 into each
equation gives the Sarus chick weighing about
120 grams and the hooded chick weighing about
92 grams. The weight of the Sarus chick is closer to
130 grams than the weight of the hooded chick is.

2.3 Skill Practice 1. like terms **3.** $10x^2 - 8$ **5.** $14y - 8$
7. $7s^3 - 2s^2 + 8s + 10$ **9.** $2c^3 + 5c^2 + c + 9$
11. $-2b^4 - 15b^3 + 5b + 7$ **13.** $2x^4 - x^3$
17. $30x^3 + 10x^2$ **19.** $3z^2 - 8z - 3$ **21.** $2a^3 - 23a^2 +$
$26a + 6$ **23.** $-x^4 + 12x^3 - 34x^2 + 4x + 3$

25. $12y^4 - 9y^3 - 85y^2 - 19y + 5$ **27.** The cube of a binomial $(a - b)^3$ is found by $a^3 - 3a^2b + 3ab^2 - b^3$; $(2x - 7)^3 = (2x)^3 - 3(2x)^2(7) + 3(2x)(7)^2 - (7)^3 = 8x^3 - 84x^2 + 294x - 343$. **29.** $x^3 - 3x^2 - 25x - 21$
31. $2a^3 - 5a^2 - 37a - 30$ **33.** $-2b^3 + 7b^2 - 7b + 2$
35. $-12w^3 + 95w^2 - 143w + 30$ **37.** $-27q^3 + 132q^2 - 172q + 32$ **39.** $w^2 - 18w + 81$ **41.** $4c^2 + 20c + 25$
43. $25p^2 - 9$ **45.** $4a^2 - 81b^2$ **49.** $2\pi x^3 - 13\pi x^2 + 8\pi x + 48\pi$ **51.** $4x^3 - \frac{20}{3}x^2 - 7x + 12$ **53.** $(a + b)^2 = (a + b)(a + b) = a^2 + ab + ab + b^2 = a^2 + 2ab + b^2$
55. $(a - b)^3 = (a - b)(a - b)(a - b) = (a - b)(a^2 - 2ab + b^2) = a^3 - 2a^2b + ab^2 - a^2b + 2ab^2 - b^3 = a^3 - 3a^2b + 3ab^2 - b^3$
57. a. $(x - 1)(x^4 + x^3 + x^2 + x + 1)$; $(x - 1)(x^5 + x^4 + x^3 + x^2 + x + 1)$
b. $(x - 1)(x^{n-1} + x^{n-2} + x^{n-3} + \dots + 1)$

2.3 Problem Solving 59. $0.281t^3 - 16.8t^2 + 460t + 8600$ **61.** $P = 0.0000310s^3 + 0.00211s$; about 0.0521 horsepower **63.** $N = -1.52t^4 - 25.5t^3 + 216t^2 + 128t + 9860$; calculate $L_m \cdot S_m + L_w \cdot S_w$.

2.4 Skill Practice 1. quadratic
3. $7x(2x - 3)$ **5.** $c(c + 3)(c + 6)$
7. $3y^3(y - 4)(y + 4)$ **11.** $(y - 4)(y^2 + 4y + 16)$
13. $(5n + 6)(25n^2 - 30n + 36)$
15. $(2c + 7)(4c^2 - 14c + 49)$
17. $-5(z - 4)(z^2 + 4z + 16)$ **19.** $(y - 7)(y^2 + 4)$
21. $(3m - 1)(m^2 + 3)$ **23.** $(c + 2)(2c - 3)(2c + 3)$
25. $(a^2 + 1)(a^2 + 6)$ **27.** $2z(2z - 1)(2z + 1)(4z^2 + 1)$
29. $3x(x^2 - 6)(5x^2 + 6)$ **31.** The factor $3x$ should also be set equal to 0; $x = 0$ or $x = -4$ or $x = 4$.
33. $0, -1\frac{2}{3}, 1\frac{2}{3}$ **35.** $2, -2, -6$ **37.** $0, -\sqrt{21}, \sqrt{21}$
39. $-\sqrt{3}, \sqrt{3}, 2, -2$ **43.** $(n^2 - 10)(n^2 + 6)$
45. $(12a - 5)(3a^2 + 7)$ **47.** $(d + 3)(d - 3)(2d^2 + 5)$
49. $2y^2(y^2 - 5)(4y^2 + 1)$ **51.** 2 **53.** 5
55. $(c + d)(c - d)(7a + b)$

2.4 Problem Solving 59. 3 cm by 9 cm by 18 cm
61. length: 10 in., width: 5 in., height: 5 in.

63. The volume cannot be $\frac{7}{3}$ because the only x value that corresponds to that volume is about -1.37, which would yield a negative side length.

2.4 Problem Solving Workshop 1. 4 **3.** 6 **5.** about 1.4, 4 **7.** 2.5 **9.** height: 12 in., width: 8 in., length: 18 in.

2.5 Skill Practice 1. If a polynomial $f(x)$ is divided by $x - k$, then the remainder is $r = f(k)$.

3. $x + 5 + \frac{3}{x - 4}$ **5.** $x^2 + 4x + 7 + \frac{9}{x - 1}$
7. $3x + 8 + \frac{-4x + 1}{x^2 + x}$ **9.** $5x^2 - 12x + 37 + \frac{-122x + 109}{x^2 + 2x - 4}$

11. $2x + 3 + \frac{25}{x - 5}$ **13.** $x + 4 + \frac{-15}{x + 4}$
15. $x^2 - x - 4 + \frac{-18}{x - 4}$ **17.** $x^3 + x^2 - 2x + 1 + \frac{-6}{x - 6}$
19. The degree of the answer should be reduced by 1; $x^2 + 2x - 1 + \frac{1}{x - 2}$. **21.** $(x - 6)(x - 5)(x + 1)$
23. $(x - 8)(x + 2)(x + 4)$ **25.** $(x - 4)(x - 3)(x + 9)$
27. $(2x - 7)(x - 3)(x - 1)$ **29.** $-1, 6$ **31.** $-0.4, 1.5$
33. $\frac{-4 \pm \sqrt{14}}{2}$ **37.** $x + 8$

2.5 Problem Solving 41. 1 million T-shirts
43. $f(x) = -0.132x^2 + 11.2x - 560.9 + \frac{408,803}{14.8x + 725}$
45. $-0.00233x^3 + 0.249x^2 - 21.0x + 1740 + \frac{-445,000}{3.10x + 256}$; divided the overnight stays function by the total visits function

2.6 Skill Practice 1. constant, leading coefficient
3. $\pm 1, \pm 2, \pm 4, \pm 7, \pm 14, \pm 28$ **5.** $\pm 1, \pm 3,$
$\pm 9, \pm \frac{1}{2}, \pm \frac{3}{2}, \pm \frac{9}{2}$ **7.** $\pm 1, \pm 2, \pm 7, \pm 14, \pm \frac{1}{2}, \pm \frac{7}{2}, \pm \frac{1}{4},$
$\pm \frac{7}{4}$ **9.** $\pm 1, \pm 3, \pm 5, \pm 15, \pm \frac{1}{2}, \pm \frac{3}{2}, \pm \frac{5}{2}, \pm \frac{15}{2}, \pm \frac{1}{4}, \pm \frac{3}{4},$
$\pm \frac{5}{4}, \pm \frac{15}{4}, \pm \frac{1}{8}, \pm \frac{3}{8}, \pm \frac{5}{8}, \pm \frac{15}{8}$ **11.** $1, 3, 8$ **13.** $-5, -1, 6$
15. $-2, -1$ **17.** $-4, -1, 1, 2$ **19.** $1, \frac{-1 \pm \sqrt{17}}{2}$
21. $-3, -\frac{5}{3}, \frac{1}{2}$ **25.** $-1, \frac{3}{2}, 3$ **27.** $-4, -\frac{1}{3}, 3$
29. $-3.5, -1, 2$ **31.** $-2, 2$ **33.** $-2, 1, \frac{5}{2}, 3$ **35.** $-3, \frac{1}{2}, 1$
37. p should be factors of 5 and q should be factors of 6; possible zeros: $\pm 1, \pm 5, \pm \frac{1}{2}, \pm \frac{5}{2}, \pm \frac{1}{3}, \pm \frac{5}{3}, \pm \frac{1}{6}, \pm \frac{5}{6}$.
41. $-1, 1, 2$; B **43.** -2; A

2.6 Problem Solving 45. length: 3 in., width: 3 in., height: 7 in. **47.** $x^3 - 3x^2 + 2x - 24 = 0$; $\pm 1, \pm 2, \pm 3, \pm 4, \pm 6, \pm 8, \pm 12, \pm 24$ **49. a.** $-10t^3 + 140t^2 - 20t - 2150 = 0$ **b.** 1, 2, 5 **c.** 5; 1999

2.7 Skill Practice 1. repeated **3.** 4 **5.** 6
7. 7 **11.** $-5, -3, 1, 2$ **13.** $-5, -2, 2$ **15.** $-2, 1, 2i, -2i$
17. $1, -1, 1 + \sqrt{3}, 1 - \sqrt{3}$ **19.** $-4, -2, -\frac{3}{2}, 1$
21. $f(x) = x^3 - 2x^2 - 5x + 6$ **23.** $f(x) = x^3 - 4x^2 - 15x + 18$ **25.** $f(x) = x^4 - 4x^3 + 14x^2 - 36x + 45$
27. $f(x) = x^4 - 18x^3 + 122x^2 - 370x + 425$
29. $f(x) = x^4 - x^3 - 18x^2 + 10x + 8$
31. $f(x) = x^5 - 13x^4 + 60x^3 - 82x^2 - 144x + 360$
33. *Sample answer:* $f(x) = x^5 - 4x^4 + 6x^3 - 6x^2 + 5x - 2$ **35.** positive: 1, negative: 0, imaginary: 2
37. positive: 2 or 0, negative: 3 or 1, imaginary: 4, 2, or 0 **39.** positive: 3 or 1, negative: 2 or 0, imaginary: 4, 2, or 0 **41.** positive: 2 or 0, negative: 1, imaginary: 6 or 4 **43.** $x \approx -1.1, x \approx 1.3$ **45.** $x \approx -0.58, x \approx 1.9$

47. $x \approx -0.42$, $x \approx 2.0$ **49.** $x \approx -3.5$, $x \approx -1.1$, $x = -1$, $x \approx 2.1$, $x \approx 3.6$ **51.** There could be 3, 2, 1, or 0 positive zeros, 3, 2, 1, or 0 negative zeros, and 2 or 0 imaginary zeros. **53.** Positive real zeros: 1, negative real zeros: 2, imaginary zeros: 0; the graph crosses the positive x-axis once and the negative x-axis twice. **55.** Positive real zeros: 0, negative real zeros: 1, imaginary zeros: 4; the graph does not cross the positive x-axis and it crosses the negative x-axis once. Since the function has degree 5, the remaining 4 zeros must be imaginary.

2.7 Problem Solving 59. year 3 and year 9 **61.** about 16.4 g per 100 mL **63.** 0 in., about 59 in.; the bookshelf would have nearly 0 inches of deflection near each end because of the supports holding the bookshelf, so the answers make sense because they represent each end of a 60 inch bookshelf.

2.8 Skill Practice 1. turning

3.

5.

13. The x-intercepts should be at -2 and 1.

15–19. Sample answers are given. **15.** local maximum: $(-0.3, 0.3)$, local minimum: $(0.9, -1.3)$; zeros: -0.75, 0, 1.4, least degree: 3 **17.** local maximums: $(1, 0)$, $(3, 0)$, local minimum: $(2, -2)$; zeros: 1, 3, least degree: 4 **19.** local maximums: $(-1.1, 0.8)$, $(1.9, 8)$, local minimums: $(-2.2, -38)$, $(0.3, -40)$, $(2.8, -13)$; zeros: -2.6, -1.2, -1, 1.5, 2.2, 3, least degree: 6 **23.** x-intercept: -2.5; local maximum: $(-1.2, 4.0)$; local minimum: $(1.2, 0.96)$ **25.** x-intercepts: -2.2, 1, 1.7; local maximums: $(-1.6, 10.5)$, $(0.17, 2.0)$; local minimums: $(0, 2)$, $(1.5, -1.7)$ **27.** x-intercepts: -0.77, 4.5; local maximum: $(0.47, -2.6)$; local minimums: $(-0.16, -3.1)$, $(3.4, -39.4)$ **29.** x-intercepts: -0.77, 0, 0.82; local maximum: $(0.47, 1.6)$; local minimum: $(-0.46, -1.5)$ **31.** *Sample answer:* Quadratic functions only have one turning point, therefore one maximum or minimum value of the function. Cubic functions can have two turning points, therefore one local maximum and one local minimum, and the end behavior is to positive and negative infinity, so there is no real maximum or minimum value of the function.

35. 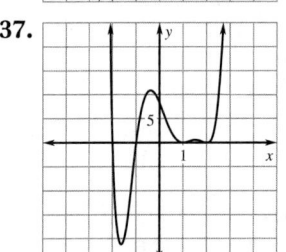 domain: all real numbers, range: all real numbers

37. 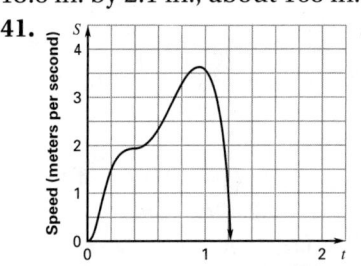 domain: all real numbers, range: $y \geq -21.3$

2.8 Problem Solving 39. maximum: about 5.8 in. by 13.8 in. by 2.1 in.; about 168 in.[3]

41. after about 0.95 sec

43. a.

b. Maximum: $(11.7, 44{,}971)$, minimum: $(29.8, 40{,}078)$. *Sample answer:* The maximum indicates that in 1972 the number of students enrolled was about 44,971,000. The minimum indicates that in 1990 there were about 40,078,000 students enrolled. **c.** $36{,}300 \leq S \leq 47{,}978$

Chapter Review **1.** local maximum, local minimum **3.** If it is in the form $c \times 10^n$ where $1 \le c < 10$ and n is an integer. **5.** 128; product of powers property **7.** $\dfrac{y^{10}}{x^4}$; power of a power property, negative exponent property **9.** $\dfrac{16}{9}$; quotient of powers property, negative exponent property **11.** $\dfrac{1}{x^8 y^8}$; power of a quotient property, negative exponent property

13. 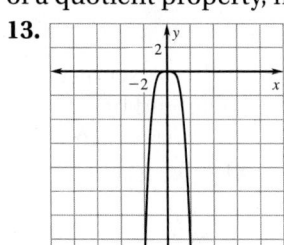 **15.**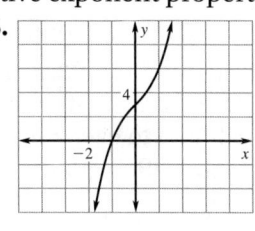

17. $6x^3 - 9x^2 + 3x + 3$ **19.** $5x^3 - 29x^2 - 14x + 48$
21. $8(2x - 1)(4x^2 + 2x + 1)$ **23.** $(x - 2)(x + 2)(2x - 7)$
25. $x - 6 + \dfrac{18x - 16}{x^2 + 3x - 1}$ **27.** $2x^2 - x + 8 + \dfrac{-4}{x - 5}$
29. $(x + 2)(x - 3)(x - 4)$ **31.** $(x - 1)(3x - 2)(3x + 2)$
33. $-3, 2, 5$ **35.** $x^3 - 2x^2 - 19x + 20$
37. $x^4 - 15x^3 + 72x^2 - 120x + 56$
39. x-intercept: -1.7; local maximum: $(0, -1)$; local minimum: $(-1, -2)$

Chapter 2
Extra Practice

1. 9.52×10^{11} **3.** 5×10^1 **5.** $\dfrac{b^6}{64a^{15}}$; quotient of powers property; power of a product property, negative exponent property **7.** $7x^2 y^2$; product of powers property, quotient of powers property, negative exponent property

9. 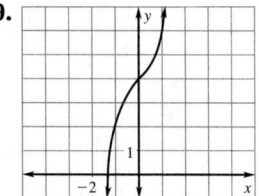 **11.**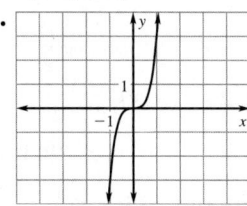

13. $-3x^2 + 3x - 8$ **15.** $3x^2(x + 3)^2$

17. $(x - 2)(x + 2)(2x + 1)$ **19.** ± 4

21. $2x^2 + 10x + 25 + \dfrac{91}{x - 3}$ **23.** $-3, \dfrac{1}{2}, 1$

25. $-3 \pm \sqrt{5}, \dfrac{1}{2}, 5$ **27.** $-1, -3, \pm 2i$

29. positive: 2 or 0, negative: 1, imaginary: 2 or 0
31. positive: 1, negative: 1, imaginary: 2 **33.** $(-1.5, -4)$ local minimum, $(0, 0)$ local maximum, $(1.5, -4)$ local minimum; $(-2, 0), (0, 0), (0, 0), (2, 0)$, degree 4

Chapter 3

3.1 Skill Practice 1. index **7.** $12^{1/3}$
9. $x^{5/2}$ **11.** $\sqrt[4]{5}$ **13.** $\sqrt[3]{2t}$ **15.** ± 8 **17.** 0 **19.** no real
roots **21.** 2 **23.** 64 **25.** 9 **27.** $\frac{1}{4}$ **29.** $\frac{1}{128}$ **31.** $\frac{1}{16}$
35. 2.89 **37.** 2.10 **39.** 12 **41.** 0.01 **43.** 0.02
45. -0.18 **47.** 3 and 4; $3^4 = 81$ and $4^4 = 256$,
and $81 < 125 < 256$ **49.** There are two real solutions;
$x = \pm 3$. **51.** 6 **53.** 1, 9 **55.** ± 1.68 **57.** -7.66

3.1 Problem Solving 61. about 4.30 in.
63. $\frac{3}{12,282,500,000}$; about 1800 RPM **65. a.** 4096 mm^3
b. tetrahedron: about 32.6 mm, octahedron:
about 20.6 mm, dodecahedron: about 8.12 mm,
icosahedron: about 12.3 mm **c.** No. *Sample answer:*
The icosahedron has the greatest number of faces, 20,
and an edge length of 12.3 millimeters which is
greater than the edge length of the dodecahedron,
which has 12 faces.

3.2 Skill Practice 1. No; they do not have the same
index. **3.** 25 **5.** 3 **7.** $2 \cdot 5^{1/2}$ **9.** $\frac{\sqrt[5]{1331}}{11}$
11. $7^{3/4}$ **13.** $\frac{\sqrt[3]{50}}{16,000}$ **15.** 10 **17.** $2\sqrt{2}$ **19.** 2 **21.** 3
25. $2\sqrt[3]{2}$ **27.** $40\sqrt[4]{2}$ **29.** $\frac{\sqrt{3}}{2}$ **31.** $\sqrt[15]{3}$ **33.** $\frac{2}{5}\sqrt[3]{5}$
35. $\frac{1}{2}\sqrt[4]{7}$ **37.** $-2\sqrt[7]{2}$ **39.** $-6\sqrt[4]{2}$ **41.** The radicands
are not the same, so they cannot be combined;
$2\sqrt[3]{10} + 6\sqrt[3]{5}$. **43.** $x^{7/12}$ **45.** $3x$ **47.** $\frac{y^{4/3}}{x^{3/5}}$ **49.** $\frac{1}{x^4}$
51. *Sample answer:* $x^{5/4}$ and $x^{1/2}$ **53.** $yz^3\sqrt[4]{12x^2y^2}$
55. $x^2z^4\sqrt{xy}$ **57.** $\frac{x\sqrt[3]{y^2}}{y^2}$ **59.** $\sqrt[14]{x^{11}}$ **61.** $\frac{1}{2}y^{3/2}$
63. $2x^2y^{1/2}$ **65.** $(2xy + 3y)\sqrt[4]{2x^2}$ **67.** perimeter:
$24x^{1/4}$,
area: $35x^{1/2}$ **71.** $\frac{1}{y^{6.6}}$ **73.** $\frac{1}{x^{1.2}}$ **75.** $\frac{1}{y^{1.3}}$ **77.** $7z^{0.3}$
79. $x^{\sqrt{6}}$ **81.** $4x^2y^{\sqrt{2}}$

3.2 Problem Solving 83. a. about 580 cm^2
b. about 16,671 cm^2 **85.** about 0.45 mm **87. a.** about
2 times fainter **b.** about 1.6 times fainter **c.** about
3 times fainter **89. a.** $r = \sqrt[3]{\frac{3V}{4\pi}}$ **b.** $S = 4\pi\left(\sqrt[3]{\frac{3V}{4\pi}}\right)^2 =$
$4\pi\left(\frac{3V}{4\pi}\right)^{2/3} = \frac{4\pi(3V)^{2/3}}{(4\pi)^{2/3}} = (4\pi)^{1/3}(3V)^{2/3}$ **c.** The balloon
with twice as much water will have $\sqrt[3]{4}$, or about 1.59,
times the surface area of the balloon with less water.

3.3 Skill Practice 1. composition **3.** $2x^{1/3} + 8x^{1/2}$,
all nonnegative real numbers **5.** $-6x^{1/3} + 8x^{1/2}$,
all nonnegative real numbers **7.** $-8x^{1/3}$, all
nonnegative real numbers **9.** 0, all nonnegative real
numbers **13.** $20x^{7/6}$, nonnegative real numbers
15. $25x$, all nonnegative real numbers

17. $\frac{5}{4x^{1/6}}$, positive real numbers **19.** 1, positive real
numbers **21.** -64 **23.** $-\frac{36}{25}$ **25.** 71 **27.** -625
29. $\frac{6}{x} - 7$, all real numbers except $x = 0$ **31.** $\frac{2x - 13}{3}$,
all real numbers **33.** x, all real numbers except $x = 0$
35. $4x - 21$, all real numbers **37.** 4 should be
distributed to each term, not just the first term;
$4x^2 - 12$. **39.** *Sample answer:* $f(x) = 3x, g(x) = 2x$

3.3 Problem Solving 43. $r(w) = 220w^{-0.266}$;
about 134 breaths per minute, about 48.3 breaths
per minute, about 11.3 breaths per minute **45. a.** \$63
b. \$61.50 **c.** Apply the 10% discount before the
\$15 discount; you pay \$61.50 using this method and
\$63 using the other method.

3.4 Skill Practice 1. An inverse relation interchanges
the input and output values of the original relation.
3. $y = \frac{x + 1}{4}$ **5.** $y = \frac{x + 6}{7}$
7. $y = \frac{x - 7}{12}$ **9.** $y = \frac{1}{5}x - \frac{1}{15}$ **11.** $y = \frac{7 - 5x}{3}$
13. Switching the roles of x and y does not include
switching the sign of the variables;
$x = -y + 3, x - 3 = -y, 3 - x = y$.
15. $f(g(x)) = x - 4 + 4 = x, g(f(x)) = x + 4 - 4 = x$
17. $f(g(x)) = \frac{1}{4}((4x)^{1/3})^3 = \frac{1}{4}(4x) = x, g(f(x)) =$
$\left(4\left(\frac{1}{4}x^3\right)\right)^{1/3} = (x^3)^{1/3} = x$ **19.** $f(g(x)) = 4\left(\frac{1}{4}x - \frac{9}{4}\right) +$
$9 = x - 9 + 9 = x, g(f(x)) = \frac{1}{4}(4x + 9) - \frac{9}{4} = x + \frac{9}{4} -$
$\frac{9}{4} = x$ **23.** $f^{-1}(x) = \sqrt[4]{\frac{x}{4}}$ **25.** $f^{-1}(x) = \frac{\sqrt[5]{x}}{2}$
27. $f^{-1}(x) = -\frac{5}{4}\sqrt{x}$ **29.** function **31.** not a function
33. function **35.** not a function **37.** not a function
39. $f^{-1}(x) = \sqrt[3]{x + 2}$ **41.** $f^{-1}(x) = -\sqrt[6]{\frac{40 - 5x}{2}}$
43. $f^{-1}(r) = \sqrt[4]{x + 9}$

3.4 Problem Solving 47. a. $w = 2\ell - 6$ **b.** 7 lb
49. $\ell = \left(\frac{v}{1.34}\right)^2$; about 31.3 ft

Selected Answers

3.5 Skill Practice 1. radical

3. 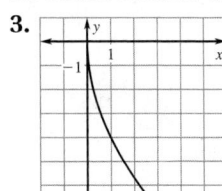 domain: $x \geq 0$, range: $y \leq 0$

5. 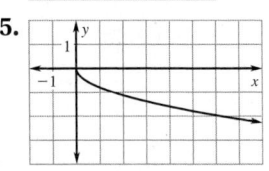 domain: $x \geq 0$, range: $y \leq 0$

11. 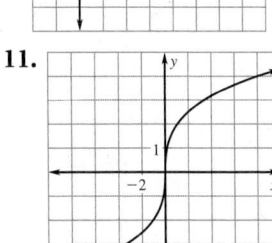 domain: all real numbers, range: all real numbers

13. domain: all real numbers, range: all real numbers

17. 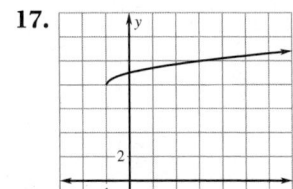 domain: $x \geq -1$, range: $y \geq 8$

19. 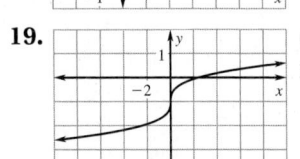 domain: all real numbers, range: all real numbers

25. The domain is limited because the square root of a negative number is not a real number. The range is limited because the square root of a number is nonnegative. **29.** Domain: $x \geq 12$, range: $y \geq 0$; the expression under the radical sign must be greater than or equal to 0, so substitute the least value of x into the equation and find y. **31.** Domain: all real numbers, range: all real numbers; there are no restrictions on finding the cube root of a number and therefore no restrictions on the range. **33.** Domain: $x \geq 3$, range: $f(x) \geq 6$; the expression

under the radical sign must be greater than or equal to 0, so substitute the least value of x into the equation and find $f(x)$.

3.5 Problem Solving 35. about 43 ft above sea level **37. a.** $v = 331.5\sqrt{1 + \dfrac{C}{273.15}}$ **b.** domain: $C \geq -273.15$, range: $v \geq 0$ **39. a.** $v_t = 33.7\sqrt{\dfrac{165}{A}}$

b. *Sample answer:*

A	2	4	6	8	10
v_t	306.1	216.44	176.72	153.05	136.89

c.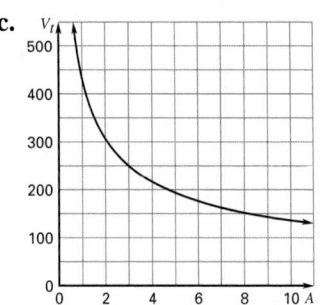

3.6 Skill Practice 1. extraneous **3.** 7
5. 1 **7.** 6 **9.** 29 **11.** $-70\frac{1}{2}$ **13.** 343 **15.** 18 **17.** 8
19. 11 **21.** -37 **23.** ± 64 **25.** ± 32 **27.** 40 **29.** 108
31. $-\dfrac{107}{3}$, 7 **33.** Both sides must be raised to the power; $\left((x+7)^{1/2}\right)^2 = 5^2$, $x + 7 = 25$, $x = 18$.
35. 25 **37.** 3, 8 **39.** $-2\frac{1}{10}$ **41.** $\frac{1}{2}$ **45.** 3 **47.** 4 **49.** $\frac{1}{4}$
51. $-2, 2$ **53.** (4, 25)

3.6 Problem Solving 57. about 391 min
59. *Sample answer:* The elephant with a shoulder height of 250 centimeters is about 20 years older than the elephant with a shoulder height of 150 centimeters. **61. a.** about 0.162 mi/h **b.** about 80.4 mi/h **c.** $0.162 \leq s \leq 80.4$

3.6 Problem Solving Workshop 1. -39
3. about 55.7 **5.** about 97 ft **7.** about 37.5 cm

3.6 Extension 1. $x \geq 16$ **3.** $0 \leq x \leq 4$ **5.** $x \geq 1$
7. $0 \leq x \leq 6.25$ **9.** $0 \leq x < 1.3$ **11.** $0 \leq x < 4$ **13.** about 413 m^2

Chapter Review 1. 4 **3.** power **5.** If a horizontal line crosses the graph of the function more than once, the inverse is not a function.
7. Take the square root of each side; raise each side to the $\frac{3}{2}$ power. **9.** 0 **11.** 5 **13.** $\frac{1}{9}$ **15.** -8 **17.** $\frac{1}{15}$
19. $\dfrac{3x^2y^2\sqrt{2z}}{7z^2}$ **21.** $3x - 14$ **23.** $4x + 26$ **25.** $y = \dfrac{\sqrt{x-9}}{2}$

27. 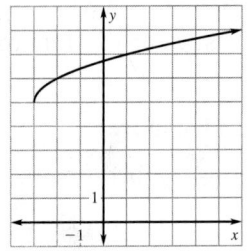 domain: $x \geq -3$, range: $y \geq 5$

29. 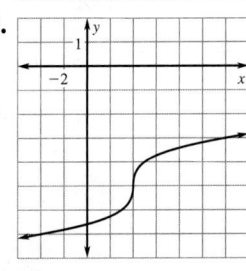 domain: all real numbers, range: all real numbers

31. 16

Chapter 3
Extra Practice

1. ± 3 **3.** -3 **5.** 32 **7.** 16 **9.** ± 3

11. ± 2.15 **13.** $\dfrac{1}{17^{1/7}}$ **15.** 3 **17.** $9\sqrt[3]{2}$ **19.** $48\sqrt[3]{2}$

21. $y^2 z^4 \sqrt[5]{18x^3 y^4}$ **23.** $2x^2 y^2 \sqrt[3]{12x^2 y}$ **25.** $x^3 + x - 4$, all real numbers **27.** $\dfrac{-x + 4}{x^3}$, all real numbers except $x = 0$ **29.** $\dfrac{x^3}{64}$, all real numbers **31.** x, all real numbers

33. $f(g(x)) = 3\left(\left(\dfrac{x-1}{3}\right)^{1/2}\right)^2 + 1 = x - 1 + 1 = x$,

$g(f(x)) = \left(\dfrac{(3x^2 + 1) - 1}{3}\right)^{1/2} = \left(\dfrac{3x^2}{3}\right)^{1/2} = x$

35. $f^{-1}(x) = \dfrac{3}{4}x - \dfrac{3}{2}$ **37.** $f^{-1}(x) = -\sqrt[6]{-x + 2}$

39. $f^{-1}(x) = \dfrac{\sqrt[5]{x - 4}}{2}$

41. 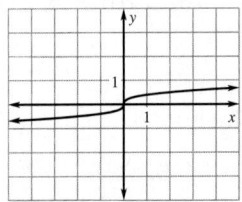 domain: all real numbers, range: all real numbers

43. 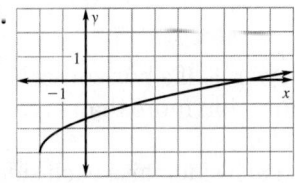 domain: $x \geq -2$, range: $y \geq -3$

49. 3 **51.** -1 **53.** 3 **55.** 1, 3

Mastering the Standards

for Mathematical Practice

The topics described in the Standards for Mathematical Content will vary from year to year. However, the *way* in which you learn, study, and think about mathematics will not. The Standards for Mathematical Practice describe skills that you will use in all of your math courses.

Mathematical Practices

1. Make sense of problems and persevere in solving them.
2. Reason abstractly and quantitatively.
3. Construct viable arguments and critique the reasoning of others.
4. Model with mathematics.
5. Use appropriate tools strategically.
6. Attend to precision.
7. Look for and make use of structure.
8. Look for and express regularity in repeated reasoning.

① Make sense of problems and persevere in solving them.

Mathematically proficient students start by explaining to themselves the meaning of a problem... They analyze givens, constraints, relationships, and goals. They make conjectures about the form... of the solution and plan a solution pathway...

In your book

Verbal Models and the **Problem Solving Plan** help you translate the information in a problem into a model and then analyze your solution.

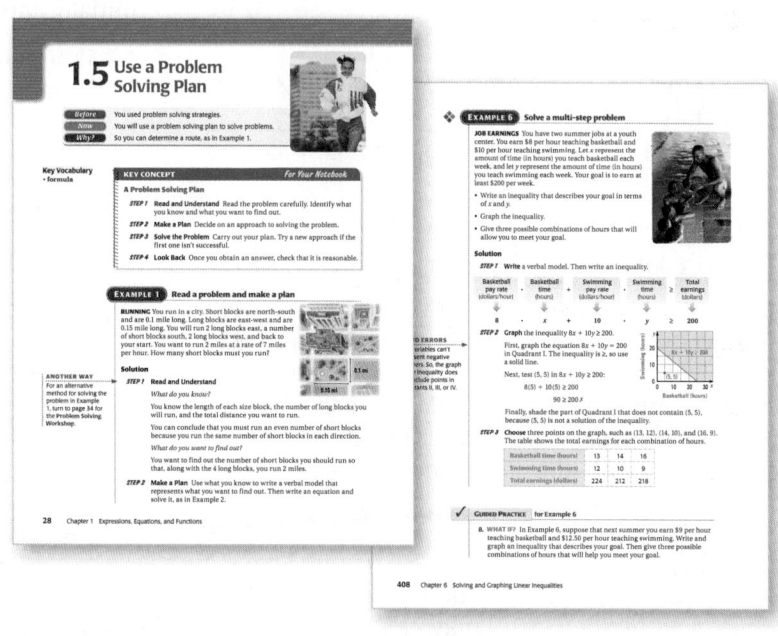

Selected Answers

Chapter 4

4.1 Skill Practice 1. 2.4, 1.5, 50%

7.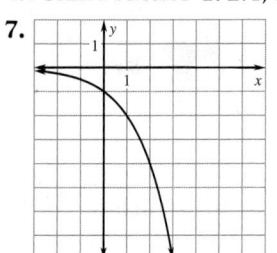

9.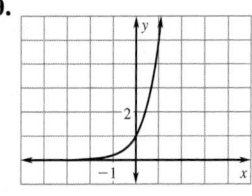

15. 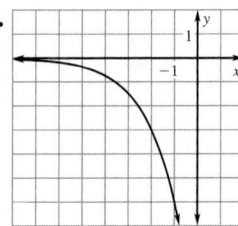 domain: all real numbers, range: $y < 0$

17. 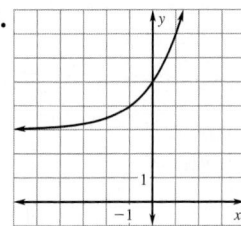 domain: all real numbers, range: $y > 3$

27. The power of $(x - 3)$ translates the parent graph 3 units to the right, not to the left.

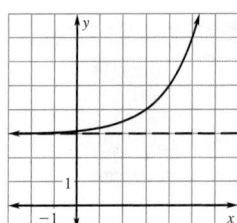

29. $A = 800\left(1 + \frac{0.02}{365}\right)^{365t}$, where A represents the amount in the account after t years. **31. a.** $1844.81 **b.** 18 yr **33. a.** The graph no longer has a vertical stretch of 2. **b.** The graph will increase slower. **c.** The graph will be translated 3 units to the right instead of 4 units to the left. **d.** The graph will be translated 1 unit down instead of 3 units up.

4.1 Problem Solving
35. a. 0.42 million, 2.47, 147%

b. 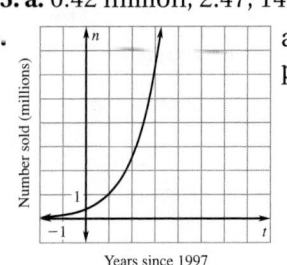 about 16 million DVD players

37. a. $2479.38 **b.** $2406.98 **c.** $2383.23
39. a. $P = 494.29(1.03)^t$; 664,284 people

b. 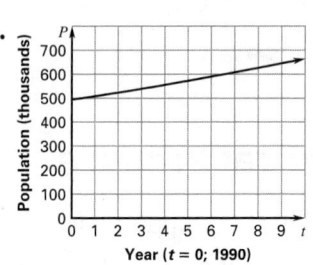 domain: $t \ge 0$, range: $P \ge 494.29$

c. 1996 **41. a.** $p = 48.28(1.06)^t$

b. 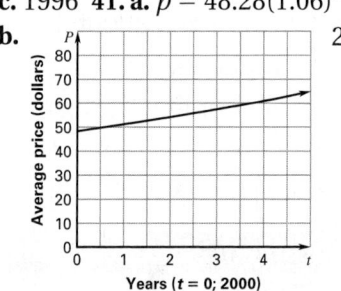 2003

c. *Sample answer:* Since the function is only defined when t is between 0 and 4, you can look at the graph between these values to determine the minimum or maximum that gives meaningful results. **43.** No. *Sample answer:* The amounts are not equal except initially and one year after the investments are made.

4.2 Skill Practice 1. 1250, 0.85, 15%
3. exponential decay **5.** exponential growth

7. 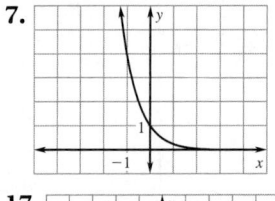 **9.**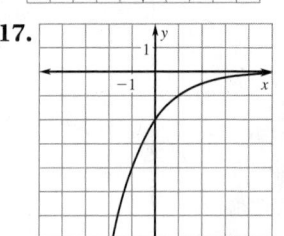

17. 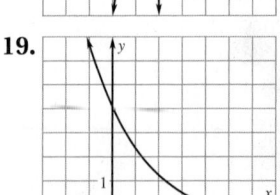 domain: all real numbers, range: $y < 0$

19. domain: all real numbers, range: $y > -1$

25. a. The graph is a vertical stretch by a factor of $\frac{4}{3}$.
b. The graph will be steeper because the decay factor

SA14

Selected Answers

is smaller. **c.** The graph moves 5 units to the right instead of 2 units to the right. **d.** The horizontal asymptote moves to $y = 3$.

4.2 Problem Solving 31. a. $y = 200(0.75)^t$; about $84.38

b.

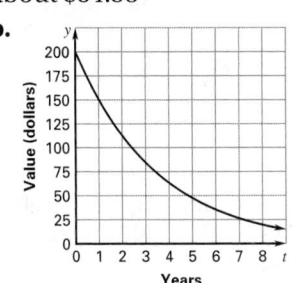

c. after about 2.5 yr

33. a.

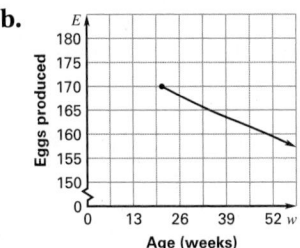

after 5 yr **b.** $5.29; no. *Sample answer:* A car does not normally last 50 years.

35. a. 0.89, 11%

b.

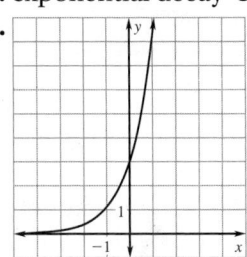

c. about 134 eggs per yr **d.** Change the exponent to just w.

4.2 Extension 1. about 0.0028, or about 0.28% **3.** about 0.00090, or about 0.090% **5.** about 0.0718, or about 7.18%

4.3 Skill Practice 1. e **3.** e^7 **5.** $8e^{9x}$ **7.** $\dfrac{1}{3e^{5x}}$
9. $3e^3$ **11.** $3e^{1-x}$ **13.** $2e^{3x}$ **17.** The 3 should be raised to the second power also; $(3e^{5x})^2 = 3^2 e^{(5x)(2)} = 9e^{10x}$.
19. about 20.086 **21.** about 9.025 **23.** about 0.670 **25.** about 1096.633 **27.** about 1.482 **29.** about -66.139 **31.** exponential decay **33.** exponential decay **35.** exponential decay **37.** exponential growth

43.

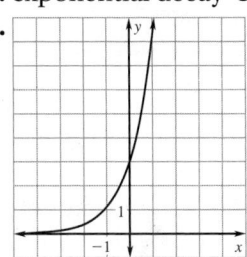

domain: all real numbers, range: $y > 0$

45.

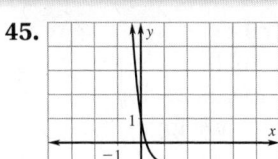

domain: all real numbers, range: $y > -1$

51. 10,000,000,000. *Sample answer:* Since small values of n were increasing the function very slowly, I checked larger intervals. I noticed that every power of 10 gave an answer one digit closer to the actual value of e. **53.** *Sample answer:* $f(x) = \frac{1}{2}e^{-3x}, g(x) = \frac{2}{3}e^{-5x}$

4.3 Problem Solving 55. about 895 million camera phones **57.** $2442.81
59. a. $L(x) = 100e^{-0.02x}$

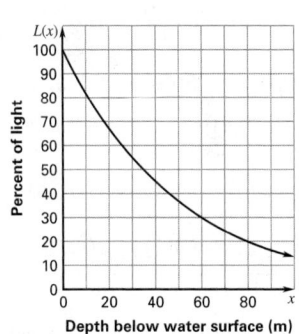

b. about 45% **c.** about 35 m **61.** about 1.986 cm^2

4.4 Skill Practice 1. common **3.** $4^2 = 16$
5. $6^{-2} = \frac{1}{36}$ **7.** *Sample answer:* The -3 and $\frac{1}{8}$ are switched around; $\log_2 \frac{1}{8} = -3$. **9.** 2 **11.** 6 **13.** -3
15. $-\frac{1}{2}$ **17.** 3 **19.** 2 **21.** about 1.792 **23.** about 0.793
25. about 1.683 **27.** about 4.700 **29.** x **31.** 8 **33.** $4x$
35. $5x$ **37.** $y = 8^x$ **39.** $y = \log_{0.4} x$ **41.** $y = \ln x - 2$
43. $y = e^x - 1$

45.

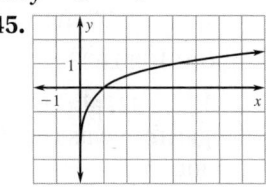

domain: $x > 0$, range: all real numbers

47.

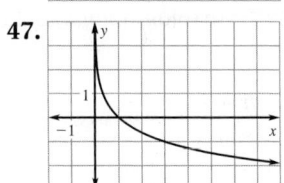

domain: $x > 0$, range: all real numbers

4.4 Problem Solving 59. 2.3 **61. a.** about 6.4 **b.** $E = e^{(M+9.9)/0.29}$; the inverse represents the amount of energy released, in ergs, as a function of the energy magnitude.

SA15

Selected Answers

4.5 Skill Practice 1. product **7.** 0.477
9. 1.204 **11.** 2.158 **13.** -0.602 **15.** $\log_3 4 + \log_3 x$
17. $\log 3 + 4\log x$ **19.** $\log_2 2 - \log_2 5$ **21.** $\log_4 x -$
$\log_4 3 - \log_4 y$ **23.** $\log_7 5 + 3\log_7 x + \log_7 y + 2\log_7 z$
25. $2\ln x + \frac{1}{3}\ln y$ **27.** $\frac{1}{2}\log_2 x$ **29.** $\frac{3}{4}\ln x$ **31.** The two
parts should be added, not multiplied; $\log_2 5 + \log_2 x$.
33. $\log_4 \frac{7}{10}$ **35.** $\log 11x^2$ **37.** $\log \frac{x^5}{y^4}$ **39.** $\ln 10x$
41. $\ln \frac{64}{y^4}$ **45.** about 1.404 **47.** about 2.465 **49.** about
1.631 **51.** about 1.581 **53.** about 1.513 **55.** 1.5
57. about 0.875 **59.** about -1.358 **61.** When using
the change of base formula, the base goes in the
denominator; $\frac{\log 7}{\log 3}$. **63.** 150 decibels

4.5 Problem Solving 69. about 76 decibels
71. 10; $L(10I) - L(I) = 10\log\frac{10I}{I_0} - 10\log\frac{I}{I_0} =$
$10\left(\log\frac{10I}{I_0} - \log\frac{I}{I_0}\right) = 10\left(\log 10 + \log\frac{I}{I_0} - \log\frac{I}{I_0}\right) =$
$10\log 10 = 10(1) = 10$ **73. a.** $s = 2\log_2 f$

b.

f	1.414	2.000	2.828	4.000
s	about 1	2	about 3	4

f	5.657	8.000	11.314	16.000
s	about 5	6	about 7	8

Sample answer: The amount of light increases by
about 1 each time. **c.** About 22.627; if you set up the
equation $9 = 2\log_2 f$ and solve for f, the result is $2^{9/2}$.

4.6 Skill Practice 1. exponential **3.** 8
5. $\frac{7}{12}$ **7.** $-\frac{5}{7}$ **9.** $-\frac{5}{3}$ **11.** -2 **13.** about -1.609
15. about 0.292 **17.** about -0.723 **19.** about 0.650
21. about -0.378 **23.** about -0.203 **25.** 6 **27.** no
solution **29.** $\frac{31}{15}$ **31.** $\frac{1}{3}$ **33.** e^7 or about 1096.633
35. about 35.601 **37.** 4 **39.** about 0.729 **41.** about
2.720 **43.** about 10.243 **45.** The logarithm was not
simplified correctly, $x\log_3 6 \neq 2x$; $\log_3 6 \approx 1.631$,
$x = 1.585$. **47.** *Sample answer:* $3^x = 81$, $\log_5 (x + 4) = 0$

4.6 Problem Solving
55. about 24°F **57.** about 6967 yr

59. a.

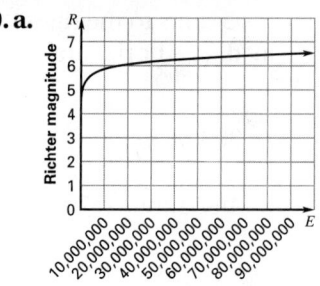

Energy released
(kilowatt-hours)

Japan: about
127,000,000 kilowatt-
hours, Greece: about
11,500,000 kilowatt-
hours, USA: about
23,500 kilowatt-hours

b. Japan: $6.6 = 0.67\log (0.37E) + 1.46$, 126,893,702
kilowatt-hours; Greece: $5.9 = 0.67\log (0.37E) + 1.46$,
11,446,269 kilowatt-hours; USA; $4.1 = 0.67\log (0.37E)$
$+ 1.46$, 23,556 kilowatt-hours

4.6 Problem Solving Workshop 1. about 0.799
3. about 2.10 **5.** 0.8 **7.** about 4.48 **9.** 2001
11. about 251.19 mm **13.** about 0.03225°C

Extension 1. $x \leq 2.727$ **3.** $x \leq 1.51$ **5.** $x \leq 6.03$
7. $x \geq 27$ **9.** $0 < x \leq 36$ **11.** $0 < x < 32$ **13.** after 5.25 yr

4.7 Skill Practice 1. exponential
3. $y = \frac{3}{4} \cdot 4^x$ **5.** $y = \frac{1}{8} \cdot 2^x$ **7.** $y = \frac{2}{5} \cdot 5^x$
9. $y = 4.99 \cdot 0.499^x$
11.

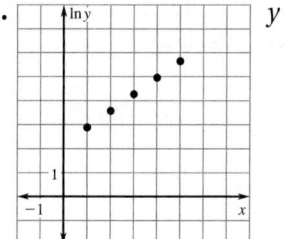

$y = 9(2)^x$

13.

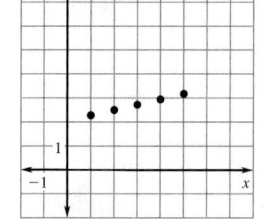

$y = 7.83(1.25)^x$

15. $y = 0.12x^{2.32}$ **17.** $y = 1.25x^{1.26}$ **19.** $y = 0.569x^{1.91}$
21. $y = 0.241x^{2.34}$
23.

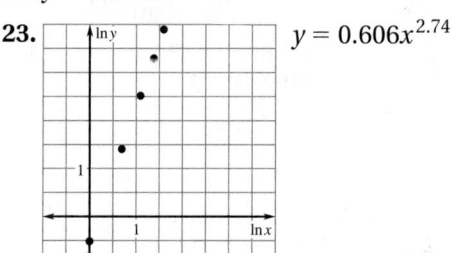

$y = 0.606x^{2.74}$

25.
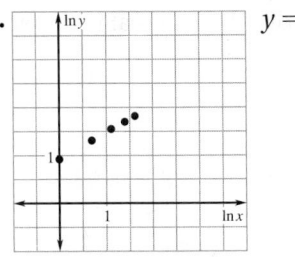
$y = 2.50x^{0.567}$

29. The x should be raised to the 3, not multiplied by it; $\ln y = \ln x^3 - 2$, $y = e^{\ln x^3 - 2}$, $y = e^{\ln x^3} \cdot e^{-2}$, $y = e^{\ln x^3} \cdot e^{-2}$, $y = 0.135x^3$

4.7 Problem Solving

31. a.
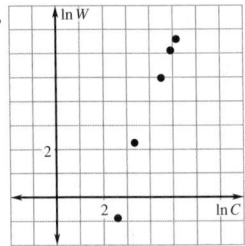
b. $y = 0.000467x^{2.80}$
c. about 65.0 kg

33. a. $y = 0.475(2.08)^x$ **b.** Graph the transformed data pairs (x, y), $(x, \ln y)$, and $(\ln x, \ln y)$. If the graph of (x, y) is most linear, then a linear function is best. If the graph of $(x, \ln y)$ is most linear, then an exponential function is best. If the graph of $(\ln x, \ln y)$ is most linear, then a power function is best. If the graphs seem equally linear, use a graphing calculator to perform a linear regression on each set of transformed data pairs. Choose the type of model whose correlation coefficient is closest to 1. Then perform this type of regression on the original data; the best-fitting model is the power function $y = 55.7x^{0.793}$.

35. a.
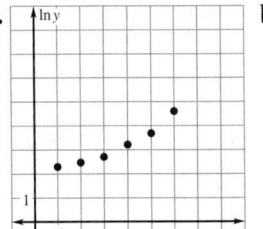
b.
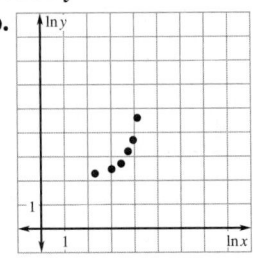

c. Exponential function; the points for $(x, \ln y)$ appear more linear than the points $(\ln x, \ln y)$, so an exponential model appears to be the best fit for the data. **d.** $y = 4.98(1.05)^x$; about 247 cm

Chapter Review 1. $y = 5$ **3.** *Sample answer:* $\log_b y = x$ if and only if $b^x = y$. **5.** Exponential function. *Sample answer:* The variable is in the exponent.

7.
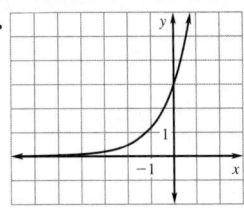
domain: all real numbers, range: $y > 0$

9. \$1725.39

11.
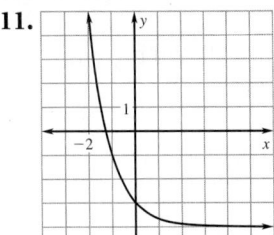
domain: all real numbers, range: $y > -4$

13.
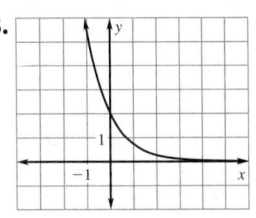
domain: all real numbers, range: $y > 0$

15.
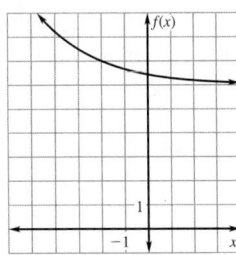
domain: all real numbers, range: $f(x) > 6$

17. 5 **19.** -3

21.
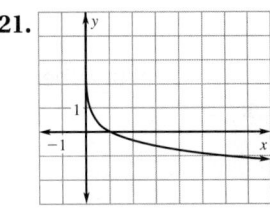
domain: $x > 0$, range: all real numbers

23.
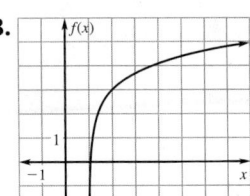
domain: $x > 1$, range: all real numbers

25. $\log_8 3 + \log_8 x + \log_8 y$ **27.** $\log 8 - 4\log y$ **29.** $\log_7 384$ **31.** $\ln 36$ **33.** 7 **35.** $y = 64\left(\frac{1}{2}\right)^x$

37. $y = \frac{1}{4} \cdot 6x$

Chapter 4
Extra Practice

1. 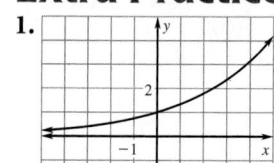 domain: all real numbers, range: $y > 0$

3. 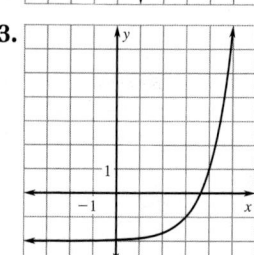 domain: all real numbers, range: $y > -2$

5. 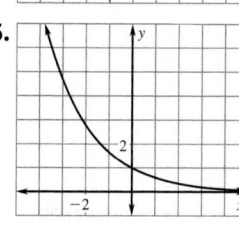 domain: all real numbers, range: $y > 0$

7. 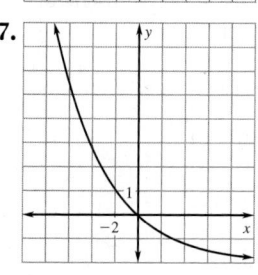 domain: all real numbers, range: $y > -2$

9. $\dfrac{1}{e^{11}}$ 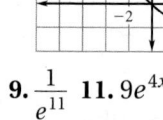 **11.** $9e^{4x}$

13. 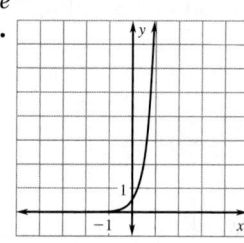 domain: all real numbers, range: $y > 0$

15. 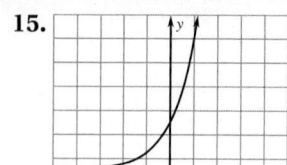 domain: all real numbers, range: $y > 3$

17. -2 **19.** 3 **21.** x **23.** $2x$

25. 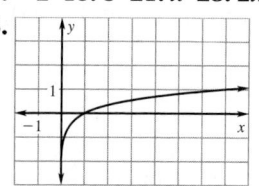 domain: $x > 0$, range: all real numbers

27. 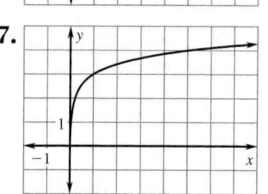 domain: $x > 0$, range: all real numbers

29. $\log_5 2 + \log_5 x - 1$ **31.** $\ln 20 + 3 \ln x + 2 \ln y$

33. $\log_4 20x^4$ **35.** $\ln \dfrac{10y^8}{x^2}$ **37.** about 3.161

39. about 1.694 **41.** 1 **43.** no solution **45.** 3

47. $y = \dfrac{3}{2} \cdot 2^x$ or $y = -\dfrac{3}{2} \cdot (-2)^x$ **49.** $y = 4 \cdot 1^x$

51. $y = \dfrac{1}{3} \cdot x^4$ **53.** $y = 0.538 \cdot x^{2.611}$

Mastering the Standards

for Mathematical Practice

The topics described in the Standards for Mathematical
Content will vary from year to year. However, the *way* in
which you learn, study, and think about mathematics will
not. The Standards for Mathematical Practice describe skills
that you will use in all of your math courses.

Mathematical Practices

1. *Make sense of problems and persevere in solving them.*
2. *Reason abstractly and quantitatively.*
3. *Construct viable arguments and critique the reasoning of others.*
4. *Model with mathematics.*
5. *Use appropriate tools strategically.*
6. *Attend to precision.*
7. *Look for and make use of structure.*
8. *Look for and express regularity in repeated reasoning.*

4 Model with mathematics.

*Mathematically proficient
students can apply...
mathematics... to... problems...
in everyday life, society, and
the workplace...*

In your book

Application exercises and **Mixed Reviews of Problem
Solving** apply mathematics to other disciplines and in
real-world scenarios.

Chapter 5

5.1 Skill Practice 1. jointly **3.** inverse variation
5. direct variation **7.** inverse variation
9. direct variation **13.** $y = \dfrac{9}{x}$; 3 **15.** $y = \dfrac{14}{x}$; $\dfrac{14}{3}$
17. $y = \dfrac{5}{x}$; $\dfrac{5}{3}$ **19.** $y = \dfrac{-35}{3x}$; $-\dfrac{35}{9}$ **21.** direct variation
23. inverse variation **25.** $z = \dfrac{1}{4}xy$; -5 **27.** $z = \dfrac{1}{14}xy$;
$\dfrac{-10}{7}$ **29.** $z = -5xy$; 100 **31.** $x = \dfrac{ay}{z}$ **33.** $w = \dfrac{axz}{y}$
35. *Sample answer:* $f(x) = 2x$, $g(x) = \dfrac{2}{x}$

5.1 Problem Solving 37. $n = \dfrac{103.68}{s}$;
26 photos **39.** $P = \dfrac{172}{A}$; about 2.87 lb/in.^{2}
41. a. $F = \dfrac{Gm_1m_2}{d^2}$ **b.** 6.7×10^{-11} **c.** It increases;
it decreases.

5.2 Skill Practice 1. range; domain

3.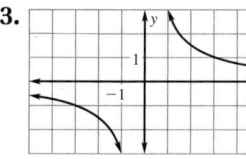
The graph lies farther from the axes than the graph of $y = \dfrac{1}{x}$. Both graphs lie in the 1st and 3rd quadrants and have the same asymptotes, domain, and range.

5.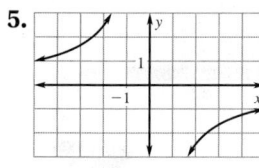
The graph lies farther from the axes than the graph of $y = \dfrac{1}{x}$ and is located in quadrants 2 and 4. Both graphs have the same asymptotes, domain, and range.

11.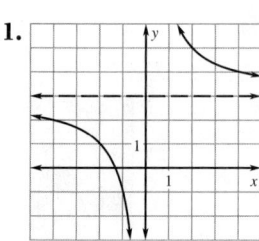
domain: all real numbers except 0, range: all real numbers except 3

13.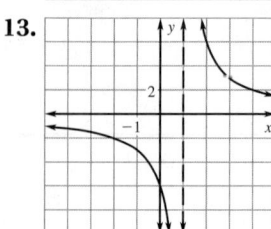
domain: all real numbers except 1, range: all real numbers except 0

25. The graph should be $y = \dfrac{-8}{x}$ not $y = \dfrac{8}{x}$.

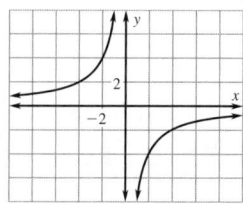

27.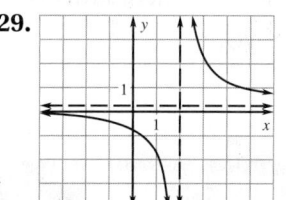
domain: all real numbers except 3, range: all real numbers except 1

29.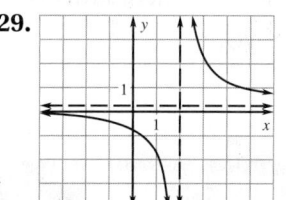
domain: all real numbers except 2, range: all real numbers except $\dfrac{1}{4}$

35. *Sample answer:* $y = \dfrac{3x + 1}{x + 8}$

5.2 Problem Solving

37. $c = \dfrac{43m + 50}{m}$; 5 mo

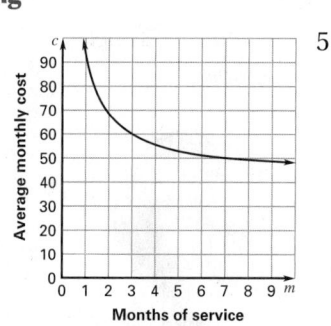

39. a. About 14.5 sec. *Sample answer:* Substitute 25 for T to find $t \approx 2.89$. Since you are 5 kilometers away, multiply t by 5 to get $5(2.89) \approx 14.5$ seconds.
b. 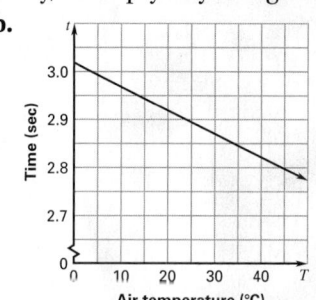 about 3.9°C

41. a. approaching: $f_1 = \dfrac{1{,}480{,}000}{740 - r}$,
moving away: $f_1 = \dfrac{1{,}480{,}000}{740 + r}$

b. 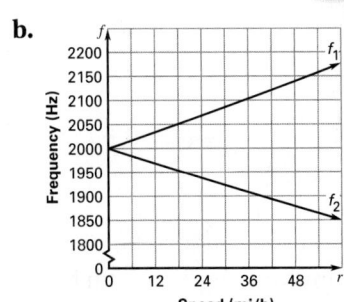 **c.** The frequency of a sound that is approaching is greater than that of a sound moving away.

15.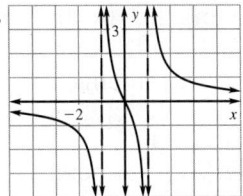

17. 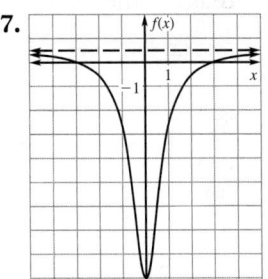 **25.** $0 < y \le 7.5$
27. all real numbers except $-4.791 < y < -0.209$

5.2 Extension 1. $y = \dfrac{2}{x - 3} + 2$

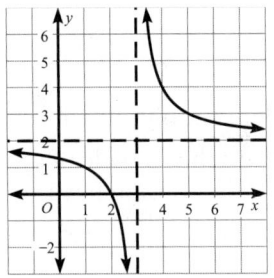

3. $y = \dfrac{1}{x + 1} + 3$

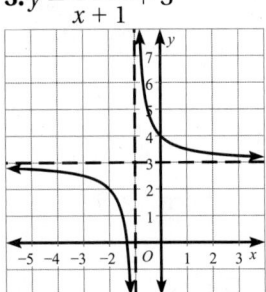

5. $y = \dfrac{6}{x - 1} + 3x + 5$ **7.** $y = \dfrac{-4x - 11}{x^2 + 2x + 1 + 2}$

9. $C = \dfrac{35}{n} + 10$

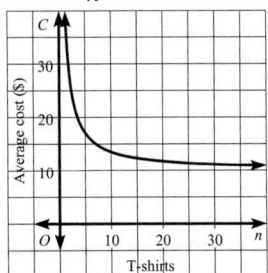

5.3 Skill Practice 1. horizontal asymptote
3. C **5.** B **7.** none; $x = 1$ and $x = -1$ **9.** none; $x = 5$ and $x = -3$ **11.** -3; $x = 0$ and $x = -\dfrac{1}{3}$ **13.** The vertical asymptote occurs at the zeros of the denominator not the numerator; the vertical asymptotes occur at the zeros of the denominator $x^2 - 8x + 7$. So, the vertical asymptotes are at $x = 7$ and $x = 1$.

5.3 Problem Solving 31. a. $\ell = \dfrac{100}{\pi r^2}$
b. $S = 2\pi r^2 + \dfrac{200}{r}$ **c.** $r \approx 2.515$ ft, $\ell \approx 5.032$ ft

33. a.

Depth (m)	Mean Temperature (°C)
1000	4.763
1050	4.580
1100	4.409
1150	4.251
1200	4.104
1250	3.967
1300	3.839

b. 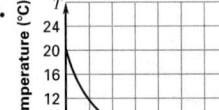 about 1238 m

35. a.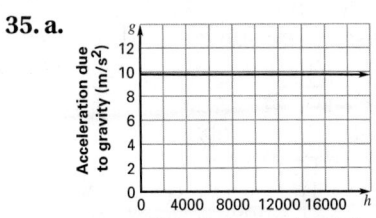

b. about 9.78 m/sec^2 **c.** about 9.47 m/sec^2
d. *Sample answer:* g decreases, but at a very small rate.

5.4 Skill Practice 1. reciprocal **3.** B **5.** C
7. simplified form **9.** $\dfrac{x - 3}{x + 5}$ **11.** $\dfrac{2(x - 1)}{x - 7}$ **13.** $\dfrac{x - 6}{x + 6}$
15. $\dfrac{4x - 1}{3x + 2}$ **17.** $\dfrac{x^2 - 3}{x - 3}$ **19.** You can only divide out

common factors. Since the factors that are divided out are not common factors of the entire numerator and denominator, you cannot divide them out; $\dfrac{x^2 + 16x + 48}{x^2 + 8x + 16} = \dfrac{(x+4)(x+12)}{(x+4)(x+4)} = \dfrac{x+12}{x+4}$ **21.** $\dfrac{2}{x}$

23. Exercise 21. *Sample answer:* The perimeter of Exercise 21 is smaller and the areas are the same.

25. $\dfrac{8x^4}{y^2}$ **27.** $\dfrac{2(x+1)}{x}$ **29.** $\dfrac{x+4}{2(x-5)}$ **31.** $(x+2)(x+7)$

33. $\dfrac{4(x+5)(x+4)}{x}$ **35.** $\dfrac{4x^4y}{5z}$ **37.** $\dfrac{16x(x-4)}{(x+4)}$

39. $\dfrac{x-5}{(x+5)^2}$ **41.** $\dfrac{5(x+1)}{x-1}$ **43.** $\dfrac{(x+8)(x-7)}{6x}$

45.

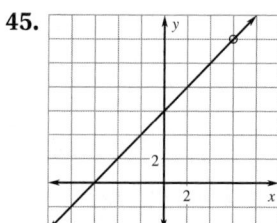

5.4 Problem Solving

49. $\dfrac{S}{A} = \dfrac{(-6420t + 292{,}000)(5.92t^2 - 131t + 1000)}{(6.02t^2 - 125t + 1000)(-407t + 7220)};$

$50.21 **51. a.** $V_{\text{sphere}} = \dfrac{4}{3}\pi r^3$, $V_{\text{cylinder}} = \pi r^2 h$, since the volumes are the same, set the equations equal to each other resulting in $h = \dfrac{4}{3}r$. **b.** $S_{\text{sphere}} = 4\pi r^2$, $S_{\text{cylinder}} = \dfrac{14}{3}\pi r^2$ **c.** $\dfrac{6}{7}$. *Sample answer:* The spherical tank uses less material.

5.5 Skill Practice

1. complex fraction

3. $\dfrac{5}{x}$ **5.** $\dfrac{9 - 2x}{x+1}$ **7.** 5 **9.** $3x(x-2)$ **11.** $2x(x-5)$

13. $x(x-5)(x+5)$ **17.** $\dfrac{32 - 15x}{12x^2}$ **19.** $\dfrac{3(x+12)}{(x+8)(x-3)}$

21. $\dfrac{2x^2 + 3x + 9}{(x+1)(x-3)}$ **23.** $\dfrac{-3(x+16)}{(x-4)^2}$ **25.** You must have a common denominator before you can add values in the numerator; $\dfrac{x(x-5) + 4(x+2)}{(x+2)(x-5)} = \dfrac{x^2 - x + 8}{(x-5)(x+2)}$.

27. $\dfrac{(2x+3)(x-1)}{(x-3)(x+3)^2}$ **29.** $\dfrac{8x^3 - 9x^2 - 28x + 8}{x(x-4)(3x-1)}$

31. $\dfrac{x(x-18)}{6(5x+2)}$ **33.** $\dfrac{8x(x+1)}{(x-2)(5x+3)}$ **35.** $\dfrac{3x}{4(x-1)}$

37. *Sample answer:* $\dfrac{\frac{x^2 - x - 6}{x^2 + 4x}}{\frac{x+2}{x}}$, $\dfrac{\frac{x^2 + 3x - 18}{4}}{\frac{x^2 + 10x + 24}{4}}$

5.5 Problem Solving

41. $T = \dfrac{2da}{(a-j)(a+j)};$ about 10.2 h **43. a.** $M = \dfrac{Pi}{1 - \left(\frac{1}{1+i}\right)^{12t}} = \dfrac{Pi}{1 - \frac{1}{(1+i)^{12t}}} = \dfrac{Pi}{\frac{(1+i)^{12t} - 1}{(1+i)^{12t}}} = \dfrac{Pi(1+i)^{12t}}{(1+i)^{12t} - 1}$ **b.** $364.02

5.6 Skill Practice

1. cross multiplying **3.** Graph both sides of the equation. If the graphs intersect at a possible solution, then it is a solution. If the graphs do not intersect at a possible solution, then it is an extraneous solution. **5.** 6 **7.** 2 **9.** -1

11. no solution **15.** 4 **17.** $-\dfrac{7}{3}$ **19.** $\dfrac{-1 \pm \sqrt{79}}{3}$ **21.** 1

23. $-\dfrac{5}{2}, 8$ **25.** $0, 7$ **27.** The student simply added numerators and denominators on the left side of the equation. Both sides of the equation should have been multiplied by the LCD, $6x$; $6x\left(\dfrac{5}{x} + \dfrac{23}{6}\right) = 6x\left(\dfrac{45}{x}\right)$, $30 + 23x = 270$. **29.** *Sample answer:* $\dfrac{6}{x+5} = \dfrac{2x}{x-1};$ $\dfrac{4}{x} + \dfrac{5}{3} = \dfrac{12}{x}$

5.6 Problem Solving **33.** 26 serves

35. 1995 **37.** $\dfrac{1 + \sqrt{5}}{2}$

5.6 Problem Solving Workshop **1.** about ± 5.6
3. 9 **5.** about ± 3.2 **7. a.** 99 ft **b.** 33 ft

Extension 1. $x < 2$ **3.** $x < 3$ **5.** $-1.5 < x < 4$
7. $x > -5$ **9.** $-1 \le x \le 1$ **11.** $0 < x < 1$ **13.** $x > -2$
15. $-4 < x < -3$ or $x > -2$ **17.** $-3 < x < -2$ or $x \ge 2$
19. 1999 to 2002 **21.** at least 13 mo

5.7 Skill Practice **1.** even
3.

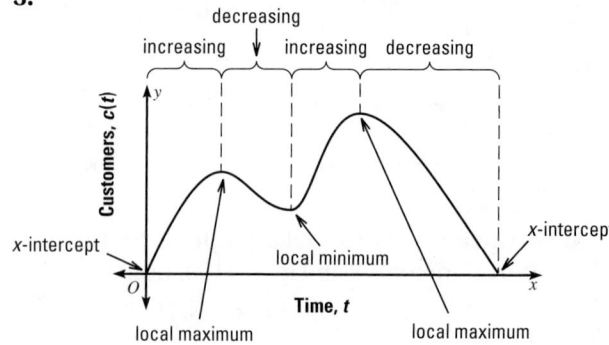

5.

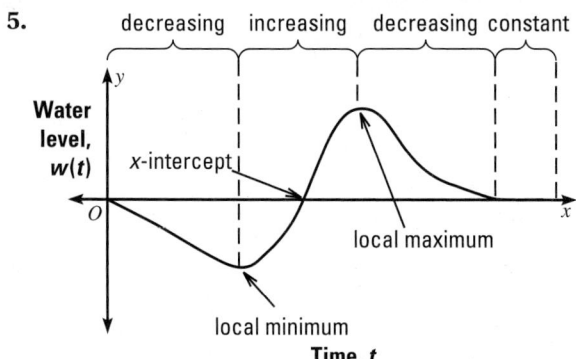

decreasing   increasing   decreasing   constant

Water
level,
$w(t)$

x-intercept

local maximum

local minimum

Time, t

7. $-1, -\frac{1}{2}, -\frac{1}{4}, -\frac{1}{8}$; As x increases, the graph of $f(x)$ falls less and less steeply. **9.** over $\left[\frac{7}{3}, 3\right]$: $\frac{3}{2}$; over $[3, 5]$: $\frac{1}{2}$; over $[5, 11]$: $\frac{1}{6}$; over $[11, 29]$: $\frac{1}{18}$; As x increases, the graph of $f(x)$ rises less and less steeply.
15. odd **17.** even **19.** odd **21.** even **23.** neither

5.7 Problem Solving 27. The y-intercept for the value of the sports utility vehicle is 30,000, while the y-intercept for the value of the minivan is 25,000. This means that the sports utility vehicle had a greater initial cost. The average rate of decrease for the value of the minivan is greater than the average rate of decrease for the value of the sports utility vehicle. So, the value of the minivan is decreasing at a greater rate. **29. a.** 1028; 1056.78; 1086.37; 1116.79; 1148.06 **b.** Your sister's initial investment is greater than yours. The average rate of increase for your account is greater than that of your sister's account. So, your balance is increasing faster than her balance. **31. a.** Pattern 1: $y = x^4$; Pattern 2: $y = 4^x$

b.

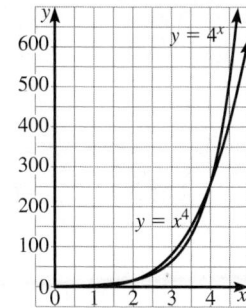

Yes, the exponential function $y = 4^x$ exceeds the polynomial function $y = x^4$ when $x > 4$, and then rises much more rapidly than the polynomial function. **c.** yes **33.** $y = 5x + 31$ **35.** $3\sqrt{3}$ **37.** $5\sqrt{6}$ **39.** $11\sqrt{2}$ **41.** $5x - 3y^2$ **43.** $\frac{3\sqrt[5]{y}}{xy}$

Chapter Review 1. inverse variation **3.** rational function **5.** cross multiplying **7.** $y = \frac{24}{x}$; -8 **9.** $y = \frac{-8}{x}$; $\frac{8}{3}$

11.

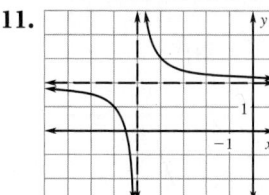

domain: all real numbers except $x = -5$, range: all real numbers except $y = 2$

13.

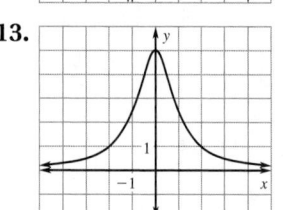

15.

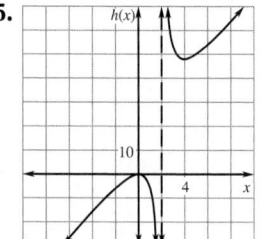

$h(x)$

17.

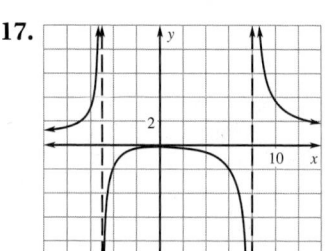

19. $\frac{16x^3}{y^2}$ **21.** $\frac{3x(4x - 1)}{(x - 4)(x - 3)}$ **23.** $\frac{3x^2 + 26x + 36}{6x(x + 3)}$ **25.** $\frac{-2(2x^2 + 3x + 3)}{(x - 3)(x + 3)(x + 1)}$ **27.** $-5, -3$ **29.** 0 **31.** odd **33.** even

Chapter 5 Extra Practice

1. inverse variation **3.** neither variation

5.

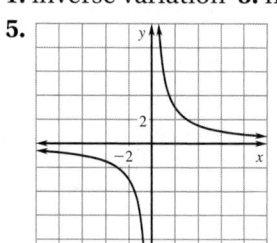

domain: all real numbers except $x = 0$, range: all real numbers except $y = 0$

7.

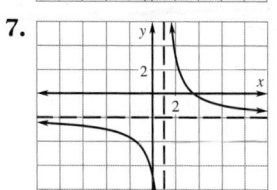

domain: all real numbers except $x = 1$, range: all real numbers except $y = -2$

9. 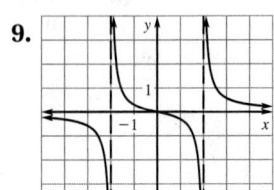 **11.**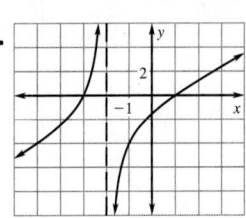

13. $\dfrac{x-2}{x+6}$ **15.** $\dfrac{x-12}{2(x-7)}$ **17.** $\dfrac{3x(x+5)^2}{x-6}$

19. $\dfrac{(x+4)(2x-3)}{x}$ **21.** $\dfrac{x^2+4x-4}{(x+6)(x-2)}$ **23.** $\dfrac{x^2}{(5x+3)(2x+1)}$

25. $\dfrac{3(x-3)}{(x-2)(x-7)}$ **27.** -3 **29.** $-\dfrac{4}{3}$ **31.** 2, 0.4, about 0.171, about 0.095 **33.** even **35.** odd

Mastering *the* Standards

for Mathematical Practice

The topics described in the Standards for Mathematical Content will vary from year to year. However, the *way* in which you learn, study, and think about mathematics will not. The Standards for Mathematical Practice describe skills that you will use in all of your math courses.

Mathematical Practices

1. *Make sense of problems and persevere in solving them.*
2. *Reason abstractly and quantitatively.*
3. *Construct viable arguments and critique the reasoning of others.*
4. *Model with mathematics.*
5. *Use appropriate tools strategically.*
6. *Attend to precision.*
7. *Look for and make use of structure.*
8. *Look for and express regularity in repeated reasoning.*

⑤ Use appropriate tools strategically.

Mathematically proficient students consider the available tools when solving a... problem... [and] are... able to use technological tools to explore and deepen their understanding...

In your book

Problem Solving Workshops explore alternative methods as tools for problem solving. A variety of **Activities** use concrete and technological tools to explore mathematical concepts.

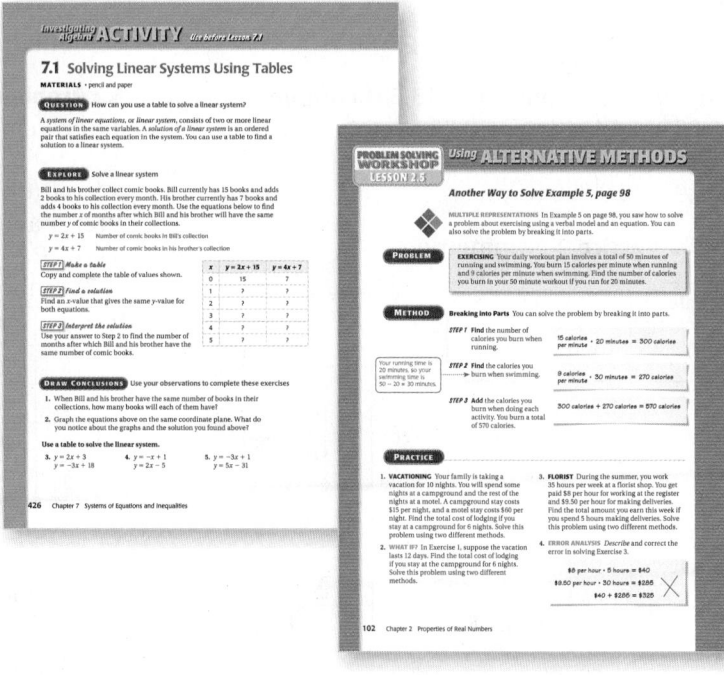

Getty Images/Image Source

Chapter 6

6.1 Skill Practice 1. Binomial Theorem **3.** 10 **5.** 84
7. 1 **9.** 21 **11.** The denominator should have been

multiplied by 2!; $\dfrac{6!}{(6-2)! \cdot 2!} = \dfrac{720}{48} = 15$.

13. 792 hands **15.** 778,320 hands **17.** 2,490,624 hands
19.

```
            1    6    15   20   15    6    1
        1    7   21   35   35   21    7    1
     1    8   28   56   70   56   28    8    1
  1    9   36   84  126  126   84   36    9    1
1   10   45  120  210  252  210  120   45   10    1
```

21. $y^{10} - 30y^9z + 405y^8z^2 - 3240y^7z^3 + 17{,}010y^6z^4 - 61{,}236y^5z^5 + 153{,}090y^4z^6 - 262{,}440y^3z^7 + 295{,}245y^2z^8 - 196{,}830yz^9 + 59{,}049z^{10}$ **23.** $128s^7 - 448s^6t^4 + 672s^5t^8 - 560s^4t^{12} + 280s^3t^{16} - 84s^2t^{20} + 14st^{24} - t^{28}$ **25.** $c^5 - 20c^4 + 160c^3 - 640c^2 + 1280c - 1024$ **27.** $4096p^6 - 6144p^5q + 3840p^4q^2 - 1280p^3q^3 + 240p^2q^4 - 24pq^5 + q^6$ **29.** $32s^{20} + 400s^{16} + 2000s^{12} + 5000s^8 + 6250s^4 + 3125$
31. $x^{12} - 4x^9y^2 + 6x^6y^4 - 4x^3y^6 + y^8$ **33.** 1080
37. The sum along each diagonal segment is equal to the sum of the two previous diagonal segment sums. **39.** combinations; 13,836,130,056 ways
41. $1 = {}_nC_n = \dfrac{n!}{(n-n)! \cdot n!} = \dfrac{n!}{0! \cdot n!} = \dfrac{1}{0!}$, so 0! must equal 1.

6.1 Problem Solving

49. 816 combinations **51. a.** 15,504 combinations
b. 3,003 combinations **c.** 252 combinations;
10 combinations; 3 combinations
d. 351,982,350,720 ways

6.2 Skill Practice 1. symmetric

3.

x (value)	1	2	3
P(x)	$\frac{1}{2}$	$\frac{3}{10}$	$\frac{1}{5}$

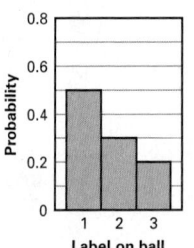

Label on ball

5.

x (value)	1	2	3
P(x)	$\frac{1}{100}$	$\frac{9}{100}$	$\frac{9}{10}$

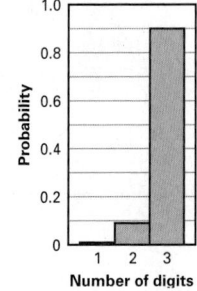

Number of digits

7. 3 **11.** about 0.00018 **13.** about 0.037
15. about 0.120 **17.** about 0.00018 **19.** about 0.0086
21. about 0.055 **23.** about 0.00000024 **25.** about
0.00000000000000000087 **27.** The ${}_5C_3$ was left out of

the equation; ${}_5C_3\left(\dfrac{1}{6}\right)^3\left(\dfrac{5}{6}\right)^{5-3} \approx 0.03$. **29.** about 0.594

31. about 0.852

33.

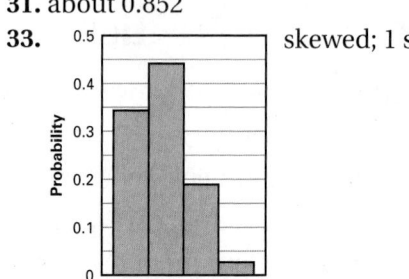

skewed; 1 success

35.

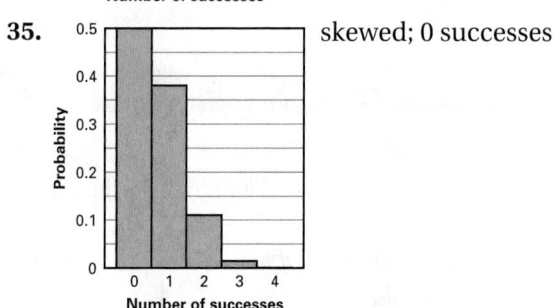

skewed; 0 successes

41. ${}_nC_k$; since order does not matter, find the combination of n things taken k at a time.

6.2 Problem Solving 43. about 0.196

45. a. about 0.143 **b.** about 0.276
c. about 0.124 **d.** about 0.999
47. a. $P(0) =$ about 0.099, $P(1) =$ about 0.271,
$P(2) =$ about 0.319, $P(3) = 0.208$, $P(4) =$ about
0.081, $P(5) =$ about 0.019, $P(6) =$ about 0.0025,
$P(7) =$ about 0.00014
b.

x	P(x)
0	0.099
1	0.271
2	0.319
3	0.208
4	0.081
5	0.019
6	0.0025
7	0.00014

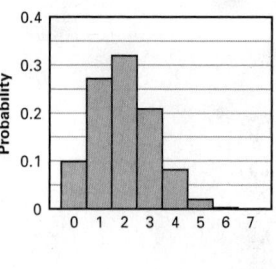

6.3 Skill Practice 1. normal curve

3. 0.16 **5.** 0.84 **7.** 0.68 **9.** 16% **11.** 0.68 **13.** 0.9735
15. 0.84 **19.** 0.7257 **21.** 0.0035 **23.** 0.5 **25.** 0.0548
27. 0.5363 **29.** The table was interpreted incorrectly;
$P(z \geq -0.8) = 1 - 0.2119 = 0.7881$.

6.3 Problem Solving 31. 0.16 **33. a.** -2.4, 1.6 **b.** 0.0082 **c.** 0.937; $P(z \le 1.6) - P(z \le -2.4)$ **35. a.** 2.4 **b.** 1.2 **c.** Lisa; in a standard normal distribution Lisa's score is higher.

6.4 Skill Practice 1. random **3.** Systematic; unbiased; the sample is representative of the customers. **5.** Random; unbiased; each student has an equal change of being selected. **7.** $\pm 3.2\%$ **9.** $\pm 1.3\%$ **11.** $\pm 4.4\%$ **13.** $\pm 1.0\%$ **15.** 1111 people **17.** 100 people **19.** 319 people **21.** 237 people **25.** about 453 people

6.4 Problem Solving 27. a. about $\pm 4.8\%$ **b.** between 9.2% and 18.8% **29.** No. *Sample answer:* Since the margin of error is $\pm 5\%$, Kosta could have 49% of the votes and Murdock could have 51% of the votes. **31. a.** 47%, 53% **b.** about $\pm 4.5\%$ **c.** between 42.5% and 51.5%, between 48.5% and 57.5% **d.** no; 273 people

6.5 Skill Practice 1. observational study **3.** This question may be biased because it assumes that the respondent is familiar with the proposed budget cuts. The responses from people who are unfamiliar with the proposed budget cuts may not accurately reflect their opinions. **5.** This question may be biased because the question is phrased to encourage a "yes" response. **7.** Observational study; the researcher gathers data without controlling the individuals or applying a treatment. **9.** B **11.** The study is a randomized comparative experiment.

6.5 Problem Solving 13. Observational study **15.** No; individuals were not randomly assigned to control/ treatment groups.

21.

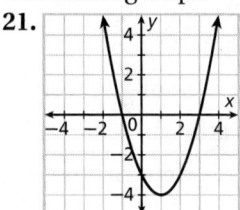

Chapter Review 1. $t^6 + 18t^5 + 135t^4 + 540t^3 + 1215t^2 + 1458t + 729$ **3.** $4096v^4 - 2048v^3w + 384v^2w^2 - 32vw^3 + w^4$ **5.** 32,192 combinations **7.** about 0.273 **9.** about 0.0039 **11.** about 0.0548 **13.** about 0 **15.** about 0.0179 **17.** $\pm 2\%$ **19.** $\pm 1.4\%$ **21.** survey **23.** randomized controlled experiment

Chapter 6
Extra Practice

1. 35 **3.** 10 **5.** $x^3 - 9x^2 + 27x - 27$ **7.** $p^{10} + 20p^8 + 160p^6 + 640p^4 + 1280p^2 + 1024$ **9.** about 0.000458 **11.** about 0.196 **13.** 0.84 **15.** 0.05 **17.** 0.16 **19.** Systematic; not biased; the owner took a random selection of customers. **21.** $\pm 10\%$ **23.** $\pm 1.9\%$ **25.** 10,000 **27.** 331 **29.** This question may be biased first because the referendum is not stated or explained, and the respondent may not be familiar with it. Also, the language of keeping your money in your own pocket biases the answer toward a "yes" response. To remove bias, the referendum could be read fully and clearly to the respondent, and the question could ask simply whether the person leans more toward a "yes" or "no" vote based on his or her current understanding of the referendum. **31.** Observational study; the researcher gathers data without controlling the individuals or applying a treatment.

Selected Answers

Chapter 7

7.1 Skill Practice 1. sigma notation **3.** 3, 4, 5, 6, 7, 8
5. 1, 4, 9, 16, 25, 36 **7.** 1, 4, 16, 64, 256, 1024

9. $-4, -1, 4, 11, 20, 31$ **11.** $-4, -2, -\frac{4}{3}, -1, -\frac{4}{5}, -\frac{2}{3}$

13. $\frac{2}{3}, 1, \frac{6}{5}, \frac{4}{3}, \frac{10}{7}, \frac{3}{2}$ **15.** You can write the terms as
$(5 \cdot 1 - 4), (5 \cdot 2 - 4), (5 \cdot 3 - 4), (5 \cdot 4 - 4), a_5 = 21,$
$a_n = 5n - 4.$ **17.** You can write the terms as
$(-1)^1(4 \cdot 1), (-1)^2(4 \cdot 2), (-1)^3(4 \cdot 3), (-1)^4(4 \cdot 4),$
$a_5 = -20, a_n = (-1)^n(4 \cdot n).$ **19.** You can write the
terms as $\frac{2}{3(1)}, \frac{2}{3(2)}, \frac{2}{3(3)}, \frac{2}{3(4)}, a_5 = \frac{2}{15}, a_n = \frac{2}{3n}.$ **21.** You
can write the terms as $\frac{1}{4}, \frac{2}{4}, \frac{3}{4}, \frac{4}{4}, \frac{5}{4}, a_6 = \frac{6}{4}, a_n = \frac{n}{4}.$
23. You can write the terms as $0.7(1) + 2.4, 0.7(2) + 2.4,$
$0.7(3) + 2.4, 0.7(4) + 2.4, a_5 = 5.9, a_n = 0.7n + 2.4.$
25. You can write the terms as $1^2 + 0.2, 2^2 + 0.2,$
$3^2 + 0.2, 4^2 + 0.2, a_5 = 25.2, a_n = n^2 + 0.2.$

29. 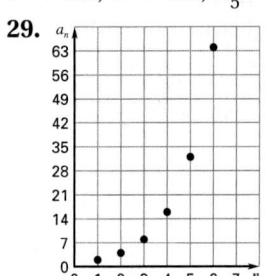 **31.**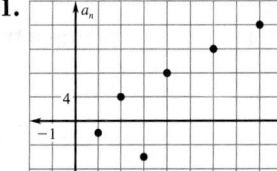

37. $\displaystyle\sum_{i=1}^{5} (3i + 4)$ **39.** $\displaystyle\sum_{i=1}^{\infty} (2i - 3)$ **41.** $\displaystyle\sum_{i=1}^{\infty} (7i - 4)$

43. $\displaystyle\sum_{i=1}^{7} \frac{i}{3 + i}$ **45.** 42 **47.** 100 **49.** 82 **51.** $\frac{761}{140}$ **53.** 35

55. 325 **57.** The lower limit is zero, so the first term
should be 3; $3 + 5 + 7 + 9 + 11 + 13 = 48.$

7.1 Problem Solving 63. $60°, 90°, 108°, 120°,$ about
$128.57°; T_n = 180(n - 2); 1800°$ **65.** $a_n = 2^n - 1; 63$
moves, 127 moves, 255 moves **67. a.** 15 balls **b.** 35
balls **c.** Except for layer 1, there are always more
balls in the same layer of the square pyramid. The
difference in the number of balls is $\frac{n(n - 1)}{2}.$

7.2 Skill Practice 1. common difference
3. Arithmetic; there is a common difference of 3
between consecutive terms. **5.** Arithmetic; there is a
common difference of 9 between consecutive terms.
7. Arithmetic; there is a common difference of 0.5
between consecutive terms. **9.** Not arithmetic; there is
not a common difference between consecutive terms.
11. Arithmetic; there is a common difference of 1.5
between consecutive terms. **13.** $a_n = -1 + 6n; 119$
15. $a_n = -5 + 2n; 35$ **17.** $a_n = 36 - 11n; -184$

19. $a_n = \frac{7}{3} - \frac{1}{3}n; -\frac{13}{3}$ **21.** The equation for an
arithmetic sequence is not correct; $a_n = a_1 + (n - 1)d,$
$a_n = 37 + (n - 1)(-13), a_n = 50 - 13n.$

23. $a_n = -28 + 5n;$

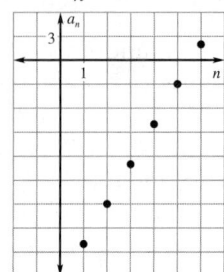

25. $a_n = 152 - 14n;$

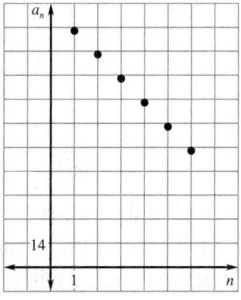

31. $a_n = 9 + 5n$ **33.** $a_n = 22 - 4n$ **35.** $a_n = 13 + 2n$
37. $a_n = \frac{15}{4} + \frac{9}{4}n$ **41.** -96 **43.** 2585 **45.** 315 **47.** 132
49. $a_n = -3 + 5n$ **51.** $a_n = -1 - 2n$ **53.** False.
Sample answer: Doubling the common difference
alone does not double the sum. **55.** 12 **57.** 25
59. 15 **61.** 22,500

7.2 Problem Solving 63. a. $a_n = 6n$
b. 271 cells **65. a.** $a_n = -4 + 8n$ **b.** 576 blocks
67. $100

7.3 Skill Practice 1. common ratio
3. Not geometric; there is no common ratio.
5. Geometric; there is a common ratio of $\frac{1}{6}.$ **7.** Not
geometric; there is no common ratio. **9.** Geometric;
there is a common ratio of $\frac{1}{2}.$ **11.** Geometric; there
is a common ratio of $-3.$ **13.** Not geometric; there
is no common ratio. **15.** $a_n = (-4)^{n-1}; 4096$
17. $a_n = 4(6)^{n-1}; 186,624$ **19.** $a_n = 2\left(\frac{3}{4}\right)^{n-1}; \frac{729}{2048}$
21. $a_n = 4\left(\frac{1}{2}\right)^{n-1}; \frac{1}{16}$ **23.** $a_n = -2(0.4)^{n-1}; -0.008192$
25. $a_n = 5(-2.8)^{n-1}; 2409.45152$

29. $a_n = -2(6)^{n-1}$;

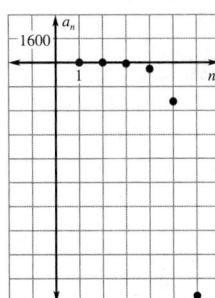

31. $a_n = 30\left(\frac{1}{2}\right)^{n-1}$;

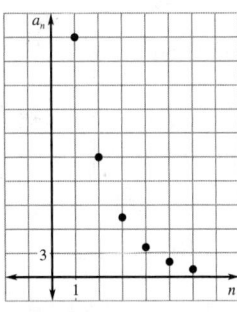

37. The exponent should be $n - 1$ instead of n; $a_n = 3(2)^{n-1}$. **39.** $a_n = 3(2)^{n-1}$ or $a_n = 3(-2)^{n-1}$ **41.** $a_n = \left(-\frac{1}{4}\right)(4)^{n-1}$ **43.** $a_n = -80\left(\frac{1}{2}\right)^{n-1}$ or $a_n = 80\left(-\frac{1}{2}\right)^{n-1}$ **45.** $a_n = 6(3)^{n-1}$ **47.** $a_n = \frac{32}{27}\left(\frac{3\sqrt[3]{12}}{4}\right)^{n-1}$

49. 131,070 **51.** $\frac{1365}{256}$ **53.** 838,861 **55.** *Sample answer:*

The graph of $f(x)$ is a curve defined for all real numbers, and the graph of a_n is each point from the graph of $f(x)$ for positive integer values of x.

7.3 Problem Solving 57. a. $a_n = 5(2)^{n-1}$

b. 75 skydivers **59. a.** $a_n = 512\left(\frac{1}{2}\right)^{n-1}$ **b.** 10.

Sample answer: On the 10th pass, there is only 1 term to choose from so it must be the answer **61. a.** $a_n =$ $19{,}000 + 1000n$, arithmetic; $b_n = 20{,}000(1.04)^{n-1}$, geometric

b.

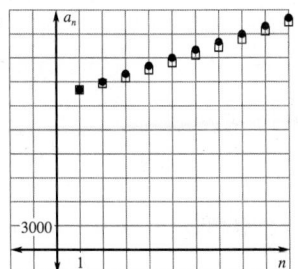

c. Company A: $590,000; Company B: about $595,562
d. 19 yr

7.4 Skill Practice 1. partial sum
3. $S_1 = 0.5, S_2 \approx 0.67, S_3 \approx 0.72, S_4 \approx 0.74, S_5 \approx 0.75$; S_n appears to be approaching 0.75.

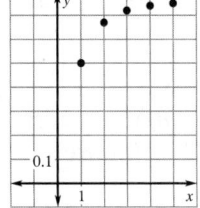

5. $S_1 = 4, S_2 = 6.4, S_3 = 7.84, S_4 \approx 8.71, S_5 \approx 9.22$; S_n appears to be approaching 10.

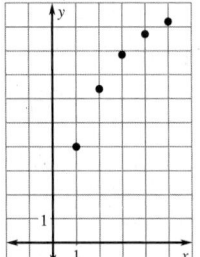

7. 10 **9.** no sum **11.** $\frac{12}{5}$ **13.** $\frac{63}{17}$ **15.** no sum **17.** $\frac{7}{10}$ **19.** Since $r > 1$, the infinite geometric series has no sum. **21.** $\frac{1}{2}$ **23.** 18 **25.** $\frac{4}{9}$ **27.** $\frac{625}{999}$ **29.** $\frac{130{,}000}{999}$ **31.** $\frac{5}{18}$ **33.** $\frac{0.9}{1-0.1} = \frac{0.9}{0.9} = 1$

7.4 Problem Solving 37. 70 ft **41. a.** 12 ft; 9 ft **b.** $\sum_{i=1}^{\infty} 12(0.75)^{i-1}$ **c.** 56 ft **d.** $\frac{2(0.75h)}{1-0.75} + h = 7h$

7.5 Skill Practice 1. iteration **3.** 1, 4, 7, 10, 13 **5.** -1, $-6, -11, -16, -21$ **7.** 2; 5; 26; 677; 458,330 **9.** 2, 8, 10, 18, 22 **11.** 2, 3, 6, 18, 108 **13.** $a_1 = 21, a_n = a_{n-1} - 7$ **15.** $a_1 = 4, a_n = -3a_{n-1}$ **17.** $a_1 = 44, a_n = \frac{1}{4}a_{n-1}$ **19.** $a_1 = 54, a_n = a_{n-1} - 11$ **21.** $a_1 = 16, a_2 = 9$, $a_n = a_{n-2} - a_{n-1}$ **23.** The rule does not work for all of the terms of the sequence; $a_1 = 5, a_2 = 2$, $a_n = a_{n-2} - a_{n-1}$. **25.** $-4, -14, -64$ **27.** $-2, -4, -5$ **29.** 5, 21, 437 **31.** 2, 4, 14 **35.** $a_1 = 1$, $a_2 = 2, a_n = 4(a_{n-2} + a_{n-1})$ **37.** $a_1 = 2, a_2 = 5$, $a_n = 3a_{n-2} + a_{n-1}$ **39.** $a_1 = -3, a_2 = -2$, $a_n = -1(a_{n-2} + a_{n-1})$ **41.** *Sample answer:* If the first two iterates are 2, the third iterate must also be 2.

7.5 Problem Solving 43. a. $a_1 = 5000$, $a_n = 0.8a_{n-1} + 500$; 3524 fish **b.** The population of the lake approaches 2500 fish.
45. $a_1 = 2000, a_n = 1.014a_{n-1} - 100$; 24 mo. *Sample answer:* As long as Gladys does not add anything to her credit card and continues her payments, her 24th payment will only be $62.14.

47. a. $a_1 = 20$, $a_n = 0.7 a_{n-1} + 20$ **b.** $66\frac{2}{3}$ mg
c. The maintenance level of the drug doubles as well; $a_1 = 40$, $a_n = 0.7 a_{n-1} + 40$

7.5 Problem Solving Workshop
1. The sequence approaches 400. **3.** The number of members approaches 15,000. **5.** *Sample answer:* 2% of the books are lost of discarded so 98% are retained; $a_n = 0.98 a_{n-1} + 1150$.

7.5 Extension 1. $a_1 = 13$, $a_n = a_{n-1} - 4$ **3.** $a_1 = 16$, $a_n = 3 a_{n-1}$ **5.** $a_n = 16n - 28$ **7.** $a_n = 2(-6)^{n-1}$
9. $a_1 = 82$, $a_n = a_{n-1} + 30$ **11.** $a_1 = 35{,}000$, $a_n = 1.04 a_{n-1}$

Chapter Review 1. terms **3.** explicit
5. 133 **7.** 153 **9.** $a_n = 11 - 3n$ **11.** $a_n = 3 + 6n$
13. -403 **15.** 1200 **17.** $a_n = 256 \left(\frac{1}{4} \right)^{n-1}$
19. $a_n = 144 \left(\frac{1}{3} \right)^{n-1}$ or $a_n = 144 \left(-\frac{1}{3} \right)^{n-1}$
21. 4088 **23.** $\frac{635}{8}$ **25.** 4 **27.** -0.4 **29.** $\frac{182}{333}$ **31.** $\frac{388}{495}$
33. 8, 40, 200, 1000, 5000 **35.** $a_1 = 6$, $a_n = 3 a_{n-1}$
37. $a_1 = 7$, $a_n = a_{n-1} + 6$

Chapter 7
Extra Practice
1. perfect squares listed in order starting at 3, 49, $a_n = (n + 2)^2$ **3.** each term is decreased by 5.5, -9.5, $a_n = 18 - 5.5n$

5. $\displaystyle\sum_{n=1}^{\infty} \frac{n}{5 + n}$ **7.** 220 **9.** 1071

11. $a_n = -10n + 22$

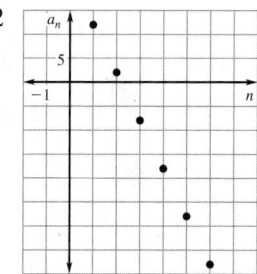

13. $a_n = 9n + 2$; 137 **15.** $a_n = -\frac{2}{3}n + \frac{11}{3}$; $-\frac{19}{3}$
17. $a_n = 2.5 + n$ **19.** $a_n = \frac{1}{27} \cdot 3^{n-1}$; 729
21. $a_n = 4 \cdot \left(\frac{4}{3} \right)^{n-1}$; about 53.3 **23.** 273.5
25. about 25.8 **27.** no sum **29.** $\frac{1}{3}$ **31.** $\frac{7}{33}$ **33.** $a_1 = 2.5$, $a_n = 2(a_{n-1})$ **35.** $a_1 = 1$ and $a_2 = 2$, $a_n = (a_{n-2})(a_{n-1})$
37. -10, -10, -10

Mastering the Standards

for Mathematical Practice

The topics described in the Standards for Mathematical Content will vary from year to year. However, the *way* in which you learn, study, and think about mathematics will not. The Standards for Mathematical Practice describe skills that you will use in all of your math courses.

Mathematical Practices

1. *Make sense of problems and persevere in solving them.*
2. *Reason abstractly and quantitatively.*
3. *Construct viable arguments and critique the reasoning of others.*
4. *Model with mathematics.*
5. *Use appropriate tools strategically.*
6. *Attend to precision.*
7. *Look for and make use of structure.*
8. *Look for and express regularity in repeated reasoning.*

① Make sense of problems and persevere in solving them.

Mathematically proficient students start by explaining to themselves the meaning of a problem... They analyze givens, constraints, relationships, and goals. They make conjectures about the form... of the solution and plan a solution pathway...

In your book

Verbal Models and the **Problem Solving Plan** help you translate the information in a problem into a model and then analyze your solution.

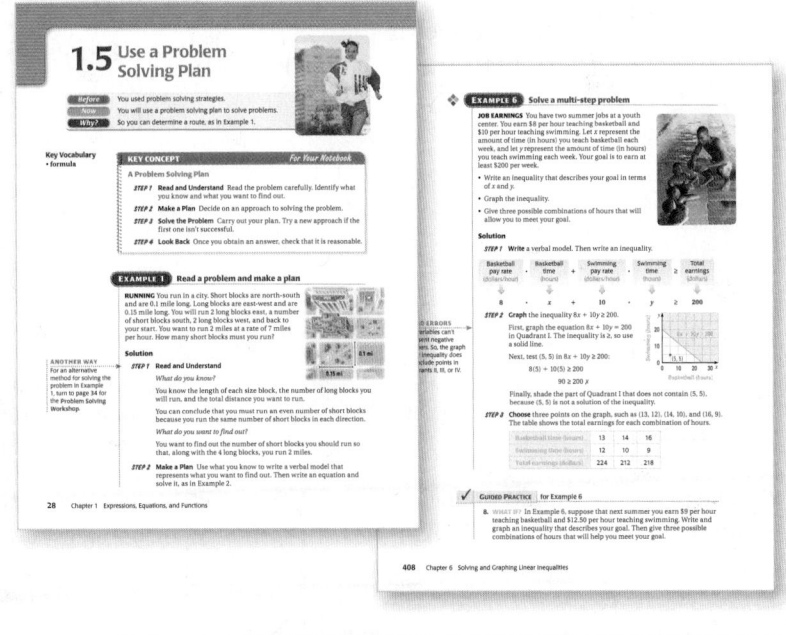

Selected Answers

Chapter 8

8.1 Skill Practice

1. The distance d between (x_1, y_1) and (x_2, y_2) is $d = \sqrt{(x_2 - x_1)^2 + (y_2 - y_1)^2}$; the midpoint of the line segment joining $A(x_1, y_1)$ and $B(x_2, y_2)$ is $M\left(\dfrac{x_1 + x_2}{2}, \dfrac{y_1 + y_2}{2}\right)$. **3.** $17; \left(4, \dfrac{15}{2}\right)$ **5.** $5\sqrt{5}; \left(\dfrac{5}{2}, 1\right)$

7. $4\sqrt{2}; (4, -3)$ **9.** $12\sqrt{2}; (2, 2)$ **11.** $\sqrt{145}; \left(\dfrac{1}{2}, 0\right)$

13. $\sqrt{449}; \left(5, \dfrac{9}{2}\right)$ **15.** $2\sqrt{194}; (1.2, 2)$ **17.** $\dfrac{\sqrt{3221}}{10}$ or about 5.68; $(0.35, -6)$ **21.** The squares of the differences should be added not subtracted; $d = \sqrt{(2 - (-4))^2 + (8 - 3)^2} = \sqrt{36 + 25} = \sqrt{61}$.
23. isosceles **25.** scalene **27.** scalene **29.** scalene
31. $y = -\dfrac{2}{3}x + \dfrac{43}{3}$ **33.** $y = -\dfrac{1}{4}x - \dfrac{5}{2}$ **35.** $y = -4x + \dfrac{17}{2}$
37. *Sample answer:* $(6, 4), (2, 0)$ **39.** $y = -\dfrac{5}{4}x + \dfrac{55}{4}$
41. ± 6 **43.** $-10, 2$ **45.** $d(x) = \sqrt{5x^2 - 16x + 13}$; $\left(\dfrac{1}{5}, \dfrac{2}{5}\right), (3, 6)$

8.1 Problem Solving
47. 17 m **49.** about 6.02 mi
51. about 4.55 mi **53. a.** $(-1.5, 8)$ **b.** about 1.32 mi
c. about 1.68 mi **55.** about 550 ft

8.2 Skill Practice
1. focus, directrix
3. 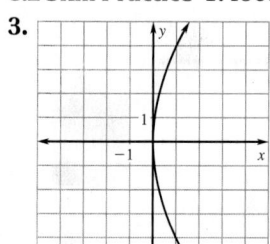 $(4, 0), x = -4, y = 0$

5. 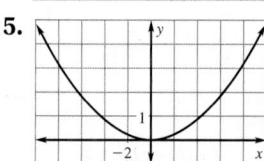 $(0, 5), y = -5, x = 0$

23. The parabola should open to the right rather than up;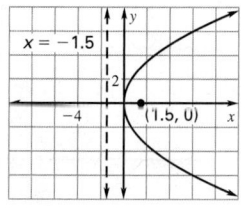

27. $y^2 = -20x$ **29.** $x^2 = -16y$ **31.** $x^2 = -40y$
33. $y^2 = -36x$ **35.** $x^2 = -\dfrac{3}{2}y$ **37.** $y^2 = -\dfrac{9}{4}x$

39. $y^2 = -12x$ **41.** $y^2 = 20x$ **43.** $x^2 = 16y$
45. $x^2 = -24y$ **47.** $y^2 = 6x$ **49.** $x^2 = \dfrac{22}{3}y$

51. a. The new focus will be located at $(0, 1)$ rather than $\left(0, \dfrac{1}{4}\right)$. The new directrix will be $y = -1$ rather than $y = -\dfrac{1}{4}$. The parabola will be wider.
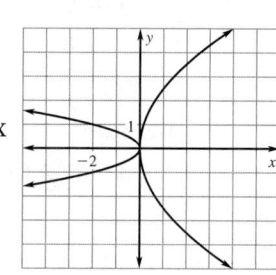
b. The new focus will be located at $\left(-\dfrac{1}{8}, 0\right)$ rather than $\left(\dfrac{3}{2}, 0\right)$. The new directrix will be at $x = \dfrac{1}{8}$ rather than $x = -\dfrac{3}{2}$. The parabola will open left rather than right and be narrower.
53. The graph gets wider. *Sample answer:* As the value of $|p|$ increases, then the focus and directrix (each of which lie $|p|$ units from the vertex) get further and further away from the vertex and from each other. Since each point on a parabola is equidistant from the focus and the directrix, this has the effect of making the parabola wider and wider as $|p|$ increases.

8.2 Problem Solving
55. $x^2 = 24y$; about 3 ft

57. a.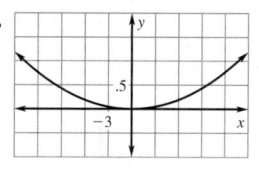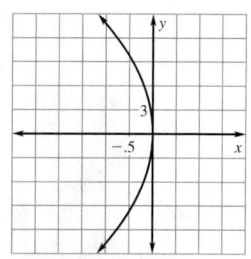

b. $x^2 = 192y, y^2 = -192x$ **c.** About 27.8 in.; no. *Sample answer:* Except for the direction they open, they are identical. **59. a.** about 20 in. **b.** *Sample answer:* $x^2 = 50y$; choose a value for p such that $4p > 10.5$; about 43.6 in. **c.** *Sample answer:* $x^2 = 8y$; choose a value for p such that $0 < 4p < 10.5$; about 17.4 in.

8.3 Skill Practice
1. center **3.** C **5.** A **7.** F
9. 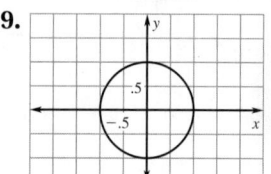 1

SA32

11. 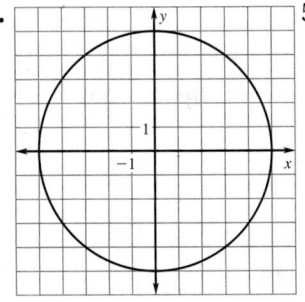 5

23. $x^2 + y^2 = 64$ **25.** $x^2 + y^2 = 256$ **27.** $x^2 + y^2 = 15$
29. $x^2 + y^2 = 96$ **31.** $x^2 + y^2 = 36$ **33.** $x^2 + y^2 = 25$
35. $x^2 + y^2 = 100$ **37.** $x^2 + y^2 = 116$ **39.** $x^2 + y^2 = 260$
41. $x^2 + y^2 = 242$

45. 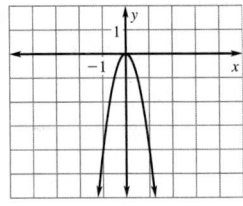 **47.**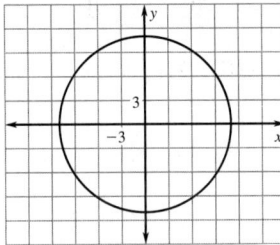

53. $y = -\frac{1}{4}x + \frac{17}{4}$ **55.** $y = \frac{5}{3}x + \frac{34}{3}$ **57.** $y = \frac{5}{9}x + \frac{106}{9}$
59. *Sample answer:* $x^2 + y^2 = 35$, $x^2 + y^2 = 36$,
$x^2 + y^2 = 38$

8.3 Problem Solving 63. yes **65. a.** about 28.9 mi
b. about 18.3 mi **c.** 6 mi **67.** about 7.94 ft

8.3 Skill Practice 1. foci

3. 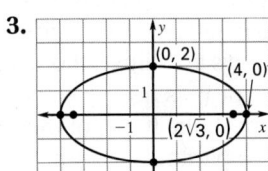 $(\pm 4, 0), (0, \pm 2), (\pm 2\sqrt{3}, 0)$

5. 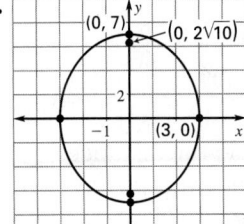 $(0, \pm 7), (\pm 3, 0), (0, \pm 2\sqrt{10})$

15. The major axis should be
the y-axis, not the x-axis.

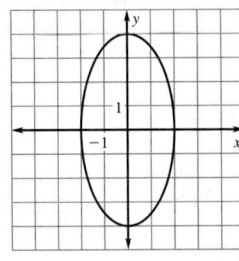

17. $\frac{x^2}{25} + \frac{y^2}{9} = 1$ **19.** $\frac{x^2}{196} + \frac{y^2}{81} = 1$ **21.** $\frac{x^2}{121} + \frac{y^2}{144} = 1$
23. $\frac{x^2}{28} + \frac{y^2}{64} = 1$ **25.** $\frac{x^2}{49} + \frac{y^2}{81} = 1$ **27.** $\frac{x^2}{4} + \frac{y^2}{16} = 1$
29. $\frac{x^2}{16} + \frac{y^2}{7} = 1$ **31.** $\frac{x^2}{400} + \frac{y^2}{175} = 1$ **33.** $\frac{x^2}{60} + \frac{y^2}{256} = 1$

37. 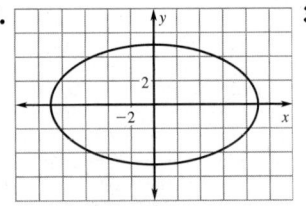 **39.**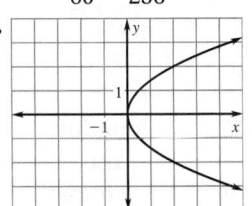

45. The conic changes from
an ellipse elongated along the
y-axis to a circle to an ellipse
elongated along the x-axis.

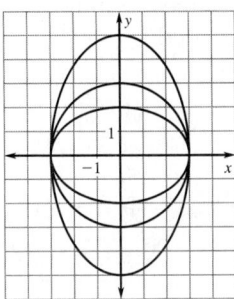

8.4 Problem Solving

49. $\frac{x^2}{(77.5)^2} + \frac{y^2}{(92.5)^2} = 1$, $\frac{x^2}{(55)^2} + \frac{y^2}{(67.5)^2} = 1$;
about $11{,}700 \le A \le 22{,}500$

51. 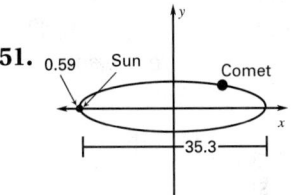 *Sample answer:*
$\frac{x^2}{322} + \frac{y^2}{20.8} = 1$

8.4 Problem Solving Workshop 1. About 66,100 m²;
better. *Sample answer:* More rectangles means there
is less area of the ellipse not included.

3. a. $\frac{x^2}{125^2} + \frac{y^2}{100^2} = 1$ **b.** about 39,000 m²

8.5 Skill Practice
1. vertices, transverse axis

3. 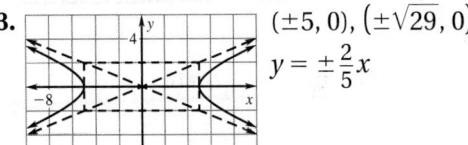 $(\pm 5, 0), (\pm\sqrt{29}, 0),$
$y = \pm\frac{2}{5}x$

5. 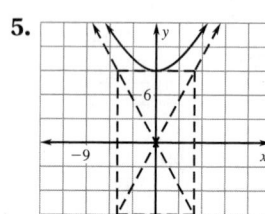 $(0, \pm 9)$, $\left(0, \pm\sqrt{106}\right)$, $y = \pm\frac{9}{5}x$

17. The equation of a hyperbola must equal one, so the hyperbola's vertices should be located at $(\pm 4, 0)$.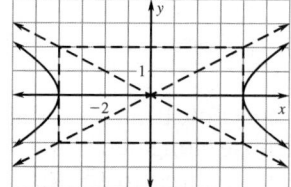

19. $\frac{x^2}{4} - \frac{y^2}{32} = 1$ **21.** $\frac{y^2}{49} - \frac{x^2}{95} = 1$ **23.** $\frac{y^2}{16} - \frac{x^2}{64} = 1$

25. $\frac{x^2}{4} - \frac{y^2}{50} = 1$

27. 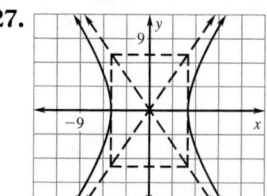 **29.**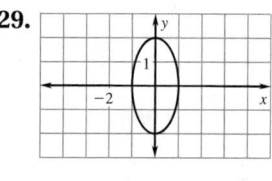

33. a. The hyperbola will be narrower, the vertices are the same, but the foci move to $\left(\pm\sqrt{13}, 0\right)$. **b.** The hyperbola will be wider, the vertices are the same, but the foci move to $\left(0, \pm\sqrt{41}\right)$. **35.** *Sample answer:* $x^2 - \frac{y^2}{4} = 1, \frac{x^2}{4} - \frac{y^2}{16} = 1, \frac{x^2}{9} - \frac{y^2}{36} = 1$; as the value of a gets larger the hyperbola is stretched vertically.

8.5 Problem Solving 39. $\dfrac{x^2}{\frac{1}{2}} - \dfrac{y^2}{\frac{1}{4}} = 1$

41. a. $(30.5, 0)$, $(85, -40)$ **b.** $\dfrac{x^2}{930.25} - \dfrac{y^2}{236.45} = 1$

c. about 54.6 ft **43. a.** $\dfrac{x^2}{16} - \dfrac{y^2}{20} = 1$ **b.** *Sample answer:* Choose any point on the graph and observe that the difference of the distances from that point and the foci remain constant.

8.6 Skill Practice 1. The intersection of a plane and a double-napped cone form them.

3. 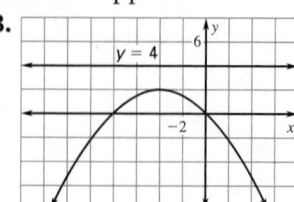 parabola with vertex $(-4, 2)$, focus $(-4, 0)$, and directrix $y = 4$

5. 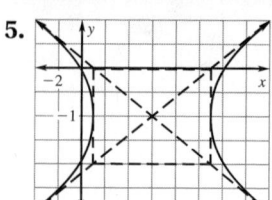 hyperbola with center $(6, -1)$, vertices $(11, -1)$ and $(1, -1)$, asymptotes $y = \frac{1}{5}x - \frac{11}{5}$ and $y = -\frac{1}{5}x + \frac{1}{5}$

13. $(x + 5)^2 + (y - 1)^2 = 36$ **15.** $(y + 3)^2 = 20(x + 4)$

17. $\dfrac{(x - 1)^2}{16} + \dfrac{(y - 4)^2}{12} = 1$ **19.** $\dfrac{(y + 1)^2}{4} - \dfrac{(x - 6)^2}{21} = 1$

21. The center is at $(-2, 3)$, not $(2, -3)$; $\dfrac{(x + 2)^2}{25} + \dfrac{(y - 3)^2}{9} = 1$. **23.** $y = 4$ **25.** $x = 3, y = 5$

27. any line passing through the point $(-2, -1)$

29. circle **31.** ellipse **33.** parabola **35.** hyperbola

37. circle, $(x - 7)^2 + (y + 2)^2 = 64$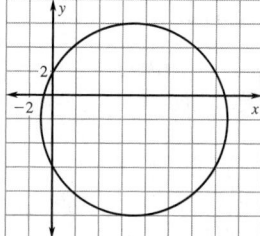

39. parabola, $(x - 8)^2 = 8(y - 2)$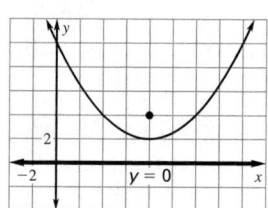

45. If the non-zero coefficients of x^2 and y^2 are the same it's a circle. If the non-zero coefficients of x^2 and y^2 are both positive and different it's an ellipse. If one of the non-zero coefficients of x^2 or y^2 is negative and the other one is positive it's a hyperbola. If one of the coefficients of x^2 or y^2 is zero it's a parabola.

8.6 Problem Solving

49. $(x - 5)^2 = -4\left(y - \frac{25}{4}\right)$; $6\frac{1}{4}$ ft, 10 ft

51. a. $(x - 100)^2 + (y + 60)^2 \le 150^2$, $(x + 80)^2 + (y + 70)^2 \le 100^2$

b.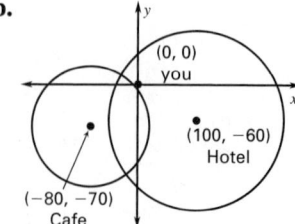

One; the distance from your position to the hotel is less than the radius of the hotel's transmitter, but you are about 106 yards from the café's transmitter which is out of range.

c. *Sample answer:* Find the distance from the hotel to the cafe. If it's greater than 250 yards they do not overlap. It's less than or equal to 250 yards they overlap.

8.7 Skill Practice 1. quadratic
3. $(-4, -4)$, $(4, 4)$ **5.** $(0.472, -2.58)$, $(3.53, 6.58)$
7. $(-2.18, -3.36)$, $(1.38, 3.76)$ **9.** $(3, -3)$, $(-2, 2)$
11. $\left(\dfrac{-64 - 2\sqrt{106}}{17}, \dfrac{8 - 4\sqrt{106}}{17} \right), \left(\dfrac{-64 + 2\sqrt{106}}{17}, \dfrac{4 + 2\sqrt{106}}{17} \right)$
13. $(0, 2)$, $\left(\dfrac{4}{3}, \dfrac{2}{3} \right)$ **15.** $(-1, -4)$, $\left(-\dfrac{13}{2}, 7 \right)$ **17.** no solution
19. $\left(\dfrac{7 + 3\sqrt{3}}{11}, \dfrac{-1 + 9\sqrt{3}}{11} \right), \left(\dfrac{7 - 3\sqrt{3}}{11}, \dfrac{-1 - 9\sqrt{3}}{11} \right)$
23. $\left(0, \pm\sqrt{5} \right)$, $(-5, 0)$ **25.** $\left(\dfrac{1}{2}, \dfrac{1}{2} \right)$ **27.** no solution
29. no solution **31.** $(4, 0)$ **33.** $(-1, -2)$, $(2, 1)$ **35.** When $(1 - y^2)^2$ was expanded, the last term should have been y^4; $1 - 2y^2 + y^4 + y^2 - 2 + 2y^2 - 2y = -1$, $y^4 + y^2 - 2y = 0$; $(0, 1)$, $(1, 0)$. **37.** about $(-2.32, -2.02)$, $(-0.296, -2.82)$

8.7 Problem Solving 39. $d = 0.8t$, $d = 2.5t^2$, 0.32 min
41. a. $x^2 + y^2 = 1$, $y = -\dfrac{1}{7}x + \dfrac{5}{7}$ **b.** $\left(-\dfrac{3}{5}, \dfrac{4}{5} \right)$, $\left(\dfrac{4}{5}, \dfrac{3}{5} \right)$
c. about 1.41 mi **43. a.** $(1, 1)$
b. about $(-8.94, -2.68)$

8.7 Extension 1. 0 **3.** $\dfrac{\sqrt{15}}{8} \approx 0.484$ **5.** 1
7. $\dfrac{x^2}{36} + \dfrac{25(y - 4)^2}{756} = 1$ **9.** $\dfrac{x^2}{49} + \dfrac{25(y - 5)^2}{1176} = 1$
11. $\dfrac{(x - 4)^2}{9} - \dfrac{25(y + 4)^2}{504} = 1$ **13.** *Sample answer:*
$\dfrac{x^2}{30.25} + \dfrac{y^2}{13.19} = 1$ **15.** In the ellipse $0 < c < a$, therefore $0 < \dfrac{c}{a} < 1$. In the hyperbola $0 < a < c$, therefore $\dfrac{c}{a} > 1$.

Chapter Review 1. parabola **3.** transverse axis **5.** $2\sqrt{17}$; $(-2, -4)$ **7.** $\sqrt{106}$; $\left(-\dfrac{1}{2}, \dfrac{1}{2} \right)$
9.
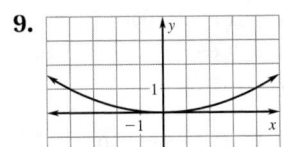
$(0, 4)$, $y = -4$, $x = 0$
11.
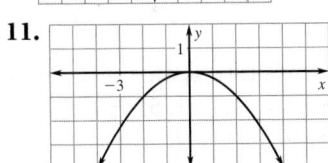
$(0, -1)$, $y = 1$, $x = 0$
13. $x^2 = 12y$

15.
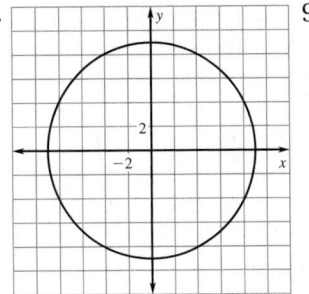
9

17.
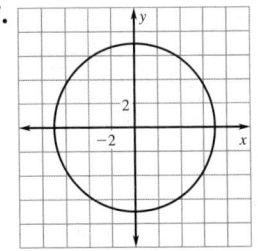
7

19. $x^2 + y^2 = 68$
21.
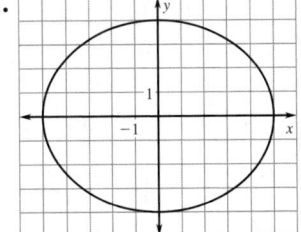
$(\pm 5, 0)$, $(0, \pm 4)$, $(\pm 3, 0)$

23.
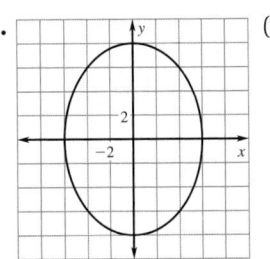
$(0, \pm 8)$, $(\pm 6, 0)$, $\left(0, \pm 2\sqrt{7} \right)$

25. $\dfrac{y^2}{64} + \dfrac{x^2}{39} = 1$
27.
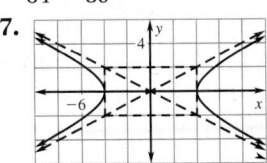
$(\pm 4, 0)$, $\left(\pm 2\sqrt{5}, 0 \right)$, $y = \pm\dfrac{1}{2}x$

29. $\dfrac{y^2}{4} - \dfrac{x^2}{21} = 1$
31. ellipse, $\dfrac{(x + 5)^2}{9} + \dfrac{(y + 4)^2}{4} = 1$
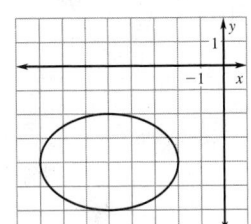

33. hyperbola,

$$\frac{(x-1)^2}{\frac{10}{9}} - \frac{(y+2)^2}{10} = 1$$

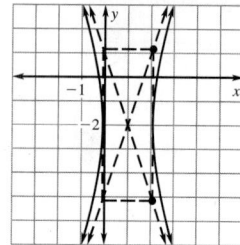

35. $(16, 8), (1, 2)$ **37.** $(2, 0)$

Chapter 8
Extra Practice

1. $2\sqrt{29}; (0, 2)$ **3.** $2\sqrt{233}; (1, 4)$

5. 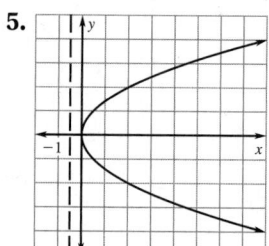 $\left(\frac{1}{2}, 0\right), x = -\frac{1}{2}, y = 0$

7. 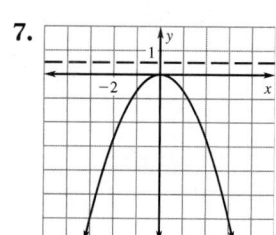 $\left(0, -\frac{3}{8}\right), y = \frac{3}{8}, x = 0$

9. 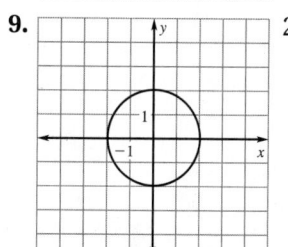 2

11. 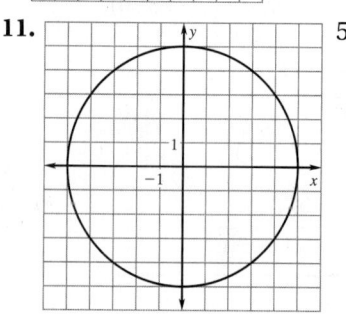 5

13. $x^2 + y^2 = 64$ **15.** $x^2 + y^2 = 50$

17. 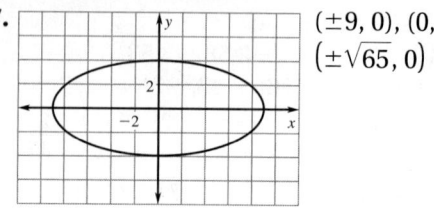 $(\pm 9, 0), (0, \pm 4),$
$(\pm\sqrt{65}, 0)$

19. 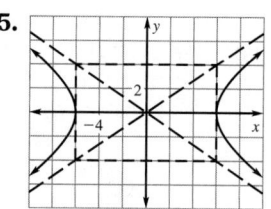 $(0, \pm 12), (\pm 8, 0), (0, \pm 4\sqrt{5})$

21. $\frac{x^2}{16} + \frac{y^2}{4} = 1$ **23.** $\frac{x^2}{81} + \frac{y^2}{72} = 1$

25. 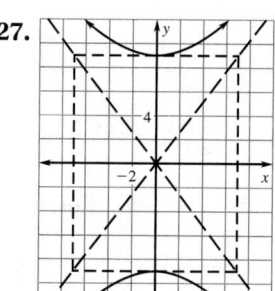 $(\pm 6, 0), (\pm 2\sqrt{13}, 0),$
$y = \pm\frac{2}{3}x$

27. 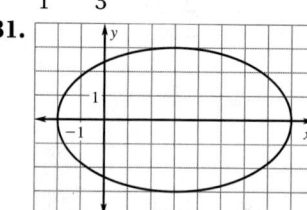 $(0, \pm 9), (0, \pm\sqrt{130}),$
$y = \pm\frac{9}{7}x$

29. 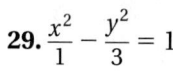 $\frac{x^2}{1} - \frac{y^2}{3} = 1$

31. 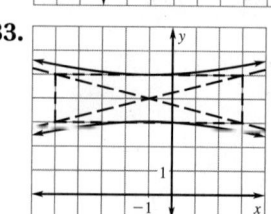 center: $(3, 0)$,
vertices: $(-2, 0)$ $(8, 0)$,
co-vertices:
$(3, 3)$ $(3, -3)$,
foci: $(-1, 0)$ $(7, 0)$

33. center: $(-1, 4)$,
vertices: $(-1, 5)$ $(-1, 3)$,
foci: $\left(-1, 4 + \sqrt{17}\right)$
$\left(-1, 4 - \sqrt{17}\right)$,
asymptotes: $y = \pm\frac{1}{4}x$

35. ellipse,
$$\frac{(x-4)^2}{16} + \frac{(y+2)^2}{36} = 1$$

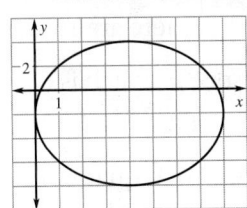

37. parabola,
$(x-3)^2 = 4(y-2)$

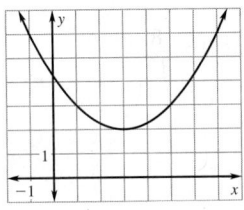

39. $(0, -2)$ $(7, 5)$

Selected Answers

Chapter 9

9.1 Skill Practice 1. The angle formed by the line of sight to an object and a line parallel to the ground. **3.** $\sin\theta = \frac{12}{13}$, $\cos\theta = \frac{5}{13}$, $\tan\theta = \frac{12}{5}$, $\csc\theta = \frac{13}{12}$, $\sec\theta = \frac{13}{5}$, $\cot\theta = \frac{5}{12}$

5. $\sin\theta = \frac{8}{11}$, $\cos\theta = \frac{\sqrt{57}}{11}$, $\tan\theta = \frac{8\sqrt{57}}{57}$, $\csc\theta = \frac{11}{8}$, $\sec\theta = \frac{11\sqrt{57}}{57}$, $\cot\theta = \frac{\sqrt{57}}{8}$

7. $\sin\theta = \frac{\sqrt{115}}{14}$, $\cos\theta = \frac{9}{14}$, $\tan\theta = \frac{\sqrt{115}}{9}$, $\csc\theta = \frac{14\sqrt{115}}{115}$, $\sec\theta = \frac{14}{9}$, $\cot\theta = \frac{9\sqrt{115}}{115}$

9. $\cos\theta = \frac{\sqrt{11}}{6}$, $\tan\theta = \frac{5\sqrt{11}}{11}$, $\csc\theta = \frac{6}{5}$, $\sec\theta = \frac{6\sqrt{11}}{11}$, $\cot\theta = \frac{\sqrt{11}}{5}$ **11.** $\sin\theta = \frac{7\sqrt{58}}{58}$, $\cos\theta = \frac{3\sqrt{58}}{58}$, $\csc\theta = \frac{\sqrt{58}}{7}$, $\sec\theta = \frac{\sqrt{58}}{3}$, $\cot\theta = \frac{3}{7}$ **13.** $\sin\theta = \frac{\sqrt{119}}{12}$, $\cos\theta = \frac{5}{12}$, $\tan\theta = \frac{\sqrt{119}}{5}$, $\csc\theta = \frac{12\sqrt{119}}{119}$, $\cot\theta = \frac{5\sqrt{119}}{119}$ **17.** $x = 8\sqrt{3}$, $y = 16$ **19.** $x = 4\sqrt{3}$, $y = 8\sqrt{3}$ **21.** $B = 55°$, $a \approx 9.18$, $b \approx 13.11$ **23.** $A = 72°$, $a \approx 22.83$, $b \approx 7.42$ **25.** $A = 15°$, $b \approx 55.98$, $c \approx 57.96$ **27.** $B = 26°$, $a \approx 65.61$, $c \approx 73.0$

9.1 Problem Solving 31. about 63.4 cm **33.** About 652 ft. *Sample answer:* The larger the angle the deeper the final depth. **35. a.** about 22,818 mi **b.** about 7263 mi

9.2 Skill Practice
1. origin, initial side **3.** B **5.** A
7. **9.**

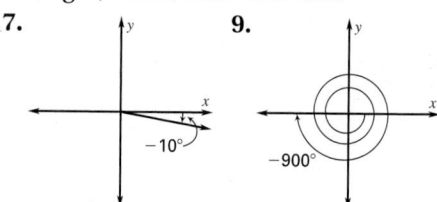

15–21. Sample answers are given. **15.** 430°, −290° **17.** 235°, −485° **19.** $\frac{\pi}{2}$, $-\frac{3\pi}{2}$ **21.** $\frac{10\pi}{9}$, $-\frac{8\pi}{9}$ **23.** $\frac{2\pi}{9}$ **25.** $-\frac{13\pi}{9}$ **27.** 20° **29.** 900° **33.** about 3.93 m, about 5.89 m² **35.** about 31.4 ft, about 188 ft² **37.** about 118 in., about 1470 in.² **39.** $\frac{1}{2}$ **41.** $\frac{\sqrt{3}}{3}$ **43.** about 2.41 **45.** about 0.975

9.2 Problem Solving 49. 72,000°, 400π

51. a. $\frac{\pi}{2}$ **b.** about 45.6 ft **53. a.** about 16.5 in. **b.** 360°. *Sample answer:* Since each step has a central

angle of $\frac{\pi}{8}$ and there are 16 steps, the staircase will cover $16\left(\frac{\pi}{8}\right)$ or 2π, which is equivalent to 360°. **c.** about 5195.4 in.²

9.3 Skill Practice 1. quadrantal angle

3. $\sin\theta = \frac{15}{17}$, $\cos\theta = \frac{8}{17}$, $\tan\theta = \frac{15}{8}$, $\csc\theta = \frac{17}{15}$, $\sec\theta = \frac{17}{8}$, $\cot\theta = \frac{8}{15}$ **5.** $\sin\theta = -\frac{24}{25}$, $\cos\theta = -\frac{7}{25}$, $\tan\theta = \frac{24}{7}$, $\csc\theta = -\frac{25}{24}$, $\sec\theta = -\frac{25}{7}$, $\cot\theta = \frac{7}{24}$

7. $\sin\theta = -\frac{\sqrt{2}}{2}$, $\cos\theta = \frac{\sqrt{2}}{2}$, $\tan\theta = -1$, $\csc\theta = -\sqrt{2}$, $\sec\theta = \sqrt{2}$, $\cot\theta = -1$ **9.** $\sin\theta = -\frac{5\sqrt{34}}{34}$, $\cos\theta = -\frac{3\sqrt{34}}{34}$, $\tan\theta = \frac{5}{3}$, $\csc\theta = -\frac{\sqrt{34}}{5}$, $\sec\theta = -\frac{\sqrt{34}}{3}$, $\cot\theta = \frac{3}{5}$ **13.** $\sin\theta = 1$, $\cos\theta = 0$, $\tan\theta =$ undefined, $\csc\theta = 1$, $\sec\theta =$ undefined, $\cot\theta = 0$ **15.** $\sin\theta = -1$, $\cos\theta = 0$, $\tan\theta =$ undefined, $\csc\theta = -1$, $\sec\theta =$ undefined, $\cot\theta = 0$

17. 30° **19.** 10°

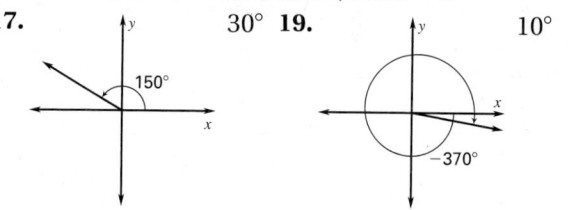

25. $\sqrt{3}$ **27.** $-\frac{2\sqrt{3}}{3}$ **29.** $\frac{\sqrt{3}}{3}$ **31.** $\frac{2\sqrt{3}}{3}$ **33.** $\tan\theta = \frac{\sin\theta}{\cos\theta}$; $\sin 90° = 1$ and $\cos 90° = 0$ so $\tan 90°$ is undefined because you cannot divide by zero but $\cot\theta = \frac{0}{1} = 0$.

9.3 Problem Solving 35. about 10 ft **37.** About 104 ft; no. *Sample answer:* If your starting height above the ground is not doubled, the entire height is not doubled.

39. a.

Angle of sprinkler, θ	25°	30°	35°	40°	45°
Horizontal distance water travels, d	15.0	16.9	18.4	19.2	19.5

Angle of sprinkler, θ	50°	55°	60°	65°
Horizontal distance water travels, d	19.2	18.4	16.9	15.0

b. 45°; since $\frac{v^2}{32}$ is constant, the maximum distance traveled will occur when $\sin 2\theta$ is as large as possible. The maximum value of $\sin 2\theta$ occurs when $2\theta = 90°$, that is, when $\theta = 45°$. **c.** The distances are the same.

9.4 Skill Practice 1. inverse **3.** $\frac{\pi}{2}$, 90° **5.** $\frac{\pi}{2}$, 90° **7.** $\frac{\pi}{3}$, 60° **9.** $-\frac{\pi}{6}$, −30° **13.** about 1.20, about 69.0°

15. about 1.98, about 113.6° **17.** about −0.20, about −11.5° **19.** about 0.14, about 8.1° **21.** about 206.7° **23.** about 252.6° **25.** about 284.5° **27.** about 38.7° **29.** 120° **31.** *Sample answer:* 600°

9.4 Problem Solving

35.

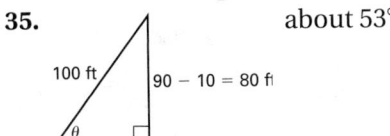

100 ft, 90 − 10 = 80 ft, θ   about 53°

37. About 32.9°; about 46.4 ft. *Sample answer:* The pile is 15 feet high and the angle of repose is about 32.9°, the base of the right triangle formed is about 23.2 feet. Since this represents the radius of the pile, you need to multiply by 2 to get the diameter.

39. $\theta = \tan^{-1}\left(\dfrac{44t}{100}\right)$

9.5 Skill Practice

1. two angle measures and the length of a side, or the lengths of two sides and the measure of an angle opposite one of the two sides **3.** SSA; one triangle **5.** SSA; no triangle **7.** ASA; one triangle **9.** SSA; no triangle **11.** SSA; one triangle **13.** $A \approx 37.6°$, $B \approx 38.4°$, $a \approx 15.7$ **15.** $B = 65°$, $a \approx 23.8$, $b \approx 32.2$ **17.** $C = 95°$, $a \approx 17.6$, $b \approx 37.8$ **19.** $B = 119°$, $a \approx 6.5$, $c \approx 8.5$ **21.** $B \approx 54.1°$, $C \approx 87.9°$, $c \approx 30.8$, or $B \approx 125.9°$, $C \approx 16.1°$, $c \approx 8.6$ **23.** $B \approx 37.5°$, $C \approx 28.5°$, $c \approx 7.8$ **25.** $C = 99°$, $a \approx 62.7$, $c \approx 82.0$ **27.** The sides were not paired with their opposite angles; $\dfrac{\sin C}{5} = \dfrac{\sin 55°}{6}$, $\sin C = \dfrac{\sin 55°}{6} \approx 0.6826$, $C \approx 43.0°$. **29.** about 41.0 **31.** about 291.9 **33.** about 18.9 **35.** about 176.2 **37.** about 285.6 **39.** about 205.3

9.5 Problem Solving

43. about 193.6 ft, about 212.9 ft

45. a.

C, 54 ft, 62 ft, 58°, A, B   **b.** third side: about 70.4 ft; other angles: about 47.6°, about 74.4° **c.** 9 bags **47. a.** about 152.9 m

9.6 Skill Practice

1. semiperimeter **3.** law of cosines **5.** law of sines **7.** law of sines **9.** $B \approx 30.7°$, $C \approx 35.3°$, $a \approx 41.1$ **11.** $A \approx 110.4°$, $C \approx 44.6°$, $b \approx 3.60$ **13.** $A \approx 30.3°$, $B \approx 128.4°$, $C \approx 21.3°$ **15.** $A \approx 55.7°$, $B \approx 76.3°$, $c \approx 15.3$ **17.** $A \approx 42.6°$, $B \approx 11.7°$, $C \approx 125.7°$ **19.** $A \approx 36.7°$, $B \approx 47.3°$, $c \approx 58.2$ **21.** about 104 **23.** about 1108.6 **25.** about 25 **27.** about 131.9 **29.** about 2259.7 **31.** about 994.3 **35.** Since you are looking for A the equation should

be $a^2 = b^2 + c^2 - 2bc \cos A$; $18^2 = 15^2 + 10^2 - 2(15)(10) \cos A$, $A \approx \cos^{-1} 0.0033 \approx 89.8°$. **37.** $A = 45°$, $b \approx 25.2$, $c \approx 15.3$ **39.** $A \approx 68.2°$, $C \approx 21.8°$, $b \approx 16.2$ **41.** $A \approx 93.7°$, $B \approx 33.9°$, $C \approx 52.4°$

9.6 Problem Solving

43. about 119.6° **45.** About 19.8 acres. *Sample answer:* Find $\overline{AC}$ then find the area of $\triangle ACD$ and $\triangle ABC$ using Heron's formula. **47. a.** about 2.6 mi **b.** about 3 h 45 min **c.** About 1 h 46 min; 79.2° W of N. *Sample answer:* The angle at hiker 1 is 79.2° and you have parallel lines at each hiker pointing in the North direction. The angle at hiker 2 is then an alternate interior angle, and is congruent.

9.6 Problem Solving Workshop

1. about 81.9 **3.** about 4619.5 **5.** about 792.6 ft^2

Chapter Review 1. An angle in standard position has its vertex at the origin, and its initial side lies on the positive x-axis. **3.** unit circle **5.** *Sample answer:* The law of sines is a ratio relating the sine of an angle and its corresponding side to the other angles and corresponding sides. **7.** about 26.6 m **9.** $-\dfrac{4\pi}{9}$ **11.** 330° **13.** $-\sqrt{2}$ **15.** 2 **17.** about 19.5° **19.** $A \approx 31.7°$, $C \approx 44.3°$, $a \approx 13.5$ **21.** $A = 47°$, $a \approx 16.9$, $c \approx 22.1$ **23.** $A \approx 58.7°$, $C \approx 46.3°$, $b \approx 22.6$

Chapter 9
Extra Practice

1. $\cos \theta = \dfrac{4}{5}$, $\tan \theta = \dfrac{3}{4}$, $\csc \theta = \dfrac{5}{3}$, $\sec \theta = \dfrac{5}{4}$, $\cot \theta = \dfrac{4}{3}$ **3.** $\sin \theta = \dfrac{\sqrt{3}}{2}$, $\cos \theta = \dfrac{1}{2}$, $\tan \theta = \sqrt{3}$, $\csc \theta = \dfrac{2\sqrt{3}}{3}$, $\cot \theta = \dfrac{\sqrt{3}}{3}$ **5.** $B = 69°$, $a \approx 2.867$, $b \approx 7.469$ **7.** $A = 30°$, $a = 10$, $b = 10\sqrt{3}$ **9.** $B = 72°$, $a \approx 5.562$, $b \approx 17.119$ **11.** $\dfrac{5\pi}{9}$ **13.** 135° **15.** $\dfrac{5\pi}{2}$ ft, $\dfrac{25\pi}{4}$ ft^2 **17.** 12π cm, 72π cm^2

19.   30° **21.**

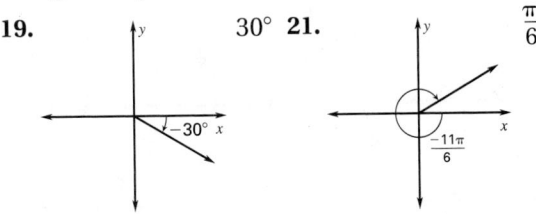

−30°, $\dfrac{\pi}{6}$, $-\dfrac{11\pi}{6}$

23. $-\dfrac{2\sqrt{3}}{3}$ **25.** $-\dfrac{\sqrt{2}}{2}$ **27.** $\dfrac{5\pi}{6}$, 150° **29.** $\dfrac{\pi}{4}$, 45° **31.** about 334.16 **33.** $B \approx 40.7°$, $C \approx 105.3°$, $c \approx 10.35$ or $B \approx 139.3°$, $C \approx 6.72°$, $c \approx 1.26$ **35.** $A \approx 36.4°$, $C \approx 57.6°$, $a \approx 7.73$ **37.** about 24.1 **39.** $A \approx 44.1°$, $B \approx 88.3°$, $C \approx 47.6°$ **41.** $B \approx 61.3°$, $C \approx 38.7°$, $a \approx 7.86$ **43.** about 189

Chapter 10
10.1 Skill Practice

1. period **3.** $1, \frac{\pi}{2}$ **5.** 1, 2

7. 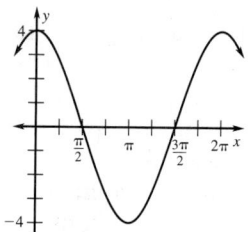 **9.**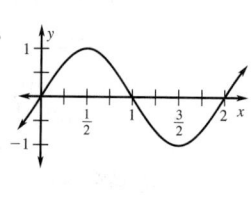

17. 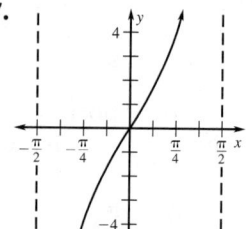 **19.**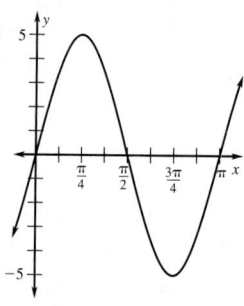

25. *Sample answer:* The rise and fall of the tides versus time.

10.1 Problem Solving

29. 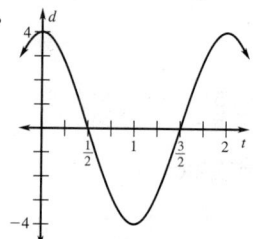 8 in.

31. a. $y = 1.75 \cos \frac{\pi}{3} t$ **b.** Since the high point occurs at $t = 0$, the cosine function best represents situation.

10.2 Skill Practice
1. 3 **3.** E **5.** D **7.** A

9. 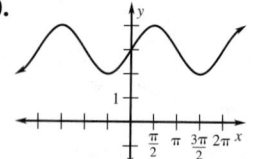 **11.**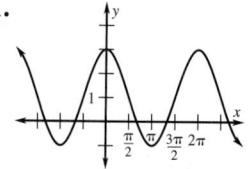

23. 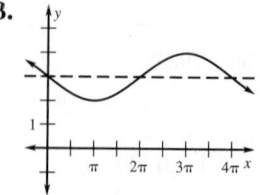 **25.**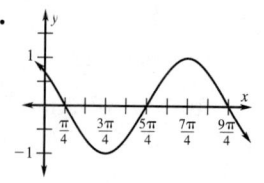

37. 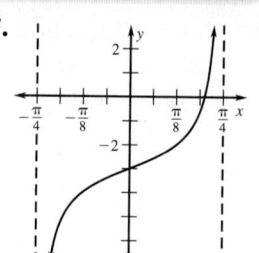 **39.**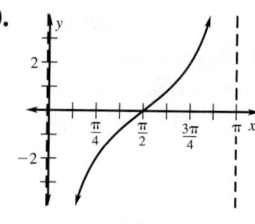

43. $y = 3 \sin (x - \pi) + 2$ **45.** $y = -\frac{1}{3} \cos \pi x - 1$

47. The graph of $y = \cos x$ can be obtained by translating the graph of $y = \sin x$ either to the left by $\frac{\pi}{2}$ or to the right $\frac{3\pi}{2}$.

10.2 Problem Solving
51. $h = 3.75 \cos (200\pi t)$ **53. a.** $d = -300 \tan \theta + 200$

b. 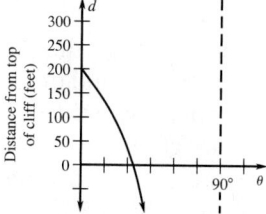 **c.** about 18.4°

10.3 Skill Practice
1. A trigonometric equation that is true for all values of θ in its domain

3. $\cos \theta = \frac{2\sqrt{2}}{3}$, $\tan \theta = \frac{\sqrt{2}}{4}$, $\csc \theta = 3$, $\sec \theta = \frac{3\sqrt{2}}{4}$, $\cot \theta = 2\sqrt{2}$ **5.** $\sin \theta = -\frac{\sqrt{11}}{6}$, $\tan \theta = -\frac{\sqrt{11}}{5}$, $\csc \theta = -\frac{6\sqrt{11}}{11}$ $\sec \theta = \frac{6}{5}$, $\cot \theta = -\frac{5\sqrt{11}}{11}$

7. $\sin \theta = \frac{5\sqrt{29}}{29}$, $\cos \theta = -\frac{2\sqrt{29}}{29}$, $\tan \theta = -\frac{5}{2}$, $\csc \theta = \frac{\sqrt{29}}{5}$, $\sec \theta = -\frac{\sqrt{29}}{2}$ **11.** $-\tan \theta$

13. $\sec \theta$ **15.** $\sin^2 x$ **17.** 1 **19.** $\sin x$ **21.** -1

23. $\tan (-x) = -\tan (x)$, so Step 1 used an incorrect substitution; $-\frac{\sin x}{\cos x} \cdot \frac{1}{\sin x} = -\frac{1}{\cos x} = -\sec x$.

25. $\sin x \csc x = \sin x \left(\frac{1}{\sin x} \right) = 1$

27. $\frac{\left(\cos \frac{\pi}{2} - \theta \right) + 1}{1 - \sin (-\theta)} = \frac{\sin \theta + 1}{1 - (-\sin \theta)} = \frac{\sin \theta + 1}{1 + \sin \theta} = 1$

29. $\frac{\csc^2 \theta - \cot^2 \theta}{1 - \sin^2 \theta} = \frac{1}{\cos^2 \theta} = \sec^2 \theta$

31. $\sin x + \cos x \cot x = \sin x + \cos x \left(\frac{\cos x}{\sin x} \right) = \sin x + \frac{\cos^2 x}{\sin x} = \frac{\sin^2 x + \cos^2 x}{\sin x} = \frac{1}{\sin x} = \csc x$

33. $\dfrac{1 + \cos x}{\sin x} + \dfrac{\sin x}{1 + \cos x} =$

$\dfrac{1 + 2\cos x + \cos^2 x + \sin^2 x}{(1 + \cos x)(\sin x)} = \dfrac{1 + 2\cos x + 1}{(1 + \cos x)(\sin x)} =$

$\dfrac{2 + 2\cos x}{(1 + \cos x)(\sin x)} = \dfrac{2(1 + \cos x)}{(1 + \cos x)(\sin x)} = \dfrac{2}{\sin x} =$

$2 \csc x$

35. $\sin x,\ \csc x,\ \tan x,\ \cot x;\ \cos x,\ \sec x$

37. $\ln|\tan\theta| = \ln\left|\dfrac{\sin\theta}{\cos\theta}\right| = \ln|\sin\theta| - \ln|\cos\theta|$

10.3 Problem Solving

39. $\sec x \tan x - \sin x = \dfrac{1}{\cos x} \cdot \dfrac{\sin x}{\cos x} - \sin x =$

$\dfrac{\sin x}{\cos^2 x} - \dfrac{\sin x \cos^2 x}{\cos^2 x} = \dfrac{\sin x - \sin x \cos^2 x}{\cos^2 x} =$

$\dfrac{\sin x\,(1 - \cos^2 x)}{\cos^2 x} = \dfrac{\sin x\,(\sin^2 x)}{\cos^2 x} = \sin x \tan^2 x$

41. a. $r = \dfrac{1.069}{1 - 0.97\cos\theta}$ **b.**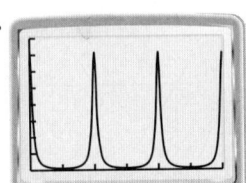

c.

θ	0	$\frac{\pi}{4}$	$\frac{\pi}{2}$	$\frac{3\pi}{4}$	π	$\frac{5\pi}{4}$	$\frac{3\pi}{2}$
r	35.6	3.40	1.07	0.634	0.543	0.634	1.07

about 50.5 million mi, about 3.31 billion mi

43. The unit circle shows that $\sin\theta$ and $\cos\theta$ are positive in the first quadrant, or the intervals $0 \pm 2\pi < \theta < \frac{\pi}{2} \pm 2\pi$. On these intervals, $\sin\theta$ is increasing and $\cos\theta$ is decreasing. Since $\tan\theta = \dfrac{\sin\theta}{\cos\theta}$ has a positive, increasing numerator and a positive, decreasing denominator, $\tan\theta$ is increasing on these intervals.

10.4 Skill Practice 1. A trigonometric identity is true for *all* values of the variable for which both sides of the equation are defined.

3. $2 + 3\cos(4\pi) - 5 = 2 + 3(1) - 5 = 0$

5. $12\sin^2\left(\frac{\pi}{6}\right) - 3 = 12\left(\frac{1}{2}\right)^2 - 3 = 0$

7. $2\cos^4\left(\frac{\pi}{2}\right) - \cos^2\left(\frac{\pi}{2}\right) = 2(0)^4 - (0)^2 = 0$

9. $\frac{\pi}{6} + 2n\pi$ or $\frac{5\pi}{6} + 2n\pi$ **11.** $\frac{\pi}{6} + n\pi$

13. $\frac{\pi}{6} + n\pi$ or $\frac{5\pi}{6} + n\pi$ **17.** $\frac{\pi}{6}, \frac{7\pi}{6}$ **19.** $\frac{\pi}{4}, \frac{3\pi}{4}, \frac{5\pi}{4}, \frac{7\pi}{4}$

21. $\frac{\pi}{3}, \frac{2\pi}{3}, \frac{4\pi}{3}, \frac{5\pi}{3}$ **23.** When two negative values are divided, the quotient is positive; $\cos x = \frac{1}{2}, x = \frac{\pi}{3}$.

25. $\frac{\pi}{6} + n\pi$ **27.** $\frac{\pi}{3} + n\pi$ or $\frac{2\pi}{3} + n\pi$ **29.** $\frac{\pi}{3} + 2n\pi$ or $\pi + 2n\pi$ **31.** $\frac{\pi}{3}$ **33.** about 0.572 **35.** $\frac{5\pi}{3}$ **37.** (0, 1)

39. $\left(\frac{\pi}{6}, \frac{\sqrt{3}}{3}\right), \left(\frac{2\pi}{3}, 3\sqrt{3}\right), \left(\frac{7\pi}{6}, \frac{\sqrt{3}}{3}\right), \left(\frac{5\pi}{3}, 3\sqrt{3}\right)$

10.4 Problem Solving 41. July 26 and November 26 **43. a.** $S = \dfrac{27}{4} + \dfrac{27}{32}\left(\dfrac{\sqrt{3} - \cos\theta}{\sin\theta}\right)$

b. *Sample:*

θ	16	17	18	19
S	9.1095	8.9887	8.8825	8.7884

θ	120	121	122	123
S	8.9246	8.9619	9.0005	9.0405

about 17° and about 122°

c. 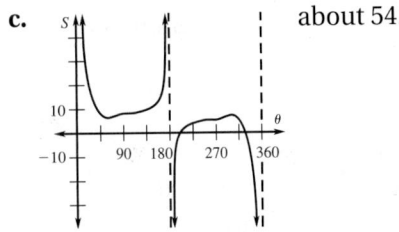 about 54.7°

10.4 Problem Solving Workshop 1. about 0.987, about 3.01 **3.** about 0.298, about 0.702 **5.** about 22.6, about 37.4 **7.** 1:32 AM, 10:52 AM, 1:56 PM, 11:16 PM **9.** about 0.17 sec and about 0.83 sec

10.5 Skill Practice 1. The graph of a sine or cosine function **3.** *Sample answer:* $y = 3\sin 2x$

5. *Sample answer:* $y = -2\cos\frac{\pi}{2}x + 4$

7. To determine the amplitude, you must take half of the difference between the maximum and the minimum; $\dfrac{10 - (-6)}{2} = 8$.

9–17. Sample answers are given. **9.** $y = 6\sin\frac{1}{2}x$

11. $y = -\cos 3x + 4$ **13.** $y = 2\cos\frac{4}{5}\left(x - \frac{3\pi}{4}\right) + 7$

15. $y = 2\sin\frac{1}{4}(x + 2\pi) - 2$ **17.** $y = -6\cos\frac{3}{2}x - 6$

21. $y = 3\cos 4\left(x - \frac{\pi}{8}\right) + 2;$

$y = 3\cos\left(4x - \frac{\pi}{2}\right) + 2$ (Dist. property);

$y = 3\cos\left(\frac{\pi}{2} - 4x\right) + 2$ (Neg. angle identity);

$y = 3\sin 4x + 2$ (Cofunction identity)

10.5 Problem Solving

23. $V = 100\sin 4\pi t$ **25.** $h = -2.5\cos\pi t + 6.5$
27. a. $N = 3.68\sin(0.776t - 0.703) + 20.4$
b. about 23,100 employees

10.6 Skill Practice 1. $\sin(a + b) =$ $\sin a \cos b + \cos a \sin b$, $\sin(a - b) = \sin a \cos b - \cos a \sin b$, $\cos(a + b) = \cos a \cos b - \sin a \sin b$, $\cos(a - b) = \cos a \cos b + \sin a \sin b$, $\tan(a + b) =$

$\dfrac{\tan a + \tan b}{1 - \tan a \tan b}$, $\tan(a - b) = \dfrac{\tan a - \tan b}{1 + \tan a \tan b}$

3. $\sqrt{3} - 2$ **5.** $2 - \sqrt{3}$ **7.** $\dfrac{\sqrt{2} - \sqrt{6}}{4}$ **9.** $\dfrac{\sqrt{6} - \sqrt{2}}{4}$

11. $\sin\left(\dfrac{\pi}{2} - \theta\right) = \sin\dfrac{\pi}{2}\cos\theta - \cos\dfrac{\pi}{2}\sin\theta = 1(\cos\theta) -$

$0(\sin\theta) = \cos\theta$ **13.** $\dfrac{77}{85}$ **15.** $\dfrac{84}{85}$ **17.** $-\dfrac{84}{13}$ **19.** $\tan x$

21. $\cos x$ **23.** $\cos x$ **25.** $-\cos x$ **27.** $-\cot x$
29. $-\cot x$ **31.** The sign in the denominator should be negative when using the sum formula;

$\dfrac{\tan x + \tan\dfrac{\pi}{4}}{1 - \tan x \tan\dfrac{\pi}{4}} = \dfrac{\tan x + 1}{1 - \tan x}$. **33.** $\dfrac{3\pi}{2}$ **35.** about 3.757,

about 5.668 **37.** $0, \dfrac{\pi}{3}, \pi, \dfrac{5\pi}{3}$

10.6 Problem Solving 41. about 15 min

48 sec **43. a.** $\dfrac{f(1 + \tan^2 t)}{h(1 + \tan\theta\tan t)}$ **b.** $\dfrac{f(1 + \tan^2 0)}{h(1 + \tan\theta\tan 0)} = \dfrac{f}{h}$

10.7 Skill Practice 1. double angle

3. $\dfrac{\sqrt{2 + \sqrt{3}}}{2}$ **5.** $2 - \sqrt{3}$ **7.** $\dfrac{\sqrt{\sqrt{2} + 2}}{2}$ **9.** $\sqrt{2} + 1$

13. $\dfrac{\sqrt{3}}{3}, -\dfrac{\sqrt{6}}{3}, -\dfrac{\sqrt{2}}{2}$ **15.** $\dfrac{3\sqrt{10}}{10}, -\dfrac{\sqrt{10}}{10}, -3$

17. $\dfrac{4}{5}, -\dfrac{3}{5}, -\dfrac{4}{3}$ **19.** $\dfrac{4\sqrt{5}}{9}, \dfrac{1}{9}, 4\sqrt{5}$ **21.** 1 **23.** $\dfrac{2\tan\theta}{1 + \tan\theta}$
25. $\cos\theta - 1$ **29.** The correct half angle formula is

$\pm\sqrt{\dfrac{1 - \cos a}{2}}; \sqrt{\dfrac{1 - \dfrac{\sqrt{2}}{2}}{2}} = \sqrt{\dfrac{\dfrac{2 - \sqrt{2}}{2}}{2}} = \sqrt{\dfrac{2 - \sqrt{2}}{4}} = \dfrac{\sqrt{2 - \sqrt{2}}}{2}$

31. $\sin 3\theta = \sin(2\theta + \theta) = \sin 2\theta \cos\theta +$
$\cos 2\theta \sin\theta = 2\sin\theta\cos\theta\cos\theta + (2\cos^2\theta - 1)\sin\theta$
$= 2\sin\theta\cos^2\theta + (2\cos^2\theta - 1)\sin\theta =$
$\sin\theta(2\cos^2\theta + 2\cos^2\theta - 1) = \sin\theta(4\cos^2\theta - 1)$

33. $2\sin^2 x \tan\dfrac{x}{2} = 2\sin^2 x\left(\dfrac{1 - \cos x}{\sin x}\right) =$
$2\sin x(1 - \cos x) = 2\sin x - 2\sin x\cos x =$
$2\sin x - \sin 2x$ **35.** $\cos 4\theta = \cos(2\theta + 2\theta) =$
$\cos 2\theta\cos 2\theta - \sin 2\theta\sin 2\theta = (\cos^2\theta - \sin^2\theta)^2 -$
$(2\sin\theta\cos\theta)^2 = \cos^4\theta - 2\cos^2\theta\sin^2\theta + \sin^4\theta -$
$4\sin^2\theta\cos^2\theta = \cos^4\theta - 6\sin^2\theta\cos^2\theta + \sin^4\theta$

37. $\dfrac{4\pi}{3}$ **39.** $\dfrac{\pi}{4}, \dfrac{7\pi}{4}$ **41.** $\dfrac{\pi}{3}, \dfrac{\pi}{2}, \dfrac{2\pi}{3}, \dfrac{4\pi}{3}, \dfrac{3\pi}{2}, \dfrac{5\pi}{3}$

43. $0 + 2n\pi$ or $\dfrac{\pi}{2} + n\pi$ **45.** $\dfrac{\pi}{3} + 2n\pi$ or $\dfrac{5\pi}{3} + 2n\pi$ or

$\pi + 2n\pi$ **47.** $\pi + 4n\pi$ or $\dfrac{7\pi}{3} + 4n\pi$ or $\dfrac{11\pi}{3} + 4n\pi$

10.7 Problem Solving
51. $24.3° \le \theta \le 65.7°$ **53.** about $47.2°$

55. a. $y = -\dfrac{16}{(40)^2\cos^2\theta}(41.75)^2 + \tan\theta(41.75) + 6$

b. $y = -\dfrac{1743.0625}{100\cos^2\theta} + \tan\theta(41.75) + 6$; about $36.7°$ or

about $58.8°$ **c.** *Sample answer:* The person aims toward the basket and the ball does not bounce off the rim.

Chapter Review 1. cycles **3.** period **5.** frequency
7.

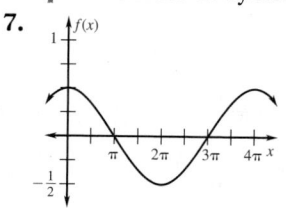

9.

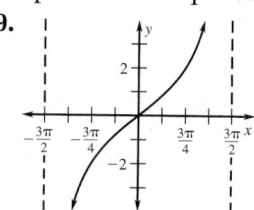

11.

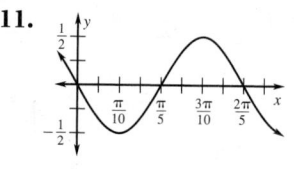

13.

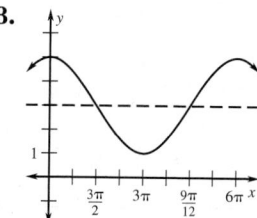

15.

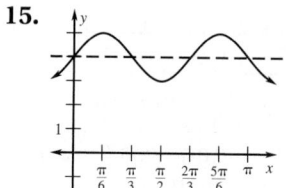

17. $\sec^3 x$ **19.** $\dfrac{\sin^2(-x) - 1}{\cot^2 x} = \dfrac{-(1 - \sin^2 x)}{\dfrac{\cos^2 x}{\sin^2 x}} = \dfrac{-\cos^2 x}{\dfrac{\cos^2 x}{\sin^2 x}} =$

$-\sin^2 x$ **21.** $\dfrac{\pi}{3}, \dfrac{2\pi}{3}, \dfrac{4\pi}{3}, \dfrac{5\pi}{3}$ **23.** $\dfrac{\pi}{12}, \dfrac{\pi}{6}, \dfrac{\pi}{3}, \dfrac{5\pi}{12}, \dfrac{7\pi}{12}, \dfrac{2\pi}{3}, \dfrac{5\pi}{6},$

$\dfrac{11\pi}{12}, \dfrac{13\pi}{12}, \dfrac{7\pi}{6}, \dfrac{4\pi}{3}, \dfrac{17\pi}{12}, \dfrac{19\pi}{12}, \dfrac{5\pi}{3}, \dfrac{11\pi}{6}, \dfrac{23\pi}{12}$ **25.** *Sample*

answer: $y = \cos\pi x - 2$ **27.** $2 + \sqrt{3}$ **29.** $-\dfrac{\sqrt{3}}{2}$

31. $\dfrac{\sqrt{2 + \sqrt{3}}}{2}$ **33.** $\dfrac{\sqrt{2 + \sqrt{3}}}{2}$ **35.** $\dfrac{\sqrt{3}}{2}, \dfrac{\sqrt{3}}{2}$

Chapter 10
Extra Practice

1. 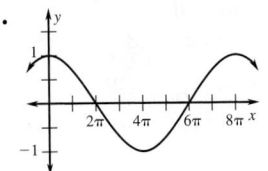 **3.**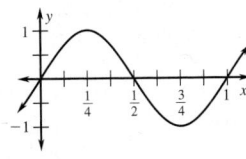

5. 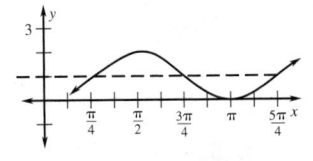 **7.**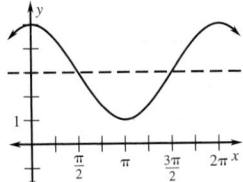

9.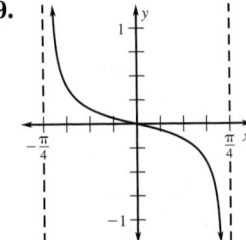

11. 1 **13.** -1 **15.** $\dfrac{\cos^2 x + \sin^2 x}{\tan^2 x + 1} = \dfrac{1}{\sec^2 x} = \cos^2 x$

17. $\dfrac{\pi}{6} + n\pi, \dfrac{5\pi}{6} + n\pi$ **19.** $\dfrac{\pi}{4} + n\pi$ **21.** $\dfrac{7\pi}{6}, \dfrac{11\pi}{6}$

23. about 1.2995 **25.** $y = 3 + \dfrac{1}{2}\cos \pi x$

27. $\dfrac{-\sqrt{2} - \sqrt{6}}{4}$ **29.** $\dfrac{\sqrt{2} + \sqrt{6}}{4}$ **31.** $\dfrac{9\sqrt{19}}{50}, \dfrac{31}{50}, \dfrac{9\sqrt{19}}{31}$

33. $\dfrac{2\pi}{3} + 2n\pi, \dfrac{4\pi}{3} + 2n\pi, 0 + 2n\pi$ **35.** $\dfrac{3\pi}{4} + n\pi$

Selected Answers

Skills Review Handbook

Operations with Positive and Negative Numbers
1. -6 **3.** -60 **5.** 2 **7.** 8 **9.** 44 **11.** -4 **13.** 12 **15.** -72
17. -2 **19.** -3 **21.** 9 **23.** 6 **25.** -15 **27.** -12 **29.** 5
31. 42 **33.** -17 **35.** 2

Fractions, Decimals, and Percents **1.** $\frac{13}{20}$ **3.** $\frac{3}{2}$
5. $\frac{7}{10}$ **7.** $\frac{13}{50}$ **9.** $\frac{19}{20}$ **11.** 0.25 **13.** 1.2 **15.** 0.375 **17.** 1.42
19. 0.3 **21.** 60% **23.** 130% **25.** 45% **27.** 80% **29.** 250%

Calculating with Percents **1.** 196 **3.** 38.4 **5.** 17
7. 1 **9.** 54% **11.** 10% **13.** 20% **15.** 2% **17.** 80 **19.** 60
21. 70 **23.** 8 **25.** 25% decrease **27.** 50% increase
29. 96% increase **31.** 79% decrease

Factors and Multiples **1.** $2 \cdot 3 \cdot 7$ **3.** $3 \cdot 5^2$
5. $2 \cdot 5 \cdot 7$ **7.** $2^3 \cdot 3^2$ **9.** prime **11.** $2^3 \cdot 11$ **13.** prime
15. 2^5 **17.** 8 **19.** 11 **21.** 4 **23.** 3 **25.** 10 **27.** 3 **29.** 1
31. 16 **33.** 30 **35.** 24 **37.** 6 **39.** 36 **41.** 30 **43.** 40
45. 891 **47.** $\frac{7}{16}$ **49.** $\frac{5}{6}$ **51.** $\frac{37}{40}$ **53.** $\frac{1}{3}$ **55.** $\frac{17}{30}$ **57.** $\frac{13}{20}$
59. $\frac{9}{20}$ **61.** $\frac{13}{16}$ **63.** $\frac{23}{30}$ **65.** $\frac{59}{80}$ **67.** $\frac{17}{20}$ **69.** $\frac{11}{18}$

Ratios and Proportions **1.** 1 to 3, $1:3$, $\frac{1}{3}$
3. 5 to 4, $5:4$, $\frac{5}{4}$ **5.** 5 to 6, $5:6$, $\frac{5}{6}$ **7.** 1 to 1, $1:1$, $\frac{1}{1}$
9. 4 to 9, $4:9$, $\frac{4}{9}$ **11.** 7 to 1, $7:1$, $\frac{7}{1}$ **13.** 7 **15.** 20 **17.** 2
19. 5 **21.** 40 **23.** 6.75 **25.** 99 **27.** 72

Converting Units of Measurement **1.** 6000
3. 5 **5.** 7.7 **7.** 16 **9.** 4000 **11.** 0.8 **13.** 6 **15.** 1.5
17. 3600 **19.** 3 **21.** $\frac{1}{8}$ **23.** $63{,}360$ **25.** 2 **27.** 4000

Scientific Notation **1.** 6×10^{-1} **3.** 8×10^{-2}
5. 4.08×10^{1} **7.** 3.85×10^{-4} **9.** 4.1236×10^{4}
11. 4.86×10^{5} **13.** 1.002×10^{-2} **15.** 7.0505×10^{3}
17. 9.85×10^{3} **19.** 8.05×10^{2} **21.** 5000 **23.** 0.82
25. 0.0032 **27.** $734{,}500$ **29.** 1.814 **31.** $1{,}000{,}000$
33. 0.000008 **35.** $1{,}870{,}000{,}000$ **37.** $6{,}080{,}000$
39. $34{,}010{,}000$

Significant Digits **1.** 600 **3.** 81 **5.** 1.885
7. 4.9 **9.** $.195$ **11.** 0.036 **13.** 1009 **15.** 18 **17.** $\$17.40$
19. 2.5 pints per student **21.** 2543 books per library
23. $\$1250$

Writing Algebraic Expressions **1.** $n + 8$ **3.** $2n$
5. $\frac{1}{5}n$ **7.** $5n$ **9.** $0.25n$ **11.** $n - 2$ **13.** $c - 4$ yr
15. $x + 5$ dollars **17.** $45 - m$ min **19.** $10x$ dollars

Binomial Products **1.** $a^2 + 8a + 15$

3. $t^2 + 15t + 56$ **5.** $y^2 + 6y + 8$ **7.** $y^2 - 4y + 4$
9. $z^2 - 8z + 16$ **11.** $y^2 - 4y - 21$ **13.** $25x^2 - 16$
15. $2c^2 + 3c - 35$ **17.** $-z^2 + 49$ **19.** $16a^2 + 24a + 9$
21. $-x^2 - 4x + 32$ **23.** $-a^2 + 18a - 81$
25. $10x^2 - 21x - 10$ **27.** $-24z^2 + 22z - 3$

LCDs of Rational Expressions **1.** $2a^2b$ **3.** z^3
5. $126m$ **7.** $3y^2$ **9.** $(n + 2)(n - 2)$ **11.** $5(n + 1)$
13. $6(m - 3)$ **15.** $(x - 4)^2$ **17.** $2n^3(5n + 4)$ **19.** $(k + 3)^4$
21. $70(n + 2)$ **23.** $(a + 2)^2$ **25.** $(k - 3)(k - 2)$
27. $(m - 7)(m - 4)(m^2 + 5m - 45)$

The Coordinate Plane
1–20.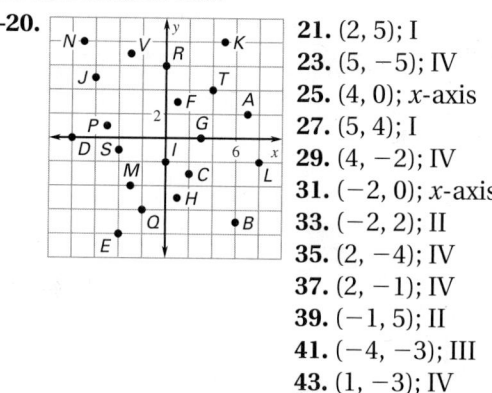
21. $(2, 5)$; I
23. $(5, -5)$; IV
25. $(4, 0)$; x-axis
27. $(5, 4)$; I
29. $(4, -2)$; IV
31. $(-2, 0)$; x-axis
33. $(-2, 2)$; II
35. $(2, -4)$; IV
37. $(2, -1)$; IV
39. $(-1, 5)$; II
41. $(-4, -3)$; III
43. $(1, -3)$; IV

Transformations
1. $(3, -8)$ **3.** $(-3, 11)$ **5.** $(8, 3)$ **7.** $(-8, -3)$
9. 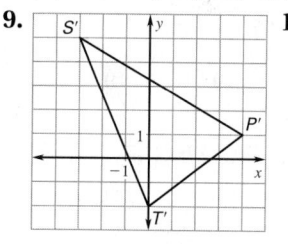 **11.**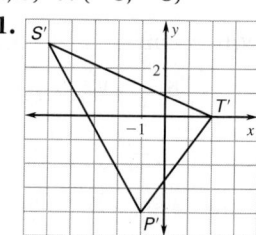
19. 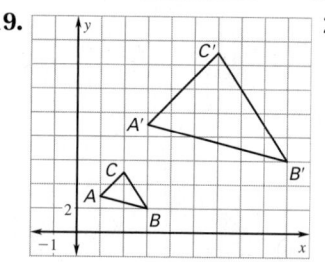 **21.**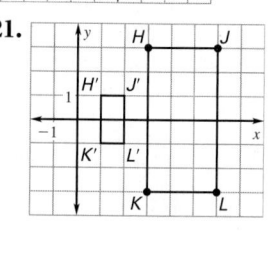

Line Symmetry 1. none **3.** 1 **5.** none **7.** 2
9. $(-4, -1)$ **11.** $(-2, 2)$

Perimeter and Area 1. 10 cm, 6 cm^2 **3.** 26 in.,
24 in.^{2} **5.** 48 yd, 84 yd^2 **7.** 14 m, 10.8 m^2

Circumference and Area of a Circle
1. $C = 10\pi$ in. or about 31 in., $A = 25\pi$ in.^{2} or about
79 in.^{2} **3.** $C = 8\pi$ in. or about 25 in., $A = 16\pi$ in.^{2}

or about 50 in.^{2} **5.** $C = 24\pi$ ft or about 75 ft, $A = 144\pi$ ft^2 or about 452 ft^2 **7.** $C = 6\pi$ ft or about 19 ft, $A = 9\pi$ ft^2 or about 28 ft^2 **9.** $C = 2\pi$ cm or about 6 cm, $A = \pi$ cm^2 or about 3 cm^2 **11.** $C = 22\pi$ in. or about 69 in., $A = 121\pi$ in.^{2} or about 380 in.^{2}

Surface Area and Volume 1. 158 in.^{2}, 120 in.^{3} **3.** 54 cm^2, 27 cm^3 **5.** 154π yd^2 or about 484 yd^2, 196π yd^3 or about 616 yd^3

Angle Relationships 1. 39 **3.** 8 **5.** 16 **7.** 23 **9.** 29

Triangle Relationships 1. 40 **3.** 60 **5.** 50 cm **7.** 12 ft **9.** 55°

Congruent and Similar Figures 1. similar **3.** congruent **5.** congruent **7.** neither **9.** congruent **11.** 11.5 **13.** 14 **15.** 40 **17.** 7

More Problem Solving Strategies 1. 4:15 P.M. **3.** 6 ways **5.** 40 parts **7.** 8 dimes, 5 nickels

Logical Argument 1. valid; Chain Rule **3.** invalid **5.** valid; *And* Rule **7.** valid; *Or* Rule **9.** invalid **11.** true **13.** false **15.** true **17.** true **19.** false **21.** true

Conditional Statements and Counterexamples 1. If you have the equation $y = mx + b$, then you have the graph of a line; if you have the graph of a line, then you have the equation $y = mx + b$, false. **3.** If Abby finishes her homework, then she can go swimming; if Abby goes swimming, then she finished her homework, false. **5.** If $4x + 8 = 28$, then $x = 5$; if $x = 5$, then $4x + 8 = 28$, true. **7.** True; if two lines are perpendicular, then they intersect to form a right angle and if two lines intersect to form a right angle, then they are perpendicular. **9.** False; not all orange vegetables are carrots. **11.** False; the converse is not true. **13.** False; zero is neither positive nor negative. **15.** False. *Sample answer:* An octagon could have exactly 5 congruent sides. **17.** False; A could be in between B and C and therefore would only be 2 inches from C. **19.** False. *Sample answer:* Charlie could have 10 dimes.

Venn Diagrams

1.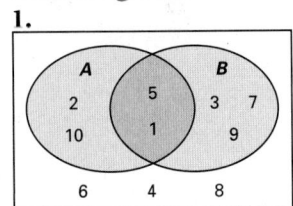

3.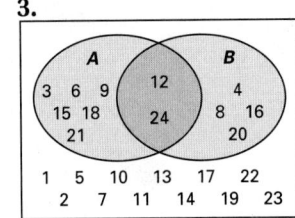

5. False. *Sample answer:* 10 is even, but it is not a multiple of 3 or 4. **7.** False; 1 is a positive odd integer and a factor of 10. **9.** True; 2 is the only even prime number.

Mean, Median, Mode, and Range 1. about $664, $675, $650, $300 **3.** 685 min, 713 min, none, 611 min **5.** 48 cookies, 48 cookies, 48 cookies and 60 cookies, 24 cookies **7.** $9.20, $8.90, none, $5.85 **9.** 15 people, 14 people, 10 people and 18 people and 22 people, 25 people

Graphing Statistical Data 1. 6 P.M. **3.** 5 diners; yes **5.** 14 diners **7.** winter and summer **9.** natural gas **11.** 50 homes

13.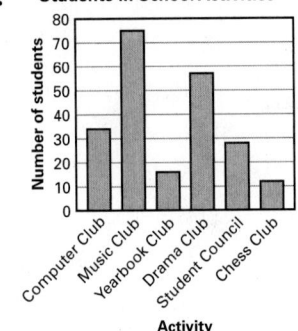

Organizing Statistical Data

1.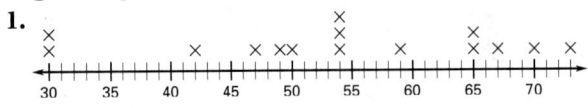

3. Stem | Leaves

Stem	Leaves
3	0 0
4	2 7 9
5	0 4 4 4 9
6	5 5 7
7	0 3

Key: 3 | 0 = 30

5.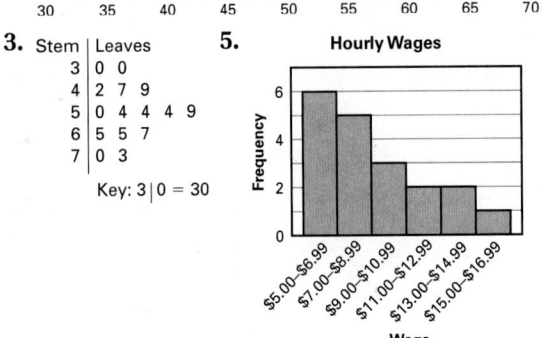

7.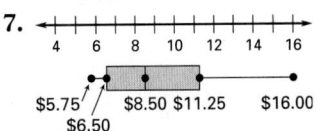

9. 5 **11.** 23 dogs **13.** 43 lb **15.** 25 children **17.** 12 songs **19.** 10 songs; 18 songs

Selected answers for the Extra Practice section are at the end of each chapter.